"Dan Appleman's previous works have established him as the leading authority on the use of Windows API from Visual Basic applications. I fully expect Dan's newest work to quickly become the bible for how millions of Visual Basic developers access the Win32 API in their Visual Basic applications on Windows 95 and Windows NT."

Jon Roskill
Visual Basic Director of Product Management and Marketing
Microsoft Corporation

"This is it: the eagerly awaited Win32 update to a Win 3.1 classic. If you call Win32 APIs directly or just want to know what VB is doing under the hood, you need this book."

Keith Pleas
Contributing Editor, *Visual Basic Programmer's Journal* and *Windows NT Magazine*

"Every serious VB programmer should keep this book within arm's reach at all times. Dan Appleman completely bridges the gap between Visual Basic and the Windows operating system. Don't even think about not buying this book, you can't afford to pass it up."

Carl Franklin
Carl & Gary's Visual Basic Home Page

"Once again, Dan has paved the way for the Visual Basic programmer to successfully plunge into the intricacies of the Win32 API. *PC Magazine Visual Basic Programmer's Guide to the Win32 API* is destined to achieve rare status of being known simply as the authoritative reference, 'Appleman/32'."

Brad McLane
President, Caladonia Systems, Inc.

"Dan Appleman has long been known, with good reason, as Mr. API. Visual Basic programmers couldn't be in better hands as they sally forth into the world of Win32 API."

Paul Bonner
Columnist, *Windows Sources* and *Computer Shopper*

Dan Appleman's Visual Basic 5.0 Programmer's Guide to the Win32 API

Dan Appleman's
Visual Basic 5.0
Programmer's
Guide to the
Win32 API

Dan Appleman

Ziff-Davis Press
An imprint of Macmillan Computer Publishing USA
Emeryville, California

Publisher	Stacy Hiquet
Associate Publisher	Steven Sayre
Acquisitions Editor	Lysa Lewallen
Copy Editor	Patrick Bevin
Proofreaders	Joe Sadusky and Jeff Barash
Cover Illustration and Design	Megan Gandt
Book Design	Laura Lamar/MAXX, San Francisco
Page Layout	M. D. Barrera
Indexer	Carol Burbo

Ziff-Davis Press, ZD Press, and the Ziff-Davis Press logo are trademarks or registered trademarks of, and are licensed to Macmillan Computer Publishing USA by Ziff-Davis Publishing Company, New York, New York.

Ziff-Davis Press imprint books are produced on a Macintosh computer system with the following applications: FrameMaker®, Microsoft® Word, QuarkXPress®, Adobe Illustrator®, Adobe Photoshop®, Adobe Streamline™, MacLink®Plus, Aldus® FreeHand™, Collage Plus™.

Ziff-Davis Press, an imprint of
Macmillan Computer Publishing USA
200 Tamal Plaza, Suite 101
Corte Madera, CA 94925

ISBN 1-56276-446-2

Manufactured in the United States of America
10 9 8 7 6 5 4 3 2

CONTENTS AT A GLANCE

TABLE OF CONTENTS

Part 2   Windows API Functions

Part 3   Windows Messages

Part 4   Real World API Programming Revisited

The following three chapters appear on the CD-ROM included with this book:

ACKNOWLEDGMENTS

Alot of people put in a great deal of work into making this book a reality. I could easily spend an entire chapter thanking them, but I think the folks at Ziff-Davis Press would have my head if I proposed adding so much as a single page to this already long book. Fortunately, this book includes a CD-ROM, so I ask that you take the time later to explore the acknowledgments chapter where you will have a chance to meet many of the people who contributed directly to this book.

To the wonderful folks at Ziff-Davis Press: We've been through a lot on this one, with you needing to deal with both corporate reorganization and occasionally obstinate authors such as me. Thanks to: Juliet Langley, who stayed—and was always there to talk about whatever issues came up. Margo Hill, with her gentle editing. Madhu Prasher, for pulling it all together. Sarah Ishida, for once again making my drawings look good. Lysa Lewallen—you were caught between the demands of your publishing schedule and the limitations of my schedule and somehow kept your sanity, and helped me keep mine. Cindy Johnson, for your moral support and other help. And Cindy Hudson (now at Mindscape), for starting it all.

Thanks to Hank Wallace who handled the outside technical editing—you made time in a schedule that was as bad as mine to help maintain this book's accuracy.

This book is dedicated first to the people who work at my company, Desaware. Each and every one of them was involved in one way or another, including taking over some of my responsibilities so that I could work on the book. Without their help, this book would never have been written. A special thanks to Franky Wong, who acted as the inside technical editor, reviewing every chapter before it was submitted to the publisher. He also helped with the reference sections of Chapters 16–18 and Appendix B. To Clint Chaplin who also helped with Appendix B. To Levy Ring who helped with formatting the reference sections and verifying functions against both the declaration files and the original 16-bit book. To Mark Rabkin who helped tech-edit part of the book and wrote several of the sample programs. To Gabriel Appleman (my father) who reviewed each chapter for grammar and readability before submission. To Stjepan Pejic, lead programmer on the API class library included in the book, and his assistant, Rami Nagel. To Roan Bear, for support both moral and practical. To Marian Kicklighter, Karyn Duncan, Josh Peck, Michael Dickman, and Yaniv Soha, who all helped keep the company going. To Dr. Seuss AZA for help with mailing the bulletin. To my mother for providing the chicken soup (and much, much more). To Desaware as a company for providing thousands of dollars in labor and technical resources to bring this book to completion.

This book is also dedicated to the many readers of the original *Visual Basic Programmer's Guide to the Windows API*. Without your support, patronage, encouragement, and suggestions, I would not have even attempted this project in the first place.

FOREWORD

STOP! Please read the following important message before you purchase this book!

A substantial amount of the contents of this book was also published under the title PC Magazine *Visual Basic Programmer's Guide to the Win32 API*. The title change is in part due to the change to Visual Basic 5.0, and in part because the book really has no association with *PC Magazine* (and never did).

This edition contains numerous changes to take both Visual Basic 5.0 and Windows NT 4.0 into account. It includes two new chapters on the CD-ROM. It includes all of the source code in both Visual Basic 4.0 and Visual Basic 5.0 formats (with modifications to support new VB5 features where appropriate). It also includes new articles on various Win32 and Visual Basic related subjects. However, if you already own the original book, you are likely to find that the changes do not justify the price of a new book.

In order to provide a solution to this problem, I have arranged with the publisher to make the updated CD-ROM for this book available to owners of the original book at a substantially lower cost. Update sales are being handled directly by Desaware Inc. For further information including price and verification requirements, see the notice on www.desaware.com, or contact Desaware directly at (408) 377-4770 or by e-mail: support@desaware.com.

Daniel Appleman

Once upon a Time, There Was the Visual Basic Programmer's Guide to the Windows API....

I decided to write that book after seeing Visual Basic 1.0. Here at last was a language that allowed ordinary human beings to write Windows programs—a task that had been a complex and frustrating art until then. Visual Basic encapsulated the power of Windows in an easy-to-use language. At the same time, it still allowed programmers to access the power of Windows using API and DLL calls.

But I found that many Visual Basic programmers could not take full advantage of the power of Windows. The problem was that all of the documentation on Windows was written for C and C++ programmers—there was nothing available to help Visual Basic programmers take advantage of the power that was now available to them. At that time in my life, I was ready to leave the job that I held (well, more than ready, actually—but that's another story), and had decided to create a company to develop add-on products for Visual Basic. But I didn't want to do ordinary add-on products—I wanted to create products that would let Visual Basic programmers take advantage of all of the capabilities of Windows—to blow away the limitations of the language itself and to educate programmers about the possibilities that exist. So, in addition to founding Desaware to handle software products, I approached Cindy Hudson, who at the time was the publisher at Ziff-Davis Press, and proposed that I write a book about the Windows API purely from the perspective of the Visual Basic programmer. The result was the original Visual Basic Programmer's Guide to the Windows API.

To say that I was surprised by the response is an understatement. The amount of encouragement and support that I have received from readers still astonishes me.

In mid-1995, when it became clear that a 32-bit version of Visual Basic was under development, I faced a dilemma and a challenge. Desaware's customers expected (correctly) that we upgrade our controls to the new OLE control model as quickly as possible. To lead in that task and simultaneously run a company would be a full-time job. To write a 32-bit API book would be another full-time job. The logical answer, to tell the truth, would be not to do the book—even if it is a bestseller, it is unlikely to ever pay back the investment in time and money. A 32-bit API book would, by necessity, be a nearly complete rewrite of the original.

But sometimes logic isn't everything. The problem of providing a Visual Basic specific reference for Win32 still existed, and a lot of people were looking to me to follow through. If I hadn't received all of those kind messages from readers on the first book, it would have been easy to walk away from the task, but that was not the case. So I said good-bye to weekends, vacations, holidays, and sleep for the last eight months, and the results are here before you.

What Is in This Book: the New and the Old

In writing this book, I followed the same principles and goals that I had for the original *Visual Basic Programmer's Guide to the Windows API*.

First, I designed this edition for programmers who are acquainted with Visual Basic but do not necessarily have any Windows API knowledge. As such, it contains a fairly thorough windows primer that is based on the knowledge that you already have about Visual Basic. No knowledge of C or C++ is assumed—all of the code in the book is written in Visual Basic. While accessible to beginners, the book goes into enough depth to satisfy most experienced programmers.

Second, I did not want it to be simply a set of techniques and boilerplate code to copy blindly. I believe that most programmers would like a real understanding of the code that they are placing in their application. In order to help provide this, the book is divided into general subject areas, each of which is self-contained with an introduction, one or two sample programs, and a Function Reference listing the Windows functions that are related to that subject. The introduction not only describes the underlying theory of how and why the Windows API functions work, but how Visual Basic fits into the picture.

At the same time, with the Win32 book I faced certain new challenges. The first is that the Win32 API is enormous—far larger than I could fit into a single book no matter how long I worked. In fact, I suspect that the Win32 API is continuing to grow at a faster pace than I can learn about it, much less write about it. As a result, with this book I introduced the following changes:

- If the book cannot document every Win32 API function (which is the case), the alternative is to teach API programming in sufficient depth so that Visual Basic programmers will be able to understand the C or C++ documentation well enough to convert and apply it. To accomplish this, the amount of text discussing the Visual Basic-to-Windows interface has grown from a single chapter to two larger chapters plus additional text scattered throughout the book.

- Many Visual Basic programmers are still in the process of supporting 16-bit applications as well as 32-bit applications. As a result, this book provides in-depth information on porting from 16-bit to 32-bit API calls. It also includes information and samples to help you write applications that are compatible with both 16- and 32-bit platforms, if you are still using Visual Basic 4.0.

- The explanatory text and number of sample applications have grown substantially.

- The CD-ROM includes a full text searchable electronic edition of the book to make it easier to find the information that you need.

I've also made every effort to ensure the technical accuracy of this book, especially with regard to Visual Basic compatibility issues where much of the information is based on experimentation and deduction.

Nevertheless, you may find some shortcomings in the form of errors, omissions, or areas where difficult concepts are not explained clearly enough. I hope you will feel free to contact me with any suggestions so that they can be incorporated into future editions of this book. I can be reached via e-mail at dan@desaware.com or CompuServe mail at 70303,2252, and by fax at Desaware: (408) 371-3530. If you don't have access to any of these, write me at the following address:

Ziff-Davis Press
Macmillan Computer Publishing USA
200 Tamal Plaza, Suite 101
Corte Madera, CA 94925

How to Use This Book (Please Read!)

This is a big book.

Okay, it is a very big book.

But please don't let this scare you—you don't have to read the whole thing to take full advantage of what's here.

You see, most of the chapters in this book are divided into three parts. They start out with a discussion of the subject being introduced in the chapter. This is the tutorial part of the chapter that introduces key concepts and summarizes the API functions relating to that subject. Next, you'll find some sample programs that demonstrate the functions introduced earlier in the chapter. Finally, you'll find a Function Reference section that describes how to use those API functions.

That said, here are my recommendations for what you really should read to take full advantage of this book.

First, read Chapters 1 through 4 completely. These chapters cover all of the core information that you'll need to take full advantage of the Windows API—not to mention porting your Win16 applications to Win32.

Next, read the explanatory parts of Chapters 5 through 15. These chapters cover the core API functions—the things that you'll really want to know as you work with the Win32 API. Chapter 15 also contains advanced information that you'll be ready for by the time you've read what I've listed so far.

After that, you can go back to those subjects that you are particularly interested in.

Common Questions

I'm a beginning programmer, will this book help me?

This book is very suitable for beginners. No, really—I'm serious! Of course, I'm referring to beginning Windows programmers. This book does assume that you already know how to program in Visual Basic.

Should I read the chapters in order, or can I just jump to particular subjects?

This book is not a tips and techniques book, though it probably covers thousands of techniques. It is not intended to be an encyclopedia of stand-alone code fragments that you can plug in to your applications without thought, though it has numerous examples that can be used that way.

This book is intended to teach you to use the Win32 API from Visual Basic effectively even if you have never used it before. It is intended to turn you into a Win32 expert if you choose to go that far.

In order to accomplish this, the book is structured like a text book: Each chapter presumes that you have knowledge gained in previous chapters. As such, you will gain the most from this book if you read the explanatory parts of each chapter starting at the beginning and continuing in sequence to the end.

How do the Function Reference sections work?

Most of the chapters include a Function Reference section that contains detailed information for those API functions that relate to the chapter subject. Each section contains the following information:

VB Declaration

This is the Visual Basic declaration found in the file API32.TXT.

Description

Contains a brief description of the function.

Use with VB

This section indicates whether there are any VB-related issues that you should consider when using this function. "No problem" means that there are no known problems with using this function, but despite many hours of testing API functions under VB, this is not an absolute guarantee that you won't run into difficulty.

Parameter Table

This is a table containing a list of parameters used with this function.

Return Value

This describes the value returned by this function. Some common terms you will see include:

True (nonzero)—Listed this way to emphasize the fact that under Windows True is usually not the –1 value used by Visual Basic (See Chapter 3).

Sets GetLastError—Indicates that the function sets an internal error value that can be read by the GetLastError API function (See Chapter 6).

Platform

This indicates the platform that this function will work with as follows:

Windows NT—This function works on Windows NT 3.51 or later.

Windows NT 4.0—This function works on Windows NT 4.0 or later.

Windows 95—This function works on Windows 95. It may also work on Windows NT using the Windows 95 shell.

Win16—This function has an equivalent Win16 function available. Refer to the *Visual Basic Programmer's Guide to the Windows API* (16-bit edition) for information on the Win16 version of the function, and file API16.TXT for the declaration. This information is provided for your convenience only; all of the information in the Function Reference section of this book applies only to the Win32 function and you should assume that the Win16 function has differences.

Comments

I include any additional comments that may help you.

Porting Notes

This section describes any unusual issues relating to porting the function from Win16. It is not intended to be an in-depth explanation of how to port the function—only a place to point out any subtle issues or changes that are not readily apparent from comparison of the Win32 function description and the Win16 function description.

Example

This section lists the sample programs which demonstrate the use of this function or a closely related function. It does not include every use of the function in all sample programs in the book. Some functions have short code fragments included.

Most of the functions without examples are so simple to use that an example should not be necessary even for beginners, as long as they have read the first three chapters of this book.

Why should I use your API32.TXT declaration file when Microsoft provides a perfectly good WIN32API.TXT file with VB?

Because frankly, WIN32API.TXT is not perfectly good. In fact, it's not even close. It was created using a file parsing tool generated by Microsoft, but it did not undergo any extensive testing. API32.TXT incorporates literally hundreds of corrections to WIN32API.TXT. It is based not only on WIN32API.TXT, but also on the actual export tables from the various Win32 dynamic link libraries, Microsoft's Win32 Software Development Kit API database, The Microsoft Developer's Network CD-ROM, and most important of all, hundreds of hours of actual use by other Desaware software engineers and myself.

That said, I am quite certain that it is not perfect—I have no doubt that errors will continue to be found by readers and by me. Nevertheless, it's what we use, and what I ask you to use—or at least try before you decide that one of the book's code samples doesn't work.

Why did you leave out...?

Despite the increased size of this book, there wasn't room for everything that I wanted to include. In the process of adding to the explanatory text and incorporating the new core API functions, something had to give. Most NT specific functionality was left out, as were most of the extension libraries. Communications was left out (though some information is included on the CD-ROM) because most people just use controls to support communications. Palette information was left out for now because of the clear trend toward 16- and 24-bit graphic cards (especially on the higher end systems that support Win32). Most of the information in the original *Visual Basic Programmer's Guide to the Windows API* on palettes still applies.

I've been gradually offering additional information on these subjects and others through articles, through Desaware's products, and on our Web page at www.desaware.com, so stay in touch. Also, with the increased information on how to interpret Win32 documentation, you should find it easier than you expect to make use of the C/C++ documentation under Visual Basic.

What is the story with these demonstration controls for callbacks, subclassing, and hooks? Why can't they be used in real applications the way the cbk.vbx control was in the original book?

There is one unavoidable fact: There are many capabilities provided by the Win32 API that require use of callbacks, subclassing, hooks, or an interface DLL.

The question then is: How do I deal with this?

In the original 16-bit book, I included a limited version of the cbk.vbx callback control that was fully functional. The problem is that as the commercial version of the control became widely distributed, applications that used it would (correctly) overwrite the older version of the control included with the book. As a result, readers could no longer load the sample applications; they were not licensed for the newer control. They could either run the sample program, or run the program that depended on the new control, but not both—an unacceptable situation.

In the ideal world, I would be able to include all of these controls at no cost and provide ongoing support and upgrades for them as well. Unfortunately, I simply can't afford to do so. You would be shocked if you knew how little income an author actually makes even on a successful technical book.

I could also leave the controls out completely and avoid discussing any API functions that require their use. But doing so eliminates an important part of API technology, and one that you are likely to run into on many occasions. A discussion of the Win32 API and Visual Basic simply cannot be complete without discussing these issues.

So what's left? The only real choice that remained was to create fully functional demonstration versions of these controls that would run only within the Visual Basic design time environment. This will give you the tools that you need to experiment and learn the technology.

I realize that there are a lot of books that promise gobs and gobs of "free" software. But it often turns out to be crippled software or demo programs that have little value and are not supported. I don't want you to purchase this book because you think you'll be getting a great value in free software. I want you to purchase this book because it contains information and explanations that you will find worthwhile. As far as I'm concerned, this book has no free software—just a lot of information that I hope you'll find valuable, more valuable than the purchase cost.

Here's the bottom line: As a professional software developer, I would never stake an application that I wrote on some free unsupported controls that I found in a book. I won't insult you by suggesting that you do something that I would not do myself.

If you want to take advantage of the capabilities provided by these demonstration controls in your own applications, you're going to have to obtain controls for yourself. You can purchase the SpyWorks controls (which I would personally appreciate, and besides which are, in my humble opinion, the best in the business), or find another offering by another vendor. Regardless of which controls you use, please—for your own sake—use commercial-quality supported controls from a reputable vendor. Subclassing is easy to do poorly, and notoriously difficult to do correctly (even with the AddressOf operator in Visual Basic 5.0). The same applies to callbacks in Visual Basic 4.0 and earlier. The long-term cost of "free" controls can be enormous.

I'm Stuck and Desperate and I Need Help

I see an e-mail message like this or its equivalent almost daily. I wish I could answer them all, but this is simply not feasible. You see, if I tried to do so I would not be able to make a living. But I hate to just say no because I know what it's like to have a critical project blocked by a problem and how difficult it is sometimes to get accurate answers.

So, here's what happens when a question comes in.

If it's something that I can answer in a few lines off the top of my head, I frequently answer, even if it is only to try to point the person in the right direction.

If it's a question from a Desaware customer, I try to give it extra attention even if it does not relate directly to the use of one of our products (or I turn it over to someone else on our technical staff to look at).

If it's a problem that I find intriguing and I have some time available, I might take a look at it just for the educational value.

In some cases I might offer to look at it on a consulting basis, but I try to avoid that approach (and you don't want to know what I charge for that kind of work).

If your problem relates at all to use of another vendor's products, you'll need to call that vendor—I have no information on products other than Desaware's and Visual Basic itself, and no ability to answer questions or provide support in those areas. (And if that vendor cannot provide you adequate support, I regret that there is nothing that I can do to help.)

Also, please do not e-mail long listings and ask that I debug them—it won't happen.

Finally, Desaware supports a Web page and list server to help provide more frequent updates, information, and application notes for this book on an ongoing basis. If you would like to be on a mailing list, simply send a message to listserv@desaware.com with the word "Subscribe" in the topic or message. To receive further information, please send an e-mail request to Desaware at support@desaware.com or on CompuServe (Go Desaware) or 74431.3534@compuserve.com.

DLLs and APIs

Getting a Handle on Windows

The Visual Basic-Windows Interface

Real World API Programming

1

The Windows API

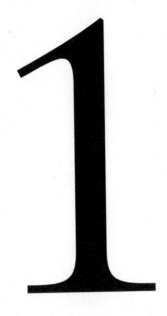

C H A P T E R

1

DLLs and APIs

N 1991, MICROSOFT RELEASED VERSION 1.0 OF A NEW LANGUAGE CALLED Visual Basic. By doing so, they have literally revolutionized Windows programming, and in many ways advanced the art of programming in general. By some estimates over 1 million copies of Visual Basic have been sold, making it one of the most popular programming languages of all time. Perhaps the most important reason for this is that Visual Basic is the first programming tool that truly allows people to write Windows applications without being a Windows expert.

Moving from DOS to Windows

Visual Basic is a comprehensive programming language. It is certainly adequate for a great many applications. There is a good chance, however, that sooner or later you will run into a requirement that Visual Basic does not support directly. For example, sound support, I/O port access, and many bitmap operations are not part of the Visual Basic language.

But this is not really a flaw in Visual Basic. No language can contain every command and function that might be needed by every programmer. In the DOS world, this problem is solved by creating and using libraries of functions that extend the capabilities of the language. These functions can be linked into your programs as needed.

In the Windows world, things are a bit more complex. For one thing, the operating environment is considerably more complicated than DOS—the simple act of displaying a line on the screen involves the use of objects known as Windows handles, display contexts, and pens. The process of linking in external functions is also different—Windows applications often use a technique known as dynamic linking instead of the static linking common in DOS (linking will be described in detail later in this chapter).

As long as you are using only Visual Basic functions and commands, this complexity remains mostly in the background. As soon as you are ready to go beyond the built-in features of the language, however, you are sure to face some of these issues.

Don't panic.

Like any serious programming language, Visual Basic is highly extensible. While a great deal of press has been devoted to the third-party add-ons and libraries available for VB, the fact is that the greatest add-on library of them all is included automatically with every copy of the language. That is Windows itself.

There has been a great deal of talk about how complex Windows programming is—and it is, for people writing entire programs in C++, C, or Pascal. As a Visual Basic programmer, though, you already have a good general understanding of how Windows works (though you may not realize it). That is because Visual Basic is very closely tied to Windows. VB events correspond closely to Windows messages. VB properties often correspond closely to

Windows styles and properties. In a sense, Visual Basic is a programmable shell for Windows.

The first part of this book covers the relationship between Windows and Visual Basic. This chapter focuses on the transition from DOS to Windows in general, the 32-bit versions of Windows in particular, and discusses the subject of extensibility. Chapter 2 looks inside Windows and shows how it corresponds to Visual Basic. Chapter 3 is a thorough review of everything you need to know to access Windows functions and DLL functions from Visual Basic. Chapter 4 examines specific techniques for writing programs that will work on the different types of Windows operating systems and goes into further detail on how to translate typical C language documentation into Visual Basic.

To appreciate the differences between DOS and Windows programming, it is a good idea to take a moment and review the three big differences between DOS and Windows itself.

First, Windows is multitasking—it's able to run more than one program at the same time. Multitasking poses an interesting set of problems. Which program gets access to the screen? How is memory shared? If more than one program is using the screen, which program gets keyboard input? Which one gets mouse input? What if two programs want to use the same serial port? Almost every difference between DOS and Windows programming relates in some way to multitasking.

Second, Windows is event driven. Many DOS programs are written as loops that perform I/O operations as needed. The programmer decides when it is time to check for keyboard or mouse input. Windows programs can receive external events at almost any time and should not use continuous loops, which on some operating systems can tie up the system and prevent other applications from running.

Third, Windows is device independent. DOS programs frequently need to take into account every possible printer or graphics device type. It is not unusual for a DOS program to ship with dozens of printer drivers, and separate graphics drivers for EGA, VGA, monochrome, and Super VGA graphics mode—and sometimes even for different brands of VGA cards! Windows provides a graphics device interface (called GDI) that makes it possible to support virtually any graphics device—Windows takes care of providing the individual drivers. GDI translates graphics commands so that they appear identical (or at least as similar as possible) on all devices.

Many of the programming issues that will be discussed here derive from these differences. The development of dynamic linking is one such issue.

Dynamic Link Libraries (DLLs)

Linking refers to the process in which external functions are incorporated into an application. There are two types of linking: *static* and *dynamic*. Static linking takes place during creation of the program. Dynamic linking takes place when the program is running.

Static Linking

Programming languages are typically extended in two ways. First, most languages provide access to the underlying operating system. In DOS, this is accomplished with interrupt 21 calls to DOS. Second, most languages allow you to create libraries of functions that can be merged into your program. These functions then appear to the programmer as if they were built into the language.

Program modules containing functions are precompiled into object (.OBJ) files. These object files are often grouped into library (.LIB) files using a program called a librarian (such as LIB.EXE).

When it is time to create a final executable version of an application, a program known as a linker scans your application's object files for references to functions that are not defined. It then searches through any specified library files for the missing functions. The linker extracts any program modules containing the required functions and copies them into the new executable file, "linking" them to your program. This process, shown in Figure 1.1, is known as *static linking* because all of the addressing information needed by your program to access the library functions is fixed when the executable file is created, and remains unchanged (static) when the program is running.

Linkers traditionally include entire modules when linking in an executable file, thus functions F2 and F5 in Figure 1.1 are included in the application even though they are not called by module YourApp. Newer compilers and linkers, especially those used by the C++ language, allow inclusion of functions on an individual basis.

Static linking has one minor drawback. Consider the example in Figure 1.2. Imagine you have a function called ShowMessage that displays a message on the screen and requests a user prompt. Say this function is 20K in size and you use it in five different programs.

As Figure 1.2 shows, 80K of disk space is essentially wasted in copies of the same function. If a typical application uses library functions totaling 100K, it is clear that this can quickly add up. Since Windows applications tend to make heavy use of common functionality and function libraries, it is not unusual for applications to use many hundreds of kilobytes of functions and grow into the megabyte range.

Still, it's only disk space. It's almost impossible today to find a disk with a capacity under 500 megabytes, so this really isn't much of a problem.

That is, until you start writing Windows applications. Windows is multitasking, meaning that it is quite possible for all five programs to be running at the same time. Now that 80K of wasted space is tying up scarce memory as well.

Figure 1.1
Static linking

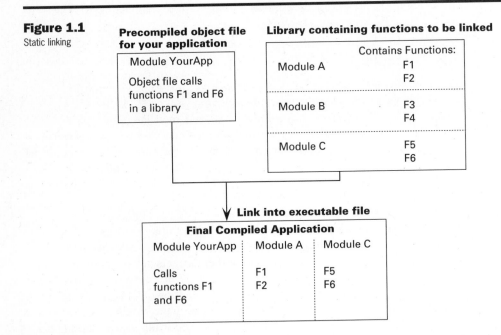

Precompiled object file for your application

Module YourApp

Object file calls functions F1 and F6 in a library

Library containing functions to be linked

	Contains Functions:
Module A	F1
	F2
Module B	F3
	F4
Module C	F5
	F6

↓ **Link into executable file**

Final Compiled Application

| Module YourApp | Module A | Module C |
| Calls functions F1 and F6 | F1 F2 | F5 F6 |

Figure 1.2
Disk space used under static linking

| Program #1 | Program #2 | Program #3 | Program #4 | Program #5 |
| Function ShowMessage 20K | Function ShowMessage 20K | Function ShowMessage 20K | Function ShowMessage 20K | Function ShowMessage 20K |

Total space used by function ShowMessage = 100K

Another problem that arises with Windows is the issue of accessing the underlying system. With DOS applications, a few dozen operating system commands can be accessed through a simple interrupt scheme. Windows has hundreds of commands. Microsoft addressed these problems by implementing a technique called *dynamic linking* which is described in the next section.

Dynamic Linking

With dynamic linking, program modules containing functions are also precompiled into object (.OBJ) files. Instead of grouping them into library files, they are linked into a special form of Windows executable file known as a *dynamic link library* (DLL). When a DLL is created, the programmer specifies which of the functions included should be accessible from other running applications. This is known as *exporting* the function.

When you create a Windows-executable file, the linker scans your program's object files and makes a list of those functions that are not present and the DLL in which they can be found. The process of specifying where each function can be found is known as *importing* the function.

The dynamic linking process is shown in Figure 1.3.

Figure 1.3

Dynamic linking

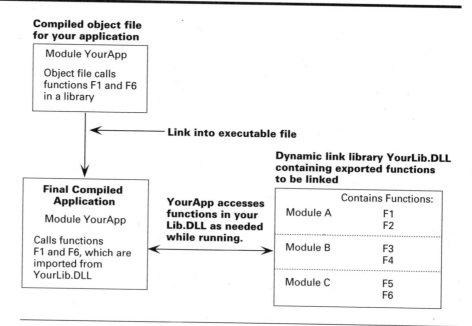

When your application runs, any time it needs a function that is not in the executable file, Windows loads the dynamic link library so that all of its functions become accessible to your application. At that time, the address of each function is resolved and dynamically linked into your application—hence the term *dynamic* linking. Figure 1.4 updates the example shown in Figure 1.2, illustrating how memory is saved by having all applications share the same dynamic link library.

Dynamic link libraries typically have the extension .DLL, but this is not a requirement. Visual Basic custom controls and OLE controls are also DLLs (though they have some special features) and use the extension .VBX or .OCX. Windows device drivers are DLLs and typically have the extension .DRV. Some Windows system DLLs use the standard executable extension .EXE, especially in the 16-bit environments.

Figure 1.4
Disk space used
under dynamic
linking

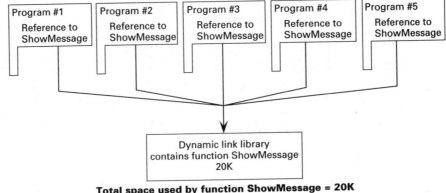

Total space used by function ShowMessage = 20K

Visual Basic and DLLs

Visual Basic provides two mechanisms for programmers to specify import information for a program. The Declare statement tells Windows which DLL contains a desired function and what parameters it expects. You can also add a reference to a Windows API type library which contains the same information. The tradeoffs involved with these two choices is discussed further in Chapter 3.

Visual Basic does not allow you to directly export functions that can be directly called from other applications. DLLs created using Visual Basic expose OLE automation interfaces—not individual functions.

For those situations where you just have to create your own dynamic link libraries that export functions, you will either need a third party tool that adds this capability to Visual Basic (such as Desaware's SpyWorks) or a more traditional development system and language. The most common tool for DLL development at this time is Visual C++ from Microsoft. This is a rapidly changing field, however, and new tools appear frequently, so you may want to do additional research if you choose to take this approach.

Application Programmer's Interface (API)

API is one of those acronyms that seems to be used primarily to intimidate people. An API is simply a set of functions available to an application programmer. The DOS interrupt functions can technically be considered the DOS API. If you write database programs in dBase, the dBase functions you use can be considered the dBase API.

The term is most often used to describe a set of functions that are part of one application but are being accessed by another application. When a Visual Basic program uses OLE Automation to execute an Excel spreadsheet function, you can say that it is accessing the Excel API.

So, the Windows API refers to the set of functions that are part of Windows and are accessible to any Windows application. It is difficult to overstate the significance of this concept. Consider the following example.

Bring up the Windows Program Manager (NT) or Windows Explorer (Windows 95) and invoke the About command from the Help menu. A dialog box will come up showing information about the system, including the amount of physical memory that is free or available.

Obviously there is a method within Windows for determining these values. As it turns out, that function is called GlobalMemoryStatus and is exported by Windows. Thus it is part of the API and is available to any Windows application.

Try the following trivial Visual Basic program:

```
' Create a new project
' In the global module place the following statements:
Type MEMORYSTATUS
    dwLength As Long           ' 32
    dwMemoryLoad As Long       ' percent of memory in use
    dwTotalPhys As Long        ' bytes of physical memory
    dwAvailPhys As Long        ' free physical memory bytes
    dwTotalPageFile As Long    ' bytes of paging file
    dwAvailPageFile As Long    ' free bytes of paging file
    dwTotalVirtual As Long     ' user bytes of address space
    dwAvailVirtual As Long     ' free user bytes
End Type
Declare Sub GlobalMemoryStatus Lib "kernel32" (lpmstMemStat As MEMORYSTATUS)
' In the form_Click event for form1 place the following lines:
Dim ms As MEMORYSTATUS
    ms.dwLength = Len(ms)
    GlobalMemoryStatus ms
    Print "Total physical memory: "; ms.dwTotalPhys
    Print "Available physical memory: "; ms.dwAvailPhys
```

Now run the program. When you click anywhere on the form, it will display the physical memory statistics for the system. Almost every aspect of the Windows environment and the API functions associated with it are accessible from Visual Basic.

The Windows API and Visual Basic

When you consider that the Windows API has literally thousands of functions, it becomes apparent that there is a great deal of capability available.

This may seem overwhelming—after all, learning thousands of functions can be somewhat time-consuming, almost as time-consuming as trying to figure out which ones to use in any given case. Fortunately, there are a number of factors that help bring this down to size. From the point of view of the Visual Basic programmer, the Windows API functions can be divided into four categories:

1. *API functions that correspond to Visual Basic features.* Many API functions are already built into Visual Basic, so there is no need to access them via the Declare statement. These functions will be covered briefly, as they are of little use to the VB programmer.

2. *API functions that cannot be used from Visual Basic.* There are a number of API functions that, for reasons that will become clear later, simply cannot be accessed from Visual Basic. In most cases, this is because they require parameters that are incompatible with VB. In other cases, they implement operations that are necessary for an independent Windows program that VB handles behind the scenes. Most of these will also be mentioned briefly in Appendix E, but will not be covered in any detail.

3. *API functions that are useful for Visual Basic programmers.* Most of these functions will be covered in detail with examples.

4. *API functions that cannot be called directly from Visual Basic, but can be accessed through a simple interface that performs certain parameter conversions or allows access to information that cannot be obtained directly.* The CD-ROM provided with this book includes the dynamic link library APIGID32.DLL (described in Appendix A), which provides support for these functions; thus they will also be covered in detail with examples. As an added bonus, the APIGID32.DLL library also contains a number of extra functions (such as port I/O support) that help fill in some of the few remaining gaps.

The Different Flavors of Windows

Between 1991 and 1995, Visual Basic evolved from version 1.0 to 3.0, and Windows evolved from version 3.0 to 3.11. This period saw a dramatic improvement in features and performance in both Windows and Visual Basic, yet the Windows API itself remained fundamentally the same. True, the number of functions increased as Microsoft added new dynamic link libraries to Windows that extended the capability of the operating system, but the core API remained constant, and you could write your Visual Basic programs to take advantage of the capability provided by the Windows API knowing that your program would run on any Windows system.

In 1995, with the appearance of Visual Basic 4.0, this situation changed. The root of this change lies in this simple, but crucial fact: The Windows API is *not* the same thing as Windows. Or to put it differently: an API is not an operating system. Up until Visual Basic 4.0, Windows programmers did not have to worry about this difference. Windows was essentially a single operating system—from the programmer's point of view the differences between Windows 3.0 and Windows 3.11 were minor. That single operating system had a single API.

Visual Basic 4.0 provides support for three different operating systems: Windows 3.*x*, Windows NT, and Windows 95, and is likely to support additional operating systems soon. As the underlying operating systems have evolved, the Windows API has evolved as well. Instead of a single 16-bit API, there is now a 16-bit Windows API called the "Win16" API, and several variations of a 32-bit API as well.

These changes mean that it is no longer possible to write code for a single operating system and API. As long as you are writing pure Visual Basic code, VB hides most of the differences between environments from you. However, in order to preserve compatibility with older operating systems, it also prevents you from taking advantage of many of the new operating system and API features. Once you start accessing the Windows API, it becomes necessary to consider which operating system and API you intend your program to support. In some cases, you may need to write functions that perform differently depending on the operating environment. Fortunately, Visual Basic 4.0 contains new features to make this possible. Visual Basic 5.0, on the other hand, only supports 32-bit operating systems and thus only accesses the Win32 API.

Table 1.1 lists the versions of the Windows API that work with each of the Microsoft operating systems that are available today.

Table 1.1   **The Windows APIs**

API	Description
Win16	The original Windows 16-bit API. This is the native API for Windows and Windows for Workgroups 3.*x*. It is also supported by Windows 95 and Windows NT in 16-bit mode. You can access this API from the 16-bit editions of Visual Basic (including VB 3.0 and 4.0). Documentation on using this API from Visual Basic can be found in *The Visual Basic Programmer's Guide to the Windows API*—the predecessor to this book.
Win32	The full 32-bit API. This is the native API for Windows NT. You can access this API from any 32-bit edition of Visual Basic or Visual Basic for Applications.

Table 1.1	**The Windows APIs (Continued)**	
	API	**Description**
	Win32c Windows 95	This is a subset of Win32 that is supported by Windows 95 (the "c" stands for the original code name of Windows 95, which was Chicago). You can call any Win32 function under this API, but many of the functions are not implemented—especially those that relate to NT-specific features that are not built into Windows 95. There may be some operating system-specific API functions in Win32c that are not yet incorporated into the latest implementation of Win32 on Windows NT.
	Win32s	This is a smaller subset of Win32 that is supported under Windows and Windows for Workgroups 3.x. It is not supported by Visual Basic 4.0 or 5.0.

This book will focus on the Win32 API and will emphasize those features supported in Win32c, as it seems likely that Windows 95 will become the dominant operating system platform for the foreseeable future. It will not cover Win32s at all, as this API subset is unlikely to see widespread use. You will also learn how to write programs that are compatible with multiple operating systems, including how to write Visual Basic 4.0 programs that can compile successfully on both Win16 and Win32 platforms.

Let me stress once again the importance of the fact that a particular API is NOT the same thing as an operating system. For example, in many cases functions or constants in this book are defined as Windows 95 only. This does not necessarily mean that the function will not work on Windows NT. Win32 is rapidly incorporating many new Windows 95 features and can run the Windows 95 desktop—meaning that many Windows 95-only functions are available in some NT environments.

The Major Windows DLLs

The core functionality of the Win32 API is divided into three major dynamic link libraries and a number of smaller DLLs as shown in Table 1.2.

Table 1.2	**Windows DLLs**	
	DLL Name	**Description**
	KERNEL32.DLL	Low-level operating functions. Memory management, task management, resource handling, and related operations are found here.
	USER32.DLL	Functions relating to Windows management. Messages, menus, cursors, carets, timers, communications, and most other nondisplay functions can be found here.

Table 1.2	Windows DLLs (Continued)	
DLL Name	**Description**	
GDI32.DLL	The Graphics Device Interface library. This DLL contains functions relating to device output. Most drawing, display context, metafile, coordinate, and font functions are in this DLL.	
COMDLG32.DLL LZ32.DLL VERSION.DLL	These DLLs provide additional capabilities including support for common dialogs, file compression, and version control. In some cases the capabilities are accessible directly; in others you will need to use APIGID32.DLL.	
APIGID32.DLL	Provided on the CD-ROM that comes with this book. This DLL provides VB interfaces for some incompatible Windows API functions, plus a few additional utility functions.	

A Universe of Extension Libraries

You have already seen how Windows is made up of several core dynamic link libraries. One of the curious effects of this operating system architecture is that it makes it possible to change Windows incrementally. When Microsoft wanted to add electronic mail capability to the operating system, they did not need to update the entire Windows system, all they had to do was add a new dynamic link library. As it turns out, most of the new features that have appeared in Windows over the past few years have actually taken the form of new DLLs, and with these new DLLs came new extensions to the API. Table 1.3 lists some of the most important extension DLLs and the functionality that they provide.

Table 1.3	Major Extension Libraries	
DLL Name	**Description**	
COMCTL32.DLL	This DLL implements a new set of Windows controls, such as the tree list and rich text edit control. This DLL was initially created for Windows 95, but is now available for Windows NT as well.	
MAPI32.DLL	This DLL provides a set of functions that lets any application work with electronic mail.	
NETAPI32.DLL	This DLL provides a set of API functions for the access and control of networks.	
ODBC32.DLL	This is one of the DLLs that implements ODBC—Open Database Connectivity. These functions provide a standard API that can be used to work with different types of databases.	
WINMM.DLL	This DLL provides access to a system's multimedia capabilities.	

The Windows API (be it Win16 or Win32) is evolving rapidly. The complexity and number of functions are growing so quickly that it is nearly impossible to keep up with them. Fortunately, it is not necessary to become an expert in the entire Windows API to use it effectively. It is important to become acquainted with the general architecture of Windows and the fundamental concepts that make it possible to understand the various API functions. It is also important to learn how to read API documentation and function declarations so that you can create the declarations necessary to access those functions from Visual Basic. The rest of Part 1 tackles these two critical subjects.

The Different Flavors of Visual Basic

Even as Windows was evolving, an interesting thing was happening to Visual Basic itself. You see, Visual Basic actually consists of two separate parts that closely interact. There is the form engine—the part of the language that manages windows and controls and provides a development environment—and the language engine—the part of Visual Basic that compiles the code that you write into a low-level pseudo code, then executes it.

In versions 1.0 through 3.0 of Visual Basic, parts of the language engine were written in assembly language, which provided good performance but made it very unportable and difficult to extend to 32 bits. At the same time, a group at Microsoft was working on a new language engine called "Object Basic," which was designed from scratch to be portable, to support both 16- and 32-bit platforms, and to include support for the new OLE technology. The resulting language engine, now referred to as VBA (Visual Basic for Applications), first saw use in Microsoft Excel, and is gradually spreading to other Microsoft applications. It is becoming, in effect, the "macro" language for Microsoft's applications. This term, however, is misleading—"macro" language suggests that it is limited as compared to a real language, while in reality VBA is a full-featured Basic language.

How full featured? It turns out that VBA is the language engine for Visual Basic 4.0 and above.

Now add to this statement the additional fact that the ability of Visual Basic to call Windows API and DLL functions is part of the VBA language engine, and a rather astonishing truth emerges: Virtually all of the techniques described in this book can be applied not only to Visual Basic, but to every Microsoft tool or application that uses the VBA language engine!

This book will continue to focus on the standalone Visual Basic language due to time and space limitations, but several examples for other Microsoft VBA-based applications can be found in the VBPG32\SAMPLES\VBA directory on the CD-ROM that comes with this book.

2

**Getting a Handle
on Windows**

S A VISUAL BASIC PROGRAMMER, YOU ALREADY HAVE A GOOD UNDER-
standing of how Windows works. As you read this chapter you will
start to acquire the background that will enable you to use the
Win32 API effectively.

Relating Visual Basic to Windows

Visual Basic is more than just a language that runs in the Windows environment. It is closely tied to Windows. Visual Basic features and characteristics
almost always have a close correspondence to a feature or characteristic of
Windows. This chapter takes advantage of these similarities to allow you to
use your knowledge of Visual Basic to understand Windows.

An Overview of Visual Basic

Before discussing Windows itself, it's worth taking a moment to review the architecture of Visual Basic. The point here is not to teach Visual Basic (which
you know already), but to identify some of its key concepts with an eye toward showing the corresponding Windows concepts.

Multitasking

A Visual Basic program can run at the same time as other Visual Basic programs and other Windows applications, a process known as multitasking.
Moreover, unless you specify otherwise, it is possible to run more than one
copy of the same program at one time. For example, if you create a clock program in VB and run it more than once (without closing the previous copy),
you can have more than one clock on the screen running simultaneously.
Each "clock" is considered an instance of the clock program.

Each Visual Basic program or instance owns its own forms, and each
form may contain controls.

Forms and Controls

In Visual Basic, forms and controls are objects that represent a rectangular
area of the screen. A form can contain controls that can be considered "child"
controls. Some controls (like the frame and picture controls) can contain
other controls as children in a similar manner. Each form and control has the
following capabilities:

- *Properties.* Properties reflect attributes of the form or control. Some at-
tributes are simple, like the position of the object or whether it is visible.
Others are more sophisticated and trigger a complex set of operations.
For example, setting the Path property for a directory control causes the
control to be updated based on the path you specified and generates a
Change event.

- *Events*. Each form or control object can generate events. You have the option of attaching program code to these events. The code will be executed each time the event occurs.

- *Methods*. Each form or control object can be acted on by special functions known as methods. For example, the Refresh method causes a form or control to be erased and then redrawn.

System Objects

Visual Basic contains a number of other system objects, for example: Menu, Clipboard, Screen, and Printer objects. Each of these objects allows you to access some underlying capability in Windows. These objects can also have properties and methods associated with them.

An Overview of Windows

Visual Basic really has a very simple and straightforward architecture. You create forms and controls, define their attributes using properties, and write code to handle the various events that occur. Additional code can be written to add functionality (using the command language along with form and control methods) and to work with additional systems objects. Finally, Visual Basic can create an executable file that can run in a multitasking environment.

Now consider the other Windows applications you are acquainted with. They incorporate the following features of the Windows environment.

Multitasking

The earlier definition of multitasking used the clock application as an example. It is possible to not only run different applications at the same time, but multiple instances of those applications that allow it. Every application can have virtually any number of windows.

Windows and Controls

Like Visual Basic's form, a window is an object that represents a rectangular area of the screen. A window can contain other windows known as child windows. Windows have functionality associated with them, which can be defined by the application programmer. Alternatively, the programmer can assign the attributes and functionality of a standard built-in window such as the list box or edit box. Child windows used in dialog boxes typically use one of the standard window definitions or one defined in a DLL, and are usually called *controls*.

A window has the following features:

- *Attributes*. The concept of a window is extremely flexible; thus it is not surprising that a window has many attributes. These vary from attributes related to appearance, such as size, position, and visibility, to functional attributes that define the performance of the window, how it handles keystrokes and mouse events, and so on.

- *Messages*. Every window has associated with it a special function called a Windows function. This function receives messages from a variety of sources, the most important in most cases being event messages from the Windows environment itself.

- *Functionality*. Each window has some underlying functionality. This can be quite sophisticated, as is the case with an edit control, or quite simple as in the case of a window that simply displays text (such as an About box). The functionality of a window can be triggered by external messages through the Windows function, or directly through API function calls.

System and Environment Calls

Windows supports a vast array of underlying system resources and tools. Some are obvious: printer support, menus, and the clipboard come to mind. Some are less known: information functions, drawing tools, memory management, communications, and sound support only begin the list. As important as these features are, most are incidental to understanding the architecture of the Windows operating environment. Once you understand the basic concepts of the system, these features will fall quickly into place.

Translating Visual Basic Concepts to Windows

Visual Basic and Windows are very similar. A Visual Basic form corresponds very closely to a window in Windows. Visual Basic controls correspond closely to Windows controls. Visual Basic properties and events reflect Windows attributes and messages. Visual Basic system objects provide an interface to Windows system capabilities.

In truth, the similarity is far closer than you might expect. Yes, Visual Basic forms correspond to windows, but that's because they *are* windows. Visual Basic controls often contain standard Windows controls. Many VB properties and events correspond on a one-to-one basis with standard Windows attributes and messages.

This correspondence between Visual Basic and Windows is critical, and one of the things that make Visual Basic the powerful tool that it is. Because a VB form is a window, virtually every Windows API function or message can be used with a VB form. When a VB control encapsulates a standard Windows control, virtually every API function or message that accesses the underlying Windows control will also work on the Visual Basic control. As a result, a very large percentage of the hundreds of functions provided by Windows is not only accessible but is also useful to the Visual Basic programmer.

Inside Windows

It is one thing to say that Visual Basic and Windows are similar. Taking advantage of it is something else. Visual Basic provides a very easy-to-use interface. The attributes of a form or control are accessed easily through a limited number of properties. A window actually has a great many attributes beyond those accessible through the standard Visual Basic properties. The API interface to that information is correspondingly more complex.

In the next section we'll look in greater detail at the internal workings of Windows. This will help you better understand both the API and Visual Basic itself.

What Is a Window?

The most important thing to recognize about Windows is this: If it is on the screen, it is in a window. If it is not on the screen, it is probably still in a window. Forms are windows. Controls such as scroll bars, edit controls, list boxes, and buttons are windows. The icons in the Program Manager are windows, as are the ones on your desktop (which are actually two windows—one for the icon, one for the text label!). In fact, the background desktop is also a window.

This leads to an interesting question. How can two objects as different as a scroll bar and an edit control be windows? How does the system differentiate between the two?

To understand this, it is necessary to look at the different types of attributes that a window can have.

Windows Have Class

All Windows belong to a class. When a window is assigned to a class, it is given a set of attributes that define fundamental aspects of its functionality and appearance, as shown in Table 2.1.

Table 2.1   **Class Attributes**

Class Attribute	Description
Class Style	Defines various fundamental attributes of each window in the class. Examples include whether the window can receive double clicks, if it should be automatically redrawn when the window size changes, and others (see Chapter 5).
Class Function	The default Windows function for the class.

Table 2.1   **Class Attributes (Continued)**

Class Attribute	Description
Class and Window Extra Bytes	Class extra bytes are used to hold data that is shared by all windows in a class. Window extra bytes specify extra data area allocated with each window in a class.
Instance	Specifies which instance owns the class. Most classes that you will deal with in Visual Basic belong either to the system or to the Visual Basic runtime library.
Icon	Specifies the default icon that appears on the Windows desktop when a window of this class is minimized.
Cursor	Specifies the default cursor that is used when the mouse is positioned over a window in this class.
Background	Specifies the default background color for windows in this class.
Menu	Specifies the default menu for windows in this class.

Class information is helpful in determining the type of window you are looking at; however, since changing a class attribute changes the characteristics of every window in the class, it has little utility for the Visual Basic programmer.

For example, let's say you change the cursor for a class. You can use API functions to load any cursor or create your own, and set it as the default cursor for a class. Unfortunately, doing so changes the cursor for every window of the class. Since Visual Basic classes are shared by all VB applications, changing the cursor in this manner may affect every application written in Visual Basic that is currently running.

Changes made to a class in this manner affect the current runtime environment only (since the information for a class is kept in memory once loaded). It does not modify any application files. The original class definition will be restored when the class is reloaded after being unloaded from the system (or *registered*, as it is called in Windows). When this occurs depends on whether the class is defined to be specific to one application or shared by the entire system. Application-specific classes are unregistered when the application terminates. Shared classes (also known as *Global* classes) are registered when Windows loads, so you may need to exit Windows to reload a system class that has been modified. It's enough to say that it is a good idea for any application that modifies a class to restore the original state when it terminates. Table 2.2 describes commonly used system classes that are built into Windows.

Table 2.2   **Standard Windows Classes**

Class Name	Description
BUTTON	Used for buttons, option buttons, and check boxes
COMBOBOX	Used for windows that combine an edit control and list box
EDIT	Used for single and multiline edit controls
LISTBOX	Used for single- and multiple-select list boxes
SCROLLBAR	Used for scroll bars
STATIC	Used for windows that display text
MDICLIENT	Used for Multiple Document Interface (MDI) windows

Windows 95 introduced a new set of standard controls, called *common controls*, which significantly extend the set of controls available to Windows programmers. Visual Basic 4.0 introduced a set of OLE controls that encapsulate most of these standard controls and makes them available to Visual Basic programmers. Table 2.3 describes these new classes.

Table 2.3   **Common Control Windows Classes**

Class Name	Description
BUTTONSLISTBOX	A list box that contains buttons.
HOTKEY_CLASS	A control that makes it easy for a user to specify a particular keyboard key combination. This is typically used to specify hot keys.
PROGRESS_CLASS	A control that displays a progress bar. These are typically used during long operations such as software installation.
STATUSCLASSNAME	A control that makes it easy to implement status bars.
RICHEDIT	A rich text format (RTF) edit control.
TOOLBARCLASSNAME	A control that implements toolbars.
TOOLTIPS_CLASS	A control that implements tooltips—those increasingly ubiquitous yellow windows that appear when you leave your cursor over a control for more than a few seconds.
TRACKBARCLASS	A scrollbar-type control that allows the user to set a range of values.

Table 2.3	**Common Control Windows Classes (Continued)**	
	Class Name	**Description**
	UPDOWN_CLASS	Implements an UpDown control, which consists of an up and down arrow along with an edit control that contains a value. Clicking on the arrows increments and decrements the value in the edit control.
	WC_HEADER	A header control—typically used at the top of columns of data to specify column headings.
	WC_LISTVIEW	Implements a ListView control which is a list box that includes text and icons.
	WC_TABCONTROL	This control is used to create tabbed dialog boxes.
	WC_TREEVIEW	Similar to the ListView control, except that entries appear in a hierarchy.

Windows Have Style

Every window has a class defined when the window is created; however, class alone is not enough to define a window. For example, the LISTBOX class includes both single-select and multiple-select list boxes. The EDIT class includes single and multiline edit controls, with and without scroll bars.

Windows uses an attribute called the window style to define the characteristics of a window within a class. The window style is a 32-bit flag that is passed to the Windows operating system during the creation process. Figure 2.1 shows some of the common variations determined by the window Style. A window's style also helps determine its appearance attributes such as border style, presence of a caption and system menu, modality, presence of scroll bars, text alignment, and more.

Chapter 5 goes into detail on how you can examine and in some cases modify the style of Visual Basic forms and controls.

Other Windows Attributes

Windows have a large number of other attributes that can be determined and set by a variety of Windows API calls. Many of these, like position and size, are self-explanatory. A few deserve a closer look.

Parent and Child Relationship

Every window may have a parent window and child windows. This relationship is crucial for managing windows in an application.

Figure 2.1

Common window variations based on class and Style

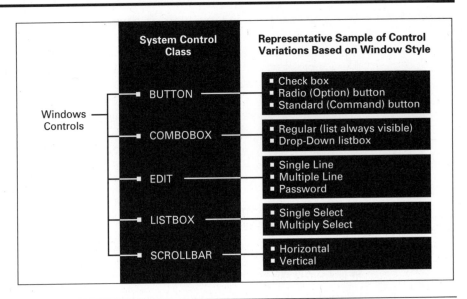

A window without a parent is a top level window. An application typically has a single top level window, which is the main window for the application. When it is minimized, an icon for that window appears on the desktop. It is possible for an application to have several top level windows, though that requires additional effort on the part of the programmer. Visual Basic stand-alone forms and MDI forms are all top level windows, but Visual Basic takes care of any overhead that this requires.

There are two types of windows that have parents. Owned windows may appear anywhere on the screen. The most common type of owned window, the Pop-up window, is frequently used for dialog boxes. Child windows are confined to the display area of the window to which they belong.

When a window has a parent, it is affected by the parent window in a number of ways:

- When a parent window is shown (made visible), all visible child and owned windows are displayed after the parent window.

- When a parent window is hidden, all child and owned windows are hidden.

- When a parent window is destroyed, all child and owned windows are automatically destroyed first.

- When a parent window is moved, child windows are moved with the parent.

Sibling Relationships and the Z-Order

When a parent window is made visible, all of its child windows that are visible are displayed. As long as windows have a parent-child relationship, the order in which windows are displayed is clear. However, in many cases, child windows share the same parent; for example, in Visual Basic all controls drawn directly on a form window have that form as a parent. These windows are called *sibling* windows and are at the same level in the parent-child window hierarchy.

If any of these child windows overlap each other, the order in which they are displayed becomes important. The display order of sibling windows is called the *Z-Order*. This term is derived from the concept of windows appearing in layers stacked up on an imaginary Z axis rising up from the screen as shown in Figure 2.2. A window at the top of the Z-Order is drawn after its sibling windows and thus appears above them if there is any overlap.

The Z-Order can be controlled using Windows API functions and the Visual Basic Z-Order method.

Figure 2.2

Illustration of Z-Order

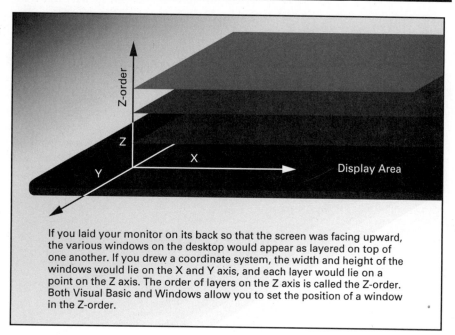

If you laid your monitor on its back so that the screen was facing upward, the various windows on the desktop would appear as layered on top of one another. If you drew a coordinate system, the width and height of the windows would lie on the X and Y axis, and each layer would lie on a point on the Z axis. The order of layers on the Z axis is called the Z-order. Both Visual Basic and Windows allow you to set the position of a window in the Z-order.

Focus

Dozens of individual windows can be on the display screen at a time, but there is only one keyboard. How does Windows know which window or control should receive keyboard input?

Keyboard input can go to only one window at a time. The window receiving keyboard input is considered to have the *input focus*. The way a window indicates focus varies with the type of the window. A button displays a dashed rectangle around the button text and a solid rectangle around the outside edge of the button. An edit control shows a blinking vertical line called a *caret* (which indicates the text insertion point) when it has the focus. Focus is usually shifted with the Tab key, but you can control the focus directly using Windows API calls and Visual Basic methods. There are some significant differences between Win16 and Win32 with regard to input focus and window activation. These are discussed in Chapter 5.

The Windows Function

Every window has a Windows function that processes messages very much like a Visual Basic program contains code to process events. Each Windows message has a message number assigned to it. For example, the message that a window receives when it receives the input focus is the WM_SETFOCUS message, which is assigned number seven. This event corresponds to the Visual Basic GotFocus event.

The Windows function receives four parameters. The first parameter is the window handle, which will be described later in this chapter. The second parameter is the message number. The third and fourth parameters are 32-bit parameters that vary depending on the message. For example, when a window receives the WM_SETFOCUS message, the third parameter contains a handle identifying the window that has just lost the input focus.

Windows functions are usually written in C; however, if it were possible to write a Windows function in Visual Basic, it would look something like this:

```
' Typical Windows Function
Function WindowsProc&(ByVal hwnd&, ByVal message&, ByVal wparam&, ByVal lparam&)
    Select Case message&
        Case WM_PAINT
            ' The window receives this message when it is
            ' time to update the screen.
        Case WM_SETFOCUS
            ' Place code here describing what to do when
            ' the window receives the focus.
        ' Add cases for additional messages as needed
    End Select
    ' Function DefWindowProc& provides a default response
    ' for each Windows message that needs one.
    WindowProc& = DefWindowProc&(hwnd&, message& wparam&, lparam&)
End Function
```

There is one outstanding benefit of this simple message-passing protocol. A Windows function can be called directly by the application programmer, in many cases even if the caller belongs to a different application. This can be

done in Visual Basic via the SendMessage and PostMessage Windows API functions. Part 3 of this book describes this technique in detail.

Superclassing and Visual Basic Controls

Each class provides a default Windows function that is used by every window in the class. However, a window need not use that default function. It is possible for a window to call a user-defined Windows function. This user-defined function can process any messages necessary, and can then call the original default Windows function. This technique is called *subclassing* of a window, because the subclassed window exhibits some of the characteristics of the original class along with those that are newly defined.

When a new class is created it can define a default Windows function from scratch or it can make use of the default function of an existing class. This new class function can handle some messages directly, and pass the rest to the existing class function. This in effect allows creation of a *superclass* of the original class. All windows created in this new class will have a default Windows function that has some of the characteristics of the base class along with whatever functionality was created by the new class function.

There is no limit to this capability. A class can be a superclass of another superclass. Windows of a superclass can in turn be subclassed.

Figure 2.3 illustrates the program flow for a standard control or a window that belongs to a class defined by an application. The window function for each window is set when it is created by taking the default window function for the class and storing it in a separate data structure that belongs to that window. In Figures 2.3 through 2.5, solid lines with arrows indicate program flow, dotted lines with arrows indicate that a value (typically a function address) was copied from one place to another.

Creating a superclass of a standard function is not supported by Visual Basic 4.0, but can theoretically be accomplished using the AddressOf operator in later versions of Visual Basic. It is best implemented in a dynamic link library using tools such as Visual Basic 5.0 or Visual C++ , but Visual Basic itself uses this technique with many of its standard controls. When a superclass is created, as shown in Figure 2.4, the default window function for each window in the new class is loaded from class information provided by the superclass. In the case of Visual Basic, Visual Basic provides a new class window function. However, it still keeps a pointer to the original class window function. When a message arrives at a window, the new class window function will be called—this function is provided by Visual Basic. If Visual Basic does not recognize the message, or does not need to perform any special processing for the message, it will call the original class window function that was provided by Windows. For example, if you send a ListBox message that the Visual Basic list box control does not implement, the message will still be processed by the standard list box window function.

Figure 2.3

Program flow for a
standard window
function

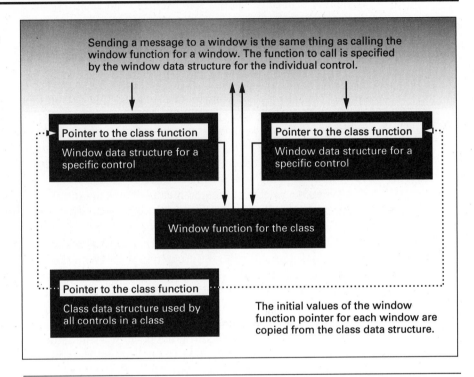

Sending a message to a window is the same thing as calling the
window function for a window. The function to call is specified
by the window data structure for the individual control.

Pointer to the class function
Window data structure for a
specific control

Pointer to the class function
Window data structure for a
specific control

Window function for the class

Pointer to the class function
Class data structure used by
all controls in a class

The initial values of the window
function pointer for each window are
copied from the class data structure.

Consider this simple example that allows you to quickly find a string inside a list control.

```
VERSION 5.00
Begin VB.Form ch02
    Caption         =   "ListBox Search Example"
    ClientHeight    =   6030
    ClientLeft      =   1095
    ClientTop       =   1515
    ClientWidth     =   6720
    Height          =   6435
    Left            =   1035
    LinkTopic       =   "Form1"
    ScaleHeight     =   6030
    ScaleWidth      =   6720
    Top             =   1170
    Width           =   6840
    Begin VB.CommandButton Command2
        Caption         =   "Find String"
        Height          =   495
        Left            =   3360
        TabIndex        =   2
```

Figure 2.4

Program flow for a
superclass window
function

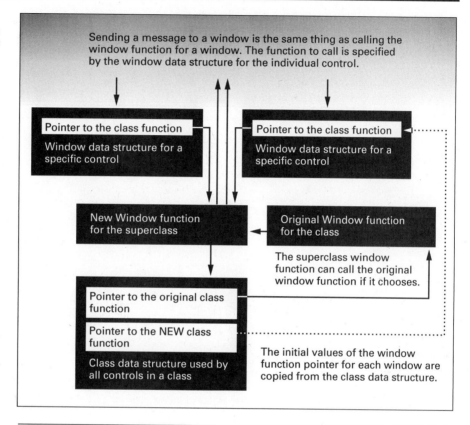

```
    Top              =    1320
    Width            =    1575
End
Begin VB.CommandButton Command1
    Caption          =    "Load List"
    Height           =    495
    Left             =    3360
    TabIndex         =    1
    Top              =    720
    Width            =    1575
End
Begin VB.ListBox List1
    Height           =    2565
    Left             =    360
    TabIndex         =    0
    Top              =    720
    Width            =    2175
End
```

```
End
Attribute VB_Name = "ch02"
Attribute VB_GlobalNameSpace = False
Attribute VB_Creatable = False
Attribute VB_PredeclaredId = True
Attribute VB_Exposed = False
Option Explicit
'
' Fill the listbox with some sample text
'
Sub Command1_Click()
    Dim x%
    For x% = 1 To 500
        List1.AddItem "Listbox entry #" + Str$(x%)
    Next x%
End Sub
'
' This code demonstrates a fast search for a string in
' the list box
'
Sub Command2_Click()
    Dim hw&, t&
    hw& = List1.hWnd      ' Get the window handle for the list box
    t& = SendMessageByString&(hw&, LB_FINDSTRINGEXACT, -1, "Listbox entry # _
    200")
    MsgBox "Listbox entry found at " + Str$(t&)
End Sub
' In a separate module, add the following declarations:
Global Const LB_FINDSTRINGEXACT = &H1A2&
Declare Function SendMessageByString& Lib "user32" Alias "SendMessageA" (ByVal
hWnd As Long, ByVal wMsg As Long, ByVal wParam As Long, ByVal lParam As String)
```

The form for this small sample program contains a list box and two command buttons. Clicking on the Command1 button causes the list box to be loaded with sample data strings. Clicking on the Command2 button causes an API function to be called that searches for a specific string and displays the number of the entry that contains that string.

This example also illustrates one advantage of using Windows messages to work with Visual Basic controls. Searching for a string in a list control using Visual Basic requires a loop similar to the one shown in the listing for the Command1_Click event to fill the list control. This process can be quite slow on list controls with many entries. The message-based technique is extremely fast. The actual example on disk (project CH02.VDP and associated files) includes a routine that performs a set value of random list box searches using a Visual Basic loop and again using the LB_FINDSTRINGEXACT message and compares the relative performance of the two methods. The API-based search typically measured over five times faster than the loop-based algorithm.

Figure 2.5 illustrates a technique called subclassing. With subclassing, the window function for a particular window is replaced with your own window function. You then have the option of processing any incoming messages yourself, or passing them on to the original window function. Subclassing is a powerful technique because not only does it allow you to modify the standard behavior of controls and forms, it lets you respond to messages that are not normally reflected to VB programmers in the form of events. Visual Basic 5.0 and later support subclassing using the AddressOf operator, however it can be difficult to do correctly. Several third party controls, such as Desaware's SpyWorks, provide commercial-quality subclassing solutions.

Table 2.4 shows the class names for the standard VB controls for Visual Basic and known base classes.

Figure 2.5

Program flow for a
subclassed window
function

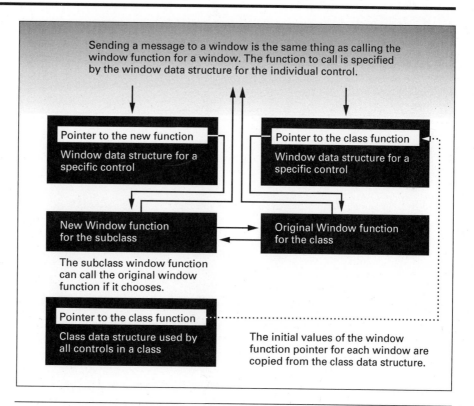

NOTE   *Visual Basic class names shown below are for design time. At runtime VB class names have a prefix depending on the version of Visual Basic, for example: ThunderCheckBox might become ThunderRTCheckBox at runtime. You can use the GetClassName API function described in Chapter 5 to determine the class name for a window.*

Table 2.4   **Visual Basic Class Names**

Control	Class Name	Windows Base Class
Check	ThunderCheckBox	BUTTON
Combo	ThunderComboBox	COMBOBOX
Command	ThunderCommandButton	BUTTON
Dir	ThunderDirListBox	LISTBOX
Drive	ThunderDriveListBox	COMBOBOX
File	ThunderFileListBox	LISTBOX
Form	ThunderForm	—
Frame	ThunderFrame	BUTTON
Label	ThunderLabel	—
List	ThunderListBox	LISTBOX
MDIForm	ThunderMDIForm	—
Option	ThunderOptionButton	BUTTON
Picture	ThunderPictureBox	—
Scroll (Horiz)	ThunderHScrollBar	SCROLLBAR
Scroll (Vert)	ThunderVScrollBar	SCROLLBAR
Text	ThunderTextBox	EDIT
Timer	ThunderTimer	—

The Visual Basic-Windows Connection Revisited

From the above description, it may seem that defining classes and Windows functions is a fairly complex proposition. As a matter of fact, it is. This is why the smallest "Hello World" program written in C can take over a hundred lines of code.

Fortunately, Visual Basic handles all of this overhead for you. Some of these tasks (like creating classes, subclassing, and directly creating windows) cannot easily be accomplished from within Visual Basic, and cannot be done at all with Visual Basic 4.0 and earlier without extensive DLL support. Nevertheless, while the concepts introduced in this chapter will be indispensable when it comes to using the API functions and messages effectively, by and large you will be able to let Visual Basic do its work, adding API functions only as needed.

When Is a Window Not a Window?

Version 2.0 of Visual Basic introduced a new type of control called a *graphical control*. Graphical controls are unique in that they are not actually windows, even though they often act like them. A graphical control is an object defined within Visual Basic itself that defines the characteristics of a part of a form or control. For example, the line graphical control describes how a line should be drawn; the label graphical control describes a block of text.

Graphical controls do not support many of the capabilities of a window; for example, they cannot receive the input focus and so cannot accept keyboard input. However, these limitations are offset by the fact that they require much less overhead than a standard control.

The real catch with this type of control is that since it is not a window, it does not have a window handle—an identifier used by Windows to identify a particular window. This means that, generally, it is not possible to use API functions with graphical controls even though they do have a Windows function. Some OLE Controls also do not have window handles. The APIGID32.DLL library included in this book contains a number of functions that allow you to work with these types of controls.

System Objects

The system objects in Visual Basic (such as the Clipboard, Screen, and Printer objects) have no direct corresponding entity in Windows. These system resources are accessed by API functions and are covered in detail in later chapters.

There is, however, one other area of Windows that deserves some attention as it affects almost everything related to display and drawing operations. That is the subject of graphic output and device contexts.

Graphic Output in Windows

One of the great advantages of Windows over other operating environments is that Windows provides a *graphical user interface* (GUI) to the user. With features such as "point and click" with a mouse, dragging of objects, toolbars, and menus, applications written for GUIs tend to be easier to use and understand than traditional character-based applications.

The Graphical Device Interface

It is possible to write a GUI program that runs directly under DOS without Windows, just as it is possible to incorporate graphics into any DOS program, but this involves considerably more work than doing so under Windows.

Consider the task of drawing a colored line across a screen. Conceptually, the task can be divided into several steps.

1. Figure out the screen resolution (pixel height and width).

2. Determine which pixels are in the line and thus need to be set to the specified color.

3. Set the pixels by accessing the graphics hardware.

Not too difficult—until you consider one problem with the typical DOS system; that is, there is no such thing as a typical DOS system. Unless you are willing to limit yourself to one hardware configuration, your line-drawing program must include hardware support for CGA, EGA, MGA, VGA, SVGA, and untold numbers of ultra-VGAs with color support ranging from monochrome to full 24-bit color.

Of course, there are drawing function libraries that help by providing a general interface to the graphics hardware, but what happens when you want to send your output to a printer? Many printers have their own proprietary command languages. Some printer languages like PCL5 and Postscript can take quite a lot of work to support.

Clearly, writing code that supports every probable output device is unacceptable.

Windows therefore provides a device-independent graphics library called the *Graphical Device Interface* (GDI). GDI provides an intermediate layer between your code and the hardware. It supports a large set of drawing functions and graphical objects along with the ability to determine the characteristics of the device to which you are drawing. It also provides mapping capabilities that allow you to draw using any coordinate system, with GDI performing any scaling or conversion necessary to map your coordinate system to the target device. Above all, Windows provides drivers for literally hundreds of display and print devices, and GDI is able to convert your drawing commands into the language or command stream necessary for each one of them.

Device Contexts

At any given time when you are drawing under Windows, the area being drawn to has a number of specific characteristics. The size of the area available (window size or page size when printing), the color you are using, the background color, and the type of device (display or printer) are just some of these characteristics. They represent the current drawing context. In Windows, this drawing context is described by an object known as a *device context* (DC). A device context that represents a window on the display screen is sometimes referred to as a *display context*.

Figure 2.6 provides a graphical view of the process of drawing under Windows.

A device context describes the characteristics of the current drawing environment for a particular device or window. Table 2.5 describes the more important attributes of a device context.

Figure 2.6

Graphical view of drawing under Windows

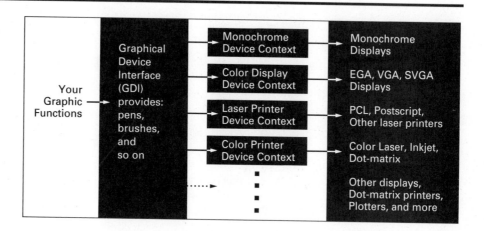

Table 2.5 **Device Context Attributes**

DC Attribute	Description
Background Color	Used for the background of styled lines and hatched brushes, and when converting bitmaps from color to monochrome and vice versa.
Bitmap	A DC may have a bitmap selected into it. This bitmap can then be transferred to another DC or to the device.
Brush	Brushes are used for filling graphic objects.
Clipping	A clipping region specifies the area within the context that can be drawn on.
Coordinate System	The mapping mode (similar to VB scale mode) and coordinate system to use (see Chapter 7).
Font	The font to be used for text output.
Pen	Pens are used for all line drawing. Pens have several attributes including width, color, and style (solid or dashed).
Pen Position	The current location (start point) for drawing operations.
Text Color	Color of text.

All the attributes shown in Table 2.5 are described in detail elsewhere in the book (especially Chapter 7). Windows provides a large set of API functions to get and set device context attributes.

Consider once again the task of drawing a color line—this time under Windows. The steps are as follows:

1. Get a device context to use for drawing to a window.

2. Determine the start position and use a GDI API function to set the start position for the line (function MoveToEx).

3. Set the drawing color by selecting a pen of the desired color into the DC.

4. Call the appropriate GDI API function to draw a line (function LineTo).

Windows takes care of accessing the display hardware regardless of the type of display being used. If the display is monochrome, Windows automatically converts the line to monochrome. If the display cannot handle the exact pen color you requested, Windows chooses the closest color available.

The real power of this technique comes into play when it is time to print. If you have a function that draws a line to the display, the same function can be used to draw a line to a printer. All that is necessary is to use a printer device context in place of the window device context. This works on more complex tasks as well. You can create a subroutine that draws a pie chart that accepts a device context as a parameter. If you pass it a device context for a window, it will draw the pie chart on the window. If you pass it a device context for a printer, it will draw the pie chart on the printer. You can even arrange things so that the function will automatically scale the pie chart based on the area available for drawing.

Visual Basic provides access to device contexts for forms, picture controls, and the Printer object, making it easy to call advanced GDI drawing functions for those objects.

Memory Device Contexts

A special type of device context available under Windows is a memory device context. A memory device context essentially simulates a device in memory. A common use of memory DCs is to prepare images in memory before sending them to a device. A complex image can be prepared and saved in a memory bitmap (a block of memory set aside to hold pixels of image data). Once the image is complete, it can be transferred to a compatible physical device context using an extremely fast BitBlt transfer (BitBlt is short for bit block transfer—a very fast function for copying bitmaps).

A Handle for Every Object

Windows, device contexts, program instances, pens, brushes, bitmaps, cursors—these represent some of the most important objects in the Windows environment. They can all be accessed or used in one way or another via Windows API functions. This means that there must be some way to identify these objects and to pass them as parameters to a function.

Windows identifies each of these objects with a 32-bit integer known as a *handle* (handles were 16-bit integers under Win16). Each handle has a type identifier starting with a lowercase "h", which is typically used when passing the parameter as a function; for example, a window handle is referred to as hWnd, so the definition of a function like SetFocus that accepts a window handle will typically be SetFocus(hWnd). Function definitions and type identifiers will be discussed further in Chapters 3 and 4. Table 2.6 provides a brief summary of the most important handles, their common type identifiers, and their use.

Table 2.6   **Windows Handles**

Object	Identifier	Description
Bitmap	hBitmap	An area in memory that holds image information.
Brush	hBrush	Used during drawing to fill areas.
Cursor	hCursor	A mouse cursor. Up to a 32x32 monochrome image that can be assigned to represent the mouse position.
Device Context	hDC	Device context.
File	hFile	Disk file object.
Font	hFont	Represents a text font.
Icon	hIcon	An icon. Typically a 32x32 color or monochrome image.
Instance	hInstance	Represents an instance of a running Windows application.
Memory	hMem	Refers to a block of memory.
Menu	hMenu	Menu bar or pop-up menu.
Metafile	hMFhMetaFile	An object in which you can record drawing operations for later playback.

Table 2.6	**Windows Handles (Continued)**	

Object	Identifier	Description
Module	hModulehLibModule	Refers to a code module such as a DLL or application module. Often used to access resources within a module such as fonts, icons, cursors, and so on.
Object (Kernel)	hObject	Win32 defines a number of synchronization objects including events, semaphores, and mutexes. Each of these has a corresponding handle.
Palette	hPalette	Color palette.
Pen	hPen	Determines the type of line during drawing.
Process	hProcess	Identifies a single executing process. Win32 also provides Thread objects where a process can run multiple threads of execution at once.
Region	hRgn	An area on the window—usually used to specify clipping (the part of the window on which one can draw).
Window	hWndhDlghCtl	Represents a window on the display. hDlg is sometimes used if the window is a dialog box and hCtl if the window is a control—but they are still window handles and can be used interchangeably.

There are a number of other handles that are used less frequently. These will be described along with the functions that use them elsewhere in this book.

Objects can be created under program control or, in some cases, loaded from existing program modules (application modules or dynamic link libraries). When an object (such as a font, bitmap, or icon) is available to be loaded from a module, it is called a *resource*.

Objects used by the Windows API should not be confused with Visual Basic objects such as forms or controls, or OLE 2.0 objects such as those retrieved by the Visual Basic GetObject command. These objects are manipulated by OLE or by Visual Basic itself and are not part of the core Windows API.

Using Handles

Handles refer to objects that are managed by the Windows environment. As such, you must be cautious when using them. The term object is possibly one of the most overused words in the Windows and Visual Basic vocabulary. Not only are there many different types of objects, but they differ dramatically in how they are used and the types of requirements and restrictions that one must follow when using them. For example: Drawing objects such as pens and brushes are implemented by GDI—not surprising as they relate to graphic

operations. There are certain rules that one must follow when using GDI objects in order to prevent loss of resources available for your application or the system. GDI objects are created and used by individual applications—they cannot be shared (this is a big change from the Win16 API).

Other objects are owned by the *kernel*—the operating system itself. One must follow a completely different set of rules when using them. For example, a File Mapping object can have a name associated with it and can be shared by multiple processes. If you are not careful to delete it, it may remain active even after your application is closed.

For now, though, you don't need to worry about all of these different types of objects. They will be covered as needed in the appropriate chapters later on. The most important thing to keep in mind now is that when it comes to working with the Windows API, all of these objects have handles that identify them, and these handles are all 32-bit long values.

The Next Step

There is a lot more to be said about Windows, but this brief overview should be helpful. In Part 2 you will find in-depth explanations of many of the concepts introduced here along with the API functions and messages that are necessary to put this information to use. With a good understanding of the material covered in this chapter, you should have no trouble deciphering many of the otherwise cryptic API calls.

One more step is needed before diving into the reference material—that is a thorough review of the interface between Visual Basic and Windows (or other dynamic link libraries). Since it is not possible to cover the entire Win32 API and all of the rapidly evolving extension libraries in one book, it is essential that you have a good understanding of how Visual Basic calls DLL or API functions so that you will be able to translate the common C oriented documentation on your own. Chapter 3 covers the theory of the VB to DLL/API interface and introduces the fundamental programming techniques that you will be using. Chapter 4 addresses real-world programming issues such as porting 16-bit applications and allowing 16- and 32-bit code to coexist (under Visual Basic 4.0—version 5.0 and later do not support 16-bit application development). It also includes a number of in-depth examples to help you become comfortable with the process of interpreting API documentation for Visual Basic.

3

The Visual Basic-Windows Interface

HERE ARE TWO APPROACHES TO TAKE IN LEARNING TO CALL DLL FUNC-
tions from Visual Basic. One is simply to look at a set of "boilerplate" definitions for the Windows API and use them as given. This
approach is certainly fast and easy, but can lead to difficulty when
things don't work right, and provides little help in dealing with other dynamic
link libraries.

This chapter will present the second approach by helping you understand
the procedures involved in accessing dynamic link libraries from Visual Basic.
It will begin with an in-depth review of the Visual Basic Declare statement,
followed by an analysis of the parameter-passing conventions, with emphasis
on understanding how Visual Basic data types correspond to those frequently
used in DLLs and how to convert from one to another. Finally, this chapter
will explore what actually happens when a DLL function is called and how
the parameters are passed on the internal Visual Basic stack.

A thorough understanding of the Visual Basic to DLL interface is even
more important for the Win32 API than it was for Win16. Since Win32 is
evolving rapidly, and runs across multiple platforms, you are increasingly
likely to run into API functions that are not covered in this book or other VB-
specific documentation. A good understanding of the mechanism by which
DLL and API calls work will also help you resolve problems that might occur
when porting your 16-bit applications to 32 bits. Finally, you may also need to
work with other dynamic link libraries that have limited documentation available, and whose documentation is limited to the C or C++ language. Fortunately, you only need to know a minimal amount of C or C++ in order to
translate function declarations and constants into Visual Basic. This chapter
focuses on the underlying data types and theory for performing these conversions. Chapter 4 shows how to apply these techniques in real world applications and includes several practical examples.

The Declare Statement

The Visual Basic Declare statement is used to import a DLL function into Visual Basic. It informs VB where a DLL function may be found, and serves to
let Visual Basic know what types of parameters a DLL function expects and
what type of value it returns. Once a DLL function is properly declared, it appears to the VB programmer like any other Basic function or subroutine.

Visual Basic 4.0 and above can also accept function declarations that are
defined in *type libraries*. A type library is a special kind of OLE resource that
can be added to your application via the Visual Basic References menu command. It is likely that third party DLLs will gradually become available with
type libraries. Type libraries have several advantages, the most important of
which is the ability to view the functions and constants defined in the library
using the object browser. They are also quite efficient, taking up little space in

the executable file. They have the disadvantage of not being divisible—when you load a type library all of the functions and constants become available to your program. You cannot modify individual declarations to suit the needs of your application or fix bugs that might exist. As you read further, you will see that there are cases where you will need to change a declaration from the one provided in the declaration file for this book—even when the declaration provided is "correct" for the majority of applications. With the Declare statement, you will typically include in your application only those declarations that are required by your program. This reduces executable size and improves performance.

Finally, the Declare statement is more accessible to Visual Basic programmers—creating a type library requires you to edit an ODL file and use a program called MkTypLib which comes with Visual Basic 5.0 and Visual C++. This book will therefore focus almost entirely on the Declare method of importing API and DLL functions. Further information on creating type libraries for your own DLLs can be found in Chapter 23 (CD-ROM only).

The most important consideration with regard to either method of declaring API or DLL functions is that they be properly declared. The function declaration in Visual Basic must correspond exactly to the DLL function in terms of numbers and types of parameters and the type of value returned. Any errors in this declaration are likely to lead to a fatal exception (or general protection fault), which will, at the very least, cause you to lose all work done in your Visual Basic project since it was last saved.

The syntax for the Visual Basic Declare statement is as follows for subroutines that do not return a value:

```
[Public | Private] Declare Sub globalname Lib libname$ [Alias aliasname$]
[(argument list)]
```

For functions that return a value it is:

```
[Public | Private] Declare Function globalname Lib libname$ [Alias aliasname$]
[(argument list)]
```

In the Declare statement, *globalname* is the name of the function as it will be called from your Visual Basic program. In most cases, this is also the name by which the function is identified in the dynamic link library itself, though, as you will see, this is not always the case. If you are defining a function, you should append a type specifier to the name (for example, *globalname%*, *globalname&*, and so forth) to indicate the type of value returned by the function. Alternatively, you can add the *AS typename* specifier to the end of the function declaration, where *typename* is one of Byte, Boolean, Integer, Long, Single, Double, Currency, Date, String, Object, Variant, a user-defined type, or an object type. In most cases, this book uses the type specifier character appended to the variable name to specify type. This tends to encourage stronger typing throughout the program, improves clarity, and keeps lines shorter (which can be an issue for some of the longer DLL declarations).

libname$ is the name of the dynamic link library that contains the function and specifies to Visual Basic where to look for that function. This is a string type and thus must be enclosed in quotes. The name must include the file extension of the DLL unless it is one of the three Windows DLLs USER32, kERNEL32, or GDI32, in which case no extension is needed.

These two examples illustrate use of the *globalname* and *libname* parameters:

```
Declare Function agGetInstance& Lib "apigid32.dll"()
Declare Function GetVersion& Lib "kernel32" ()
```

Unicode, ANSI, and Aliases

The next part of the Declare statement is the Alias term. This option allows you to identify a Windows API or DLL function by a different name within your Visual Basic application. In the Win16 API, this served primarily to allow access to functions whose names were not valid in Visual Basic. For example, the lOpen function has a leading underscore, which is legal in C, but not permitted for Visual Basic function names. Also, there are a few Windows API functions such as SetFocus and GetObject which are keywords in Visual Basic. Aliasing is used to define a new function name that VB can use to identify functions whose names would conflict with reserved commands or function names. These cases, fortunately, were few and far between. Even if you include other uses of Alias to promote type safe declarations (more on this later), only a small fraction of API function declarations under Win16 used the Alias command. With Win32, this is no longer the case.

One of the most significant differences between the Win32 API and the Win16 API relates to the way that functions dealing with text strings are identified. The Win32 API supports three different types of character sets. The first two are the single-byte and double-byte character sets. In a single-byte character set, each text character is represented by one byte; thus, the system can support up to 256 characters. In a double-byte character set (DBCS), some byte values are reserved as DBCS "lead bytes" which indicate that the byte that follows should be combined to form a single character. This allows the character set to support over 256 characters—which is crucial for languages such as Japanese which have hundreds of characters. The Win16 API supports both single- and double-byte character sets.

The third type of character set is actually just one character set called Unicode. It is a wide character set, meaning that each character is represented by a 16-bit integer. Unicode can have up to 65,535 characters, enough to support all of the characters in all of the languages in use today. The impact of Unicode support on using the Win32 API is far-reaching and will be covered further in this chapter and throughout the rest of the book.

To start with, every Win32 API function that uses text must have a way to determine if that text is in DBCS or Unicode format. This poses an interesting challenge. One solution might have been to create a new standard string format that somehow included a character set identifier, but this would have required substantial changes to languages and applications in order to create programs that would run on Win32. Microsoft could also have added a new parameter to each function that used strings to identify the character set, but this would have impacted performance and once again posed a compatibility nightmare. Instead, they chose to provide two separate functions for each API function that uses strings. For example, the GetWindowText API function actually exists in two forms: GetWindowTextA and GetWindowTextW, where the A suffix signifies ANSI (the default single-byte character set) and the W suffix signifies "wide" for the Unicode character set. Not every Win32 implementation defines both functions. Windows NT uses Unicode internally, thus if you call the GetWindowTextA API function, Windows actually calls GetWindowTextW and converts the resulting string into ANSI before returning. Windows 95 does not support Unicode at all—calling GetWindowTextW will lead to an error. Visual Basic always uses the ANSI version of the API. Visual Basic uses Unicode internally, but always converts strings into ANSI before using them as parameters to API or DLL functions defined using the Declare statement, so this book will focus exclusively on the ANSI function declarations. It is possible to access the Unicode functions from Visual Basic, but only if you reference them using a type library.

Under the Hood—Visual Basic, ANSI, and Unicode

The information in this section is intended to help you gain a better understanding of how and why Visual Basic works the way it does with regard to the ANSI and Unicode character sets. You don't really need this information in order to proceed, so feel free to skip this section if you wish.

Figure 3.1 illustrates the process that a text string goes through when it is passed as a parameter to a Win32 API function or DLL. Keep in mind that this information only applies to Win32 and the 32-bit version of Visual Basic. Before passing a string to a DLL, Visual Basic converts the string to ANSI in the current environment. Whether this will be a single-byte or double-byte (DBCS) character set depends on the locale. If you are running U.S. standard Windows, it will be a single-byte character set. If you are on Japanese Windows it will be a double-byte character set. In either case it will not be Unicode.

Since the string is ANSI, you should always specify the ANSI API function. Under Windows NT, in most cases all this function will do is convert the string back to Unicode and call the Unicode version of the function. This is necessary

Figure 3.1

Internal string conversions for Windows NT and Windows 95

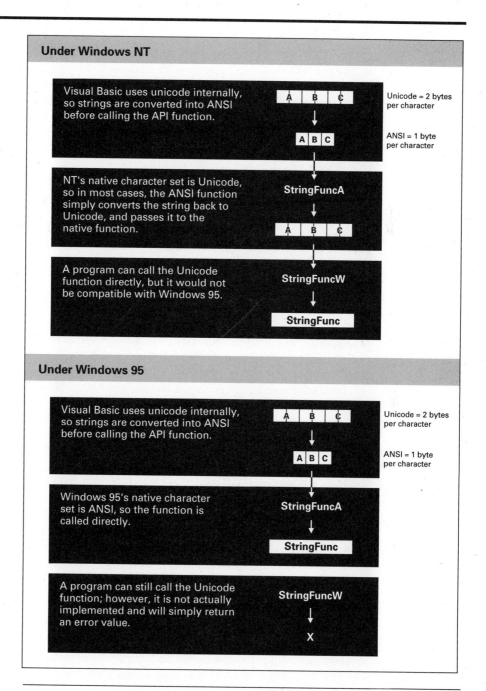

because Unicode is the native character set for Windows NT. Under Windows 95, the ANSI function will execute directly as the Unicode version is not implemented. On return, this process is reversed for each string, so it is possible for the API or DLL function to modify the contents of the string parameter.

Figure 3.1 raises some interesting questions. Isn't it inefficient to perform all of these conversions under Windows NT? Why does Visual Basic use Unicode internally? After all, if it used ANSI at least it could avoid conversions under Windows 95. And why doesn't Windows 95 implement Unicode?

The answers to these questions can be determined both from published Microsoft technical information and some astute guesswork. The choice of Unicode for Windows NT was reasonable—Windows NT is a large operating system that is intended to run on machines with lots of available memory. It was written from scratch with Unicode in mind, so there was no need to convert existing code. Unicode solves many of the problems of dealing with multiple code pages that made internationalization of software difficult. By providing ANSI entry points as well, the developers of Windows NT ensured compatibility with current applications and provided developers with a choice of which character set to use. Windows 95, on the other hand, was designed to run on smaller systems. Because Unicode effectively doubles the length of every string, it substantially increases the amount of memory needed by both the applications and operating systems that use it. Windows 95 also uses a great deal of existing 16-bit code that was written for the ANSI character set; conversion to Unicode would have increased the scope of the project considerably.

Given the operating systems, it is clear why Visual Basic uses ANSI to call API functions; it is necessary in order to work correctly on Windows 95. You actually can call the Unicode versions of API functions under Windows NT and perform the conversion yourself, if you wish, or use a type library to bypass the conversions entirely. It is less clear why Visual Basic uses Unicode internally. One reason is that the 32-bit VBA language engine was also written from scratch with Unicode in mind, and that good international support was an important criterion in its development. Another reason is that VBA makes heavy use of the capabilities of OLE 2.0, and the OLE 2.0 API is also implemented in Unicode. It is likely that the performance benefits of using Unicode within Visual Basic more than offsets the penalties associated with string format conversions during API calls.

Accessing the Right Function

The existence of two separate function names for each function poses some problems. Let's say you wanted to retrieve the caption of a window. Under Win16 you would call GetWindowText. Under Win32 you would call GetWindowTextA or GetWindowTextW depending on the character set you wanted to use. Clearly it would be extremely difficult to use the same source code on multiple platforms. In order to avoid this problem, it is advisable to use the standard Windows API name, while having Visual Basic somehow know that it must call the real API name. The Alias *aliasname$* option in the Declare statement is used when you wish the function to be called in Visual Basic by a name other than the one defined in the dynamic link library. Here is the declaration for the GetWindowText function:

```
Declare Function GetWindowText Lib "user32" Alias "GetWindowTextA" (ByVal hWnd _
As Long, ByVal lpString As String, ByVal aint As Long) As Long
```

When you call GetWindowText in your Visual Basic program, Visual Basic will actually call the GetWindowTextA function in the user32 DLL. You could specify GetWindowTextW as an alias, or leave out the alias entirely. This means that even if you use the GetWindowText function hundreds of times in your program, you would only need to change the declaration once in order to find the correct function on any operating system. Keep in mind, though, that changing the function name is not all that is involved in converting code between platforms—more on this later in this chapter and in Chapter 4. Aliasing can also be used to provide improved type checking for DLL functions that can accept parameters that reflect multiple types. This will be described later in this chapter.

One important final note: Under the Win32 API, function names within DLLs or the Windows API are case sensitive. This is a change from Win16. Be sure the capitalization in the declaration is correct.

API Call Results

Almost every Win32 API function returns a result. In many cases the result provides information that you requested; for example, the GetFocus function returns a window handle. In many other cases the result tells you whether or not the function succeeded. In most cases a nonzero result (TRUE) indicates success and a zero result (FALSE) indicates failure. Note that the Win32 definition of TRUE (nonzero) does not match the Visual Basic definition (−1). This means that you must compare the result to zero explicitly when testing the result of API functions. This issue is discussed further later in this chapter in the section on working with unsigned 32-bit integers.

When a Win32 API function fails, you can often obtain additional error information using the GetLastError API function which is accessed in Visual Basic by using the LastDLLError property of the Err object. This function is explained further in Chapter 6. Note that the result of GetLastError for some operating systems is not reset when a function succeeds. In other words, you should only call it if the result of an API call indicates that an error occurred. A few functions set an error value even on success to provide additional information. These cases are described in the documentation for the individual functions.

DLL Parameters

In order to understand how to create argument lists for dynamic link libraries, it is necessary to first examine the types of function parameters that DLLs may use. Since dynamic link libraries are typically written in C, they can use a wide variety of parameters that are not supported directly by Visual Basic. The choice of appropriate Visual Basic variable types is not always obvious and an incorrect choice can lead to a fatal exception or runtime error.

Argument Lists

An argument list is a list of dummy parameter names indicating the parameters that are passed to the function. The terms *argument* and *parameter* both have the same meaning in this context. Visual Basic tends to use the term argument in its documentation, while Windows uses parameter. This book follows the Windows convention.

The "dummy" variable names in a parameter list are merely placeholders—they have no significance outside of the declaration. This means that if you define a parameter list like this:

```
ByVal dummy1&, ByVal dummy2&
```

dummy1& and *dummy2&* are not significant outside of this line, nor will they conflict with other variables of the same name elsewhere in the program.

Call by Reference versus Call by Value (Numeric Parameters)

The default calling convention for Visual Basic is *call by reference*. This means that Visual Basic passes to the DLL a pointer to the argument variable itself. The DLL can modify the actual parameter because it has a pointer indicating where in memory the parameter is located.

Call by value is a calling convention in which a copy of the parameter value is passed to the DLL. This is specified for numeric data types by preceding the parameter with the word ByVal. Figure 3.2 illustrates the differences between these calling conventions.

Calling Conventions for String Parameters

Visual Basic is somewhat inconsistent in the use of ByVal with string variables.

There are two types of strings supported in the interface between Visual Basic and the DLL interface. If the ByVal keyword is absent, Visual Basic will pass to the DLL function a pointer to an OLE 2.0 string (known as the BSTR data type). This type of string is not generally used by Windows API functions except for those that are part of the OLE 2.0 API. They may also be supported by other dynamic link libraries.

Figure 3.2

Call by value versus
call by reference

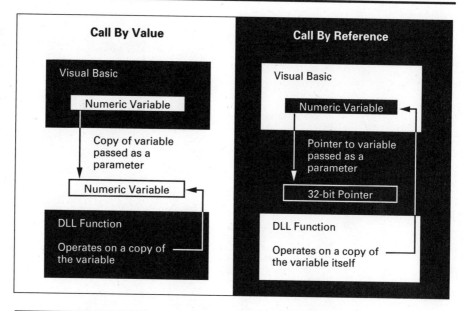

Windows API functions expect string parameters to be passed as a pointer to a *NULL terminated string*, that is, a string of characters, where the end of the string is identified by a character with the ASCII value of 0. This is the string format used by the C programming language. When the ByVal keyword is used with a string parameter, Visual Basic converts the string into C language format by adding a NULL termination character. Because the parameter is a pointer, the DLL is capable of modifying the string even though the ByVal keyword is specified. Figure 3.3 shows the differences between the two string calling conventions.

In some cases, a DLL function is designed to load data into a string that is passed as a parameter. It is critical that the Visual Basic string variable be pre-assigned a string length long enough to hold the data before it is passed as a parameter to the DLL function. This can be done by using a fixed length string, or by setting the string length using the String$ function. Additional issues relating to string parameters will be covered later in this chapter.

The calling convention specified in the Declare statement must match that expected by the DLL function (this applies to both numeric and string data types). The most common cause of fatal exceptions or "bad DLL calling convention" errors is the failure to include the ByVal keyword when it is needed, or failure to omit it when omission is necessary. How to determine if a DLL expects a parameter to be called by value or by reference will be discussed later in this chapter.

Figure 3.3

Calling conventions
for string parameters

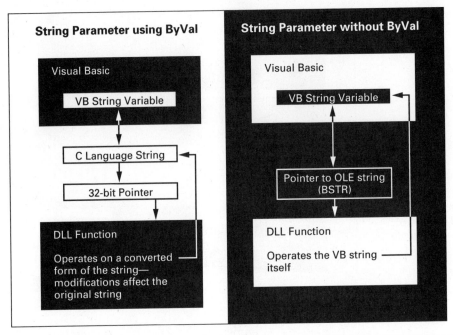

DLL Parameter Types and Notation

Table 3.1 lists parameter types that are available to DLLs created using the C or C++ programming language. Some understanding of these data types and the notation used to describe them is an essential first step in learning how to convert typical C or C++ declarations and documentation into Visual Basic. The type listed indicates the C language data type—information that is frequently provided as part of the documentation for DLL functions. The data type is also used in the C language declarations for DLL functions. The Prefix column lists the prefix that is added to variable names when using "Hungarian Notation" (more on this later). This table shows both the Win32 and Win16 data types. This will help clarify the process of writing code that will run on both platforms—a subject for Chapter 4.

Keep in mind that the most significant difference between Win16 and Win32 is that under Win16 an integer is 16 bits, and under Win32 it is 32 bits. Also remember that this difference applies only to the Windows API—the integer data type within Visual Basic is always 16 bits.

The LPSTR (string) type is also listed under Win32 as LPCSTR, LPCT-STR, and LPTSTR. The "C" qualifier indicates that the string is a constant, meaning that it will not be modified by the called function. The "T" qualifier

Table 3.1   **C/C++ Data Types Commonly Used in DLLs**

Type	Prefix	Description (Win32)	Description (Win16)
BOOL	b	32-bit Boolean value—zero is FALSE, all other values TRUE	16-bit Boolean value
BYTE	ch	Eight-bit unsigned integer	Eight-bit unsigned integer
char	ch	Eight-bit signed integer	Eight-bit signed integer
TCHAR	ch	Eight- or 16-bit signed integer, depending on whether using ANSI or Unicode	Eight-bit signed integer
FARPROC	lpfn	32-bit (far) pointer to a function or procedure	32-bit (far) pointer to a function or procedure
HANDLE	h	Handle to a Windows object—a 32-bit unsigned integer	Handle to a Windows object—a 16-bit unsigned integer
int	n	32-bit signed integer	16-bit signed integer
short	n	16-bit signed integer	16-bit signed integer
long	l	32-bit signed integer (VB Long integer)	32-bit signed integer (VB Long integer)
LP....	lp	32-bit (Long) pointer to a structure or other data item	32-bit (Long) pointer to a structure or other data item
LPINT	lpi	32-bit (Long) pointer to a 32-bit signed integer	32-bit (Long) pointer to a 16-bit signed integer
LPSTR LPCSTR LPTSTR	lpsz	32-bit (Long) pointer to a C type NULL terminated string (see note below regarding T and C qualifiers)	32-bit (Long) pointer to a C type NULL terminated string
NP....	p	Not applicable	16-bit (Near) pointer to a structure or other data item
NPSTR	np	Not applicable	16-bit (Near) pointer to a C type NULL terminated string
unsigned int, UINT	n	32-bit unsigned integer	16-bit unsigned integer
unsigned short, WORD	w	16-bit unsigned integer	16-bit unsigned integer

Table 3.1   **C/C++ Data Types Commonly Used in DLLs (Continued)**

Type	Prefix	Description (Win32)	Description (Win16)
unsigned long, DWORD	dw	32-bit unsigned integer—also referred to as a "double word"	32-bit unsigned integer—also referred to as a "double word"
flags	f	Indicates a flag bit within a 16- or 32-bit variable	Indicates a flag bit within a 16- or 32-bit variable
LPUNKNOWN		A 32-bit pointer to an IUnknown OLE 2.0 interface	A 32-bit pointer to an IUnknown OLE 2.0 interface

is used to indicate that the string may be either ANSI or Unicode, depending on whether the ANSI or Unicode entry point for the function is called. As far as Visual Basic is concerned, you can simply ignore both of these qualifiers.

Hungarian Notation

Table 3.1 includes a column for the Hungarian notation prefix for each variable type. This type of notation is used extensively in most Windows and DLL documentation to help make variables self-documenting. For example, if you have a variable named Visible which is a Boolean, it will typically be named bVisible. This way a programmer can tell at a glance that Visible is a 16-bit variable that can take on a TRUE or FALSE value.

Many Visual Basic programmers have adopted the Hungarian Notation style over the traditional Basic typing, which consists of adding a special character after the variable name (for example, "%" indicates an integer, "&" indicates a long, "$" indicates a string, and so forth). You will find that the code samples in this book tend to use the traditional Basic type characters instead of Hungarian notation. This choice is not meant to discourage you from using Hungarian notation or to suggest that the Basic method is superior—each has its advantages. The main reason that I prefer to use the Basic type characters is that while Hungarian notation is better in terms of being self-documenting, the Basic type characters have semantic meaning to the compiler. For example, if you have a function declaration that accepts any type of parameter (ByVal As Any), the variable will be passed in its current type to the function. Let's say the function in this case requires an integer parameter. As long as you have correctly dimensioned the parameter as an integer, there will be no problems; but what happens if you accidentally declared it as a long, or forgot to add a type to the Dim statement (in which case it will default to a variant). With the Hungarian notation approach, you would use variable nMyVariable to the function. The compiler considers the "n" prefix to be part of the name, so an invalid parameter is passed to the function. If, however, you had used

MyVariable% as a parameter, the compiler detects an error and reports this as an attempt to redeclare a variable. I have run into this problem often enough to justify staying with the Basic notation; however, there is nothing to prevent you from using both if you choose.

The exception to this usage are variables that are intended to change types based on a conditional compilation—for example, a variable that is an integer for 16-bit compilations and a long for 32-bit compilations. In this case, the type character would cause a conflict in one environment or the other.

Introduction to Parameter Types

The remainder of this section reviews interface techniques for each of the various parameter types. Each type will be described along with a C sample, followed by the common Visual Basic parameter declaration for that type. The final section in this chapter contains a more advanced technical discussion of exactly what happens when parameters are passed to dynamic link libraries. This theoretical discussion is not necessary for using the Windows API effectively or understanding the rest of this book; however, the information provided there should make it easier to track down bugs in your programs that use API or DLL calls. You may also find it advantageous to read through the interface techniques for each parameter type a second time after reading the theoretical discussion.

Eight-Bit Numeric Parameters

The eight-bit numeric parameters include the char, uchar, and BYTE parameter types. These are all 8-bit data types that are called by value. Thus the Visual Basic parameter for this type will usually be (ByVal param As Byte).

C Declaration	VB Parameter (Win32)	VB Parameter (Win16)
char chMyChar	ByVal chMyChar As Byte	ByVal chMyChar As Byte
BYTE chMyByte	ByVal chMyByte As Byte	ByVal chMyByte As Byte

Eight-bit signed numbers can range from –128 to 127. Eight-bit unsigned integers can range from 0 to 255. The Visual Basic Byte data type is always unsigned. In most cases when working with bytes, you will be dealing with unsigned information, so VB's lack of support for signed bytes will not be an issue. This is especially true when you consider that the Windows API itself rarely uses 8-bit data types. In the unlikely event that you need to convert to and from 8-bit signed values, you can apply the conversion techniques described later in this chapter for use with unsigned integers, only use the value

&H100 instead of &H10000&, &H0ff instead of &H0ffff&, and perform the conversions either using integers or longs instead of just longs.

Note that if you are writing code that you wish to remain compatible with Visual Basic 3.0, you may use the VB Integer data type instead of the Byte data type. Refer to the Visual Basic Programmer's Guide to the Windows API (16-bit edition) for further information.

16-Bit Numeric Parameters

The 16-bit numeric parameters include the following DLL parameter types: short, unsigned short, and WORD. These are all 16-bit data types that are called by value. Thus the Visual Basic parameter for this type will usually be (ByVal param As Integer) or (ByVal paramname%)

C Declaration	VB Parameter (Win32)	VB Parameter (Win16)
short nMyShort	ByVal nMyShort As Integer	ByVal nMyShort As Integer
WORD wMyWord	ByVal wMyWord As Integer	ByVal wMyWord As Integer

16-Bit Signed Numeric Parameters

The signed short data type is one of the easiest data types to handle from Visual Basic. The Visual Basic integer data type works perfectly.

16-Bit Unsigned Numeric Parameters

The Visual Basic signed integer has a range of –32768 to 32767. An unsigned 16-bit number (unsigned short, WORD) has a range of 0 to 65535. Converting to and from signed variables can be accomplished as follows: To pass an unsigned 16-bit integer value from 32768 to 65535 to a DLL that expects an unsigned value, use a signed long value from 32768 to 65535, inclusive. (The value is likely to be in a long, anyway, as Visual Basic cannot handle this range of values in the Integer data type.) Subtract 65536 from the value (hex value &h10000&). The result is a negative number that corresponds to the required unsigned value.

```
SignedEquivalent%= cint(UnsignedNumber&-&h10000&)
```

The trick here is this: The DLL function expects an unsigned 16-bit value. Even though Visual Basic interprets SignedEquivalent% as a negative number, the function will interpret the same 16 bits as a positive number in the 32768 to 65535 range.

The same situation exists in reverse when a DLL function returns an unsigned value. The 16 bits returned will be interpreted by Visual Basic as a negative number. When using a function that can return 16-bit unsigned values greater than 32767, the integer returned should be loaded into a long integer using the following equation:

```
LongResult& = (Clng(IntegerResult%) and &h0ffff&)
```

In this case the negative number is first converted into a Long via the Clng function. This results in a long negative number. The value is then masked to remove the high 16 bits. The result is a positive 16-bit number in a long variable.

32-Bit Numeric Parameters

The 32-bit numeric parameters include the following DLL parameter types: int, unsigned int, long, unsigned long, BOOL, and DWORD. These are all 32-bit data types that are called by value. Thus the Visual Basic parameter for this type will always be (ByVal param As Long) or (ByVal paramname&)

C Declaration	VB Parameter (Win32)	VB Parameter (Win16)
int nMyInt	ByVal nMyInt As Long	ByVal nMyInt As Integer
UINT wMyUInt	ByVal nMyUInt As Long	ByVal nMyUInt As Integer
BOOL bMyBool	ByVal nMyBool As Long	ByVal nMyBool As Integer
DWORD dwMyDWord	ByVal dwMyDWord As Long	ByVal dwMyDWord As Long
LONG lMyLong	ByVal lMyLong As Long	ByVal lMyLong As Long

Note that those C variable types that are based on the C integer data type are declared differently for Win32 and Win16. These include integers, unsigned integers, and Booleans. The LONG and DWORD data types are based on the C long data type, which is 32 bits under both environments.

32-Bit Signed Integers

The Visual Basic Long data type is fully compatible with this data type and can be used directly without conversion both as a parameter and as a function return value.

32-Bit Unsigned Integers

A 32-bit signed integer has a range of –2,147,483,648 to 2,147,483,647 whereas a 32-bit unsigned integer has a range of 0 to 4,294,967,295. In the unlikely event that you need to perform an unsigned to signed conversion in the range 2,147,483,647 to 4,294,967,295, use the same technique as that shown for 16-bit values, but use the Currency or Double data type to hold the intermediate values. The single precision type does not provide enough precision.

Booleans

Both Visual Basic and C define a Boolean FALSE as zero, and all nonzero values as TRUE. It is important to note, however, that in C programming the value for TRUE is typically 1, whereas in Visual Basic the value of TRUE is typically –1. This difference can lead to confusion in cases where a programmer makes assumptions about the value of the TRUE condition. For example, to determine if a window is visible using the IsWindowVisible() API, use:

```
If IsWindowVisible(hWnd%) then .... '
or
If IsWindowVisible(hWnd%)<>Ø then .... '
```

The following won't work:

```
If IsWindowVisible(hWnd%) = -1 then ....
or
If Not IsWindowVisible(hWnd%) then
```

The latter examples may not work because Windows does not specify that IsWindowVisible will return –1 when a window is visible, only that the result will be nonzero. If IsWindowVisible returns the value 1, you have the incredible situation in Visual Basic where:

```
if IsWindowVisible And (Not IsWindowVisible) Then
   ' This code will execute!!!  The condition is TRUE
```

For those who are curious, the reason this difference exists relates to differences between the C and C++ languages and Visual Basic. C and C++ include both logical and Boolean operations. Consider the NOT operation (used to determine if something is NOT TRUE). The logical NOT operation in C is indicated by the "~" symbol in front of a variable name. The Boolean Not operation is indicated by the "!" symbol.

~1 is &HFFFE—both values that are nonzero and logically TRUE.

But !1 is 0, and !&HFFFF is 0 as well. Since logical operations would always be used on results, it does not matter what the value of TRUE is, as long as it is nonzero.

Visual Basic does not have a Boolean operator. The only way for NOT TRUE to be FALSE is if TRUE is always –1 and FALSE is always 0. Purists might argue that this means that all values other than 0 and –1 are undefined with regard to Boolean operations (since it becomes possible for NOT TRUE

to be TRUE—a Boolean impossibility). Pragmatists such as I will be satisfied with a warning: Be careful how you use Boolean results from API functions.

Currency Parameters

The Windows API does not use the Visual Basic Currency data type. Any dynamic link libraries that use this data type should pose no conversion problems (assuming they work correctly). Treat Currency as any other numeric type.

Floating-Point Parameters

The core Windows API does not use floating-point variables (this fact is surprising to many). Any dynamic link libraries that use the Single (Float) or Double data type can be converted easily, assuming the DLLs work correctly. In general, you may treat singles and doubles as any other numeric type.

C Declaration	VB Parameter (Win32)	VB Parameter (Win16)
float MyFloat	ByVal MyFloat As Single	ByVal MyFloat As Single
double MyDouble	ByVal MyDouble As Double	ByVal MyDouble As Double

There are, however, two areas where caution may be needed. First, be careful that your Declare statement matches the DLL function parameters and return type correctly—Single and Double are *not* interchangeable.

Second, be sure that the DLL you are using is compatible with Visual Basic in terms of floating-point calling conventions. There are two issues to be concerned with relating to the floating-point calling convention. First, the compiler must use the IEEE floating-point standard. Second, the compiler must use the Microsoft calling convention for floating-point numbers. Microsoft languages pass floating-point values using CPU registers for singles, and by passing a pointer to a temporary area on the stack for doubles. Some other compilers pass floating-point numbers using coprocessor registers. These are not compatible with Visual Basic.

Variants

The core Windows API does not use the Visual Basic Variant data type. The Visual Basic variant data type is, however, compatible with the OLE 2.0 variant type. Any dynamic link library that is specifically designed to use OLE 2.0 variants should pose no conversion problem.

C Declaration	VB Parameter (Win32)	VB Parameter (Win16)
VARIANT MyVar	ByVal MyVar As VARIANT	ByVal MyVar As VARIANT
VARIANTARG MyVar	ByVal MyVar As VARIANT	ByVal MyVar As VARIANT

One caveat here: The Variant data type supported under Visual Basic 3.0 is *not* compatible with the OLE 2.0 variants used by Visual Basic 4.0 and later. This change should have no affect on most people; however, if you are still using VB 3.0 and attempt to call a DLL that expects OLE 2.0 variants, or are using DLLs that support Variants that were written specifically for VB 3.0, you may run into incompatibilities.

Handles (Windows Objects)

The term "object" is perhaps one of the most overused words when it comes to programming Visual Basic and Windows. The problem is that *object* means so many things, and it is sometimes difficult to distinguish between the different types of objects and where they are used. Throughout the course of this book you will be introduced to many of the objects that are used by Windows and that can be manipulated using the Windows API. These objects are identified by a 32-bit number called a *handle*. These objects should not be confused with Visual Basic objects such as forms and controls. Visual Basic objects may or may not have a windows object handle associated with them that has meaning to Windows.

Since Windows object handles are all 32 bits long, the Visual Basic Long data type is used when passing handles as parameters. The following table shows a few of the common Windows API object types. As you can see, handles are another case where declarations differ between Win32 and Win16.

C Declaration	VB Parameter (Win32)	VB Parameter (Win16)
HWND hWnd (window handle)	ByVal hWnd As Long	ByVal hWnd As Integer
HPEN hPen (handle to a pen)	ByVal hPen As Long	ByVal hPen As Integer
HGLOBAL hgbl (handle to memory block)	ByVal hglbl As Long	ByVal hglbl As Integer

Keep in mind that object handles are identifiers to internal Windows objects and that no mathematical operations should be performed on them.

Objects (Visual Basic and OLE)

OLE 2.0 is not part of the core Windows API and will not be covered extensively in this book. However, there are some DLLs available that are designed to work with OLE 2.0 objects. These functions will typically expect a 32-bit parameter called an LPUNKNOWN or LPDISPATCH—a pointer to an interface called IUnknown, or an OLE automation interface. Visual Basic can pass these objects using the (ByVal hObj As Object) convention.

Don't worry if you don't understand terms such as interfaces and IUnknown. These are not part of the core Windows API and are not something that you are likely to be using. If they do come up, it will probably be in the context of a custom DLL that includes documentation on how to use it from Visual Basic. OLE 2.0 is a vast subject and outside of the scope of this book. The information included here is intended only for the sake of completeness and for those advanced users who are possibly writing their own OLE 2.0-compatible dynamic link libraries.

Flags and Bitfields

Many DLL functions interpret individual bits in an integer parameter or result as flags, each with its own meaning. It is therefore important to know how to set and retrieve the values of individual bits and groups of bits in a 16-bit or 32-bit integer.

Bit Numbering

Bits are numbered in an integer from the least significant bit (rightmost) to the most significant bit. Bits are numbered starting at 0, as shown in Figure 3.4.

Using Hexadecimal

This book makes extensive use of hexadecimal numbers when discussing flags and bitfields. This is because it is much easier to determine which bits are being manipulated in hex than in decimal. Table 3.2 shows the bit patterns and values for hex numbers one through &H0F.

Table 3.2 shows that if you wanted a number in which only bit 2 was set, number 4 satisfies that condition. At first glance, hexadecimal seems to be no easier than decimal.

Now consider the case where you want a 16-bit integer in which only bit 6 is set.

Figure 3.4
Bit numbering within
numeric variables

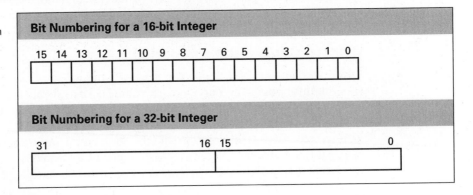

Table 3.2   **Hexadecimal Bit Patterns and Decimal Values**

Hex Value	Bit Pattern	Decimal Equivalent
0	0000	0
1	0001	1
2	0010	2
3	0011	3
4	0100	4
5	0101	5
6	0110	6
7	0111	7
8	1000	8
9	1001	9
A	1010	10
B	1011	11
C	1100	12
D	1101	13
E	1110	14
F	1111	15

In decimal, this requires a fair amount of math. Each binary position represents a power of two (bit 0 is 2^0, bit 1 is 2^1, and so on), so bit 6 is 2^6, which is 64.

In hexadecimal, the solution is much easier. A 16-bit hexadecimal number is made up of four hexadecimal digits. The first digit represents bits 0 through 3, the second digit represents bits 4 through 7, and so on. Bit 6 is the third bit (bit 2) in the second digit. Bit 2 is represented by the number 4—thus the solution is &H40.

Assume that you wanted to set bit 3 as well. In decimal, a number with bits 6 and 3 set is calculated via 2^6+2^3 = 72. In hexadecimal, the second hex digit remains the same, and bit 3 is set in the first hex digit leading to the result &H48.

If you are still not convinced of the advantages of hexadecimal, consider the problem of determining which bits are set in the following 32-bit number 6029316 (decimal). Not a pleasant prospect. Now consider the same number portrayed in hex: &H05C0004. Each hex digit represents four bits, so the bits set can be determined easily by using Table 3.2 to find the bits set for each hex digit, and taking into account which bits in the 32-bit number are represented by that digit. This is shown in Table 3.3.

Table 3.3 **Determining Bit Values in a Number (Example &H05C0004)**

Hex Digit	Hex Value	Bits Included	Bits Set
0	4	0–3	2
1	0	4–7	None
2	0	8–11	None
3	0	12–15	None
4	C	16–19	19 and 18
5	5	20–23	22 and 20

Three Boolean operators are used frequently in manipulating bits in numbers. These are the OR, AND, and NOT operators and are described in the Visual Basic manuals.

Setting, Retrieving, and Testing a Flag Bit

Bits are set using the Visual Basic OR operator. This is a case where hexadecimal notation comes in very handy—as it makes it easy to see the location of the bits being set. Consider the following examples where f% represents any integer variable:

```
f% = f% or &h0001%          ' Set bit 0
f% = f% or &h0200%          ' Set bit 9
f% = f% or &h0001 or &h0200% ' Set bit 0 and 9
f% = f% or &h0405&          ' Set bits 0,2 and 10
```

Testing of bit values is made easy by the definition that a FALSE condition is described by the value zero. A mask can be created that has set only those bits that need to be tested, as shown here:

```
if f% and &h0001% then ...  ' TRUE if bit 0 is set
if f% and &h0200% then ...  ' TRUE if bit 9 is set
if ((f% and &H0001%)<>0) And ((f% and &H0200%)<>0) then ... ' TRUE if bit 0
and 9 are both set.
if (f% and &h0001%) or (f% and &h0200%) then ... ' TRUE if bit 0 is set or bit
9 is set.
```

Clearing flag bits is accomplished by using the Visual Basic AND operator and the complement of the bit you wish to reset. For example:

```
f% = f% and (not &h0001%)  ' Clear bit 0
f% = f% and (not &h0200%)  ' Clear bit 9
f% = f% and (not (&h0200% or &h001%)) ' Clear bits 0 and 9
f% = f% and (not &h0201%)  ' Same as above
```

Working with Bitfields

Many DLL functions use pointers to structures that contain bitfields. A bitfield is simply a group of bits within a 16-bit or 32-bit integer. When one of these bitfields consists of a single bit, it is a flag bit and can be dealt with as shown in the previous section.

When a bitfield has more than one bit, it becomes necessary to perform a shift operation to access it. Consider an example in which bits 2 through 4 are a bitfield in an integer. With three bits, this bitfield can have a value from 0 to 7.

To set the value of this bitfield it is necessary to first clear the previous value, then combine the two values using the OR operator. The value can be cleared using:

```
f% = f% and (not &h001c%) ' Bits 2,3,4 are cleared
```

The new value must be shifted left two spaces, then merged with the existing value. Visual Basic does not have built-in shift operators, but this task is easily accomplished through multiplication:

```
f% = f% or (newval% * 4)
```

The multiplier needed to shift n spaces to the left is 2^n.

To determine the existing value, it is necessary to extract the bitfield and shift it to the right. This is done using division:

```
groupval% = (f% and &h001c)\4  ' Get value of group
```

Problems occur when you attempt to access the high order bit (bit 15) of a 16-bit integer. If you begin to get overflow errors, you should convert the variable into a long integer and perform long integer arithmetic.

The Visual Basic function Hex$() is quite useful in determining hexadecimal values when working with individual bits—especially when it comes to reviewing intermediate results during debugging.

Bitfield Definitions

When you refer to the DLL documentation for a bitfield, you will see it defined in a C structure as follows:

```
struct tagStructName {
    unsigned short field1:1  ' Single bitfield
    unsigned short field2:1  ' Another single bitfield
    unsigned short field3:3  ' 3 bit bitfield
    unsigned short fieldx:n  ' n = # of bits in field
}
```

Bitfields in Microsoft C are assigned from the low order bits; thus, in this example, field1 will be in bit 0, field2 in bit 1, field3 a 3-bit bitfield including bits 2 through 4, and so on.

Strings

Strings are represented in C by the LPSTR data type (pointer to characters). As mentioned earlier, most dynamic link libraries expect NULL terminated C language strings. Visual Basic can pass these parameters by using the (ByVal paramname As String) or (ByVal paramname$) conventions.

These DLL functions cannot return Visual Basic strings. They do on occasion return LPSTR pointers, which can then be copied into Visual Basic strings or user-defined types using API functions. This process is covered in "Inside Strings and Structures" in Chapter 15.

API Functions That Modify Strings

DLL functions may not return VB strings directly, but they can modify strings that are passed to them. It is therefore absolutely essential that you predefine the length of any VB string parameter that may be changed by a DLL call.

This can be accomplished by either defining a fixed-length string or using the String$ function to set the initial length of the string. DLL functions that can change string parameters will allow you to specify the maximum length of the buffer as one of the parameters, or the DLL will provide another function that allows you to determine the length of the string buffer required.

When allocating string length, be sure to allocate enough space for the NULL termination character used in C language strings. If a string is to hold N characters, you must allocate a string buffer of length N+1.

Note that Visual Basic strings may contain NULL characters, but C language strings may not (since they use the NULL character to indicate the end of the string). If you find that strings are being truncated, you may have NULL characters hidden in them.

There are some additional subtleties to working with fixed length strings that are inside of user-defined types. These are described further in Chapter 15.

Visual Basic Strings

The core Windows API uses C language NULL terminated strings exclusively. Some dynamic link libraries that are designed for use with Visual Basic (such as APIGID32.DLL, for example) and other OLE 2.0 compatible DLLs can accept Visual Basic strings as parameters. To pass a VB string directly use the (param As String) or (param $) convention; do not use the ByVal keyword.

Be sure that the DLL specifically states that the parameter expects a Visual Basic string (or pointer to a BSTR) format—VB string and C language string parameters are not generally interchangeable.

It is also possible for a function to return a Visual Basic string, in which case the function name will have the string type specifier ($), or the declaration will be followed by the As String specifier.

NULL Strings versus NULL Values

Some DLL functions that accept string parameters can also accept a NULL value in place of the string. It is important to recognize the difference between a NULL string and a NULL (or zero) value. A NULL string is an empty string. An empty string can be assigned in VB using

```
stringname$ = ""
```

When you pass a NULL string pointer to a DLL function using ByVal, you are passing a pointer to a string that contains only the NULL terminating character. When passing it without the ByVal specifier, you are passing a pointer to a valid BSTR containing an empty string. In both cases you are passing a valid pointer to the DLL function. This pointer will definitely not have the value zero.

When a DLL function accepts a NULL value in place of a string, it expects the actual value zero rather than a pointer or handle to an empty string. There are two ways to accomplish this. One way is to create a second declaration for the function that uses the long data type instead of the string data type. The other is to use the special constant string vbNULLString which

passes a TRUE NULL value to the DLL function. If the API function accepts a string or long value other than NULL, you will need a way to declare a DLL function as a parameter that effectively supports both the String and Long data types. Methods for handling functions that accept more than one data type are covered later in this chapter.

Pointers to Numeric Values

Pointers to numeric values include the LPINT, LPSHORT data types, and other pointers to numeric types as defined by the individual DLL functions. It is extremely common for pointers to be used in this way as parameters.

Visual Basic can pass a pointer to a numeric data type simply by not using the ByVal keyword (call by reference). The DLL function can then use this pointer to access the actual variable, and may also modify this variable in some cases. This technique can be used with any numeric data type.

Be very careful, however, that the size of the variable that you are pointing to matches what is expected by the DLL. If you pass a pointer to a VB integer (16 bits) to an API function that expects a pointer to a C integer (32 bits), the API function will go ahead and write data not only into the integer that you provided, but into the next 16 bits of memory. This could cause anything from a tiny data error to a fatal exception, and this type of problem can be notoriously difficult to track down.

Pointers to Structures

A DLL structure is the same as a Visual Basic user-defined type as created with the Type keyword. This book will tend to use the term "structure" in place of "user-defined type" in order to remain consistent with the C/C++ documentation that you are likely to be exposed to elsewhere. In many cases it is possible to create a VB user-defined type that exactly matches the structure expected by the DLL. In other cases, that becomes somewhat tricky.

Once you have a compatible VB type definition, it can be passed by reference as a parameter (you cannot pass a user-defined type by value to a DLL).

Converting a DLL Structure to a VB Structure

A DLL structure can contain any number of variables, each with any data type. The standard Windows API structures are defined in the file API32.TXT, which is provided with this book; however, if you use other commercial or shareware DLLs, you may need to adapt a DLL structure to VB yourself. Table 3.4 shows how various DLL structure data types can be handled in a VB user-defined type.

One of the changes to note here from Visual Basic 3.0 is the use of the Byte data type in place of a fixed length string of length 1. Since Visual Basic

Table 3.4   **DLL Data Types in a VB User-Defined Type**

Data Type	Entry in VB User-Defined Type
BYTE	Byte.
16-bit number (short, WORD, int on Win16)	Integer.
32-bit number (long, DWORD, int on Win32)	Long.
Bitfields	Combine every 16 bits of bitfields into an Integer. Use techniques described in this chapter to access the bitfields.
Character Array (fixed length)	Fixed length string if Unicode, Byte array otherwise.
Binary Data Array (fixed length)	Byte array.
FARPROC (pointer to a function)	Long. Not supported directly by VB. For details, refer to the discussion on FARPROCs later in this chapter.
Handle	Long for Win32, Integer for Win16.
BSTR (OLE string handle)	Variable length string.
LPSTR (pointer to C string)	Long. Use techniques described in Chapter 15 and Appendix A to obtain a long value to use as an address for a VB string.
Number Array (fixed length)	Numeric array of the appropriate type.
Pointer to structure	Long. See LPSTR.
Single or Double	Single or Double (type must match).

4.0 and above uses Unicode internally, a fixed length string that is one character long actually takes up two bytes. This can be seen by running the following small Visual Basic program:

```
Dim s As String * 1
Print Len(s), LenB(s)
```

As you will see, the length is one character, the byte length is two.

The way data is organized internally within a data structure by Visual Basic differs from the way it is organized when a structure is passed as a parameter to a DLL function or written to a file. Internally, the string is stored as two bytes—when the structure is passed as a parameter to an API function it is converted to one byte. This conversion can lead to erroneous results with binary data so you should always use the Byte data type for binary data within structures.

On rare occasions, when you are accessing a structure directly (not as a DLL parameter), you may need to consider data alignment issues, as Visual Basic will add extra space in a structure if necessary to meet the natural alignment requirements of each data type. A byte can be located anywhere in a structure, but an integer must be located at an address that is divisible by two (since it is two bytes long). A long variable, which is 4 bytes long, must be aligned at an address divisible by 4. The structure itself must also meet this requirement.

Consider the following user-defined type:

```
Private Type mytype
    a As Byte
    b As Integer
End Type

Dim v As mytype
```

How long is this structure? If you print Len(v) you will get 3, suggesting that it is 3 bytes long, but if you use the LenB structure (which is designed to measure the length of objects in bytes) you will get 4. Visual Basic adds an extra byte in order to allow the integer variable to be placed at a legal location. If you change b to a Long, you will get Len(v) as 5 and LenB(v) as 8, once again demonstrating this point.

The good news is that most structures used by Windows are designed to follow these natural alignment rules, so you will find that when you convert API structures to Visual Basic user-defined types, the alignment works out correctly without requiring any special action on your part. Third party DLLs (including those in Desaware's SpyWorks) are available to handle structure packing and unpacking for those few cases where an API function requires a structure that does not follow natural alignment rules.

A more in-depth look at how Visual Basic structures work, especially with regard to placing strings inside of structures, can be found in Chapter 15. More information and examples on converting C/C++ structures into Visual Basic can be found in Chapter 4.

Pointers to Arrays

Some DLL functions accept pointers to arrays of numbers or structures. These can be handled by specifying the parameter data type as that of the array data type and using the call by reference convention. You can then use the first element of the array as the parameter. This passes a pointer to the start of the array.

In cases where the DLL function can modify the contents of the array, it is critical that the array be predefined to be large enough to hold any changes. Refer to the documentation on the specific API function to determine its array size requirements.

The following example shows how to pass the first element of an array to a DLL function:

```
' Declaration is:
Declare Sub SendToDLL Lib "alib.dll" (x As Byte)

' In the subroutine use:
ReDim x(10) As Byte
SendToDLL x(0)
```

This illustrates a common technique for working with API functions that require access to a buffer of memory. Such a buffer can easily be defined as a byte array. A pointer to the buffer can be passed to the API function by declaring the parameter 'As Byte' and passing the first byte of the array as a parameter.

It is also possible to pass an array to a DLL function using the standard array passing syntax as follows:

```
' Declaration
Declare Sub SendToDLL Lib "alib.dll" (x() As Integer)

' In subroutine use:
SendToDLL x()
```

This technique passes a pointer to a pointer to an OLE 2.0 SAFEARRAY structure to the DLL function and should not be used with Windows API functions. Only dynamic link libraries that are specifically designed to work with Visual Basic or OLE 2.0 arrays can use this method.

Pointers to Functions

Pointers to functions include FARPROC, DLGPROC, and other data types that define 32-bit pointers to functions. Many Windows API functions use pointers to functions as parameters in order to allow Windows to call a function in a user application. The user function that is called by Windows is referred to as a *callback* function.

Visual Basic 5.0 and later allows you to obtain a pointer to a function defined in a standard module by using the AddressOf operator.

Visual Basic 4.0 and earlier provides no support for callback functions; thus DLL functions and structures that have pointers to functions as parameters cannot normally be used with those versions of Visual Basic.

The disk accompanying this book includes an OLE custom control called DWCBK32D.OCX, which will enable you to use pointers to functions with earlier editions of Visual Basic in most situations by providing a 32-bit pointer to an internal function that in turn triggers a control event when called by Windows. Refer to Appendix A for information on using this control.

Parameters Accepting More Than One Type

In some cases DLL functions are defined to accept more than one type. An example of this is the LoadCursor function, which is defined as follows:

```
HCURSOR LoadCursor(hInstance, lpCursorName)
```

where HCURSOR is a 32-bit handle to a cursor object, hInstance is a 32-bit instance handle, and lpCursorName is either the name of the cursor or a 32-bit integer ID for the cursor resource. To support both types of lpCursor-Name parameters it would take the following two declarations:

```
Declare Function LoadCursor& Lib "user32" Alias "LoadCursorA" (ByVal _
hInstance&, ByVal lpCursorName As string)
and
Declare Function LoadCursor& Lib "user32" Alias "LoadCursorA" (ByVal _
hInstance&, ByVal lpCursorName As long)
```

Of course, both of these definitions cannot coexist in the same program, as Visual Basic would flag a duplicate declaration error if they did.

In order to allow use of functions that accept more than one data type for a parameter, Visual Basic defines the special data type Any to declare a parameter that has no type checking. The type of parameter passed is always that of the parameter passed when the function is called. The declaration for LoadCursor would therefore be:

```
Declare Function LoadCursor& Lib "user32" Alias "LoadCursorA" (ByVal hInstance& _
lpCursorName As Any)
```

In this case, to call LoadCursor with a string parameter you would use the command:

```
res& = LoadCursor&(hmodule&, ByVal cursorname$)
```

where *hmodule* is the handle of the module that contains the cursor and *cursorname$* is the name of the cursor resource. Note the necessity of using the ByVal keyword to force the string to be passed correctly as a NULL terminated C language string.

To use the cursor resource ID you would use the command:

```
res& = LoadCursor&(hmodule&, ByVal cursorid&)
```

where *cursorid* is the long value identifying a cursor resource. Note that both the ByVal and & specifiers must be included. ByVal forces the call by value convention to be used. The & type specifier informs Visual Basic that the value is a 32-bit Long.

Neglecting to use the ByVal in either case, or the & type specifier in the latter case, will lead to an error, and can cause a fatal exception or general protection fault.

The As Any type forces the parameter passing convention and data type to be defined entirely by the calling procedure. Any data type can be passed to the DLL either by reference or by value. It is the programmer's responsibility to be certain that the DLL function can accept the parameter as it is passed—Visual Basic does not perform any conversions.

It is possible to move the ByVal specifier into the declaration for cases where a parameter is always called by value. The following declaration of LoadCursor accomplishes this:

```
Declare Function LoadCursor& Lib "user32" Alias "LoadCursorA" (ByVal _
hInstance&, ByVal _
lpCursorName As Any)
```

It is still necessary to include a type specifier with the *lpCursorName* parameter. See "Aliasing" in Chapter 4 for a better solution to this problem.

Under the Hood—How API/DLL Calls Work

You may have noticed a strong emphasis in this chapter on the sizes of parameters. No issue is more important when it comes to correctly declaring API and DLL functions for use with Visual Basic. This section will briefly cover the mechanism by which parameters are passed to, and returned from, DLL functions.

Stack Frames

Every application has an internal stack data structure which is used to implement parameter passing and function calls. A stack can be thought of as a block of memory in which you can place data. Data is pushed onto the stack one item at a time. The last piece of data pushed onto the stack is considered to be on the top of the stack. You can look at data that is below the top of the stack, but you can only remove the topmost item. When a function is called, the parameters and return address are pushed onto the stack. If that function calls another function, it pushes additional parameters and another return address onto the stack. When a function completes, it pops the return address from the stack and jumps to that location. This allows the stack to essentially unwind. A stack also contains variables that are local to a function—this assures that each time you call a function it has its own set of local variables—even when a function calls itself.

Clearly it is essential that the calling function place parameters onto the stack in exactly the correct order and size, otherwise the called function will not be able to find the correct data items. Figure 3.5 shows a typical stack frame for a function that expects a 16-bit short integer and a string parameter for both Win32 and Win16. Note that the order of parameters on the stack differs between Win16, in which parameters are pushed onto the stack from left to right, and Win32, in which parameters are pushed onto the stack from right to left.

Figure 3.5

Normal stack frame

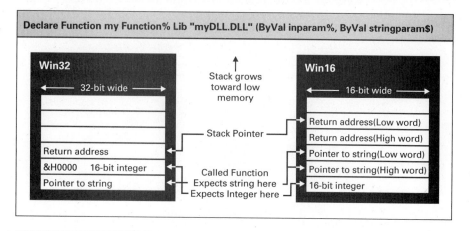

As you can see, the amount of space that each item actually takes on the stack depends on the width of the stack. In Win32, an integer takes up the low 16-bit word of a stack entry—the high word is ignored. In Win16, however, an integer takes up an entire stack entry. The 32-bit wide Win32 stack can place a pointer in a single stack entry. This pointer entry contains a memory address for the location in memory that contains the first character of a NULL terminated string. It takes two stack entries in Win16 to hold a 32-bit address. The stack frame in Figure 3.5 is correct—you can see that the called function references each parameter in the location where it actually exists. The stack pointer—a CPU register that points to the top of the stack—correctly points to the return address—the location in memory where execution will continue after the function returns. When the function is complete, the called function restores the program execution location from this return address and sets the Stack Pointer to point to the previous top of stack—an entry below those shown in the figure. A key point to keep in mind here is this: Even though the *calling* program sets the top of stack location when a new function is called, it is the *called* function that restores the top of stack to its original location when it is finished executing.

Figure 3.6 shows what can happen when a declaration is incorrect. In this example the declaration left out the integer parameter. The stack frame on the top section shows the first problem: The parameters are not in the locations expected by the called function. In Win32, it will interpret the low 16 bits of the string address as a short integer. A potentially more serious problem is that it will interpret the previous value of the stack pointer for the function as a string! While it might be able to read the information, if the function tries to write data into the string, it is certain to cause an error or a fatal exception, as that value might be a code address or a saved memory segment value. In Win16 the situation is similar. Due to the different parameter ordering, the string parameter is correct; however, the integer parameter contains garbage. In either case, there is no way to anticipate what might occur, but you can be sure it will not be pleasant.

Figure 3.6

Stack frame with missing parameter in the declaration

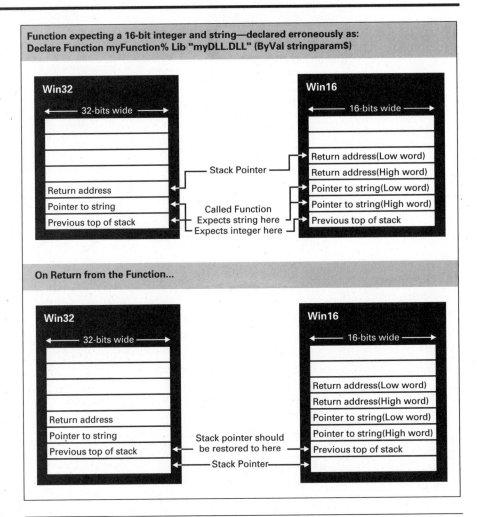

The lower section of Figure 3.6 illustrates a second problem. On the Win32 side, the calling function had pushed two 32-bit values onto the stack, setting the top of stack pointer to an address 8 bytes higher than the previous top of stack. However, the called function has no way of knowing that an incorrect number of bytes were pushed on the stack, and it is the *called* function's responsibility to restore the stack pointer to its prior value. It expected three 32-bit values (12 bytes) on the stack, so when it is complete, the stack pointer will be 12 bytes below the return address—4 bytes below where it actually was.

The good news is that Visual Basic is able to detect this situation; it records the original top of stack before it calls the DLL function. When the function returns it checks to verify that the stack pointer has been restored to its original value. If it has not, Visual Basic triggers the notorious "Bad DLL Calling Convention" error. The same problem occurs with Win16.

Now refer to Figure 3.7. Here you can see what happens when you set the wrong data type and use a long value instead of an integer. Under Win16, you have a similar problem to the one in Figure 3.6—the called function does not find the correct information and the stack pointer is in the wrong place. You once again run the risk of a fatal exception in addition to the program not running correctly, plus you will once again receive the "Bad DLL Calling Convention" error. On Win32, however, a strange thing happens. Since every variable takes up at least 32 bits, Visual Basic sign extends the 16-bit value into a long before pushing it onto the stack. As a result, the called function will in fact see the correct parameter value. In other words, the declaration will work correctly.

Figure 3.7

Stack frame with parameter type error

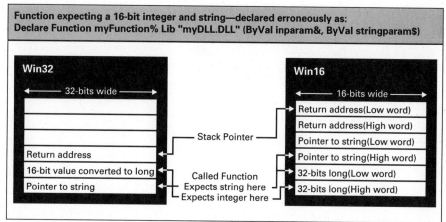

In previous versions of Visual Basic, the Byte data type did not exist. For DLL calls that required Byte parameters, you would use an integer parameter, depending on Visual Basic to extend it to an integer. This worked because the smallest parameter size on Win16 is 16 bits. For the same reason, you can actually use a long parameter declaration for integers or bytes. Still, it is preferable to keep your parameter types correct to insure future compatibility and prevent potential errors due to the conversion process.

Figure 3.8 illustrates the single most common error that people make when declaring API or DLL functions: forgetting to include the ByVal specifier. This is another situation where Win32 differs from Win16. When you forget the ByVal specifier, Visual Basic pushes a memory address where the integer variable can be located instead of the value of the integer. Under Win16, this problem is quickly detected. Because the pointer is 32 bits instead of 16 bits, not only is the integer value in error, but the called function reads an incorrect string address as well. The stack pointer is again in the wrong location and the "Bad DLL Calling Convention" error is bound to occur.

Figure 3.8
Stack frame with missing ByVal

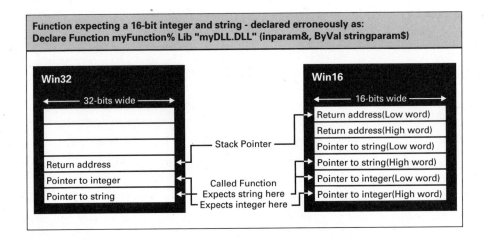

Under Win32 the situation is trickier. Because the numeric variable and the memory address both take up 32 bits, the size of the stack frame is correct and only the single parameter is affected. The called function will see an incorrect parameter value for the integer, but no error will be detected by Visual Basic due to side effects from other parameters. The only way to detect this type of error will be through side effects from the erroneous parameter value. If the called function does not use this parameter, you will never see any effects from this error.

This means that in some ways Win32 actually may make it harder to detect certain types of declaration errors, and makes it even more important that you make certain that your declarations are accurate.

Return Values

There is little difference between the way values are returned in Win32 and Win16. Numeric variables and all other 8-, 16-, and 32-bit values are returned in CPU registers. The only issue to be concerned about is the possibility of overflow errors. For example, if a function returns a long value and you assign it to an integer, the possibility of an overflow exists if the value in the long variable is outside of the legal range for an integer. However, this is the same problem that occurs any time you assign a long to an integer—it is not unique to DLL calls.

The only case where serious problems will occur is if you forget to define the function return type or where the return type is incorrectly declared when a data type larger than 32 bits is involved (for example, variants and doubles). The problem with forgetting to define a return type is that the function will by default return a variant.

In these cases, in order to return a value over 32-bits long, the stack frame will contain an extra pointer to a space allocated on the stack to hold the return value. In order for this protocol to work correctly, the calling function must allocate this pointer and space correctly, and the called function must expect it to be there. If the declaration does not match the expectations of the called function, an error will occur—and since the error includes misallocation of data on the stack, a "Bad DLL Calling Convention" error will occur.

Beyond Theory

This concludes the introduction to the Windows API/DLL interface. The vast and rapidly changing nature of the Win32 API increases the likelihood that you will need to use this information at some point to create your own declarations. So far you have seen a fairly comprehensive description of how to handle the various parameter types and an in-depth look at how stack frames are used to implement the API/DLL calling convention.

As important as this information is, there is no substitute for experience and examples. Chapter 4 will show you how to apply the information and theory to solve actual interfacing problems, and addresses the real-world issues that you are likely to face. It also demonstrates how to write code that will run on both Win16 and Win32 under Visual Basic 4.0, and how to port Windows API code from Win16 to Win32 for Visual Basic 4.0 and 5.0.

4

Real World API Programming

API Programming Techniques

This chapter is intended to help you gain a practical understanding of how to declare and use Windows API functions. This section introduces the idea of type-safe declarations and describes a number of other technologies that can help you when working with API functions. The next four sections walk you through a number of exercises that demonstrate the techniques covered in Chapter 3. Finally, the chapter will close with API debugging hints along with a newly revised edition of the ten commandments for safe Windows API programming.

Type-Safe Declarations

As shown earlier, the As Any declaration in an argument list allows any parameter type to be passed as a DLL parameter. This makes it possible to support API and DLL functions that can accept more than one data type for a particular parameter.

This does have one disadvantage, however. Using As Any turns off all type checking for the specified parameter. Consider once again the definition for LoadCursor:

```
Declare Function LoadCursor& Lib "user32" Alias "LoadCursorA" (ByVal _
hInstance&, ByVal lpCursorName As Any)
```

It is true that lpCursorName can now be a string or long parameter. It is also true that lpCursorName can be a 16-bit integer, a double, a control, a variant, or any other data type. This opens the door to all sorts of disastrous possibilities, including fatal exceptions. All it takes is to call the function accidentally with a variable that has an incorrect data type.

One way to enforce strict type checking and help prevent these problems is to use the Alias technique in the function declaration. Consider the following two declarations:

```
Declare Function LoadCursorByName& Lib "user32" _
Alias "LoadCursorA" (ByVal hInstance&, ByVal _
lpCursorName As String)
```

and

```
Declare Function LoadCursorByID& Lib "user32" _
Alias "LoadCursorA" (ByVal hInstance&, ByVal _
lpCursorName As Long)
```

LoadCursorByName accesses the API function LoadCursor using a string as the lpCursorName parameter. LoadCursorByID accesses the same LoadCursor DLL function, but uses a long integer as the lpCursorName parameter. Each of these functions enforces strict type checking on the lpCursorName parameter allowing Visual Basic to detect incorrect variable types before calling the API function and minimizing the chance of a fatal exception or other system crash.

The Advantages of Type-Safe Declarations

The availability of aliasing poses the Visual Basic programmer with an interesting philosophical dilemma. A look at the WIN31API.TXT and WIN32API.TXT files that are provided with the professional version of Visual Basic shows that Microsoft has chosen the first approach for the declaration library that they provide. In cases where a Windows API function parameter accepts multiple data types, the declaration either specifies the more common data type or uses the As Any type specifier.

This book advocates using the second approach. The API32.TXT and API16.TXT files provided on the included disk include type-safe declarations for many common Windows API functions.

There are two overwhelming reasons why type-safe declarations are worth the extra effort of keeping track of multiple declarations. The first is simple: it will reduce the number of bugs that you run into during development. The second is somewhat more subtle. Use of the As Any specifier places all of the responsibility for accurately defining API parameters in the program code itself. Each time an API function is used, there is the possibility of an error. Not only that, but even an error as minor as a missing type specifier or incorrect use of a ByVal command can lead to a system crash or a hard-to-find data corruption error. As long as you are a single programmer working on a small project, this may not be a problem. But once you create a declaration file that is intended to be shared among programmers, or used to develop a larger application, the advantages become clear. Which is better: to define the declaration once in such a way that Visual Basic will catch any errors in its use, or to define it in such a way that every time it is used there is a risk of errors that may corrupt data or cause a fatal exception? Let the compiler do its job—use type-safe declarations wherever possible.

Aliasing and Function Ordinal Numbers

Most functions in Windows dynamic link libraries have associated with them a number called an *ordinal number*. It is possible to access functions by ordinal number instead of the function name by specifying the number in the alias string preceded with a "#" sign. This technique can provide a slight improvement in performance. For example, the GetVersion API function is normally declared as:

```
Declare Function GetVersion& Lib "kernel32"()
```

The GetVersion function has the ordinal value of 311 under Windows NT and 443 under Windows 95. Under Windows NT it can thus be accessed using this declaration:

```
Declare Function GetVersion& Lib "kernel32" Alias "#311" ()
```

Ordinal values for functions can be determined using a utility program that analyzes the header of an executable file or DLL, for example, the DUMPBIN.EXE program that comes with Microsoft Visual C++. Unfortunately, ordinal values for functions can vary from one operating system to the next, so this ability to use ordinal numbers has little practical use with regard to the Windows API, though it can provide slightly improved performance for other DLLs that do have consistent values across different platforms.

Sending Messages

Chapter 2 discussed the fact that Visual Basic has the ability to send messages to controls. There are actually two approaches to sending windows messages, and it is important to understand the difference between them. The Windows API functions that are commonly used to send messages are SendMessage andPostMessage. They are declared as follows:

```
Declare Function SendMessage Lib "user32" Alias _
"SendMessageA" (ByVal hwnd As Long, ByVal wMsg As _
Long, ByVal wParam As Long, lParam As Any) As Long
Declare Function PostMessage Lib "user32" Alias _
"PostMessageA" (ByVal hwnd As Long, ByVal wMsg As _
Long, ByVal wParam As Long, lParam As Any) As Long
```

SendMessage sends a message by immediately calling the Windows function for the window specified. The function does not return until the window function has finished executing, and it is possible for the window function to return a value to the calling routine.

PostMessage sends a message by posting a message into the message queue for the window (that is, the list of messages that are in line to be processed by the window). Messages sent via PostMessage will be processed by the window at some future time. The PostMessage function returns immediately, so it is not possible for the window function to return a value—it probably has not even begun to execute when the PostMessage function returns. Note that on Windows NT or Windows 95, a posted message may be processed immediately, depending on when a task switch occurs. This differs from 16-bit Windows where a posted message cannot be processed until regular message processing occurs due to completion of an event or execution of a DoEvents statement.

Part 3 of this book covers the use of these functions in detail and introduces several variations of these functions that support advanced Win32 features. In addition, it provides type-safe declarations for these functions.

Modular Programming

Modular programming, the division of large projects into smaller functional units, is a good idea in general and is used extensively by programmers. This methodology is even more important when it comes to API programming. If you can group API functions into a single module which is called from the rest of your program, your program will be easier to support in the long term, especially on multiple platforms.

Many API functions require support code in order to work and prevent fatal exceptions from occurring: for example, functions that load data into strings require that the strings be initialized to a sufficient length before the function is called. If you use this type of function, you have a choice to make. You can use the API function directly every time it is needed, remembering to define and initialize the necessary string each time, or you can create a new VB function that takes care of the initialization, calls the API function, and returns a string. Once you have debugged this function, it can be used safely anywhere in your program. Any effort needed to use this API function under multiple operating systems is isolated to this function alone.

The VB4INI and VB5INI examples that follows later in this chapter demonstrates this technique. Since the focus of this book is teaching the Windows API, the examples throughout the book tend to be smaller programs that are not designed to be supported by programming teams or to be reusable. As such, most of the examples do not bother to create an additional interface layer between the API and the core of the program itself. Nonetheless, for intermediate and large projects, and those that are intended to be supported over the long term or by multiple programmers, isolating your API calls to a few modules is strongly recommended.

A more sophisticated form of modular programming involves creating a class library to encapsulate Windows API functionality. This approach is discussed in Part 4 of this book, which revisits the subject of real world programming from a more advanced perspective—one that assumes that you have already explored this book and are well acquainted with API programming techniques.

API Declaration Files and Tools

The disk that comes with this book contains a number of files that should prove useful as you incorporate Windows API calls into your Visual Basic projects.

Visual Basic Declaration Files

Files API16.TXT and API32.TXT contain the function declarations and the structure and constant definitions that are necessary to access the Windows API from Visual Basic. They are based on the files WIN31API.TXT and WIN32API.TXT that are provided with the professional and enterprise versions of Visual Basic; however, several changes have been incorporated into these files to make them easier to use and to help reduce overhead.

The original files suffer from several problems. First, it is impossible to include the entire file in an application module without running out of memory. Programmers need to extract only those declarations and definitions needed for the application using an editor. Second, the file makes extensive use of As Any instead of providing type-safe declarations. Third, the files contain declarations for many API functions that are not usable under Visual Basic.

The API16.TXT and API32.TXT files include type-safe declarations for the most frequently used Windows API functions. The original declarations were left in to ensure compatibility with the Microsoft files and sample projects, but you are encouraged to use the type-safe declarations in their place. These files also fix numerous errors in the Microsoft files that were discovered during the course of writing this book.

Visual Basic 4.0 and later improved on version 3.0 by providing the APILOD16.EXE and APILOD32.EXE programs that can build a database of API functions, types and constants, and which make it possible to quickly search and copy the definitions you need onto the clipboard. Unfortunately, Microsoft did not include the source code for these tools—it would have come in handy for adding new features. To help solve this problem, this book includes the APITOOLS package, a tool kit that among other things lets you build a database that holds both 16- and 32-bit definitions and add both into your program at once using the necessary conditional compilation commands. It also includes the APIDATA.MDB database which contains all of the information from the declaration files plus information on which functions are not implemented under Win32c (for Windows 95). It also lists which chapter in the book contains the reference information for the function, if applicable.

APIGID32.DLL

Many of the Windows API functions require parameters that are difficult to obtain directly from Visual Basic. APIGID32.DLL contains a set of support functions that can dramatically extend the number of API functions that are accessible under Visual Basic. This DLL is described in detail in Appendix A, though other functions will be introduced as needed.

APIGID32.DLL also contains functions that demonstrate the Visual Basic to DLL interface from the C++ point of view. Advanced technical information on writing DLLs for use with VB can be found in Appendix D. To help facilitate this, the full source code for APIGID32.DLL is included.

DWCBK32D.OCX, DWSBC32D.OCX, DWSHK32D.OCX

DWCBK32D.OCX is a fully functional demonstration version of an OLE control that allows you to use pointers to functions from Visual Basic 4.0 (this control is not required for Visual Basic 5.0, though it does work). This is necessary for API functions that use function pointers to directly call into your application. (The term "callback" function is used to describe the function referenced by a function pointer. DWCBK32D.OCX essentially provides a pool of these callback functions that you can use.) This is a demonstration version of the DWCBK32.OCX callback control included in Desaware's Spy-Works package, and is limited to use under the Visual Basic design environment (meaning that it will not work with compiled programs). Details on use of this control will also be introduced as needed and are covered in Appendix A.

Fully functional demonstration versions of two other SpyWorks controls, the DWSBC32D.OCX subclassing control and DWSHK32D.OCX window hook control, are also included and described in Appendix A. Several examples throughout this book make use of these controls to teach advanced API programming techniques.

The Desaware API Class Library

Building a class library is an excellent way to deploy API functionality safely in large applications or for the use of programming teams. Through a special arrangement with Desaware, this book includes version 1.1 of the Desaware API Classes, a commercial quality class library that covers the core API functionality. This class library includes full source code and can either be incorporated directly into your own applications or turned into an OLE DLL server, in which case it provides easy access to the Win32 API by way of OLE automation. This class library, and the subject of class libraries in general, is covered in Part 4 of this book.

Translating API Documentation to Visual Basic (Part 1—Functions)

Chapter 3 described in detail the theory behind the Visual Basic to DLL interface, use of the Declare statement, and the various data types involved. But there is nothing like practice when it comes to learning how to correctly declare API functions for use with Visual Basic. This is especially important with Win32, where even this book, which attempts to be as comprehensive as possible, nevertheless leaves out hundreds of functions that belong to that rapidly increasing array of extension libraries that are still referred to as the Windows API.

Example: Private Initialization Files

This example will address two of the most frequently used API functions; those that work with private initialization files. The sample code for the VB4INI.VBP project can be found in the Ch04 directory on your CD-ROM. A version of the project updated to Visual Basic 5.0 is also provided under the name VB5INI.VBP. These projects (which are essentially identical) will be referred to as VB?INI throughout this chapter.

In the original Windows system, there were two initialization files: SYSTEM.INI, which contained information on how Windows itself is configured, and WIN.INI, which contained information on how individual applications were configured along with user configurations such as printers and desktop colors—the type of configuration information typically set via the control panel.

WIN.INI was originally used by every application that wanted to store initialization information. However, later versions of Windows added support for private initialization files. These allowed each application to maintain its own set of configuration information. With Win32, Microsoft recommends using the registration database for storing configuration information instead of initialization files. It is not clear at this time whether or not this recommendation is going to catch on. The registration database is not known for its reliability under Windows 3.1, and is both harder to use and sometimes slower than private initialization files under Windows 95 and Windows NT. The registration database does effectively replace WIN.INI—API calls that access this file modify the registration database as well, but it is likely that private initialization files will continue to be used by many programmers for some time to come.

Specifying the Declaration

This example will concern itself with the two most important functions: GetPrivateProfileString, which retrieves a string, and WritePrivateProfileString, which writes a string into a private initialization file. The declaration for GetPrivateProfileString in the Win32 documentation is as follows:

```
DWORD GetPrivateProfileString(

    LPCTSTR  lpszSection, // address of section name
    LPCTSTR  lpszKey, // address of key name
    LPCTSTR  lpszDefault, // address of default string
            // address of destination buffer
    LPTSTR  lpszReturnBuffer,

            // size of destination buffer
    DWORD   cchReturnBuffer,
    LPCTSTR  lpszFile // address of initialization filename
    );
```

The first step is to identify the source DLL that contains this function. If you have the dumpbin utility that comes with Visual C++ or its equivalent, you can determine the API functions exported from each dynamic link library. If you are working with a third party library, you should be provided with the name of the DLL and the name under which the function is exported. If worse comes to worse, you can simply declare the function for a number of different DLLs until you find one that does not cause a "function not found" error.

In this case, GetPrivateProfileString is in KERNEL32.DLL. Since it has string parameters, you can anticipate the possibility that there will be separate Unicode and ANSI entry points for the function. Sure enough, the ANSI version of this function is exported as GetPrivateProfileStringA. This means that you will need to use an alias to identify the exported function name. The function returns a DWORD which is a 32-bit value (per the table in Chapter 3). Based on these facts, the declare statement will be structured as follows:

```
Declare Function GetPrivateProfileString& Lib _
"kernel32" Alias "GetPrivateProfileStringA" _
(parameters here)
```

You may wonder, why not use the typical form of the declaration:

```
Declare Function GetPrivateProfileString Lib _
"kernel32" Alias "GetPrivateProfileStringA" _
(parameters here) As Long
```

Either one is just fine. I prefer the former as I have a tendency to forget to specify the function return type if I leave it for the end. Since forgetting to specify a type is equivalent to declaring it to return a variant, this oversight invariably leads to a bad DLL calling convention error or fatal exception.

Specifying the Parameters

At first glance, the parameters look straightforward—there are four strings, a long and a final string. This would suggest the following declaration:

```
Declare Function GetPrivateProfileString& Lib _
"kernel32" Alias "GetPrivateProfileStringA" (ByVal _
lpszSection$, ByVal lpszKey$, ByVal lpszDefault$, _
ByVal lpszReturnBuffer$, ByVal cchReturnBuffer&, _
ByVal lpszFile$)
```

Once again, the Visual Basic type characters are used instead of the full As String declarations primarily in order to save space and improve readability.

So, is this declaration actually correct? In order to find out, it is necessary to look at the actual meaning of each of these parameters. The lpszDefault$, lpszReturnBuffer$ and lpszFile$ parameters are always strings. The lpszSection$ parameter will be left for a later exercise. Now look at the description for the lpszKey$ parameter:

```
lpszKey
Points to the null-terminated string containing the key name whose associated
string is to be retrieved. If this parameter is NULL, all key names in the
section specified by the lpszSection parameter are copied to the buffer
specified by the lpszReturnBuffer parameter.
```

This poses a problem. The lpszKey parameter can be a string, but can also be a NULL value. This situation was discussed in Chapter 3 as well. The

NULL value is not the same thing as a null string. If you pass the NULL string "" as a parameter to this function, you would be passing a pointer to a location in memory containing a null character. The NULL value can only be passed as a 32-bit long. The declaration for GetPrivateProfileString from the WIN32API.TXT file addresses this issue by declaring the function as follows:

```
Declare Function GetPrivateProfileString Lib _
"kernel32" Alias "GetPrivateProfileStringA" _
(ByVal lpApplicationName As String, lpKeyName As Any, _
ByVal lpDefault As String, ByVal lpReturnedString _
As String, ByVal nSize As Long, ByVal lpfilename _
As String) As Long
```

The first thing you might notice is that they used the word lpKeyName instead of lpszKey as the parameter name. This does not matter—these are dummy parameter names that have no meaning or use other than as placeholders. Even the Windows API documentation uses different dummy parameter names depending on the version of the documentation and which API it is written for.

As you see, they chose to specify the lpszKey parameter As Any to allow you to pass either a string or a long value to the function. If you wish to pass a string to the function, you must call it as follows:

```
res = GetPrivateProfileString(mysection$, ByVal mykey$, .......
```

If you wish to pass a NULL value to the function, you do it thus:

```
res = GetPrivateProfileString(mysection$, ByVal 0&, .....
```

If you forget the ByVal keyword, or forget to use a variable of the correct type, or forget to coerce a constant to the correct type, you will cause an error. This can range from an incorrect result, to a "Bad DLL Calling Convention" error, to a fatal exception.

The situation can be improved somewhat by adding a ByVal to the original declaration as follows:

```
Declare Function GetPrivateProfileString Lib _
"kernel32" Alias "GetPrivateProfileStringA" (ByVal _
lpApplicationName As String, ByVal lpKeyName As Any, _
ByVal lpDefault As String, ByVal lpReturnedString As _
String, ByVal nSize As Long, ByVal lpfilename As _
String) As Long
```

At least this form of the declaration forces the parameter to be passed by value, however, it does not coerce the parameter to the correct type, so errors can still occur. The type-safe approach advocated by this book recommends that you create two different declarations as follows:

```
Declare Function GetPrivateProfileStringByKeyName& Lib "kernel32" Alias _
```

```
"GetPrivateProfileStringA" (ByVal lpszSection$, ByVal lpszKey$, ByVal _
lpszDefault$, ByVal lpszReturnBuffer$, ByVal cchReturnBuffer&, ByVal lpszFile$)
Declare Function GetPrivateProfileStringKeys& Lib "kernel32" Alias _
"GetPrivateProfileStringA" (ByVal lpszSection$, ByVal lpszKey&, ByVal _
lpszDefault$, ByVal lpszReturnBuffer$, ByVal cchReturnBuffer&, ByVal lpszFile$)
```

The first of these functions is used to retrieve the value of a key, the second is designed to pass a long value as the key which should always be the value zero, thus passing a NULL to the function. The cost of having an extra declaration and remembering two different function names is offset by the safety provided by two virtually foolproof functions.

A second solution that avoids creating a second declaration is to use the first declaration (where all of the parameters are strings) and simply pass the constant vbNullString as the value of lpszKey any time you wish to obtain a list of keys. While more efficient, the nice thing about the dual function approach used here is that it allows each function to have a more descriptive name, leading to more readable code. Use of aliasing and vbNullString will be mixed throughout the book depending on the needs of the application and programmer's whim.

The VB?INI.BAS file contains additional declarations for writing initialization files as follows:

```
Declare Function WritePrivateProfileStringByKeyName% Lib "kernel32" Alias _
 "WritePrivateProfileStringA" (ByVal lpApplicationName As String, ByVal _
lpKeyName _As String, ByVal lpString As String, ByVal lplFileName As String)
Declare Function WritePrivateProfileStringToDeleteKey% Lib "kernel32" Alias _
 "WritePrivateProfileStringA" (ByVal lpApplicationName As String, ByVal _
lpKeyName As String, ByVal lpString As Long, ByVal lplFileName As String)
Declare Function  WritePrivateProfileStringToDeleteSection% Lib "kernel32" _
Alias "WritePrivateProfileStringA" (ByVal lpApplicationName As _
String, ByVal lpKeyName As Long, ByVal lpString As Long, ByVal lplFileName _
As String)
```

Using the API Functions

Comprehensive documentation for using the private initialization file functions can be found in Chapter 13. This section will focus on just one or two common tasks.

First, consider the problem of obtaining a list of keys for a particular section. The code for this can be found in the cmdListKeys_Click( ) function in file VB?INI.FRM.

```
Private Sub cmdListKeys_Click()
Dim characters As Long
Dim KeyList$

    KeyList$ = String$(128, 0)
    lstKeys.Clear

    ' Retrieve the list of keys in the section
    characters = GetPrivateProfileStringKeys("FirstSection", 0, "", KeyList$, _
    127, FileName$)

    ' Load sections into the list box
    Dim NullOffset%
    Do
        NullOffset% = InStr(KeyList$, Chr$(0))
        If NullOffset% > 1 Then
            lstKeys.AddItem Mid$(KeyList$, 1, NullOffset% - 1)
            KeyList$ = Mid$(KeyList$, NullOffset% + 1)
        End If
    Loop While NullOffset% > 1

End Sub
```

The GetPrivateProfileStringKeys alias for GetPrivateProfileString is used here in order to pass a NULL value as the second parameter. The return value of the function is the number of characters loaded into the KeyList$ buffer. GetPrivateProfileString, like all other Windows API functions that load data into a string, simply write data into a buffer that you provide. It is the calling function's responsibility to make sure that the buffer is large enough to hold the data. The function does this by initializing the string with the String$ function. The choice of 128 characters is arbitrary in this case; you should choose a buffer large enough for your particular application. The GetPrivateProfileString function allows you to specify the length of the buffer. You will note that the number is one less than the actual buffer length. The reason for this has to do with the way Windows handles strings. API functions treat strings as an array of characters that are terminated by the NULL character—chr$(0). If the function loads a word such as "Test" into a buffer, it will actually set five characters—the word "Test" followed by a null character. The question arises: Does the buffer length specified in the cchReturnBuffer& parameter include the NULL character or not? In other words, if you specify a buffer length of 4, will the function interpret that as 4 characters and assume that you have provided space for the null character, or will it interpret the 4 as the total length of the buffer including the null character? The documentation on this is vague for most functions, and it is not guaranteed to be consistent among all functions. The cost of allowing an extra character in the buffer is negligible and might potentially save you from a fatal error, thus many programmers will routinely allocate a buffer one character larger than the maximum buffer size specified to API functions just to be safe and avoid having to worry about it.

In order to make it possible to safely work with strings, API functions that load string buffers will always use one of the following techniques:

- Include a parameter that allows you to specify a maximum buffer size.

- Provide a function that allows you to determine the necessary buffer size before you call the function that loads the buffer.

- Document a maximum buffer length—the function is guaranteed to never need more than the space indicated.

Finally, this function parses the string. When you specify a null value as the key, the returned buffer contains all of the key strings, each one separated from the other by a single NULL character. The final string is followed by two NULL characters.

Reading Key Values

The technique shown here for reading a list of keys can easily be adapted to reading values for an individual key simply by using the GetPrivateProfileStringByKeyName alias of the function and substituting the name of the key for the lpszKey parameter. However, if your application needs to read more than one value from the initialization file, it will be necessary to remember to initialize the string buffer each time the function is used. This increases the risk of error. In addition, as you will see, some changes are needed to declare these functions for use under Win16, and these changes would have to be applied everywhere that the function is used.

These facts make this an excellent candidate for applying modular programming techniques. This is demonstrated in the VB?INI.BAS file in the VB-GetPrivateProfileString function.

```
' An example of modular programming - This provides a safer interface to
' GetPrivateProfileString
Function VBGetPrivateProfileString(section$, key$, File$) As String
    Dim KeyValue$
    Dim characters As Long
    KeyValue$ = String$(128, 0)

    characters = GetPrivateProfileStringByKeyName(section$, key$, "", _
    KeyValue$, 127, File$)

    If characters > 1 Then
        KeyValue$ = Left$(KeyValue$, characters)
    End If

    VBGetPrivateProfileString = KeyValue$
End Function
```

Once this function is written correctly and debugged, it provides a very safe interface to the API function that can be called throughout your program. This function also takes advantage of the characters' result value to trim off the trailing null character and return a string that contains only the text loaded by the function.

Suggestions for Further Practice

The Win32 documentation for GetPrivateProfileString is as follows:

```
lpszSection
Points to a null-terminated string that specifies the section containing the
key name. If this parameter is NULL, the GetPrivateProfileString function
copies all section names in the file to the supplied buffer.
```

- Create an alias for GetPrivateProfileString that will allow you to extract all of the section names from an INI file.

- Create a stand-alone class that exposes the private initialization functions in a form that can be used under both Win16 and Win32. You should be able to create a reusable module that can be added into any project to provide easy-to-use and safe access to these functions.

- Finally, this sample project could form the basis for a complete INI file browser and editor.

Writing Programs for 16- and 32-bit Platforms (VB 4 only)

Sometimes you may get the impression from the press and advertisements that Microsoft wants everyone to throw out all of their 16-bit software and tools and switch over immediately to pure 32-bit programming. This is probably because (near as I can tell) Microsoft actually does want everyone to throw out all of their 16-bit software and tools and switch over immediately to pure 32-bit programming.

Unfortunately, many programmers will not have the luxury of offering only 32-bit versions of their programs for some time to come—too many computers will continue to run Windows 3.1 and require 16-bit software. This means that many programmers will not be able to switch immediately to Visual Basic 5.0 and later—these versions of VB only support 32-bit development.

Programmers who must support both 16- and 32-bit platforms face two alternatives. They can support two separate code bases—A 16-bit code base for Visual Basic 3.0 or 4.0 and a 32-bit code base for Visual Basic 5.0. Or they can use Visual Basic 4.0's ability to create both 16- and 32-bit versions of applications from a single source code base. The remainder of this section shows you how a feature called *conditional compilation* makes this possible.

Conditional Compilation

The conditional compilation commands, #if, #else, #elseif, and #endif look very much like the standard if, else, elseif, and endif statements, and work in a similar fashion. The big difference between them lies in when the conditional operation is performed. The conditional compilation commands act on a program once—only during the compilation process. Regular conditional commands are executed while the program is running each time the program is running; they produce actual executable code. Consider the simple example from project CH04.VBP:

```
Option Explicit

' Compile time constant
#Const UCASECTCONSTANT = True
' Runtime constant
Dim UCASERTVARIABLE As Boolean

Private Sub Command1_Click()
Dim a$, b$

UCASERTVARIABLE = True

a$ = "This Was A Mixed Case String"
b$ = "This Was Another Mixed Case String"

#If UCASECTCONSTANT Then
    a$ = UCase$(a$)
#Else
    a$ = LCase$(a$)
#End If

If UCASERTVARIABLE Then
    b$ = UCase$(b$)
Else
    b$ = LCase$(b$)
End If

Print a$
Print b$

End Sub
```

When you execute this program, both strings are converted into uppercase and print as uppercase strings. Both types of conditionals seem to behave identically. However, there is a significant difference, which is shown in Figure 4.1.

Figure 4.1
Conditional
compilations versus
standard conditional
operators

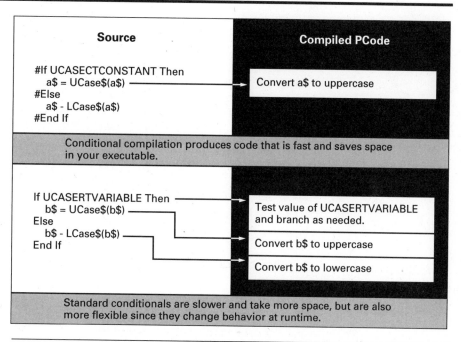

As you can see, in this example the conditional compilation causes only the a$ = UCase$(a$) to be compiled into P-Code and loaded into the executable file. When the program is run, the constant UCASECTCONSTANT does not exist, and no comparison operation is performed. With the standard comparison, both the upper- and lowercase options are compiled into P-Code along with the comparison test. Each time the command is executed, the comparison is performed and the appropriate code branch taken. This approach has the advantage of allowing you to change the UCASERTVARIABLE variable as the program is running—something that is not possible with compile time conditionals. In other words: Conditional compilation commands execute while Visual Basic is compiling the program, and standard conditional commands execute while the compiled program is running.

You may be wondering what happens when you use regular constants defined with the Const keyword (as compared to the #Const keyword). Regular constants also do not change at runtime, so it should in theory be possible for Visual Basic to remove any code that will never run. For example, if we defined UCASERTVARIABLE as

```
Const UCASERTVARIABLE = True
```

the lowercase term would never execute and it would be safe to remove the comparison and lowercase term, in effect producing the exact same code as produced when using conditional compilation. This is, in fact, exactly the kind of thing that smart optimizing compilers such as Visual C++ do to improve performance, though it does tend to reduce compilation speed. There is, unfortunately, no documentation on whether Visual Basic performs this particular optimization, or what other optimizations it does perform.

What makes conditional compilation so important with regard to creating code that will compile under both Win16 and Win32? Consider the following declaration example:

```
#If Win32 Then
Declare Function GetPrivateProfileStringByKeyName& Lib "kernel32" Alias _
"GetPrivateProfileStringA" (ByVal lpszSection$, ByVal lpszKey$, ByVal _
lpszDefault$, ByVal lpszReturnBuffer$, ByVal cchReturnBuffer&, ByVal lpszFile$)
#Else
Declare Function GetPrivateProfileStringByKeyName% Lib "Kernel" Alias _
"GetPrivateProfileString" (ByVal lpSection$, ByVal lpKeyName$, ByVal _
lpDefault$, ByVal lpReturnedString$, ByVal nSize%, ByVal lpfilename$)
#Endif
```

In this case you have two different declarations for the same function name. Each has a different set of parameter types and a different return value. Visual Basic, like most languages, reports an error when you create a duplicate definition for a function or variable, and if you tried to use standard conditional operators here, you would run into that problem, aside from the fact that you can't place code in the declaration section of your module.

Not only are conditional compilation operators allowed in the declaration section of a module, but since the False condition is never compiled, it is not detected as a duplicate definition—it simply doesn't exist in your program. This allows you to create code such as that shown above, where one declaration exists during a 32-bit compilation, and a completely different declaration exists during a 16-bit compilation with no possibility of conflict between them.

The Win32 and Win16 constants are predefined by Visual Basic according to the environment that you are using.

Platform-Sensitive Coding

Conditional compilation was made necessary by the differences between Win16 and Win32. These differences fall into two different categories with regard to writing source code that can compile on both Win16 and Win32.

First, there is the problem that you have already seen: Many variables, function return parameters, constant values, and function parameter data types have changed from 16 bits to 32 bits. In addition, the names of the dynamic link libraries that contain the Windows API functions have themselves changed. This means that every API function declaration is different under Win32, even if the function name and parameters remain identical. The parameter changes go beyond those caused by the change from 16-bit to 32-bit handles. In some cases the amount of data that can be handled by the API call is no longer subject to a previous 64K limit. This means that parameters that specify buffer length or functions that return a buffer size need to be 32 bits as well. In many cases, not only will the API function declaration need to be changed, but the data types of the Visual Basic variables that are used to work with that function. In some cases you may need to perform type conversions based on the platform that you are using.

A second, sometimes more subtle issue relates to functional differences between Win16 and Win32. The Win32 API is larger than the Win16 API and contains many more features. If you wish to write code for both systems you have two choices. You can write your program using a common subset of the Windows API—only using those functions that appear in a substantially compatible form in both APIs. Or you can take advantage of additional functions in Win32, using conditional compilation to remove those features from your program when creating a 16-bit application.

Example: Private Initialization Files—Revisited

The first part of this chapter illustrated the process of declaring and calling Win32 APIs through the example of implementing some of the private initialization file API functions. This example will now be extended to work under both Win16 and Win32.

Updating the Declarations

The first step is to create a set of 16-bit declarations to correspond to the 32-bit declarations used earlier. The resulting code can be found in file VB4INI.BAS:

```
#If Win32 Then
Declare Function GetPrivateProfileStringByKeyName& Lib "kernel32" Alias _
"GetPrivateProfileStringA" (ByVal lpApplicationName$, ByVal lpszKey$, ByVal _
lpszDefault$, ByVal lpszReturnBuffer$, ByVal cchReturnBuffer&, ByVal lpszFile$)
Declare Function GetPrivateProfileStringKeys& Lib "kernel32" Alias _
"GetPrivateProfileStringA" (ByVal lpApplicationName $, ByVal lpszKey&, ByVal _
lpszDefault$, ByVal lpszReturnBuffer$, ByVal cchReturnBuffer&, ByVal lpszFile$)
Declare Function GetPrivateProfileStringSections& Lib "kernel32" Alias _
```

```
"GetPrivateProfileStringA" (ByVal lpApplicationName &, ByVal lpszKey&, _
ByVal lpszDefault$, ByVal lpszReturnBuffer$, ByVal cchReturnBuffer&, ByVal _
lpszFile$)
Declare Function WritePrivateProfileStringByKeyName& Lib "kernel32" Alias _
 "WritePrivateProfileStringA" (ByVal lpApplicationName As String, ByVal _
lpKeyName As  String, ByVal lpString As String, ByVal lplFileName As String)
Declare Function _WritePrivateProfileStringToDeleteKey& Lib "kernel32" Alias_
 "WritePrivateProfileStringA" (ByVal lpApplicationName As String, ByVal _
lpKeyName As String, ByVal_
 lpString As Long, ByVal lplFileName As String)
Declare Function WritePrivateProfileStringToDeleteSection& Lib "kernel32" Alias _
 "WritePrivateProfileStringA" (ByVal lpApplicationName As String, ByVal _
lpKeyName As Long, ByVal lpString As Long, ByVal lplFileName As String)
#Else
Declare Function GetPrivateProfileStringByKeyName% Lib "Kernel" Alias _
"GetPrivateProfileString" (ByVal lpApplicationName$, ByVal lpKeyName$, _
ByVal lpDefault$, ByVal lpReturnedString$, ByVal nSize%, ByVal lpfilename$)
Declare Function WritePrivateProfileStringByKeyName% Lib "Kernel" Alias _
 "WritePrivateProfileString" (ByVal lpApplicationName $, ByVal lpKeyName$, _
ByVal lpString$, ByVal lplFileName$)
Declare Function GetPrivateProfileStringKeys% Lib "Kernel" Alias + _
"GetPrivateProfileString" (ByVal lpApplicationName $, ByVal lpKeyName&, ByVal _
lpDefault$, ByVal lpReturnedString$, ByVal nSize%, ByVal lpfilename$)
Declare Function WritePrivateProfileStringToDeleteKey% Lib "Kernel" Alias _
 "WritePrivateProfileString" (ByVal lpApplicationName $, ByVal lpKeyName$, _
ByVal lpString&, ByVal lplFileName$)
Declare Function WritePrivateProfileStringToDeleteSection% Lib "Kernel" Alias _
 "WritePrivateProfileString" (ByVal lpApplicationName $, ByVal lpKeyName&, _
ByVal lpString&, ByVal lplFileName$)
#End If
```

The latter section (after the #Else statement) contains the Win16 declarations. Note that these functions all return integers whereas those Win32 declarations that return a character count return longs instead. We could actually cheat here and change the Win32 declarations to all return integers. Why? Because it is not possible for a line or value in an initialization file to contain over 32K characters. This means that the high word of the result will always be zero. This would let us avoid having to use different types of variables to hold the results when the functions are called.

The reverse is not true: You cannot set the Win16 declarations to return long values. While it is true that the declaration will not cause a DLL calling convention error or exception, the Win16 API does not guarantee that the high word of the result would be set to zero. Of course you could explicitly clear the high word of the result using the AND operation, but this approach is less efficient than simply using conditional compilation.

Even if you change the return type, the only benefit would be a possible savings in some conditionally compiled code when the function is called. You will still need two separate declarations due to the differences in DLL name and parameters. This example, and all other examples in this book, will follow the convention of having the Visual Basic return type correspond to the actual return type specified by the API documentation. The intent here is to demonstrate a general and reliable approach to writing dual platform code; doing otherwise creates additional risk of error and provides very little benefit.

Updating the Code

Consider now the VBGetPrivateProfileString function from file VB?INI.BAS that was demonstrated earlier. The only change that is required is in the "characters" variable, which will contain the returned data. This variable will be a long value under Win32 and an integer under Win16.

```
Function VBGetPrivateProfileString(section$, key$, File$) As String
    Dim KeyValue$
    #If Win32 Then
        Dim characters As Long
    #Else
        Dim characters As Integer
    #End If
    KeyValue$ = String$(128, 0)
    characters = GetPrivateProfileStringByKeyName(section$, key$, "", _
    KeyValue$, 127, File$)
    If characters > 1 Then
        KeyValue$ = Left$(KeyValue$, characters)
    End If

    VBGetPrivateProfileString = KeyValue$
End Function
```

The actual call to GetPrivateProfileStringByKeyName remains identical, since the only parameter that differs is the constant 127, and Visual Basic will automatically convert that number to the appropriate type according to the declaration.

You might be wondering, why bother with conditional compilation for the characters variable? Couldn't you use an integer variable? In general, this would be dangerous because a truncation can occur (with a possible overflow error) when converting the 32-bit number to 16 bits. To be fair, in this case using an integer would be safe because the result will always be zero to a relatively small number of characters.

Then perhaps you could always use a long value? The answer here, surprisingly, is yes. In the 32-bit program you would obviously have no problems, and in the 16-bit program Visual Basic will always be able to successfully convert the integer result from the function into a 32-bit long data type. The only trade-off would be a very slight impact on performance due to the extra conversion that would be needed, but this should be extremely small. This can be seen in the beginning part of the cmdListKeys_Click( ) function from VB?INI.FRM

```
Private Sub cmdListKeys_Click()
    Dim characters As Long
    Dim KeyList$

    KeyList$ = String$(128, 0)
    lstKeys.Clear

    ' Retrieve the list of keys in the section
    ' Note that characters is always a long here -      ' in 16 bit mode
    ' VB will convert the integer result of the API      ' function into
    ' a long - no problem.
    characters = GetPrivateProfileStringKeys("FirstSection", 0, "", KeyList$, _
    127, FileName$)
```

So in this particular case you could easily create a function that runs correctly under both platforms without requiring conditional compilation. When would this not be possible? Any time the function returns a handle. In that case using a long in a 16-bit environment is not generally a good idea. Returning a handle and assigning it to a long variable will work correctly, but when you try to use that long value as a parameter to another function that expects an integer handle, there is a strong probability that an overflow error will occur during the conversion.

Functional Differences

You have already seen that it is possible to use the GetPrivateProfileString API to obtain a list of available keys for a section in an INI file (refer to the Reading Key Values section earlier in this chapter). One feature that the Win32 API provides with regard to initialization files is the ability to obtain a list of all of the sections in an initialization file. How then can you incorporate this functionality into only the 32-bit version of the program while keeping it from interfering with the compilation, operation, and user interface of the 16-bit program?

The first thing that you should consider is how to handle the different functionality from a design perspective. Should the differences between editions be apparent to the user? If so, how? In some cases you can accomplish the same functionality on both platforms using different techniques and there will be no differences from the user's perspective.

For this example, it was decided to provide an additional button on the main form that would list all of the sections in the file into a message box. A more robust application might provide a separate form to specify which section to edit as the basis of a complete initialization file editor, but that will be left as an exercise to the reader.

Figure 4.2 shows the main form for the VB4INI project. The List Keys button causes the list box to be loaded with a list of the keys for section "SampleKeys1" (this value is hard coded into the program for this example). Clicking on any of these keys causes the key and value to be displayed in the corresponding text boxes. You can edit the value for a key, or create a new key and value and have them added into the section by choosing the Edit Entry button. Finally, you can delete the highlighted key by clicking on the Delete Key button. Listing 4.1 contains the complete program listing for file VB5INI.FRM. File VB?INI.BAS, which is also part of the project, contains the API declarations and function VBGetPrivateProfileString, the listings for which can be found earlier in this section.

Figure 4.2
Layout of
VB4INI.FRM

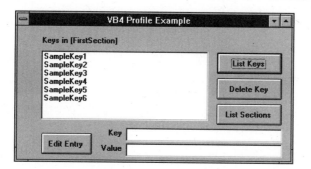

The VB5INI.VBP project code shown here still includes the conditional compilation support present in the Visual Basic 4.0 project. Because conditional compilation removes unused code from the project, this code has no impact on the VB5 project, thus VB5 programmers may disregard those sections and remove them from the project if they wish.

Listing 4.1   VB5INI.FRM: Private Initialization File Sample

```
VERSION 5.00
Begin VB.Form frmVB5INI
   Caption        =    "VB5 Profile Example"
   ClientHeight   =    3135
```

Listing 4.1   **VB5INI.FRM: Private Initialization File Sample (Continued)**

```
ClientLeft       =   1095
ClientTop        =   1485
ClientWidth      =   6600
BeginProperty Font
   name          =   "MS Sans Serif"
   charset       =   1
   weight        =   700
   size          =   8.25
   underline     =   0     'False
   italic        =   0     'False
   strikethrough =   0     'False
EndProperty
Height           =   3540
Left             =   1035
LinkTopic        =   "Form1"
ScaleHeight      =   3135
ScaleWidth       =   6600
Top              =   1140
Width            =   6720
Begin VB.CommandButton cmdShowSections
   Caption       =   "List Sections"
   Height        =   495
   Left          =   4800
   TabIndex      =   9
   Top           =   1800
   Width         =   1575
End
Begin VB.CommandButton cmdDeleteKey
   Caption       =   "Delete Key"
   Height        =   495
   Left          =   4800
   TabIndex      =   8
   Top           =   1200
   Width         =   1575
End
Begin VB.CommandButton cmdAdd
   Caption       =   "Edit Entry"
   Height        =   495
   Left          =   600
   TabIndex      =   7
   Top           =   2520
   Width         =   1215
End
Begin VB.TextBox txtNewValue
   Height        =   285
   Left          =   2640
   TabIndex      =   6
   Top           =   2760
```

Listing 4.1   VB5INI.FRM: Private Initialization File Sample (Continued)

```
      Width           =   3735
   End
   Begin VB.TextBox txtNewKey
      Height          =   285
      Left            =   2640
      TabIndex        =   5
      Top             =   2400
      Width           =   3735
   End
   Begin VB.CommandButton cmdListKeys
      Caption         =   "List Keys"
      Height          =   495
      Left            =   4800
      TabIndex        =   2
      Top             =   600
      Width           =   1575    .
   End
   Begin VB.ListBox lstKeys
      Height          =   1590
      Left            =   600
      TabIndex        =   0
      Top             =   600
      Width           =   3975
   End
   Begin VB.Label Label3
      Alignment       =   1  'Right Justify
      Caption         =   "Value"
      Height          =   255
      Left            =   1920
      TabIndex        =   3
      Top             =   2760
      Width           =   615
   End
   Begin VB.Label Label2
      Alignment       =   1  'Right Justify
      Caption         =   "Key"
      Height          =   255
      Left            =   1920
      TabIndex        =   4
      Top             =   2400
      Width           =   615
   End
   Begin VB.Label Label1
      Caption         =   "Keys in [FirstSection]"
      Height          =   255
      Left            =   600
      TabIndex        =   1
      Top             =   240
```

Listing 4.1   **VB5INI.FRM: Private Initialization File Sample (Continued)**

```
        Width           =   2415
    End
End
Attribute VB_Name = "frmVB4INI"
Attribute VB_GlobalNameSpace = False
Attribute VB_Creatable = False
Attribute VB_PredeclaredId = True
Attribute VB_Exposed = False
Option Explicit

Dim FileName$
Const INIFILE = "private.ini"

'
' Add a new key and value into the INI file section
'
Private Sub cmdAdd_Click()
    Dim success%

    If Len(txtNewKey.Text) = 0 Or Len(txtNewValue.Text) = 0 Then
        MsgBox "Key and value must both be specified"
        Exit Sub
    End If

    ' Write the new key
    success% = WritePrivateProfileStringByKeyName%("FirstSection", _
    txtNewKey.Text, txtNewValue.Text, FileName$)

    If success% = 0 Then
        Dim msg$
        msg$ = "Edit failed - this is typically caused by a write protected INI _
        file"
        msg$ = msg$ & Chr$(10) & "Try copying the file and project to your hard _
        disk."
        MsgBox msg$
        Exit Sub
    End If

    cmdListKeys_Click    ' Refresh the list box

End Sub

'
' Delete the selected key
'
Private Sub cmdDeleteKey_Click()
    Dim success%
```

Listing 4.1   **VB5INI.FRM: Private Initialization File Sample (Continued)**

```
If lstKeys.ListIndex < 1 Then
    MsgBox "No selected entries in the list box"
    Exit Sub
End If
' Delete the selected key
success% = WritePrivateProfileStringToDeleteKey ("FirstSection", _
lstKeys.Text, 0, FileName$)

If success% = 0 Then
    Dim msg$
    msg$ = "Delete failed - this is typically caused by a write protected _
    INI file"
    msg$ = msg$ & Chr$(10) & "Try copying the file and project to your hard _
    disk."
    MsgBox msg$
    Exit Sub
End If

cmdListKeys_Click    ' Refresh the list box

End Sub
```

Win16 does not provide the ability to list all of the sections in a private initialization file. The code in the cmdListKeys_Click( ) function will never execute because the command button that triggers it is hidden during the Form_Load( ) event. However, you can still use conditional compilation to make the event code conditional on being compiled in the 32-bit environment. The advantage of this approach is that it strips the extra code from your 16-bit executable, which will provide a slight reduction in memory usage and load times.

```
' List all of the keys in a particular section
'
Private Sub cmdListKeys_Click()
    Dim characters As Long
    Dim KeyList$

    KeyList$ = String$(128, 0)
    lstKeys.Clear

    ' Retrieve the list of keys in the section
    ' Note that characters is always a long here - in 16 bit mode
    ' VB will convert the integer result of the API function
    ' into a long - no problem.
    characters = GetPrivateProfileStringKeys ("FirstSection", 0, "", KeyList$, _
    127, FileName$)
```

```
    ' Load sections into the list box
    Dim NullOffset%
    Do
        NullOffset% = InStr(KeyList$, Chr$(0))
        If NullOffset% > 1 Then
            lstKeys.AddItem Mid$(KeyList$, 1, NullOffset% - 1)
            KeyList$ = Mid$(KeyList$, NullOffset% + 1)
        End If
    Loop While NullOffset% > 1

End Sub

Private Sub cmdShowSections_Click()
#If Win32 Then
    Dim characters As Long
    Dim SectionList$

    SectionList$ = String$(128, 0)

    ' Retrieve the list of keys in the section
    characters = GetPrivateProfileStringSections(0, 0,  "", SectionList$, 127, _
    FileName$)

    ' Load sections into the list box
    Dim NullOffset%
    Dim MsgString$
    Do
        NullOffset% = InStr(SectionList$, Chr$(0))
        If NullOffset% > 1 Then

            MsgString$ = MsgString$ & Chr$(10) & Mid$(SectionList$, 1, _
            NullOffset% - 1)
            SectionList$ = Mid$(SectionList$, NullOffset% + 1)
        End If
    Loop While NullOffset% > 1
    MsgBox MsgString$, 0, "Sections in file"
#endif
End Sub
```

During the Form_Load( ) event you can hide the command button that triggers the display of section names. This illustrates one way that you can use conditional compilation to change the user interface between the two environments. In an extreme case you could actually create two different forms, one for the 16-bit version and another for the 32-bit version of your program, and only load the one that you need.

```
'
' This sample expects to see the INI file in the application
' directory. At design time, the current directory is VB, so
' we add the app.path to make sure we choose the right ' place.
```

```
' The \ handling deals with the unlikely event that the INI ' file is in the _
root directory.
'
Private Sub Form_Load()
    FileName$ = App.Path
    If Right$(FileName$, 1) <> "\" Then FileName$ = FileName$ & "\"
    FileName$ = FileName$ & INIFILE
#If Win16 Then
    ' We can't show sections on Win16
    cmdShowSections.Visible = False
#End If


End Sub

Private Sub lstKeys_Click()
    Dim KeyValue$
    ' Retrieve the list of keys in the section
    KeyValue$ = VBGetPrivateProfileString("FirstSection", lstKeys.Text, _
    FileName$)

    txtNewKey.Text = lstKeys.Text
    txtNewValue.Text = KeyValue$
End Sub
```

When Conditional Compilation Is Not Available

The Visual Basic language is now the underlying language for platforms other than Visual Basic itself. Visual Basic Applications (VBA) is now part of Excel, Access, FoxPro, Project, and Word. Unfortunately, older versions of some of these applications do not support conditional compilation. In this case, you will need to take advantage of declaration aliasing to come up with different function names for the 16- and 32-bit functions.

```
Declare Function GetPrivateProfileStringByKeyName32& Lib "kernel32" Alias _
"GetPrivateProfileStringA" (ByVal lpszSection$, ByVal lpszKey$, ByVal _
lpszDefault$, ByVal lpszReturnBuffer$, ByVal cchReturnBuffer&, ByVal lpszFile$)

Declare Function GetPrivateProfileStringByKeyName16% Lib "Kernel" Alias _
"GetPrivateProfileString" (ByVal lpSection$, ByVal lpKeyName$, ByVal _
lpDefault$, ByVal lpReturnedString$, ByVal nSize%, ByVal lpfilename$)
```

You'll need to find out how your particular platform can determine at runtime whether it is running in 32-bit or 16-bit mode. In most cases you can use the OperatingSystem property of the Application object to determine if it is 16 or 32 bits and call the correct function accordingly. For example:

```
If instr(Application.OperatingSystem,"32") then
     res = GetPrivateProfileStringByKeyName32 (......
else
     res = GetPrivateProfileStringByKeyName16 (......
Endif
```

Porting Existing 16-Bit Code

You have already seen some of the issues that need to be addressed in writing code that supports both 16- and 32-bit applications. In the private initialization file example, you actually saw the less common approach—essentially porting a 32-bit application to also run on 16-bit Windows. This section will address the more common concern: how to port 16-bit applications to 32 bits.

This section will briefly introduce the principles involved in doing this type of porting and the changes that exist between the 16- and 32-bit API. Examples of the porting process itself will be scattered throughout the book. You will see how some of the examples from the original Visual Basic Programmer's Guide to the Windows API (16 bit) were ported to 32 bits for this book.

This section is intended for readers who are new to Win32 but have experience with API programming under earlier 16-bit editions of Visual Basic. If you are not yet acquainted with 16-bit API programming, much of this section will prove cryptic and confusing. You are strongly encouraged to skip this part of the chapter and return to it after you have read further through this book.

This section should also prove useful in creating Visual Basic 4.0 programs that are intended to be compiled for both 16- and 32-bit platforms.

Functions That Have Changed

Most of the changes to existing API functions have to do with the evolution of handles from 16- to 32-bit values. Many Win16 functions, for example, would return two 16-bit values packed into a single 32-bit long return value. This is no longer possible with Win32 in cases where the function needs to return two 32-bit values. In order to provide the same functionality, many of these functions now have an "Ex" version of the function, which has an additional parameter which points to a structure that is loaded with the two 32-bit result values on return. Many of these Ex suffixed functions also exist under Win16, so it is relatively easy to implement a solution that runs on both platforms. Table 4.1 summarizes functions that have changed due to parameter changes or changes due to the way Win32 loads modules.

Table 4.1 **Functions with Changed Parameters**

Function	Summary of Change
AddFontResource	No longer accepts a handle to a loaded module as a parameter.
GetAspectRatioFilter	Use GetAspectRatioFilterEx.
GetBitmapDimension	Use GetBitmapDimensionEx.
GetBrushOrg	Use GetBrushOrgEx.
GetClassWord	Many of the values that could be retrieved using this function under Win16 are now 32-bit long values under Win32, thus GetClassLong is used to retrieve them instead. The previous constant values that describe offsets of the information to retrieve have changed as well. Refer to Chapter 5 for additional information.
GetCurrentPosition	Use GetCurrentPositionEx.
GetDCOrg	Use GetDCOrgEx.
GetMetaFileBits	Use GetMetaFileBitsEx.
GetModuleUsage	Under Win32 there is a greater separation between modules. This means that one application has no knowledge of whether modules are used by other applications. Refer to Chapter 14 for further information.
GetTextExtent	Use GetTextExtentPoint.
GetTextExtentEx	Use GetTextExtentPoint.
GetViewportExt	Use GetViewportExtEx.
GetViewportOrg	Use GetViewportOrgEx.
GetWindowExt	Use GetWindowExtEx.
GetWindowOrg	Use GetWindowOrgEx.
GetWindowWord	Many of the values that could be retrieved using this function under Win16 are now 32-bit long values under Win32, thus GetWindowLong is used to retrieve them instead. The previous constant values that describe offsets of the information to retrieve have changed as well. Refer to Chapter 5 for additional information.
MoveTo	Use MoveToEx.
OffsetViewportOrg	Use OffsetViewportOrgEx.
OffsetWindowOrg	Use OffsetWindowOrgEx.
RemoveFontResource	No longer accepts a handle to a loaded module as a parameter.

Table 4.1   **Functions with Changed Parameters (Continued)**

Function	Summary of Change
ScaleViewportExt	Use ScaleViewportExtEx.
ScaleWindowExt	Use ScaleWindowExtEx.
SetBitmapDimension	Use SetBitmapDimensionEx.
SetClassWord	See notes for GetClassWord.
SetMetaFileBits	Use SetMetaFileBitsEx.
SetViewportExt	Use SetViewportExtEx.
SetViewportOrg	Use SetViewportOrgEx.
SetWindowExt	Use SetWindowExtEx.
SetWindowOrg	Use SetWindowOrgEx.
SetWindowWord	See notes for SetWindowWord.

Functions that Have Vanished

Win32 does provide a high level of compatibility with Win16, but some functions have been completely dropped. In most cases new functions exist to provide similar or improved functionality. Table 4.2 lists these functions. This list is not a complete list of all functions dropped from Win16 to Win32, but includes those functions that are accessible and useful to Visual Basic programmers.

Table 4.2   **Functions That Are No Longer Supported**

Function	Summary of Change
AccessResource	Use LoadResource, LockResource, and FindResource instead.
AllocResource	Use LoadResource, LockResource, and FindResource instead.
CloseComm	Win32 has new communications support.
CloseSound	The old synthesizer-based sound system that was defined by Windows 1.0, actually worked in Windows 2.0, and was rendered obsolete (though still supported) by Windows 3.x, is finally dead and gone.
CountVoiceNotes	See CloseSound.

Table 4.2   **Functions That Are No Longer Supported (Continued)**

Function	Summary of Change
DeviceMode	Replaced by DocumentProperties.
ExtDeviceMode	Replaced by DocumentProperties.
FlushComm	Win32 has new communications support.
GetCommError	Win32 has new communications support.
GetCurrentPDB	Use GetCommandLine or GetEnvironmentStrings.
GetKBCodePage	Refer to Chapter 6 for information on new locale functions.
GetTempDrive	Use GetTempPath.
GetThresholdEvent	See CloseSound.
GetThresholdStatus	See CloseSound.
OpenComm	Win32 has new communications support.
OpenSound.	See CloseSound.
ReadComm	Win32 has new communications support.
SetCommEventMask	Win32 has new communications support.
SetSoundNoise	See CloseSound.
SetVoiceAccent	See CloseSound.
SetVoiceEnvelope	See CloseSound.
SetVoiceNote	See CloseSound.
SetVoiceQueueSize	See CloseSound.
SetVoiceSound	See CloseSound.
SetVoiceThreshold	See CloseSound.
StartSound	See CloseSound.
StopSound	See CloseSound.
SyncVoices	See CloseSound.
UngetCommChar	Win32 has new communications support.
WaitSoundState	See CloseSound.

Porting Messages

Regardless of whether you are sending or posting a message, the parameters received by the window function for a window are the same. There is a window handle, message number, and two parameters, wParam and lParam. Here you can see the differences between the parameter types for a windows message under 16- and 32-bit windows based on the SendMessage API function.

```
#If Win16 Then
Declare Function SendMessage Lib "User" (ByVal hWnd As Integer, ByVal wMsg As _
Integer, ByVal wParam As Integer, lParam As Any) As Long
#else
Declare Function SendMessage Lib "user32" Alias "SendMessageA" (ByVal hwnd As _
Long, ByVal wMsg As Long, ByVal wParam As Long, lParam As Any) As Long
#End if
```

When converting from 16-bit code, the window handle and message both become 32 bits—this is the easy part. The wParam and lParam properties are bigger issues. In some cases, windows messages used the lParam parameter to pass two different values to a windows function (one in the high word, the other in the low word). If one of those values was a handle, that handle under Win32 requires the full 32 bits of the parameter. This tells you that the meanings of the lParam and wParam parameters for some Windows messages have been changed.

Table 4.3 lists those messages where the meanings of the wParam and lParam parameters have changed. Refer to Part 3 of this book for reference information on each of these messages.

Table 4.3   Messages Impacted by the Conversion to Win32

WM_ACTIVATE

WM_CHARTOITEM

WM_COMMAND

WM_CTLCOLOR

WM_MDIACTIVATE

WM_MDISETMENU

WM_MENUCHAR

WM_MENUSELECT

WM_PARENTNOTIFY

Table 4.3	**Messages Impacted by the Conversion to Win32 (Continued)**
	WM_VKEYTOITEM
	EM_GETSEL
	EM_LINESCROLL
	EM_SETSEL
	WM_HSCROLL
	WM_VSCROLL

Fortunately, only a few of these messages are used by API programmers within Visual Basic. However, if you are using a subclassing control in your application, you may need to adapt your code to handle the new meanings of the wParam and lParam parameters. Your control vendor should provide information on the porting process with the 32-bit versions of their controls.

One very important change that is both easy to fix and easy to overlook is that the actual message numbers have in some cases changed. For example, the message number for the LB_FINDSTRINGEXACT message is &H423 under Win16 and &H1A2 under Win32. The WM_xxx message numbers have remained the same, but all of the message numbers for controls have changed. When writing code to run under both Win16 and Win32, you will need to define these constants using conditional compilation as shown below:

```
#if WIN32 Then
Const LB_FINDSTRINGEXACT& =  & H1A2
#else
Const LB_FINDSTRINGEXACT& =  ( WM_USER+35 )
#endif 'WIN32
```

Porting Issues Related to Changes to the Windows Architecture

If the only concern when porting 16-bit code to Win32 was the change of handles from 16 bits to 32 bits and an occasional rearrangement of message parameters, porting would indeed be a simple process. If only that were the case. There are some architectural differences between Win32 and Win16 that can have a major impact in some cases.

The biggest change is in how Windows manages memory. Under 16-bit Windows, memory is shared among all applications. This means that applications are able to read and write memory that is used by other applications. This is most often done by dynamic link libraries, which can be used by multiple applications simultaneously. It is also possible for applications to easily exchange blocks of memory.

Under Win32, dynamic link libraries can still be used by multiple applications simultaneously, but Windows builds a wall between the data space available to the different applications. Applications cannot easily read or write another application's memory, nor can they easily exchange blocks of data. It can still be done, but it requires substantial effort to do so and it is unlikely to happen through an accident or bug. Applications can no longer share graphic objects such as bitmaps, pens, and brushes without explicitly transferring ownership of the object to the other application.

Any programs that depend on the ability to find out information about another application are potentially impacted by this change in architecture. This subject will be covered in more depth in Chapter 14.

The input queue is also impacted by the multitasking nature of Win32 operating systems. Applications can only set and retrieve focus to windows within their own application (though low-level third-party tools are available to provide these types of capabilities). Mouse capture is impacted as well. Issues relating to capture and focus are covered further in Chapter 5.

Translating API Documentation to Visual Basic (Part 2—Files and Structures)

Up until now, this chapter has focused on functions—function declarations and usage under both Win32 and Win16. Another extremely important aspect of Windows API programming relates to data structures and file formats.

Why include data structures and file formats together? Because as soon as you examine one of the many file format standards supported by Windows, you find that they almost always consist of a very sophisticated collection of data structures. The process of reading and interpreting a file using Visual Basic requires that you not only translate the various C/C++ structures to Visual Basic user defined types, but that you also understand the internal organization of variables within a structure. This subject will be revisited again in Chapter 15 with a more in-depth examination of the behavior of strings within data structures.

Example: TrueType Font Browser

When you install a font under Windows several things happen. Windows creates a font resource file (with the extension .FOT) which it uses to access the font information. Windows also adds information describing the font to the WIN.INI file and/or system registry and loads the font resource when Windows is booted. This makes the font available to all applications and causes it to appear in the various font combo boxes and font common dialogs—depending on the application. Windows provides API functions that let you create a font resource and install a TrueType font on your system. It also provides functions to retrieve information about a font that is installed on the system, and even functions to remove fonts from the system. These are discussed further in Chapter 11. But what if you want to create a font management program or font loading program that can browse through a list of fonts that are on disk? There are no API functions that let you extract information directly from a font file.

The documentation for the TrueType file format (.TTF) is not included with any of the standard Windows API documentation (16 or 32 bits). It can, however, be downloaded from CompuServe or Microsoft's FTP site—look for file TTF_SPEC.HLP. The documentation is rather extensive (to put it mildly), but the important information for this exercise can be found in Chapter 4 of the help file. The file format description begins thus:

```
The Table Directory

The TrueType font file begins at byte 0 with the Offset Table.
```

Type	Name	Description
Fixed	sfntversion	0x00010000 for version 1.0.
USHORT	numTables	Number of tables.
USHORT	searchRange	(Maximum power of 2 <= numTables) x 16.
USHORT	entrySelector	Log2(maximum power of 2 <= numTables).
USHORT	rangeShift	NumTables x 16-searchRange.

In C/C++ this might appear like this:

```
struct OffsetTable {
    Fixed       sfntversion;
    USHORT      numTables;
    USHORT      searchRange;
    USHORT      entrySelector;
    USHORT      rangeShift;
};
```

As you can see, the first 12 bytes of the file correspond exactly to a structure. You could load the structure by opening the TrueType file in binary mode and reading the structure directly using a Get operation, which is exactly what the sample FontInfo project that follows will do. The USHORT data type is clear from Chapter 3: It is an unsigned short (16-bit) integer. The Fixed data type is not as obvious. It is, in fact, defined earlier in the TrueType specification file as two 16-bit integers that represent the version number of the file. Now the translation to Visual Basic becomes clear:

```
Type OffsetTable
  sfntVersionA As Integer
```

```
    sfntVersionB As Integer
    numTables As Integer
    searchRange As Integer
    entrySelector As Integer
    rangeShift As Integer
End Type
```

Now that you have a structure, a good first step is to examine some actual font files and try loading the structure for those files and examining some of the fields to make sure that they make sense. This helps verify the accuracy of the conversion to VB.

The FontInfo project in the source\ch04 directory on your CD-ROM contains a form with a standard drive, directory, and file list control, set up to allow you to choose a font file. When you click on the font file in the file list control, function LoadFontInfo in FONTINFO.BAS is called with a mode parameter based on the Option1 option buttons. LoadFontInfo loads information about the selected font into the List1 control. Figure 4.3 shows the layout of the FontInfo project in run mode. Refer to Listing 4.2 later in this chapter for a complete program listing including form header information.

Figure 4.3
Layout of form
FONTINFO.FRM

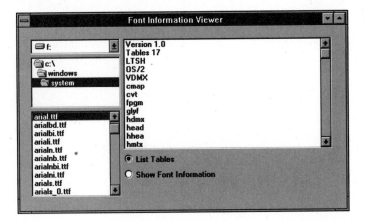

For now, consider this small code fragment extracted from LoadFontInfo that loads the OffsetTable structure and adds the version information and number of tables to the list box:

```
Global OT As OffsetTable   ' Found in FontInfo.Bas

#If Win32 Then
Declare Function GetWindowsDirectory Lib "kernel32" Alias _
"GetWindowsDirectoryA" (ByVal lpBuffer As String, ByVal nSize As Long) As Long
```

```
Declare Function GetVersion Lib "kernel32" () As Long
#Else
Declare Function GetVersion& Lib "Kernel" ()
Declare Function GetWindowsDirectory% Lib "Kernel" (ByVal lpBuffer$, ByVal _
nSize%)
#End If


Sub LoadFontInfo(filename$, list1 As ListBox, mode%)

    list1.Clear
    fileid% = FreeFile   ' Get a file ID

    Open filename$ For Binary Access Read As #fileid%
    Get #fileid%, , OT ' Retrieve the offset table
```

Note: These two lines differ from the code in the FontInfo project—the reasons for this will quickly become apparent.

```
list1.AddItem "Version " & OT.sfntVersionA & "." & OT.sfntVersionB
list1.AddItem "Tables " & OT.numTables
```

If you execute this code fragment the results will be interesting. The version number for most fonts will be 256.0, and the number of tables will vary but will typically be in the thousands. Since it is logically impossible for a font whose total size is only a few thousand bytes to have thousands of tables, it is clear that something is seriously wrong.

An Aside on Byte Ordering

This section is about to cover a subject that few Visual Basic programmers have ever needed to consider and that the vast majority of VB programmers will be able to continue to avoid. The only people who will run into this are those who are working with files or structures that are in some way compatible with or convertible to non-PC-based operating systems. With the advent of 32-bit Visual Basic and VBA, the chances of this occurring have increased substantially, as Visual Basic is becoming available on an increasing number of non-PC platforms (keep in mind that the applications edition of Visual Basic, VBA, is already found on the Macintosh).

If you are not concerned with sharing files or code across platforms, the issues that are about to be raised with regard to byte ordering are unlikely to impact your own programming efforts and you should be able to safely skip this section.

The question raised by the peculiar results of the LoadFontInfo function is this: How can a font that is probably version 1.0 show up as version 256.0? To see this, it is necessary to look at the hexadecimal values for these version numbers. 1 in hex is still &H0001. 256 in hex is &H0100. The difference between them is the order of the bytes within an integer.

That the issue here is byte ordering is confirmed in the TrueType specification by the following line in the DataTypes section of the help file:

```
"All TrueType fonts use Motorola-style byte ordering (Big Endian):"
```

Motorola, which developed the 68000 series processors used in the Macintosh, differed from Intel and its 8086 line in many ways, including the order of bytes in a number. Consider the following four bytes in memory starting from address zero:

```
00 01 02 03
```

How are these bytes organized into integers and longs? On a Motorola processor, you would get the two integers 0x0001 and 0x0203 or the long value 0x00010203. On an Intel processor, you would get the two integers 0x0100 and 0x0302 or the long value 0x03020100. Don't be misled by the fact that the Motorola ordering looks like it makes more sense on paper; the choice of organization goes to the lowest level hardware architecture of the processors and neither ordering has an inherent superiority over the other. However, the fact that they don't agree means that conversions are necessary. Since TrueType files were meant to be readable on both Macintosh and PC type computers, they had to choose one byte ordering or the other. They chose Motorola's, so it is up to your program to perform its own byte swapping. To do this you'll need the following three functions:

```
' Note that we swap the low order bytes in a long ' so that
' we don't have to worry about overflow problems
'
Function SwapInteger (ByVal i As Long) As Long
    SwapInteger = ((i \ &H100) And &HFF) Or ((i And &HFF) * &H100&)
End Function
'
' Swap a long value from Motorola to Intel format or vice versa
'
Function SwapLong (ByVal l As Long) As Long
    Dim addbit%
    Dim newlow&, newhigh&

    newlow& = l \ &H10000
    newlow& = SwapInteger(newlow& And &HFFFF&)

    newhigh& = SwapInteger(l And &HFFFF&)
    If newhigh& And &H8000& Then
        ' This would overflow
        newhigh& = newhigh And &H7FFF
        addbit% = True
    End If
    newhigh& = (newhigh& * &H10000) Or newlow&
    If addbit% Then newhigh = newhigh Or &H80000000
```

```
    SwapLong = newhigh&

End Function
' Swap every other byte in a Unicode string
Sub SwapArray(namearray() As Byte)
    Dim u%, p%
    Dim b As Byte
    u% = UBound(namearray)
    For p = 0 To u - 1 Step 2
        b = namearray(p)
        namearray(p) = namearray(p + 1)
        namearray(p + 1) = b
    Next p
End Sub
```

Note the extra effort that had to be put in to avoid overflow situations. On the integer side, a simple solution was to work entirely in longs. On the long side it is necessary to handle the high bit separately to avoid overflows. A more efficient solution that avoids all risk of overflow is to use the agSwap-Bytes and agSwapWords functions from APIGID32.DLL. The SwapArray function reverses all of the byte pairs in a Unicode string (which consists of 16-bit integers instead of 8-bit bytes).

A small change in the LoadFontInfo function now produces the correct results of version 1.0 and 17 tables for ARIAL.TTF.

```
list1.AddItem "Version " & SwapInteger (OT.sfntVersionA) & "." & SwapInteger _
(OT.sfntVersionB)
list1.AddItem "Tables " & SwapInteger(OT.numTables)
```

The Table Directory

The OffsetTable is followed by a series of structures called TableDirectories. The TrueType specification describes them as follows:

```
This is followed at byte 12 by the Table Directory entries. Entries in the
Table Directory must be sorted in ascending order by tag.
```

Type	Name	Description
ULONG	tag	4 -byte identifier.
ULONG	checkSum	CheckSum for this table.
ULONG	offset	Offset from beginning of TrueType font file.
ULONG	length	Length of this table.

```
Tags are the names given to tables in the TrueType font file. At present, all
tag names consist of four characters, though this need not be the case. Names
with less than four letters are allowed if followed by the necessary trailing
spaces.
```

In C/C++ this structure would probably look like this:

```
struct TableDirectory {
  BYTE   tag[4];
```

```
    ULONG checkSum;
    ULONG offset;
    ULONG length;
};
```

Why is the tag field specified as a long in the original specification and as a byte array in C? This choice is made based on an interpretation of the description for the field. It may use the 32-bit long type in the definition, but the description clearly states that this field will contain a 4-byte "name" for the table. Both definitions use 32 bits, so the choice is really dictated by which is easier for the application program to use. The Visual Basic type would thus be as follows:

```
Type TableDirectoryEntry
      tag(3) As Byte
      checkSum As Long
      offset As Long
      length As Long
End Type
```

The first thing you might notice here is that the tag Byte array is defined as three bytes, not four as shown in the C structure. This illustrates a very important issue relating to the definition of byte arrays, especially in structures. On a simple array declaration such as this one, Visual Basic always allocates entries in the array starting from index zero. Thus this array actually does contain four bytes numbered zero through three. If you used tag(4) As Byte, you would actually allocate five bytes which would lead to erroneous results.

The choice of a Byte array instead of a fixed length string ensures the allocation of individual bytes. The 32-bit edition of Visual Basic has the option of allocating fixed length strings in Unicode, in which case the string would take 8 bytes instead of 4.

Table 4.4 lists the following possible tags for table directory structures.

Table 4.4   **Tag Names for TableDirectory Structures**

Tag Name	Description
'cmap'	Character to glyph mapping
'glyf'	Glyph data
'head'	Font header
'hhea'	Horizontal header
'hmtx'	Horizontal metrics

Table 4.4	Tag Names for TableDirectory Structures (Continued)	
Tag Name	**Description**	
'loca'	Index to location	
'maxp'	Maximum profile	
'name'	Naming table	
'post'	PostScript information	
'OS/2'	OS/2 and Windows specific metrics	
'cvt '	Control Value Table	
'fpgm'	Font program	
'hdmx'	Horizontal device metrics	
'kern'	Kerning	
'LTSH'	Linear threshold table	
'prep'	CVT Program	
'PCLT '	PCL5	
'VDMX'	Vertical Device Metrics table	

The LoadFontInfo function in mode 1 displays the names of all of the tables in the font file as shown in the following fragment from the function:

```
Dim TD As TableDirectoryEntry
For n& = 1 To SwapInteger(OT.numTables)
  Get #fileid%, , TD
  ' We used to be able to add the string directly    ' (Win16), but
  ' Using a byte array requires a conversion
  list1.AddItem TagToString(TD)
Next n&
```

TagToString is a function that converts an array of bytes into a string so that it can be loaded into the list box as follows:

```
Public Function TagToString(TD As TableDirectoryEntry)
    Dim tagstr As String * 4
    Dim x%
    For x% = 1 To 4
        Mid(tagstr, x%, 1) = Chr$(TD.tag(x% - 1))
    Next x%
    TagToString = tagstr
End Function
```

The Naming Table

For the purposes of this example, only one of these tables is important—the Naming table. This table contains text descriptions of various attributes of the font. The TrueType specification describes the contents of this table as follows:

```
The Naming Table is organized as follows:

Type     Description
USHORT   Format selector (=0).
USHORT   Number of NameRecords that follow n.
USHORT   Offset to start of string storage (from start of table).
n NameRecords      The NameRecords.
(Variable)   Storage for the actual string data .

Each NameRecord looks like this:

Type     Description
USHORT   Platform ID.
USHORT   Platform-specific encoding ID.
USHORT   Language ID.
USHORT   Name ID.
USHORT   String length (in bytes).
USHORT   String offset from start of storage area (in bytes).
```

This description is a little bit confusing at first glance. What you really have here are two different structures. The first is a NamingTable structure that actually contains only three integer fields. The "n NameRecords" label actually just indicates that each NamingTable structure is followed by some number of NameRecord structures.

In C/C++ these structures might be defined as follows:

```
struct NamingTable {
    USHORT FormatSelector;
    USHORT NameRecords;
    USHORT offsStrings;
};

struct Type NameRecord {
    USHORT PlatformID;
    USHORT PlatformSpecific;
    USHORT LanguageID;
    USHORT NameID;
    USHORT StringLength;
    USHORT StringOffset;
};
```

As with the other C declarations in this section, you won't actually find these declarations in the TrueType specification file. They are included here only to help illustrate the correspondence between C structure declarations and Visual Basic type declarations. In this case, the conversions are trivial—all 16-bit integers as follows:

```
Type NamingTable
    FormatSelector As Integer
    NameRecords As Integer
    offsStrings As Integer
End Type

Type NameRecord
    PlatformID As Integer
    PlatformSpecific As Integer
    LanguageID As Integer
    NameID As Integer
    StringLength As Integer
    StringOffset As Integer
End Type
```

Before writing the code to scan through these functions, there are a few utility functions that would be handy in terms of improving the readability of the display. The PlatformID is a value from zero to three that indicates the platform encoding for this particular string. This is important because different systems use different character sets. The NameID field is a value currently defined to be from zero to seven that indicates the meaning of the string. Thus NameID 0 is always the copyright notice for the font. The GetPlatform-ForID and GetNameForID functions return string descriptions for the various values as follows:

```
Function GetPlatformForID (ByVal id As Long) As String
    Dim s$
    Select Case id
        Case Ø
            s$ = "Apple Unicode"
        Case 1
            s$ = "Macintosh"
        Case 2
            s$ = "ISO"
        Case 3
            s$ = "Microsoft"
    End Select
    GetPlatformForID = s$
End Function

Function GetNameForID (ByVal id As Long) As String
    Dim s$
    Select Case id
        Case Ø
            s$ = "Copyright"
        Case 1
            s$ = "Font Family"
```

```
        Case 2
            s$ = "Font subfamily"
        Case 3
            s$ = "Font Identifier"
        Case 4
            s$ = "Full Font Name"
        Case 5
            s$ = "Version"
        Case 6
            s$ = "Postscript name"
        Case 7
            s$ = "Trademark"
        Case Else
            s$ = "Unknown"
    End Select
    GetNameForID = s$
End Function
```

The character set issue will be quite important, as you will see. Visual Basic's ability to handle Unicode strings will become quite useful, as the NameRecord structure supports strings in both ANSI and Unicode formats.

The entire LoadFontInfo function is shown in Listing 4.2. Passing 1 as the value for the mode parameter displays the various strings for the font in the list box.

Listing 4.2   The LoadFontInfo Function

```
Sub LoadFontInfo(filename$, list1 As ListBox, mode%)
    Dim fileid%
    Dim TD As TableDirectoryEntry
    Dim NT As NamingTable
    Dim NR As NameRecord
    Dim n&
    Dim NTStart&     ' Start of naming table
    Dim CurrentLoc& ' Current location in file
    Dim nrnum&
    Dim nameinfo() As Byte
    Dim nPlatformID&
    Dim stroffset&

    list1.Clear
    fileid% = FreeFile   ' Get a file ID

    Open filename$ For Binary Access Read As #fileid%
    Get #fileid%, , OT ' Retrieve the offset table
    list1.AddItem "Version " & SwapInteger(OT.sfntVersionA) & "." & _
    SwapInteger(OT.sfntVersionB)
    list1.AddItem "Tables " & SwapInteger(OT.numTables)
```

Listing 4.2   The LoadFontInfo Function (Continued)

```
Select Case mode%
    Case 0  ' List all tables
        For n& = 1 To SwapInteger(OT.numTables)
            Get #fileid%, , TD
            ' We used to be able to add the string _
            directly (Win16), but
            ' Using a byte array requires a conversion
            list1.AddItem TagToString(TD)
        Next n&
    Case 1  ' Name Information
        For n& = 1 To SwapInteger(OT.numTables)
            Get #fileid%, , TD
            If TagToString(TD) = "name" Then
            ' Seek to the specified location in the file
            NTStart& = SwapLong(TD.offset) + 1
            Seek #fileid%, NTStart&
            Get #fileid%, , NT
          list1.AddItem "NumRecords " & SwapInteger(NT.NameRecords)
            For nrnum& = 1 To SwapInteger(NT.NameRecords)
                Get #fileid%, , NR
                list1.AddItem "NameRecord # " & nrnum&
                list1.AddItem "  Platform ID: " &  GetPlatformForID( _
                SwapInteger( NR.PlatformID))
                list1.AddItem "  NameID: " & _
                GetNameForID$(SwapInteger(NR.NameID))
                nPlatformID = SwapInteger(NR.PlatformID)
                If (nPlatformID = 1 Or nPlatformID = 3) And _
                NR.StringLength <> 0 Then
                 ' Mark the current location in the file
                 CurrentLoc& = Seek(fileid%)
                 ' Calculate the length of the string
                 ReDim nameinfo(SwapInteger ( NR.StringLength) - 1)
                 ' Calculate the location of the string
                 ' It should be possible to use the NT.offsStrings field _
                 to determine the
                 ' start location of the string table, but it turns out _
                 some fonts get this
                 ' wrong, so we calculate it based on the number of _
                 NameRecord structures
                 ' and the size of the structures.
                 stroffset = 6 + SwapInteger(NT.NameRecords) * 12
                 ' Get #fileid%, NTStart& + SwapInteger(NT.offsStrings) _
                  +SwapInteger (NR.StringOffset), nameinfo
                 Get #fileid%, NTStart& + stroffset + _
                 SwapInteger(NR.StringOffset), nameinfo
                 Select Case nPlatformID
```

Listing 4.2   The LoadFontInfo Function (Continued)

```
                        Case 1  ' Macintosh (ANSI)
                            #If Win32 Then
                                list1.AddItem "  " & StrConv(nameinfo, _
                                vbUnicode)
                            #Else
                                list1.AddItem "  " & CStr(nameinfo)
                            #End If
                        Case 3  ' Microsoft (Unicode)
                            #If Win32 Then
                                SwapArray nameinfo()
                                list1.AddItem "  " & CStr(nameinfo)
                            #Else
                                list1.AddItem "  " & "Not supported in 16 bit _
                                environments"
                            #End If
                    End Select
                    ' Restore the previous location
                    Seek #fileid%, CurrentLoc&
                Else
                        list1.AddItem "  - This program only diplays Macintosh _
                        and  Microsoft strings"
                End If
            Next nrnum&

            Exit For
        End If
    Next n&
End Select


    Close #fileid%

End Sub
```

The function is largely documented by the comments in the code. Note how it is necessary to swap both the bytes within integers and the words with long variables in order to properly calculate offsets in the file. When dealing with most Windows structures and file formats this type of byte and word swapping is not necessary. In fact, it is frequently necessary for people programming on the Macintosh platform to swap variables when reading Windows file formats.

You can also see the problem that Unicode can cause within a file. A byte array is used to load the string data from the file. Visual Basic can convert a byte array into a string, but it assumes that the byte array is already in the same format that is used internally by Visual Basic, which is Unicode under 32 bits. The VB StrConv function is used to convert the ANSI string into Unicode when reading ANSI strings. Under 16 bits, this step is not necessary as the 16-bit Visual Basic uses ANSI internally. When reading Microsoft formatted strings, the array is already in Unicode format, however every 16-bit character is byte swapped and needs to be changed into the correct format using the SwapArray function. On a 16-bit system it would be necessary to convert this string to ANSI, but since Unicode to ANSI conversions are not supported by 16-bit Visual Basic, this functionality is disabled for 16-bit environments. It is possible to convert the string using VB code one character at a time if necessary.

The listings shown to this point are from file FONTINFO.BAS. The remaining listings for the FontInfo project (file FONTINFO.FRM) are shown in Listing 4.3.

Listing 4.3   **FONTINFO.FRM**

```
VERSION 5.00
Begin VB.Form frmFontInfo
    Caption         =   "Font Information Viewer"
    ClientHeight    =   4305
    ClientLeft      =   825
    ClientTop       =   1905
    ClientWidth     =   7935
    BeginProperty Font
        name            =   "MS Sans Serif"
        charset         =   1
        weight          =   700
        size            =   8.25
        underline       =   0       'False
        italic          =   0       'False
        strikethrough   =   0       'False
    EndProperty
    Height          =   4710
    Left            =   765
    LinkTopic       =   "Form1"
    ScaleHeight     =   4305
    ScaleWidth      =   7935
    Top             =   1560
    Width           =   8055
    Begin VB.OptionButton Option1
        Caption         =   "Show Font Information"
        Height          =   315
        Index           =   1
        Left            =   2580
        TabIndex        =   5
```

Listing 4.3 **FONTINFO.FRM (Continued)**

```
      Top              =    3300
      Width            =    2595
   End
   Begin VB.OptionButton Option1
      Caption          =    "List Tables"
      Height           =    315
      Index            =    0
      Left             =    2580
      TabIndex         =    4
      Top              =    2940
      Value            =    -1  'True
      Width            =    2595
   End
   Begin VB.ListBox List1
      Height           =    2565
      Left             =    2580
      TabIndex         =    3
      Top              =    300
      Width            =    4995
   End
   Begin VB.FileListBox File1
      Height           =    1980
      Left             =    300
      Pattern          =    "*.ttf"
      TabIndex         =    2
      Top              =    1980
      Width            =    2175
   End
   Begin VB.DirListBox Dir1
      Height           =    1155
      Left             =    300
      TabIndex         =    1
      Top              =    720
      Width            =    2175
   End
   Begin VB.DriveListBox Drive1
      Height           =    315
      Left             =    300
      TabIndex         =    0
      Top              =    300
      Width            =    2175
   End
End
Attribute VB_Name = "frmFontInfo"
Attribute VB_GlobalNameSpace = False
Attribute VB_Creatable = False
Attribute VB_PredeclaredId = True
Attribute VB_Exposed = False
```

Listing 4.3   **FONTINFO.FRM (Continued)**

```
Option Explicit

Dim CurrentOption%

Private Sub Dir1_Change()
    file1.Path = Dir1.Path
End Sub

Private Sub Drive1_Change()
    Dir1.Path = Drive1.Drive
End Sub

Private Sub file1_Click()
    LoadFontInfo file1.Path & "\" & file1.filename, list1, CurrentOption
End Sub

Private Sub Form_Load()
    Dim d$, r&
    d$ = String$(255, 0)
    r& = GetWindowsDirectory(d$, 254)
    d$ = Left$(d$, r)
    If GetVersion() > 0 Then d$ = d$ & "\system" Else d$ = d$ & "\fonts"
    Dir1.Path = d$
    file1.ListIndex = 0
End Sub

Private Sub Option1_Click(Index As Integer)
    CurrentOption% = Index
    file1_Click
End Sub
```

Porting Notes

Some of you may recognize the FontInfo project from an article I wrote in 1995 for use with Visual Basic 3.0. One of the most astonishing things about this project was how trivial it was to port from Win16 to Win32. One of the reasons for this is that the project does not use any Windows API calls. Another is that all of the data types in these structures were defined originally to an absolute size—none of the sizes changed from Win16 to Win32. If they had, the data files would become virtually unreadable between one system and another (or would have required complex conversion code).

Structures used in memory are not always as cooperative, and there have been changes to some of the standard API structures as you will see in examples that follow in later chapters.

Debugging API Code

One of the nice things about Visual Basic is that it is a safe environment to program in. It allows you to experiment and test your code interactively without worrying about sudden exceptions or general protection faults that could cause you to lose your work or possibly corrupt the system. This safety is increased further with the transition to 32-bit operating systems which limit the ability of one application to harm another.

This safety takes an equally important though more subtle form within your own application. Languages that allow more direct access to memory using features such as pointers make it possible for your code to introduce tough-to-find bugs caused by various types of memory corruption. For example, if you pass a pointer to an integer variable to a function that expects a pointer to a long variable, that function can overwrite the memory next to the integer value that was passed. While this may cause the program to fail, it is equally likely that the problem will remain undetected. This can lead to errors in results, to intermittent errors that only occur under very specific circumstances, or to errors that are not detected until long after the data overwrite occurs. These types of bugs can be incredibly difficult to track down.

The Visual Basic language, and the way that Visual Basic encapsulates a large part of the Windows API, provide this safety and this in turn is one of the reasons that Visual Basic is such an efficient programming environment. But the price of this safety includes some limitations in capability. Fortunately, VB makes it possible to avoid those limitations and go directly to the Windows API or custom dynamic link libraries. Unfortunately, when you do so you lose part of that blanket of protection provided by Visual Basic.

Used correctly, calling Windows API functions from Visual Basic is absolutely safe.

Used incorrectly, calling Windows API functions can make your program unstable and lead to exactly the kind of bugs described at the start of this section—bugs that can crash your program and bugs that can cause subtle or intermittent errors in your software's operation or results.

The vast majority of API programming errors fall into a few categories, mostly relating to improper function declaration. In 1993 I came up with ten principles, or "commandments," for safe API programming which became the subject for several conferences and an article or two. The following revised edition of these commandments is based on several years of answering questions and seeing the same problems arise over and over again in the public CompuServe and Internet forums.

Ten Commandments for Safe API Programming (Revised)

I. Remember ByVal and keep it wholly.

I would guess that about 90 percent of all Windows API programming errors are due to either a missing ByVal statement or (on rare occasions) the addition of an unnecessary ByVal statement.

This point cannot be stressed enough. If there is one thing that you gain from this entire book, let it be this: **Double-check and triple-check your declarations to make sure the ByVal statement is used where needed**. If you are using the "As Any" term in any declarations (see commandment 5), this becomes even more important.

The consequences of a missing ByVal statement are usually dire; it almost always results in corrupted memory and frequently leads to a fatal exception.

II. Thou shalt check thy parameter types.

If a missing ByVal statement causes 90 percent of all API errors, incorrect parameter types in declarations surely cause 50 percent of all other API errors. This is even more important under Win32 because 8-, 16-, and 32-bit numeric variables are all passed as 32 bits, and errors can be subtle if they show up at all. Be extra careful for cases where the parameter type is missing. If you forget to type a parameter you are likely to see a "Bad DLL Calling Convention" error as VB tries to pass a Variant to the API function.

III. Thou shalt check thy return types.

It is quite common for people to forget to add a type specification to a function declaration. In this case Visual Basic will assume that the function returns a variant. Since API functions do not return variants, this is yet another source for "Bad DLL Calling Convention" errors.

IV. Thou shalt preinitialize thy strings, lest ye become corrupted.

If you pass a string variable to an API function that is expecting a pointer to a buffer that it can load with data, be very careful to initialize your string to the proper length before calling the function. If you are using a Byte array, be sure to redimension it to sufficient length. The API functions have no way of knowing how long the buffer is that you provided—they assume that the calling program has allocated enough space.

If you do not provide a large enough buffer, the API function may overwrite the end of the buffer, thus trampling over whatever lies after that string in memory—be it other strings, internal Visual Basic data structures, and so on. The result can range from an immediate exception to an intermittent problem that won't show up until you have shipped your program to thousands of customers, at which point it will probably appear on every one of their systems at once.

V. Thou shalt not use "As Any," for it is evil.

The case for "As Any" was made at the beginning of this chapter. At least another 50 percent of all API errors are caused by people who forget to use a ByVal or type specifier when calling a function that was declared with the "As Any" type.

VI. Thou shalt specify "option explicit."

The very first thing you should do when installing Visual Basic is to make sure that the "Require Variable Declaration" environment option is turned on (which inserts the line Option Explicit into the first line of each module). Allowing Visual Basic to create a variable every time you enter a simple typographical error is a sure road to disaster when it comes to API programming. Especially since all of the new variables will probably be created as variants— meaning that Visual Basic's ability to convert variable types will prevent errors being triggered when API functions are called. Instead, VB will happily pass NULL values for strings, longs, integer, and every other type. The result will once again vary from total disaster to your program simply not working.

VII. Honor thy VB integers and thy Win32 integers— for they are not alike.

Always remember that "Integer" means 16 bits under Visual Basic and when reading Win16 C/C++ documentation, but means 32 bits when reading C/C++ Win32 documentation. Keep this in mind whenever looking at documentation or application notes relating to Windows API functions or 32-bit dynamic link libraries. When you hear or read about integers, be sure you understand the context that the source is referring to. This will help you to create correct API function declarations and data structures, and help you use them safely.

VIII. Always recheck your function names, for they are now case-sensitive and may have suffixes.

Windows API Function names are case-sensitive under Win32, and are not case-sensitive under Win16. If a function cannot be found in a DLL, there is a chance that you entered it incorrectly. Also keep in mind the use of the A and W suffixes on those functions that handle strings.

IX. Thou shalt check parameter and return values.

Part of Visual Basic's efficiency as a programming environment derives from the fact that it is an interpreter. This means that you can break at any line and test and modify values of variables. You can change the next instruction to execute commands (including API functions) in immediate mode and test their return values.

When an API function fails to do what you expect, the reason is frequently that one of the parameters is of the wrong type or has an incorrect value. If an API function expects a handle to a device context, a window handle is guaranteed not to work.

Trace through your program and see where each parameter comes from, verify that it is the correct type of object and that it has a reasonable value for the function in question. This is especially true in Visual Basic 4.0 which has added a new feature that is sometimes referred to as "evil type coersion." Consider the example of a function that expects a string parameter. If you accidently pass it a numeric value, Visual Basic will now happily convert the number to a string, which in the case of API calls is almost certainly not what you want to do.

Many API functions return a result to indicate whether or not they succeeded in their operation. Test this result. If it failed, there is a good chance that one of your parameters is incorrect in some way. Many API functions set an internal Win32 variable that provides extended error information which can be read using the LastDllError method of the Visual Basic Err object. This allows you to retrieve the GetLastError API function result for the API call and is documented in Chapter 6. A list of error code constants can be found in the API32.TXT file (look for the constants with the prefix ERROR_). Do not call GetLastError for a function unless you receive a result from the function that indicates that an error occurred; the internal error variable is not always cleared when an API function succeeds. Also note that not all functions set this variable. The reference section for this book indicates which functions are documented as setting the GetLastError function.

Once again, don't forget to recheck the original declaration if you are still having difficulty getting a function to work.

X. Save thy work often.

When a problem occurs with an API function call, it can lead to a fatal exception or can corrupt or freeze Visual Basic itself. You are strongly encouraged to save your project before testing code that accesses Windows API functions.

Moving On

This concludes the introductory portion of this book. Most of the remaining chapters of this book follow a consistent structure. Each chapter addresses a functional aspect of the Windows API. The chapter begins with an explanation of that part of the Windows API and any issues that relate specifically to Visual Basic. It also summarizes the API functions that are most closely related to the subject being covered. The chapter continues with one or more sample programs that illustrate the use of many of these functions. It concludes with a reference section that provides more in-depth information for each function.

While you can skip directly to chapters that cover subjects that interest you most, you should be aware that each chapter does build on the information provided earlier. More important, earlier chapters provide a more comprehensive explanation of basic concepts and include additional examples of porting techniques and dual platform techniques that are not necessarily directly related to the subject of the chapter.

Windows Control and Information Functions

Hardware and System Functions

Device Contexts

Drawing Functions

Bitmaps, Icons, and Raster Operations

Working with Menus

Text and Fonts

Printing

File Operations

Processes and Threads

Memory, Strings, Structures, and Resources

PART

2

Windows API Functions

5

Windows Control and Information Functions

T HIS CHAPTER COVERS THE WINDOWS API FUNCTIONS THAT DEAL DIRECTLY with the Windows objects that were introduced in Chapter 2. In Visual Basic, these include both forms and controls. In addition, two sample programs are presented. The RectPlay program demonstrates use of rectangle functions with Windows. The WinView program allows you to determine the hierarchy of windows in an application and obtain various types of information about them.

Rectangle and Point Functions

Before we discuss Windows objects themselves, it is important for you to understand two data structures that are used extensively in Windows: the rectangle (RECT) and the point (POINTAPI). These structures are used as parameters to many API functions. Keep in mind that the term "structure" is the API equivalent to the Visual Basic "user defined type" as created with the Type command.

A window by its very nature represents a rectangular area on the screen, so many functions that involve specification of all or part of a window's area use the RECT structure. The POINTAPI structure is frequently used in cases where an X,Y coordinate needs to be specified.

The RECT Structure

The RECT structure is defined in Visual Basic as follows:

```
Type RECT
     left As Long
     top As Long
     right As Long
     bottom As Long
End Type
```

The RECT structure is used to represent a rectangular area. The *left* and *top* fields describe the location of the first corner of the rectangle (normally the upper left corner). The *right* and *bottom* fields determine the size of the rectangle. The units and coordinate system for these fields can vary depending on the scaling in effect, the object being described, and the API function being called.

In most cases, the field names are merely conventions and have no functional connotations. For example, there is no absolute requirement that the contents of the bottom field be greater than the contents of the top field. The two locations described may be located anywhere, and may in fact be negative. Figure 5.1 shows some possible rectangles.

Note that the RECT structure has been changed from its WIN16 definition in which the four fields are defined as 16-bit integers. This means that

Figure 5.1

Sample rectangle

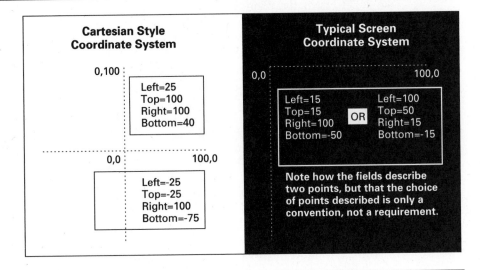

you will almost always need to change to this new definition when porting from 16-bit to 32-bit code.

Determining Rectangle Size

One of the slightly confusing subtleties in dealing with RECT structures is that the point specified by the right and bottom fields is generally not part of the rectangle. Consider the rectangle left=0, top=0, right=1, bottom=1, where the units are screen pixels. Intuitively, one might expect this to be a rectangle that is two units on each side (thus the rectangle would contain four pixels).

In fact, this rectangle describes a single pixel located at 0,0. The second point (1,1) is not part of the rectangle. This has two very important consequences for the programmer.

First, calculating the height and width of a rectangle is simple:

```
' rc is defined as type RECT
' Note that this example assumes a typical screen
' coordinate system in which the right, bottom fields
' do in fact describe the lower right corner.
' For other coordinate systems, you would need to take
' the absolute value of width& and height&
width& = rc.right - rc.left
height& = rc.bottom - rc.top
```

Second, the rectangle describes an empty rectangle (one that contains no pixels).

Using RECT Parameters

RECT structures are passed to Windows functions by reference. The parameter list for a RECT parameter will contain the entry (rcname As RECT). Do not try to use ByVal here.

The POINTAPI Structure

The POINTAPI structure is defined in Visual Basic as follows:

```
Type POINTAPI
    x As Long
    y As Long
End Type
```

The POINTAPI structure corresponds to the Windows POINT structure, but is defined as POINTAPI in Visual Basic to avoid conflict with the VB Point keyword.

POINTAPI is used to describe a location. As with the RECT structure, the units of the x and y fields depend on the object and API function being used.

Though a simple structure, the POINTAPI type illustrates some of the subtle concerns involved in both porting from Win16 to Win32, and writing code that can run on both platforms. To understand them, let's first look at the original Win16 POINTAPI definition, which is duplicated in Win32 with a "small" point structure called POINTS, which is defined as follows:

```
Type POINTS ' POINTAPI under Win16 has the same definition
    x As Integer
    y As Integer
End Type
```

Under Win16, where the POINTAPI structure uses integers instead of longs, Windows functions that accept POINTAPI structures as parameters often expect them as a 32-bit long value with the x field in the low order 16 bits and the y field in the high order 16 bits. This works because even though the POINTAPI structure differs from a long variable from a language viewpoint, it is stored exactly the same way in memory, with the x field followed in memory by the y field. This proved to be a very efficient way for returning point information as well—more efficient than passing the information by reference (for example, passing the address of the structure).

Functions often return a long value that has the x and y information packed into it in the same way. In fact, many Win16 functions use this technique to return two integer values efficiently. You can convert the Win16 POINTAPI structure or Win32 POINTS structure to a long mathematically as follows:

```
' EndPoint is defined as a POINTS structure
tlong& = EndPoint.x + CLng(EndPoint.y) * &H10000
```

Alternatively, you can use the agPOINTStoLong() function in the apigid32 DLL provided with this book to convert a POINTS or 16-bit POINTAPI structure directly to a long.

This technique will not work with the Win32 POINTAPI structure because it is not possible to place two 32-bit longs into a 32-bit long variable. How, then, does Win32 handle those functions which previously transferred point structures as longs? First consider the case of returning values: Most of the functions that returned two integers as a long under Win16 can still be used in Win32, but they truncate the return value, removing the high 16 bits from each integer value before returning the result. As long as the return values fit into an integer, this will work without any problems; however, if one of the return values exceeds the range of an integer (–32768 to 32767) the result will be in error. In order to provide a better solution, Win32 added new functions for each of these Win16 functions. These functions either accept two pointers to long variables or a pointer to a POINTAPI or SIZE structure in which the function can store the result. These new functions typically either return a status result or no result at all. Most of the new Win32 functions that have an "Ex" suffix work in this manner. An example of this type of function is the GetViewportOrgEx function which is the successor to the GetViewportOrg function. You will read more about this and similar functions in Chapter 6.

Passing POINTAPI structures to functions which used to take a long parameter is somewhat more complex. Under C and C++, it is possible to pass an entire structure by value to a function. This is the solution that was used for handling point structures in many cases. For example, the C declaration for the PtInRect API function, a function that determines if a particular point is within a specified rectangle, is as follows:

```
BOOL PtInRect(RECT *lprc, POINT pt);
```

The C declaration for the function is the same for both Win16 and Win32—though the declarations for the data types used (BOOL, RECT, and POINT) are different. Figure 5.2 shows how a POINT structure appears on the stack when passed as a parameter. As you see, the organization of the x and y field is the same on the two platforms except for the width of each field. Moreover, you can see how, on Win16, the two fields are organized in exactly the way the low and high word of a long variable would be arranged in memory.

The Visual Basic declaration for the 16-bit PtInRect function is:

```
Declare Function PtInRect Lib "User" (lpRect As RECT,_
  ByVal pt As Long) As Integer
```

How do we convert this to Win32? The return value is easy—the integer becomes a long. The library name changes to "user32" from "User." The lpRect parameter remains the same as well—since it is being passed by reference, a 32-bit address to the RECT structure is passed to the function.

Figure 5.2

Passing a POINT
structure on the
stack

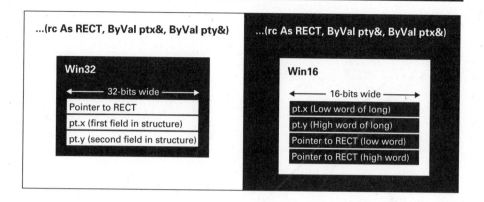

Though the definition of the RECT structure changes, pointers are 32 bits regardless of the platform. As you can see, the POINT structure is passed by value (there is no "*" character to indicate that a C pointer is being passed). This means that a C program using this API actually places the entire structure, two 32-bit values, onto the system stack to be used by the function as shown in Figure 5.2.

Your first reaction might be to create the following Visual Basic declaration:

```
Declare Function PtInRect Lib "user32" (lpRect As RECT, ByVal pt _
As POINTAPI) As Long
```

But there's a catch. Visual Basic cannot pass user defined types by value. Fortunately, it is not too difficult to trick Visual Basic into placing the entire structure onto the stack. You just have to do it one item at a time as follows:

```
Declare Function PtInRect Lib "user32" (lpRect As RECT, ByVal _
ptx As Long, ByVal pty As Long) As Long
```

It turns out that you can actually use this same approach under Win16 to pass a long parameter to a function by passing two integer parameters, thus making it easier to share code between the two platforms. However, note that the order of fields within the declaration differs between the two platforms. This happens because under the PASCAL calling convention used by the Win16 API, parameters are placed on the stack from left to right instead of the right to left order used by Win32.

Rectangle Functions and the RectPlay Example

Table 5.1 describes the Windows API functions that directly manipulate rectangles. Note that rectangles are used extensively by many other functions as well. These functions are described in full detail in the reference section of this chapter.

Table 5.1 **Rectangle Functions**

Function	Description
CopyRect	Copies the contents of one rectangle to another.
EqualRect	Returns TRUE (nonzero) if two rectangles are equal.
InflateRect	Increases or decreases the size of a rectangle.
IntersectRect	Obtains a rectangle that represents the intersection of two rectangles. This means that all points in the new rectangle are present in both source rectangles.
IsRectEmpty	Returns TRUE (nonzero) if a rectangle is empty.
OffsetRect	Moves the location of a rectangle by the offset specified.
PtInRect	Determines if a specified point is in a rectangle.
SetRect	Sets the fields of a rectangle via function (instead of assigning the fields directly).
SetRectEmpty	Sets a rectangle to empty by setting all fields to 0.
SubtractRect	Subtracts one rectangle from another. It effectively uses one rectangle to "cut off" part of another.
UnionRect	Obtains a rectangle that represents the union of two rectangles. This is the smallest rectangle that fully contains both source rectangles.

RectPlay is a program designed to illustrate use of some of the Windows API rectangle functions. Equally important, RectPlay demonstrates the process of porting a simple Win16 application to Win32. In fact, the program can be loaded and compiled successfully under both Win16 and Win32. Figure 5.3 shows the RectPlay program in action.

The RectPlay program defines two global RECT variables: Rect1 and Rect2. It lets you draw the rectangles using the mouse. It can display both rectangles as well as the corresponding intersection and union rectangles. A point mode brings up a message box describing whether the point is in any of these rectangles. As an aside, many of the figures in this book show the Win3.x interface rather than the new Windows 95 interface. This is in part because most of the development of this book was done on Windows NT using the older interface. Rest assured that the samples are all developed and

Figure 5.3
RectPlay program
screen

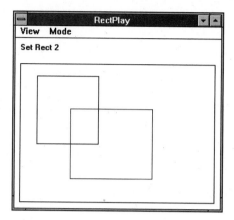

tested for Win32, and tested under both Windows NT 3.51, Windows NT 4.0 and Windows 95.

Project Description

The RectPlay project includes two files. RECTPLAY.FRM is the only form used by the program. RECTPLAY.BAS is the only module in the program and contains the constant type, global, and API definitions.

Form Description

Listing 5.1 contains the header from file RECTPLAY.FRM that describes the control setup for the form. The form contains a picture box on which you will be able to draw rectangles. No special action is required to convert the form to Win32—loading the 16-bit project into 32-bit Visual Basic suffices.

Listing 5.1   **Header for RECTPLAY.FRM**

```
VERSION 5.00
Begin VB.Form RectPlay
    Appearance      =   0  'Flat
    BackColor       =   &H80000005&
    Caption         =   "RectPlay"
    ClientHeight    =   3990
    ClientLeft      =   1095
    ClientTop       =   1770
    ClientWidth     =   4950
    BeginProperty Font
        name            =   "MS Sans Serif"
```

Listing 5.1   Header for RECTPLAY.FRM (Continued)

```
        charset       =  1
        weight        =  700
        size          =  8.25
        underline     =  Ø      'False
        italic        =  Ø      'False
        strikethrough =  Ø      'False
     EndProperty
     ForeColor     =  &H80000008&
     Height        =  4680
     Left          =  1035
     LinkMode      =  1 'Source
     LinkTopic     =  "Form1"
     ScaleHeight   =  3990
     ScaleWidth    =  4950
     Top           =  1140
     Width         =  5070
     Begin VB.PictureBox Picture1
        Appearance    =  Ø 'Flat
        BackColor     =  &H80000005&
        ForeColor     =  &H00000000&
        Height        =  3255
        Left          =  120
        ScaleHeight   =  215
        ScaleMode     =  3 'Pixel
        ScaleWidth    =  311
        TabIndex      =  Ø
        Top           =  600
        Width         =  4695
     End
     Begin VB.Label Label1
        Appearance    =  Ø 'Flat
        BackColor     =  &H80000005&
        Caption       =  "Label1"
        ForeColor     =  &H80000008&
        Height        =  255
        Left          =  120
        TabIndex      =  1
        Top           =  120
        Width         =  3735
     End
```

Checking the menu entry in the MenuViewBar pop-up menu causes the corresponding rectangle to be displayed.

```
Begin VB.Menu MenuViewBar
     Caption        =   "View"
     Begin VB.Menu MenuView
```

```
        Caption        =    "Rect&1"
        Checked        =    -1  'True
        Index          =    0
     End
     Begin VB.Menu MenuView
        Caption        =    "Rect&2"
        Checked        =    -1  'True
        Index          =    1
     End
     Begin VB.Menu MenuView
        Caption        =    "&Union"
        Index          =    2
     End
     Begin VB.Menu MenuView
        Caption        =    "&Intersect"
        Index          =    3
     End
  End
```

Each menu command in the ModeViewBar menu sets the global variable SettingState% to specify the action of the mouse on the picture control.

```
Begin VB.Menu ModeViewBar
     Caption          =    "Mode"
     Begin VB.Menu MenuMode
        Caption        =    "Point"
        Index          =    0
     End
     Begin VB.Menu MenuMode
        Caption        =    "SetRect1"
        Index          =    1
     End
     Begin VB.Menu MenuMode
        Caption        =    "SetRect2"
        Index          =    2
     End
End
```

Using RectPlay

The Mode menu defines the three operating modes for the RectPlay program. The three entries in this menu set the SettingState% global variable to one of its three allowed values. When SettingState% is 1 (the initial value), it is possible to draw a rectangle on the picture control by clicking the left mouse button at the first point, dragging the mouse while holding the button down, then releasing the mouse button at the second point. This defines a rectangle that is stored in variable Rect1. SettingState% of 2 is similar, except that the rectangle defined is stored in variable Rect2.

When SettingState% is 0, it is possible to click anywhere in the picture control. If the click position is anywhere within either of the two rectangles, their intersection, or their union, that information is displayed in a message box.

The View menu has four entries: Rect1, Rect2, Union, and Intersection, which indicate which rectangles will be displayed. Each rectangle is displayed in a different color.

RectPlay Program Listings

Before we look at our first program example, let's briefly review the conventions followed in presenting the listings. (See "How to Use This Book" for a full discussion of conventions.)

Program listings appear as saved in Visual Basic version 5.0 ASCII file format. While several of the programs are written to work under both 16- and 32-bit Visual Basic, the majority of the programs in this book are intended to run only under Win32. The listings divide into two parts. The header section describes the properties of both the form and the controls on the form. This header is fairly intuitive as can be seen from Listing 5.1 above, which shows the header for the RectPlay program. A detailed description of this format can be found in the appendix of the *Visual Basic Programmer's Guide*.

The balance of the listing describes the variables and procedures of the form or module. Use the declaration of each Sub or function to determine the object to which a subroutine is attached if you are using the Visual Basic editor to type in the code. For example,

```
Sub MenuView_Click(Index As Integer)
```

is code attached to the MenuView menu array.

All of the listings and executable programs provided with this book are compatible with version 5.0 of Visual Basic. Samples compatible with version 4.0 are also included on the CD-ROM. Applications which support both 16- and 32-bit code under Visual Basic 4.0 still include the 16-bit code in the VB 5.0 sample—however it is never used and is removed by the compiler based on the conditional compilation constants. In cases where applications contain long listings of constants, some of the constants may be left out of the printed book; however, they will be found in the sample program. In many cases the order of functions in the listing in the book will differ from the actual order of functions in the file. This is because the functions in the book have been rearranged to help make the listing explanations more coherent.

Listing 5.2 provides the code for module RECTPLAY.BAS. Listing 5.3 provides the code listing for form RECTPLAY.FRM.

Rect1 and Rect2 hold two rectangles set by the user. RectUnion and RectIntersect are set to the union and intersection of the rectangle. StartPoint and EndPoint are used during mouse tracking when the user is drawing the

Listing 5.2   Module RECTPLAY.BAS

```
Attribute VB_Name = "RECTPLAY1"
Option Explicit

' Rectplay
'
' Chapter 5 demonstration of rectangle operations

'-----------------------------------------------------------
'
'                      API Declarations
'
'-----------------------------------------------------------

#If Win32 Then
' 32-Bit declarations
Type RECT
        left As Long
        top As Long
        right As Long
        bottom As Long
End Type

Type POINTAPI
        X As Long
        Y As Long
End Type

Declare Function SetRect Lib "user32" (lpRect As RECT, ByVal X1 As Long, ByVal _
Y1 As Long, ByVal X2 As Long, ByVal Y2 As Long) As Long
Declare Function SetRectEmpty Lib "user32" (lpRect As RECT) As Long
Declare Function CopyRect Lib "user32" (lpDestRect As RECT, lpSourceRect As _
RECT) As Long
Declare Function InflateRect Lib "user32" (lpRect As RECT, ByVal X As Long, _
ByVal Y As Long) As Long
Declare Function IntersectRect Lib "user32" (lpDestRect As RECT, lpSrc1Rect As _
RECT, lpSrc2Rect As RECT) As Long
Declare Function UnionRect Lib "user32" (lpDestRect As RECT, lpSrc1Rect As _
RECT, lpSrc2Rect As RECT) As Long
Declare Function SubtractRect Lib "user32" (lprcDst As RECT, lprcSrc1 As RECT, _
lprcSrc2 As RECT) As Long
Declare Function OffsetRect Lib "user32" (lpRect As RECT, ByVal X As Long, _
ByVal Y As Long) As Long
Declare Function IsRectEmpty Lib "user32" (lpRect As RECT) As Long
```

Listing 5.2   **Module RECTPLAY.BAS (Continued)**

```
Declare Function EqualRect Lib "user32" (lpRect1 As RECT, lpRect2 As RECT) As _
Long
Declare Function PtInRect Lib "user32" (lpRect As RECT, ByVal ptx As Long, _
ByVal pty As Long) As Long

#Else
' 16-bit declarations
Type RECT
    left As Integer
    top As Integer
    right As Integer
    bottom As Integer
End Type

Type POINTAPI
    X As Integer
    Y As Integer
End Type

Declare Sub SetRect Lib "User" (lpRect As RECT, ByVal X1 As Integer, ByVal Y1 _
As Integer, ByVal X2 As Integer, ByVal Y2 As Integer)
Declare Sub SetRectEmpty Lib "User" (lpRect As RECT)
Declare Function CopyRect Lib "User" (lpDestRect As RECT, lpSourceRect As RECT) _
As Integer
Declare Sub InflateRect Lib "User" (lpRect As RECT, ByVal X As Integer, ByVal Y _
As Integer)
Declare Function IntersectRect Lib "User" (lpDestRect As RECT, lpSrc1Rect As _
RECT, lpSrc2Rect As RECT) As Integer
Declare Function UnionRect Lib "User" (lpDestRect As RECT, lpSrc1Rect As RECT, _
lpSrc2Rect As RECT) As Integer
Declare Sub OffsetRect Lib "User" (lpRect As RECT, ByVal X As Integer, ByVal Y _
As Integer)
Declare Function IsRectEmpty Lib "User" (lpRect As RECT) As Integer
Declare Function EqualRect Lib "User" (lpRect1 As RECT, lpRect2 As RECT) As _
Integer
Declare Function PtInRect Lib "User" (lpRect As RECT, ByVal pty As Integer, _
ByVal ptx As Integer) As Integer
Declare Function PtInRectByNum Lib "User" Alias "PtInRect" (lpRect As RECT, _
ByVal ptRect As Long) As Integer

#End If
```

Listing 5.2 Module RECTPLAY.BAS (Continued)

```
'----------------------------------------------------------
'
'                         Application Globals
'
'----------------------------------------------------------

' Global rectangles

Global Rect1 As RECT
Global Rect2 As RECT
Global RectUnion As RECT
Global RectIntersect As RECT

Global SettingState%     ' Ø = Point detect mode
                         ' 1 = Setting rect1
                         ' 2 = Setting rect2

Global StartPoint As POINTAPI
Global EndPoint As POINTAPI
Global HasCapture%  ' Indicates that tracking is in effect
```

Listing 5.3 RECTPLAY.FRM

```
Attribute VB_Name = "RectPlay"
Attribute VB_GlobalNameSpace = False
Attribute VB_Creatable = False
Attribute VB_PredeclaredId = True
Attribute VB_Exposed = False
' One of the first changes from the original code
' was to add Option Explicit here.  The original
' program goes back to VB 1.Ø!
'
Option Explicit
'    Displays information about the point in the EndPoint
'    global variable (which is set during the Picture1
'    MouseUp event).
'
Private Sub Form_Load()
    SettingState% = 1    ' Set the initial value
End Sub

'    Set the Label1 control based on the SettingState%
'    global variable to indicate to the user what the
'    operating mode is.
'
```

Listing 5.3   RECTPLAY.FRM (Continued)

```
Private Sub Form_Paint()
    Select Case SettingState%
        Case 0
            Label1.Caption = "Point Detect"
        Case 1
            Label1.Caption = "Set Rect 1"
        Case 2
            Label1.Caption = "Set Rect 2"
    End Select

End Sub

'   Set the SettingState% variable according to the
 mode command selected.
'
Private Sub MenuMode_Click(Index As Integer)
    SettingState% = Index
    RectPlay.Refresh
End Sub

'   Check or uncheck the item to view
'   Then redraw the picture box
'
Private Sub MenuView_Click(Index As Integer)
    If MenuView(Index).Checked Then
        MenuView(Index).Checked = 0
    Else MenuView(Index).Checked = -1
    End If
    Picture1.Refresh
End Sub
```

rectangles. Note how conditional compilation is used to support both Win16 and Win32 functions.

The MouseDown, MouseMove, and MouseUp events demonstrate a well-known technique for drawing a rectangle by dragging the mouse. The Mouse-Down event records the start location, or anchor, of the rectangle. The drawing mode is set to exclusive OR, meaning that drawing inverts the pixels on the screen. For example, on a white screen, the inversion process will draw a black line. However, if the same line is drawn a second time, the inversion process will restore the previous state—erasing the line.

The MouseMove event erases any existing rectangle using this technique, then draws a new rectangle from the anchor point to the current mouse position. Finally, the MouseUp procedure erases the final rectangle, records it in the appropriate global variable, and forces the entire display to be updated.

```
'    Record the current mouse location in StartPoint, and
'    set the drawing mode to exclusive or
'
Private Sub Picture1_MouseDown(Button As Integer, Shift As Integer, X As _
Single, Y As Single)
    ' This conversion is safe, as we are in pixels

    ' Note: The original RectPlay program used explicit type
    ' conversions such as "StartPoint.X = CInt(X)"
    ' Because the point fields can be integers or longs depending
    ' on platform, it's better to just let VB do its automatic
    ' conversion than to coerce it to the wrong one or use conditional _
    compilation.
    StartPoint.X = X
    StartPoint.Y = Y
    EndPoint.X = X
    EndPoint.Y = Y
    ' Drawing will be exclusive Or
    Picture1.DrawMode = vbNotXorPen
    HasCapture% = -1
End Sub


'    If mouse tracking is in effect, and a rectangle
'    is being drawn, erase the prior rectangle and draw
'    one based on the new location.
'
Private Sub Picture1_MouseMove(Button As Integer, Shift As Integer, X As _
Single, Y As Single)
    If SettingState% <> 0 And HasCapture% Then
        Picture1.Line (StartPoint.X, StartPoint.Y)-(EndPoint.X, EndPoint.Y), , B
        Picture1.Line (StartPoint.X, StartPoint.Y)-(X, Y), , B
    End If
    EndPoint.X = X
    EndPoint.Y = Y
End Sub

'    Erase the prior rectangle and save the information
'    in the appropriate global rectangle.
'
'
Private Sub Picture1_MouseUp(Button As Integer, Shift As Integer, X As Single, _
Y As Single)

    ' If we're not mouse tracking, exit the subroutine
    If Not HasCapture% Then Exit Sub

    If SettingState% <> 0 Then
        Picture1.Line (StartPoint.X, StartPoint.Y) - (EndPoint.X, EndPoint.Y), _
        , B
    End If
    EndPoint.X = X
    EndPoint.Y = Y
```

```
        Select Case SettingState%
            Case Ø
                DoPointDisplay   ' Show point information
            Case 1
                SetRect Rect1, StartPoint.X, StartPoint.Y, EndPoint.X, EndPoint.Y
            Case 2
                SetRect Rect2, StartPoint.X, StartPoint.Y, EndPoint.X, EndPoint.Y
        End Select
        HasCapture% = Ø
        ' Restore the original drawing mode
        Picture1.DrawMode = vbCopyPen
        Picture1.Refresh
End Sub


'   Draw each of the rectangles that are requested,
'   each in a different color.
'
Private Sub Picture1_Paint()
    Dim dl&

    ' Find the union and intersection rectangles
    ' Using API calls
    dl& = IntersectRect(RectIntersect, Rect1, Rect2)
    dl& = UnionRect(RectUnion, Rect1, Rect2)

    If MenuView(Ø).Checked Then ' Rect1
        Picture1.Line (Rect1.left, Rect1.top)-(Rect1.right, Rect1.bottom), _
        QBColor(1), B
    End If
    If MenuView(1).Checked Then ' Rect2
        Picture1.Line (Rect2.left, Rect2.top)-(Rect2.right, Rect2.bottom), _
        QBColor(2), B
    End If
    If MenuView(2).Checked Then ' Union
        Picture1.Line (RectUnion.left, RectUnion.top) - (RectUnion.right, _
        RectUnion.bottom)_
        , QBColor(8), B
    End If
    If MenuView(3).Checked Then
        Picture1.Line (RectIntersect.left, RectIntersect.top) - _
        (RectIntersect.right, RectIntersect.bottom), QBColor(4), B
    End If

End Sub
```

The DoPointDisplay function tests the contents of the EndPoint POINTAPI structure to see if the point that it defines lies in any of the four rectangles (RECT1, RECT2, the union, or the intersection). This function posed the greatest porting challenge due to its use of the PtInRect function. The technique for using two parameters to pass a structure as a parameter was described earlier. Two temporary variables, usex and usey, are defined both to differentiate between integer and long, and more important in this case, to define the order in which the parameters are passed. On Win16, the order is reversed so the first parameter (usex) is assigned the Y value of the structure. Fortunately, the POINTAPI structure is one of the very few cases where this type of problem occurs when working with the Windows API.

```
Private Sub DoPointDisplay()
    Dim outstring$, crlf$
    Dim tlong&

    ' Unfortunately, the order in which elements are
    ' placed on the stack differs for Win16 and Win32.
    ' So we have to do a swap as follows
#If Win32 Then
    Dim usex&, usey&
    usex = EndPoint.X
    usey = EndPoint.Y
#Else
    Dim usex%, usey%
    usex = EndPoint.Y
    usey = EndPoint.X
#End If


    ' Define a newline string
    crlf$ = Chr$(13) + Chr$(10)

    ' Here we changed the PtInRect to accept the two
    ' POINTAPI fields individually instead of converting it first
    ' into a long as was done in the original 16-bit example.
    Debug.Print usex, usey
    If PtInRect(Rect1, usex, usey) Then
        outstring$ = "is in Rect1" + crlf$
    End If
    If PtInRect(Rect2, usex, usey) Then
        outstring$ = outstring$ + "is in Rect2" + crlf$
    End If
    If PtInRect(RectUnion, usex, usey) Then
        outstring$ = outstring$ + "is in RectUnion" + crlf$
    End If
    If PtInRect(RectIntersect, usex, usey) Then
        outstring$ = outstring$ + "is in RectIntersect" + crlf$
    End If
    If outstring$ = "" Then outstring$ = "is not in any rectangle"
    MsgBox outstring$, 0, "Selected Point"
End Sub
```

Suggestions for Further Practice

You should consider the following suggestions for improving RectPlay to gain additional experience working with the rectangle API functions.

- Add a command (menu or button) to clear Rect1 or Rect2 (use SetRect-Empty).

- Add a RectSubtract rectangle similar to the RectUnion and RectIntersect so that you can experiment with the SubtractRect API function.

- Add a text field that allows you to enter offset information (x and y) that can then be used to offset or change the size of Rect1 and Rect2 (use InflateRect and OffsetRect).

- Implement a warning box that notifies you if Rect1 and Rect2 are equal.

Windows Control and Information Functions

This section describes the Windows API functions that relate to the control and identification of Windows objects.

Many of the functions described here can work on any window in the system. This fact has far-reaching ramifications. It means that it is possible for a VB program to directly manipulate the windows of any running application. It is possible to find out if a particular application is running, and launch it if it is not. It is possible to rearrange all of the windows on the screen, or to minimize or maximize other applications.

This means that the VB programmer must use these API functions very cautiously. One of the nice features of the Visual Basic environment is that it protects you from yourself—in theory it is impossible for VB to crash the system or crash other applications (but in practice, there are a number of bugs that can cause exceptions). When used incorrectly, the API functions can cause many kinds of exceptions in both Visual Basic and other applications. Read the function reference carefully before using these functions.

Many functions that worked on any window in the system under Win16 now return errors when you attempt to use them with Windows belonging to other applications. You will see this effect later in this chapter in the WinView application, where you can no longer obtain as much information about windows as before.

You will also see that there are some potentially significant differences between the way these functions work under Win32 and the way they worked under Win16. The WinView sample application that follows later in this chapter was ported from the original 16-bit version, and illustrates some of these changes and how you can deal with them.

All of the functions described in this section are usable, if not always useful, to the Visual Basic programmer. There are a number of functions that relate primarily to creation of windows that are either not compatible with Visual Basic, or can be used only with great difficulty or risk. Some of these are described in Appendix E.

Some functions and constants are marked as being "Windows 95 only". This means that these are new functions that were added to Windows 95 and are part of the Windows 95 (a.k.a. Win32c) API. Functions and constants marked specifically for Windows NT 4.0 are not supported under earlier versions of Windows NT.

Window Hierarchy and Identification Functions

The Windows API provides a number of functions that allow you to obtain information about windows. This includes both information relating to the attributes of a window and information relating to the relationship of windows to each other.

Identifying Windows

Chapter 2 introduced the idea of a "handle"—a long integer that uniquely identifies an object in the system. Every window in the system has a window handle that is typically referred to as an Hwnd (often pronounced "H-Wind"). All the functions in this section require a window handle as one of their parameters. Visual Basic forms and most VB controls provide the window handle via the hWnd property of the form or control.

On rare occasions you will find a control that has a window but does not provide an hWnd property. In these cases you may be able to obtain a window handle for the control by setting the focus to the control (more on focus later), then using the GetFocus API function to retrieve the handle of the window that currently has the focus. Under Win16 there were many third-party DLLs available (including the 16-bit apiguide.dll) that provided a function that could directly obtain a window handle from a control passed as a parameter to the function. These DLLs relied on a special Visual Basic API that was used for the development of VBX custom controls. In the transition to OLE custom controls, this internal Visual Basic API vanished, making some of that functionality either impossible or extremely difficult to implement. Some third-party products have 32-bit compatible versions of these functions—contact your DLL vendor for their latest information.

Fortunately, in this case, almost all window-based controls now include an hWnd property, so this particular problem should occur rarely. Though as you will soon see, new problems have appeared to replace it.

It is possible for more than one window to be associated with a control. A control can implement a main window and have any number of child windows within the control. The API functions described in this section can be used to examine the hierarchy of windows within a control. An example of this is the standard combo box control, which consists of both a list box and an edit control (text box).

Identifying a Form or Control from Its Window Handle

Many of the functions in this section enable you to find or search for windows in various way. But what do you do when you have found a window handle and want to work with the underlying control? This is another case where the disappearance of the underlying Visual Basic API used to create VBXs has complicated matters. Win16-based DLLs could tap into a Visual Basic API function called "VBGetControlName" which would let you easily determine a form or control name given a window handle to the form or control handle. Contact your DLL vendor to see if they have implemented a 32-bit replacement for this function if you need it. The good news is that under the latest edition of Visual Basic, the Name property can be read at runtime.

This means that the best option is to search through the form and control collection for your project, comparing the hWnd property of each form and control with the window handle that you are looking for. You can then return the Name property for the object for which you found a match. This solution is shown in the WinView sample later in this chapter. An interesting variation of this exists—once you find a match you can actually return a reference to the object itself, meaning that you can access any of its properties or methods.

Graphical Controls

The important thing to remember about graphical controls is that they are not actually windows. They do not have an associated window handle or hWnd property. As such, they cannot be used with the API functions described in this chapter. A graphical control can best be thought of as an object, internal to Visual Basic, that provides VB with instructions for drawing something onto a window. Thus a label control is nothing more than an instruction to Visual Basic to draw some text at a certain location using a certain color and font. As far as Windows is concerned, graphical controls do not exist.

ActiveX Controls

ActiveX controls (previously known as OLE Controls) have their own unique characteristics that are seemingly designed to confuse the issue even more. Some ActiveX controls appear and work just like regular Visual Basic controls such as the picture box or text control. These controls have windows that always exist and hWnd properties that are always valid. You can use Windows API functions with these controls without any problems.

Some ActiveX controls look like regular windows-based controls, but in fact only have real windows when they are visible and have the focus. When this type of control is active it has a window handle and usually a valid hWnd property—and you can use Windows API functions to work with it. However, as soon as this type of control becomes inactive or invisible, its window may be destroyed. You may still see the control because it has the ability to draw itself into any window when requested by Visual Basic. At this time its hWnd property may not be valid and the control should return a 0 as the hWnd property. To be safe, use the IsWindow API to determine if the value provided by the hWnd property is valid. Do not try to save the hWnd property in a variable—with this type of ActiveX control the window handle may change every time the control becomes active. The behavior of these types of controls may also vary among containers. Even ActiveX controls that are windows based may not have a window handle at design time within the Visual Basic design environment.

Finally, some ActiveX controls behave like graphical controls and never have a window handle. Like graphical controls, they do not exist as far as the Windows system is concerned.

How do you tell what type of ActiveX Control you are working with in a given situation? You can experiment (the WinView sample application can help), but the most reliable way to determine its behavior is to contact your control vendor for this information.

Window Hierarchy

Chapter 2 discussed how windows exist in a hierarchy of top level windows, owned windows, and child windows. Windows maintains an internal list of every window in the system. The Windows API provides a number of functions that make it possible to search for particular windows and list windows, and otherwise determine the hierarchy of every window in the system.

These functions, listed in Table 5.2, are covered in detail in the reference section of this chapter.

Table 5.2   Window Hierarchy Functions

Function	Description
EnumChildWindows	Requires the dwcbk32d.ocx custom control provided with this book under VB 4.0. Enumerates child windows of a specified window by invoking a callback function for each child window.
EnumThreadWindows	Requires the dwcbk32d.ocx custom control under VB 4.0. Enumerates all windows that belong to a specified thread by invoking a callback function for each window.

Table 5.2   **Window Hierarchy Functions**

EnumWindows	Requires the dwcbk32d.ocx custom control under VB 4.0. Enumerates all top level and owned windows in the system by invoking a callback function for each window.
FindWindow	Finds a window by class name and/or window name (the window caption).
FindWindowEx	Similar to FindWindow with additional functionality.
GetLastActivePopup	Obtains the handle of the last active pop-up window for a specified window.
GetNextWindow	This Win16 function has been superseded by the GetWindow API function. It is now implemented within the Win32 software development kit as a macro and is not actually present in the 32-bit DLLs. From VB you must use the GetWindow API instead.
GetParent	Obtains the handle of the parent window of the specified window.
GetSysModalWindow	This Win16 API function is not supported under Win32 and there is no equivalent.
GetTopWindow	Obtains the handle of the first (highest-level) child window for the specified window.
GetWindow	Given a window handle, this function obtains the handle to another window that has a specified relationship, for example: the first child window, the parent window, or the next or previous window in the window list.
SetParent	Allows you to change the parent window of any window.
SetSysModalWindow	This Win16 API function is not supported under Win32 and there is no direct equivalent within the API, though you may gain the same effect using third party add-ins.

Examples of many of these functions can be found in the sample program WinView that is presented later in this chapter.

MDI Hierarchy

One of the subtle aspects of relationships between MDI forms and MDI child forms is that an MDI child form is not a child of an MDI form. Each MDI form actually has a child window that fills the client area of the MDI form. This window, which belongs to class MDIClient, is the real parent of any MDI child forms that belong to the MDI form. There are two common ways to obtain the window handle of the MDI client window. One is to use the GetWindow API to obtain the first child window of the form, the other is to use the GetParent API to obtain the parent of one of the MDI child forms.

Be sure to take the MDI client window into account when using Windows hierarchy functions with MDI applications.

Window Location and Size Functions

Each window has location and size characteristics regardless of whether it is visible or not. The Windows API functions described here always use screen pixel units. If the window is a VB form or control, the ScaleMode property has no effect on the parameters, or the values returned by these functions.

This section refers to screen, window, and client coordinates. *Screen coordinates* are measured in pixels, with the upper left corner of the screen being 0,0. The *client area* of a window is the usable space of the window (not counting the borders, caption, and menu bars). The term *client coordinates* refers to pixel coordinates within the client area, with the upper left corner of the window being 0,0. These three coordinate systems are shown in Figure 5.4. It is very important to remember that all coordinate parameters used by these functions (and other functions in the USER32.DLL dynamic link library) are device coordinates—which in the case of a screen or window is always expressed in pixels. The functions that relate to graphics and drawing have a great deal of flexibility in terms of coordinate systems that you can use. Chapter 7 will go into more detail on the different coordinate systems available under Windows.

The functions listed in Table 5.3 relate to window location and size and are covered in detail in the reference section of this chapter.

Table 5.3   **Window Location and Size Functions**

Function	Description
ArrangeIconicWindows	Can be used to rearrange iconic (minimized) windows that are contained in another window.
AdjustWindowRect AdjustWindowRectEx	Calculate the required size of a window to obtain a specified client area size.
BeginDeferWindowPos DeferWindowPos EndDeferWindowPos	Make it possible to reposition a group of windows at once by building a window position list. BeginDeferWindowPos creates a window list handle. Each call to DeferWindowPos specifies the new location or visibility of a specified window. When EndDeferWindowPos is called, all of the changes will be made at once.
BringWindowToTop	Brings the specified window to the top of the list of visible windows, making it visible if it is wholly or partially obscured. The window is also activated. This function only takes effect when called from the foreground thread.

Figure 5.4

Screen, Window, and Client coordinate systems

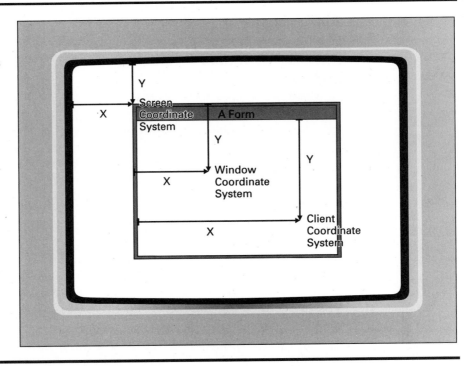

Table 5.3   Window Location and Size Functions (Continued)

ChildWindowFromPoint	Obtains the handle of the child window at the specified coordinates if one exists. The coordinates are client coordinates relative to the parent window.
ChildWindowFromPointEx	Similar to ChildWindowFromPoint with some additional functionality.
ClientToScreen	Determines the screen coordinates for the specified point in a window's client area.
GetClientRect	Obtains a rectangle that describes the client area of a window. This is a convenient way to determine the size of the client area in pixels.
GetWindowPlacement	Retrieves a WINDOWPLACEMENT structure for the specified window showing the state of the window, and its location when minimized, maximized, and normal.
GetWindowRect	Used to obtain a rectangle describing the location and size of the window rectangle in screen coordinates. The window rectangle includes the border, caption, menu bars, and so on.
MapWindowPoints	Converts one or more points in the client coordinates of one window into the client coordinates of a second window.

Table 5.3	**Window Location and Size Functions (Continued)**

MoveWindow	Allows you to move and change the size of the specified window.
OpenIcon	Restores a minimized window to its previous state.
ScreenToClient	Determines the client coordinates in a particular window for the specified point on the screen.
SetWindowPos	Allows you to change the position and size of a window, and to modify its position in the internal windows list that controls display order.
SetWindowPlacement	Sets characteristics for the specified window according to a WINDOW-PLACEMENT structure. This structure provides the state of the window, and its location when minimized, maximized, and normal.
WindowFromPoint	Determines which window is under a specified point in screen coordinates.

Window Information Functions

The Windows API contains a number of functions that provide information on the current state of the window. These are listed in Table 5.4 and are described in further detail in the reference section of this chapter.

Table 5.4	**Window Information Functions**

Function	Description
GetClassInfo	Retrieves the class information structure for the specified window's class.
GetClassInfoEx	Similar to GetClassInfo with additional capability.
GetClassLong	Use to retrieve or set information from a window's class.
GetClassWord	
SetClassLong	
SetClassWord	
GetClassName	Use to obtain the name of a window's class.
GetDesktopWindow	Obtains the window handle of the entire desktop (or screen).

Table 5.4	Window Information Functions (Continued)	
GetWindowLong	Use to retrieve or set information about a window.
GetWindowWord	
SetWindowLong	
SetWindowWord	
GetWindowText	Obtains the window text. This is roughly equivalent to the Text property for a form or control.
GetWindowTextLength	Obtains the length of the window text in characters.
IsChild	Use to determine if one window is a child window or descendent of a second window.
IsIconic	Use to determine if a window is minimized.
IsWindow	Use to determine if a specified handle is a window handle.
IsWindowEnabled	Use to determine if a window is enabled.
IsWindowVisible	Use to determine if a window is visible.
IsZoomed	Use to determine if a window is maximized.
SetWindowText	Sets the window text. This is roughly equivalent to the Text property for a form or control.

Every class has a class style word associated with it that can be accessed with the GetClassLong and SetClassLong functions. This style word is defined with the WNDCLASS structure listed in Appendix B.

Every window has a 32-bit style and a 32-bit extended style that can be accessed with the GetWindowLong and SetWindowLong API commands. These are described later in this chapter.

Focus, Foreground, and Input States

The concept of "Input Focus" is fundamental to Windows and is actually quite simple to understand. Windows can be running a large number of applications at one time, and these applications may have one or more windows visible on the screen at once. The question then arises: When you type on the keyboard or click with the mouse, which window (and hence, which application) will receive that keystroke or mouse click?

Under Windows 3.11 and below, the answer was clear: One application can be active at a time. One of the windows belonging to that application will be active as indicated by a system-defined caption color. The active window, or any of its child windows, is given the input focus. Focus can be indicated many different ways depending on the type of child window. An EDIT control (TextBox) indicates focus by displaying a small vertical caret at the character insertion point. A button displays a small focus rectangle around the caption, and so forth for each control.

　　Under Win16, you could use Windows API functions to easily determine or set focus and activation state. For example, the SetFocus API function could be called on a text control in a different application to both set the focus to that control and at the same time activate the other application.

　　Mouse input was also very straightforward under Win16. The mouse input would always go to the window under the mouse pointer unless another window "captured" mouse input—using the SetCapture API call to force all mouse input to a particular window regardless of where it is on the screen.

　　From the above few paragraphs you can probably infer that the situation under Win32 is not quite as straightforward.

　　Consider what happens under 16-bit Windows when an application freezes. This can be demonstrated easily using the TIMWASTE.EXE sample application in the Chapter 5 samples directory on the CD-ROM. This simple program has a single text box on a form with the following code in its Change event.

```
Sub Text1_Change ()
    Static z%
    Dim l&
    If z% = 0 Then
        For l& = 1 To 10000000
        Next l&
        z% = 1
    End If
End Sub
```

　　This routine simulates a frozen system by inserting a very long delay the first time you try to change the contents of the text box. As an experiment, launch two instances of this program, reposition them so that they are side by side (if using Windows NT, do NOT specify that the applications run in separate memory spaces). Next, click on one of the text boxes and enter a character, then immediately try performing any operation with the other instance of the application (or any other application if you are trying this under Win16). You will see that you cannot activate the second instance of the application until the loop has completed on the first one (note that the loop constant has been set to provide a comfortably long delay on a 90 MHz Pentium—you may wish to choose a lower number if your system is slower).

　　The reason for this is that under 16-bit Windows, all input is posted immediately into the message queue for the currently active application. Freezing the application using a long loop prevents message processing from occurring—the keyboard messages pile up in the queue until the application is ready to handle them. Try the same experiment as before, except this time try typing in five or six characters then clicking on the text box of the other application. Once the timer expires you will see that all of the characters that you typed in go to the first text box—the activation of the second text box does not occur until after those characters are processed.

So under Windows 3.x not only do long delays in one application prevent you from using other applications, but if an application completely hangs it serves to freeze the entire system. One of the major goals of Win32 (both under Windows NT and Windows 95) is to prevent this kind of problem from occurring.

This is accomplished by changing the way Windows processes both keyboard and mouse input. Try the same experiment using the TIMWST32.EXE application (which is identical to TIMWASTE.EXE except that it was compiled with 32-bit Visual Basic 5.0). You will see that one instance of the application does not freeze the other. Under Win32, each application has its own input queue. Windows watches the keyboard input stream for keys that change between applications (such as Alt-Tab) and when it sees one, switches input to the next application's input queue. Windows also limits the ability of one application to capture the mouse, making it possible to use the mouse at any time to switch among applications.

As a result, the behavior of those API functions that work with input and focus have changed. Win32 adds the concept of a foreground application. It is analogous to the active window under Win16—the application that has the focus and is currently active. Each application maintains its own internal focus and activation state. If you try to set the focus to a different application using the SetFocus or SetActiveWindow functions, it will have no effect. If you try to determine the focus using the GetFocus or GetActiveWindow functions while another application is in the foreground, you will read a zero result—as if no window is active!

This is part of a conscious attempt on the part of Microsoft to protect applications from each other and limit their ability to interfere with the normal operation of Windows. It is still possible to activate other applications, but to do so you must use the SetForegroundWindow function.

But what if you have two applications that you wish to have cooperate with one another—to work in the same way as they did under Win16 and share the same input queue? The new AttachThreadInput API function lets you attach a second application to your application's input queue. In fact, you could attach every application in the system to your application's input queue and thus go back completely to the behavior and associated problems of Windows 3.x—but please don't do this—your customers will not appreciate your applications reintroducing to their computer the ability of one application to freeze the entire system.

Table 5.5 lists the functions that affect Windows input state.

Table 5.5   **Windows Input State Functions**

Function	Description
GetActiveWindow	Returns the handle of the active window. The active window is the top level window that is associated with the input focus.
GetCapture	Determines which window (if any) in the current thread has captured mouse input.
GetFocus	Returns the handle of the window that has the input focus.
GetForegroundWindow	Returns the handle of the active window from the thread that is in the foreground.
ReleaseCapture	Releases mouse capture set earlier using the SetCapture API function.
SetActiveWindow	Sets the active window if called from the foreground thread.
SetCapture	Captures all mouse input to the specified window.
SetForegroundWindow	Sets the foreground window.
SetFocus	Selects a window to receive the input focus if called from the foreground thread. Note the need to use the SetFocusAPI alias to avoid conflicts with the Visual Basic SetFocus keyword.

A Note for Advanced Programmers

Purists will note that Windows does not, in fact, maintain separate input queues on an application basis but rather on a per thread basis. Chapter 14 discusses the differences between threads and processes. Visual Basic 4.0 and 5.0 support only a single thread; thus from a VB programmer's point of view there is no practical difference between a thread and a process. If you wish to use these functions on other applications that use multiple threads (possible, if you attach their input to your application), you should first review Chapter 14.

The Statevw Example

The Statevw example allows you to experiment with the input state API functions. Figure 5.5 shows the main window for the program.

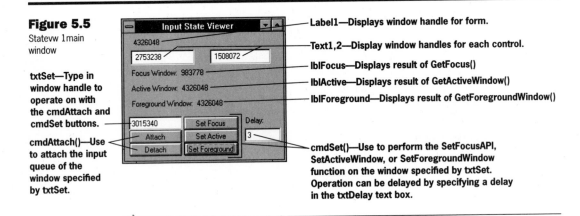

Figure 5.5
Statevw 1main window

txtSet—Type in window handle to operate on with the cmdAttach and cmdSet buttons.

cmdAttach()—Use to attach the input queue of the window specified by txtSet.

Label1—Displays window handle for form.

Text1,2—Display window handles for each control.

lblFocus—Displays result of GetFocus()

lblActive—Displays result of GetActiveWindow()

lblForeground—Displays result of GetForegroundWindow()

cmdSet()—Use to perform the SetFocusAPI, SetActiveWindow, or SetForegroundWindow function on the window specified by txtSet. Operation can be delayed by specifying a delay in the txtDelay text box.

Form Description

The form, which is shown in Listing 5.4 and 5.5, has two timers. Timer1 triggers periodically to show the current results from the GetFocus, GetActiveWindow, and GetForegroundWindow API functions. The form also displays the window handle of the form and two additional text boxes. These handle values are displayed so that you can use them to experiment with other API functions.

Listing 5.4   Header for STATEVW.FRM

```
VERSION 5.00
Begin VB.Form frmInput
    Caption        =   "Input State Viewer"
    ClientHeight   =   3000
    ClientLeft     =   2340
    ClientTop      =   2055
    ClientWidth    =   3885
    Height         =   3405
    Left           =   2280
    LinkTopic      =   "Form1"
    ScaleHeight    =   3000
    ScaleWidth     =   3885
    Top            =   1710
    Width          =   4005
    Begin VB.CommandButton cmdAttach
        Caption    =   "Detach"
        Height     =   315
        Index      =   1
        Left       =   120
```

Listing 5.4   Header for STATEVW.FRM (Continued)

```
        TabIndex        -    13
        Top             -    2580
        Width           -    1275
     End
     Begin VB.CommandButton cmdAttach
        Caption         -    "Attach"
        Height          -    315
        Index           -    0
        Left            -    120
        TabIndex        -    12
        Top             -    2280
        Width           -    1275
     End
     Begin VB.Timer tmrDelayOp
        Enabled         -    0      'False
        Left            -    3300
        Top             -    1440
     End
     Begin VB.TextBox txtDelay
        Height          -    285
        Left            -    2940
        TabIndex        -    10
        Text            -    "0"
        Top             -    2280
        Width           -    855
     End
     Begin VB.CommandButton cmdSet
        Caption         -    "Set Foreground"
        Height          -    315
        Index           -    2
        Left            -    1440
        TabIndex        -    9
        Top             -    2580
        Width           -    1335
     End
     Begin VB.CommandButton cmdSet
        Caption         -    "Set Active"
        Height          -    315
        Index           -    1
        Left            -    1440
        TabIndex        -    8
        Top             -    2280
        Width           -    1335
     End
     Begin VB.CommandButton cmdSet
        Caption         -    "Set Focus"
        Height          -    315
        Index           -    0
```

Listing 5.4   **Header for STATEVW.FRM (Continued)**

```
      Left            =    1440
      TabIndex        =    7
      Top             =    1980
      Width           =    1335
   End
   Begin VB.TextBox txtSet
      Height          =    285
      Left            =    120
      TabIndex        =    6
      Top             =    1980
      Width           =    1275
   End
   Begin VB.Timer Timer1
      Interval        =    500
      Left            =    3300
      Top             =    780
   End
   Begin VB.TextBox Text2
      Height          =    315
      Left            =    2100
      TabIndex        =    1
      Text            =    "Text2"
      Top             =    420
      Width           =    1455
   End
   Begin VB.TextBox Text1
      Height          =    315
      Left            =    180
      TabIndex        =    0
      Text            =    "Text1"
      Top             =    420
      Width           =    1515
   End
   Begin VB.Label Label1
      Caption         =    "Delay:"
      Height          =    195
      Left            =    2940
      TabIndex        =    11
      Top             =    1980
      Width           =    855
   End
   Begin VB.Label lblForm
      Caption         =    "Label1"
      Height          =    255
      Left            =    180
      TabIndex        =    5
      Top             =    120
      Width           =    3375
```

Listing 5.4   Header for STATEVW.FRM (Continued)

```
      End
      Begin VB.Label lblForeground
         Height          =   255
         Left            =   180
         TabIndex        =   4
         Top             =   1560
         Width           =   3495
      End
      Begin VB.Label lblActive
         Height          =   255
         Left            =   180
         TabIndex        =   3
         Top             =   1200
         Width           =   3495
      End
      Begin VB.Label lblFocus
         Height          =   255
         Left            =   180
         TabIndex        =   2
         Top             =   840
         Width           =   3495
      End
   End
   Attribute VB_Name = "frmInput"
   Attribute VB_GlobalNameSpace = False
   Attribute VB_Creatable = False
   Attribute VB_PredeclaredId = True
   Attribute VB_Exposed = False
```

Listing 5.5   STATEVW.FRM

```
Option Explicit
Dim OpToDo%
Dim WndToDo&


Private Declare Function AttachThreadInput Lib "user32" (ByVal idAttach As _
Long, ByVal idAttachTo As Long, ByVal fAttach As Long) As Long
Private Declare Function GetActiveWindow Lib "user32" () As Long
Private Declare Function GetCurrentThreadId Lib "kernel32" () As Long
Private Declare Function GetFocus Lib "user32" () As Long
Private Declare Function GetForegroundWindow Lib "user32" () As Long
Private Declare Function GetWindowThreadProcessId Lib "user32" (ByVal hwnd As _
Long, lpdwProcessId As Long) As Long
Private Declare Function IsWindow Lib "user32" (ByVal hwnd As Long) As Long
```

Listing 5.5   **STATEVW.FRM (Continued)**

```
Private Declare Function SetFocusAPI Lib "user32" Alias "SetFocus" (ByVal hwnd _
As Long) As Long
Private Declare Function SetActiveWindow Lib "user32" (ByVal hwnd As Long) As _
Long
Private Declare Function SetForegroundWindow Lib "user32" (ByVal hwnd As Long) _
As Long
```

The txtSet text box is used to enter a window handle. You can then use the cmdAttach and cmdSet buttons to perform operations on that window.

Using Statevw

To work with the Statevw application, launch two instances of the program and position them beside each other. You have a total of six window handles available to work with: the main form and two text boxes for each instance. The functionality of the program is extremely simple—type the handle of the window that you wish to work with in the txtSet text box, then execute one of the operations and see what happens.

Here are a few of the more interesting operations you should try:

■ Use the SetFocus or SetActive commands to set the focus or activate a window in the other instance. You'll see that they have no effect. The SetForegroundWindow command, on the other hand, will activate the other instance.

■ Use the SetFocus command with a five-second delay to set the focus to one of the text boxes in the first instance of the application. Before the delay expires, click on one of the text boxes in the second instance. Try this a few times. You should easily be able to reach a state where both applications have an active window and a text box with the focus showing the caret! How is this possible? Each application instance has its own focus and active windows. You can use the SetFocus API to make a window active or have the focus from the application's point of view even when it is not the foreground application. Even though the window has the focus, it will not actually receive any input until it becomes the foreground application. You should avoid doing this because of the confusion that can arise when two applications seem to have the focus at the same time.

■ Type the window handle of the second application instance into the first application's txtSet text box, then use the Attach button to attach the second instance to the input queue of the first. Now try the first two experiments. You will see that the API functions now behave as they did under

Win16—the focus and activation of both applications behave as if they were a single application.

In most cases, you will place declarations in a module where they can be shared among all of the forms and modules in your application. In the case of a simple single form application such as this one you can place the declarations in the form by specifying them as private.

```
Private Sub Form_Load()
    Text1.TEXT = Str$(Text1.hwnd)
    Text2.TEXT = Str$(Text2.hwnd)
    lblForm.Caption = Str$(hwnd)
End Sub


Private Sub Timer1_Timer()
    lblActive = "Active Window: " & Str$(GetActiveWindow())
    lblFocus = "Focus Window: " & Str$(GetFocus())
    lblForeground = "Foreground Window: " & Str$(GetForegroundWindow())
End Sub
```

The display and setting operations are both very straightforward. If a delay is specified, the type of operation to perform is stored in a global variable to be executed when the timer is triggered. Clearly this is not a robust application, in that it does not prevent a user from clicking on a command button while another operation is pending, but for experimentation it serves its purpose nicely.

```
Private Sub cmdSet_Click(Index As Integer)
    Dim UseDelay&
    WndToDo = Val(txtSet.TEXT)
    OpToDo = Index
    UseDelay = Val(txtDelay.TEXT)
    If UseDelay <> 0 Then
        tmrDelayOp.Interval = UseDelay * 1000
        tmrDelayOp.Enabled = True
    Else
        DoOperation
    End If

End Sub



Public Sub DoOperation()
    Dim dl&
    Select Case OpToDo
        Case 0
            dl& = SetFocusAPI(WndToDo)
        Case 1
```

```
                  dl& = SetActiveWindow(WndToDo)
          Case 2
                  dl& = SetForegroundWindow(WndToDo)
      End Select
      tmrDelayOp.Enabled = False     ' Make sure timer is off

End Sub

Private Sub tmrDelayOp_Timer()
    DoOperation
End Sub
```

The GetWindowThreadProcessId function retrieves a handle to the process and thread that own a specified window. This function and the concept of threads in general are discussed in Chapter 14.

```
Private Sub cmdAttach_Click(Index As Integer)
    Dim wnd&
    Dim dl&
    Dim pid&
    Dim destid&
    Dim fAttach%
    wnd = Val(txtSet.TEXT)
    destid& = GetWindowThreadProcessId(wnd, pid)
    ' Make sure values are valid
    ' Note the need to compare with zero!
    If destid& = 0 Or IsWindow(wnd) = 0 Then
        MsgBox "Invalid hWnd"
        Exit Sub
    End If
    If Index = 0 Then fAttach = True
    dl& = AttachThreadInput(destid&, GetCurrentThreadId(), fAttach)
    If dl& Then
        MsgBox "Operation succeeded"
    Else
        MsgBox "Operation failed"
    End If
End Sub
```

Other Window Functions

The Windows API functions listed in Table 5.6 relate to window objects but don't fall cleanly into any of the categories presented so far. They are described in detail in the reference section of this chapter.

Let's look closer at the InvalidateRect, ValidateRect, and Update-Window commands. Each window maintains information internally on whether any part of it needs to be drawn. For example, when a window is created the entire window needs updating. When part of a window is revealed due to the closing of a higher-level window or dialog box, only part of the win-

Table 5.6   **Miscellaneous Window Object Functions**

Function	Description
AnyPopup	Use to determine if any popup window is visible.
CascadeWindows	Cascades windows within a parent window.
CloseWindow	Use to minimize the specified window if it is a top level window. It has no effect on pop-up and child windows.
DestroyWindow	Destroys the specified window and all child and owned windows for which that window is the parent.
DrawAnimatedRects	Creates an animated effect of a window opening or closing.
EnableWindow	Enables or disables the specified window.
FlashWindow	Flashes the caption of the specified window.
GetUpdateRect	Determines the portion of a window that needs to be updated.
GetWindowContextHelpId	Retrieves the help context associated with a window.
InvalidateRect	Specifies that all or part of the client area of a window needs to be updated.
IsWindowUnicode	Determines if a window expects text messages to be in Unicode.
LockWindowUpdate	Enables or disables drawing for the specified window.
RedrawWindow	A powerful function to control the redrawing of all or part of a window.
ScrollWindow ScrollWindowEx	Use to scroll all or part of the client area of a window.
SetWindowContextHelpId	Sets the help context associated with a window.
ShowOwnedPopups	Hides or shows all owned pop-up windows belonging to the window specified.
ShowWindow	Use to set the state of a window, including hiding, showing, minimizing, maximizing, and activating the window.
ShowWindowAsync	Similar to ShowWindow, with the additional ability to work on windows in other processes.
TileWindows	Tiles windows within a parent window.
UpdateWindow	Causes an immediate update of any portions of a window that require updating.
ValidateRect	Specifies that all or part of a rectangle has been updated or no longer requires updating.

dow may need to be updated. The process of notifying a window that an update is needed is called *invalidating*, and is done with the InvalidateRect function.

When all or part of a window is invalidated, it is not drawn immediately. Instead, the window keeps track of the area and combines the area specified by multiple InvalidateRect calls into a single invalid area.

When the Windows system has idle time available, it generates a WM_PAINT message to the window, which tells the window to update the specified area. A program can force an immediate update by using the UpdateWindow function. If a program draws all or part of a window, it may use the ValidateRect function to inform Windows that part of the window no longer needs updating. The RedrawWindow API function also provides a great deal of flexibility in invalidating and redrawing all or part of a window.

The WinView Example

WinView is a program that illustrates some of the Windows API functions described in this chapter. It includes several functions from each category discussed, with an emphasis on the hierarchy functions. Figure 5.6 shows the WinView program in action.

Figure 5.6

WinView main
program

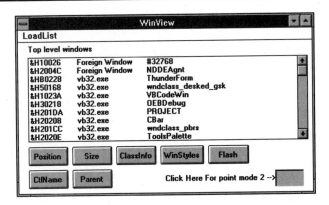

The list box shown in Figure 5.6 contains a list of the windows in the system. Menu commands can be used to display lists of all top level windows, or of the owned or child windows for a selected window. Alternatively, it is possible to point to any window on the screen and add it to the list.

Once a window in the list is selected, command buttons are used to bring up message boxes containing various types of information on the windows selected.

Project Description

The WinView system includes four files. WINVIEW.FRM is the only form used in the program. WINVIEW.BAS is the only module in the program and contains the constant type and public variables along with API declarations and some program code. APIGID32.BAS contains the declarations for the APIGID32.DLL dynamic link library. dwcbk32d.ocx is the generic callback custom control, included on the program disk of this book, that enables use of callback functions with Visual Basic 4.0. This custom control is described in detail in Appendix A. Refer to the VB 4.0 compatible examples on the CD-ROM for an implementation of the WinView project that uses this control and is thus compatible with VB 4.0.

The WinView example was ported from the original WinView sample application in the Visual Basic Programmer's Guide to the Windows API (16-bit edition). In this particular example, no effort was made to support both 16- and 32-bit code—it is a straight port. However, most of the original code was commented out and left in place to help you see the porting process. In this case, much of the porting process was done through the simple brute force method of replacing the 16-bit API declarations with their 32-bit equivalents, updating all of the Win32 constants to make sure the correct value is defined, then attempting to compile and run the program. The Visual Basic compiler caught many of the errors, especially with regard to declarations. Many more errors were found at runtime while exercising the code. Only a few functional problems remained after those errors detectable by Visual Basic were fixed.

This sample also illustrates some unique problems brought about by trying to port very old code: The original WinView application was written for Visual Basic 1.0—thus one of the first steps was to add the Option Explicit statement to each form and module.

Form Description

Listing 5.6 contains the header from file WINVIEW.FRM that describes the control setup for the form.

Listing 5.6   **WINVIEW.FRM**

```
VERSION 5.00
Begin VB.Form Winview
    Appearance      =   Ø 'Flat
    BackColor       =   &H80000005&
    Caption         =   "WinView"
    ClientHeight    =   3555
    ClientLeft      =   3600
    ClientTop       =   2475
    ClientWidth     =   7140
```

Listing 5.6   **WINVIEW.FRM (Continued)**

```
BeginProperty Font
    name            =   "MS Sans Serif"
    charset         =   Ø
    weight          =   7ØØ
    size            =   8.25
    underline       =   Ø    'False
    italic          =   Ø    'False
    strikethrough   =   Ø    'False
EndProperty
ForeColor           =   &H8ØØØØØØ8&
Height              =   4245
Left                =   354Ø
LinkMode            =   1    'Source
LinkTopic           =   "Form1"
ScaleHeight         =   237
ScaleMode           =   3    'Pixel
ScaleWidth          =   476
Top                 =   1845
Width               =   726Ø
```

The picPoint2 control is used to implement a variation on point mode that allows you to obtain information about Windows in other applications. You will see later in the text why this is necessary.

```
Begin VB.PictureBox picPoint2
    Height          =   375
    Left            =   624Ø
    ScaleHeight     =   345
    ScaleWidth      =   645
    TabIndex        =   9
    Top             =   3Ø6Ø
    Width           =   675
End
```

The List1 list box is loaded with lists of windows. Each entry includes a window handle, followed by the name of the application that owns the window (if available), and then by the name of the class to which the window belongs. The selected window in the list (if any) can be operated on by the command buttons.

```
Begin VB.ListBox List1
    Appearance      =   Ø    'Flat
    Height          =   198Ø
    Left            =   24Ø
    TabIndex        =   8
    Top             =   36Ø
```

```
    Width          =   6795
End
```

The command buttons are used to obtain information about the window
selected in the List1 box. The CmdPosition and CmdSize buttons display the location and size of the selected window. The CmdClassInfo button displays the
class style of the selected window. The CmdWinStyles button displays the window styles of the selected window that are common to all classes. The CmdFlash
button demonstrates the FlashWindow API function. The CmdName button is
used to display the Visual Basic form name or control name if the window is a
Visual Basic form or control.

```
Begin VB.CommandButton CmdPosition
    Appearance     =   0  'Flat
    BackColor      =   &H80000005&
    Caption        =   "Position"
    Height         =   435
    Left           =   240
    TabIndex       =   2
    Top            =   2460
    Width          =   975
End
Begin VB.CommandButton CmdSize
    Appearance     =   0  'Flat
    BackColor      =   &H80000005&
    Caption        =   "Size"
    Height         =   435
    Left           =   1320
    TabIndex       =   3
    Top            =   2460
    Width          =   975
End
Begin VB.CommandButton CmdClassInfo
    Appearance     =   0  'Flat
    BackColor      =   &H80000005&
    Caption        =   "ClassInfo"
    Height         =   435
    Left           =   2400
    TabIndex       =   4
    Top            =   2460
    Width          =   975
End
Begin VB.CommandButton CmdWinStyles
    Appearance     =   0  'Flat
    BackColor      =   &H80000005&
    Caption        =   "WinStyles"
    Height         =   435
    Left           =   3480
    TabIndex       =   5
    Top            =   2460
    Width          =   1035
```

```
    End
    Begin VB.CommandButton CmdFlash
        Appearance      =   0   'Flat
        BackColor       =   &H80000005&
        Caption         =   "Flash"
        Height          =   435
        Left            =   4620
        TabIndex        =   6
        Top             =   2460
        Width           =   975
    End
    Begin VB.CommandButton CmdCtlName
        Appearance      =   0   'Flat
        BackColor       =   &H80000005&
        Caption         =   "CtlName"
        Height          =   435
        Left            =   240
        TabIndex        =   7
        Top             =   3000
        Width           =   975
    End
    Begin VB.CommandButton CmdParent
        Appearance      =   0   'Flat
        BackColor       =   &H80000005&
        Caption         =   "Parent"
        Height          =   435
        Left            =   1320
        TabIndex        =   1
        Top             =   3000
        Width           =   975
    End
Begin VB.Label lblHere
        Alignment       =   1   'Right Justify
        BackColor       =   &H00FFFFFF&
        Caption         =   "Click Here For point mode 2 -->"
        Height          =   255
        Left            =   3420
        TabIndex        =   10
        Top             =   3120
        Width           =   2835
    End
```

The Label1 control displays the type of windows being displayed in the List1 control. In Point mode, this label indicates the window that is being pointed to.

```
    Begin VB.Label Label1
        Appearance      =   0   'Flat
        BackColor       =   &H80000005&
        ForeColor       =   &H80000008&
        Height          =   195
        Left            =   240
```

```
        TabIndex        -   Ø
        Top             -   6Ø
        Width           -   5415
    End
```

The MenuLoadList popup menu contains menu commands to fill the List1 control with lists of all top level windows, all owned windows of a selected window, and all child windows of a selected window. The MenuPointed menu entry causes the program to enter point mode in which you can move the cursor over the screen and add any window into the window list, though as you will see, its behavior has changed from the 16-bit edition. The Menu-Clear menu entry can be used to clear the window list.

```
    Begin VB.Menu MenuLoadList
        Caption          -   "LoadList"
        Begin VB.Menu MenuTopLevel
            Caption          -   "&TopLevel"
            Shortcut         -   ^T
        End
        Begin VB.Menu MenuChildren
            Caption          -   "&Children"
            Shortcut         -   ^C
        End
        Begin VB.Menu MenuOwned
            Caption          -   "&Owned"
            Shortcut         -   ^O
        End
        Begin VB.Menu MenuPointed
            Caption          -   "&Pointed"
            Shortcut         -   ^P
        End
        Begin VB.Menu MenuClear
            Caption          -   "C&lear"
        End
    End
End
Attribute VB_Name - "Winview"
Attribute VB_GlobalNameSpace - False
Attribute VB_Creatable - False
Attribute VB_PredeclaredId - True
Attribute VB_Exposed - False
```

Using WinView

WinView is a windows information viewer designed to demonstrate some of the API functions that deal with windows objects. WinView operations fall into two categories: finding or selecting a window, and viewing information about the window.

Finding and selecting windows is accomplished with the LoadList menu, which has five commands in a pop-up menu. The TopLevel command loads the list box with a list of every top level window in the system (see Figure 5.6). The window information includes the window handle, application name, and class name. The Children command loads the list box with a list of child windows for the currently selected window. The Owned command loads the list box with a list of owned windows for the currently selected window. Note that since owned windows may also be top level windows, these windows may also appear in the top level window list.

The Pointed command allows you to point to any window in your application and add it to the list box by clicking on it. In the original Win16 version, point mode would work with any window in the system, but Win32 does not allow you to capture the mouse input for other applications, thus eliminating that capability. The picPoint2 picture box does, however, provide a way of obtaining the same functionality even with other applications. While it is true that Win32 does not allow you to capture most mouse input to other applications, there is one slight exception. If you set the mouse capture while a mouse button is held down, the capture will affect the entire system until the mouse button is released. This was necessary to preserve the behavior of most Windows applications—for example, drag-and-drop demands that mouse input be connected to a single input message queue during the duration of the drag regardless of which application the mouse pointer is over. It is possible to implement true mouse capture under Win32 using third party tools such as Desaware's SpyWorks. Command buttons and other controls also rely on the ability to capture mouse input while the mouse button is held down. WinView takes advantage of this capability with the picPoint2 control—simply click on the picture box, hold the mouse button down and move it over other windows on the system. The Label1 control will display information on the window under the mouse pointer. When you release the mouse button, information on the window at that position will be added to the list box.

Once a window is in the list box, it may be selected. Information about the selected window can be obtained by clicking on any of the command buttons. The Clear command clears the list box.

WinView Program Listings

Module WINVIEW.BAS, which is shown in Listing 5.7, contains the constant declarations and global variables used by the program. Listing 5.8 shows the code listing for form WINVIEW.FRM.

PointMode% is used to determine if the system is in point mode. When in point mode, the WinView form has the mouse capture (explained in the next listing) and is using the form's MouseMove event to update the Label1 control with information about the window that the cursor is over. PointMode can take the values –1 and –2 to indicate point mode #1 or point mode #2. Zero indicates normal operation.

Listing 5.7   WINVIEW.BAS

```
Attribute VB_Name = "WinView1"
Option Explicit
' Winview sample program
' Copyright (c) 1992-1997 by Desaware
' Constants based on file api32.txt
'
'-------------------------------------------------------
'           Application global constants
'-------------------------------------------------------
Public PointMode%


'-------------------------------------------------------
'           API type definitions
'-------------------------------------------------------
Type POINTAPI
        X As Long
        Y As Long
End Type
```

Listing 5.8   WINVIEW.FRM

```
Option Explicit
```

```
'-------------------------------------------------------
'           API constants
'-------------------------------------------------------
```

The API Constants used by this sample application can be found in the sample program on the CD-ROM and in file API32.txt. This application uses constants with the following prefixes: GWL_, GCL_, WS_, CS_, GW_, ES_, BS_, SS_, LBS_, CBS_, and SBS. The values of these constants have changed from Win16. During the port of this project, it turned out to be easiest to simply delete all of the old constants and add the new ones, counting on the Visual Basic compiler to find any undeclared constants (be sure to set Option Explicit for each module and form).

The constants have been left out of the book in order to save space.

```
Global Const WM_USER = &H400

' Watch out here - control message numbers have changed!
Public Const LB_RESETCONTENT = &H184
Public Const LB_SETTABSTOPS = &H192
```

```
Declare Function IsWindowVisible Lib "user32" Alias "IsWindowVisible" (ByVal _
hwnd As Long) As Long
Declare Function IsWindowEnabled Lib "user32" Alias "IsWindowEnabled" (ByVal _
hwnd As Long) As Long
Declare Function IsZoomed Lib "user32" Alias "IsZoomed" (ByVal hwnd As Long) As _
Long
Declare Function IsIconic Lib "user32" (ByVal hwnd As Long) As Long
Declare Function GetClientRect Lib "user32" (ByVal hwnd As Long, lpRect As _
RECT) As Long
Declare Function GetWindowRect Lib "user32" (ByVal hwnd As Long, lpRect As _
RECT) As Long
Declare Function ClientToScreen Lib "user32" (ByVal hWnd As Long, lpPoint As _
POINTAPI) As Long
Declare Function EnumWindows Lib "user32" (ByVal lpEnumFunc As Long, ByVal _
lParam As Long) As Long
Declare Function EnumChildWindows Lib "user32" (ByVal hWndParent As Long, ByVal _
lpEnumFunc As Long, ByVal lParam&) As Long
Declare Function FlashWindow Lib "user32" (ByVal hWnd As Long, ByVal bInvert As _
Long) As Long
Declare Function GetCapture Lib "user32" () As Long
Declare Function GetClassLong Lib "user32" Alias "GetClassLongA" (ByVal hWnd As _
Long, ByVal nIndex As Long) As Long
Declare Function GetClassName Lib "user32" Alias "GetClassNameA" (ByVal hWnd As _
Long, ByVal lpClassName As String, ByVal nMaxCount As Long) As Long
Declare Function GetCurrentProcessId Lib "kernel32" () As Long
Declare Function GetDesktopWindow Lib "user32" () As Long
Declare Function GetModuleFileName Lib "kernel32" Alias "GetModuleFileNameA" _
(ByVal hModule As Long, ByVal lpFileName As String, ByVal nSize As Long) As Long
Declare Function GetParent Lib "user32" (ByVal hWnd As Long) As Long
Declare Function GetWindow Lib "user32" (ByVal hWnd As Long, ByVal wCmd As _
Long) As Long
Declare Function GetWindowLong Lib "user32" Alias "GetWindowLongA" (ByVal hWnd _
As Long, ByVal nIndex As Long) As Long
Declare Function GetWindowThreadProcessId Lib "user32" (ByVal hWnd As Long, _
lpdwProcessId As Long) As Long
Declare Function ReleaseCapture Lib "user32" () As Long
' We create a special SendMessage alias that accepts a long value by reference
Declare Function SendMessageLongByRef Lib "user32" Alias "SendMessageA" (ByVal _
hWnd As Long, ByVal wMsg As Long, ByVal wParam As Integer, lParam As Long) As Long
Declare Function SendMessage Lib "user32" Alias "SendMessageA" (ByVal hWnd As _
Long, ByVal wMsg As Long, ByVal wParam As Integer, ByVal lParam As Long) As Long
Declare Function SetCapture Lib "user32" (ByVal hWnd As Long) As Long
' Note the use of two longs to transfer a POINTAPI structure.
Declare Function WindowFromPoint Lib "user32" (ByVal X As Long, ByVal Y As _
```

```
Long) As Long

'    lpData was passed by the EnumWindows call and contains
'    the parent window handle that we are looking for.
Public Function Callback1_EnumWindows(ByVal hwnd As Long, ByVal lpData As Long) _
As Long
    ' If hWnd is owned by window in lpData,
    ' Add it to the listbox
    If GetParent(hwnd) = lpData Then
        Winview.List1.AddItem Winview.GetWindowDesc$(hwnd)
    End If
    Callback1_EnumWindows = 1  ' Continue enumeration
End Function
```

During the Form_Load event, a message is sent to the list box to set internal tab stops. This operation is documented further in Chapter 18. This is also the first of many places where an integer variable or array had to be changed to longs during the port to Win32. Also, now would be a good time to make sure you have Option Explicit defined at the start of every form and module.

```
Private Sub Form_Load()
    Dim tabsets&(2) ' Change to an array of longs
    Dim dl&
    tabsets(0) = 45
    tabsets(1) = 110
    dl = SendMessageLongByRef&(List1.hWnd, LB_SETTABSTOPS, 2, tabsets(0))
End Sub
```

The MenuTopLevel_Click( ) event demonstrates the first of several methods for enumerating windows. It starts by obtaining the handle of the desktop window—the window that represents the entire screen. All windows in the system are considered children of the desktop—which is not the same as saying that they are child windows. It's best to think of the desktop window as a special window that provides certain special capabilities, one of which is to help you enumerate other windows in the system. The MenuChildren_Click( ) event uses the same technique, except that it starts from a selected window instead of the desktop.

Porting these functions was quite straightforward. The biggest change was converting the window handles and associated functions from integers to longs. Since this code was originally written for Visual Basic 1.0, clearing the list boxes was accomplished using the LB_RESETCONTENT windows message—the Clear method did not exist at the time. The port to 32 bits provided a good opportunity to clean up the code and use the Clear method instead. There are relatively few cases where you should use an API function instead of a built-in Visual Basic method—this isn't one of them (look in the "Use

with VB" section in the function reference section for suggested usage for
individual functions).

```
'    Loads the listbox with a list of all top level windows.
'
Private Sub MenuTopLevel_Click()
    Dim hWnd&

    ' Clear the listbox
    ' Was: dummy% = SendMessage&(agGetControlHwnd(List1), LB_RESETCONTENT, Ø, _
    Ø&)
    ' Could be: dummy& = SendMessage&(agGetControlHwnd(List1), LB_RESETCONTENT, _
    Ø, Ø&)
    ' But we might as well use:
    List1.Clear

    ' The desktop is the highest window
    hWnd& = GetDesktopWindow()

    ' It's first child is the 1st top level window
    hWnd& = GetWindow(hWnd&, GW_CHILD)

    ' Now load all top level windows
    Do
        List1.AddItem GetWindowDesc$(hWnd&)
        hWnd& = GetWindow(hWnd&, GW_HWNDNEXT)
    Loop While hWnd& <> Ø
    Label1.Caption = "Top level windows"

End Sub


Private Sub MenuChildren_Click()
    Dim hWnd&    ' Changed to long
    Dim windowdesc$

    ' Is there a window selected?
    If List1.ListIndex < Ø Then
        MsgBox "No Window Selected", Ø, "Error"
        Exit Sub
    End If
    windowdesc$ = List1.TEXT

    hWnd = GetHwnd(windowdesc$)    ' Extract window handle

    ' It's first child is the specified window
    hWnd = GetWindow(hWnd, GW_CHILD)

    If hWnd = Ø Then
        MsgBox "No children found for this window", Ø, "Error"
        Exit Sub
    End If
```

```
        ' Clear the listbox
        List1.Clear

        ' Now load all the child windows
        Do
            List1.AddItem GetWindowDesc$(hWnd)
            hWnd = GetWindow(hWnd, GW_HWNDNEXT)
        Loop While hWnd <> 0
        Label1.Caption = "Children of: " + "&" + windowdesc$

End Sub


'    Just clear the listbox
'
Private Sub MenuClear_Click()
    ' Clear the listbox
    ' Was:   dummy% = SendMessageBynum&(agGetControlHwnd(List1), _
    LB_RESETCONTENT, 0, 0&)
    List1.Clear

End Sub
```

The MenuOwned_Click( ) function demonstrates another method of enumerating windows, in this case to list all of the windows that are owned by the specified window. The EnumWindows function is a special type of windows function known as an "enumeration" function. These functions require that you pass to windows the address of a function in your own application. Windows will then call that "enumeration function" for each object that is being enumerated. In the case of EnumWindows, Windows calls the function that you specify for each top level window in the system. During the enumeration function, you simply check if the window has a parent, and if so, if the parent matches the one that you are looking for. EnumWindows allows you to pass a parameter to the enumeration functions. In this case the handle of the selected window is used.

There is one catch, however: Under Visual Basic 5.0, the enumeration function must be in a standard module. The Callback1_EnumWindows event is thus placed in the WINVIEW1.BAS module. You must use great care to define the enumeration function with the correct parameters and return type. Failure to do so can lead to a memory exception that can crash your application (and even the system under Windows 95).

Visual Basic 4.0 supports enumeration using the dwcbk32d.ocx custom control included with this book. It is a generic callback control that contains a pool of function addresses that you can draw on to use with enumeration functions. When windows calls the function, the dwcbk32d.ocx control triggers an event in Visual Basic.

```
'   Show owned windows of the currently selected window
```

```
'
'
Private Sub MenuOwned_Click()
    Dim hWnd&      ' Switch to Long
    Dim dl&
    Dim windowdesc$

    ' Is there a window selected?
    If List1.ListIndex < 0 Then
        MsgBox "No Window Selected", 0, "Error"
        Exit Sub
    End If
    windowdesc$ = List1.TEXT

    hWnd = GetHwnd(windowdesc$)      ' Extract window handle

    ' Clear the listbox
    List1.Clear

    ' This uses VB5's support for callbacks to a callback
    ' address for EnumWindows.
    ' This will trigger the Callback1_EnumWindows function
    ' for each top level window.  This technique could
    ' also have been used in place of the GetWindow loop
    ' in the MenuTopLevel_Click event.
    ' In prior versions of VB, this sample used the dwCBK.ocx or cbk.vbx
    ' callback control
    dl& = EnumWindows(AddressOf Callback1_EnumWindows, hwnd)

    If List1.ListCount = 0 Then
        MsgBox "No owned windows found for this window", 0, "Error"
        Label1.Caption = ""
        Exit Sub
    End If

    Label1.Caption = "Owned windows of: " + "&" + windowdesc$

End Sub
```

Point mode captures the mouse input. This means that all mouse input goes to the specified window regardless of which window the mouse is over—as long as the mouse is over a window in your application (under Win16 you could capture the input for every application in the system). The code to implement the two point modes described earlier is straightforward. This is one case where the porting process was simple as far as syntax goes, but complex due to changes in architecture for Win32. Aside from attaching the input of every application in the system to Winview (which is not a good idea), the only way to duplicate the original Win16 functionality would be to intercept mouse clicks on a system-wide basis—something that requires a third-party hook control to do from Visual Basic.

```
Private Sub MenuPointed_Click()
    Dim dl&
    ' Let system know that we're in point mode
    PointMode% = -1
    dl& = SetCapture(Winview.hWnd)
End Sub


Private Sub picPoint2_MouseDown(Button As Integer, Shift As Integer, X As
Single, Y As Single)
    Dim dl&
    ' Let system know that we're in point mode
    PointMode% = -2
    dl& = SetCapture(Winview.hWnd)
    ' Initialize the label
    Label1.Caption = GetWindowDesc$(picPoint2.hWnd)

End Sub


'   If we're in point mode, record the current window
'   in the listbox
'
Private Sub Form_MouseDown(Button As Integer, Shift As Integer, X As Single, Y _
As Single)
    If PointMode% <> -1 Then Exit Sub
    List1.AddItem Label1.Caption
    PointMode% = 0
    Label1.Caption = ""
    ' If capture is still held, release it - this is
    ' actually not necessary in VB 1.0 as it seems to
    ' release the capture anyway!
    If GetCapture() = Winview.hWnd Then ReleaseCapture
End Sub
```

The MouseMove event receives coordinates X,Y in client coordinates based on the ScaleMode property, which for this form is set as pixels. Because the form has the capture (see the description for the MenuPointed_Click event), it will receive MouseMove events regardless of where the cursor is within the application or on the screen depending on the point mode in use. The coordinates are converted from client to screen coordinates by function ClientToScreen; then function WindowFromPoint is used to determine the window for that position. One technique for understanding this better is to create a label control on the form and set the caption to display the client and screen coordinate values as the mouse moves.

```
Private Sub Form_MouseMove(Button As Integer, Shift As Integer, X As Single, Y _
As Single)
```

```
    Dim pt As POINTAPI
    Dim foundhWnd&    ' Now a long

    ' Only record window if we're in point mode
    If PointMode% = 0 Then Exit Sub
    pt.X = X
    pt.Y = Y
    ClientToScreen Winview.hWnd, pt
    ' Was: foundhWnd% = WindowFromPointBynum%(agPOINTAPItoLong&(pt))
    foundhWnd& = WindowFromPoint(pt.X, pt.Y)
    Label1.Caption = GetWindowDesc$(foundhWnd)

End Sub

Private Sub Form_MouseUp(Button As Integer, Shift As Integer, X As Single, Y As _
Single)
    If PointMode% <> -2 Then Exit Sub
    List1.AddItem Label1.Caption
    PointMode% = 0
    Label1.Caption = ""
    ' If capture is still held, release it - this is
    ' actually not necessary in VB 1.0 as it seems to
    ' release the capture anyway!
    If GetCapture() = Winview.hWnd Then ReleaseCapture

End Sub
```

Obtaining the control name for a window is not as easy a process as it was under 16-bit Visual Basic. The underlying Visual Basic API that made it possible to easily determine the control name for a window handle is no longer available. The GetControlNameFromWindow function shows another way to find the name of a control given the window handle. The other information functions are quite straightforward. Style information is extracted using the AND operator—refer to the information on bitfields in Chapter 3 for additional information on bitwise operations.

```
Public Function GetControlNameFromWindow(ByVal hWnd&)
    Dim formnum%
    Dim ctlnum%
    For formnum% = 0 To Forms.Count - 1
        If Forms(formnum%).hWnd = hWnd& Then
            GetControlNameFromWindow = Forms(formnum%).Name
            Exit Function
        End If
        For ctlnum% = 0 To Forms(formnum%).Controls.Count - 1
            On Error Resume Next
            If Forms(formnum%).Controls(ctlnum%).hWnd = hWnd& Then
                If Err.Number = 0 Then
                    GetControlNameFromWindow = _
                    Forms(formnum%).Controls(ctlnum%).Name
                End If
```

```
            Exit Function
        End If
      Next ctlnum%
   Next formnum%
End Function


' Show class styles for the selected window
'
Private Sub CmdClassInfo_Click()
    Dim clsextra&, wndextra&      ' Change to long, though probably unnecessary
    Dim style&        ' Changed to long
    Dim useHwnd&      ' Changed to long
    Dim crlf$

    Dim outstring$, titlestring$

    crlf$ = Chr$(13) + Chr$(10)

    If List1.ListIndex < 0 Then
        MsgBox "No windows selected", 0, "Error"
        Exit Sub
    End If

    titlestring$ = List1.TEXT
    useHwnd& = GetHwnd(titlestring$)

    ' Get the class info
    ' These all used to be GetClassWord and GCW_ constants
    clsextra& = GetClassLong(useHwnd&, GCL_CBCLSEXTRA)
    wndextra& = GetClassLong(useHwnd&, GCL_CBWNDEXTRA)
    style& = GetClassLong(useHwnd&, GCL_STYLE)

    outstring$ = "Class & Word Extra = " + Str$(clsextra&) + ","+ _
    Str$(wndextra&) + crlf$
    If style& And CS_BYTEALIGNCLIENT Then
        outstring$ = outstring$ + "CS_BYTEALIGNCLIENT" + crlf$
    End If
    If style& And CS_BYTEALIGNWINDOW Then
        outstring$ = outstring$ + "CS_BYTEALIGNWINDOW" + crlf$
    End If
    If style& And CS_CLASSDC Then
        outstring$ = outstring$ + "CS_CLASSDC" + crlf$
    End If
    If style& And CS_DBLCLKS Then
        outstring$ = outstring$ + "CS_DBLCLKS" + crlf$
    End If
    ' Was CS_GLOBALCLASS (has same value)
    If style& And CS_PUBLICCLASS Then
        outstring$ = outstring$ + "CS_GLOBALCLASS" + crlf$
    End If
    If style& And CS_HREDRAW Then
```

```
            outstring$ = outstring$ + "CS_HREDRAW" + crlf$
        End If
        If style& And CS_NOCLOSE Then
            outstring$ = outstring$ + "CS_NOCLOSE" + crlf$
        End If
        If style& And CS_OWNDC Then
            outstring$ = outstring$ + "CS_OWNDC" + crlf$
        End If
        If style& And CS_PARENTDC Then
            outstring$ = outstring$ + "CS_PARENTDC" + crlf$
        End If
        If style& And CS_SAVEBITS Then
            outstring$ = outstring$ + "CS_SAVEBITS" + crlf$
        End If
        If style& And CS_VREDRAW Then
            outstring$ = outstring$ + "CS_VREDRAW" + crlf$
        End If

        MsgBox outstring$, 0, titlestring$

End Sub


' Obtains the control name or form name of a Visual
' Basic form or control given the window handle.
' Non VB windows will have no form or control name
'
Private Sub CmdCtlName_Click()
    Dim titlestring$
    Dim outputstring$
    Dim useHwnd&

    If List1.ListIndex < 0 Then
        MsgBox "No windows selected", 0, "Error"
        Exit Sub
    End If

    titlestring$ = List1.TEXT
    useHwnd& = GetHwnd(titlestring$)

    ' Was: outputstring$ = agGetControlName$(useHwnd&)
    ' See text for reason for this change
    outputstring$ = GetControlNameFromWindow(useHwnd&)

    If outputstring$ = "" Then
        MsgBox "Not a VB Form or Control", 0, titlestring$
    Else
        MsgBox "CtlName or FormName = " + outputstring$, 0, titlestring$
    End If

End Sub
```

```
' Flashes the caption of the selected window. This feature
' is typically attached to a timer when the code needs to
' "flash" a window caption to attract the user's attention.
' Try clicking this button several times quickly for a
' visible window that has a caption to see the effect
'
Private Sub CmdFlash_Click()
    Dim titlestring$
    Dim useHwnd&
    Dim dl&

    If List1.ListIndex < 0 Then
        MsgBox "No windows selected", 0, "Error"
        Exit Sub
    End If

    titlestring$ = List1.TEXT
    useHwnd& = GetHwnd(titlestring$)
    dl& = FlashWindow(useHwnd&, -1)

End Sub

Private Sub CmdParent_Click()
    Dim hWnd&, newhwnd& ' Changed to long
    Dim windowdesc$

    If List1.ListIndex < 0 Then
        MsgBox "No Window Selected", 0, "Error"
        Exit Sub
    End If
    hWnd& = GetHwnd(List1.TEXT)
    newhwnd& = GetParent(hWnd&)
    If newhwnd& = 0 Then
        MsgBox "Window has no parent", 0, "Window &H" + Hex$(hWnd&)
        Exit Sub
    End If
    windowdesc$ = GetWindowDesc$(newhwnd&)
    MsgBox windowdesc$, 0, "Parent of &H" + Hex$(hWnd&) + " is"
End Sub

'   Show the position of the selected window
'
Private Sub CmdPosition_Click()
    Dim WindowRect As RECT
    Dim useHwnd&
    Dim crlf$

    Dim outstring$, titlestring$

    crlf$ = Chr$(13) + Chr$(10)

    If List1.ListIndex < 0 Then
```

```
        MsgBox "No windows selected", 0, "Error"
        Exit Sub
    End If

    titlestring$ = List1.TEXT
    useHwnd& = GetHwnd(titlestring$)

    ' Get the rectangle describing the window
    GetWindowRect useHwnd&, WindowRect

    If IsIconic&(useHwnd&) Then
        outstring$ = "Is Iconic" + crlf$
    End If

    If IsZoomed&(useHwnd&) Then
        outstring$ = outstring$ + "Is Zoomed" + crlf$
    End If

    If IsWindowEnabled&(useHwnd&) Then
        outstring$ = outstring$ + "Is Enabled" + crlf$
    Else
        outstring$ = outstring$ + "Is Disabled" + crlf$
    End If

    If IsWindowVisible&(useHwnd&) Then
        outstring$ = outstring$ + "Is Visible" + crlf$
    Else
        outstring$ = outstring$ + "Is NOT Visible" + crlf$
    End If

    outstring$ = outstring$ + "Rect: " + Str$(WindowRect.Left) + ","
    outstring$ = outstring$ + Str$(WindowRect.TOP) + ","
    outstring$ = outstring$ + Str$(WindowRect.Right) + ","
    outstring$ = outstring$ + Str$(WindowRect.bottom)

    MsgBox outstring$, 0, titlestring$


End Sub

'   Show the size of the selected window
'
Private Sub CmdSize_Click()
    Dim WindowClientRect As RECT
    Dim useHwnd&
    Dim crlf$

    Dim outstring$, titlestring$

    crlf$ = Chr$(13) + Chr$(10)

    If List1.ListIndex < 0 Then
```

```
        MsgBox "No windows selected", 0, "Error"
        Exit Sub
    End If

    titlestring$ = List1.TEXT
    useHwnd& = GetHwnd(titlestring$)

    ' Get the rectangle describing the window
    GetClientRect useHwnd&, WindowClientRect

    outstring$ = "Horiz Pixels: " + Str$(WindowClientRect.Right) + crlf$
    outstring$ = outstring$ + "Vert Pixels: " + Str$(WindowClientRect.bottom)

    MsgBox outstring$, 0, titlestring$


End Sub

' Show window styles for the selected window
'
Private Sub CmdWinStyles_Click()
    Dim style&
    Dim useHwnd&       ' Was integer
    Dim crlf$

    Dim outstring$, titlestring$

    crlf$ = Chr$(13) + Chr$(10)

    If List1.ListIndex < 0 Then
        MsgBox "No windows selected", 0, "Error"
        Exit Sub
    End If

    titlestring$ = List1.TEXT
    useHwnd& = GetHwnd(titlestring$)

    ' Get the class info
    style& = GetWindowLong&(useHwnd&, GWL_STYLE)

    If style& And WS_BORDER Then
        outstring$ = outstring$ + "WS_BORDER" + crlf$
    End If
    If style& And WS_CAPTION Then
        outstring$ = outstring$ + "WS_CAPTION" + crlf$
    End If
    If style& And WS_CHILD Then
        outstring$ = outstring$ + "WS_CHILD" + crlf$
    End If
    If style& And WS_CLIPCHILDREN Then
        outstring$ = outstring$ + "WS_CLIPCHILDREN" + crlf$
    End If
```

```
If style& And WS_CLIPSIBLINGS Then
    outstring$ = outstring$ + "WS_CLIPSIBLINGS" + crlf$
End If
If style& And WS_DISABLED Then
    outstring$ = outstring$ + "WS_DISABLED" + crlf$
End If
If style& And WS_DLGFRAME Then
    outstring$ = outstring$ + "WS_DLGFRAME" + crlf$
End If
If style& And WS_GROUP Then
    outstring$ = outstring$ + "WS_GROUP" + crlf$
End If
If style& And WS_HSCROLL Then
    outstring$ = outstring$ + "WS_HSCROLL" + crlf$
End If
If style& And WS_MAXIMIZE Then
    outstring$ = outstring$ + "WS_MAXIMIZE" + crlf$
End If
If style& And WS_MAXIMIZEBOX Then
    outstring$ = outstring$ + "WS_MAXIMIZEBOX" + crlf$
End If
If style& And WS_MINIMIZE Then
    outstring$ = outstring$ + "WS_MINIMIZE" + crlf$
End If
If style& And WS_MINIMIZEBOX Then
    outstring$ = outstring$ + "WS_MINIMIZEBOX" + crlf$
End If
If style& And WS_POPUP Then
    outstring$ = outstring$ + "WS_POPUP" + crlf$
End If
If style& And WS_SYSMENU Then
    outstring$ = outstring$ + "WS_SYSMENU" + crlf$
End If
If style& And WS_TABSTOP Then
    outstring$ = outstring$ + "WS_TABSTOP" + crlf$
End If
If style& And WS_THICKFRAME Then
    outstring$ = outstring$ + "WS_THICKFRAME" + crlf$
End If
If style& And WS_VISIBLE Then
    outstring$ = outstring$ + "WS_VISIBLE" + crlf$
End If
If style& And WS_VSCROLL Then
    outstring$ = outstring$ + "WS_VSCROLL" + crlf$
End If

' Note: We could tap the style& variable for class
' styles as well (especially since it is easy to
' determine the class for a window), but that is
' beyond the scope of this sample program.

MsgBox outstring$, 0, titlestring$
```

```
End Sub


' If source$ is a path, this function retrieves the
' basename, or filename sans path
' source$ MUST be a valid filename
'
Private Function GetBaseName$(ByVal source$)
    Do While InStr(source$, "\") <> 0
        source$ = Mid$(source$, InStr(source$, "\") + 1)
    Loop
    If InStr(source$, ":") <> 0 Then
        source$ = Mid$(source$, InStr(source$, ":") + 1)
    End If
    GetBaseName$ = source$
End Function
```

The GetWindowDesc$ function is another case where a change in architecture to Win32 had an impact on the functionality of the application. Before, you could use the GetWindowWord function to retrieve the instance handle of a window, then use the GetModuleFileName function to obtain the executable name for that instance. Unlike Win16, under Win32, instance handles do NOT uniquely identify an application in the system. They are valid only within the context of their own application. This means that we can only find the module names for the executable and any windows owned by dynamic link libraries and custom controls that are used by the current application. The GetWindowThreadProcessId function is used to obtain the unique identifier of the process that owns a window. The module file name is retrieved only for cases where that identifier matches the identifier of the current process.

When an API function loads a string into a buffer as is done with functions GetClassName and GetModuleFileName, it simply copies the data into the string buffer with a null character to indicate the end of the string. It does not actually change the length of the string as known to Visual Basic. In order to set the VB string to the correct length, you may use the InStr function to determine the position of the terminating NULL character. The APIGID32.DLL dynamic link library also provides function agGetStringFromLPSTR$, which performs the same task.

```
'   Builds a string describing the window in format
'   handle, source application, class
'   separated by tabs
'   Used to take an integer parameter, now a long
'
Private Function GetWindowDesc$(hWnd&)
    Dim desc$
    Dim tbuf$
```

```
Dim inst&    ' Now a long
Dim dl&
Dim hWndProcess&

' Include the windows handle first
desc$ = "&H" + Hex$(hWnd) + Chr$(9)

' Get name of source app
tbuf$ = String$(256, 0) ' Predefine string length

' Handling of process is different in Win32 - see text
dl& = GetWindowThreadProcessId(hWnd, hWndProcess)
If hWndProcess = GetCurrentProcessId() Then
    ' Get instance for window
    ' Was: inst% = GetWindowWord(hwnd%, GWW_HINSTANCE)

    inst& = GetWindowLong(hWnd&, GWL_HINSTANCE)
    ' Get the module filename
    ' Was: dummy% = GetModuleFileName(inst%, tbuf$, 255)
    dl& = GetModuleFileName(inst, tbuf$, 255)

    tbuf$ = GetBaseName(tbuf$)

    ' The following two lines are equivalent
    tbuf$ = agGetStringFromLPSTR$(tbuf$)
    ' If InStr(tbuf$, Chr$(0)) Then tbuf$ = Left$(tbuf$, InStr(tbuf$, _
    Chr$(0)) - 1)
Else
    tbuf$ = "Foreign Window"
End If

' And add it to the description
desc$ = desc$ + tbuf$ + Chr$(9)

' Finally, add the class name
tbuf$ = String$(256, 0) ' Initialize space again
dl& = GetClassName(hWnd&, tbuf$, 255)
tbuf$ = agGetStringFromLPSTR$(tbuf$)

desc$ = desc$ + tbuf$

' And return the description
GetWindowDesc$ = desc$

End Function
```

Astute observers who look at the original 16-bit WinView application will note that it used to be possible to extract the window handle from the description string simply by using the Val statement. Val would stop scanning upon reaching a space or tab character, so it would work fine. This turned out to be a bug in Visual Basic 3.0—the command specification actually called for spaces and tabs to be ignored. This was fixed with Visual Basic 4.0, thus breaking the original program. For example: the string "&HD04   Foreign window" used to be interpreted as &HD04. With VB4, the tab character was ignored, causing the value to be interpreted as Val(&HD04F) which was the sign extended to the 32-bit value &HFFFFD04F. The solution was to explicitly extract the hex value using the code below.

```
Private Function GetHwnd&(title$)
    Dim p%
    p% = InStr(title$, Chr$(9))
    If p% > 0 Then GetHwnd& = Val(Left$(title$, p% - 1))
End Function
```

Suggestions for Further Practice

You may wish to consider the following list of exercises for improving Win-View and gaining additional experience working with Windows API functions:

Add a menu command to move up one level in the hierarchy. Given a selected window, this command would add the parent window and all its siblings to the list box. The GetWindow function will help here.

Extend the window style viewer to take into account the window style bits unique to each of the standard classes.

Add a Find Window command that looks for the handle of a window given its caption.

Create a tiling program that will divide the screen among all running applications. Use the DeferWindowPos functions. Hint for determining the screen size: What happens when you use the GetWindowRect on the desktop window?

Create a project where you print text to the form, then randomly scroll rectangular areas on the form from one part of the form to another. The result will be a jumble, but a good demonstration of the use of the ScrollWindow and ScrollWindowEx API calls.

Window Style Reference

The 32-bit window style data is divided into two parts. The high 16 bits are used to define general window styles common to all classes. The interpretation of the low 16 bits depends on the class. Chapter 2 discusses how Visual Basic controls correspond to the standard windows classes listed below.

Style bits do generally reflect the current state of a window; however, changing a style bit via SetWindowLong does not cause a corresponding change in the window—at least not immediately. Some style bits may be changed at runtime successfully (frequently taking effect when the window is redrawn), but most take effect correctly only when the window is created (meaning that they cannot be set from VB). Microsoft does not document which style bits may be changed safely at runtime; thus you should do so at your own risk and only after thorough experimentation.

By the same token, experimentation is the best way to learn about style bits. Simply retrieve the current style for a form or control, use the bit setting techniques described in Chapter 3 to modify the style, and set the new style. It is beyond the scope of this book to completely characterize the style combinations for every Visual Basic control. Instead, this chapter documents all of the standard window styles, and points out particular cases that are useful. If you see a feature that interests you, try it out and see if it works. If you find something particularly interesting, please send it to the publisher for incorporation into future editions of this book. Also, keep in mind that the WinView project provides a powerful tool for examining window styles.

Windows does provide API functions to perform most tasks that affect a window style (such as controlling visibility, window state, and so on), so it should rarely be necessary to directly modify the window style.

Each style bit is represented by a constant name and a value in hexadecimal that indicates the bit that is set. Normal style bits are retrieved via:

```
GetWindowLong(hWnd&, GWL_STYLE)
and set via:
SetWindowLong(hWnd&, GWL_STYLE, value&)
```

To access the extended Windows style bits, substitute

```
GWL_EXSTYLE
for
GWL_STYLE
```

Keep in mind that each time a program is run, the style bits are reset from the VB project files; thus any changes to style bits must take place at runtime. This is often done in the form Load event.

The values and meanings of style bits are the same in Win16 and Win32 except for cases where a style is unique to one platform or the other. See Tables 5.7 and 5.8 below.

Table 5.7   **General Windows Style Bits Table**

Constant Name	Hex Value	Description
WS_BORDER	800000	Window has a border.
WS_CAPTION	C00000	Window has a title bar.

Table 5.7 **General Windows Style Bits Table (Continued)**

WS_CHILD	40000000	Window is a child window.
WS_CLIPCHILDREN	2000000	Prevents drawing to a parent window from drawing over a child window. This bit is controlled by the Visual Basic ClipControls property for forms and controls that can contain other controls.
WS_CLIPSIBLINGS	4000000	Prevents drawing into one child window from drawing over the client area of another child window that shares the same parent window.
WS_DISABLED	8000000	Window is disabled.
WS_DLGFRAME	400000	Window has a double border but no title bar.
WS_GROUP	20000	Window is the beginning of a group of controls in a dialog box.
WS_HSCROLL	100000	Window has a horizontal scroll bar.
WS_MAXIMIZE	1000000	Window is maximized.
WS_MAXIMIZEBOX	10000	Window has a maximize box to the right of its title bar.
WS_MINIMIZE	20000000	Window is minimized.
WS_MINIMIZEBOX	20000	Window has a minimize box to the right of its title bar.
WS_OVERLAPPED	0	Default (no bits set) is an overlapped top level window with a caption and border.
WS_POPUP	80000000	Window is a pop-up window.
WS_SYSMENU	80000	Window has a system menu box at the left of its title bar.
WS_TABSTOP	10000	Window has a tab stop. This means that you may use the tab key to set the focus to this control in a dialog box.
WS_THICKFRAME	40000	Window has a thick frame (or border) that can be used to size the window.
WS_VISIBLE	10000000	Window is visible.
WS_VSCROLL	200000	Window has a vertical scroll bar.

Of these, the most intriguing are the WS_EX_ACCEPTFILES and WS_EX_TRANSPARENT styles. Unfortunately, both cannot be used under VB without resorting to a custom control or DLL (both require subclassing to implement). Still, you might want to try setting the

Table 5.8   **Extended Windows Style Bits Table**

Constant Name	HexValue	Description
WS_EX_ACCEPTFILES	10	Window accepts drag-drop files from file manager.
WS_EX_DLGMODALFRAME	1	Window has a double border. If WS_CAPTION is also specified, it will have a title bar.
WS_EX_NOPARENTNOTIFY	4	Windows will not send a WM_PARENTNOTIFY message to the parent when destroyed.
WS_EX_TOPMOST	8	This window should be placed over all windows (except others with this bit set). The SetWindowPos API function can be used to change this attribute.
WS_EX_TRANSPARENT	20	Creates a transparent window that does not obscure windows below it.

WS_EX_TRANSPARENT bit on a form (such as the form for the RectPlay project)—the results are interesting, especially if you minimize and then restore the program.

New Window Extended Class Style Bits Table

These extended styles are supported by Windows 95 and later (including NT 4.0).

Tables 5.9 through 5.13 list the styles for the standard Windows controls.

Constant Name	Hex Value	Description
WS_EX_MDICHILD	40	Creates a button that holds a bitmap instead of text.
WS_EX_TOOLWINDOW	80	Gives window a smaller caption and prevents it from appearing in the task bar.
WS_EX_WINDOWEDGE	100	Gives window a raised edge border.
WS_EX_CLIENTEDGE	200	Window has sunken edge.
WS_EX_CONTEXTHELP	400	Adds question mark to window caption which, when clicked, changes the cursor to a question mark. A WM_HELP message is sent to the next window that is clicked.
WS_EX_RIGHT	1000	If WS_EX_RTLREADING is set, sets right text alignment.
WS_EX_RTLREADING	2000	For Hebrew and Arabic, sets text to display right to left.

Constant Name	Hex Value	Description
WS_EX_LEFTSCROLLBAR	4000	If WS_EX_RTLRREADING is set, moves scrollbar to the left.
WS_EX_CONTROLPARENT	10000	Causes tab key to switch between child windows on this window.
WS_EX_STATICEDGE	20000	Sets a 3D style common to static controls.
WS_EX_APPWINDOW	40000	Forces minimized application into the taskbar.

Table 5.9   **Button Class Style Bits Table**

Constant Name	Hex Value	Description
BS_3STATE	5	A check box that has a third "gray" state.
BS_AUTO3STATE	6	A 3 State check box that cycles through the three states, changing each time it is selected.
BS_AUTOCHECKBOX	3	Specifies a check box that toggles the selection state each time the user selects the control.
BS_AUTORADIOBUTTON	9	A radio button that automatically checks itself and un-checks all other radio buttons in its group when it is se-lected.
BS_CHECKBOX	2	Button is a check box.
BS_DEFPUSHBUTTON	1	Creates a default button. Similar to setting the Default property on the VB command button.
BS_GROUPBOX	7	Similar to the VB Frame control.
BS_LEFTTEXT (also known as BS_RIGHTBUTTON)	20	Places text to the left of a check box or radio button. This bit may be changed on a VB check box or option button as shown below.
BS_OWNERDRAW	B	A button that must be drawn by the application. This feature is not available from VB though it can be used with the help of third party products.
BS_RADIOBUTTON	4	Similar to a VB Option Button control.

Here is an example of how you can use the BS_LEFTTEXT style bits to move the text for a Visual Basic checkbox or option button to the left of the indicator.

```
Dim f&, d1&
```

Table 5.10   **ComboBox Class Style Bits Table**

Constant Name	HexValue	Description
CBS_AUTOHSCROLL	40	See ES_HSCROLL for edit control.
CBS_DISABLENOSCROLL	800	Vertical scroll is always shown (instead of being shown only when there are more entries than fit).
CBS_DROPDOWN	2	List box is displayed only when user selects the dropdown icon.
CBS_DROPDOWNLIST	3	Like CBS_DROPDOWN except that instead of an edit control, there is a static control that reflects the selected list box entry.
CBS_LOWERCASE	4000	All text in the combo box is forced to lowercase.
CBS_NOINTEGRALHEIGHT	400	Combo box can be any size. Normally the box is sized so that partial lines are not shown.
CBS_OEMCONVERT	80	See ES_OEMCONVERT.
CBS_OWNERDRAWFIXED	10	Styles for combo boxes drawn under application control. Not used in VB without the aid of a third-party control.
CBS_OWNERDRAWVARIABLE	20	
CBS_HASSTRINGS	200	
CBS_SIMPLE	1	List box is displayed at all times.
CBS_SORT	100	List box entries are sorted.
CBS_UPPERCASE	2000	All text in the combo box is forced to uppercase. Unsupported in NT 3.51

```
f& = GetWindowLong(Option1.hwnd, GWL_STYLE)
f& = f& OR BS_LEFTTEXT
dl& = SetWindowLong(Option1.hwnd, GWL_STYLE, f&)
Option1.Refresh
```

New Button Class Style Bits Table

These button styles are supported by Windows 95, NT 4.0 and later. The Btnplay example provided on disk demonstrates many of these styles.

Constant Name	Hex Value	Description
BS_BITMAP	80	Creates a button that holds a bitmap instead of text.
BS_BOTTOM	800	Places the caption at the bottom of the button.

Constant Name	Hex Value	Description
BS_CENTER	300	Centers the caption within the button.
BS_ICON	40	Creates a button that holds an icon instead of text.
BS_LEFT	100	Left justifies the caption within the button, or text area of an option or check box.
BS_MULTILINE	2000	Allows multiline text within a button.
BS_NOTIFY	4000	Causes the new Windows 95 notifications: BN_DISABLED, BN_PUSHED, BN_KILLFOCUS, BN_PAINT, BN_SETFOCUS, BN_UNPUSHED to be sent to the parent of the button control.
BS_PUSHLIKE	1000	Forces a check box or option button to look and behave like a standard button.
BS_RIGHT	200	Right justifies the caption within the button, or text area of an option or check box.
BS_TOP	400	Places the caption at the top of the button.
BS_VCENTER	C00	Centers the caption vertically within the button.

Table 5.11 Edit Class Style Bits Table

Constant Name	Hex Value	Description
ES_AUTOHSCROLL	80	Control automatically scrolls horizontally when typing at the end of a line. Without this bit, the text length is limited to what will fit in the box.
ES_AUTOVSCROLL	40	Control automatically scrolls up a page when the Enter key is pressed on the last line.
ES_CENTER	1	Text is centered.
ES_LEFT	0	Default: Text is left-justified.
ES_LOWERCASE	10	Characters are converted to lowercase as they are typed in.
ES_MULTILINE	4	Multiline edit control.
ES_NOHIDESEL	100	Normally, when a control loses the focus the selected text no longer appears selected. This bit disables that behavior.
ES_NUMBER	2000	Only allows numbers in this edit control. Unsupported in NT 3.51
ES_OEMCONVERT	400	Text in the control is converted to the OEM character set. See Chapter 6.

Table 5.11   Edit Class Style Bits Table (Continued)

Constant Name	Hex Value	Description
ES_PASSWORD	20	The asterisk character (*) is displayed in the box as characters are typed in.
ES_READONLY	800	Text in this control cannot be edited by the user.
ES_RIGHT	2	Text is right-justified.
ES_UPPERCASE	8	Characters are converted to uppercase as they are typed in.
ES_WANTRETURN	1000	Pressing the Enter key inserts a carriage return into the text on multiline edit controls. This overrides the default push button if present.

The bad news is that many of these styles need to be set when the control is created and thus modifying them for an existing VB text control has no effect. The good news is that many of them can be simulated by intercepting the VB KeyDown and KeyPressed events. Also, many third-party edit controls take advantage of these features.

Table 5.12   ListBox Class Style Bits Table

Constant Name	Hex Value	Description
LBS_DISABLENOSCROLL	1000	Vertical scroll is always shown (instead of being shown only when there are more entries than fit in the control window).
LBS_EXTENDEDSEL	800	Shift and control combinations can be used to select multiple entries. See LBS_MULTIPLESEL.
LBS_MULTICOLUMN	200	List box supports multiple columns. See LBS_MULTIPLESEL.
LBS_MULTIPLESEL	8	List box allows multiple selections.
LBS_NODATA	2000	The list box does not contain data. Only valid for owner draw list boxes and thus is not usable under VB.
LBS_NOINTEGRALHEIGHT	100	List box can be any size. Normally the box is sized so that partial lines are not shown.
LBS_NOREDRAW	4	Prevents update of the list box while changes are made. See Chapters 17 and 19.
LBS_NOSEL	4000	Items cannot be selected—only viewed. Unsupported in NT 3.51

Table 5.12	**ListBox Class Style Bits Table (Continued)**		
	LBS_NOTIFY	1	Parent window receives event notification for this control.
	LBS_OWNERDRAWFIXED	10	Used for list boxes drawn under program control. Not usable under VB without third party support.
	LBS_OWNERDRAWVARIABLE	20	
	LBS_HASSTRINGS	40	
	LBS_SORT	2	List box is sorted.
	LBS_USETABSTOPS	80	Allows alignment by tab stops. This is set by default in VB list box controls.
	LBS_WANTKEYBOARDINPUT	400	List box receives all keyboard input allowing special processing for keyboard input.

Table 5.13	**ScrollBar Class Style Bits Table**		
	Constant Name	**HexValue**	**Description**
	SBS_HORZ	0	Default: Horizontal scroll bar.
	SBS_SIZEBOX	8	Creates a size box (maximize or minimize button).
	SBS_TOPALIGN	2	Used during creation of the scroll bar to align the scroll bar to the specified side of a rectangle. Top and Bottom apply to horizontal scroll bars, Left and Right to vertical.
	SBS_LEFTALIGN	2	
	SBS_BOTTOMALIGN	4	
	SBS_RIGHTALIGN	4	
	SBS_VERT	1	Vertical scroll bar.
	SBS_SIZEBOXTOPLEFT- ALIGN	2	Used to align size boxes to the top left or bottom right of a rectangle.
	SBS_SIZEBOXBOTTOM- RIGHTALIGN	4	
	SBS_SIZEGRIP	10	Like SBS_SIZEBOX, except using the Windows 95 style. Unsupported in NT 3.51

Static Class Style Bits Table

None of the standard Visual Basic controls are based on the STATIC class. However these styles are included both for completeness, and due to the possibility of finding STATIC-based controls in other VBA-based environments or in custom controls.

Constant Name	Hex Value	Description
SS_BLACKFRAME	7	Box whose frame is in the color used to draw window frames (default=black).
SS_BLACKRECT	4	Solid rectangle in the color used to draw window frames (default=black).
SS_CENTER	1	Text is centered.
SS_CENTERIMAGE	200	Centers text vertically in the control. If the control contains an image, uses the upper-left pixel to fill any empty space in the control.
SS_GRAYFRAME	8	Box whose frame is in the color used to draw the screen background (default=gray).
SS_GRAYRECT	5	Solid rectangle in the color used to draw the screen background (default=gray).
SS_ICON	3	When used in a dialog box, this displays an icon. The text contains a resource ID to the icon in the file.
SS_LEFT	0	Default: left-aligned.
SS_LEFTNOWORDWRAP	C	Same as SS_SIMPLE except that tabs are expanded.
SS_NOPREFIX	80	The & character does not cause the next character to be underlined. Normally, &Hello would display as Hello.
SS_RIGHT	2	Text is right-aligned.
SS_SIMPLE	B	Simple box containing fixed text to display.
SS_WHITEFRAME	9	Box whose frame is in the color used to fill windows backgrounds (default=white).
SS_WHITERECT	6	Solid rectangle in the color used to fill window backgrounds (default=white).

New Static Class Style Bits Table

These styles are supported by Windows 95 and later (including NT 4.0).

Constant Name	Hex Value	Description
SS_OWNERDRAW	D	A control that must be drawn by the application. This feature is not available from VB though it can be used with the help of third-party products.

Constant Name	Hex Value	Description
SS_ENHMETAFILE	F	Displays a metafile in the control. The control's text specifies the metafile.
SS_ETCHEDHORZ	10	Uses the EDGE_ETCHED style of the DrawEdge function to draw the controls frame.
SS_ETCHEDVERT	11	Uses the EDGE_ETCHED style of the DrawEdge function to draw the left and right sides of the control's border.
SS_ETCHEDFRAME	12	Uses the EDGE_ETCHED style of the DrawEdge function to draw the top and bottom of the control's border.
SS_NOTIFY	100	Causes the new Windows 95 notifications: STN_DBLCLICK, STN_DISABLE, and STN_ENABLE to be sent to the parent of the STATIC control STN_CLICKED.
SS_RIGHTJUST	400	When the control is resized to fit a new image, the top and left edges of the control are moved instead than the bottom and right edges.
SS_REALSIZEIMAGE	800	Prevents resizing of the static control to fit the image.
SS_SUNKEN	1000	Draws a sunken 3D style border around the control.

Dialog styles

Visual Basic manages its own forms instead of using the standard Windows dialog manager. As such, it is extremely unlikely that you would find the dialog styles useful. These are included in the API32.TXT file with the prefix DS_. Refer to the original Win32 documentation from Microsoft if you need information on these constants.

Suggestions for Further Practice

Try extending the BtnPlay sample program to experiment with style bits for other controls.

Function Reference

A complete explanation of how to interpret the information in the function reference sections of this book can be found in the "How to Use This Book" part of the introduction. You may also wish to review the definition of the GetLastError API function which can be found in the Function Reference for Chapter 6.

■ AdjustWindowRect, AdjustWindowRectEx

VB Declaration
```
Declare Function AdjustWindowRect& Lib "user32" (lpRect As RECT, ByVal dwStyle _
As Long, ByVal bMenu As Long)
Declare Function AdjustWindowRectEx& Lib "user32" (lpRect As RECT, ByVal _
dwStyle As Long, ByVal bMenu As Long, ByVal dwEsStyle As Long)
```

Description
Calculates the size of a window rectangle needed to obtain a specified client rectangle given a window style.

Use with VB
No problem.

Parameter	Type/Description
lpRect	RECT—Initially contains the desired client area. Is set by the function to the target window rectangle size.
dwStyle	Long—Window style.
bMenu	Long—Set TRUE (nonzero) if window has a menu.
dwEsStyle	Long—(AdjustWindowRectEx only) The extended window style.

Return Value
Long—Nonzero on success, zero on failure. Sets GetLastError.

Platform
Windows 95, Windows NT, Win16

Comments
Use GetWindowLong to retrieve the style of a form before calling this function.

The function will not correctly calculate sizes when the menu takes up two rows. If your application uses a multirow caption, you can use the GetSystemMetrics function.

There is a known bug in which this function returns invalid results with large font video modes on NT 3.5.

Example
See Ex5a.vbp

■ AnyPopup

VB Declaration
```
Declare Function AnyPopup& Lib "user32" ()
```

Description
Determines if a pop-up window exists anywhere on the screen.

Use with VB
No problem.

Return Value
Long—TRUE (nonzero) if a pop-up exists.

Platform	Windows 95, Windows NT, Win16
Comments	A pop-up for this function includes any visible, owned top level windows, both pop-up and overlapped. Though present for compatibility reasons, I have not heard of a useful purpose for this function.

■ ArrangeIconicWindows

VB Declaration

```
Declare Function ArrangeIconicWindows& Lib "user32" (ByVal hwnd As Long)
```

Description   Arranges the minimized child windows of a parent window.

Use with VB   Useful for arranging icons on the desktop. Use the GetDesktopWindow function to obtain a handle to the desktop window.

Parameter	Type/Description
hwnd	Long—Handle of the parent window.

Return Value   Long—The height of a row of icons. Zero on failure. Sets GetLastError.

Platform   Windows 95, Windows NT, Win16

Comments   You may also be able to use this on a custom control that can contain iconized child windows.

Example   Arranges the icons on the desktop—See Ex5a.vbp
      dl& = ArrangeIconicWindows(GetDesktopWindow())

■ AttachThreadInput

VB Declaration

```
Declare Function AttachThreadInput& Lib "user32" (ByVal idAttach As Long, ByVal _
idAttachTo As Long, ByVal fAttach As Long)
```

Description   Normally, each thread in the system has its own input queue. This function allows threads and processes to share input queues. Focus, window activation, mouse capture, keyboard state, and input queue status are shared when threads are attached, allowing related input functions to work as in Win16.

Use with VB   No problem.

Parameter	Type/Description
idAttach	Long—Identifier of thread to attach.
idAttachTo	Long—Identifier of thread to which thread idAttach is attached.
fAttach	Long—TRUE (nonzero) to attach, FALSE to detach.

Return Value   Long—Nonzero on success, zero on failure. Sets GetLastError.

Platform	Windows 95, Windows NT
Comments	Refer to Chapter 14 for information on threads and processes.
	The keyboard state is reset when this function is called (See GetKeyState and GetKeyboardState in Chapter 6).
Example	See Statevw.vbp.

■ BeginDeferWindowPos

VB Declaration `Declare Function BeginDeferWindowPos& Lib "user32" (ByVal nNumWindows As Long)`

Description Begins the process of building a list of new window positions for simultaneous updating. This function returns a handle to an internal structure that will hold the window positions. This structure is then filled by calls to DeferWindowPos. When you are ready to update all the window positions, a call to EndDeferWindowPos changes all of the window positions in the structure simultaneously.

Use with VB No problem.

Parameter	Type/Description
nNumWindows	Long—Initial number of windows to allocate space for in the structure. The structure will automatically be resized if necessary during each DeferWindowPos call.

Return Value Long—Handle to the internal structure. Zero on error.

Platform Windows 95, Windows NT, Win16

Comments See DeferWindowPos, EndDeferWindowPos.

Example See Ex5a.vbp.

■ BringWindowToTop

VB Declaration `Declare Function BringWindowToTop& Lib "user32" (ByVal hwnd As Long)`

Description Brings the specified window to the top of the window list, uncovering it if it is partially or entirely obscured by other windows. Pop-up, top level, and MDI child windows are also activated by this function.

Use with VB No problem.

Parameter	Type/Description
hwnd	Long—The handle of the window to bring to the top.

Return Value Long—Nonzero on success, zero on failure. Sets GetLastError.

Platform Windows 95, Windows NT, Win16

Comments   This function may be used with child windows as well. This function is local to a specific input thread—in other words, calling this function on a window that is not part of the foreground application will still bring the window to the top of the list of windows within its own application, but will not bring that application to the foreground. This means that the window may remain hidden even after calling this function.

Porting Notes   Under Win16 this function would activate the application that owns the window. This change is closely related to the changes in the SetFocus and SetActiveWindow functions described earlier in this chapter.

Example   Ex5A.vbp

■ CascadeWindows, CascadeWindowsBynum

VB Declaration
```
Declare Function CascadeWindows% Lib "user32" (ByVal hwndParent As Long, ByVal _
wHow As Long, lpRect As RECT, ByVal cKids As Long, lpKids As Long)
Declare Function CascadeWindowsBynum% Lib "user32" Alias "CascadeWindows" _
(ByVal hwndParent As Long, ByVal wHow As Long, ByVal lpRect As Long, ByVal _
cKids As Long, ByVal lpKids As Long)
```

Description   Arranges windows in cascade order.

Use with VB   No problem for top level windows or owned windows.

Parameter	Type/Description
hwndParent	**Long**—Parent window whose children are to be arranged. Use **GetDesktopWindow** to obtain the top level window handle.
wHow	**Long**—MDITILE_SKIPDISABLED—does not arrange disabled MDI children.
lpRect	**RECT**—Rectangle within which to cascade the windows. May be NULL to use the entire client area.
cKids	**Long**—Number of child windows specified in the lpKids array.
lpKids	**Long**—First element in list of child windows to arrange. Pass NULL (be sure to define parameter as ByVal). Long, to arrange all child windows.

Return Value   Integer—The number of windows arranged on success, zero on failure.

Platform   Windows 95, Windows NT 4.0

Comments   The original Win32 documentation for this function is incorrect. The parameters here are based on the actual Win32 C header files. The function does not work on child windows such as controls—only top level windows and MDI children. Note in the case of MDI forms, the parent window specified should be the handle of the MDIClient window, not the window handle of the MDI form itself. You can use the GetParent API to obtain this handle based on the handle of an MDI child form.

Example   Ex5a.vbp

■ ChildWindowFromPoint, ChildWindowFromPointEx

VB Declaration   Declare Function ChildWindowFromPoint& Lib "user32" (ByVal hWnd As Long, ByVal _
X As Long, ByVal Y As Long)
Declare Function ChildWindowFromPointEx& Lib "user32" (ByVal hWndParent As _
Long, ByVal ptx As Long, ByVal pty As Long, ByVal uFlags As Long)

Description   Returns the handle of the first child window in a parent window that contains the specified point.

Use with VB   No problem.

Parameter	Type/Description
hWnd	Long—Handle of parent window.
X	Long—X value of the point in pixels.
Y	Long—Y value of the point in pixels.
uFlags	Long—(ChildWindowFromPointEx only) Controls the search for windows as follows: CWP_ALL = Tests all windows. CWP_SKIPINVISIBLE = Ignores invisible windows. CWP_SKIPDISABLED = Ignores disabled windows. CWP_SKIPTRANSPARENT = Ignores transparent windows.

Return Value   Long—Window handle of the first child window found containing the specified point. If no window is found, returns hWnd (the handle of the parent window). If the point is outside of the parent window, returns 0.

Platform   Windows 95, Windows NT, Win16

Example   WinView.vbp

■ ClientToScreen

VB Declaration   Declare Function ClientToScreen& Lib "user32" (ByVal hwnd As Long, lpPoint As _
POINTAPI)

Description   Determines the screen coordinates for a point given in the client coordinates of a window.

Use with VB   No problem.

Parameter	Type/Description
hwnd	Long—Handle of the window that determines the client coordinates to use.
lpPoint	POINTAPI—Point in client coordinates of hWnd. On return, this parameter will contain the same point in screen coordinates.

Return Value   Long—Nonzero on success, zero on failure.

Platform   Windows 95, Windows NT, Win16

Example   WinView
                     CloseWindow

VB Declaration   `Declare Function CloseWindow& Lib "user32" (ByVal hwnd As Long)`

Description   Minimizes the specified window. The window is not destroyed.

Use with VB   Use the WindowState property to minimize VB forms.

Parameter	Type/Description
hwnd	Long—Handle of the window to minimize.

Return Value   Long—Nonzero on success, zero on failure. Sets GetLastError.

Platform   Windows 95, Windows NT, Win16

Comments   This function has no effect on pop-up and child windows.

■ CopyRect

VB Declaration   `Declare Function CopyRect& Lib "user32" (lpDestRect As RECT, lpSourceRect As _`
                     `RECT)`

Description   The contents of rectangle lpSourceRect are copied into rectangle lpDestRect.

Use with VB   No problem.

Parameter	Type/Description
lpDestRect	RECT—Destination rectangle structure.
LpSourceRect	RECT—Source rectangle.

Return Value   Long—Nonzero on success, zero on failure. Sets GetLastError.

Platform   Windows 95, Windows NT, Win16

Example   Rectplay.vbp

■ DeferWindowPos

VB Declaration   `Declare Function DeferWindowPos& Lib "user32" (ByVal hWinPosInfo As Long, ByVal _`
                     `hwnd As Long, ByVal hWndInsertAfter As Long, ByVal x As Long, ByVal y As Long, _`
                     `ByVal cx As Long, ByVal cy As Long, ByVal wFlags As Long)`

Description   This function specifies a new window position for the specified window and enters it into the
                     structure created by BeginDeferWindowPos for update during execution of the EndDeferWin-
                     dowPos function.

Use with VB   No problem.

Parameter	Type/Description
hWinPosInfo	Long—Handle of structure returned by BeginDeferWindowPos for subsequent calls to DeferWindowPos.
Hwnd	Long—Window to position.
HWndInsertAfter	Long—Window handle. Window hWnd will be placed after this window handle in the window list. May also be one of the following values: HWND_BOTTOM: Place window at bottom of the window list. HWND_TOP: Place window at the top of the Z-order, the order in which windows are displayed for the given level of the window in the hierarchy. HWND_TOPMOST: Place window at the top of the list, ahead of any topmost windows (see WS_EX_TOPMOST style bit). HWND_NOTOPMOST: Place window at the top of the list, behind any topmost windows.
X	Long—The new x coordinate of the window. If hWnd is a child window, x is given in the client coordinates of the parent window
y	Long—The new y coordinate of the window. If hWnd is a child window, y is given in the client coordinates of the parent window
cx	Long—Specifies the new window width.
Cy	Long—Specifies the new window height
wFlags	Long—An integer containing flags from the following: SWP_DRAWFRAME: Draws a frame around the window. SWP_HIDEWINDOW: Hides the window. SWP_NOACTIVATE: Does not activate the window. SWP_NOMOVE: Retains current position (x and y are ignored). SWP_NOREDRAW: Window is not automatically redrawn. SWP_NOSIZE: Retains current size (cx and cy are ignored). SWP_NOZORDER: Retains current position in the window list (hWndInsertAfter is ignored). SWP_SHOWWINDOW: Displays the window. SWP_NOOWNERZORDER: Does not change owners Z-order. (Win32) SWP_NOSENDCHANGING: Window is not sent a WM_WINDOWPOSCHANGING message.

Return Value   Long—Returns a new handle to the structure containing the position update information. This handle should be used on further calls to DeferWindowPos and the ending call to EndDeferWindowPos. Returns zero on error.

Platform   Windows 95, Windows NT, Win16

Comments   See comments for the SetWindowPos function. See BeginDeferWindowPos, EndDeferWindowPos.

Example   See Ex5a.vbp

■ DestroyWindow

VB Declaration   Declare Function DestroyWindow& Lib "user32" (ByVal hwnd As Long)

Description   Destroys the specified window and all its child windows.

Use with VB   No problem, though it is unlikely to be of much use.

Parameter	Type/Description
hwnd	Long—Handle of window to destroy.

Return Value   Long—Nonzero on success, zero on failure. Sets GetLastError.

Platform   Windows 95, Windows NT, Win16

■ DrawAnimatedRects

VB Declaration   Declare Function DrawAnimatedRects& Lib "user32" (ByVal hWnd As Long, ByVal _
idAni As Long, lprcFrom As RECT, lprcTo As RECT)

Description   Draws an animated series of rectangles between lprcFrom and lprcTo.

Use with VB   No problem.

Parameter	Type/Description
hWnd	Long—Window within which to draw the rectangles. Zero to use the desktop.
IdAni	Long—0 for Windows 95.
LprcFrom	RECT—Origin rectangle.
LprcTo	RECT—Destination rectangle

Return Value   Long—Nonzero on success, zero on failure.

Platform   Windows 95, Windows NT 4.0

■ EnableWindow

VB Declaration   Declare Function EnableWindow& Lib "user32" (ByVal hwnd As Long, ByVal fEnable _
As Long)

Description   Enables or disables all mouse and keyboard input to the specified window.

Use with VB   Use the Enabled property on VB forms and controls.

Parameter	Type/Description
hwnd	Long—Window handle.
FEnable	Long—Nonzero to enable the window, zero to disable.

Return Value	Long—Nonzero on success, zero on failure. Sets GetLastError.
Platform	Windows 95, Windows NT, Win16

■ EndDeferWindowPos

VB Declaration `Declare Function EndDeferWindowPos& Lib "user32" (ByVal hWinPosInfo As Long)`

Description Simultaneously updates the positions and states of all windows specified by calls to DeferWindowPos.

Use with VB No problem.

Parameter	Type/Description
hWinPosInfo	Long—Structure handle as returned by the most recent call to DeferWindowPos.

Return Value Long—Nonzero on success, zero on failure. Sets GetLastError.

Platform Windows 95, Windows NT, Win16

Example See Ex5a.vbp.

■ EnumChildWindows

VB Declaration `Declare Function EnumChildWindows& Lib "user32" (ByVal hWndParent As Long, _`
`ByVal lpEnumFunc As Long, ByVal lParam As Long)`

Description Enumerates the child windows for the specified parent window.

Use with VB Requires the dwcbkd32.ocx custom control under Visual Basic 4.0.

Parameter	Type/Description
hWndParent	Integer—Handle of parent window for which to enumerate child windows.
lpEnumFunc	Long—Pointer to function to call for each child window. Use the Addressof operator to obtain the address of a function in a standard module. Use the ProcAddress property of the dwcbkd32.ocx custom control to obtain a function pointer for callbacks under VB 4.0.
lParam	Long—Value that is passed to the EnumWindows event of the dwcbkd32.ocx custom control during enumeration. The meaning of this value is defined by the programmer.

Return Value Long—Nonzero on success, zero on failure.

Platform Windows 95, Windows NT, Win16

Comments Refer to Appendix A for details on using the dwcbkd32.ocx custom control with enumeration functions under VB 4.0. Child windows of child windows are also enumerated by this function.

Example WinView.vbp

■ EnumThreadWindows

VB Declaration   `Declare Function EnumThreadWindows& Lib "user32" (ByVal dwThreadID As Long, _`
`ByVal lpfn As Long, ByVal lParam As Long)`

Description   Enumerates the windows associated with the specified task.

Use with VB   Requires the dwcbkd32.ocx custom control included on the CD-ROM under VB 4.0.

Parameter	Type/Description
dwThreadID	Long—Identifier of the thread whose windows will be enumerated.
lpfn	Long—Pointer to function to call for each child window. Use the Addressof operator to obtain the address of a function in a standard module. Use the ProcAddress property of the dwcbkd32.ocx custom control to obtain a function pointer for callbacks under VB 4.0.
lParam	Long—Value that is passed to the EnumWindows event of the dwcbkd32.ocx custom control during enumeration. The meaning of this value is defined by the programmer.

Return Value   Long—Nonzero on success, zero on failure.

Platform   Windows 95, Windows NT

Comments   Refer to Appendix A for details on using the dwcbkd32.ocx custom control with enumeration functions under VB 4.0. Child windows of child windows are also enumerated by this function.

Porting Notes   This function corresponds roughly to the Win16 EnumTaskWindows API function.

Example   WinView.vbp

■ EnumWindows

VB Declaration   `Declare Function EnumWindows& Lib "user32" (ByVal lpEnumFunc As Long, ByVal _`
`lParam As Long)`

Description   Enumerates all parent windows (top level and owned) in the window list.

Use with VB   Requires the dwcbkd32.ocx custom control under VB 4.0.

Parameter	Type/Description
lpEnumFunc	Long—Pointer to function to call for each child window. Use the Addressof operator to obtain the address of a function in a standard module. Use the ProcAddress property of the dwcbkd32.ocx custom control to obtain a function pointer for callbacks under VB 4.0.
lParam	Long—Value that is passed to the EnumWindows event of the dwcbkd32.ocx custom control during enumeration. The meaning of this value is defined by the programmer.

Return Value   Long—Nonzero on success, zero on failure.

Platform   Windows 95, Windows NT, Win16

Comments   Refer to Appendix A for details on using the dwcbkd32.ocx custom control with enumeration functions under VB 4.0.

Example   WinView.vbp

■ EqualRect

VB Declaration   `Declare Function EqualRect& Lib "user32" (lpRect1 As RECT, lpRect2 As RECT)`

Description   Determines if two rectangles structures are equal.

Use with VB   No problem.

Parameter	Type/Description
lpRect1	RECT—Rectangle to compare.
lpRect2	RECT—Rectangle to compare.

Return Value   Long—Nonzero on success, zero on failure. Sets GetLastError.

Platform   Windows 95, Windows NT, Win16

Example   Rectplay.vbp

■ FindWindow

VB Declaration   `Declare Function FindWindow& Lib "user32" Alias "FindWindowA" (ByVal _`
`lpClassName As String, ByVal lpWindowName As String)`

Description   Finds the first top level window in the window list that meets the specified conditions.

Use with VB   No problem. One common use of FindWindow is to obtain the handle of the hidden window of class ThunderRTMain that is part of every running Visual Basic executable. You can then use the GetWindowText API to retrieve the window name of this window which is also the application title.

Parameter	Type/Description
lpClass-Name	String—Pointer to null terminated (C language) string containing the name of the class for the window, or zero to accept any class.
lpWin-dowName	String—Pointer to null terminated (C language) string containing the window text (or title), or zero to accept any window title.

Return Value   Long—Handle of the window found. Zero if no window was found. Sets GetLastError.

Platform   Windows 95, Windows NT, Win16

Comments   You will rarely search by both class and window name at the same time. The easiest way to pass a zero to the parameter that you are not searching for is to pass the vbNullString constant.

Porting Notes vbNullString did not exist under VB 3.0, thus aliases of this function were frequently used. You can continue to use aliases if you wish, adjusting the declarations as needed for Win32.

Example See Ex5a.vbp:

```
Dim hw&, cnt&
Dim rttitle As String * 256
hw& = FindWindow("ThunderRT5Main", vbNullString) ' ThunderRTMain under VB4
cnt = GetWindowText(hw&, rttitle, 255)
MsgBox Left$(rttitle, cnt), 0, "RTMain title"
```

■ FindWindowEx

VB Declaration
```
Declare Function FindWindowEx& Lib "user32" Alias "FindWindowExA" (ByVal _
hWndParent As Long, ByVal hWndChildAfter As Long, ByVal lpClassName As String, _
ByVal lpWindowName As String)
```

Description Finds the first child window in the window list that meets the specified conditions.

Use with VB No problem.

Parameter	Type/Description
hWndParent	Long—Parent window whose children will be searched. Zero to use the desktop window (in which case top level windows, which are considered child windows of the desktop, will be searched as well).
hWndChildAfter	Long—Begins search after this window. This allows multiple calls of FindWindow to be used to find all child windows that meet the specified criteria. Zero to start with the first child window.
lpClassName	String—Class name to search for. Zero to ignore.
lpWindowName	String—Window name to search for. Zero to ignore.

vbNullString?

Return Value Long—Handle of the window found. Zero if no window was found. Sets GetLastError.

Platform Windows 95, Windows NT 4.0

Comments See FindWindow.

Example See FindWindow.

■ FlashWindow

VB Declaration
```
Declare Function FlashWindow& Lib "user32" (ByVal hwnd As Long, ByVal bInvert _
As Long)
```

Description Flashes the specified window. This means that the title or caption is changed as if switching from active to inactive or vice versa. This function is commonly used for inactive windows to attract the user's attention.

Use with VB	No problem.	
	Parameter	**Type/Description**
	hwnd	Long—Handle of the window to flash.
	bInvert	Long—TRUE (nonzero) to toggle the window caption. FALSE to return to the original state.

Return Value Long—TRUE (nonzero) if the window was active before the call.

Platform Windows 95, Windows NT, Win16

Comments This function is frequently used in combination with a timer to cause repeated flashing. bInvert is ignored on minimized windows under Windows NT and Windows for Workgroups (Win16). It is not ignored under Windows 95.

Example WinView.vbp

■ GetActiveWindow

VB Declaration `Declare Function GetActiveWindow& Lib "user32" ()`

Description Obtains the handle of the active window.

Use with VB No problem.

Return Value Long—The handle of the active window, or zero if no window is active.

Platform Windows 95, Windows NT, Win16

Comments This function is discussed at length within the chapter text.

Porting Notes Unlike Win16, it is common for no window to be active. This is because the active window state is kept on a per-application instead of system-wide basis. Refer to the chapter text for details.

Example Statevw.vbp.

■ GetCapture

VB Declaration `Declare Function GetCapture& Lib "user32" ()`

Description Retrieves the handle of the window within the current input thread that has the mouse capture, if any exists.

Use with VB No problem.

Return Value Long—The handle of the window that has the capture. Zero if no window within the current thread has the capture.

Platform Windows 95, Windows NT, Win16

Porting Notes   Capture under Win32 is kept on a per thread basis—not a system-wide basis. Refer to the chapter text for further information.

Example   WinView.vbp

■ GetClassInfo, GetClassInfoEx

VB Declaration
```
Declare Function GetClassInfo& Lib "user32" Alias "GetClassInfoA" (ByVal _
hInstance As Long, ByVal lpClassName As String, lpWndClass As WNDCLASS)
Declare Function GetClassInfoEx& Lib "user32" Alias "GetClassInfoExA" (ByVal _
hInstance As Long, ByVal lpClassName As String, lpWndClassEx As WNDCLASSEX)
```

Description   Retrieves a copy of the WNDCLASS structure (or WNDCLASSEX structure) containing information about the specified class.

Use with VB   No problem.

Parameter	Type/Description
hInstance	Long—A handle to the instance that owns the class. NULL to obtain information on standard Windows classes.
lpClassName	String—The name of the class to search for. May also be a Long value where the low word is a global atom containing the class name.
lpWndClass	WNDCLASS—(GetClassInfo) structure to contain the results
lpWndClassEx	WNDCLASSEX—(GetClassInfoEx) structure to contain the result.

Return Value   Long—Nonzero on success, zero on failure. Sets GetLastError.

Platform   Windows 95, Windows NT, Win16 (GetClassInfo only)

Comments   Refer to Appendix B for information on the WNDCLASS and WNDCLASSEX data structures. Be sure to set the cbSize field in the WNDCLASSEX structure before using it as a parameter to this function.

■ GetClassLong

VB Declaration
```
Declare Function GetClassLong& Lib "user32" Alias "GetClassLongA" (ByVal hwnd _
As Long, ByVal nIndex As Long)
```

Description   Obtains one of the Long variable entries for the window class.

Use with VB   No problem.

Parameter	Type/Description
hwnd	Long—Window handle for which to obtain class information.

Parameter	Type/Description
nIndex	Long—Information to retrieve, may be one of the following constants: Positive values represent a byte offset used to obtain class information allocated in the extra bytes for this class. GCL_CBCLSEXTRA: Number of extra bytes allocated in this class structure. GCL_CBWNDEXTRA: Number of extra bytes allocated in the window structure for each window in this class. GCL_HBRBACKGROUND: Handle to the default brush to use when painting the background of each window of this class (see Chapter 7). GCL_HCURSOR: Handle to the default cursor for windows in this class. GCL_HICON: Handle to the default icon for windows in this class. GCL_HICONSM: Small icon for this class. GCL_HMODULE: Handle to the module for this class. GCL_MENUNAME: Retrieves the name or resource ID for the class menu. GCL_STYLE: Style of this class. Positive values obtain class information allocated in the extra bytes for this class. GCL_WNDPROC: Retrieves the address of the class window function (the default window function for windows in this class).

Return Value   Long—As specified by nIndex. Zero on error. Sets GetLastError.

Platform   Windows 95, Windows NT, Win16

Porting Notes   Many of the nIndex options to this function are changed from Win16 where they had the GCW_xxx prefix and were used with the GetClassWord and SetClassWord functions.

Example   WinView.vbp

■ GetClassName

VB Declaration   ```
Declare Function GetClassName& Lib "user32" Alias "GetClassNameA" (ByVal hwnd _
As Long, ByVal lpClassName As String, ByVal nMaxCount As Long)
```

**Description**     Retrieves the class name for the specified window.

**Use with VB**     No problem.

| Parameter | Type/Description |
|---|---|
| hwnd | Long—Window handle for which to obtain the class name. |
| lpClassName | String—Buffer to load with the class name. Must be preallocated to at least nMaxCount+1 characters. |
| nMaxCount | Long—Length of the buffer provided by lpClassName. |

**Return Value**     Long—The length in bytes of the class name excluding the final null terminating character. Zero on error. Sets GetLastError.

**Platform**     Windows 95, Windows NT, Win16
```

Example   WinView.vbp

■ GetClassWord

VB Declaration   `Declare Function GetClassWord% Lib "user32" (ByVal hwnd As Long, ByVal nIndex _`
                     `As Long)`

Description   Obtains one of the Integer variable entries for the window class.

Use with VB   No problem.

Parameter	Type/Description
hwnd	Long—Window handle for which to obtain class information.
nIndex	Long—Positive offset to class information allocated in the extra bytes for this class.

Return Value   Integer—As specified by nIndex. Zero on error. Sets GetLastError.

Platform   Windows 95, Windows NT, Win16

Porting Notes   This function used to support a number of standard indexes with the GCW_ prefix which are now
                     32-bit values accessed using the GetClassLong function (with the prefix GCL_).

■ GetClientRect

VB Declaration   `Declare Function GetClientRect& Lib "user32" (ByVal hwnd As Long, lpRect As _`
                     `RECT)`

Description   Returns the size of the client rectangle for the specified window.

Use with VB   No problem.

Parameter	Type/Description
hwnd	Long—Window for which to obtain the size.
lpRect	RECT—Rectangle to load with the size of the client area in pixels.

Return Value   Long—Nonzero on success, zero on failure. Sets GetLastError.

Platform   Windows 95, Windows NT, Win16

Comments   The left and top fields of lpRect are always set to zero by this function.

Example   WinView.vbp

■ GetDesktopWindow

VB Declaration   `Declare Function GetDesktopWindow& Lib "user32" ()`

Description	Obtains a window handle representing the entire screen.
Use with VB	No problem.
Return Value	Long—Handle of the desktop window.
Platform	Windows 95, Windows NT, Win16
Comments	All desktop icons are drawn on this window. It is also used for screen savers.
Example	WinView.vbp, Ex5a.vbp

■ GetFocus

VB Declaration	`Declare Function GetFocus& Lib "user32" ()`
Description	Obtains the handle of the window that has the input focus.
Use with VB	No problem.
Return Value	Long—Handle of the window with the focus. Zero if no window has the focus.
Platform	Windows 95, Windows NT, Win16
Comments	This function is discussed at length in the chapter text.
Porting Notes	Unlike Win16, it is common for no window to have the focus. This is because the focus state is kept on a per-application instead of system-wide basis. Refer to the chapter text for details.
Example	Statevw.vbp

■ GetForegroundWindow

VB Declaration	`Declare Function GetForegroundWindow& Lib "user32" ()`
Description	Obtains the handle of the foreground window. This is the active window in the foreground application.
Use with VB	No problem.
Return Value	Long—The handle of the foreground window.
Platform	Windows 95, Windows NT Windows NT supports multiple desktops that are independent of each other (for example, the login window is a separate desktop). Each desktop has its own foreground window.
Comments	The concept of foreground and background windows is new to Win32. Refer to the chapter text for further information.
Example	Statevw.vbp

GetLastActivePopup

VB Declaration   `Declare Function GetLastActivePopup& Lib "user32" (ByVal hwndOwnder As Long)`

Description   Obtains the handle of the most recently used popup window for a given parent window.

Use with VB   Visual Basic applications do not use pop-up windows, so this function is not particularly useful.

Parameter	Type/Description
hwndOwnder	Long—Parent window.

Return Value   Long—Handle to most recently used pop-up window. hwndOwner if no pop-up was found.

Platform   Windows 95, Windows NT, Win16

GetParent

VB Declaration   `Declare Function GetParent& Lib "user32" (ByVal hwnd As Long)`

Description   Determines the parent window of the specified window.

Use with VB   No problem.

Parameter	Type/Description
hwnd	Long—Handle of the window to test.

Return Value   Long—Handle of the parent window. Zero if the window has no parent or if an error occurs. Sets GetLastError.

Platform   Windows 95, Windows NT, Win16

Example   WinView.vbp

GetTopWindow

VB Declaration   `Declare Function GetTopWindow& Lib "user32" (ByVal hwnd As Long)`

Description   Searches the internal window list for the handle of the first child window belonging to the specified window.

Use with VB   No problem.

Parameter	Type/Description
hwnd	Long—Window for which to find the top level child. Zero to find the top level window on the desktop.

Return Value   Long—The handle of the top level child window for the window specified.

Platform   Windows 95, Windows NT, Win16

Comments   The Top level window in the Z-order is also the first window in the internal window list.

■ GetUpdateRect

VB Declaration   `Declare Function GetUpdateRect& Lib "user32" (ByVal hwnd As Long, lpRect As _`
`RECT, ByVal bErase As Long)`

Description   Obtains a rectangle describing the portion of the specified window that needs to be updated.

Use with VB   Unfortunately, by the time the Paint event occurs for a VB form or control, the update area has already been cleared, making this function useless for VB. However, you can use a subclasser to intercept the WM_PAINT event for a form or control to determine the update area before VB clears it. This is described further in Chapter 17.

Parameter	Type/Description
hwnd	Long—Window for which to determine the update area.
lpRect	RECT—Rectangle to load with the update coordinates.
bErase	Long—Set TRUE (nonzero) to erase the update area.

Return Value   Long—Nonzero on success, zero on failure.

Platform   Windows 95, Windows NT, Win16

Comments   If the window class style has CS_OWNDC set and the window mapping mode is not MM_TEXT, the update rectangle will be in logical coordinates. Refer to Chapter 7 for a description of these terms. VB form and picture controls do have CS_OWNDC set, but are almost always set to MM_TEXT.

■ GetWindow

VB Declaration   `Declare Function GetWindow& Lib "user32" (ByVal hwnd As Long, ByVal wCmd As _`
`Long)`

Description   Obtains the handle of a window with a specified relationship to a source window.

Use with VB   No problem.

Parameter	Type/Description
hwnd	Long—Source window.

Parameter	Type/Description
wCmd	Long—Specifies the relationship of the result window to the source window based on the following constants: GW_CHILD: Find the first child window of the source window. GW_HWNDFIRST: Find the first sibling window for a source child window, or the first top level window. GW_HWNDLAST: Find the last sibling for a source child window, or the last top level window. GW_HWNDNEXT: Find the next sibling window for the source window. GW_HWNDPREV: Find the previous sibling window for the source window. GW_OWNER: Find the owner of the window.

Return Value   Long—Window handle as specified by wCmd. Zero if none found or on error. Sets GetLastError.

Platform   Windows 95, Windows NT, Win16

Comments   Sibling windows refer to windows on the same level of the hierarchy. If a window has five child windows, those five windows are siblings. While GetWindow can be used to enumerate windows, EnumWindows and EnumChildWindows are more reliable in cases where windows are being repositioned, created, or destroyed during the enumeration process.

Example   WinView.vbp

■ GetWindowContextHelpId

VB Declaration   `Declare Function GetWindowContextHelpId& Lib "user32" (ByVal hWnd As Long)`

Description   Retrieves the help context ID associated with a window.

Use with VB   This function does not retrieve the Help context ID set for a VB form or control from within the Visual Basic environment.

Parameter	Type/Description
hWnd	Long—Window handle for which to obtain a help context.

Return Value   Long—The help context Id if present. Zero otherwise.

Platform   Windows 95, Windows NT 4.0

■ GetWindowLong

VB Declaration   `Declare Function GetWindowLong& Lib "user32" Alias "GetWindowLongA" (ByVal hwnd _`
`As Long, ByVal nIndex As Long)`

Description   Obtains information from the window structure for the specified window.

Use with VB   No problem.

Parameter	Type/Description
hwnd	Long—Handle of window for which to obtain information.
nIndex	Long—Information to retrieve; may be one of the following constants: GWL_EXSTYLE: The extended window style. GWL_STYLE: The window style. GWL_WNDPROC: The address of the window function for this window. GWL_HINSTANCE: The handle of the instance that owns the window. GWL_HWNDPARENT: The handle of the parent of this window. Do not use SetWindowWord to change this value. GWL_ID: The identifier of a child window within a dialog box. GWL_USERDATA: Defined by the application. Dialog boxes also specify the following constants: DWL_DLGPROC: Address of the dialog function for this window. DWL_MSGRESULT: Value returned by a message processed within the dialog function. DWL_USER: Defined by the application. Positive values obtain window information allocated in the extra bytes for this window.

Return Value   Long—As specified by nIndex. Zero on error. Sets GetLastError.

Platform   Windows 95, Windows NT, Win16

Porting Notes   Many of the nIndex options to this function are changed from Win16 where they had the GWW_xxx prefix and were used with the GetWindowWord and SetWindowWord functions.

Example   WinView.vbp

■ GetWindowPlacement

VB Declaration   `Declare Function GetWindowPlacement& Lib "user32" (ByVal hwnd As Long, lpwndpl _`
                      `As WINDOWPLACEMENT)`

Description   Obtains window state and location information for a window.

Use with VB   No problem.

Parameter	Type/Description
hwnd	Long—Handle of window for which to obtain the information.
lpwndpl	WINDOWPLACEMENT—Structure containing location and state information for the window. See Appendix B for details.

Return Value   Long—Nonzero on success, zero on failure. Sets GetLastError.

Platform   Windows 95, Windows NT, Win16

Comments   Be sure to set the length field of the WINDOWPLACEMENT structure before calling this function.

■ GetWindowRect

VB Declaration   `Declare Function GetWindowRect& Lib "user32" (ByVal hwnd As Long, lpRect As _`
`RECT)`

Description   Obtains the bounding rectangle for the entire window including borders, title bars, scroll bars, menus, and so on.

Use with VB   No problem.

Parameter	Type/Description
hwnd	Long—Handle of window for which to obtain the bounding rectangle.
lpRect	RECT—Rectangle to load with the window dimensions in screen coordinates.

Return Value   Long—Nonzero on success, zero on failure. Sets GetLastError.

Platform   Windows 95, Windows NT, Win16

Comments   Use this with the handle obtained from GetDesktopWindow to obtain a rectangle describing the entire visible display.

Example   WinView.vbp

■ GetWindowText

VB Declaration   `Declare Function GetWindowText& Lib "user32" Alias "GetWindowTextA" (ByVal hwnd _`
`As Long, ByVal lpString As String, ByVal cch As Long)`

Description   Retrieves the title (caption) text of a window or contents of a control.

Use with VB   Use the Caption or Text property (as appropriate) for VB forms or controls.

Parameter	Type/Description
hwnd	Long—Handle of window for which to obtain the text.
lpString	String—Predefined string buffer of at least cch+1 characters to load with the window text.
cch	Long—Length of lpString buffer.

Return Value   Long—The length of the string copied into lpString not including the null terminating character. Sets GetLastError.

Platform   Windows 95, Windows NT, Win16

Porting Notes   Cannot be used to retrieve text from an edit control in another application.

Example   Ex5a.vbp

■ GetWindowTextLength

VB Declaration `Declare Function GetWindowTextLength& Lib "user32" Alias "GetWindowTextLengthA" _`
`(ByVal hwnd As Long)`

Description Retrieves the length of the title (caption) text of a window or contents of a control.

Use with VB Use the Caption or Text property (as appropriate) for VB forms or controls.

Parameter	Type/Description
hwnd	Long—Handle of window for which to obtain the text.

Return Value Long—The length of the string not including the null terminating character.

Platform Windows 95, Windows NT, Win16

■ GetWindowWord

VB Declaration `Declare Function GetWindowWord% Lib "user32" (ByVal hwnd As Long, ByVal nIndex _`
`As Long)`

Description Obtains information from the window structure for the specified window.

Use with VB No problem.

Parameter	Type/Description
hwnd	Long—Handle of window for which to obtain information.
nIndex	Long—Positive offset indicating the Information to retrieve from the space allocated in the extra bytes for this window.

Return Value Integer—As specified by nIndex.

Platform Windows 95, Windows NT, Win16

Porting Notes This function used to support a number of standard indexes with the GWW_ prefix which are now 32-bit values accessed using the GetWindowLong function (with the prefix GWL_).

■ InflateRect

VB Declaration `Declare Function InflateRect& Lib "user32" (lpRect As RECT, ByVal x As Long, _`
`ByVal y As Long)`

Description This function increases or decreases the size of a rectangle. X is added to the right field and subtracted from the left field. This serves to increase the width of the rectangle if X is positive, and reduce it if X is negative. Y does the same for the top and bottom fields.

	Parameter	Type/Description
Use with VB	No problem.	
	lpRect	RECT—Rectangle structure to modify.
	x	Long—Inflate width by this number.
	y	Long—Inflate height by this number.

Return Value   Long—Nonzero on success, zero on failure. Sets GetLastError.

Platform   Windows 95, Windows NT, Win16

Comments   Note that the actual change in width and height will be twice the value of the X and Y parameters.

Example   Scroll.vbp

■ IntersectRect

VB Declaration
```
Declare Function IntersectRect& Lib "user32" (lpDestRect As RECT, lpSrc1Rect As _
RECT, lpSrc2Rect As RECT)
```

Description   This function loads into rectangle lpDestRect a rectangle that describes the intersection of lpSrc1Rect and lpSrc2Rect. This is the rectangle that includes all points that are common to both rectangles. If the two source rectangles do not overlap at all, lpDestRect will be set to be an empty rectangle.

Use with VB   No problem.

	Parameter	Type/Description
	lpDestRect	RECT—Destination rectangle that will contain the intersection of lpSrc1Rect and lpSrc2Rect.
	lpSrc1Rect	RECT—First source rectangle.
	lpSrc2Rect	RECT—Second source rectangle.

Return Value   Long—Nonzero on success, zero on failure. Sets GetLastError.

Platform   Windows 95, Windows NT, Win16

Example   Rectplay.vbp

■ InvalidateRect, InvalidateRectBynum

VB Declaration
```
Declare Function InvalidateRect& Lib "user32" (ByVal hwnd As Long, lpRect As _
RECT, ByVal bErase As Long)
Declare Function InvalidateRectBynum& Lib "user32" Alias "InvalidateRect" _
(ByVal hwnd As Long, ByVal lpRect As Long, ByVal bErase As Long)
```

Description   This function invalidates all or part of the client area of a window. This will cause that part of the window to be redrawn in due course.

Use with VB   No problem.

Parameter	Type/Description
hwnd	Long—Handle of window to invalidate.
lpRect	RECT—Rectangle structure describing the part of the rectangle to invalidate. Use InvalidateRectBynum with lpRect set to zero (Long data type) to invalidate the entire window.
bErase	Long—TRUE (nonzero) to cause the specified area to be erased before it is redrawn.

Return Value   Long—Nonzero on success, zero on failure.

Platform   Windows 95, Windows NT, Win16

Comments   Windows causes the window to be redrawn when the system has some idle time available in which to update the screen.

■ IsChild

VB Declaration
```
Declare Function IsChild& Lib "user32" (ByVal hWndParent As Long, ByVal hwnd As _
Long)
```

Description   Determines if one window is the child or descendent of another.

Use with VB   No problem.

Parameter	Type/Description
hWndParent	Long—Window handle of parent.
hwnd	Long—Window handle to test.

Return Value   Long—Nonzero on success, zero on failure.

Platform   Windows 95, Windows NT, Win16

■ IsIconic

VB Declaration   `Declare Function IsIconic& Lib "user32" (ByVal hwnd As Long)`

Description   Determines if the window is minimized.

Use with VB   No problem.

Parameter	Type/Description
hwnd	Long—Handle of window to test.

Return Value   Long—Nonzero on success, zero on failure.

Platform   Windows 95, Windows NT, Win16

■ IsRectEmpty

VB Declaration   `Declare Function IsRectEmpty& Lib "user32" (lpRect As RECT)`

Description   Determines if a rectangle is empty.

Use with VB   No problem.

Parameter	Type/Description
lpRect	RECT—Rectangle to check.

Return Value   Long—Nonzero on success, zero on failure. Sets GetLastError.

Platform   Windows 95, Windows NT, Win16

■ IsWindow

VB Declaration   `Declare Function IsWindow& Lib "user32" (ByVal hwnd As Long)`

Description   Determines if a window handle is valid.

Use with VB   No problem.

Parameter	Type/Description
hwnd	Long—Handle to test.

Return Value   Long—Nonzero on success, zero on failure.

Platform   Windows 95, Windows NT, Win16

Comments   This function is especially useful in cases where you are holding a window handle in a program variable to make sure that it is still valid.

■ IsWindowEnabled

VB Declaration   `Declare Function IsWindowEnabled& Lib "user32" (ByVal hwnd As Long)`

Description   Determines if the window is enabled.

Use with VB   No problem. Use the VB Enabled property for Visual Basic forms and controls.

Parameter	Type/Description
hwnd	Long—Handle of window to test.

Return Value	Long—Nonzero on success, zero on failure.
Platform	Windows 95, Windows NT, Win16
Example	WinView.vbp

■ IsWindowUnicode

VB Declaration   Declare Function IsWindowUnicode& Lib "user32" (ByVal hwnd As Long)

Description   Allows you to determine if a window is a native Unicode window. This means that the window receives Unicode text for all text-based messages.

Use with VB   You need not worry about this. Windows automatically converts messages that reference text to meet the needs of the window receiving the message.

Parameter	Type/Description
hwnd	Long—Window handle

Return Value   Long—Nonzero if the window is a Unicode window. Zero if the window is a native ANSI window.

Platform   Windows 95, Windows NT

■ IsWindowVisible

VB Declaration   Declare Function IsWindowVisible& Lib "user32" (ByVal hwnd As Long)

Description   Determines if the window is visible.

Use with VB   No problem.

Parameter	Type/Description
hwnd	Long—Handle of window to test.

Return Value   Long—TRUE (nonzero) if the window is visible.

Platform   Windows 95, Windows NT, Win16

Comments   A window can be visible and still obscured by other visible windows that are on top of it (precede it in the internal window list).

Example   WinView.vbp

■ IsZoomed

VB Declaration   Declare Function IsZoomed& Lib "user32" (ByVal hwnd As Long)

Description   Determines if the window is maximized.

Use with VB	No problem.	
	Parameter	**Type/Description**
	hwnd	Long—Handle of window to test.

Return Value Long—Nonzero on success, zero on failure.

Platform Windows 95, Windows NT, Win16

Example WinView.vbp

■ LockWindowUpdate

VB Declaration `Declare Function LockWindowUpdate& Lib "user32" (ByVal hwndLock As Long)`

Description Locks the specified window from being updated. Only one window may be locked at a time.

Use with VB	No problem.	
	Parameter	**Type/Description**
	hwndLock	Long—Handle of window to lock. Specify zero to unlock the window.

Return Value Long—Nonzero on success, zero on failure (for example, if another window is already locked).

Platform Windows 95, Windows NT, Win16

Comments Windows keeps track of areas in the locked window that are invalid and causes them to be redrawn after the window is unlocked. You can draw into a locked window by using GetDCEx to obtain a special device context that will work with locked windows. One application of this is to create tracking rectangles (such as those used to size windows).

■ MapWindowPoints

VB Declaration `Declare Function MapWindowPoints& Lib "user32" (ByVal hwndFrom As Long, ByVal _`
`hwndTo As Long, lppt As POINTAPI, ByVal cPoints As Long)`

Description Converts points in the client coordinates of one window into the client coordinates of a second window.

Use with VB Be careful to pass to the function either a single point, or the first POINTAPI structure in an array, and that the number of entries in the array is at least equal to the number specified by the cPoints parameter.

Parameter	**Type/Description**
hwndFrom	Long—Handle of window that defines the source coordinates. Use zero or the desktop window handle to specify screen coordinates
hwndTo	Long—Handle of window that defines the destination coordinates. Use zero or the desktop window handle to specify screen coordinates.

Parameter	Type/Description
lppt	POINTAPI—First entry in an array of point structures to convert. Note that a RECT structure is organized in memory as two consecutive POINTAPI structures—thus you can create an alias for this function that uses RECT structures instead of POINTAPI structures. If you do so, be sure to double the cPoints value.
cPoints	Long—The number of points to convert.

Return Value   Long—The low word is the horizontal offset added to each point during the mapping, the high word is the vertical offset.

Platform   Windows 95, Windows NT, Win16

■ MoveWindow

VB Declaration
```
Declare Function MoveWindow& Lib "user32" (ByVal hwnd As Long, ByVal x As Long, _
ByVal y As Long, ByVal nWidth As Long, ByVal nHeight As Long, ByVal bRepaint As _
Long)
```

Description   Used to change the position and size of the specified window. Top level windows may be bound by minimum or maximum sizes that will override the parameters provided.

Use with VB   No problem.

Parameter	Type/Description
hwnd	Long—Handle of the window to move.
x	Long—New left position for the window.
y	Long—New top position for the window.
nWidth	Long—New width for the window.
nHeight	Long—New height for the window.
bRepaint	Long—TRUE (nonzero) if window should be redrawn. FALSE (zero) indicates that the application will explicitly redraw the window.

Return Value   Long—Nonzero on success, zero on failure.

Platform   Windows 95, Windows NT, Win16

Example   Ex5a.vbp

■ OffsetRect

VB Declaration
```
Declare Function OffsetRect& Lib "user32" (lpRect As RECT, ByVal x As Long, _
ByVal y As Long)
```

Description	This function moves a rectangle by applying a specified offset. X is added to the right and left fields, Y to the top and bottom fields. The direction of offset depends on whether the parameters are positive or negative, and on the coordinate system in use.
Use with VB	No problem.

Parameter	Type/Description
lpRect	RECT—Rectangle to be offset.
x	Long—Horizontal offset.
y	Long—Vertical offset.

Return Value	Long—Nonzero on success, zero on failure. Sets GetLastError.
Platform	Windows 95, Windows NT, Win16

■ OpenIcon

VB Declaration	`Declare Function OpenIcon& Lib "user32" (ByVal hwnd As Long)`
Description	Restores a minimized program and activates it.
Use with VB	No problem. The VB WindowState property should be used for Visual Basic forms.

Parameter	Type/Description
hwnd	Long—The window to restore.

Return Value	Long—TRUE (nonzero) on success, Zero on error. Sets GetLastError.
Platform	Windows 95, Windows NT, Win16
Comments	The restored window does not become the foreground window.

■ PtInRect

VB Declaration	`Declare Function PtInRect& Lib "user32" (lpRect As RECT, ByVal _` `ptx As Long, ByVal pty As Long)`
Description	This function determines if the specified point is located in rectangle lpRect.
Use with VB	No problem.

Parameter	Type/Description
lpRect	RECT—Rectangle to use for test.
ptx	Long—X point value
pty	Long—Y point value.

Return Value	Long—Nonzero on success, zero on failure. Sets GetLastError.

Platform   Windows 95, Windows NT, Win16

Comments   A point is considered to be inside a rectangle if it is within the four boundaries of the rectangle, or on the top or left side of the rectangle. A point located on the right or bottom side is not considered to be in the rectangle.

Example   Rectplay.vbp

■ RedrawWindow

VB Declaration
```
Declare Function RedrawWindow& Lib "user32" (ByVal hwnd As Long, lprcUpdate As _
RECT, ByVal hrgnUpdate As Long, ByVal fuRedraw As Long)
```

Description Redraws all or part of a window according to the fuRedraw flag.

Use with VB No problem.

Parameter	Type/Description
hwnd	Long—Handle of the window to redraw. Zero to update the desktop window.
lprcUpdate	RECT—Rectangle describing the area in the window to redraw.
hrgnUpdate	Long—Handle to a region describing the area to redraw. (Regions are described in Chapter 7.)
fuRedraw	Long—Flags specifying the redraw operation to perform. The constants in the following table may be combined to specify the redraw operation.

fuRedraw Constant	Description
RDW_ERASE	The background of the redraw area is erased before drawing. RDW_INVALIDATE must also be specified.
RDW_FRAME	Updates the nonclient area if included in the redraw area. RDW_INVALIDATE must also be specified.
RDW_INTERNALPAINT	A WM_PAINT message is posted to the window even if it is not invalid.
RDW_INVALIDATE	Invalidates the redraw area.
RDW_NOERASE	Prevents the background of the redraw area from being erased.
RDW_NOFRAME	Prevents the nonclient area from being redrawn if it is part of the redraw area. RDW_VALIDATE must also be specified.
RDW_NOINTERNALPAINT	Prevents any pending WM_PAINT messages that were generated internally or by this function. WM_PAINT messages will still be generated for invalid areas.
RDW_VALIDATE	Validates the redraw area.

Parameter	Type/Description
RDW_ERASENOW	Erases the specified redraw area immediately.
RDW_UPDATENOW	Updates the specified redraw area immediately.
RDW_ALLCHILDREN	Redraw operation includes child windows if present in the redraw area.
RDW_NOCHILDREN	Redraw operation excludes child windows if present in the redraw area.

Return Value   Long—Nonzero on success, zero on failure. Sets GetLastError.

Platform   Windows 95, Windows NT, Win16

Comments   If this function is used on the desktop window, the application must use the RDW_ERASE flag to redraw the desktop.

■ ReleaseCapture

VB Declaration   `Declare Function ReleaseCapture& Lib "user32" ()`

Description   Releases the mouse capture for the current application.

Use with VB   No problem.

Return Value   Long—TRUE (nonzero) on success, zero on error.

Platform   Windows 95, Windows NT, Win16

Porting Notes   The behavior of mouse capture has changed significantly from Win16. Refer to the chapter text for further information on mouse capture.

Example   WinView.vbp

■ ScreenToClient

VB Declaration   `Declare Function ScreenToClient& Lib "user32" (ByVal hwnd As Long, lpPoint As _`
`POINTAPI)`

Description   Determines the client coordinates for a given point on the screen.

Use with VB   No problem.

Parameter	Type/Description
hwnd	Long—Handle of window defining the client coordinate system to use.
lpPoint	POINTAPI—Structure containing the point on the screen in screen coordinates. This function loads the structure with the corresponding client coordinates based on hWnd.

Return Value   Long—Nonzero on success, zero on failure.

Platform   Windows 95, Windows NT, Win16

■ ScrollWindow

VB Declaration
```
Declare Function ScrollWindow& Lib "user32" (ByVal hWnd As Long, ByVal XAmount _
As Long, ByVal YAmount As Long, lpRect As RECT, lpClipRect As RECT)
```

Description   Scrolls all or part of a window's client area. ScrollWindowBynum specifies the rectangle pointers as Long to facilitate passing zero as a parameter.

Use with VB   No problem.

Parameter	Type/Description
hWnd	Long—Handle of the window to scroll.
XAmount	Long—Distance to scroll horizontally. Positive values scroll right, negative values scroll left.
YAmount	Long—Distance to scroll vertically. Positive values scroll down, negative values scroll up.
lpRect	RECT—Rectangle in client coordinates defining the portion of the client area to scroll. When NULL, the entire client area is scrolled. When NULL, child windows and controls are offset as well, along with any invalid areas. Otherwise child windows and invalid areas are not offset; thus it is advisable to call the UpdateWindow function before scrolling when lpRect is specified.
lpClipRect	RECT—Clipping rectangle. Only the area within this rectangle may be scrolled. This rectangle takes priority over lpRect. May be NULL.

Return Value   Long—Nonzero on success, zero on failure. Sets GetLastError.

Platform   Windows 95, Windows NT, Win16

Comments   ScrollWindowBynum provides a declaration that calls for Long variables containing pointers to the specified rectangles. This allows you to specify zero (NULL) as the rectangle parameters. You may use agGetAddressForObject to obtain a Long pointer to a rectangle object. For example, to scroll the part of a window specified by rectangle rcname up ten pixels without specifying a clipping rectangle use.

```
ScrollWindowBynum(formname.hWnd, 0, -10, agGetAddressForObject(rcname.left), 0&)
```

Example   Scroll.vbp

■ ScrollWindowEx

VB Declaration
```
Declare Function ScrollWindowEx& Lib "user32" (ByVal hwnd As Long, ByVal dx As _
Long, ByVal dy As Long, lprcScroll As RECT, lprcClip As RECT, ByVal hrgnUpdate _
As Long, lprcUpdate As RECT, ByVal fuScroll As Long)
```

Description   Scrolls all or part of a window's client area with additional options. ScrollWindowExBynum speci-
                      fies the rectangle pointers as Long to facilitate passing zero as a parameter.

Use with VB   See comments for ScrollWindow.

Parameter	Type/Description
hwnd	Long—Handle of the window to scroll.
dx	Long—Distance to scroll horizontally. Positive values scroll right, negative values scroll left.
dy	Long—Distance to scroll vertically. Positive values scroll down, negative values scroll up.
lprcScroll	RECT—Rectangle in client coordinates defining the portion of the client area to scroll. When zero, the entire client area is scrolled.
lprcClip	RECT—Clipping rectangle. Only the area within this rectangle may be scrolled. This rectangle takes priority over lpRect. May be zero, in which case no clipping takes place.
hrgnUpdate	Long—Region to load with the area invalidated during scrolling. May be zero. Refer to Chapter 7 for information on regions.
lprcUpdate	RECT—Rectangle structure that will be loaded with a rectangle defining the area invalidated during scrolling. May be zero.
fuScroll	Long—Flags that control scrolling. May be a combination of the following constants: SW_ERASE: Erases the background of the newly invalidated area. SW_INVALDATE: Invalidates the area uncovered by scrolling. SW_SCROLLCHILDREN: Child windows within the scroll area are moved by the amount scrolled. To prevent invalid results be sure that child windows or controls are either entirely in the scroll area or entirely outside the scroll area when using this function.

Return Value   Long—Constant values SIMPLEREGION, COMPLEXREGION, or NULLREGION that
                      describes the type of region that was invalidated.

Platform   Windows 95, Windows NT, Win16

Comments   See comments for ScrollWindow.

Example   Scroll.vbp

■ SetActiveWindow

VB Declaration   `Declare Function SetActiveWindow& Lib "user32" (ByVal hwnd As Long)`

Description   Activates the specified window.

Use with VB Use with caution. This function does not change the input focus, thus it is possible for the focus to be set to an inactive window—generally an undesirable situation. It is preferable to use the SetFocusAPI function to activate a window.

Parameter	Type/Description
hwnd	Long—Handle of window to activate.

Return Value Long—Handle of the previously active window.

Platform Windows 95, Windows NT, Win16

Comments Has no effect if the window specified does not belong to the current input thread.

Porting Notes The behavior and use of this function has changed considerably from Win16. Refer to the chapter text for detailed information on use of this function.

Example Statevw.vbp

■ SetCapture

VB Declaration `Declare Function SetCapture& Lib "user32" (ByVal hwnd As Long)`

Description Sets the mouse capture to the specified window. This window will receive all mouse input for the current application, or the entire system while the mouse button is pressed.

Use with VB No problem.

Parameter	Type/Description
hwnd	Long—The handle of the window to receive all mouse input.

Return Value Long—The handle of the window that previously had the mouse capture.

Platform Windows 95, Windows NT, Win16

Porting Notes The behavior and use of this function has changed considerably from Win16. Refer to the chapter text for detailed information on use of this function.

Example WinView.vbp.

■ SetClassLong

VB Declaration `Declare Function SetClassLong& Lib "user32" Alias "SetClassLongA" (ByVal hwnd _`
`As Long, ByVal nIndex As Long, ByVal dwNewLong As Long)`

Description Sets one of the Long variable entries for the window class.

Use with VB	No problem.	
	Parameter	**Type/Description**
	hwnd	Long—Window handle for which to set class information.
	nIndex	Long—See description for the nIndex parameter to the GetClassLong function.
	dwNewLong	Long—New value for the class information specified by nIndex.

Return Value Long—The previous value for the class information specified by nIndex. Zero on error. Sets GetLastError.

Platform Windows 95, Windows NT, Win16

Comments Use with care. Remember that changes affect all windows of the specified class, but that changes may not take effect until the window is redrawn.

Porting Notes See GetClassLong.

■ SetClassWord

VB Declaration
```
Declare Function SetClassWord% Lib "user32" (ByVal hwnd As Long, ByVal nIndex _
As Long, ByVal wNewWord As Integer)
```

Description Sets one of the Integer variable entries for the window class.

Use with VB	See comments.	
	Parameter	**Type/Description**
	hwnd	Long—Window handle for which to obtain class information.
	nIndex	Long—Positive number offset into the extra allocated space in the class information structure.
	wNewWord	Long—New value for the class information specified by nIndex.

Return Value Integer—The previous value for the class information specified by nIndex. Zero may indicate an error. Sets GetLastError.

Platform Windows 95, Windows NT, Win16

Comments Use with care. Remember that changes affect all windows of the specified class, but that changes may not take effect until the window is redrawn.

Porting Notes See GetClassWord.

■ SetFocusAPI

VB Declaration
```
Declare Function SetFocusAPI& Lib "user32" Alias "SetFocus" (ByVal hwnd As Long)
```

Description Sets the input focus to the specified window. Activates the window if necessary.

Use with VB   The SetFocus method is preferred for VB forms and controls.

Parameter	Type/Description
hwnd	Long—Handle of the window that will receive the focus.

Return Value   Long—Handle of the window that previously had the focus.

Platform   Windows 95, Windows NT, Win16

Comments   This function has no effect if the window specified is not owned by the current input thread.
     This function uses the alias SetFocusAPI to avoid conflicts with the Visual Basic SetFocus method.

Porting Notes   The behavior and use of this function has changed considerably from Win16. Refer to the chapter text for detailed information on use of this function.

Example   Statevw.vbp

■ SetForegroundWindow

VB Declaration   `Declare Function SetForegroundWindow& Lib "user32" (ByVal hwnd As Long)`

Description   Sets the window to be the foreground window for the system. This function can be used to change the application that the user is currently working with. It should not be done haphazardly, as it can be disconcerting to the user to have an application suddenly appear from the background.

Use with VB   No problem.

Parameter	Type/Description
hwnd	Long—Window to bring to the foreground.

Return Value   Long—Nonzero on success, zero on failure. Sets GetLastError.

Platform   Windows 95, Windows NT

Porting Notes   The concept of foreground and background windows is new to Win32. Refer to the chapter text for further information.

Example   Statevw.vbp

■ SetParent

VB Declaration   `Declare Function SetParent& Lib "user32" (ByVal hWndChild As Long, ByVal _`
     `hWndNewParent As Long)`

Description   Specifies the new parent for a window.

Use with VB	Makes it possible for VB to support child windows in many cases. For example: you can move controls from one container to another on a form. Using this function to move controls between forms is risky, but has been known to work. If you do this, be sure to SetParent the control back to its original form before closing either form.

Parameter	Type/Description
hWndChild	Long—Handle of child window.
hWndNewParent	Long—New parent for hWndChild.

Return Value	Long—The handle of the previous parent window.
Platform	Windows 95, Windows NT, Win16
Comments	This function can be used to place VB controls inside of container controls at runtime (such as making a button a child window of a picture or frame control), or moving controls from one container control to another. When a control is moved to another parent, its position is based on the coordinate system of the new parent, thus it may be necessary to reposition the control in order for it to appear in the desired location.
Porting Notes	Be sure to test your application thoroughly under each destination platform if you use this function.
Example	Ex5a.vbp

■ SetRect

VB Declaration	```Declare Function SetRect& Lib "user32" (lpRect As RECT, ByVal X1 As Long, ByVal _ Y1 As Long, ByVal X2 As Long, ByVal Y2 As Long)```
Description	Sets the contents of the specified rectangle.
Use with VB	No problem.

Parameter	Type/Description
lpRect	RECT—Rectangle to set.
X1	Long—Value for left field.
Y1	Long—Value for top field.
X2	Long—Value for right field.
Y2	Long—Value for bottom field.

Return Value	Long—Nonzero on success, zero on failure. Sets GetLastError.
Platform	Windows 95, Windows NT, Win16
Example	Rectplay.vbp

■ SetRectEmpty

VB Declaration `Declare Function SetRectEmpty& Lib "user32" (lpRect As RECT)`

Description Sets lpRect to be an empty rectangle (all fields=0).

Use with VB No problem.

Parameter	Type/Description
lpRect	RECT—Rectangle to set to empty.

Return Value Long—Nonzero on success, zero on failure. Sets GetLastError.

Platform Windows 95, Windows NT, Win16

Example Rectplay.vbp

■ SetWindowContextHelpId

VB Declaration `Declare Function SetWindowContextHelpId& Lib "user32" (ByVal hWnd As Long, _`
`ByVal dwContextHelpId As Long)`

Description Sets the help context Id for the specified window.

Use with VB No problem, but not particularly useful since Visual Basic provides its own help context support.

Parameter	Type/Description
hWnd	Long—Window handle.
dwCon-textHelpId	Long—New help context Id.

Return Value Long—Non zero on success, zero on failure.

Platform Windows 95, Windows NT 4.0

■ SetWindowLong

VB Declaration `Declare Function SetWindowLong& Lib "user32" Alias "SetWindowLongA" (ByVal hwnd _`
`As Long, ByVal nIndex As Long, ByVal dwNewLong As Long)`

Description Sets information in the window structure for the specified window.

	Parameter	**Type/Description**
Use with VB	See comments.	
	hwnd	Long—Handle of window for which to obtain information.
	nIndex	Long—See description for the nIndex parameter to the GetWindowLong function.
		Do not use this function with the GWL_HWNDPARENT index (use the SetParent API function instead).
	dwNewLong	Long—New value for the window information specified by nIndex.

Return Value   Long—The previous value of the specified data.

Platform   Windows 95, Windows NT, Win16

Comments   Changing the GWL_WNDPROC data is dangerous and should not be done by a VB application. Refer to the style reference in this chapter for information on windows style bits that may be changed.

■ SetWindowPlacement

VB Declaration   `Declare Function SetWindowPlacement& Lib "user32" (ByVal hwnd As Long, lpwndpl _`
`As WINDOWPLACEMENT)`

Description   Sets window state and location information for a window.

Use with VB   No problem.

	Parameter	**Type/Description**
	hwnd	Long—Handle of window for which to set placement information.
	lpwndpl	WINDOWPLACEMENT—Structure containing location and state information for the window. See Appendix B for details.

Return Value   Long—Nonzero on success, zero on failure. Sets GetLastError.

Platform   Windows 95, Windows NT, Win16

■ SetWindowPos

VB Declaration   `Declare Function SetWindowPos& Lib "user32" (ByVal hwnd As Long, ByVal _`
`hWndInsertAfter As Long, ByVal x As Long, ByVal y As Long, ByVal cx As Long, _`
`ByVal cy As Long, ByVal wFlags As Long)`

Description   This function specifies a new position and state for a window. It can also change the position of the window in the internal window list. This function is similar to the DeferWindowPos function, except that it takes effect immediately.

Use with VB   Visual Basic forms reset the topmost state when they are deactivated or minimized under Win32. Use a subclasser to reset the topmost state when necessary.

Parameter	Type/Description
hwnd	Long—Window to position.
hWndInsertAfter	Long—Window handle. Window hWnd will be placed after this window handle in the window list. May also be one of the following values: HWND_BOTTOM: Place window at bottom of the window list. HWND_TOP: Place window at the top of the Z-order, the order in which windows are displayed for the given level of the window in the hierarchy. HWND_TOPMOST: Place window at the top of the list, ahead of any topmost windows (see WS_EX_TOPMOST style bit). HWND_NOTOPMOST: Place window at the top of the list, behind any topmost windows.
x	Long—The new x coordinate of the window. If hWnd is a child window, x is given in the client coordinates of the parent window.
y	Long—The new y coordinate of the window. If hWnd is a child window, y is given in the client coordinates of the parent window.
cx	Long—Specifies the new window width.
cy	Long—Specifies the new window height.
wFlags	Long—An integer containing flags from the following: SWP_DRAWFRAME: Draws a frame around the window. SWP_HIDEWINDOW: Hides the window. SWP_NOACTIVATE: Does not activate the window. SWP_NOMOVE: Retains current position (x and y are ignored). SWP_NOREDRAW: Window is not automatically redrawn. SWP_NOSIZE: Retains current size (cx and cy are ignored). SWP_NOZORDER: Retains current position in the window list (hWndInsertAfter is ignored). SWP_SHOWWINDOW: Displays the window. SWP_FRAMECHANGED: Forces a WM_NCCALCSIZE message to go to the window even if its size does not change.

Return Value   Long—Nonzero on success, zero on failure. Sets GetLastError.

Platform   Windows 95, Windows NT, Win16

Comments   When a window is made into a topmost window, all its owned windows are also made topmost. When it is made non-topmost, all of its owned and owner windows are also made non-topmost. Z-order refers to the order of windows from the top to the bottom of an imaginary Z-axis extending outward from the screen.

Example   See Ex5a.vbp.

■ SetWindowText

VB Declaration   `Declare Function SetWindowText& Lib "user32" Alias "SetWindowTextA" (ByVal hwnd _`

```
As Long, ByVal lpString As String)
```

Description   Sets the title (caption) text of a window or contents of a control.

Use with VB   Use the Caption or Text property (as appropriate) for VB forms or controls.

Parameter	Type/Description
hwnd	Long—Handle of a window for which to set the text.
lpString	String—Text to set into hWnd.

Return Value   Long—Nonzero on success, zero on failure. Sets GetLastError.

Platform   Windows 95, Windows NT, Win16

■ SetWindowWord

VB Declaration
```
Declare Function SetWindowWord% Lib "user32" (ByVal hwnd As Long, ByVal nIndex _
As Long, ByVal wNewWord As Integer)
```

Description   Sets information in the window structure for the specified window.

Use with VB   Use with caution.

Parameter	Type/Description
hwnd	Long—Handle of window for which to obtain information.
nIndex	Long—See description for the nIndex parameter to the GetWindowWord function.
wNewWord	Long—New value for the window information specified by nIndex.

Return Value   Long—The previous value of the specified data.

Platform   Windows 95, Windows NT, Win16

Porting Notes   A number of standard indexes with the prefix GWW_ have become long indexes with the prefix GWL_. Use the SetWindowLong function to set these under Win32.

■ ShowOwnedPopups

VB Declaration
```
Declare Function ShowOwnedPopups& Lib "user32" (ByVal hwnd As Long, ByVal fShow _
As Long)
```

Description   Shows or hides all pop-up windows owned by the specified window.

Use with VB No problem, though not particularly useful, as Visual Basic does not use pop-up windows.

Parameter	Type/Description
hwnd	Long—Handle to parent window.
fShow	Long—TRUE (nonzero) to show all pop-up windows owned by hWnd; FALSE (zero) to hide them.

Return Value Long—Nonzero on success, zero on failure. Sets GetLastError.

Platform Windows 95, Windows NT, Win16

■ ShowWindow

VB Declaration
```
Declare Function ShowWindow& Lib "user32" (ByVal hwnd As Long, ByVal nCmdShow _
As Long)
```

Description Use to control the visibility of a window.

Use with VB Use the VB property that corresponds to a ShowWindow command for VB forms and controls.

Parameter	Type/Description
hwnd	Long—Handle of the window on which to apply the command specified by nCmdShow.
nCmdShow	Long—Specifies a visibility command for the window. Use one of the following constants: SW_HIDE: Hides the window. Activation passes to another window. SW_MINIMIZE: Minimizes the window. Activation passes to another window. SW_RESTORE: Displays a window at its original size and location and activates it. SW_SHOW: Displays a window at its current size and location, and activates it. । SW_SHOWMAXIMIZED: Maximizes a window and activates it. SW_SHOWMINIMIZED: Minimizes a window and activates it. SW_SHOWMINNOACTIVE: Minimizes a window without changing the active window. SW_SHOWNA: Displays a window at its current size and location. Does not change the active window. SW_SHOWNOACTIVATE: Displays a window at its most recent size and location. Does not change the active window. SW_SHOWNORMAL: Same as SW_RESTORE.

Return Value Long—TRUE (nonzero) if window was previously visible. FALSE (zero) otherwise.

Platform Windows 95, Windows NT, Win16

■ ShowWindowAsync

VB Declaration
```
Declare Function ShowWindowAsync& Lib "user32" (ByVal hwnd As Long, ByVal _
nCmdShow As Long)
```

Description
Similar to ShowWindow, except that the ShowWindow command is posted to the specified window for asynchronous processing. This allows you to control the visibility of windows belonging to another process without risking having your own application hang if the other process is hung.

Use with VB
No problem.

Parameter	Type/Description
hwnd	Long—The window that will receive the ShowWindow command.
nCmdShow	Long—Same as ShowWindow.

Return Value
Long—TRUE (nonzero) if window was previously visible. FALSE (zero) otherwise.

Platform
Windows 95, Windows NT 4.0

■ SubtractRect

VB Declaration
```
Declare Function SubtractRect& Lib "user32" (lprcDst As RECT, lprcSrc1 As RECT, _
lprcSrc2 As RECT)
```

Description
This function loads into rectangle lpDestRect, a rectangle that describes the result when rectangle lpSrc2Rect is subtracted from lpSrc1Rect.

Use with VB
No problem.

Parameter	Type/Description
lprcDst	RECT—Destination rectangle that will contain the result of lpSrc2Rect subtracted from lpSrc1Rect.
lprcSrc1	RECT—First source rectangle.
lprcSrc2	RECT—Second source rectangle.

Return Value
Long—TRUE (nonzero) if the function was successful, zero otherwise.

Platform
Windows 95, Windows NT, Win16

Comments
lpSrc2Rect must completely intersect lpSrc1Rect either horizontally or vertically. In other words, when the part of lpSrc1Rect that intersects lpSrc2Rect is removed from lpSrc1Rect, the result must be a rectangle. If it is not, lpDestRect is simply set to lpSrc1Rect.

■ TileWindows, TileWindowsBynum

VB Declaration
```
Declare Function TileWindows% Lib "user32" (ByVal hwndParent As Long, ByVal _
wHow As Long, lpRect As RECT, ByVal cKids As Long, lpKids As Long)
Declare Function TileWindowsBynum% Lib "user32" Alias "TileWindows" (ByVal _
```

```
hwndParent As Long, ByVal wHow As Long, ByVal lpRect As Long, ByVal cKids As _
Long, ByVal lpKids As Long)
```

Description   Arranges windows in tiled order.

Use with VB   No problem for top level windows or owned windows.

Parameter	Type/Description
hwndParent	Long—Parent window whose children are to be arranged. Use GetDesktopWindow to obtain the top level window handle.
wHow	Long—MDITILE_HORIZONTAL or MDITILE_VERTICAL —Sets tiling direction
lpRect	RECT—Rectangle within which to tile the windows. May be NULL to use the entire client area.
cKids	Long—Number of child windows specified in the lpKids array.
lpKids	Long—First element in list of child windows to arrange. Pass NULL (be sure to define parameter as ByVal—Long), to arrange all child windows.

Return Value   Integer—The number of windows arranged on success, zero on failure.

Platform   Windows 95, Windows NT 4.0

Comments   The original Win32 documentation for this function is incorrect. The parameters here are based on the actual Win32 C header files. The function does not work on child windows such as controls—only top level windows and MDI children. Note in the case of MDI forms, the parent window specified should be the handle of the MDIClient window, not the window handle of the MDI form itself. You can use the GetParent API to obtain this handle based on the handle of an MDI child form.

Example   Ex5a.vbp

■ UnionRect

VB Declaration   Declare Function UnionRect& Lib "user32" (lpDestRect As RECT, lpSrc1Rect As _
RECT, lpSrc2Rect As RECT)

Description   This function loads into rectangle lpDestRect a rectangle that describes the union of lpSrc1Rect and lpSrc2Rect. This is the rectangle that includes all points in both rectangles.

Use with VB   No problem.

Parameter	Type/Description
lpDestRect	RECT—Destination rectangle that will contain the union of lpSrc1Rect and lpSrc2Rect.
lpSrc1Rect	RECT—First source rectangle.
lpSrc2Rect	RECT—Second source rectangle.

Return Value	Long—Nonzero on success, zero on failure. Sets GetLastError.
Platform	Windows 95, Windows NT, Win16
Comments	The RectPlay example program provides a graphical illustration of this function in action.
Example	Rectplay.vbp

■ UpdateWindow

VB Declaration
```
Declare Function UpdateWindow& Lib "user32" (ByVal hwnd As Long)
```

Description
Forces an immediate update of a window. All areas in the window that were previously invalidated are redrawn.

Use with VB
If any part of a VB form or control needs updating, this is similar to the Refresh method.

Parameter	Type/Description
hwnd	Long—Handle of the window to update.

Return Value
Long—Nonzero on success, zero on failure.

Platform
Windows 95, Windows NT, Win16

■ ValidateRect, ValidateRectBynum

VB Declaration
```
Declare Function ValidateRect& Lib "user32" (ByVal hwnd As Long, lpRect As RECT)
Declare Function ValidateRectBynum& Lib "user32" Alias "ValidateRect" (ByVal _
hwnd As Long, ByVal lpRect As Long)
```

Description
Validates all or part of the client area of a window. This informs Windows that the specified area does not need to be redrawn.

Use with VB
No problem, though not particularly useful with VB applications.

Parameter	Type/Description
hwnd	Long—Handle of window to validate.
lpRect	RECT—Rectangle structure describing the part of the rectangle to be validated. Use ValidateRectBynum with lpRect set to zero (Long data type) to validate the entire window.

Return Value
Long—Nonzero on success, zero on failure.

Platform
Windows 95, Windows NT, Win16

■ WindowFromPoint

VB Declaration
```
Declare Function WindowFromPoint& Lib "user32" (ByVal X As Long, ByVal Y As Long)
```

Description   Returns the handle of the window that contains the specified point. Ignores disabled, hidden, and transparent windows.

Use with VB   No problem. Can be used to identify forms and controls given their position in screen coordinates.

Parameter	Type/Description
X	Long—X point value.
Y	Long—Y point value.

Return Value   Long—Handle of the window that contains the specified point. Zero if no window exists at the point specified.

Platform   Windows 95, Windows NT, Win16

Example   WinView.vbp

Hardware and System Functions

THE WINDOWS API PROVIDES ACCESS TO A VARIETY OF SYSTEM information and hardware functions that can be useful to the Visual Basic programmer. This chapter reviews those functions relating to the mouse and cursor, the caret, keyboard input, time, and other system information. Compared with Win16, Win32 adds a wealth of new information functions. However, some of the functions with which you may be familiar have become obsolete or have even disappeared.

Mouse, Cursor, and Caret Functions

Visual Basic provides support for the mouse and the cursor it controls (or MousePointer, as it is called in Visual Basic). Each input thread has an associated cursor, thus it is not generally possible for an application to control the cursor on a system-wide basis. This is a change from Win16, where a single cursor is shared by the entire system.

The caret is used to indicate a position within a control. Like the cursor, each input thread can have a single caret.

Unless otherwise noted, all mouse and cursor positions are specified in pixel screen coordinates.

Cursor Clipping

Windows provides the ability to restrict the mouse to a specified area on the screen, a process called *clipping*. The cursor clipping functions are shown in Table 6.1.

Table 6.1   **Cursor Clipping Functions**

Function	Description
ClipCursor	Specifies the clipping rectangle
GetClipCursor	Retrieves the current cursor clipping area if one is present

The following code fragment from file Ex6a.vbp demonstrates how you can clip the cursor to the client area of a window. Note the use of the ClientToScreen function to convert from client coordinates to screen coordinates.

```
Dim myRect As RECT, myPoint As POINTAPI
Dim dl&
myPoint.x = Ø
myPoint.Y = Ø
dl& = ClientToScreen&(pctCursor.hwnd, myPoint)
```

```
myRect.Top = myPoint.Y
myRect.Left = myPoint.x
myRect.Right = myRect.Left + pctCursor.ScaleWidth
myRect.Bottom = myRect.Top + pctCursor.ScaleHeight
dl& = ClipCursor&(myRect)
```

The ClipCursor function requires a null parameter in order to clear the clipping state. The standard ClipCursor function expects a RECT parameter. In order to pass it a NULL value, you should use an alias of the function that uses a long parameter and pass it a zero.

```
dl& = ClipCursorBynum&(0)
```

Cursor Position

Table 6.2 describes the Windows API functions that may be used to set and retrieve the cursor position.

Table 6.2   **Cursor Position Functions**

Function	Description
SetCursorPos	Moves the cursor to the location specified
GetCursorPos	Retrieves the current cursor position

The following example from Ex6a.vbp shows how you can set the cursor to a location within a form or control (specified in pixels).

```
Dim myPoint As POINTAPI
Dim dl&
myPoint.x = 12
myPoint.Y = 12
dl& = ClientToScreen&(pctCursor.hwnd, myPoint)
dl& = SetCursorPos&(myPoint.x, myPoint.Y)
```

Other Mouse and Cursor Functions

Windows provides a number of other mouse related functions that—with limitations—may be used with Visual Basic.

Custom Cursors

A cursor is made up of a pair of bitmaps whose dimensions may be up to 32x32 pixels. It is very similar internally to an icon. Like other Windows objects, a cursor object is represented by a 32-bit handle.

Windows provides functions to create cursors and select them for use. Unfortunately, Visual Basic is not truly compatible with these API functions. When a custom cursor is selected using the SetCursor API function, VB tends to reset the cursor to the original value without notice. Fortunately, Visual Basic 4.0 added a new custom MouseIcon property that allows most controls to use any icon or cursor as a mouse pointer.

You can use the SetCursor API function to change the cursor only during uninterrupted operations in a procedure. As soon as normal event processing takes place through use of the DoEvents function or exiting an event procedure, the cursor is changed to the value appropriate for the form or control over which it appears. Setting the cursor in this manner only affects the calling application—other applications still have control over their own cursor.

Cursor resources may be loaded from program files or DLL files or may be created directly using the CreateCursor API function, which is described in Chapter 9.

Table 6.3 summarizes the remaining API functions relating to the mouse and cursor.

Table 6.3   **Additional Mouse and Cursor Functions**

Function	Description
CopyCursor	This Win16 function has been replaced by CopyIcon (which works just fine for cursors)
CreateCursor	Creates a cursor from two bitmaps (see Chapter 9 function reference)
DestroyCursor	Destroys a cursor and frees all system resources that it uses (see Chapter 9) function reference
GetCursor	Retrieves the handle of the current cursor
GetDoubleClickTime	Determines the time during which two consecutive mouse clicks will be considered a double click
LoadCursor	Loads a cursor resource from a file (see Chapter 9 function reference)
mouse event	Generates a simulated mouse event
SetCursor	Selects the cursor to use
SetDoubleClickTime	Sets the time during which two consecutive mouse clicks will be considered a double click
SetSystemCursor	Allows you to change any of the system standard cursors

Table 6.3	**Additional Mouse and Cursor Functions (Continued)**	
ShowCursor	Controls the visibility of the cursor
SwapMouseButton	Swaps the meanings of the right and left mouse buttons

Caret Functions

The *caret* is a resource that is commonly used to indicate a position with text. It is generally a flashing line or block, though any bitmap can be used as the caret. There can be only one caret associated with a given input thread at a time.

The caret API functions are of limited use under Visual Basic. Normally, a window should set the caret when it receives the input focus, and destroy it when it loses the focus. Unfortunately, in Visual Basic the GotFocus and Lost-Focus events occur only when a control loses focus to another control in the current application. They do not occur when the focus is switched to other applications. This makes it difficult to know when to set the caret for a particular control. It is of course possible to use a timer to detect when a control has the focus and to set the caret based on the results, but this is a cumbersome technique.

The SysInfo project described later in this chapter demonstrates use of a custom caret in an edit box. The caret functions are listed in Table 6.4.

Table 6.4	**Caret Functions**	
Function	**Description**
CreateCaret	Creates and selects a caret
DestroyCaret	Destroys a caret
GetCaretBlinkTime	Gets the flash rate for the caret
GetCaretPos	Determines the position of the caret in logical coordinates
HideCaret	Hides the caret
SetCaretBlinkTime	Sets the flash rate for the caret
SetCaretPos	Sets the position of the caret in logical coordinates
ShowCaret	Makes the caret visible

Keyboard and Other Input Functions

The Windows API provides a number of functions that can be used to control and process keyboard input. This chapter focuses on those character and keyboard functions that are closely related to the underlying hardware or locale settings. Those character and string conversion functions that are hardware and system independent are covered in Chapters 11 and 15. Many of these functions were available under Win16 but were rarely used by Visual Basic programmers. With the increased emphasis toward internationalizing software, these functions are likely to become more important.

Character Sets Revisited

In order to understand how to use the keyboard functions, it is first necessary to know a little bit about the way that Windows processes characters. The idea of character sets was introduced in Chapter 3. This chapter takes a second look at how character sets work under Windows. This subject will be revisited several more times throughout this book—in the context of fonts and text processing in Chapter 11, and of string operations in Chapter 15.

A character is generally represented in Windows as either an 8-bit unsigned value or a 16-bit unsigned value. String data is made up of a sequence of these characters. An 8-bit character is sufficient to define 256 characters. Many of these characters are defined by a standard known as ASCII (American Standard Code for Information Interchange); for example, ASCII character #10 is defined as a line feed character that indicates a break between lines.

Windows also provides support for extended two-byte character sets such as those used to represent Kanji (a Japanese alphabet). With these double-byte character sets (DBCS), a few special character values, called lead bytes, are used to indicate that the following byte is part of the same character.

Unicode is a 16-bit character set which is large enough to hold all of the characters of all of the world's languages, thus eliminating the problem of multiple character sets and code pages forever. Or at least it will, if it ever becomes the standard character set for every operating system and application. For the time being, Unicode is the standard character set only for Windows NT. Windows 95 is still based on 8-bit character sets.

A character set describes the appearance of each of the characters defined for the character set. Different languages frequently have different character sets in order to provide support for the characters unique to that language. The MS-DOS and Windows 95 operating systems describe a character set as a *code page*, and provide standard code pages for a number of different languages. Computer manufacturers will generally provide a keyboard that matches the default code page for a particular system, thus a DOS-based computer sold in Germany will have a German keyboard and default to the German MS-DOS code page. Windows refers to this character set as the OEM (original equipment manufacturer) character set. All DOS-related activities, such as command lines and file names, use the OEM character set on traditional FAT (file allocation table) file systems such as that used by Windows 3.*x* and Windows 95. The NT file system is able to use Unicode file names.

Both Windows 3.x and Windows 95 use their own internal character set based on ANSI (American National Standards Institute), called the ANSI or Windows character set. There are several ANSI code pages available. The current one can be identified using the GetACP function. A number of translation functions exist to convert OEM to ANSI and vice versa. They are typically used when working with file names, since these are always in the OEM character set on FAT file systems. The mapping from one character set to another is not one-to-one, thus, if you convert a string from OEM to ANSI and back, it may not match the original string.

One example of this is the "Ê" character (ASCII #202 decimal). This character does not exist in the MS-DOS code page #437 (U.S. standard). An attempt to save a file using this character would lead to an error, or a file that could not be accessed from the keyboard. The CharToOem API function will convert this character to the letter E. The OemToChar function will obviously not convert the letter E back to Ê.

The API conversion functions for OEM and ANSI character sets are shown in Table 6.5.

Table 6.5   **OEM and ANSI Conversion Functions**

Function	Description
CharToOem CharToOemBuff	Converts a string from the ANSI character set to the OEM character set. Replaces the Win16 AnsiToOem and AnsiToOemBuff functions.
OemToChar OemToCharBuff	Converts a string from the OEM character set to the ANSI character set. Replaces the Win16 OemToAnsi and OemToAnsiBuff functions.

Scan Codes and Virtual Keys

Keys on the keyboard produce different scan codes based on their position. A scan code is a hardware-dependent code that the keyboard sends to the computer to indicate that a keyboard operation took place. Scan codes can vary by the type of keyboard and type of computer being used, so software that uses scan codes directly may not be compatible with every computer that runs Windows. The meaning of scan codes and their locations on the keyboard are defined by keyboard layouts. Windows 95 and Windows NT support multiple keyboard layouts, and API functions are available to load and select keyboard layouts. Where might this be useful? Imagine that you have written a text editor that can edit two languages simultaneously. You could instantly select keyboard layouts based on the language being edited. Windows 95 and NT 4.0 allow each thread to have its own keyboard layout defined. Windows NT 3.51 defines the keyboard layout on a system-wide basis.

In order to provide low-level access to the keyboard that does not depend on the scan code, Windows defines *virtual keys*. Virtual keys are defined by constants with a VK_ prefix and are listed in Table 6.7 later in this chapter. They are also defined in the API32.TXT file provided with this book.

An overview of character processing can be seen in Figure 6.1.

Table 6.6 lists the keyboard processing API functions.

Table 6.6   **Keyboard Processing API Functions**

Function	Description
ActivateKeyboardLayout	Allows you to select a keyboard layout from those defined by the system.
EnumSystemCodePages	Used to obtain a list of all code pages supported or installed on a system.
GetACP	Retrieves the identifier of the ANSI code page that is currently in effect.
GetAsyncKeyState	Retrieves the state of the specified virtual key at the time the function is called.
GetCPInfo	Obtains information about a code page.
GetKBCodePage	Equivalent to and replaced by GetOEMCP.
GetKeyboardLayout	Determines the keyboard layout in use by a specified thread.
GetKeyboardLayoutList	Retrieves a list of available keyboard layouts.
GetKeyboardLayoutName	Retrieves the name of a keyboard layout.
GetKeyboardState	Retrieves the current state of all 256 virtual keys.
GetKeyboardType	Determines the type of keyboard in use.
GetKeyNameText	Determines the name of a particular virtual key. For example, the spacebar on U.S. keyboards is called "Space."
GetKeyState	Retrieves the state of the specified virtual key.

Figure 6.1

An overview of character processing under Windows

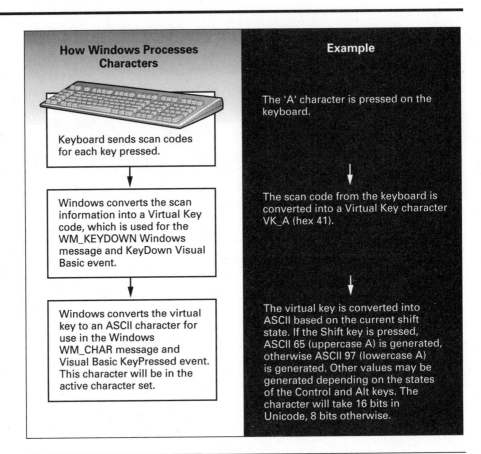

How Windows Processes Characters

Keyboard sends scan codes for each key pressed.

Windows converts the scan information into a Virtual Key code, which is used for the WM_KEYDOWN Windows message and KeyDown Visual Basic event.

Windows converts the virtual key to an ASCII character for use in the Windows WM_CHAR message and Visual Basic KeyPressed event. This character will be in the active character set.

Example

The 'A' character is pressed on the keyboard.

The scan code from the keyboard is converted into a Virtual Key character VK_A (hex 41).

The virtual key is converted into ASCII based on the current shift state. If the Shift key is pressed, ASCII 65 (uppercase A) is generated, otherwise ASCII 97 (lowercase A) is generated. Other values may be generated depending on the states of the Control and Alt keys. The character will take 16 bits in Unicode, 8 bits otherwise.

Table 6.6   **Keyboard Processing API Functions (Continued)**

GetOEMCP	Retrieves the identifier of the OEM code page that is currently in effect.
keybd_event	Generates a simulated keystroke to the system.
LoadKeyboardLayout	Loads a new keyboard layout.
MapVirtualKeyMapVirtualKeyEx	Converts characters to and from virtual keys, scan codes, and ASCII values.
OemKeyScan	Converts ASCII codes to OEM scan codes and shift states.

Table 6.6 **Keyboard Processing API Functions (Continued)**

SetKeyboardState	Sets the state of the 256 virtual keys as perceived by Windows.
ToAsciiToAsciiEx	Converts a scan code and shift state to an ASCII character.
ToUnicode	Converts a scan code and shift state to a Unicode character.
UnloadKeyboardLayout	Unloads a keyboard layout previously loaded by LoadKeyboardLayout.
VkKeyScan VkKeyScanEx	Converts ASCII codes to virtual key codes and shift states.

Virtual Key Codes

Table 6.7 shows the virtual key codes used in Windows.

Table 6.7 **Virtual Key Codes**

Virtual Key Code	Value
VK_LBUTTON	&H01
VK_RBUTTON	&H02
VK_CANCEL	&H03
VK_MBUTTON	&H04
VK_BACK	&H08
VK_TAB	&H09
VK_CLEAR	&H0C
VK_RETURN	&H0D
VK_SHIFT	&H10
VK_CONTROL	&H11
VK_MENU	&H12
VK_PAUSE	&H13
VK_CAPITAL	&H14
VK_ESCAPE	&H1B

Table 6.7 **Virtual Key Codes (Continued)**

VK_SPACE	&H20
VK_PRIOR	&H21
VK_NEXT	&H22
VK_END	&H23
VK_HOME	&H24
VK_LEFT	&H25
VK_UP	&H26
VK_RIGHT	&H27
VK_DOWN	&H28
VK_SELECT	&H29
VK_PRINT	&H2A
VK_EXECUTE	&H2B
VK_SNAPSHOT	&H2C
VK_INSERT	&H2D
VK_DELETE	&H2E
VK_HELP	&H2F
VK_NUMPAD0	&H60
VK_NUMPAD1	&H61
VK_NUMPAD2	&H62
VK_NUMPAD3	&H63
VK_NUMPAD4	&H64
VK_NUMPAD5	&H65
VK_NUMPAD6	&H66
VK_NUMPAD7	&H67
VK_NUMPAD8	&H68
VK_NUMPAD9	&H69
VK_MULTIPLY	&H6A

Table 6.7	**Virtual Key Codes (Continued)**
VK_ADD	&H6B
VK_SEPARATOR	&H6C
VK_SUBTRACT	&H6D
VK_DECIMAL	&H6E
VK_DIVIDE	&H6F
VK_F1	&H70
VK_F2	&H71
VK_F3	&H72
VK_F4	&H73
VK_F5	&H74
VK_F6	&H75
VK_F7	&H76
VK_F8	&H77
VK_F9	&H78
VK_F10	&H79
VK_F11	&H7A
VK_F12	&H7B
VK_F13	&H7C
VK_F14	&H7D
VK_F15	&H7E
VK_F16	&H7F
VK_F17	&H80
VK_F18	&H81
VK_F19	&H82
VK_F20	&H83
VK_F21	&H84
VK_F22	&H85

Table 6.7	Virtual Key Codes (Continued)
VK_F23	&H86
VK_F24	&H87
VK_NUMLOCK	&H90
VK_SCROLL	&H91
VK_A—VK_Z	Same as ASCII values for A–Z
VK_0—VK_9	Same as ASCII values for 0–9

The following six virtual keys are recognized only by the GetKeyState and GetAsyncKeyState functions to distinguish between left and right shift, control, and alt keys. No other functions recognize these codes.

VK_LSHIFT	&HA0
VK_RSHIFT	&HA1
VK_LCONTROL	&HA2
VK_RCONTROL	&HA3
VK_LMENU	&HA4
VK_RMENU	&HA5

Locales

Software is already a worldwide market, and it is becoming increasingly common for programmers to need to consider international issues. Win32 provides extensive API support for localizing software and determining the underlying platform on which your software is running.

A *Locale* is a 32-bit value that identifies the language and platform for the thread or system. Bits 0 through 15 (the low order word) identify the language. Bits 16 through 19 specify how sorting works under this language. It is typically 0, but may be set to 1 for Far East Unicode environments. Figure 6.2 shows the structure of a Locale identifier.

The low order word is divided into two parts. The low 10 bits (bits 0 through 9) indicate the language. The high 6 bits (bits 10 through 15) indicate a subset of the language—to differentiate, for example, between U.S. English and U.K. English. The values for the supported languages can be found in the file API32.TXT; look for the constants with the prefix LANG_. The subsets, or sublanguage constants are identified with the prefix SUBLANG_. Many

Figure 6.2
Locale Identifier

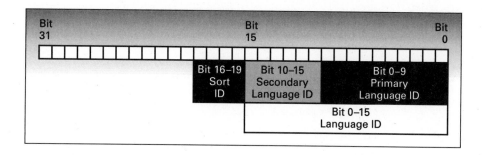

functions take the default system or user locales, which are given the special constant values:

```
Public Const LOCALE_SYSTEM_DEFAULT = &H800
Public Const LOCALE_USER_DEFAULT = &H400
```

A great deal of information is associated with locales. For example, the country name, names of days and months (and their abbreviations), the symbol used for local currency, the format used for dates and times, and other information that tends to vary from country to country. This information can go a long way to helping you create truly international applications using Visual Basic.

Table 6.8 lists the functions used to work with locales.

Table 6.8   **Locale Functions**

Function	Description
ConvertDefaultLocale	Converts a special default locale identifier such as LOCALE_SYSTEM_DEFAULT or LOCALE_USER_DEFAULT to an actual locale value
EnumSystemLocales	Obtains a list of all locales installed or supported on a system
GetCurrencyFormat	Formats a currency value according to the specified locale
GetDateFormat	Formats a date value according to the specified locale
GetLocaleInfo	Obtains detailed information about a locale
GetNumberFormat	Formats a number according to the specified locale
GetSystemDefaultLangID	Retrieves the default language identifier for the system

Table 6.8   **Locale Functions (Continued)**

GetSystemDefaultLCID	Retrieves the default locale identifier for the system
GetThreadLocale	Retrieves the default locale identifier for a thread
GetTimeFormat	Formats a time according to a specified locale
GetUserDefaultLangID	Retrieves the default language identifier for the current user
GetUserDefaultLCID	Retrieves the default locale identifier for the current user
IsValidLocale	Determines if a specified locale value is valid
SetLocaleInfo	Allows a user to customize some of the characteristics of the specified locale
SetThreadLocale	Allows you to change the locale for a specific thread

Input Control Functions

Windows provides a number of additional input control functions, which are listed in Table 6.9.

Table 6.9   **Input Control Functions**

Function	Description
EnableHardwareInput	This Win16 function is not supported by Win32
GetInputState	Determines if any keyboard or mouse events are in the system queue ready to be processed
GetQueueStatus	Determines what types of messages are in the application queue ready to be processed
LockInput	This Win16 function is not supported by Win32

Time Functions

Win32 provides improved support for keeping track of time as compared to Win16. Internally, Windows works with system time, which is always in Coordinated Universal Time (UTC, also known as GMT or Greenwich Mean Time, as it is based on the time in Greenwich, England). Windows converts between system time and local time by applying an adjustment based on the

time zone setting for the system. Win32 allows you to work with both local time and system time and to convert between them. Win32 also provides a set of functions to work with file time and dates, which relate to the date and time of files as they are stored in the file system. File dates and times will be covered in Chapter 13.

This book includes a sample project Time.vbp that demonstrates many of these functions. This project is included on the CD-ROM that comes with the book but is not listed here.

The functions listed in Table 6.10 are used to retrieve information on Windows timing. Note that systems measure time internally by timer ticks, the duration of which can vary based on the operating system and processor in use. Timing intervals for Win32 are typically 10 to 15 milliseconds. The timer tick duration determines the resolution of the time results returned by these functions.

Table 6.10   **Windows Time Functions**

Function	Description
EnumCalendarInfo	Enumerates locale-specific calendar information for the system.
EnumDateFormats	Enumerates date formats available for the specified locale.
EnumTimeFormats	Enumerates time formats available for the specified locale.
GetCurrentTime	This Win16 function has been replaced by GetTickCount, which has identical functionality.
GetLocalTime	Retrieves the current local time.
GetMessageTime	Returns the time (measured in milliseconds) that the most recent message was posted to the application message queue. Measured from when the current Windows session was started.
GetSystemTime	Retrieves the current system standard time.
GetSystemTimeAdjustment	Determines if the system is applying a periodic time adjustment to help maintain accurate system time.
GetTickCount	Retrieves the number of milliseconds that the current Windows session has been running.
GetTimeFormat	Formats a time according to a specified locale.
GetTimerResolution	This Win16 function is not supported under Win32, which is a shame.
GetTimeZoneInformation	Retrieves information about the current time zone.

Table 6.10	Windows Time Functions (Continued)	
	SetLocalTime	Sets the local time.
	SetSystemTime	Sets the system time.
	SetSystemTimeAdjustment	Sets the periodic time adjustment that the system applies to help maintain accuracy.
	SetTimeZoneInformation	Specifies the time zone.
	SystemTimeToTzSpecificLocalTime	Converts a system time into a local time.

The Windows API also includes functions to control the internal Windows timers; however, these should not be used by Visual Basic applications. The Visual Basic timer control duplicates their functionality.

Suggestions for Further Practice

The Time.vbp project is quite simple, but could be combined with the Locale examples in Ex6b.vbp and SysInfo to produce some interesting utilities. Try creating a world clock program that displays local time for other countries in the language of each country. Sorry, we don't have a database with countries, time zones, and languages spoken available. You'll have to solve that one on your own!

System Information and Control Functions

The Windows API includes a number of functions that make it possible to obtain information about the Windows system and to control various features in Windows. Some of these functions duplicate the functionality of the Windows Control Panel application.

The functions listed in Table 6.11 may be used to determine information about the Windows system and perform various system operations. Among these is an extended set of functions for manipulating environment variables that are significantly improved over those in Win16.

Example: Environ.vbp—A Class for Working with Environment Variables

Despite its increased use of the registry, Win32 systems still make use of environment variables to control some system behavior and to allow creation of environment blocks that can be inherited by newly created processes. It is

Table 6.11   System Information Functions

Function	Description
Beep	Sounds a tone on the internal speaker.
ExitWindowsEx	Exits Windows. Has a variety of restart options.
ExpandEnvironmentStrings	Helps build environment strings.
FreeEnvironmentStrings	Frees a block of environment strings allocated by GetEnvironment-Strings.
GetCommandLine	Retrieves the command line that launched the application.
GetComputerName	Retrieves the name of this computer.
GetEnvironmentStrings	Obtains an environment block which provides access to environment variables.
GetEnvironmentVariable	Obtains a single environment variable within an environment block.
GetFreeSpace	This Win16 function has been replaced by the GlobalMemoryStatus function. See Chapter 15 for further information.
GetFreeSystemResources	This Win16 function is not supported under Win32.
GetLastError	Obtains extended error information for the last API function call. Use the LastDLLError property of the Err object to obtain this value in Visual Basic.
GetSysColor	Determines the current color setting for a Windows object (for example, the color of a button or the color of the title bar of an active window).
GetSystemInfo	Retrieves information about the hardware platform.
GetSystemMetrics	Determines a variety of system metrics such as the height of a menu bar or window caption, the width of a vertical scroll bar, the minimum size of a window, etc.
GetSystemPowerStatus	Retrieves information about the power source and state of the system.
GetUserName	Gets the name of the current user.
GetVersion, GetVersionEx	Determines the versions of Windows and DOS that are running.
MessageBeep	Generates one of the standard system sounds.
SetComputerName	Sets the computer name.
SetEnvironmentVariable	Sets an environment variable within an environment block.

Table 6.11   **System Information Functions (Continued)**

SetSwapAreaSize	This Win16 function is not supported under Win32.
SetSysColors	Sets the current color setting for a Windows object (for example, the color of a scroll bar or the color of the title bar of an inactive window).
SystemParametersInfo	This powerful function can be used to retrieve and set a large number of system parameters such as the Windows screen saver, the desktop wallpaper, the keyboard delay and repeat rate, and more. Refer to the function reference for details.

worth taking a closer look at these functions because they illustrate additional techniques for working with memory buffers from Visual Basic.

The Environ project consists of a single form and a class module which provides a wrapper for the Win32 environment functions. The project also references APIGID32.BAS, the declaration file for the APIGID32.DLL library included with this book. Listing 6.1 shows the listing for the class module.

Listing 6.1   **Class Module Environ.cls**

```
VERSION 1.0 CLASS
BEGIN
  MultiUse = -1  'True
END
Attribute VB_Name = "EVClass"
Attribute VB_Creatable = True
Attribute VB_Exposed = True
Option Explicit

#If Win32 Then
Private Declare Function GetEnvironmentStrings& Lib "kernel32" Alias _
"GetEnvironmentStringsA" ()
Private Declare Function GetEnvironmentVariable& Lib "kernel32" Alias _
"GetEnvironmentVariableA" (ByVal lpName As String, ByVal lpBuffer _
As String, ByVal nSize As Long)
Private Declare Function SetEnvironmentVariable& Lib "kernel32" Alias _
"SetEnvironmentVariableA" (ByVal lpName As String, ByVal lpValue As String)
Private Declare Function ExpandEnvironmentStrings& Lib "kernel32" Alias _
"ExpandEnvironmentStringsA" (ByVal lpSrc As String, ByVal lpDst As String, _
ByVal nSize As Long)
Private Declare Function FreeEnvironmentStrings Lib "kernel32" Alias _
```

Listing 6.1   Class Module Environ.cls (Continued)

```
"FreeEnvironmentStringsA" (ByVal lpsz As String) As Long
#End If 'WIN32

Private datEVBlock&
```

The datEVBlock& variable is a private variable that is loaded with the address of the environment block when the class is initialized. This block contains all of the environment strings of the application separated by null characters. The final string is terminated with a double null character. One of the great advantages of using a class in this case is that the class can free the environment string block when it terminates. This means that the user of the class need not remember to call the FreeEnvironmentStrings function when done.

```
Private Sub Class_Initialize()
    datEVBlock& = GetEnvironmentStrings&()
End Sub


Private Sub Class_Terminate()
    Dim dl&
    dl& = FreeEnvironmentStrings(datEVBlock)
End Sub
```

Visual Basic does not provide a way to work directly with memory blocks given an address. The easiest way to work with such memory blocks is to copy them into a Visual Basic string. There is a complex way to do this by using the lstrcpy API function to copy the strings one at a time. An easier way is to use the agGetStringFrom2NullBuffer function that is included in APIGID32.DLL. This function copies all information from a buffer until it finds two nulls. Since it returns a Visual Basic string, you need not worry about pre-initializing buffers. Chapter 15 goes into more detail on working with strings and memory blocks.

The GetString function only returns the name of the environment string—not its value. It strips off everything after the "=" sign. Note that if the first character is an "=" sign, that character is part of the environment string name.

```
Public Function GetString$(idx%)
    Dim e$, e2$
    Dim startpos%, newpos%
    e$ = agGetStringFrom2NullBuffer(datEVBlock)
    e2$ = ParseAnyString(e$, idx%, Chr$(0))
    If Left$(e2$, 1) = "=" Then startpos% = 2 Else startpos% = 1
    newpos% = InStr(startpos%, e2$, "=")
    If newpos% > 0 Then e2$ = Left$(e2$, newpos% - 1)
```

```
        GetString$ = e2$
End Function
```

ParseAnyString is an incredibly useful function for parsing strings that
are divided by a separator. In this case it is used to extract individual strings
from the environment block.

```
'Extracts the idx%'th string from source$, where the
'substrings are separated by character sep$
'idx%=0 is the first string
Function ParseAnyString$(source$, ByVal idx%, ByVal sep$)
    Dim nexttab%, basepos%, thispos%
    Dim res$
    basepos% = 1
    thispos% = 0
    If (Len(source$) = 0) Then
        ParseAnyString$ = ""
        Exit Function
    End If
    Do
        nexttab% = InStr(basepos%, source$, sep$)
        If nexttab% = 0 Then nexttab% = Len(source$) + 1
        'Now points to next tab or 1 past end of string
        'The following should never happen
        'If nexttab% = basepos% Then GoTo ptsloop1

        If thispos% = idx% Then
            If nexttab% - basepos% - 1 < 0 Then
                res$ = ""
            Else
                res$ = Mid$(source$, basepos%, nexttab% - basepos%)
            End If
            Exit Do
        End If
ptsloop1:
        basepos% = nexttab% + 1
        thispos% = thispos% + 1
    Loop While (basepos% <= Len(source$))
    ParseAnyString$ = res$
End Function


' Determine the number of strings
Public Function GetStringCount%()
    Dim e$, e2$
    Dim strcnt%
    e$ = agGetStringFrom2NullBuffer(datEVBlock)
    Do
        e2$ = ParseAnyString(e$, strcnt%, Chr$(0))
        Debug.Print e2$
        If e2$ <> "" Then strcnt% = strcnt% + 1
    Loop While e2$ <> ""
```

```
    GetStringCount = strcnt%
End Function
```

GetStringValue provides a simple mapping of the GetEnvironmentVariable function. The advantage of implementing it is twofold: First it does all of the work of preinitializing string buffers and returning a string of the correct length. Second, it is logically related to the environment class, thus making the program more modular and turning Environ.cls into a comprehensive and easily reusable block of code.

```
' Retrieves the value of an environment string
'
Public Function GetStringValue$(ByVal envstr$)
    Dim dl&
    Dim buf$
    buf$ = String$(2048, 0)
    dl& = GetEnvironmentVariable(envstr$, buf$, 2047)
    If dl& > 0 Then GetStringValue$ = Left$(buf$, dl&)
End Function
```

The remainder of the project is very straightforward and need not be listed here.

Suggestions for Further Practice

Environ.cls is a first step toward what could be a very useful class. Here are some ways that it can be improved:

- Modify GetStringValue so that it is not limited to 2,048 character environment strings. (Hint: Look at the result value of the GetEnvironmentVariable function.)

- Turn Environ.frm into a full environment string editor using SetEnvironmentVariable.

- Use ExpandEnvironmentStrings to provide an option that expands environment strings that depend on other environment strings.

Example: SysInfo—A System Information Viewer

SysInfo is a program designed to illustrate some of the Windows API functions described in this chapter. It includes several functions from each category presented above. The program allows you to determine current system colors, system metrics, and other Windows system parameters. It can be easily extended to provide other kinds of information.

SysInfo also demonstrates some of the keyboard and caret functions. Refer to the WinView program in Chapter 5 for examples of some of the mouse functions.

Figure 6.3 shows the SysInfo program when retrieving system metrics information.

Figure 6.3

SysInfo system metrics screen

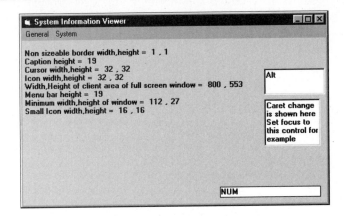

Using SysInfo

A list box and associated label control are visible on the screen only when checking system colors after invoking the System-Colors menu command. Selecting an entry causes the background color of the label control to be set to the system color for the specified object.

Two text controls are present on the form. When the upper text control has the focus, pressing any key will cause the key name to appear in the control. When the lower text control receives the input focus, a square caret will be created and shown.

A label control at the lower right of the form is used in conjunction with a timer control to show the current state of the CapsLock, NumLock, and ScrollLock keys.

Project Description

The SysInfo project includes three files; SYSINFO.FRM is the only form used in the program. SYSINFO.BAS is the only module in the program and contains the constant type, constant, and function declarations. The program also uses file VBPGUTIL.BAS, a collection of general purpose functions provided with this book.

The SysInfo is ported from the original 16-bit SysInfo application from the Visual Basic Programmers Guide to the Windows API. The VB4 version of the program is still compatible with 16-bit Visual Basic 4.0. This helps illustrate the differences between the two platforms.

Form Description

Listing 6.2 contains the header from file SYSINFO.FRM that describes the control setup for the form. Figure 6.4 shows the SysInfo form during design time (to help identify control locations).

Figure 6.4

SysInfo design time screen

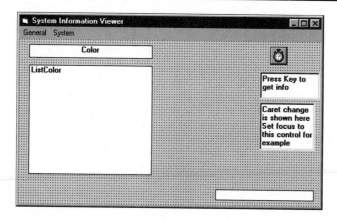

Listing 6.2 **SYSINFO.FRM**

```
VERSION 5.00
Begin VB.Form SysInfo
   BackColor        =    &H00E0E0E0&
   Caption          =    "System Information Viewer"
   ClientHeight     =    3870
   ClientLeft       =    1275
   ClientTop        =    1965
   ClientWidth      =    7365
   BeginProperty Font
      name          =    "MS Sans Serif"
      charset       =    0
      weight        =    700
      size          =    8.25
      underline     =    0     'False
      italic        =    0     'False
      strikethrough =    0     'False
```

Listing 6.2   **SYSINFO.FRM (Continued)**

```
EndProperty
ForeColor      =   &H80000008&
Height         =   4560
Left           =   1215
LinkMode       =   1  'Source
LinkTopic      =   "Form1"
ScaleHeight    =   3870
ScaleWidth     =   7365
Top            =   1335
Width          =   7485
```

Timer1 is used to update the key state description in the LabelKeyState control. If you are currently using a custom control in order to display the key state, you are highly encouraged to rip it out and replace it with the code in this project. Replacing the control with a few simple API calls will save memory and resources, and improve your application's performance—not to mention reducing the number of controls you need to distribute with your application.

```
Begin VB.Timer Timer1
    Interval     =   250
    Left         =   6120
    Top          =   120
End
```

When the MenuColor menu command is selected, the ListColor list box will be made visible and will show a list of Windows objects that have associated colors.

```
Begin VB.ListBox ListColor
    Appearance    =   0  'Flat
    Height        =   2565
    Left          =   240
    TabIndex      =   2
    Top           =   600
    Visible       =   0   'False
    Width         =   3015
End
```

When the KeyCheck control has the focus, any keystroke causes the name of the key found to be displayed in the control. For letters, the key name is the same as the character. For control keys and function keys, the key name describes the key.

```
Begin VB.TextBox KeyCheck
    Height       =   615
    Left         =   5880
    MultiLine    =   -1  'True
```

```
        TabIndex       =   0
        Text           =   "SYSINFO.frx":0000
        Top            =   720
        Width          =   1455
    End

Begin VB.TextBox Text1
        Height         =   1095
        Left           =   5880
        MultiLine      =   -1   'True
        TabIndex       =   1
        Text           =   "SYSINFO.frx":0016
        Top            =   1440
        Width          =   1335
    End
```

The background color of the LabelColor control is set to the system color for the object selected in the ListColor list box.

```
Begin VB.Label LabelColor
        Alignment      =   2   'Center
        Appearance     =   0   'Flat
        BackColor      =   &H00FFFFFF&
        BorderStyle    =   1   'Fixed Single
        Caption        =   "Color"
        ForeColor      =   &H80000008&
        Height         =   315
        Left           =   240
        TabIndex       =   3
        Top            =   120
        Visible        =   0    'False
        Width          =   3015
End
```

The LabelKeyState control will be updated with the state of the CapsLock, NumLock, and ScrollLock keys during each timer event.

```
Begin VB.Label LabelKeyState
        Appearance     =   0   'Flat
        BackColor      =   &H80000005&
        BorderStyle    =   1   'Fixed Single
        ForeColor      =   &H80000008&
        Height         =   255
        Left           =   4800
        TabIndex       =   4
        Top            =   3480
        Width          =   2415
End
```

The MenuGeneral menus commands are used to obtain statistics on the system. The first of these commands is not implemented for Win32. The other two display time information and the type of hardware in use.

```
Begin VB.Menu MenuGeneral
    Caption         =   "General"
    Begin VB.Menu MenuFreeSpace
        Caption         =   "Free&Space"
    End
    Begin VB.Menu MenuTimes
        Caption         =   "&Times"
    End
    Begin VB.Menu MenuFlags
        Caption         =   "&Flags"
    End
End
```

The MenuSystem menu commands can be used to determine the colors of various system objects and to view other system metrics including standard object size information, locale information, and additional system parameters.

```
Begin VB.Menu MenuSystem
    Caption         =   "System"
    Begin VB.Menu MenuColors
        Caption         =   "&Colors"
    End
    Begin VB.Menu MenuMetrics
        Caption         =   "&Metrics"
    End
    Begin VB.Menu MenuParameters
        Caption         =   "&Parameters"
    End
    Begin VB.Menu MenuKeyboard
        Caption         =   "&Keyboard"
    End
    Begin VB.Menu MenuLocale
        Caption         =   "&Locale"
    End
End
End
Attribute VB_Name = "SysInfo"
Attribute VB_GlobalNameSpace = False
Attribute VB_Creatable = False
Attribute VB_PredeclaredId = True
Attribute VB_Exposed = False
Option Explicit
```

SysInfo Listing
Module SYSINFO.BAS, shown in Listing 6.3, contains the constant declarations and global variables used by the program.

Listing 6.3 SYSINFO.BAS

```
Attribute VB_Name = "SYSINFO1"
Option Explicit

' Sysinfo.txt sample program
' Copyright (c) 1992-1997 by Desaware
' Constants based on file API32.TXT

'--------------------------------
'   API Type Definitions
'--------------------------------

Public Type SYSTEM_INFO
        dwOemID As Long
        dwPageSize As Long
        lpMinimumApplicationAddress As Long
        lpMaximumApplicationAddress As Long
        dwActiveProcessorMask As Long
        dwNumberOfProcessors As Long
        dwProcessorType As Long
        dwAllocationGranularity As Long
        wProcessorLevel As Integer
        wProcessorRevision As Integer
End Type

Public Type OSVERSIONINFO ' 148 bytes
        dwOSVersionInfoSize As Long
        dwMajorVersion As Long
        dwMinorVersion As Long
        dwBuildNumber As Long
        dwPlatformId As Long
        szCSDVersion As String * 128
End Type

Type FILETIME
        dwLowDateTime As Long
        dwHighDateTime As Long
End Type

Public Const MAX_DEFAULTCHAR = 2
Public Const MAX_LEADBYTES = 12

Type CPINFO
        MaxCharSize As Long        ' max length (Byte) of a char
        DefaultChar(MAX_DEFAULTCHAR) As Byte    ' default character
        LeadByte(MAX_LEADBYTES) As Byte         ' lead byte ranges
End Type

Public Const KL_NAMELENGTH = 9
```

Listing 6.3   SYSINFO.BAS (Continued)

```
'----------------------------------------------------

'                Application Global Variables

'----------------------------------------------------


' Holder for the original caret blink time
Global OriginalCaretBlinkTime%

' Holder for version information. Set on form load
Global myVer As OSVERSIONINFO



' Chapter 6 demonstration program

#If Win32 Then
Declare Function CreateCaret Lib "user32" (ByVal hWnd As Long, ByVal hBitmap As _
Long, ByVal nWidth As Long, ByVal nHeight As Long) As Long
Declare Function GetCaretBlinkTime Lib "user32" () As Long
Declare Function GetACP Lib "kernel32" () As Long
Declare Function GetOEMCP Lib "kernel32" () As Long
Declare Function GetCPInfo Lib "kernel32" (ByVal CodePage As Long, lpCPInfo As _
CPINFO) As Long
' Obsolete: Declare Function GetKBCodePage Lib "user32" () As Long
Declare Function GetKeyboardLayoutName Lib "user32" Alias _
"GetKeyboardLayoutNameA" (ByVal pwszKLID As String) As Long
Declare Function GetKeyState Lib "user32" (ByVal nVirtKey As Long) As Integer
Declare Function GetAsyncKeyState Lib "user32" (ByVal vKey As Long) As Integer
Declare Function GetDoubleClickTime Lib "user32" () As Long
Declare Function GetKeyboardState Lib "user32" (pbKeyState As Byte) As Long
Declare Function SetKeyboardState Lib "user32" (lppbKeyState As Byte) As Long
Declare Function GetKeyboardType Lib "user32" (ByVal nTypeFlag As Long) As Long
Declare Function GetKeyNameText Lib "user32" Alias "GetKeyNameTextA" (ByVal _
lParam As Long, ByVal lpBuffer As String, ByVal nSize As Long) As Long
Declare Function GetLocaleInfo Lib "kernel32" Alias "GetLocaleInfoA" (ByVal _
Locale As Long, ByVal LCType As Long, ByVal lpLCData As String, _
ByVal cchData As Long) As Long
Declare Function GetMessageTime Lib "user32" () As Long
Declare Function GetSysColor Lib "user32" (ByVal nIndex As Long) As Long
Declare Sub GetSystemInfo Lib "kernel32" (lpSystemInfo As SYSTEM_INFO)
Declare Function GetSystemMetrics Lib "user32" (ByVal nIndex As Long) As Long
Declare Function GetTickCount Lib "kernel32" () As Long
Declare Function GetVersion Lib "kernel32" () As Long
```

Listing 6.3   SYSINFO.BAS (Continued)

```
Declare Function GetVersionEx Lib "kernel32" Alias "GetVersionExA" _
(lpVersionInformation As OSVERSIONINFO) As Long
Declare Function MapVirtualKey Lib "user32" Alias "MapVirtualKeyA" (ByVal wCode _
As Long, ByVal wMapType As Long) As Long
Declare Function SetCaretBlinkTime Lib "user32" (ByVal wMSeconds As Long) As Long
Declare Function SetDoubleClickTime Lib "user32" (ByVal wCount As Long) As Long
Declare Function ShowCaret Lib "user32" (ByVal hWnd As Long) As Long
Declare Function SystemParametersInfo Lib "user32" Alias "SystemParametersInfoA" _
(ByVal uAction As Long, ByVal uParam As Long, lpvParam As Any, ByVal _
fuWinIni As Long) As Long
#Else    'Win16 here
Declare Function GetKeyState% Lib "User" (ByVal nVirtKey%)
Declare Function GetKeyboardState% Lib "User" (LpKeyState As Any)
Declare Function GetFreeSpace& Lib "Kernel" (ByVal wFlags%)
Declare Function GetFreeSystemResources% Lib "User" (ByVal fuSysResource%)
Declare Function GetCaretBlinkTime% Lib "User" ()
Declare Function GetCurrentTime& Lib "User" ()
Declare Function GetTickCount& Lib "User" ()
Declare Function GetMessageTime& Lib "User" ()
Declare Function GetDoubleClickTime% Lib "User" ()
Declare Function GetTimerResolution& Lib "User" ()
Declare Function GetWinFlags& Lib "Kernel" ()
Declare Function GetVersion& Lib "Kernel" ()
Declare Function GetSysColor& Lib "User" (ByVal nIndex%)
Declare Function GetSystemMetrics% Lib "User" (ByVal nIndex%)
Declare Function SystemParametersInfo% Lib "User" (ByVal uAction%, ByVal _
uParam%, lpvParam As Any, ByVal fuWinIni%)
Declare Function SystemParametersInfoByval% Lib "User" Alias _
"SystemParametersInfo" (ByVal uAction%, ByVal uParam%, ByVal lpvParam _
As Any, ByVal fuWinIni%)
Declare Sub CreateCaret Lib "User" (ByVal hWnd%, ByVal hBitmap%, ByVal nWidth%, _
ByVal nHeight%)
Declare Sub ShowCaret Lib "User" (ByVal hWnd%)
Declare Sub SetCaretBlinkTime Lib "User" (ByVal wMSeconds%)
Declare Function GetKeyNameText% Lib "Keyboard" (ByVal lParam&, ByVal
lpBuffer$, ByVal nSize%)
Declare Function MapVirtualKey% Lib "Keyboard" (ByVal wCode%, ByVal wMapType%)

#End If


'------------------------------------------------------------
'          API constants
'------------------------------------------------------------


Global Const WM_USER = &H400
```

The API Constants used by this sample application can be found in the sample program on the CD-ROM and in file API32.TXT. Win16 constants (which are mixed in) can be found in file API16.TXT. This application uses constants with the following prefixes: GFSR, WF, VK, COLOR, SM, VER, SPI, SPIF, EWX, PROCESSOR, and LOCALE. The values of these constants have changed from Win16. During the port of this project, it turned out to be easiest to simply delete all of the old constants and add the new ones, counting on the Visual Basic compiler to find any undeclared constants (be sure to set Option Explicit for each module and form).

The constants have been left out of the book in order to save space. Listing 6.4 shows the code listing for SYSINFO.FRM.

Listing 6.4   SYSINFO.FRM

```
Private Sub Form_Load()
    Dim dl&

    #If Win32 Then
        ' Preload version information
        dl& = GetVersionEx&(myVer)
    #End If

    ListColor.AddItem "COLOR_ACTIVEBORDER"
    ListColor.AddItem "COLOR_ACTIVECAPTION"
    ListColor.AddItem "COLOR_APPWORKSPACE"
    ListColor.AddItem "COLOR_BACKGROUND"
    ListColor.AddItem "COLOR_BTNFACE"
    ListColor.AddItem "COLOR_BTNHIGHLIGHT"
    ListColor.AddItem "COLOR_BTNSHADOW"
    ListColor.AddItem "COLOR_BTNTEXT"
    ListColor.AddItem "COLOR_CAPTIONTEXT"
    ListColor.AddItem "COLOR_GRAYTEXT"
    ListColor.AddItem "COLOR_HIGHLIGHT"
    ListColor.AddItem "COLOR_HIGHLIGHTTEXT"
    ListColor.AddItem "COLOR_INACTIVEBORDER"
    ListColor.AddItem "COLOR_INACTIVECAPTION"
    ListColor.AddItem "COLOR_INACTIVECAPTIONTEXT"
    ListColor.AddItem "COLOR_MENU"
    ListColor.AddItem "COLOR_MENUTEXT"
    ListColor.AddItem "COLOR_SCROLLBAR"
    ListColor.AddItem "COLOR_WINDOW"
    ListColor.AddItem "COLOR_WINDOWFRAME"
    ListColor.AddItem "COLOR_WINDOWTEXT"
    ' These are new for Windows 95. Even though they
    ' are defined for Win32, they will also work on Win16 on Win95!
    ListColor.AddItem "COLOR_3DDKSHADOW"
    ListColor.AddItem "COLOR_3DLIGHT"
```

Listing 6.4   **SYSINFO.FRM (Continued)**

```
        ListColor.AddItem "COLOR_INFOBK"
        ListColor.AddItem "COLOR_INFOTEXT"

End Sub

'   Display in the edit control the name of the key
'
Private Sub KeyCheck_KeyDown(KeyCode As Integer, Shift As Integer)
    Dim dummy&
    Dim scancode&
    Dim keyname As String * 256

    ' Get the scancode
    scancode& = MapVirtualKey(KeyCode, 0)
    ' Shift the scancode to the high word and get the
    ' key name
    dummy = GetKeyNameText(scancode& * &H10000, keyname, 255)
    KeyCheck.Text = keyname
End Sub

Private Sub KeyCheck_KeyPress(KeyAscii As Integer)
    KeyAscii = 0     ' Ignore keys in this control
End Sub

Private Sub KeyCheck_LostFocus()
    KeyCheck.Text = "Press key to get info"
End Sub

'
' Display the selected color in the label control.
Private Sub ListColor_Click()
    Dim colindex%
    Select Case ListColor.ListIndex
        Case 0
            colindex% = COLOR_ACTIVEBORDER
        Case 1
            colindex% = COLOR_ACTIVECAPTION
        Case 2
            colindex% = COLOR_APPWORKSPACE
        Case 3
            colindex% = COLOR_BACKGROUND
        Case 4
            colindex% = COLOR_BTNFACE
        Case 5
            colindex% = COLOR_BTNHIGHLIGHT
        Case 6
            colindex% = COLOR_BTNSHADOW
        Case 7
```

Listing 6.4   SYSINFO.FRM (Continued)

```
                colindex% = COLOR_BTNTEXT
        Case 8
            colindex% = COLOR_CAPTIONTEXT
        Case 9
            colindex% = COLOR_GRAYTEXT
        Case 10
            colindex% = COLOR_HIGHLIGHT
        Case 11
            colindex% = COLOR_HIGHLIGHTTEXT
        Case 12
            colindex% = COLOR_INACTIVEBORDER
        Case 13
            colindex% = COLOR_INACTIVECAPTION
        Case 14
            colindex% = COLOR_INACTIVECAPTIONTEXT
        Case 15
            colindex% = COLOR_MENU
        Case 16
            colindex% = COLOR_MENUTEXT
        Case 17
            colindex% = COLOR_SCROLLBAR
        Case 18
            colindex% = COLOR_WINDOW
        Case 19
            colindex% = COLOR_WINDOWFRAME
        Case 20
            colindex% = COLOR_WINDOWTEXT
        Case 21
            colindex% = COLOR_3DDKSHADOW
        Case 22
            colindex% = COLOR_3DLIGHT
        Case 23
            colindex% = COLOR_INFOBK
        Case 24
            colindex% = COLOR_INFOTEXT
    End Select
    LabelColor.BackColor = GetSysColor&(colindex%) And &HFFFFFF

End Sub

Private Sub MenuColors_Click()
    SysInfo.Cls
    ShowColors -1
End Sub
```

The MenuFlags command is used to obtain information about the system hardware. As you can see, Win32 provides much greater access to hardware information than Win16. However, it does so in a manner that is completely incompatible with Win16. This requires two completely different approaches, both of which are implemented here.

```
Private Sub MenuFlags_Click()
    Dim flagnum&
    Dim dl&, s$

    Dim vernum&, verword%
    #If Win32 Then
        Dim mySys As SYSTEM_INFO
    #End If

    ShowColors Ø
    SysInfo.Cls
    Print

    ' Get the windows flags and version numbers
    #If Win32 Then
        myVer.dwOSVersionInfoSize = 148
        dl& = GetVersionEx&(myVer)
        If myVer.dwPlatformId = VER_PLATFORM_WIN32_WINDOWS Then
            s$ = " Windows95 "
        ElseIf myVer.dwPlatformId = VER_PLATFORM_WIN32_NT Then
            s$ = " Windows NT "
        End If
        Print s$ & myVer.dwMajorVersion & "." & myVer.dwMinorVersion & " Build " _
        & (myVer.dwBuildNumber And &HFFFF&)
        s$ = LPSTRToVBString(myVer.szCSDVersion)
        If Len(s$) > Ø Then Print s$
        GetSystemInfo mySys
        Print " Page size is " & mySys.dwPageSize; " bytes"
        Print " Lowest memory address: &H" & _
        Hex$(mySys.lpMinimumApplicationAddress)
        Print " Highest memory address: &H" & _
        Hex$(mySys.lpMaximumApplicationAddress)
        Print " Number of processors: "; mySys.dwNumberOfProcessors
        Print " Processor: ";
        Select Case mySys.dwProcessorType
            Case PROCESSOR_INTEL_386
                    Print "Intel 386"
            Case PROCESSOR_INTEL_486
                    Print "Intel 486"
            Case PROCESSOR_INTEL_PENTIUM
                    Print "Intel Pentium"
            Case PROCESSOR_MIPS_R4ØØØ
                    Print "MIPS R4ØØØ"
            Case PROCESSOR_ALPHA_21Ø64
                    Print "Alpha 21Ø64"
        End Select
```

```
        #Else
            flagnum& = GetWinFlags&()
            vernum& = GetVersion&()
            verword% = CInt(vernum& / &H10000)

            Print " Running MS-DOS version "; verword% / 256; "."; verword% And &HFF
            verword% = CInt(vernum& And &HFFFF&)
            Print " Running Windows version "; verword% And &HFF; "."; _
            CInt(verword% / 256)

            If flagnum& And WF_80x87 Then Print " 80x87 coprocessor present"
            If flagnum& And WF_CPU086 Then Print " 8086 present"
            If flagnum& And WF_CPU186 Then Print " 80186 present"
            If flagnum& And WF_CPU286 Then Print " 80286 present"
            If flagnum& And WF_CPU386 Then Print " 80386 present"
            If flagnum& And WF_CPU486 Then Print " 80486 present"
            If flagnum& And WF_ENHANCED Then Print " Windows 386-enhanced mode"
        #End If

End Sub
```

Win32 does provide ways to obtain information about system memory use that are as flexible or more flexible than those provided under Win16. However, their use requires a more in-depth understanding of the memory architecture under Win32—a subject that will be covered (with new examples) in Chapter 15. Including those functions here would only serve to confuse the issue, so for now SysInfo simply reports that the code is not implemented.

```
Private Sub MenuFreeSpace_Click()
    ShowColors 0
    SysInfo.Cls
    Print
    ' These functions are obsolete under Win32
    #If Win16 Then
        Print GetFreeSpace&(0); "Bytes free in Global Heap"
        Print GetFreeSystemResources%(GFSR_SYSTEMRESOURCES); _
        "% free system resources."
        Print GetFreeSystemResources%(GFSR_GDIRESOURCES); _
        "% free GDI resources."
        Print GetFreeSystemResources%(GFSR_USERRESOURCES); _
        "% free USER resources."
    #Else
        Print " Refer Chapter 15 examples for information"
        Print " on retrieving memory statistics for Win32"
    #End If

End Sub


'
' Display keyboard related information.
'
```

```vb
Private Sub MenuKeyboard_Click()
    Dim cp As CPINFO
    Dim cpAnsi&, cpOEM&
    Dim dl&
    Dim layoutname As String * KL_NAMELENGTH
    Print

    SysInfo.Cls
    #If Win32 Then
        cpAnsi = GetACP()
        cpOEM = GetOEMCP()
        Print " ANSI code page: " & cpAnsi
        dl& = GetCPInfo(cpAnsi, cp)
        Print " Max byte length is " & cp.MaxCharSize
        dl& = GetCPInfo(cpOEM, cp)
        Print " OEM code page: " & cpOEM
        Print " Max byte length is " & cp.MaxCharSize
        dl& = GetKeyboardLayoutName(layoutname)
        Print " Keyboard layout: " & LPSTRToVBString(layoutname)
        dl& = GetKeyboardType(0)
        Select Case dl&
            Case 0
                Print " PC 83 key keyboard"
            Case 3
                Print " AT 84 key keyboard"
            Case 4
                Print " Enhanced 101 or 102 key keyboard"
            Case Else
                Print " Special keyboard"
        End Select
        dl& = GetKeyboardType(2)
        Print " Keyboard has " & dl & " function keys."
    #Else
        Print " Not implemented under Win16 at this time"
    #End If


End Sub

'
' Locale specific information
'
Private Sub MenuLocale_Click()
    Dim buffer As String * 100
    Dim dl&

    SysInfo.Cls

    #If Win32 Then
        dl& = GetLocaleInfo(LOCALE_USER_DEFAULT, LOCALE_SENGLANGUAGE, buffer, _
        99)
        Print " Language: " & LPSTRToVBString(buffer)
```

```
        dl& = GetLocaleInfo(LOCALE_USER_DEFAULT, LOCALE_SENGCOUNTRY, buffer, 99)
        Print " Country: " & LPSTRToVBString(buffer)
        dl& = GetLocaleInfo(LOCALE_USER_DEFAULT, LOCALE_SCURRENCY, buffer, 99)
        Print " Currency Symbol: " & LPSTRToVBString(buffer)
        dl& = GetLocaleInfo(LOCALE_USER_DEFAULT, LOCALE_SLONGDATE, buffer, 99)
        Print " Long date format: " & LPSTRToVBString(buffer)
        dl& = GetLocaleInfo(LOCALE_USER_DEFAULT, LOCALE_SDAYNAME3, buffer, 99)
        Print " Long name for Wednesday: " & LPSTRToVBString(buffer)
        dl& = GetLocaleInfo(LOCALE_USER_DEFAULT, LOCALE_SABBREVDAYNAME3, _
        buffer, 99)
        Print " Abbreviation for Wednesday: " & LPSTRToVBString(buffer)
    #Else
        Print " Not implemented under Win16"
    #End If


End Sub



'   The following is a selection of the system metrics
'   that can be determined - see the reference section
'   under the GetSystemMetrics function for more.
'
Private Sub MenuMetrics_Click()
    ShowColors 0
    SysInfo.Cls
    Print
    Print " Non sizeable border width,height = "; _
    GetSystemMetrics(SM_CXBORDER); ","; _
    GetSystemMetrics(SM_CYBORDER)
    Print " Caption height = "; GetSystemMetrics(SM_CYCAPTION)
    Print " Cursor width,height = "; GetSystemMetrics(SM_CXCURSOR);  ","; _
    GetSystemMetrics(SM_CYCURSOR)
    Print " Icon width,height = "; GetSystemMetrics(SM_CXICON); ","; _
    GetSystemMetrics(SM_CYICON)
    Print " Width,Height of client area of full screen window = "; _
    GetSystemMetrics(SM_CXFULLSCREEN); ","; GetSystemMetrics(SM_CYFULLSCREEN)
    Print " Menu bar height = "; GetSystemMetrics(SM_CYMENU)
    Print " Minimum width,height of window = "; GetSystemMetrics(SM_CXMIN); _
    ","; GetSystemMetrics(SM_CYMIN)
    ' Here is a sample Windows 95 specific metric
    #If Win32 Then
        If myVer.dwPlatformId = VER_PLATFORM_WIN32_WINDOWS Then
            Print " Small Icon width,height = "; GetSystemMetrics(SM_CXSMICON); _
            ","; GetSystemMetrics(SM_CYSMICON)
        End If
    #End If


End Sub
```

```
'    A few examples of the many system parameters that can
'    be set and retreived using the SystemParametersInfo
'    function
'
Private Sub MenuParameters_Click()
    Dim dummy&

    SysInfo.Cls
    #If Win32 Then
        Dim intval&
    #Else
        Dim intval%
    #End If
    ShowColors 0
    SysInfo.Cls
    Print
    dummy = SystemParametersInfo(SPI_GETKEYBOARDDELAY, 0, intval, 0)
    Print " Keyboard Delay is "; intval
    dummy = SystemParametersInfo(SPI_GETKEYBOARDSPEED, 0, intval, 0)
    Print " Keyboard Speed is "; intval
    dummy = SystemParametersInfo(SPI_GETSCREENSAVEACTIVE, 0, intval, 0)
    If intval Then Print " Screen Saver is Active"
    dummy = SystemParametersInfo(SPI_GETSCREENSAVETIMEOUT, 0, intval, 0)
    Print " Screen Save Delay is "; intval; " seconds"


End Sub

Private Sub MenuTimes_Click()
    Dim curtime&
    ShowColors 0
    SysInfo.Cls
    Print
    Print " Caret blinks every "; GetCaretBlinkTime(); " ms"
    #If Win16 Then
        curtime& = GetCurrentTime()
    #Else
        curtime& = GetTickCount()
    #End If
    Print " It's been "; curtime&; " ms since Windows was started"
    Print " The last Windows message was processed at "; GetMessageTime&(); _
    " ms"
    Print " Two clicks within "; GetDoubleClickTime(); _
    " ms of each other are a double click"
    #If Win16 Then
        Print " Timer resolution is "; GetTimerResolution&(); _
        "microseconds per tick"
    #End If

End Sub

'   Use to show or hide the colors listbox and label
```

```vb
'
Private Sub ShowColors(bflag%)
    If bflag% Then   ' Show them
        ListColor.Visible = -1
        LabelColor.Visible = -1
    Else      ' Hide them
        ListColor.Visible = 0
        LabelColor.Visible = 0
    End If

End Sub

'   This shows how a custom caret can be used in a text
'   box. Note that an arbitrary bitmap could be used as
'   well (refer to the function reference for the
'   CreateCaret function - also chapter 8 for information
'   on bitmaps).
'   Also note that VB may change the caret back to the
'   default without notice (like when a menu or other
'   application is selected)
'
Private Sub Text1_GotFocus()

    ' Save the original blink time - it will be used to
    ' restore the original value during the LostFocus event
    OriginalCaretBlinkTime% = GetCaretBlinkTime()

    ' Create a different shaped caret
    CreateCaret Text1.hWnd, 0, 10, 15

    ' Creating the new caret caused the prior one (the
    ' default for the edit control) to be destroyed and
    ' thus hidden. So we must show the new caret.
    ShowCaret Text1.hWnd

    ' And change to an obnoxiously fast blink time - just
    ' to show how it's done.
    SetCaretBlinkTime 150
End Sub

'   Be sure to set the caret blink time back to its
'   original value when the control loses the focus
'
Private Sub Text1_LostFocus()
    SetCaretBlinkTime OriginalCaretBlinkTime%
End Sub

'   Update a label field to show the current state
'   of the capslock, numlock, and scroll lock keys
'
Private Sub Timer1_Timer()
    Dim numlock%, scrolllock%, capslock%
```

```
        Dim keyarray(256) As Byte
        Dim dl&
        Dim res$

        capslock% = GetKeyState%(VK_CAPITAL)
        numlock% = GetKeyState%(VK_NUMLOCK)

        ' Here's another way to do it - take a snapshot
        ' of the entire keyboard
        dl& = GetKeyboardState(keyarray(0))
        scrolllock% = keyarray(VK_SCROLL) ' GetKeyState%(VK_SCROLL)

        ' The low bit indicates the state of the toggle
        If capslock% And 1 Then res$ = res$ + "CAPS   "
        If numlock% And 1 Then res$ = res$ + "NUM   "
        If scrolllock% And 1 Then res$ = res$ + "SCROLL"

        LabelKeyState.Caption = res$
End Sub
```

Suggestions for Further Practice

SysInfo barely touches on the possibilities of what a real system information viewer utility could include. The intent of this sample was to include a few tidbits of information from each category covered in the chapter. This opens the door to a vast number of possible improvements, a few of which are listed here.

A real system information utility would never let the user see that certain information or commands were unavailable for a particular platform. It would simply hide those commands that are not supported. Only a program with a terrible user interface, or one that specifically intended to show the differences between platforms, would make all commands visible at all times. This sample clearly falls into the latter category, and the author makes no claims one way or another as to whether it falls into the former. (The author does, however, humbly suggest that a tabbed dialog would be a superior implementation by today's standards to the menu selection approach shown here.)

- Extend this program to show all of the information available under each category, rather than the small subset currently implemented.

- Extend the program to allow editing of system parameters.

The author hereby accepts neither the blame nor the credit should these suggestions spawn an entire subindustry of thousands of shareware system information utility programs.

Simulating Keystrokes and Mouse Events

At times the Win32 API seems overwhelming. And once you know the API functions that are available, how do you tie them together to actually accomplish something useful? This chapter has focused on system information functions, and at first glance it might seem that the only thing these API functions might be good for is figuring out system settings and maybe allowing some user configuration. But hidden among these gems are some powerful functions that accomplish three tasks that are often requested: simulating keystrokes, simulating mouse movements, and performing screen captures.

Bringing It All Together: The SimKeys Example

The SimKeys example demonstrates how the system functions described in this chapter can be tied together to accomplish these tasks. Figure 6.5 shows the appearance of the SimKeys main screen under Windows NT. The program works under Windows 95 as well, though as you will see, there are differences in implementation between the two platforms.

Figure 6.5

The SimKeys main screen

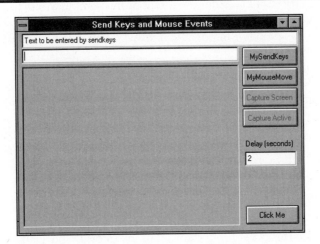

There are two text boxes. The upper text box contains a source string for the simulated send keys that is implemented by the program. This SendKeys is a very low-level implementation and is not as fully implemented as the SendKeys built into Visual Basic; however, it also does not suffer from some of the limitations of the Visual Basic SendKeys, as it works directly with virtual keys. The lower text box is intended as a convenient destination for the keystrokes—it has no other functionality.

The picture control is used to display the contents of the clipboard after a screen capture. There are four buttons that implement four different operations. All of them will take effect either immediately or after a specified delay. The default is a two-second delay. The reason for this is to demonstrate the fact that these operations are system-wide in nature. For example: you can press the MySendKeys button with a five-second delay, activate a word processor, and see that the keystrokes are entered into the word processor.

The MyMouseMove command demonstrates simulated mouse movement. The mouse is moved down to the Click Me button and clicks it. This brings up a message box that indicates that the button was clicked. The Capture Screen and Capture Active buttons implement the screen capture functions, also after the specified delay. You'll notice that these buttons are disabled in the figure. This is because screen capture can be a rather long operation, and disabling the buttons prevents additional button clicks from being queued while the operation is in progress. And yes, Figure 6.5 was captured for this book using this program.

Project Description

The SimKeys project includes two files; SIMKEYS.FRM is the only form used in the program. SIMKEYS.BAS is the only module in the program and contains the constant type, constant, and function declarations. This program is designed for 32-bit use only.

Form Description

Listing 6.5 contains the header from file SIMKEYS.FRM that describes the control setup for the form. Listing 6.6 contains the listing for the SIMKEYS.BAS file. The code for the form is shown in Listing 6.7.

Listing 6.5   SIMKEYS.FRM

```
VERSION 5.00
Begin VB.Form frmSimKeys
   Caption         =   "Send Keys and Mouse Events"
   ClientHeight    =   4725
   ClientLeft      =   1095
   ClientTop       =   1515
   ClientWidth     =   6870
   Height          =   5130
   Left            =   1035
   LinkTopic       =   "Form1"
   ScaleHeight     =   4725
   ScaleWidth      =   6870
   Top             =   1170
   Width           =   6990
```

Listing 6.5   SIMKEYS.FRM (Continued)

```
Begin VB.CommandButton cmdClickMe
    Caption         =   "Click Me"
    Height          =   435
    Left            =   5520
    TabIndex        =   9
    Top             =   4140
    Width           =   1275
End
Begin VB.Timer Timer1
    Left            =   5880
    Top             =   3480
End
Begin VB.TextBox txtDelay
    Height          =   315
    Left            =   5520
    TabIndex        =   7
    Text            =   "2"
    Top             =   2880
    Width           =   1215
End
Begin VB.TextBox txtTarget
    Height          =   315
    Left            =   120
    TabIndex        =   6
    Top             =   420
    Width           =   5235
End
Begin VB.CommandButton cmdCaptureActive
    Caption         =   "Capture Active"
    Height          =   435
    Left            =   5460
    TabIndex        =   5
    Top             =   1860
    Width           =   1335
End
Begin VB.CommandButton cmdCaptureAll
    Caption         =   "Capture Screen"
    Height          =   435
    Left            =   5460
    TabIndex        =   4
    Top             =   1380
    Width           =   1335
End
Begin VB.CommandButton cmdMouseMove
    Caption         =   "MyMouseMove"
    Height          =   435
    Left            =   5460
    TabIndex        =   3
```

Listing 6.5   **SIMKEYS.FRM (Continued)**

```
            Top             =   900
            Width           =   1335
         End
         Begin VB.CommandButton cmdSendKeys
            Caption         =   "MySendKeys"
            Height          =   435
            Left            =   5460
            TabIndex        =   2
            Top             =   420
            Width           =   1335
         End
         Begin VB.TextBox txtSource
            Height          =   315
            Left            =   120
            TabIndex        =   1
            Text            =   "Text to be entered by sendkeys"
            Top             =   60
            Width           =   6675
         End
         Begin VB.PictureBox Picture1
            Height          =   3735
            Left            =   120
            ScaleHeight     =   3675
            ScaleWidth      =   5175
            TabIndex        =   0
            Top             =   840
            Width           =   5235
         End
         Begin VB.Label Label1
            Caption         =   "Delay (seconds)"
            Height          =   255
            Left            =   5520
            TabIndex        =   8
            Top             =   2580
            Width           =   1155
         End
      End
      Attribute VB_Name = "frmSimKeys"
      Attribute VB_GlobalNameSpace = False
      Attribute VB_Creatable = False
      Attribute VB_PredeclaredId = True
      Attribute VB_Exposed = False
      Option Explicit
```

In addition to the constants and declarations listed above, the file contains all of the constants from file API32.TXT with the VK_ and MOUSEEVENTF prefix. That portion of the listing was removed to save space.

Listing 6.6   **LSIMKEYS.BAS**

```vb
Attribute VB_Name = "simKeysModule"
Option Explicit

Type POINTAPI
        x As Long
        y As Long
End Type

Public Const KEYEVENTF_EXTENDEDKEY = &H1
Public Const KEYEVENTF_KEYUP = &H2

Declare Sub keybd_event Lib "user32" (ByVal bVk As Byte, ByVal bScan As Byte, _
ByVal dwFlags As Long, ByVal dwExtraInfo As Long)


Declare Sub mouse_event Lib "user32" (ByVal dwFlags As Long, ByVal dx As Long, _
ByVal dy As Long, ByVal cButtons As Long, ByVal dwExtraInfo As Long)

Declare Function OemKeyScan Lib "user32" (ByVal wOemChar As Integer) As Long
Declare Function CharToOem Lib "user32" Alias "CharToOemA" (ByVal lpszSrc As _
String, ByVal lpszDst As String) As Long
Declare Function VkKeyScan Lib "user32" Alias "VkKeyScanA" (ByVal cChar As _
Byte) As Integer
Declare Function MapVirtualKey Lib "user32" Alias "MapVirtualKeyA" (ByVal wCode _
As Long, ByVal wMapType As Long) As Long
Declare Function ClientToScreen Lib "user32" (ByVal hwnd As Long, lpPoint As _
POINTAPI) As Long
Declare Function GetSystemMetrics Lib "user32" (ByVal nIndex As Long) As Long
Declare Function GetCursorPos Lib "user32" (lpPoint As POINTAPI) As Long
Declare Function GetForegroundWindow Lib "user32" () As Long
Declare Function SetForegroundWindow Lib "user32" (ByVal hwnd As Long) As Long
Declare Function GetDesktopWindow Lib "user32" () As Long


Type OSVERSIONINFO
        dwOSVersionInfoSize As Long
        dwMajorVersion As Long
        dwMinorVersion As Long
        dwBuildNumber As Long
        dwPlatformId As Long
        szCSDVersion As String * 128        ' Maintenance string for PSS
End Type

'  dwPlatformId defines:
'
```

Listing 6.6   **LSIMKEYS.BAS (Continued)**

```
Public Const VER_PLATFORM_WIN32s = 0
Public Const VER_PLATFORM_WIN32_WINDOWS = 1
Public Const VER_PLATFORM_WIN32_NT = 2

Declare Function GetVersionEx Lib "kernel32" Alias "GetVersionExA" _
(lpVersionInformation As OSVERSIONINFO) As Long

Public Const SM_CXSCREEN = 0
Public Const SM_CYSCREEN = 1
```

The SendAKey function simulates a single keystroke. The function that actually performs the simulation is the keybd event function; however, additional code is required to determine the correct parameters to use. The c$ parameter to the function is an ASCII character, so the first step is to determine the virtual key code for the character. This is accomplished with the VkKeyScan function. The keybd event function also requires the hardware scan code for the character. This is obtained using the CharToOem function (which obtains the OEM character code) followed by the OemKeyScan function which obtains the hardware scan code. This operation could have been performed in one step using the MapVirtualKey function—this technique will be shown later.

To simulate a key it is actually necessary to call the keybd event function twice; once to simulate the keypress, and again for the keyup condition.

All key events triggered by this function will appear in lowercase. Determining shift and control key states and simulating them is left as an exercise for the reader. The capture routine shown later demonstrates how to simulate an Alt key press—a technique that can easily be extended to work with the shift and control keys.

The MySendKeys function that follows simply loops through a string, calling the SendAKey function for each character.

```
' Sends a single character using keybd_event
'    Note that this function does not set shift state
'    (By pressing down the shift key or setting the shift keys state)
'    and it doesn't handle extended keys.
'
Public Sub SendAKey(ByVal c$)
    Dim vk%
    Dim scan%
    Dim oemchar$
    Dim dl&
    ' Get the virtual key code for this character
    vk% = VkKeyScan(Asc(c$)) And &HFF
```

```
        oemchar$ = "  "   ' 2 character buffer
        ' Get the OEM character - preinitialize the buffer
        CharToOem Left$(c$, 1), oemchar$
        ' Get the scan code for this key
        scan% = OemKeyScan(Asc(oemchar$)) And &HFF
        ' Send the key down
        keybd_event vk%, scan%, 0, 0
        ' Send the key up
        keybd_event vk%, scan%, KEYEVENTF_KEYUP, 0
End Sub

Public Sub MySendKeys(ByVal c$)
        Dim x&
        For x& = 1 To Len(c$)
                SendAKey Mid$(c$, x&)
        Next x&
End Sub
```

Listing 6.7   **SIMKEYS.FRM**

The SimKeys program has two form level variables. The OperationInProgress is a state flag that informs the system that an operation has been selected and is pending on expiration of the timer. While this flag is set, no other commands can be processed. The IsWindows95 variable is set if running under Windows 95.

```
' 0 if no operation is in progress
' 1 if sending keys
' 2 if sending mouse commands
' 3 if capturing the whole screen
' 4 if capturing the active window
Dim OperationInProgress%

Dim IsWindows95%
```

The cmdSendKeys, cmdMouseMove, cmdCaptureAll, and cmdCapture-Active are all similar. They first check to see that no operation is in progress, then either enable the timer for a deferred operation, or call the function to perform their associated operation directly.

```
Private Sub cmdSendKeys_Click()
        Dim delay&
        If OperationInProgress Then
                MsgBox "Wait for prior operation to finish"
                Exit Sub
        End If
        delay& = Val(txtDelay)
        If delay& = 0 Then
                MySendKeys txtSource.Text
        Else
```

```
                OperationInProgress = 1
                timer1.Interval = delay& * 1000
                timer1.Enabled = True
            End If


End Sub

Private Sub cmdMouseMove_Click()
        Dim delay&
        If OperationInProgress Then
            MsgBox "Wait for prior operation to finish"
            Exit Sub
        End If
        delay& = Val(txtDelay)
        If delay& = 0 Then
            MyMouseMove
        Else
            OperationInProgress = 2
            timer1.Interval = delay& * 1000
            timer1.Enabled = True
        End If

End Sub

Private Sub cmdCaptureAll_Click()
        Dim delay&
        If OperationInProgress Then
            MsgBox "Wait for prior operation to finish"
            Exit Sub
        End If
        delay& = Val(txtDelay)
        If delay& = 0 Then
            MyCapture 0
        Else
            OperationInProgress = 3
            timer1.Interval = delay& * 1000
            timer1.Enabled = True
        End If

End Sub

Private Sub cmdCaptureActive_Click()
        Dim delay&
        If OperationInProgress Then
            MsgBox "Wait for prior operation to finish"
            Exit Sub
        End If
        delay& = Val(txtDelay)
        If delay& = 0 Then
            MyCapture 1
        Else
```

```
        OperationInProgress = 4
        timer1.Interval = delay& * 1000
        timer1.Enabled = True
    End If

End Sub


Private Sub cmdClickMe_Click()
    MsgBox "Button has been clicked"
End Sub
```

On load, the program determines if it is running under Windows 95. This is the same technique used earlier in the SysInfo program.

```
Private Sub Form_Load()
    Dim dl&
    Dim osinfo As OSVERSIONINFO
    osinfo.dwOSVersionInfoSize = Len(osinfo)
    dl& = GetVersionEx(osinfo)
    If osinfo.dwPlatformId = VER_PLATFORM_WIN32_WINDOWS Then IsWindows95 = True
End Sub
```

The timer is triggered after a user-specified delay. It uses the OperationIn-Progress state variable to determine which operation to execute. MySend-Keys is implemented in SIMKEYS.BAS, the other functions in the form.

```
Private Sub timer1_Timer()
    timer1.Enabled = False
    Select Case OperationInProgress
        Case 1
            MySendKeys txtSource.Text
        Case 2
            MyMouseMove
        Case 3
            MyCapture 0
        Case 4
            MyCapture 1
    End Select
    OperationInProgress = 0
End Sub
```

The Win32 documentation for the keybd event function suggests that performing a screen capture is quite simple. Just use the VK_SNAPSHOT virtual key as the first parameter, and set the second parameter (the scan code) to zero for a full screen capture and 1 to capture just the active window.

It is an unfortunate truth that sometimes the documentation is not quite accurate, and so it turned out in this case.

Under Windows NT, a full screen capture was not a problem; however, setting the scan code to 1 had no effect. The only solution was to simulate more closely the actual screen capture process, where one can press the Alt key at the same time as the print screen key in order to capture the active window. It took several hours of experimentation to find a reliable solution to this problem. Before taking the snapshot, the keybd event function "presses" the Alt key, which is represented by the virtual key VK_MENU. The MapVirtualKey function is used to obtain the correct scan code for this key. After the screen capture, the key is released. The snapshot needed to be bracketed with DoEvents commands to make this work correctly—probably due to some interaction between the keyboard queue and the print screen mechanism, but there is no documentation anywhere to suggest why this should be the case. The DoEvents is not needed for full screen captures in this case, but it does no harm, and seems to make things more reliable under Windows 95.

Speaking of Windows 95: It turned out that under Windows 95 the scan parameter to the keybd event function does control whether it is a full screen or active screen capture. However, the value of the parameter is the exact opposite of what the Win32 documents suggest. A value of 1 enables full screen capture.

After the capture, the contents of the clipboard are copied into the picture box.

This code works. It has been tested on Windows NT 3.51, NT4.0 and Windows 95.

```
' Setting mode to 1 causes capture of the active window only
'
Public Sub MyCapture(ByVal mode%)
    Dim altscan%
    Dim dl&
    Dim snapparam%
    altscan% = MapVirtualKey(VK_MENU, 0)
    cmdCaptureAll.Enabled = False
    cmdCaptureActive.Enabled = False
    Screen.MousePointer = vbHourglass
    If mode Then
        keybd_event VK_MENU, altscan, 0, 0
        ' It seems necessary to let this key get processed before
        ' taking the snapshot.
    End If

    ' Why does this work?  Who knows!
    If mode = 0 And IsWindows95 Then snapparam = 1

    DoEvents    ' These seem necessary to make it reliable

    ' Take the snapshot
    keybd_event VK_SNAPSHOT, snapparam, 0, 0

    DoEvents
```

```
    Picture1.Picture = Clipboard.GetData(vbCFBitmap)
    If mode Then keybd_event VK_MENU, altscan, KEYEVENTF_KEYUP, 0

    cmdCaptureAll.Enabled = True
    cmdCaptureActive.Enabled = True
    Screen.MousePointer = vbDefault
End Sub
```

Simulating a mouse movement is accomplished using the mouse event function and is somewhat simpler than simulating keyboard events. However, it does pose its own interesting challenges and makes use of many of the functions introduced in Chapter 5.

The coordinates required by the mouse event function are based on yet another coordinate system—one used internally by the mouse driver. The screen is divided horizontally and vertically into 65,535 mouse units. The routine first finds the destination location by choosing a point within the cmd-ClickMe button—in this case, point 10,10 in the client coordinates of the button. The ClientToScreen function converts the button window's client coordinates into screen coordinates. The GetSystemMetrics command is determined to find the total size of the desktop—this size corresponds to the 65535 x 65535 size of the mouse coordinate system. The GetCursorPos function is used to obtain the current location.

From these values it is possible to determine the current and destination location in mouse coordinates. It is also possible to estimate the vertical and horizontal mouse units per pixel. This lets us move two pixels at a time towards the final point, stopping when the mouse has reached its final location.

The actual movement is triggered by calling the mouse event function with the MOUSEEVENTF_MOVE flag. The MOUSEEVENTF_ABSOLUTE flag tells the function that absolute coordinates are being specified, otherwise movement is relative to the current location. Once the mouse has reached the desired location, a left button down and left button up are simulated, causing the mouse click.

```
' Try to move the mouse to click the "click me" button
'
Public Sub MyMouseMove()
    Dim pt As POINTAPI
    Dim dl&
    Dim destx&, desty&, curx&, cury&
    Dim distx&, disty&
    Dim screenx&, screeny&
    Dim finished%
    Dim ptsperx&, ptspery&
    ' Get screen coordinates first
    ' 10 by 10 pixels into the button
    pt.x = 10
    pt.y = 10
```

```
    dl& = ClientToScreen(cmdClickMe.hwnd, pt)
    screenx& = GetSystemMetrics(SM_CXSCREEN)
    screeny& = GetSystemMetrics(SM_CYSCREEN)

    destx& = pt.x * &HFFFF& / screenx&
    desty& = pt.y * &HFFFF& / screeny&

    ' About how many mouse points per pixel
    ptsperx& = &HFFFF& / screenx&
    ptspery& = &HFFFF& / screeny&

    ' Now move it
    Do
        dl& = GetCursorPos(pt)
        curx& = pt.x * &HFFFF& / screenx&
        cury& = pt.y * &HFFFF& / screeny&
        distx& = destx& - curx&
        disty& = desty& - cury&
        If (Abs(distx&) < 2 * ptsperx& And Abs(disty&) < 2 * ptspery) Then
            ' Close enough, go the rest of the way
            curx& = destx&
            cury& = desty&
            finished% = True
        Else
            ' Move closer
            curx& = curx& + Sgn(distx&) * ptsperx * 2
            cury& = cury& + Sgn(disty&) * ptspery * 2
        End If
        mouse_event MOUSEEVENTF_ABSOLUTE Or MOUSEEVENTF_MOVE, curx, cury, 0, 0
    Loop While Not finished
    ' We got there, click the button
    mouse_event MOUSEEVENTF_ABSOLUTE Or MOUSEEVENTF_LEFTDOWN,  curx, cury, 0, 0
    mouse_event MOUSEEVENTF_ABSOLUTE Or MOUSEEVENTF_LEFTUP, curx,  cury, 0, 0

End Sub
```

This concludes the SimKeys example. As you can see, it ties together many unrelated functions from both this chapter and Chapter 5 to perform a useful task that cannot be accomplished using Visual Basic alone.

Suggestions for Further Practice

- First a relatively easy suggestion: Try creating a program that checks the state of the CapsLock, NumLock, and ScrollLock keys and forces them to a desired state. (Hint: Look at the GetKeyState function.)

- Here's a challenge for someone who is really ambitious: Try creating a complete implementation of the Visual Basic SendKeys function using the keybd event function.

*Function Reference

■ ActivateKeyboardLayout

VB Declaration Declare Function ActivateKeyboardLayout& Lib "user32" (ByVal HKL As Long, ByVal _
flags As Long)

Description Activates a new keyboard layout. A keyboard layout defines the locations and meanings of keys on a physical keyboard.

Use with VB No problem.

Parameter	Type/Description
HKL	Long—A handle to a keyboard layout loaded by LoadKeyboardLayout or GetKeyboardLayoutList functions. Or use the constants HKL_NEXT to activate the next loaded layout, or HKL_PREV to load the previous layout.
flags	Long—Moves the specified keyboard to the start of the internal keyboard layout list.

Return Value Long—The handle of the previous keyboard layout on success, zero on error. Sets GetLastError.

Platform Windows 95, Windows NT

■ Beep

VB Declaration Declare Function Beep& Lib "kernel32" (ByVal dwFreq As Long, ByVal dwDuration _
As Long)

Description Used to generate simple sounds.

Use with VB No problem.

Parameter	Type/Description
dwFreq	Long—Frequency of the sound from 37hz to 32767Hz. Ignored on Windows 95.
dwDuration	Long—The duration of the sound in milliseconds, –1 to play the sound until the function is called again. Ignored on Windows 95.

Return Value Long—TRUE (nonzero) on success, zero on error. Sets GetLastError.

Platform Windows 95, Windows NT

Comments On Windows 95 this command simply sounds the default system beep.

Example Beep 1000,1000
  Try it.

■ CharToOem, CharToOemBuff

VB Declaration
```
Declare Function CharToOem& Lib "user32" Alias "CharToOemA" (ByVal lpszSrc As _
String, ByVal lpszDst As String)
Declare Function CharToOemBuff& Lib "user32" Alias "CharToOemBuffA" (ByVal _
lpszSrc As String, ByVal lpszDst As String, ByVal cchDstLength As Long)
```

Description
Converts a string from the ANSI character set to the OEM character set. CharToOemBuff allows you to specify the number of characters in the string to convert.

Use with VB
No problem.

Parameter	Type/Description
lpszSrc	String—String to convert.
lpszDst	String—String to load with the OEM equivalent. Be sure to pre-initialize the string to the required length. You may pass the same string to both parameters to perform the conversion in place.
cchDstLength	Long—Number of characters in string lpszSrc to convert.

Return Value
Long—Always TRUE.

Platform
Windows 95, Windows NT

Comments
If you are using a Win32 type library to access the wide character function CharToOemW, lpszSrc is a Unicode string and the lpszDst parameter must not be the same as lpszSrc.

Example
SimKeys.vbp

■ ClipCursor, ClipCursorBynum

VB Declaration
```
Declare Function ClipCursor& Lib "user32" (lpRect As RECT)
Declare Function ClipCursorBynum& Lib "user32" Alias "ClipCursor" (ByVal lpRect _
As Long)
```

Description
Restricts the cursor to the area specified. ClipCursorBynum is an alias that lets you clear a previously set cursor clipping region.

Use with VB
No problem.

Parameter	Type/Description
lpRect	RECT—RECT: specifies the rectangle, describing in pixel screen coordinates the area in which the cursor may be positioned. LONG uses the value 0 to the ClipCursorBynum form of the function to disable cursor clipping and restore normal operation.

Return Value
Long—Nonzero on success, zero on failure. Sets GetLastError.

Platform
Windows 95, Windows NT, Win16

Porting Notes Cursor clipping is one of those rare cases under Win32 where an application can interfere with the operation of another application. Clearly, if a program locks the cursor to an area within its own windows, it will prevent you from clicking on another application. For this reason, pressing Ctrl-Alt-Del clears the cursor clipping area.

Example Ex6a.vbp

■ ConvertDefaultLocale

VB Declaration `Declare Function ConvertDefaultLocale& Lib "kernel32" (ByVal Locale As Long)`

Description Converts one of the special locale identifiers to a true locale ID.

Use with VB No problem.

Parameter	Type/Description
Locale	Long—The constants LOCALE_SYSTEM_DEFAULT, LOCALE_USER_DEFAULT retrieve the default system or user locales. Zero to retrieve the language neutral locale. A primary language ID to retrieve the locale for that language using the default sublanguage.

Return Value Long—The actual locale ID on success. The value passed to the Locale parameter on error.

Platform Windows 95, Windows NT

Comments The results of this function when called with the values LOCALE_SYSTEM_DEFAULT and LOCALE_USER_DEFAULT are the same as the results for the GetSystemDefaultLCID and GetUserDefaultLCID functions.

Example Ex6b.vbp

■ CreateCaret

VB Declaration `Declare Function CreateCaret& Lib "user32" (ByVal hwnd As Long, ByVal hBitmap _`
`As Long, ByVal nWidth As Long, ByVal nHeight As Long)`

Description Creates a caret as specified and selects it as the caret for the specified window. The caret is a line, block, or bitmap that is generally used to indicate text position within a text box.

Use with VB Works, but the standard VB text controls do not process GotFocus and LostFocus events when switching between applications, thus it is difficult to know when to set the caret for a control. Also, VB controls the position of the caret based on the assumption that it is a vertical line, so other carets may not be positioned correctly.

Parameter	Type/Description
hwnd	Long—Handle of the window that will own the caret.
hBitmap	Long—Handle to a bitmap to use as the caret. May be zero or one, in which case a caret is created using the nWidth and nHeight parameters. If one, the new caret will be gray instead of black.

Parameter	Type/Description
nWidth	Long—The width of the caret in logical units (see Chapter 7 for more on logical units).
nHeight	Long—The height of the caret in logical units.

Return Value   Long—Nonzero on success, zero on failure. Sets GetLastError.

Platform   Windows 95, Windows NT, Win16

Comments   Creating a new caret destroys the previous caret, as does the DestroyCaret function. Do not attempt to destroy a caret using DestroyCaret during the Visual Basic LostFocus event. This is because the LostFocus event in VB is not received until another window already has the focus, so calling DestroyCaret at that time will destroy the other window's caret. You can (and should) destroy the caret during the WM_KILLFOCUS message when using a subclasser if you are managing carets on your own.

Porting Notes   The Win32 documentation suggests that there can be only one caret in the system (as was the case with Win16). This is not strictly true—in some multithreading situations, such as when you attach a second application to the same input thread, it is possible for two windows to have a caret visible. You can duplicate this effect with the Chapter 5 Statevw.vbp sample program.

Example   SysInfo.vbp

■ DestroyCaret

VB Declaration   `Declare Function DestroyCaret& Lib "user32" ()`

Description   Destroys a caret.

Use with VB   Can be used to eliminate a caret from a control. Otherwise, it does not seem to have any practical use.

Return Value   Long—Nonzero on success, zero on failure. Sets GetLastError.

Platform   Windows 95, Windows NT, Win16

Comments   See comments for the CreateCaret function.

■ EnumCalendarInfo

VB Declaration   `Declare Function EnumCalendarInfo& Lib "kernel32" Alias "EnumCalendarInfoA" _`
                       `(ByVal lpCalInfoEnumProc As Long, ByVal Locale As Long, ByVal Calendar As Long, _`
                       `ByVal CalType As Long)`

Description   Enumerates information about the calendars available under a given locale.

Use with VB   Requires the dwcbkd32.ocx custom control under Visual Basic 4.0.

Parameter	Type/Description
lpCalInfoEnumProc	Long—Pointer to function to call for each calendar. Use the Addressof operator to obtain the address of a function in a standard module. Use the ProcAddress property of the dwcbkd32.ocx custom control to obtain a function pointer for callbacks under VB 4.0.
Locale	Long—The locale to use to determine which calendars to enumerate.
Calendar	Long—The constant ENUM_ALL_CALENDARS to enumerate all calendars, 1 for localized Gregorian, 2 for English Gregorian, 3 for Japanese era, 4 for Chinese, 5 for Korean.
CalType	Long—One of the CAL_ functions that indicate the type of information to enumerate.

Return Value   Long—TRUE (nonzero) on success, zero on error. Sets GetLastError on error to one of the following constants:

1. ERROR_BADDB

2. ERROR_INVALID_FLAGS

3. ERROR_INVALID_PARAMETER

Platform   Windows 95, Windows NT

Comments   Refer to Appendix A for details on using the dwcbkd32.ocx custom control with enumeration functions under VB 4.0.

Example   Ex6b.vbp

■ EnumDateFormats

VB Declaration
```
Declare Function EnumDateFormats& Lib "kernel32" Alias "EnumDateFormatsA" _
(ByVal lpDateFmtEnumProc As Long, ByVal Locale As Long, ByVal dwFlags As Long)
```

Description   Enumerates the short and long date formats that are available for a specified locale.

Use with VB   Requires the dwcbkd32.ocx custom control under Visual Basic 4.0.

Parameter	Type/Description
lpDateFmtEnumProc	Long—Pointer to function to call for each date format. Use the Addressof operator to obtain the address of a function in a standard module. Use the ProcAddress property of the dwcbkd32.ocx custom control to obtain a function pointer for callbacks under VB 4.0.
Locale	Long—The locale to use to determine which formats to enumerate.

Parameter	Type/Description
dwFlags	Long—One of the constants DATE_SHORTDATE or DATE_LONGDATE to enumerate the short or long date formats.

Return Value Long—TRUE (nonzero) on success, zero on error. Sets GetLastError on error to one of the following constants:

1. ERROR_BADDB

2. ERROR_INVALID_FLAGS

3. ERROR_INVALID_PARAMETER

Platform Windows 95, Windows NT

Comments Refer to Appendix A for details on using the dwcbkd32.ocx custom control with enumeration functions under VB 4.0.

Example Ex6b.vbp

■ EnumSystemCodePages

VB Declaration
```
Declare Function EnumSystemCodePages& Lib "kernel32" Alias _
"EnumSystemCodePagesA" (ByVal lpCodePageEnumProc As Long, ByVal dwFlags As Long)
```

Description Enumerates the code pages that are installed or supported on the system.

Use with VB Requires the dwcbkd32.ocx custom control under Visual Basic 4.0.

Parameter	Type/Description
lpCodePageEnumProc	Long—Pointer to function to call for each code page. Use the Addressof operator to obtain the address of a function in a standard module. Use the ProcAddress property of the dwcbkd32.ocx custom control to obtain a function pointer for callbacks under VB 4.0.
dwFlags	Long—The constant CP_INSTALLED to enumerate all installed code pages, CP_SUPPORTED to enumerate all those that are supported.

Return Value Long—TRUE (nonzero) on success, zero on error. Sets GetLastError on error to one of the following constants:

1. ERROR_BADDB

2. ERROR_INVALID_FLAGS

3. ERROR_INVALID_PARAMETER

Platform Windows 95, Windows NT

Comments   Refer to Appendix A for details on using the dwcbkd32.ocx custom control with enumeration functions under VB 4.0.

Example   Ex6b.vbp

■ EnumSystemLocales

VB Declaration
```
Declare Function EnumSystemLocales& Lib "kernel32" Alias "EnumSystemLocalesA" _
    (ByVal lpLocaleEnumProc As Long, ByVal dwFlags As Long)
```

Description   Enumerates the locales that are installed or supported on the system.

Use with VB   Requires the dwcbkd32.ocx custom control under Visual Basic 4.0.

Parameter	Type/Description
lpLocaleEnumProc	Long—Pointer to function to call for each locale. Use the Addressof operator to obtain the address of a function in a standard module. Use the ProcAddress property of the dwcbkd32.ocx custom control to obtain a function pointer for callbacks under VB 4.0.
dwFlags	Long—The constant LCID_INSTALLED to enumerate all installed locales, LCID_SUPPORTED to enumerate all those that are supported.

Return Value   Long—TRUE (nonzero) on success, zero on error. Sets GetLastError on error to one of the following constants:

1. ERROR_BADDB
2. ERROR_INVALID_FLAGS
3. ERROR_INVALID_PARAMETER

Platform   Windows 95, Windows NT

Comments   Refer to Appendix A for details on using the dwcbkd32.ocx custom control with enumeration functions under VB 4.0.

Example   Ex6b.vbp

■ EnumTimeFormats

VB Declaration
```
Declare Function EnumTimeFormats& Lib "kernel32" Alias "EnumTimeFormatsA" _
    (ByVal lpTimeFmtEnumProc As Long, ByVal Locale As Long, ByVal dwFlags As Long)
```

Description   Enumerates the time formats that are available for a specified locale.

Use with VB   Requires the dwcbkd32.ocx custom control under Visual Basic 4.0.

Parameter	Type/Description
lpTimeFmtEnumProc	Long—Pointer to function to call for each time format. Use the Addressof operator to obtain the address of a function in a standard module. Use the ProcAddress property of the dwcbkd32.ocx custom control to obtain a function pointer for callbacks under VB 4.0.
Locale	Long—The locale to use to determine which formats to enumerate.
dwFlags	Long—Unused, set to zero.

Return Value   Long—TRUE (nonzero) on success, zero on error. Sets GetLastError on error to one of the following constants:

1. ERROR_BADDB

2. ERROR_INVALID_FLAGS

3. ERROR_INVALID_PARAMETER

Platform   Windows 95, Windows NT

Comments   Refer to Appendix A for details on using the dwcbkd32.ocx custom control with enumeration functions under VB 4.0.

Example   Ex6b.vbp

■ ExitWindowsEx

VB Declaration
```
Declare Function ExitWindowsEx& Lib "user32" (ByVal uFlags As Long, ByVal _
dwReserved As Long)
```

Description   Allows you to exit and optionally restart windows.

Use with VB   No problem.

Parameter	Type/Description
uFlags	Long—Specify one or more of the following flags (combined using the OR operation): EWX_FORCE—Forcibly terminates processes that do not respond. EWX_LOGOFF—Terminates processes, then logs off. EWX_SHUTDOWN—Powers the system off, if possible. EWX_REBOOT—Reboots the system. EWX_SHUTDOWN—Shuts the system down.
dwReserved	Long—Reserved—set to zero.

Return Value   Long—Nonzero on success, zero on error. Sets GetLastError.

Platform   Windows 95, Windows NT

Comments   This function returns immediately and the shutdown proceeds in the background. Be sure to terminate your own application to help the shutdown proceed smoothly. Your process must have sufficient privilege to execute this operation.

Porting Notes   Replaces the ExitWindows API call in Win16.

Example   ExitWindowsEx EWX_LOGOFF, 0
        Unload Me

■ ExpandEnvironmentStrings

VB Declaration
```
Declare Function ExpandEnvironmentStrings& Lib "kernel32" Alias _
"ExpandEnvironmentStringsA" (ByVal lpSrc As String, ByVal lpDst As String, _
ByVal nSize As Long)
```

Description   Expands environment strings in much the same way that the command line processor does by converting any occurrence of an environment variable name that is bracketed by percent signs to the contents of that variable. For example: "%path%" is expanded into the full path.

Use with VB   No problem. Most often used to create an environment block for a new process.

Parameter	Type/Description
lpSrc	String—The string to expand.
lpDst	String—The expanded string.
nSize	Long—The length of lpDst. Be sure lpDst is preinitialized to at least this length.

Return Value   Long—The size of buffer required for lpDst. If nSize is smaller than this number (that is, the buffer is too small for the expanded string), lpDst will not be loaded. This result can then be used to resize the string. Zero on error. Sets GetLastError.

Platform   Windows 95, Windows NT

Example
```
Dim s$, dl&
Dim y As String * 500
s$ = "%PATH%"
dl& = ExpandEnvironmentStrings(s$, y, 499)
Print y
```

■ FreeEnvironmentStrings

VB Declaration
```
Declare Function FreeEnvironmentStrings& Lib "kernel32" Alias _
"FreeEnvironmentStringsA" (ByVal lpsz As Long)
```

Description   Frees the specified environment string block.

Use with VB	No problem.	

Parameter	Type/Description
lpsz	Long—A handle to a block of memory previously obtained using the GetEnvironmentStrings function.

Return Value Long—Nonzero on success, zero on failure. Sets GetLastError.

Platform Windows 95, Windows NT

Example Environ.vbp

■ GetACP

VB Declaration `Declare Function GetACP& Lib "kernel32" ()`

Description Determines the ANSI code page that is currently in effect.

Use with VB No problem.

Return Value Long—Identifies the ANSI code page that is active. There can be more than one code page for a particular language. Available code pages include are listed below.

874	Thai
932	Japanese
936	Chinese
949	Korean
950	Chinese (Taiwan & Hong Kong)
1200	Unicode
1250	Eastern European
1251	Cyrillic
1252	US & Western Europe
1253	Greek
1254	Turkish
1255	Hebrew
1256	Arabic
1257	Baltic

Platform Windows 95, Windows NT

Comments Do not confuse ANSI code pages—which are used to define the standard ANSI 8-bit character set for different versions of Windows—with the OEM code page, which specifies the underlying DOS code page used by the file system and keyboard.

Example SysInfo.vbp

■ GetAsyncKeyState

VB Declaration `Declare Function GetAsyncKeyState% Lib "user32" (ByVal vKey As Long)`

Description Determines the state of the specified virtual key at the time the function is called.

Use with VB No problem.

Parameter	Type/Description
vKey	Long—The key code of the virtual key to test.

Return Value Integer—Bit 0 is 1 if the key has been pressed since the last call to GetAsyncKeyState, 0 otherwise. Bit 15 is 1 if the key is currently down, 0 if up.

The Microsoft Win32 documentation suggests that the result is always zero if the focus belongs to a different input thread than the one calling the function (for example, if another application has focus, it should return zero). Evidence suggests that in fact the function works on a system-wide basis.

Platform Windows 95, Windows NT, Win16

Comments If VK_LBUTTON or VK_RBUTTON is specified, the button state is reported based on the actual button regardless of whether the mouse buttons were swapped with SwapMouseButton.

Win32 provides additional virtual key codes such as VK_LSHIFT and VK_RSHIFT to let you distinguish between the left and right of two identical keys (including Ctrl and Alt).

■ GetCaretBlinkTime

VB Declaration `Declare Function GetCaretBlinkTime& Lib "user32" ()`

Description Determines the flash or blink rate of the caret.

Use with VB No problem.

Return Value Long—The time between flashes of the caret in milliseconds. Zero on failure. Sets GetLastError.

Platform Windows 95, Windows NT, Win16

Example SysInfo.vbp

■ GetCaretPos

VB Declaration `Declare Function GetCaretPos& Lib "user32" (lpPoint As POINTAPI)`

Description Determines the current position of the caret.

Use with VB No problem.

Parameter	Type/Description
lpPoint	POINTAPI—This structure is loaded with the position of the caret in client coordinates of the window containing the caret.

Return Value	Long—Nonzero on success, zero on failure. Sets GetLastError.
Platform	Windows 95, Windows NT, Win16

■ GetClipCursor

VB Declaration `Declare Function GetClipCursor& Lib "user32" (lprc As RECT)`

Description Retrieves a rectangle describing the current clipping area for the cursor as defined by the SetClipCursor function.

Use with VB No problem.

Parameter	Type/Description
lprc	RECT—Rectangle to load with the current clipping rectangle in screen coordinates. The rectangle will reflect the size of the display screen if no clipping is in effect.

Return Value Long—Nonzero on success, zero on failure. Sets GetLastError.

Platform Windows 95, Windows NT, Win16

Example Ex6a.vbp

■ GetCommandLine

VB Declaration `Declare Function GetCommandLine& Lib "kernel32" Alias "GetCommandLineA" ()`

Description Obtains a pointer to the current command line buffer.

Use with VB The Visual Basic Command function is easier to use for retrieving parameters, but it does not provide the executable name. Using this function requires a memory copy operation.

Return Value Long—The address in memory of the command line buffer.

Platform Windows 95, Windows NT

Comments You can use the agGetStringFromPointer function in apigid32.dll to retrieve the command line in a Visual Basic string.

Example `s$ = agGetStringFromPointer(GetCommandLine())`

■ GetComputerName

VB Declaration `Declare Function GetComputerName& Lib "kernel32" Alias "GetComputerNameA" _`
`(ByVal lpBuffer As String, nSize As Long)`

Description Retrieves the name of this computer.

Use with VB   No problem.

Parameter	Type/Description
lpBuffer	String—String buffer to load with the computer name.
nSize	Long—The length of the buffer. This variable is loaded with the actual length of the computer name on return.

Return Value   Long—TRUE (nonzero) on success, zero on error. Sets GetLastError.

Platform   Windows 95, Windows NT

Comments   Note that the nSize parameter is not passed by value. See API32.TXT for the value of the MAX_COMPUTER_NAME constant.

Example
```
Dim s$
s$ = String$(MAX_COMPUTERNAME_LENGTH+1, 0)
Dim dl&
Dim sz&
sz& = MAX_COMPUTERNAME_LENGTH+1
dl& = GetComputerName(s$, sz)
```

■ GetCPInfo

VB Declaration   `Declare Function GetCPInfo& Lib "kernel32" (ByVal CodePage As Long, lpCPInfo As _`
`CPINFO)`

Description   Retrieves information about the specified code page.

Use with VB   No problem.

Parameter	Type/Description
CodePage	Long—The identifier of the code page for which to load information. This can be an ANSI or OEM code page.
lpCPInfo	CPINFO—Structure in which to load information on this code page.

Return Value   Long—Nonzero on success, zero on failure. Sets GetLastError.

Platform   Windows 95, Windows NT

Comments   The CPINFO structure is defined as follows:

```
Type CPINFO
        MaxCharSize As Long
        DefaultChar(MAX_DEFAULTCHAR) As Byte
        LeadByte(MAX_LEADBYTES) As Byte
End Type
```

MaxCharSize is loaded with the maximum size of a character in this character set. This will be one or two.

DefaultChar is the character that is placed in a string when converting from this code page to another if the character does not exist in the other code page.

LeadByte is an array of byte pairs, where each pair specifies a range of lead bytes for a double-byte character set (DBCS). For example, if the first two bytes in this array were 89 and 93, this would mean that byte values 89 through 93 in this code page are lead bytes, and that the byte that follows is part of the same character. A character set with five lead bytes would have a total of (256-5) + 5 * 256 possible characters.

Example   SysInfo.vbp

■ GetCurrencyFormat, GetCurrencyFormatBynum

VB Declaration
```
Declare Function GetCurrencyFormat& Lib "kernel32" Alias "GetCurrencyFormatA" _
(ByVal Locale As Long, ByVal dwFlags As Long, ByVal lpValue As String, lpFormat _
As CURRENCYFMT, ByVal lpCurrencyStr As String, ByVal cchCurrency As Long)
Declare Function GetCurrencyFormatBynum& Lib "kernel32" Alias _
"GetCurrencyFormatA" (ByVal Locale As Long, ByVal dwFlags As Long, ByVal _
lpValue As String, ByVal lpFormat As Long, ByVal lpCurrencyStr As String, ByVal _
cchCurrency As Long)
```

Description   Formats a number according to the currency format for the locale specified.

Use with VB   No problem if using an alias in which lpFormat is NULL. Properly initializing a CURRENCY-FMT structure is quite challenging—see Chapter 15.

Parameter	Type/Description
Locale	Long—The locale ID to use to determine the format. Any information specified in the lpFormat parameter (if not NULL) overrides the locale specific information.
dwFlags	Long—If lpFormat is specified, this should be zero. Otherwise, may be set to LOCALE_NOUSEROVERRIDE to force the system locale parameters to be used even if they have been overridden by the user.
lpValue	String—The number to format. Number may only have digits, a preceding "-" sign, and a single decimal point.
lpFormat	CURRENCYFMT—May be NULL to use the locale specific values (use GetCurrencyFormatBynum which passes this parameter ByVal as long). Otherwise may reference a CURRENCYFMT structure that has every field loaded with the formatting information to use. This structure is tricky to use from Visual Basic—refer to the chapter text for more information.
lpCurrencyStr	String—Buffer to load with the formatted string. Be sure to preinitialize the string.
cchCurrency	Long—The length of the lpCurrencyStr buffer. If zero, the function will return the length of buffer needed.

Return Value	Long—The length of the formatted string. Zero on error. Sets GetLastError to the following:

1. ERROR_INSUFFICIENT_BUFFER
2. ERROR_INVALID FLAGS
3. ERROR_INVALID_PARAMETER

Platform	Windows 95, Windows NT
Comments	Refer to Chapter 15 for information on using the CURRENCYFMT and similar structures.
Example	Ex6b.vbp

■ GetCursor

VB Declaration	`Declare Function GetCursor& Lib "user32" ()`
Description	Retrieves the handle of the currently selected cursor.
Use with VB	No problem.
Return Value	Long—The handle of the cursor currently in use. Zero if no cursor exists.
Platform	Windows 95, Windows NT, Win16
Comments	This function returns the cursor for the current input thread—it will not retrieve the cursor for other applications.
Porting Notes	Under Win16 the cursor was a system-wide resource. Refer to the chapter text for further information.
Example	SimKeys.vbp

■ GetCursorPos

VB Declaration	`Declare Function GetCursorPos& Lib "user32" (lpPoint As POINTAPI)`
Description	Retrieves the current position of the cursor.
Use with VB	No problem.

Parameter	Type/Description
lpPoint	POINTAPI—Structure to load with the position of the cursor in screen pixel coordinates.

Return Value	Long—Nonzero on success, zero on failure. Sets GetLastError.
Platform	Windows 95, Windows NT, Win16
Example	`Dim dl&`

```
Dim pt As POINTAPI
dl& = GetCursorPos(pt)
```

GetDateFormat

VB Declaration
```
Declare Function GetDateFormat& Lib "kernel32" Alias "GetDateFormatA" (ByVal _
Locale As Long, ByVal dwFlags As Long, lpDate As SYSTEMTIME, ByVal lpFormat As _
String, ByVal lpDateStr As String, ByVal cchDate As Long)
```

Description   Formats a system date according to the format for the locale specified.

Use with VB   No problem.

Parameter	Type/Description
Locale	Long—The locale ID to use to determine the format. Any information specified in the lpFormat parameter (if not NULL) overrides the locale specific information.
dwFlags	Long—If lpFormat is specified, this should be zero. Otherwise, may be set to LOCALE_NOUSEROVERRIDE to force the system locale parameters to be used even if they have been overridden by the user. Use DATE_SHORTDATE or DATE_LONGDATE to choose between date formats.
lpDate	SYSTEMTIME—A structure containing a system time. Refer to Appendix B for more information.
lpFormat	String—May be NULL to use the locale specific values (use vbNullString to pass a NULL). Otherwise contains a time format string. The codes d, dd, ddd, dddd, m, mm, mmm, mmmm, y, yy, and yyyy are used in formatting in the same way as in the Visual Basic format command (refer to your VB documentation). gg is used to specify the era.
lpDateStr	String—Buffer to load with the formatted string. Be sure to preinitialize the string.
cchDate	Long—The length of the lpCurrencyStr buffer. If zero, the function will return the length of buffer needed.

Return Value   Long—The length of the formatted string. Zero on error. Sets GetLastError to the following:

1. ERROR_INSUFFICIENT_BUFFER

2. ERROR_INVALID FLAGS

3. ERROR_INVALID_PARAMETER

Platform   Windows 95, Windows NT

GetDoubleClickTime

VB Declaration   `Declare Function GetDoubleClickTime& Lib "user32" ()`

Description	Determines the time between two consecutive mouse clicks that will cause them to be considered a single double-click event.
Use with VB	No problem.
Return Value	Long—The double-click time in milliseconds.
Platform	Windows 95, Windows NT, Win16

■ GetEnvironmentStrings

VB Declaration	```Declare Function GetEnvironmentStrings& Lib "kernel32" Alias _``` ```"GetEnvironmentStringsA" ()```
Description	Allocates and returns a handle to a block of memory containing the current environment string settings. This block of memory contains all of the environment strings separated by NULLs, with two consecutive NULLs indicating the end of the list.
Use with VB	No problem, though you will need to use the function agGetStringFrom2NullBuffer from apigid32.dll to convert the pointer returned into a Visual Basic string.
Return Value	Long—A pointer to a memory block containing the environment strings. Zero on error. Sets GetLastError.
Platform	Windows 95, Windows NT
Comments	Be sure to release this block of memory using the FreeEnvironmentStrings function.
Porting Notes	Replaces the GetDOSEnvironment API.
Example	Environ.vbp

■ GetEnvironmentVariable

VB Declaration	```Declare Function GetEnvironmentVariable& Lib "kernel32" Alias _```
	```"GetEnvironmentVariableA" (ByVal lpName As String, ByVal lpBuffer As String, _```
	```ByVal nSize As Long)```

Description	Retrieves the value of an environment variable.
Use with VB	No problem.

Parameter	Type/Description
lpName	String—The name of the environment string to read.
lpBuffer	String—A buffer to load with the string. Be sure to pre-initialize to an adequate length.
nSize	Long—The length of lpBuffer.

Return Value	Long—The length of the environment variable loaded. Zero if the specified environment string does not exist. If lpBuffer is not long enough to hold the string, the function returns the total length of the string which can then be used to allocate a buffer that is large enough.
Platform	Windows 95, Windows NT
Porting Notes	Supersedes the Win16 GetDosEnvironment function.
Example	Environ.vbp

■ GetInputState

VB Declaration	Declare Function GetInputState& Lib "user32" ()
Description	Determines if there are any mouse or keyboard events pending.
Use with VB	No problem.
Return Value	Long—Nonzero on success, zero on failure.
Platform	Windows 95, Windows NT, Win16
Porting Notes	Unlike Win16, under Win32 this function only returns the state for the current input thread. Refer to Chapter 5 for an explanation of input threads.

■ GetKBCodePage

VB Declaration	Declare Function GetKBCodePage& Lib "user32" ()
Description	Identical to and superseded by GetOEMCP described later in this section.

■ GetKeyboardLayout

VB Declaration	Declare Function GetKeyboardLayout& Lib "user32" (ByVal dwLayout As Long)
Description	Retrieves a handle that describes the keyboard layout for the specified application.
Use with VB	No problem.

Parameter	Type/Description
dwLayout	Long—The identifier of the thread to check. Zero to obtain the keyboard layout for the current thread.

Return Value	Long—A handle to a keyboard layout.
Platform	Windows 95, Windows NT 4.0, Win16
Comments	Refer to the chapter text for additional information on keyboard layouts.
Example	Sysinfo.vbp

■ GetKeyboardLayoutList

VB Declaration Declare Function GetKeyboardLayoutList& Lib "user32" (ByVal nBuff As Long, _
lpList As Long)

Description Obtains a list of all of the keyboard layouts available to the system.

Use with VB No problem.

Parameter	Type/Description
nBuff	Long—The number of entries in the lpList array. Zero to retrieve the number of keyboard layouts available.
lpList	Long—The first element in an array of longs that is at least nBuff elements long. This array will be loaded with the handles to the available keyboard layouts.

Return Value Long—The number of keyboard layout handles loaded into the array.

Platform Windows 95, Windows NT 4.0

■ GetKeyboardLayoutName

VB Declaration Declare Function GetKeyboardLayoutName& Lib "user32" Alias _
"GetKeyboardLayoutNameA" (ByVal pwszKLID As String)

Description Retrieves the name of the active keyboard layout.

Use with VB No problem.

Parameter	Type/Description
pwszKLID	String—String of length KL_NAMELENGTH characters.

Return Value Long—TRUE (nonzero) on success, zero on error. Sets GetLastError.

Platform Windows 95, Windows NT
On NT the keyboard layout is specific to the application. On Windows 95 it is specific to a thread.

Example Sysinfo.vbp

■ GetKeyboardState

VB Declaration Declare Function GetKeyboardState& Lib "user32" (pbKeyState As Byte)

Description Retrieves the current state of each virtual key on the keyboard.

Use with VB	No problem.

Parameter	Type/Description
pbKeyState	Byte—The first item in a 256-entry byte array. Each byte will be loaded with the state of its corresponding virtual key. Bit 0 is 1 for toggle keys (CapsLock, NumLock, and ScrollLock) if the key is toggled (on). Bit 7 is 1 if the key is currently down, 0 if up.

Return Value Long—Nonzero on success, zero on failure. Sets GetLastError.

Platform Windows 95, Windows NT, Win16

Comments The virtual key code constants VK_? work as indexes into the array. This function takes a snapshot of the keystate—the array is not automatically updated as keys are pressed.

Porting Notes Under Win16 this function takes a fixed length string. Use a byte array in Win32 to avoid possible errors due to Visual Basic's internal conversion into Unicode.

Example SysInfo.vbp

■ GetKeyboardType

VB Declaration `Declare Function GetKeyboardType& Lib "user32" (ByVal nTypeFlag As Long)`

Description Determines information about the keyboard in use.

Use with VB No problem.

Parameter	Type/Description
nTypeFlag	Long—One of the following: 0—Return the type of keyboard. 1—Return the subtype of the keyboard 2—Return the number of function keys on the keyboard.

Return Value Long—Zero on error. Otherwise as shown here:

nTypeFlag=0

1	PC or compatible 83-key keyboard
2	Olivetti 102-key keyboard
3	AT or compatible 84-key keyboard
4	Enhanced (IBM) 101- or 102-key keyboard
5	Nokia 1050 keyboard
6	Nokia 9140 keyboard
7	Japanese keyboard

nTypeFlag=1

Any value	Depends on the manufacturer

nTypeFlag=2

1	10 function keys
2	12 or 18 function keys
3	10 function keys
4	12 function keys
5	10 function keys
6	24 function keys
7	Depends on the manufacturer

Platform   Windows 95, Windows NT, Win16

Example   SysInfo.vbp

■ GetKeyNameText

VB Declaration `Declare Function GetKeyNameText& Lib "user32" Alias "GetKeyNameTextA" (ByVal _`
`lParam As Long, ByVal lpBuffer As String, ByVal nSize As Long)`

Description Determines the name of a key given the scan code.

Use with VB No problem.

Parameter	Type/Description
lParam	Long—Bits 0–5 = 0.
	Bits 16–23 = the scan code of the key.
	Bit 24 = extended bit on enhanced keyboards.
	Bit 25 = set to 1 to ignore differentiation between the left and right shift and control keys.
lpBuffer	String—String preinitialized to at least nSize+1 bytes that will be loaded with the key name.
nSize	Long — Maximum length of the string.

Return Value Long—Actual length of the key name loaded into lpBuffer.

Platform   Windows 95, Windows NT, Win16

Example   SysInfo.vbp

■ GetKeyState

VB Declaration `Declare Function GetKeyState% Lib "user32" (ByVal nVirtKey As Long)`

Description Determines the state of the specified virtual key at the time the most recent input message for that key was processed.

Use with VB   No problem.

Parameter	Type/Description
nVirtKey	Long—The key code of the virtual key to test. Use the actual ASCII value for alphanumeric characters (A–Z, a–z, and 0–9).

Return Value   Integer—Bit 0 is 1 for toggle keys (CapsLock, NumLock, and ScrollLock) if the key is toggled (on). Bit 15 is 1 if the key is currently down, 0 if up.

Platform   Windows 95, Windows NT, Win16

Example   SysInfo.vbp

■ GetLastError

VB Declaration   `Declare Function GetLastError& Lib "kernel32" ()`

Description   This function is used to retrieve extended error information for the previously called API functions.

Use with VB   Use the LastDLLError property of the Err object to obtain the GetLastError value under Visual Basic. This is necessary because Visual Basic sometimes resets the GetLastError value between the time the API call returns and the time your Visual Basic call continues to execute.

Return Value   Long—Depends on the API function. Refer to the API32.TXT file for a list of error constants starting with the ERROR_ prefix. Some API functions list those errors that they set; most, unfortunately, do not, so you may need to experiment to determine which error codes are likely in your application. Some of the most common error codes are:

- ERROR_INVALID_HANDLE—Invalid handle is passed as a parameter.

- ERROR_CALL_NOT_IMPLEMENTED—Typically occurs when calling a Win32 API under Windows 95 that is only implemented for Windows NT.

- ERROR_INVALID_PARAMETER—One of the function parameters is incorrect.

Platform   Windows 95, Windows NT

Comments   The value returned by GetLastError is set by calling SetLastError or SetLastErrorEx within the API function. Functions are not required to set the last error information, thus a zero result from a GetLastError call does not guarantee that a function succeeded. By the same token, an error result from this function is only valid if the function call returned an error result.

In general, you should access the GetLastError value only after a function has returned an error result and if the function is known to set the GetLastError variable. The return value documentation for each function lists those functions that set this information.

The SetLastError API function is intended for use in DLL functions that emulate API functions and thus is not useful for VB applications and is not documented further here.

■ GetLocaleInfo

VB Declaration   `Declare Function GetLocaleInfo& Lib "kernel32" Alias "GetLocaleInfoA" (ByVal _`
`Locale As Long, ByVal LCType As Long, ByVal lpLCData As String, ByVal cchData _`

```
As Long)
```

Description   Retrieves information relating to the specified locale.

Use with VB   No problem.

Parameter	Type/Description
Locale	Long—The locale ID for which to obtain information.
LCType	Long—The type of information to retrieve. Refer to the API32.TXT file for constants with the LOCALE_ prefix. Use the OR operation to combine in the LOCALE_NOUSEROVERRIDE to force use of the system default information even if overridden by the current user.
lpLCData	String—Buffer to load with the requested information. Be sure the string is preinitialized to the required length.
cchData	Long—The length of the lpLCData buffer, or zero to obtain the necessary buffer length.

Return Value   Long—The number of characters loaded into the buffer or the required buffer size of cchData is zero. Zero on error. Sets GetLastError to the following:

1. ERROR_INSUFFICIENT_BUFFER

2. ERROR_INVALID_FLAGS

3. ERROR_INVALID_PARAMETER

Platform   Windows 95, Windows NT

Example   SysInfo.vbp

■ GetLocalTime

VB Declaration   `Declare Sub GetLocalTime Lib "kernel32" (lpSystemTime As SYSTEMTIME)`

Description   Loads the lpSystemTime structure with the local date and time.

Use with VB   No problem.

Parameter	Type/Description
lpSystemTime	SYSTEMTIME—Structure to load with the local time.

Platform   Windows 95, Windows NT

Example   Time.vbp

■ GetNumberFormat

VB Declaration   `Declare Function GetNumberFormat& Lib "kernel32" Alias "GetNumberFormatA" _`
`(ByVal Locale As Long, ByVal dwFlags As Long, ByVal lpValue As String, lpFormat _`

```
As NUMBERFMT, ByVal lpNumberStr As String, ByVal cchNumber As Long)
Declare Function GetNumberFormatBynum& Lib "kernel32" Alias "GetNumberFormatA" _
(ByVal Locale As Long, ByVal dwFlags As Long, ByVal lpValue As String, ByVal _
lpFormat As Long, ByVal lpNumberStr As String, ByVal cchNumber As Long)
```

Description   Formats a number according to the number format for the locale specified.

Use with VB   No problem, if using an alias in which lpFormat is NULL. Properly initializing a NUMBERFMT structure is quite challenging—see Chapter 15.

Parameter	Type/Description
Locale	Long—The locale ID to use to determine the format. Any information specified in the lpFormat parameter (if not NULL) overrides the locale specific information.
dwFlags	Long—If lpFormat is specified, this should be zero. Otherwise, may be set to LOCALE_NOUSEROVERRIDE to force the system locale parameters to be used even if they have been overridden by the user.
lpValue	String—The number to format. Number may only have digits, a preceding "-" sign, and a single decimal point.
lpFormat	NUMBERFMT—May be NULL to use the locale specific values (use GetNumberFormatBynum which passes this parameter ByVal as long). Otherwise may reference a NUMBERFMT structure that has every field loaded with the formatting information to use. This structure is tricky to use from Visual Basic—refer to Chapter 15 for more information.
lpNumberStr	String—Buffer to load with the formatted string. Be sure to pre-initialize the string.
cchNumber	Long—The length of the lpCurrencyStr buffer. If zero, the function will return the length of buffer needed.

Return Value   Long—The length of the formatted string. Zero on error. Sets GetLastError to the following:

1. ERROR_INSUFFICIENT_BUFFER
2. ERROR_INVALID FLAGS
3. ERROR_INVALID_PARAMETER

Platform   Windows 95, Windows NT

Comments   Refer to Chapter 15 for information on using the CURRENCYFMT structure (it is similar to the NUMBERFMT structure).

Example   Ex6b.vbp demonstrates the GetCurrencyFormat function, which is similar.

■ GetOEMCP

VB Declaration   `Declare Function GetOEMCP& Lib "kernel32" ()`

Description   Determines the Windows code page used to translate between the OEM and ANSI character sets.

Use with VB   No problem.

Return Value   Long—Identifies the OEM code page that is active. There can be more than one code page for a particular language. Available code pages include:

437	Default: United States
708-720	Arabic code pages
737	Greek
775	Baltic
850	International
852	Slavic
855	Cyrillic
857	Turkish
860	Portuguese
861	Icelandic
862	Hebrew
863	French Canadian
864	Arabic
865	Norway/Denmark
866	Russian
874	Thai
932	Japanese
936	Chinese
949	Korean
950	Chinese (Taiwan & Hong Kong)
1361	Korean

Platform   Windows 95, Windows NT

Example   SysInfo.vbp

■ GetQueueStatus

VB Declaration   `Declare Function GetQueueStatus& Lib "user32" (ByVal fuFlags As Long)`

Description   Determines the type of messages that are pending in an application's message queue.

| **Use with VB** | Not particularly useful. |

Parameter	**Type/Description**
fuFlags	Long—A flag word indicating which messages to check for. The flag bits are defined by the following constants: QS_KEY: WM_CHAR messages (will cause VB KeyPressed events). QS_MOUSE: Any mouse message. QS_MOUSEMOVE: MouseMove message or event. QS_MOUSEBUTTON: Mouse button message or related event. QS_PAINT: Paint message pending. QS_POSTMESSAGE: Other posted message. QS_SENDMESSAGE: Message sent from another application. QS_TIMER: Timer message. QS_HOTKEY: A Hotkey message is in the queue.

Return Value   Long—The high word is a 16-bit flag word containing the messages pending. Bits are determined by the same constants defined for the fuFlags parameter. The low word is a matching flag word, where each bit indicates unprocessed messages added since the last call to this function, or since messages were last processed.

Platform   Windows 95, Windows NT, Win16

Porting Notes   QS_HOTKEY is new to Win32.

■ GetSysColor

VB Declaration   `Declare Function GetSysColor& Lib "user32" (ByVal nIndex As Long)`

Description   Determines the color of the specified Windows display object.

Use with VB   No problem.

Parameter	**Type/Description**
nIndex	Long—Constant specifying a Windows display object as shown in the table that follows.

Constant Definition	**Windows Object**
COLOR_ACTIVEBORDER	Border of active window
COLOR_ACTIVECAPTION	Caption of active window
COLOR_APPWORKSPACE	Background of MDI desktop
COLOR_BACKGROUND	Windows desktop
COLOR_BTNFACE	Button
COLOR_BTNHIGHLIGHT	3D highlight of button
COLOR_BTNSHADOW	3D shading of button
COLOR_BTNTEXT	Button text
COLOR_CAPTIONTEXT	Text in window caption

Constant Definition	Windows Object
COLOR_GRAYTEXT	Gray text, or zero if dithering is used
COLOR_HIGHLIGHT	Selected item background
COLOR_HIGHLIGHTTEXT	Selected item text
COLOR_INACTIVEBORDER	Border of inactive window
COLOR_INACTIVECAPTION	Caption of inactive window
COLOR_INACTIVECAPTIONTEXT	Text of inactive window
COLOR_MENU	Menu
COLOR_MENUTEXT	Menu text
COLOR_SCROLLBAR	Scroll Bar
COLOR_WINDOW	Window background
COLOR_WINDOWFRAME	Window frame
COLOR_WINDOWTEXT	Window text
COLOR_3DDKSHADOW	3D dark shadow*
COLOR_3DFACE	Face color for 3D shaded objects*
COLOR_3DHILIGHT	3D Highlight color (Win95)
COLOR_3DLIGHT	Light color for 3D shaded objects*
COLOR_INFOBK	Tooltip background color*
COLOR_INFOTEXT	Tooltip text color*

*Constants with an asterisk are not be supported under NT 3.51

Return Value   Long—RGB color of the specified object.

Platform   Windows 95, Windows NT, Win16

Comments   Refer to file API32.TXT for the current values for the COLOR_ constants. Note that at this time some of these constants share the same value.

Windows 95 uses four levels of shading for many buttons. See Chapter 8 for a more in-depth description and example of 3D effects.

Porting Notes   Constants marked with an asterisk are available under Win16 as well as Win32 when running under Windows 95.

Example   SysInfo.vbp

■ GetSystemDefaultLangID

VB Declaration   `Declare Function GetSystemDefaultLangID% Lib "kernel32" ()`

Description   Retrieves the default language ID for the system.

Use with VB	No problem.
Return Value	Integer—The default language ID for the system.
Platform	Windows 95, Windows NT
Example	Ex6b.vbp

■ GetSystemDefaultLCID

VB Declaration	`Declare Function GetSystemDefaultLCID& Lib "kernel32" ()`
Description	Retrieves the current default system locale.
Use with VB	No problem.
Return Value	Long—The default system locale ID.
Platform	Windows 95, Windows NT
Example	Ex6b.vbp

■ GetSystemInfo

VB Declaration	`Declare Sub GetSystemInfo Lib "kernel32" (lpSystemInfo As SYSTEM_INFO)`
Description	Loads a SYSTEM INFO structure with information about the underlying hardware platform.
Use with VB	No problem.

Parameter	Type/Description
lpSystemInfo	SYSTEM INFO—Structure to be loaded with system information. See Appendix B for a description of this structure.

Platform	Windows 95, Windows NT
Example	SysInfo.vbp

■ GetSystemMetrics

VB Declaration	`Declare Function GetSystemMetrics& Lib "user32" (ByVal nIndex As Long)`
Description	Returns information about the Windows environment.
Use with VB	No problem.

Parameter	Type/Description
nIndex	Long—Constant specifying information to retrieve as shown in the table that follows.

Constant Definition	Information Retrieved
SM_ARRANGE	Flags that set how Windows arranges minimized windows. See the ARW constants in file API32.TXT for details.
SM_CLEANBOOT	Boot mode. 0 = normal, 1 = safe, 2 = safe with network.
SM_CMETRICS	Number of available system metrics.
SM_CMOUSEBUTTON	Number of mouse buttons. Zero if no mouse.
SM_CXBORDER, SM_CYBORDER	Dimensions of non-sizeable borders.
SM_CXCURSOR, SM_CYCURSOR	Standard cursor dimensions.
SM_CXDLGFRAME, SM_CYDLGFRAME	Dimensions of dialog box borders.
SM_CXDOUBLECLK, SM_CYDOUBLECLK	Size of double click area (see comments).
SM_CXFRAME, SM_CYFRAME	Dimensions of sizeable border (use SM_C?FIXEDFRAME for Win 95 and NT 4.0).
SM_CXFULLSCREEN, SM_CYFULLSCREEN	Size of client area of maximized window.
SM_CXHSCROLL, SM_CYHSCROLL	Dimensions of arrow on horizontal scroll bar.
SM_CXHTHUMB, SM_CYHTHUMB	Dimensions of scroll box on horizontal scroll bar.
SM_CXICON, SM_CYICON	Size of standard icon.
SM_CXICONSPACING, SM_CYICONSPACING	Space between desktop icons. Large icon spacing for Win95 and NT4.0.
SM_CXMAXIMIZED, SM_CYMAXIMIZED	Default size of maximized window.
SM_CXMAXTRACK, SM_CYMAXTRACK	Maximum tracking width when resizing window.
SM_CXMENUCHECK, SM_CYMENUCHECK	Size of menu checkmark bitmap.
SM_CXMENUSIZE, SM_CYMENUSIZE	Size of button on menu bar.
SM_CXMIN, SM_CYMIN	Minimum size of a window.
SM_CXMINIMIZED, SM_CYMINIMIZED	Rectangle in which minimized windows must fit. Smaller or equal to SM_C?ICONSPACING.
SM_CXMINTRACK, SM_CYMINTRACK	Minimum tracking size of window.
SM_CXSCREEN, SM_CYSCREEN	Size of screen.

Constant Definition	Information Retrieved
SM_CXSIZE, SM_CYSIZE	Size of title bar bitmaps.
SM_CXSIZEFRAME, SM_CYSIZEFRAME	Size of window with WS_THICKFRAME style.
SM_CXSMICON, SM_CYSMICON	Size of small icon.
SM_CXSMSIZE, SM_CYSMSIZE	Size of small caption button.
SM_CXVSCROLL, SM_CYVSCROLL	Size of arrow in vertical scroll bar.
SM_CYCAPTION	Height of window caption.
SM_CYKANJIWINDOW	Height of Kanji window.
SM_CYMENU	Height of menu.
SM_CYSMCAPTION	Height of small caption.
SM_CYVTHUMB	Height of scroll box on vertical scroll bar.
SM_DBCSENABLED	TRUE if double byte characters are supported.
SM_DEBUG	TRUE if debugging version of Windows is running.
SM_MENUDROPALIGNMENT	Zero if pop-up menus are aligned to the left of the menu bar item. TRUE if the pop-up menu is aligned to the right of the menu bar item.
SM_MIDEASTENABLED	Hebrew and Arabic enabled.
SM_MOUSEPRESENT	TRUE if a mouse is present.
SM_MOUSEWHEELPRESENT	TRUE if a mouse with a wheel is installed. NT 4.0 only.
SM_NETWORK	Bit 0 is set if a network is present. Other bits are reserved.
SM_PENWINDOWS	The handle of the pen windows supports DLL if loaded.
SM_SECURE	TRUE if security is present.
SM_SHOWSOUNDS	Forces visible prompt along with sound.
SM_SLOWMACHINE	System is too slow for effective use but is being run anyway.
SM_SWAPBUTTON	TRUE if left and right mouse buttons are swapped.

Return Value   As specified for each index.

Platform   Windows 95, Windows NT, Win16
   Constants SM_ARRANGE, SM_CLEANBOOT, SM_CMETRICS, SM_C?MAXIMIZED, SM_C?MAXTRACK, SM_C?SIZEFRAME, SM_C?SMICON, SM_C?SMSIZE, SM_CYSMCAPTION, SM_SECURE, SM_SHOWSOUNDS, and SM_SLOWMACHINE are not supported on NT 3.51 and earlier.

Comments	The double-click area specifies the proximity in which two mouse clicks must take place on the display to be considered a double click.
Porting Notes	With Windows 3.x applications, GetSystemMetrics returns one less than the actual size for the following constants: SM_CYVSCROLL, SM_CYHSCROLL, SM_CYCAPTION, SM_CYFULLSCREEN. It returns one more than the actual size for constants: SM_CXDLGFRAME, SM_CYDLGFRAME, SM_CYMENU. This is because on earlier systems, the scroll bars overlapped the border by one pixel. On Windows 95 and NT 4.0, these constants return the actual sizes.
Example	SysInfo.vbp

■ GetSystemPowerStatus

VB Declaration	`Declare Function GetSystemPowerStatus& Lib "kernel32" (lpSystemPowerStatus As _` `SYSTEM_POWER_STATUS)`
Description	Obtains information about the power status of the current system. This is especially useful with laptop machines where you can use this function to determine information on power source and battery life.
Use with VB	No problem.

Parameter	Type/Description
lpSystemPowerStatus	SYSTEM POWER STATUS—Structure to load with power status information. See Appendix B for information on this structure.

Return Value	Long—TRUE (nonzero) on success, zero on failure.
Platform	Windows 95
Comments	The accuracy of the results depends on the underlying power management capability of the system.

■ GetSystemTime

VB Declaration	`Declare Sub GetSystemTime Lib "kernel32" (lpSystemTime As SYSTEMTIME)`
Description	Loads a SYSTEMTIME structure with the current system time. This time is given in Coordinated Universal Time (UTC, also known as GMT).
Use with VB	No problem.

Parameter	Type/Description
lpSystemTime	SYSTEMTIME—Structure to load with the current time.

Platform	Windows 95, Windows NT
Example	Time.vbp

■ GetSystemTimeAdjustment

VB Declaration   Declare Function GetSystemTimeAdjustment& Lib "kernel32" (lpTimeAdjustment As _
Long, lpTimeIncrement As Long, lpTimeAdjustmentDisabled As Long)

Description   Win32 makes it possible for the internal system clock to be synchronized to an external source by adding an adjustment value periodically. All times specified by this function are 100ns increments (0.1 microseconds).

Use with VB   No problem.

Parameter	Type/Description
lpTimeAdjustment	Long—Amount of time added to the internal system clock.
lpTimeIncrement	Long—Time between adjustments. Equal to the interrupt clock time.
lpTimeAdjustmentDisabled	Long—TRUE if time adjustments are disabled.

Return Value   Long—TRUE (nonzero) on success, zero on error.

Example
```
Dim lpTimeAdjustment&, lpTimeIncrement&, lpTimeAdjustmentDisabled&
GetSystemTimeAdjustment lpTimeAdjustment, lpTimeIncrement, _
    lpTimeAdjustmentDisabled
Print "Time adjustment: " & lpTimeAdjustment & "Increment: " & lpTimeIncrement _
    & "Adjustment Disabled: " & lpTimeAdjustmentDisabled
```

■ GetThreadLocale

VB Declaration   Declare Function GetThreadLocale& Lib "kernel32" ()

Description   Retrieves the Locale ID for the current thread.

Use with VB   No problem. Under VB, current thread means the current application except when called from a multithreading EXE server.

Return Value   Long—Locale identifier.

Platform   Windows 95, Windows NT

Example   SysInfo.vbp

■ GetTickCount

VB Declaration   Declare Function GetTickCount& Lib "kernel32" ()

Description   Used to retrieve the number of milliseconds that have elapsed since Windows was started.

Use with VB   No problem.

Return Value Long—Elapsed time in milliseconds.

Platform Windows 95, Windows NT, Win16

Porting Notes Replaces the Win16 GetCurrentTime function.

Example SysInfo.vbp

■ GetTimeFormat

VB Declaration
```
Declare Function GetTimeFormat& Lib "kernel32" Alias "GetTimeFormatA" (ByVal _
Locale As Long, ByVal dwFlags As Long, lpTime As SYSTEMTIME, ByVal lpFormat As _
String, ByVal lpTimeStr As String, ByVal cchTime As Long)
```

Description Formats a system time according to the format for the locale specified.

Use with VB No problem.

Parameter	Type/Description
Locale	Long—The locale ID to use to determine the format. Any information specified in the lpFormat parameter (if not NULL) overrides the locale-specific information.
dwFlags	Long—If lpFormat is specified, this should be zero. Otherwise, may be set to LOCALE_NOUSEROVERRIDE to force the system locale parameters to be used even if they have been overridden by the user. Use the self-explanatory constants TIME_NOMINUTESORSECONDS, TIME_NOSECONDS, or TIME_FORCE24HOURFORMAT to choose between date formats. Constant TIME_NOMARKER removes the AM or PM marker.
lpTime	SYSTEMTIME—A structure containing a system time. Refer to Appendix B for more information.
lpFormat	String—May be NULL to use the locale specific values (use vbNullString to pass a NULL). Otherwise contains a time format string. The codes h, hh, H, HH, m, mm, s, and ss are used in formatting in the same way as in the Visual Basic format command (refer to your VB documentation). t and tt are used to specify the marker (A or AM, P or PM).
lpTimeStr	String—Buffer to load with the formatted string. Be sure to preinitialize the string.
cchTime	Long—The length of the lpCurrencyStr buffer. If zero, the function will return the length of buffer needed.

Return Value Long—The length of the formatted string. Zero on error. Sets GetLastError to the following:

1. ERROR_INSUFFICIENT_BUFFER

2. ERROR_INVALID FLAGS

3. ERROR_INVALID_PARAMETER

Platform	Windows 95, Windows NT
Example	Time.vbp

■ GetTimeZoneInformation

VB Declaration   `Declare Function GetTimeZoneInformation& Lib "kernel32" (lpTimeZoneInformation _`
                               `As TIME_ZONE_INFORMATION)`

Description   Loads a TIME ZONE INFORMATION structure with information about the time zone setting for the system.

Use with VB   No problem.

Parameter	Type/Description
lpTimeZoneInformation	TIME ZONE INFORMATION—Structure to load with time zone information. See Appendix B for further information.

Return Value   Long—One of the following constants:

1. TIME_ZONE_ID_INVALID—Function failed—Sets GetLastError.
2. TIME_ZONE_ID_UNKNOWN—Time zone is unknown (bias value may still be specified).
3. TIME_ZONE_ID_STANDARD—Standard time is in effect.
4. TIME_ZONE_ID_DAYLIGHT—Daylight savings time is in effect.

Platform   Windows 95, Windows NT

Comments   Add the bias information in the lpTimeZoneInformation structure to the local time to obtain the system time.
     The DaylightName and StandardName strings inside the TIME_ZONE_INFORMATION structure are always in Unicode.

Example   Time.vbp

■ GetUserDefaultLangID

VB Declaration   `Declare Function GetUserDefaultLangID% Lib "kernel32" ()`

Description   Retrieves the default language ID for the current user.

Use with VB   No problem.

Return Value   Long—The language ID for the current user.

Platform   Windows 95, Windows NT

Example   Ex6b.vbp

■ GetUserDefaultLCID

VB Declaration   `Declare Function GetUserDefaultLCID& Lib "kernel32" ()`

Description   Retrieves the default locale for the current user.

Use with VB   No problem.

Return Value   Long—The default locale ID for the current user.

Platform   Windows 95, Windows NT

Example   Ex6b.vbp

■ GetUserName

VB Declaration   `Declare Function GetUserName& Lib "advapi32.dll" Alias "GetUserNameA" (ByVal _`
`lpBuffer As String, nSize As Long)`

Description   Retrieves the name of the current user.

Use with VB   No problem.

Parameter	Type/Description
lpBuffer	String—A string buffer preinitialized to length nSize. It will be loaded with the user name.
nSize	Long—A long variable initialized to the length of lpBuffer. On return it will contain the number of characters loaded into lpBuffer

Return Value   Long—TRUE (nonzero) on success, zero on error. Sets GetLastError.

Platform   Windows 95, Windows NT

Example
```
Dim s$, cnt&, dl&
cnt& = 199
s$ = String$(200, 0)
dl& = GetUserName(s$, cnt)
Debug.Print Left$(s$, cnt); cnt
```

■ GetVersion

VB Declaration   `Declare Function GetVersion& Lib "kernel32" ()`

Description   Determines the version of Windows and DOS currently running.

Use with VB   No problem.

Return Value   Long—The low 16 bits contain the Windows version; the low byte contains the major version number (3 for Windows 3.10, 4 for NT 4.0); and the high byte contains the minor version as a two-digit

decimal number (10 for Windows 3.10, 95 for Windows 95). The high 16 bits contain platform information. The high bit is set to 0 for Windows NT; 1 for Win32s on Windows for Workgroups.

Platform   Windows 95, Windows NT, Win16

Porting Notes   GetVersionEx is the preferred function to use under Win32. Note that unlike Win16, the high word under Win32 does not return the DOS version.

Example   SysInfo.vbp

■ GetVersionEx

VB Declaration   `Declare Function GetVersionEx& Lib "kernel32" Alias "GetVersionExA" (_lpVersionInformation As OSVERSIONINFO)`

Description   Loads an OSVERSIONINFO structure with version information about the platform and operating system.

Use with VB   No problem.

Parameter	Type/Description
lpVersionInformation	OSVERSIONINFO—OSVERSIONINFO structure to load with version information. You must set the dwOSVersionInfoSize field of this structure to the size of the structure (148) before calling this function.

Return Value   Long—TRUE (nonzero) on success, zero on error.

Platform   Windows 95, Windows NT

Porting Notes   Supersedes the GetVersion function.

Example   SysInfo.vbp

■ HideCaret

VB Declaration   `Declare Function HideCaret& Lib "user32" (ByVal hwnd As Long)`

Description   Hides the caret in the specified window.

Use with VB   Works, but be aware that Visual Basic will reset and redisplay the caret when a control obtains the focus.

Parameter	Type/Description
hwnd	Long—Handle of the window that contains the caret. May be zero, in which case the caret will be hidden only if it is contained in a window that is owned by the active task (see Chapter 14 for information on tasks).

Return Value   Long—Nonzero on success, zero on failure. Sets GetLastError.

Platform   Windows 95, Windows NT, Win16

Comments   Windows maintains an internal counter for caret display similar to that used for the ShowCursor function. Thus calls to HideCaret and ShowCaret must be balanced.

Example   SysInfo.vbp

■ IsValidCodePage

VB Declaration   `Declare Function IsValidCodePage& Lib "kernel32" (ByVal CodePage As Long)`

Description   Determines if the specified code page is valid.

Use with VB   No problem.

Parameter	Type/Description
CodePage	Long—Identifier of a code page. Refer to the GetACP and GetOEMCP functions for lists of code pages.

Return Value   Long—TRUE (nonzero) if the code page is valid, zero otherwise.

Platform   Windows 95, Windows NT

■ IsValidLocale

VB Declaration   `Declare Function IsValidLocale& Lib "kernel32" (ByVal Locale As Long, ByVal _`
`dwFlags As Long)`

Description   Determines if a Locale identifier is valid.

Use with VB   No problem.

Parameter	Type/Description
Locale	Long—Locale identifier to check.
dwFlags	Long—One of the following constants: LCID_SUPPORTED: Checks if the locale is supported by the system. LCID_INSTALLED: Checks if the locale is supported and installed.

Return Value   Long—TRUE (nonzero) if the locale is valid according to the test condition, zero otherwise.

Platform   Windows 95, Windows NT

■ keybd_event

VB Declaration   `Declare Sub keybd_event Lib "user32" (ByVal bVk As Byte, ByVal bScan As Byte, _`
`ByVal dwFlags As Long, ByVal dwExtraInfo As Long)`

Description   This function simulates keyboard action.

Use with VB   No problem.

Parameter	Type/Description
bVk	Byte—The virtual key code to simulate.
bScan	Byte—The OEM scan code for the key.
dwFlags	Long—Zero, or one of the two following flags: KEYEVENTF_EXTENDEDKEY—Indicates that the key is an extended key and prefixed by the 0xE0 code. KEYEVENTF_KEYUP—Simulates a key release.
dwExtraInfo	Long—A value that is typically unused. The GetMessageExtraInfo API can retrieve this value. Allowed values depend on the driver.

Platform   Windows 95, Windows NT

Comments   This function supports screen capture. Read the comments in the listing for SIMKEYS.FRM in this chapter for further information.

Porting Notes   Be sure to test programs using this function on Windows 95 and Windows NT. Behavior may not be identical between the two.

Example   SimKeys.vbp

■ LoadKeyboardLayout

VB Declaration
```
Declare Function LoadKeyboardLayout& Lib "user32" Alias "LoadKeyboardLayoutA" _
(ByVal pwszKLID As String, ByVal flags As Long)
```

Description   Loads a keyboard layout.

Use with VB   No problem.

Parameter	Type/Description
pwszKLID	String—An 8-character string describing the name of the keyboard layout. See comments.
flags	Long—A combination of the following constants: KLF_ACTIVATE: Loads and activates the specified layout. KLF_NOTELLSHELL: Prevents a shell hook procedure from receiving a HSHELL_LANGUAGE notification. Use this if you are loading a sequence of keyboard layouts to improve performance (don't set this flag on the last one loaded). KLF_REORDER: Moves the specified active layout to the start of the internal keyboard layout list. KLF_REPLACELANG: If a keyboard layout with the specified language already exists, replace it with this one. Win95 only. KLF_SUBSTITUTE_OK: Uses substitution information in the registry to cause a user-specified substitute keyboard layout for this language (if one exists) to be loaded instead of this one. KLF_UNLOADPREVIOUS: NT only—unloads the previous layout if KLF_ACTIVATE is specified and succeeds.

Return Value   Long—The handle of the keyboard layout. Zero on error.

Platform   Windows 95, Windows NT

Comments   A keyboard layout name takes the form "ddddnnnn," where nnnn is a string representation of a language ID and dddd is a string representation of a device code. The standard U.S. keyboard name is "00000409."

Porting Notes   Keyboard layouts are thread specific on Windows 95, system-wide on Windows NT.

■ MapVirtualKey

VB Declaration
```
Declare Function MapVirtualKey& Lib "user32" Alias "MapVirtualKeyA" (ByVal _
wCode As Long, ByVal wMapType As Long)
```

Description   Performs various scan code and character conversions depending on the mapping type specified.

Use with VB   No problem.

Parameter	Type/Description
wCode	Long—The source character or scan code to convert.
wMapType	Long—Controls the type of mapping as follows: 0—wCode is a virtual key code. The function returns the corresponding scan code. 1—wCode is a scan code. The function returns the corresponding virtual key code. 2—wCode is a virtual key code. The function returns the corresponding ASCII value (unshifted).

Return Value   Long—As specified by the wMapType parameter.

Platform   Windows 95, Windows NT, Win16

Example   SimKeys.vbp

■ MapVirtualKeyEx

VB Declaration
```
Declare Function MapVirtualKeyEx& Lib "user32" Alias "MapVirtualKeyExA" (ByVal _
uCode As Long, ByVal uMapType As Long, ByVal dwhkl As Long)
```

Description   Performs various scan code and character conversions depending on the mapping type specified.

Use with VB   No problem.

Parameter	Type/Description
uCode	Long—The source character or code to convert.

Parameter	Type/Description
uMapType	Long— Controls the type of mapping as follows: 0—uCode is a virtual key code. The function returns the corresponding scan code. 1—uCode is a scan code. The function returns the corresponding virtual key code. 2—uCode is a virtual key code. The function returns the corresponding ASCII value (unshifted). The high bit is set to 1 on dead keys. Returns NULL on error. 3 —uCode is a scan code. The function returns the corresponding virtual key code, correctly distinguishing between left and right keys.
dwhkl	Long—A handle to a keyboard layout.

Return Value   Long—Depends on uMapType.

Platform   Windows 95, Windows NT 4.0

Comments   This function makes it possible to convert between scan codes and additional virtual key codes such as VK_LSHIFT and VK_RSHIFT that let you distinguish between the left and right of two identical keys (including Ctrl and Alt).

■ MessageBeep

VB Declaration
```
Declare Function MessageBeep& Lib "user32" (ByVal wType As Long)
```

Description   Plays a system sound. System sound assignments are made using the control panel.

Use with VB   No problem.

Parameter	Type/Description
wType	Long—One of the following values: 0xffffffff: Standard beep MB_ICONASTERISK: System asterisk sound. MB_ICONEXCLAMATION: System exclamation sound. MB_ICONHAND: System hand sound. MB_ICONQUESTION: System question sound.

Return Value   Long—TRUE (nonzero) on success, FALSE on error. Sets GetLastError.

Platform   Windows 95, Windows NT, Win16

■ mouse_event

VB Declaration
```
Declare Sub mouse_event Lib "user32" (ByVal dwFlags As Long, ByVal dx As Long, _
ByVal dy As Long, ByVal cButtons As Long, ByVal dwExtraInfo As Long)
```

Description   Simulates a mouse event.

Use with VB	No problem.	

Parameter	Type/Description
dwFlags	Long—A combination of the following flags: MOUSEEVENTF_ABSOLUTE: dx and dy specify an absolute position in mouse coordinates which divide the screen into 65,535 units horizontally and vertically. MOUSEEVENTF_MOVE: Moves the mouse. MOUSEEVENTF_LEFTDOWN: Simulates a left button down. MOUSEEVENTF_LEFTUP: Simulates a left button up. MOUSEEVENTF_RIGHTDOWN: Simulates a right button down. MOUSEEVENTF_RIGHTUP: Simulates a right button up. MOUSEEVENTF_MIDDLEDOWN: Simulates a middle button down. MOUSEEVENTF_MIDDLEUP: Simulates a middle button up.
dx	Long—Specifies the absolute position or relative movement depending on whether the MOUSEEVENTF_ABSOLUTE flag is specified.
dy	Long — Specifies the absolute position or relative movement depending on whether the MOUSEEVENTF_ABSOLUTE flag is specified.
cButtons	Long — Unused.
dwEx-traInfo	Long — A value that is typically unused. The GetMessageExtraInfo API can retrieve this value. Allowed values depend on the driver.

Platform   Windows 95, Windows NT

Comments   When performing relative movement, the system mouse tracking speed as specified by the SystemParametersInfo function is applied to control the speed of mouse movement.

Example   SimKeys.vbp

■ OemKeyScan

VB Declaration   `Declare Function OemKeyScan& Lib "user32" (ByVal wOemChar As Integer)`

Description   Determines the scan code and shift states for an ASCII character in the OEM character set.

Use with VB   No problem.

Parameter	Type/Description
wOemChar	Integer—ASCII value of the character to convert.

Return Value   Long—The low word contains the scan code. The high word contains the following flags: Bit 0 indicates that the shift key is down; bit 1 indicates that the control key is down; bit 2 indicates that the Alt key is down. If both words are –1, the character is not defined in the OEM character set.

Platform   Windows 95, Windows NT, Win16

Comments   This function only translates keys that can be typed with a single keystroke. Keys that are entered using the ALT + 3-digit entry cannot be converted with this function.

■ OemToChar, OemToCharBuff

| **VB Declaration** | ```
Declare Function OemToChar& Lib "user32" Alias "OemToCharA" (ByVal lpszSrc As _
String, ByVal lpszDst As String)
Declare Function OemToCharBuff& Lib "user32" Alias "OemToCharBuffA" (ByVal _
lpszSrc As String, ByVal lpszDst As String, ByVal cchDstLength As Long)
``` |

Description Converts a string from the OEM character set to the ANSI character set. OemToCharBuff allows you to specify the number of characters in the string to convert.

Use with VB No problem.

Parameter	Type/Description
lpszSrc	String—String to convert.
lpszDst	String—String to load with the ANSI equivalent. Be sure to pre-initialize the string to the required length. You may pass the same string to both parameters to perform the conversion in place.
cchDstLength	Long—The number of characters in the string to convert.

Return Value Long—Always TRUE.

Platform Windows 95, Windows NT

Comments If you are using a Win32 type library to access the wide character function CharToOemW, lpszSrc is a Unicode string and the lpszDst parameter must not be the same as lpszSrc.

■ SetCaretBlinkTime

VB Declaration `Declare Function SetCaretBlinkTime& Lib "user32" (ByVal wMSeconds As Long)`

Description Specifies the flash or blink rate of the caret.

Use with VB No problem.

Parameter	Type/Description
wMSeconds	Long—The new time between flashes of the caret in milliseconds.

Return Value Long—Nonzero on success, zero on failure. Sets GetLastError.

Platform Windows 95, Windows NT, Win16

Comments The caret is a shared resource, so the blink time affects the caret for all applications. You can use the GetCaretBlinkTime function to obtain the initial blink time setting, which can be used then to restore the initial value when appropriate. See the comments for the CreateCaret function.

Example SysInfo.vbp
```

■ SetCaretPos

VB Declaration   Declare Function SetCaretPos& Lib "user32" (ByVal x As Long, ByVal y As Long)

Description   Specifies the position of the caret.

Use with VB   No problem.

Parameter	Type/Description
x	Long—X position for the caret in client coordinates.
y	Long—Y position for the caret in client coordinates.

Return Value   Long—Nonzero on success, zero on failure. Sets GetLastError.

Platform   Windows 95, Windows NT, Win16

Comments   The caret is a shared resource. Programmers should be sure that the caret is in a window owned by the current task before changing its position. See the notes for the CreateCaret function.

■ SetComputerName

VB Declaration   Declare Function SetComputerName& Lib "kernel32" Alias "SetComputerNameA" _
(ByVal lpComputerName As String)

Description   Sets the new computer name.

Use with VB   No problem.

Parameter	Type/Description
lpComputerName	String—The new computer name. May have up to MAX_COMPUTERNAME_LENGTH characters.

Return Value   Long—TRUE (nonzero) on success, zero on error. Sets GetLastError.

Platform   Windows 95, Windows NT

Comments   Windows 95 changes any illegal characters into the standard character set. Windows NT reports an error in this case.

■ SetCursor

VB Declaration   Declare Function SetCursor& Lib "user32" (ByVal hCursor As Long)

Description   Selects the specified cursor to be the current cursor.

Use with VB   Does not work well with Visual Basic due to VB's habit of changing the cursor back at various times.

Parameter	Type/Description
hCursor	Long—Handle of the cursor to set as the current cursor. Zero to specify that no cursor will be displayed.

Return Value   Long—The value of the previous cursor.

Platform   Windows 95, Windows NT, Win16

Porting Notes   Refer to Chapter 5 for information on changes to cursor processing from Win16.

■ SetCursorPos

VB Declaration   Declare Function SetCursorPos& Lib "user32" (ByVal x As Long, ByVal y As Long)

Description   Sets the cursor position.

Use with VB   No problem.

Parameter	Type/Description
x	Long—X position for the cursor in screen pixel coordinates.
y	Long— Y position for the cursor in screen pixel coordinates.

Return Value   Long—Nonzero on success, zero on failure. Sets GetLastError.

Platform   Windows 95, Windows NT, Win16

Example   Ex6a.vbp

■ SetDoubleClickTime

VB Declaration   Declare Function SetDoubleClickTime& Lib "user32" (ByVal wCount As Long)

Description   Sets the time between two consecutive mouse clicks that will cause them to be considered a single double click event.

Use with VB   No problem.

Parameter	Type/Description
wCount	Long—The new DoubleClick time delay in milliseconds.

Return Value   Long—Nonzero on success, zero on failure.

Platform   Windows 95, Windows NT, Win16

Comments   Changing the double-click time affects the entire system.

■ SetEnvironmentVariable

VB Declaration   Declare Function SetEnvironmentVariable& Lib "kernel32" Alias _
"SetEnvironmentVariableA" (ByVal lpName As String, ByVal lpValue As String)

Description   Sets an environment variable to the value specified.

Use with VB   No problem.

Parameter	Type/Description
lpName	String—The name of the environment variable to set. If an environment variable with this name does not yet exist, this function will create it.
lpValue	String—The new value for the variable. NULL to clear an existing value (use the vbNullString constant to pass a NULL to this function).

Return Value   Long—TRUE (nonzero) on success, zero on error. Sets GetLastError.

Platform   Windows 95, Windows NT

■ SetKeyboardState

VB Declaration   Declare Function SetKeyboardState& Lib "user32" (lppbKeyState As Byte)

Description   Sets the current state of each virtual key on the keyboard.

Use with VB   No problem.

Parameter	Type/Description
lppbKeyState	Byte—A 256-character fixed-length string. Each character in the internal Windows keyboard state table will be set according to the state of its corresponding virtual key in this table. The state of each key is the same as the result of the GetKeyState function.

Return Value   Long—Nonzero on success, zero on failure. Sets GetLastError.

Platform   Windows 95, Windows NT, Win16

Comments   This function can be used to set the states of the CapsLock, NumLock, and ScrollLock keys.

■ SetLocaleInfo

VB Declaration   Declare Function SetLocaleInfo& Lib "kernel32" Alias "SetLocaleInfoA" (ByVal _
Locale As Long, ByVal LCType As Long, ByVal lpLCData As String)

Description   Changes the user locale setting information.

Use with VB No problem.

Parameter	Type/Description
Locale	Long—The locale ID for which to change information.
LCType	Long—The type of information to change. Refer to the API32.TXT file for constants with the LOCALE_ prefix.
lpLCData	String—New setting for this locale information item.

Return Value Long—TRUE (nonzero) on success, zero on error. Sets GetLastError to one of the following values:

1. ERROR_INVALID_ACCESS
2. ERROR_INVALID_FLAGS
3. ERROR_INVALID_PARAMETER

Platform Windows 95, Windows NT

Comments This function does not change system locale settings.

■ SetLocalTime

VB Declaration `Declare Function SetLocalTime& Lib "kernel32" (lpSystemTime As SYSTEMTIME)`

Description Sets the current local time.

Use with VB No problem.

Parameter	Type/Description
lpSystemTime	SYSTEMTIME—A SYSTEMTIME structure specifying the new local time. The wDayOfWeek entry in this structure is ignored.

Return Value Long—TRUE (nonzero) on success, zero on error. Sets GetLastError.

Platform Windows 95, Windows NT

■ SetSysColors

VB Declaration `Declare Function SetSysColors& Lib "user32" (ByVal nChanges As Long, lpSysColor _`
`As Long, lpColorValues As Long)`

Description Sets the color of the specified Windows display object.

Use with VB No problem.

Parameter	Type/Description
nChanges	Long—Number of objects to change.

Parameter	Type/Description
lpSysColor	Long—Passed by reference. This is the first element in an integer array with nChanges elements. Each entry contains a constant specifying a Windows display object. Refer to the GetSysColors function for a complete list of objects whose colors may be set.
lpColorValues	Long—Passed by reference. This is the first element in a long array of RGB values that will be used to set the colors of the objects in the lpSysColor array.

Return Value   Long—Nonzero on success, zero on failure. Sets GetLastError.

Platform   Windows 95, Windows NT, Win16

■ SetSystemCursor

VB Declaration   `Declare Function SetSystemCursor& Lib "user32" (ByVal hcur As Long, ByVal id As _`
`Long)`

Description   Allows you to change any of the standard system cursors.

Use with VB   No problem.

Parameter	Type/Description
hcur	Long—The new cursor.
id	Long—One of the constants beginning with the prefix OCR_ that specifies a standard system cursor.

Return Value   Long—Nonzero on success, zero on failure. Sets GetLastError.

Platform   Windows 95, Windows NT

Comments   Do not destroy the cursor specified by hcur—it will be destroyed (if necessary) by the system.

■ SetSystemTime

VB Declaration   `Declare Function SetSystemTime& Lib "kernel32" (lpSystemTime As SYSTEMTIME)`

Description   Sets the current system time.

Use with VB   No problem.

Parameter	Type/Description
lpSystemTime	SYSTEMTIME—A SYSTEMTIME structure specifying the new local time. The wDayOfWeek entry in this structure is ignored.

Return Value   Long—Nonzero on success, zero on failure. Sets GetLastError.

Platform   Windows 95, Windows NT

■ SetSystemTimeAdjustment

VB Declaration   Declare Function SetSystemTimeAdjustment& Lib "kernel32" (ByVal _
dwTimeAdjustment As Long, ByVal bTimeAdjustmentDisabled As Long)

Description   Win32 makes it possible for the internal system clock to be synchronized to an external source by
adding an adjustment value periodically. All times specified by this function are 100ns increments
(0.1 microseconds).

Use with VB   No problem.

Parameter	Type/Description
dwTimeAdjustment	Long—Amount of time to add to the internal system clock at each clock interrupt.
bTimeAdjustmentDisabled	Long—TRUE to disable time adjustments.

Return Value   Long—TRUE (nonzero) on success, zero on error. Sets GetLastError.

■ SetThreadLocale

VB Declaration   Declare Function SetThreadLocale& Lib "kernel32" (ByVal Locale As Long)

Description   Sets the locale for the current thread.

Use with VB   No problem.

Parameter	Type/Description
Locale	Long—The locale ID to use for this thread.

Return Value   Long—TRUE (nonzero) on success, zero on error. Sets GetLastError.

Platform   Windows NT

■ SetTimeZoneInformation

VB Declaration   Declare Function SetTimeZoneInformation& Lib "kernel32" (lpTimeZoneInformation _
As TIME_ZONE_INFORMATION)

Description   Sets the system time zone information.

Use with VB   No problem.

Parameter	Type/Description
lpTimeZoneInformation	TIME ZONE INFORMATION—Structure from which to set the current time zone information. See Appendix B for further information

Return Value   Long—TRUE (nonzero) on success, zero on error. Sets GetLastError.

Platform   Windows 95, Windows NT

Comments   See GetTimeZoneInformation.

■ ShowCaret

VB Declaration   `Declare Function ShowCaret& Lib "user32" (ByVal hwnd As Long)`

Description   Shows the caret in the specified window.

Use with VB   See the description of the HideCaret function.

Parameter	Type/Description
hwnd	Long—Handle of the window that contains the caret. May be zero, in which case the caret will be shown only if it is contained in a window that is owned by the active task (see Chapter 14 for information on tasks).

Return Value   Long—Nonzero on success, zero on failure. Sets GetLastError.

Platform   Windows 95, Windows NT, Win16

Comments   See the description of the HideCaret function.

■ ShowCursor

VB Declaration   `Declare Function ShowCursor& Lib "user32" (ByVal bShow As Long)`

Description   Controls the visibility of the cursor.

Use with VB   No problem.

Parameter	Type/Description
bShow	Long—TRUE (nonzero) to display the cursor, FALSE to hide it.

Return Value   Long—The display count (see comments).

Platform   Windows 95, Windows NT, Win16

Comments   Windows maintains an internal display count that is incremented for each call of this function if bShow is TRUE and decremented if bShow is FALSE. The cursor will be displayed when this count is greater than or equal to zero.

Example   Ex6a.vbp

■ SwapMouseButton

VB Declaration   `Declare Function SwapMouseButton& Lib "user32" (ByVal bSwap As Long)`

Description   Determines if the functions of the left and right mouse buttons are reversed.

Use with VB   No problem.

Parameter	Type/Description
bSwap	Long—When TRUE (nonzero), the functions of the mouse buttons are swapped (meaning that the left button triggers right button events and vice versa). FALSE restores normal operation.

Return Value   Long—TRUE (nonzero) if the mouse buttons were swapped before calling this function, zero otherwise.

Platform   Windows 95, Windows NT, Win16

Comments   The mouse is a shared resource so this function affects all applications in the system.

■ SystemParametersInfo, SystemParametersInfoByval

VB Declaration
```
Declare Function SystemParametersInfo& Lib "user32" Alias _
"SystemParametersInfoA" (ByVal uAction As Long, ByVal uParam As Long, lpvParam _
As Any, ByVal fuWinIni As Long)
Declare Function SystemParametersInfoByVal& Lib "user32" Alias _
"SystemParametersInfoA" (ByVal uAction As Long, ByVal uParam As Long, ByVal _
lpvParam As Any, ByVal fuWinIni As Long)
```

Description   Allows the retrieval and setting of a number of Windows system parameters.

Use with VB   This is one of the few cases where a single function takes so many different parameters that it might make sense to use the As Any parameter type. Use extreme caution to be sure that the lpvParam parameter is of the correct data type before calling this function. It is strongly recommended that you create type safe aliases for your own application for those parameter types that you need.

Parameter	Type/Description
uAction	Long—Specifies the parameter to set. Refer to the constants in the table that follows.
uParam	Long—Refer to uAction table below.
lpvParam	Any—Integer, Long, and data structures are called by reference. Use SystemParametersInfoByval with String data. Refer to uAction table below for use.
fuWinIni	Long—Depending on parameter and operating system, user configuration parameters set with this function are stored in the file WIN.INI, the registration database, or both. This parameter specifies whether the user settings should be updated when setting system parameters. May be zero (to prevent the update) or one of the following constants: SPIF_UPDATEINIFILE: Updates the user profile in win.ini and/or the registration database. SPIF_SENDWININICHANGE: Causes a WM_WININICHANGE message to be sent to all applications when SPIF_UPDATEINIFILE is also set. Otherwise has no effect. This message informs applications that the user configuration settings have been changed.

uAction Table   Refer to your Windows manual for information on these parameters and the registration data-base or WIN.INI file. Parameters that are not specified for an action are not used. In many cases a system parameter has corresponding GET and SET actions, for example, SPI_GETACCESSTIMEOUT and SPI_SETACCESSTIMEOUT. In these cases, unless other-wise specified, the only difference between them is that one retrieves the information and the other sets it. Only parameter differences will be listed for the SET action entry.

SPI_GETACCESSTIMEOUT	lpvParam is an ACCESSTIMEOUT structure that will be loaded with accessibility features timing information. uParam must be set to the size of the ACCESSTIMEOUT structure be-fore calling the function.
SPI_GETANIMATION	lpvParam is an ANIMATIONINFO structure that will be loaded with minimize and restore animation information. No NT 3.51.
SPI_GETBEEP	lpvParam is a long that will be set TRUE if the beep sound is on.
SPI_GETBORDER	lpvParam is a long that receives a multiplier that controls the sizeable window border size.
SPI_GETDEFAULTINPUTLANG	lpvParam is a long that receives a 32-bit handle to the default keyboard layout. No NT 3.51.
SPI_GETDRAGFULLWINDOWS	lpvParam is a long that will be set TRUE if dragging moves the entire window. FALSE if only a rectangle outline is dragged. Requires NT 4.0 or Windows 95 with Plus! Pack.
SPI_GETFASTTASKSWITCH	lpvParam is a long that will be set TRUE if fast task switching is enabled. Always TRUE for Windows 95 and NT4.0
SPI_GETFILTERKEYS	lpvParam is an FILTERKEYS structure that will be loaded with keyboard-related accessi-bility feature information.
SPI_GETFONTSMOOTHING	lpvParam is a long that will be set TRUE if anti-aliasing is turned on to make fonts look smoother. NT 4.0 and Windows 95 with Plus! pack only.
SPI_GETGRIDGRANULARITY	lpvParam is a long that will be set to the grid granularity value.
SPI_GETHIGHCONTRAST	lpvParam is a HIGHCONTRAST structure that will be loaded with user display-related accessibility feature information. Win95 only.
SPI_GETICONMETRICS	lpvParam is an ICONMETRICS structure that will be loaded with information relating to the scaling and arrangement of icons. Windows 95 and NT 4.0.

SPI_GETICONTITLELOGFONT	lpvParam points to a LOGFONT structure that will be set according to the font used for icon titles.
SPI_GETICONTITLEWRAP	lpvParam is a long that will be set TRUE if icon title wrapping is enabled.
SPI_GETKEYBOARDDELAY	lpvParam is a long that will be set to the keyboard repeat delay.
SPI_GETKEYBOARDPREF	lpvParam is a long that will be set TRUE if the user prefers to use the keyboard over the mouse. When this parameter is true, Windows displays additional keyboard interface information. Win95 only.
SPI_GETKEYBOARDSPEED	lpvParam is a long that will be set to the keyboard repeat speed.
SPI_GETMENUDROPALIGNMENT	lpvParam is a long that will be set FALSE if pop-up menus are left aligned (default), TRUE for right aligned.
SPI_GETMINIMIZEDMETRICS	lpvParam is a MINIMIZEDMETRICS structure that will be loaded with information relating to the scaling and arrangement of minimized windows. Win95 only.
SPI_GETMOUSE	lpvParam is the first entry in a three-element long array. Entry 0 is set to the user configuration MouseThreshold1 field, entry 1 to MouseThreshold2, and entry 2 to MouseSpeed.
SPI_GETMOUSEKEYS	lpvParam is a MOUSEKEYS structure that will be loaded with mouse-related accessibility feature information. No NT 3.51.
SPI_GETNONCLIENTMETRICS	lpvParam is a NONCLIENTMETRICS structure that will be loaded with information about the fonts and metrics involved in drawing the non-client area of a window (borders, captions, etc.). Win95 only.
SPI_GETSCREENSAVEACTIVE	lpvParam points to an integer that will be set TRUE if the screen saver is active, FALSE otherwise.
SPI_GETSCREENSAVETIMEOUT	lpvParam points to an integer that will be set to the screen save time-out in seconds.
SPI_GETSERIALKEYS	lpvParam is a SERIALKEYS structure that will be loaded with accessibility feature information related to input devices that simulate keyboard input. Win95 only.

SPI_GETSHOWSOUNDS	lpvParam is a long that will be set TRUE if applications should use visual cues in place of sound. This is the same as the SM_GETSHOWSOUNDS option of the GetSystemMetrics function.
SPI_GETSNAPTODEFBUTTON	lpvParam is a long that will be set TRUE if the mouse will automatically move to the default button on a new dialog. NT 4.0 only.
SPI_GETSOUNDSENTRY	lpvParam is a SOUNDSENTRY structure that will be loaded with accessibility feature information related to having Windows provide visual indications in place of system sounds. uParam must be set to the size of the SOUNDSENTRY structure before the call.
SPI_GETSTICKYKEYS	lpvParam is a STICKYKEYS structure that will be loaded with accessibility feature information related to allowing a user to press keys in sequence instead of simultaneously (for example: shift+, control+, alt+). uParam must be set to the size of the STICKYKEYS structure before the call.
SPI_GETTOGGLEKEYS	lpvParam is a TOGGLEKEYS structure that will be loaded with accessibility feature information relating to the tone generated when pressing a toggle key (NumLock, CapsLock, ScrollLock). Windows will use a different tone to indicate the on and off states. uParam must be set to the size of the TOGGLEKEYS structure before the call.
SPI_GETWORKAREA	lpvParam is a RECT structure that is loaded with the working area of the screen.
SPI_ICONHORIZONTALSPACING	If lpvParam is NULL, uParam is the new width for icon spacing on the desktop in pixels.
SPI_ICONVERTICALSPACING	Same as SPI_ICONHORIZONTALSPACING for the vertical icon spacing.
SPI_LANGDRIVER	lpvParam is a string with the new language driver file name.
SPI_SETACCESSTIMEOUT	Same parameters as SPI_GETACCESSTIMEOU.
SPI_SETANIMATION	Same parameters as SPI_GETANIMATION.
SPI_SETBEEP	uParam is TRUE to turn the beep sound on, FALSE to turn it off.
SPI_SETBORDER	uParam is the multiplier that controls the sizeable window border size.

SPI_SETDEFAULTINPUTLANG	Same parameters as SPI_GETDEFAULTINPUTLANG.
SPI_SETDESKPATTERN	Forces windows to restore the current desktop pattern from the registration database or WIN.INI.
SPI_SETDESKWALLPAPER	lpvParam is a string containing the name of a bitmap file to use as the desktop wallpaper.
SPI_SETDOUBLECLICKTIME	uParam is the number of milliseconds between two clicks within which they will be considered a single double click.
SPI_SETDOUBLECLKHEIGHT	uParam is the new double-click height. See the comments for the GetSystemMetrics function for details.
SPI_SETDOUBLECLKWIDTH	uParam is the new double-click width. See the comments for the GetSystemMetrics function for details.
SPI_DRAGFULLWINDOWS	uParam is TRUE to turn on full window dragging, FALSE otherwise. Win95 only.
SPI_SETDRAGHEIGHT	uParam is the height in pixels of the rectangle that determines if a drag operation is starting. Win95 only.
SPI_SETDRAGWIDTH	uParam is the width in pixels of the rectangle that determines if a drag operation is starting. Win95 only.
SPI_SETFASTTASKSWITCH	uParam is TRUE to turn on fast task switching, FALSE to turn it off.
SPI FILTERKEYS	Same parameters as SPI_GETFILTERKEYS.
SPI_SETFONTSMOOTHING	uParam is TRUE to turn on font smoothing. NT 4.0 and Win95 with Plus! pack only.
SPI_SETGRIDGRANULARITY	uParam is the new grid granularity.
SPI_SETHIGHCONTRAST	Same parameters as SPI_GETHIGHCONTRAST.
SPI_SETICONMETRICS	Same parameters as SPI_GETICONMETRICS.
SPI_SETICONTITLELOGFONT	lpvParam is a LOGFONT structure that will define the font to use for icon titles. uParam is the size of the LOGFONT structure. If both are NULL, the font defined during system startup will be used.
SPI_SETICONTITLEWRAP	uParam is TRUE to turn on icon title wrapping.
SPI_SETKEYBOARDDELAY	uParam is the new keyboard repeat delay.

SPI_SETKEYBOARDPREF	uParam is TRUE to indicate that the user prefers to use the keyboard over the mouse. See SPI_GETKEYBOARDPREF.
SPI_SETKEYBOARDSPEED	uParam is the new keyboard repeat speed.
SPI_SETLANGTOGGLE	Causes windows to reload the hotkey information for switching between keyboard layouts from the system registry.
SPI_SETLOWPOWERACTIVE	uParam is TRUE to enable the low power screen saver mode. Win95 only.
SPI_SETLOWPOWERTIMEOUT	uParam is the new low power screen saver time-out. Win95 only.
SPI_SETMENUDROPALIGNMENT	uParam is FALSE to set left aligned pop-up menus, TRUE for right aligned.
SPI_SETMINIMIZEDMETRICS	Same parameters as SPI_GETMINIMIZEDMETRICS.
SPI_SETMOUSE	lpvParam is the first entry in a three-element integer array containing mouse settings. See SPI_GETMOUSE for details.
SPI_SETMOUSEBUTTONSWAP	uParam is TRUE to swap the meaning of the left and right mouse buttons, FALSE to use original values.
SPI_SETMOUSEKEYS	Same parameters as SPI_GETMOUSEKEYS.
SPI_SETNONCLIENTMETRICS	Same parameters as SPI_GETNONCLIENTMETRICS.
SPI_SETPENWINDOWS	uParam is TRUE to load pen windows, FALSE to unload.
SPI_SETPOWEROFFACTIVE	uParam is TRUE to enable the power down screen saver mode. Win95 only.
SPI_SETPOWEROFFTIMEOUT	uParam is the new power down screen saver time-out. Win95 only.
SPI_SETSCREENREADER	uParam is TRUE if a screen reader utility is running. See SPI_GETSCREENREADER.
SPI_SETSCREENSAVEACTIVE	uParam is TRUE to activate the screen saver, FALSE to deactivate.
SPI_SETSCREENSAVETIMEOUT	uParam is the new screen save time-out in seconds.
SPI_SETSERIALKEYS	Same parameters as SPI_GETSERIALKEYS.
SPI_SETSHOWSOUNDS	uParam is TRUE to enable the windows showsounds accessibility features. See SPI_GETSHOWSOUNDS.

SPI_SETSNAPTODEFBUTTON	uParam is a TRUE if the mouse should automatically move to the default button on a new dialog. NT 4.0 only.
SPI_SETSOUNDSENTRY	Same as SPI_GETSOUNDSENTRY.
SPI_SETSTICKYKEYS	Same as SPI_GETSTICKYKEYS.
SPI_SETTOGGLEKEYS	Same as SPI_GETTOGGLEKEYS.
SPI_SETWORKAREA	Same as SPI_GETWORKAREA.

Return Value Long—Nonzero on success, zero on failure. Sets GetLastError.

Platform Windows 95, Windows NT, Win16 (see individual parameters)
   Refer to the latest Win32 documentation for the new constants supported by this function. Microsoft may add constants with each version of NT and Windows 95 including service pack and extension pack updates. This table has been updated as of NT 4.0, but does not include constants referring to the new mouse wheel support for NT 4.0.

Porting Notes Be careful: In many cases where lpvParam pointed to an integer variable under Win16 (for example, with booleans), it now points to a long.

Example SysInfo.vbp

■ SystemTimeToTzSpecificLocalTime

VB Declaration
```
Declare Function SystemTimeToTzSpecificLocalTime& Lib "kernel32" _
(lpTimeZoneInformation As TIME_ZONE_INFORMATION, lpUniversalTime As SYSTEMTIME, _
lpLocalTime As SYSTEMTIME)
```

Description Converts a system time to local time.

Use with VB No problem.

Parameter	Type/Description
lpTimeZoneInformation	TIME ZONE INFORMATION—Structure containing time zone information.
lpUniversalTime	SYSTEMTIME—Structure containing the system time.
lpLocalTime	SYSTEMTIME—Structure to load with the local time.

Return Value Long—TRUE (nonzero) on success, zero on error. Sets GetLastError.

Platform Windows NT

■ ToAscii, ToAsciiEx

VB Declaration
```
Declare Function ToAscii& Lib "user32" (ByVal uVirtKey As Long, ByVal uScanCode _
As Long, lpbKeyState As Byte, lpwTransKey As Integer, ByVal fuState As Long)
```

```
Declare Function ToAsciiEx& Lib "user32" (ByVal uVirtKey As Long, ByVal _
uScanCode As Long, lpKeyState As Byte, lpwTransKey As Integer, ByVal fuState As _
Long, ByVal dwhkl As Long)
```

Description   Converts a virtual key into an ASCII character based on current scan and keyboard information.

Use with VB   No problem.

Parameter	Type/Description
uVirtKey	Long—The virtual key code to convert.
uScanCode	Long—The scan code of the key. The high bit is set if the key is up, clear if down.
lpbKeyState	Byte—The first entry in a 256-byte array indicating the keyboard state. Refer to the GetKeyboardState function for more information on this array.
lpwTransKey	Integer—An integer variable to load with the translated character. Use the chr$() function to convert this value into a string.
fuState	Long—Set to 1 if a menu is active.
dwhkl	Long—Handle to a keyboard layout to use for the translation.

Return Value   Long—Negative indicates that the key is dead—it does not translate by itself into a character (accent keys are an example of this). Zero if the key cannot be translated given the current keyboard state. 1 if a single character was loaded into lpwTransKey. 2 if lpwTransKey was loaded with two characters (you will need to split it into two bytes). This might occur if a dead key or accent key combination supported by the keyboard cannot be represented by a single character in the current character set.

Platform   Windows 95, Windows NT (ToAsciiEx is Windows 95 or Windows NT 4.0 only)

Comments   The state of the NUM-LOCK key is ignored, since the virtual key code includes that information.

The Microsoft Win32 documentation for ToAsciiEx suggests that the lpwTransKey parameter of ToAsciiEx is a long instead of an integer. The declaration shown here is based on the actual C language headers which define it as a 16-bit Word (VB integer).

■ ToUnicode

VB Declaration
```
Declare Function ToUnicode& Lib "user32" (ByVal wVirtKey As Long, ByVal _
wScanCode As Long, lpKeyState As Byte, ByVal pwszBuff As String, ByVal cchBuff _
As Long, ByVal wFlags As Long)
```

Description   Converts a virtual key into an Unicode character based on current scan and keyboard information.

Use with VB   No problem.

Parameter	Type/Description
wVirtKey	Long—The virtual key code to convert.

Parameter	Type/Description
wScanCode	Long—The scan code of the key. The high bit is set if the key is up, clear if down.
lpKeyState	Byte—The first entry in a 256-byte array indicating the keyboard state. Refer to the GetKeyboardState function for more information on this array.
pwszBuff	String—A string buffer to load with the Unicode character(s). Be sure to preinitialize the string.
cchBuff	Long—The length of the pwszBuff string buffer.
wFlags	Long—Set to 1 if a menu is active.

Return Value   Long——1 indicates that the key is dead—it does not translate by itself into a character (accent keys are an example of this). Zero if the key cannot be translated given the current keyboard state. 1 if a single character was loaded into pwszBuff. 2 if two or more characters were loaded into the pwszBuff string. This might occur if a dead key or accent key combination supported by the keyboard cannot be represented by a single character in the current character set.

Platform   Windows NT

■ UnloadKeyboardLayout

VB Declaration   `Declare Function UnloadKeyboardLayout& Lib "user32" (ByVal HKL As Long)`

Description   Unloads the specified keyboard layout. Refer to the LoadKeyboardLayout function for additional information.

Use with VB   No problem.

Parameter	Type/Description
HKL	Long—The handle of the keyboard layout to unload.

Return Value   Long—The handle of the keyboard layout on success, zero on error. Sets GetLastError.

Platform   Windows 95, Windows NT

Comments   Under Windows 95, this function will never unload the default system keyboard layout.

■ VkKeyScan, VkKeyScanEx

VB Declaration   `Declare Function VkKeyScan% Lib "user32" Alias "VkKeyScanA" (ByVal cChar As _`
`Byte)`
`Declare Function VkKeyScanEx% Lib "user32" Alias "VkKeyScanExA" (ByVal ch As _`
`Byte, ByVal dwhkl As Long)`

Description   Determines the virtual key code and shift states for an ASCII character in the Windows character set.

Use with VB   No problem.

Parameter	Type/Description
cChar	Byte—ASCII value of the character to convert.
dwhkl	Long—The keyboard layout on which to base the conversion.

Return Value   Integer—The low word contains the virtual key code. The high word contains the following flags:

- Bit 0 indicates that the shift key is down.

- Bit 1 indicates that the control key is down.

- Bit 2 indicates that the alt key is down.

- If both words are –1, the character is not defined.

Platform   Windows 95, Windows NT, Win16 (VkKeyScanEx is Windows 95 and Windows NT 4.0 only).

Comments   Translations for the numeric keypad are ignored. This function can be used to obtain the correct parameters to use when sending WM_KEYDOWN and WM_KEYUP messages.

Example   SimKeys.vbp

CHAPTER

7

Device Contexts

WINDOWS SUPPORTS A NUMBER OF DIFFERENT TYPES OF DEVICES FOR both input and output. The two most common devices are the display screen and the printer, although Windows also supports other devices such as plotter and image acquisition devices.

Windows is a graphical environment, so it is not surprising that there are many functions that deal with the process of generating graphic output on various types of devices. The next three chapters deal exclusively with this subject—and that's not even getting into text output and printing, subjects that are covered in later chapters.

The Windows graphic system is incredibly flexible and powerful. It is also surprisingly simple—once you understand certain fundamental concepts and rules that must be followed. This chapter concentrates on three of these concepts: device contexts, clipping regions, and coordinate systems. You may find the temptation to go straight to Chapter 8 nearly overwhelming—it deals with the graphic operations themselves, which are certainly more exciting, if not literally colorful. But make no mistake—a good understanding of the subject matter discussed in this chapter will change the way you look at graphic programming under Windows forever. It will even lead you to a better understanding of graphic programming under Visual Basic—even if you never use a single API call.

Introduction to Device Contexts

A *device context* (DC) is a Windows object that allows drawing to a window or device. All graphic and text output to a device take place through a device context. Device contexts for windows are sometimes referred to in the Windows documentation as "display contexts."

Device contexts were also briefly discussed in Chapter 2 (which you may wish to review before continuing).

The Philosophy behind the Device Context

The two most frequently used devices under Windows are the display screen and the printer. There obviously needs to be some mechanism for sending data to these devices. Under Windows, this data will most frequently be graphics information such as lines and fills, and text information.

Under MS-DOS, when you write data to a device, you are accessing all parts of the device at all times. In other words, a program drawing graphics on a VGA screen has access to the entire screen, and a program sending output to a printer has access to the entire page. If you wish a program to draw only on a portion of the display or page, it is the responsibility of the program itself to calculate where it may or may not draw. Consider the following example.

You have written a word processing program that needs to display and print a page that contains text, a graphic logo, and an image. The page contains a graphic logo area, a text area, and an image (or picture) area.

MS-DOS provides no protection when drawing in one area to prevent the program from drawing over the other areas. Thus the application program must be very careful to draw the image only in the picture area. If the image is too large to fit, the program must either scale it or check each pixel to make sure that it falls within the picture area before drawing it. This applies to the text and graphic logo areas as well. Also, the program must calculate the position on the screen for each element in each area. If the picture image is offset by 15 pixels from the top of the screen, the position of each pixel in the image must be offset by 15 pixels before it is drawn. All of the coordinate calculations must be performed manually by the program. Figure 7.1a illustrates the drawing coordinates that a DOS program would need to use to draw this sample page.

Consider then what happens when you take the code that draws a page to the screen and try to adapt it to a printer. The printer resolution is different from that of the display screen. The aspect ratio is probably different as well. This adds considerable complexity to a program, and does not even take into account the fact that you will probably want the program to support a number of different display devices and printers. Figure 7.1b shows how drawing coordinates might change when going to a printed page. You can see how the code that draws each of the elements on this page would need to calculate drawing locations based on the resolution and coordinate system of each printer or graphic resolution.

Windows provides two features that eliminate much of this complexity: built-in *clipping* and *coordinate transformation*.

Clipping

With clipping, every time a program calls a graphics or text output function, Windows checks to see if the output falls within a clipping area. It does this on a pixel-by-pixel basis. With regard to our word processing example, this means that each area may be protected from the other. When you are drawing the graphic logo, you can specify that the graphic logo area be the clipping region. If the graphic image extends beyond that area it will automatically be clipped and there is no risk of it affecting other areas. This makes it easy to handle the problem described earlier of images that exceed the picture area—if the image is too large it will automatically be clipped to the desired space.

The most common use of clipping is within Windows to prevent drawing in one window from affecting others. You can see this by creating a Visual Basic form and placing a command button in the center. Use the Line command to draw a line that starts at one end of the form and passes through the command button to the other side. Note how the line appears on both sides

Figure 7.1

Drawing under
MS-DOS

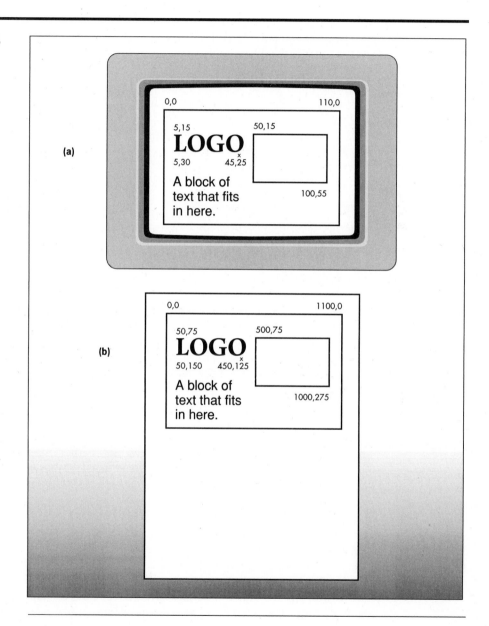

of the command button but does not appear on the command button itself. This is because the command button is a window that is not part of the clipping region for the form.

The default clipping region for any window is the window itself. It is important to note, however, that the clipping region may be set to any portion of a window. In the same way, clipping may be used to allow drawing onto only part of a printer page. The Region example program shows how this is done. Win32 also introduces the SetWindowRng function which allows you to change the clipping region for an entire window. This makes it possible to create windows that are not rectangular.

Coordinate Transformation

Windows also provides the ability to translate a coordinate system from one used by the physical device to any coordinate system you choose. This is an extremely powerful technique as can be seen once again with our word processing example.

Consider the graphic logo. Assume that you want this logo to always appear in the same relative location and size on the window or page regardless of which output device you are using.

Without coordinate transformations, you must first determine the pixel location on the screen of the start of the logo area. Then it is necessary to calculate the height and width of the logo area. All of these figures will vary from device to device. The actual drawing routine must be designed to use these calculated values to draw the graphic.

With coordinate transformation, all of these calculations become unnecessary. Your program need only define the coordinate system for the graphic logo area. It can specify, for example, that the lower left corner of the area will be the coordinates 0,0, and that the width of the area will always be 800 units and the height will always be 200 units. These units are called *logical units*. The Windows drawing functions always use logical units, and it is the responsibility of Windows to convert these logical units into the actual device physical units.

Now the graphic logo drawing routine can be simplified—it can be set up to always draw into an 800x200 unit area. Windows will perform the coordinate transformations required to draw the logo correctly on any device once the coordinate system has been set up. This process is illustrated in Figure 7.2. The logical window that you define, shown as the 800x200 logical window in the upper left of the figure, will actually draw into a physical area that you define on the screen, printer, or other device. Windows takes care of translating the coordinates for each dot as needed. By setting up the clipping region to 800x200, your code does not have to worry about accidentally writing to other areas on the device. Windows restricts all graphic output to the area that you specify.

Figure 7.2

Drawing under
Windows

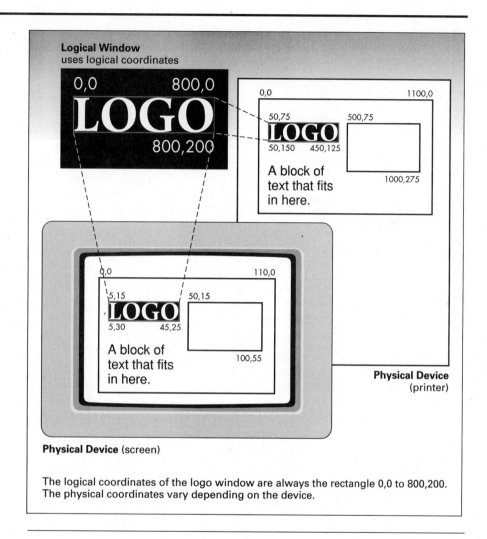

Logical Window
uses logical coordinates

The logical coordinates of the logo window are always the rectangle 0,0 to 800,200. The physical coordinates vary depending on the device.

Device Contexts Revisited

So far this section has shown how specifying a clipping area and a coordinate system can both simplify output to a device and provide device independence. The question then is how do you specify the clipping area and coordinate system for a device?

You are already acquainted with Windows objects from Chapter 5. Windows objects can provide automatic clipping to other windows as shown in the example where a line was drawn "through" a command button, but a window provides no ability to specify a clipping region within the window. Nor does a window help with regard to printed output. A window is only useful for specifying an area on the display screen (which is a very important "only"—but still does not address the current problem).

Windows therefore provides an object known as a device context. A device context may be associated with a window, with a device, or with a block of memory that simulates a device (called a memory device context). A device context may also have associated with it a clipping region and a coordinate system.

All drawing under Windows takes place through a device context rather than directly to a window or device. This provides the mechanism by which clipping and coordinate transformations may take place. You can think of a device context as a black box—graphics and text output commands go in one side, are processed and translated according to the attributes that are selected for the device context, and then are sent to the actual window or device.

Here is yet another way to look at a device context: Imagine an art studio where you are an artist who is working on a number of different paintings at one time. Each painting uses a different sized canvas, and has a different style. Perhaps one painting is large and uses heavy textured paints with many dark colors. Another is a smaller work, with bright colors and fine lines. While working, you hold in your hand an artist's palette that holds a number of paints and a selection of brushes (for those of you who are not artists, imagine the picture of a rather disheveled looking artist in an paint-splattered smock, holding a tray containing a few containers of paints in different colors, with a small selection of pencils and brushes scattered among the paints—this tray is the artist's palette). At any given time you can only hold one of these palettes—and you obviously can't work on a painting without one. If you were a poor artist, you might make do with a single palette—but imagine the work needed to remix the colors and reselect brushes each time you wanted to work on a different painting. A better approach might be to have a different artist's palette for each work. All you would need to do when switching between paintings is pick up a different palette. You might even keep a few general purpose palettes around that could be shared among similar works.

A device context is the Windows equivalent to the artist's palette. Any time you wish to draw onto a window or printer, you need that palette that holds the brush that you are using, defines the colors that are available, and in the case of Windows, defines many other characteristics relating to drawing.

But don't follow this analogy too far: The artist's palette defined here has little to do with the color palettes used by Windows.

Introduction to Using Device Contexts

Windows provides a pool of built-in device contexts that are available for use to draw into windows or devices. When you wish to draw to a window or device, you request a device context from this pool, specify the attributes for the context, and then use it for drawing. Once you no longer need it, you release it. The device context is returned to the pool and becomes available for use by this or other applications.

Windows also provides the capability of creating device contexts in cases where you do not wish to use one from the general context pool. You can also specify that each window in a specific class have its own device context or that all windows in a class share a device context. These possibilities are described later in this chapter.

So far only two device context attributes have been discussed: clipping regions and coordinate systems. In fact, a device context has a number of other important attributes. These are listed in Table 7.1 along with the default values assigned to a device context when it is newly created or retrieved from the device context pool. Don't worry if some of these attributes are unclear—they will all be explained later in this chapter and in Chapter 8.

Table 7.1   **Default Device Context Attributes**

Attribute	Default Value	See Chapter
Background color	White	8
Background mode	Opaque	8
Bitmap	None	9
Brush	White brush	8
Brush origin	0,0	8
Clipping region	Entire window or device surface	7
Color palette	Default palette	
Pen position	0,0	8
Drawing mode	R2_COPYPEN	8
Font	System font	11
Intercharacter spacing	0	11
Mapping mode	MM_TEXT	7
Pen	Black	8
Polygon-filling mode	ALTERNATE	8

Table 7.1   **Default Device Context Attributes (Continued)**

Attribute	Default Value	See Chapter
Stretching mode	BLACKONWHITE	9
Text color	Black	11
Viewport origin	0,0	7
Viewport extents	1,1	7
Window origin	0,0	7
Window extents	1,1	7

Obtaining a Device Context

A device context handle is used as a parameter to most Windows drawing functions. The device context itself is an internal Windows data structure. Windows provides several ways to create or obtain device contexts:

- *Private device contexts* When a window belongs to a class with the CS_OWNDC, CS_PARENTDC, or CS_CLASSDC class style bits set, it is given a private device context. In the case of CS_CLASSDC, a single device context is shared by all windows in a class. The CS_PARENTDC style gives a window the device context of its parent window. In the case of CS_OWNDC, each window has its own device context. The advantage of this is that the device context is always available for drawing into the window. The Windows system does not modify the device context in any way. The disadvantage lies in the extra memory taken up by each window—memory that is taken out of windows resource space. This is not a big issue on Windows NT, but resource space is still limited under Windows 95. Visual Basic forms and picture controls have the CS_OWNDC style. The handle for a private device context is obtained using the GetDC or GetDCEx function and is returned by the hDC property for a Visual Basic form or picture control.

- *Cached device contexts* In order to conserve resources, Windows provides a cache of internal device contexts that are shared by all applications and that may be used with any window. These contexts are also obtained using the GetDC or GetDCEx function. When a cached DC is obtained, it is initialized to the default attributes shown in Table 7.1. It is essential, when using cached DCs, to release them when they are no longer needed using the ReleaseDC function. This is necessary in order to prevent the system from locking up due to lack of available device contexts.

- *Created device contexts* It is possible to create a device context using the CreateDC and CreateCompatibleDC functions. You may create as many of these as needed.

Table 7.2 describes the API functions used in obtaining and freeing device contexts.

Table 7.2   **Device Context API Functions**

Function	Description
CreateCompatibleDC	Creates a memory device context that is compatible to a source DC. A memory device context can be considered a simulation of a device in memory. Selecting a bitmap into the device allows creation of a memory image that is compatible with the device.
CreateDC	Creates a device context for the specified device. It is most often used to create a DC for a printer.
CreateIC	Creates an information context (IC) for the specified device. An IC is similar to a device context, except that it takes less overhead. It can be used to obtain information about a device but may not be used for drawing operations.
DeleteDC	Deletes a created device context. This should be used to free device contexts created using the CreateDC, CreateIC, and CreateCompatibleDC functions.
GetDC GetDCEx	Obtains a device context for the specified window. If the window's class uses a private DC, that device context is retrieved by this function. Otherwise the function obtains a DC from the Windows cache. The GetDCEx function makes it possible to obtain a cached context even for windows that normally use private DCs.
GetWindowDC	This function is similar to GetDC except that it retrieves a device context for the entire window rectangle (not just the client area of the window).
ReleaseDC	Releases a window obtained using GetDC, GetDCEx, or GetWindowDC. If the DC is a private device context, this function has no effect. Otherwise, the DC is returned to the cache.
WindowFromDC	Determines the window handle that is associated with a specified device context.

It's important to differentiate between the device contexts retrieved by the GetDC and GetDCEx functions and the CreateDC and CreateCompatibleDC functions. The former retrieve a device context from the Windows device context pool. This is a pool of device contexts that are available to any Windows application. Device contexts obtained using these functions must never be destroyed—they must be released using the ReleaseDC function, which causes the device context to be returned to the Windows device context pool when it is no longer needed. They must be returned as soon as possible, as these DCs are shared by all Windows applications, and their number is limited.

When the CreateDC and CreateCompatibleDC functions are used to obtain a device context, a new device context is actually created. This involves a fair amount of overhead in both time and memory, but contexts created in this manner may be held as long as you wish. When they are no longer needed they should be destroyed using the DeleteDC function, which frees up the memory allocated during the creation process.

Device Context Attributes

Table 7.1 lists the attributes of a device context. All of these attributes may be set using API function calls. Generally speaking, it is necessary to set the DC attributes before drawing into a device context. If a window uses cached device contexts, the attributes need to be set each time a DC is obtained for drawing.

Drawing Objects

Drawing objects are selected into a DC using the SelectObject API function described in Chapter 8. For example, it is possible to select a red pen into a DC in order to draw a red line in a window. The SelectObject function returns as its result a handle to the original drawing object for that DC. It is very important to select that original object back into the device context before releasing or destroying the device context.

Drawing Attributes and Mapping Modes

A device context describes drawing attributes such as the drawing mode and intercharacter spacing. It also defines the mapping mode and coordinate system to use for drawing. Unlike drawing objects there is no need to clear these settings before releasing or destroying the device context.

Color Palettes

With version 2.0 and greater, Visual Basic supports the use of color palettes to provide a selection of up to 256 colors to use from the millions available on many super-VGA devices.

Using Device Contexts with Visual Basic

Visual Basic forms and picture controls use private device contexts. You can retrieve a DC for a form or picture control using the hDC property or the GetDC function (both techniques return the same handle when the Auto-Redraw property is FALSE).

Saving the Device Context State

It is absolutely essential that a Visual Basic device context be restored to its original state before returning control to Visual Basic. Windows provides two handy API functions (shown in Table 7.3) that allow you to save and restore the state of a device context.

Table 7.3   **Device Context Stack Functions**

Function	Description
SaveDC	Saves the state and attributes of the specified device context on a device context stack.
RestoreDC	Restores the state and attributes of a device context from the Windows device context stack.

The following sequence of operations is commonly used when using Windows API functions to draw to a VB form or control:

1. Retrieve a device context handle using the hDC property.

2. Save the state of the device context using the SaveDC function.

3. Select the desired drawing objects and coordinate system.

4. Perform the drawing operations.

5. Restore the state of the device context using the RestoreDC function.

This process is described in further detail in the example programs in Chapter 8.

Device Contexts and the AutoRedraw Property

To effectively use the Windows API drawing functions, it is important to understand how Visual Basic uses device contexts and bitmaps internally. Figure 7.3 shows the architecture of the VB drawing environment.

Each form or picture control may have two bitmap images associated with it. The background bitmap image contains a bitmap that is to be used as the background for the window. The handle to this bitmap may be set and retrieved by the Picture property. The persistent image bitmap is used only when the AutoRedraw property is set to TRUE (–1). In this case, all drawing goes to a memory bitmap that is compatible with the window. This technique allows the VB programmer to draw an image once, and let VB automatically copy the persistent image bitmap to the window whenever the window needs updating. This also means that when AutoRedraw is 0, the persistent image

Figure 7.3
Visual Basic drawing
and the AutoRedraw
property

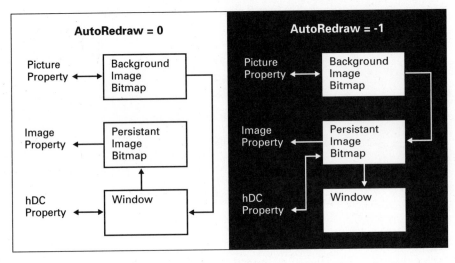

bitmap does not exist and is not modified during drawing. You can still retrieve an image bitmap by reading the Image property, in which case Visual Basic will create a bitmap containing the background picture and return a handle to that bitmap.

When the AutoRedraw property is FALSE, all drawing goes directly to the window. This is much faster and requires less overhead, since the extra memory for the persistent bitmap is not required and drawing to a window is frequently faster than copying a bitmap—especially if the bitmap is large. However, since VB does not maintain a persistent image for the window, it is necessary for the VB program to detect paint events and draw the window upon receipt of a Paint event.

Tables 7.4 and 7.5 describe the values of the VB properties associated with drawing and the process of updating a window.

Table 7.4   **Drawing with AutoRedraw = FALSE**

hDC property	Handle to a device context for the window.
Image property	Handle to a bitmap for the persistent image for the window. This image is not changed during drawing.
Picture property	Handle to the background image bitmap for the window.

Table 7.4	**Drawing with AutoRedraw = FALSE (Continued)**
Effect of Cls method	Clears the window to the background color or bitmap.
Window update process	Windows copies the Picture bitmap (if one exists) to the window, then sends a Paint event. All drawing goes directly to the window by way of the hDC device context.

Table 7.5	**Drawing with AutoRedraw = –1**
hDC property	Handle to a device context for a memory device context that is compatible with the window and contains a bitmap the size of the window. This bitmap is called the persistent image bitmap, or screen, for the window.
Image property	Handle to a bitmap for the persistent image for the window. This is the bitmap selected into the device context described by the hDC property.
Picture property	Handle to the background image bitmap for the window. Changing this property causes the persistent image bitmap to be immediately updated to reflect this bitmap.
Effect of Cls method	Clears the persistent bitmap to the background color and copies the background image bitmap (if one exists) to the persistent bitmap.
Window update process	Windows copies the persistent image bitmap to the window. All drawing goes directly to the persistent image bitmap by way of the hDC device context. No Paint events are sent.

The Windows API drawing functions can be used in either drawing mode. When drawing to the device context retrieved by the hDC property, drawing will go to the persistent bitmap or the window, depending on the state of the AutoRedraw property.

There are some subtleties to be aware of when drawing to the persistent image bitmap when AutoRedraw is TRUE. First, unlike the VB drawing functions, the API functions do not inform VB that the window needs to be updated. Therefore it is necessary to invoke the Refresh method on the window or to invalidate the window to cause the persistent image to be transferred to the window. This also means that creating a complex drawing using API functions when AutoRedraw is TRUE is much faster than using the VB functions that update the display after each drawing operation.

Second, when AutoRedraw is set to TRUE, it is still possible to obtain a device context to the window itself using the GetDC API function and draw directly to the window. This is a subtle difference that is important to understand. When you use the hDC property to retrieve a device context when AutoRedraw is TRUE and draw into it, you are drawing into a memory device context that contains the persistent image bitmap. When you use the GetDC function to obtain a device context for a window, you are accessing the window itself.

Images drawn in this manner will not be placed in the persistent image bitmap. Due to the lack of Paint events, your program will have no way of knowing when that information is overwritten due to an update from the persistent image bitmap.

You should make no assumptions regarding the state of the device context retrieved using the GetDC function when AutoRedraw is TRUE. You should save the device context state and select any needed drawing objects before drawing into this DC. The state of the device context returned by the GetDC function or hDC property when AutoRedraw is FALSE depends on the values of the properties of the form or control.

The ClipControls Property and Graphical Controls

The Windows API drawing functions work identically to the Visual Basic drawing methods with regard to the ClipControls property and Graphical controls.

Forms, picture controls, and frame controls can be containers of other controls. This means that they can have child windows or controls contained within their client area. The ClipControls and AutoRedraw properties combine to determine whether the control is excluded from the clipping region. When the control is excluded from the clipping region, any drawing on the area of that control will be prevented. Tables 7.6 and 7.7 indicate whether drawing over a control will take place or not.

Table 7.6   Drawing over a Window-Based Child Control

	AutoRedraw = TRUE	AutoRedraw = FALSE
ClipControls = TRUE	No	No
ClipControls = FALSE	No	Yes

Table 7.7   Drawing over a Graphical Child Control

	AutoRedraw = TRUE	AutoRedraw = FALSE
ClipControls = TRUE	No	Yes
ClipControls = FALSE	No	Yes

Visual Basic graphical controls do not have a window associated with them. This means that you cannot obtain a device context for a graphical control. You can draw into the area occupied by a graphical control by obtaining a device context for the container control and drawing into it as long as Auto-Redraw is set to FALSE for the container.

If you expect to be drawing on container objects, you will probably want to experiment with the various drawing methods and properties.

Device Context Information Functions

The Windows General Device Interface (GDI) provides a mechanism for obtaining information about devices in the form of the GetDeviceCaps function. The most important information from the programmer's point of view are the various device dimensions, including resolution, aspect ratio, and colors supported. The RASTERCAPS capabilities field allows the programmer to determine if a device supports certain raster capabilities such as the BitBlt operation, device-independent bitmap functions, and bitmaps that are greater than 64K in size. A plotter, for example, is usually unable to handle raster operations.

GetDeviceCaps also allows you to determine which GDI functions are supported internally by the device. For example, some devices are able to draw lines and circles using built-in hardware accelerators. In such cases, GDI will usually allow the driver to perform the operation. Otherwise, GDI will perform the graphic function itself. This information is usually not important to the programmer.

Example: DevView—A Device Information Viewer

DevView is a program that can display information about a given device. It does not include all of the information provided by the GetDeviceCaps function, but is easily extensible.

Figure 7.4 shows the DevView program in action and shows the location of the project's controls on the form.

Using DevView
This simple program has only two controls. The Form button obtains a device context for the form and displays information for that context. The Printer button does the same for the default printer.

Porting DevView
DevView is one of the sample applications that was ported from the original 16-bit example in the Visual Basic Programmers Guide to the Windows API (16-bit edition). This was one of the easiest programs to port, mostly because it

Figure 7.4

Main screen for
DevView.frm

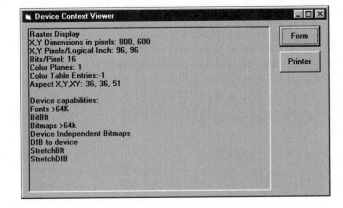

relies on a single Windows API function. The current version works under both Win16 and Win32. The conversion involved using conditional compilation for the function declaration and the device context and result variable types.

Project Description

The DevView project includes two files. DEVVIEW.FRM is the only form used in the program. DEVVIEW.BAS is the only module in the program and contains the constant, type, and function definitions.

Listing 7.1 contains the header from file DEVVIEW.FRM that describes the control setup for the form.

Listing 7.1   **Header from file DEVVIEW.FRM**

```
VERSION 5.00
Begin VB.Form Devview
    Caption        =   "Device Context Viewer"
    ClientHeight   =   4065
    ClientLeft     =   1095
    ClientTop      =   1485
    ClientWidth    =   7365
    BeginProperty Font
        name           =   "MS Sans Serif"
        charset        =   0
        weight         =   700
        size           =   8.25
        underline      =   0   'False
        italic         =   0   'False
        strikethrough  =   0   'False
```

Listing 7.1   Header from file DEVVIEW.FRM (Continued)

```
EndProperty
ForeColor      =   &H80000008&
Height         =   4470
Left           =   1035
LinkMode       =   1   'Source
LinkTopic      =   "Form1"
ScaleHeight    =   4065
ScaleWidth     =   7365
Top            =   1140
Width          =   7485
Begin VB.TextBox Text1
   BackColor      =   &H00C0C0C0&
   Height         =   3855
   Left           =   120
   MultiLine      =   -1   'True
   TabIndex       =   0
   Top            =   120
   Width          =   5895
End
Begin VB.CommandButton Command1
   Caption        =   "Form"
   Height         =   495
   Left           =   6240
   TabIndex       =   1
   Top            =   120
   Width          =   975
End
Begin VB.CommandButton Command2
   Caption        =   "Printer"
   Height         =   495
   Left           =   6240
   TabIndex       =   2
   Top            =   720
   Width          =   975
End
End
Attribute VB_Name = "Devview"
Attribute VB_GlobalNameSpace = False
Attribute VB_Creatable = False
Attribute VB_PredeclaredId = True
Attribute VB_Exposed = False
```

DevView Listing

Module DEVVIEW.BAS (Listing 7.2) contains the constant declarations and global variables used by the program.

Listing 7.2   Module DEVVIEW.BAS

```
Attribute VB_Name = "DEVVIEW1"
#If Win32 Then
Declare Function GetDeviceCaps Lib "gdi32" (ByVal hDC As Long, _
ByVal nIndex As Long) As Long
#Else
Declare Function GetDeviceCaps% Lib "GDI" (ByVal hDC%, ByVal _
nIndex%)
#End If

' Global Constants used in devview
Global Const DRIVERVERSION = 0
Global Const TECHNOLOGY = 2
Global Const HORZSIZE = 4
Global Const VERTSIZE = 6
Global Const HORZRES = 8
Global Const VERTRES = 10
Global Const BITSPIXEL = 12
Global Const PLANES = 14
Global Const NUMBRUSHES = 16
Global Const NUMPENS = 18
Global Const NUMMARKERS = 20
Global Const NUMFONTS = 22
Global Const NUMCOLORS = 24
Global Const PDEVICESIZE = 26
Global Const CURVECAPS = 28
Global Const LINECAPS = 30
Global Const POLYGONALCAPS = 32
Global Const TEXTCAPS = 34
Global Const CLIPCAPS = 36
Global Const RASTERCAPS = 38
Global Const ASPECTX = 40
Global Const ASPECTY = 42
Global Const ASPECTXY = 44
Global Const LOGPIXELSX = 88
Global Const LOGPIXELSY = 90
Global Const SIZEPALETTE = 104
Global Const NUMRESERVED = 106
Global Const COLORRES = 108
```

This module also includes constants with the prefixes DT_, CC_, LC_, PC_, CP_, TC_ and RC_ which are not included here in order to save space. These constant definitions can be found in the API32.TXT file on your CD-ROM.

The DevView project displays the device information in a text control. This technique was chosen in order to make it easy to scroll information should you choose to expand the program to display additional information (you are encouraged to do so). In the DEVVIEW.FRM listing (Listing 7.3), note the use of crlf$ to insert line breaks into the text string.

Listing 7.3   **Module DEVVIEW.FRM**

```
Private Sub Command1_Click()
    LoadInfo Devview.hDC
End Sub

Private Sub Command2_Click()
    LoadInfo Printer.hDC
End Sub

'   Loads the edit box with information about the DC
'
Private Sub LoadInfo(usehDC&)
    Dim a$
    #If Win32 Then
    Dim r As Long
    Dim nhDC As Long
    #Else
    Dim r As Integer
    Dim nhDC As Integer
    #End If
    nhDC = usehDC
    Dim crlf$

    crlf$ = Chr$(13) + Chr$(10)

    r = GetDeviceCaps(nhDC, TECHNOLOGY)
    If r And DT_RASPRINTER Then a$ = "Raster Printer"
    If r And DT_RASDISPLAY Then a$ = "Raster Display"
    ' You can detect other technology types here - see the
    ' GetDeviceCaps function description for technology types
    If a$ = "" Then a$ = "Other technology"
    a$ = a$ + crlf$
    a$ = a$ + "X,Y Dimensions in pixels:" + Str$(GetDeviceCaps(nhDC, HORZRES)) _
    + "," + Str$(GetDeviceCaps(nhDC, VERTRES)) + crlf$
    a$ = a$ + "X,Y Pixels/Logical Inch:" + Str$(GetDeviceCaps(nhDC, _
    LOGPIXELSX)) + "," + Str$(GetDeviceCaps(nhDC, LOGPIXELSY)) + crlf$
    a$ = a$ + "Bits/Pixel:" + Str$(GetDeviceCaps(nhDC, BITSPIXEL)) + crlf$  '
    a$ = a$ + "Color Planes:" + Str$(GetDeviceCaps(nhDC, PLANES)) + crlf$
    a$ = a$ + "Color Table Entries:" + Str$(GetDeviceCaps(nhDC, NUMCOLORS)) + _
    crlf$
    a$ = a$ + "Aspect X,Y,XY:" + Str$(GetDeviceCaps(nhDC, ASPECTX)) + "," + _
    Str$(GetDeviceCaps (nhDC, ASPECTY)) + "," + Str$(GetDeviceCaps(nhDC, _
    ASPECTXY)) + crlf$
```

Listing 7.3   Module DEVVIEW.FRM (Continued)

```
        r = GetDeviceCaps(nhDC, RASTERCAPS)
        a$ = a$ + crlf$ + "Device capabilities:" + crlf$
        If r And RC_BANDING Then a$ = a$ + "Banding" + crlf$
        If r And RC_BIGFONT Then a$ = a$ + "Fonts >64K" + crlf$
        If r And RC_BITBLT Then a$ = a$ + "BitBlt" + crlf$
        If r And RC_BITMAP64 Then a$ = a$ + "Bitmaps >64k" + crlf$
        If r And RC_DI_BITMAP Then a$ = a$ + "Device Independent Bitmaps" + crlf$
        If r And RC_DIBTODEV Then a$ = a$ + "DIB to device" + crlf$
        If r And RC_FLOODFILL Then a$ = a$ + "Flood fill" + crlf$
        If r And RC_SCALING Then a$ = a$ + "Scaling" + crlf$
        If r And RC_STRETCHBLT Then a$ = a$ + "StretchBlt" + crlf$
        If r And RC_STRETCHDIB Then a$ = a$ + "StretchDIB" + crlf$
        Text1.Text = a$
End Sub
```

Scaling and Coordinate Systems

GDI provides extensive coordinate transformation and scaling capabilities. This is critical to providing device independence. Without such capabilities, it would be necessary for a program to take into account the resolution of each device.

Consider the task of drawing a bar chart. Without scaling and coordinate transformations, it would be necessary to determine the coordinate value of the origin, the direction of the scales, and the number of pixels or bits on each scale. A screen would typically have the origin at the upper-left corner of the screen with coordinate values increasing to the right and down. A printer might have the origin at the lower-left corner of the page with coordinate values increasing toward the top and right. The screen resolution might be anything from 640x350 to 1280x1024 or more. The printer resolution may range from a few hundred dots per inch on each axis to thousands of dots per inch on a high resolution laser printer. The complexity of the bar chart drawing program is increased by the need to determine the information about the device and then adjust every drawing operation accordingly.

Logical versus Device Coordinates

GDI solves this problem by having drawing take place into a device context that provides its own coordinate system that is independent of the actual physical device. This coordinate system is referred to as the *logical coordinate system* and it defines a *logical window* as compared to *device coordinates* that define a physical or device window.

Consider again the task of drawing a bar chart. Instead of creating a bar chart routine that handles every possible device, it is possible to create a bar chart routine that draws to a logical window. For example, the routine can be designed to draw into a 4000x3000 pixel logical coordinate system with the origin at the lower left. It is then possible to use the API scaling functions to map this logical window to any device. This principle was shown earlier in the logo example in Figures 7.1 and 7.2.

The advantage of using a very-high-resolution logical window is that it allows the graphic routines to automatically take advantage of a high-resolution device such as a printer, while still producing the best possible image on lower-resolution devices such as monitors. In the case of this bar chart routine, if the chart was designed to fit into an area 4 inches wide by 3 inches high, you would be able to take full advantage of a high resolution laser printer or low resolution image typesetting system which supports 1,000 dots-per-inch resolution. That same 4-inch display might only take up 400 pixels or so on a 100-dots-per-inch monitor. Windows will draw the image at the highest quality possible for the output device.

The bar chart routine could also be designed to use full 24-bit color. Windows will then attempt to find the nearest color match that the device supports.

This coordinate mapping system provides an additional feature that can be extremely useful to a programmer. It is possible to choose a coordinate system that is based on real physical dimensions, such as inches, centimeters, or twips (1/1440 inch). This makes it easy for a programmer to create graphics that are accurately scaled.

The accuracy of the output will vary by device. A device such as a printer, which has an exact physical resolution expressed as the number of dots per inch, can produce extremely accurate output. If the program draws a line that is one inch long in the logical coordinate system, it will appear exactly one inch long on paper.

Display monitors do not have the same precision. A 640x480 pixel display will appear different on a 13-inch monitor than it does on a 21-inch monitor. Windows does not know the size of the monitor you are using, so it defines a logical inch for displays that are usually close to a physical inch. The determination of how many display pixels are in a logical inch is made by the device driver, and can be determined using the GetDeviceCaps DC information function.

To help you understand logical inches better, run Word for Windows, or another word processing program that displays a ruler on the screen—set the scaling to 100 percent to display the document in its "actual" size. Now take a ruler and measure the length of one inch on the ruler. It is very unlikely that they will match. Now try adjusting the horizontal and vertical width of the display—the size of an inch on the screen has changed! How can this be?

The ruler on the screen is showing logical inches. If you draw a line that is one inch long on the screen, the actual display length will vary because Windows cannot know exactly how many pixels there are in an inch on the display—it has no control over your monitor size or adjustments. But if you print the line, you will see that it is exactly one inch long—Windows can determine the exact number of dots in a printed inch and can use that information to accurately render the image.

It is important to differentiate between logical and device coordinates when using Windows API functions. Logical coordinates are used for most GDI drawing operations and describe the logical window that you are drawing to. Physical or device coordinates are used for most Windows management functions and describe actual physical pixels or bits on a device. Device coordinates on a display screen are usually given as client coordinates—these coordinates are based on the client area of a window and have an origin at the upper-left corner of the client area. This contrasts with window rectangle coordinates that describe the entire window rectangle including scroll bars, captions, and menus. The different physical coordinate systems (screen, window, and client area) were described in detail in Chapter 5. The necessary parameters for each Windows function are described in the function reference.

It is possible to convert logical coordinates to and from device coordinates using the functions in Table 7.8.

Table 7.8   **Logical to Physical Coordinate Conversion Functions**

Function	Description
DPtoLP	Converts a point in the device coordinate system to the logical coordinate system for a device context
LPtoDP	Converts a point in the logical coordinate system for a device context to the physical or device coordinate system

Mapping Modes

Windows provides a number of mapping modes that define or partially define the logical coordinate system for a device context. Even though all drawing takes place in logical coordinates, the default mapping mode, MM_TEXT, is often confused with using device coordinates because it provides an exact mapping between the two. In MM_TEXT, one logical unit is equal to one device unit. The MM_ANISOTROPIC and MM_ISOTROPIC mapping modes allow you to arbitrarily define how many logical units map into a given number of physical pixels or dots. The remaining mapping modes allow you to work in real world units such as inches or millimeters. Keep in mind that images drawn in these modes will be scaled accurately only when printed—

when displayed they will use logical inches (or centimeters) whose size will depend on the display in use.

More detailed information on these mapping modes is shown in Table 7.9.

Table 7.9 **Windows Mapping Modes**

Mapping Mode	Description
MM_ANISOTROPIC	This is similar to the VB ScaleMode property being set to 0. The mapping between the logical coordinate system and the device coordinate system is completely arbitrary. Images in the logical window may be stretched or shifted in any direction when drawn.
MM_HIENGLISH	Each unit in the logical coordinate system is 0.001 inch long. The origin is at the lower-left corner of the device, with values incrementing toward the top and right.
MM_HIMETRIC	Each unit in the logical coordinate system is 0.01 millimeter long. The origin is at the lower-left corner of the device, with values incrementing toward the top and right.
MM_ISOTROPIC	The mapping between the logical coordinate system and the device coordinate system is completely arbitrary with one exception: Windows guarantees that the horizontal and vertical units represent the same physical length. For example, a line 100 units long will appear the same length regardless of whether it is horizontal or vertical. Thus a square in the logical window will appear square when drawn. Images in the logical window may be scaled and shifted in any manner.
MM_LOENGLISH	Each unit in the logical coordinate system is 0.01 inch long. The origin is at the lower-left corner of the device, with values incrementing toward the top and right.
MM_LOMETRIC	Each unit in the logical coordinate system is 0.1 millimeter long. The origin is at the lower-left corner of the device, with values incrementing toward the top and right.
MM_TEXT	This is the default mapping for a device context and is the mapping used in Visual Basic forms or picture controls regardless of the value of the VB ScaleMode property. This is similar to the ScaleMode property being set to 3. Each unit in the logical coordinate system represents one pixel in the device coordinate system. The origin is at the upper-left corner of the device increasing toward the bottom and right. The logical and device coordinate systems are thus effectively the same.
MM_TWIPS	This is similar to the VB ScaleMode property being set to 1. Each unit represents one twip (or 1/1440 inch). The origin is at the lower-left corner of the device increasing toward the top and right.

Keep in mind that setting the mapping mode and coordinate system for a device context only affects future drawing operations onto that context. Any existing image on the device remains unchanged.

Some of the Windows mapping modes correspond to the mapping modes provided by Visual Basic using the ScaleMode property. There are some critical differences between them and some subtleties when using Windows mapping modes on Visual Basic controls. One of the key differences is that Visual Basic uses floating point values to describe coordinates (thus in the VB inches scale, each unit represents one inch and fractional units are possible). Windows uses integer arithmetic in almost every case. For this reason, Windows API functions will tend to have better performance than VB drawing functions when extensive scaling is used. Another advantage of using API coordinate conversions over the Visual Basic Scaling system is that it is compatible with metafiles—one of the standard windows picture formats that is often used to build complex, scaleable images or to exchange scaleable image data between applications. Metafiles will be discussed in Chapter 8.

Windows and Viewports—Extents and Origins

The idea of a logical window has already been introduced. The height and width of the logical window are known as the *extents* of the window. It is also possible to define where in the logical window the origin lies. The origin of a logical window is the point that has X,Y coordinates of 0,0 (see Figure 7.5). This point may be located anywhere in the logical window.

The area on the device that corresponds exactly to the logical window is known as the *viewport*. The height and width of the viewport are called the viewport extents. The offset of the viewport from the device origin is known as the viewport origin.

It is essential to note that the extents and origin of the logical window do not restrict drawing to that window. In other words, it is possible to draw outside of the logical window using the same logical coordinate system. In this case, the drawing will also appear outside of the viewport. The window and viewport extents are used only to define the scaling on each axis. The window and viewport origins are used only to define the offset. The equations describing the logical-to-physical mapping are as follows:

Variable Definitions

```
DevX = device X coordinate
DevY = device Y coordinate
LogX = logical X coordinate
LogY = logical Y coordinate
xWO = logical window origin on the X axis
yWO = logical window origin on the Y axis
xWE = Logical window extents on the X axis
```

Figure 7.5

Original logo example in the context of windows and viewports

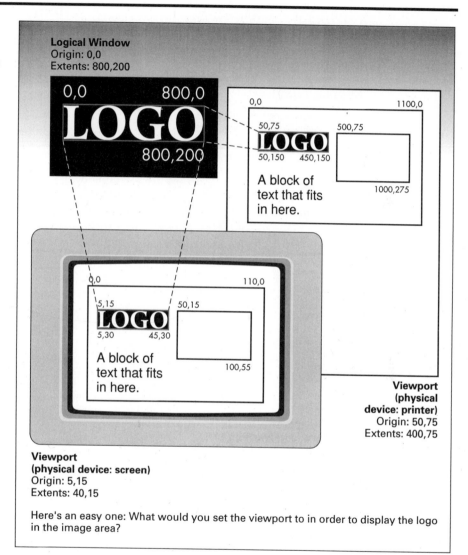

Logical Window
Origin: 0,0
Extents: 800,200

0,0   800,0

LOGO

800,200

0,0   1100,0

50,75   500,75

LOGO
50,150   450,150

A block of
text that fits
in here.

1000,275

0,0   110,0

5,15   50,15

LOGO
5,30   45,30

A block of
text that fits
in here.

100,55

**Viewport
(physical
device: printer)**
Origin: 50,75
Extents: 400,75

**Viewport
(physical device: screen)**
Origin: 5,15
Extents: 40,15

Here's an easy one: What would you set the viewport to in order to display the logo in the image area?

```
yWE = Logical window extents on the Y axis
xVO = viewport origin on the X axis (device coordinates)
yVO = viewport origin on the Y axis (device coordinates)
xVE = viewport extents on the X axis (device coordinates)
yVE = viewport extents on the Y axis (device coordinates)
```

Mapping Equations

```
DevX = (LogX - xWO) * xVE/xWE+xVO
DevY = (LogY - yWO) * yVE/yWE+yVO
LogX = (DevX - xVO) * xWE/xVE+xWO
LogY = (DevY - yVO) * yWE/yVE+yWO
```

Windows and viewport extents are used only with the
MM_ANISOTROPIC and MM_ISOTROPIC modes. The scaling in the other
mapping modes is fixed by Windows. Figures 7.6 and 7.7 illustrate possible
use of the MM_ANISOTROPIC and MM_ISOTROPIC mapping modes.

Figure 7.6

The MM_ISOTROPIC
mapping mode

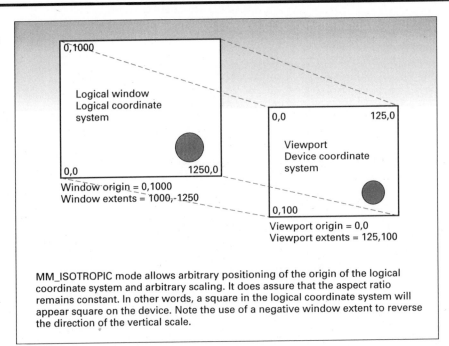

MM_ISOTROPIC mode allows arbitrary positioning of the origin of the logical
coordinate system and arbitrary scaling. It does assure that the aspect ratio
remains constant. In other words, a square in the logical coordinate system will
appear square on the device. Note the use of a negative window extent to reverse
the direction of the vertical scale.

As shown in Figure 7.6, the MM_ISOTROPIC mode allows arbitrary positioning of the origin of the logical coordinate system and arbitrary scaling. It
assures that the aspect ratio remains constant. In other words, a square in the

logical coordinate system will appear square on the device. In this figure, the viewport takes up a 125 by 100 unit area in device coordinates starting at the upper-left corner of the page or window. Only the viewport is shown in the figure. Figure 7.7 shows the viewport as part of a larger device area. Note the use of a negative window extent to reverse the direction of the vertical scale. In fact, most of the physical mapping modes place the origin at the lower-left instead of the upper-left.

Figure 7.7

The MM_ANISOTROPIC mapping mode

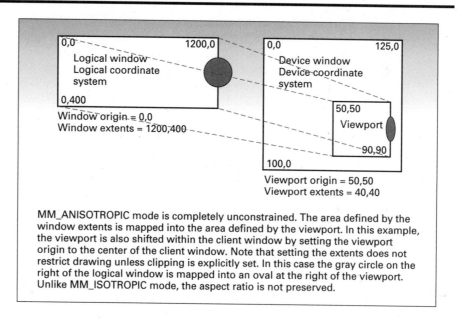

MM_ANISOTROPIC mode is completely unconstrained. The area defined by the window extents is mapped into the area defined by the viewport. In this example, the viewport is also shifted within the client window by setting the viewport origin to the center of the client window. Note that setting the extents does not restrict drawing unless clipping is explicitly set. In this case the gray circle on the right of the logical window is mapped into an oval at the right of the viewport. Unlike MM_ISOTROPIC mode, the aspect ratio is not preserved.

MM_ANISOTROPIC mode, shown in Figure 7.7, is completely unconstrained. The area defined by the window extents is mapped into the area defined by the viewport. In Figure 7.7, the viewport is also shifted within the client window by setting the viewport origin to the center of the client window. Note that setting the extents does not restrict drawing unless clipping is explicitly set. In this case the gray circle on the right of the logical window is mapped into an oval at the right of the viewport. Unlike the MM_ISOTROPIC mode, the aspect ratio is not preserved.

World Transforms

So far you have read about two layers of transformation: first, from logical window coordinates to device coordinates, where the device coordinates are defined by a viewport and are relative to the client area of a window or a printed page; and next, the internal transformation that Windows uses to convert from client coordinates to the actual screen coordinates where it ultimately needs to draw.

Windows NT adds yet another higher level coordinate system called *world coordinates*. This provides a level of transformation that lets you scale, shift, and rotate an image before drawing. The result of this transformation is logical window coordinates. For example, if you have a pixel to draw at location 20,20 in world coordinates and transform it using a world transform to location 100,100—that 100,100 refers to coordinates in the logical window. Those coordinates will then be transformed to device coordinates according to the viewport settings. Figure 7.8 illustrates the complete windows transformation scheme from world coordinates to physical device coordinates.

World coordinate transformations are one of the few places where Windows uses floating point values. The world transformation is based on a structure called the XFORM structure which is defined as follows:

```
Private Type XFORM
        eM11 As Single
        eM12 As Single
        eM21 As Single
        eM22 As Single
        eDx As Single
        eDy As Single
End Type
```

Coordinates are translated according to the following equations:

```
xNew = x * eM11 + y * eM21 + eDx
yNew = x * eM12 + y * eM22 + eDy
```

The mathematicians among you will see this as the following transformation matrix:

$$
|\ xNew,\ yNew,\ 1\ | = |\ x,\ y,\ 1\ | * \begin{vmatrix} eM11 & eM12 & 0 \\ eM21 & eM22 & 0 \\ eDx & eDy & 1 \end{vmatrix}
$$

For those of us who are not mathematicians, suffice it to say that this set of equations allows for sophisticated transformations that are not possible with the standard logical window translation scheme. The eDX and eDy terms are the easy ones—they simply offset the image by the specified amount. If you only use the eM11 and eM22 terms, simple scaling will occur—the image will be enlarged or shrunk on each access according to the values in the structure.

Figure 7.8
From world transforms to device coordinates

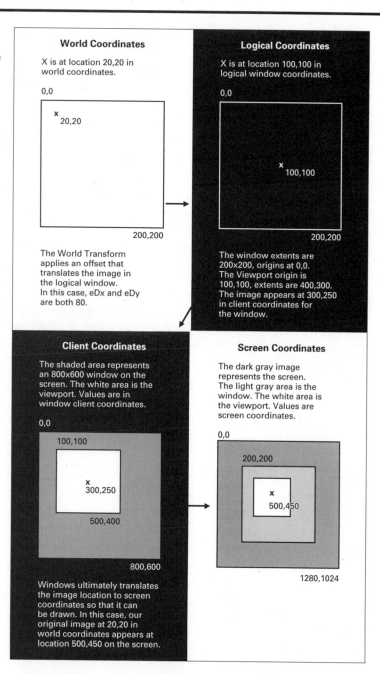

World Coordinates

X is at location 20,20 in world coordinates.

0,0

x
20,20

200,200

The World Transform applies an offset that translates the image in the logical window. In this case, eDx and eDy are both 80.

Logical Coordinates

X is at location 100,100 in logical window coordinates.

0,0

x
100,100

200,200

The window extents are 200x200, origins at 0,0. The Viewport origin is 100,100, extents are 400,300. The image appears at 300,250 in client coordinates for the window.

Client Coordinates

The shaded area represents an 800x600 window on the screen. The white area is the viewport. Values are in window client coordinates.

0,0

100,100

x
300,250

500,400

800,600

Windows ultimately translates the image location to screen coordinates so that it can be drawn. In this case, our original image at 20,20 in world coordinates appears at location 500,450 on the screen.

Screen Coordinates

The dark gray image represents the screen. The light gray area is the window. The white area is the viewport. Values are screen coordinates.

0,0

200,200

x
500,450

1280,1024

Scaling and offsets are nothing special—the standard mapping modes handle these without any problem. However, if A is an angle (specified in radians) and you assign the structure variables as follows:

```
eM11 = cos(A)
eM12 = sin(A)
eM21 = -sin(A)
eM22 = cos(A)
```

The image will be rotated by the angle specified by A. If you set the eM11 and eM22 terms to one, then use a scale factor in the eM12 and eM21 term, the image will appear sheared.

In order to use world transformation, you must first use the SetGraphicsMode function to turn on the advanced mapping mode capability of Win32. You can then use the SetWorldTransform function to specify the transform to use. The CombineTransform function allows you to combine two different transforms. This allows you to use one XFORM structure to specify rotation, a second to specify offset and scaling, and allows Windows to calculate the resulting final transform.

World transforms are very flexible, and an in-depth review of the mathematics involved is beyond the scope of this book. However, you will find a sample program called Spin.vbp in the Chapter 7 directory on the CD-ROM that comes with this book (the Spin example is not included in the chapter text). This sample allows you to experiment with different values of terms in an XFORM structure.

Beyond that, a good high school or college text on trigonometry and analytic geometry should be enough to let you take full advantage of these capabilities.

Table 7.10 summarizes the Windows API functions that are used to control the mapping of logical to device coordinates.

Table 7.10   Windows Mapping Functions

Function	Description
CombineTransform	Combines two world transforms (NT only)
GetDCOrgEx	Determines the position of the origin of the client area of a window in screen coordinates. Replaces the Win16 GetDCOrg function
GetGraphicsMode	Determines if advanced mapping modes are enabled
GetMapMode	Determines the current mapping mode of a device context
GetViewportExtEx	Obtains the extents of the specified viewport
GetViewportOrgEx	Obtains the origins of the specified viewport

Table 7.10   Windows Mapping Functions (Continued)

Function	Description
GetWindowExtEx	Obtains the extents of the specified logical window
GetWindowOrgEx	Obtains the origins of the specified logical window
GetWorldTransform	Determines the current world transform (NT only)
ModifyWorldTransform	Modifies a world transform (NT only)
OffsetViewportOrgEx	Offsets the origin of the specified viewport
OffsetWindowOrgEx	Offsets the origin of the specified window
ScaleViewportExtEx	Scales the extents of the specified viewport
ScaleWindowExtEx	Scales the extents of the specified logical window
SetGraphicsMode	Allows selection of the advanced graphics mode (NT only)
SetMapMode	Sets the mapping mode for the specified device context
SetViewportExtEx	Sets the extents of the specified viewport
SetViewportOrgEx	Sets the origin of the specified viewport
SetWindowExtEx	Sets the extents of the specified logical window
SetWindowOrgEx	Sets the origin of the specified window
SetWorldTransform	Sets the current world transform (NT only)

Windows Coordinate Systems and Visual Basic

All of the coordinate transformations described in this section work with Visual Basic windows. However, it is important to understand how Visual Basic handles scaling so as not to interfere with the correct operation of Visual Basic.

Visual Basic does not use the Windows mapping modes to control scaling. It leaves device contexts in the MM_TEXT mapping mode and does all scaling internally. This allows VB to handle floating point coordinates (unlike Windows, which uses integer coordinate values in almost every case).

As a result, when using device context mapping it is absolutely critical to restore the device context mapping mode to its original value once you are finished using API drawing functions. The easiest way to do this is by using the SaveDC and RestoreDC functions to save the original device context information. If you do not restore the original mapping mode, you will almost certainly interfere with the correct operation of Visual Basic and the display of Visual Basic graphics and some controls.

Examples of this technique, along with examples of the use of Windows mapping modes during drawing, can be found in the Viewport example, and in Chapter 8, which discusses drawing with API functions.

Platform Differences

The Windows coordinate system functions are almost identical under Win16 and Win32, and under Windows 95 and Windows NT—but there is one important difference. The Graphic Device Interface system (GDI) is implemented fully in 32 bits under Windows NT, but is still implemented in 16 bits under Windows 95. This means that while logical coordinates are specified in Win32 as 32 bit longs, allowing you to theoretically define coordinate systems with ranges up to ±2147483647 units on a side, Windows 95 only looks at the low 16 bits, limiting your coordinate systems to ±32765 units on a side. This limitation applies, naturally, to Win16 API calls as well.

Windows 95 also does not support advanced graphic modes, including, unfortunately, world transforms. Hopefully this will be changed in the future.

The Viewport Example

The Viewport example is designed to provide you with a tool for experimenting with windows and viewports under the MM_ANISOTROPIC mapping mode. Figure 7.9 shows the main program screen for this sample. The figure is shown under Windows NT in order to demonstrate coordinate rotation—a feature that was discussed earlier in this chapter and that is not supported by Windows 95.

Figure 7.9

The Viewport example main form

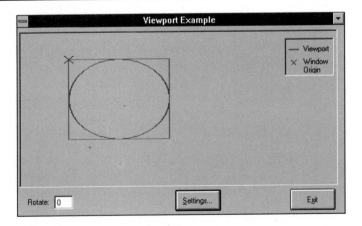

Using Viewport

Click on the main window and drag the mouse in order to define the viewport to use on the main picture control of the program. Initially the program defines the window origin as 0,0 and the extents as 100,100. The program draws a border around the window area in light blue. It then draws a rectangle and an ellipse that are 100x100 and starts at location 0,0—which serves to fill the window as well. The default is thus for the full area of the window to fill the viewport area. The Settings button brings up the frmSettings dialog box which allows you to change these default settings. This form is shown in Figure 7.10.

Figure 7.10

Viewport example dialog frmSettings dialog box

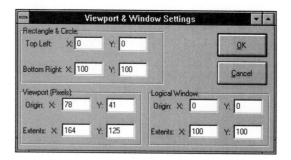

Try adjusting the rectangle origin (top,left) to 5,5 and the bottom right to 80,80. You will see how the rectangle and circle fit within the logical window. Now change the X origin of the window to 5. See how the rectangle is now bordered against the left of the window? If you set the window X origin to 5, and start drawing at an x coordinate of 5, you are clearly drawing at the left side of the window, which will in turn be mapped to the left of the viewport.

Now try changing the bottom right of the rectangle to 110, 110. See how it draws outside of the defined viewport area? This is possible because coordinate systems alone perform no clipping. Clipping will be covered later in this chapter.

Now try changing viewport values without modifying the window extents. See how the window area is placed on the picture control according to the viewport values?

Project and Form Description

The Viewport project includes two files, VIEWPORT.FRM, the main window of the program shown in Listing 7.4, and VIEWSET.FRM, the settings dialog box shown in Listing 7.5. This program is designed for 32-bit use only.

The rotation text box allows you to enter a number in degrees to use to rotate the image using the Windows NT world transformations.

Listing 7.4   **VIEWPORT.FRM**

```
VERSION 5.00
Begin VB.Form frmViewport
    BorderStyle     =   1  'Fixed Single
    Caption         =   "Viewport Example"
    ClientHeight    =   4410
    ClientLeft      =   1380
    ClientTop       =   2040
    ClientWidth     =   7920
    Height          =   4815
    Left            =   1320
    LinkTopic       =   "Form1"
    MaxButton       =   0   'False
    ScaleHeight     =   294
    ScaleMode       =   3  'Pixel
    ScaleWidth      =   528
    Top             =   1695
    Width           =   8040
    Begin VB.CommandButton cmdSettings
        Caption     =   "&Settings..."
        Default     =   -1 'True
        Height      =   495
        Left        =   3840
        TabIndex    =   4
        Top         =   3840
        Width       =   1095
    End
```

```
    Begin VB.TextBox txtRotate
        Alignment   =   1  'Right Justify
        Height      =   285
        Left        =   900
        MaxLength   =   3
        TabIndex    =   3
        Text        =   "0"
        Top         =   3960
        Visible     =   0   'False
        Width       =   435
    End
    Begin VB.CommandButton cmdExit
        Cancel      =   -1 'True
        Caption     =   "E&xit"
        Height      =   495
        Left        =   6600
        TabIndex    =   1
        Top         =   3840
        Width       =   1095
    End
```

The pctScreen control provides the main drawing area for the program.
Note that the drawing mode is set to invert mode with a dotted line. This sets
it up correctly for the rectangle dragging mode. Also note the use of the pixel
ScaleMode. This eliminates the need to convert to and from twips and makes
it easier to mix VB drawing commands with API functions.

```
Begin VB.PictureBox pctScreen
        DrawMode        =   7   'Invert
        DrawStyle       =   2   'Dot
        FillColor       =   &H00C0C0C0&
        ForeColor       =   &H000000FF&
        Height          =   3615
        Left            =   60
        ScaleHeight     =   239
        ScaleMode       =   3   'Pixel
        ScaleWidth      =   510
        TabIndex        =   0
        TabStop         =   0   'False
        Top             =   120
        Width           =   7680
```

This picture box provides a legend explaining the meanings of the symbols drawn by the program.

```
Begin VB.PictureBox Picture1
        Height          =   855
        Left            =   6420
        ScaleHeight     =   825
        ScaleWidth      =   1125
        TabIndex        =   5
        Top             =   180
        Width           =   1155
        Begin VB.Line Line3
            BorderColor     =   &H00FF0000&
            X1              =   240
            X2              =   120
            Y1              =   480
            Y2              =   600
        End
        Begin VB.Line Line2
            BorderColor     =   &H00FF0000&
            X1              =   120
            X2              =   240
            Y1              =   480
            Y2              =   600
        End
        Begin VB.Label Label2
            Caption         =   "Window Origin"
            Height          =   375
            Left            =   420
            TabIndex        =   7
```

```
         Top             =    420
         Width           =    615
         WordWrap        =    -1   'True
      End
      Begin VB.Line Line1
         BorderColor     =    &H00FFFF00&
         BorderWidth     =    2
         X1              =    60
         X2              =    300
         Y1              =    240
         Y2              =    240
      End
      Begin VB.Label Label1
         Caption         =    "Viewport"
         Height          =    255
         Left            =    420
         TabIndex        =    6
         Top             =    120
         Width           =    675
      End
   End
 End
 Begin VB.Label lblRotate
    Caption         =    "Rotate:"
    Height          =    255
    Left            =    240
    TabIndex        =    2
    Top             =    3990
    Visible         =    0     'False
    Width           =    615
 End
End
Attribute VB_Name = "frmViewport"
Attribute VB_GlobalNameSpace = False
Attribute VB_Creatable = False
Attribute VB_PredeclaredId = True
Attribute VB_Exposed = False
' Viewport example
' Copyright (c) 1995-1997, Desaware

Option Explicit
```

The current window and viewport origins and extents are kept in global variables. They are only used for drawing during the paint event itself. The XFORM structure is used for world transforms.

```
Dim dummy&
Public dviewX1!, dviewX2!, dviewY1!, dviewY2! ' anchors for the _
viewport drag
Public savedDC&, RotAngle%
Dim mySize As SIZE, myPoint As POINTAPI
Public viewOrgX&, viewOrgY&, viewExtX&, viewExtY&
```

```
Public WinOrgX&, WinOrgY&, WinExtX&, WinExtY&
Public RectX1&, RectY1&, RectX2&, RectY2&
'********************************
'**  Type Definitions:

#If Win32 Then
Private Type XFORM
        eM11 As Single
        eM12 As Single
        eM21 As Single
        eM22 As Single
        eDx As Single
        eDy As Single
End Type

Private Type SIZE
    cx As Long
    cy As Long
End Type

Private Type POINTAPI
    X As Long
    Y As Long
End Type

Private Type RECT
    Left As Long
    Top As Long
    Right As Long
    Bottom As Long
End Type
Const PS_SOLID& = 0
```

This sample is designed to run under Win32 only. No conditional compilation is necessary.

```
'********************************
'**  Function Declarations:

Private Declare Function LineTo& Lib "gdi32" (ByVal hdc As Long, ByVal X2 As _
Long, ByVal Y2 As Long)
Private Declare Function MoveToEx& Lib "gdi32" (ByVal hdc As Long, ByVal X As _
Long, ByVal Y As Long, oldPoint As POINTAPI)
Private Declare Function Rectangle& Lib "gdi32" (ByVal hdc As Long, ByVal X1 As _
Long, ByVal Y1 As Long, ByVal X2 As Long, ByVal Y2 As Long)
Private Declare Function SetWorldTransform& Lib "gdi32" (ByVal hdc As Long, _
lpXform As XFORM)
Private Declare Function ModifyWorldTransform& Lib "gdi32" (ByVal hdc As Long, _
lpXform As XFORM, ByVal iMode As Long)
```

```
Private Declare Function GetWorldTransform& Lib "gdi32" (ByVal hdc As Long, _
lpXform As XFORM)
Private Declare Function SetGraphicsMode& Lib "gdi32" (ByVal hdc As Long, ByVal _
iMode As Long)
Private Declare Function SetMapMode& Lib "gdi32" (ByVal hdc As Long, ByVal _
nMapMode As Long)
Private Declare Function LPtoDP& Lib "gdi32" (ByVal hdc As Long, lpPoint As _
POINTAPI, ByVal nCount As Long)
Private Declare Function DPtoLP& Lib "gdi32" (ByVal hdc As Long, lpPoint As _
POINTAPI, ByVal nCount As Long)
Private Declare Function GetViewportExtEx& Lib "gdi32" (ByVal hdc As Long, _
lpSize As SIZE)
Private Declare Function GetViewportOrgEx& Lib "gdi32" (ByVal hdc As Long, _
lpPoint As POINTAPI)
Private Declare Function SetViewportExtEx& Lib "gdi32" (ByVal hdc As Long, _
ByVal nX As Long, ByVal nY As Long, lpSize As SIZE)
Private Declare Function ScaleViewportExtEx& Lib "gdi32" (ByVal hdc As Long, _
ByVal nXnum As Long, ByVal nXdenom As Long, ByVal _
nYnum As Long, ByVal nYdenom As Long, lpSize As SIZE)
Private Declare Function SetViewportOrgEx& Lib "gdi32" (ByVal hdc As Long, _
ByVal nX As Long, ByVal nY As Long, lpPoint As POINTAPI)
Private Declare Function Ellipse& Lib "gdi32" (ByVal hdc As Long, ByVal X1 As _
Long, ByVal Y1 As Long, ByVal X2 As Long, ByVal Y2 As Long)
Private Declare Function SetWindowExtEx& Lib "gdi32" (ByVal hdc As Long, ByVal _
nX As Long, _
ByVal nY As Long, lpSize As SIZE)
Private Declare Function SetWindowOrgEx& Lib "gdi32" (ByVal hdc As Long, ByVal _
nX As Long, ByVal nY As Long, lpPoint As POINTAPI)
Private Declare Function GetWindowExtEx& Lib "gdi32" (ByVal hdc As Long, lpSize _
As SIZE)
Private Declare Function GetWindowOrgEx& Lib "gdi32" (ByVal hdc As Long, _
lpPoint As POINTAPI)
Private Declare Function CreatePen& Lib "gdi32" (ByVal nPenStyle As Long, ByVal _
nWidth As Long, ByVal crColor As Long)
Private Declare Function SelectObject& Lib "gdi32" (ByVal hdc As Long, ByVal _
hObject As Long)
Private Declare Function DeleteObject& Lib "gdi32" (ByVal hObject As Long)
Private Declare Function SaveDC& Lib "gdi32" (ByVal hdc As Long)
Private Declare Function RestoreDC& Lib "gdi32" (ByVal hdc As Long, ByVal _
nSavedDC As Long)
Private Declare Function ClipCursor& Lib "user32" (lpRect As RECT)
```

```
Private Declare Function ClipCursorBynum& Lib "user32" Alias "ClipCursor" _
(ByVal lpRect As Long)
Private Declare Function ClientToScreen& Lib "user32" (ByVal hWnd As Long, _
lpPoint As POINTAPI)
Private Declare Function SetROP2& Lib "gdi32" (ByVal hdc As Long, ByVal _
nDrawMode As Long)
Const GM_ADVANCED& = 2
Const MWT_IDENTITY& = 1
Const MM_ANISOTROPIC& = 8
Const MM_HIENGLISH& = 5
Const MM_HIMETRIC& = 3
Const MM_ISOTROPIC& = 7
Const R2_COPYPEN& = 13
Private Type OSVERSIONINFO
        dwOSVersionInfoSize As Long
        dwMajorVersion As Long
        dwMinorVersion As Long
        dwBuildNumber As Long
        dwPlatformId As Long
        szCSDVersion As String * 128
End Type

Const VER_PLATFORM_WIN32_NT& = 2
Const VER_PLATFORM_WIN32_WINDOWS& = 1
Private Declare Function GetVersionEx& Lib "kernel32" Alias "GetVersionExA" _
(lpVersionInformation As OSVERSIONINFO)
#End If 'WIN32

Private Sub cmdExit_Click()
    Unload Me
End Sub


Private Sub cmdSettings_Click()
    frmSettings.Show 1
End Sub
```

This sample provides a good demonstration of how to have an application degrade cleanly when a platform does not support a certain level of functionality. In this case, the code checks to see if it is running under Windows NT. If so, world transforms are possible, so the rotation option is enabled.

```
Private Sub Form_Load()
    Dim myVer As OSVERSIONINFO
    myVer.dwOSVersionInfoSize = 148
    dummy& = GetVersionEx&(myVer) 'Get all the version info
    If myVer.dwPlatformId = VER_PLATFORM_WIN32_NT Then
        txtRotate.Visible = True
        lblRotate.Visible = True
    End If
'Set the default values for all the variables controlling the painting:
```

```
                  'Viewport
                  viewOrgX& = 200&
                  viewOrgY& = 75&
                  viewExtX& = 100&
                  viewExtY& = 100&

                  'Logical Window
                  WinOrgX& = 0
                  WinOrgY& = 0
                  WinExtX& = 100
                  WinExtY& = 100

                  'Rectangle & Ellipse Dimensions
                  RectX1& = 0
                  RectY1& = 0
                  RectX2& = 100
                  RectY2& = 100

         End Sub
```

This method for dragging rectangles was introduced in the RectPlay example in Chapter 5. Note the additional use of the ClipCursor function to prevent the user from moving the cursor outside of the window while drawing the rectangle. The rectangle that is drawn defines the new viewport.

```
Private Sub pctScreen_MouseDown(Button As Integer, Shift As Integer, X As _
Single, Y As Single)
    Dim clipR As RECT, clipP As POINTAPI
    If Button And vbLeftButton Then
        'The first corner of the rectangle is recorded in the viewX1
        'and dviewY1 variables. The other corner is set to the same point.
        dviewX1! = X
        dviewY1! = Y
        dviewX2! = dviewX1!
        dviewY2! = dviewY1!

'Clip the cursor to the picture control:

        'Get the SCREEN coordinates of the form's origin
        clipP.X = 0
        clipP.Y = 0
        dummy& = ClientToScreen(Me.hWnd, clipP)

        'Set the clip rectangle
        clipR.Top = pctScreen.Top + clipP.Y ' Top of pctScreen + top of form
        clipR.Left = pctScreen.Left + clipP.X ' left of pctScreen + left of _
        form, etc.
        clipR.Right = pctScreen.Left + pctScreen.Width + clipP.X
        clipR.Bottom = pctScreen.Top + pctScreen.Height + clipP.Y
        dummy& = ClipCursor&(clipR) ' Clip the cursor to the clipR rectangle
    End If
```

```
End Sub


Private Sub pctScreen_MouseMove(Button As Integer, Shift As Integer, X As _
Single, Y As Single)
    If Button And vbLeftButton Then ' If the button is down then
        'Draw mode is XOR. We will draw a second box in the place of the
        'previous one, erasing it.
        pctScreen.Line (dviewX1!, dviewY1!)-(dviewX2!, dviewY2!), QBColor(10), B

        ' Record where we are.
        dviewX2! = X
        dviewY2! = Y

        'Draw a dotted box to simulate a dragging rectangle
        pctScreen.Line (dviewX1!, dviewY1!)-(dviewX2!, dviewY2!), QBColor(10), B
    End If
End Sub


Private Sub pctScreen_MouseUp(Button As Integer, Shift As Integer, X As Single, _
Y As Single)
    'Unclip the cursor
    dummy& = ClipCursorBynum&(0&)

    'If any of the box's dimensions are 0, then quit
    If dviewX1 = dviewX2 Or dviewY1 = dviewY2 Then Exit Sub

    'Erase the box from the screen by re-drawing it.
    pctScreen.Line (dviewX1!, dviewY1!)-(dviewX2!, dviewY2!), QBColor(10), B

    'Set the Viewport Variables to the box dimensions
    viewOrgX& = CLng(dviewX1!)
    viewOrgY& = CLng(dviewY1!)
    viewExtX& = CLng(dviewX2!) - CLng(dviewX1!)
    viewExtY& = CLng(dviewY2!) - CLng(dviewY1!)

    'Redraw the screen.
    pctScreen.Refresh
End Sub
```

The real work for this program is performed in the Paint event. The routine first saves the current state of the device context. It is then free to modify the device context attributes. The program works directly with the hDC property provided by the picture control. Since the control has the CS_OWNDC style set, it has a dedicated device context available at all times that is not shared with any other window. Even though this takes additional resources, it does improve performance since Visual Basic does not need to reinitialize the drawing attributes each time drawing takes place.

If Windows NT is running, the program first applies the world transformation, rotating the image if requested.

The routine then sets the window and viewport extents. It draws a rectangle and ellipse according to the current rectangle settings. It draws the border of the viewport by drawing a rectangle whose origin is the window origin and whose size is the windows' extents—this will by definition result in a rectangle that borders the entire logical window which will appear as bordering the entire defined viewport.

The final act of this routine is to restore the original device context settings.

```
Private Sub pctScreen_Paint()
    Dim myXform As XFORM, PI As Double, color&
    Dim cosvalue As Double, sinvalue As Double

    ' Save the DC in order not to mess up VB drawing functions
    savedDC& = SaveDC&(pctScreen.hdc)

    'Make sure the drawing mode is MM_ANISOTROPIC ( no proportions)
    dummy& = SetMapMode&(pctScreen.hdc, MM_ANISOTROPIC)

    If txtRotate.Visible Then ' If we're in NT
        ' Set the graphics mode to advanced (Enable transformations)
        dummy& = SetGraphicsMode&(pctScreen.hdc, GM_ADVANCED)

        If RotAngle% = 0 Then ' No rotate
            dummy& = ModifyWorldTransform&(pctScreen.hdc, myXform, MWT_IDENTITY)
        Else
            PI = 3.14159265358979
            ' No translation up or down
            myXform.eDx = 0!
            myXform.eDy = 0!

            'Set the matrix to the correct values
            cosvalue = Cos(CDbl(RotAngle%) * PI / CDbl(180))
            sinvalue = Sin(CDbl(RotAngle%) * PI / CDbl(180))
            myXform.eM11 = cosvalue
            myXform.eM12 = sinvalue
            myXform.eM21 = -sinvalue
            myXform.eM22 = cosvalue

            ' Enable the transformation
            dummy& = SetWorldTransform&(pctScreen.hdc, myXform)
        End If
    End If

    'Set the Logical Window to the global variables
    dummy& = SetWindowOrgEx&(pctScreen.hdc, WinOrgX&, WinOrgY&, myPoint)
    dummy& = SetWindowExtEx&(pctScreen.hdc, WinExtX&, WinExtY&, mySize)

    'Set the viewport
```

```
    dummy& = SetViewportOrgEx&(pctScreen.hdc, viewOrgX&, viewOrgY&, myPoint)
    dummy& = SetViewportExtEx&(pctScreen.hdc, viewExtX&, viewExtY&, mySize)

    'Make sure drawing mode is NOT xor (see the other Ch. 7 example)
    dummy& = SetROP2&(pctScreen.hdc, R2_COPYPEN)

    'Make sure we don't draw dotted.
    pctScreen.DrawStyle = 0 'Solid


    'Draw the rectangle with dimensions specified in global variables
    dummy& = Rectangle&(pctScreen.hdc, RectX1&, RectY1&, RectX2&, RectY2&)
    dummy& = Ellipse&(pctScreen.hdc, RectX1&, RectY1&, RectX2&, RectY2&)

    'Draw the Viewport Rectangle in a different color
    color& = pctScreen.ForeColor
    pctScreen.ForeColor = QBColor(11)
    dummy& = Rectangle&(pctScreen.hdc, WinOrgX&, WinOrgY&, _
            WinOrgX& + WinExtX&, WinOrgY& + WinExtY&)
    pctScreen.ForeColor = color&

    'Draw the Window Origin in a different color
    color& = pctScreen.ForeColor
    pctScreen.ForeColor = QBColor(1)
    dummy& = MoveToEx&(pctScreen.hdc, -4&, -4&, myPoint)
    dummy& = LineTo&(pctScreen.hdc, 4&, 4&)
    dummy& = MoveToEx&(pctScreen.hdc, -4&, 4&, myPoint)
    dummy& = LineTo&(pctScreen.hdc, 4&, -4&)
    pctScreen.ForeColor = color&


    'Restore all the changed settings.
    pctScreen.DrawStyle = 2 'Dot
    dummy& = RestoreDC(pctScreen.hdc, savedDC&)
End Sub
```

You may have noticed a few curious things about this code. First: How is it possible to change the drawing color with Visual Basic commands while using API drawing functions?

Because the subject of pens, brushes, and other drawing tools will not be covered until Chapter 8, this program cheats. It takes advantage of the fact that Visual Basic assigns a dedicated device context to each form or picture control. When you set the drawing color to a picture control by setting the ForeColor property, Visual Basic immediately creates a pen of the appropriate color and selects it for use in the device context. This means that both API calls and Visual Basic routines both start using the new color for all further drawing operations.

But the routine goes ahead and sets the color back when it is finished. Why is this necessary? Because at the end of the function the device context is restored to the state that it was in at the beginning of the function. Let's say you set the ForeColor property to blue. The device context is immediately given a blue pen to work with. Next you restore the device context to its original state. The device context goes back to its original pen, which might be black. Now you have a situation where the device context has a black pen, but the ForeColor property still thinks it's blue! This can confuse Visual Basic and lead to additional errors. This illustrates why it is so critical to undo any operations that you perform—and why (as you will see) it is often easier to use API functions to set the drawing colors when doing API drawing instead of mixing the two as shown here.

The remainder of this sample program is fairly straightforward.

```
Private Sub txtRotate_Change()
    If txtRotate = "" Then
        txtRotate = "0"
    End If
    If CInt(txtRotate) > 360 Then
        txtRotate = CStr(CInt(txtRotate Mod 360))
    End If
    RotAngle% = CInt(txtRotate)
    pctScreen.Refresh
End Sub

Private Sub txtRotate_KeyPress(KeyAscii As Integer)
    If (KeyAscii < Asc("0") Or KeyAscii > Asc("9")) And KeyAscii <> 8 Then
        KeyAscii = 0
    End If
End Sub


Private Sub txtRotate_LostFocus()
    If txtRotate = "" Then
        txtRotate = "0"
    End If
    If CInt(txtRotate) > 360 Then
        txtRotate = CStr(CInt(txtRotate Mod 360))
    End If
    RotAngle% = CInt(txtRotate)
End Sub
```

Listing 7.5   **VIEWSET.FRM**

```
VERSION 5.00
Begin VB.Form frmSettings
    Caption         =   "Viewport & Window Settings"
    ClientHeight    =   2955
    ClientLeft      =   1815
```

Listing 7.5   VIEWSET.FRM (Continued)

```
ClientTop          =    2220
ClientWidth        =    6240
Height             =    3360
Left               =    1755
LinkTopic          =    "Form1"
ScaleHeight        =    2955
ScaleWidth         =    6240
Top                =    1875
Width              =    6360
Begin VB.Frame Frame3
    Caption            =    "Rectangle && Circle:"
    Height             =    1335
    Left               =    60
    TabIndex           =    0
    Top                =    60
    Width              =    3495
    Begin VB.TextBox txtRectY2
        Height             =    315
        Left               =    2400
        TabIndex           =    4
        Text               =    "100"
        Top                =    840
        Width              =    675
    End
    Begin VB.TextBox txtRectX2
        Height             =    285
        Left               =    1320
        TabIndex           =    3
        Text               =    "100"
        Top                =    840
        Width              =    675
    End
    Begin VB.TextBox txtRectY1
        Height             =    315
        Left               =    2400
        TabIndex           =    2
        Text               =    "0"
        Top                =    240
        Width              =    675
    End
    Begin VB.TextBox txtRectX1
        Height             =    285
        Left               =    1320
        TabIndex           =    1
        Text               =    "0"
        Top                =    240
        Width              =    675
    End
```

Listing 7.5 **VIEWSET.FRM (Continued)**

```
Begin VB.Label Label7
   Caption        =   "Y: "
   Height         =   255
   Left           =   2160
   TabIndex       =   28
   Top            =   900
   Width          =   135
End
Begin VB.Label Label6
   Caption        =   "Y: "
   Height         =   255
   Left           =   2160
   TabIndex       =   27
   Top            =   300
   Width          =   135
End
Begin VB.Label Label1
   Caption        =   "Bottom Right:  X:"
   Height         =   195
   Index          =   5
   Left           =   60
   TabIndex       =   26
   Top            =   900
   Width          =   1275
End
Begin VB.Label Label1
   Caption        =   "Top Left:        X:"
   Height         =   195
   Index          =   4
   Left           =   120
   TabIndex       =   25
   Top            =   300
   Width          =   1155
End
End
Begin VB.CommandButton cmdCancel
   Cancel         =   -1  'True
   Caption        =   "&Cancel"
   Height         =   555
   Left           =   4860
   TabIndex       =   14
   Top            =   840
   Width          =   1215
End
Begin VB.CommandButton cmdOK
   Caption        =   "&OK"
   Default        =   -1  'True
   Height         =   555
```

Listing 7.5   VIEWSET.FRM (Continued)

```
            Left            =    4860
            TabIndex        =    13
            Top             =    180
            Width           =    1215
         End
         Begin VB.Frame Frame2
            Caption         =    "Viewport (Pixels):"
            Height          =    1335
            Left            =    60
            TabIndex        =    20
            Top             =    1500
            Width           =    2955
            Begin VB.TextBox txtViewOrgX
               Height       =    285
               Left         =    1020
               TabIndex     =    5
               Text         =    "200"
               Top          =    240
               Width        =    675
            End
            Begin VB.TextBox txtViewOrgY
               Height       =    315
               Left         =    2100
               TabIndex     =    6
               Text         =    "75"
               Top          =    240
               Width        =    675
            End
            Begin VB.TextBox txtViewExtX
               Height       =    285
               Left         =    1020
               TabIndex     =    7
               Text         =    "100"
               Top          =    840
               Width        =    675
            End
            Begin VB.TextBox txtViewExtY
               Height       =    315
               Left         =    2100
               TabIndex     =    8
               Text         =    "100"
               Top          =    840
               Width        =    675
            End
            Begin VB.Label Label1
               Caption      =    "Origin:   X: "
               Height       =    195
               Index        =    3
```

Listing 7.5   VIEWSET.FRM (Continued)

```
                Left            =    120
                TabIndex        =    24
                Top             =    300
                Width           =    855
             End
             Begin VB.Label Label1
                Caption         =    "Extents:    X:"
                Height          =    195
                Index           =    2
                Left            =    60
                TabIndex        =    23
                Top             =    900
                Width           =    915
             End
             Begin VB.Label Label5
                Caption         =    "Y: "
                Height          =    255
                Left            =    1860
                TabIndex        =    22
                Top             =    300
                Width           =    135
             End
             Begin VB.Label Label4
                Caption         =    "Y: "
                Height          =    255
                Left            =    1860
                TabIndex        =    21
                Top             =    900
                Width           =    135
             End
          End
          Begin VB.Frame Frame1
             Caption            =    "Logical Window:"
             Height             =    1335
             Left               =    3180
             TabIndex           =    15
             Top                =    1500
             Width              =    2955
             Begin VB.TextBox txtWinExtY
                Height          =    315
                Left            =    2100
                TabIndex        =    12
                Text            =    "100"
                Top             =    840
                Width           =    675
             End
             Begin VB.TextBox txtWinExtX
                Height          =    285
```

Listing 7.5   VIEWSET.FRM (Continued)

```
            Left          =    1020
            TabIndex      =    11
            Text          =    "100"
            Top           =    840
            Width         =    675
         End
         Begin VB.TextBox txtWinOrgY
            Height        =    315
            Left          =    2100
            TabIndex      =    10
            Text          =    "0"
            Top           =    240
            Width         =    675
         End
         Begin VB.TextBox txtWinOrgX
            Height        =    285
            Left          =    1020
            TabIndex      =    9
            Text          =    "0"
            Top           =    240
            Width         =    675
         End
         Begin VB.Label Label3
            Caption       =    "Y: "
            Height        =    255
            Left          =    1860
            TabIndex      =    19
            Top           =    900
            Width         =    135
         End
         Begin VB.Label Label2
            Caption       =    "Y: "
            Height        =    255
            Left          =    1860
            TabIndex      =    18
            Top           =    300
            Width         =    135
         End
         Begin VB.Label Label1
            Caption       =    "Extents:   X:"
            Height        =    195
            Index         =    1
            Left          =    60
            TabIndex      =    17
            Top           =    900
            Width         =    915
         End
         Begin VB.Label Label1
```

Listing 7.5   VIEWSET.FRM (Continued)

```
                Caption        =   "Origin:    X: "
                Height         =   195
                Index          =   0
                Left           =   120
                TabIndex       =   16
                Top            =   300
                Width          =   855
            End
        End
    End
Attribute VB_Name = "frmSettings"
Attribute VB_GlobalNameSpace = False
Attribute VB_Creatable = False
Attribute VB_PredeclaredId = True
Attribute VB_Exposed = False
Option Explicit


Private Sub cmdCancel_Click()
    Unload Me
End Sub


Private Sub cmdOK_Click()
    frmViewport.viewOrgX = CLng(txtViewOrgX)
    frmViewport.viewOrgY = CLng(txtViewOrgY)
    frmViewport.viewExtX = CLng(txtViewExtX)
    frmViewport.viewExtY = CLng(txtViewExtY)
    frmViewport.WinOrgX = CLng(txtWinOrgX)
    frmViewport.WinOrgY = CLng(txtWinOrgY)
    frmViewport.WinExtX = CLng(txtWinExtX)
    frmViewport.WinExtY = CLng(txtWinExtY)
    frmViewport.RectX1 = CLng(txtRectX1)
    frmViewport.RectY1 = CLng(txtRectY1)
    frmViewport.RectX2 = CLng(txtRectX2)
    frmViewport.RectY2 = CLng(txtRectY2)
    frmViewport!pctScreen.Refresh
    Unload Me
End Sub


Private Sub Form_Load()
    txtViewOrgX = CStr(frmViewport.viewOrgX&)
    txtViewOrgY = CStr(frmViewport.viewOrgY&)
    txtViewExtX = CStr(frmViewport.viewExtX&)
    txtViewExtY = CStr(frmViewport.viewExtY&)

    txtWinOrgX = CStr(frmViewport.WinOrgX&)
```

Listing 7.5 **VIEWSET.FRM (Continued)**

```
        txtWinOrgY = CStr(frmViewport.WinOrgY&)
        txtWinExtX = CStr(frmViewport.WinExtX&)
        txtWinExtY = CStr(frmViewport.WinExtY&)

        txtRectX1 = CStr(frmViewport.RectX1&)
        txtRectY1 = CStr(frmViewport.RectY1&)
        txtRectX2 = CStr(frmViewport.RectX2&)
        txtRectY2 = CStr(frmViewport.RectY2&)
End Sub
```

The following code attached to each function allows entry of numbers only. In hindsight, a control array might have been a better approach for this form. This change is left as an exercise for the reader.

```
Private Sub txtViewExtX_KeyPress(KeyAscii As Integer)
    If (KeyAscii < Asc("0") Or KeyAscii > Asc("9")) And KeyAscii <> 8 Then
        KeyAscii = 0
    End If
End Sub


Private Sub txtViewExtY_KeyPress(KeyAscii As Integer)
    If (KeyAscii < Asc("0") Or KeyAscii > Asc("9")) And KeyAscii <> 8 Then
        KeyAscii = 0
    End If
End Sub


Private Sub txtViewOrgX_KeyPress(KeyAscii As Integer)
    If (KeyAscii < Asc("0") Or KeyAscii > Asc("9")) And KeyAscii <> 8 Then
        KeyAscii = 0
    End If
End Sub


Private Sub txtViewOrgY_KeyPress(KeyAscii As Integer)
    If (KeyAscii < Asc("0") Or KeyAscii > Asc("9")) And KeyAscii <> 8 Then
        KeyAscii = 0
    End If
End Sub


Private Sub txtWinExtX_KeyPress(KeyAscii As Integer)
    If (KeyAscii < Asc("0") Or KeyAscii > Asc("9")) And KeyAscii <> 8 Then
        KeyAscii = 0
    End If
End Sub
```

```
Private Sub txtWinExtY_KeyPress(KeyAscii As Integer)
    If (KeyAscii < Asc("0") Or KeyAscii > Asc("9")) And KeyAscii <> 8 Then
        KeyAscii = 0
    End If
End Sub


Private Sub txtWinOrgX_KeyPress(KeyAscii As Integer)
    If (KeyAscii < Asc("0") Or KeyAscii > Asc("9")) And KeyAscii <> 8 Then
        KeyAscii = 0
    End If
End Sub


Private Sub txtWinOrgY_KeyPress(KeyAscii As Integer)
    If (KeyAscii < Asc("0") Or KeyAscii > Asc("9")) And KeyAscii <> 8 Then
        KeyAscii = 0
    End If
End Sub
```

Suggestions for Further Practice

- Try extending the Viewport example to handle the MM_ISOTROPIC mode. Remember to read the actual window and viewport settings—Windows may correct them in order to preserve the correct aspect ratio.

- Try adding a shear capability to supplement the rotation option.

Clipping, Regions, and Other Device Context Functions

Windows provides a number of functions for controlling the process of drawing into device contexts. These require a mechanism for specifying an area in a device context.

Regions

Just as rectangles are important for controlling Windows, regions are important for controlling device contexts. A region is a GDI object that describes an area in a device context. Each region has an object handle and, like any GDI object, should be deleted using the DeleteObject API function when it is no longer needed (see Chapter 8). This area can be as simple as a rectangle, or arbitrarily complex. It can include several areas that are detached from each other. It can include polygons and circles.

One important fact to keep in mind when working with regions is that region functions always use device client coordinates. In the course of creating graphic output, Windows applies all of the coordinate transforms (world to logical window, logical window to viewport), then tests each pixel against the current clipping region to see if it is valid to actually draw it. You saw earlier how it is possible to draw outside of the viewport (see Figure 7.7 and the Viewport example). If you wish to restrict drawing to the area of the viewport, all you need to do is create a rectangular clipping region that matches the area of the viewport, and select it as the current clipping region.

But what if you want to create complex graphic objects similar to regions for drawing in logical coordinates? To accomplish this, Win32 introduces a new drawing object called a *path*—but this is a subject for Chapter 8.

The functions used to create and manipulate regions are shown in Table 7.11.

Table 7.11 **Region Functions**

Function	Description
CombineRgn	Combines two regions in the manner specified
CreateEllipticRgn	Creates circular and elliptical regions
CreateEllipticRgnIndirect	
CreatePolygonRgn	Creates a region out of one or more polygons
CreatePolyPolygonRgn	
CreateRectRgn	Creates rectangular regions
CreateRectRgnIndirect	
CreateRoundRectRgn	Creates a region from a rectangle with rounded corners
EqualRgn	Determines if two regions are equal
ExtCreateRegion	Allows you to apply a transform to a region
GetRgnBox	Obtains a rectangle that bounds the specified region

Table 7.11   **Region Functions (Continued)**

Function	Description
GetRegionData	Retrieves data describing a region
OffsetRgn	Offsets the specified region
PtInRegion	Determines if a point is inside the specified region
RectInRegion	Determines if any part of a rectangle is in the specified region
SetRectRgn	Changes the specified region to describe a rectangular area

Clipping

It is possible to restrict the drawing to a device context to specific parts of the logical window. This can be intuitively seen by the fact that when you draw graphics onto a Visual Basic form, it will not draw over the form's controls unless clipping is explicitly disabled by setting the ClipControls property to FALSE. Windows excludes the area covered by controls from the drawing area of the form's device context. This process is known as *clipping* and the drawing area is referred to as the *clipping region*. Clipping is also useful during drawing to create a variety of graphic events. This will be illustrated in the Region project that is described later in this chapter.

Clipping was discussed earlier in this chapter. Table 7.12 lists the device context clipping functions.

Table 7.12   **Region Clipping Functions**

Function	Description
ExcludeClipRect	Excludes the specified rectangle from the clipping region
ExtSelectClipRegion	Combines a region with the current clipping region
GetClipBox	Retrieves a rectangle that bounds the clipping region
GetClipRgn	Retrieves the current clipping region
GetWindowRgn	Retrieves the clipping area for a window
IntersectClipRect	Sets the clipping region to the intersection of the current region and the specified rectangle

Table 7.12 **Region Clipping Functions (Continued)**

Function	Description
OffsetClipRgn	Offsets the clipping region by a specified amount
PtVisible	Determines if the specified point is visible (lies within the current clipping region)
RectVisible	Determines if any part of the specified rectangle is visible (lies within the current clipping region)
SelectClipPath	Selects a path to be the clipping region for the specified device context
SelectClipRgn	Selects a region to be the clipping region for the specified device context
SetWindowRgn	Sets the clipping area for a window; lets you create arbitrarily shaped windows

Validation and Other Device Context Functions

Chapters 2 and 5 discussed the process of updating windows and described how part of a window may be invalidated for update at some future time. Just as rectangle functions are used to invalidate all or part of a window, region functions can be used to invalidate or validate all or part of a device context. Table 7.13 lists these functions.

Table 7.13 **Device Context Validation Functions**

Function	Description
ExcludeUpdateRgn	Excludes the invalidated parts of the window (the update region) from the clipping region. This can be used to prevent drawing to those parts of the window that will be updated later by Windows.
FillRgn	Fills a region with a specified color.
FrameRgn	Draws a border around a region.
GetBoundsRect	Retrieves the bounding rectangle. Refer to the function reference in this chapter for information on this function.
GetUpdateRgn	Obtains a region describing the invalid area in the window.
InvalidateRgn	Invalidates the specified region in the device context.

Table 7.13   **Device Context Validation Functions**

Function	Description
PaintRgn	Fills a region with the current background color.
ScrollDC	Scrolls a region within a device context.
SetBoundsRect	Sets (or clears) the bounding rectangle.
ValidateRgn	Validates the specified region in the device context.

Performance Considerations

When Windows is drawing into a device context, it is necessary to check every pixel to see if it is within the clipping region. This means that clipping may have a significant impact on performance. This is, in fact, the reason that Visual Basic provides a ClipControls property. Setting this property to FALSE can dramatically improve drawing speed on a form or picture control that contains child controls. When clipping is used, it is always advisable to use rectangular clipping regions if possible.

Example: Region

Those of you who have the original Visual Basic Programmer's Guide to the Windows API (16-bit edition) have probably noticed that this book has many new examples in addition to 32-bit versions of the original sample programs. In this case, the original ClipView sample program has been completely discarded to make way for a more sophisticated region demonstration program. The Region example illustrates how to create regions, how to combine them, and how to perform clipping with them in order to create interesting graphic effects. Figure 7.11 shows the main form of the region program in action. Figure 7.12 shows the results of the "Combine and Clip Selected" option.

Using Region

The main screen of the region program shows five different regions, a simple rectangular region, an ellipse, a polygon (in this case, a star), and a rounded rectangle. It also shows a complex polygon region. You can select or deselect any of these regions by clicking on them—selected regions are indicated by a thick outline around the region. Be patient when you click on the complex region—it can take quite a while for the region border to be drawn, especially on a slower system.

When you click on the "Combine and Clip Selected" button, all of the selected regions are combined into a single region that is made into the clipping

Figure 7.11

Main form for the
Region example

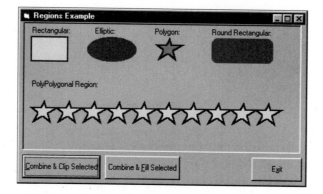

Figure 7.12

Form demonstrating
graphic effects
possible with clipping

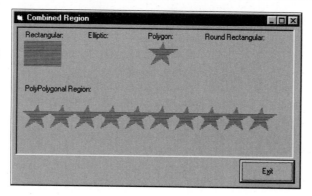

region for the frmCombine form. The paint event for the form proceeds to draw a series of horizontal lines across the form which will be clipped to the clipping region producing the image shown in Figure 7.12. When you click on the "Combine and Fill Selected" button, the regions are combined and filled.

Project and Form Description

The Region project includes three files (Listing 7.6, Listing 7.7, and Listing 7.8). REGION.FRM is the main form of the project. FRMCOMB.FRM is the form used to show region combination effects and MODREG.BAS contains the API constant and function declarations. Region is designed to run on both 16- and 32-bit versions of Visual Basic, providing yet another example of a common code base running on both platforms.

Listing 7.6   **MODREG.BAS**

```
Attribute VB_Name = "modRegion"
Option Explicit

Public Const rRECT = 0
Public Const rROUNDRECT = 1
Public Const rELLIPTIC = 2
Public Const rPOLYGON = 3
Public Const rPOLYPOLYGON = 4
```

In most cases, constants are the same under Win16 and Win32. If you use the ListAPI add-in that comes with this book to generate constant and function declarations, you may wish to remove some of the conditional compilation terms where the constants are identical. Note, however, that due to the nature of conditional compilation, all this will do is reduce the size of your source file. It will have no effect on the executable, as constants outside of the scope of the current compilation are simply ignored.

```
'*****************************************************************
#If Win32 Then
Public Const ALTERNATE = 1
Public Const WINDING = 2
Public Const RGN_AND = 1
Public Const RGN_COPY = 5
Public Const RGN_DIFF = 4
Public Const RGN_OR = 2
Public Const RGN_XOR = 3
#Else
Public Const ALTERNATE = 1
Public Const WINDING = 2
Public Const RGN_AND = 1
Public Const RGN_COPY = 5
Public Const RGN_DIFF = 4
Public Const RGN_OR = 2
Public Const RGN_XOR = 3
#End If 'WIN32


#If Win32 Then

Public Type POINTAPI
    X As Long
    Y As Long
End Type
```

```vb
Public Type RECT
    Left As Long
    Top As Long
    Right As Long
    Bottom As Long
End Type
#Else
Public Type RECT
    Left As Integer
    Top As Integer
    Right As Integer
    Bottom As Integer
End Type

Public Type POINTAPI
    X As Integer
    Y As Integer
End Type
#End If 'WIN32 Types



#If Win32 Then
Public Declare Function RestoreDC& Lib "gdi32" (ByVal hDC As Long, ByVal _
nSavedDC As Long)
Public Declare Function SaveDC& Lib "gdi32" (ByVal hDC As Long)
Public Declare Function PaintRgn& Lib "gdi32" (ByVal hDC As Long, ByVal hRgn As _
Long)
Public Declare Function CombineRgn& Lib "gdi32" (ByVal hDest As Long, ByVal _
hSrc1 As Long, ByVal hsrc2 As Long, ByVal fHow As Long)
Public Declare Function CreateEllipticRgn& Lib "gdi32" (ByVal X1 As Long, ByVal _
Y1 As Long, ByVal X2 As Long, ByVal Y2 As Long)
Public Declare Function CreatePolygonRgn& Lib "gdi32" (lpPoint As POINTAPI, _
ByVal nCount As Long, ByVal nPolyFillMode As Long)
Public Declare Function CreatePolyPolygonRgn& Lib "gdi32" (lpPoint As POINTAPI, _
lpPolyCounts As Long, ByVal nCount As Long, ByVal nPolyFillMode As Long)
Public Declare Function CreateRectRgn& Lib "gdi32" (ByVal X1 As Long, ByVal Y1 _
As Long, ByVal X2 As Long, ByVal Y2 As Long)
Public Declare Function CreateRoundRectRgn& Lib "gdi32" (ByVal X1 As Long, _
ByVal Y1 As Long, ByVal X2 As Long, ByVal Y2 As Long, ByVal X3 As Long, _
ByVal Y3 As Long)
Public Declare Function FrameRgn& Lib "gdi32" (ByVal hDC As Long, ByVal hRgn As _
```

```
Long, ByVal hBrush As Long, ByVal nWidth As Long, ByVal nHeight As Long)
Public Declare Function SelectClipRgn& Lib "gdi32" (ByVal hDC As Long, ByVal _
hRgn As Long)
Public Declare Function PtInRegion& Lib "gdi32" (ByVal hRgn As Long, ByVal X As _
Long, ByVal Y As Long)
Public Declare Function DeleteObject& Lib "gdi32" (ByVal hObject As Long)
Public Declare Function CreateSolidBrush& Lib "gdi32" (ByVal crColor As Long)
#Else
Public Declare Function SaveDC% Lib "GDI" (ByVal hDC As Integer)
Public Declare Function RestoreDC% Lib "GDI" (ByVal hDC As Integer, ByVal _
nSavedDC As Integer)
Public Declare Function CombineRgn% Lib "GDI" (ByVal hDestRgn As Integer, ByVal _
hSrcRgn1 As Integer, ByVal hSrcRgn2 As Integer, ByVal nCombineMode As Integer)
Public Declare Function CreateEllipticRgn% Lib "GDI" (ByVal X1 As Integer, _
ByVal Y1 As Integer, ByVal X2 As Integer, ByVal Y2 As Integer)
Public Declare Function CreatePolygonRgn% Lib "GDI" (lpPoints As POINTAPI, _
ByVal nCount As Integer, ByVal nPolyFillMode As Integer)
Public Declare Function CreatePolyPolygonRgn% Lib "GDI" (lpPoints As POINTAPI, _
lpPolyCounts As Integer, ByVal nCount As Integer, ByVal nPolyFillMode As Integer
Public Declare Function CreateRectRgn% Lib "GDI" (ByVal X1 As Integer, ByVal Y1 _
As Integer, ByVal X2 As Integer, ByVal Y2 As Integer)
Public Declare Function CreateRoundRectRgn% Lib "GDI" (ByVal X1 As Integer, _
ByVal Y1 As Integer, ByVal X2 As Integer, ByVal Y2 As Integer, ByVal X3 _
As Integer, ByVal Y3 As Integer)
Public Declare Function CreateSolidBrush% Lib "GDI" (ByVal crColor As Long)
Public Declare Function DeleteObject% Lib "GDI" (ByVal hObject As Integer)
Public Declare Function FrameRgn% Lib "GDI" (ByVal hDC As Integer, ByVal hRgn _
As Integer, ByVal hBrush As Integer, ByVal nWidth As Integer, ByVal nHeight _
As Integer)
Public Declare Function PtInRegion% Lib "GDI" (ByVal hRgn As Integer, ByVal X _
As Integer, ByVal Y As Integer)
Public Declare Function SelectObject% Lib "GDI" (ByVal hDC As Integer, ByVal _
hObject As Integer)
Public Declare Function PaintRgn% Lib "GDI" (ByVal hDC As Integer, ByVal hRgn _
As Integer)
Public Declare Function SelectClipRgn% Lib "GDI" (ByVal hDC%, ByVal hRgn%)
#End If 'WIN32
```

Listing 7.7   REGION.FRM

As common in many of these sample programs, the ScaleMode is set to pixels in order to make it easy to combine Visual Basic functions with API functions.

```
VERSION 5.00
Begin VB.Form frmRegion
    Caption         =   "Regions Example"
    ClientHeight    =   3735
    ClientLeft      =   1185
    ClientTop       =   1575
    ClientWidth     =   6840
    Height          =   4140
    Left            =   1125
    LinkTopic       =   "Form1"
    ScaleHeight     =   249
    ScaleMode       =   3   'Pixel
    ScaleWidth      =   456
    Top             =   1230
    Width           =   6960
    Begin VB.CommandButton cmdExit
        Cancel      =   -1  'True
        Caption     =   "E&xit"
        Height      =   555
        Left        =   5580
        TabIndex    =   8
        Top         =   3120
        Width       =   1215
    End
    Begin VB.CommandButton cmdCombine
        Caption     =   "Combine && &Fill Selected"
        Height      =   555
        Index       =   0
        Left        =   2040
        TabIndex    =   7
        Top         =   3120
        Width       =   1815
    End
    Begin VB.CommandButton cmdCombine
        Caption     =   "&Combine && Clip Selected"
        Default     =   -1  'True
        Height      =   555
        Index       =   1
        Left        =   60
        TabIndex    =   6
        Top         =   3120
        Width       =   1875
    End
    Begin VB.PictureBox picOut
```

Listing 7.7 **REGION.FRM (Continued)**

```
DrawWidth        =    2
FillColor        =    &H0000FFFF&
FillStyle        =    0    'Solid
ForeColor        =    &H00FF00FF&
Height           =    3015
Left             =    60
ScaleHeight      =    197
ScaleMode        =    3    'Pixel
ScaleWidth       =    442
TabIndex         =    0
Top              =    0
Width            =    6690
Begin VB.Label Label1
   Caption       =    "PolyPolygonal Region:"
   Height        =    195
   Left          =    180
   TabIndex      =    5
   Top           =    1320
   Width         =    1695
End
Begin VB.Label lblRoundRect
   Caption       =    "Round Rectangular:"
   Height        =    195
   Left          =    4500
   TabIndex      =    4
   Top           =    60
   Width         =    1515
End
Begin VB.Label lblPolygon
   Caption       =    "Polygon:"
   Height        =    195
   Left          =    3120
   TabIndex      =    3
   Top           =    60
   Width         =    1275
End
Begin VB.Label lblElliptic
   Caption       =    "Elliptic:"
   Height        =    195
   Left          =    1680
   TabIndex      =    2
   Top           =    60
   Width         =    855
End
Begin VB.Label lblRect
   Caption       =    "Rectangular:"
   Height        =    195
   Left          =    180
```

Listing 7.7   **REGION.FRM (Continued)**

```
            TabIndex       =  1
            Top            =  60
            Width          =  1035
         End
      End
End
Attribute VB_Name = "frmRegion"
Attribute VB_GlobalNameSpace = False
Attribute VB_Creatable = False
Attribute VB_PredeclaredId = True
Attribute VB_Exposed = False
' region sample program
' Copyright (c) 1996-1997 by Desaware Inc.
```

We keep a number of handles around during the execution of the program. There is an array of five regions that is used to display the regions in the main form, and a variable to hold the combined region.

```
Option Explicit
Dim rSelected%(4) ' Array indicating selection state
#If Win32 Then
Dim hRegions(4) As Long ' Array of regions
Dim hCombined&  ' Combined region
#Else
Dim hRegions(4) As Integer
Dim hCombined As Integer
#End If
```

Polygon regions are among the more complex—they are made up of arrays of points. You should always create regions from closed polygons (the final point coordinate is the same as the first). The CreatePolyPolygonRgn function in Win32 will automatically close the polygon for you, but the Win16 version will not. Detailed information for working with polygons will be presented in Chapter 8 along with the polygon drawing functions.

```
'
' Initialize a bunch of regions
'
Private Sub Form_Load()
    Dim myPolygon(5) As POINTAPI
    Dim myPolyPolygon() As POINTAPI
    #If Win32 Then
        Dim myPolyCount() As Long
        Dim hPPRegion As Long, hTRegion As Long
    #Else
        Dim myPolyCount() As Integer
        Dim hPPRegion As Integer, hTRegion As Integer
```

```
#End If
Dim PPCount%
Dim i%, j%

'Polygon region  - This draws a star
myPolygon(0).X = 233:  myPolygon(0).Y = 19
myPolygon(1).X = 212:  myPolygon(1).Y = 57
myPolygon(2).X = 257:    myPolygon(2).Y = 31
myPolygon(3).X = 209:    myPolygon(3).Y = 31
myPolygon(4).X = 244:    myPolygon(4).Y = 57
myPolygon(5).X = 233:    myPolygon(5).Y = 19
hRegions(rPOLYGON) = CreatePolygonRgn(myPolygon(0), 6, WINDING)

'Poly-Polygon region

PPCount% = 10
ReDim myPolyPolygon(PPCount% * 6 - 1)
ReDim myPolyCount(PPCount% - 1)

' Copy the star 10 times
For i% = 0 To 5
    For j% = 0 To PPCount% - 1
        myPolyPolygon(i% + j% * 6).X = myPolygon(i%).X - 200 + 40 * j%
        myPolyPolygon(i% + j% * 6).Y = myPolygon(i%).Y + 100
    Next j%
     myPolyPolygon(i% + 5).X = myPolygon(i%).X - 200
     myPolyPolygon(i% + 5).Y = myPolygon(i%).Y + 100
Next i%

For i% = 0 To PPCount% - 1
    myPolyCount(i%) = 6
Next i%

hRegions(rPOLYPOLYGON) = CreatePolyPolygonRgn(myPolyPolygon(0), _
myPolyCount(0), _
PPCount%, WINDING)

'Rectangle
hRegions(rRECT) = CreateRectRgn(10, 20, 70, 60)

'Ellipse
hRegions(rELLIPTIC) = CreateEllipticRgn(100, 20, 180, 60)

'Round-Rect
hRegions(rROUNDRECT) = CreateRoundRectRgn(300, 20, 400, 60, 20, 20)
End Sub
```

The PtInRegion function allows you to quickly determine if a point is in a region. This technique could easily be extended to perform complex hit detection in a graphic program.

```
Private Sub picOut_MouseDown(Button As Integer, Shift As Integer, X As Single, _
```

```
Y As Single)
    Dim myX As Long, myY As Long, i%, inAny%
    myX = CLng(X)
    myY = CLng(Y)

    For i% = 0 To 4
        If PtInRegion(hRegions(i%), myX, myY) Then
            rSelected%(i%) = Not rSelected%(i%)
            inAny% = True
            Exit For
        End If
    Next i%

    ' Right button on non-region area deselects all
    If (Not inAny%) And (Button And vbRightButton) Then
        For i% = 0 To 4
            rSelected%(i%) = 0
        Next i%
    End If

    picOut.Refresh
End Sub
```

The Paint routine demonstrates how regions can be used for drawing. The PaintRgn function uses the background color brush currently selected into the device context which is set by the FillColor property in much the same way as the drawing pen color is set by the ForeColor property. The FrameRgn function, which is used to draw a border around a region, requires a brush object which is created using the CreateSolidBrush function. Drawing objects such as brushes is discussed in detail in Chapter 8. You might notice that no effort is made to save the current state of the device context and restore it afterward. This is because none of the API functions in this routine modify the state of the device context. Setting the FillColor does, but it is a VB property—and it is quite obvious that changing the state of a device context using a Visual Basic property cannot possibly conflict with Visual Basic.

```
Private Sub picOut_Paint()
#If Win32 Then
    Dim hBrush As Long
#Else
    Dim hBrush As Integer
#End If

    hBrush = CreateSolidBrush(QBColor(0))

    picOut.FillColor = QBColor(14) 'Yellow
    dl = PaintRgn(picOut.hDC, hRegions(rRECT))
    If rSelected%(rRECT) Then dl = FrameRgn(picOut.hDC, hRegions(rRECT), _
    hBrush, 2, 2)
```

```
    picOut.FillColor = QBColor(12) 'Red
    dl = PaintRgn(picOut.hDC, hRegions(rELLIPTIC))
    If rSelected%(rELLIPTIC) Then dl = FrameRgn(picOut.hDC, _
    hRegions(rELLIPTIC), hBrush, 2, 2)

    picOut.FillColor = QBColor(10) 'Green
    dl = PaintRgn(picOut.hDC, hRegions(rPOLYGON))
    If rSelected%(rPOLYGON) Then dl = FrameRgn(picOut.hDC, hRegions(rPOLYGON), _
    hBrush, 2, 2)

    picOut.FillColor = QBColor(11) 'Cyan
    dl = PaintRgn(picOut.hDC, hRegions(rROUNDRECT))
    If rSelected%(rROUNDRECT) Then dl = FrameRgn(picOut.hDC, _
    hRegions(rROUNDRECT), hBrush, 2, 2)

    picOut.FillColor = QBColor(9) 'Blue
    dl = PaintRgn(picOut.hDC, hRegions(rPOLYPOLYGON))
    Screen.MousePointer = vbHourglass
    picOut.Enabled = False
    If rSelected%(rPOLYPOLYGON) Then dl = FrameRgn(picOut.hDC, _
    hRegions(rPOLYPOLYGON), hBrush, 2, 2)
    picOut.Enabled = True
    Screen.MousePointer = vbDefault

    dl = DeleteObject(hBrush)
End Sub
```

If more than one region is selected when one of the combined region commands is invoked, a single region is chosen, and the others are combined with it using the CombineRgn command.

```
'
' Combine selected regions into one region
' Index 0 means combine and fill the selected regions
' Index 1 means clip to the combined region
Private Sub cmdCombine_Click(Index As Integer)
    Dim i%, fAnySelected As Integer, WhichSelected%
    WhichSelected% = -1

    ' Count the number selected, and determine which is first
    For i% = 0 To 4
        If rSelected%(i%) = True Then
            fAnySelected = fAnySelected + 1
            If WhichSelected% = -1 Then WhichSelected% = i%
        End If
    Next i%
```

```
        Select Case fAnySelected
            Case 0:
                MsgBox "No regions are selected!", vbCritical, "Error:"
            Case 1:
                Load frmCombine
                ' Debug.Print hRegions(WhichSelected%)
                frmCombine.Initialize Index, hRegions(WhichSelected%)
            Case Else:
                If hCombined <> 0 Then
                    dl = DeleteObject(hCombined)
                End If
                hCombined = CreateRectRgn(0, 0, 0, 0)
                ' This is one way to copy a region
                dl = CombineRgn(hCombined, hRegions(WhichSelected%), hCombined, _
                RGN_DIFF)
                ' Combine in the rest of the regions
                For i% = WhichSelected% + 1 To 4
                    If rSelected%(i%) = True Then
                        dl = CombineRgn(hCombined, hCombined, hRegions(i%), RGN_OR)
                    End If
                Next i%
                Load frmCombine
                frmCombine.Initialize Index, hCombined
        End Select
End Sub

Private Sub cmdExit_Click()
    Unload Me
End Sub
```

Regions are GDI objects, which are not automatically deleted under Win16, so it is absolutely necessary to delete any objects you create to avoid resource leaks. Under Win32, resources are associated to applications where possible, so the risk of resource leaks is lessened, but this is nonetheless good programming practice and should be followed even under Win32.

```
'
' Be sure to delete objects
'
Private Sub Form_Unload(Cancel As Integer)
    Dim i%
    For i% = 0 To 4
        dl = DeleteObject(hRegions(i%))
    Next i%
    ' Delete combined region if it exists
    If hCombined <> 0 Then dl = DeleteObject(hCombined)
End Sub
```

Listing 7.8   **FRMCOMB.FRM**

The labels on this form duplicate those on the Region form.

```
VERSION 5.00
Begin VB.Form frmCombine
   Caption         =   "Combined Region"
   ClientHeight    =   3735
   ClientLeft      =   1500
   ClientTop       =   3465
   ClientWidth     =   6870
   Height          =   4140
   Left            =   1440
   LinkTopic       =   "Form2"
   ScaleHeight     =   249
   ScaleMode       =   3  'Pixel
   ScaleWidth      =   458
   Top             =   3120
   Width           =   6990
   Begin VB.PictureBox picCombined
      FillColor    =   &H0000FFFF&
      FillStyle    =   0  'Solid
      ForeColor    =   &H00FF00FF&
      Height       =   3015
      Left         =   60
      ScaleHeight  =   197
      ScaleMode    =   3  'Pixel
      ScaleWidth   =   442
      TabIndex     =   1
      Top          =   60
      Width        =   6690
      Begin VB.Label Label1
         Caption   =   "PolyPolygonal Region:"
         Height    =   195
         Left      =   180
         TabIndex  =   6
         Top       =   1320
         Width     =   1695
      End
      Begin VB.Label lblRoundRect
         Caption   =   "Round Rectangular:"
         Height    =   195
         Left      =   4500
         TabIndex  =   5
         Top       =   60
         Width     =   1515
      End
      Begin VB.Label lblPolygon
         Caption   =   "Polygon:"
         Height    =   195
         Left      =   3120
```

Listing 7.8   FRMCOMB.FRM (Continued)

```
                TabIndex      =    4
                Top           =    60
                Width         =    1275
            End
            Begin VB.Label lblElliptic
                Caption       =    "Elliptic:"
                Height        =    195
                Left          =    1680
                TabIndex      =    3
                Top           =    60
                Width         =    855
            End
            Begin VB.Label lblRect
                Caption       =    "Rectangular:"
                Height        =    195
                Left          =    180
                TabIndex      =    2
                Top           =    60
                Width         =    1035
            End
        End
        Begin VB.CommandButton cmdExit
            Cancel        =    -1   'True
            Caption       =    "E&xit"
            Default       =    -1   'True
            Height        =    555
            Left          =    5460
            TabIndex      =    0
            Top           =    3120
            Width         =    1335
        End
    End
Attribute VB_Name = "frmCombine"
Attribute VB_GlobalNameSpace = False
Attribute VB_Creatable = False
Attribute VB_PredeclaredId = True
Attribute VB_Exposed = False
Option Explicit
Dim fClip As Integer, dl
Dim hCombinedRegion As Long

Public Sub Initialize(CmdButton As Integer, useRegion As Long)
    Select Case CmdButton
        Case 0
            fClip = False
        Case 1
            fClip = True
    End Select
```

Listing 7.8 **FRMCOMB.FRM (Continued)**

```
        ' Don't delete this copy - it's owned by the other form.
        hCombinedRegion = useRegion
        Me.Show 1
    End Sub

    Private Sub cmdExit_Click()
        Unload Me
    End Sub
```

Once a clipping region is selected into a device context, only graphic output within the clipping region will appear, as demonstrated by this function. Selecting a clipping region does change the state of the device context, so it is necessary to restore the previous DC state before exiting the function.

```
Private Sub picCombined_Paint()
    Dim savedDC, i%
    If Not fClip Then
        picCombined.FillColor = QBColor(13) 'Magenta
        dl = PaintRgn(picCombined.hDC, hCombinedRegion)
    Else
        savedDC = SaveDC(picCombined.hDC)
        dl = SelectClipRgn(picCombined.hDC, hCombinedRegion)
        picCombined.ForeColor = QBColor(13)
        ' Draw a bunch of horizontal lines to illustrate clipping
        For i% = 1 To 300 Step 2
            picCombined.Line (0, i%)-(500, i%)
        Next i%
        picCombined.ForeColor = QBColor(0)
        dl = RestoreDC(picCombined.hDC, savedDC)
    End If
End Sub
```

Suggestions for Further Practice

- Extend the Viewport example by using a clipping region to restrict output to the actual viewport.

- Create a clipping region that you can drag around by clicking on it and moving the mouse.

- Create a single window that takes up two separate areas on the screen. (Hint: Look in the Function Reference at the SetWindowRgn function and the Round.vbp project.)

Function Reference

■ CombineRgn

VB Declaration
```
Declare Function CombineRgn& Lib "gdi32" (ByVal hDestRgn As Long, ByVal _
hSrcRgn1 As Long, ByVal hSrcRgn2 As Long, ByVal nCombineMode As Long)
```

Description Combines two regions to form a new region.

Use with VB No problem.

Parameter	Type/Description
hDestRgn	Long—Handle to a region that will contain the combined result.
hSrcRgn1	Long—First source region.
hSrcRgn2	Long—Second source region.
nCombineMode	Long—Method in which to combine the two regions. May be one of the following constants defined in API32.TXT: RGN_AND: hDestRgn is set to the intersection of the two source regions (the area common to both). RGN_COPY: hDestRgn is set to a copy of hSrcRgn1. RGN_DIFF: hDestRgn is set to the area in hSrcRgn1 that is not present in hSrcRgn2. RGN_OR: hDestRgn is set to the union of the two source regions (the area that appears in either source region). RGN_XOR: hDestRgn is the exclusive OR (XOR) of the two source regions (the area that appears in either source region, but not both).

Return Value Long—Returns one of the following constants:

1. COMPLEXREGION: If the region has borders that overlap each other.

2. SIMPLEREGION: If the borders of the region do not overlap each other.

3. NULLREGION: If the region is empty.

4. ERRORAPI: If the combined region could not be created.

Platform Windows 95, Windows NT, Win16

Example Region.vbp

■ CombineTransform

VB Declaration
```
Declare Function CombineTransform& Lib "gdi32" (lpxformResult As xform, _
lpxform1 As xform, lpxform2 As xform)
```

Description Derives a world transformation that is equivalent to applying two transforms in sequence.

Use with VB	No problem.	
	Parameter	**Type/Description**
	lpxformResult	xform—Structure to hold resulting transform.
	lpxform1	xform—First transform in sequence.
	lpxform2	xform—Second transform in sequence.

Return Value	Long—TRUE (nonzero) on success, zero on failure.
Platform	Windows NT

■ CreateCompatibleDC

VB Declaration   `Declare Function CreateCompatibleDC& Lib "gdi32" (ByVal hdc As Long)`

Description   Creates a memory device context that is compatible with the specified device context.

Use with VB   Refer to "Using Device Contexts with Visual Basic," earlier in this chapter.

	Parameter	**Type/Description**
	hdc	Long—Handle to a device context. The new device context will be compatible with this one. May be zero to create a device context compatible with the screen.

Return Value   Long—A handle to the new device context or zero on error.

Platform   Windows 95, Windows NT, Win16

Comments   A bitmap needs to be selected for this device context before it can be drawn on. The device context should be deleted with the DeleteDC function when it is no longer needed. All objects selected into the DC should be unselected and replaced with the original selected objects before the device context is deleted.

Example   Puzzle.vbp in Chapter 9.

■ CreateDC, CreateDCBynum

VB Declaration
```
Declare Function CreateDC& Lib "gdi32" Alias "CreateDCA" (ByVal lpDriverName As _
String, ByVal lpDeviceName As String, ByVal lpOutput As String, lpInitData As _
DEVMODE)
Declare Function CreateDCBynum& Lib "gdi32" Alias "CreateDCA" (ByVal _
lpDriverName As String, ByVal lpDeviceName As String, ByVal lpOutput As String, _
lpInitData As Long)
```

Description   Creates a device context for the specified device.

Use with VB   Refer to "Using Device Contexts with Visual Basic," earlier in this chapter.

Parameter	Type/Description
lpDriverName	String—Use vbNullString to pass a null to this parameter unless: 1—Use DISPLAY to retrieve a device context to the entire screen; 2—Use WINSPOOL to access the printer driver.
lpDeviceName	String—The name of the particular device to use. This is the name assigned in and displayed by the print manager.
lpOutput	String—Use vbNullString to pass a null to this parameter.
lpInitData	DEVMODE—A DEVMODE structure containing initialization values to use. Use CreateDCBynum and pass zero (NULL) to use default settings.

Return Value   Long—A handle to the new device context or zero on error.

Platform   Windows 95, Windows NT, Win16

Comments   The device context should be deleted with the DeleteDC function when it's no longer needed. All objects selected into the DC should be unselected and replaced with the original selected objects before the device context is deleted. The DocumentProperties API function can be used to load a DEVMODE structure if the initial settings are for a device (see Chapter 12).

Use screen device contexts (DISPLAY) with great caution as they can interfere with the appearance of other applications.

Porting Notes Use of the lpDriverName and lpOutput parameters has changed from Win16. Refer to the Visual Basic Programmers Guide to the Windows API (16-bit edition) for Win16 information.

Example   Picprint.vbp in Chapter 12.

Draw a rectangle near the upper left corner of the screen.

```
dc& = CreateDCBynum("DISPLAY", vbNullString, vbNullString, 0)
dl& = Rectangle(dc&, 5, 5, 100, 100)
```

■ CreateEllipticRgn

VB Declaration
```
Declare Function CreateEllipticRgn& Lib "gdi32" (ByVal X1 As Long, ByVal Y1 As _
Long, ByVal X2 As Long, ByVal Y2 As Long)
```

Description   Creates a region in the shape of an ellipse that fits in the rectangle described by the points X1,Y1 and X2,Y2.

Use with VB   No problem.

Parameter	Type/Description
X1,Y1	Long—X,Y coordinates describing the upper-left corner of the bounding rectangle.
X2,Y2	Long—X,Y coordinates describing the lower-right corner of the bounding rectangle. This point is not included in the calculation.

Return Value	Long—A region handle on success, zero on error.
Platform	Windows 95, Windows NT, Win16
Comments	Be sure to delete the region with the DeleteObject function when it is no longer needed. An ellipse drawn using the Ellipse API function will not match an elliptic region exactly, as this function does not include the bottom and right side of the rectangle in its drawing calculations.
Example	Region.vbp

■ CreateEllipticRgnIndirect

VB Declaration
```
Declare Function CreateEllipticRgnIndirect& Lib "gdi32" (lpRect As RECT)
```

Description   Creates a region in the shape of an ellipse that fits in the specified rectangle.

Use with VB   No problem.

Parameter	Type/Description
lpRect	RECT—Rectangle that specifies the size of the elliptic region to create.

Return Value   Long—A region handle on success, zero on error.

Platform   Windows 95, Windows NT, Win16

Comments   Be sure to delete the region with the DeleteObject function when it is no longer needed.

■ CreateIC

VB Declaration
```
Declare Function CreateIC& Lib "gdi32" Alias "CreateICA" (ByVal lpDriverName As _
String, ByVal lpDeviceName As String, ByVal lpOutput As String, lpInitData As _
DEVMODE)
Declare Function CreateICBynum& Lib "gdi32" Alias "CreateICA" (ByVal _
lpDriverName As String, ByVal lpDeviceName As String, ByVal lpOutput As String, _
lpInitData As Long)
```

Description   Creates an information context for the specified device. An information context can be used to quickly retrieve information about a device without the overhead of creating a device context. It can be passed as a parameter to information functions such as GetDeviceCaps in place of the device context parameter.

Use with VB   Refer to "Using Device Contexts with Visual Basic," earlier in this chapter.

Parameter	Type/Description
lpDriverName	String—Use vbNullString to pass a null to this parameter unless: 1—Use DISPLAY to retrieve a device context to the entire screen; 2—Use WINSPOOL to access the printer driver.
lpDeviceName	String—The name of the particular device to use. This is the name assigned in and displayed by the print manager.

Parameter	Type/Description
lpOutput	String—Use vbNullString to pass a null to this parameter.
lpInitData	DEVMODE—A DEVMODE structure containing initialization values to use. Use CreateICBynum and pass zero (NULL) to use default settings.

Return Value   Long—A handle to the information context or zero on error.

Platform   Windows 95, Windows NT, Win16

Comments   The device context should be deleted with the DeleteDC function when it's no longer needed. Refer to comments for the CreateDC function for further information.

In early versions of the Win32 SDK, the documentation for this function's parameters is incorrect. The parameters match those of CreateDC.

Porting Notes   Use of the lpDriverName and lpOutput parameters has changed from Win16. Refer to the Visual Basic Programmers Guide to the Windows API (16-bit edition) for Win16 information.

Example   To retrieve an information context for a printer named "Color Stylus":

```
dc& = CreateICBynum("WINSPOOL", "Color Stylus", vbNullString, 0)
```

■ CreatePolygonRgn

VB Declaration
```
Declare Function CreatePolygonRgn& Lib "gdi32" (lpPoint As POINTAPI, ByVal _
nCount As Long, ByVal nPolyFillMode As Long)
```

Description   Creates a region out of an arbitrary series of points. Windows automatically closes the polygon by connecting the last and first points if necessary.

Use with VB   No problem.

Parameter	Type/Description
lpPoint	POINTAPI—The first POINTAPI structure in an array of nCount POINTAPI structures.
nCount	Long—Number of points in the polygon.
nPolyFillMode	Long—Describes the polygon filling mode. May be either the ALTERNATE or the WINDING constant. Refer to the SetPolyFillMode function in Chapter 8 for an explanation of polygon fill modes.

Return Value   Long—The handle of the region created, or zero on error.

Platform   Windows 95, Windows NT, Win16

Comments   Be sure to delete the region with the DeleteObject function when it's no longer needed.

Example   Region.vbp

■ CreatePolyPolygonRgn

VB Declaration Declare Function CreatePolyPolygonRgn& Lib "gdi32" (lpPoint As POINTAPI, _
lpPolyCounts As Long, ByVal nCount As Long, ByVal nPolyFillMode As Long)

Description Creates a region made up of any number of polygons. Each polygon must be closed.

Use with VB No problem.

Parameter	Type/Description
lpPoint	POINTAPI—The first POINTAPI structure in an array of nCount POINTAPI structures.
lpPolyCounts	Long—The first entry in an array of Longs. Each entry contains the number of points that make up a closed polygon. The lpPoints array consists of a series of closed polygons, each of which has an entry in the lpPolyCounts array.
nCount	Long—Total number of points in the lpPoints array.
nPolyFillMode	Long—Describes the polygon filling mode. May be either the ALTER-NATE or the WINDING constant. Refer to the SetPolyFill-Mode function in Chapter 8 for an explanation of polygon fill modes.

Return Value Long—The handle of the region created, or zero on error.

Platform Windows 95, Windows NT, Win16

Comments Be sure to delete the region with the DeleteObject function when it's no longer needed.

Porting Notes Under Win16, each of the polygons must be explicitly closed, in other words, the last point in the polygon must match the first point. This requirement does not exist in Win32 (it will close each polygon if necessary). The Region example uses closed polygons in order to remain Win16 compatible.

Example Region.vbp

■ CreateRectRgn

VB Declaration Declare Function CreateRectRgn& Lib "gdi32" (ByVal X1 As Long, ByVal Y1 As _
Long, ByVal X2 As Long, ByVal Y2 As Long)

Description Creates a region in the shape of a rectangle described by the points X1,Y1 and X2,Y2.

Use with VB No problem.

Parameter	Type/Description
X1,Y1	Long—X,Y coordinates describing the upper-left corner of the rectangle.
X2,Y2	Long—X,Y coordinates describing the lower-right corner of the rectangle.

Return Value Long—A region handle on success, zero on error.

Platform	Windows 95, Windows NT, Win16
Comments	Be sure to delete the region with the DeleteObject function when it's no longer needed. 　　The bottom and right edges of the rectangle described by X1,Y1–X2,Y2 are not included in the region.
Example	Region.vbp

■ CreateRectRgnIndirect

VB Declaration	`Declare Function CreateRectRgnIndirect& Lib "gdi32" (lpRect As RECT)`
Description	Creates a region in the shape of a rectangle described by lpRect.
Use with VB	No problem.

Parameter	Type/Description
lpRect	RECT—Rectangle that defines the region to create.

Return Value	Long—A region handle on success, zero on error.
Platform	Windows 95, Windows NT, Win16
Comments	See comments for CreateRectRgn.
Example	Region.vbp

■ CreateRoundRectRgn

VB Declaration	`Declare Function CreateRoundRectRgn& Lib "gdi32" (ByVal X1 As Long, ByVal Y1 As _` `Long, ByVal X2 As Long, ByVal Y2 As Long, ByVal X3 As Long, ByVal Y3 As Long)`
Description	Creates a region in the shape of a rectangle with rounded corners described by the points X1,Y1 and X2,Y2. X3 and X4 define the ellipse used to round the corners.
Use with VB	No problem.

Parameter	Type/Description
X1,Y1	Long—X,Y coordinates describing the upper-left corner of the rectangle.
X2,Y2	Long—X,Y coordinates describing the lower-right corner of the rectangle.
X3	Long—The width of the ellipse used to round the corners. Ranges from zero for no rounding, to the width of the rectangle for full rounding.
Y3	Long—The height of the ellipse used to round the corners. Ranges from zero for no rounding, to the height of the rectangle for full rounding.

Return Value	Long—A region handle on success, zero on error.
Platform	Windows 95, Windows NT, Win16

Comments	Be sure to delete the region with the DeleteObject function when it's no longer needed. A region created with this function will not exactly match a rounded rectangle drawn with the RoundRect API function due to the fact that the bottom and right edge of the rectangle is not included in the region calculations.
Example	Region.vbp

■ DeleteDC

VB Declaration	Declare Function DeleteDC& Lib "gdi32" (ByVal hdc As Long)
Description	Deletes the specified device context or information context and frees all associated windows resources. Do not use with device contexts obtained using the GetDC function.
Use with VB	Do not use on device context handles obtained using the VB hDC property.

Parameter	Type/Description
hdc	Long—Device context to delete.

Return Value	Long—Nonzero on success, zero on failure.
Platform	Windows 95, Windows NT, Win16
Comments	If objects have been selected into the device context, they should be selected out before calling this function. This is done by selecting the original objects back into the DC or by using a SaveDC, RestoreDC pair to restore the DC to its state when it was created.
Example	Picprint.vbp in Chapter 12.

■ DPtoLP

VB Declaration	Declare Function DPtoLP& Lib "gdi32" (ByVal hdc As Long, lpPoint As POINTAPI, _ ByVal nCount As Long)
Description	Converts an array of points from device coordinates into logical coordinates in the specified device context.
Use with VB	Refer to "Scaling and Coordinate Systems," earlier in this chapter.

Parameter	Type/Description
hdc	Long—Handle to a device context that defines a logical coordinate system.
lpPoint	POINTAPI—The first entry in an array of one or more POINTAPI structures containing points in device coordinates. Each entry will be converted to logical coordinates (world coordinates if world transforms are in effect).
nCount	Long — The number of entries in the lpPoints array.

Return Value	Long—Nonzero on success, zero on failure.

Platform	Windows 95, Windows NT, Win16
Example	Viewport.vbp

■ EqualRgn

VB Declaration	Declare Function EqualRgn& Lib "gdi32" (ByVal hSrcRgn1 As Long, ByVal hSrcRgn2 _ As Long)
Description	Determines if two regions are equivalent.
Use with VB	No problem.

Parameter	Type/Description
hSrcRgn1	Long—Handle to a region.
hSrcRgn2	Long—Handle to a region.

Return Value	Long—TRUE (nonzero) if the two regions are equal. Zero if they are not equal. ERRORAPI if one of the regions is not valid.
Platform	Windows 95, Windows NT, Win16

■ ExcludeClipRect

VB Declaration	Declare Function ExcludeClipRect& Lib "gdi32" (ByVal hdc As Long, ByVal X1 As _ Long, ByVal Y1 As Long, ByVal X2 As Long, ByVal Y2 As Long)
Description	Excludes the rectangle defined by points X1,Y1 and X2,Y2 from the clipping area in the specified device context. Drawing will not take place inside this rectangle.
Use with VB	No problem.

Parameter	Type/Description
hdc	Long—Device context to modify.
X1,Y1	Long—X,Y coordinates describing the upper-left corner of the rectangle in logical coordinates.
X2,Y2	Long—X,Y coordinates describing the lower-right corner of the rectangle in logical coordinates. The bottom and right edges of the rectangle are not removed from the clipping region.

Return Value Long—Returns one of the following constants that describe the resulting clipping region:

1. COMPLEXREGION: If the region has borders that overlap each other.

2. SIMPLEREGION: If the borders of the region do not overlap each other.

3. NULLREGION: If the region is empty.

4. ERRORAPI: If an error occurred.

Platform   Windows 95, Windows NT, Win16

■ ExcludeUpdateRgn

VB Declaration   `Declare Function ExcludeUpdateRgn& Lib "user32" (ByVal hdc As Long, ByVal hwnd _`
`As Long)`

Description   Excludes the update region of the specified window from the clipping region of the specified device context. This prevents drawing into areas that are invalid (and are thus due to be updated at a later time).

Use with VB   Let's say you have a long or complex drawing operation to perform. This function allows you to avoid drawing into an area that has recently been uncovered and will thus be drawn later, possibly improving performance and eliminating a flicker effect. Refer to the WM_PAINT message description in Chapter 16 for additional information. Also refer to "Clipping, Regions, and Other Device Context Functions," earlier in this chapter.

Parameter	Type/Description
hdc	Long—Device context. The clipping region of this device context will be modified by excluding the update region of window hWnd.
hwnd	Long—Handle to a window.

Return Value   Long—See function ExcludeClipRect for return values.

Platform   Windows 95, Windows NT, Win16

■ ExtCreateRegion

VB Declaration   `Declare Function ExtCreateRegion& Lib "gdi32" (lpXform As xform, ByVal nCount _`
`As Long, lpRgnData As RGNDATA)`

Description   Allows you to modify a region according to a world transform.

Use with VB   The RGNDATA structure can be difficult to work with. In most cases you may prefer to use an alias in which lpRgnData is defined as a byte array which can be dynamically allocated. Refer to "Dynamically Sized Structures" in Chapter 9 for information and examples of working with structures whose size varies. Refer to the GetRegionData function definition in this chapter for additional information.

Parameter	Type/Description
lpXform	xform—A transform to apply to the region specified by lpRgnData.
nCount	Long—The size in bytes of the lpRgnData structure or buffer.
lpRgnData	RGNDATA—A RGNDATA structure that has been loaded with the definition of a region using the GetRegionData function.

Return Value   Long—A handle to a transformed region on success. Zero on error.

Platform Windows 95, Windows NT
Under Windows 95, only scaling and translation (offsets) transformations are possible with this function. Rotation and shearing are not supported.

■ ExtSelectClipRgn

VB Declaration `Declare Function ExtSelectClipRgn& Lib "gdi32" (ByVal hdc As Long, ByVal hRgn _`
`As Long, ByVal fnMode As Long)`

Description Allows you to combine a specified region into the current clipping region for a device context.

Use with VB No problem.

Parameter	Type/Description
hdc	Long—The device context whose clipping region will be modified.
hRgn	Long—A handle to a source region. May be NULL if fnMode is RGN_COPY.
fnMode	Long—One of the following constants: RGN_AND: The new clipping region includes those areas that are in region hRgn and the current clipping region. RGN_COPY: The new clipping region is set to region hRgn. RGN_DIFF: The new clipping region consists of the current clipping region excluding those areas that are in region hRgn. RGN_OR: The new clipping region includes those areas that are in region hRgn or the current clipping region. RGN_XOR: The new clipping region includes those areas that are in region hRgn or the current clipping region, but excludes those that are in both.

Return Value Long—Returns one of the following constants that describe the resulting clipping region:

1. COMPLEXREGION: If the region has borders that overlap each other.

2. SIMPLEREGION: If the borders of the region do not overlap each other.

3. NULLREGION: If the region is empty.

4. ERRORAPI: If an error has occurred.

Platform Windows 95, Windows NT

Comments Region hRgn is not affected by this function and may be destroyed afterwards.

■ FillRgn

VB Declaration `Declare Function FillRgn& Lib "gdi32" (ByVal hdc As Long, ByVal hRgn As Long, _`
`ByVal hBrush As Long)`

Description Fills the specified region using the specified brush. Brushes are described in Chapter 8.

Use with VB	No problem.	
	Parameter	**Type/Description**
	hdc	Long—Handle to a device context.
	hRgn	Long—Handle to a region to fill in device coordinates.
	hBrush	Long—Handle of the brush to use.

Return Value Long—Nonzero on success, zero on failure.

Platform Windows 95, Windows NT, Win16

Example Region.vbp

■ FrameRgn

VB Declaration
```
Declare Function FrameRgn& Lib "gdi32" (ByVal hdc As Long, ByVal hRgn As Long, _
ByVal hBrush As Long, ByVal nWidth As Long, ByVal nHeight As Long)
```

Description Draws a frame around the specified region using the specified brush. Brushes are discussed in Chapter 8.

Use with VB	No problem.	
	Parameter	**Type/Description**
	hdc	Long—Handle to a device context.
	hRgn	Long—Handle to a region to fill in device coordinates.
	hBrush	Long—Handle of the brush to use.
	nWidth	Long—Width in device units of the vertical borders.
	nHeight	Long—Height in device units of the horizontal borders.

Return Value Long—Nonzero on success, zero on failure.

Platform Windows 95, Windows NT, Win16

Example Region.vbp

■ GetBoundsRect

VB Declaration
```
Declare Function GetBoundsRect& Lib "gdi32" (ByVal hdc As Long, lprcBounds As _
RECT, ByVal flags As Long)
```

Description Retrieves the bounding rectangle for the specified device context. Each device context has a bounding rectangle that may be used by the programmer to accumulate information representing the bounds of the current image.

Use with VB	No problem.

Parameter	Type/Description
hdc	Long—Device context for the bounding rectangle.
lprcBounds	RECT—Rectangle to load with the current bounding rectangle for device context hDC.
flags	Long—May be set to constant DCB_RESET to clear the bounding rectangle. Otherwise set to zero.

Return Value   Long—Zero on error or one of the following constants:

1. DCB_SET: If the bounding rectangle is not empty.

2. DCB_RESET: If the bounding rectangle is empty.

3. DCB_ENABLE: If a bounding rectangle is being accumulated.

4. DCB_DISABLE: If a bounding rectangle is not being accumulated.

Platform   Windows 95, Windows NT, Win16

Comments   See SetBoundsRect for further information.

■ GetClipBox

VB Declaration   `Declare Function GetClipBox& Lib "gdi32" (ByVal hdc As Long, lpRect As RECT)`

Description   Retrieves the smallest rectangle that completely contains the clipping region for the specified device context.

Use with VB   Refer to "Clipping, Regions, and Other Device Context Functions," earlier in this chapter.

Parameter	Type/Description
hdc	Long—Handle to a device context.
lpRect	RECT—Rectangle structure to load with a rectangle that contains the clipping region for device context hDC.

Return Value   Long—Returns one of the following constants that describe the current clipping region:

1. COMPLEXREGION: If the region has borders that overlap each other.

2. SIMPLEREGION: If the borders of the region do not overlap each other.

3. NULLREGION: If the region is empty.

4. ERRORAPI: If an error has occurred.

Platform   Windows 95, Windows NT, Win16

■ GetClipRgn

VB Declaration   Declare Function GetClipRgn& Lib "gdi32" (ByVal hdc As Long, ByVal hRgn As Long)

Description   Retrieves the current clipping region for a device context.

Use with VB   No problem.

Parameter	Type/Description
hdc	Long—The device context for whose clipping region you wish to read.
hRgn	Long—A handle to an existing region. This region will be set to the current clipping region for the device context.

Return Value   Long—1 on success if a clipping region exists, 0 on success if no clipping region is defined. –1 on error.

Platform   Windows 95, Windows NT

Comments   hRgn is loaded with a copy of the clipping region. Later changes to hRgn will not affect the clipping region. This function only loads the clipping region if set by the application. Internal clipping regions, such as those set by the BeginPaint function, are not read by this function.

■ GetDC

VB Declaration   Declare Function GetDC& Lib "user32" (ByVal hwnd As Long)

Description   Retrieves a device context for the specified window.

Use with VB   Refer to "Using Device Contexts with Visual Basic" earlier in this chapter.

Parameter	Type/Description
hwnd	Long—Handle of window for which a device context is obtained. Zero to retrieve a DC for the entire screen.

Return Value   Long—The handle of a device context to the specified window. Zero on error.

Platform   Windows 95, Windows NT, Win16

Comments   If the window belongs to a class with the CS_OWNDC, CS_CLASSDC, or CS_PARENTDC style bits set, the context retrieved will be that of the window or class. This is the case with VB forms and picture controls where the result of this function will be identical to the hDC property for the control when AutoRedraw is FALSE. You should make no assumptions regarding the default attributes of the retrieved device context for a form or picture control, especially with regard to drawing objects. In addition, the default attributes will differ depending on the setting of the AutoRedraw property for the control or form. You must restore the attributes of the device context to their original values before the device context is released. Device contexts for windows that do not have the CS_OWNDC, CS_CLASSDC, or CS_PARENTDC style bits set will be retrieved from the general Windows cache and will have all attributes set to their default values. There are a limited number of device contexts available in the cache, so be sure to release the device context as soon as possible.

Be sure to use ReleaseDC to release device contexts allocated using this function—do not use DeleteDC.

Example

Most of the examples in this book work with forms or picture controls where the AutoRedraw property is FALSE; thus they use the hDC property directly.

■ GetDCEx

VB Declaration

```
Declare Function GetDCEx& Lib "user32" (ByVal hwnd As Long, ByVal hrgnclip As _
Long, ByVal fdwOptions As Long)
```

Description

Retrieves a device context for the specified window. This function provides additional options as compared to GetDC.

Use with VB

Refer to "Using Device Contexts with Visual Basic," earlier in this chapter.

Parameter	Type/Description
hwnd	Long—Handle of window for which a device context is obtained.
hrgnclip	Long—A clipping region to use with the window.
fdwOptions	Long—A flag word with bits set according to the following constants: DCX_CACHE: The device context is retrieved from the Windows cache regardless of the class style setting for the window. DCX_CLIPCHILREN: The area of all visible child windows is excluded from the DC's clipping region. DCX_CLIPSIBLINGS: The area of all visible sibling windows above window hWnd is excluded from the DC's clipping region. DCX_EXCLUDERGN: Excludes the region specified by hrgnClip from the DC's clipping region. DCX_EXCLUDEUPDATE: Excludes the update region from the clipping region for the device context. DCX_INTERSECTRGN: Intersects the region specified by hrgnClip with the clipping region for the device context. DCX_INTERSECTUPDATE: Intersects the region specified with the update region for the device context. DCX_LOCKWINDOWUPDATE: This flag allows drawing to the window even if it is locked due to a call to LockWindowUpdate. DCX_NORESETATTRS: The device context is not reset to its default attributes after it is released. DCX_PARENTCLIP: Overrides the CS_PARENTDC class style setting. The DC's origin is set to the upper-left corner of window hWnd.

Return Value

Long—The handle of a device context to the specified window. Zero on error.

Platform

Windows 95, Windows NT, Win16

Comments

If the window belongs to a class with the CS_OWNDC, CS_CLASSDC, or CS_PARENTDC style bits set, the context retrieved will be that of the window or class. In this case, the attributes of the device context will be unchanged from their previous values. This is usually the case with VB forms and controls. Otherwise, the DCX_CACHE bit must be set to retrieve a device context from the general

Windows cache. If it is not set, this function will return zero. The DC will have all attributes set to their default values. Device contexts from the cache must be released after use with the ReleaseDC function to prevent the system from locking up, as Windows only has five cached DCs available.

Refer to the comments for the GetDC function for additional information.

Porting Notes   Win32 adds several new DCX flags.

■ GetDCOrgEx

VB Declaration   Declare Function GetDCOrgEx& Lib "gdi32" (ByVal hdc As Long, lpPoint As _
POINTAPI)

Description   Retrieves the location of the origin of the specified device context in screen coordinates. For example, if the DC origin is the upper-left corner of a window client area, this function retrieves the position of that corner on the screen in screen pixel coordinates.

Use with VB   No problem.

Parameter	Type/Description
hdc	Long—The handle to a device context.
lpPoint	POINTAPI—A POINTAPI structure to load with the screen coordinates of the device context origin.

Return Value   Long—TRUE (nonzero) on success, zero otherwise.

Platform   Windows 95, Windows NT

Porting Notes   Supersedes the Win16 GetDCOrg function.

Example   When placed in a form module, this code loads the pt structure with the upper-left coordinate of the client area of the form in screen coordinates. This is also the origin of the form's hDC property.

```
Dim dl&
Dim pt As POINTAPI
dl& = GetDCOrgEx(hDC, pt)
```

■ GetDeviceCaps

VB Declaration   Declare Function GetDeviceCaps& Lib "gdi32" (ByVal hdc As Long, ByVal nIndex As _
Long)

Description   Retrieves information regarding the capabilities of the device for the specified device context.

Use with VB   No problem.

Parameter	Type/Description
hdc	Long—Device context for the device for which information is requested.
nIndex	Long—Specifies the type of information to retrieve based on constants shown in Table 7.14.

Return Value   Long—Refer to Table 7.14.

Table 7.14   **GetDeviceCaps Index Table**

Constant	Information Returned
DRIVERVERSION	Device driver version.
TECHNOLOGY	One of the following constants: DT_PLOTTER: Plotter; DT_RASDISPLAY: Raster display; DT_RASPRINTER: Raster printer; DT_RASCAMERA: Raster camera; DT_CHARSTREAM: Character stream; DT_METAFILE: Metafile; DT_DISPFILE: Display file.
HORZSIZE	Display width in millimeters.
VERTSIZE	Display height in millimeters.
HORZRES	Display width in pixels.
VERTRES	Display height in pixels.
LOGPIXELSX	Pixels/logical inch (horizontal).
LOGPIXELSY	Pixels/logical inch (vertical).
BITSPIXEL	Bits/pixel (on each color plane).
PLANES	Number of color planes.
NUMBRUSHES	Number of built-in device brushes.
NUMPENS	Number of built-in device pens.
NUMMARKERS	Number of built-in device markers.
NUMFONTS	Number of built-in device fonts.
NUMCOLORS	Entries in the device color table.
ASPECTX	Width of device pixel (see ASPECTXY).
ASPECTY	Height of device pixel (see ASPECTXY).
ASPECTXY	Diagonal size of device pixel. These values are relative to each other such that the $((ASPECTX^2)+(ASPECTY^2))^{.5} = ASPECTXY$.
PDEVICESIZE	Size of PDEVICE internal structure.
CLIPCAPS	One of the following constants: CP_NONE: Device has no built-in clipping; CP_RECTANGLE: Device can clip to rectangles; CP_REGION: Device can clip to regions.
SIZEPALETTE	Entries in the system palette (see RASTERCAPS RC_PALETTE flag).
NUMRESERVED	Reserved entries in the system palette.
BLTALIGNMENT	Some display devices perform image operations faster if the image is aligned on a particular address boundary specified by this value. Zero if it makes no difference.

Table 7.14   GetDeviceCaps Index Table (Continued)

Constant	Information Returned
COLORRES	Color resolution in bits/pixel (see RASTERCAPS RC_PALETTE flag).
DESKTOPHORIZRES DESKTOPVERTRES	Horizontal and vertical resolution of the desktop (NT only). Some devices support virtual desktops that are larger than the physical display.
PHYSICALOFFSETX	Horizontal offset to the printable area of a printer.
PHYSICALOFFSETY	Vertical offset to the printable area of a printer.
PHYSICALHEIGHT	Physical height of a printed page in device units.
PHYSICALWIDTH	Physical width of a printed page in device units.
SCALINGFACTORX SCALINGFACTORY	A printer's horizontal and vertical scaling factor.
VREFRESH	Vertical refresh of display (NT only).
RASTERCAPS	A flag made up of the following values: R_BANDING: Device supports banding; RC_BIGFONT: Fonts larger than 64K supported; RC_BITBLT: BitBlt is supported; RC_BITMAP64K: Bitmaps larger than 64K okay; RC_DI_BITMAP: SetDIBits and GetDIBits functions are supported; RC_DIBTODEV: SetDIBitsToDevice supported; RC_FLOODFILL: FloodFill API supported; RC_NONE: No raster operations supported; RC_PALETTE: Palette-based device; RC_SAVEBITMAP: Can save bitmaps; RC_SCALING: Scaling is built-in; RC_STRETCHBLT: StretchBlt supported; RC_STRETCHDIB: StretchDIBits supported.
CURVECAPS	A flag describing built-in curve-generation capabilities. Refer to the CC_xxx constants in file API32.TXT for a complete list.
LINECAPS	A flag describing built-in line-generation capabilities. Refer to the LC_xxx constants in file API32.TXT for a complete list.
POLYGONCAPS	A flag describing built-in polygon generation capabilities. Refer to the PC_xxx constants in file API32.TXT for a complete list.
TEXTCAPS	A flag made up of the following values: TC_OP_CHARACTER: Fonts can be placed in any location; TC_OP_STROKE: Device can omit any stroke on a built-in font; TC_CP_STROKE: Built-in fonts can be clipped at any pixel. TC_CR_90: Characters can be rotated 90 degrees; TC_CR_ANY: Character rotation supported; TC_SF_X_YINDEP: Separate X and Y scaling of characters is supported; TC_SA_DOUBLE: Built-in fonts may be doubled in size; TC_SA_INTEGER: Built-in fonts may be scaled by integer multipliers; TC_SA_CONTIN: Built-in fonts may be scaled continuously; TC_EA_DOUBLE: Device can create bold fonts; TC_IA_ABLE: Device can create italic fonts; TC_UA_ABLE: Device can underline fonts; TC_SO_ABLE: Device can strikeout fonts; TC_RA_ABLE: Supports raster fonts; TC_SCROLLBLT: Supports raster fonts; TC_VA_ABLE: Supports vector fonts.

Platform   Windows 95, Windows NT, Win16

Example   Devview.vbp

■ GetGraphicsMode

VB Declaration	Declare Function GetGraphicsMode& Lib "gdi32" (ByVal hdc As Long)
Description	Determines whether advanced graphic modes (world transforms) are enabled.
Use with VB	No problem.

Parameter	Type/Description
hdc	Long—The device context whose mode is being tested.

Return Value	Long—One of the following constants:

1. GM_COMPATIBLE—Graphics mode is compatible with Win16.
2. GM_ADVANCED—World transforms are enabled.

Platform	Windows 95, Windows NT. World transforms are supported only by Windows NT.
Example	Spin.vbp, Viewport.vbp

■ GetMapMode

VB Declaration	Declare Function GetMapMode& Lib "gdi32" (ByVal hdc As Long)
Description	Retrieves the mapping mode for the specified device context.
Use with VB	Refer to "Scaling and Coordinate Systems," earlier in this chapter.

Parameter	Type/Description
hdc	Long—Handle to the device context to check.

Return Value	Long—The current mapping mode for the device context. Refer to the SetMapMode function for a description of mapping modes.
Platform	Windows 95, Windows NT, Win16.

■ GetRegionData

VB Declaration	Declare Function GetRegionData& Lib "gdi32" (ByVal hRgn As Long, ByVal dwCount _ As Long, lpRgnData As RgnData)
Description	Loads a RgnData structure or buffer with information describing a region.
Use with VB	See comments below.

Parameter	Type/Description
hRgn	Long—The handle of the region for which to obtain information.
dwCount	Long—The size of the RGNDATA structure.
lpRgnData	RgnData—A RGNDATA structure to load with the region information.

Return Value   Long—1 if the structure is large enough to load with the region data. 0 on failure. The required size of the structure if lpRgnData is not large enough to hold the region data.

Platform   Windows 95, Windows NT

Comments   The RGNDATA structure is defined as follows:

```
Type RGNDATA
        rdh As RGNDATAHEADER
        Buffer As Byte
End Type
```

The RGNDATAHEADER is a fixed-size structure that describes the region (see Appendix B). The Buffer is a buffer that will hold the region data. The actual size of the buffer required depends on the complexity of the region (one byte is obviously never enough). This leaves you with two approaches:

1. Redefine RGNDATA to be as large as you will ever need it to be. This is necessary as Visual Basic does not let you resize structures dynamically.

2. Allocate a byte array and use it in place of the RGNDATA structure. This requires changing the function declaration for APIs using this structure from...As RGNDATA to...As Byte, and passing the first element of the byte array. If you then need to access elements of the RGNDATAHEADER structure, you will need to use a memory copy routine to copy data to and from the buffer and a separately defined RGNDATAHEADER structure.

Examples of this process along with a more in-depth explanation can be found in Chapter 9 in the section on Dynamically Sized Structures and Device Independent bitmaps, and in Chapter 15 which discusses advanced string and structure techniques. It is not illustrated here because, frankly, the odds of your ever using this function and its related ExtCreateDC function are quite slim.

■ GetRgnBox

VB Declaration   `Declare Function GetRgnBox& Lib "gdi32" (ByVal hRgn As Long, lpRect As RECT)`

Description   Retrieves the smallest rectangle that completely contains the specified region.

Use with VB   No problem.

Parameter	Type/Description
hRgn	Long—Handle to a region.
lpRect	RECT—Rectangle structure to load with a rectangle that completely contains the specified region.

Return Value   Long—Returns one of the following constants that describe the current clipping region:

1. COMPLEXREGION: If the region has borders that overlap each other.

2. SIMPLEREGION: If the borders of the region do not overlap each other.

3. NULLREGION: If the region is empty.

4. ERRORAPI: If an error occurred.

Platform   Windows 95, Windows NT, Win16

■ GetUpdateRgn

VB Declaration   Declare Function GetUpdateRgn& Lib "user32" (ByVal hwnd As Long, ByVal hRgn As _
Long, ByVal fErase As Long)

Description   Determines the update region of the specified window. This is the region that is currently invalid
and needs to be updated.

Use with VB   No problem.

Parameter	Type/Description
hwnd	Long—Handle of window for which to determine the update region.
hRgn	Long—Handle to a region to load with the update region for window hWnd.
fErase	Long—TRUE (nonzero) to specify that the window background should be erased and parts of the window outside of the client area should be redrawn.

Return Value   Long—Returns one of the following constants that describe the resulting region:

1. COMPLEXREGION: If the region has borders that overlap each other.

2. SIMPLEREGION: If the borders of the region do not overlap each other.

3. NULLREGION: If the region is empty.

4. ERRORAPI: If an error occurred.

■ GetViewportExtEx

VB Declaration   Declare Function GetViewportExtEx& Lib "gdi32" (ByVal hdc As Long, lpSize As _
SIZE)

Description   Retrieves the extents of the device context's viewport.

Use with VB   Refer to "Scaling and Coordinate Systems," earlier in this chapter.

Parameter	Type/Description
hdc	Long—Handle to a device context.
lpSize	SIZE—SIZEAPI structure to load with the horizontal and vertical extents of the DC viewport in device units.

Return Value   Long—Nonzero on success, zero on failure.

Platform   Windows 95, Windows NT, Win16

Example   Viewport.vbp

■ GetViewportOrgEx

VB Declaration   Declare Function GetViewportOrgEx& Lib "gdi32" (ByVal hdc As Long, lpPoint As _
POINTAPI)

Description   Retrieves the origins of the device context's viewport.

Use with VB   Refer to "Scaling and Coordinate Systems," earlier in this chapter.

Parameter	Type/Description
hdc	Long—Handle to a device context.
lpPoint	POINTAPI—POINTAPI structure to load with the viewport origin.

Return Value   Long—Nonzero on success, zero on failure.

Platform   Windows 95, Windows NT, Win16

Example   Viewport.vbp

■ GetWindowDC

VB Declaration   Declare Function GetWindowDC& Lib "user32" (ByVal hwnd As Long)

Description   Retrieves a device context for the entire window specified (including borders, scroll bars, captions, menus, and so on).

Use with VB   Works, but is not recommended.

Parameter	Type/Description
hwnd	Long—Handle of a window for which to retrieve a device context.

Return Value   Long—Device context for the window, zero on error.

Platform   Windows 95, Windows NT, Win16

Comments   Be sure to release the context when done using the ReleaseDC function.

■ GetWindowExtEx

VB Declaration   Declare Function GetWindowExtEx& Lib "gdi32" (ByVal hdc As Long, lpSize As SIZE)

Description   Retrieves the window extents of the specified device context.

| **Use with VB** | Refer to "Scaling and Coordinate Systems," earlier in this chapter. |

Parameter	Type/Description
hdc	Long—Handle to a device context.
lpSize	SIZE—SIZEAPI structure to load with the horizontal and vertical extents of the device context logical window in logical units.

| **Return Value** | Long—Nonzero on success, zero on failure. |

| **Platform** | Windows 95, Windows NT, Win16 |

| **Example** | Viewport.vbp |

■ GetWindowOrgEx

VB Declaration
```
Declare Function GetWindowOrgEx& Lib "gdi32" (ByVal hdc As Long, lpPoint As _
POINTAPI)
```

Description Retrieves the logical window origin for the specified device context.

Use with VB Refer to "Scaling and Coordinate Systems," earlier in this chapter.

Parameter	Type/Description
hdc	Long—Handle to a device context.
lpPoint	POINTAPI—POINTAPI structure to load with the origin of the logical window.

Return Value Long—Nonzero on success, zero on failure.

Platform Windows 95, Windows NT, Win16

Example Viewport.vbp

■ GetWindowRgn

VB Declaration
```
Declare Function GetWindowRgn& Lib "user32" (ByVal hWnd As Long, ByVal hRgn As _
Long)
```

Description Retrieves the window region as defined earlier by the SetWindowRgn function.

Use with VB No problem.

Parameter	Type/Description
hWnd	Long—The window whose region you wish to retrieve.
hRgn	Long—A handle to a region. This region will be loaded with a copy of the current window region if one has been set.

Return Value   Long—Returns one of the following constants that describe the resulting region:

   1. COMPLEXREGION: If the region has borders that overlap each other.

   2. SIMPLEREGION: If the borders of the region do not overlap each other.

   3. NULLREGION: If the region is empty.

   4. ERRORAPI: If an error occurred.

Platform   Windows 95, Windows NT

Comments   Refer to the SetWindowRgn function for additional information.

Example   Round.vbp

■ GetWorldTransform

VB Declaration   `Declare Function GetWorldTransform& Lib "gdi32" (ByVal hdc As Long, lpXform As _`
`XFORM)`

Description   Retrieves the current world transform for a device context if one is in effect.

Use with VB   No problem.

Parameter	Type/Description
hdc	Long—The device context to examine.
lpXform	xform—An XFORM structure to load with the current world transform for this device context.

Return Value   Long—Nonzero on success, zero on failure.

Platform   Windows NT

Example   Viewport.vbp, Spin.vbp

■ IntersectClipRect

VB Declaration   `Declare Function IntersectClipRect& Lib "gdi32" (ByVal hdc As Long, ByVal X1 As _`
`Long, ByVal Y1 As Long, ByVal X2 As Long, ByVal Y2 As Long)`

Description   Specifies a new clipping region for the specified device context from the intersection of the current clipping region and the rectangle defined by points X1,Y1 and X2,Y2.

Use with VB   Refer to "Clipping, Regions, and Other Device Context Functions," earlier in this chapter.

Parameter	Type/Description
hdc	Long—Device context to modify.

Parameter	Type/Description
X1,Y1	Long—X,Y coordinates describing the upper-left corner of the rectangle in logical coordinates.
X2,Y2	Long—X,Y coordinates describing the lower-right corner of the rectangle in logical coordinates.

Return Value   Long—Returns one of the following constants that describe the new clipping region:

1. COMPLEXREGION: If the region has borders that overlap each other.

2. SIMPLEREGION: If the borders of the region do not overlap each other.

3. NULLREGION: If the region is empty.

4. ERRORAPI: If an error occurred.

Platform   Windows 95, Windows NT, Win16

■ InvalidateRgn

VB Declaration
```
Declare Function InvalidateRgn& Lib "user32" (ByVal hwnd As Long, ByVal hRgn As _
Long, ByVal bErase As Long)
```

Description   Invalidates the specified region in a window, adding it to the update region of the window so that it may be redrawn in due course.

Use with VB   No problem.

Parameter	Type/Description
hwnd	Long—Handle of window to invalidate.
hRgn	Long—Handle to region defining the area to invalidate. The region is specified in window client coordinates. Zero to invalidate the entire window (client area).
bErase	Long—TRUE (nonzero) if the region is to be erased before being updated.

Return Value   Long—TRUE

Platform   Windows 95, Windows NT, Win16

Comments   If bErase is TRUE, the entire update area will be erased before update, not just the specified region.

■ InvertRgn

VB Declaration
```
Declare Function InvertRgn& Lib "gdi32" (ByVal hdc As Long, ByVal hRgn As Long)
```

Description   Inverts the specified region on a device context by inverting the value of each pixel. Refer to Chapter 9 for an in-depth discussion of pixel value.

Use with VB	No problem.	
	Parameter	**Type/Description**
	hdc	Long—A handle to a device context.
	hRgn	Long—The region on the device to invert.

Return Value Long—Nonzero on success, zero on failure.

Platform Windows 95, Windows NT, Win16

Example Region.vbp

■ LPtoDP

VB Declaration `Declare Function LPtoDP& Lib "gdi32" (ByVal hdc As Long, lpPoint As POINTAPI, _`
`ByVal nCount As Long)`

Description Converts an array of points from logical coordinates in the specified device context to device coordinates.

Use with VB Refer to "Scaling and Coordinate Systems," earlier in this chapter.

Parameter	**Type/Description**
hdc	Long—Handle to a device context that defines a logical coordinate system.
lpPoint	POINTAPI—The first entry in an array of one or more POINTAPI structures containing points in logical coordinates. Each entry will be converted to device coordinates.
nCount	Long—The number of entries in the lpPoints array.

Return Value Long—Nonzero on success, zero on failure.

Platform Windows 95, Windows NT, Win16

Comments If a world transform is in effect, the points in the lpPoint array are assumed to be in world coordinates.

Example See DPtoLP

■ ModifyWorldTransform

VB Declaration `Declare Function ModifyWorldTransform& Lib "gdi32" (ByVal hdc As Long, lpXform _`
`As XFORM, ByVal iMode As Long)`

Description Modifies the current world transform according to the mode specified.

Use with VB No problem.

Parameter	**Type/Description**
hdc	Long—Device context whose transform is being modified.

Parameter	Type/Description
lpXform	xform—XFORM structure containing additional transform to work with according to the iMode parameter.
iMode	Long—One of the following constants: MWT_IDENTITY—Sets the world transform to the default identity transform (with the identity transform, the world transform has no effect). lpXform is ignored. MWT_LEFTMULTIPLY—The lpXform transform is multiplied by the current transform and the result set to be the new world transform. MWT_RIGHTMULTIPLY—The current transform is multiplied by the lpXform transform and the result set to be the new world transform.

Return Value Long—Nonzero on success, zero on failure.

Platform Windows NT

Comments Unlike normal multiplication, the results of a matrix multiplication depend on the order of the matrices. In MW_LEFTMULTIPLY, the lpXform transform is the left operand. A complete tutorial on matrix multiplication is beyond the scope of this book, but can be found in any good advanced algebra book.

The GM_ADVANCED graphic mode must be set using the SetGraphicsMode function before calling this function.

■ OffsetClipRgn

VB Declaration `Declare Function OffsetClipRgn& Lib "gdi32" (ByVal hdc As Long, ByVal x As _`
`Long, ByVal y As Long)`

Description Moves the clipping region of the specified device context by the amount specified.

Use with VB No problem.

Parameter	Type/Description
hdc	Long—Device context.
x	Long—Horizontal offset in logical units.
y	Long—Vertical offset in logical units.

Return Value Long—Returns one of the following constants that describe the new clipping region:

1. COMPLEXREGION: If the region has borders that overlap each other.

2. SIMPLEREGION: If the borders of the region do not overlap each other.

3. NULLREGION: If the region is empty.

4. ERRORAPI: If an error occurred.

Platform Windows 95, Windows NT, Win16

■ OffsetRgn

VB Declaration Declare Function OffsetRgn& Lib "gdi32" (ByVal hRgn As Long, ByVal x As Long, _
ByVal y As Long)

Description Moves the specified region by the offset specified.

Use with VB No problem.

Parameter	Type/Description
hRgn	Long—Handle to a region.
x	Long—Horizontal offset in logical units.
y	Long—Vertical offset in logical units.

Return Value Long—Returns one of the following constants that describe the new region:

1. COMPLEXREGION: If the region has borders that overlap each other.

2. SIMPLEREGION: If the borders of the region do not overlap each other.

3. NULLREGION: If the region is empty.

4. ERRORAPI: If an error occurred.

Platform Windows 95, Windows NT, Win16

■ OffsetViewportOrgEx

VB Declaration Declare Function OffsetViewportOrgEx& Lib "gdi32" (ByVal hdc As Long, ByVal nX _
As Long, ByVal nY As Long, lpPoint As POINTAPI)

Description Offsets the origin of the device context's viewport.

Use with VB Refer to "Scaling and Coordinate Systems," earlier in this chapter.

Parameter	Type/Description
hdc	Long—Handle to a device context.
nX, nY	Long—Horizontal and vertical offset to add to the viewport origins in device coordinates.
lpPoint	POINTAPI—POINTAPI structure to load with the previous horizontal and vertical origins of the device context viewport in device coordinates.

Return Value Long—Nonzero on success, zero on failure.

Platform Windows 95, Windows NT, Win16

■ OffsetWindowOrgEx

VB Declaration Declare Function OffsetWindowOrgEx& Lib "gdi32" (ByVal hdc As Long, ByVal nX As _

```
Long, ByVal nY As Long, lpPoint As POINTAPI)
```

Description   Offsets the window origin for the specified device context.

Use with VB   Refer to "Scaling and Coordinate Systems," earlier in this chapter.

Parameter	Type/Description
hdc	Long—Handle to a device context.
nX, nY	Long—Horizontal and vertical window origins in logical coordinates.
lpPoint	POINTAPI—POINTAPI structure to load with the previous horizontal and vertical origins of the DC window in logical coordinates.

Return Value   Long—Nonzero on success, zero on failure.

Platform   Windows 95, Windows NT, Win16

■ PaintRgn

VB Declaration   `Declare Function PaintRgn& Lib "gdi32" (ByVal hdc As Long, ByVal hRgn As Long)`

Description   This function fills the specified region using the current brush background color. Brushes are described in Chapter 8.

Use with VB   No problem.

Parameter	Type/Description
hdc	Long—Device context to draw on.
hRgn	Long—A handle to the region to fill.

Return Value   Long—Nonzero on success, zero on failure.

Platform   Windows 95, Windows NT, Win16

Example   Region.vbp

■ PtInRegion

VB Declaration   `Declare Function PtInRegion& Lib "gdi32" (ByVal hRgn As Long, ByVal x As Long, _`
`ByVal y As Long)`

Description   Determines if a point is in a specified region.

Use with VB   No problem. Very useful for hit testing on complex images.

Parameter	Type/Description
hRgn	Long—Handle to a region.

Parameter	Type/Description
x	Long—X coordinate of a point in logical coordinates.
y	Long—Y coordinates of a point in logical coordinates.

Return Value   Long—TRUE (nonzero) if the point is in the region, zero otherwise.

Platform   Windows 95, Windows NT, Win16

Example   Region.vbp

■ PtVisible

VB Declaration
```
Declare Function PtVisible& Lib "gdi32" (ByVal hdc As Long, ByVal _
x As Long, ByVal y As Long)
```

Description   Determines if the specified point is visible (that is, inside the clipping region of the specified device context).

Use with VB   No problem.

Parameter	Type/Description
hdc	Long—Handle to a device context.
x, y	Long—The X,Y coordinates of the point to check

Return Value   Long—TRUE (nonzero) if the point is within the clipping region of the specified device context, zero otherwise.

Platform   Windows 95, Windows NT, Win16

■ RectInRegion

VB Declaration   `Declare Function RectInRegion& Lib "gdi32" (ByVal hRgn As Long, lpRect As RECT)`

Description   Determines if any part of a rectangle is in a specified region.

Use with VB   No problem.

Parameter	Type/Description
hRgn	Long—Handle to a region.
lpRect	RECT—Rectangle structure to test against region hRgn.

Return Value   Long—TRUE (nonzero) if any part of the rectangle is in the specified region, zero otherwise.

Platform   Windows 95, Windows NT, Win16

Comments   The bottom and right edges of the rectangle are not included in the rectangle for the purposes of this function.

■ RectVisible

VB Declaration `Declare Function RectVisible& Lib "gdi32" (ByVal hdc As Long, lpRect As RECT)`

Description Determines if any part of the specified rectangle is visible (that is, inside the clipping region of the specified device context).

Use with VB No problem.

Parameter	Type/Description
hdc	Long—Handle to a device context.
lpRect	RECT—The rectangle to test for visibility. The rectangle is specified in logical coordinates.

Return Value Long—TRUE (nonzero) if any part of the rectangle is within the clipping region for the specified device context, zero otherwise.

Platform Windows 95, Windows NT, Win16

Comments The bottom and right edge of the rectangle are not included in the rectangle for the purposes of this function

■ ReleaseDC

VB Declaration `Declare Function ReleaseDC& Lib "user32" (ByVal hwnd As Long, ByVal hdc As Long)`

Description Releases the specified device context that was obtained through calls to GetDC or GetWindowDC. It has no affect on class or private device contexts (however, there is no harm in calling it in these cases).

Use with VB Refer to "Using Device Contexts with Visual Basic," earlier in this chapter.

Parameter	Type/Description
hwnd	Long—The window handle associated with the device context being released.
hdc	Long—Handle to the device context to release.

Return Value Long—1 on success, 0 otherwise.

Platform Windows 95, Windows NT, Win16

Comments Do not use this function on device contexts that were created using a DC creation function such as CreateDC.

Example TextMsgs.vbp in Chapter 17

■ RestoreDC

VB Declaration   ```
Declare Function RestoreDC& Lib "gdi32" (ByVal hdc As Long, ByVal nSavedDC As _
Long)
```

**Description**    Restores a previously saved device context from the device context stack.

**Use with VB**    Refer to "Using Device Contexts with Visual Basic," earlier in this chapter.

| Parameter | Type/Description |
|-----------|-----------------|
| hdc | Long—Handle of the device context to restore. |
| nSavedDC | Long—ID number of the device context to restore as returned by the SaveDC function. Use –1 to restore the most recently saved device context. |

**Return Value**    Long—Nonzero on success, zero on failure.

**Platform**    Windows 95, Windows NT, Win16

**Comments**    If nSavedDC refers to a DC that is not on the top of the stack, all device contexts above nSavedDC on the stack are removed from the stack as well. See the SaveDC function for additional information.

**Example**    Viewport.vbp, Spin.vbp

# ■ SaveDC

**VB Declaration**    ```
Declare Function SaveDC& Lib "gdi32" (ByVal hdc As Long)
```

Description   Saves the state of the specified device context on the Windows device context stack. The DC mapping mode, window and viewport scaling, clipping region, and list of selected objects are saved. This function is often used before making a temporary change to the device context. The DC attributes are restored by the RestoreDC function.

Use with VB   Refer to "Using Device Contexts with Visual Basic," earlier in this chapter.

Parameter	Type/Description
hdc	Long—Handle of the device context to save.

Return Value   Long—An integer identifying the device context so that it may be restored using the RestoreDC function. Zero on error.

Platform   Windows 95, Windows NT, Win16

Comments Device contexts are saved on an internal stack. This means that you can perform multiple saves of a device context's state. For example, you might save the device context state on entry to a function, perform some API calls, save it again, perform some more calls, restore the previous state, make additional API function calls, then finally restore the device context to its original state before exiting the function. The number of device contexts that may be saved is limited only by memory.

Example Viewport.vbp, Spin.vbp

■ ScaleViewportExtEx

VB Declaration
```
Declare Function ScaleViewportExtEx& Lib "gdi32" (ByVal hdc As Long, ByVal _
nXnum As Long, ByVal nXdenom As Long, ByVal nYnum As Long, ByVal nYdenom As _
Long, lpSize As SIZE)
```

Description Scales the extents of the device context's viewport.

Use with VB Refer to "Scaling and Coordinate Systems," earlier in this chapter.

Parameter	Type/Description
hdc	Long—Handle to a device context.
nXnum, nYnum	Long—The current X and Y extents are multiplied by these numbers.
nXdenom nYdenom	Long—The product of the current X and Y extents multiplied by nXnum and nYnum is divided by these numbers.
lpSize	SIZE—SIZEAPI structure to load with the previous horizontal and vertical viewport extents.

Return Value Long—Nonzero on success, zero on failure.

Platform Windows 95, Windows NT, Win16

Comments Refer to the chapter text for an explanation of viewport and window extents and origins. Only valid in the MM_ISOTROPIC and MM_ANISOTROPIC mapping modes. In MM_ISOTROPIC mode you must set the window extents before the viewport extents.

■ ScaleWindowExtEx

VB Declaration
```
Declare Function ScaleWindowExtEx& Lib "gdi32" (ByVal hdc As Long, ByVal nXnum _
As Long, ByVal nXdenom As Long, ByVal nYnum As Long, ByVal nYdenom As Long, _
lpSize As SIZE)
```

Description Scales the window extents for the specified device context.

Use with VB Refer to "Scaling and Coordinate Systems," earlier in this chapter.

Parameter	Type/Description
hdc	Long—Handle to a device context.
nXnum, nYnum	Long—The current X and Y extents are multiplied by these numbers.

Parameter	Type/Description
nXdenom nYdenom	Long—The product of the current X and Y extents multiplied by nXnum and nYnum is divided by these numbers.
lpSize	SIZE—SIZEAPI structure to load with the previous horizontal and vertical window extents of the device context viewport in logical units.

Return Value   Long—Nonzero on success, zero on failure.

Platform   Windows 95, Windows NT, Win16

Comments   Refer to "Windows and Viewpoints—Extents and Origins," earlier in this chapter. Only valid in the MM_ISOTROPIC and MM_ANISOTROPIC mapping modes. In MM_ISOTROPIC mode you must set the window extents before the viewport extents.

■ ScrollDC

VB Declaration
```
Declare Function ScrollDC& Lib "user32" (ByVal hdc As Long, ByVal dx As Long, _
ByVal dy As Long, lprcScroll As RECT, lprcClip As RECT, ByVal hrgnUpdate As _
Long, lprcUpdate As RECT)
```

Description   Scrolls a rectangle in a window represented by a device context horizontally and/or vertically.

Use with VB   Refer to "Scaling and Coordinate Systems," earlier in this chapter.

Parameter	Type/Description
hdc	Long—Handle to a device context.
dx	Long—Horizontal units to scroll.
dy	Long—Vertical units to scroll.
lprcScroll	RECT—The rectangle to scroll.
lprcClip	RECT—A rectangle that specifies the clipping rectangle. Scrolling only occurs within this rectangle.
hrgnUpdate	Long—This region will be set to the area uncovered by the scrolling operation in the client coordinate system. May be zero, in which case the update region will not be set.
lprcUpdate	RECT—This rectangle will be set to the area uncovered by the scrolling operation in the client coordinate system. May be zero (this requires that the VB declaration be modified to accept a long parameter such as lprcUpdate).

Return Value   Long—Nonzero on success, zero on failure. Sets GetLastError.

Platform   Windows 95, Windows NT, Win16

Comments   If both hrgnUpdate and lprcUpdate are NULL, Windows will not compute the update region for this DC.

Example   Similar to the ScrollWindow function shown in Scroll.vbp in Chapter 5.

SelectClipRgn

VB Declaration   `Declare Function SelectClipRgn& Lib "gdi32" (ByVal hdc As Long, ByVal hRgn As _`
`Long)`

Description   Selects a new clipping region for the specified device context.

Use with VB   Refer to "Clipping, Regions, and Other Device Context Functions," earlier in this chapter.

Parameter	Type/Description
hdc	Long—Device context for which to set a new clipping region.
hRgn	Long—Handle to a clipping region to set for the device context. This region uses device coordinates.

Return Value   Long—Returns one of the following constants that describe the new region:

1. COMPLEXREGION: If the region has borders that overlap each other.

2. SIMPLEREGION: If the borders of the region do not overlap each other.

3. NULLREGION: If the region is empty.

4. ERRORAPI: If an error occurred (the previous clipping region remains).

Platform   Windows 95, Windows NT, Win16

Comments   This function makes a copy of the specified region; thus the same region may be used on multiple device contexts or deleted without affecting the clipping region on each device context. Some printers have different coordinate systems for text and graphics; in these cases, use the coordinate system that provides the higher resolution—for example, a dot-matrix printer that uses dithering. The text resolution will be higher than the graphics resolution. In this case the text coordinate system should be used.

  If using subclassing of the WM_PAINT message, you cannot use this function to increase the clipping region beyond the invalid area of the window while processing this message.

Example   Region.vbp

SetBoundsRect

VB Declaration   `Declare Function SetBoundsRect& Lib "gdi32" (ByVal hdc As Long, lprcBounds As _`
`RECT, ByVal flags As Long)`

Description   Sets the bounding rectangle for the specified device context. Each device context has a bounding rectangle that may be used by the programmer to accumulate information representing the bounds of the current image. When bounding rectangle accumulation is enabled, every time Windows draws into the device context the drawing location is tested against the bounding rectangle. The bounding rectangle is then expanded if necessary to include the drawing location. This provides one method of determining what parts of a device context have been drawn into.

Use with VB   No problem.

Parameter	Type/Description
hdc	Long—Device context for the bounding rectangle.

Parameter	Type/Description
lprcBounds	RECT—Rectangle from which to set the bounding rectangle.
flags	Long—Flag integer that may be a combination of the following constants: DCB_ACCUMULATE: The new bounding rectangle is the union of the current bounding rectangle and lprcBounds. DCB_DISABLE: Turns off bounds accumulation. This is the default. DCB_ENABLE: Turns on bounds accumulation. DCB_RESET: Clears the previous bounding rectangle. Use with DCB_ACCUMULATE to set the new bounding rectangle to lprcBounds.

Return Value   Long—The bounding settings before calling this function:

1. DCB_SET: If the bounding rectangle was not empty.

2. DCB_RESET: If the bounding rectangle was empty.

3. DCB_ENABLE: If a bounding rectangle was being accumulated.

4. DCB_DISABLE: If a bounding rectangle was not being accumulated.

Platform   Windows 95, Windows NT, Win16

■ SetGraphicsMode

VB Declaration   `Declare Function SetGraphicsMode& Lib "gdi32" (ByVal hdc As Long, ByVal iMode _`
`As Long)`

Description   Enables or disables advanced graphic mode support including world transforms.

Use with VB   No problem.

Parameter	Type/Description
hdc	Long—The device context whose mode you are setting.
iMode	Long—One of the following values: GM_COMPATIBLE to set Win16 compatible mode or GM_ADVANCED to enable advanced graphics mode including world transforms.

Return Value   Long—The previous graphics mode, zero on error.

Platform   Windows 95, Windows NT. World transforms are only supported on Windows NT.

Comments   If you have entered advanced graphics mode and have set a world transform, you must set the world transform back to default identity transform using SetWorldTransform or ModifyWorldTransform before you can set the graphics mode back to GM_COMPATIBLE. See ModifyWorldTransform for more information on the identity transform.

Example   Viewport.vbp, Spin.vbp.

■ SetMapMode

VB Declaration
```
Declare Function SetMapMode& Lib "gdi32" (ByVal hdc As Long, ByVal nMapMode As _
Long)
```

Description
Sets the mapping mode for the specified device context.

Use with VB
Refer to "Scaling and Coordinate Systems," earlier in this chapter. Changing the mapping mode without the proper precautions will lead to incorrect drawing on the part of VB drawing functions.

Parameter	Type/Description
hdc	Long—Handle to the device context to change.
nMapMode	Long—One of the following constants: MM_ANISOTROPIC: Viewport and window extents may be completely arbitrary. MM_HIENGLISH: Logical units are 0.001 inch. Origin is the lower-left corner. MM_HIMETRIC: Logical units are 0.01 millimeter. Origin is the lower-left corner. MM_ISOTROPIC: Viewport and window extents are arbitrary except that the X and Y logical units are the same size. MM_LOENGLISH: Logical units are 0.01 inch. Origin is the lower-left corner. MM_HIMETRIC: Logical units are 0.1 millimeter. Origin is the lower-left corner. MM_TEXT: Logical units are one pixel. MM_TWIPS: Logical units are one twip (1/1440 inch). Origin is the lower-left corner.

Return Value
Long—The previous mapping mode for the device context. Zero on error.

Platform
Windows 95, Windows NT, Win16

Comments
Refer to "Scaling and Coordinate Systems," earlier in this chapter.

Example
Viewport.vbp

■ SetRectRgn

VB Declaration
```
Declare Function SetRectRgn& Lib "gdi32" (ByVal hRgn As Long, ByVal X1 As Long, _
ByVal Y1 As Long, ByVal X2 As Long, ByVal Y2 As Long)
```

Description
Sets the specified region to a rectangle described by the points X1,Y1 and X2,Y2.

Use with VB
No problem.

Parameter	Type/Description
hRgn	Long—This region is set to the specified rectangle.
X1,Y1	Long—X,Y coordinates describing the upper-left corner of the rectangle.

Parameter	Type/Description
X2,Y2	Long—X,Y coordinates describing the lower-right corner of the rectangle

Return Value   Long—Nonzero on success, zero on failure.

Platform   Windows 95, Windows NT, Win16

Comments   This function is similar to CreateRectRgn except that it sets an existing region rather than creating a new region.
The bottom and right edges of the rectangle are not included in the region.

Example   Region.vbp

■ SetViewportExtEx

VB Declaration   ```
Declare Function SetViewportExtEx& Lib "gdi32" (ByVal hdc As Long, ByVal nX As _
Long, ByVal nY As Long, lpSize As SIZE)
```

**Description**    Sets the extents of the device context's viewport.

**Use with VB**    Refer to "Scaling and Coordinate Systems," earlier in this chapter.

| Parameter | Type/Description |
|---|---|
| hdc | Long—Handle to a device context. |
| nX, nY | Long—Horizontal and vertical viewport extents. |
| lpSize | SIZE—SIZEAPI structure to load with the previous horizontal and vertical extents of the DC viewport in device units. |

**Return Value**    Long—Nonzero on success, zero on failure.

**Platform**    Windows 95, Windows NT, Win16

**Comments**    Refer to "Windows and Viewpoints—Extents and Origins," earlier in this chapter. Only valid in the MM_ISOTROPIC and MM_ANISOTROPIC mapping modes. In MM_ISOTROPIC mode you must set the window extents before the viewport extents.

**Example**    Viewport.vbp

# ■ SetViewportOrgEx

**VB Declaration**    ```
Declare Function SetViewportOrgEx& Lib "gdi32" (ByVal hdc As Long, ByVal nX As _
Long, ByVal nY As Long, lpPoint As POINTAPI)
```

Description   Sets the origin of the device context's viewport.

Use with VB   Refer to "Scaling and Coordinate Systems," earlier in this chapter.

Parameter	Type/Description
hdc	Long—Handle to a device context.

Parameter	Type/Description
nX, nY	Long—Horizontal and vertical viewport origins in device coordinates.
lpPoint	POINTAPI—A POINTAPI structure to load with the previous viewport origins.

Return Value   Long—Nonzero on success, zero on failure.

Platform   Windows 95, Windows NT, Win16

Comments   Refer to "Windows and Viewpoints—Extents and Origins," earlier in this chapter.

Example   Viewport.vbp

■ SetWindowExtEx

VB Declaration
```
Declare Function SetWindowExtEx& Lib "gdi32" (ByVal hdc As Long, ByVal nX As _
Long, ByVal nY As Long, lpSize As SIZE)
```

Description   Sets the window extents for the specified device context.

Use with VB   Refer to "Scaling and Coordinate Systems," earlier in this chapter.

Parameter	Type/Description
hdc	Long—Handle to a device context.
nX, nY	Long—Horizontal and vertical window extents.
lpSize	SIZE—SIZEAPI structure to load with the previous horizontal and vertical window extents of the device context viewport in logical units.

Return Value   Long—Nonzero on success, zero on failure.

Platform   Windows 95, Windows NT, Win16

Comments   Refer to "Windows and Viewpoints—Extents and Origins," earlier in this chapter. Only valid in the MM_ISOTROPIC and MM_ANISOTROPIC mapping modes. In MM_ISOTROPIC mode you must set the window extents before the viewport extents.

Example   Viewport.vbp

■ SetWindowOrgEx

VB Declaration
```
Declare Function SetWindowOrgEx& Lib "gdi32" (ByVal hdc As Long, ByVal nX As _
Long, ByVal nY As Long, lpPoint As POINTAPI)
```

Description   Sets the window origin for the specified device context.

Use with VB   No problem.

Parameter	Type/Description
hdc	Long—Handle to a device context.

Parameter	Type/Description
nX, nY	Long—Horizontal and vertical window origins in logical coordinates.
lpPoint	POINTAPI—A POINTAPI structure to load with the previous window origins.

Return Value   Long—Nonzero on success, zero on failure.

Platform   Windows 95, Windows NT, Win16

Comments   Refer to "Windows and Viewpoints—Extents and Origins," earlier in this chapter.

Example   Viewport.vbp

■ SetWindowRgn

VB Declaration
```
Declare Function SetWindowRgn& Lib "user32" (ByVal hWnd As Long, ByVal hRgn As _
Long, ByVal bRedraw As Long)
```

Description   This is one of those hidden API functions that hardly anyone notices, yet has enormous implications for programmers. SetWindowRgn allows you to change the region for a window.

Normally, all windows are rectangular—they have an implied region in which they exist, which is a rectangle. This function allows you to override that region. This means that you can create windows that are round, star-shaped, fragmented into two or more different sections—virtually anything.

Use with VB   No problem—you can change the shape of forms and other Visual Basic controls without any trouble.

Parameter	Type/Description
hWnd	Long—The window whose region you wish to set.
hRgn	Long—The handle of the region to set. Once you set this region, you should not use or modify this region handle. Do not delete it.
bRedraw	Boolean—TRUE to redraw the window immediately.

Return Value   Long—TRUE (nonzero) on success, zero on error.

Platform   Windows 95, Windows NT

Comments   All coordinates specified for the region are in window coordinates (NOT client coordinates). They are relative to the upper-left corner of the entire window including captions and borders if present.

Example   Round.vbp

■ SetWorldTransform

VB Declaration
```
Declare Function SetWorldTransform& Lib "gdi32" (ByVal hdc As Long, lpXform As _
XFORM)
```

Description   Sets the world transform. See the section on World Transforms earlier in the chapter.

Use with VB   No problem.

Parameter	Type/Description
hdc	Long—The device context to set.
lpXform	XFORM—An XFORM structure containing the world transform to apply.

Return Value   Long—Nonzero on success, zero on failure.

Platform   Windows NT

Comments   You must set the graphics mode to GM_ADVANCED using the SetGraphicsMode function before using world transforms.

Example   Viewport.vbp, Spin.vbp

■ ValidateRgn

VB Declaration
```
Declare Function ValidateRgn& Lib "user32" (ByVal hwnd As Long, ByVal hRgn As _
Long)
```

Description   Validates the specified region in a window, removing it from the update region.

Use with VB   No problem.

Parameter	Type/Description
hwnd	Long—Handle of window to validate.
hRgn	Long—Handle to region defining the area to validate. The region is specified in window client coordinates.

Return Value   Long—Nonzero on success, zero on failure.

Platform   Windows 95, Windows NT, Win16

■ WindowFromDC

VB Declaration
```
Declare Function WindowFromDC& Lib "user32" (ByVal hdc As Long)
```

Description   Retrieves the handle of the window associated with a device context.

Use with VB   No problem.

Parameter	Type/Description
hdc	Long—The device context to test.

Return Value   Long—The handle of the window associated with this device context. Zero on error.

Platform   Windows 95, Windows NT

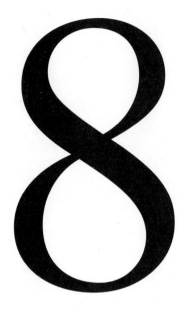

Drawing Functions

WINDOWS IS A GRAPHICAL ENVIRONMENT, AND THIS CHAPTER discusses one of the most interesting parts of the Win32 API—those functions dealing with graphic output. In a sense, all of the preceding chapters are just a prelude to this subject—a subject that draws on everything that has come before and ties it all together. This is also an area where Win32 has added some intriguing new features when compared to Win16.

In fact, the drawing capabilities available under Win32 are so sophisticated that it would probably take an entire book to describe them in the kind of depth that they deserve. Since that is not possible, this chapter focuses on giving you the tools that you will need to do your own experimentation with these API functions. The chapter begins by discussing the principles and rules for drawing under Windows and gives a brief summary of the functions that are available. This is followed by an in-depth analysis of several sample programs. The best way for you to learn to use these functions is to experiment, and the sample programs demonstrate how you can create your own programs for experimenting with these drawing functions. They also provide a base which you can extend in order to try out functions that are not covered in detail.

Overview of Graphic Output

The process of drawing in Windows involves a number of different objects:

- *Device:* This can be a display window, a printer page, or any other output device for which a device context can be obtained.

- *Device context:* This determines all aspects of drawing onto a device. The drawing objects listed below are selected into a device context before drawing. The DC also specifies the coordinate system to use when drawing.

- *Pen:* A pen is an object that defines the way that lines are drawn. Pens have several attributes, including width, color, and dashing.

- *Brush:* A brush is an object that defines the way that areas are filled. Brushes may be solid, hatched, or defined using a bitmap pattern.

- *Drawing attributes:* These define how the line or area being drawn on by the pen or brush is combined with the existing image on a device.

- *Clipping area:* This defines the area in the device context that can actually be drawn on. Clipping is discussed in Chapter 7.

- *Color palette:* This GDI object defines the colors that are visible on a window.

- *Path:* An object that defines a complex shape which can be drawn or filled.

Figure 8.1 illustrates the process of drawing onto a device.

Figure 8.1

How Windows draws
onto a device

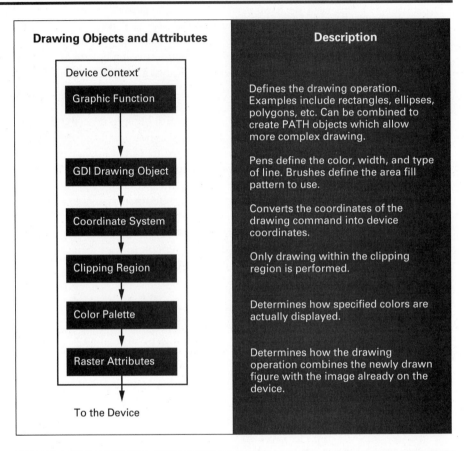

Drawing Objects and Attributes	Description
Device Context	
Graphic Function	Defines the drawing operation. Examples include rectangles, ellipses, polygons, etc. Can be combined to create PATH objects which allow more complex drawing.
GDI Drawing Object	Pens define the color, width, and type of line. Brushes define the area fill pattern to use.
Coordinate System	Converts the coordinates of the drawing command into device coordinates.
Clipping Region	Only drawing within the clipping region is performed.
Color Palette	Determines how specified colors are actually displayed.
Raster Attributes	Determines how the drawing operation combines the newly drawn figure with the image already on the device.
To the Device	

This figure also clarifies the issues of coordinate systems under Windows and shows how Windows is built in layers. The upper two boxes, *Graphic Function* and *GDI Drawing Object*, indicate processes that occur before the coordinate transformation occurs. The implications of this are far-reaching. It means that all parameters to GDI drawing functions and GDI object creation and manipulation functions that have to do with positions or size are specified in logical or world coordinates—not device coordinates. They are all subject to coordinate transformations.

Those boxes that appear under the coordinate System box indicate processes that occur after coordinate transformations have occurred—thus all parameters to those functions that relate to position or size are specified in device coordinates. This is why region functions, which were described in Chapter 7, all use parameters that are specified in device coordinates. Regions are tied in closely to clipping regions and to devices. GDI provides a similar object for manipulation of complex shapes that use logical coordinates called paths. Paths are described later in this chapter.

GDI Drawing Objects

A GDI drawing object is an internal Windows object that defines an aspect of the drawing operation. In this chapter, the focus is on pens and brushes, though much of the discussion also applies to GDI objects such as paths, regions, and metafiles. These objects are collectively referred to as GDI resources, and there are a number of rules that you should follow when using them.

Creation of GDI Drawing Objects

Pens and brushes are obtained using one of the functions listed in Table 8.1.

Table 8.1   **Pen and Brush Creation Functions**

Function	Description
CreateBrushIndirect	Creates a brush using a LOGBRUSH data structure.
CreateDIBPatternBrush CreateDIBPatternBrushPt	Creates a brush based on a device-independent bitmap pattern.
CreateHatchBrush	Creates a hatched brush.
CreatePatternBrush	Creates a brush based on a bitmap pattern.
CreatePen	Creates a pen.
CreatePenIndirect	Creates a pen based on a LOGPEN data structure.
CreateSolidBrush	Creates a solid color brush.
ExtCreatePen	Creates an extended pen.
GetStockObject	Retrieves a system pen or brush.
GetSysColorBrush	Retrieves a brush for a specified system color.

Selection and Deletion Rules for GDI Objects

In order to use a pen or a brush it is necessary to select it into a device context using the SelectObject function. A device context may have only one object of each type selected at a time. When an object is selected into a DC, the Select-Object function returns as a result the object of that type that was previously selected into the device context. For example, when a pen is selected into a DC, a handle to the previously selected pen is returned.

This handle should be saved so that it may be restored into the device context before the DC is deleted. *Always restore the original GDI objects into a device context before that context is deleted.* It is also possible to use the SaveDC and RestoreDC functions to accomplish this. If you save the state of a device context, select some new GDI objects into the DC, then restore the previous state of the device context using RestoreDC, the original objects will be reselected into the device context. Remember that you can make no assumptions regarding the initial settings of a device context except in certain specific cases discussed later in this chapter in the section on use of GDI objects under Visual Basic.

Under Win16 GDI objects were owned by GDI and were shared on a systemwide basis. This not only severely limited available resources, but made it absolutely essential that you delete any resources that you allocated in your program. Under Win32, resources are private to each application. This makes it possible for both Windows 95 and Windows NT to automatically free any resources allocated by your application. Nevertheless, it is good practice to delete any GDI objects that you create. It is essential if you are writing applications for both 16- and 32-bit platforms, as Windows 95 cannot always free resources automatically when a program exits.

Never delete a GDI object that is selected into a device context!

Another result of GDI objects being private to an application is that in Win32 you cannot share GDI objects among applications. This was possible under Win16.

The GetStockObject function retrieves a stock system object. Objects returned by this function must not be deleted with the DeleteObject function.

Table 8.2 shows the API functions used when working with GDI objects.

Table 8.2   **GDI Object Control**

Function	Description
DeleteObject	Deletes a GDI object.
EnumObjects	Enumerates the objects available to a device context.
GetCurrentObject	Retrieves a handle to the currently selected object of a specified type.
GetObjectAPI	Retrieves information about a GDI object.
GetObjectType	Determines the type of a GDI object.

Table 8.2 **GDI Object Control (Continued)**

Function	Description
IsGDIObject	Not supported under Win32. Use GetObjectType.
SelectObject	Selects a GDI object into a device context.

Pens

A pen is a GDI object that defines how lines are drawn. Pens are selected into a device context using the SelectObject function. Win32 defines two different types of pens. The standard pen type has three attributes: color, width, and style.

A pen's color specifies the desired RGB color for lines. The actual color used will depend on the device. GDI will always choose the closest color that the device can actually render.

The width attribute specifies the width of a line in logical coordinates.

Standard pens can be created with a number of styles including solid, invisible, and several varieties of dashed and dotted lines. Only the solid and invisible styles may be used with line widths greater than one.

Under Win32 it is also possible to create two types of extended pen styles. A cosmetic pen always has a width of one logical unit, and can be solid, have a standard dash or dot pattern, or have a user-defined dash or dot pattern. A geometric pen can have a variety of widths, styles, and dot patterns, and provides enhanced control over the way two lines are joined. The ExtPen example described later in this chapter goes into more detail on how to create and use extended pens.

Table 8.1 describes the API functions used to create pens.

Brushes

A brush is a GDI object that defines how areas are filled. A brush defines a small area (typically 8 x 8 pixels) which is replicated over the area that is being filled. On Windows 95 and Windows 3.x, a brush can never be larger than 8 x 8 pixels.

Attributes

Brush attributes define the contents of the pixel area defined by the brush. In the case of pattern brushes, the area contains a user-defined bitmap. For solid brushes, the entire area is a single solid color. For hatched brushes, a bitmap is defined such that a cross-hatched pattern is created when the area is filled.

A brush's color specifies the desired RGB color for the brush. The actual color used will depend on the device. GDI will always choose the closest color that the device can actually render.

Table 8.1 describes the API functions used to create brushes.

Origins

A brush, as mentioned earlier, represents an area used in filling areas on a display device. Imagine an 8 x 8 pixel brush that consists of a pair of diagonal lines, and consider what happens when you fill a window using that brush. If the brush begins filling from the upper-left corner of a window, the window will be filled as shown in the top example of Figure 8.2. It doesn't matter where you start painting on the window—the diagonal lines will always match up. This is because the brush origin is aligned with the top of the window. But what if you wanted the diagonal lines to start at the second or third pixel from the top of the window? This might be necessary if a window has been scrolled by a number of pixels that is not divisible by 8 as shown in the second example in Figure 8.2. If you then try to fill the exposed area, the pattern painted in that area will not be properly aligned with the scrolled area.

Figure 8.2

Illustration of brush alignment

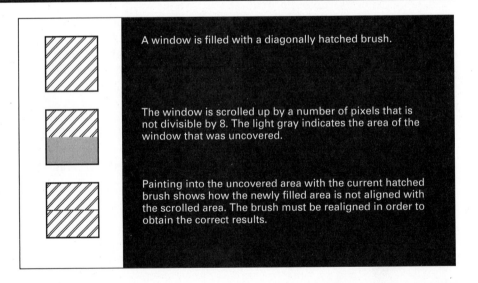

A window is filled with a diagonally hatched brush.

The window is scrolled up by a number of pixels that is not divisible by 8. The light gray indicates the area of the window that was uncovered.

Painting into the uncovered area with the current hatched brush shows how the newly filled area is not aligned with the scrolled area. The brush must be realigned in order to obtain the correct results.

You could create a new brush where the diagonal lines start at the second or third row in the 8 x 8 area, but an easier solution is to offset the origin of the brush to start at the desired row. Windows NT does this automatically for you, but under Windows 95 (which is still using Win16 GDI internally) you must manage the brush origins yourself.

This is a two-part process. First, the origin of the brush is changed using the SetBrushOrgEx function. Next, the UnrealizeObject function is used on the brush. This function tells Windows to delete any existing physical representation of the brush. This is necessary because Windows actually uses the logical brush object to create a physical brush that is used internally to do the actual drawing.

The exact process for aligning brushes is as follows:

1. Be sure that the brush to be realigned is not selected into a device context. If necessary, select a different brush into the device context temporarily.

2. Use the SetBrushOrg function to set the new brush origin.

3. Use the UnrealizeObject function to realign the brush. This informs Windows that it should re-create the internal bitmap based on the new origin when the brush is selected into a device context.

4. Select the realigned brush into the device context.

Do not change the origin of the system stock brushes (those obtained by the GetStockObject function).

Table 8.3 shows the API functions used when working with brushes.

Table 8.3   **API Brush Origin Functions**

Function	Description
GetBrushOrgEx	Retrieves the origin of a brush
SetBrushOrgEx	Realigns the origin of a brush
UnrealizeObject	Forces Windows to re-create the internal brush bitmap when a brush is selected into a DC

GDI Objects and Visual Basic

As mentioned in Chapter 7, Visual Basic forms and picture controls use private device contexts. Visual Basic always has a pen or brush selected into this device context. The pen and brush selected depends on the various properties of the VB control. These include the FillColor, FillStyle, DrawStyle, and DrawWidth properties.

It is important to restore these original objects into the device context if other pens or brushes are used during API drawing operations. This is because Visual Basic does not reselect drawing objects each time it draws. If you leave a different object selected into the device context, Visual Basic will continue to use that object, leading to results that do not match the VB property settings.

When using API drawing functions, you should use the following sequence of operations:

1. Create drawing objects (pens, brushes, and so on). You can create them immediately before use, or when your program starts (or any time in between).

The key thing to remember is to destroy them when you are done. For example, if you create a set of drawing objects when your application starts, destroy them when your program terminates. If you create drawing objects at the beginning of a function, destroy them before the function returns.

2. Before drawing, consider how you will go about restoring the previous state of the device context. Two common approaches are to use SaveDC to save the state of the device context and to use RestoreDC to restore it later. Another is to create variables to store the values of the current drawing objects as you select new objects.

3. Select the objects that you wish to draw with. If you are storing the original objects in temporary variables, assign those variables with the result of the SelectObject function. For example: *oldpen = SelectObject(hDC, newpen)* stores the handle of the original pen into variable oldpen.

4. Perform any drawing operations. You can select additional drawing objects at any time.

5. Select the original objects back into the device context. This can be done using the SelectObject function: *dummyvar = SelectObject (hDC, oldpen)* or using RestoreDC (if you used SaveDC earlier).

Because Visual Basic selects pens and brushes based on VB properties, you can often mix VB property setting and API drawing commands at will. However, API drawing commands provide far more capability than is available under Visual Basic alone, and you will generally obtain better performance.

Generally speaking, with Visual Basic forms and picture boxes, when you obtain the private device context for a control it will have objects selected according to the Visual Basic properties. Device context properties such as the drawing mode will also be set according to VB properties. These settings can lead to unexpected side effects in your own drawing routines if you do not take them into account. This is demonstrated in the XOR_COPY sample program that is included on the CD-ROM that comes with this book. In one case the picture control's drawing mode is set to exclusive or mode. Try dragging a second window over the control and watch as the lines appear and disappear. This occurs because every time a paint event arrives, those areas of the window that were cleared are drawn correctly, and those areas of the window where the lines are still visible are inverted. The paint event draws the entire control each time it is received—Visual Basic does not set a clipping area to restrict drawing only to those areas that were uncovered. The copy pen example changes the drawing mode during the paint event to prevent this problem from occurring.

Those of you who study the example and are particularly observant might notice something interesting. Hint: Replace the Rectangle API drawing command with the Visual Basic Line command (for example, picture1.line

(0,0)-(1000,1000),RGB(255,255,255),F). The problem still occurs! While it is true that this book focuses on the Win32API, keep in mind one of the key points from Chapter 2: that Visual Basic and Windows are tightly coupled. The problem illustrated in the XOR_COPY sample program is a general Windows programming issue and not limited to direct use of API functions (though, obviously, VB is using those same functions internally). Even if you never use API functions, a good understanding of how these functions work is directly transferable to Visual Basic programming.

Which brings us once again to stress an important rule of API drawing: Make no assumptions about the state of the device context that you obtain. If you want to draw a black line, be sure to select a black pen into the device context or, if appropriate, to the VB control in question, verify that the VB properties are set correctly to obtain the result that you want.

This is also a good time to add a second reminder: Restoring the device context to its initial state is important not only with regard to GDI object selections but also with regard to other device context settings such as those relating to coordinate systems. Visual Basic always assumes that the mapping mode is MM_TEXT; if you change the coordinate system and forget to set it back, Visual Basic will not be able to draw correctly.

Drawing Attributes

A device context also specifies a number of drawing attributes. These define the way that brushes and pens interact with the current contents of the window or device surface. Table 8.4 lists the API functions that are used to control drawing attributes.

Table 8.4　　**Drawing Attribute Control Functions**

Function	Description
GetArcDirection	Determines the direction used for drawing arcs and rectangles.
GetBkColor	Retrieves the current background color.
GetBkMode	Retrieves the current background mode.
GetCurrentPositionEx	Retrieves the current pen position.
GetMiterLimit	Retrieves the miter limit used for drawing miters on geometric pens.
GetNearestColor	Given a color, obtains the nearest color that can actually be rendered by a device.

Table 8.4 **Drawing Attribute Control Functions (Continued)**

Function	Description
GetPolyFillMode	Retrieves the current polygon filling mode. See SetPolyFillMode in the Function Reference section of this chapter for details.
GetROP2	Retrieves the current line raster operation mode.
MoveToEx	Sets the pen position.
SetArcDirection	Sets the direction used for drawing arcs and rectangles.
SetBkColor	Sets the background color.
SetBkMode	Sets the background mode.
SetMiterLimit	Sets the miter limit used for drawing miters on geometric pens.
SetPolyFillMode	Sets the current polygon filling mode. Refer to the description of this function in the function reference section of this chapter for details.
SetROP2	Sets the line raster operation mode.

Line Raster Operations

Normally, when you think of drawing with a pen, you assume that the pen color is simply drawn on the display or device. Windows actually supports 16 different line drawing modes that define how a line is combined with information already present on the display. These modes are called *line raster operations* (also known as raster-ops, binary raster operations, or ROP2 mode) and are referred to in Visual Basic as the drawing mode. The ROP2 raster operations are identical to the VB DrawMode property.

One commonly used raster operation is the exclusive-or mode. Drawing a line once in this mode causes a line to appear in which the pixels are inverted wherever the line is drawn. Drawing the line again causes the original display to be restored. This technique is used in the RectPlay program in Chapter 5 to allow creation of a rectangle by dragging the mouse.

Background Mode

Hatched brushes, dashed pens, and text all have a background. For hatched brushes it is the area between the hatch lines. For dashed pens it is the area between the dots or dashes. For text it is the background of each character cell.

The background mode defines how Windows handles this background area. It can be opaque or transparent. When opaque, the background area is set to the background color. When transparent, the background area remains undisturbed.

Current Position

Each device context has a current pen position specified. You can set the pen position using the MoveToEx function. Drawing functions that end with the suffix "To" (such as LineTo and ArcTo) set the pen position to the final point in the drawing command. Drawing commands without this suffix do not change the current pen position. Win32 provides substantially more functions that change the pen position in order to support the new path capability, which will be described shortly.

Drawing Functions

Windows provides a robust set of drawing functions beyond those provided by Visual Basic. Each function is described in detail in the function reference section of this chapter. Among the most interesting are the new Win32 functions that allow you to create complex spline curves called Bézier curves. Table 8.5 lists the Win32 general purpose drawing functions.

Table 8.5   **Windows API Drawing Functions**

Function	Description
AngleArc	Draws a line that ends with an arc.
Arc	Draws an arc.
ArcTo	Draws an arc and updates the current position.
CancelDC	Aborts long drawing operations.
Chord	Draws a chord (an ellipse bisected by a line).
Ellipse	Draws an ellipse.
ExtFloodFill	Fills an area on the screen.
FillRect	Fills a rectangle.
FloodFill	Fills an area on the screen.
FrameRect	Draws a frame around a rectangle.
GetPixel	Retrieves the color of a pixel.
InvertRect	Inverts the image in a rectangle.
LineDDA	Retrieves a list of all pixels that will be set by a specified line.

Table 8.5   **Windows API Drawing Functions (Continued)**

Function	Description
LineTo	Draws a line and sets the current position.
Pie	Draws a pie shape.
PolyBezier	Draws a series of Bézier curves.
PolyBezierTo	Draws a series of Bézier curves and sets the current position.
PolyDraw	Draws a series of Bézier curves and line segments.
Polygon	Draws a polygon.
Polyline	Draws a series of connected line segments.
PolyLineTo	Draws a series of connected line segments. Sets the current position.
PolyPolygon	Draws a series of polygons.
PolyPolyline	Draws a series of Polyline line segment groups.
Rectangle	Draws a rectangle.
RoundRect	Draws a rectangle with rounded corners.
SetPixel	Sets the color of a single pixel.
SetPixelV	Sets the color of a single pixel without returning the color actually set.

Windows also provides a number of more specialized drawing functions that are used less frequently. They give you the ability to tap into the same API functions that Windows uses internally to draw system objects such as frames, captions, 3D controls, and the desktop. These functions are shown in Table 8.6.

Table 8.6   **Win32 API Additional Drawing Functions**

Function	Description
DrawEdge	Draws edges of a rectangle according to a specified style (including 3D effects).
DrawEscape	Allows you to bypass GDI to access the underlying capabilities of a video device.
DrawFocusRect	Draws a rectangle with a fine dotted line as commonly used to indicate the control that has the focus.

Table 8.6	**Win32 API Additional Drawing Functions (Continued)**

Function	Description
DrawFrameControl	Draws a standard control frame according to a specified style.
DrawState	Allows you to apply effects to complex drawing operations.
GdiFlush	Flushes the queue of pending drawing operations. Refer to the comments in the Function Reference section for this function for an explanation of the GDI batch system.
GdiGetBatchLimit	Determines the maximum number of drawing operations that may be queued for the current application.
GdiSetBatchLimit	Sets the maximum number of drawing operations that may be queued for the current application.
PaintDesktop	Paints the specified device context with the pattern used by the Windows desktop.

Paths

Paths are one of the most exciting new capabilities of the Win32 API. A path is not a drawing object in the sense that a pen or brush is a GDI object. You cannot obtain a handle to a path which you create and which then needs to be destroyed. A path can best be thought of as a series of drawing commands executed for a device context that are temporarily stored and not actually drawn. A device context can contain only one path at a time.

You create a path by calling the BeginPath API. This throws away any existing path in the device context and begins recording API drawing commands. You can use the following commands within a path:

AngleArc, Arc, ArcTo, Chord, Ellipse, ExtTextOut, LineTo, MoveToEx, Pie, PolyBezier, PolyBezierTo, PolyDraw, Polygon, Polyline, PolylineTo, Poly-Polygon, PolyPolyline, Rectangle, RoundRect, and TextOut.

The EndPath function informs the system that the path is complete.

A path can be made up of one or more subpaths or figures. Figure 8.3 illustrates how this works. *Subpaths* are groups of line segments that are unconnected. Each subpath (also known as an open figure) can be turned into a closed figure by the CloseFigure function or by filling the path.

So what are paths good for? After all, there is no real difference between drawing a path which is then outlined (stroked) and filled, and using individual drawing commands, is there?

There are several obvious uses for paths. They allow you to create complex shapes using logical coordinates. Remember that regions are defined in device

Figure 8.3

Paths, subpaths, and figures

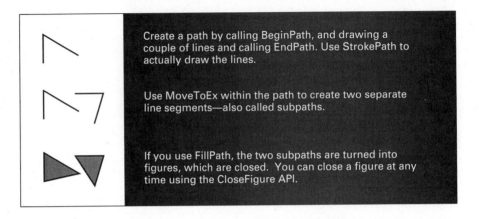

Create a path by calling BeginPath, and drawing a couple of lines and calling EndPath. Use StrokePath to actually draw the lines.

Use MoveToEx within the path to create two separate line segments—also called subpaths.

If you use FillPath, the two subpaths are turned into figures, which are closed. You can close a figure at any time using the CloseFigure API.

coordinates, and thus are not subject to the mapping mode and transformations that are in effect. Paths are always defined in logical coordinates; thus you can set your mapping mode, window, viewport, and world transformations, then create a path in logical or world coordinates. This path can then be converted into a region or clipping region, allowing you to take advantage of complex fills or use complex clipping regions that are based on logical coordinates.

A second obvious use for paths is to create complex shapes using line segments, arcs, and Bézier curves which can then be filled.

There are two other equally important but less obvious uses for paths. In addition to the drawing commands described in this chapter, you can draw text into a path. As long as that text is drawn using a TrueType or vector font, the path will be loaded with the outline of the text. This allows you to fill text with arbitrary patterns or even create clipping regions out of text! The Path.vbp example demonstrates this capability.

Another use for paths derives from the way paths handle line segments internally. Normally when you draw a series of lines, each line is independent even though one may start where another ends. Within a path, line segments that meet in this way are considered joined, and if you are using a geometric pen, Windows can use a number of special effects to draw the transition between the lines, including beveling and mitering. These effects are shown in the ExtPen.vbp example that follows later in this chapter.

All drawing operations into paths use logical coordinates; however, the transformation to device coordinates occurs as the path is being created (path information is stored internally in device coordinates). Thus you should stroke or fill a path using the same coordinate system and transformation settings that are in effect when the path is created.

Table 8.7 lists the functions that relate to paths.

Table 8.7 **Win32 Path Functions**

Function	Description
AbortPath	Removes the current path from a device context.
BeginPath	Starts creating a path in the specified device context.
CloseFigure	Turns the current path segment into a closed figure.
EndPath	Ends creation of a path on a device context.
FillPath	Closes any open figures in the path for the specified device context. It then fills them using the current brush.
FlattenPath	Converts all curves in the path for the specified device context into lines.
GetPath	Retrieves information about the path for the specified device context.
PathToRegion	Converts a path into a region.
SelectClipPath	Combines the path of a device context with its clipping region.
StrokeAndFillPath	Draws the segments of the path for the specified device context, closing and filling the figures in the path.
StrokePath	Draws the segments of the path for the specified device context.
WidenPath	Converts the path into lines, widening the path according to the pen selected into the device context.

Platform Issues

By now you may be quite excited about the possibilities unleashed by the new Win32 drawing functions. Unfortunately, it is necessary to throw a slight damper on things. First, many of the new drawing functions are not supported under Windows 95. Next, many of the features of geometric pens are also not supported under Windows 95. Finally, because GDI is still 16 bits under Windows 95, the performance of some of the graphic operations described here is significantly slower under Windows 95 than Windows NT. For example, in the Path.vbp example that follows there is a demonstration of clipping in which radial circles are drawn within a clipping region. The drawing is nearly instantaneous under Windows NT (tested on a 90Mhz Pentium system), and so slow as to be almost impractical under Windows 95.

Bringing It All Together: Learning through Examples

The best way to become acquainted with the Win32 drawing functions is through experimentation in code. Each of the examples that follow combines most of the principles described in this chapter, from creating and selecting objects to draw-ing and using paths. Some of the examples also draw on functions that will be de-scribed in later chapters, but their use here should be fairly self-explanatory. The first of these examples is Path.vbp, which demonstrates how paths can be used to create complex clipping regions to generate some impressive graphical effects.

Example: Path.vbp

Path.vbp is a very simple example that draws some text into a path, then turns the path into the clipping region for the device context. It then draws a pattern into the device context which appears clipped to the text. There are four but-tons on the main form of the project, three of them fill the clipping area with different patterns, the fourth uses the StrokePath API to outline the path. Fig-ure 8.4 shows one of the clipping effects supported by this example.

Figure 8.4
Clipping ellipses to text

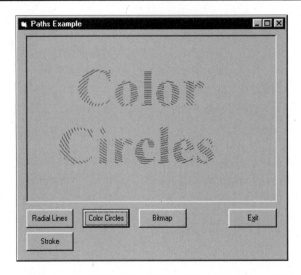

Project and Form Description
The Path.vbp project contains only one file, PATH.FRM (two if you count the frx file that contains the bitmap used by the picture control). Listing 8.1 shows the form header and program listing.

Listing 8.1 **PATH.FRM**

```
VERSION 5.00
Begin VB.Form frmPaths
```

Listing 8.1   **PATH.FRM (Continued)**

```
Caption          =   "Paths Example"
ClientHeight     =   5355
ClientLeft       =   1095
ClientTop        =   1515
ClientWidth      =   6465
ClipControls     =   0    'False
Height           =   5760
Left             =   1035
LinkTopic        =   "Form1"
ScaleHeight      =   5355
ScaleWidth       =   6465
Top              =   1170
Width            =   6585
Begin VB.CommandButton cmdWhich
   Caption       =   "Stroke"
   Height        =   435
   Index         =   3
   Left          =   180
   TabIndex      =   6
   Top           =   4740
   Width         =   1155
End
Begin VB.CommandButton cmdExit
   Caption       =   "E&xit"
   Height        =   435
   Left          =   5100
   TabIndex      =   5
   Top           =   4200
   Width         =   1155
End
Begin VB.CommandButton cmdWhich
   Caption       =   "Bitmap"
   Height        =   435
   Index         =   2
   Left          =   2940
   TabIndex      =   4
   Top           =   4200
   Width         =   1155
End
Begin VB.CommandButton cmdWhich
   Caption       =   "Color Circles"
   Height        =   435
   Index         =   1
   Left          =   1560
   TabIndex      =   3
   Top           =   4200
   Width         =   1155
End
```

Listing 8.1   PATH.FRM (Continued)

```
Begin VB.CommandButton cmdWhich
    Caption        =   "Radial Lines"
    Height         =   435
    Index          =   0
    Left           =   180
    TabIndex       =   2
    Top            =   4200
    Width          =   1155
End
```

The "out" picture box is loaded with the 256-color.bmp bitmap that has been included with Windows and Windows NT in the past. The data for this bitmap is kept in the PATH.FRX file.

```
Begin VB.PictureBox Out
    ClipControls     =   0    'False
    FillColor        =   &H000000FF&
    BeginProperty Font
        name         =   "Times New Roman"
        charset      =   0
        weight       =   700
        size         =   63.75
        underline    =   0    'False
        italic       =   0    'False
        strikethrough =  0    'False
    EndProperty
    FontTransparent  =   -1   'True
    ForeColor        =   &H00FF0000&
    Height           =   3915
    Left             =   180
    ScaleHeight      =   259
    ScaleMode        =   3    'Pixel
    ScaleWidth       =   403
    TabIndex         =   0
    Top              =   120
    Width            =   6075
End
Begin VB.PictureBox pctBmp
    AutoRedraw       =   -1   'True
    AutoSize         =   -1   'True
    Height           =   1830
    Left             =   60
    Picture          =   "path.frx":0000
    ScaleHeight      =   120
    ScaleMode        =   3    'Pixel
    ScaleWidth       =   160
    TabIndex         =   1
    Top              =   60
```

```
        Visible       =   0    'False
        Width         =   2430
     End
End
Attribute VB_Name = "frmPaths"
Attribute VB_GlobalNameSpace = False
Attribute VB_Creatable = False
Attribute VB_PredeclaredId = True
Attribute VB_Exposed = False
```

The WhichDrawing module variable keeps track of what type of fill pattern the program uses. There are two arrays that hold sine and cosine values. Preloading the arrays improves performance by eliminating the need to recalculate the values each time they are used.

```
Option Explicit
Public dl&, savedDC&, WhichDrawing%
Private allCos!(90), allSin!(90)
'*********************************
'** Type Definitions:

#If Win32 Then
Private Type RECT
    left As Long
    top As Long
    right As Long
    bottom As Long
End Type

Private Type POINTAPI
    x As Long
    y As Long
End Type

#End If 'WIN32 Types

#If Win32 Then
Private Const SRCPAINT& = &HEE0086
Private Const SRCCOPY& = &HCC0020
Private Const SRCAND& = &H8800C6
Private Const SRCERASE& = &H440328
Private Const SRCINVERT& = &H660046
Private Const TRANSPARENT& = 1
Private Const RGN_COPY& = 5
Private Const RGN_AND& = 1
Private Const RGN_DIFF& = 4
Private Const RGN_XOR& = 3
Private Const RGN_OR& = 2
Private Const BLACK_BRUSH = 4
Private Const BLACK_PEN = 7
'  Pen Styles
```

```
Private Const PS_SOLID = 0
Private Const PS_DASH = 1                        '  -------
Private Const PS_DOT = 2                         '  .......
Private Const PS_DASHDOT = 3                     '  _._._._
Private Const PS_DASHDOTDOT = 4                  '  _.._.._
Private Const PS_NULL = 5
Private Const PS_INSIDEFRAME = 6
Private Const PS_USERSTYLE = 7
Private Const PS_ALTERNATE = 8
Private Const PS_STYLE_MASK = &HF
#End If 'WIN32
```

You can place API function declarations into a form; however, you must declare them as Private.

```
'**********************************
'**  Function Declarations:

#If Win32 Then
Private Declare Function SelectObject& Lib "gdi32" (ByVal hdc As Long, ByVal _
hObject As Long)
Private Declare Function DeleteObject& Lib "gdi32" (ByVal hObject As Long)
Private Declare Function CreatePen& Lib "gdi32" (ByVal nPenStyle As Long, ByVal _
nWidth As Long, ByVal crColor As Long)
Private Declare Function GetStockObject& Lib "gdi32" (ByVal nIndex As Long)
Private Declare Function TextOut& Lib "gdi32" Alias "TextOutA" (ByVal hdc As _
Long, ByVal x As Long, ByVal y As Long, ByVal lpString As String, _
ByVal nCount As Long)
Private Declare Function Ellipse& Lib "gdi32" (ByVal hdc As Long, ByVal X1 As _
Long, ByVal Y1 As Long, ByVal X2 As Long, ByVal Y2 As Long)
Private Declare Function MoveToEx& Lib "gdi32" (ByVal hdc As Long, ByVal x As _
Long, ByVal y As Long, Prev As POINTAPI)
Private Declare Function LineTo& Lib "gdi32" (ByVal hdc As Long, ByVal x As _
Long, ByVal y As Long)
Private Declare Function GetLastError& Lib "kernel32" ()
Private Declare Function GetRgnBox& Lib "gdi32" (ByVal hdc As Long, bounds As _
RECT)
Private Declare Function GetClipRgn& Lib "gdi32" (ByVal hdc As Long, ByVal _
hRegion As Long)
Private Declare Function SaveDC& Lib "gdi32" (ByVal hdc As Long)
Private Declare Function RestoreDC& Lib "gdi32" (ByVal hdc As Long, ByVal _
nSavedDC As Long)
Private Declare Function DrawText& Lib "user32" Alias "DrawTextA" (ByVal hdc As _
Long, ByVal lpStr As String, ByVal nCount As Long, lpRect As RECT, _
ByVal wFormat As Long)
Private Declare Function BeginPath& Lib "gdi32" (ByVal hdc As Long)
Private Declare Function EndPath& Lib "gdi32" (ByVal hdc As Long)
Private Declare Function AbortPath& Lib "gdi32" (ByVal hdc As Long)
```

```
Private Declare Function CloseFigure& Lib "gdi32" (ByVal hdc As Long)
Private Declare Function StrokeAndFillPath& Lib "gdi32" (ByVal hdc As Long)
Private Declare Function StrokePath& Lib "gdi32" (ByVal hdc As Long)
Private Declare Function GetPath& Lib "gdi32" (ByVal hdc As Long, lpPoint As _
POINTAPI, lpTypes As Byte, ByVal nSize As Long)
Private Declare Function FlattenPath& Lib "gdi32" (ByVal hdc As Long)
Private Declare Function SelectClipPath& Lib "gdi32" (ByVal hdc As Long, ByVal _
iMode As Long)
Private Declare Function PathToRegion& Lib "gdi32" (ByVal hdc As Long)
Private Declare Function CreateRectRgn& Lib "gdi32" (ByVal X1 As Long, ByVal Y1 _
As Long, ByVal X2 As Long, ByVal Y2 As Long)
Private Declare Function SelectClipRgn& Lib "gdi32" (ByVal hdc As Long, ByVal _
hRgn As Long)
Private Declare Function FillRgn& Lib "gdi32" (ByVal hdc As Long, ByVal hRgn As _
Long, ByVal hBrush As Long)
Private Declare Function BitBlt& Lib "gdi32" (ByVal hDestDC As Long, ByVal x As _
Long, ByVal y As Long, ByVal nWidth As Long, ByVal nHeight As Long, ByVal _
hSrcDC As Long, ByVal xSrc As Long, ByVal ySrc As Long, ByVal dwRop As Long)
#End If 'WIN32
```

The allCos and allSin arrays are loaded with the values of the sine and co-sine of zero through 90 degrees in one-degree increments. The equation converts degrees to the radian values required by these functions.

```
Private Sub Form_Load()
    Dim i%
    Screen.MousePointer = 11
    For i% = 1 To 90
        allCos!(i%) = Cos(CSng(i%) / 180! * 3.14159)
        allSin!(i%) = Sin(CSng(i%) / 180! * 3.14159)
    Next i%
    Screen.MousePointer = 0
End Sub
```

All of the buttons are in a control array, which simply records the index of the button that was clicked and redraws the output window.

```
Private Sub cmdWhich_Click(Index As Integer)
    WhichDrawing% = Index
    out.Refresh
End Sub
```

This function performs different operations depending on the button that was pressed as reflected by the WhichDrawing variable. The function starts by using the SaveDC function to save the current device context state. It then opens a path bracket (another way of saying that it starts the creation of a path). It then draws two lines of text onto the window. After closing the path bracket (ending the path), the SelectClipPath function combines the path with the clipping region—in this case, the RGN_COPY parameter causes the path to be copied into the clipping region.

Case 0 uses a stock object—a black pen which is selected into the device context. Since it is a stock object there is no need to destroy it afterward—it is automatically selected out of the device context by the RestoreDC operation at the end of the function.

Case 1 creates a solid color pen. Note how the current value of the pen is saved when the new pen is selected into the device context. The old pen is selected back into the device context after the ellipses are drawn. The purpose here is not to restore the device context to its previous state—that is accomplished later by the RestoreDC function. The issue here is that you need to destroy the pen, and you should never destroy an object that is selected into a device context. Selecting the old pen into the device context also serves to select the new pen out of the device context—so it is safe to destroy.

```
Private Sub out_Paint()
    Dim usepen&, oldpen&
    Dim dl&
    Dim myRect As RECT, radius&, i%, j%, myPoint As POINTAPI
    savedDC& = SaveDC&(out.hdc)

    Select Case WhichDrawing%
    Case Ø ' Lines ( black on gray)
        dl& = BeginPath&(out.hdc)
        dl& = TextOut&(out.hdc, 5Ø&, 3Ø&, "Radial", 6)
        dl& = TextOut&(out.hdc, 8Ø&, 12Ø&, "Lines", 5)
        dl& = EndPath&(out.hdc)

        dl& = SelectClipPath&(out.hdc, RGN_COPY)
        radius& = 6ØØ


        ' Don't delete stock pens
        usepen = GetStockObject(BLACK_PEN)
        oldpen = SelectObject(out.hdc, usepen)

        For i% = 1 To 9Ø
            dl& = MoveToEx&(out.hdc, out.ScaleWidth, Ø, myPoint)
            dl& = LineTo&(out.hdc, out.ScaleWidth - allCos!(i%)  * _
            CSng(radius&), _
            Ø + allSin!(i%) * CSng(radius&))
        Next i%


    Case 1 ' Color Circles:
```

```
        dl& = BeginPath&(out.hdc)
            dl& = TextOut&(out.hdc, 80&, 30&, "Color", 5)
            dl& = TextOut&(out.hdc, 50&, 120&, "Circles", 7)
        dl& = EndPath&(out.hdc)

        dl& = SelectClipPath&(out.hdc, RGN_COPY)

        usepen = CreatePen(PS_SOLID, 1, QBColor(12))
        oldpen = SelectObject(out.hdc, usepen)
        For i% = 0 To 40
            dl& = Ellipse&(out.hdc, i% * out.ScaleWidth / 80, i% * _
                out.ScaleHeight / 80, out.ScaleWidth - (i% * out.ScaleWidth / 80), _
                out.ScaleHeight - (i% * out.ScaleHeight / 80))
        Next i%
        ' Select out the pen before deleting
        dl = SelectObject(out.hdc, oldpen)
        dl = DeleteObject(usepen)

    Case 2 ' Bitmap:
        dl& = BeginPath&(out.hdc)
        dl& = TextOut&(out.hdc, 80&, 30&, "Color", 5)
        dl& = TextOut&(out.hdc, 50&, 120&, "Bitmap", 6)
        dl& = EndPath&(out.hdc)

        dl& = SelectClipPath&(out.hdc, RGN_COPY)

        TileBitmaps
    Case 3
        dl& = BeginPath&(out.hdc)
        dl& = TextOut&(out.hdc, 50&, 30&, "Stroke", 6)
        dl& = TextOut&(out.hdc, 80&, 120&, "Path", 4)
        dl& = EndPath&(out.hdc)
        StrokeThePath
    End Select


    dl& = RestoreDC&(out.hdc, savedDC&)
End Sub
```

The TileBitmaps function performs an image copy from the bitmap in the prtBmp picture control onto the output picture. The bitmap is tiled—drawn repeatedly to fill the output bitmap. This is not a good example of tiling; the dimensions of the bitmap are hardcoded. However, the functions that are needed to determine the size of a bitmap are not covered until the next chapter and doing so here would only confuse the issue more. Replacing this function with a reliable tiling function that will work with any bitmap is thus left as an exercise for the reader—after you read Chapter 9.

```
' Tile the bitmap onto the output picture
'
```

```
Public Sub TileBitmaps()
    Dim dl&, i%, j%
    For i% = 0 To 5
        For j% = 0 To 5
            dl& = BitBlt&(out.hdc, 0 + i% * 160, 0 + j% * 120, 160, 120, _
            pctBmp.hdc, _
            0, 0, SRCCOPY)
        Next j%
    Next i%

End Sub
```

This function strokes the path using a green pen that is three units wide. When a path is created out of text, the path consists of the curves that make up the text outline. Stroking the path serves to draw the outline using the selected pen. The WidenPath API function can be used to widen the path further—it works by increasing the size of the path to take into account the width of the pen. Experimenting with the WidenPath function is left as an exercise for the reader.

```
Public Sub StrokeThePath()
    Dim dl&, usepen&, oldpen&
    ' Create a green pen
    usepen = CreatePen(PS_SOLID, 3, RGB(0, 255, 0))
    oldpen = SelectObject(out.hdc, usepen)
    dl = StrokePath(out.hdc)
    ' Select out the pen before deleting
    dl = SelectObject(out.hdc, oldpen)
    dl = DeleteObject(usepen)

End Sub

Private Sub cmdExit_Click()
    Unload Me
End Sub
```

Example: ExtPen.vbp

The ExtPen.vbp example serves two purposes. First, it demonstrates in great detail how to use cosmetic and geometric pens, the new pen types available under Win32. But it also serves a second purpose that is perhaps even more important, especially if you never use extended pen styles yourself. ExtPen.vbp demonstrates how to create a program for experimenting with API functions and parameters. It is the ideal tool for learning API techniques and can be applied to many other functions.

Figure 8.5 shows the main screen of the ExtPen.vbp project. Extended pens have a number of characteristics which ExtPen lets you experiment with:

- **Style**: Solid, standard dash pattern or user-defined dash pattern. ExtPen allows you to specify a solid or dashed pen, and demonstrates how to use a user-defined style which can be changed by modifying the program code.

Figure 8.5

Main program screen for ExtPen.vbp

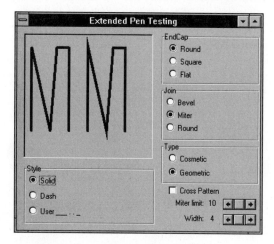

- **Type**: Cosmetic or geometric. Cosmetic pens always have a width of 1 unit. The width of the geometric pen is set using the Width scrollbar.

- **Brush**: Solid or with a specified pattern. ExtPen allows you to select a standard hatched pattern brush by checking the "Cross Pattern" check box. You can modify the brush using code to choose from among one of the other standard pattern brushes. You can use the techniques demonstrated in Chapter 9 to create a brush from any bitmap.

- **EndCap**: The end of a geometric pen can be round, square, or flat as shown in Figure 8.6. ExtPen allows you to choose the endcap to use.

Figure 8.6

Geometric pen end caps

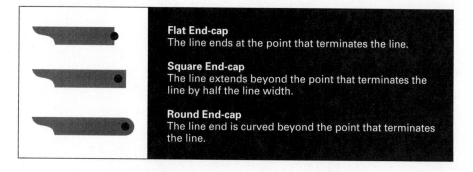

■ **Join**: ExtPen allows you to specify how joined line segments are connected. Note that in order for two line segments to be joined they either need to be part of a single object, such as a rectangle, or part of a path. Just drawing a line from the end point of another line does not create a joined effect—they must both be drawn into a path and then rendered using the StrokePath or StrokeAndFillPath function. Figure 8.7 shows the three possible joins.

Figure 8.7

Geometric pen joins

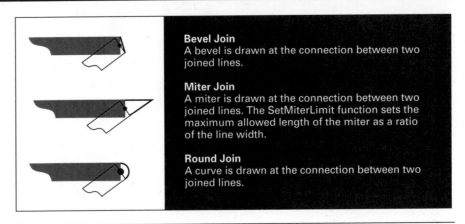

Bevel Join
A bevel is drawn at the connection between two joined lines.

Miter Join
A miter is drawn at the connection between two joined lines. The SetMiterLimit function sets the maximum allowed length of the miter as a ratio of the line width.

Round Join
A curve is drawn at the connection between two joined lines.

The ExtPen.vbp project uses a single form, EXTPEN.FRM. Listing 8.2 contains the heading and functions for the project.

Listing 8.2   EXTPEN.FRM

The layout of the form is straightforward. It uses three groups of option buttons in control arrays.

```
VERSION 5.00
Begin VB.Form frmExtPen
    Caption         =   "Extended Pen Testing"
    ClientHeight    =   4785
    ClientLeft      =   1095
    ClientTop       =   1515
    ClientWidth     =   5865
    Height          =   5190
    Left            =   1035
    LinkTopic       =   "Form1"
    ScaleHeight     =   4785
    ScaleWidth      =   5865
    Top             =   1170
    Width           =   5985
```

Listing 8.2   **EXTPEN.FRM (Continued)**

```
Begin VB.CheckBox chkCross
    Caption         =   "Cross Pattern"
    Height          =   195
    Left            =   3660
    TabIndex        =   22
    Top             =   3720
    Width           =   1755
End
Begin VB.HScrollBar scrMiter
    Height          =   255
    Left            =   4980
    Max             =   20
    Min             =   1
    TabIndex        =   18
    Top             =   4020
    Value           =   10
    Width           =   795
End
Begin VB.Frame Frame4
    Caption         =   "Join"
    Height          =   1275
    Left            =   3480
    TabIndex        =   14
    Top             =   1380
    Width           =   2355
    Begin VB.OptionButton chkJoin
        Caption         =   "Round"
        Height          =   255
        Index           =   2
        Left            =   120
        TabIndex        =   17
        Top             =   840
        Width           =   2175
    End
    Begin VB.OptionButton chkJoin
        Caption         =   "Miter"
        Height          =   255
        Index           =   1
        Left            =   120
        TabIndex        =   16
        Top             =   540
        Width           =   2175
    End
    Begin VB.OptionButton chkJoin
        Caption         =   "Bevel"
        Height          =   255
        Index           =   0
        Left            =   120
```

Listing 8.2   EXTPEN.FRM (Continued)

```
                TabIndex        =    15
                Top             =    240
                Value           =    -1   'True
                Width           =    2175
            End
        End
        Begin VB.Frame Frame3
            Caption         =    "EndCap"
            Height          =    1215
            Left            =    3480
            TabIndex        =    10
            Top             =    120
            Width           =    2355
            Begin VB.OptionButton chkEndcap
                Caption         =    "Flat"
                Height          =    255
                Index           =    2
                Left            =    180
                TabIndex        =    13
                Top             =    840
                Width           =    1635
            End
            Begin VB.OptionButton chkEndcap
                Caption         =    "Square"
                Height          =    255
                Index           =    1
                Left            =    180
                TabIndex        =    12
                Top             =    540
                Width           =    1635
            End
            Begin VB.OptionButton chkEndcap
                Caption         =    "Round"
                Height          =    255
                Index           =    0
                Left            =    180
                TabIndex        =    11
                Top             =    240
                Value           =    -1   'True
                Width           =    1635
            End
        End
        Begin VB.HScrollBar scrWidth
            Height          =    255
            Left            =    4980
            Max             =    10
            Min             =    1
            TabIndex        =    8
```

Listing 8.2   **EXTPEN.FRM (Continued)**

```
         Top              =    4380
         Value            =    1
         Width            =    795
      End
      Begin VB.Frame Frame2
         Caption          =    "Style"
         Height           =    1395
         Left             =    180
         TabIndex         =    4
         Top              =    3240
         Width            =    3135
         Begin VB.OptionButton chkStyle
            Caption        =    "User ___ . . _"
            Height         =    255
            Index          =    2
            Left           =    120
            TabIndex       =    7
            Top            =    960
            Width          =    1695
         End
         Begin VB.OptionButton chkStyle
            Caption        =    "Dash"
            Height         =    255
            Index          =    1
            Left           =    120
            TabIndex       =    6
            Top            =    600
            Width          =    1695
         End
         Begin VB.OptionButton chkStyle
            Caption        =    "Solid"
            Height         =    255
            Index          =    0
            Left           =    120
            TabIndex       =    5
            Top            =    240
            Value          =    -1   'True
            Width          =    1695
         End
      End
      Begin VB.Frame Frame1
         Caption          =    "Type"
         Height           =    975
         Left             =    3480
         TabIndex         =    1
         Top              =    2700
         Width            =    2355
         Begin VB.OptionButton chkType
```

Listing 8.2   **EXTPEN.FRM (Continued)**

```
        Caption       =   "Geometric"
        Height        =   315
        Index         =   1
        Left          =   180
        TabIndex      =   3
        Top           =   540
        Width         =   1455
    End
    Begin VB.OptionButton chkType
        Caption       =   "Cosmetic"
        Height        =   255
        Index         =   0
        Left          =   180
        TabIndex      =   2
        Top           =   240
        Value         =   -1   'True
        Width         =   1635
    End
End
Begin VB.PictureBox Picture1
    Height        =   2895
    Left          =   180
    ScaleHeight   =   191
    ScaleMode     =   3   'Pixel
    ScaleWidth    =   203
    TabIndex      =   0
    Top           =   180
    Width         =   3075
End
Begin VB.Label lblWidth
    Caption       =   "1"
    Height        =   255
    Left          =   4620
    TabIndex      =   21
    Top           =   4380
    Width         =   315
End
Begin VB.Label lblMiter
    Caption       =   "10"
    Height        =   255
    Left          =   4620
    TabIndex      =   20
    Top           =   4020
    Width         =   315
End
Begin VB.Label Label2
    Alignment     =   1   'Right Justify
    Caption       =   "Miter limit:"
```

Listing 8.2   EXTPEN.FRM (Continued)

```
      Height          =     255
      Left            =     3720
      TabIndex        =     19
      Top             =     4020
      Width           =     795
   End
   Begin VB.Label Label1
      Alignment       =     1    'Right Justify
      Caption         =     "Width:"
      Height          =     255
      Left            =     3660
      TabIndex        =     9
      Top             =     4380
      Width           =     855
   End
End
Attribute VB_Name = "frmExtPen"
Attribute VB_GlobalNameSpace = False
Attribute VB_Creatable = False
Attribute VB_PredeclaredId = True
Attribute VB_Exposed = False
```

The module variables include the extended pen handle and an array that defines the custom style. The BrushInfo structure contains the information used to define the color and brush styles for the geometric pen.

```
Option Explicit

Dim ExtendedPen&
Dim CustomStyle(8) As Long
Private Const CustomStyleLength = 8
Dim BrushInfo As LOGBRUSH

Private Declare Function BeginPath Lib "gdi32" (ByVal hdc As Long) As Long
Private Declare Function EndPath Lib "gdi32" (ByVal hdc As Long) As Long
Private Declare Function StrokePath Lib "gdi32" (ByVal hdc As Long) As Long
Private Declare Function ExtCreatePen Lib "gdi32" (ByVal dwPenStyle As Long, _
ByVal dwWidth As Long, lplb As LOGBRUSH, ByVal dwStyleCount As Long, _
lpStyle As Any) As Long
Private Declare Function MoveToEx Lib "gdi32" (ByVal hdc As Long, ByVal x As _
Long, ByVal y As Long, lpPoint As POINTAPI) As Long
Private Declare Function LineTo Lib "gdi32" (ByVal hdc As Long, ByVal x As _
Long, ByVal y As Long) As Long
Private Declare Function Ellipse Lib "gdi32" (ByVal hdc As Long, ByVal X1 As _
Long, ByVal Y1 As Long, ByVal X2 As Long, ByVal Y2 As Long) As Long
```

```vb
Private Declare Function SelectObject Lib "gdi32" (ByVal hdc As Long, ByVal _
hObject As Long) As Long
Private Declare Function DeleteObject Lib "gdi32" (ByVal hObject As Long) As _
Long
Private Declare Function SetMiterLimit Lib "gdi32" (ByVal hdc As Long, ByVal _
eNewLimit As Single, peOldLimit As Single) As Long
Private Declare Function Rectangle Lib "gdi32" (ByVal hdc As Long, ByVal X1 As _
Long, ByVal Y1 As Long, ByVal X2 As Long, ByVal Y2 As Long) As Long


Private Type POINTAPI
        x As Long
        y As Long
End Type

Private Type LOGBRUSH
        lbStyle As Long
        lbColor As Long
        lbHatch As Long
End Type


Private Const PS_SOLID = 0
Private Const PS_DASH = 1            ' -------
Private Const PS_DOT = 2            ' .......
Private Const PS_DASHDOT = 3            ' _._._._
Private Const PS_DASHDOTDOT = 4            ' _.._.._
Private Const PS_NULL = 5
Private Const PS_INSIDEFRAME = 6
Private Const PS_USERSTYLE = 7
Private Const PS_ALTERNATE = 8
Private Const PS_STYLE_MASK = &HF

Private Const PS_ENDCAP_ROUND = &H0
Private Const PS_ENDCAP_SQUARE = &H100
Private Const PS_ENDCAP_FLAT = &H200
Private Const PS_ENDCAP_MASK = &HF00

Private Const PS_JOIN_ROUND = &H0
Private Const PS_JOIN_BEVEL = &H1000
Private Const PS_JOIN_MITER = &H2000
Private Const PS_JOIN_MASK = &HF000

Private Const PS_COSMETIC = &H0
Private Const PS_GEOMETRIC = &H10000
Private Const PS_TYPE_MASK = &HF0000
Private Const BS_SOLID = 0
Private Const BS_NULL = 1
Private Const BS_HOLLOW = BS_NULL
```

```
Private Const BS_HATCHED = 2
Private Const BS_PATTERN = 3
Private Const BS_INDEXED = 4
Private Const BS_DIBPATTERN = 5
Private Const BS_DIBPATTERNPT = 6
Private Const BS_PATTERN8X8 = 7
Private Const BS_DIBPATTERN8X8 = 8


'  Hatch Styles
Private Const HS_HORIZONTAL = 0         '  -----
Private Const HS_VERTICAL = 1           '  |||||
Private Const HS_FDIAGONAL = 2          '  \\\\\
Private Const HS_BDIAGONAL = 3          '  /////
Private Const HS_CROSS = 4              '  +++++
Private Const HS_DIAGCROSS = 5          '  xxxxx
```

The check boxes and option buttons simply force the picture box to be redrawn—the drawing routines do all the work.

```
Private Sub chkCross_Click()
    Picture1.Refresh

End Sub

Private Sub chkEndcap_Click(Index As Integer)
    Picture1.Refresh
End Sub

Private Sub chkJoin_Click(Index As Integer)
    Picture1.Refresh
End Sub


Private Sub chkStyle_Click(Index As Integer)
    Picture1.Refresh
End Sub

Private Sub chkType_Click(Index As Integer)
    Picture1.Refresh
End Sub

Private Sub scrMiter_Change()
    lblMiter.Caption = Str$(scrMiter.Value)
    Picture1.Refresh
End Sub

Private Sub scrWidth_Change()
    lblWidth.Caption = Str$(scrWidth.Value)
    Picture1.Refresh
End Sub
```

The CustomStyle array contains long values indicating the length of each dot or dash segment. The first entry is the length of the first dash, the second is the length of the space to the next dash, and so on. In this example, there is a 3-unit dash, followed by a 1-unit space, a 1-unit dot, a 2-unit space, and so forth. The lengths are specified in logical units for the current coordinate system settings. The lbColor field of the BrushInfo structure is set to green in this case. The default hatching style is HS_CROSS, but it is only used when a hatch mode is specified.

```
Private Sub Form_Load()
    CustomStyle(0) = 3
    CustomStyle(1) = 1
    CustomStyle(2) = 1
    CustomStyle(3) = 2
    CustomStyle(4) = 1
    CustomStyle(5) = 2
    CustomStyle(6) = 1
    CustomStyle(7) = 2
    BrushInfo.lbColor = RGB(0, 255, 0)
    BrushInfo.lbHatch = HS_CROSS
End Sub
```

The DoPenUpdate function is called when the picture control is painted. The function starts by destroying any existing pen. It then scans the various checkboxes and option buttons to build a style variable. It handles some special cases: cosmetic pens are limited to one pixel. When the custom style option is chosen, the routine calls the appropriate version of the ExtCreatePen function. Note how the styles are joined using the Or operation.

```
Private Sub DoPenUpdate()
    Dim di&
    Dim pentype&, penstyle&, endcap&, join&
    Dim usewidth&
    ' Delete the pen if it exists
    If ExtendedPen Then di = DeleteObject(ExtendedPen)
    If chkType(0).Value Then pentype = PS_COSMETIC Else pentype = PS_GEOMETRIC
    If chkStyle(0).Value Then penstyle = PS_SOLID
    If chkStyle(1).Value Then penstyle = PS_DASH
    If chkStyle(2).Value Then penstyle = PS_USERSTYLE
    If chkEndcap(0).Value Then endcap = PS_ENDCAP_ROUND
    If chkEndcap(1).Value Then endcap = PS_ENDCAP_SQUARE
    If chkEndcap(2).Value Then endcap = PS_ENDCAP_FLAT
    If chkJoin(0).Value Then join = PS_JOIN_BEVEL
    If chkJoin(1).Value Then join = PS_JOIN_MITER
    If chkJoin(2).Value Then join = PS_JOIN_ROUND
    ' Set the pen style
    If chkCross.Value = 1 Then BrushInfo.lbStyle = BS_HATCHED Else _
    BrushInfo.lbStyle = BS_SOLID
    If pentype = PS_COSMETIC Then usewidth = 1 Else usewidth = scrWidth.Value
    If penstyle = PS_USERSTYLE Then
```

```
        ExtendedPen = ExtCreatePen(pentype Or penstyle Or endcap Or join, _
            usewidth, BrushInfo, CustomStyleLength, CustomStyle(0))
    Else
        ExtendedPen = ExtCreatePen(pentype Or penstyle Or endcap Or join, _
            usewidth, BrushInfo, 0, ByVal 0&)
    End If

End Sub
```

Two sets of line segments are drawn in the picture control. The one on the left is made up of line segments drawn directly on the control. The one on the right is made up of line segments drawn into a path and then rendered using StrokePath. This allows you to clearly see the difference between line segments that happen to meet at the same point, and those that are joined by virtue of being part of a path.

```
Private Sub Picture1_Paint()
    Dim di&
    Dim pt As POINTAPI
    Dim oldpen&
    Dim oldmiter As Single
    Dim newmiter As Single
    DoPenUpdate
    newmiter = scrMiter
    di = SetMiterLimit(Picture1.hdc, newmiter, oldmiter)
    oldpen = SelectObject(Picture1.hdc, ExtendedPen&)
    di = MoveToEx(Picture1.hdc, 10, 150, pt)
    di = LineTo(Picture1.hdc, 10, 20)
    di = LineTo(Picture1.hdc, 40, 150)
    di = LineTo(Picture1.hdc, 50, 20)
    di = LineTo(Picture1.hdc, 70, 20)
    di = LineTo(Picture1.hdc, 70, 150)
    di = BeginPath(Picture1.hdc)
    di = MoveToEx(Picture1.hdc, 100, 150, pt)
    di = LineTo(Picture1.hdc, 100, 20)
    di = LineTo(Picture1.hdc, 130, 150)
    di = LineTo(Picture1.hdc, 140, 20)
    di = LineTo(Picture1.hdc, 160, 20)
    di = LineTo(Picture1.hdc, 160, 150)
    di = EndPath(Picture1.hdc)
    di = StrokePath(Picture1.hdc)


    di = SelectObject(Picture1.hdc, oldpen)
    di = SetMiterLimit(Picture1.hdc, oldmiter, newmiter)
End Sub
```

The pen should always be deleted on exit.

```
Private Sub Form_Unload(Cancel As Integer)
    Dim di&
    If ExtendedPen Then di = DeleteObject(ExtendedPen)
End Sub
```

As you experiment with this program, one of the things you should try is to choose the miter join and adjust the miter limit. Depending on the line width, you can reach a setting where the miter is turned into a bevel because the length of the miter is too long relative to the width of the line.

Example: Bezier.vbp

Bézier curves are a special type of spline curve which is defined by four points. Support for Bézier curves is one of the most useful new features in Win32 GDI. Two of the points specify the start and end point of the curve. The other two points are control points that determine the direction and curvature of the line segment as it connects with these two points. Figure 8.8 shows the main form of the Bézier program which illustrates a Bézier curve with two points.

Figure 8.8

Bézier example main form

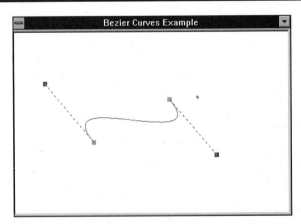

The blue rectangles represent the start and end points, the magenta rectangles show the control points. The dashed lines connect the control point with its associated curve point. The direction of the dashed line indicates the direction from which the line segment connects to the curve point. The length of the control line defines the curvature from that point. In the Bezier example, you can click and drag any of these rectangles to experiment with these curves. The program itself is quite straightforward and demonstrates a number of Win32 programming techniques. The Bezier.vbp project contains a single form—BEZIER.FRM (Listing 8.3).

| Listing 8.3 | **BEZIER.FRM** |

```
VERSION 5.00
Begin VB.Form frmBezier
    BorderStyle     =   1  'Fixed Single
    Caption         =   "Bezier Curves Example"
    ClientHeight    =   4380
    ClientLeft      =   1140
    ClientTop       =   1515
    ClientWidth     =   6720
    Height          =   4785
    Left            =   1080
    LinkTopic       =   "Form1"
    MaxButton       =   0  'False
    ScaleHeight     =   4380
    ScaleWidth      =   6720
    Top             =   1170
    Width           =   6840
    Begin VB.PictureBox Out
        BackColor       =   &H00FFFFFF&
        ClipControls    =   0  'False
        DrawMode        =   7  'Invert
        FillStyle       =   0  'Solid
        Height          =   4275
        Left            =   0
        ScaleHeight     =   283
        ScaleMode       =   3  'Pixel
        ScaleWidth      =   443
        TabIndex        =   0
        Top             =   60
        Width           =   6675
    End
End
Attribute VB_Name = "frmBezier"
Attribute VB_GlobalNameSpace = False
Attribute VB_Creatable = False
Attribute VB_PredeclaredId = True
Attribute VB_Exposed = False
```

The Points array contains the four points that define the Bézier curve. Note that a Visual Basic array with a dimension of three actually has four entries starting at entry zero. The Rects array defines the four rectangles that are used to allow the user to move the Bézier points. The current point and dragging flags are used for the dragging operation. Entries zero and three are the start and end point, respectively. Entries one and two are the two control points. The PT_ constants are used by the program to help clarify the code.

```
Option Explicit
```

```
Dim Points(3) As POINTAPI
Dim Rects(3) As RECT

Dim dl&
Dim curPt%
Dim fDragging%
Const PT_START = 0
Const PT_C1 = 1
Const PT_C2 = 2
Const PT_END = 3


'*********************************
'**  Type Definitions:

#If Win32 Then
Private Type RECT
        Left As Long
        Top As Long
        Right As Long
        Bottom As Long
End Type

Private Type POINTAPI
        X As Long
        Y As Long
End Type

#End If 'WIN32 Types

'*********************************
'**  Function Declarations:

#If Win32 Then
Private Declare Function PolyBezier& Lib "gdi32" (ByVal hdc As Long, lppt As _
POINTAPI, ByVal cPoints As Long)
Private Declare Function PolyBezierTo& Lib "gdi32" (ByVal hdc As Long, lppt As _
POINTAPI, ByVal cCount As Long)
Private Declare Function Rectangle& Lib "gdi32" (ByVal hdc As Long, ByVal X1 As _
Long, ByVal Y1 As Long, ByVal X2 As Long, ByVal Y2 As Long)
Private Declare Function SaveDC& Lib "gdi32" (ByVal hdc As Long)
Private Declare Function RestoreDC& Lib "gdi32" (ByVal hdc As Long, ByVal _
nSavedDC As Long)
Private Declare Function PtInRect& Lib "user32" (lpRect As RECT, ByVal ptx As _
Long, ByVal pty As Long)
Private Declare Function SetRect& Lib "user32" (lpRect As RECT, ByVal X1 As _
```

```
Long, ByVal Y1 As Long, ByVal X2 As Long, ByVal Y2 As Long)
#End If 'WIN32
```

The points are set to arbitrary initial values. The SetPtRect function sets the values of the Rects structures based on the point values.

```
Private Sub Form_Load()
    SetPoint Points(PT_START), 100, 140
    SetPoint Points(PT_C1), 50, 80
    SetPoint Points(PT_C2), 350, 200
    SetPoint Points(PT_END), 300, 140
    SetPtRect PT_START
    SetPtRect PT_C1
    SetPtRect PT_C2
    SetPtRect PT_END
End Sub

Private Sub SetPtRect(ByVal Index As Integer)
        Rects(Index).Left = Points(Index).X - 3
        Rects(Index).Top = Points(Index).Y - 3
        Rects(Index).Right = Rects(Index).Left + 6
        Rects(Index).Bottom = Rects(Index).Top + 6
' dl& = SetRect(Rects(Index), Points(Index).X - 3, Points(Index).Y - 3, _
Rects(Index).Left + 6, Rects(Index).Top + 6)
End Sub
```

The MouseDown routine's primary task is to start the drag operation. It uses the PtInRect API function to see if you clicked in any of the rectangles (this is an extremely efficient way to determine if a point is in a rectangle). If so, the dragging flag is set to TRUE. If you click on the right mouse button, the curve is set to its initial values. Why is this important? Because this program intentionally allows you to drag outside of the window area in order to allow more flexibility in adjusting the curves. However, once set outside of the window, there is no way to bring the control or curve points back into the window—hence the right mouse button option. Not a good design for a real application—but good for an example.

```
Private Sub Out_MouseDown(Button As Integer, Shift As Integer, X As Single, Y _
As Single)
    Dim fAny%, i%
    If Button And vbRightButton Then
        Form_Load
        Out.Refresh
        Exit Sub
    End If
    For i% = 0 To 3
        If PtInRect(Rects(i%), X, Y) Then
            curPt = i%
            fAny% = True
            fDragging% = True
```

```
            Exit For
        End If
    Next i%
End Sub
```

The MouseMove function performs the actual dragging. All drawing in this program is in XOR pen mode—which inverts the current display. In order to obtain a particular color in this mode, you actually need to choose the inverted color. When it draws in XOR mode, the actual color will be drawn. The first drawing operation uses the current point values and erases the previous curve and control information. Next it draws in the new curve and control information. The same process is used to erase and then redraw the rectangles.

```
Private Sub Out_MouseMove(Button As Integer, Shift As Integer, X As Single, Y _
As Single)
    Dim i%
    If Not fDragging% Then Exit Sub

    Out.ForeColor = (Not (QBColor(8)) And &HFFFFFF)
    dl& = PolyBezier(Out.hdc, Points(0), 4)
    Out.ForeColor = QBColor(10)
    Out.DrawStyle = 2 'Dot
    Out.Line (Points(PT_C1).X, Points(PT_C1).Y)-(Points(PT_START).X, _
    Points(PT_START).Y)
    Out.Line (Points(PT_C2).X, Points(PT_C2).Y)-(Points(PT_END).X, _
    Points(PT_END).Y)
    Out.DrawStyle = 0

    SetPoint Points(curPt), X, Y

    Out.ForeColor = (Not (QBColor(8)) And &HFFFFFF)
    dl& = PolyBezier(Out.hdc, Points(0), 4)
    Out.ForeColor = QBColor(10)
    Out.DrawStyle = 2 'Dot
    Out.Line (Points(PT_C1).X, Points(PT_C1).Y)-(Points(PT_START).X, _
    Points(PT_START).Y)
    Out.Line (Points(PT_C2).X, Points(PT_C2).Y)-(Points(PT_END).X, _
    Points(PT_END).Y)
    Out.DrawStyle = 0

    For i% = 0 To 3
        Out.ForeColor = QBColor(IIf(i% = 0 Or i% = 3, 12, 10))
        Out.FillColor = QBColor(IIf(i% = 0 Or i% = 3, 12, 10))
        DrawRect Out.hdc, Rects(i%)
        If i% = curPt Then
            SetPtRect curPt
        End If
        DrawRect Out.hdc, Rects(i%)
    Next i%
End Sub
```

```
Private Sub Out_MouseUp(Button As Integer, Shift As Integer, X As Single, Y As _
Single)
    If fDragging% Then
        SetPoint Points(curPt), X, Y
        SetPtRect curPt
        fDragging% = False
    End If
End Sub
```

The Paint event draws the curve, control lines, and rectangles.

```
Private Sub Out_Paint()
    Out.ForeColor = (Not (QBColor(8)) And &HFFFFFF)
    dl& = PolyBezier(Out.hdc, Points(0), 4)
    Out.ForeColor = QBColor(12)
    Out.FillColor = QBColor(12)
    DrawRect Out.hdc, Rects(PT_START)
    DrawRect Out.hdc, Rects(PT_END)
    Out.ForeColor = QBColor(10)
    Out.FillColor = QBColor(10)
    DrawRect Out.hdc, Rects(PT_C1)
    DrawRect Out.hdc, Rects(PT_C2)
    Out.DrawStyle = 2 'Dot
    Out.ForeColor = QBColor(10)
    Out.Line (Points(PT_C1).X, Points(PT_C1).Y)-(Points(PT_START).X, _
    Points(PT_START).Y)
    Out.Line (Points(PT_C2).X, Points(PT_C2).Y)-(Points(PT_END).X, _
    Points(PT_END).Y)
    Out.DrawStyle = 0
End Sub


Private Sub SetPoint(myPt As POINTAPI, ByVal X As Long, ByVal Y As Long)
        myPt.X = X
        myPt.Y = Y
End Sub


Private Sub DrawRect(ByVal hdc As Long, myRect As RECT)
    Out.Line (myRect.Left, myRect.Top)-(myRect.Right, myRect.Bottom), , BF
End Sub
```

Suggestions for Further Practice

- Modify the TileBitmaps function in the Path.vbp example to work with any bitmap (read Chapter 9 first).

- Can you modify the Path.vbp so that the pattern (lines, circles, or bitmaps) appears everywhere except where the text is drawn? Demonstrate this once using regions, and once without using regions.

- Use the WidenPath API function to widen the text outlines in the Path.vbp example.

- Extend ExtPen.vbp to allow you to experiment with all of the available styles.

- Experiment with ExtPen.vbp under both Windows 95 and Windows NT to see those areas where the Windows 95 implementation is limited.

- Extend the Bezier.vbp example so that you can manipulate a Bézier curve containing two or more line segments instead of one as shown.

- The Bezier.vbp example works, but has several obvious design flaws. How would you change it to make it more modular?

Metafiles

A *metafile* is an object that can record GDI drawing operations for later playback. Metafiles can be stored in memory or on disk and are useful for any situation where an image needs to be saved. Metafiles have an advantage over bitmaps in that they usually consume less space, are device-independent, and are scalable. Their main disadvantage is that they are often slower, since rendering a metafile requires that each of the GDI commands recorded in the metafile be executed.

Each record in a metafile contains a single GDI output command. A complete list of GDI commands that can be represented by metafile records can be found in Appendix B under the METARECORD and ENHMETARECORD data structures.

Win32 supports two different types of metafiles: standard Windows metafiles and Enhanced metafiles. The Win32 documentation strongly recommends that you use enhanced metafiles as they support all of the Win32 drawing functions, the full 32-bit coordinate system, and additional functionality that is not part of standard metafiles. There is one catch, however—enhanced metafiles are not compatible with 16-bit Windows. In fact, despite Microsoft's encouragement, enhanced metafiles are not yet widely supported by graphic programs or clip-art libraries. A quick scan of two disks, one with a Windows NT installation and the other with a Windows 95 installation, found several hundred standard metafiles, and not one single enhanced metafile. For this reason, while this book does document enhanced metafiles, the examples still focus on standard Windows metafiles.

You are much more likely to run into standard metafiles in your own applications, and this will probably be the case for some time to come. If you are using metafiles within your own application only, enhanced metafiles are probably a better way to go. The good news is that enhanced metafiles are

used in almost the same manner as standard metafiles, they just have additional features; so once you know how to use one type of metafile, you can easily adapt to the other type.

There are also functions to convert from one type of metafile to another. The term "metafile" refers to a concept—an object that contains GDI graphic commands. A metafile can exist on disk or in memory. A metafile in memory can also be transferred to the clipboard. There are API commands for storing and loading standard metafiles on disk, but you should avoid using them. The metafile format used by those API functions goes back to version 1.0 of Windows and has not become a standard. The standard metafile file format, which typically has the extension .WMF (Windows metafile), is actually a format called a "Placeable Metafile" because it has an additional structure at the beginning of the file that contains information about the recommended size and resolution for which the picture was created. The QuikDraw.vbp sample application demonstrates how to read and write placeable metafiles. The enhanced metafile functions that read and write disk-based metafiles do not suffer from this limitation and can be used directly.

A metafile is created by using the CreateMetaFile or CreateEnhMetaFile function to create a metafile device context. Note that a metafile device context is not the same thing as a metafile handle. Your application can draw on a metafile device context in the same way as it would draw on any other device context. When the drawing is complete, the CloseMetaFile function is called to close the metafile device context and create a metafile handle. This metafile handle can then be used to play back the drawing commands on another device context.

There are two catches to keep in mind when using metafiles. First, not every GDI function is supported within a metafile. Check Appendix B under the METARECORD and ENHMETRECORD structure definitions for a list of which records are supported under standard and enhanced metafiles. Standard metafiles do not support new Win32 drawing such as paths and Bézier curves. Next, remember that metafiles are a recording of GDI commands—like any fixed recording, there is no mechanism for computation within a metafile. GDI commands that return results are therefore either not supported or ignored. This is not to say that an application cannot modify a metafile that is playing—the Analyze.vbp application shows how this can be done—just that this capability must be implemented as part of an application; it is not part of the metafile itself.

Table 8.8 lists the metafile functions.

Metafiles and Coordinate Systems

If you load a metafile into a picture control, you may notice that it is almost always scaled to match the size of the picture control. How can this be

Table 8.8 **Metafile Functions**

Function	Description
CloseEnhMetaFile	Closes an enhanced metafile device context and retrieves the metafile handle.
CopyEnhMetaFile	Copies an enhanced metafile.
CloseMetaFile	Closes a metafile device context. Retrieves a metafile handle.
CopyMetaFile	Copies a metafile.
CreateEnhMetaFile	Creates an enhanced metafile device context that is ready to be drawn on.
CreateMetaFile	Creates a metafile device context that is ready to be drawn on.
DeleteEnhMetaFile	Deletes an enhanced metafile.
DeleteMetaFile	Deletes a metafile.
EnumEnhMetaFile	Enumerates records in an enhanced metafile.
EnumMetaFile	Enumerates records in a metafile.
GdiComments	Adds a comment into an enhanced metafile.
GetEnhMetaFile	Obtains a metafile handle for a specified disk metafile.
GetEnhMetaFileBits	Extracts the data from an enhanced metafile into a block of memory.
GetEnhMetaFileDescription	Retrieves a description for an enhanced metafile if one exists.
GetEnhMetaFileHeader	Retrieves the ENHMETAHEADER structure for an enhanced metafile.
GetEnhMetaFilePaletteEntries	Retrieves palette entries for an enhanced metafile.
GetMetaFile	Retrieves a metafile handle to a DOS file containing a metafile.
GetMetaFileBitsEx	Extracts the data from a metafile into a block of memory.
GetWinMetaFileBits	Converts an enhanced metafile into a standard metafile.
PlayEnhMetaFile	Plays back the commands in an enhanced metafile.
PlayEnhMetaFileRecord	Plays back a single enhanced metafile record.
PlayMetaFile	Plays back the commands in a metafile.
PlayMetaFileRecord	Plays back a single metafile record.

Table 8.8	Metafile Functions (Continued)	
Function	**Description**	
SetEnhMetaFileBits	Creates an enhanced metafile handle for a block of memory that contains a metafile.	
SetMetaFileBitsEx	Creates a metafile handle for a block of memory that contains a metafile.	
SetWinMetaFileBits	Converts a standard metafile into an enhanced metafile.	

accomplished if a metafile is nothing but a set of GDI drawing commands whose parameters, including drawing locations and coordinates, are fixed? After all, there is no way for the metafile to know in advance how large the image area will be or what its coordinate system will be set to—or is there?

You have already seen the answer. There *is* no possible way for a metafile to know how big the image area will be on which it is to be drawn, and no way for the metafile to read the size of the image area and adjust its graphic commands accordingly. However, it does not need to know this information.

Metafiles contain a sequence of GDI commands, and all GDI commands use parameters that are in logical or world coordinates. But logical coordinates have absolutely nothing to do with where an image appears on a device or how large it is. *That's the job of the viewport definition!*

As long as an application displaying a metafile sets the viewport information, and the metafile sets the logical window information (and draws only into the logical window), the metafile will draw itself into whatever viewport the application sets.

The placeable header in the metafile allows an application to determine how large the metafile was on its original device. It includes the dimensions of a bounding rectangle that specifies the total size of the area used by the metafile in metafile units. It also includes the number of metafile units per inch. An application can use this information to determine the optimal window extents and viewport settings for a metafile if the metafile has set the values in the placeable header correctly.

This leads to the following common practices for creating and displaying metafiles:

When Creating a Metafile...

You can set the bounding box in the METAFILEHEADER structure to the window extents used by the metafile. Many metafiles set the logical window extents themselves and set the mapping mode to MM_ANISOTROPIC to force the metafile to be drawn to the full viewport as set by the drawing application. When you call the SetWindowExtEx and SetMapMode functions within a metafile, those functions will be executed when the metafile is played back, thus setting the logical window coordinate system.

When Playing a Metafile...

Before playing a metafile, you may wish to set the map mode to MM_ANISOTROPIC in case the metafile has not done so. You can also set the window extents based on the bounding box information in the metafile header, but this setting will be overridden if the metafile sets its own window extents (which is common). Finally, set the Viewport origin and extents to define the viewport where you wish the metafile to be drawn.

Coordinate Systems and Advanced Metafiles

It may seem that this sequence requires a great deal of cooperation on the part of the metafile and the drawing application, and this is true. It also illustrates why Microsoft developed the enhanced metafile format. Enhanced metafiles contain detailed information about the original resolution of the device; thus if you create a metafile to specific physical dimensions, the drawing application can determine that fact, though it is not required to use it. More important, the metafile drawing routines are much more capable, taking care of setting up the coordinate system for you so that the information need not be included in the metafile itself.

Bringing It All Together II: Additional Examples

The QuikDraw and Analyze programs that follow illustrate how to apply many of the API drawing routines discussed in this chapter and demonstrate how to work with metafiles.

Example: QuikDraw-A Simple Drawing Application

QuikDraw is a program that ties together many of the concepts illustrated in the past few chapters. It is a very simple drawing program, that despite a primitive and limited user interface, nevertheless incorporates many of the techniques that are used to implement full featured drawing program. The major features that are not included here are text and bitmap manipulation, both of which are subjects for later chapters. Those of you who have the original *Visual Basic Programmer's Guide to the Windows API* will recognize this example as a port of the original QuikDraw program with additional metafile features. The version presented is compatible with both Win32 and Win16 (under 16 bit VB 4.0).

Figure 8.9 shows the design-time screen of the QuikDraw program.

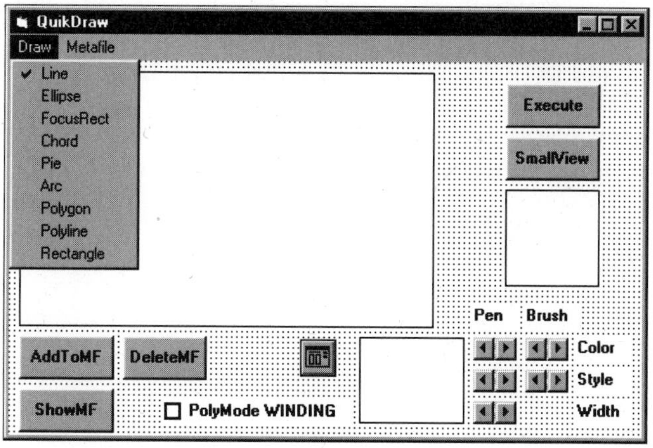

Figure 8.9

The QuikDraw.vbp designtime screen

Using QuikDraw

The QuikDraw menu allows you to specify a Windows API drawing command to execute when the Execute button is pressed. The drawing command is specified using the Draw menu. Each drawing command needs two or more points as parameters. The points are specified by clicking the mouse in the large picture control. The maximum number of points that can be specified depends on the type of figure selected; for example, a line only has two points.

The Execute command button causes the current figure to be drawn. Clicking in the large picture control after the Execute button is pressed starts the definition of a new object.

The SmallView command button causes the current figure to be drawn into the small picture control. The figure is scaled so that the entire area of the large picture control is mapped into the smaller picture control. This shows how coordinate system transformations can be used to scale images.

The five scroll bars at the lower right of the screen allow you to specify the pen and brush style, pen and brush color, and pen width for drawing. The current figure will be drawn using these drawing objects. Click on the Execute or SmallView button after changing the drawing objects to show the current figure drawn with the new attributes. The small rectangle picture control (Picture3) shows a rectangle drawn with the currently selected pen and brush.

The AddToMF button adds the current figure to a global metafile. The ShowMF button plays the metafile on the large and small picture controls. These two commands allow you to build a more complex image. The DeleteMF button deletes the current metafile. The PolyMode WINDING check box sets the polygon fill mode. Refer to Figure 8.15 in the function reference section for this chapter for a description of this value. Figure 8.10 shows the QuikDraw runtime program screen after drawing a complex metafile created with the program.

The Metafile menu contains options to load and save disk metafiles, and to copy the current global metafile to the clipboard.

Figure 8.10

The QuikDraw.vbp runtime screen

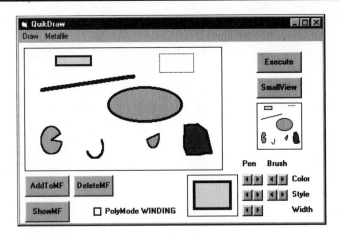

Project Description

The QuikDraw project includes three files. QUIKDRAW.FRM is the only form used in the program. QUIKDRAW.BAS is the only module in the program and contains the constant type and global definitions. APIGID32.BAS is the declaration file for the APIGID32.DLL dynamic link library which contains several utility functions used by this application.

Listing 8.4 shows the form header for the QUICKDRAW.FRM form.

Listing 8.4   **Header for form QUICKDRAW.FRM**

```
VERSION 5.00
Object = "{F9043C88-F6F2-101A-A3C9-08002B2F49FB}#1.1#0"; "COMDLG32.OCX"
Begin VB.Form QuikDraw
    Appearance      =   0  'Flat
    BackColor       =   &H80000005&
    Caption         =   "QuikDraw"
    ClientHeight    =   4245
    ClientLeft      =   1110
    ClientTop       =   1770
    ClientWidth     =   7365
    BeginProperty Font
```

Listing 8.4   Header for form QUICKDRAW.FRM (Continued)

```
        name            =   "MS Sans Serif"
        charset         =   0
        weight          =   700
        size            =   8.25
        underline       =   0    'False
        italic          =   0    'False
        strikethrough   =   0    'False
    EndProperty
    ForeColor       =   &H80000008&
    Height          =   4935
    Left            =   1050
    LinkMode        =   1  'Source
    LinkTopic       =   "Form1"
    ScaleHeight     =   4245
    ScaleWidth      =   7365
    Top             =   1140
    Width           =   7485
```

The five scroll bars in QuikDraw are in a control array with property Ctl-Name = ScrollObject. Their design-time property settings are shown in Table 8.9. The color values are indexes into the QBColor function that returns an RGB color. These scroll bars have code attached to their Change event that causes them to wrap around. In other words, when the value of the scroll is set to Max, the code will immediately set the value to Min+1.

Table 8.9   QuikDraw Scroll Bar Controls

Index	Min	Max	Value	Description
0	-1	16	0	Pen color
1	-1	16	15	Brush color
2	-1	5	0	Pen style
3	-1	7	6	Brush style; 0-4 are hatch styles, 5 for a solid brush
4	0	9	1	Pen width

```
Begin VB.HScrollBar ScrollObject
    Height      =   255
    Index       =   4
    Left        =   5400
```

```
         Max          =    9
         TabIndex     =    16
         Top          =    3840
         Value        =    1
         Width        =    495
      End
Begin VB.HScrollBar ScrollObject
         Height       =    255
         Index        =    3
         Left         =    6000
         Max          =    7
         Min          =    -1
         TabIndex     =    11
         Top          =    3480
         Value        =    6
         Width        =    495
      End
      Begin VB.HScrollBar ScrollObject
         Height       =    255
         Index        =    2
         Left         =    5400
         Max          =    5
         Min          =    -1
         TabIndex     =    10
         Top          =    3480
         Width        =    495
      End
      Begin VB.HScrollBar ScrollObject
         Height       =    255
         Index        =    1
         Left         =    6000
         Max          =    16
         Min          =    -1
         TabIndex     =    9
         Top          =    3120
         Value        =    15
         Width        =    495
      End
      Begin VB.HScrollBar ScrollObject
         Height       =    255
         Index        =    0
         Left         =    5400
         Max          =    16
         Min          =    -1
         TabIndex     =    8
         Top          =    3120
         Width        =    495
      End
      Begin VB.CheckBox ChkPoly
         Appearance   =    0    'Flat
         BackColor    =    &H80000005&
         Caption      =    "PolyMode WINDING"
```

```
        ForeColor      =    &H80000008&
        Height         =    255
        Left           =    1800
        TabIndex       =    18
        Top            =    3840
        Width          =    2175
      End
      Begin VB.CommandButton CmdShowMF
        Appearance     =    0   'Flat
        BackColor      =    &H80000005&
        Caption        =    "ShowMF"
        Height         =    495
        Left           =    120
        TabIndex       =    6
        Top            =    3720
        Width          =    1095
      End
    Begin VB.PictureBox Picture3
        Appearance     =    0   'Flat
        BackColor      =    &H80000005&
        ForeColor      =    &H80000008&
        Height         =    975
        Left           =    4080
        ScaleHeight    =    945
        ScaleWidth     =    1185
        TabIndex       =    7
        Top            =    3120
        Width          =    1215
      End
      Begin VB.CommandButton CmdDeleteMF
        Appearance     =    0   'Flat
        BackColor      =    &H80000005&
        Caption        =    "DeleteMF"
        Height         =    495
        Left           =    1320
        TabIndex       =    5
        Top            =    3120
        Width          =    975
      End
      Begin VB.CommandButton CmdExecute
        Appearance     =    0   'Flat
        BackColor      =    &H80000005&
        Caption        =    "AddToMF"
        Height         =    495
        Index          =    2
        Left           =    120
        TabIndex       =    4
        Top            =    3120
        Width          =    1095
      End
      Begin VB.PictureBox Picture2
        Appearance     =    0   'Flat
```

```
        BackColor       =   &H80000005&
        ForeColor       =   &H80000008&
        Height          =   1095
        Left            =   5760
        ScaleHeight     =   71
        ScaleMode       =   3   'Pixel
        ScaleWidth      =   71
        TabIndex        =   3
        Top             =   1440
        Width           =   1095
    End
    Begin VB.CommandButton CmdExecute
        Appearance      =   0   'Flat
        BackColor       =   &H80000005&
        Caption         =   "SmallView"
        Height          =   495
        Index           =   1
        Left            =   5760
        TabIndex        =   2
        Top             =   840
        Width           =   1095
    End
    Begin VB.CommandButton CmdExecute
        Appearance      =   0   'Flat
        BackColor       =   &H80000005&
        Caption         =   "Execute"
        Height          =   495
        Index           =   0
        Left            =   5760
        TabIndex        =   1
        Top             =   240
        Width           =   1095
    End
```

Picture1 is the main control for drawing. The ScaleMode is set to pixels to make it easier to work with the API functions since it eliminates the need for Twips to Pixels conversions.

```
    Begin VB.PictureBox Picture1
        Appearance      =   0   'Flat
        BackColor       =   &H80000005&
        ForeColor       =   &H80000008&
        Height          =   2895
        Left            =   120
        ScaleHeight     =   191
        ScaleMode       =   3   'Pixel
        ScaleWidth      =   319
        TabIndex        =   0
        Top             =   120
        Width           =   4815
    End
    Begin MSComDlg.CommonDialog CMDialogMF
```

```
      Left            =     3360
      Top             =     3120
      _Version        =     65536
      _ExtentX        =     847
      _ExtentY        =     847
      _StockProps     =     0
      Filter          =     "Metafiles (*.wmf)|*.wmf"
      Flags           =     4100
   End
   Begin VB.Label Label5
      Appearance      =     0    'Flat
      BackColor       =     &H80000005&
      Caption         =     "Width"
      ForeColor       =     &H80000008&
      Height          =     255
      Left            =     6600
      TabIndex        =     17
      Top             =     3840
      Width           =     615
   End
   Begin VB.Label Label4
      Appearance      =     0    'Flat
      BackColor       =     &H80000005&
      Caption         =     "Style"
      ForeColor       =     &H80000008&
      Height          =     255
      Left            =     6600
      TabIndex        =     15
      Top             =     3480
      Width           =     615
   End
   Begin VB.Label Label3
      Appearance      =     0    'Flat
      BackColor       =     &H80000005&
      Caption         =     "Color"
      ForeColor       =     &H80000008&
      Height          =     255
      Left            =     6600
      TabIndex        =     14
      Top             =     3120
      Width           =     615
   End
   Begin VB.Label Label2
      Appearance      =     0    'Flat
      BackColor       =     &H80000005&
      Caption         =     "Brush"
      ForeColor       =     &H80000008&
      Height          =     255
      Left            =     6000
      TabIndex        =     13
      Top             =     2760
      Width           =     615
```

```
End
Begin VB.Label Label1
    Appearance      =    Ø   'Flat
    BackColor       =    &H8ØØØØØØ5&
    Caption         =    "Pen"
    ForeColor       =    &H8ØØØØØØ8&
    Height          =    255
    Left            =    54ØØ
    TabIndex        =    12
    Top             =    276Ø
    Width           =    495
End
Begin VB.Menu MenuDraw
    Caption         =    "Draw"
    Begin VB.Menu MenuDrawType
        Caption         =    "Line"
        Checked         =    -1   'True
        Index           =    Ø
    End
    Begin VB.Menu MenuDrawType
        Caption         =    "Ellipse"
        Index           =    1
    End
    Begin VB.Menu MenuDrawType
        Caption         =    "FocusRect"
        Index           =    2
    End
    Begin VB.Menu MenuDrawType
        Caption         =    "Chord"
        Index           =    3
    End
    Begin VB.Menu MenuDrawType
        Caption         =    "Pie"
        Index           =    4
    End
    Begin VB.Menu MenuDrawType
        Caption         =    "Arc"
        Index           =    5
    End
    Begin VB.Menu MenuDrawType
        Caption         =    "Polygon"
        Index           =    6
    End
    Begin VB.Menu MenuDrawType
        Caption         =    "Polyline"
        Index           =    7
    End
    Begin VB.Menu MenuDrawType
        Caption         =    "Rectangle"
        Index           =    8
    End
End
```

```
      Begin VB.Menu mnu_Metafile
         Caption         =   "Metafile"
         Begin VB.Menu mnu_MetafileSave
            Caption       =   "Save"
         End
         Begin VB.Menu mnu_MetafileLoad
            Caption       =   "Load"
         End
         Begin VB.Menu mnu_MetafileCopy
            Caption       =   "Copy to Clipboard"
         End
      End
   End
End
Attribute VB_Name = "QuikDraw"
Attribute VB_GlobalNameSpace = False
Attribute VB_Creatable = False
Attribute VB_PredeclaredId = True
Attribute VB_Exposed = False
DefStr A-Z
```

The listings for the QuikDraw module are divided into two sections. List-ing 8.5 covers the declaration section. The rest of the module contains meta-file functions which follow in Listing 8.6. This arrangement should make the code listings easier to understand.

One of the important yet subtle changes between Win16 and Win32 is that many Win32 functions return values whereas the equivalent Win16 func-tion is defined as a subroutine. In order to minimize changes to the code it-self, it proved easiest in this case to simply change the Win16 declarations from Subs to Functions. Since numeric return values are returned in registers rather than on the stack (see Chapter 3), this does not impact the calling con-vention. As long as you ignore the return values (at least under Win16), it will not affect the execution of the program.

Listing 8.5   Declarations section for QUICKDRAW.BAS

```
Attribute VB_Name = "QUICKDRAW1"
Option Explicit
' QuikDraw program example

' Porting notes:
'   Win16 APIs defined as Sub are changed to functions returning
'     integers. This is safe (we ignore the values) as sub vs return
'     integer or long has same stack frames.


#If Win32 Then
```

Listing 8.5   Declarations section for QUICKDRAW.BAS (Continued)

```
Type RECT
        Left As Long
        Top As Long
        Right As Long
        Bottom As Long
End Type

Type POINTAPI
        X As Long
        Y As Long
End Type

Type SIZE
        cx As Long
        cy As Long
End Type

Type METAFILEPICT
        mm As Long
        xExt As Long
        yExt As Long
        hMF As Long
End Type

Type METARECORD
        rdSize As Long
        rdFunction As Integer
        rdParm(1) As Integer
End Type

Declare Function Arc& Lib "gdi32" (ByVal hDC As Long, ByVal X1 As Long, ByVal _
Y1 As Long, ByVal X2 As Long, ByVal Y2 As Long, ByVal X3 As Long, ByVal Y3 _
As Long, ByVal X4 As Long, ByVal Y4 As Long)
Declare Function Chord& Lib "gdi32" (ByVal hDC As Long, ByVal X1 As Long, ByVal _
Y1 As Long, ByVal X2 As Long, ByVal Y2 As Long, ByVal X3 As Long, ByVal _
Y3 As Long, ByVal X4 As Long, ByVal Y4 As Long)
Declare Function CloseClipboard& Lib "user32" ()
Declare Function CloseMetaFile& Lib "gdi32" (ByVal hMF As Long)
Declare Function CreateHatchBrush& Lib "gdi32" (ByVal nIndex As Long, ByVal _
crColor As Long)
Declare Function CreateMetaFile& Lib "gdi32" Alias "CreateMetaFileA" (ByVal _
lpstring As String)
Declare Function CreatePen& Lib "gdi32" (ByVal nPenStyle As Long, ByVal nWidth _
As Long, ByVal crColor As Long)
```

Listing 8.5   **Declarations section for QUICKDRAW.BAS (Continued)**

```
Declare Function CreateSolidBrush& Lib "gdi32" (ByVal crColor As Long)
Declare Function DeleteMetaFile& Lib "gdi32" (ByVal hMF As Long)
Declare Function DeleteObject& Lib "gdi32" (ByVal hObject As Long)
Declare Function DrawFocusRect& Lib "user32" (ByVal hDC As Long, lpRect As RECT)
Declare Function Ellipse& Lib "gdi32" (ByVal hDC As Long, ByVal X1 As Long, _
ByVal Y1 As Long, ByVal X2 As Long, ByVal Y2 As Long)
Declare Function EmptyClipboard& Lib "user32" ()
Declare Function EnumMetaFile Lib "gdi32" (ByVal hDC As Long, ByVal hMF As _
Long, ByVal lpCallbackFunc As Long, ByVal lpClientData As Long) As Long
Declare Function GetClientRect& Lib "user32" (ByVal hWnd As Long, lpRect As _
RECT)
Declare Function GetMetaFileBitsEx& Lib "gdi32" (ByVal hMF As Long, ByVal nSize _
As Long, lpvData As Any)
Declare Function GlobalAlloc& Lib "kernel32" (ByVal wFlags As Long, ByVal _
dwBytes As Long)
Declare Function GlobalFree& Lib "kernel32" (ByVal hMem As Long)
Declare Function GlobalLock& Lib "kernel32" (ByVal hMem As Long)
Declare Function GetObjectType& Lib "gdi32" (ByVal hgdiobj As Long)
Declare Function GlobalSize Lib "kernel32" (ByVal hMem As Long) As Long
Declare Function GlobalUnlock& Lib "kernel32" (ByVal hMem As Long)
Declare Function InflateRect& Lib "user32" (lpRect As RECT, ByVal X As Long, _
ByVal Y As Long)
Declare Function LineTo& Lib "gdi32" (ByVal hDC As Long, ByVal X As Long, ByVal _
Y As Long)
Declare Function MoveToEx Lib "gdi32" (ByVal hDC As Long, ByVal X As Long, _
ByVal Y As Long, lpPoint As POINTAPI) As Long
Declare Function OpenClipboard& Lib "user32" (ByVal hWnd As Long)
Declare Function Pie& Lib "gdi32" (ByVal hDC As Long, ByVal X1 As Long, ByVal _
Y1 As Long, ByVal X2 As Long, ByVal Y2 As Long, ByVal X3 As Long, ByVal _
Y3 As Long, ByVal X4 As Long, ByVal Y4 As Long)
Declare Function PlayMetaFile& Lib "gdi32" (ByVal hDC As Long, ByVal hMF As _
Long)
Declare Function PlayMetaFileRecord& Lib "gdi32" (ByVal hDC As Long, ByVal _
lpHandletable As Long, lpMetaRecord As Any, ByVal nHandles As Long)
Declare Function Polyline& Lib "gdi32" (ByVal hDC As Long, lpPoint As POINTAPI, _
ByVal nCount As Long)
Declare Function Polygon& Lib "gdi32" (ByVal hDC As Long, lpPoint As POINTAPI, _
```

Listing 8.5   **Declarations section for QUICKDRAW.BAS (Continued)**

```
ByVal nCount As Long)
Declare Function Rectangle& Lib "gdi32" (ByVal hDC As Long, ByVal X1 As Long, _
ByVal Y1 As Long, ByVal X2 As Long, ByVal Y2 As Long)
Declare Function RestoreDC& Lib "gdi32" (ByVal hDC As Long, ByVal nSavedDC As _
Long)
Declare Function SaveDC& Lib "gdi32" (ByVal hDC As Long)
Declare Function SelectObject& Lib "gdi32" (ByVal hDC As Long, ByVal hObject As _
Long)
Declare Function SetClipboardData& Lib "user32" (ByVal wFormat As Long, ByVal _
hMem As Long)
Declare Function SetMapMode& Lib "gdi32" (ByVal hDC As Long, ByVal nMapMode As _
Long)
Declare Function SetMetaFileBitsEx& Lib "gdi32" (ByVal nSize As Long, lpData As _
Byte)
Declare Function SetMetaFileBitsBuffer& Lib "gdi32" Alias "SetMetaFileBitsEx" _
(ByVal nSize As Long, ByVal lpData As Long)

Declare Function SetPolyFillMode& Lib "gdi32" (ByVal hDC As Long, ByVal _
nPolyFillMode As Long)
Declare Function SetRect& Lib "user32" (lpRect As RECT, ByVal X1 As Long, ByVal _
Y1 As Long, ByVal X2 As Long, ByVal Y2 As Long)
Declare Function SetViewportExtEx& Lib "gdi32" (ByVal hDC As Long, ByVal nX As _
Long, ByVal nY As Long, lpSize As SIZE)
Declare Function SetViewportOrgEx& Lib "gdi32" (ByVal hDC As Long, ByVal nX As _
Long, ByVal nY As Long, lpPoint As POINTAPI)
Declare Function SetWindowOrgEx& Lib "gdi32" (ByVal hDC As Long, ByVal nX As _
Long, ByVal nY As Long, lpPoint As POINTAPI)
Declare Function SetWindowExtEx& Lib "gdi32" (ByVal hDC As Long, ByVal nX As _
Long, ByVal nY As Long, lpSize As SIZE)

Declare Function lopen Lib "kernel32" Alias "_lopen" (ByVal lpPathName As _
String, ByVal iReadWrite As Long) As Long
Declare Function lclose Lib "kernel32" Alias "_lclose" (ByVal hFile As Long) As _
Long
Declare Function lcreat Lib "kernel32" Alias "_lcreat" (ByVal lpPathName As _
String, ByVal iAttribute As Long) As Long
Declare Function llseek Lib "kernel32" Alias "_llseek" (ByVal hFile As Long, _
ByVal lOffset As Long, ByVal iOrigin As Long) As Long
```

Listing 8.5   Declarations section for QUICKDRAW.BAS (Continued)

```
Declare Function lread Lib "kernel32" Alias "_lread" (ByVal hFile As Long, _
lpBuffer As Any, ByVal wBytes As Long) As Long
Declare Function lwrite Lib "kernel32" Alias "_lwrite" (ByVal hFile As Long, _
lpBuffer As Any, ByVal wBytes As Long) As Long

Declare Function hread Lib "kernel32" Alias "_hread" (ByVal hFile As Long, _
lpBuffer As Any, ByVal lBytes As Long) As Long
Declare Function hwrite Lib "kernel32" Alias "_hwrite" (ByVal hFile As Long, _
lpBuffer As Any, ByVal lBytes As Long) As Long

#Else

Type RECT
        Left As Integer
        Top As Integer
        Right As Integer
        Bottom As Integer
End Type

Type POINTAPI
        X As Integer
        Y As Integer
End Type

Type SIZE
        cx As Integer
        cy As Integer
End Type

Type METAFILEPICT        '8 Bytes
    mm As Integer
    xExt As Integer
    yExt As Integer
    hMF As Integer
End Type

Declare Function Arc% Lib "GDI" (ByVal hDC%, ByVal X1%, ByVal Y1%, ByVal X2%, _
ByVal Y2%, ByVal X3%, ByVal Y3%, ByVal X4%, ByVal Y4%)
Declare Function Chord% Lib "GDI" (ByVal hDC%, ByVal X1%, ByVal Y1%, ByVal X2%, _
ByVal Y2%, ByVal X3%, ByVal Y3%, ByVal X4%, ByVal Y4%)
Declare Function CloseClipboard% Lib "User" ()
Declare Function CloseMetaFile% Lib "GDI" (ByVal hMF%)
```

Listing 8.5   Declarations section for QUICKDRAW.BAS (Continued)

```
Declare Function CreateHatchBrush% Lib "GDI" (ByVal nIndex%, ByVal crColor&)
Declare Function CreateMetaFile% Lib "GDI" (ByVal lpstring$)
Declare Function CreatePen% Lib "GDI" (ByVal nPenStyle%, ByVal nWidth%, ByVal _
crColor&)
Declare Function CreateSolidBrush% Lib "GDI" (ByVal crColor&)
Declare Function DeleteMetaFile% Lib "GDI" (ByVal hMF%)
Declare Function DeleteObject% Lib "GDI" (ByVal hObject%)
Declare Function DrawFocusRect% Lib "User" (ByVal hDC%, lpRect As RECT)
Declare Function Ellipse% Lib "GDI" (ByVal hDC%, ByVal X1%, ByVal Y1%, ByVal _
X2%, ByVal Y2%)
Declare Function EmptyClipboard% Lib "User" ()
Declare Function GetClientRect% Lib "User" (ByVal hWnd%, lpRect As RECT)
Declare Function GetMetaFileBits% Lib "GDI" (ByVal hMF%)
Declare Function GlobalAlloc% Lib "Kernel" (ByVal wFlags%, ByVal dwBytes&)
Declare Function GlobalFree% Lib "Kernel" (ByVal hMem%)
Declare Function GlobalLock& Lib "Kernel" (ByVal hMem%)
Declare Function GlobalSize& Lib "Kernel" (ByVal hMem%)
Declare Function GlobalUnlock% Lib "Kernel" (ByVal hMem%)
Declare Function InflateRect% Lib "User" (lpRect As RECT, ByVal X%, ByVal Y%)
Declare Function LineTo% Lib "GDI" (ByVal hDC%, ByVal X%, ByVal Y%)
Declare Function MoveToEx& Lib "GDI" (ByVal hDC%, ByVal X%, ByVal Y%, lpPoint _
As POINTAPI)
Declare Function OpenClipboard% Lib "User" (ByVal hWnd%)
Declare Function Pie% Lib "GDI" (ByVal hDC%, ByVal X1%, ByVal Y1%, ByVal X2%, _
ByVal Y2%, ByVal X3%, ByVal Y3%, ByVal X4%, ByVal Y4%)
Declare Function PlayMetaFile% Lib "GDI" (ByVal hDC%, ByVal hMF%)
Declare Function Polygon% Lib "GDI" (ByVal hDC%, lpPoints As POINTAPI, ByVal _
nCount%)
Declare Function Polyline% Lib "GDI" (ByVal hDC%, lpPoints As POINTAPI, ByVal _
nCount%)
Declare Function Rectangle% Lib "GDI" (ByVal hDC%, ByVal X1%, ByVal Y1%, ByVal _
X2%, ByVal Y2%)
Declare Function RestoreDC% Lib "GDI" (ByVal hDC%, ByVal nSavedDC%)
Declare Function SaveDC% Lib "GDI" (ByVal hDC%)
Declare Function SelectObject% Lib "GDI" (ByVal hDC%, ByVal hObject%)
Declare Function SetClipboardData% Lib "User" (ByVal wFormat%, ByVal hMem%)
Declare Function SetMapMode% Lib "GDI" (ByVal hDC%, ByVal nMapMode%)
Declare Function SetMetaFileBitsBetter% Lib "GDI" (ByVal hMF%)
Declare Function SetPolyFillMode% Lib "GDI" (ByVal hDC%, ByVal nPolyFillMode%)
Declare Function SetViewportExtEx% Lib "GDI" (ByVal hDC%, ByVal nX%, ByVal nY%, _
lpSize As SIZE)
Declare Function SetViewportOrgEx% Lib "GDI" (ByVal hDC%, ByVal X%, ByVal Y%, _
lpSize As SIZE)
Declare Function SetWindowExtEx% Lib "GDI" (ByVal hDC%, ByVal X%, ByVal Y%, _
lpSize As SIZE)
```

Listing 8.5   **Declarations section for QUICKDRAW.BAS (Continued)**

```
Declare Function SetWindowOrgEx% Lib "GDI" (ByVal hDC%, ByVal X%, ByVal Y%, _
lpSize As SIZE)
Declare Function SetRect% Lib "User" (lpRect As RECT, ByVal X1%, ByVal Y1%, _
ByVal X2%, ByVal Y2%)

Declare Function lopen% Lib "Kernel" Alias "_lopen" (ByVal lpPathName$, ByVal _
iReadWrite%)
Declare Function lclose% Lib "Kernel" Alias "_lclose" (ByVal hFile%)
Declare Function lcreat% Lib "Kernel" Alias "_lcreat" (ByVal lpPathName$, ByVal _
iAttribute%)
Declare Function lseek& Lib "Kernel" Alias "_llseek" (ByVal hFile%, ByVal _
lOffset&, ByVal iOrigin%)
Declare Function lread% Lib "Kernel" Alias "_lread" (ByVal hFile%, lpBuffer As _
Any, ByVal wBytes%)
Declare Function lwrite% Lib "Kernel" Alias "_lwrite" (ByVal hFile%, lpBuffer _
As Any, ByVal wBytes%)
Declare Function hread& Lib "Kernel" Alias "_hread" (ByVal hf%, hpvBuffer As _
Any, ByVal cbBuffer&)
Declare Function hwrite& Lib "Kernel" Alias "_hwrite" (ByVal hf%, hpvBuffer As _
Any, ByVal cbBuffer&)

#End If
```

The RECTS structure is necessary because standard Windows metafiles need a 16-bit based rectangle, and file formats do not change between Win16 and Win32.

```
Type RECTS
        Left As Integer
        Top As Integer
        Right As Integer
        Bottom As Integer
End Type

' Note how RECT does not change within a structure
' that is saved on disk and is Win16 compatible!
Type METAFILEHEADER      ' 22 bytes
    key As Long
    hMF As Integer
    bbox As RECTS
    inch As Integer
```

```
    reserved As Long
    checksum As Integer
End Type
```

A number of constant groups that are included in the file have been removed from the listing to save space. These include constants with the prefixes: OBJ_, R2_, PS_, MM_, and HS_.

```
' Application global variables

#If Win32 Then
    ' Metafile to hold objects
    Public hndMetaFile&

    ' Private Pen and Brush to use
    Public hndPen&
    Public hndBrush&
#Else
    ' Metafile to hold objects
    Public hndMetaFile%

    ' Private Pen and Brush to use
    Public hndPen%
    Public hndBrush%

#End If

' Application global variables
Public MaxPoints%    ' Maximum points to use this drawing mode
Public PointsUsed%   ' Number of points used.
' Array of points
Public PointArray(32) As POINTAPI

' Current drawing mode - most recent Draw menu index
Public LastDrawIndex%

' This flag is set to -1 after the Execute button is pressed.
' This is an indication that the next click in Picture1 should
' start a new object.
Public LastWasExecute%


Public Const ALTERNATE = 1
Public Const WINDING = 2
Public Const TRANSPARENT = 1
Public Const OPAQUE = 2
Public Const ABSOLUTE = 1
Public Const RELATIVE = 2
Public Const WHITE_BRUSH = 0
Public Const LTGRAY_BRUSH = 1
Public Const GRAY_BRUSH = 2
Public Const DKGRAY_BRUSH = 3
```

```
Public Const BLACK_BRUSH = 4
Public Const NULL_BRUSH = 5
Public Const HOLLOW_BRUSH = NULL_BRUSH
Public Const WHITE_PEN = 6
Public Const BLACK_PEN = 7
Public Const NULL_PEN = 8
Public Const OEM_FIXED_FONT = 10
Public Const ANSI_FIXED_FONT = 11
Public Const ANSI_VAR_FONT = 12
Public Const SYSTEM_FONT = 13
Public Const DEVICE_DEFAULT_FONT = 14
Public Const DEFAULT_PALETTE = 15
Public Const SYSTEM_FIXED_FONT = 16

Public Const GMEM_MOVEABLE = &H2
Public Const CF_METAFILEPICT = 3
Public Const GMEM_ZEROINIT = &H40
```

Listing 8.6   QUICKDRAW.FRM

```
Option Explicit

'
' We default to the line mode with no points defined.
'
Private Sub Form_Load()
    MaxPoints% = 2
    PointsUsed% = 0
    ' Force the selection of a valid pen and brush
    ScrollObject_Change 0
End Sub


'
'    It is important to delete these GDI objects (if they
'    were created) before closing the application so that
'    the Windows resources may be properly freed.
'
Private Sub Form_Unload(Cancel As Integer)
    Dim di&
    If hndMetaFile <> 0 Then di = DeleteMetaFile(hndMetaFile)
    If hndPen <> 0 Then di = DeleteObject(hndPen)
    If hndBrush <> 0 Then di = DeleteObject(hndBrush)

End Sub
```

Listing 8.6   **QUICKDRAW.FRM (Continued)**

```
'   This function handles the menu commands. Each one defines
'   a different object to draw when the Execute command button
'   is selected.
'
Private Sub MenuDrawType_Click(Index As Integer)
    Dim X%
    ' Clear out the current object.
    PointsUsed% = 0
    picture1.Cls
    ' LastDrawIndex is a global that shows which GDI drawing
    ' function is being tested.
    LastDrawIndex% = Index
    ' Uncheck all of the menu entries
    For X% = 0 To 8
        MenuDrawType(X%).Checked = 0
        Next X%
    ' And check this one only..
    MenuDrawType(Index).Checked = -1
    ' Each GDI drawing tool has a maximum number of points
    ' that it needs in order to perform the drawing.
    Select Case Index
        Case 0, 1, 2, 8
            MaxPoints% = 2
        Case 3, 4, 5
            MaxPoints% = 4
        ' Polygons are limited to the size of the point data array
        Case 6, 7
            MaxPoints% = 32
        End Select
End Sub
```

The ScrollObject_Change event sets the pen and brush according to the scroll bar settings. It then refreshes the picture3 object which displays a rectangle using the current brush and pen. Notice how the function deletes the previous pen and brush before creating the new ones.

```
'   These scroll bars are used to select colors, styles, and
'   pen widths.  The Min and Max properties are selected
'   such that the Scrollbar value parameter may be used
'   directly in the GDI object creation function.
'
Private Sub ScrollObject_Change(Index As Integer)

    Dim di%
    ' Wrap around when increasing
    If ScrollObject(Index).value = ScrollObject(Index).Max Then
        ScrollObject(Index).value = ScrollObject(Index).Min + 1
```

```
        Exit Sub
    End If
    ' Wrap around when decrementing
    If ScrollObject(Index).value = ScrollObject(Index).Min Then
        ScrollObject(Index).value = ScrollObject(Index).Max - 1
        Exit Sub
    End If


    ' Delete the current objects
    If hndPen Then di = DeleteObject(hndPen)
    If hndBrush Then di = DeleteObject(hndBrush)

    ' Now create the new pen
    hndPen = CreatePen(ScrollObject(2).value, ScrollObject(4).value, _
    QBColor(ScrollObject(0).value))

    ' Now create the new brush
    ' Value 6 indicates that we should create a solid brush
    ' 0-5 indicate styles of hatched brushes.
    If ScrollObject(3).value = 6 Then
        hndBrush = CreateSolidBrush(QBColor(ScrollObject(1).value))
    Else
        hndBrush = CreateHatchBrush(ScrollObject(3).value, _
        QBColor(ScrollObject(1).value))
    End If

    ' Draw a sample rectangle using the current pen&Brush
    ' This forces the Paint event to be triggered.
    Picture3.Refresh

End Sub
```

The Picture3_Paint event calculates the rectangle that it draws based on the actual size of the control. It starts by loading a rectangle with the dimensions of the control using the GetClientRect function. It then uses the Inflate-Rect function to shrink the rectangle.

As always, the function is careful to restore the original objects to the device context.

```
'
'   This picture control shows a rectangle drawn in the
'   current pen and brush.
'
Private Sub Picture3_Paint()
    Dim rc As RECT
    #If Win32 Then
        Dim hWnd&
        Dim oldpen&, oldbrush&
        Dim di&
    #Else
```

```
        Dim hWnd%
        Dim oldpen%, oldbrush%
        Dim di%
#End If


' Get the window handle for Picture2
hWnd = Picture3.hWnd
' Get a rectangle with the client area size...
GetClientRect hWnd, rc
'.. and shrink it by 10 pixels on a side.
InflateRect rc, -10, -10


' Select in our private pen and brush
If hndPen <> 0 And hndBrush <> 0 Then
    oldpen = SelectObject(Picture3.hDC, hndPen)
    oldbrush = SelectObject(Picture3.hDC, hndBrush)
End If


' Draw the rectangle
di = Rectangle(Picture3.hDC, rc.Left, rc.Top, rc.Right, rc.Bottom)


' Be sure to restore the original GDI objects!
If oldpen <> 0 Then di = SelectObject(Picture3.hDC, oldpen)
If oldbrush <> 0 Then di = SelectObject(Picture3.hDC, oldbrush)


End Sub
```

When the mouse is clicked on the picture1 control, an internal array of points is updated based on the location of the mouse click. A small + symbol is drawn to indicate the locations of the points.

```
'
'   Mouse clicks in Picture1
'
Private Sub Picture1_MouseDown(Button As Integer, Shift As Integer, X As _
Single, Y As Single)
    Dim pt%, px%, py%

    ' If last command was an execute, clear the points to
    ' start a new image
    If LastWasExecute% Then
        PointsUsed% = 0
        LastWasExecute% = 0
    End If


    ' If the maximum number of points has been exceeded
    ' Shift all of the points down
    If PointsUsed% >= MaxPoints% Then
        For pt% = 1 To MaxPoints%
            PointArray(pt% - 1) = PointArray(pt%)
```

```
        Next pt%
        PointsUsed% = PointsUsed% - 1
    End If
    ' Add the current point to the list
    PointArray(PointsUsed%).X = CInt(X)
    PointArray(PointsUsed%).Y = CInt(Y)
    PointsUsed% = PointsUsed% + 1
    picture1.Cls

    ' Draw small + indicators to show where the points are.
    For pt% = 0 To PointsUsed% - 1
        px% = PointArray(pt%).X
        py% = PointArray(pt%).Y
        picture1.Line (px% - 2, py%)-(px% + 3, py%)
        picture1.Line (px%, py% - 2)-(px%, py% + 3)
    Next pt%
End Sub
```

There are three execution command buttons in a control array. Button 0 simply draws the object selected by the Draw menu. Button 1 draws into the picture3 control, showing how scaling is accomplished. Button 2 adds the drawing into the current metafile.

In any case, the first step is to set the coordinate system. When drawing into picture1, the mapping mode is left as MM_TEXT because all of the points and drawing coordinates are the same as the device coordinates for this control. For drawing into picture2, the small picture control, we need to scale the image. The window extents are set to the size of the picture1 control, since all of the point coordinates are set for that control. The viewport extents are set to the device coordinates of the picture2 control. For drawing into the metafile, no extents or viewports are set—this routine is performing a simple recording of GDI commands. There is no easy way to add commands to a metafile, so the first step for the metafile operation is to create a new metafile, draw the previous metafile into the new metafile device context, then delete the original metafile.

The device context to use is placed in variable dc. The drawing commands that follow do not care which device they are drawing into.

After the drawing operation is complete, the function cleans up after itself. In the case of the metafile option, the function closes the metafile. This destroys the metafile device context and returns a handle to the metafile which can then be played.

```
'   Draw the current object on the picture
'   Index = 0 is the Execute button which draws the current
'   object into the large Picture1 control
'
'   Index = 1 is the SmallView button which draws the
'   current object into the small Picture2 control
'
```

```
'    Index = 2 is the AddToMF button which adds the current
'    object into the current metafile.
'
Private Sub CmdExecute_Click(Index As Integer)
    #If Win32 Then
        Dim dc&, saved&, di&, dl&
        Dim oldpen&, oldbrush&, oldpolymode&
    #Else
        Dim dc%, saved%, di%, dl&
        Dim oldpen%, oldbrush%, oldpolymode%
    #End If
    Dim rc As RECT
    Dim oldsize As SIZE
    Dim oldpoint As POINTAPI

    Select Case Index
        Case 0  ' Execute button - draw into Picture1 after
                ' clearing the control.
            dc = picture1.hDC
            picture1.Cls
        Case 1  ' SmallView button - draw into Picture2
            picture2.Cls
            dc = picture2.hDC
            ' We're going to be changing the scaling, better
            ' save the current state of the DC or the VB
            ' drawing routines will no longer draw correctly.
            saved = SaveDC(dc)

            ' The entire area of Picture1 is scaled to fit
            ' Picture2 exactly - this requires a change of
            ' the mapping mode.
            di = SetMapMode(dc, MM_ANISOTROPIC)

            ' The logical window is the size of Picture1.
            ' Mapping this to the area of Picture2 is done
            ' by making all of Picture2 the viewport.
            dl& = SetWindowExtEx(dc, picture1.ScaleWidth, _
            picture1.ScaleHeight, oldsize)
            dl& = SetViewportExtEx(dc, picture2.ScaleWidth, _
            picture2.ScaleHeight, oldsize)

        Case 2  ' AddToMeta button - Add the current object
                ' to the global metafile.
            ' First create a new metafile device context.
            dc = CreateMetaFile(vbNullString)
            If hndMetaFile <> 0 Then
                ' If a global metafile already exists,
                ' first play the existing metafile into the new one.
                di = PlayMetaFile(dc, hndMetaFile)
                ' Then delete the existing metafile.
                di = DeleteMetaFile(hndMetaFile)
                hndMetaFile = 0
```

```
                    ' The drawing commands that follow will add
                    ' the current object to the new metafile
                    ' device context.
            End If

        End Select

    ' Select in the private pen and brush if we're using them
    If hndPen <> 0 And hndBrush <> 0 Then
        oldpen = SelectObject(dc, hndPen)
        oldbrush = SelectObject(dc, hndBrush)
    End If
    ' Also change the polygon filling mode to winding if necessary
    If ChkPoly.value = 1 Then oldpolymode = SetPolyFillMode(dc, WINDING)

    ' The object drawn depends on global LastDrawIndex which
    ' was set by the Draw menu commands.
    ' The PointsUsed global indicates how many points have
    ' been drawn in Picture1.
    Select Case LastDrawIndex
        Case 0  ' Draw a line
            If PointsUsed = 2 Then
                ' Set the current position of the pen
                dl = MoveToEx(dc, PointArray(0).X, PointArray(0).Y, oldpoint)
                ' and draw to the specified point.
                di = LineTo(dc, PointArray(1).X, PointArray(1).Y)
            End If
        Case 1  ' Draw an ellipse
            If PointsUsed% = 2 Then
                di = Ellipse(dc, PointArray(0).X, PointArray(0).Y, _
                PointArray(1).X, PointArray(1).Y)
            End If
        Case 2 ' Draw a focus rectangle
            If PointsUsed% = 2 Then
                SetRect rc, PointArray(0).X, PointArray(0).Y, PointArray(1).X, _
                PointArray(1).Y
                DrawFocusRect dc, rc
            End If
        Case 3  ' Draw a chord
            If PointsUsed% = 4 Then
                di = Chord(dc, PointArray(0).X, PointArray(0).Y, _
                PointArray(1).X,
                PointArray(1).Y, PointArray(2).X, PointArray(2).Y, _
                PointArray(3).X,
                PointArray(3).Y)
            End If
        Case 4  ' Draw a pie
            If PointsUsed% = 4 Then
                di = Pie(dc, PointArray(0).X, PointArray(0).Y, PointArray(1).X, _
                PointArray(1).Y, PointArray(2).X, PointArray(2).Y, _
```

```
                          PointArray(3).X, PointArray(3).Y)
                End If
            Case 5  ' Draw an arc
                If PointsUsed% = 4 Then
                    di = Arc(dc, PointArray(0).X, PointArray(0).Y, PointArray(1).X, _
                        PointArray(1).Y, PointArray(2).X, PointArray(2).Y, _
                        PointArray(3).X, PointArray(3).Y)
                End If
            Case 6 ' Draw a polygon
                If PointsUsed% > 1 Then
                    di = Polygon(dc, PointArray(0), PointsUsed%)
                End If
            Case 7 ' Draw a polyline
                If PointsUsed% > 1 Then
                    di = Polyline(dc, PointArray(0), PointsUsed%)
                End If
            Case 8 ' Draw a rectangle
                If PointsUsed% = 2 Then
                    di = Rectangle(dc, PointArray(0).X, PointArray(0).Y, _
                        PointArray(1).X, PointArray(1).Y)
                End If

        End Select


    ' Be sure to restore the original GDI objects!
    If oldpen <> 0 Then di = SelectObject(dc, oldpen)
    If oldbrush <> 0 Then di = SelectObject(dc, oldbrush)
    If ChkPoly.value = 1 Then di = SetPolyFillMode(dc, oldpolymode)

    Select Case Index
        Case 0
            ' Notify the mouse down routine that the last
            ' command was an execute
            ' This informs the system that the next mouse
            ' click in Picture1 is the start of a new object.
            LastWasExecute% = -1
        Case 1  ' Restore the previous state of the Picture2 DC
            di = RestoreDC(dc, saved)
        Case 2  ' Close the metafile device context and
                ' objtain a metafile handle.
            hndMetaFile = CloseMetaFile(dc)
            dc = picture1.hDC
        End Select
End Sub




'
' Delete the current metafile
'
```

```
Private Sub CmdDeleteMF_Click()
    Dim di& ' Change to long - will work in Win16 too.

    If hndMetaFile Then
        di = DeleteMetaFile(hndMetaFile)
        hndMetaFile = 0
    End If

End Sub
```

The CmdShowMF_Click routine draws the metafile onto the picture1 control. During porting it was necessary to change the window and viewport extents calls to use the extended versions of the functions (SetWindowExtEx instead of SetWindowExt) in order to share code between the 16- and 32-bit versions without additional use of conditional compilation. The metafile can be played directly into picture1 because the drawing coordinates are recorded in the same mapping mode and window size as they are being drawn in. In order to scale the metafile to draw into the small picture control, it is necessary to set the mapping mode, window extents, and viewport extents.

```
'
'
' Show the current global metafile if one exists. It will
'   be shown in both Picture1 and Picture2
'
' Porting notes:
'
'   Conditionally define the variable types.
'   Remove type characters % and & from variable usage to avoid
'       conflicts between 16 and 32 bits environments
'   Change SetViewportEx and SetWindowExt to SetViewportExtEx and
'       SetWindowExtEx for Win32 compatibility.
'
'
'
Private Sub CmdShowMF_Click()
    #If Win32 Then
        Dim saved&, dc&, di&, dl&
    #Else
        Dim saved%, dc%, di%, dl&
    #End If
    Dim oldsize As SIZE
    ' Because the original drawing was into Picture1,
    ' playing the metafile into Picture1 is trivial.
    picture1.Cls

    di = PlayMetaFile(picture1.hDC, hndMetaFile)

    ' Picture 2 is trickier. First we clear it and save the
    ' current DC state.
    picture2.Cls
```

```
dc = picture2.hDC
saved = SaveDC(dc)
' Now set the new coordinate system. See the CmdExecute()_Click
' command for further explanation
di = SetMapMode(dc, MM_ANISOTROPIC)
dl = SetWindowExtEx(dc, picture1.ScaleWidth, picture1.ScaleHeight, oldsize)
dl = SetViewportExtEx(dc, picture2.ScaleWidth, picture2.ScaleHeight, _
oldsize)
' All of the drawing objects that were used on the original
' objects were saved with the metafile, thus the metafile
' will automatically draw each object in the correct color
' and style.
di = PlayMetaFile(dc, hndMetaFile)
' And restore the original DC state
di = RestoreDC(dc, saved)

End Sub
```

The Metafile Copy command copies the current metafile into the clipboard. In order to do this, it must load a METAFILEPICT structure.

While the current metafile object could be copied into the clipboard, it would not serve much purpose since the coordinates are hardcoded into the metafile. A clipboard metafile should be scalable. In addition, a copy is necessary because a metafile handle should not be used by an application once it has been placed into the clipboard. The solution is to create a new metafile and copy the current metafile into it. The first step is to create the new metafile and set the window extents to match the dimensions of the picture1 control. Next, the existing metafile is played into the new metafile and the metafile is closed. The METAFILEPICT structure is loaded with the requested mapping mode and the extents of the metafile. A global memory block is then allocated to hold the METAFILEPICT structure. The structure is copied into the allocated memory block using the agCopyData function.

Memory blocks and methods for using them will be demonstrated further in Chapter 9 and discussed in detail in Chapter 15. The clipboard is used by opening the clipboard, emptying the current contents of the clipboard, setting the new clipboard data, and then closing the clipboard. The metafile object that was created during the copy process is now owned by the clipboard and must not be deleted by the application.

```
Private Sub mnu_MetafileCopy_Click()

    #If Win32 Then
        Dim hdcMeta&
        Dim dl&, di&
        Dim newmf&
        Dim hgmem&

    #Else
```

```
        Dim hdcMeta%
        Dim dl&, di%
        Dim newmf%
        Dim hgmem%
#End If

Dim mfp As METAFILEPICT
Dim GlblAddr&
Dim oldsize As SIZE

If hndMetaFile = 0 Then
    MsgBox "Metafile must be defined before saving"
    Exit Sub
End If

hdcMeta = CreateMetaFile(vbNullString)
dl& = SetWindowExtEx(hdcMeta, picture1.ScaleWidth, picture1.ScaleHeight, _
oldsize)
di = PlayMetaFile(hdcMeta, hndMetaFile)
newmf = CloseMetaFile(hdcMeta)

mfp.mm = MM_ANISOTROPIC
mfp.xExt = picture1.ScaleWidth
mfp.yExt = picture1.ScaleHeight
mfp.hMF = newmf

' Take out hardcoded sizes - used to be 8 instead of len(mfp)
hgmem = GlobalAlloc(GMEM_MOVEABLE, Len(mfp))

GlblAddr = GlobalLock(hgmem)
agCopyData mfp, ByVal GlblAddr&, Len(mfp)
di = GlobalUnlock(hgmem)

' Place the metafile into the clipboard
di = OpenClipboard(picture1.hWnd)
di = EmptyClipboard()
di = SetClipboardData(CF_METAFILEPICT, hgmem)
di = CloseClipboard()

End Sub
```

The menu commands that load and save metafiles use the common dialog control to select a file. The drawing that takes place in the metafile load routine is similar to what you've seen earlier in this listing. The real work is performed in the LoadTheMetafile and SaveTheMetafile routines which are shown in Listing 8.7

```
Private Sub mnu_MetafileLoad_Click()
    Dim usefile$
    #If Win32 Then
        Dim saved&
```

```
        Dim dc&
        Dim usemf&
        Dim di&, dl&
    #Else
        Dim saved%
        Dim dc%
        Dim usemf%
        Dim di%, dl&
    #End If
    Dim oldsize As SIZE

    CMDialogMF.DialogTitle = "Load a metafile"
    CMDialogMF.Action = 1
    usefile$ = CMDialogMF.FileName
    If usefile$ <> "" Then
        usemf = LoadTheMetafile(usefile$)
        If usemf <> 0 Then
            ' Now draw the metafile
            picture1.Cls
            dc = picture1.hDC
            saved = SaveDC(dc)
            ' Now set the new coordinate system. See the CmdExecute()_Click
            ' command for further explanation
            ' Most metafiles will set their own extents, but we need
            ' to set the viewport to match the scalemode of the
            ' entire screen to fill the window
            di = SetMapMode(dc, MM_ANISOTROPIC)
            dl = SetViewportExtEx(dc, picture1.ScaleWidth, _
            picture1.ScaleHeight, oldsize)
            ' All of the drawing objects that were used on the original
            ' objects were saved with the metafile, thus the metafile
            ' will automatically draw each object in the correct color
            ' and style.
            di = PlayMetaFile(dc, usemf)
            ' And restore the original DC state
            di = RestoreDC(dc, saved)
            di = DeleteMetaFile(usemf)
        End If
    End If

End Sub

Private Sub mnu_MetafileSave_Click()
    Dim di&
    Dim usefile$
    If hndMetaFile = 0 Then
        MsgBox "Metafile must be defined before saving"
        Exit Sub
    End If
    CMDialogMF.DialogTitle = "Save a metafile"
    CMDialogMF.Action = 2
    usefile$ = CMDialogMF.FileName
```

```
    If usefile$ <> "" Then
        di = SaveTheMetafile(usefile$, hndMetaFile, CInt(picture1.ScaleWidth), _
        CInt(picture1.ScaleHeight))
    End If

End Sub
```

Loading a metafile takes place in two parts. It is first necessary to determine if the file is a placeable metafile. This is accomplished by reading the first 22 bytes of the file into a MEATFILEHEADER structure. A special key value in the structure determines if it is a placeable metafile header. If not, the program seeks back to the start of the file to read the non-placeable metafile. A global memory block is allocated that is large enough to hold the entire file. The GlobalLock function retrieves the memory address of the block. The hread function then reads the entire file into the memory block. Under Win32 there is no difference between hread and lread, and, in fact you, will see that there are other preferred file I/O routines that will be described in Chapter 13. However, under Win16, hread is able to read blocks of data over 64K in size, which is necessary to support very large metafiles.

It would also be possible to use byte arrays instead of memory blocks under Win32, since the Win32 metafile functions expect pointers to memory blocks. However, since the Win16 metafile code actually uses global handles during the conversion, it seemed easier to use global memory for both platforms. To do this, an alias for SetMetaFileBitsEx (which expects a byte array) was created called SetMetaFileBitsBuffer (which expects a long variable containing a memory address).

The two SetMetaFileBits functions both perform the same task—they convert the data in a block of memory into a metafile handle. The memory block is then discarded, the file closed, and the handle returned as the function result.

Listing 8.7   **QUICKDRAW.BAS—Metafile routines**

```
'
' Yes, it is possible for function declarations to change as well
'
#If Win32 Then
Function LoadTheMetafile(FileName$) As Long
#Else
Function LoadTheMetafile(FileName$) As Integer
#End If
    #If Win32 Then
        Dim fhnd&
        Dim di&, dl&
        Dim mfglbhnd&
        Dim mfhnd&
    #Else
```

Listing 8.7   QUICKDRAW.BAS—Metafile routines (Continued)

```
        Dim fhnd%
        Dim di%, dl&
        Dim mfglbhnd%
        Dim mfhnd%
#End If
Dim mfile As METAFILEHEADER

Dim mfinfosize&
Dim currentfileloc&
Dim gptr&

' Open the file to read
fhnd = lopen(FileName$, 0)
If fhnd < 0 Then Exit Function


' First read the placeable header file header
di = lread(fhnd, mfile, Len(mfile))
If mfile.key <> &H9AC6CDD7 Then
    ' It's not a placeable metafile - so just seek to the start
    di = llseek(fhnd, 0, 0)
End If

' Now we need a buffer that will contain the metafile data
currentfileloc& = llseek(fhnd, 0, 1)
mfinfosize& = llseek(fhnd, 0, 2) - currentfileloc&


' Now allocate a buffer to hold the data
' We use the Global memory pool because this buffer
' could easily be above 64k bytes.
mfglbhnd = GlobalAlloc(GMEM_MOVEABLE, mfinfosize)
gptr& = GlobalLock&(mfglbhnd)
dl = llseek(fhnd, currentfileloc, 0)

dl = hread(fhnd, ByVal gptr, mfinfosize)

' Win32 does not support the SetMetaFileBitsBetter function
#If Win32 Then
    ' If we were using a byte array, we could use
    ' the original definition of SetMetaFileBitsEx, but
    ' we want to preserve 16-bit compatibility
    mfhnd = SetMetaFileBitsBuffer(mfinfosize, gptr)
    di = GlobalUnlock(mfglbhnd)
#Else
    di = GlobalUnlock(mfglbhnd)
    mfhnd = SetMetaFileBitsBetter(mfglbhnd)
#End If
```

Listing 8.7   QUICKDRAW.BAS—Metafile routines (Continued)

```
    di = lclose(fhnd)

    ' Don't delete the global handle - it holds the metafile data
    LoadTheMetafile = mfhnd
End Function
```

The SaveTheMetafile function reverses the operations in the LoadTheMetafile function. It begins by creating a file, then loading a METAFILEHEADER structure. It initializes the structure with the key, extents, and an arbitrary value for the number of metafile units per inch (the Windows documentation suggests that you use a number under 1,440). A checksum is included in the structure and can be used by a program loading a metafile to verify that it is not corrupt (or at least that the header is not corrupt). The checksum is generated by performing an exclusive OR (XOR) operation on the first 10 integers in the structure. You'll note that the code here does not bother to include the left and top fields of the bounding rectangle in this calculation. This is because those values are always set to zero, and zero exclusive OR'd with any value is equal to that value.

The METAFILEHEADER is then written to the file. A copy of the global metafile is created in much the same way as shown in the Clipboard copy routine in Listing 8.6.

Here the 16-bit and 32-bit editions of the code part company. Win16 provides the GetMetaFileBits function which allocates a global handle for a metafile. This handle can then be locked to obtain a memory address, and the buffer written directly to the disk file. Under Win32, it is necessary to first use GetMetaFileBitsEx to determine how large a buffer is necessary, then to allocate the buffer and call the function a second time to load it. The buffer can then be written to disk.

```
    '
    '
    ' Even though xExt and yExt are longs, they are limited to integer
    ' values to stay compatible with the METAFILEHEADER structure
    '
#If Win32 Then
Function SaveTheMetafile(FileName$, mfhnd&, xExt&, yExt&)
#Else
Function SaveTheMetafile(FileName$, mfhnd%, xExt%, yExt%)
#End If

    #If Win32 Then
        Dim fhnd&
        Dim di&, dl&
        Dim mfglbhnd&
```

```
        Dim newmf&
        Dim dc&
#Else
        Dim fhnd%
        Dim di%, dl&
        Dim mfglbhnd%
        Dim newmf%
        Dim dc%
#End If
Dim mfile As METAFILEHEADER

Dim mfinfosize&
Dim currentfileloc&
Dim gptr&

Dim oldsize As SIZE

' Open the file to write
fhnd = lcreat(FileName$, 0)
If fhnd >= 0 Then Call lclose(fhnd) ' Close the open handle
fhnd = lopen(FileName$, 2)
If fhnd < 0 Then Exit Function
If mfhnd = 0 Then Exit Function


' First write a placeable header file header
mfile.key = &H9AC6CDD7  ' The key - required
mfile.hMF = 0               ' Must be 0
mfile.bbox.Left = 0
mfile.bbox.Top = 0
' These should be calculated using GetDeviceCaps
mfile.bbox.Right = xExt + 1 ' Size in metafile units of bounding area
mfile.bbox.Bottom = yExt + 1
mfile.inch = 1000 ' Number of metafile units per inch

mfile.reserved = 0
' Build the checksum
mfile.checksum = &H9AC6 Xor &HCDD7 ' 9ac6 xor cdd7
mfile.checksum = mfile.checksum Xor mfile.bbox.Right
mfile.checksum = mfile.checksum Xor mfile.bbox.Bottom
mfile.checksum = mfile.checksum Xor mfile.inch


' Write the buffer
di = lwrite(fhnd, mfile, Len(mfile))

' Now we retrieve a handle that will contain the
' metafile  - We make a copy, but first we set the
' extents so that it can be properly displayed
dc = CreateMetaFile(vbNullString)
dl = SetWindowExtEx(dc, xExt, yExt, oldsize)
di = SetMapMode(dc, MM_ANISOTROPIC)
```

```
    di = PlayMetaFile(dc, mfhnd)
    newmf = CloseMetaFile(dc)

    #If Win32 Then
        ' Find out how big the buffer needs to be
        mfinfosize = GetMetaFileBitsEx(newmf, 0, ByVal 0)
        If mfinfosize = 0 Then
            di = lclose(fhnd)
            Exit Function
        End If
        mfglbhnd = GlobalAlloc(GMEM_MOVEABLE Or GMEM_ZEROINIT, mfinfosize)
        gptr = GlobalLock(mfglbhnd)
        dl = GetMetaFileBitsEx(newmf, mfinfosize, ByVal gptr)
    #Else
        mfglbhnd = GetMetaFileBits(newmf)
        gptr = GlobalLock(mfglbhnd)
        mfinfosize = GlobalSize(mfglbhnd)
    #End If


    dl = hwrite(fhnd, ByVal gptr, mfinfosize)

    di = GlobalUnlock(mfglbhnd)
    di = GlobalFree(mfglbhnd)
    di = lclose(fhnd)

End Function
```

Suggestions for Further Practice

Like the other example programs in this book, QuikDraw was designed to illustrate the use of API functions. As such, it is far from a polished application. You may wish to add some of these features for practice:

- Support for additional GDI drawing functions.

- The ability to preview the current object with the metafile before adding it to the metafile.

- Support for different ROP2 (line drawing) and background modes.

- A more sophisticated user interface.

- The ability to delete an object from a metafile (Hint: first look at the Analyze example that follows).

- The ability to load a metafile and make it into the current global metafile.

Example: Analyze—Inside a Metafile

A metafile is a recording of GDI graphic commands—but, like any good recording, it is subject to editing. You can examine the individual records within a metafile using a process called enumeration, which is shown in the Analyze.vbp program. This program makes use of an enumeration function, which under Visual Basic 4.0 requires the use of the dwcbk32d.ocx demonstration OLE control that is included with this book.

This program allows you to select a metafile on disk and play it into a picture control. You can obtain a complete list of all of the commands in the metafile, and even play the metafile one object at a time, discarding those that you do not wish to include in the drawing.

Figure 8.11 shows the Analyze program in action.

Figure 8.11

Analyze.frm main
screen (runtime)

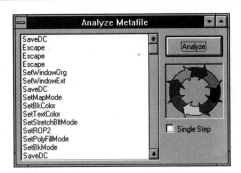

The Analyze program uses five files. ANALYZE.FRM (Listing 8.8) is the main form for the program and includes a list box that is loaded with the metafile commands, and a small picture box in which the metafile is drawn. A single step option determines if the file is stepped through one command at a time or all at once. The Analyze button brings up a common dialog from which to choose a metafile to load. The ANALYZE.BAS module contains the callback function, which must be in a standard module. The ANPROMPT.FRM form (Listing 8.9) is used during the single stepping process. APIGID32.BAS is the declaration file for the APIGID32.DLL dynamic link library included with this book. QUICK-DRAW.BAS is used by this program to load metafiles and was described earlier in this chapter. Unlike QuikDraw.vbp, this particular sample was designed for 32-bit use only, though it should be easily adaptable if necessary.

The analyze routine starts by loading a metafile in much the same way as the QuikDraw example. The mapping mode for the picture1 device context is set in preparation for drawing the metafile. The EnumMetafile function does the enumeration. While this function is executing, the Callback1_EnumMetaFile

---

Listing 8.8   **ANALYZE.FRM and ANALYZE.BAS**

```
VERSION 5.00
Object = "{F9043C88-F6F2-101A-A3C9-08002B2F49FB}#1.1#0"; "COMDLG32.OCX"
Begin VB.Form frmAnalyze
   Caption         =   "Analyze Metafile"
   ClientHeight    =   3180
   ClientLeft      =   1095
   ClientTop       =   1515
   ClientWidth     =   5160
   Height          =   3585
   Left            =   1035
   LinkTopic       =   "Form1"
   ScaleHeight     =   3180
   ScaleWidth      =   5160
   Top             =   1170
   Width           =   5280
   Begin VB.CheckBox chkSingle
      Caption      =   "Single Step"
      Height       =   255
      Left         =   3660
      TabIndex     =   3
      Top          =   2220
      Width        =   1395
   End
   Begin VB.PictureBox Picture1
      Height       =   1275
      Left         =   3660
      ScaleHeight  =   83
      ScaleMode    =   3   'Pixel
      ScaleWidth   =   91
      TabIndex     =   2
      Top          =   840
      Width        =   1395
   End
   Begin VB.CommandButton cmdAnalyze
      Caption      =   "Analyze"
      Height       =   495
      Left         =   3660
      TabIndex     =   1
      Top          =   180
      Width        =   1395
   End
   Begin VB.ListBox List1
      Height       =   2955
      Left         =   120
      TabIndex     =   0
      Top          =   120
      Width        =   3375
   End
```

Listing 8.8   **ANALYZE.FRM and ANALYZE.BAS (Continued)**

```
Begin MSComDlg.CommonDialog CMDialogMF
   Left            =   3660
   Top             =   2580
   _Version        =   65536
   _ExtentX        =   847
   _ExtentY        =   847
   _StockProps     =   0
   Filter          =   """Metafiles (*.wmf)|*.wmf"""
   Flags           =   4100
End
End
Attribute VB_Name = "frmAnalyze"
Attribute VB_GlobalNameSpace = False
Attribute VB_Creatable = False
Attribute VB_PredeclaredId = True
Attribute VB_Exposed = False
Option Explicit
' Set by frmPrompt to include or discard a record
Public IncludeRecord%
```

---

function will be called once for each metafile record. The EnumMetafile function will not return until either all of the metafiles are enumerated, or the enumeration function returns FALSE.

```
Private Sub cmdAnalyze_Click()
    Dim usefile$
    #If Win32 Then
        Dim saved&
        Dim dc&
        Dim usemf&
        Dim di&, dl&
    #Else
        Dim saved%
        Dim dc%
        Dim usemf%
        Dim di%, dl&
    #End If
    Dim oldsize As SIZE

    IncludeRecord = True     ' Initialize value
    List1.Clear              ' Clear list box

    CMDialogMF.DialogTitle = "Load a metafile"
    CMDialogMF.Action = 1
    usefile$ = CMDialogMF.FileName
    If usefile$ <> "" Then
        usemf = LoadTheMetafile(usefile$)
        If usemf <> 0 Then
```

```
              ' Now draw the metafile
          picture1.Cls
          dc = picture1.hDC
          saved = SaveDC(dc)
          ' Now set the new coordinate system. See the CmdExecute()_Click
          ' command for further explanation
          ' Most metafiles will set their own extents, but we need
          ' to set the viewport to match the scalemode of the
          ' entire screen to fill the window
          di = SetMapMode(dc, MM_ANISOTROPIC)
          dl = SetViewportExtEx(dc, picture1.ScaleWidth, _
          picture1.ScaleHeight, oldsize)
          ' All of the drawing objects that were used on the original
          ' objects were saved with the metafile, thus the metafile
          ' will automatically draw each object in the correct color
          ' and style.
          di = EnumMetaFile(dc, usemf, AddressOf Callback1_EnumMetaFile, 0)
          ' di = PlayMetaFile(dc, usemf)
          ' And restore the original DC state
          di = RestoreDC(dc, saved)
          di = DeleteMetaFile(usemf)
      End If

  End If
End Sub
```

The Callback1_EnumMetaFile function is called for each record in the metafile. Its parameters include the device context that you are enumerating, a pointer to a table containing handles to any GDI objects currently in use, a pointer to the actual metafile record, the number of handles in the handle table, and a user-defined variable (which is not used in this example). The return value can be set to FALSE to stop the enumeration. It must be set to TRUE to allow the enumeration to continue to the next record.

The function begins by loading a local METARECORD structure with the contents of the first part of the metafile record. This can be used to obtain the name of the command using the GetFunctionName function. If you are single stepping through the metafile, the frmPrompt form is brought up modally. When the form is unloaded, it will have set the IncludeRecord variable for this form (which is public) to indicate whether the current record should be drawn or not.

The record is drawn using the PlayMetaFileRecord command which draws a single metafile record into the device context. The function then adds the name of the command into the list box.

Next, the function examines the handle table. If any GDI objects are defined, they are described in the list box as well. This is done by copying the handles into an array that is redimensioned to match the size of the handle table. Keep in mind that handles are 32 bits under Win32 and 16 bits under Win16 (in case you decide to add 16-bit compatibility to this program).

```
' In ANALYZE.BAS

Public Objlist() As Long

Public Function Callback1_EnumMetaFile(ByVal hDC As Long, ByVal lpHTable As _
Long, ByVal lpMFR As Long, ByVal nObj As Long, ByVal lpClientData As Long) As Long
    Dim di&
    Dim f$, od$
    Dim x%
    Dim foundone%
    ReDim Objlist(nObj)
    Dim mr As METARECORD
    agCopyData ByVal lpMFR, mr, Len(mr)
    f$ = frmAnalyze.GetFunctionName(mr.rdFunction)
    If frmAnalyze.chkSingle.value Then
        frmPrompt.lblFunc.Caption = f$
        frmPrompt.Show 1
    End If
    If frmAnalyze.IncludeRecord Then
        di& = PlayMetaFileRecord(hDC, ByVal lpHTable, ByVal lpMFR, ByVal nObj) _
        frmAnalyze.List1.AddItem f$
        If nObj > 0 Then
            agCopyData ByVal lpHTable, Objlist(0), nObj * 4
            For x% = 0 To nObj
                od$ = frmAnalyze.GetObjDescription(GetObjectType(Objlist(x)))
                If od$ <> "" Then
                    If Not foundone% Then frmAnalyze.List1.AddItem "-- Objects _
                    in table"
                    foundone% = True
                    frmAnalyze.List1.AddItem "    " & od$
                End If
            Next x%
        End If

    End If
    Callback1_EnumMetaFile = True
End Function


' In ANALYZE.FRM
Public Function GetFunctionName$(fnum As Integer)
    Select Case fnum
        Case &H817: GetFunctionName = "Arc"
        Case &H830: GetFunctionName = "Chord"
        Case &H418: GetFunctionName = "Ellipse"
        Case &H415: GetFunctionName = "ExcludeClipRect"
        Case &H419: GetFunctionName = "FloodFill"
        Case &H416: GetFunctionName = "IntersectClipRect"
        Case &H213: GetFunctionName = "LineTo"
        Case &H214: GetFunctionName = "MoveTo"
        Case &H220: GetFunctionName = "OffsetClipRgn"
        Case &H211: GetFunctionName = "OffsetViewportOrg"
        Case &H20F: GetFunctionName = "OffsetWindowOrg"
```

```
Case &H211: GetFunctionName = "OffsetViewportOrg"
Case &H61D: GetFunctionName = "PatBlt"
Case &H81A: GetFunctionName = "Pie"
Case &H35:  GetFunctionName = "RealizePalette"
Case &H41B: GetFunctionName = "Rectangle"
Case &H139: GetFunctionName = "ResizePalette"
Case &H127: GetFunctionName = "RestoreDC"
Case &H61C: GetFunctionName = "RoundRect"
Case &H1E:  GetFunctionName = "SaveDC"
Case &H412: GetFunctionName = "ScaleViewportExt"
Case &H400: GetFunctionName = "ScaleWindowExt"
Case &H61C: GetFunctionName = "RoundRect"
Case &H201: GetFunctionName = "SetBkColor"
Case &H102: GetFunctionName = "SetBkMode"
Case &H103: GetFunctionName = "SetMapMode"
Case &H231: GetFunctionName = "SetMapperFlags"
Case &H41F: GetFunctionName = "SetPixel"
Case &H106: GetFunctionName = "SetPolyFillMode"
Case &H104: GetFunctionName = "SetROP2"
Case &H107: GetFunctionName = "SetStretchBltMode"
Case &H12E: GetFunctionName = "SetTextAlign"
Case &H108: GetFunctionName = "SetTextCharExtra"
Case &H209: GetFunctionName = "SetTextColor"
Case &H20A: GetFunctionName = "SetTextJustification"
Case &H20E: GetFunctionName = "SetViewportExt"
Case &H20D: GetFunctionName = "SetViewportOrg"
Case &H20C: GetFunctionName = "SetWindowExt"
Case &H20B: GetFunctionName = "SetWindowOrg"
Case &H2FC: GetFunctionName = "CreateBrushIndirect"
Case &H2FB: GetFunctionName = "CreateFontIndirect"
Case &HF7:  GetFunctionName = "CreatePalette"
Case &H922: GetFunctionName = "BitBlt (DDB)"
Case &H940: GetFunctionName = "BitBlt (DIB)"
Case &H1F9: GetFunctionName = "CreateBrushIndirect (DDB)"
Case &H142: GetFunctionName = "CreateBrushIndirect (DIB)"
Case &H2FA: GetFunctionName = "CreatePenIndirect"
Case &H6FF: GetFunctionName = "CreateRegion"
Case &H1F0: GetFunctionName = "DeleteObject"
Case &H626: GetFunctionName = "Escape"
Case &HA32: GetFunctionName = "ExtTextOut"
Case &H324: GetFunctionName = "Polygon"
Case &H538: GetFunctionName = "PolyPolygon"
Case &H325: GetFunctionName = "Polyline"
Case &H12C: GetFunctionName = "SelectClipRgn"
Case &H12D: GetFunctionName = "SelectObject"
Case &H234: GetFunctionName = "SelectPalette"
Case &HD33: GetFunctionName = "SetDIBitsToDevice"
Case &H37:  GetFunctionName = "SetPaletteEntries"
Case &HB23: GetFunctionName = "StretchBlt (DDB)"
Case &HB41: GetFunctionName = "StretchBlt (DIB)"
Case &HF43: GetFunctionName = "StretchDIBits"
Case &H521: GetFunctionName = "TextOut"
```

```
        End Select
End Function

Public Function GetObjDescription$(objnum)
    Select Case objnum
        Case OBJ_PEN:    GetObjDescription$ = "Pen"
        Case OBJ_BRUSH:   GetObjDescription$ = "Brush"
        Case OBJ_DC:    GetObjDescription$ = "Device Context"
        Case OBJ_METADC:   GetObjDescription$ = "Metafile Device Context"
        Case OBJ_PAL:    GetObjDescription$ = "Palette"
        Case OBJ_FONT:   GetObjDescription$ = "Font"
        Case OBJ_BITMAP:   GetObjDescription$ = "Bitmap"
        Case OBJ_REGION:   GetObjDescription$ = "Region"
        Case OBJ_METAFILE:   GetObjDescription$ = "Metafile"
        Case OBJ_MEMDC:   GetObjDescription$ = "Memory device context"
        Case OBJ_EXTPEN:   GetObjDescription$ = "Extended Pen"
        Case OBJ_ENHMETAFILE:   GetObjDescription$ = "Enhanced metafile"
    End Select
End Function
```

Listing 8.9   ANPROMPT.FRM

The prompt form is fairly straightforward—it sets the main form's public IncludeRecord variable based on the button that is pressed. The form positions itself directly under the main form whenever it is shown.

```
VERSION 5.00
Begin VB.Form frmPrompt
    BorderStyle    =    1 'Fixed Single
    ClientHeight   =    705
    ClientLeft     =    1095
    ClientTop      =    5100
    ClientWidth    =    5145
    ControlBox     =    0    'False
    Height         =    1110
    Left           =    1035
    LinkTopic      =    "Form1"
    MaxButton      =    0    'False
    MinButton      =    0    'False
    ScaleHeight    =    705
    ScaleWidth     =    5145
    Top            =    4755
    Width          =    5265
    Begin VB.CommandButton cmdNo
        Caption     =    "Discard"
        Height      =    435
        Left        =    4140
        TabIndex    =    1
        Top         =    120
        Width       =    855
    End
```

```
    Begin VB.CommandButton cmdYes
        Caption         =    "Include"
        Height          =    435
        Left            =    3060
        TabIndex        =    0
        Top             =    120
        Width           =    915
    End
    Begin VB.Label lblFunc
        Caption         =    "Label1"
        Height          =    255
        Left            =    120
        TabIndex        =    2
        Top             =    180
        Width           =    2775
    End
End
Attribute VB_Name = "frmPrompt"
Attribute VB_GlobalNameSpace = False
Attribute VB_Creatable = False
Attribute VB_PredeclaredId = True
Attribute VB_Exposed = False
Option Explicit

Private Sub cmdNo_Click()
    frmAnalyze.IncludeRecord = False
    Me.Hide
End Sub

Private Sub cmdYes_Click()
    frmAnalyze.IncludeRecord = True
    Me.Hide
End Sub

Private Sub Form_Load()
    Me.Move frmAnalyze.Left, frmAnalyze.Top + frmAnalyze.Height,
frmAnalyze.Width
End Sub
```

Suggestions for Further Practice

The Analyze program could form the basis for a complete metafile editor. However, before doing so you'll need to understand more about the internal structure of metafile records. This will require that you study the METARECORD structure described in Appendix B and that you learn more about working with data structures and memory buffers, a subject that is covered thoroughly in Chapter 15. So consider these suggestions—for later use, or for the ambitious reader.

- Improve the Analyze program so that it not only shows the command being executed in a metafile record, but also shows the parameters for the command.

- Extend the Analyze program so that it not only lists the types of objects in the handle table for the metafile, but information about each object as well, for example, the color of a pen or brush.

- Create a color filter that removes all objects of a certain color from a metafile while it is being drawn. Or take this a step further and convert them from one color to another.

Function Reference

◼ AbortPath

VB Declaration   `Declare Function AbortPath& Lib "gdi32" (ByVal hdc As Long)`

Description   Discards any path selected into the specified device context. Also cancels creation of any paths that are in progress.

Use with VB   No problem.

Parameter	Type/Description
hdc	Long—Device context.

Return Value   Long—Nonzero on success, zero on failure. Sets GetLastError.

Platform   Windows 95, Windows NT

◼ AngleArc

VB Declaration   `Declare Function AngleArc& Lib "gdi32" (ByVal hdc As Long, ByVal x As Long, _`
`ByVal y As Long, ByVal dwRadius As Long, ByVal eStartAngle As Single, ByVal _`
`eSweepAngle As Single)`

Description   Draws a line with an attached arc. See Figure 8.12.

Use with VB   No problem.

Parameter	Type/Description
hdc	Long—The device context to draw into.
x,y	Long—The center coordinate of a circle describing the arc.
dwRadius	Long—The radius of the circle.
eStartAngle	Single—The angle in degrees where the line connects to the circle.
eSweepAngle	Single—The sweep of the arc along the circle in degrees.

Return Value   Long—Nonzero on success, zero on failure.

Platform   Windows NT

Comments   Note that the eStartAngle and eSweepAngle parameters are specified in degrees and are singles (not doubles).

Example   Ex8a.vbp

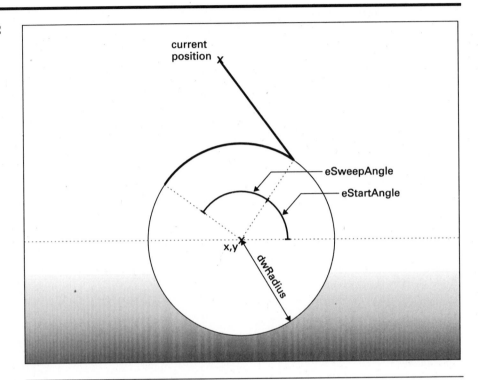

Figure 8.12
Illustration of the
AngleArc function

■ Arc, ArcTo

VB Declaration

```
Declare Function Arc& Lib "gdi32" (ByVal hdc As Long, ByVal X1 As Long, ByVal _
Y1 As Long, ByVal X2 As Long, ByVal Y2 As Long, ByVal X3 As Long, ByVal Y3 As _
Long, ByVal X4 As Long, ByVal Y4 As Long)
Declare Function ArcTo& Lib "gdi32" (ByVal hdc As Long, ByVal X1 As Long, ByVal _
Y1 As Long, ByVal X2 As Long, ByVal Y2 As Long, ByVal X3 As Long, ByVal Y3 As _
Long, ByVal X4 As Long, ByVal Y4 As Long)
```

Description

Draws an arc as shown in Figure 8.13. X1,Y1,X2,Y2 specify a bounding rectangle of an ellipse. The point at which a line drawn from the center of the rectangle to points X3,Y3 intersects the ellipse determines the start of the arc. A similar line through X4,Y4 determines the end of the arc.

The ArcTo function sets the current pen position to the end of the arc. The Arc function does not affect the current pen position.

Use with VB

No problem.

Parameter	Type/Description
hdc	Long—Handle to a display context.
X1,Y1	Long—Specify the upper-left corner of a rectangle that bounds an ellipse.

Figure 8.13

Arc Chord and Pie functions

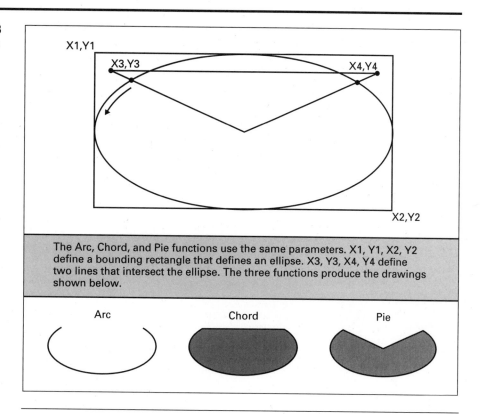

The Arc, Chord, and Pie functions use the same parameters. X1, Y1, X2, Y2 define a bounding rectangle that defines an ellipse. X3, Y3, X4, Y4 define two lines that intersect the ellipse. The three functions produce the drawings shown below.

Parameter	Type/Description
X2,Y2	Long—Specify the lower-right corner of a rectangle that bounds an ellipse.
X3,Y3	Long—Specify the arc starting point.
X4,Y4	Long—Specify the arc ending point.

Return Value   Long—Nonzero on success, zero on failure.

Platform   Windows 95, Windows NT, Win16

Win16 and Windows 95: The width and height of the bounding rectangle must be between 3 and 32,766 units in size. The drawing direction is always counterclockwise.

Windows NT: The drawing direction is set by the SetArcDirection function. Default is counterclockwise.

Example   Quikdraw.vbp

■ BeginPath

VB Declaration   `Declare Function BeginPath& Lib "gdi32" (ByVal hdc As Long)`

Description   Begins a path bracket. GDI drawing commands that are executed after this command become part of the path. Connecting line segments are joined (see chapter text). Any existing path in the device context is discarded. Refer to Table 8.10 for a list of functions that can be recorded into a path.

Use with VB   No problem.

Parameter	Type/Description
hdc	Long—The device context on which to record the path.

Return Value   Long—Nonzero on success, zero on failure. Sets GetLastError.

■ Platform

Windows 95, Windows NT. Refer to Table 8.10 for a list of functions that can be recorded into a path for each platform.

Table 8.10   Legal Path Functions

Function	Windows NT	Windows 95
AngleArc	Yes	No
Arc	Yes	No
ArcTo	Yes	No
Chord	Yes	No
Ellipse	Yes	No
ExtTextOut	Yes	Yes
LineTo	Yes	Yes
MoveToEx	Yes	Yes
Pie	Yes	No
PolyBezier	Yes	Yes
PolyBezierTo	Yes	Yes
PolyDraw	Yes	No
Polygon	Yes	Yes
Polyline	Yes	Yes
PolylineTo	Yes	Yes
PolyPolygon	Yes	Yes

Table 8.10	**Legal Path Functions (Continued)**		
Function	**Windows NT**	**Windows 95**	
PolyPolyline	Yes	Yes	
Rectangle	Yes	No	
RoundRect	Yes	No	
TextOut	Yes	Yes	

Example Path.vbp, ExtPen.vbp

■ CancelDC

VB Declaration `Declare Function CancelDC& Lib "gdi32" (ByVal hdc As Long)`

Description Allows you to cancel long drawing operations in another thread.

Use with VB Not useful with Visual Basic.

Parameter	**Type/Description**
hdc	Long—Device context whose drawing is canceled.

Return Value Long—Nonzero on success, zero on failure.

Platform Windows NT

Comments Sometimes drawing operations can be quite time-consuming. In a multithreading application, this command allows one thread to stop the drawing operation in progress in another thread.

■ Chord

VB Declaration
```
Declare Function Chord& Lib "gdi32" (ByVal hdc As Long, ByVal X1 As Long, ByVal _
Y1 As Long, ByVal X2 As Long, ByVal Y2 As Long, ByVal X3 As Long, ByVal Y3 As _
Long, ByVal X4 As Long, ByVal Y4 As Long)
```

Description Draws a chord as shown in Figure 8.13. X1,Y1,X2,Y2 specify a bounding rectangle of an ellipse. The chord is the area between the ellipse and the line defined by X3,Y3 and X4,Y4.

Use with VB No problem.

Parameter	**Type/Description**
hdc	Long—Handle to a display context.
X1,Y1	Long—Specify the upper-left corner of a rectangle that bounds an ellipse.
X2,Y2	Long—Specify the lower-right corner of a rectangle that bounds an ellipse.

Parameter	Type/Description
X3,Y3	Long—Specify one point of a line that intersects the ellipse.
X4,Y4	Long—Specify the second point of a line that intersects the ellipse.

Return Value Long—Nonzero on success, zero on failure. Sets GetLastError.

Platform Windows 95, Windows NT, Win16

Comments The width and height of the bounding rectangle must be between 3 and 32,766 units in size in Windows 95 and Win16.

Example Quikdraw.vbp

■ CloseEnhMetaFile

VB Declaration `Declare Function CloseEnhMetaFile& Lib "gdi32" (ByVal hdc As Long)`

Description Closes the specified enhanced metafile device context and returns a handle to the newly created metafile.

Use with VB No problem.

Parameter	Type/Description
hdc	Long—A metafile device context as returned by the CreateEnhMetaFile function.

Return Value Long—A handle to the enhanced metafile. The PlayEnhMetaFile function may be used to play the metafile. Zero on error.

Platform Windows 95, Windows NT

Example See CloseMetafile.

■ CloseFigure

VB Declaration `Declare Function CloseFigure& Lib "gdi32" (ByVal hdc As Long)`

Description Closes the current open figure when drawing into a path.

Use with VB No problem.

Parameter	Type/Description
hdc	Long—The device context containing an open Path bracket.

Return Value Long—Nonzero on success, zero on failure. Sets GetLastError.

Platform Windows 95, Windows NT

Comments   If you are drawing a series of lines into a path, you have an open figure. When you call this function, Windows draws a line between the current position and the start of the figure (typically where the last MoveToEx operation set the pen position). This line and the first line in the figure are joined. Note that if you drew this line yourself, the figure would still be open, even though the start and end points are the same. This makes a difference with geometric pens. Using CloseFigure, the lines are joined—otherwise they will be displayed using the end caps. Once you close a figure, the next line you draw into the path starts a new figure. Open figures are closed automatically by those functions that fill a path.

■ CloseMetaFile

VB Declaration   `Declare Function CloseMetaFile& Lib "gdi32" (ByVal hMF As Long)`

Description   Closes the specified metafile device context and returns a handle to the newly created metafile.

Use with VB   No problem.

Parameter	Type/Description
hMF	Long—A metafile device context as returned by the CreateMetaFile function.

Return Value   Long—A handle to the metafile. The PlayMetaFile function may be used to play the metafile. Zero on error.

Platform   Windows 95, Windows NT, Win16

Comments   Be sure to use the DeleteMetaFile function to delete the metafile and free its resources when the metafile is no longer needed.

Example   QuikDraw.vbp

■ CopyEnhMetaFile

VB Declaration   `Declare Function CopyEnhMetaFile& Lib "gdi32" Alias "CopyEnhMetaFileA" (ByVal _`
`hemfSrc As Long, ByVal lpszFile As String)`

Description   Makes a copy of the specified enhanced metafile.

Use with VB   No problem.

Parameter	Type/Description
hemfSrc	Long—A handle to the enhanced metafile to copy.
LpszFile	String—The file name for the copy (creates a new disk-based metafile). Use vbNullString to pass a NULL to this parameter to create a copy in memory.

Return Value   Long—A handle to the copy on success. Zero on error. Sets GetLastError.

Platform   Windows 95, Windows NT

■ CopyMetaFile

VB Declaration   Declare Function CopyMetaFile& Lib "gdi32" Alias "CopyMetaFileA" (ByVal hMF As _
Long, ByVal lpFileName As String)

Description   Makes a copy of the specified metafile. CopyMetaFileBynum is used to copy a metafile to a memory metafile.

Use with VB   No problem.

Parameter	Type/Description
hMF	Long—Handle to a metafile to copy.
lpFileName	String—File name for the new metafile. Use vbNullString to pass a NULL to this parameter to create a copy in memory.

Return Value   Long—A handle to the new metafile. Zero on error. Sets GetLastError.

Platform   Windows 95, Windows NT, Win16

■ CreateBrushIndirect

VB Declaration   Declare Function CreateBrushIndirect& Lib "gdi32" (lpLogBrush As LOGBRUSH)

Description   Creates a brush based on a LOGBRUSH data structure.

Use with VB   No problem.

Parameter	Type/Description
lpLogBrush	LOGBRUSH—LOGBRUSH data structure as defined in Appendix B.

Return Value   Long—A handle to the new brush on success, zero otherwise.

Platform   Windows 95, Windows NT, Win16

Comments   Use the DeleteObject function to delete the brush when it is no longer needed. Refer also to the CreateBrush function whose parameters correspond to the fields in the LOGBRUSH structure.

Example   Extpen.vbp (uses the LOGBRUSH structure to create a geometric pen—a very similar operation).

■ CreateDIBPatternBrush, CreateDIBPatternBrushPt

VB Declaration   Declare Function CreateDIBPatternBrush& Lib "gdi32" (ByVal hPackedDIB As Long, _
ByVal wUsage As Long)
Declare Function CreateDIBPatternBrushPt& Lib "gdi32" (lpPackedDIB As Any, _
ByVal wUsage As Long)

Description   Creates a brush using a device-independent bitmap to specify the brush pattern.

Use with VB	No problem.

Parameter	Type/Description
hPackedDIB lpPackedDIB	Long—hPackedDIB is a global memory handle to a block of memory containing a BITMAPINFO structure followed by a device-independent bitmap. lpPackedDIB is the memory address of a block of memory with the same configuration. If a monochrome DIB is specified, the DIB colors are ignored and the text and background colors are used instead. Refer to Chapter 9 for information on device-independent bitmaps and Chapter 15 for information on using global memory blocks and memory addresses.
wUsage	Long—One of the following constants: DIB_PAL_COLORS: The DIB color table contains indexes to the current logical palette. DIB_RGB_COLORS: The DIB color table contains 32-bit RGB color values.

Return Value	Long—A handle to the brush on success. Zero on error.
Platform	Windows 95, Windows NT, Win16. Bitmap dimensions may not be larger than 8x8 for Windows 95 and Win16.
Comments	CreateDIBPatternBrushPt is preferred for Win32 applications.
Example	Puzzle.vbp in Chapter 9.

■ CreateEnhMetaFile

VB Declaration	`Declare Function CreateEnhMetaFile& Lib "gdi32" Alias "CreateEnhMetaFileA" _`
	`(ByVal hdcRef As Long, ByVal lpFileName As String, lpRect As RECT, ByVal _`
	`lpDescription As String)`

Description	Creates an enhanced metafile device context. Drawing operations may be performed on this device context. When the CloseEnhMetaFile function is called to close this device context, a metafile handle is created that contains the recorded sequence of drawing commands, which can then be played back into any device context.
Use with VB	No problem.

Parameter	Type/Description
hdcRef	Long—A reference device context. This function will use this device context to store in the metafile information about the resolution of the device on which the metafile was created. Use zero to use the display as a reference.
lpFileName	String—The name of the disk file for this metafile. This file should have the extension .EMF. Use vbNullString to pass a NULL to create a memory metafile.

Parameter	Type/Description
lpRect	RECT—A bounding rectangle that describes the size and location of the metafile in .01mm units. It is used to define the ideal physical size of the metafile.
lpDescription	String—A description of the metafile consisting of the name of the creating application, a NULL character, a description of the metafile, and two NULL characters. For example: "My app" & chr$(0) & "my metafile" & chr$(0) & chr$(0). May also be vbNullString if you do not wish to include a description.

Return Value   Long—An enhanced metafile device context. Zero on error. This device context should not be confused with a metafile handle. The metafile device context is used to draw the metafile—it is used like any other device context as a parameter to GDI drawing functions. The actual metafile handle is obtained later when the CloseEnhMetafile function is called.

Platform   Windows 95, Windows NT

Comments   One of the advantages of enhanced metafiles over standard metafiles is that they include information that describes accurately the size and location of the metafile as it was originally created. This information can be read by Windows and the drawing application to render the metafile accurately on any device.

Example   See CreateMetafile.

■ CreateHatchBrush

VB Declaration   `Declare Function CreateHatchBrush& Lib "gdi32" (ByVal nIndex As Long, ByVal _`
`crColor As Long)`

Description   Creates a brush with a hatched pattern as shown in Figure 8.14.

Figure 8.14
Hatched brush types

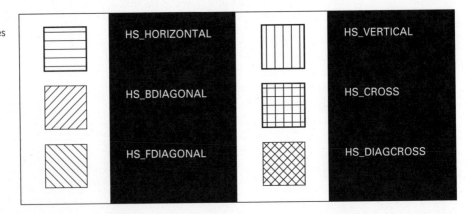

Use with VB	No problem.	

Parameter	Type/Description
nIndex	Long—Specifies the type of hatching as shown in Figure 8.14.
crColor	Long—Specifies the RGB foreground color of the brush.

Return Value   Long—A handle to the new brush on success, zero otherwise. Use DeleteObject to destroy the brush when you no longer need it.

Platform   Windows 95, Windows NT

Comments   Use the DeleteObject function to delete the brush when it is no longer needed.

Example   Quikdraw.vbp, ExtPen.vbp

■ CreateMetaFile

VB Declaration
```
Declare Function CreateMetaFile& Lib "gdi32" Alias "CreateMetaFileA" (ByVal _
lpString As String)
```

Description   Creates a metafile device context. Drawing operations may be performed on this device context. When the CloseMetaFile function is called to close this device context, a metafile handle is created that contains the recorded sequence of drawing commands, which can then be played back into any device context.

Use with VB   No problem.

Parameter	Type/Description
lpString	String—The name of the file to hold the metafile. Use vbNullString to pass a zero value to create a memory metafile.

Return Value   Long—A handle to the metafile device context. Zero on error. This device context should not be confused with a metafile handle. The metafile device context is used to draw the metafile—it is used like any other device context as a parameter to GDI drawing functions. The actual metafile handle is obtained later when the CloseMetafile function is called.

Platform   Windows 95, Windows NT, Win16

Comments   While this function can create disk-based metafiles, these metafiles are NOT the standard placeable metafile format that is commonly used under Windows. To create a placeable metafile, you should use this function to create a memory-based metafile, then use the techniques shown in the QuikDraw application to transfer the metafile to disk.

Example   QuikDraw.vbp

■ CreatePatternBrush

VB Declaration
```
Declare Function CreatePatternBrush& Lib "gdi32" (ByVal hBitmap As Long)
```

Description   Creates a brush using a bitmap to specify the brush pattern.

Parameter	Type/Description
Use with VB	No problem.

Parameter	Type/Description
hBitmap	Long—A handle to a bitmap. If a monochrome bitmap is specified, the text and background colors are used in the pattern. Refer to Chapter 9 for information on bitmaps.

Return Value   Long—A handle to the new brush on success, zero otherwise.

Platform   Windows 95, Windows NT, Win16

The bitmap dimensions should be no more than 8x8 pixels under Windows 95 or Win16.

Comments   Use the DeleteObject function to delete the brush when it is no longer needed. Do not use bitmaps created as DIB sections with this function.

Example   Ex8a.vbp. Note: Sample uses a bitmap that is larger than 8x8, so only part of the bitmap will be used if run on Windows 95.

■ CreatePen

VB Declaration
```
Declare Function CreatePen& Lib "gdi32" (ByVal nPenStyle As Long, ByVal nWidth _
As Long, ByVal crColor As Long)
```

Description   Creates a pen with the specified style, width, and color.

Use with VB   No problem.

Parameter	Type/Description
nPenStyle	Long—Specifies the pen style based on the following constants: PS_SOLID: Pen is a solid color. PS_DASH: Pen is dashed (nWidth must be 1). PS_DOT: Pen is dotted (nWidth must be 1). PS_DASHDOT: Pen alternates dashes and dots (nWidth must be 1). PS_DASHDOTDOT: Pen alternates dashes and double dots (nWidth must be 1). PS_NULL: Pen does not draw. PS_INSIDEFRAME: Pen draws inside the frame of closed objects produced by Ellipse, Rectangle, RoundRect, Pie, and Chord. If the exact RGB color specified does not exist, dithering is used.
nWidth	Long—Width of the pen in logical units.
crColor	Long—RGB color of the pen.

Return Value   Long—A handle to the new pen on success, zero otherwise.

Platform   Windows 95, Windows NT, Win16

Comments   Use the DeleteObject function to delete the pen when it is no longer needed.

Example   QuikDraw.vbp

■ CreatePenIndirect

VB Declaration   `Declare Function CreatePenIndirect& Lib "gdi32" (lpLogPen As LOGPEN)`

Description   Creates a pen based on the specified LOGPEN structure.

Use with VB   No problem.

Parameter	Type/Description
lpLogPen	LOGPEN—Logical pen structure. Contents of this structure correspond closely to the parameters of the CreatePen function. Refer also to Appendix B.

Return Value   Long—A handle to the new pen on success, zero otherwise.

Platform   Windows 95, Windows NT, Win16

Comments   Use the DeleteObject function to delete the pen when it's no longer needed.

Example   QuikDraw.vbp demonstrates the CreatePen function, which is similar.

■ CreateSolidBrush

VB Declaration   `Declare Function CreateSolidBrush& Lib "gdi32" (ByVal crColor As Long)`

Description   Creates a brush with a solid color.

Use with VB   No problem.

Parameter	Type/Description
crColor	Long—RGB color of the brush.

Return Value   Long—A handle to the new brush on success, zero otherwise.

Platform   Windows 95, Windows NT, Win16

Comments   Use the DeleteObject function to delete the brush when it is no longer needed.

Example   QuikDraw.vbp

■ DeleteEnhMetaFile

VB Declaration   `Declare Function DeleteEnhMetaFile& Lib "gdi32" (ByVal hemf As Long)`

Description   Deletes the specified enhanced metafile.

Use with VB   No problem.

Parameter	Type/Description
hemf	Long—A handle to an enhanced metafile.

Return Value   Long—Nonzero on success, zero on failure.

Platform   Windows 95, Windows NT

Comments   If the metafile is based on a disk file, the file itself is not deleted by this function. It may thus be reopened with the GetEnhMetaFile function.

Example   QuikDraw.vbp demonstrates the DeleteMetaFile function, which is similar.

■ DeleteMetaFile

VB Declaration   `Declare Function DeleteMetaFile& Lib "gdi32" (ByVal hMF As Long)`

Description   Deletes the specified metafile.

Use with VB   No problem.

Parameter	Type/Description
hMF	Long—A handle to a metafile.

Return Value   Long—Nonzero on success, zero on failure.

Platform   Windows 95, Windows NT, Win16

Comments   If the metafile is based on a disk file, the file itself is not deleted by this function. It may thus be reopened with the GetMetaFile function. However, this metafile does not follow the standard placeable metafile format.

Example   QuikDraw.vbp

■ DeleteObject

VB Declaration   `Declare Function DeleteObject& Lib "gdi32" (ByVal hObject As Long)`

Description   This function is used to delete GDI objects such as pens, brushes, fonts, bitmaps, regions, and palettes. All system resources used by the object are released.

Use with VB   No problem.

Parameter	Type/Description
hObject	Long—Handle to a GDI object (pen, brush, font, bitmap, region, or palette).

Return Value   Long—Nonzero on success, zero on failure.

Platform   Windows 95, Windows NT, Win16

Comments   Do not delete a pen, brush, or bitmap that is selected into a device context.
    If you delete a bitmap-based pattern brush, the bitmap is not deleted by this function—only the brush.

Example   QuikDraw.vbp, ExtPen.vbp, Path.vbp, Ex8A.vbp, and many other samples throughout this book.

■ DrawEdge

VB Declaration
```
Declare Function DrawEdge& Lib "user32" (ByVal hdc As Long, qrc As RECT, ByVal _
edge As Long, ByVal grfFlags As Long)
```

Description   Draws the edge of a rectangle using the specified style.

Use with VB   Recommended. This function can eliminate the need to use many 3D frames and panels, and is far more efficient than controls in terms of resources and memory. It will improve performance.

Parameter	Type/Description
hdc	Long—Device context to draw into.
qrc	RECT—Rectangles whose edges are to be drawn.
edge	Long—A combination of two constants with the prefix BDR_, one that specifies if the inner edge is raised or sunken, the other that specifies the outer edge. The constants with the EDGE_ prefix may be used instead. The constant name is self-descriptive.
grfFlags	Long—A combination of constants with the prefix BF_. These constants are mostly self-descriptive.

Return Value   Long—TRUE (nonzero) on success, Zero on error. Sets GetLastError.

Platform   Windows 95, Windows NT

Comments   Keep in mind that since this is a GDI function, the rectangle coordinates are logical coordinates.

Example   Ex8a.vbp. This would be an excellent function to demonstrate using the principles shown in the ExtPen.vbp example.

■ DrawEscape

VB Declaration
```
Declare Function DrawEscape& Lib "gdi32" (ByVal hdc As Long, ByVal nEscape As _
Long, ByVal cbInput As Long, ByVal lpszInData As String)
```

Description   The escape function sends data directly to the video device driver. Refer to the description of the Escape function in Chapter 12 for a list of available escapes.

Use with VB   Works, but Escapes are device-specific and should be avoided if at all possible. They are a last resort.

Parameter	Type/Description
hdc	Long—The device context for the display device.
Nescape	Long—A constant specifying the escape to execute.
CbInput	Long—The length of the input buffer.
LpszInData	String—The input string or buffer.

Return Value   Long—Nonzero on success, zero on error (except for the QUERYESCSUPPORT escape which returns TRUE if the escape is supported, zero if not).

Platform   Windows 95, Windows NT

Comments   Use the QUERYESCSUPPORT escape to determine if a particular escape is supported by the current video driver.

■ DrawFocusRect

VB Declaration
```
Declare Function DrawFocusRect& Lib "user32" (ByVal hdc As Long, _
lpRect As RECT)
```

Description   Draws a focus rectangle. The rectangle is drawn using the exclusive-or operation in the style used to indicate the focus (typically a dotted line). Call this function a second time with the same parameters to erase the focus rectangle.

Use with VB   No problem.

Parameter	Type/Description
hdc	Long—Handle to a device context.
lpRect	RECT—Rectangle to draw in logical coordinates.

Return Value   Long—Nonzero on success, zero on failure. Sets GetLastError.

Platform   Windows 95, Windows NT, Win16

Example   QuikDraw.vbp

■ DrawFrameControl

VB Declaration
```
Declare Function DrawFrameControl Lib "user32" (ByVal hDC As Long, lpRect As _
RECT, ByVal un1 As Long, ByVal un2 As Long)
```

Description   This function draws a standard control. For example, you can draw the frame of a button or scrollbar.

Use with VB   No problem. In fact, the possibilities boggle the mind.

Parameter	Type/Description
hDC	Long—The device context to draw into.
lpRect	RECT—A rectangle specifying the location and size of the frame.
un1	Long—A constant specifying the type of frame. The constants include: DFC_BUTTON, DFC_CAPTION, DFC_MENU, and DFC_SCROLL.
un2	Long—A constant specifying the state of the frame to draw. Consists of a constant with the prefix DFCS_.

Return Value   Long—TRUE (nonzero) on success. Zero on error. Sets GetLastError.

Platform   Windows 95, Windows NT

Example   Ex8a.vbp

■ DrawState

VB Declaration
```
Declare Function DrawState& Lib "user32" Alias "DrawStateA" (ByVal hDC As Long, _
ByVal hBrush As Long, ByVal lpDrawStateProc As Long, ByVal lParam As Long, _
ByVal wParam As Long, ByVal n1 As Long, ByVal n2 As Long, ByVal n3 As Long, _
ByVal n4 As Long, ByVal un As Long)
```

Description   This complex function applies a variety of effects to an image or drawing operation.

It is used by Windows 95 to obtain some of the effects that you see applied to images; for example, bitmaps or other images that look disabled or dithered. For bitmaps and icons, it simply applies an effect to the bitmap or icon while drawing it. For text, you can either allow the function to draw the text, or perform your own drawing in a callback function. For complex (user-defined) images, you must use a callback function. During the callback function, your own code draws whatever you wish onto the device context, after which the DrawState function applies the desired effect.

Use with VB   No problem. Some options require use of the dwcbk32d.ocx callback control.

Parameter	Type/Description
hDC	Long—Device context to draw in.
hBrush	Long—A brush handle if the state (specified in parameter un) is DSS_MONO.
lpDrawStateProc	Long—A pointer to a function address. Must be provided for image type DST_COMPLEX. Optional for DST_TEXT.
lParam	Long—Depends on the type of image.
wParam	Long—Depends on the type of image.
n1	Long—Horizontal location of the image.
n2	Long—Vertical location of the image.
n3	Long—Width of the image. Required for image type DST_COMPLEX. For others, may be zero, in which case it will be calculated based on the image.
n4	Long—Height of the image. Required for image type DST_COMPLEX. For others, may be zero, in which case it will be calculated based on the image.

Parameter	Type/Description
un	Long—A combination of image type and state. Image types include: DST_BITMAP: Handle in lParam. DST_COMPLEX: Drawing is performed during the callback function specified by the lpDrawStateProc parameter. lParam and wParam are passed to the callback event. DST_ICON: lParam contains the icon handle. DST_TEXT: lParam is an address of text (you may use a string alias). wParam is the length of the string. DST_PREFIXTEXT: Same as DST_TEXT except that the & character indicates that the next character is underlined. The image state constants are: DSS_NORMAL: Draw normally. DSS_UNION: The image is dithered. DSS_DISABLED: The image is embossed. DSS_MONO: Use hBrush to draw the image. DSS_RIGHT: Undocumented—experimentation seems to show no effect.

Return Value   Long—TRUE (nonzero) on success, FALSE on error.

Platform   Windows 95, Windows NT 4.0

Comments   Use the cbxLLLLL callback type for the dwcbk32d.ocx control with Visual Basic 4.0. The five long callback function parameters have the following meanings.

lval1 = A handle to the device context. The device context has a memory bitmap of width lval4 and height lval5 selected into it.

lval2 = lParam from the DrawState function.

lval3 = wParam from the DrawState function.

lval4, lval5 = the width and height to draw in.

Example   Ex8b.vbp

■ Ellipse

VB Declaration
```
Declare Function Ellipse& Lib "gdi32" (ByVal hdc As Long, ByVal X1 As Long, _
ByVal Y1 As Long, ByVal X2 As Long, ByVal Y2 As Long)
```

Description   Draws an ellipse that is bounded by the specified rectangle. The ellipse is drawn using the currently selected pen and filled using the currently selected brush.

Use with VB   No problem.

Parameter	Type/Description
hdc	Long—Handle to a device context.
X1,Y1	Long—Upper-left point in logical coordinates of the bounding rectangle.
X2,Y2	Long—Lower-right point in logical coordinates of the bounding rectangle.

Return Value   Long—Nonzero on success, zero on failure. Sets GetLastError.

Platform	Windows 95, Windows NT, Win16
Example	QuikDraw.vbp

■ EndPath

VB Declaration   `Declare Function EndPath& Lib "gdi32" (ByVal hdc As Long)`

Description   Call to stop defining a path. On success, the drawing operations that occurred between the Begin-Path function call and this function become the path for the specified device context.

Use with VB   No problem.

Parameter	Type/Description
hdc	Long—Device context.

Return Value   Long—Nonzero on success, zero on failure. Sets GetLastError to one of the following: ERROR_CAN_NOT_COMPLETE or ERROR_INVALID_PARAMETER.

Platform   Windows 95, Windows NT

Example   Path.vbp, ExtPen.vbp

■ EnumEnhMetaFile

VB Declaration   `Declare Function EnumEnhMetaFile& Lib "gdi32" (ByVal hdc As Long, ByVal hemf As _`
`Long, ByVal lpEnhMetaFunc As Long, ByVal lpData As Long, lpRect As RECT)`

Description   Enumerates the individual metafile records for an enhanced metafile. Each metafile record contains a single GDI command. This can be used along with the PlayEnhMetaFileRecord function to selectively play portions of a metafile.

Use with VB   Requires use of the dwcbk32d.ocx demonstration callback control included with this book with Visual Basic 4.0.

Parameter	Type/Description
hdc	Long—Handle of the device context to use for output. Required only if the callback function will be performing drawing operations.
hemf	Long—Handle to an enhanced metafile to enumerate.
lpEnhMetaFunc	Long—Pointer to function to call for each metafile command. Use the ProcAddress property of the dwcbk32d.ocx custom control to obtain a function pointer for callbacks with Visual Basic 4.0.
lpData	Long—User-defined value.
lpRect	RECT—A rectangle defining the boundaries of the metafile.

Return Value   Long—TRUE (nonzero) if all the records in the metafile are enumerated. Zero otherwise.

Platform   Windows 95, Windows NT

Comments   Refer to the chapter text describing the analyze.vbp program for further details.
Refer to Appendix A for details on using the dwcbk32d.ocx custom control with enumeration functions with Visual Basic 4.0.

Example   Analyze.vbp demonstrates enumeration of a standard metafile, which is virtually identical.

■ EnumMetaFile

VB Declaration   `Declare Function EnumMetaFile Lib "gdi32" (ByVal hDC As Long, ByVal hMetafile _`
`As Long, ByVal lpMFEnumProc As Long, ByVal lParam As Long)`

Description   Enumerates the individual metafile records for a standard Windows metafile. Each metafile record contains a single GDI command. This can be used along with the PlayMetaFileRecord function to selectively play portions of a metafile.

Use with VB   Requires use of the dwcbk32d.ocx demonstration callback control included with this book, with Visual Basic 4.0.

Parameter	Type/Description
hDC	Long—Handle of the device context to use for output. Required only if the callback function will be performing drawing operations.
hMetafile	Long—Handle to a standard metafile to enumerate.
lpMFEnumProc	Long—Pointer to function to call for each metafile command. Use the ProcAddress property of the dwcbk32d.ocx custom control to obtain a function pointer for callbacks with Visual Basic 4.0.
lParam	Long—User-defined value.

Return Value   Long—Nonzero on success, zero on failure.

Platform   Windows 95, Windows NT, Win16

Comments   Refer to the chapter text describing the analyze.vbp program for further details.
Refer to Appendix A for details on using the dwcbk32d.ocx custom control with enumeration functions with Visual Basic 4.0.

Example   Analyze.vbp

■ EnumObjects

VB Declaration   `Declare Function EnumObjects& Lib "gdi32" (ByVal hDC As Long, ByVal n As Long, _`
`ByVal lpGOBJEnumProc As Long, ByVal lpVoid As Long)`

Description   Enumerates the pens and brushes that may be used with the specified device context.

Use with VB   Requires use of the dwcbk32d.ocx demonstration callback control included with this book, with Visual Basic 4.0.

Parameter	Type/Description
hDC	Long—Handle to a device context.

Parameter	Type/Description
n	Long—The type of object to enumerate. Refer to the constants with the prefix OBJ_ for a list of objects. The Win32 document suggests that only OBJ_PEN and OBJ_BRUSH are supported.
lpGOBJEnum-Proc	Long—Pointer to function to call for each GDI object. Use the ProcAddress property of the dwcbk32d.ocx custom control to obtain a function pointer for callbacks, with Visual Basic 4.0.
lpVoid	Long—Value that is passed to the callback function during enumeration.

Return Value   Long— –1 if there are too many objects for the function to enumerate. User-defined (as returned from the last call of the EnumObjects event in the dwcbk32d.ocx control or VB5 callback function).

Platform   Windows 95, Windows NT, Win16

Comments   Refer to Appendix A for information on using callbacks with the dwcbk32d.ocx custom control.

■ ExtCreatePen

VB Declaration
```
Declare Function ExtCreatePen& Lib "gdi32" (ByVal dwPenStyle As Long, ByVal _
dwWidth As Long, lplb As LOGBRUSH, ByVal dwStyleCount As Long, lpStyle As Long)
```

Description   Creates an extended pen (cosmetic or geometric).

Use with VB   No problem.

Parameter	Type/Description
dwPenStyle	Long—The pen style is a combination (OR operation) of one constant from each of the following groups: PS_COSMETIC or PS_GEOMETRIC—The type of pen. PS_ALTERNATE, PS_SOLID, PS_DASH, PS_DOT, PS_DASHDOT, PS_DASHDOTDOT, PS_NULL, PS_USERSTYLE, PS_INSIDEFRAME—The style of the pen. PS_ENDCAP_???—The endcap of the pen. PS_JOIN_???—The join to use to connect line segments in a figure or joined lines in a path.
dwWidth	Long—The width of the line. Always 1 for cosmetic pens.
lplb	LOGBRUSH—The lbColor is the pen color. lbStyle is PS_SOLID for cosmetic, the actual style for geometric pens. All other fields must be set for geometric pens (see Appendix B for information on this structure).
dwStyleCount	Long—Number of entries in the lpStyle array if PS_USERSTYLE is specified.
lpStyle	Long—Line/space pairs for PS_USERSTYLE.

Return Value   Long—A handle to an extended pen on success. Zero on error. Use DeleteObject to destroy the pen when it is no longer needed.

Platform	Windows 95, Windows NT
	PS_ALTERNATE and PS_USERSTYLE are NT only.
	PS_DASH, PS_DOT, PS_DASHDOT, PS_DASHDOTDOT only work with cosmetic pens on Windows 95.
	Endcap and Join styles are only supported in Windows 95 when drawing in a path.
Comments	Refer to the chapter text for additional information on extended pens.
Example	ExtPen.vbp

■ ExtFloodFill

VB Declaration

```
Declare Function ExtFloodFill& Lib "gdi32" (ByVal hdc As Long, ByVal x As Long, _
ByVal y As Long, ByVal crColor As Long, ByVal wFillType As Long)
```

Description   Fills an area in the specified device context using the currently selected brush.

Use with VB   No problem.

Parameter	Type/Description
hdc	Long—Handle to a device context.
x,y	Long— Point at which to begin filling in logical coordinates.
crColor	Long—Boundary color to use.
wFillType	Long—Type of filling to perform based on one of the following constants: FLOODFILLBORDER: Same as performed by the FloodFill function. FLOODFILLSURFACE: Fills outward from the specified point as long as color crColor is found (use if the border is more than one color).

Return Value   Long—Nonzero on success, zero on failure. Sets GetLastError.

Platform   Windows 95, Windows NT, Win16

Comments   If FLOODFILLBORDER is specified, point X,Y must not have color crColor. If FLOODFILLSUR-FACE is specified, point X,Y must have color crColor. This function only works on raster devices.

Hints: When FLOODFILLBORDER is specified, be sure the initial point does not have color crColor. When FLOODFILLSURFACE is used, be sure the initial point has the color cr-Color (these are two reasons that the function typically fails). Be sure the initial point is inside the clipping region.

Use the GetDeviceCaps function to determine if the device supports this function.

Example   None provided, but it is an easy function to use and ideal for experimentation.

■ FillPath

VB Declaration   `Declare Function FillPath& Lib "gdi32" (ByVal hdc As Long)`

Description   Closes any open figures in the path and fills them with the current brush.

Use with VB	No problem.	
	Parameter	**Type/Description**
	hdc	Long—Device context to operate on.

Return Value   Long—Nonzero on success, zero on failure. Sets GetLastError to one of the following:

1. ERROR_CAN_NOT_COMPLETE
2. ERROR_INVALID_PARAMETER
3. ERROR_NOT_ENOUGH_MEMORY

Platform   Windows 95, Windows NT

Comments   The selected path is destroyed after this function is completed.

■ FillRect

VB Declaration
```
Declare Function FillRect& Lib "user32" (ByVal hdc As Long, lpRect As RECT, _
ByVal hBrush As Long)
```

Description   Fills a rectangle using the specified brush.

Use with VB	No problem.	
	Parameter	**Type/Description**
	hdc	Long—Handle to a device context.
	lpRect	RECT—Rectangle describing the area to fill in logical coordinates.
	hBrush	Long—Handle of the brush to use.

Return Value   Long—Nonzero on success, zero on failure. Sets GetLastError.

Platform   Windows 95, Windows NT, Win16

Comments   The right and bottom edges of the rectangle are not drawn.

Example   Ex8a.vbp, Ex8b.vbp

■ FlattenPath

VB Declaration
```
Declare Function FlattenPath& Lib "gdi32" (ByVal hdc As Long)
```

Description   Converts all curves in a path into line segments.

Use with VB	No problem.	
	Parameter	**Type/Description**
	hdc	Long—The device context containing the path.

Return Value   Long—Nonzero on success, zero on failure. Sets GetLastError to one of the following:

1. ERROR_CAN_NOT_COMPLETE
2. ERROR_INVALID_PARAMETER
3. ERROR_NOT_ENOUGH_MEMORY

Platform   Windows 95, Windows NT

■ FloodFill

VB Declaration   `Declare Function FloodFill& Lib "gdi32" (ByVal hdc As Long, ByVal x As Long, _`
`ByVal y As Long, ByVal crColor As Long)`

Description   Fills an area in the specified device context using the currently selected brush. The area is defined by color crColor.

Use with VB   No problem.

Parameter	Type/Description
hdc	Long—Handle to a device context.
x,y	Long—Point at which to begin filling in logical coordinates.
crColor	Long— Boundary color to use. The surface bounded by this color is filled.

Return Value   Long—Nonzero on success, zero on failure. Sets GetLastError.

Platform   Windows 95, Windows NT, Win16

Comments   Point X,Y must not have color crColor, and must be within the clipping region. This function only works on raster devices.

Example   See ExtFloodFill for comments.

■ FrameRect

VB Declaration   `Declare Function FrameRect& Lib "user32" (ByVal hdc As Long, lpRect As RECT, _`
`ByVal hBrush As Long)`

Description   Draws a border one logical unit wide around a rectangle using the specified brush.

Use with VB   No problem.

Parameter	Type/Description
hdc	Long—Handle to a device context.
lpRect	RECT—Rectangle specifying the border to draw. This is identical to the border drawn using the Rectangle function when the pen is one unit wide.
hBrush	Long—Handle of the brush to use.

Return Value Long—Nonzero on success, zero on failure. Sets GetLastError.

Platform Windows 95, Windows NT, Win16

Comments The value of the top field of lpRect must be smaller than that of the bottom field. The value of the left field of lpRect must be smaller than that of the right field.

■ GdiComment

VB Declaration ```
Declare Function GdiComment& Lib "gdi32" (ByVal hdc As Long, ByVal cbSize As _
Long, lpData As Any)
```

**Description** Adds a comment into the specified enhanced metafile device context.

**Use with VB** No problem.

| Parameter | Type/Description |
|---|---|
| hdc | Long—An enhanced metafile device context. |
| cbSize | Long—The size of the data to embed into the metafile. |
| lpData | Byte—A comment structure or long memory address of a buffer containing a comment buffer. |

**Return Value** Long—Nonzero on success, zero on failure.

**Platform** Windows 95, Windows NT

**Comments** While you can embed any private data into a metafile, there are several public data formats that can be embedded. If you consider the buffer as an array of 32-bit long values, the values for public comments are as follows:

The first entry is the constant GDICOMMENT_IDENTIFIER.
The second entry is one of the following:
GDICOMMENT_WINDOWS_METAFILE—Embeds a standard metafile into the enhanced metafile. It is followed by:

- The version number of the standard metafile.

- A checksum value: The sum of all the metafile data, including this value, must be zero.

- Zero.

- The size of the windows metafile data that follows.

GDICOMMENT_BEGINGROUP—Marks the beginning of a group of drawing commands in the enhanced metafile. It is followed by:

- Four Long values defining a RECT structure that contains the bounding rectangle for the drawing commands.

- The length of an optional Unicode string that follows containing a description of the group. May be zero if no description is present.

GDICOMMENT_ENDGROUP—Marks the end of a group of drawing commands in the enhanced metafile.
```

GDICOMMENT_MULTIFORMATS—Embeds a rendering of an image in a different format. For example, you can embed an encapsulated postscript image into an enhanced metafile using this comment. Windows will render the first format that it is able to draw when it plays this record. It is followed by:

- Four Long values defining a RECT structure that contains the bounding rectangle for the drawing commands.

- The number of formats included in this comment.

- A series of EMRFORMAT structures, one for each format. Refer to Appendix B for details on the EMRFORMAT structure.

■ GdiFlush

VB Declaration   `Declare Function GdiFlush& Lib "gdi32" ()`

Description   Executes any pending drawing operations.

Use with VB   No problem.

Return Value   Long—TRUE (nonzero) if all of the pending drawing operations succeed. Zero if any of the operations failed.

Platform   Windows 95, Windows NT

Comments   The Win32 graphics subsystem (GDI) can improve drawing performance by combining drawing operations into a batch. If you call a sequence of drawing operations that all return boolean values (TRUE on success, zero otherwise), they can be placed in an internal GDI queue and the functions can return immediately. These pending drawing commands are then executed by the GDI subsystem. Consider the common situation where a system has a graphics card with its own on board processor or graphics accelerator. When drawing, GDI simply sends graphic commands to the card which performs the actual drawing. If it were necessary to wait for each drawing operation to complete, system and application performance would be limited by the drawing speed of the card. Instead, GDI places the drawing commands in a queue called "batch," and the system and applications can continue to run while the graphic card is drawing.

The GdiFlush command causes the application to wait until all pending drawing operations are complete. This also occurs in cases where you execute a GDI drawing command that does not return a boolean value; for example, the GetPixel function needs to be able to read a pixel value, something that cannot be reliably done until all pending drawing has completed.

Example   See the discussion of DIBSections in Chapter 9 for examples of where this function is applied.

■ GdiGetBatchLimit

VB Declaration   `Declare Function GdiGetBatchLimit& Lib "gdi32" ()`

Description   Determines how many GDI drawing operations may be queued.

Use with VB   No problem.

Return Value   Long—The maximum number of pending drawing operations. Zero on error. Sets GetLastError.

Platform   Windows 95, Windows NT

Comments   See the comments for the GdiFlush command.

■ GdiSetBatchLimit

VB Declaration   `Declare Function GdiSetBatchLimit& Lib "gdi32" (ByVal dwLimit As Long)`

Description   Specifies how many GDI drawing operations may be queued.

Use with VB   No problem.

Parameter	Type/Description
dwLimit	Long—The maximum number of drawing operations that may be queued. Zero to restore the default. One to disable queuing of drawing commands.

Return Value   Long—The previous limit on success. Zero on error. Sets GetLastError.

Platform   Windows 95, Windows NT

Comments   See the comments for the GdiFlush command.

■ GetArcDirection

VB Declaration   `Declare Function GetArcDirection& Lib "gdi32" (ByVal hdc As Long)`

Description   Determines the current direction used when drawing arcs.

Use with VB   No problem.

Parameter	Type/Description
hdc	Long—The device context to query.

Return Value   Long—The constant AD_COUNTERCLOCKWISE or AD_CLOCKWISE. Zero on error.

Platform   Windows 95, Windows NT

■ GetBkColor

VB Declaration   `Declare Function GetBkColor& Lib "gdi32" (ByVal hdc As Long)`

Description   Retrieves the current background color for the specified device context.

Use with VB   No problem.

Parameter	Type/Description
hdc	Long—A device context to query for the background color.

Return Value   Long—RGB value of the current background color.

Platform   Windows 95, Windows NT, Win16

■ GetBkMode

VB Declaration   `Declare Function GetBkMode& Lib "gdi32" (ByVal hdc As Long)`

Description   Retrieves the current background filling mode for the specified device context.

Use with VB   No problem.

Parameter	Type/Description
hdc	Long—Handle to a device context.

Return Value   Long—One of the following constants:

1. OPAQUE: The background of text, hatched brushes, and dashed pen lines is set to the current background color.

2. TRANSPARENT: The background of text, hatched brushes, and dashed pen lines is not modified.

   Zero on error.

Platform   Windows 95, Windows NT, Win16

■ GetBrushOrgEx

VB Declaration   `Declare Function GetBrushOrgEx& Lib "gdi32" (ByVal hDC As Long, lpPoint As _`
`POINTAPI)`

Description   Retrieves the origin of the currently selected brush in the specified device context. Refer to "Brushes," earlier in this chapter.

Use with VB   No problem.

Parameter	Type/Description
hDC	Long—Handle to a device context.
lpPoint	POINTAPI—POINTAPI structure to load with the current brush origin.

Return Value   Long—Nonzero on success, zero on failure. Sets GetLastError.

Platform   Windows 95, Windows NT, Win16

■ GetCurrentObject

VB Declaration   `Declare Function GetCurrentObject& Lib "gdi32" (ByVal hdc As Long, ByVal _`
`uObjectType As Long)`

Description   Use to obtain the currently selected object of the specified type.

Use with VB   No problem.

Parameter	Type/Description
hdc	Long—The device context to query.
uObjectType	Long—The type of object. May be one of the constants: OBJ_PEN, OBJ_BRUSH, OBJ_PAL, OBJ_FONT, or OBJ_BITMAP.

Return Value   Long—The handle to the currently selected object. Zero on error.

Platform   Windows 95, Windows NT

■ GetCurrentPositionEx

VB Declaration   `Declare Function GetCurrentPositionEx& Lib "gdi32" (ByVal hdc As Long, lpPoint _ As POINTAPI)`

Description   Retrieves the current pen position in the specified device context.

Use with VB   No problem.

Parameter	Type/Description
hdc	Long—Handle to a device context.
lpPoint	POINTAPI—POINTAPI structure to load with the current position.

Return Value   Long—Nonzero on success, zero on failure.

Platform   Windows 95, Windows NT, Win16

■ GetEnhMetaFile

VB Declaration   `Declare Function GetEnhMetaFile& Lib "gdi32" Alias "GetEnhMetaFileA" (ByVal _ lpszMetaFile As String)`

Description   Retrieves a metafile handle to an enhanced metafile contained in a disk file.

Use with VB   No problem.

Parameter	Type/Description
lpszMetaFile	String—The name of a disk file containing an enhanced Windows metafile.

Return Value   Long—A handle to the metafile. Zero on error.

Platform   Windows 95, Windows NT

■ GetEnhMetaFileBits

VB Declaration   `Declare Function GetEnhMetaFileBits& Lib "gdi32" (ByVal hemf As Long, ByVal _`
`cbBuffer As Long, lpbBuffer As Byte)`

Description   Copies the specified enhanced metafile into a memory buffer. This function may be used to retrieve the raw data for a metafile in order to save it to a disk file.

Use with VB   No problem.

Parameter	Type/Description
hemf	Long— A handle to an enhanced metafile.
cbBuffer	Long—The length of lpbBuffer.
lpbBuffer	Byte—The first byte in a buffer of length cbBuffer. Use an alias that defines this parameter ByVal As Long to pass a memory address.

Return Value   Long—The length of buffer required if lpbBuffer is zero (use ByVal As Long to pass a NULL parameter in this case). The number of bytes actually loaded into the buffer on success, zero on error.

Platform   Windows 95, Windows NT

Comments   The metafile handle hemf remains valid after this function is called.

Example   Similar to GetMetaFileBitsEx, which is demonstrated in quikdraw.vbp.

■ GetEnhMetaFileDescription

VB Declaration   `Declare Function GetEnhMetaFileDescription& Lib "gdi32" Alias _`
`"GetEnhMetaFileDescriptionA" (ByVal hemf As Long, ByVal cchBuffer As Long, _`
`ByVal lpszDescription As String)`

Description   Retrieves the description of an enhanced metafile.

Use with VB   No problem.

Parameter	Type/Description
hemf	Long—A handle to an enhanced metafile.
cchBuffer	Long—The length of the lpszDescription buffer.
lpszDescription	String—A preinitialized string buffer to load with the metafile description. Refer to the CreateEnhMetafile function for a description of the format of an enhanced metafile description string.

Return Value   Long—The length of buffer required if lpszDescription is NULL (use vbNullString). The number of bytes actually loaded into the buffer on success, zero if no description is present. GDI_ERROR on error.

Platform   Windows 95, Windows NT

GetEnhMetaFileHeader

VB Declaration
```
Declare Function GetEnhMetaFileHeader& Lib "gdi32" (ByVal hemf As Long, ByVal _
    cbBuffer As Long, lpemh As ENHMETAHEADER)
```

Description Retrieves the metafile header for an enhanced metafile.

Use with VB No problem.

Parameter	Type/Description
hemf	Long—A handle to an enhanced metafile.
cbBuffer	Long—The size of the ENHMETAHEADER structure.
lpemh	ENHMETAHEADER—Refer to Appendix B for a description of this structure.

Return Value Long—The length of buffer required if lpemh is zero (use ByVal As Long to pass a NULL parameter in this case). The number of bytes actually loaded into the buffer on success, zero on error.

Platform Windows 95, Windows NT

GetEnhMetaFilePaletteEntries

VB Declaration
```
Declare Function GetEnhMetaFilePaletteEntries& Lib "gdi32" (ByVal hemf As Long, _
    ByVal cEntries As Long, lppe As PALETTEENTRY)
```

Description Retrieves all or part of the palette for an enhanced metafile.

Use with VB No problem.

Parameter	Type/Description
hemf	Long—A handle to an enhanced metafile.
cEntries	Long—The number of entries to retrieve.
lppe	PALETTEENTRY—An array of PALETTEENTRY structures to load with the palette entries for the enhanced metafile. Must contain at least cEntries structures.

Return Value Long—The length of buffer required if lppe is zero (use ByVal As Long to pass a NULL parameter in this case). The number of entries actually loaded into the buffer on success, zero if no palette exists in the metafile. GDI_ERROR on error.

Platform Windows 95, Windows NT

GetMetaFile

VB Declaration
```
Declare Function GetMetaFile& Lib "gdi32" Alias "GetMetaFileA" (ByVal _
    lpFileName As String)
```

Description	Retrieves a metafile handle to a metafile contained in a disk file.
Use with VB	No problem, but next to useless because Windows metafiles are typically stored in placeable metafile format, which cannot be read by this function.

Parameter	Type/Description
lpFileName	String—Name of the disk file containing a metafile.

Return Value	Long—A handle to the loaded metafile. Zero on error.
Platform	Windows 95, Windows NT, Win16

■ GetMetaFileBitsEx

VB Declaration	Declare Function GetMetaFileBitsEx& Lib "gdi32" (ByVal hMF As Long, ByVal nSize _ As Long, lpvData As Any)
Description	Copies the specified metafile into a memory buffer. This function may be used to retrieve the raw data for a metafile in order to save it to a disk file.
Use with VB	No problem.

Parameter	Type/Description
hMF	Long—A handle to a standard Windows metafile.
nSize	Long—The length of the lpvData buffer.
lpvData	Any—The first entry in a byte array to load with the metafile data. Use ByVal As Long to specify NULL or the memory address of a buffer.

Return Value	Long—The length of buffer required if lpvData is zero (use ByVal As Long to pass a NULL parameter in this case). The number of bytes actually loaded into the buffer on success, zero on error.
Platform	Windows 95, Windows NT, Win16
Example	QuikDraw.vbp

■ GetMiterLimit

VB Declaration	Declare Function GetMiterLimit& Lib "gdi32" (ByVal hdc As Long, peLimit As _ Single)
Description	Retrieve the current miter limit setting for the device context.
Use with VB	No problem.

Parameter	Type/Description
hdc	Long—A device context to query.
peLimit	Single—A single to load with the current miter limit.

Return Value	Long—Nonzero on success, zero on failure. Sets GetLastError.
Platform	Windows 95, Windows NT
Comments	The miter limit is the ratio between the miter length and the width of the line.
Example	ExtPen.vbp

■ GetNearestColor

VB Declaration   Declare Function GetNearestColor& Lib "gdi32" (ByVal hdc As Long, ByVal crColor _
As Long)

Description   Retrieves the closest solid color to the specified color that the device can actually display.

Use with VB   No problem.

Parameter	Type/Description
hdc	Long—Handle to a device context.
crColor	Long—RGB color to test.

Return Value   Long—Retrieves the nearest color to the one specified that can actually be rendered by the device context given the current system palette. CLR_INVALID on error. Sets GetLastError.

Platform   Windows 95, Windows NT, Win16

■ GetObjectAPI

VB Declaration   Declare Function GetObjectAPI& Lib "gdi32" Alias "GetObjectA" (ByVal hObject As _
Long, ByVal nCount As Long, lpObject As Any)

Description   Retrieves a structure describing the specified object.

Use with VB   No problem. The Windows documentation refers to this function by the name GetObject. GetObjectAPI is used in VB in order to avoid conflict with the GetObject keyword.

Parameter	Type/Description
hObject	Long—Handle to a pen, brush, font, bitmap, or palette.
nCount	Long—Number of bytes of data to retrieve. Usually the size of the structure defined by lpObject.
lpObject	Any—Structure with object data. This will typically be a LOGPEN structure for pens, EXTLOGPEN for extended pens. LOGBRUSH for fonts, LOGFONT for fonts, and BITMAP for bitmaps. DIBSECTION for DIB-Section bitmap (see Chapter 9). For palettes, this should point to an integer variable that will be loaded with the number of entries in the palette.

Return Value   Long—The length of buffer required if lpObject is zero (use ByVal As Long to pass a NULL parameter in this case). The number of bytes actually loaded into the structure on success, zero on error.

Platform	Windows 95, Windows NT, Win16
Comments	Refer to Appendix B for information on logical object data structures. The bmBits field of the BITMAP data structure is not valid when retrieving information for a bitmap; however, the bm-Bits field within the BITMAP structure contained in a DIBSECTION structure will be valid.

■ GetObjectType

VB Declaration   `Declare Function GetObjectType& Lib "gdi32" (ByVal hgdiobj As Long)`

Description   Retrieves the type of GDI object referenced by the specified handle.

Use with VB   No problem.

Parameter	Type/Description
hgdiobj	Long—A GDI object handle.

Return Value   Long—A constant with the prefix OBJ_ indicating the type of object. Zero on error.

Platform   Windows 95, Windows NT

Example   Analyze.vbp

■ GetPath

VB Declaration   `Declare Function GetPath& Lib "gdi32" (ByVal hdc As Long, lpPoint As POINTAPI, _`
`lpTypes As Byte, ByVal nSize As Long)`

Description   Retrieves a set of data that defines the current path.

Use with VB   No problem.

Parameter	Type/Description
hdc	Long—The device context containing the path.
lpPoint	POINTAPI—The first element in an array of POINTAPI structures to load with coordinate data for each segment in the path. This information is provided in logical coordinates.
lpTypes	Byte—The first element in a byte array that defines the type of operation corresponding to each coordinate. These include: PT_MOVETO: Coordinate is start of a new subpath. PT_LINETO: Coordinate is the end point of a line from the previous coordinate. PT_BEZIERTO: Always appears in groups of three. The first two of these points are the control points, the third is the end point of a Bézier curve. PT_LINETO and PT_BEZIERTO may be combined with PT_CLOSEFIGURE, in which case this is the last point in a figure. The path is closed by connecting this point to the first point in the subpath.
nSize	Long—The size of the lpPoint and lpTypes array. Set to zero to retrieve the required array size.

| Return Value | Long—The number of points loaded into the array (or the number of entries required if nSize is zero). –1 if the array is not large enough to hold the points. Sets GetLastError to one of the following: |

1. ERROR_CAN_NOT_COMPLETE

2. ERROR_INVALID_PARAMETER

3. ERROR_BUFFER_OVERFLOW

Platform   Windows 95, Windows NT

Comments   Even though path information is stored internally in device coordinates, this function returns all co-ordinates in logical coordinates based on the current coordinate system and transformation settings.

You can use the FlattenPath function to force all of the points in the path to be of type PT_MOVETO and PT_LINETO.

■ GetPixel

VB Declaration
```
Declare Function GetPixel& Lib "gdi32" (ByVal hdc As Long, ByVal x As Long, _
ByVal y As Long)
```

Description   Retrieves the RGB value of a pixel in the specified device context.

Use with VB   No problem.

Parameter	Type/Description
hdc	Long—Handle to a device context.
x,y	Long—Point to check in logical coordinates.

Return Value   Long—RGB color of the specified point. CLR_INVALID if the specified point is outside of the clipping region for the device context.

Comments   Use the GetDeviceCaps function to determine if a device supports this function.

Platform   Windows 95, Windows NT, Win16

■ GetPolyFillMode

VB Declaration   `Declare Function GetPolyFillMode& Lib "gdi32" (ByVal hdc As Long)`

Description   Retrieves the polygon filling mode for the specified device context. Figure 8.15 describes the two polygon fill modes.

Use with VB   No problem.

Parameter	Type/Description
hdc	Long—Handle to a device context.

Return Value   Long—The constant ALTERNATE or WINDING. Zero on error.

Platform   Windows 95, Windows NT, Win16

Comments   Refer to the SetPolyFillMode function description for further information.

Example   QuikDraw.vbp

Figure 8.15
Polygon fill modes

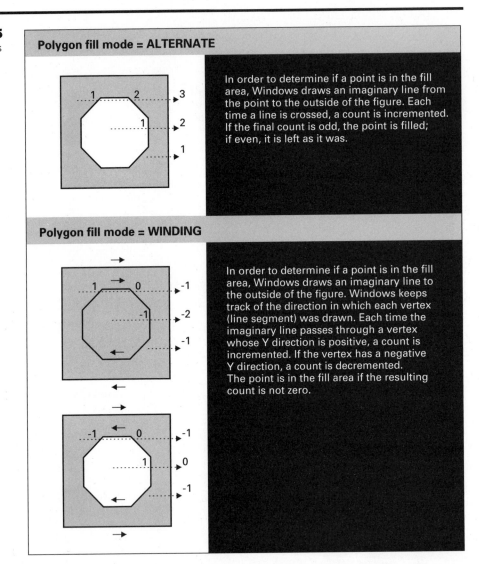

GetROP2

VB Declaration   Declare Function GetROP2& Lib "gdi32" (ByVal hdc As Long)

Description   Retrieves the current drawing mode for the specified device context. This defines how drawing operations combine with the image already on the display.

Use with VB   This is identical to reading the DrawMode property for VB forms or picture controls.

Parameter	Type/Description
hdc	Long—Handle to a device context.

Return Value   Long—Table 8.11 shows the name of the constant specifying a drawing mode from the API32.TXT file, the equivalent VB DrawMode property value, and a brief description of the drawing mode.

Platform   Windows 95, Windows NT, Win16

Comments   This function only works on raster devices. For a more thorough description of how raster operations are used to combine a color with an existing image on a device, refer to the discussion in Chapter 9 on raster operations.

Table 8.11   Drawing Mode Constants

Constant	DrawMode	Pixel Value
R2_BLACK	vbBlackness	Black
R2_WHITE	vbWhitness	White
R2_NOP	vbNop	Unchanged
R2_NOT	vbInvert	The inverse of the current display color
R2_COPYPEN	vbCopyPen	The pen color
R2_NOTCOPYPEN	vbNotCopyPen	The inverse of R2_COPYPEN
R2_MERGEPENNOT	vbMergePenNot	The inverse of the display color ORed with the pen color
R2_MASKPENNOT	vbMaskPenNot	Inverse of the display color ANDed with the pen color
R2_MERGENOTPEN	vbMergeNotPen	Inverse of the pen color Ored with the display color
R2_MASKNOTPEN	vbMaskNotPen	Inverse of the pen color ANDed with the display color
R2_MERGEPEN	vbMergePen	The pen color ORed with the display color
R2_NOTMERGEPEN	vbNotMergePen	Inverse of R2_MERGEPEN
R2_MASKPEN	vbMaskPen	The display color ANDed with the pen color

---

Table 8.11   Drawing Mode Constants (Continued)

Constant	DrawMode	Pixel Value
R2_NOTMASKPEN	vbNotMaskPen	Inverse of R2_MASKPEN
R2_XORPEN	vbXorPen	The exclusive-or of the display and pen colors
R2_NOTXORPEN	vbNotXorPen	The inverse of R2_XORPEN

Example   Viewport.vbp in Chapter 7 demonstrates SetROP2

■ GetStockObject

VB Declaration   `Declare Function GetStockObject& Lib "gdi32" (ByVal nIndex As Long)`

Description   Retrieves a stock object. This is one of the standard Windows objects that may be used by any application.

Use with VB   No problem.

Parameter	Type/Description
nIndex	Long—One of the constants specified in the following table:
Value of nIndex	**System Object Retrieved**
BLACK_BRUSH	Black brush.
DKGRAY_BRUSH	Dark gray brush.
GRAY_BRUSH	Gray brush.
HOLLOW_BRUSH	Hollow brush.
LTGRAY_BRUSH	Light gray brush.
NULL_BRUSH	Empty brush.
WHITE_BRUSH	White brush.
BLACK_PEN	Black pen.
NULL_PEN	Empty pen.
WHITE_PEN	White pen.
ANSI_FIXED_FONT	Fixed pitched font using the Windows (ANSI) character set.
ANSI_VAR_FONT	Variable width font using the Windows (ANSI) character set.
DEVICE_DEFAULT_FONT	Default font used by the device (NT).
DEFAULT_GUI_FONT	Default font for the user interface, including menus and dialog boxes (Windows 95).

Value of nIndex	System Object Retrieved
OEM_FIXED_FONT	Fixed font in the OEM character set.
SYSTEM_FONT	Screen system font. This is the default variable width font used for menus, dialog boxes, and so on.
SYSTEM_FIXED_FONT	Screen system font. This is the default fixed pitch font used for menus, dialog boxes, and so on, before Windows 3.0.
DEFAULT_PALETTE	Default color palette.

Return Value Long—A handle to the specified object, zero on error.

Platform Windows 95, Windows NT, Win16

Comments Origins of stock brushes may not be changed. These objects should not be deleted using Delete-Object. Do not use the DK_GRAY_BRUSH, GRAY_BRUSH, and LTGRAY_BRUSH brushes on windows that do not have the CS_HREDRAW and CS_VREDRAW class styles.

Example Path.vbp

■ GetSysColorBrush

VB Declaration `Declare Function GetSysColorBrush& Lib "user32" (ByVal nIndex As Long)`

Description Retrieves a brush for one of the standard system colors. Refer to the description of the Get-SysColor function in Chapter 6 for further information on system colors.

Use with VB No problem.

Parameter	Type/Description
nIndex	Long—An index to a system color from among the constants with the COLOR_ prefix. Refer to the table under the definition of the Get-SysColor function in Chapter 6 for a list of available colors.

Return Value Long—The handle to a stock brush for a system color. Zero on error.

Platform Windows 95, Windows NT

Comments Do not delete these brushes using the DeleteObject function. They are stock objects that are owned by the system. Do not assign these brushes to be the default brush for a window class.

■ GetWinMetaFileBits

VB Declaration `Declare Function GetWinMetaFileBits& Lib "gdi32" (ByVal hemf As Long, ByVal _`
`cbBuffer As Long, lpbBuffer As Byte, ByVal fnMapMode As Long, ByVal hdcRef As _`
`Long)`

Description Converts an enhanced metafile into a standard Windows metafile by filling a buffer with the data for the standard metafile.

Use with VB	No problem.

Parameter	Type/Description
hemf	Long—A handle to the enhanced metafile to convert. This handle remains valid after this function is called.
cbBuffer	Long—The length of the destination buffer.
lpbBuffer	Byte—The first byte in a byte array to use as the destination buffer. This array must be at least cbBuffer bytes long.
fnMapMode	Long—The mapping mode to use for the conversion. Typically MM_ANISOTROPIC to create a scalable metafile.
hdcRef	Long—A reference device context that is used to determine the reference resolution to use for the new metafile.

Return Value　Long—The size in bytes of the metafile. If lpbBuffer is NULL (use an alias with the parameter specified ByVal as Long to pass NULL to this function) returns the required size of the byte array. Zero on error.

Platform　Windows 95, Windows NT

Comments　Some enhanced metafile commands have no standard metafile equivalents. These commands will be converted to the closest available command or discarded. The resulting metafile has window extents specified. The window origin will be 0,0.

■ InvertRect

VB Declaration　`Declare Function InvertRect& Lib "user32" (ByVal hdc As Long, lpRect As RECT)`

Description　Inverts the specified rectangle on a device context by inverting the value of each pixel.

Use with VB　No problem.

Parameter	Type/Description
hdc	Long—A handle to a device context
lpRect	RECT—The rectangle to invert specified in logical coordinates

Return Value　Long—Nonzero on success, zero on failure. Sets GetLastError.

Platform　Windows 95, Windows NT, Win16

Comments　Refer to Chapter 9 for information on raster operations such as inversion.

■ LineDDA

VB Declaration　`Declare Function LineDDA& Lib "gdi32" (ByVal n1 As Long, ByVal n2 As Long, _`
`ByVal n3 As Long, ByVal n4 As Long, ByVal lpLineDDAProc As Long, ByVal lParam _`
`As Long)`

Description   Enumerates all points in the specified line.

Use with VB   Requires the dwcbk32d.ocx custom control provided with this book with Visual Basic 4.0.

Parameter	Type/Description
n1,n2	Long—The X,Y start coordinates for the line.
n3,n4	Long—The X,Y end coordinates for the line.
lpLineDDAProc	Long—A function address in VB5. The value of the ProcAddress property from the dwcbk32d.ocx control with Visual Basic 4.0.
lParam	Long—User-defined value that is passed to the callback function during enumeration.

Return Value   Long——Nonzero on success, zero on failure.

Platform   Windows 95, Windows NT, Win16

Comments   Refer to Appendix A for details on using the dwcbk32d.ocx custom control with enumeration functions with Visual Basic 4.0.

            Typical uses for this function are to perform custom line drawing—you can, for example, set every other pixel in a line to a different color.

            In MM_TEXT mode, each point corresponds to a pixel on the device—in this mode you can use the function for hit testing on a line as well.

            The last point in the line is not enumerated.

■ LineTo

VB Declaration
```
Declare Function LineTo& Lib "gdi32" (ByVal hdc As Long, ByVal x As Long, ByVal _
y As Long)
```

Description   Draws a line using the current pen from the current position to the point specified. The new current position will be point X,Y after this function is called.

Use with VB   No problem.

Parameter	Type/Description
hdc	Long—Handle to a device context.
x,y	Long—End position for the point in logical coordinates. This point is not drawn; it's not part of the line.

Return Value   Long—Nonzero on success, zero on failure.

Platform   Windows 95, Windows NT, Win16

Comments   If you create a sequence of line segments using repeated calls to this function and a geometric pen, the segments are not considered joined unless called within the context of a path.

Example   QuikDraw.vbp, ExtPen.vbp, Path.vbp

■ MoveToEx

VB Declaration	`Declare Function MoveToEx& Lib "gdi32" (ByVal hdc As Long, ByVal x As Long, _` `ByVal y As Long, lpPoint As POINTAPI)`
Description	Specifies a new current pen position for the specified device context. The previous position is stored in lpPoint.
Use with VB	No problem.

Parameter	Type/Description
hdc	Long—Handle to a device context.
x,y	Long—New pen position in logical coordinates.
lpPoint	POINTAPI—POINTAPI in which to store the previous pen position. May be NULL (change parameter to ByVal As Long to pass a NULL parameter).

Return Value	Long—TRUE (nonzero) on success, zero otherwise.
Platform	Windows 95, Windows NT, Win16
Comments	When drawn within a path bracket, this function creates a new subpath.
Example	QuikDraw.vbp, Path.vbp, ExtPen.vbp

■ PaintDesktop

VB Declaration	`Declare Function PaintDesktop Lib "user32" (ByVal hdc As Long)`
Description	Draws the desktop wallpaper pattern onto the device context specified.
Use with VB	No problem.

Parameter	Type/Description
hdc	Long—The device context to fill

Return Value	Long—TRUE (nonzero) on success, FALSE on error.
Platform	Windows 95, Windows NT 4.0

■ PathToRegion

VB Declaration	`Declare Function PathToRegion& Lib "gdi32" (ByVal hdc As Long)`
Description	Converts the current selected path into a region.

Use with VB   No problem.

Parameter	Type/Description
hdc	Long—Device context containing the path to convert

Return Value   Long—A handle to the new region. Zero on error. Sets GetLastError to one of the following values:

1. ERROR_CAN_NOT_COMPLETE

2. ERROR_INVALID_PARAMETER

3. ERROR_NOT_ENOUGH_MEMORY

Platform   Windows 95, Windows NT

Comments   The path is destroyed after this function is executed.

■ Pie

VB Declaration
```
Declare Function Pie& Lib "gdi32" (ByVal hdc As Long, ByVal X1 As Long, ByVal _
Y1 As Long, ByVal X2 As Long, ByVal Y2 As Long, ByVal X3 As Long, ByVal Y3 As _
Long, ByVal X4 As Long, ByVal Y4 As Long)
```

Description   Draws a pie as shown in Figure 8.13. X1,Y1,X2,Y2 specify a bounding rectangle of an ellipse. The point at which lines drawn from the center of the rectangle to points X3,Y3 and X4,Y4 defines the wedge in the pie figure.

Use with VB   No problem.

Parameter	Type/Description
hdc	Long—Handle to a display context
X1,Y1	Long—Specify the upper-left corner of a rectangle that bounds an ellipse
X2,Y2	Long—Specify the lower-right corner of a rectangle that bounds an ellipse
X3,Y3	Long—Specify one side of the pie wedge
X4,Y4	Long—Specify the side of the pie wedge not specified by X3,Y3

Return Value   Long—Nonzero on success, zero on failure. Sets GetLastError.

Platform   Windows 95, Windows NT, Win16. The width and height of the bounding rectangle must be between 3 and 32,766 units in size on Windows 95 and Win16.

Example   QuikDraw.vbp

■ PlayEnhMetaFile

VB Declaration
```
Declare Function PlayEnhMetaFile& Lib "gdi32" (ByVal hdc As Long, ByVal hemf As _
Long, lpRect As RECT)
```

Description	Draws an enhanced metafile into the specified device context. Unlike standard metafiles, enhanced metafiles restore the previous state of the device context when they are finished playing.
Use with VB	No problem.

Parameter	Type/Description
hdc	Long—Destination device context
hemf	Long—A handle to the enhanced metafile to draw
lpRect	RECT—A bounding rectangle defining where to draw the metafile

Return Value	Long—Nonzero on success, zero on failure. Sets GetLastError.
Platform	Windows 95, Windows NT
Example	QuikDraw.vbp, which uses the similar PlayMetaFile function.

■ PlayEnhMetaFileRecord

| **VB Declaration** | ```
Declare Function PlayEnhMetaFileRecord& Lib "gdi32" (ByVal hdc As Long, _
lpHandletable As HANDLETABLE, lpEnhMetaRecord As ENHMETARECORD, ByVal nHandles _
As Long)
``` |
| **Description** | Plays a single enhanced metafile record. This can be used in combination with the EnumEnhMetaFile function to play only selected metafile records. The parameters to this function are similar to those returned by the EnumMetaFile event of the dwcbk32d.ocx custom control. |
| **Use with VB** | No problem. |

Parameter	Type/Description
hdc	Long—A device context for drawing
lpHandletable	HANDLETABLE—An array of handles used
lpEnh-MetaRecord	ENHMETARECORD—A structure (or pointer to a structure) containing the enhanced metafile record
nHandles	Long—The number of handles in the handle table

Return Value	Long—No zero on success, zero on failure.
Platform	Windows 95, Windows NT
Comments	Refer to the chapter text for further information on use of the PlayMetaFileRecord function.
Example	Analyze.vbp demonstrates the EnumMetafileRecord function, which is nearly identical.
```

■ PlayMetaFile

VB Declaration   `Declare Function PlayMetaFile& Lib "gdi32" (ByVal hdc As Long, ByVal hMF As _`
`Long)`

Description   Plays a metafile into the specified device context. The GDI operations that were recorded in the metafile are executed for the DC.

Use with VB   A metafile is capable of changing objects and mapping modes for a device context. Be sure to save the state of a VB form or picture control DC before calling this function.

Parameter	Type/Description
hdc	Long—Handle to a device context on which to play the metafile.
hMF	Long—Handle to a metafile to play.

Return Value   Long—Nonzero on success, zero on failure.

Platform   Windows 95, Windows NT, Win16

Comments   Refer to the chapter text for further information on use of this function.

Example   Analyze.vbp

■ PlayMetaFileRecord

VB Declaration   `Declare Function PlayMetaFileRecord& Lib "gdi32" (ByVal hdc As Long, _`
`lpHandletable As HANDLETABLE, lpMetaRecord As METARECORD, ByVal nHandles As _`
`Long)`

Description   Plays a single record from a metafile (each record contains a single GDI drawing command). This can be used in combination with the EnumMetaFile function to play only selected metafile records. The parameters to this function are similar to those returned by the EnumMetaFile callback function.

Use with VB   No problem.

Parameter	Type/Description
hdc	Long—Handle to a device context on which to play the metafile record's GDI command.
lpHandletable	HANDLETABLE—The first entry in an integer array of handles to GDI objects used by the metafile.
lpMetaRecord	METARECORD—A single metafile record. Appendix B contains a description of this data structure.
nHandles	Long—The number of handles in the metafile's handle table.

Return Value   Long—Nonzero on success, zero on failure.

Platform   Windows 95, Windows NT, Win16

Comments   Refer to the chapter text for further information.

Example   Analyze.vbp

■ PolyBezier, PolyBezierTo

VB Declaration
```
Declare Function PolyBezier& Lib "gdi32" (ByVal hdc As Long, lppt As POINTAPI, _
ByVal cPoints As Long)
Declare Function PolyBezierTo& Lib "gdi32" (ByVal hdc As Long, lppt As _
POINTAPI, ByVal cCount As Long)
```

Description   Draws one or more Bézier curves. PolyBezierTo sets the current pen position to the end point of the last curve.

Use with VB   No problem.

Parameter	Type/Description
hdc	Long—Device context in which to draw.
lppt	POINTAPI—An array of POINTAPI structures. The first structure specifies the starting point. The remaining points are in groups of three, consisting of two control points and an end point.
cPoints	Long—The total number of points in the lppt array.

Return Value   Long—Nonzero on success, zero on failure.

Platform   Windows 95, Windows NT

Comments   Refer to the chapter text for a complete description of Bézier curves.

Example   Bezier.vbp

■ PolyDraw

VB Declaration
```
Declare Function PolyDraw& Lib "gdi32" (ByVal hdc As Long, lppt As POINTAPI, _
lpbTypes As Byte, ByVal cCount As Long)
```

Description   Draws a complex curve consisting of line segments and Bézier curves.

Use with VB   No problem.

Parameter	Type/Description
hdc	Long—The device context for drawing.
lppt	POINTAPI—The first element in an array of POINTAPI structures to load with coordinate data for each segment to draw. This information is provided in logical coordinates.

Parameter	Type/Description
lpbTypes	Byte—The first element in a byte array that defines the type of operation corresponding to each coordinate. These include: PT_MOVETO: Coordinate is start of a new open figure. PT_LINETO: Coordinate is the end point of a line from the previous coordinate. PT_BEZIERTO: Always appears in groups of three. The first two of these points are the control points, the third is the end point of a Bézier curve. PT_LINETO and PT_BEZIERTO may be combined with PT_CLOSEFIGURE, in which case this is the last point in a figure. The figure is closed by connecting this point to the first point in the figure.
cCount	Long—The size of the lpPoint and lpTypes array. Set to zero to retrieve the required array size.

Return Value

Long—Nonzero on success, zero on failure.

Comments

The current pen position is set to the end point of the last line segment or curve in the lppt array.

Platform

Windows NT

■ Polygon

VB Declaration

```
Declare Function Polygon& Lib "gdi32" (ByVal hdc As Long, lpPoint As POINTAPI, _
ByVal nCount As Long)
```

Description

Draws a polygon consisting of an arbitrary series of two or more points. Windows automatically closes the polygon by connecting the last and first points. The border of the polygon is drawn with the currently selected pen. The polygon is filled using the currently selected brush.

Use with VB

No problem.

Parameter	Type/Description
hdc	Long—Device context for drawing.
lpPoint	POINTAPI—The first POINTAPI structure in an array of nCount POINTAPI structures.
nCount	Long—Number of points in the polygon.

Return Value

Long—Nonzero on success, zero on failure. Sets GetLastError.

Platform

Windows 95, Windows NT, Win16

Comments

The GetPolyFillMode and SetPolyFillMode functions determine how the polygon is filled.

Example

QuikDraw.vbp

■ Polyline, PolyLineTo

VB Declaration `Declare Function Polyline& Lib "gdi32" (ByVal hdc As Long, lpPoint As POINTAPI, _`
`ByVal nCount As Long)`

Description Draws a series of lines using the current pen. The current position is set to the end point of the last line segment when using the PolyLineTo function. It is not modified by the PolyLine function.

Use with VB No problem.

Parameter	Type/Description
hdc	Long—Device context for drawing.
lpPoint	POINTAPI—The first POINTAPI structure in an array of nCount POINTAPI structures.
nCount	Long—Number of points in the lpPoints array. A line is drawn from the first point to the second, and so on.

Return Value Long—Nonzero on success, zero on failure.

Platform Windows 95, Windows NT, Win16

Example QuikDraw.vbp

■ PolyPolygon

VB Declaration `Declare Function PolyPolygon& Lib "gdi32" (ByVal hdc As Long, lpPoint As _`
`POINTAPI, lpPolyCounts As Long, ByVal nCount As Long)`

Description Draws two or more polygons using the currently selected pen. Fills them using the currently selected brush based on the polygon fill mode specified by the SetPolyFillMode function. Each polygon must be closed.

Use with VB No problem.

Parameter	Type/Description
hdc	Long—Device context for drawing.
lpPoint	POINTAPI—The first POINTAPI structure in an array of nCount POINTAPI structures.
lpPolyCounts	Long—The first entry in an array of long values. Each entry contains the number of points that make up a closed polygon. The lpPoints array consists of a series of closed polygons, each one of which has an entry in the lpPolyCounts array.
nCount	Long—Total number of polygons to be drawn (which is the size of the lpdwPolyPoints array). Must be at least 2.

Return Value Long—Nonzero on success, zero on failure. Sets GetLastError.

Platform Windows 95, Windows NT, Win16

Example   Region.vbp in Chapter 7 uses the CreatePolyPolygonRgn function which works identically to this function except that it creates a region instead of drawing. Refer also to the Chapter 7 text that describes this example.

■ PolyPolyline

VB Declaration
```
Declare Function PolyPolyline& Lib "gdi32" (ByVal hdc As Long, lppt As _
POINTAPI, lpdwPolyPoints As Long, ByVal cCount As Long)
```

Description   Draws two or more polygons using the currently selected pen.

Use with VB   No problem.

Parameter	Type/Description
hdc	Long—Device context for drawing.
lppt	POINTAPI—The first POINTAPI structure in an array of nCount POINTAPI structures.
lpdwPolyPoints	Long—The first entry in an array of long values. Each entry contains the number of points that make up a polygon. The lpPoints array consists of a series of polygons, each one of which has an entry in the lpPolyCounts array.
cCount	Long—Total number of polygons to be drawn (which is the size of the lpdwPolyPoints array).

Return Value   Long—Nonzero on success, zero on failure.

Platform   Windows 95, Windows NT

Comments   This function is virtually identical to the PolyPolygon function except that the polygons are not filled and need not be closed.

Example   Region.vbp in Chapter 7 uses the CreatePolyPolygonRgn function which works identically to this function except that it creates a region instead of drawing. Refer also to the Chapter 7 text that describes this example.

■ Rectangle

VB Declaration
```
Declare Function Rectangle& Lib "gdi32" (ByVal hdc As Long, ByVal X1 As Long, _
ByVal Y1 As Long, ByVal X2 As Long, ByVal Y2 As Long)
```

Description   Draws the rectangle specified with the currently selected pen and fills it with the currently selected brush.

Use with VB   No problem.

Parameter	Type/Description
hdc	Long—Handle to a device context.

Parameter	Type/Description
X1,Y1	Long—Point specifying the upper-left corner of the rectangle.
X2,Y2	Long—Point specifying the lower-right corner of the rectangle.

Return Value   Long—Nonzero on success, zero on failure. Sets GetLastError.

Platform   Windows 95, Windows NT, Win16

Example   QuikDraw.vbp

■ RoundRect

VB Declaration
```
Declare Function RoundRect& Lib "gdi32" (ByVal hdc As Long, ByVal X1 As Long, _
ByVal Y1 As Long, ByVal X2 As Long, ByVal Y2 As Long, ByVal X3 As Long, ByVal _
Y3 As Long)
```

Description   Draws the rectangle with rounded corners with the currently selected pen and fills it with the currently selected brush. X3 and Y3 define the ellipse used to round the corners.

Use with VB   No problem.

Parameter	Type/Description
hdc	Long—Device context for drawing.
X1,Y1	Long—X,Y coordinates describing the upper-left corner of the rectangle.
X2,Y2	Long—X,Y coordinates describing the lower-right corner of the rectangle.
X3	Long—The width of the ellipse used to round the corners. Ranges from zero for no rounding, to the width of the rectangle for full rounding.
Y3	Long—The height of the ellipse used to round the corners. Ranges from zero for no rounding, to the height of the rectangle for full rounding.

Return Value   Long—Nonzero on success, zero on failure. Sets GetLastError.

Platform   Windows 95, Windows NT, Win16

Example   Region.vbp in Chapter 7 illustrates use of the CreateRoundRectRgn function, which is virtually identical except that it creates a region instead of drawing.

■ SelectClipPath

VB Declaration
```
Declare Function SelectClipPath& Lib "gdi32" (ByVal hdc As Long, ByVal iMode As _
Long)
```

Description   Merges the current path in a device context into the clipping region.

Use with VB	No problem.

Parameter	Type/Description
hdc	Long—Handle to a device context containing a path to merge into the clipping region.
iMode	Long—Determines how the path is combined with the current clipping region. May be one of the following constants: RGN_AND—The new clipping region contains only points present in the path and the current clipping region. RGN_COPY—The new clipping region is set to the path. RGN_DIFF—The new clipping region contains only points present in the current clipping region that are not in the path. RGN_OR—The new clipping region contains only points present in both the path and the current clipping region. RGN_XOR—The new clipping region contains only points present in either the path or the current clipping region, but not in both.

Return Value   Long—TRUE (nonzero) on success, zero on error. Sets GetLastError to one of the following values:

1. ERROR_CAN_NOT_COMPLETE

2. ERROR_INVALID_PARAMETER

3. ERROR_NOT_ENOUGH_MEMORY

Platform   Windows 95, Windows NT

Example   Path.vbp

■ SelectObject

VB Declaration   `Declare Function SelectObject& Lib "gdi32" (ByVal hdc As Long, ByVal hObject As _`
`Long)`

Description   Each device context may have graphics objects selected into it. These include bitmaps, brushes, fonts, pens, and regions. Only one of each object may be selected into a device context at a time. The selected object is used during drawing to the device context; for example, the currently selected pen determines the color and style of lines drawn into the device context.

Use with VB   No problem.

Parameter	Type/Description
hdc	Long—A handle to a device context.
hObject	Long—A handle to a bitmap, pen, brush, font, or region.

Return Value   Long—A handle to the object of the same type of hObject that was previously selected into the device context, zero on error. If the object being selected is a region, the result is one of the constants: SIMPLEREGION, COMPLEXREGION, NULLREGION describing the region, or GDI_ERROR on error.

Platform   Windows 95, Windows NT, Win16

Comments   The return value is typically used to obtain the original value of the objects selected into the DC when new objects are selected. This original object is usually selected back into the device context after the graphic operations are complete. It is important to restore the original objects before destroying a device context.

A bitmap can only be selected into a memory device context, and can be selected into only one device context at a time.

Example   QuikDraw.vbp and many other sample programs throughout the book.

■ SetArcDirection

VB Declaration
```
Declare Function SetArcDirection& Lib "gdi32" (ByVal hdc As Long, ByVal _
ArcDirection As Long)
```

Description   Sets the direction to use when drawing arcs.

Use with VB   No problem.

Parameter	Type/Description
hdc	Long—The device context to set.
ArcDirection	Long—AD_CLOCKWISE or AD_COUNTERCLOCKWISE.

Return Value   Long—The old arc direction on success, zero on error.

Comments   Applies to the functions: Arc, ArcTo, Chord, Ellipse, Pie, Rectangle, and RoundRect.

Platform   Windows NT

■ SetBkColor

VB Declaration
```
Declare Function SetBkColor& Lib "gdi32" (ByVal hdc As Long, ByVal crColor As _
Long)
```

Description   Sets the background color for the specified device context. The background color is used to fill the gaps in hatched brushes, dashed pens, and characters if the background mode is OPAQUE. It is also used during bitmap color conversions as described in Chapter 9.

Use with VB   No problem.

Parameter	Type/Description
hdc	Long—Handle to a device context.
crColor	Long—RGB color value of new background color.

Return Value   Long—The previous background color. CLR_INVALID on error.

Platform   Windows 95, Windows NT, Win16

Comments   The background color will actually be the closest color to crColor that the device can display.

■ SetBkMode

VB Declaration   `Declare Function SetBkMode& Lib "gdi32" (ByVal hdc As Long, ByVal nBkMode As _`
`Long)`

Description   Specifies the way that gaps in hatched brushes, dashed pens, and characters are filled.

Use with VB   No problem.

Parameter	Type/Description
hdc	Long—Handle to a device context.
nBkMode	Long—One of the following constant values: OPAQUE: Use the current background color to fill in gaps in dashed pens, hatched brushes, and characters. TRANSPARENT: Do not fill in gaps as described above.

Return Value   Long—The value of the previous background mode.

Platform   Windows 95, Windows NT, Win16

Comments   The background mode does not affect lines drawn with extended pens.

■ SetBrushOrgEx

VB Declaration   `Declare Function SetBrushOrgEx& Lib "gdi32" (ByVal hdc As Long, ByVal nXOrg As _`
`Long, ByVal nYOrg As Long, lppt As POINTAPI)`

Description   Sets the origin of the currently selected brush in the specified device context. Refer to "Brushes," earlier in this chapter.

Use with VB   Be sure to reset the device context's brush origin to 0,0 when finished. This may be done explicitly, or when the original DC is restored using the RestoreDC function.

Parameter	Type/Description
hdc	Long—Handle to a device context.
nXOrg, nYOrg	Long—New origin for the brush in device coordinates. May range from 0 to 7 (larger values are not needed, as the maximum brush size under Windows 95 is 8×8 and this function is not needed under NT).
lppt	POINTAPI—A structure that is loaded with the previous brush origin.

Return Value   Long—Nonzero on success, zero on failure. Sets GetLastError.

Platform   Windows 95, Windows NT
Windows NT automatically sets brush origins, so this function should not be used under Windows NT.

Porting Notes   Replaces the Win16 SetBrushOrg function.

Example   Refer to the chapter text.

■ SetEnhMetaFileBits

VB Declaration `Declare Function SetEnhMetaFileBits& Lib "gdi32" (ByVal cbBuffer As Long, _`
`lpData As Byte)`

Description Creates an enhanced metafile using the data contained in the specified memory buffer. This function is often used to create a metafile after reading raw metafile data from disk that had originally been obtained using the GetEnhMetaFileBitsEx function.

Use with VB No problem.

Parameter	Type/Description
cbBuffer	Long—The length of the lpData array.
lpData	Byte—The first entry in an array of bytes containing the metafile data.

Return Value Long—An enhanced metafile handle on success, zero otherwise.

Platform Windows 95, Windows NT

Example QuikDraw.vbp demonstrates the SetMetaFileBits function, which is similar.

■ SetMetaFileBitsEx

VB Declaration `Declare Function SetMetaFileBitsEx& Lib "gdi32" (ByVal nSize As Long, lpData As _`
`Byte)`

Description Creates a metafile using the data contained in the specified memory buffer. This function is often used to create a metafile after reading raw metafile data from disk that had originally been obtained using the GetMetaFileBitsEx function.

Use with VB No problem.

Parameter	Type/Description
nSize	Long—The length of the lpData array.
lpData	Byte—The first entry in an array of bytes containing the metafile data.

Return Value Long—A handle of a standard metafile on success, zero on failure.

Platform Windows 95, Windows NT

Porting Notes Replaces the SetMetaFileBits and SetMetaFileBitsBetter Win16 functions.

Example QuikDraw.vbp

■ SetMiterLimit

VB Declaration `Declare Function SetMiterLimit& Lib "gdi32" (ByVal hdc As Long, ByVal eNewLimit _`
`As Single, peOldLimit As Single)`

Description   Retrieve the current miter limit setting for the device context.

Use with VB   No problem.

Parameter	Type/Description
hdc	Long—The device context to set.
eNewLimit	Single—The new miter limit.
peOldLimit	Single—A single to load with the old miter limit.

Return Value   Long—Nonzero on success, zero on failure. Sets GetLastError.

Platform   Windows 95, Windows NT

Comments   The miter limit is the ratio between the miter length and the width of the line.

Example   ExtPen.vbp

■ SetPixel

VB Declaration
```
Declare Function SetPixel& Lib "gdi32" (ByVal hdc As Long, ByVal x As Long, _
ByVal y As Long, ByVal crColor As Long)
```

Description   Sets the RGB value of a pixel in the specified device context.

Use with VB   No problem.

Parameter	Type/Description
hdc	Long—Handle to a device context.
x,y	Long—Point to set in logical coordinates.
crColor	Long—New RGB color for the specified pixel.

Return Value   Long—The actual RGB color of the point. This will differ from crColor if the device does not support the exact color specified. It will return –1 if the point cannot be set (for example, if the point is outside of the clipping region for the device context). Sets GetLastError.

Platform   Windows 95, Windows NT, Win16

Comments   Use the GetDeviceCaps function to determine if a device supports this function.

■ SetPixelV

VB Declaration
```
Declare Function SetPixelV& Lib "gdi32" (ByVal hdc As Long, ByVal x As Long, _
ByVal y As Long, ByVal crColor As Long)
```

Description   Sets the RGB value of a pixel in the specified device context.

Use with VB   No problem.

Parameter	Type/Description
hdc	Long—Handle to a device context.
x,y	Long—Point to set in logical coordinates.
crColor	Long—New RGB color for the specified pixel.

Return Value   Long—Nonzero on success, zero on failure. Sets GetLastError.

Platform   Windows 95, Windows NT

Comments   This function is faster than SetPixel, but it does not return the actual color set.
Use the GetDeviceCaps function to determine if a device supports this function.

■ SetPolyFillMode

VB Declaration   `Declare Function SetPolyFillMode& Lib "gdi32" (ByVal hdc As Long, ByVal _`
`nPolyFillMode As Long)`

Description   Sets the filling mode for polygons. Refer to Figure 8.15 (located with the definition of the Get-PolyFillMode function) for a description of the two filling modes.

Use with VB   No problem.

Parameter	Type/Description
hdc	Long—Handle to a device context.
nPolyFillMode	Long—One of the following constants: ALTERNATE: Alternates filling. WINDING: Fills based on drawing direction. Refer to Figure 8.15 for details.

Return Value   Long—The previous polygon filling mode on success. Zero on error.

Platform   Windows 95, Windows NT, Win16

Example   QuikDraw.vbp

■ SetROP2

VB Declaration   `Declare Function SetROP2& Lib "gdi32" (ByVal hdc As Long, ByVal nDrawMode As _`
`Long)`

Description   Sets the drawing mode for the specified device context. This is identical to the VB DrawMode property.

Use with VB	No problem. This function sets the DrawMode property when used with the device context for a VB form or picture control.

Parameter	Type/Description
hdc	Long—Handle to a device context.
nDrawMode	Long—New drawing mode for the device context. Refer to Table 8.11 in the Function Reference entry for the GetROP2 function for legal values.

Return Value	Long—The previous drawing mode on success. Zero on error.
Platform	Windows 95, Windows NT, Win16
Example	Viewport.vbp in Chapter 7

■ SetWinMetaFileBits

VB Declaration	`Declare Function SetWinMetaFileBits& Lib "gdi32" (ByVal cbBuffer As Long, _` `lpbBuffer As Byte, ByVal hdcRef As Long, lpmfp As METAFILEPICT)`
Description	Converts a standard Windows metafile into an enhanced metafile.
Use with VB	No problem.

Parameter	Type/Description
cbBuffer	Long—The length of the lpbBuffer array.
lpbBuffer	Byte—The first entry in a byte array containing the standard metafile data. This data is obtained using the GetMetaFileBitsEx or GetWinMetaFileBitsEx functions.
hdcRef	Long—A reference device context used to determine the original format and resolution of the metafile. May be zero, in which case the display resolution is used.
lpmfp	METAFILEPICT—A structure defining additional reference information for the metafile. Refer to Appendix B for additional information. May be NULL (pass using an alias that defines this parameter ByVal As Long) to assume the MM_ANISOTROPIC mapping mode on the current display).

Return Value	Long—A handle to an enhanced metafile (memory based) on success. Zero on error. Sets GetLastError.
Platform	Windows 95, Windows NT

■ StrokeAndFillPath

VB Declaration	`Declare Function StrokeAndFillPath& Lib "gdi32" (ByVal hdc As Long)`
Description	Closes any open regions on the path for the specified device context. Draws the outline of a path using the current pen and fills the path using the current brush.

Use with VB	No problem.	

Parameter	Type/Description
hdc	Long—A device context containing a path to stroke and fill.

Return Value Long—TRUE (nonzero) on success, zero on error. Sets GetLastError to the following values:

1. ERROR_CAN_NOT_COMPLETE
2. ERROR_INVALID_PARAMETER
3. ERROR_NOT_ENOUGH_MEMORY

Platform Windows 95, Windows NT

Comments The path is destroyed upon completion of this function.

Example Path.vbp

■ StrokePath

VB Declaration `Declare Function StrokePath& Lib "gdi32" (ByVal hdc As Long)`

Description Draws the outline of a path using the current pen. Open figures are not closed by this function.

Use with VB No problem.

Parameter	Type/Description
hdc	Long—A device context containing a path to stroke and fill.

Return Value Long—Nonzero on success, zero on failure. Sets GetLastError to the following values:

1. ERROR_CAN_NOT_COMPLETE
2. ERROR_INVALID_PARAMETER
3. ERROR_NOT_ENOUGH_MEMORY

Platform Windows 95, Windows NT

Example Path.vbp

■ UnrealizeObject

VB Declaration `Declare Function UnrealizeObject& Lib "gdi32" (ByVal hObject As Long)`

Description This function must be called for a brush object before selecting it into a device context if the brush origin is to be changed using the SetBrushOrg function. Refer to "Brushes," earlier in this chapter.

Use with VB	No problem.	
	Parameter	**Type/Description**
	hObject	Long—Handle to a brush or logical palette.

Return Value Long—TRUE (nonzero) on success, zero on error. Sets GetLastError.

Platform Windows 95, Windows NT, Win16
Windows NT performs automatic tracking of brush origins; thus this function has no effect on Windows NT if the object is a brush. It returns TRUE in that case.

■ WidenPath

VB Declaration `Declare Function WidenPath& Lib "gdi32" (ByVal hdc As Long)`

Description Redefines the currently selected path based on the width of the selected pen. For example, if the path describes a closed rectangle that is 10x10 pixels, and it is drawn with a pen that is 3 pixels wide, the widened path will consist of a rectangle that is 12x12.

Use with VB	No problem.	
	Parameter	**Type/Description**
	hdc	Long—Handle to a device context containing a path.

Return Value Long—Nonzero on success, zero on failure. Sets GetLastError to the following values:

1. ERROR_CAN_NOT_COMPLETE

2. ERROR_INVALID_PARAMETER

3. ERROR_NOT_ENOUGH_MEMORY

Platform Windows 95, Windows NT

Comments All Bézier curves are converted into line segments by this function.

9

Bitmaps, Icons, and Raster Operations

THIS CHAPTER DESCRIBES THE WINDOWS API FUNCTIONS THAT DEAL with image areas on raster devices, specifically, the use of bitmaps and icons. Techniques for using raster operations to combine bitmaps or merge a bitmap onto an existing image are described along with a summary of the available raster operations. The chapter includes an example project called Puzzle, which implements a scrambled tiling game with any bitmap. Puzzle illustrates the creation of bitmaps, how they may be copied and stretched, and the use of device-independent bitmaps. Other samples include a program that allows you to view the stock bitmaps and icons included in Windows, and a program that lets you experiment with different raster operations.

Unlike those in other chapters, most of these sample programs require an understanding of concepts that are discussed throughout the chapter; thus the examples have all been placed at the end of the chapter instead of interspersed throughout.

Visual Basic 4.0 added a new method called PaintPicture to forms, picture controls, and the printer object. This method goes a long way toward addressing the problem of image manipulation in Visual Basic—an area which was sorely neglected in previous versions of VB. The PaintPicture method will handle most situations where you wish to transfer an image from one form or picture control to another or to the printer. However, the API approach is still preferred (or necessary) for tasks that go beyond the ability of the PaintPicture method, including:

- Copying images from windows other than forms or picture controls

- Copying images from the screen (screen capture) or other applications

- Pattern fills and pattern brushes

- Obtaining maximum performance (BitBlt is faster than PaintPicture)

- Complex masking and bitmap rotation/skewing

- Direct manipulation of bitmap palettes

- Direct manipulation (using code) of bitmap data

- And, of course, using many of the other Win32 APIs that work directly with device-independent bitmap data or bitmap objects

In other words, the trade-off is the same one that you face with any other decision to use API functions with Visual Basic: Visual Basic provides ease of use; direct API access provides maximum power, performance, and flexibility. The nice thing about Visual Basic is that it allows you to choose the balance between these trade-offs for each situation.

Bitmaps

All Windows display screens and a great many printers are *raster devices*. On a raster device, an image is made up of multiple scan lines and individual pixels may be accessed. Windows also supports non-raster devices such as plotters, but most of the operations described in this chapter will not work with those devices. The GetDeviceCaps API function described in Chapter 4 may be used to determine which raster operations a device supports.

The information that follows in this chapter focuses on display devices, as they are the most common raster devices and the devices on which raster operations are most often applied. Keep in mind, however, that most printers are also raster devices, and that color printers often look, from the programmer's point of view, just like a display device. Virtually everything that follows with regard to display devices can be applied directly to these types of printers.

A bitmap is a set of data that represents an image in a form compatible with a raster device. Under Windows, this set of data is contained in a Windows object that is called a bitmap object. In order to understand the different types of bitmaps and how they are used, it is necessary to examine how raster devices represent pixels.

Displaying Pixels

A pixel is the smallest unit that can be displayed by a raster device. On a monochrome display or printer, a pixel can be represented by a single bit of data. Typically a monochrome device will consist of a single array of bytes where each bit represents one pixel. Bits that are set to 1 will usually be displayed in white (or the current background color); bits that are set to 0 will be black (or the current foreground color). An example of a monochrome bitmap is shown in Figure 9.1.

On a color device, each pixel requires multiple bits. Table 9.1 shows the number of bits per pixel and number of colors available on various Windows devices.

Table 9.1   **Color Support in Windows**

Bits per Pixel	Number of Colors	Typical Device
1	2	Monochrome graphics, monochrome printers
4	16	Standard VGA
8	256	256-color VGA
16	32,768 or 65,535	32K- or 64K-color super VGA
24	2^{24}	TRUE 24-bit color devices

Figure 9.1

Monochrome bitmap
example

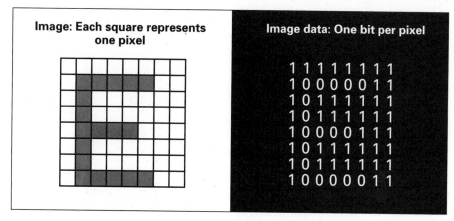

Color Planes and Device Palettes

A color on a video display is generated by combining shading of the colors red, green, and blue. The total number of possible colors depends on the number of shades of each of those primary colors. On a 24-bit color device, each primary color has eight bits. The total number of possible colors is thus $2^8 * 2^8 * 2^8$ or 16,777,216.

On a true 24-bit color device, each pixel has 24 bits; thus, the device can display all 16,777,216 colors simultaneously. The disadvantage of this technique is that it requires huge amounts of memory. For example, a 1,024 x 768 pixel 24-bit display requires $1024 * 768 * 3 = 2.36$ megabytes of video memory! One common compromise is to use a 15-bit color card that provides 32,768 colors. In this case each of the primary colors uses five bits to provide 32 shades. Since memory hardware is typically organized in 16-bit groups on these types of cards, many of them add the extra bit to one of the colors in order to support 65,535 different colors.

Until recently, most people used standard or super VGA cards that use either four or eight bits per pixel. These cards are known as palette-based devices. The contents of the pixel do not directly determine the shadings of the primary colors that determine the pixel color. Instead, the pixel value is an index into an array of 24-bit values on the video card itself. Each entry in this palette array defines the color to use for the specified pixel value. This makes it possible for a device to select from millions of possible colors, even though it can display only a limited number of those colors simultaneously. Figure 9.2 illustrates how the color for each pixel is determined for the different types of display devices.

Figure 9.2

How color output is
determined for
different devices

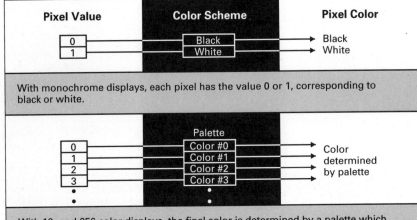

With monochrome displays, each pixel has the value 0 or 1, corresponding to black or white.

With 16- and 256-color displays, the final color is determined by a palette which is either user-defined, or defined by the system. Each entry in the palette is a 24-bit color. The pixel value on a 16-bit display ranges from 0 to 15, on a 256-color display from 0 to 255. The pixel value determines which entry in the palette to use to determine the actual color for the pixel.

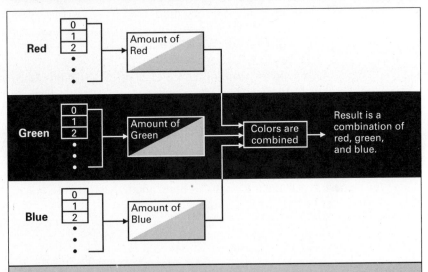

With 15-bit or 24-bit pixels, the bits are divided into groups of 5 or 8 bits. Each group specifies the level of the red, green, and blue colors in the final pixel value. There is no palette–the final colors are determined entirely by the pixel value. You can work with a display that uses 5 bits per pixel as if it were a device that uses 8 bits per pixel and just sets the lowest three bits to zero. Thus, as far as a Windows programmer is concerned, there is no difference between 15- or 16-bit color hardware and 24-bit color hardware.

Pixel Values

Consider this statement that summarizes the previous section: The number of possible colors that a device supports depends directly on the number of bits that it uses to represent a pixel.

Another way of saying this is that on any given device a pixel can take on a certain range of values. On a monochrome display, each pixel can have the value 0 or 1. On a 4-bit display, each pixel can have the value 0 to 15. On an 8-bit display, 0 to 255, and so on. In other words, every pixel has a numeric value.

As you see in Figure 9.2, the pixel value does not always directly set the output color. On displays with fewer than 15 bits per pixel, the pixel value represents an entry into a color table (palette) that contains the actual color to use for that picture value. On displays with 15 bits or more per pixel, the pixel value directly sets the output color.

If this explanation seems to be a bit belabored, it is for a good reason, as it introduces a concept that is fundamental to working with bitmaps and raster images in general.

If a pixel has an associated numeric value, then it is reasonable to expect that you can perform numeric and logical operations on pixel values.

As you will soon see, the implications of this concept are profound and the applications far reaching.

Display Configurations

It is one thing to say that a display device has a certain number of bits for each pixel. It is another to figure out how those bits are organized. The bits that are used for each pixel may be configured in a number of different ways depending on the device. For example, in a VGA card the bits are divided into four different planes. Each plane is an array of bits in a particular color. Figure 9.3 illustrates a four-bit pixel in both 4-plane and 4-bit configurations.

The left portion of Figure 9.3 shows four planes, each of which contains a single bit for each pixel. To read the value of a particular pixel, you read one bit from each plane. However, internally, the data is grouped by plane—all of the data for plane 0 comes before all of the data for plane 1, and so on.

The right part of Figure 9.3 shows a single plane device where each pixel is represented by 4 bits of data. On this type of device, all of the data for a pixel is stored together instead of being spread out among four planes.

Keep in mind that these are only two simple examples of how image memory can be organized—every device is free to set its own internal image format, so the possible bitmap image configurations are endless.

Figure 9.3

Sample display configurations

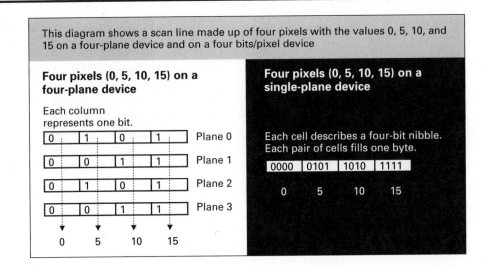

This diagram shows a scan line made up of four pixels with the values 0, 5, 10, and 15 on a four-plane device and on a four bits/pixel device

Four pixels (0, 5, 10, 15) on a four-plane device

Each column represents one bit.

0	1	0	1	Plane 0
0	0	1	1	Plane 1
0	1	0	1	Plane 2
0	0	1	1	Plane 3

0   5   10   15

Four pixels (0, 5, 10, 15) on a single-plane device

Each cell describes a four-bit nibble. Each pair of cells fills one byte.

| 0000 | 0101 | 1010 | 1111 |

0   5   10   15

The Two Types of Bitmaps

A bitmap has already been defined as an object in Windows that holds an image. When the internal format of the image depends on the configuration of the device on which it is used, the bitmap is referred to as a *device-dependent bitmap*.

As long as you are copying images on a display from one location to another, device-dependent bitmaps are fine. But what happens when you want to transfer an image between two different devices, say, between a display screen and a printer? Or if you want to save an image in a standard file format that can be read successfully on systems that do not have the same display device? What if you want to read and write the bitmap data directly under program control? With device-dependent bitmaps you would have to know detailed information about each type of hardware that your program supports and figure out how its bitmaps are configured in order to determine where each of the individual bits of each pixel is located within the bitmap data—a nightmare, to say the least. This also defeats one of the primary advantages of Windows, which is that it provides a device-independent way of working with graphic output. The only device-dependent bitmap that has a standard format is a monochrome bitmap. This is scant consolation in a world that has switched almost completely to color displays, and is rapidly switching to color printing as well.

To address these problems, Windows 3.0 introduced the concept of device-independent bitmaps—a combination of standard data structures that define how a device-independent bitmap should be stored, and a set of API functions that manipulate these structures. For example, it is possible to create a device-independent bitmap that has a full 24-bit color image, yet display or print it to any raster device knowing that Windows will render the image with the highest quality and best color support possible for the given device. The Windows bitmap file format (.BMP) uses the device-independent bitmap standard, so these bitmaps can be loaded and displayed on any video or printer device so long as a Windows driver exists for it. WIN32 extends the set of device-independent bitmap functions to provide new capabilities and dramatically improve ease of use.

If device-independent bitmaps are so great, why would anyone use device-dependent bitmaps? There is only one reason, but it's a good one. Device-dependent bitmaps are fast—very, very, very fast. That is because all Windows needs to do to move an image with a device-dependent bitmap is to copy memory, an operation called a "Bit Block Transfer" or BitBlt (pronounced *bit-blit*), for short. And since even low cost video cards have on-board hardware that can perform this type of operation, all Windows really needs to do in most cases is send a few commands to the graphic controller telling it how to transfer the image data. It can then continue processing while the graphic card does all the work. With device-independent bitmaps, Windows needs to perform a time-consuming conversion to the format of the device each time the image is displayed.

Now let's take a closer look at these two types of bitmaps.

Device-Dependent Bitmaps

All bitmaps in Windows are device-dependent unless noted otherwise. Generally speaking, a bitmap can only be used with devices that have the same internal configuration. The exception is the monochrome bitmap, which is compatible with all devices.

Windows requires that the data within a bitmap be aligned on a 16-bit or 32-bit boundary. The alignment is dictated by the driver and operating system in use—which is yet another aspect of being device-dependent. Figure 9.4 shows the internal data format of a monochrome bitmap. This is the required format for data buffers used to set or retrieve monochrome bitmap data, and more important, it is the data format used for monochrome data within icon- and device-independent bitmap files. Each scan line for a monochrome bitmap must be aligned on a 16-bit boundary.

Each pixel requires 1 bit of data; thus 8 pixels are grouped together in a single byte. Figure 9.4 shows a bitmap that is 20 pixels across and 5 pixels high. Figure 9.4 also illustrates the requirement that Windows imposes on monochrome bitmaps that each horizontal scan line lie on a 16-bit boundary.

Figure 9.5 shows the internal data format for a 16-color four-plane device-dependent bitmap.

Figure 9.4

Format of a
monochrome device-
dependent bitmap

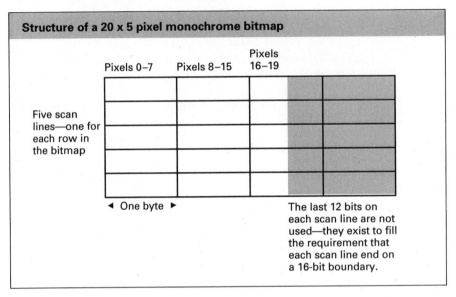

In Figure 9.5, you can see how all of the data for a given scan line is grouped together. This corresponds closely to the bitmap format shown in the upper part of Figure 9.3. Once again there is a boundary requirement.

It is not safe under Windows to make any assumptions regarding the internal data format of a color device-dependent bitmap. This is because each video device may define its own internal format for these bitmaps. Figure 9.5 is presented only as an example for clarification.

Table 9.2 lists functions used to create and load device-dependent bitmaps.

Using Device-Dependent Bitmaps

The key to using device-dependent bitmaps lies in the word "compatible." By and large, the device-dependent functions assume that the bitmaps and device contexts used by the function are compatible with each other—that they share the same internal data organization, number of image planes, bits per pixel, and so forth. The easiest way to make certain that a bitmap is compatible with a particular device context is to use the CreateCompatibleBitmap function. The easiest way to obtain a device context that is compatible with a particular device is to use the CreateCompatibleDC function to obtain a device context that is compatible with an existing device context.

Figure 9.5

Possible organization of a device-dependent bitmap

Structure of a 20 x 4 pixel 16-color device-dependent bitmap (typical VGA format)

	Pixels 0–7	Pixels 8–15	Pixels 16–19	
Four scan lines on the first color plane				
Four scan lines on the second color plane				
Four scan lines on the third color plane				
Four scan lines on the fourth color plane				

◄ One byte ►

The last 12 bits on each scan line are not used—they exist to fill the requirement that each scan line end on a 16- or 32-bit boundary.

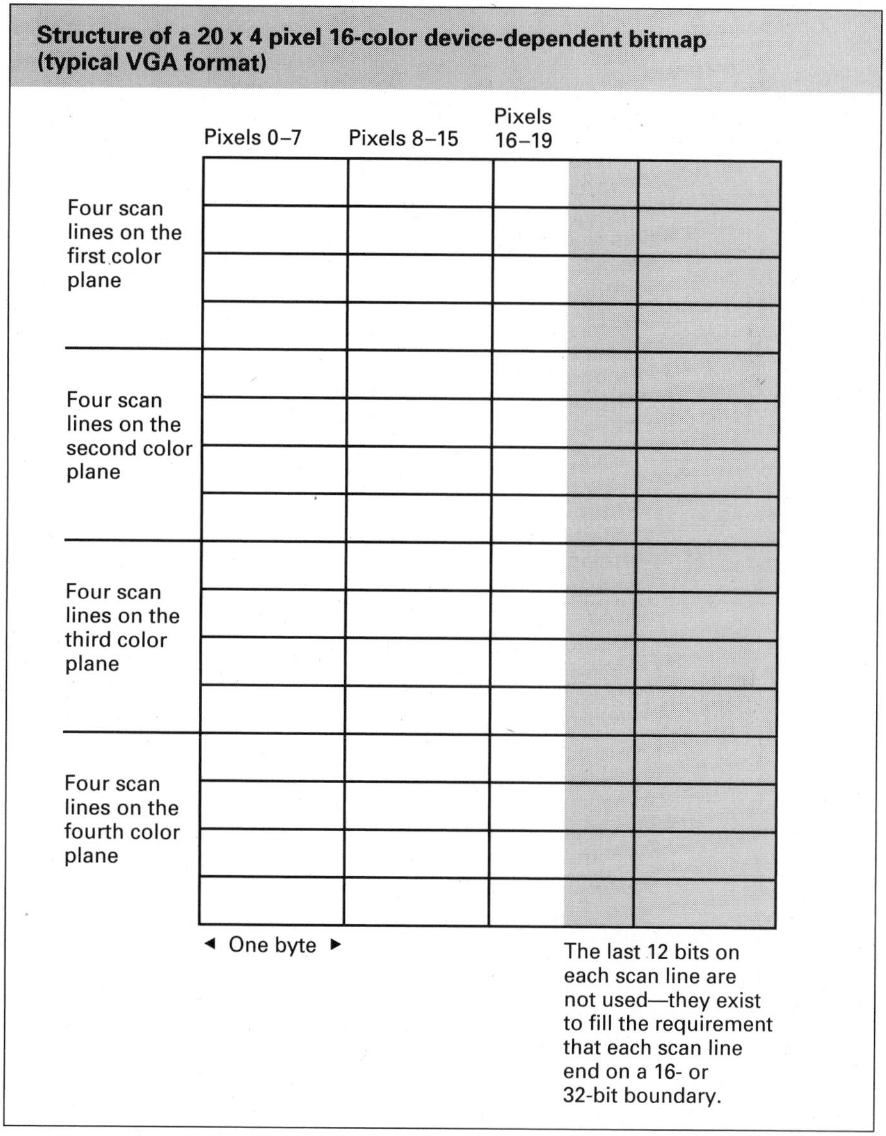

Table 9.2   **Device-Dependent Bitmap Functions**

Function	Description
CreateBitmap	Creates a bitmap and optionally initializes bitmap data.
CreateBitmapIndirect	Creates a bitmap based on a BITMAP data structure.
CreateCompatibleBitmap	Creates a bitmap that is compatible with a specified device context.
CreateDiscardableBitmap	Obsolete. Use CreateCompatibleBitmap with Win32.
GetBitmapBits	Retrieves the image data of a bitmap.
GetBitmapDimensionEx	Retrieves the dimensions of a bitmap.
LoadBitmap	Loads a bitmap from a resource file or loads a stock system bitmap.
LoadImage	A general purpose function for loading bitmaps, icons, and cursors.
SetBitmapBits	Sets the bitmap image from a data buffer.
SetBitmapDimensionEx	Sets the dimension of a bitmap.

Bitmaps are GDI objects, and, like other GDI objects, a bitmap may be selected into a device context; however, it may only be selected into a memory device context. There is a logical reason for this. A bitmap represents the image area of a device. A display screen or printer already has an image area defined—it is the physical screen or page. A memory device context simulates a device in memory. The memory device context provides the interface to access the simulated device. The bitmap provides a block of memory that represents the device surface. It is always necessary to select a bitmap into a memory device context before drawing into it—if you wish to actually generate an image. Otherwise the drawing operations will have no image space to draw on.

Consider this example: Let's say that you want to create a complex drawing, but you don't want to display all of the drawing steps on the screen. Ideally you would like to create a hidden drawing in the background which can be transferred quickly to a window in one operation.

To do this, you need to allocate an area in memory where you can create the image. This block of memory must match the internal data format of the display device in order to allow it to be copied quickly using the BitBlt operation. In other words, the bitmap must be compatible with the display device. This block of memory is the bitmap, and it can be created using the CreateCompatibleBitmap function. Windows allocates the memory and internal data structures for this bitmap object and provides you with a handle to the bitmap.

Now you have a bitmap in memory—how can you draw to it? The answer is clear: All drawing in Windows requires that you use a device context. Because you are drawing to a bitmap in memory, you need to create a memory device context—a device context that is compatible with the display driver, but which is able to draw into memory instead of the screen. The CreateCompatibleDC function creates this type of device context. When you select the compatible bitmap into the compatible device context, you have effectively created an image area in memory that simulates the display. You can draw into it and perform any operation that you could perform on the actual screen. More important, since this simulated device is compatible with the display, you can BitBlt images between the memory bitmap and the screen.

When you no longer need a bitmap, it is important to delete it using the DeleteObject API function to free the system resources and memory that it occupies. You must also use DeleteDC to destroy any device contexts that you created.

A bitmap cannot be selected into two different device contexts at the same time.

Windows provides a number of functions to transfer images on a device, or from one device to another. These functions are described in Table 9.3.

Table 9.3   **Bitmap Transfer Functions**

Function	Description
BitBlt	Bit block transfer. Transfers an image area from one area to another.
PatBlt	Pattern block transfer. Fills an image area based on a specified pattern (as represented by a brush).
GetStretchBltMode	Determines the mechanism by which Windows deletes lines or pixels when stretching takes place.
MaskBlt	Masked block transfer. Transfers an image with the aid of a mask and sophisticated raster operations.
PlgBltP	Parallelogram block transfer. Allows you to stretch, distort, and rotate an image.
SetStretchBltMode	Sets the mechanism by which Windows deletes lines or pixels when stretching takes place.
StretchBlt	Stretch block transfer. Transfers an image area from one area to another, stretching it in the process.

Since bitmaps are device-dependent objects, it is usually not possible to use these functions to transfer an image between devices that are not compatible with each other. In other words, it is rarely possible to use BitBlt to transfer an image directly from the display surface onto a printer. Windows supports device-independent bitmaps that can be used for interdevice transfers. They are described later in this chapter.

You can use the BitBlt function to move images around the screen or to stretch bitmap images.

In order to copy a bitmap to the display surface, you must first select it into a memory device context that is compatible with the display. You can then use the BitBlt or StretchBlt function to copy the image from the memory device context to the display device context. The Puzzle example program in this chapter shows how this is done.

Color Conversions

For accurate color conversions when transferring images between devices, it is necessary to use device-independent bitmaps. However, the BitBlt and StretchBlt functions do support conversions to and from monochrome bitmaps. To do this they use the foreground color, which is set by the SetText-Color function described in Chapter 11, and the background color, which is set by the SetBkColor function described in Chapter 8. (The foreground and background colors also correspond to the Visual Basic forecolor and back-color properties for picture controls and forms.)

When converting from color to monochrome, all pixels that match the current background color are set to white, and all other pixels are set to black.

When converting from monochrome to color, white pixels are set to the current background color and black pixels are set to the foreground color.

Using Bitmaps with Visual Basic

As GDI objects, bitmaps can be used with Visual Basic in much the same way as the drawing objects described in Chapter 8. As before, be sure to restore a VB device context to its original state when you are finished using it.

The form and picture control Picture and Image properties return bitmaps that may be used with Windows API functions. The Puzzle example program takes advantage of this to store a bitmap in a picture control, which it can then access when needed.

When you use BitBlt or a similar function to display a bitmap on a Visual Basic form or control, you are simply changing the display. This does not actually change the picture property of the control. You cannot assign a bitmap, icon, or metafile handle directly to the picture property of a control, though there are some third party tools that allow you to perform this type of indirect property access.

If the AutoRedraw property of a picture control or form is set to TRUE, the device context for the control references a memory device context that is owned by the control. Using BitBlt to draw into this device context does change the current contents of the control, but you will need to use the Refresh method to inform the form or control to redisplay its memory bitmap. In this, bitmap functions are identical to any other GDI drawing function.

Device-Independent Bitmaps

The key to understanding device-independent bitmaps (DIBs) lies in their description: A combination of standard data structures that define how a device-independent bitmap should be stored, and a set of API functions that manipulate these structures.

A device-independent bitmap is not a Windows object. It does not have a handle and is not created or managed by Windows. It is the responsibility of the programmer to create and manage the various data structures that make up the parts of a device-independent bitmap. Before doing that, however, it is necessary to provide a brief introduction to a subject that will be covered in depth in Chapter 15—the allocation and management of data structures.

Dynamically Sized Structures

There are several key issues to keep in mind when working with structures and arrays of structures, beginning with the nature of structures themselves.

A structure, or user-defined type, is a sequence of variables in memory. In other words, every structure has a location (also known as an address) in memory. This address has a 32-bit value. So, ultimately, every DIB function that requires a pointer to a structure is actually looking for a 32-bit address.

There are two ways to pass a structure address to a function. The first method, and the one that has been used up until now through most of the samples in this book, is to define the parameters to the function declaration in the form: *mystruct As StructureType* or *mystruct As Any*. This declaration passes the address of a Visual Basic structure to the API function.

Now what if, by some mechanism, you could load the memory address of a structure into a long variable? In that case, you could achieve exactly the same effect by defining the parameters to a function declaration as: *ByVal mystructaddress As Long*. It is extremely important that you understand the distinction between passing a structure by reference, and passing the address of a structure by value. One common error is to load an address into a long variable and pass it by reference. The result is that you pass the address of the long variable itself rather than the address of the structure.

So how do you obtain a memory address for a structure? The easiest way is to use the agGetAddressForObject function that is part of the APIGID32.DLL library that comes with this book. The parameter for this function is defined *As Any*. As you know, passing an object by reference to a parameter defined As Any passes the memory address of that object to the function. agGetAddressForObject simply returns that value as a long result.

But there is a catch, which represents a change from Visual Basic 3.0. You can't pass the structure itself to agGetAddressForObject and use the resulting memory address. Instead, you must pass the first variable in the structure to the function. There is a reason for this, and cases where this technique requires additional effort on the part of the programmer; however, the important thing to know is that it does work for the DIB structures that are covered in this chapter. The reasons for this change and pitfalls that you will face dealing with it are covered in Chapter 15.

Bytes and Buffers

One of the biggest changes between Visual Basic 3.0 and later versions of Visual Basic is that you will be using byte arrays instead of strings to hold information. This avoids Unicode conversion problems (a subject for Chapter 15). In some cases, however, you will be using memory blocks that are allocated directly using the Win32 API.

With regard to byte arrays, you can pass the memory address of the start of the array to a function by passing the first element of the array by reference. This is why some API functions that expect memory buffers have a parameter defined as *mybuffer As Byte*. Once again note the distinction: without the ByVal, you are passing the memory address of the byte (or start of a byte array). With a ByVal, you are passing the contents of the byte.

When working with API-allocated memory buffers, you will always have the memory address in a long variable, thus you will pass it using the *ByVal As Long* declaration.

As you've seen, there are three ways to reference memory with regard to DIBs: as individual structures, as byte arrays, and as memory buffers. In each case, all that changes is the way that you reference the information—the organization of data within the memory buffer can be identical. Why is this important? Because when working with DIB functions, you will need to copy information to and from structures, arrays, and memory buffers, and to combine structures together into larger structures. The main mechanism for copying data used in this book is the agCopyData function which accepts two memory addresses and copies data between the two locations specified. This is shown in Figure 9.6. Note the different uses of calling by reference and calling by value depending on the data type in use.

For example, what do you do if an API function allocates a block of memory for you that contains a structure? You could calculate the location of each field within the buffer and read them one at a time. But an easier approach is to copy that part of the memory block that contains the structure into a Visual Basic user-defined type and access the variables using the standard VB syntax. If necessary, the contents of the structure can be copied back to the memory buffer when done. This approach is used frequently throughout this book.

There is another reason to use byte arrays and memory buffers instead of structures. In some cases, the Windows API defines a structure where the exact size of the structure is unknown. For example, the BITMAPINFO structure that you will read about shortly contains a color palette. The size of this color palette

Figure 9.6

Three ways to access memory, and methods for copying between types

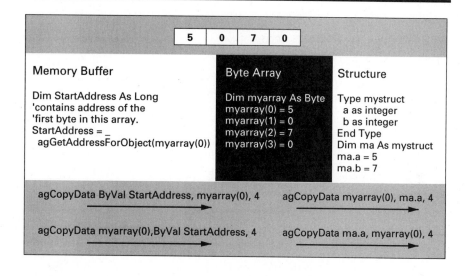

can vary from two entries (monochrome DIBs) to 256 entries (256-color display). For 24-bit color DIBs, the size is zero—there is no color table. In cases like these, it is sometimes easiest to dynamically allocate a buffer to hold the structure, or part of the structure. You will see several examples of this as well.

This concludes the introduction to dynamically sized structures, pointers, and memory management. Purists will note that we have conveniently dodged the issues of structure alignment, Unicode conversions, temporary buffers, and so on. Those issues and more will all be covered in depth in Chapter 15.

DIB Structures

Device-independent bitmaps (DIBs) are used to hold images that are compatible with any raster device. They accomplish this by providing a standard format for the bitmap data and by including within the DIB the definitions of the colors represented by that data. DIBs may be defined as having two colors (monochrome), 16 colors, or 256 colors, or they may provide true 24-bit color support.

Device-independent bitmaps actually consist of two separate data structures followed by the actual data. The BITMAPINFOHEADER structure defines the size and type of the DIB. It also indicates the type of compression in effect and the number of colors. This structure is shown below and is described in detail in Appendix B.

```
Type BITMAPINFOHEADER '40 bytes
    biSize As Long
```

```
    biWidth As Long
    biHeight As Long
    biPlanes As Integer
    biBitCount As Integer
    biCompression As Long
    biSizeImage As Long
    biXPelsPerMeter As Long
    biYPelsPerMeter As Long
    biClrUsed As Long
    biClrImportant As Long
End Type
```

The biSize field will always be set to 40 (the size of the structure). The bi-Planes field is always 1—device-independent bitmaps are always formatted as a single plane. The biBitCount field specifies the number of bits per pixel.

The biHeight field indicates the height of the bitmap and the internal coordinate system of the bitmap. By default, device-independent bitmaps set the origin at the lower-left corner of the bitmap. This can be inconvenient when using typical window coordinates that place the origin at the upper-left corner of the window. If biHeight is negative, the DIB origin is set to the upper-left. This is demonstrated in the DIBSect.vbp sample program later in the chapter. The BITMAPINFO structure consists of the BITMAPINFO-HEADER structure followed by a color table. The number of entries in the color table matches the number of colors supported by the DIB unless the DIB is a 24-bit color bitmap, in which case the color table is not present. Thus the size of a BITMAPINFO structure will vary depending on the type of DIB.

The BITMAPINFO structure is defined as follows in API32.TXT:

```
Type BITMAPINFO
        bmiHeader As BITMAPINFOHEADER
        bmiColors As RGBQUAD
End Type
```

But you will never use the structure as shown here! You can redefine the structure to use the appropriate color table size, for example:

```
Type BITMAPINFm016
        bmiHeader As BITMAPINFOHEADER
        bmiColors(15) As RGBQUAD
End Type
```

would be a good definition for a 16-color DIB. Note that the maximum array index is one fewer than the desired number of entries to take into account the fact that Visual Basic arrays start with entry zero. Alternatively, you can use the buffer approach described earlier.

The BITMAPINFO structure is the first part of a DIB. The second part consists of the bitmap data itself.

The number of bits for each pixel depends on the color configuration for the DIB. For 2-, 16-, and 256-color DIBs, the pixel describes an index into the color table that contains the color for that pixel. For 24-bit color, each pixel consists of 24 bits (three bytes) that contain the actual RGB color to use.

The data for each scan line in a DIB must be aligned to a 32-bit boundary. Figure 9.7 shows the structure of a 16-color device-independent bitmap.

The color table represents the desired palette to use with this device-independent bitmap. Each entry in the DIB color table defines the ideal color to use for pixels that have the value corresponding to the position of the entry. Windows will choose the closest available color when copying the DIB to the device. Some of the functions that use device-independent bitmaps also support palette relative color tables, in which case each entry in the color table is a 16-bit index into the currently selected logical palette for the device that the DIB is being rendered on. This is typically used to create a DIB based on an existing logical palette.

The data area is structured as a single plane bitmap with 4 bits per pixel. Note that unlike device-dependent bitmaps, DIBs require that scan lines end on 32-bit boundaries.

Several of the device-independent bitmap API functions allow you to keep only a portion of the bitmap data in memory at once. In these cases, the function allows you to specify the first horizontal line and the total number of lines in the DIB data array. These lines, which consist of a row of pixels the width of the DIB, are often referred to as scan lines.

Figure 9.8 summarizes the structure of a device-independent bitmap. Note that it is divided into two parts. Many API functions that work with DIBs require two separate memory addresses—one for the BITMAPINFO structure, and one for the data area.

When the data area of a DIB follows immediately after the BITMAP-INFO structure, the device-independent bitmap is called a "packed DIB." Packed DIBs are sometimes used by API functions, and are the standard way of organizing device-independent bitmaps within files.

As you have seen, device-independent bitmaps are contained in memory buffers—they are not GDI resources. You can create a DIB without using API functions at all.

The Windows BMP bitmap file format consists of a file header followed by a device-independent bitmap, so understanding the structure of a DIB is the first step in reading and writing these files. The Puzzle example that follows later in this chapter demonstrates many of the techniques described here. Additional DIB examples, including a demonstration of how to load a .BMP file directly from disk, are included in the picprint example in Chapter 12.

Win32 also defines a version 4 device-independent bitmap that is identical to a standard DIB except that the BITMAPINFOHEADERstructure is replaced with a BITMAPV4HEADER structure. This structure contains information on the logical color space for which a bitmap is defined. Logical color spaces are used to match colors between different devices.

Figure 9.7

Organization of the data area for a 16-color device-independent bitmap

---

Structure of a 6 x 5 pixel 16-color device-independent bitmap (DIB)

Color table for the DIB

Blue	Green	Red	Set to zero

Sixteen entries in the DIB color table

Each column represents one byte

Data for the DIB

Pixels 0 & 1	Pixels 2 & 3	Pixels 4 & 5	
Pix 0 : Pix 1			

Five scan lines—one for each row in the bitmap

Each columm represents one byte

The last byte on each scan line is not used in this case—it exists to fill the requirement that each scan line end on a 32-bit boundary.

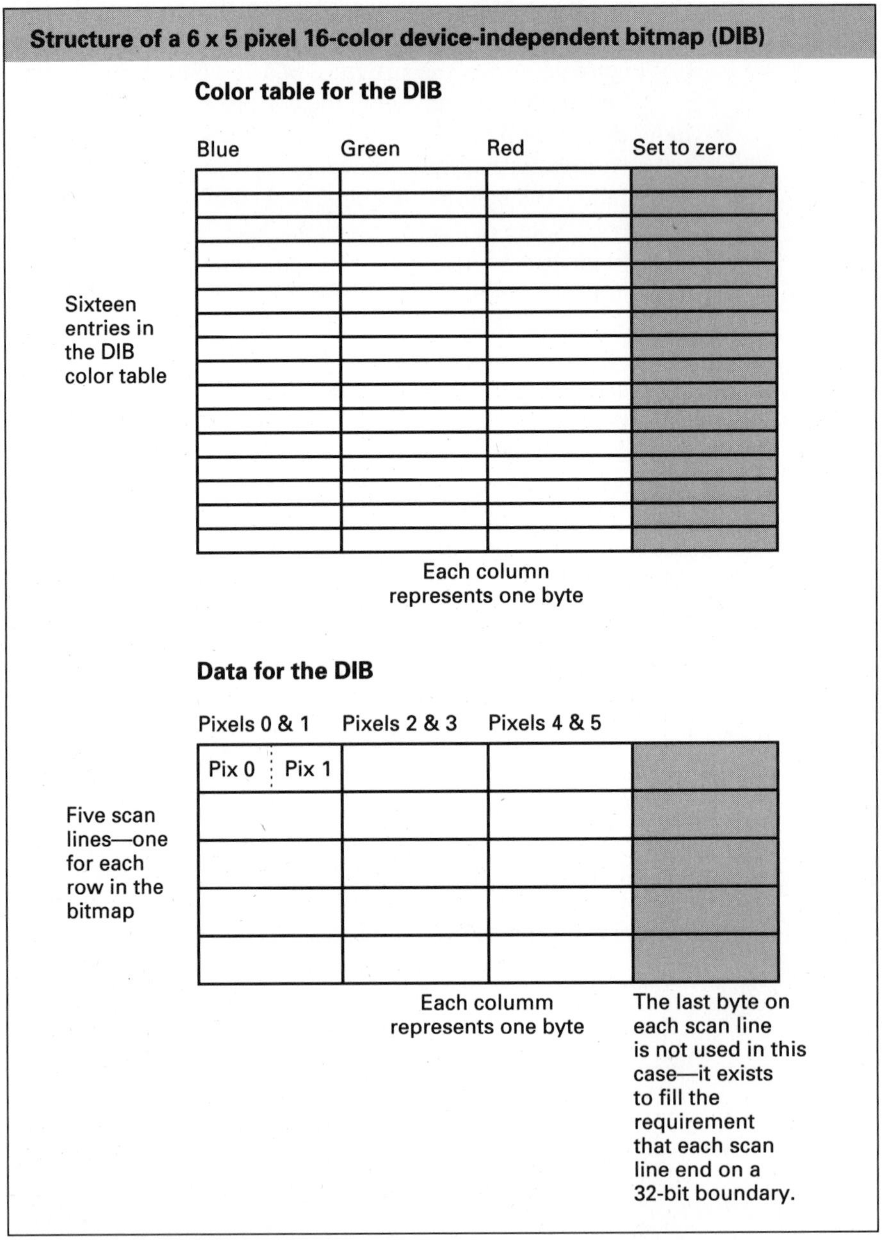

Figure 9.8

Organization of a device-independent bitmap in memory

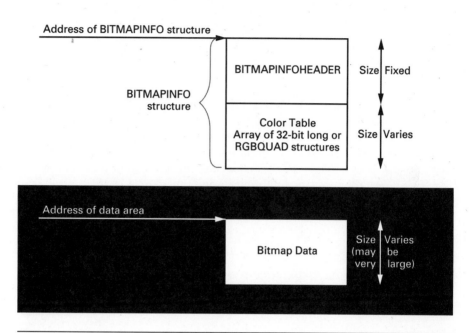

Address of BITMAPINFO structure

BITMAPINFO structure

BITMAPINFOHEADER — Size Fixed

Color Table
Array of 32-bit long or
RGBQUAD structures — Size Varies

Address of data area

Bitmap Data — Size Varies
(may be
very large)

DIBSections

As you have seen, device-independent bitmaps are more of a way to organize data than an actual Windows object. Win16 provided only a few functions to work with device-independent bitmaps—one to render a DIB on a device, one to convert a DIB into a device-dependent bitmap, and one to generate a device-independent bitmap from a device-dependent bitmap. If you wanted to use GDI graphic commands to create a DIB, you would typically create a regular device-dependent bitmap and convert it to a DIB. It was also exceedingly slow and difficult to work with the actual bitmap data, since the GetBitMapBits function retrieves data in a device-dependent format.

Win32 addressed these limitations in a way that is so elegant that it's almost frightening. It defines a new type of Windows object called a DIBSection. You create a DIBSection object in much the same way that you create a bitmap, except that you can also specify a buffer in memory to store the DIB format bitmap data for the bitmap. Alternatively, you can have Windows allocate a buffer for you.

This object can be selected directly into a device context in exactly the same way as a regular device-dependent bitmap. Once selected into a DC, you can draw into it using standard GDI graphic commands. At the same time, you can directly read and write the actual bitmap data in memory. The DIBSect sample program shows how you can mix direct memory access with GDI graphic commands to work on a DIBSection bitmap.

As nice as this may sound, when combined with other Win32 features the implications are even more far reaching. For example, you can specify that the memory buffer to use for the DIBSection be a file mapping object—a kind of shared block of memory or disk file which will be covered in Chapters 13 and 14. This means that you can create and work with bitmaps that are actually on disk, making it possible to work with huge bitmaps without loading them into memory. You can also create bitmaps that can be operated on by several applications at once (though this requires extreme caution).

Even though DIBSection objects map into device-independent bitmaps, they are true GDI objects and thus should be deleted when no longer needed.

Table 9.4 lists the API functions that are used to manipulate device-independent bitmaps.

Table 9.4   **Device-Independent Bitmap Functions**

Function	Description
CreateDIBitmap	Creates a device-dependent bitmap based on a DIB.
CreateDIBSection	Creates a DIBSection object.
GetDIBColorTable	Retrieves color table information for a DIBSection object.
GetDIBits	Loads a device-independent bitmap with data from a device-dependent bitmap.
SetDIBColorTable	Sets the color table for a DIBSection object.
SetDIBits	Sets the image in a device-dependent bitmap with data from a DIB.
SetDIBitsToDevice	Sets data from a DIB directly to a device. This can be used to transfer data directly from a DIB to the screen or to a printer.
StretchDIBits	Sets data from a DIB to a device context, stretching the image as requested. Some devices allow this function to be used to set data directly to the output device. Use the GetDeviceCaps function to determine if this is the case.

Icons and Cursors

An icon is a small bitmap that has the unique capability of allowing any pixel to be not only one of the bitmap colors, but also the screen or inverted screen color. Icons in Windows 3.x are generally 32 x 32 pixels in size, but 16 x 16- and 64 x 64-pixel icons are supported under Win32 and are quite common under Windows 95 and NT 4.0.

An icon actually contains two separate bitmaps. The first bitmap may be monochrome or color, and it contains an image that will be combined with the display image using the exclusive-OR operation. It is referred to as the XOR bitmap. The second bitmap is a monochrome bitmap called the AND bitmap, which contains a mask that will be ANDed with the display image before it is combined with the XOR bitmap. Figure 9.9 shows how the two bitmaps in an icon combine to form an image when the bitmap is drawn.

Figure 9.9
How Windows draws
an icon or cursor

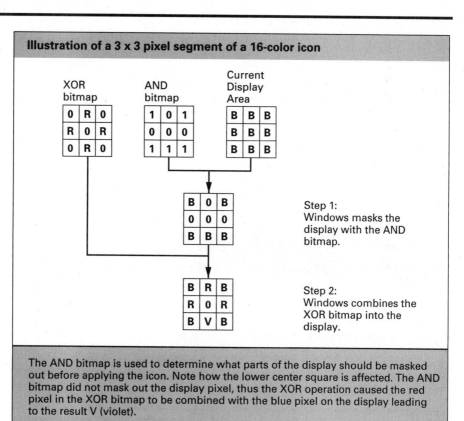

Illustration of a 3 x 3 pixel segment of a 16-color icon

The AND bitmap is used to determine what parts of the display should be masked out before applying the icon. Note how the lower center square is affected. The AND bitmap did not mask out the display pixel, thus the XOR operation caused the red pixel in the XOR bitmap to be combined with the blue pixel on the display leading to the result V (violet).

In Figure 9.9, first the AND bitmap is combined with the current display area. Display pixels that correspond to a zero in the AND bitmap are cleared—which means that the final image will be identical to the value of the pixel in the XOR bitmap. Display pixels that correspond to a one in the AND bitmap are kept and exclusive ORed with the XOR bitmap to produce the final image.

A cursor is internally identical to an icon except that it also has two fields that define the "hot-spot"—the point on the cursor that represents its exact location. Most of the functions that work with icons will work with cursors as well.

Unlike bitmaps, icons are not GDI objects; they are USER objects, meaning that they are part of the USER subsystem that is responsible for managing windows. You must use the DestroyIcon and DestroyCursor functions to destroy icon and cursor objects when they are no longer needed. Do not destroy stock system icons retrieved using the LoadIcon or LoadImage API functions. Because they are USER objects, it is possible to share icons and cursors among applications. Refer to the CopyIcon function description for more information on icon ownership.

Table 9.5 lists the API functions that are used to work with icons and to create cursors. API functions that describe how cursors are used are discussed in Chapter 6.

Table 9.5 **Icon and Cursor API Functions**

Function	Description
CopyCursor	Use CopyIcon.
CopyIcon	Copies an icon.
CreateCursor	Creates a cursor.
CreateIcon	Creates an icon.
CreatIconIndirect	Creates an icon based on an ICONINFO structure.
DestroyCursor	Destroys a cursor.
DestroyIcon	Destroys an icon.
DrawIcon	Draws an icon.
DrawIconEx	Draws an icon with additional options.
ExtractAssociatedIcon	Loads an icon that is in or associated with a specified file.
ExtractIcon	Loads an icon from an executable file or DLL.
GetIconInfo	Retrieves information about an icon.
LoadCursor	Loads a cursor from a resource file, or loads a stock system cursor. Resource files are described in Chapter 15.
LoadCursorFromFile	Creates a cursor by reading a standard cursor (.cur) or animated cursor (.ani) file.
LoadIcon	Loads an icon from a resource file, or loads a stock system icon. Resource files are described in Chapter 15.

Icons and cursors are also commonly loaded from resource files. Resources are discussed in Chapter 15.

Raster Operations

When you consider transferring a bitmap onto a device context, you might think of the simple case where the bitmap is copied to the destination. The value of each bit or pixel on the destination device context is replaced by the corresponding bit in the source bitmap.

But wait a minute! Earlier in the chapter you saw how the state of a pixel, or its value, is actually a numeric value. One can't help but wonder, what would happen if you could perform mathematical and logical operations on those values? What kind of operations would be possible? As it turns out, the BitBlt operation under Windows is not limited to a simple copy of image memory. It can also perform a wide variety of logical operations on the image data as it is being copied.

When it comes to the BitBlt operation, there are three parameters to each image operation. The first is the *source* parameter, a device context that provides access to a bitmap that provides the source image. The *destination* parameter refers to the device context that provides access to a destination bitmap. The third parameter is a *pattern* that is determined by the brush that is selected into the destination device context. For now, we will only be dealing with brushes that describe a solid color—for information on brushes that describe more complex patterns refer back to the discussion on pattern brushes in Chapter 8.

There are four possible operations that can be performed on the three parameters: AND, NOT, OR, and XOR. These operations combine 2 bits to form a result as follows:

```
NOT 0 = 1
NOT 1 = 0
0 AND 0 = 0
0 AND 1 = 0
1 AND 0 = 0
1 AND 1 = 1
0 OR 0 = 0
0 OR 1 = 1
1 OR 0 = 1
1 OR 1 = 1
0 XOR 0 = 0
0 XOR 1 = 1
1 XOR 0 = 1
1 XOR 1 = 0
```

When an operation is performed on pixels, it is performed in parallel on all of the bits in the pixel. For example, if you took a 4-bit pixel with the value 1 and performed the NOT operation on it, you would get NOT 0001 = 1110 = 14. From an image point of view on a 16-color display, a blue pixel would be converted into a light yellow pixel. This can be seen using the ROPTest sample program that follows. First select the SRCCOPY option button and click on the BitBlt command button. The left image will be copied into the destination picture box. Now select the DSTINVERT option button, and click on it several times, watching the yellow and blue rectangles. The SRCCOPY operation performs a simple copy—as a logical operation it can be described as Destination = Source. The DSTINVERT option button inverts the destination—described as the logical operation: Destination = NOT Destination. We could also have used the NOTSRCCOPY function to do the inversion while copying (Destination = NOT Source).

Windows defined a number of standard logical operations as follows:

SRCCOPY	Destination = Source
SRCPAINT	Destination = Source OR Destination
SRCAND	Destination = Source AND Destination
SRCINVERT	Destination = Source XOR Destination
SRCERASE	Destination = Source AND (NOT Destination)
NOTSRCCOPY	Destination = NOT Source
NOTSRCERASE	Destination = (NOT Source) AND (NOT Destination)
MERGECOPY	Destination = Source AND Pattern
MERGEPAINT	Destination = (NOT Source) OR Destination
PATCOPY	Destination = Pattern
PATPAINT	Destination = (NOT Source) OR Pattern OR Destination
PATINVERT	Destination = Pattern XOR Destination
DSTINVERT	Destination = NOT Destination
BLACKNESS	Destination = 0
WHITENESS	Destination = All bits set to 1

Windows actually provides 255 different ways in which the bits on the destination device context may be set—the table above shows only the most common. Windows also defines a standard equation format for describing a Boolean equation that combines the source bitmap, the currently selected brush, and the current value of the destination. These equations are known as raster operation codes or raster-ops, for short. (Chapter 8 described the 16 ROP2 line drawing raster-ops.)

The equation that determines the new value of the pixel has three possible operands, each with a single letter code:

1. D = Destination—the value of the bit in the destination bitmap.
2. S = Source—the value of the bit in the source bitmap that corresponds to a bit in the destination bitmap.
3. P = Pattern—the value of the bit in a pattern determined by the currently selected brush.

There are four Boolean operations that can be applied to these operands, each with a single letter code in lowercase:

1. a = AND operation

2. n = NOT operation (inverts the bit)

3. o = OR operation

4. x = XOR operation (exclusive OR)

The equation is written in reverse polish notation (RPN). This means that it is read from left to right, each operation affecting the operand to its left.

Consider the following example:

```
DPSaxn
```

In this example, the source bitmap is ANDed with the current pattern. The result is then XORed with the destination bitmap. The result of that operation is inverted. The result of this final operation is set into the destination.

Using Raster-Ops

The most common raster operations are those used to copy one image to another or to exclusive OR one image by another. The advantage of the exclusive OR operation is that it is reversible—repeating the operation causes the original image to be restored.

Occasionally, a more complex series of raster operations may be used to good effect. For example, you can use raster operations to extract the XOR and AND masks from an icon handle. The following steps can be used to generate those masks:

1. Create a 32 x 32-bitmap compatible with the display (or use the size of the actual icon if not 32 x 32).

2. Use the PatBlt function to set this bitmap to black.

3. Draw the icon onto this bitmap, which contains the XOR bitmap. The GetDIBits function can be used to retrieve the mask in DIB format.

4. Create a second 32 x 32-bitmap compatible with the display.

5. Use the PatBlt function to set this bitmap to white.

6. Draw the icon onto this second bitmap.

7. Draw the XOR bitmap onto this second bitmap using the XOR operation by using the SRCINVERT raster-op. After this operation the bits determined only by the icon will be black, the bits that are influenced by the display will be white.

8. Use the BitBlt function to convert this bitmap into a monochrome bitmap. This will be the mask.

Keep in mind that the bitmaps need to be selected into memory device contexts before the BitBlt and PatBlt operations can be performed.

Of course, in Win32 you can obtain the XOR and AND mask for an icon using the GetIconInfo API function.

With clever application of Boolean algebra, it is possible to convert colors, merge pictures into each other, and otherwise achieve a great many effects, some of which have no practical use whatsoever.

See Appendix G for a list of raster operations available under Windows.

Examples

The following sample programs demonstrate many of the principles and functions described in the chapter text. You will find additional device-independent bitmap examples in Chapter 12 where they are used to demonstrate advanced printing techniques.

In addition to the StockBMS, ROPTest, Puzzle, and DIBSect programs that are listed in this chapter, you will find the following functions on the CD-ROM that comes with this book in the Chapter 9 source directory:

■ BMRotate.vbp demonstrates bitmap rotation.

- Shade.vbp shows you how to shade icons or bitmaps—it's the same technique used by Windows 95 and NT 4.0 to select or disable icons.

- Combine.vbp shows you a step by step sequence for overlaying one bitmap on top of another.

StockBMs—A Stock Bitmap and Icon Viewer

StockBMs is a program that allows you to view the stock bitmaps and icons provided by Windows. It also demonstrates the loading and display of bitmaps and icons.

Figure 9.10 shows the runtime screen of the StockBMs program.

Figure 9.10
The StockBMs
runtime screen

Using StockBMs

The StockBMs screen shown in Figure 9.10 contains three controls. A list box is loaded with the constant definitions for the Windows stock bitmaps and icons. Selecting an entry in the list box causes the corresponding icon or bitmap to be loaded and displayed in the left picture control. If a stock icon is selected, the program uses the LoadImage function to load a scaled icon and display it in the right picture control.

Project Description

The StockBMs project includes two files. STOCKBMS.FRM is the only form used in the program. STOCKBMS.BAS is the only module in the program and contains the constant type, function, and constant definitions.

Listing 9.1 shows the file STOCKBMS.BAS, Listing 9.2 shows the file STOCKBMS.FRM.

Listing 9.1   **STOCKBMS.BAS**

```
Attribute VB_Name = "STOCKBMS1"
'-------------------------------------------------
'
'          Public Constants
'
Type BITMAP
        bmType As Long
        bmWidth As Long
        bmHeight As Long
        bmWidthBytes As Long
        bmPlanes As Integer
        bmBitsPixel As Integer
        bmBits As Long
End Type

Option Explicit

Public Const CBM_INIT = &H4&      '  initialize bitmap
Public Const DIB_RGB_COLORS = 0 '  color table in RGBTriples
Public Const DIB_PAL_COLORS = 1 '  color table in palette indices
```

This file also includes all constants with the following prefixes: OBM_, IDI_, BI_, IMAGE_, DI_, and LR_. It also includes the constants specifying the standard raster operations (such as SRCCOPY). These constants have been left out of the listing to conserve space.

```
Public Const TRANSPARENT = 1
Public Const OPAQUE = 2

Declare Function GetLastError& Lib "kernel32" ()
Declare Function CreateCompatibleDC& Lib "gdi32" (ByVal hdc As Long)
Declare Function LoadBitmapBynum& Lib "user32" Alias "LoadBitmapA" (ByVal _
hInstance As Long, ByVal lpBitmapName As Long)
Declare Function GetObjectAPI& Lib "gdi32" Alias "GetObjectA" (ByVal hObject As _
Long, ByVal nCount As Long, lpObject As Any)
Declare Function SelectObject& Lib "gdi32" (ByVal hdc As Long, ByVal hObject As _
Long)
Declare Function BitBlt& Lib "gdi32" (ByVal hDestDC As Long, ByVal x As Long, _
ByVal y As Long, ByVal nWidth As Long, ByVal nHeight As Long, _
ByVal hSrcDC As Long, ByVal xSrc As Long, ByVal ySrc As Long, ByVal dwRop As Long)
Declare Function DeleteDC& Lib "gdi32" (ByVal hdc As Long)
Declare Function DeleteObject& Lib "gdi32" (ByVal hObject As Long)
Declare Function LoadIconBynum& Lib "user32" Alias "LoadIconA" (ByVal hInstance _
As Long, ByVal lpIconName As Long)
```

```
Declare Function DrawIcon& Lib "user32" (ByVal hdc As Long, ByVal x As Long, _
ByVal y As Long, ByVal hIcon As Long)
Declare Function DrawIconEx& Lib "user32" (ByVal hdc As Long, ByVal xLeft As _
Long, ByVal yTop As Long, ByVal hIcon As Long, ByVal cxWidth As Long, _
ByVal cyWidth As Long, ByVal istepIfAniCur As Long, ByVal hbrFlickerFreeDraw _
As Long, ByVal diFlags As Long)
Declare Function LoadImage& Lib "user32" Alias "LoadImageA" (ByVal hInst As _
Long, ByVal lpsz As String, ByVal un1 As Long, ByVal n1 As Long, ByVal n2 _
As Long, ByVal un2 As Long)
Declare Function LoadImageBynum& Lib "user32" Alias "LoadImageA" (ByVal hInst _
As Long, ByVal lpsz As Long, ByVal un1 As Long, ByVal n1 As Long, ByVal n2 _
As Long, ByVal un2 As Long)
```

Listing 9.2   STOCKBMS.FRM

```
VERSION 5.00
Begin VB.Form StockBMS
    Caption         =   "Stock Bitmaps and Icons Viewer"
    ClientHeight    =   2985
    ClientLeft      =   1125
    ClientTop       =   1485
    ClientWidth     =   4065
    BeginProperty Font
        name        =   "MS Sans Serif"
        charset     =   0
        weight      =   700
        size        =   8.25
        underline   =   0       'False
        italic      =   0       'False
        strikethrough =  0      'False
    EndProperty
    ForeColor       =   &H80000008&
    Height          =   3390
    Left            =   1065
    LinkMode        =   1   'Source
    LinkTopic       =   "Form1"
    ScaleHeight     =   2985
    ScaleWidth      =   4065
    Top             =   1140
    Width           =   4185
    Begin VB.PictureBox Picture2
        BackColor   =   &H00FFFF80&
```

Listing 9.2   STOCKBMS.FRM (Continued)

```
        Height          =    855
        Left            =    1560
        ScaleHeight     =    55
        ScaleMode       =    3    'Pixel
        ScaleWidth      =    83
        TabIndex        =    2
        Top             =    1920
        Width           =    1275
     End
     Begin VB.PictureBox Picture1
        BackColor       =    &H00FFFFFF&
        Height          =    855
        Left            =    240
        ScaleHeight     =    825
        ScaleWidth      =    1065
        TabIndex        =    1
        Top             =    1920
        Width           =    1095
     End
     Begin VB.ListBox List1
        Height          =    1395
        Left            =    240
        TabIndex        =    0
        Top             =    360
        Width           =    3615
     End
  End
  Attribute VB_Name = "StockBMS"
  Attribute VB_GlobalNameSpace = False
  Attribute VB_Creatable = False
  Attribute VB_PredeclaredId = True
  Attribute VB_Exposed = False
  Option Explicit
  '
  '    Initialize the list box
  '
```

The list box is loaded with a list of all of the constants representing stock
bitmap and icon resources and their number.

```
Private Sub Form_Load()
    ' Load the listbox with entries for each stock
    ' bitmap and icon
    List1.AddItem "OBM_CLOSE = 32754"
    List1.AddItem "OBM_UPARROW = 32753"
    List1.AddItem "OBM_DNARROW = 32752"
    List1.AddItem "OBM_RGARROW = 32751"
    List1.AddItem "OBM_LFARROW = 32750"
```

```
        List1.AddItem "OBM_REDUCE = 32749"
        List1.AddItem "OBM_ZOOM = 32748"
        List1.AddItem "OBM_RESTORE = 32747"
        List1.AddItem "OBM_REDUCED = 32746"
        List1.AddItem "OBM_ZOOMD = 32745"
        List1.AddItem "OBM_RESTORED = 32744"
        List1.AddItem "OBM_UPARROWD = 32743"
        List1.AddItem "OBM_DNARROWD = 32742"
        List1.AddItem "OBM_RGARROWD = 32741"
        List1.AddItem "OBM_LFARROWD = 32740"
        List1.AddItem "OBM_MNARROW = 32739"
        List1.AddItem "OBM_COMBO = 32738"
        List1.AddItem "OBM_UPARROWI = 32737"
        List1.AddItem "OBM_DNARROWI = 32736"
        List1.AddItem "OBM_RGARROWI = 32735"
        List1.AddItem "OBM_LFARROWI = 32734"
        List1.AddItem "OBM_OLD_CLOSE = 32767"
        List1.AddItem "OBM_SIZE = 32766"
        List1.AddItem "OBM_OLD_UPARROW = 32765"
        List1.AddItem "OBM_OLD_DNARROW = 32764"
        List1.AddItem "OBM_OLD_RGARROW = 32763"
        List1.AddItem "OBM_OLD_LFARROW = 32762"
        List1.AddItem "OBM_BTSIZE = 32761"
        List1.AddItem "OBM_CHECK = 32760"
        List1.AddItem "OBM_CHECKBOXES = 32759"
        List1.AddItem "OBM_BTNCORNERS = 32758"
        List1.AddItem "OBM_OLD_REDUCE = 32757"
        List1.AddItem "OBM_OLD_ZOOM = 32756"
        List1.AddItem "OBM_OLD_RESTORE = 32755"
        List1.AddItem "IDI_APPLICATION = 32512"
        List1.AddItem "IDI_HAND = 32513"
        List1.AddItem "IDI_QUESTION = 32514"
        List1.AddItem "IDI_EXCLAMATION = 32515"
        List1.AddItem "IDI_ASTERISK = 32516"
        List1.AddItem "IDI_WINLOG = 32517"
End Sub


'
'   Just display the current object
'
Private Sub List1_Click()
    ShowObject
End Sub


'
'   When redrawing the picture control, show the currently
'   selected object (if any)
'
Private Sub Picture1_Paint()
    ShowObject
End Sub
```

The ShowObject function illustrates the most common method for displaying a bitmap on a picture control. A compatible device context is created and the loaded bitmap selected into it. The GetObject API function allows you to determine the size of the bitmap. BitBlt copies the image onto the control.

```
'
'   Paints the stock icon or bitmap in picture1
'
'
'   Retrieve a stock bitmap or icon for the selected list box
'   entry. Draws the bitmap or icon on the picture control.
'
Private Sub ShowObject()
    Dim ShadowDC&
    Dim isbm%
    Dim param$
    Dim idlong&
    Dim objhandle&, oldobject&
    Dim di&
    Dim bm As BITMAP

    ' Be sure there is a valid entry
    If List1.ListIndex < 0 Then Exit Sub

    picture1.Cls    ' Clear the picture control
    picture2.Cls
    param$ = List1.Text
    ' Find out if it's a bitmap or an icon
    If left$(param$, 3) = "OBM" Then isbm% = -1

    ' Extract the id value to use
    idlong& = Val(Mid$(param$, InStr(param$, "=") + 1))

    If isbm% Then    ' It's a stock bitmap

        ' Create a memory device context compatible with
        ' the picture control
        ShadowDC& = CreateCompatibleDC&(picture1.hdc)

        ' Load the bitmap
        objhandle& = LoadBitmapBynum(0, idlong&)

        ' Retrieve the height and width of the bitmap
        di = GetObjectAPI(objhandle, Len(bm), bm)

        ' Select the bitmap into the memory DC, keeping
        ' a handle to the prior bitmap.
        oldobject = SelectObject(ShadowDC, objhandle)

        ' BitBlt the bitmap into the picture control,
        ' offset by 2 pixels from the upper left corner
```

```
                    ' (just to make it look better)
                    di = BitBlt(picture1.hdc, 2, 2, bm.bmWidth, bm.bmHeight, ShadowDC&, 0, _
                    0, SRCCOPY)

                    ' Select the bitmap OUT of the memory DC
                    di = SelectObject(ShadowDC, oldobject)
                    ' and delete it (yes - even though they are system
                    ' bitmaps - this doesn't destroy them, just releases
                    ' your private copy of the bitmap.
                    di = DeleteObject(objhandle)

                    picture2.CurrentX = 2
                    picture2.CurrentY = 2
                    picture2.Print "N/A"

                    ' Finally, delete the memory DC
                    di = DeleteDC(ShadowDC)
        Else    ' It's an icon - a much easier process
                    ' Get the stock icon
                    objhandle& = LoadIconBynum(0, idlong&)

                    ' Draw it directly onto the picture control
                    di = DrawIcon(picture1.hdc, 2, 2, objhandle&)

                    ' Now try loading it as an image

                    objhandle& = LoadImageBynum(0, idlong&, IMAGE_ICON, 0, 0, _
                    LR_DEFAULTCOLOR _
                    Or LR_DEFAULTSIZE Or LR_SHARED)

                    di = DrawIconEx(picture2.hdc, 0, 0, objhandle&, picture2.ScaleWidth, _
                    picture2.ScaleHeight, 0, 0, DI_NORMAL)

        End If
End Sub
```

ROPTest—A Raster Operation Experimentation Program

ROPTest is a program that allows you to experiment with various raster operations.

Figure 9.11 shows the runtime screen of the ROPTest program.

Using ROPTest

The ROPTest program has two main picture controls. The picSource control on the left is loaded with a color bar representing the 16 standard palette entries. You can click on any of these colors to set the current brush, which will be used to fill the picBrush picture control. The picDest control on the right is the destination control. There are two ways to select a raster operation to perform. You can select one of the option buttons, or enter the numeric raster operation code

Figure 9.11

ROPTest runtime
screen

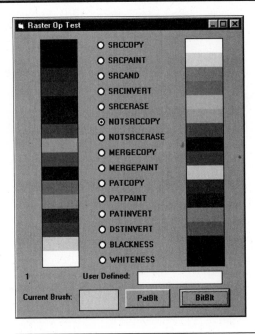

directly into the user-defined text box. The program has two operations: PatBlt
and BitBlt. PatBlt performs the specified raster operation, though it has no effect for raster operations that involve a source parameter. BitBlt performs the
specified operation combining the source, pattern brush, and destination.

Project Description

The ROPTest program contains one form only and is shown in Listing 9.3,
ROPTEST.FRM.

Listing 9.3 **ROPTest.frm**

```
VERSION 5.00
Begin VB.Form frmROPTest
    Appearance      =   0  'Flat
    BackColor       =   &H00C0C0C0&
    Caption         =   "Raster Op Test"
    ClientHeight    =   6660
    ClientLeft      =   1095
    ClientTop       =   1470
    ClientWidth     =   5490
    BeginProperty Font
```

Listing 9.3   ROPTest.frm (Continued)

```
            name            =    "MS Sans Serif"
            charset         =    0
            weight          =    700
            size            =    8.25
            underline       =    0    'False
            italic          =    0    'False
            strikethrough   =    0    'False
         EndProperty
         ForeColor          =    &H80000008&
         Height             =    7065
         Left               =    1035
         LinkTopic          =    "Form1"
         ScaleHeight        =    6660
         ScaleWidth         =    5490
         Top                =    1125
         Width              =    5610
         Begin VB.TextBox txtUserDef
            Appearance      =    0    'Flat
            Height          =    315
            Left            =    2940
            TabIndex        =    21
            Top             =    5640
            Width           =    2055
         End
         Begin VB.OptionButton Option1
            Appearance      =    0    'Flat
            BackColor       =    &H00C0C0C0&
            Caption         =    "WHITENESS"
            ForeColor       =    &H80000008&
            Height          =    315
            Index           =    14
            Left            =    1980
            TabIndex        =    20
            Top             =    5220
            Width           =    1815
         End
         Begin VB.OptionButton Option1
            Appearance      =    0    'Flat
            BackColor       =    &H00C0C0C0&
            Caption         =    "BLACKNESS"
            ForeColor       =    &H80000008&
            Height          =    315
            Index           =    13
            Left            =    1980
            TabIndex        =    19
            Top             =    4860
            Width           =    1815
         End
```

Listing 9.3   **ROPTest.frm (Continued)**

```
Begin VB.OptionButton Option1
   Appearance      =   0   'Flat
   BackColor       =   &H00C0C0C0&
   Caption         =   "DSTINVERT"
   ForeColor       =   &H80000008&
   Height          =   315
   Index           =   12
   Left            =   1980
   TabIndex        =   18
   Top             =   4500
   Width           =   1815
End
Begin VB.OptionButton Option1
   Appearance      =   0   'Flat
   BackColor       =   &H00C0C0C0&
   Caption         =   "PATINVERT"
   ForeColor       =   &H80000008&
   Height          =   315
   Index           =   11
   Left            =   1980
   TabIndex        =   17
   Top             =   4140
   Width           =   1815
End
Begin VB.OptionButton Option1
   Appearance      =   0   'Flat
   BackColor       =   &H00C0C0C0&
   Caption         =   "PATPAINT"
   ForeColor       =   &H80000008&
   Height          =   315
   Index           =   10
   Left            =   1980
   TabIndex        =   16
   Top             =   3780
   Width           =   1815
End
Begin VB.OptionButton Option1
   Appearance      =   0   'Flat
   BackColor       =   &H00C0C0C0&
   Caption         =   "PATCOPY"
   ForeColor       =   &H80000008&
   Height          =   315
   Index           =   9
   Left            =   1980
   TabIndex        =   15
   Top             =   3420
   Width           =   1815
End
```

Listing 9.3   ROPTest.frm (Continued)

```
Begin VB.OptionButton Option1
    Appearance      =   0   'Flat
    BackColor       =   &H00C0C0C0&
    Caption         =   "MERGEPAINT"
    ForeColor       =   &H80000008&
    Height          =   315
    Index           =   8
    Left            =   1980
    TabIndex        =   14
    Top             =   3060
    Width           =   1815
End
Begin VB.OptionButton Option1
    Appearance      =   0   'Flat
    BackColor       =   &H00C0C0C0&
    Caption         =   "MERGECOPY"
    ForeColor       =   &H80000008&
    Height          =   315
    Index           =   7
    Left            =   1980
    TabIndex        =   13
    Top             =   2700
    Width           =   1815
End
Begin VB.OptionButton Option1
    Appearance      =   0   'Flat
    BackColor       =   &H00C0C0C0&
    Caption         =   "NOTSRCERASE"
    ForeColor       =   &H80000008&
    Height          =   315
    Index           =   6
    Left            =   1980
    TabIndex        =   12
    Top             =   2340
    Width           =   1815
End
Begin VB.OptionButton Option1
    Appearance      =   0   'Flat
    BackColor       =   &H00C0C0C0&
    Caption         =   "NOTSRCCOPY"
    ForeColor       =   &H80000008&
    Height          =   315
    Index           =   5
    Left            =   1980
    TabIndex        =   11
    Top             =   1980
    Width           =   1815
End
```

Listing 9.3   ROPTest.frm (Continued)

```
Begin VB.OptionButton Option1
    Appearance      =   0  'Flat
    BackColor       =   &H00C0C0C0&
    Caption         =   "SRCERASE"
    ForeColor       =   &H80000008&
    Height          =   315
    Index           =   4
    Left            =   1980
    TabIndex        =   10
    Top             =   1620
    Width           =   1815
End
Begin VB.OptionButton Option1
    Appearance      =   0  'Flat
    BackColor       =   &H00C0C0C0&
    Caption         =   "SRCINVERT"
    ForeColor       =   &H80000008&
    Height          =   315
    Index           =   3
    Left            =   1980
    TabIndex        =   9
    Top             =   1260
    Width           =   1815
End
Begin VB.OptionButton Option1
    Appearance      =   0  'Flat
    BackColor       =   &H00C0C0C0&
    Caption         =   "SRCAND"
    ForeColor       =   &H80000008&
    Height          =   315
    Index           =   2
    Left            =   1980
    TabIndex        =   8
    Top             =   900
    Width           =   1815
End
Begin VB.OptionButton Option1
    Appearance      =   0  'Flat
    BackColor       =   &H00C0C0C0&
    Caption         =   "SRCPAINT"
    ForeColor       =   &H80000008&
    Height          =   315
    Index           =   1
    Left            =   1980
    TabIndex        =   7
    Top             =   540
    Width           =   1815
End
```

Listing 9.3   ROPTest.frm (Continued)

```
Begin VB.OptionButton Option1
    Appearance      =   0   'Flat
    BackColor       =   &H00C0C0C0&
    Caption         =   "SRCCOPY"
    ForeColor       =   &H80000008&
    Height          =   315
    Index           =   0
    Left            =   1980
    TabIndex        =   6
    Top             =   180
    Value           =   -1  'True
    Width           =   1815
End
Begin VB.CommandButton cmdPatBlt
    Appearance      =   0   'Flat
    BackColor       =   &H80000005&
    Caption         =   "PatBlt"
    Height          =   435
    Left            =   2640
    TabIndex        =   5
    Top             =   6060
    Width           =   1095
End
Begin VB.PictureBox picBrush
    Appearance      =   0   'Flat
    BackColor       =   &H80000005&
    ForeColor       =   &H80000008&
    Height          =   495
    Left            =   1500
    ScaleHeight     =   465
    ScaleWidth      =   945
    TabIndex        =   3
    Top             =   6060
    Width           =   975
End
Begin VB.CommandButton cmdBitBlt
    Appearance      =   0   'Flat
    BackColor       =   &H80000005&
    Caption         =   "BitBlt"
    Height          =   435
    Left            =   3960
    TabIndex        =   2
    Top             =   6060
    Width           =   1215
End
Begin VB.PictureBox picDest
    Appearance      =   0   'Flat
    BackColor       =   &H80000005&
```

Listing 9.3   ROPTest.frm (Continued)

```
    ForeColor       =   &H80000008&
    Height          =   5355
    Left            =   4140
    ScaleHeight     =   355
    ScaleMode       =   3   'Pixel
    ScaleWidth      =   59
    TabIndex        =   1
    Top             =   180
    Width           =   915
End
Begin VB.PictureBox picSource
    Appearance      =   0   'Flat
    BackColor       =   &H80000005&
    ForeColor       =   &H80000008&
    Height          =   5355
    Left            =   600
    ScaleHeight     =   355
    ScaleMode       =   3   'Pixel
    ScaleWidth      =   59
    TabIndex        =   0
    Top             =   180
    Width           =   915
End
Begin VB.Label labRes
    Appearance      =   0   'Flat
    BackColor       =   &H80000005&
    BackStyle       =   0   'Transparent
    ForeColor       =   &H80000008&
    Height          =   255
    Left            =   180
    TabIndex        =   23
    Top             =   5640
    Width           =   375
End
Begin VB.Label Label2
    Alignment       =   1   'Right Justify
    Appearance      =   0   'Flat
    BackColor       =   &H80000005&
    BackStyle       =   0   'Transparent
    Caption         =   "User Defined:"
    ForeColor       =   &H80000008&
    Height          =   255
    Left            =   960
    TabIndex        =   22
    Top             =   5640
    Width           =   1815
End
Begin VB.Label Label1
```

Listing 9.3 ROPTest.frm (Continued)

```
              Appearance      =   0   'Flat
              BackColor       =   &H80000005&
              BackStyle       =   0   'Transparent
              Caption         =   "Current Brush:"
              ForeColor       =   &H80000008&
              Height          =   315
              Left            =   120
              TabIndex        =   4
              Top             =   6120
              Width           =   1275
           End
        End
     End
     Attribute VB_Name = "frmROPTest"
     Attribute VB_GlobalNameSpace = False
     Attribute VB_Creatable = False
     Attribute VB_PredeclaredId = TrueAttribute VB_Exposed = False
     Option Explicit

     ' Globals
     Dim CellHeight&       ' Height in pixels of one color cell
     Dim CurrentMouseY&    ' Current Y location
     Dim CurrentBrush&     ' Current brush to use
     Dim CurrentOption%

     ' API calls
     Private Declare Function DeleteObject& Lib "gdi32" (ByVal hObject As Long)
     Private Declare Function CreateSolidBrush& Lib "gdi32" (ByVal crColor As Long)
     Private Declare Function PatBlt& Lib "gdi32" (ByVal hdc As Long, ByVal x As _
     Long, ByVal y As Long, ByVal nWidth As Long, ByVal nHeight As Long, _
     ByVal dwRop As Long)
     Private Declare Function BitBlt& Lib "gdi32" (ByVal hDestDC As Long, ByVal x As _
     Long, ByVal y As Long, ByVal nWidth As Long, ByVal nHeight As Long, ByVal _
     hSrcDC As Long, ByVal xSrc As Long, ByVal ySrc As Long, ByVal dwRop As Long)
     Private Declare Function SelectObject& Lib "gdi32" (ByVal hdc As Long, ByVal
     hObject As Long)


     ' The most common raster operations
     Dim RasterOps&(15)

     Const SRCCOPY = &HCC0020    ' (DWORD) dest = source
     Const SRCPAINT = &HEE0086   ' (DWORD) dest = source OR dest
     Const SRCAND = &H8800C6     ' (DWORD) dest = source AND dest
     Const SRCINVERT = &H660046  ' (DWORD) dest = source XOR dest
     Const SRCERASE = &H440328   ' (DWORD) dest = source AND (NOT dest )
     Const NOTSRCCOPY = &H330008 ' (DWORD) dest = (NOT source)
```

Listing 9.3 ROPTest.frm (Continued)

```
Const NOTSRCERASE = &H1100A6 ' (DWORD) dest = (NOT src) AND (NOT dest)
Const MERGECOPY = &HC000CA  ' (DWORD) dest = (source AND pattern)
Const MERGEPAINT = &HBB0226 ' (DWORD) dest = (NOT source) OR dest
Const PATCOPY = &HF00021     ' (DWORD) dest = pattern
Const PATPAINT = &HFB0A09    ' (DWORD) dest = (Not source) or pattern or dest
Const PATINVERT = &H5A0049   ' (DWORD) dest = pattern XOR dest
Const DSTINVERT = &H550009   ' (DWORD) dest = (NOT dest)
Const BLACKNESS = &H42&      ' (DWORD) dest = BLACK
Const WHITENESS = &HFF0062   ' (DWORD) dest = WHITE

Private Sub cmdBitBlt_Click()
    Dim di%
    Dim raster&
    Dim oldbrush&

    If Len(txtUserDef.Text) <> 0 Then
        raster& = "&H" & txtUserDef.Text
    Else
        raster& = RasterOps(CurrentOption%)
    End If

    Debug.Print raster&

    oldbrush = SelectObject(picDest.hdc, CurrentBrush&)
    di = BitBlt(picDest.hdc, 0, 0, picDest.ScaleWidth, picDest.ScaleHeight, _
    picSource.hdc, 0, 0, raster&)
    oldbrush = SelectObject(picDest.hdc, oldbrush&)

    labRes.Caption = di

End Sub

Private Sub cmdPatBlt_Click()
    Dim di&
    Dim raster&
    Dim oldbrush&

    If Len(txtUserDef.Text) <> 0 Then
        raster& = "&H" & txtUserDef.Text
    Else
        raster& = RasterOps(CurrentOption%)
    End If

    Debug.Print raster&

    oldbrush& = SelectObject(picDest.hdc, CurrentBrush&)
```

Listing 9.3   **ROPTest.frm (Continued)**

```
        di = PatBlt&(picDest.hdc, 0, 0, picDest.ScaleWidth, picDest.ScaleHeight, _
        raster&)
        oldbrush& = SelectObject(picDest.hdc, oldbrush&)

        labRes.Caption = di
End Sub

Private Sub Form_Load()

        ' Default to a white brush
        CurrentBrush& = CreateSolidBrush(QBColor(15))

        RasterOps(0) = SRCCOPY
        RasterOps(1) = SRCPAINT
        RasterOps(2) = SRCAND
        RasterOps(3) = SRCINVERT
        RasterOps(4) = SRCERASE
        RasterOps(5) = NOTSRCCOPY
        RasterOps(6) = NOTSRCERASE
        RasterOps(7) = MERGECOPY
        RasterOps(8) = MERGEPAINT
        RasterOps(9) = PATCOPY
        RasterOps(10) = PATPAINT
        RasterOps(11) = PATINVERT
        RasterOps(12) = DSTINVERT
        RasterOps(13) = BLACKNESS
        RasterOps(14) = WHITENESS


End Sub

Private Sub Form_Unload(Cancel As Integer)
        Dim di%
        If CurrentBrush& Then di = DeleteObject(CurrentBrush)
End Sub

Private Sub Option1_Click(Index As Integer)
        CurrentOption% = Index
End Sub

Private Sub picSource_Click()
        Dim usecolor%, di&
        If CurrentBrush& Then di = DeleteObject(CurrentBrush&)
        usecolor% = CInt(CurrentMouseY \ CellHeight)
        If usecolor% < 0 Then usecolor% = 0
        If usecolor% > 15 Then usecolor% = 15
        CurrentBrush& = CreateSolidBrush(QBColor(usecolor%))
        picBrush.BackColor = QBColor(usecolor%)
```

Listing 9.3   **ROPTest.frm (Continued)**

```
End Sub

Private Sub picSource_MouseUp(Button As Integer, Shift As Integer, x As Single, _
y As Single)
    CurrentMouseY = y
End Sub

Private Sub picSource_Paint()
    Dim x%

    ' Determine the height of each block of color
    CellHeight& = picSource.ScaleHeight \ 16

    For x% = 0 To 15
        picSource.Line (0, CellHeight * x)-(picSource.ScaleWidth, CellHeight * _
        (x + 1)), QBColor(x%), BF
    Next x%

End Sub

Private Sub txtUserDef_Change()
    Dim txtEmpty%
    Dim x%
    txtEmpty% = Len(txtUserDef.Text) = 0
    ' Set option button enabled status
    For x% = 0 To 14
        Option1(x%).Enabled = txtEmpty%
    Next x%

End Sub
```

This sample program allows you to enter the hexadecimal value of any of these raster operations and to quickly see the results of the operation given the 16 available colors and any brush color. Since the destination bitmap is not cleared each time, you can perform a sequence of operations to achieve a particular result.

For example, if you look at the standard VGA palette, you'll notice that the first eight colors are darker versions of the latter eight colors. Let's say you wanted to use only the eight brighter colors in an image. To do so you would need to use the OR logical operation to set the high bit of each pixel, thus pixel 0 would be set to 8, 1 would be set to 9, and so on. Doing this one pixel at a time would take an incredibly long time, but BitBlt lets us do this nearly instantly. The logical operation we want is: Destination = Source OR Pattern, where the pattern is set to color number 8. Click on color 8 (dark gray). Then set the value F3008A into the user-defined text box (this value is

obtained from the raster operation PSo). When you click on the BitBlt operation, you will see that the operation has been performed.

We could select the darker eight colors by clearing this bit using the operation: Destination = Source AND Pattern, selecting pattern number 7 (light gray). Clear the user text box and select the MERGECOPY operation, then select the BitBlt command to see this effect.

Suggestions for Further Practice

Try extending this program to allow you to experiment with the MaskBlt function.

Example: Puzzle—A Tiled Bitmap Puzzle Game

Puzzle is a simulation of a scrambled tile puzzle game. A bitmap is broken up into 25 tiles, which are then scrambled. One of the tiles is removed. It is up to the player to re-create the original bitmap by sliding the tiles one at a time into the empty space.

This program demonstrates use of device-dependent bitmaps, device-independent bitmaps, bitmap transfer and scaling, and creation of pattern brushes. It also uses a variety of device context and rectangle functions introduced in previous chapters.

Using Puzzle

The Puzzle application is extremely simple to use. When the program is loaded, it displays a scrambled version of a default bitmap (the arches bitmap provided by Windows). One of the squares in the 5x5 grid is black to indicate that it is empty. Clicking with the mouse on any of the tiles next to the empty square causes that tile to be moved into the empty square. The purpose of the game is to unscramble the image.

A menu bar shows three options. The Scramble menu option can be used to rescramble the image tiles. The Load menu option brings up a load bitmap form that allows you to load a new bitmap to descramble. The bitmap is scaled to fill the entire puzzle screen. The Empty menu option allows you to specify the look of the empty square. It can be black (the default), white, or a random color brush pattern.

Figure 9.12 shows the designtime screen of the Puzzle program. Figure 9.13 shows the runtime screen.

Project Description

The Puzzle project includes four files. PUZZLE.FRM is the main puzzle form used in the program. PUZZLE2.FRM is used to load new bitmap files and is a fairly typical example of a file load form. PUZZLE.BAS is the only module in

Figure 9.12
Designtime screen
for PUZZLE.FRM

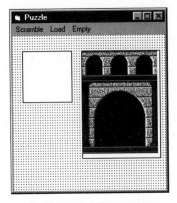

Figure 9.13
PUZZLE.FRM at
runtime

the program and contains the constant, type, and function. APIGID32.BAS contains the declarations for the APIGID32.DLL dynamic link library.

Listing 9.4 contains the header from file PUZZLE.FRM that describes the control setup for the form. The picture control on the left is Picture1; the one on the right is Picture2. Their location and size are not critical, as the program resizes them as needed.

Listing 9.4 **Header for PUZZLE.FRM**

```
VERSION 5.00
Begin VB.Form Puzzle
    Appearance      =   0  'Flat
    BackColor       =   &H80000005&
```

Listing 9.4   Header for PUZZLE.FRM (Continued)

```
Caption             =    "Puzzle"
ClientHeight        =    3645
ClientLeft          =    1095
ClientTop           =    1770
ClientWidth         =    3735
BeginProperty Font
   name             =       "MS Sans Serif"
   charset          =       0
   weight           =       700
   size             =       8.25
   underline        =       0    'False
   italic           =       0    'False
   strikethrough    =       0    'False
EndProperty
ForeColor           =    &H80000008&
Height              =    4335
Left                =    1035
LinkMode            =    1    'Source
LinkTopic           =    "Form1"
ScaleHeight         =    3645
ScaleWidth          =    3735
Top                 =    1140
Width               =    3855
Begin VB.PictureBox Picture2
   Appearance       =       0    'Flat
   BackColor        =       &H80000005&
   ForeColor        =       &H80000008&
   Height           =       2535
   Left             =       1680
   Picture          =       "PUZZLE.frx":0000
   ScaleHeight      =       2505
   ScaleWidth       =       1905
   TabIndex         =       1
   Top              =       360
   Visible          =       0    'False
   Width            =       1935
End
Begin VB.PictureBox Picture1
   Appearance       =       0    'Flat
   BackColor        =       &H80000005&
   ForeColor        =       &H80000008&
   Height           =       1215
   Left             =       240
   ScaleHeight      =       79
   ScaleMode        =       3    'Pixel
   ScaleWidth       =       79
   TabIndex         =       0
   Top              =       360
```

Listing 9.4   **Header for PUZZLE.FRM (Continued)**

```
         Width          =    1215
      End
      Begin VB.Menu MenuScramble
         Caption        =    "Scramble"
      End
      Begin VB.Menu MenuLoad
         Caption        =    "Load"
      End
      Begin VB.Menu MenuEmptyCaption
         Caption        =    "Empty"
         Begin VB.Menu MenuEmpty
            Caption      =    "Black"
            Checked      =    -1  'True
            Index        =    0
         End
         Begin VB.Menu MenuEmpty
            Caption      =    "White"
            Index        =    1
         End
         Begin VB.Menu MenuEmpty
            Caption      =    "Random"
            Index        =    2
         End
      End
   End
End
Attribute VB_Name = "Puzzle"
Attribute VB_GlobalNameSpace = False
Attribute VB_Creatable = False
Attribute VB_PredeclaredId = True
Attribute VB_Exposed = False
Option Explicit
```

The file PUZZLE.FRX is the binary part of the PUZZLE.FRM file. It contains the default image used in the puzzle, in this case, the ARCHES.BMP bitmap provided with Microsoft Windows. You can delete the line

```
Picture = Puzzle.FRX:0000
```

from the listing if you wish, in which case you should open the form in design mode and place a default bitmap of your choice into the Picture2 control.

Listing 9.5 contains the header from file PUZZLE2.FRM that describes the control setup for the form. This is a typical file load dialog box. You can click on the file list box to obtain a preview of the bitmap in question.

Listing 9.6 contains the code for module Puzzle.bas.

Listing 9.7 contains the code for Puzzle.frm.

Listing 9.5   Listing for PUZZLE2.FRM

```
VERSION 5.00
Begin VB.Form Puzzle2
    Caption         =   "Load Bitmap"
    ClientHeight    =   2535
    ClientLeft      =   1275
    ClientTop       =   2085
    ClientWidth     =   8085
    BeginProperty Font
        name            =   "MS Sans Serif"
        charset         =   0
        weight          =   700
        size            =   8.25
        underline       =   0   'False
        italic          =   0   'False
        strikethrough   =   0   'False
    EndProperty
    ForeColor       =   &H80000008&
    Height          =   2940
    Left            =   1215
    LinkMode        =   1   'Source
    LinkTopic       =   "Form1"
    ScaleHeight     =   2535
    ScaleWidth      =   8085
    Top             =   1740
    Width           =   8205
    Begin VB.PictureBox picPreview
        Height          =   2295
        Left            =   5400
        ScaleHeight     =   2265
        ScaleWidth      =   2565
        TabIndex        =   5
        Top             =   120
        Width           =   2595
    End
    Begin VB.CommandButton CmdCancel
        Caption         =   "Cancel"
        Height          =   375
        Left            =   4140
        TabIndex        =   4
        Top             =   2040
        Width           =   1095
    End
    Begin VB.CommandButton CmdLoad
        Caption         =   "Load"
        Height          =   375
        Left            =   2880
        TabIndex        =   3
        Top             =   2040
```

Listing 9.5   Listing for PUZZLE2.FRM (Continued)

```
          Width           -    1095
       End
       Begin VB.DirListBox Dir1
          Height          -    1815
          Left            -    120
          TabIndex        -    1
          Top             -    600
          Width           -    2535
       End
       Begin VB.FileListBox File1
          BackColor       -    &H00FFFFFF&
          Height          -    1785
          Left            -    2820
          Pattern         -    "*.bmp"
          TabIndex        -    2
          Top             -    120
          Width           -    2415
       End
       Begin VB.DriveListBox Drive1
          Height          -    315
          Left            -    120
          TabIndex        -    0
          Top             -    120
          Width           -    2535
       End
    End
    Attribute VB_Name - "Puzzle2"
    Attribute VB_GlobalNameSpace - False
    Attribute VB_Creatable - False
    Attribute VB_PredeclaredId - True
    Attribute VB_Exposed - False


    '
    '   Hide the form and return control to the Puzzle form
    '
    Private Sub CmdCancel_Click()
        Unload Puzzle2
    End Sub


    '
    '   Load the selected file
    '
    Private Sub CmdLoad_Click()
        LoadBitmapFile
    End Sub

    Private Sub Dir1_Change()
        File1.Path - Dir1.Path
```

Listing 9.5 **Listing for PUZZLE2.FRM (Continued)**

```
End Sub

Private Sub Drive1_Change()
    Dir1.Path = Drive1.Drive
End Sub

Private Sub File1_Click()
    Dim fname$
    Dim di&
    If File1.filename <> "" Then
        fname$ = File1.Path
        If fname$ <> "\" Then fname$ = fname$ + "\"
        fname$ = fname$ + File1.filename
        picPreview.Picture = LoadPicture(fname$)
    End If

End Sub


'
'   Load the selected file
'
Private Sub File1_DblClick()
    LoadBitmapFile
End Sub

'   Loads the bitmap file specified in the file box
'   into bitmap 2 and reinitializes.
'
Private Sub LoadBitmapFile()
    Dim fname$
    If File1.filename <> "" Then
        fname$ = File1.Path
        If fname$ <> "\" Then fname$ = fname$ + "\"
        fname$ = fname$ + File1.filename
        Puzzle.Picture2.Picture = LoadPicture(fname$)
        DoTheUpdate% = -1
    End If

    Unload Puzzle2    ' And exit this form

End Sub
```

Listing 9.6 **Module PUZZLE.BAS**

```
Attribute VB_Name = "PUZZLE1"
'--------------------------------------------------
```

Listing 9.6   **Module PUZZLE.BAS (Continued)**

```
'
'            Public Constants
'
Option Explicit

Type RECT
        Left As Long
        Top As Long
        Right As Long
        Bottom As Long
End Type

Type BITMAPINFOHEADER '40 bytes
        biSize As Long
        biWidth As Long
        biHeight As Long
        biPlanes As Integer
        biBitCount As Integer
        biCompression As Long
        biSizeImage As Long
        biXPelsPerMeter As Long
        biYPelsPerMeter As Long
        biClrUsed As Long
        biClrImportant As Long
End Type

Type RGBQUAD
        rgbBlue As Byte
        rgbGreen As Byte
        rgbRed As Byte
        rgbReserved As Byte
End Type

Type BITMAPINFO
        bmiHeader As BITMAPINFOHEADER
        bmiColors(16) As RGBQUAD
End Type

Type BITMAP
        bmType As Long
        bmWidth As Long
        bmHeight As Long
        bmWidthBytes As Long
        bmPlanes As Integer
        bmBitsPixel As Integer
        bmBits As Long
End Type
```

Listing 9.6   **Module PUZZLE.BAS (Continued)**

```
Type POINTAPI
        X As Long
        Y As Long
End Type

    '------------------------------------------------
    '
    '       Public Variables
    '
    ' Bitmap segment location in each puzzle area
    ' This represents a 5x5 square array
    ' The index represents the position on picture1
    ' The entry for each index indicates the number of the
    ' tile in the bitmap to place in position index.
    Public Position%(24)

    Public PuzzleRect As RECT

    Public ShadowDC&
    Public BMinfo As BITMAP

    Public DestRects(24) As RECT
    Public SourceRects(24) As RECT

    ' A flag set by the Puzzle2 form to let the Puzzle form
    ' know that a new bitmap was loaded.
    Public DoTheUpdate%

    ' A random brush used for the empty square
    Public EmptySquareBrush&

    ' The mode of the empty square.
    ' 0 = black, 1 = white, 2 = use EmptySquareBrush
    Public EmptySquareMode%


    Declare Function PtInRect Lib "user32" (lpRect As RECT, ByVal ptx As Long, _
    ByVal pty As Long) As Long
    Declare Function GetObjectAPI& Lib "gdi32" Alias "GetObjectA" (ByVal hObject As _
    Long, ByVal nCount As Long, lpObject As Any)
    Declare Function CreateDIBitmap Lib "gdi32" (ByVal hdc As Long, lpInfoHeader As _
    BITMAPINFOHEADER, ByVal dwUsage As Long, lpInitBits As Any, lpInitInfo As _
    BITMAPINFO, ByVal wUsage As Long) As Long
```

Listing 9.6   Module PUZZLE.BAS (Continued)

```
Declare Function CreateDIBPatternBrush Lib "gdi32" (ByVal hPackedDIB As Long, _
ByVal wUsage As Long) As Long
Declare Function CreateDIBPatternBrushPt Lib "gdi32" (lpPackedDIB As Any, ByVal _
iUsage As Long) As Long
Declare Function DeleteDC Lib "gdi32" (ByVal hdc As Long) As Long
Declare Function GetClientRect Lib "user32" (ByVal hwnd As Long, lpRect As _
RECT) As Long
Declare Function CreateCompatibleDC Lib "gdi32" (ByVal hdc As Long) As Long
Declare Function SelectObject Lib "gdi32" (ByVal hdc As Long, ByVal hObject As _
Long) As Long
Declare Function StretchBlt Lib "gdi32" (ByVal hdc As Long, ByVal X As Long, _
ByVal Y As Long, ByVal nWidth As Long, ByVal nHeight As Long, ByVal _
hSrcDC As Long, ByVal xSrc As Long, ByVal ySrc As Long, ByVal nSrcWidth As _
Long, ByVal nSrcHeight As Long, ByVal dwRop As Long) As Long
Declare Function PatBlt Lib "gdi32" (ByVal hdc As Long, ByVal X As Long, ByVal _
Y As Long, ByVal nWidth As Long, ByVal nHeight As Long, ByVal dwRop As Long) _
As Long
Declare Function CreatePatternBrush Lib "gdi32" (ByVal hBitmap As Long) As Long
Declare Function DeleteObject Lib "gdi32" (ByVal hObject As Long) As Long
Declare Function LoadImage Lib "user32" Alias "LoadImageA" (ByVal hInst As _
Long, ByVal lpsz As String, ByVal un1 As Long, ByVal n1 As Long, _
ByVal n2 As Long, ByVal un2 As Long) As Long


Public Const CBM_INIT = &H4&      ' initialize bitmap
Public Const DIB_RGB_COLORS = 0 ' color table in RGBTriples
Public Const DIB_PAL_COLORS = 1 ' color table in palette indices

Public Const SRCCOPY = &HCC0020
Public Const SRCPAINT = &HEE0086
Public Const SRCAND = &H8800C6
Public Const SRCINVERT = &H660046
Public Const SRCERASE = &H440328
Public Const NOTSRCCOPY = &H330008
Public Const NOTSRCERASE = &H1100A6
Public Const MERGECOPY = &HC000CA
Public Const MERGEPAINT = &HBB0226
Public Const PATCOPY = &HF00021
Public Const PATPAINT = &HFB0A09
Public Const PATINVERT = &H5A0049
Public Const DSTINVERT = &H550009
Public Const BLACKNESS = &H42&
```

Listing 9.6   **Module PUZZLE.BAS (Continued)**

```
Public Const WHITENESS = &HFF0062
Public Const BLACKONWHITE = 1
Public Const WHITEONBLACK = 2
Public Const COLORONCOLOR = 3
Public Const BI_RGB = 0&
Public Const BI_RLE8 = 1&
Public Const BI_RLE4 = 2&
Public Const TRANSPARENT = 1
Public Const OPAQUE = 2
```

Listing 9.7   **Listing for Puzzle.frm**

```
'
' Initialization routine
'
Private Sub Form_Load()
    Randomize
    SetPuzzleSize    ' Set the size of the puzzle window
    CalcRects        ' Calculate the window tiles
    Scramble         ' Scramble them
    CreateEmptyBrush    ' Create a random brush for the
                        ' empty square.
End Sub
```

There are many ways to set the size of controls within a form. The technique shown here is a rather roundabout way of doing it—based on the client rectangle. But since we need to initialize the PuzzleRect variable anyway, there is no harm in demonstrating the pixel to twips conversion at the same time.

```
'
'   Sets the picture1 control to the visible form area
'   Also creates a compatible bitmap to work with
'   Call this any time the size of the form changes
'
Private Sub SetPuzzleSize()
Dim rc As RECT

    Dim di&
    Picture1.BorderStyle = 0
    Picture1.Left = 0
    Picture1.Top = 0
    di = GetClientRect(Puzzle.hwnd, rc)

    ' Actually, we need not subtract off rc.left and rc.top
```

```
    ' below as these fields are always Ø after a call to
    ' GetClientRect
    ' Note the conversion to twips in order to set the
    ' picture size using the VB properties
    ' We could have used the MoveWindow API call as well - or just set it based _
      on the ScaleWidth and ScaleHeight
    ' of the form itself.
    Picture1.Width = Screen.TwipsPerPixelX * (rc.Right - rc.Left)
    Picture1.Height = Screen.TwipsPerPixelY * (rc.Bottom - rc.Top)

    ' This line is actually not necessary - we could
    ' have just used a copy of rc because we just set
    ' the client area to that specified by rc!
    GetClientRect Picture1.hwnd, PuzzleRect

    ' Create a compatible memory DC for Picture1
    If ShadowDC Then di = DeleteDC(ShadowDC)
    ShadowDC = CreateCompatibleDC(Picture1.hdc)


End Sub



'
'   Calculate all source and destination rectangles
'   Call this whenever the form size changes or the
'   image bitmap is changed.
'
Private Sub CalcRects()
    Dim x%, y%, pos%

    Dim bmsegwidth%, bmsegheight%
    Dim picsegwidth%, picsegheight%
    Dim di&

    ' Find the approx. height and width of each tile on
    ' the puzzle screen.
    picsegwidth% = (PuzzleRect.Right - PuzzleRect.Left) / 5
    picsegheight% = (PuzzleRect.Bottom - PuzzleRect.Top) / 5

    ' Get information on the bitmap in picture2
    ' This loads the BITMAP structure bmInfo with information
    ' on the bitmap.
    di = GetObjectAPI(Picture2.Picture, Len(BMinfo), BMinfo)

    bmsegwidth% = BMinfo.bmWidth / 5
    bmsegheight% = BMinfo.bmHeight / 5

    ' Fill in the rectangle description for each rectangle on
    ' the destination DC
```

```
For y% = 0 To 4
    For x% = 0 To 4
        pos% = y% * 5 + x%
        DestRects(pos%).Top = y% * picsegheight%
        DestRects(pos%).Bottom = (y% + 1) * picsegheight%
        DestRects(pos%).Left = x% * picsegwidth%
        DestRects(pos%).Right = (x% + 1) * picsegwidth%
    Next x%
Next y%


' Fill in the rectangle description for each rectangle on
' the source bitmap
For y% = 0 To 4
    For x% = 0 To 4
        pos% = y% * 5 + x%
        SourceRects(pos%).Top = y% * bmsegheight%
        SourceRects(pos%).Bottom = (y% + 1) * bmsegheight%
        SourceRects(pos%).Left = x% * bmsegwidth%
        SourceRects(pos%).Right = (x% + 1) * bmsegwidth%
        ' Make sure the rectangle does not exceed the
        ' source area for the bitmap or StretchBlt will fail
        If x% = 4 Then SourceRects(pos%).Right = BMinfo.bmWidth
        If y% = 4 Then SourceRects(pos%).Bottom = BMinfo.bmHeight
    Next x%
Next y%



End Sub
```

Function CreateEmptyBrush is one of the most important functions in
this book and is worthy of further review. The function begins by creating a
device-independent bitmap. A DIB is not a GDI object—in other words,
there is no window handle to a DIB. A DIB is simply a set of data structures
in memory that meets the specification for a device-independent bitmap.
Most of the DIB functions divide the DIB into two parts. The header information (BITMAPINFO data structure) contains the definition of the DIB and
the color table. The bitmap data itself is kept in a separate data array.

CreateEmptyBrush creates a DIB by first defining and initializing a
BITMAPINFOHEADER structure to the desired values. This structure is
copied into a BITMAPINFO structure along with a desired color table.
Finally, a separate block of memory (byte array *da*) is loaded with bitmap
data—in this case, a random pattern.

At this point the DIB is complete. It consists of structure *bi* containing
the header and string *da* containing the bitmap data.

Unlike a DIB, a regular (device-dependent) bitmap is a GDI object and
thus has a window handle. A device-dependent bitmap can be created easily

from a valid DIB using the CreateDIBitmap function as shown, and this bitmap can in turn be used to create a brush.

The principles shown here can be applied to all DIB and bitmap operations. In addition, the PicPrint sample in Chapter 12 makes extensive use of device-independent bitmaps.

```
'   Creates a brush to use for the empty square
'   This function demonstrates the creation of device-
'   independent bitmaps, converting DIBs to a device-dependent
'   bitmap and finally converting a DDB into a brush.
'
Private Sub CreateEmptyBrush()
Dim compbitmap&
Dim bih As BITMAPINFOHEADER
Dim bi As BITMAPINFO
ReDim colarray&(16)
Dim x%
Dim di&

' This used to be a string
Dim da(32) As Byte    ' Each byte contains 2 x 4bit pixels
Dim buf$
Dim bufstart&, sourceaddr&
Dim oldbm&


        ' Prepare the bitmap information header
        bih.biSize = 40        ' 40 bytes in this structure
        bih.biWidth = 8        ' 8x8 -we'll be creating a brush
        bih.biHeight = 8       ' from this bimap
        bih.biPlanes = 1       ' DIBs always 1 plane
        bih.biBitCount = 4     ' 16 colors, 4 bits/color
        bih.biCompression = BI_RGB  ' no compression
        bih.biSizeImage = 0         ' Not needed on BI_RGB
        bih.biXPelsPerMeter = 0     ' Not used
        bih.biYPelsPerMeter = 0     ' Not used
        bih.biClrUsed = 16          ' All colors used
        bih.biClrImportant = 0      ' All colors important


        ' Now fill the color array
        For x% = 0 To 15
            colarray&(x%) = QBColor(x%)
        Next x%

        ' Now we need to set the data array - for now, we're
        ' just going to put in random pixel data
        For x% = 1 To 32
            ' Note how we pack two nibbles
            ' The old way
            ' Mid$(da, x%, 1) = Chr$(Int(Rnd * 16) + Int(Rnd * 16) * 16)
            ' The new way
```

```
            da(x%) = Int(Rnd * 16) + Int(Rnd * 16) * 16
    Next x%

    ' Now we load the BITMAPINFO structure bi
    LSet bi.bmiHeader = bih
    ' Now copy the color array into the BITMAPINFO
    ' bi.bmiColors string which begins 40 characters after
    ' the start of the structure.
    ' Refer to Chapter 15 for information on the subtleties
    ' of extracting addresses for strings in a structure.
    bufstart& = agGetAddressForObject(bi.bmiHeader.biSize) + 40

    ' Get the address of the start of the colarray color array
    sourceaddr& = agGetAddressForLong(colarray&(0))
    ' And copy the 64 bytes
    agCopyDataBynum sourceaddr&, bufstart&, 64

    ' Now create the bitmap
    compbitmap& = CreateDIBitmap(Puzzle.hdc, bih, CBM_INIT, da(0), bi, _
    DIB_RGB_COLORS)


    ' Now create a brush from this bitmap
    EmptySquareBrush& = CreatePatternBrush(compbitmap)

    ' And delete the source bitmap
    di = DeleteObject&(compbitmap&)

End Sub



Private Sub DoUpdate()
'
'   Update the picture with rectangles based on the
'   puzzle array
'
    Dim x%

    For x% = 0 To 24
        UpdateOne x%
    Next x%

End Sub



'
'   When the form is resized, call SetPuzzleSize to
'   adjust the size of the picture window and rescale
'   the image.
'
Private Sub Form_Resize()
```

```
        SetPuzzleSize    ' Set the size of the puzzle window
        CalcRects        ' And recalculate the tiles
        Picture1.Refresh     ' Update the picture control
End Sub


'
'   Clean up by deleting GDI objects that are no longer
'   needed.
'
Private Sub Form_Unload(Cancel As Integer)
    Dim di&
    If ShadowDC& Then di = DeleteDC(ShadowDC)
    If EmptySquareBrush& Then di = DeleteObject(EmptySquareBrush)
End Sub


'
'   Choose the color for the empty square
'
Private Sub MenuEmpty_Click(Index As Integer)
    Dim x%
    MenuEmpty(EmptySquareMode%).Checked = 0
    MenuEmpty(Index).Checked = -1
    EmptySquareMode% = Index
    DoUpdate
End Sub


'
'   Bring up the file load dialog box to load a new
'   bitmap into the puzzle.
'
Private Sub MenuLoad_Click()
    DoTheUpdate = 0 ' Preset the update flag to false
    Puzzle2.Show 1   ' Show the file load form modal
    If DoTheUpdate Then ' A valid bitmap was loaded
        CalcRects    ' Recalculate the tiles
        Scramble     ' And refresh the image
    End If

End Sub


'
'   Rescramble the bitmap image
'
Private Sub MenuScramble_Click()
    Scramble
    DoUpdate   ' Redraw the puzzle window
End Sub


'
'   Clicking on a tile next to the empty tile causes that
'   tile to slide into the empty space.
'
```

```
Private Sub Picture1_MouseDown(Button As Integer, Shift As Integer, x As _
Single, y As Single)
    Dim pt As POINTAPI
    Dim u%
    Dim xpos%, ypos%
    Dim bxpos%, bypos%
    Dim dx%, dy%, tval%, hidden%

    pt.x = x     ' Picture1 scalemode is pixels
    pt.y = y

    ' Find the location of the black square
    ' Tile 24 in the bitmap is the missing piece.
    For hidden% = 0 To 24
        If Position%(hidden%) = 24 Then Exit For
    Next hidden%

    For u% = 0 To 24
        ' Find out which rectangle in the DestRects array
        ' contains the point specified by the mouse click.
        If PtInRect(DestRects(u%), pt.x, pt.y) Then
            Exit For
        End If
    Next u%
    ' Now find the X and Y coordinates for the mouse click
    ' and for the hidden tile.
    xpos% = u% Mod 5
    ypos% = Int(u% / 5)
    bxpos% = hidden% Mod 5
    bypos% = Int(hidden% / 5)

    ' The tile can slide into the empty square if it is
    ' one away from the empty square on the horizontal
    ' or vertical axis (but not both).
    dx% = Abs(xpos - bxpos%)
    dy% = Abs(ypos - bypos%)
    If (dx% = 1 And dy% = 0) Or (dx% = 0 And dy% = 1) Then
        tval% = Position%(u%)
        ' So simply swap this tile with the hidden one
        Position%(u%) = Position%(hidden%)
        Position%(hidden%) = tval%
        ' And update both these tiles
        UpdateOne u%
        UpdateOne hidden%

    End If
End Sub


'
'   Paint picture1 by calling the full puzzle Update routine
'
Private Sub Picture1_Paint()
```

```
        DoUpdate
End Sub


'
'    Scramble the puzzle array
'
Private Sub Scramble()
Dim x%, newpos%, hold%

        ' Initialize the positions
        For x% = 0 To 24
            Position%(x%) = x%
        Next x%
        ' Now scramble them
        For x% = 0 To 24
            ' For each source position, choose a random
            ' location and swap the two values.
            ' This is a simple and effective technique to
            ' randomize an array of numbers.
            newpos% = Int(Rnd * 25)
            hold% = Position(x%)
            Position(x%) = Position(newpos%)
            Position(newpos%) = hold%
        Next x%
End Sub
```

The UpdateOne function performs the actual drawing and demonstrates the use of the StretchBlt function to copy parts of one image to another, moving and stretching the image along the way.

```
'
'    Copies a single tile from the picture2 bitmap to the
'    appropriate space in the picture1 destination.
'    x% is the position on the puzzle to update
'
Private Sub UpdateOne(x%)
    Dim oldbm&, pos&, oldbrush&
    ' Temporary variables for copying
    Dim sx&, sy&, sw&, sh&, dx&, dy&, dw&, dh&
    Dim di&

    ' Select the bitmap into the ShadowDC
    oldbm& = SelectObject(ShadowDC&, Picture2.Picture)
    ' Select the random brush we created into the picture DC
    If EmptySquareBrush& <> 0 Then oldbrush& = SelectObject(Picture1.hdc, _
    EmptySquareBrush&)

    ' Get the position in the bitmap.
    ' Position 24 is the empty square
    pos& = Position(x)

    ' Calculate the rectangle on the puzzle display being
```

```
' updataed
dx& = DestRects(x).Left
dy& = DestRects(x).Top
dw& = DestRects(x).Right - dx&
dh& = DestRects(x).Bottom - dy&

' The bitmap locations are based on x% - the source
' location in the bitmap
sx& = SourceRects(pos&).Left
sy& = SourceRects(pos&).Top
sw& = SourceRects(pos&).Right - sx&
sh& = SourceRects(pos&).Bottom - sy&

' Now do the transfer
' Transfer all tiles from the source except for tile
' number 24 which is the black one.
If pos <> 24 Then
    di& = StretchBlt(Picture1.hdc, dx, dy, dw, dh, ShadowDC, sx, sy, sw, _
    sh, SRCCOPY)
Else ' Tile #24 is empty - use EmptySquareMode% to
    ' determine what type of square to set.
    Select Case EmptySquareMode%
        Case 0
            di = PatBlt(Picture1.hdc, dx, dy, dw, dh, BLACKNESS)
        Case 1
            di = PatBlt(Picture1.hdc, dx, dy, dw, dh, WHITENESS)
        Case 2
            di = PatBlt(Picture1.hdc, dx, dy, dw, dh, PATCOPY)
    End Select
End If

' Select the bitmap out of the shadow DC
di = SelectObject(ShadowDC, oldbm)
' And select the brush back to the original one
If EmptySquareBrush <> 0 Then di = SelectObject(Picture1.hdc, oldbrush)
End Sub
```

Suggestions for Further Practice

There are a number of ways to improve the Puzzle application. Here are some suggestions that you may wish to consider:

- Detect the winning condition automatically (Hint: It can be determined by looking at the contents of the Position array).

- Add lines to mark the tile borders. What line raster operation (ROP2) would produce the best effect?

- Add a form that allows you to edit an 8x8-pixel bitmap that will be used to create the brush pattern (instead of the random data used in the example).

■ Test whether you are running under Windows NT. If so, allow the use of a larger brush pattern than 8x8 pixels.

DIBSect—A Demonstration of Using DIBSection Objects

DIBSect is a simple program that demonstrates the use of DIBSections, a GDI object that has the internal format of a device-independent bitmap.

Figure 9.14 shows the runtime screen of the DIBSect program (though much of the impact is lost in black and white).

Figure 9.14
DIBSect runtime screen

Using DIBSect

The DIBSect program has a single picture control. When you click the Randomize button, the program sets individual pixels in a DIBSection bitmap to random colors by directly accessing the DIB memory. It then BitBlts the image to the picture control. The DrawRect button draws into the memory device context which has the DIBSection bitmap selected, demonstrating that GDI graphic commands work with DIBSection bitmaps. The Strip Red, Green, and Blue buttons perform simple image processing operations, removing the red, green, or blue components from the image. This particular task could be accomplished without too much trouble (and with better performance) using raster operations; however, it does demonstrate the fact that direct access to bitmap memory allows the ultimate flexibility in image manipulation.

Project Description

The DIBSect program contains one form only and is shown in Listing 9.8. The program also uses file APIGID32.BAS, the declaration file for the APIGID32.DLL dynamic link library that is included with this book.

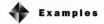

Listing 9.8   DIBSECT.FRM

```
VERSION 5.00
Begin VB.Form frmDIBSection
   Caption         =   "DIBSection Demo"
   ClientHeight    =   4515
   ClientLeft      =   1095
   ClientTop       =   1515
   ClientWidth     =   5580
   Height          =   4920
   Left            =   1035
   LinkTopic       =   "Form1"
   ScaleHeight     =   4515
   ScaleWidth      =   5580
   Top             =   1170
   Width           =   5700
   Begin VB.CommandButton cmdWhiteRect
      Caption      =   "Draw Rect"
      Height       =   435
      Left         =   1980
      TabIndex     =   6
      Top          =   2880
      Width        =   1335
   End
   Begin VB.CommandButton cmdStrip
      Caption      =   "Strip Blue"
      Height       =   495
      Index        =   2
      Left         =   480
      TabIndex     =   5
      Top          =   2820
      Width        =   1035
   End
   Begin VB.CommandButton cmdStrip
      Caption      =   "Strip Green"
      Height       =   495
      Index        =   1
      Left         =   480
      TabIndex     =   4
      Top          =   2220
      Width        =   1035
   End
   Begin VB.CommandButton cmdStrip
      Caption      =   "Strip Red"
      Height       =   495
      Index        =   0
      Left         =   480
      TabIndex     =   3
      Top          =   1620
      Width        =   1035
```

Listing 9.8   DIBSECT.FRM (Continued)

```
            End
            Begin VB.CommandButton cmdRandom
                Caption         =   "Randomize"
                Height          =   495
                Left            =   480
                TabIndex        =   2
                Top             =   900
                Width           =   1035
            End
            Begin VB.CommandButton cmdUpdate
                Caption         =   "Update"
                Height          =   495
                Left            =   480
                TabIndex        =   1
                Top             =   240
                Width           =   1035
            End
            Begin VB.PictureBox picDisplay
                Height          =   2355
                Left            =   1980
                ScaleHeight     =   155
                ScaleMode       =   3   'Pixel
                ScaleWidth      =   207
                TabIndex        =   0
                Top             =   240
                Width           =   3135
            End
        End
        Attribute VB_Name = "frmDIBSection"
        Attribute VB_GlobalNameSpace = False
        Attribute VB_Creatable = False
        Attribute VB_PredeclaredId = TrueAttribute VB_Exposed = False
        Option Explicit


        Private Type BITMAPINFOHEADER '40 bytes
                biSize As Long
                biWidth As Long
                biHeight As Long
                biPlanes As Integer
                biBitCount As Integer
                biCompression As Long
                biSizeImage As Long
                biXPelsPerMeter As Long
                biYPelsPerMeter As Long
                biClrUsed As Long
                biClrImportant As Long
        End Type
```

Listing 9.8   DIBSECT.FRM (Continued)

```vb
Private Type RGBQUAD
        rgbBlue As Byte
        rgbGreen As Byte
        rgbRed As Byte
        rgbReserved As Byte
End Type

Private Type BITMAPINFO
        bmiHeader As BITMAPINFOHEADER
        bmiColors As RGBQUAD    ' RGB, so length here doesn't matter
End Type

Dim binfo As BITMAPINFO
Dim CompDC As Long    ' Compatible DC to hold the bitmap
Dim addr As Long      ' Pointer to memory block containing bitmap data
Dim DIBSectionHandle As Long    ' Handle to DIBSection
Dim OldCompDCBM As Long         ' Original bitmap for CompDC
Dim BytesPerScanLine As Long    ' Hold this value to improve performance

Private Const BI_RGB = 0&
Private Const BI_RLE8 = 1&
Private Const BI_RLE4 = 2&
Private Const DIB_RGB_COLORS = 0 '  color table in RGBs
Private Const DIB_PAL_COLORS = 1 '  color table in palette indices
Private Const SRCCOPY = &HCC0020 ' (DWORD) dest = source

Private Declare Function CreateDIBSection Lib "gdi32" (ByVal hdc As Long, _
pBitmapInfo As BITMAPINFO, ByVal un As Long, lplpVoid As Long, ByVal _
handle As Long, ByVal dw As Long) As Long
Private Declare Function CreateCompatibleDC Lib "gdi32" (ByVal hdc As Long) As _
Long
Private Declare Function BitBlt Lib "gdi32" (ByVal hDestDC As Long, ByVal x As _
Long, ByVal y As Long, ByVal nWidth As Long, ByVal nHeight As Long, ByVal _
hSrcDC As Long, ByVal xSrc As Long, ByVal ySrc As Long, ByVal dwRop As Long) _
As Long
Private Declare Function SelectObject Lib "gdi32" (ByVal hdc As Long, ByVal _
hObject As Long) As Long
Private Declare Function DeleteDC Lib "gdi32" (ByVal hdc As Long) As Long
Private Declare Function DeleteObject Lib "gdi32" (ByVal hObject As Long) As _
Long
Private Declare Function GetLastError Lib "kernel32" () As Long
```

| **Listing 9.8** | **DIBSECT.FRM (Continued)** |

```
Private Declare Function GetStockObject Lib "gdi32" (ByVal nIndex As Long) As _
Long
Private Declare Function Rectangle Lib "gdi32" (ByVal hdc As Long, ByVal X1 As _
Long, ByVal Y1 As Long, ByVal X2 As Long, ByVal Y2 As Long) As Long
```

Creating a DIBSection is similar at first to creating any device-independent bitmap. You must first initialize the BITMAPINFOHEADER structure. This involves calculating the total size of the bitmap as well. Even though the image uses three bytes per pixel (24-bit color), it is not enough to simply multiply the height by the width and multiply the result by three. That simple calculation does not take into account the need for each scan line to end on a 32-bit boundary. Instead you must calculate the number of bytes in each scan line and multiply the result by the height (the number of scan lines). The ScanAlign function performs this operation. The number of bytes per pixel (or pixels per byte) depends on the bitmap format. The code shows the equations that you would use for other DIB formats. The number of bytes per scan line is stored in the BytesPerScanLine variable for later reference.

The height of the DIB is set to a negative number, forcing the DIB to set the upper-left corner of the bitmap as the origin (location 0,0).

Once you have the BITMAPINFO structure initialized, it can be passed as a parameter to the CreateDIBSection function. In this example, there is no need to initialize the color table—that's one advantage of using 24-bit color. As shown here, the CreateDIBSection function allocates a memory buffer to hold the bitmap and stores that information into the addr variable. This is, by the way, a good illustration of the importance of understanding how to declare API functions on your own. In the original WIN32API.TXT provided with Visual Basic, the declaration for this function specified that the address parameter be passed by value. The function would work, and would return a valid bitmap handle, but because it was passed by value, the addr variable would never be set—the function would happily load the address into the temporary copy of the addr variable made when the parameter was passed. This kind of problem can be hard to find, since the function returns (correctly) a result indicating that it succeeded. This emphasizes the reason that you are strongly encouraged to use the API32.TXT file provided with this book instead of WIN32API.TXT; there were hundreds of changes and corrections made for this book.

```
Private Sub Form_Load()
    Randomize
    ' Create a compatible DC to use
    CompDC = CreateCompatibleDC(0)
```

```
    ' Initialize the DIBSection header
    With binfo.bmiHeader
        .biSize = 40
        .biWidth = picDisplay.ScaleWidth
        .biHeight = -picDisplay.ScaleHeight
        .biPlanes = 1
        .biBitCount = 24 ' True RGB
        .biCompression = BI_RGB
        ' How many bytes per scan line?
        ' For 256 colors: ScanAlign(.biWidth)
        ' For 16 colors: ScanAlign((.biWidth+1) \ 2)
        ' For monochrome: ScanAlign((.biWidth+7) \ 8)
        ' For 24 bit color, as follows:
        BytesPerScanLine = ScanAlign(.biWidth * 3)
        .biSizeImage = BytesPerScanLine * .biHeight
    End With
    DIBSectionHandle = CreateDIBSection(CompDC, binfo, DIB_RGB_COLORS, addr, 0, _
    0)
    OldCompDCBM = SelectObject(CompDC, DIBSectionHandle)

End Sub
```

One simple way to force an alignment to 32 bits is shown here. The AND operation clears the lower two bits, which specifies a 32-bit boundary (in fact, the definition of being on a 32-bit boundary is having the two low bits set to zero). Be sure to add 3 first so that you are effectively rounding up.

```
' Scans must align on 32 bit boundary'
Public Function ScanAlign(pwidth&) As Long
    ScanAlign = (pwidth + 3) And &HFFFFFFFC
End Function
```

The cmdWhiteRect function shows how easy it is to perform standard GDI graphic commands on device contexts that have DIBSections selected.

```
Private Sub cmdWhiteRect_Click()
    Dim di&
    di = SelectObject(CompDC, GetStockObject(0))
    di = Rectangle(CompDC, 0, 0, 50, 50)
    cmdUpdate_Click
End Sub


Private Sub cmdRandom_Click()
    Dim x&
    Dim usex&, usey&
    Dim di&
    With binfo.bmiHeader
        ' Faster to access width & height in structure than pic properties
        For x& = 1 To 1000
            usex& = Int(Rnd() * .biWidth)
```

```
            ' Height can be negative for top down DIB
            usey& = Abs(Int(Rnd() * .biHeight))
            SetSectionPixel usex&, usey&, RGB(Rnd() * 256, Rnd() * 256, Rnd() * _
            256)
        Next x&
    End With

    cmdUpdate_Click

End Sub

Private Sub cmdStrip_Click(Index As Integer)
    StripColor Index
    cmdUpdate_Click
End Sub

Private Sub cmdUpdate_Click()
    Dim di&
    di& = BitBlt(picDisplay.hdc, 0, 0, picDisplay.ScaleWidth, _
    picDisplay.ScaleHeight, CompDC, 0, 0, SRCCOPY)
End Sub



'
' Clean up afterwards
'
Private Sub Form_Unload(Cancel As Integer)
    Dim di
    di = SelectObject(CompDC, OldCompDCBM)
    di = DeleteDC(CompDC)
    di = DeleteObject(DIBSectionHandle)
End Sub
```

SetSectionPixel shows how to calculate the location of a particular pixel within the data area. Watch the subtle use of the agCopyData function. When you calculate the address, you must pass it by value. But the color parameter must be passed by reference, since you need to copy the contents of that variable to the address specified.

```
'
' Calculates the location of a pixel in a DIBSection and sets it
'
Public Sub SetSectionPixel(ByVal x&, ByVal y&, ByVal color&)
    Dim ByteOffset&
    ' How would you modify this code for a 16 color, 256 color and monochrome _
    DIB?
    ByteOffset = y * BytesPerScanLine + x * 3
    agCopyData color, ByVal (addr + ByteOffset), 3

End Sub
```

The StripColor function uses the same technique shown in the SetSectionPixel function; however, it is noteworthy in its use of simple hand optimization to improve performance. Notice how each calculation is moved as far out of the loop as possible.

This illustrates an issue that does not relate so much to use of the Win32 API as to programming in general. A quick and obvious approach to this task would have been to use an double nested loop and simply call the SetSection-Pixel function within the loop. An advanced optimizing compiler such as Visual C++ would be able to take that code and improve its performance considerably, though it might not end up with as efficient an algorithm as is shown here. It is also true that this algorithm would be faster in C or C++ than it is in Visual Basic, but this is exactly the kind of routine that gains the greatest improvement from Visual Basic 5.0's native code compilation. It is important to stress that the performance benefit of redesigning the algorithm as shown here is greater than the additional performance benefit that you obtain by switching from P-code to native code compilation. In other words, the best way to improve the performance of Visual Basic code is to write good Visual Basic code—compiling code comes second.

```
'
' This strips the Red, Green, or Blue component from the image
' Could you do this in other color modes?
'
Public Sub StripColor(ByVal colorindex%)
    Dim ByteOffset&
    Dim cury&
    Dim curx&
    Dim ScanOffset&
    Dim CurrentAddr&
    Dim ByteToStrip%
    ' Reorder to match organization of bytes in DIB
    Select Case colorindex
        Case 0   ' Red
                ByteToStrip = 2
        Case 1   ' Green
                ByteToStrip = 1
        Case 2   ' Blue
                ByteToStrip = 0
    End Select

    Dim zerobyte As Byte
    ' We need to scan each line
    ' Note how we hand optimize the code to reduce calculations
    ScanOffset = addr    ' First scan line
    With binfo.bmiHeader
        For cury& = 0 To Abs(.biHeight) - 1
            ' Take into account which byte we are clearing here
            CurrentAddr& = ScanOffset& + ByteToStrip
```

```
            For curx& = 0 To .biWidth - 1
                ' Clear one byte
                agCopyData zerobyte, ByVal CurrentAddr&, 1
                CurrentAddr = CurrentAddr + 3
            Next curx&
        ScanOffset& = ScanOffset& + BytesPerScanLine
        Next cury&
    End With


End Sub

Private Sub picDisplay_Paint()
    cmdUpdate_Click
End Sub
```

Suggestions for Further Practice

This concludes the sample programs for this chapter. You are strongly encouraged to look at the other sample programs that are included on the CD-ROM. In addition, you may wish to try the following:

- Modify the DIBSection program so that it works with monochrome and 16-color and 256-color bitmaps as well.

- Modify the Shade program so that it restores the screen to its original appearance (right now you can do so by dragging the form around the screen, erasing the shading effect).

- Create a file browser that lists all of the icons available or associated with a file when you click on it.

- Create a file information viewer that displays information about .BMP files without actually loading them.

Function Reference

■ BitBlt

VB Declaration   `Declare Function BitBlt& Lib "gdi32" (ByVal hDestDC As Long, ByVal x As Long, _`
`ByVal y As Long, ByVal nWidth As Long, ByVal nHeight As Long, ByVal hSrcDC As _`
`Long, ByVal xSrc As Long, ByVal ySrc As Long, ByVal dwRop As Long)`

Description   Copies a bitmap from one device context to another. The source and destination DCs must be compatible with one another as described in the chapter text.

Use with VB   Refer to "Using Bitmaps with Visual Basic," earlier in this chapter.

Parameter	Type/Description
hDestDC	Long—Destination device context.
x, y	Long—Point describing the upper-left corner of the destination rectangle within the destination DC. This is specified in logical coordinates of the destination DC.
nWidth, nHeight	Long—Width and height of the image being transferred
hSrcDC	Long—Source device context. If the raster operation does not specify a source, this should be 0.
xSrc, ySrc	Long—Point describing the upper-left corner of the source rectangle within the source DC. This is specified in logical coordinates of the source DC.
dwRop	Long—Raster operation to use during the transfer. Refer to "Raster Operations," earlier in this chapter.

Return Value   Long—Nonzero on success, zero on failure. Sets GetLastError.

Platform   Windows 95, Windows NT, Win16
   This function will fail under NT if a world transformation that involves a shear or rotation is in effect in the source device context.

Comments   If the mapping modes of the destination and source DCs are such that the size in pixels of the rectangle must be changed during the transfer, this function will stretch, rotate, shear, fold, spindle, or mutilate the bitmap as necessary to perform the transfer. Conversions between monochrome and color bitmaps are discussed in "Color Conversions," earlier in this chapter.

Example   Puzzle, ROPTest, DIBSect

■ CopyIcon

VB Declaration   `Declare Function CopyIcon& Lib "user32" (ByVal hIcon As Long)`

Description   Makes a copy of the specified icon or cursor. The copy will belong to the calling application.

Use with VB	No problem.

Parameter	Type/Description
hIcon	Long—Handle of the icon or cursor to copy.

Return Value	Long—Handle of the new icon, zero on error. Sets GetLastError.
Platform	Windows 95, Windows NT, Win16
Porting Notes	CopyIcon can be used to copy cursors on Win32; thus Win32 does not support the Win16 Copy-Cursor function.
Comments	When you load an icon from a DLL or another application, that icon can only be used as long as the DLL or application remains loaded. This function allows you to make a copy of an icon that belongs to your application. This icon must be destroyed when it's no longer needed using the DestroyIcon API function to free up the system resources used.

■ CopyImage

VB Declaration	`Declare Function CopyImage& Lib "user32" (ByVal handle As Long, ByVal un1 As _` `Long, ByVal n1 As Long, ByVal n2 As Long, ByVal un2 As Long)`
Description	Allows you to copy a bitmap, icon, or cursor, performing some transformations on it during the copy.
Use with VB	No problem.

Parameter	Type/Description
handle	Long—A handle to the image to copy.
un1	Long—One of the constants IMAGE BITMAP, IMAGE_CURSOR, or IMAGE_ICON.
n1	Long—The width of the copy in pixels.
n2	Long—The height of the copy in pixels.
un2	Long—One or more of the following constants combined: LR_DELETEORG—Delete the original image. LR_COPYRETURNORG—Ignore n1 & n2. LR_MONOCHROME—Create a monochrome copy. LR_COPYFROMRESOURCE—Create a copy based on the original resource from which the original was loaded. Say you are trying to make a 64 x 64 copy of a 32 x 32 icon. Without this flag, CopyImage will stretch the original icon. With this flag, CopyImage will first check to see if a 64x64 version of this icon exists in the resource file—if so, it will load this higher quality image.

Return Value	Long—A handle to the new image on success, zero on error. Sets GetLastError.
Platform	Windows 95, Windows NT

Comments　　This function is often used in cases where you wish to copy a bitmap that is already selected into another device context—for example, to copy a bitmap that is part of an ImageList control. The selected bitmap is not available because bitmaps can only be selected into one device context at a time.

■ CreateBitmap

VB Declaration　　`Declare Function CreateBitmap& Lib "gdi32" (ByVal nWidth As Long, ByVal nHeight _`
`As Long, ByVal nPlanes As Long, ByVal nBitCount As Long, lpBits As Any)`

Description　　Creates a device-dependent bitmap in the format specified.

Use with VB　　Refer to "Using Bitmaps with Visual Basic," earlier in this chapter.

Parameter	Type/Description
nWidth	Long—Width of the bitmap in pixels.
nHeight	Long—Height of the bitmap in pixels.
nPlanes	Long—Number of color planes.
nBitCount	Long—Number of bits per pixel.
lpBits	Any—Pointer to data to load into the bitmap. May be zero to leave the bitmap uninitialized (remember to use ByVal to pass a zero value). The format of this data must match that required by the device. Scan lines must be aligned to 16-bit word boundaries.

Return Value　　Long—The bitmap handle on success, zero on failure.

Platform　　Windows 95, Windows NT, Win16

Comments　　Use the DeleteObject function to free the memory and resources used by the bitmap when it is no longer needed. Refer to "Using Bitmaps," earlier in this chapter.

　　Use this function to create monochrome bitmaps (1 plane, 1 bit per pixel). For color bitmaps, you should use CreateCompatibleBitmap. This function will work but using bitmaps created with this function is slower because Windows must verify the bitmap format each time it is used.

　　If nWidth and nHeight are zero, the bitmap returned will be a 1x1 monochrome bitmap.

Example　　Shade.vbp

■ CreateBitmapIndirect

VB Declaration　　`Declare Function CreateBitmapIndirect& Lib "gdi32" (lpBitmap As BITMAP)`

Description　　Creates a device-dependent bitmap.

Use with VB　　Refer to "Using Bitmaps with Visual Basic," earlier in this chapter.

Parameter	Type/Description
lpBitmap	BITMAP—Structure describing a logical bitmap. The fields inside this structure correspond closely to the parameters of CreateBitmap function. Refer also to Appendix B for further information.

Return Value	Long—The bitmap handle on success, zero on failure.
Platform	Windows 95, Windows NT, Win16
Comments	When using a BITMAP structure obtained using the GetObject API function, keep in mind that GetObject does not retrieve bitmap data—only the size and configuration of the bitmap. If nWidth and nHeight are zero, the bitmap returned will be a 1x1 monochrome bitmap. Refer also to the comments under the CreateBitmap function.
Example	See CreateBitmap.

■ CreateCompatibleBitmap

VB Declaration
```
Declare Function CreateCompatibleBitmap& Lib "gdi32" (ByVal hdc As Long, ByVal _
nWidth As Long, ByVal nHeight As Long)
```

Description   Creates a device-dependent bitmap that is compatible with the specified device context.

Use with VB   Refer to the "Using Device Dependent Bitmaps," earlier in this chapter text.

Parameter	Type/Description
hdc	Long—Handle to a device context.
nWidth	Long—Width of the bitmap in pixels.
nHeight	Long—Height of the bitmap in pixels.

Return Value   Long—The bitmap handle on success, zero on failure.

Platform   Windows 95, Windows NT, Win16

Comments   Memory device contexts are compatible with both color and monochrome bitmaps. This function creates a bitmap that is compatible with the one currently selected into hDC. The default bitmap for a memory device context is monochrome. If the memory device context has a DIBSection selected into it, this function will return a handle to a DIBSection. If hdc is a device bitmap, the resulting bitmap is always compatible with the device (that is, a color device will always result in a color bitmap).
   If nWidth and nHeight are zero, the bitmap returned will be a 1x1 monochrome bitmap.
   Use the DeleteObject function to free the memory and resources used by the bitmap when it is no longer needed. Refer to "Using Bitmaps," earlier in this chapter.

Example   Shade.vbp

■ CreateCursor

VB Declaration
```
Declare Function CreateCursor& Lib "user32" (ByVal hInstance As Long, ByVal _
nXhotspot As Long, ByVal nYhotspot As Long, ByVal nWidth As Long, ByVal nHeight _
As Long, lpANDbitPlane As Any, lpXORbitPlane As Any)
```

Description   Creates a cursor. Refer to "Icons and Cursors," earlier in this chapter, for information on how cursors and icons are created from two mask arrays.

Use with VB   Not particularly useful. Use of cursors with Visual Basic was discussed earlier in Chapter 6. You cannot directly set the MouseIcon property of a control to a cursor handle without the help of third party tools.

Parameter	Type/Description
hInstance	Long—The handle of the application instance that will own the cursor. Use the agGetWndInstance function described in Appendix A to obtain the instance to the current application. You can also use the GetWindowWord function to retrieve the handle of an instance that owns a form or control.
nXhotspot, nYhotspot	Long—The X,Y coordinate within the cursor image that represents the exact cursor location.
nWidth	Long—The width of the cursor image in pixels. Use the GetSystemMetrics function to determine the correct number for a particular device. Use 32 for VGA.
nHeight	Long—The height of the cursor image in pixels. Use the GetSystemMetrics function to determine the correct number for a particular device. Use 32 for VGA.
lpANDbitPlane	Any—Pointer to the data for the AND bitmap. Refer to "Icons and Cursors," earlier in this chapter.
lpXORbitPlane	Any—Pointer to the data for the XOR bitmap. Refer to "Icons and Cursors," earlier in this chapter.

Return Value   Long—A handle to the cursor on success, zero on error. Sets GetLastError.

Platform   Windows 95, Windows NT, Win16

Comments   Use the DestroyCursor function to free the memory and resources used by the cursor when it is no longer needed.

■ CreateDIBitmap

VB Declaration
```
Declare Function CreateDIBitmap& Lib "gdi32" (ByVal hdc As Long, lpInfoHeader _
As BITMAPINFOHEADER, ByVal dwUsage As Long, lpInitBits As Any, lpInitInfo As _
BITMAPINFO, ByVal wUsage As Long)
```

Description   Creates a device-dependent bitmap based on a device-independent bitmap.

Use with VB   Refer to "Using Bitmaps with Visual Basic," earlier in this chapter.

Parameter	Type/Description
hdc	Long—A handle to a device context defining the configuration of the device-dependent bitmap that is being created.
LpInfoHeader	BITMAPINFOHEADER—Structure that describes the format of the DIB. Refer to Appendix B for information on this structure.
dwUsage	Long—Zero if the bitmap data should not be initialized. CBM_INIT to initialize the bitmap according to the lpInitBits and lpInitInfo parameters.

Parameter	Type/Description
lpInitBits	Any—A pointer to bitmap data in DIB format as specified by lpInitInfo.
LpInitInfo	BITMAPINFO—Structure that describes the format and colors of the lpInitBits DIB. Refer to Appendix B for information on this structure.
Wusage	Long—One of the following two constants: DIB_PAL_COLORS: color table contains indexes into the currently selected palette. DIB_RGB_COLORS: color table contains RGB colors.

Return Value   Long—The bitmap handle on success, zero on failure.

Platform   Windows 95, Windows NT, Win16

Comments   Use the DeleteObject function to free the memory and resources used by the bitmap when it is no longer needed. Refer to "Using Bitmaps," earlier in this chapter.

Example   Puzzle.vbp

■ CreateDIBSection

VB Declaration
```
Declare Function CreateDIBSection& Lib "gdi32" (ByVal hDC As Long, pBitmapInfo _
As BITMAPINFO, ByVal un As Long, lplpVoid As Long, ByVal handle As Long, ByVal _
dw As Long)
```

Description   Creates a DIBSection. This is a GDI object that can be used like a device-dependent bitmap, but is stored internally as a device-independent bitmap.

Use with VB   No problem.

Parameter	Type/Description
hDC	Long—Handle to a device context. If dw specifies DIB_PAL_COLORS, the DIB color table is initialized with colors from the logical palette.
pBitmapInfo	BITMAPINFO —A BITMAPINFO structure that is initialized to the configuration of the bitmap you are creating.
un	Long—One of the following constants: DIB_PAL_COLORS: The BITMAPINFO contains an array of 16-bit palette indexes. DIB_RGB_COLORS: The BITMAPINFO contains a color table containing 32-bit colors (RGBQUAD structures).
lplpVoid	Long—A long variable that will be loaded with the memory address of the DIBSection data area.
handle	Long—An optional handle to a file mapping object on which to create the bitmap. When zero, Windows will allocate memory as needed. File mappings are discussed in Chapters 13 and 14.

Parameter	Type/Description
dw	Long—If handle is specified, specifies the offset into the file mapping object for the bitmap data.

Return Value Long—A handle to a DIBSection bitmap on success. Zero on error. Sets GetLastError.

Platform Windows 95, Windows NT

Comments Use the DeleteObject function to delete the DIBSection bitmap when no longer needed.

If Windows allocates a memory buffer, it will be freed automatically when the object is deleted. If you provided a file mapping object to use, it will not be automatically deleted.

Before accessing the DIB memory directly, you must be sure that Windows has finished drawing (remember, Windows can queue drawing operations). Call the gdiFlush command to make sure all pending drawing operations are complete.

Example DIBSect.vbp

■ CreateIcon

VB Declaration
```
Declare Function CreateIcon& Lib "user32" (ByVal hInstance As Long, ByVal _
nWidth As Long, ByVal nHeight As Long, ByVal nPlanes As Byte, ByVal nBitsPixel _
As Byte, lpANDbits As Byte, lpXORbits As Byte)
```

Description Creates an icon. Refer to the chapter text for information on how cursors and icons are created from two mask arrays.

Use with VB Refer to "Icons and Cursors," earlier in this chapter, for information on using icons with Visual Basic.

Parameter	Type/Description
hInstance	Long—The handle of the application instance that will own the cursor. Use the agGetWndInstance function described in Appendix A to obtain the instance to the current application. You can also use the GetWindowWord function to retrieve the handle of an instance that owns a form or control.
nWidth	Long—The width of the icon image in pixels. Use the GetSystemMetrics function to determine the correct number for a particular device. Use 32 for VGA.
nHeight	Long—The height of the icon image in pixels. Use the GetSystemMetrics function to determine the correct number for a particular device. Use 32 for VGA.
nPlanes	Byte—Number of color planes in the lpXORbitPlane data array.
nBitsPixel	Byte—Number of bits per pixel in the lpXORbitPlane data array.
lpANDbits	Byte—Pointer to the data for the AND bitmap. (Refer to "Icons and Cursors," earlier in this chapter.)
lpXORbits	Byte—Pointer to the data for the XOR bitmap. (Refer to "Icons and Cursors," earlier in this chapter.)

Return Value Long—A handle to the icon on success, zero on error. Sets GetLastError.

Platform	Windows 95, Windows NT, Win16
Comments	Use the DestroyIcon function to free the memory and resources used by the icon when it is no longer needed.

■ CreateIconIndirect

VB Declaration   `Declare Function CreateIconIndirect& Lib "user32" (piconinfo As ICONINFO)`

Description   Creates an icon. Refer to the chapter text for information on how cursors and icons are created from two bitmaps.

Use with VB   No problem.

Parameter	Type/Description
piconinfo	ICONINFO—A structure containing information about the icon to create along with two reference bitmaps. Note that this function allows you to create an icon given an XOR and AND bitmap handle, not the actual mask array. This structure is documented further in Appendix B.

Return Value   Long—A handle to the icon on success, zero on error. Sets GetLastError.

Platform   Windows 95, Windows NT

Comments   Use the DestroyIcon function to free the memory and resources used by the icon when it is no longer needed.

■ DestroyCursor

VB Declaration   `Declare Function DestroyCursor& Lib "user32" (ByVal hCursor As Long)`

Description   Destroys the specified cursor and frees up all system resources that it uses. Do not use this function on system cursor resources loaded with the LoadCursor function.

Use with VB   No problem.

Parameter	Type/Description
hCursor	Long—Handle to a cursor object to destroy.

Return Value   Long—Nonzero on success, zero on failure. Sets GetLastError.

Platform   Windows 95, Windows NT, Win16

■ DestroyIcon

VB Declaration   `Declare Function DestroyIcon& Lib "user32" (ByVal hIcon As Long)`

Description   Destroys an icon.

Use with VB	No problem.	

Parameter	**Type/Description**
hIcon	Long—Handle to an icon.

Return Value Long—Nonzero on success, zero on failure. Sets GetLastError.

Platform Windows 95, Windows NT, Win16

Comments Avoid using this function on system stock icons loaded with the LoadIcon function.

■ DrawIcon

VB Declaration
```
Declare Function DrawIcon& Lib "user32" (ByVal hdc As Long, ByVal x As Long, _
ByVal y As Long, ByVal hIcon As Long)
```

Description Draws an icon in the specified location.

Use with VB No problem.

Parameter	**Type/Description**
hdc	Long—Device context.
x,y	Long—Location to draw the icon (logical coordinates).
hIcon	Long—Handle to icon to draw.

Return Value Long—Nonzero on success, zero on failure. Sets GetLastError.

Platform Windows 95, Windows NT, Win16

Example StockBMs.vbp, Shade.vbp

■ DrawIconEx

VB Declaration
```
Declare Function DrawIconEx& Lib "user32" (ByVal hdc As Long, ByVal xLeft As _
Long, ByVal yTop As Long, ByVal hIcon As Long, ByVal cxWidth As Long, ByVal _
cyWidth As Long, ByVal istepIfAniCur As Long, ByVal hbrFlickerFreeDraw As Long, _
ByVal diFlags As Long)
```

Description Draws an icon or cursor. This function provides more capability than the DrawIcon function.

Use with VB No problem.

Parameter	**Type/Description**
hdc	Long—Handle to a device context to draw on.
xLeft, yTop	Long—Location for the upper-left corner of the icon in logical coordinates.
hIcon	Long—Handle of the icon to draw

Parameter	Type/Description
cxWidth, cyWidth	Long—Desired width and height of the icon. The icon will be stretched to fit.
istepIfAniCur	Long—If hIcon is an animated cursor, specifies which image in the animation to draw. Keep in mind that Win32 does not distinguish between icons and cursors.
hbrFlickerFreeDraw	Long—If set to a brush handle, the function draws the icon into a memory bitmap that is filled with this background color, then copies the image directly to the desired location. This can reduce flicker when drawing.
diFlagsw	Long— One of the following constants: DI_COMPAT: Draws the standard system cursor instead of the image specified. DI_DEFAULTSIZE: Ignores cxWidth and cyWidth and uses the original icon size. DI_IMAGE: Use the XOR part of the icon in drawing (that is, the icon has no transparent area). DI_MASK: Use the MASK part of the icon in drawing (used alone, this lets you obtain the icon mask). DI_NORMAL: Draw the icon normally (combines DI_IMAGE and DI_MASK).

Return Value   Long—TRUE (nonzero) on success, zero on error. Sets GetLastError.

Platform   Windows 95, Windows NT. You should verify Windows 95 compatibility with the flags and parameters that you specify. The Win32 documentation says the function is Windows 95 compatible, but there seem to be limitations.

Example   StockBMs.vbp

■ ExtractAssociatedIcon

VB Declaration
```
Declare Function ExtractAssociatedIcon& Lib "shell32.dll" Alias _
    "ExtractAssociatedIconA" (ByVal hInst As Long, ByVal lpIconPath As String, _
    lpiIcon As Integer)
```

Description   This function can be used to determine if there are any icons in an executable file or dynamic link library, or associated with the given file in the system registry. It then allows you to extract those icons. Chapter 15 goes into further detail on the mechanisms by which icon resources are placed into executable and DLL files.

Use with VB   No problem.

Parameter	Type/Description
hInst	Long—The instance of the current application. Use the agGetWndInstance function described in Appendix A to obtain the instance to the current application. You can also use the GetWindowWord function to retrieve the handle of an instance that owns a form or control.

Parameter	Type/Description
lpIconPath	String—The name of the file from which to extract the icon. If the file is not an executable or DLL itself, but is associated with an executable through the system registry, this string is loaded with the name of the executable.
lpiIcon	Integer—A variable that is loaded with the resource identifier of the icon in the executable file.

Return Value   Long—The handle of the icon if found, zero otherwise.

Platform   Windows 95, Windows NT

Comments   Be sure the lpIconPath string is defined to be at least MAX_PATH characters long.

■ ExtractIcon

VB Declaration   Declare Function ExtractIcon& Lib "shell32.dll" Alias "ExtractIconA" (ByVal _
                     hInst As Long, ByVal lpszExeFileName As String, ByVal nIconIndex As Long)

Description   This function can be used to determine if there are any icons in an executable file or dynamic link library and to extract those icons. Chapter 15 goes into further detail on the mechanisms by which icon resources are placed into executable and DLL files.

Use with VB   No problem.

Parameter	Type/Description
hInst	Long—The instance handle of this program. Use the agGetWndInstance function described in Appendix A to obtain the instance to the current application. You can also use the GetWindowWord function to retrieve the handle of an instance that owns a form or control.
lpszExeFileName	String—The full name of the program from which to extract an icon.
nIconIndex	Long—The index of the icon to retrieve. –1 to retrieve the total number of icons in the file.

Return Value   Long—A handle to an icon on success, zero if there are no icons in the file. If nIconIndex is –1, this will be the total number of icons in the file.

Platform   Windows 95, Windows NT, Win16

■ GetBitmapBits

VB Declaration   Declare Function GetBitmapBits& Lib "gdi32" (ByVal hBitmap As Long, ByVal _
                     dwCount As Long, lpBits As Any)

Description   Copies bits from a bitmap into a buffer.

Use with VB   No problem.

Parameter	Type/Description
hBitmap	Long—Handle to a bitmap.
dwCount	Long—Number of bytes to copy. Set to zero to retrieve the number of bytes in the bitmap.
lpBits	Any—Pointer to a buffer to hold the bitmap bits. Be sure the buffer has been preinitialized to at least dwCount bytes.

Return Value   Long—The number of bytes in the bitmap on success, zero otherwise. Sets GetLastError.

Platform   Windows 95, Windows NT, Win16. This function works, but you are strongly recommended to use device-independent bitmaps (GetDIBits).

Comments   Refer to "Device-Dependent Bitmaps," earlier in this chapter, for the required format for a device-dependent bitmap data area.

■ GetBitmapDimensionEx

VB Declaration
```
Declare Function GetBitmapDimensionEx& Lib "gdi32" (ByVal hBitmap As Long, _
lpDimension As SIZE)
```

Description   Retrieves the width and height of a bitmap as set by the SetBitmapDimensionEx function. The bitmap dimensions are not used by Windows.

Use with VB   No problem.

Parameter	Type/Description
hBitmap	Long—Handle to a bitmap.
lpDimension	SIZE—Size structure to load with the dimensions of the bitmap as set by the SetBitmapDimensionEx function. Dimensions are in tenths of a millimeter.

Return Value   Long—Nonzero on success, zero on failure. Sets GetLastError.

Platform   Windows 95, Windows NT, Win16

Comments   Refer to the SetBitmapDimensionEx function for further information.

■ GetDIBColorTable

VB Declaration
```
Declare Function GetDIBColorTable& Lib "gdi32" (ByVal hDC As Long, ByVal un1 As _
Long, ByVal un2 As Long, pRGBQuad As RGBQUAD)
```

Description   Retrieves color table information from a DIBSection that is selected into a device context.

Use with VB   No problem.

Parameter	Type/Description
hDC	Long—A device context that has a DIBSection object selected.
un1	Long—Index of the first entry to retrieve in the color table.
un2	Long—The number of entries to retrieve.
pRGBQuad	RGBQUAD—First entry in an array of RGBQUAD structures to load with color table information.

Return Value   Long—The number of color table entries retrieved. Zero on error. Sets GetLastError.

Platform   Windows 95, Windows NT

Comments   DIBSections that use over 8 bits per pixel do not have color tables.

■ GetDIBits

VB Declaration
```
Declare Function GetDIBits& Lib "gdi32" (ByVal aHDC As Long, ByVal hBitmap As _
Long, ByVal nStartScan As Long, ByVal nNumScans As Long, lpBits As Any, lpBI As _
BITMAPINFO, ByVal wUsage As Long)
```

Description   Copies bits from a bitmap into a device-independent bitmap. GetDIBitsBynum is a type-safe declaration for this function.

Use with VB   No problem.

Parameter	Type/Description
aHDC	Long—A handle to a device context defining the configuration of the device-dependent bitmap hBitmap.
hBitmap	Long—A handle to a source bitmap. This bitmap must not be selected into a device context.
nStartScan	Long—The number of the first scan line to copy into the DIB.
nNumScans	Long—The number of scan lines to copy.
lpBits	Any—A pointer to a buffer to load with the bitmap data in DIB format as specified by lpBI. If zero, lpBI is loaded with the information for the DIB, but no data is retrieved (use ByVal 0 to pass zero as this parameter).
lpBI	BITMAPINFO—Structure that describes the format and colors of the lpInitBits DIB. The biSize through biCompression fields of the BITMAP-INFOHEADER structure must be initialized. Refer to Appendix B for information on this structure.
wUsage	Long—One of the following two constants: DIB_PAL_COLORS: The color table is loaded with an array of 16-bit indexes that are relative to the currently selected palette. DIB_RGB_COLORS: The color table is loaded with RGB colors

Return Value	Long—TRUE (nonzero) on success, zero on error. On Windows 95, the return is the number of scan lines returned.
Platform	Windows 95, Windows NT, Win16
Comments	The start scan line is relative to the origin, which is at the lower left corner unless the biHeight field of the BITMAPINFOHEADER structure is negative.
Example	PicPrint.vbp in Chapter 12

■ GetIconInfo

VB Declaration
```
Declare Function GetIconInfo& Lib "user32" (ByVal hIcon As Long, piconinfo As _
    ICONINFO)
```

Description   Retrieve information about the icon.

Use with VB   No problem.

Parameter	Type/Description
hIcon	Long—A handle to an icon.
piconinfo	ICONINFO—An ICONINFO structure to load with information about the icon including the XOR and AND bitmaps.

Return Value	Long—Nonzero on success, zero on failure. Sets GetLastError.
Platform	Windows 95, Windows NT
Comments	The bitmaps that are loaded into the ICONINFO structure on return from this function must be deleted by the application.

■ GetStretchBltMode

VB Declaration   `Declare Function GetStretchBltMode& Lib "gdi32" (ByVal hdc As Long)`

Description   Determines the stretching mode for the StretchBlt and StretchDIBits functions. The stretching mode determines how Windows handles scan lines that are eliminated during stretching.

Use with VB   No problem.

Parameter	Type/Description
hdc	Long—A handle to a device context.

Return Value	Long—Retrieves the current stretching mode. Zero on error.
Platform	Windows 95, Windows NT, Win16
Comments	Refer to the SetStretchBltMode API function for further information.

■ LoadBitmap, LoadBitmapBynum

VB Declaration
```
Declare Function LoadBitmap& Lib "user32" Alias "LoadBitmapA" (ByVal hInstance _
As Long, ByVal lpBitmapName As String)
Declare Function LoadBitmapBynum& Lib "user32" Alias "LoadBitmapA" (ByVal _
hInstance As Long, ByVal lpBitmapName As Long)
```

Description
Loads a bitmap from the specified module or application instance. LoadBitmapBynum is a type-safe version of the LoadBitmap function.

Use with VB
No problem.

Parameter	Type/Description
hInstance	Long—Module handle for a dynamic link library, or instance handle that specifies the executable file that contains the bitmap.
lpBitmapName	String—As a String, specifies the name of the bitmap resource to load. As a Long, specifies the resource ID to load or a constant representing one of the stock system bitmaps. When loading a stock system bitmap, the hInstance parameter should be set to 0. The constants are specified in the API32.TXT file with the OBM_ prefix. For example, OBM_REDUCE refers to the down arrow bitmap that appears on the title bar to minimize a window. Refer to the API32.TXT file for a complete list of stock bitmaps.

Return Value
Long—A handle to the loaded bitmap, zero on error. Sets GetLastError.

Platform
Windows 95, Windows NT, Win16

Comments
You must use the DeleteObject function to delete bitmaps retrieved by this function even if they are stock system bitmaps.

Example
StockBMs.vbp

■ LoadCursor, LoadCursorBynum

VB Declaration
```
Declare Function LoadCursor& Lib "user32" Alias "LoadCursorA" (ByVal hInstance _
As Long, ByVal lpCursorName As String)
Declare Function LoadCursorBynum& Lib "user32" Alias "LoadCursorA" (ByVal _
hInstance As Long, ByVal lpCursorName As Long)
```

Description
Loads a cursor from the specified module or application instance. LoadCursorBynum is a type-safe version of the LoadCursor function.

Use with VB
No problem.

Parameter	Type/Description
hInstance	Long—Module handle for a dynamic link library, or instance handle that specifies the executable file that contains the cursor.

Parameter	Type/Description
lpCursorName	String—As a String, specifies the name of the cursor resource to load. As a Long, specifies the resource ID to load or a constant representing one of the stock system cursors. When loading a stock system cursor, the hInstance parameter should be set to 0. The constants are specified in the API32.TXT file with the IDC prefix. Refer to the API32.TXT file for a complete list of stock cursors.

Return Value   Long—A handle to the loaded cursor on success, zero on error. This function will only load standard size icons under Windows 95 and Win16.

Platform   Windows 95, Windows NT, Win16

Comments   Do not destroy stock system cursors or cursors belonging to other applications. Be careful that lpCursorName refers to a cursor resource, as this function will return a nonzero handle if the name refers to a valid resource even if it is not a cursor resource.

■ LoadCursorFromFile

VB Declaration
```
Declare Function LoadCursorFromFile& Lib "user32" Alias "LoadCursorFromFileA" _
(ByVal lpFileName As String)
```

Description   Creates a cursor from a cursor file or animated cursor file (.CUR or .ANI extensions).

Use with VB   No problem.

Parameter	Type/Description
lpFileName	String—The name of the file containing a cursor.

Return Value   Long—A handle to a cursor on success, zero on error. Sets GetLastError to the constant ERROR_FILE_NOT_FOUND on error.

Platform   Windows 95, Windows NT

Comments   If lpFileName is defined as a long (ByVal As Long), you can (in theory) pass a constant with the prefix OCR_ to obtain a stock system cursor. This was not implemented in Windows NT 3.5.

■ LoadIcon, LoadIconBynum

VB Declaration
```
Declare Function LoadIcon& Lib "user32" Alias "LoadIconA" (ByVal hInstance As _
Long, ByVal lpIconName As String)
Declare Function LoadIconBynum& Lib "user32" Alias "LoadIconA" (ByVal hInstance _
As Long, ByVal lpIconName As Long)
```

Description   Loads an icon from the specified module or application instance. LoadIconBynum is a type-safe version of the LoadIcon function.

Use with VB	No problem.

Parameter	Type/Description
hInstance	Long—Module handle for a dynamic link library, or instance handle that specifies the executable file that contains the icon.
LpIconName	String—As a String, specifies the name of the icon resource to load. As a Long, specifies the resource ID to load or a constant representing one of the stock system icons. When loading a stock system icon, the hInstance parameter should be set to 0. The constants are shown in the API32.TXT file with the constants IDI.

Return Value	Long—A handle to the loaded icon on success, zero on error. Sets GetLastError.
Platform	Windows 95, Windows NT, Win16. This function will only load standard sized icons under Windows 95 and Win16. Use GetSystemMetrics to obtain the SM_CXICON and SM_CYICON standard icon metrics. Use LoadImage to load nonstandard sized icons.
Comments	A file can contain multiple versions of the same icon resource. This function chooses the one most appropriate for the current display.
Example	StockBMs.vbp

■ LoadImage, LoadImageBynum

| **VB Declaration** | ```
Declare Function LoadImage& Lib "user32" Alias "LoadImageA" (ByVal hInst As _
Long, ByVal lpsz As String, ByVal un1 As Long, ByVal n1 As Long, ByVal n2 As _
Long, ByVal un2 As Long)
Declare Function LoadImageBynum& Lib "user32" Alias "LoadImageA" (ByVal hInst _
As Long, ByVal lpsz As Long, ByVal un1 As Long, ByVal n1 As Long, ByVal n2 As _
Long, ByVal un2 As Long)
``` |
| **Description** | Load a bitmap, icon, or cursor. |
| **Use with VB** | No problem. |

Parameter	Type/Description
hInst	Long—The module or instance handle of the DLL or application from which to load the image. Zero to load a stock image.
lpsz	String—The name of the image to load. If hInst is specified, this is the name of the resource or the identifier of the resource (the identifier is a long value). If hInst is null, and LR_LOADFROMFILE is specified, this is the name of a file (bitmap, icon, or cursor file). If a long, this is the number of the stock bitmap, icon, or cursor.
un1	Long—One of the following constants specifying the type of image to load: IMAGE_BITMAP, IMAGE_CURSOR, IMAGE_ICON.
n1, n2	Long—The requested width and height of the image. The image is stretched as needed. If zero, uses the default size for the image.
```

Parameter	Type/Description
un2	Long—A combination of the following constants from API32.TXT LR_DEFAULTCOLOR—Load the image normally. LR_LOADREALSIZE—Do not stretch the image. Ignores n1, n2. The following flags are not supported on NT prior to 4.0. LR_CREATEDIBSECTION—If IMAGE_BITMAP is specified, returns a handle to a DIBSection instead of a bitmap. LR_DEFAULTSIZE—If n1,n2 are zero, uses the default size for the image as defined by the system instead of that defined for the image itself. LR_LOADFROMFILE—If hInst is zero, lpsz is the name of a file of the appropriate type to load. Win95 only LR_LOADMAP3DCOLORS—Replaces any occurrence of dark gray, gray, and light gray in the image to the current settings for COLOR_3DSHADOW, COLOR_3DFACE, and COLOR_3DLIGHT. LR_LOADTRANSPARENT—All occurrences of pixels in the image matching the first pixel in the image are replaced with the system. COLOR_WINDOW image. LR_MONOCHROME—Converts the image to monochrome. LR_SHARED—Loads the image as a shared resource. Required to load stock resources on NT 4.0.

Return Value   Long—A handle to the object on success, zero on error.

Platform   Windows 95, Windows NT (Limited support for NT prior to version 4.0)

Example   StockBMs.vbp

■ MaskBlt

VB Declaration
```
Declare Function MaskBlt& Lib "gdi32" (ByVal hdcDest As Long, ByVal nXDest As _
Long, ByVal nYDest As Long, ByVal nWidth As Long, ByVal nHeight As Long, ByVal _
hdcSrc As Long, ByVal nXSrc As Long, ByVal nYSrc As Long, ByVal hbmMask As _
Long, ByVal xMask As Long, ByVal yMask As Long, ByVal dwRop As Long)
```

Description   Performs a complex image transfer with masking.

Use with VB   No problem.

Parameter	Type/Description
hdcDest	Long—The destination device context.
nXDest, nYDest	Long—The x,y coordinates for the upper-left corner of the destination image.
nWidth	Long—The width and height of the image in the destination device context.
hdcSrc	Long—The source device context.
nXSrc, nYSrc	Long—The x,y coordinates of the upper-left corner of the source image.

Parameter	Type/Description
hbmMask	Long— A handle to a monochrome bitmap to serve as a mask. If the dwROP code includes a source, this bitmap must be the same size as the source, otherwise it must match the destination size.
xMask, yMask	Long—An x,y offset into the monochrome mask bitmap. This allows you to create one large bitmap with multiple masks to use.
dwRop	Long—A special raster operation to use during the transfer. See comments.

Return Value   Long—Nonzero on success, zero on failure. Sets GetLastError.

Platform   Windows NT

Comments   The dwROP code is a nonstandard raster operation code made up of two regular raster operation codes: a foreground code and a background code. You create a raster operation for this function using the agMakeROP4 function in APIGID32.DLL. This function shifts the background raster-op left by 8 bits then ORs in the foreground raster operation. This is difficult to do in Visual Basic due to the likelihood of an overflow during the shift.

In every pixel where the mask bitmap is set to one, the foreground transformation is applied to the transfer. If the corresponding mask bitmap pixel is zero, the background transformation is applied. If no mask bitmap is specified, this function performs the same operation as the BitBlt operation.

If a rotation or shear transform is in effect for the source, the function fails.

Use GetDeviceCaps to determine if this function is supported by a device context.

■ PatBlt

VB Declaration
```
Declare Function PatBlt& Lib "gdi32" (ByVal hdc As Long, ByVal x As Long, ByVal _
y As Long, ByVal nWidth As Long, ByVal nHeight As Long, ByVal dwRop As Long)
```

Description   Fills the specified device context with a pattern based on the currently selected brush.

Use with VB   No problem.

Parameter	Type/Description
hdc	Long—Handle to a device context to draw on.
x, y	Long—Point describing the upper-left corner of the destination rectangle within the destination DC in logical coordinates.
nWidth, nHeight	Long—Width and height of the destination rectangle specified in logical units.
dwRop	Long—Raster operation to use during the transfer. Raster operations that refer to a source may not be used with this function. Refer to "Raster Operations," earlier in this chapter.

Return Value   Long—Nonzero on success, zero on failure. Sets GetLastError.

Platform   Windows 95, Windows NT, Win16

Comments   Use GetDeviceCaps to determine if this function is supported on a device context.

Example   ROPTest.vbp

■ PlgBlt

VB Declaration
```
Declare Function PlgBlt& Lib "gdi32" (ByVal hdcDest As Long, lpPoint As _
POINTAPI, ByVal hdcSrc As Long, ByVal nXSrc As Long, ByVal nYSrc As Long, ByVal _
nWidth As Long, ByVal nHeight As Long, ByVal hbmMask As Long, ByVal xMask As _
Long, ByVal yMask As Long)
```

Description   Copies a bitmap, transforming it into a parallelogram. This allows you to rotate a bitmap.

Use with VB   No problem.

Parameter	Type/Description
hdcDest	Long—A destination device context for the image.
lpPoint	POINTAPI—The first entry in an array of POINAPI structures. The first point corresponds to the upper-left corner of a parallelogram. The second point is the upper-right corner and the third point is the lower-left corner. The fourth corner is derived from the first three.
hdcSrc	Long—The source device context for the image.
nXSrc, nYSrc	Long—The x,y coordinates of the upper-left corner of the source image in logical coordinates.
nWidth, nHeight	Long—The size of the source image in logical coordinates.
hbmMask	Long—An optional handle to a monochrome mask. If specified, only bits that have a corresponding mask value of 1 will be transferred to the destination.
xMask, yMask	Long—The x,y coordinates for the upper-left corner of the area in the mask bitmap to use.

Return Value   Long—Nonzero on success, zero on failure. Sets GetLastError.

Platform   Windows NT

Comments   If a rotation or shear transform is in effect for the source, the function fails. Use GetDeviceCaps to determine if this function is supported by a device context.

Example   BMRotate.vbp

■ SetBitmapBits

VB Declaration
```
Declare Function SetBitmapBits& Lib "gdi32" (ByVal hBitmap As Long, ByVal _
dwCount As Long, lpBits As Any)
```

Description   Copies bits from a buffer into a bitmap.

Use with VB	No problem.	

Parameter	Type/Description
hBitmap	Long—Handle to a bitmap.
dwCount	Long—Number of bytes to copy.
lpBits	Any—Pointer to a buffer that contains the bitmap bits formatted correctly for the bitmap.

Return Value   Long—The number of bytes copied on success, zero otherwise.

Platform   Windows 95, Windows NT, Win16. Under Win32 you should use device-independent bitmaps.

Comments   Refer to "Device-Dependent Bitmaps," earlier in this chapter, for the required format for a device-dependent bitmap data area.

■ SetBitmapDimensionEx

VB Declaration
```
Declare Function SetBitmapDimensionEx& Lib "gdi32" (ByVal hbm As Long, ByVal nX _
As Long, ByVal nY As Long, lpSize As SIZE)
```

Description   Sets the width and height of a bitmap in tenths of a millimeter. This information is not used by Windows, but may be retrieved using the GetBitmapDimensionEx function.

Use with VB   No problem.

Parameter	Type/Description
hbm	Long—Handle to a bitmap.
nX, nY	Long—The recommended dimensions for the bitmap in 0.1mm units.
lpSize	SIZE—Structure to load with the previous bitmap dimensions.

Return Value   Long—Nonzero on success, zero on failure. Sets GetLastError.

Platform   Windows 95, Windows NT, Win16

■ SetDIBColorTable

VB Declaration
```
Declare Function SetDIBColorTable& Lib "gdi32" (ByVal hDC As Long, ByVal un1 As _
Long, ByVal un2 As Long, pcRGBQuad As RGBQUAD)
```

Description   Sets the color table information from a DIBSection that is selected into a device context.

Use with VB   No problem.

Parameter	Type/Description
hDC	Long—A device context that has a DIBSection object selected.
un1	Long—Index of the first entry to set in the color table.

Parameter	Type/Description
un2	Long—The number of entries to set.
pRGBQuad	RGBQUAD—First entry in an array of RGBQUAD structures containing new color table information. Must be at least un2 entries long.

Return Value Long—The number of color table entries set. Zero on error. Sets GetLastError.

Platform Windows 95, Windows NT

Comments DIBSections that use over 8 bits per pixel do not have color tables.

■ SetDIBits

VB Declaration
```
Declare Function SetDIBits& Lib "gdi32" (ByVal hdc As Long, ByVal hBitmap As _
Long, ByVal nStartScan As Long, ByVal nNumScans As Long, lpBits As Any, lpBI As _
BITMAPINFO, ByVal wUsage As Long)
```

Description Copies bits from a device-independent bitmap into a device-dependent bitmap.

Use with VB Refer to "Using Bitmaps with Visual Basic," earlier in this chapter.

Parameter	Type/Description
hdc	Long—A handle to a device context defining the configuration of the device-dependent bitmap hBitmap.
hBitmap	Long—A handle to a destination bitmap. This bitmap must not be selected into a device context.
nStartScan	Long—The number of the first scan line in the lpBits array. This scan line is counted from the bottom of the bitmap if the biHeight field in the BITMAPINFOHEADER part of the lpBl is positive, from the top if it is negative.
nNumScans	Long—The number of scan lines to copy.
lpBits	Any—A pointer to a buffer containing the bitmap data in DIB format as specified by lpBI.
lpBI	BITMAPINFO—Structure that describes the format and colors of the lpBits DIB. Refer to Appendix B for information on this structure.
wUsage	Long—One of the following two constants: DIB_PAL_COLORS: color table is an array of integers containing indexes relative to the palette currently selected into the hdc device context. DIB_RGB_COLORS: color table contains RGB colors.

Return Value Long—The number of scan lines copied on success, zero on error. Sets GetLastError.

Platform Windows 95, Windows NT, Win16

Comments Use GetDeviceCaps to determine if a device supports this function.

Example   PicPrint.vbp in Chapter 12

■ SetDIBitsToDevice

VB Declaration   `Declare Function SetDIBitsToDevice& Lib "gdi32" (ByVal hdc As Long, ByVal x As _`
`Long, ByVal y As Long, ByVal dx As Long, ByVal dy As Long, ByVal SrcX As Long, _`
`ByVal SrcY As Long, ByVal Scan As Long, ByVal NumScans As Long, lpBits As Any, _`
`lpBI As BITMAPINFO, ByVal wUsage As Long)`

Description   Copies all or part of a device-independent bitmap directly to a device. This function defines a destination rectangle on the device to receive the bitmap data. It also defines a source rectangle in the DIB from which to extract data.

Use with VB   Refer to "Using Bitmaps with Visual Basic," earlier in this chapter.

Parameter	Type/Description
hdc	Long—A handle to a device context to receive the bitmap data.
x, y	Long—Point in logical coordinates of the origin of the destination rectangle.
dx, dy	Long—Width and height in device units of the destination rectangle.
SrcX, SrcY	Long—Point in device coordinates of the origin of the source rectangle in the DIB.
Scan	Long—The number of the first scan line in the lpBits array. This scan line is counted from the bottom of the bitmap if the biHeight field in the BITMAPINFOHEADER part of the lpBI is positive, from the top if it is negative.
NumScans	Long—The number of scan lines to copy.
lpBits	Any—A pointer to a buffer containing the bitmap data in DIB format as specified by lpBI.
lpBI	BITMAPINFO—Structure that describes the format and colors of the Bits DIB. Refer to Appendix B for information on this structure.
wUsage	Long—One of the following two constants: DIB_PAL_COLORS: color table is an array of integers containing indexes relative to the palette currently selected into the hdc device context. DIB_RGB_COLORS: color table contains RGB colors.

Return Value   Long—The number of scan lines copied on success, zero on error. Sets GetLastError.

Platform   Windows 95, Windows NT, Win16

Comments   Use GetDeviceCaps to determine if a device supports this function.

Example   PicPrint.vbp in Chapter 12

■ SetStretchBltMode

VB Declaration `Declare Function SetStretchBltMode& Lib "gdi32" (ByVal hdc As Long, ByVal _`
`nStretchMode As Long)`

Description Specifies the stretching mode for the StretchBlt and StretchDIBits functions. The stretching mode determines how Windows handles scan lines that are eliminated during stretching.

Use with VB It is recommended that you restore the original StretchBlt mode for VB forms and controls if you use this function during API drawing.

Parameter	Type/Description
hdc	Long—Handle to a device context.
nStretchMode	Long—The new stretching mode based on one of the following constants as defined in file API32.TXT
	STRETCH_ANDSCANS: (default) Eliminated lines are ANDed with the remaining lines. This mode is typically used with monochrome bitmaps that have a white background.
	STRETCH_DELETESCANS: Eliminated lines are simply removed. This mode is typically used with color bitmaps.
	STRETCH_ORSCANS: Eliminated lines are ORed with the remaining lines. This mode is typically used with monochrome bitmaps that have a black background.
	STRETCH_HALFTONE: Blocks of pixels on the destination bitmap are set to an average approximation of equivalent blocks on the source bitmap. This mode is considerably slower than the others.

Return Value Long—The value of the previous stretching mode. Zero on error.

Platform Windows 95, Windows NT, Win16 (except for STRETCH_HALFTONE mode, which is not supported).

Comments As an example of the effect of stretching mode, consider what happens when a narrow black line on a white image is compressed. During the compression, pixels are removed from the image. In order to prevent the line from disappearing, it is necessary to AND pixels with a neighboring pixel before deleting them. This is accomplished with the STRETCH_ANDSCANS stretching mode.

■ StretchBlt

VB Declaration `Declare Function StretchBlt& Lib "gdi32" (ByVal hdc As Long, ByVal x As Long, _`
`ByVal y As Long, ByVal nWidth As Long, ByVal nHeight As Long, ByVal hSrcDC As _`
`Long, ByVal xSrc As Long, ByVal ySrc As Long, ByVal nSrcWidth As Long, ByVal _`
`nSrcHeight As Long, ByVal dwRop As Long)`

Description Copies a bitmap from one device context to another. The source and destination DCs must be compatible with one another as described in "Device-Dependent Bitmaps," earlier in this chapter. This function defines a destination rectangle on the device context and a source rectangle within the bitmap. The source rectangle is stretched as needed to fit into the destination rectangle.

Use with VB	Refer to "Using Bitmaps with Visual Basic," earlier in this chapter.

Parameter	Type/Description
hdc	Long—Destination device context.
x, y	Long—x,y coordinates for the upper-left corner of the destination rectangle in logical coordinates.
nWidth, nHeight	Long—Width and height of the destination rectangle in logical coordinates.
hSrcDC	Long—Source device context. If the raster operation does not specify a source, this should be 0.
xSrc, ySrc	Long—Point describing the upper-left corner of the source rectangle within the source DC. This is specified in logical coordinates of the source DC.
nSrcWidth, nSrcHeight	Long—Width and height of the image being transferred in logical units (based on the source DC). If the sign of one of these parameters does not match the sign of the corresponding destination parameter, the bitmap will be mirrored on the appropriate axis.
dwRop	Long—Raster operation to use during the transfer. Refer to "Raster Operations," earlier in this chapter. If a brush is part of the raster operation, the brush selected into the destination DC is used.

Return Value   Long—Nonzero on success, zero on failure. Sets GetLastError.

Platform   Windows 95, Windows NT, Win16

Comments   Use the GetDeviceCaps API function to determine if the device context can support this function.

A shear or rotation transform may not be selected for the source bitmap, nor can the source bitmap be a metafile device context. Conversions between monochrome and color bitmaps are discussed in "Color Conversions," earlier in this chapter.

Example   Puzzle.vbp

■ StretchDIBits

VB Declaration
```
Declare Function StretchDIBits& Lib "gdi32" (ByVal hdc As Long, ByVal x As _
Long, ByVal y As Long, ByVal dx As Long, ByVal dy As Long, ByVal SrcX As Long, _
ByVal SrcY As Long, ByVal wSrcWidth As Long, ByVal wSrcHeight As Long, lpBits _
As Any, lpBitsInfo As BITMAPINFO, ByVal wUsage As Long, ByVal dwRop As Long)
```

Description   Copies all or part of a device-independent bitmap directly to a device context. This function defines a destination rectangle on the device context to receive the bitmap data. It also defines a source rectangle in the DIB from which to extract data. The source rectangle is stretched as needed to fit into the destination rectangle using the StretchBlt mode for the device context (as set by the SetStretchBltMode function).

Use with VB   Refer to "Using Bitmaps with Visual Basic," earlier in this chapter.

Parameter	Type/Description
hdc	Long—A handle to a device context to receive the bitmap data.
x,y	Long—Point in logical coordinates of the origin of the destination rectangle.
dx, dy	Long—Width and height in logical units of the destination rectangle.
SrcX, SrcY	Long—Point in device coordinates of the origin of the source rectangle in the DIB.
wSrcWidth, wSrcHeight	Long—Width and height of the source rectangle in device coordinates. If the sign of one of these parameters does not match the sign of the corresponding destination width parameter, the bitmap will be mirrored on the appropriate axis.
lpBits	Any—A pointer to a buffer containing the bitmap data in DIB format as specified by lpBitsInfo.
lpBitsInfo	BITMAPINFO—Structure that describes the format and colors of the lpBits DIB. Refer to Appendix B for information on this structure.
wUsage	Long—One of the following two constants: DIB_PAL_COLORS: color table is an array of integers that represent entries into palette currently selected into the source device context. DIB_RGB_COLORS: color table contains RGB colors.
dwRop	Long—Raster operation to use. Refer to "Raster Operations," earlier in this chapter.

Return Value   Long—The number of scan lines copied on success, the constant GDI_ERROR on error.

Platform   Windows 95, Windows NT, Win16

Example   PicPrint.vbp in Chapter 12

10

Working with Menus

OST VISUAL BASIC APPLICATIONS USE MENUS TO ALLOW THE USER TO execute program commands. This chapter will show you how to use the Windows API functions to add to the menu capabilities provided by Visual Basic. You will learn how to create custom checkmarks for checked menus, and how to use any bitmap as a menu entry in place of a string. You will also learn how to customize floating pop-up menus that can appear anywhere on the screen. The MenuLook sample program included in this chapter demonstrates these features and shows how you can use the Windows API functions to analyze the structure of an existing menu. Finally, this chapter will demonstrate some more advanced techniques for implementing customized control menus and context menus with the aid of subclassing techniques.

Inside the Menuing System

Before reviewing the Windows API functions that deal with menus, it is important for you to understand a bit about how menus work and how Visual Basic uses menus. The Windows API functions provide some powerful capabilities, but the Visual Basic environment imposes some strict requirements on their use in order to maintain compatibility.

How Windows Menus Work

Let's first examine how the Windows menu system works outside of Visual Basic. Then you'll see how Visual Basic interacts with menus.

A menu is one of the few objects appearing on the screen that is not a window. This means that there is no window handle to a menu, nor does a menu have a window function. The appearance, visibility, and position of menus are handled entirely by the Windows environment.

There are two types of menus: top level menus and pop-up menus. A top level menu appears as a horizontal bar and may be assigned to a window. Once assigned, it will appear as the menu bar for the window. Pop-up menus appear as needed and disappear as soon as a selection is made, the Escape key is pressed, or the mouse is clicked outside of the menu. Pop-up menus may appear as dropping down from the top level menu bar or another pop-up menu, or may appear anywhere on the screen under program control. They are often used as context menus—a pop-up menu that appears when you click on an object with the right mouse button.

Each entry in a menu has attributes as shown in Table 10.1.

In Windows, a menu is built by first creating a top level menu and the associated pop-up menus. In most cases, each of the top level menu entries has a pop-up menu attached. Each entry has attributes set as needed. If an entry does not have a pop-up menu attached, it is assigned a menu ID attribute. Once the menu is built, it is assigned to a window and appears as a menu bar. Menus may also be loaded as resources from an executable module.

Table 10.1   **Attributes of a Menu Entry**

Attribute	Description
Bitmap	Bitmap to display instead of a string for a menu entry.
Checked Unchecked	An entry can be checked or unchecked. A space to the left of the entry name (or string) displays a symbol to indicate if the entry is checked or unchecked. The default is nothing when unchecked and a checkmark when checked, but any bitmap can be defined for either state.
Checkmark symbol	Bitmaps to use for the checked and unchecked state for a menu entry. The default is no mark for the unchecked state, and a checkmark for the checked state.
Enabled Disabled Grayed	If a menu entry is enabled, the user can click on that entry. When disabled, clicks on the entry are ignored. When grayed, the entry is disabled and appears in a gray color: it is not available to the user at that time.
Default (bold)	If a menu entry is the default entry, it appears in bold. By convention, when used with context menus, this is the same action that takes place for an object that is double clicked. Not supported on NT3.51.
Highlight	Top level menus only—the entry appears highlighted (inverted).
Menu ID (command)	Every entry other than separators and pop-up menus has a menu ID. This is a 16-bit integer that is sent to the window function of the menu's window when that entry is selected. Menu IDs need not be unique (that is, more than one entry may share the same menu ID).
MenuBreak MenuBarBreak	Specifies that an entry is the start of a new column (for pop-up menus) or line (for top level menus). With MenuBarBreak, a vertical separator line appears between the two columns.
OwnerDraw	Allows total customization of the appearance of a menu. Not supported by Visual Basic.
Pop-up	If an entry has a pop-up menu assigned, selecting the entry will cause that pop-up menu to appear. Pop-up entries generally have a string attribute assigned as well.
Position	The position of the entry in the menu. Positions are numbered from zero, with entry zero being the left entry (for top level menus) or top entry (for pop-up menus).
Separator	A special menu entry that appears as a separator line between entries. It is always disabled.
String (name)	The text string displayed for the entry. Also referred to as the name of the entry.

Consider what happens when the user clicks in a menu. Clicks inside of a disabled entry (such as a separator or disabled command) are ignored. Clicks inside of an entry that has a pop-up menu attached cause the pop-up menu to be displayed, from which the user may then select an entry.

When a user clicks on an enabled entry that does not have a pop-up menu attached, Windows sends a WM_COMMAND message to the window that contains the menu. This message contains the menu ID of the menu entry. Figure 10.1 illustrates the operation of menus under Windows.

Figure 10.1
Menu operation
under Windows

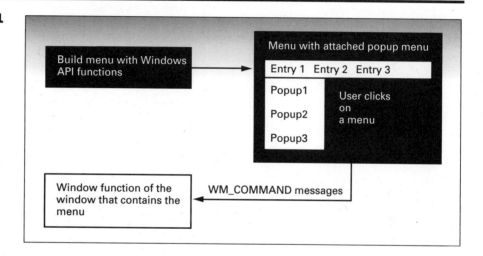

Each of the three entries in the pop-up menu has a menu ID that is sent as one of the parameters with the WM_COMMAND message. This allows the window function for the window owning the menu to determine which menu entry has been selected. The program can then take whatever action is appropriate for that menu selection.

Table 10.2 lists the API functions that deal with menus.

Table 10.2   Menu API Functions

Function	Description
AppendMenu	Adds an entry to a menu.
ChangeMenu	Obsolete: Use AppendMenu, InsertMenu, ModifyMenu, and RemoveMenu, or the new MenuItemInfo function.
CheckMenuItem	Checks or unchecks a menu entry.

Table 10.2 **Menu API Functions (Continued)**

Function	Description
CheckMenuRadioItem	Checks one of a group of menu entries, unchecking the others in the group. N/A on NT 3.51.
CreateMenu	Creates an empty top level menu.
CreatePopupMenu	Creates an empty pop-up menu.
DeleteMenu	Deletes a menu entry.
DestroyMenu	Destroys a menu.
DrawMenuBar	Updates (redraws) a menu.
EnableMenuItem	Enables, disables, or grays a menu entry.
GetMenu	Retrieves a handle to the menu for a window.
GetMenuCheckMarkDimensions	Determines the size of a menu checkmark symbol.
GetMenuContextHelpId	Retrieves a help context associated with a menu. N/A on NT 3.51.
GetMenuDefaultItem	Retrieves the default entry for a menu. N/A for NT 3.51.
GetMenuItemCount	Determines the number of entries in a menu.
GetMenuItemID	Determines the menu ID of a menu entry.
GetMenuItemInfo	New general purpose function for retrieving menu information. N/A on NT 3.51.
GetMenuItemRect	Retrieves the size and location of an entry in a menu.
GetMenuState	Retrieves information about the attributes of a menu entry.
GetMenuString	Retrieves the string (name) of a menu entry.
GetSubMenu	Retrieves a handle to the pop-up menu attached to a specified menu entry.
GetSystemMenu	Retrieves a handle to the system pop-up menu (referred to as the control menu in VB). This is the menu that appears when the ControlBox property for a form is set to TRUE.
HiliteMenuItem	Sets the highlight attribute for a top level menu entry.
InsertMenu	Inserts a menu entry into a menu.

Table 10.2   Menu API Functions (Continued)

Function	Description
InsertMenuItem	General purpose function for inserting menu entries. N/A on NT 3.51.
IsMenu	Determines if a handle is not a menu handle.
LoadMenu	Loads a menu resource.
LoadMenuIndirect	Creates a menu from a data structure.
MenuItemFromPoint	Tests whether there is a menu entry at the screen location specified.
ModifyMenu	Changes the attributes of a menu entry.
RemoveMenu	Removes a menu entry. If the entry has a pop-up menu attached, the pop-up is not destroyed (unlike the case with DeleteMenu).
SetMenu	Sets the menu for a window.
SetMenuContextHelpId	Sets a help context associated with a menu. N/A on NT 3.51.
SetMenuDefaultItem	Sets the default entry for a menu. N/A on NT 3.51.
SetMenuItemBitmaps	Sets the symbols to use to indicate the checked or unchecked state of a menu entry.
SetMenuItemInfo	New general purpose function for modifying menu entries. N/A on NT 3.51.
TrackPopupMenu	Brings up a pop-up menu anywhere on the screen.
TrackPopupMenuEx	Supports extended pop-up menu features. N/A on NT 3.51.

Standard versus Extended Menus

Windows 95 and NT 4.0 and later implement a number of changes to the traditional menu system while continuing to support the standard Win32 menu functions. These changes are summarized below:

- Context help: Allows each menu to have a help context identifier associated with it. This help context is not actually used by Windows, but can be easily retrieved by the application to implement online help.

- Context Menu support: A context menu is a pop-up menu that appears when an object such as a control is clicked. Any control can implement a context menu, and context menu support is strongly recommended for controls or other user interface objects. Windows does provide some support in the operating system for context menus in the form of the WM_CONTEXT-MENU message (see Chapter 16), but it is the responsibility of each control or the application itself to implement this capability. The TrackPopup-MenuEx function extends the original TrackPopupMenu command by supporting pop-ups that use the right mouse button as well as the left. It also provides improved control over where the pop-up menu will appear.

■ Default Entry: Windows allows one entry in a menu to be a default entry which appears in bold. This entry should represent the default command that is executed when the object associated with a pop-up context menu is double clicked.

■ New API functions. Along with individual menu API commands, Windows 95 and NT 4.0 include the GetMenuItemInfo, InsertMenuItem, and SetMenuItemInfo functions that allow you to manipulate menu entries using the MENUITEMINFO structures. Microsoft recommends using these functions instead of the standard menu function. At this time it is probably still too soon for most programmers to write off NT 3.51 and earlier. This book, therefore, advocates use of the standard menu functions, along with some of the newer functions that do not use the MENUITEMINFO structure. Not only does this reduce the amount of code needed to support all three platforms, but it turns out that the standard functions are considerably easier to use under Visual Basic.

How Visual Basic Menus Work

The Visual Basic environment includes a sophisticated menu design window that is used to create menus for Visual Basic programs. When you design a menu using the Visual Basic menu design window, you are not actually creating a Windows menu—at least not directly. The VB menu designer actually creates an internal VB menu object. VB uses this object to create the actual menu using Windows API functions. VB sets some of the attributes of the menu according to the properties you specify. Other attributes are assigned based on an internal scheme. Table 10.3 shows how VB menu control properties correspond to the Windows menu attributes.

Some of the menu attributes have no equivalent in a VB property. Table 10.4 indicates the degree of VB compatibility of these attributes.

VB menu controls manipulate the actual menu in many ways. It is important to be aware of this situation when changing menus directly. The most important fact to keep in mind when modifying menus directly through API functions is that changes to the menus do not affect the VB menu controls.

Table 10.3 **VB Menu Properties and Corresponding Attributes**

Visual Basic Property	Windows Menu Attribute
Caption	String (name).
CtlName	No equivalent.
Index	No equivalent.
Tag	No equivalent.
Checked	Checked.
Enabled/Disabled	Enabled/Grayed. There is no VB equivalent to the Disabled but Ungrayed state.
Parent	No direct equivalent. This is the handle of the window that contains the menu.
Visible	Not an attribute. Visual Basic deletes any entries or menus that are not visible.
HelpContextID	HelpContext. However, the help context property is not compatible with the help context attribute.

Table 10.4 **Menu Attributes without Corresponding VB Properties**

Windows Menu Attribute	Visual Basic Equivalent
Separator	Caption property = "-".
Bitmap	No equivalent.
Checkmark Symbol	No equivalent.
Menu ID	Chosen internally by VB. User cannot set.
MenuBreak, MenuBarBreak	No equivalent.
Pop-up	Level in the menu design window.
Position	Position in menu design window.

Figure 10.2 shows the flow of control in the Visual Basic menu system. Note how the VB menu controls set the structure of the menu, but that the menu has no corresponding arrow to set the contents of the VB menu controls. The Windows API functions bypass the VB menu controls and operate directly on the menu.

The impact of the structure of the menu system on the programmer depends on the attributes and properties in question.

Figure 10.2

Operation of menus under Visual Basic

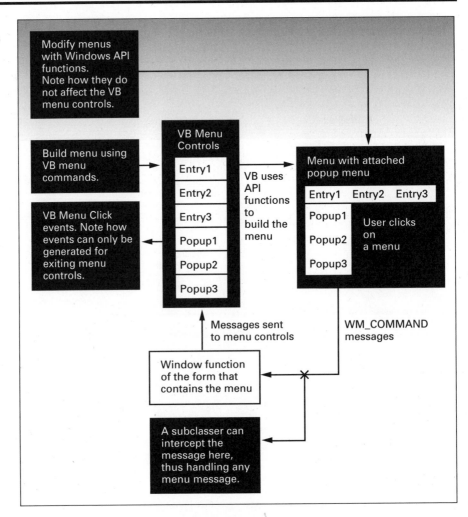

The Caption, Checked, and Enabled Properties

If you change the string attribute of a menu entry, the menu will display the new string but the VB Caption property for that menu entry will *not* reflect the new string. This applies to the Enabled and Checked properties as well. Note that if you use an API function to change the menu entry string or the enabled or checked state, the menu will work as you specify. It will display the new string and it will be checked or enabled as you specify, so in this sense these API changes are compatible with VB. However, if you choose to use the API functions to change these attributes you must avoid using the equivalent VB property to read the current state of the menu (you may use it to set the state of the menu, as setting the property will immediately update the menu to the new state).

In general, it is recommended that you use the VB property to set these three attributes.

The Visible Property—Adding and Deleting Menu Entries

It is important to be aware that hiding a menu entry does not "hide" the entry—it actually deletes it from the menu. This affects the position attribute of all menu entries below the one that was hidden. By the same token, VB assumes that menu entries are where it expects them to be. If you start adding and deleting entries directly, you can cause Visual Basic to lose track of where menu entries are located, in which case changes to properties of a menu entry will actually affect the wrong menu entry.

As a result, you should not use API functions to add or delete menu entries on any menu in the VB menu structure. You may use these API functions if you are creating a custom menu that is compatible with the VB menu structure, as described in the next section.

The correct way to add or delete entries is to use a Visual Basic menu control array, then modify each menu entry as needed using properties or API functions.

The Menu ID Attribute and Ensuring Compatibility of Menu Entries to VB

Figure 10.2 shows how the WM_COMMAND messages from the menu are sent to the VB menu controls for processing. When a VB menu control receives a WM_COMMAND message that corresponds to its own menu ID, it generates a Click event.

Since a Visual Basic program cannot intercept windows messages directly, this imposes the requirement that every menu entry have a VB control. Note that VB controls only look at the menu ID for the WM_COMMAND message, so the reverse is not true—each VB control may have more than one menu entry.

From a practical point of view, this means that you may create pop-up menus at will, assign them to entries, or use them as tracked pop-up menus, and reassign menu IDs as you wish as long as you make certain that the menu ID for each entry has a corresponding VB menu control. When a menu structure created or modified with API functions meets this condition, it is referred to in this book as a *compatible* menu structure.

If, however, you are using a subclasser, you can define any menu ID that you wish, since the subclasser can intercept the WM_COMMAND message coming in to the window. If you do this, you must be extremely careful that any menu commands due to your custom menu are blocked before they reach the destination window. Some Visual Basic controls are notoriously intolerant of unexpected WM_COMMAND or WM_MENUSELECT messages. You must also be extremely careful not to use a menu ID in this case that duplicates one that is already in use by a form or control. These issues are discussed further in the description of the SysMenu project later in this chapter. Subclassing is described further in Chapter 16.

Using the Menu API Functions with VB

This section describes a number of practical applications for the Windows menu API functions and how to safely use them with Visual Basic. Most of these examples are further illustrated in the MenuLook example program included in this chapter.

Creating Custom Checkmark Symbols

The space to the left of the menu entry text, or caption, is reserved for checkmarks. Normally, the space is empty when unchecked and displays a checkmark when the entry has been checked. Visual Basic is fully compatible with custom checkmarks; thus you could substitute another symbol such as a "+" or "–" for the standard "÷" symbol as needed by your application.

A custom checkmark must be the same size as the original checkmark. These dimensions may be obtained using the GetMenuCheckMarkDimensions API function. You may specify bitmaps for both the unchecked and checked state, and the bitmaps may be used on more than one menu entry. Note, however, that it is the programmer's responsibility to destroy the bitmap when it is no longer needed or before the program terminates.

Using Bitmaps to Customize Menus

You may replace the name (caption) of any menu entry with the bitmap of your choice. The menu entry will automatically be sized to hold the bitmap and will display color bitmaps in full color depending on the characteristics of the display. This is useful for any case where you would like to use a picture in a menu entry instead of a text string—for example, you could allow your user to choose from among hatched brushes by displaying the available hatching patterns in the menu.

One subtle use of this capability is to employ different fonts or text styles in menus. All you need to do is draw text onto a bitmap using the desired font or style. This bitmap may then be used as a menu entry.

Use the ModifyMenu API function to change a menu entry into a bitmap. Note that this will not affect the Caption property for the menu entry, which will continue to return the previous caption. Setting the Caption property will, however, remove the bitmap and replace it with the specified string.

It is important that menu entry bitmaps be preserved during the existence of the menu. VB modifies the bitmap accessed by the Image property of controls, so it is not appropriate to use the bitmap returned by the Image property of a control as a menu entry bitmap. One may, however, use the Picture property as long as the bitmap is left unchanged while it is in use. The MenuLook application solves this problem by drawing into a picture control that has the AutoRedraw property set to TRUE, and then making a copy of the image bitmap.

Bitmaps may be shared by menu entries, and should be deleted when the application exits in order to release the associated Windows resources. Chapter 9 discusses bitmaps in greater depth.

It is also possible to implement owner draw menus with the aid of a subclasser. An owner draw menu allows you to completely customize the size and contents of a menu entry using any Windows graphics command. You can see a demonstration of owner draw menus by running the SpyDemo demonstration application that is included on the CD-ROM.

Tracked Pop-up Menus

Visual Basic provides direct support for floating pop-up menus to appear anywhere on the screen using the PopupMenu command. The TrackPopupMenu API function can also be used to create pop-up menus in cases where customization is required. The only requirement is that this pop-up menu contain entries that have menu IDs that correspond to Visual Basic menu controls. One way to do this is to create a pop-up menu using the VB menu design tools, and simply hide it by setting the caption property of the top level menu for that pop-up to " " (note that this is *not* the same as setting the Visible property to zero, an action that destroys the menu). You can then use the GetSubMenu command to obtain a handle to the pop-up menu to use with TrackPopupMenu. Alternatively, you may create a new pop-up menu that is compatible with the VB menu structure.

The MenuLook application shows how to hide a top level entry and use its pop-up menu for a tracked pop-up. Note that even when a top level caption is set to the NULL string, it takes up space on the menu bar, so it is advisable to disable the menu entry as well.

Tracked pop-up menus are often used under Windows 95 and NT 4.0 to implement context menus—a small pop-up menu that appears when you right click on a control or form. The documentation for Visual Basic describes how to implement pop-up menus by using the PopupMenu command in response to the MouseDown or MouseUp event. This is fine in most cases; however, it can lead to problems with those controls that by default provide their own context menus. For example, the text box brings up its own context menu, so you would actually see two context menus if you took this approach—the standard text box context menu followed by your context menu.

The SysMenu sample program shows how you can use subclassing to detect the WM_CONTEXTMENU message going to a text box to override the default context menu and completely replace it with your own.

Creating a Pool of VB Menu Controls

If you expect to do a lot of menu customization or use many tracked pop-up menus, you will probably need a pool of menu controls to use in order to obtain menu IDs that will generate click events. The easiest way to do this is as follows:

1. Set the last entry on your top level menu to have no caption and set the Enabled property to zero.

2. Create under this entry a pop-up menu with a single entry by creating an entry indented one level in the menu design window. Make this entry a control array by setting the value of the Index property to 0.

Now, any time you need a VB menu control to use in another menu entry, simply create a new entry in the control array using the Visual Basic Load command. Because the top level entry for the control array is effectively hidden, you need not worry about the user seeing all of the menu entries you are creating in the control array. Meanwhile, new entries you create may use those menu IDs safely and will trigger Click events in the control array when selected.

Menus, System Menus, and Subclassing

Subclassing is a technique which allows you to intercept Windows messages going to a form. This technique can be used to detect the WM_COMMAND Windows message directly, eliminating the need to ensure compatibility with a Visual Basic menu structure when using menu API functions. It also allows you to intercept the WM_SYSCOMMAND message which makes it practical to customize an application's system menu. Refer to the Message Handling section in Chapter 16 for more information on subclassing and the tools required to use this powerful technique.

Obtaining Information about the VB Menu Structure

It is remarkably easy to obtain information about the existing VB menu structure. The GetMenu API function retrieves a menu handle to the top level menu for a form. The GetSubMenu function can then be used to obtain handles to the pop-up menus that it contains.

Additional API functions may be used to retrieve values of the various menu properties. The MenuLook example program shows how you may obtain a complete description of the menu structure.

Examples

This chapter includes two examples: MenuLook, which demonstrates how to customize menus and how to analyze a menu structure, and SysMenu, which demonstrates how to modify the system menu and use context menus.

MenuLook—A Menu Structure Viewer

MenuLook is a program that allows you to view the structure of the Visual Basic menu and shows how a menu may be modified. It also demonstrates many of the techniques for modifying menus described in this chapter.

This sample was ported from the 16-bit MenuLook program included in the original Visual Basic Programmer's Guide to the Windows API (16-bit edition), and has been implemented to run on both 16-bit VB4 and 32-bit VB platforms. This listing includes comments relating to some of the porting issues that came up. In addition, this program demonstrates some of the subtle issues relating to using strings inside of structures. These issues are discussed briefly here, but covered in detail in Chapter 15.

Using MenuLook

The MenuLook screen shown in Figure 10.3 demonstrates a variety of menu control techniques. The List1 list box is loaded with an analysis of the existing menu structure when the Analyze command button is selected.

The menu analysis shows the handle of each menu and a description of each menu entry. When an entry is a sub-menu, its handle is displayed along with its name. Handles are always displayed in hexadecimal; all other numbers are in decimal. Each sub-menu is analyzed in turn, with each menu entry shown along with its menu ID.

Figure 10.3
The MenuLook
program in action

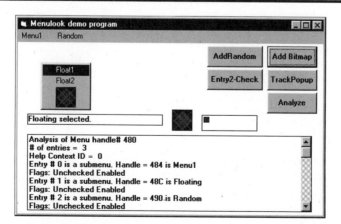

The Add Bitmap command button adds a bitmap entry into the Floating top level menu. The bitmap used is obtained from the Picture property in the Picture1 control.

When you click anywhere on the form that is not part of a control, the Floating top level menu is hidden by setting the caption to the empty string. The normal appearance of the menu bar can be seen in Figure 10.4. The program then takes a handle to the sub-menu for the Floating top level menu and displays it as a tracked pop-up menu at the cursor location. This will also take place when you select the TrackPopup command button.

Figure 10.4
Customizing popup menus using bitmaps

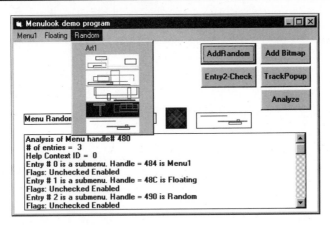

Figure 10.4 shows the effect on the Random menu of selecting the Add-Random control five times. Each time, a random set of rectangles is drawn in the Picture2 control. The image is then copied into a bitmap that is added to the Random top level menu.

Project Description
The MenuLook project includes three files. MENULOOK.FRM is the only form used in the program. MENULOOK.BAS is the only module in the program and contains the constant type, variable, and function declarations. APIGID32.BAS contains the declarations for the APIGID32.DLL dynamic link library included with this book.

Form Description
Listing 10.1 contains the header from file MENULOOK.FRM that describes the control setup for the form.

Listing 10.1   Header for file MENULOOK.FRM

```
VERSION 5.¯¯
Begin VB.Form Menulook
    Appearance      =    ¯  'Flat
    BackColor       =    &H8¯¯¯¯¯¯5&
    Caption         =    "Menulook demo program"
    ClientHeight    =    4¯2¯
    ClientLeft      =    1¯95
    ClientTop       =    177¯
    ClientWidth     =    7365
    BeginProperty Font
        name            =    "MS Sans Serif"
        charset         =    ¯
        weight          =    7¯¯
        size            =    8.25
        underline       =    ¯   'False
        italic          =    ¯   'False
        strikethrough   =    ¯   'False
    EndProperty
    ForeColor       =    &H8¯¯¯¯¯¯8&
    Height          =    471¯
    Left            =    1¯35
    LinkMode        =    1  'Source
    LinkTopic       =    "Form1"
    ScaleHeight     =    4¯2¯
    ScaleWidth      =    7365
    Top             =    114¯
    Width           =    7485
    Begin VB.ListBox List1
        Appearance      =    ¯  'Flat
        Height          =    1785
        Left            =    24¯
        TabIndex        =    ¯
        Top             =    216¯
        Width           =    6855
    End
    Begin VB.PictureBox Picture2
        Appearance      =    ¯  'Flat
        AutoRedraw      =    -1 'True
        BackColor       =    &H8¯¯¯¯¯¯5&
        ForeColor       =    &H8¯¯¯¯¯¯8&
        Height          =    375
        Left            =    444¯
        ScaleHeight     =    345
        ScaleWidth      =    13¯5
        TabIndex        =    6
        Top             =    168¯
        Width           =    1335
    End
```

File MENULOOK.FRX is the binary file for this form. It contains the definition of the Picture property for control Picture1. You may remove the line

```
Picture = MENULOOK.FRX:¯¯¯¯
```

in which case you should load a small bitmap into the control's Picture property in Visual Basic design mode. The sample program uses the bitmap AR-GYLE.BMP, which is provided with Windows.

```
Begin VB.PictureBox Picture1
      Appearance     =   ¯  'Flat
      BackColor      =   &H8¯¯¯¯¯¯5&
      ForeColor      =   &H8¯¯¯¯¯¯8&
      Height         =   495
      Left           =   372¯
      Picture        =   "MENULOOK.frx":¯¯¯¯
      ScaleHeight    =   465
      ScaleWidth     =   465
      TabIndex       =   5
      Top            =   156¯
      Width          =   495
   End
   Begin VB.CommandButton CmdAnalyze
      Appearance     =   ¯   'Flat
      BackColor      =   &H8¯¯¯¯¯¯5&
      Caption        =   "Analyze"
      Height         =   495
      Left           =   6¯¯¯
      TabIndex       =   1
      Top            =   114¯
      Width          =   1215
   End
   Begin VB.CommandButton CmdTrack
      Appearance     =   ¯  'Flat
      BackColor      =   &H8¯¯¯¯¯¯5&
      Caption        =   "TrackPop-up"
      Height         =   495
      Left           =   6¯¯¯
      TabIndex       =   2
      Top            =   6¯¯
      Width          =   1215
   End
   Begin VB.CommandButton CmdEntry2Chk
      Appearance     =   ¯  'Flat
      BackColor      =   &H8¯¯¯¯¯¯5&
      Caption        =   "Entry2-Check"
      Height         =   495
      Left           =   456¯
      TabIndex       =   8
      Top            =   6¯¯
      Width          =   1335
```

```
End
Begin VB.CommandButton CmdAddBitmap
    Appearance      =    ¯  'Flat
    BackColor       =    &H8¯¯¯¯¯¯5&
    Caption         =    "Add Bitmap"
    Height          =    495
    Left            =    6¯¯¯
    TabIndex        =    4
    Top             =    6¯
    Width           =    1215
End
Begin VB.CommandButton CmdAddRandom
    Appearance      =    ¯  'Flat
    BackColor       =    &H8¯¯¯¯¯¯5&
    Caption         =    "AddRandom"
    Height          =    495
    Left            =    456¯
    TabIndex        =    7
    Top             =    6¯
    Width           =    1335
End
Begin VB.Label Label1
    Appearance      =    ¯  'Flat
    BackColor       =    &H8¯¯¯¯¯¯5&
    BorderStyle     =    1  'Fixed Single
    ForeColor       =    &H8¯¯¯¯¯¯8&
    Height          =    255
    Left            =    24¯
    TabIndex        =    3
    Top             =    168¯
    Width           =    3255
End
Begin VB.Menu MenuTop
    Caption         =    "Menu1"
    HelpContextID   =    5¯¯
    Begin VB.Menu MenuEntry1
        Caption         =    "Entry1"
    End
    Begin VB.Menu MenuEntry2
        Caption         =    "Entry2"
    End
    Begin VB.Menu MenuEntry3
        Caption         =    "-"
    End
    Begin VB.Menu MenuArray1
        Caption         =    "Array1"
        Index           =    ¯
    End
    Begin VB.Menu MenuArray1
        Caption         =    "Array1B"
        Index           =    1
    End
```

```
      Begin VB.Menu MenuSub-menu1
         Caption        =   "Sub-menu1"
         Begin VB.Menu MenuSub1Entry1
            Caption      =    "Sub1Entry1"
         End
         Begin VB.Menu MenuSub1Entry2
            Caption      =    "Sub1Entry2"
         End
      End
   End
   Begin VB.Menu MenuFloat
      Caption       =    "Floating"
      Begin VB.Menu MenuFloat1
         Caption      =    "Float1"
         Index        =    -
      End
      Begin VB.Menu MenuFloat1
         Caption      =    "Float2"
         Index        =    1
      End
   End
   Begin VB.Menu MenuRandomTop
      Caption       =    "Random"
      Begin VB.Menu MenuArt
         Caption      =    "Art1"
         Index        =    -
      End
   End
End
```

MenuLook Listings

Module MENULOOK.BAS, shown in Listing 10.2, contains the constant,
variable, and function declarations used by the program. Listing 10.3 shows
the code for MENULOOK.FRM.

Listing 10.2   MENULOOK.BAS

```
Attribute VB_Name = "MENULOOK1"
Option Explicit

' MenuLook sample program
' Copyright (c) 1992-1997, Desaware


'-------------------------------------------------------


'        Public Constants
```

This file includes the 16- and 32-bit declarations for the following types from the file API32.TXT:

```
RECT, POINTAPI and BITMAP
```

It also includes the 32-bit declarations for OSVERSIONINFO and MENUITEMINFO. Note that MENUITEMINFO has been modified from the original WIN32API.TXT file that comes with Visual Basic for reasons that will become clear.

This file also includes constant declarations from the file API32.TXT that begin with the following prefixes: MIIM_, MF_, MFS_, MFT_, TPM_, VER_, and the standard trinary raster operations (such as SRCCOPY, SRCPAINT, and so forth).

```
Public Const WM_USER = &H4

Public Const LB_RESETCONTENT = (WM_USER + 5)


' Bitmap to use for checkmark on entry one menu

' Port: Convert to longs
Public NewCheck&

Public BMHandles&(32)

Public FloatBitmap&

#If Win32 Then
Declare Function GetLastError Lib "kernel32" () As Long
Declare Function lstrlen Lib "kernel32" Alias "lstrlenA" (ByVal lpstring As _
String) As Long
Declare Function GetMenuItemInfo Lib "user32" Alias "GetMenuItemInfoA" (ByVal _
hMenu As Long, ByVal un As Long, ByVal b As Long, lpMenuItemInfo As _
MENUITEMINFO) As Long
Declare Function GetVersionEx Lib "kernel32" Alias "GetVersionExA" _
(lpVersionInformation As OSVERSIONINFO) As Long
Declare Function CreateBitmapIndirect Lib "gdi32" (lpBitmap As BITMAP) As Long
Declare Function LoadMenu Lib "user32" Alias "LoadMenuA" (ByVal hInstance As _
Long, ByVal lpstring As String) As Long
Declare Function LoadMenuIndirect Lib "user32" Alias "LoadMenuIndirectA" (ByVal _
lpMenuTemplate As Long) As Long
Declare Function GetMenu Lib "user32" (ByVal hwnd As Long) As Long
Declare Function SetMenu Lib "user32" (ByVal hwnd As Long, ByVal hMenu As Long) _
As Long
Declare Function HiliteMenuItem Lib "user32" (ByVal hwnd As Long, ByVal hMenu _
```

```
As Long, ByVal wIDHiliteItem As Long, ByVal wHilite As Long) As Long
Declare Function GetMenuString Lib "user32" Alias "GetMenuStringA" (ByVal hMenu _
As Long, ByVal wIDItem As Long, ByVal lpstring As String, ByVal nMaxCount _
As Long, ByVal wFlag As Long) As Long
Declare Function GetMenuState Lib "user32" (ByVal hMenu As Long, ByVal wID As _
Long, ByVal wFlags As Long) As Long
Declare Function DrawMenuBar Lib "user32" (ByVal hwnd As Long) As Long
Declare Function GetSystemMenu Lib "user32" (ByVal hwnd As Long, ByVal bRevert _
As Long) As Long
Declare Function CreateMenu Lib "user32" () As Long
Declare Function CreatePop-upMenu Lib "user32" () As Long
Declare Function DestroyMenu Lib "user32" (ByVal hMenu As Long) As Long
Declare Function CheckMenuItem Lib "user32" (ByVal hMenu As Long, ByVal _
wIDCheckItem As Long, ByVal wCheck As Long) As Long
Declare Function EnableMenuItem Lib "user32" (ByVal hMenu As Long, ByVal _
wIDEnableItem As Long, ByVal wEnable As Long) As Long
Declare Function GetSubMenu Lib "user32" (ByVal hMenu As Long, ByVal nPos As _
Long) As Long
Declare Function GetMenuItemID Lib "user32" (ByVal hMenu As Long, ByVal nPos As _
Long) As Long
Declare Function GetMenuItemCount Lib "user32" (ByVal hMenu As Long) As Long

Declare Function InsertMenu Lib "user32" Alias "InsertMenuA" (ByVal hMenu As _
Long, ByVal nPosition As Long, ByVal wFlags As Long, ByVal wIDNewItem As Long, _
ByVal lpNewItem As String) As Long
Declare Function AppendMenu Lib "user32" Alias "AppendMenuA" (ByVal hMenu As _
Long, ByVal wFlags As Long, ByVal wIDNewItem As Long, ByVal lpNewItem As _
String) As Long
Declare Function AppendMenuBynum Lib "user32" Alias "AppendMenuA" (ByVal hMenu _
As Long, ByVal wFlags As Long, ByVal wIDNewItem As Long, ByVal lpNewItem As _
Long) As Long
Declare Function ModifyMenu Lib "user32" Alias "ModifyMenuA" (ByVal hMenu As _
Long, ByVal nPosition As Long, ByVal wFlags As Long, ByVal wIDNewItem As Long, _
ByVal lpstring As String) As Long
Declare Function RemoveMenu Lib "user32" (ByVal hMenu As Long, ByVal nPosition _
As Long, ByVal wFlags As Long) As Long
Declare Function DeleteMenu Lib "user32" (ByVal hMenu As Long, ByVal nPosition _
As Long, ByVal wFlags As Long) As Long
Declare Function SetMenuItemBitmaps Lib "user32" (ByVal hMenu As Long, ByVal _
nPosition As Long, ByVal wFlags As Long, ByVal hBitmapUnchecked As Long, ByVal _
hBitmapChecked As Long) As Long
```

```
Declare Function GetMenuCheckMarkDimensions Lib "user32" () As Long
Declare Function TrackPop-upMenu Lib "user32" (ByVal hMenu As Long, ByVal _
wFlags As Long, ByVal x As Long, ByVal y As Long, ByVal nReserved As Long, _
ByVal hwnd As Long, lprc As RECT) As Long
Declare Function TrackPop-upMenuBynum Lib "user32" Alias "TrackPop-upMenu" _
(ByVal hMenu As Long, ByVal wFlags As Long, ByVal x As Long, ByVal y As Long, _
ByVal nReserved As Long, ByVal hwnd As Long, ByVal lprc As Long) As Long
Declare Function GetCursorPos Lib "user32" (lpPoint As POINTAPI) As Long
Declare Function DeleteObject Lib "gdi32" (ByVal hObject As Long) As Long
Declare Function ModifyMenuBynum Lib "user32" Alias "ModifyMenuA" (ByVal hMenu _
As Long, ByVal nPosition As Long, ByVal wFlags As Long, ByVal wIDNewItem As _
Long, ByVal lpstring As Long) As Long

Declare Function GetObjectAPI Lib "gdi32" Alias "GetObjectA" (ByVal hObject As _
Long, ByVal nCount As Long, lpObject As Any) As Long
Declare Function CreateCompatibleDC Lib "gdi32" (ByVal hdc As Long) As Long
Declare Function SelectObject Lib "gdi32" (ByVal hdc As Long, ByVal hObject As _
Long) As Long
Declare Function BitBlt Lib "gdi32" (ByVal hDestDC As Long, ByVal x As Long, _
ByVal y As Long, ByVal nWidth As Long, ByVal nHeight As Long, ByVal hSrcDC As _
Long, ByVal xSrc As Long, ByVal ySrc As Long, ByVal dwRop As Long) As Long
Declare Function DeleteDC Lib "gdi32" (ByVal hdc As Long) As Long
Declare Function CreateSolidBrush Lib "gdi32" (ByVal crColor As Long) As Long
Declare Function Rectangle Lib "gdi32" (ByVal hdc As Long, ByVal X1 As Long, _
ByVal Y1 As Long, ByVal X2 As Long, ByVal Y2 As Long) As Long
Declare Function GetMenuContextHelpId Lib "user32" (ByVal hMenu As Long) As Long
Declare Function GetMenuDefaultItem Lib "user32" (ByVal hMenu As Long, ByVal _
fByPos As Long, ByVal gmdiFlags As Long) As Long
Declare Function SetMenuContextHelpId Lib "user32" (ByVal hMenu As Long, ByVal _
dw As Long) As Long
Declare Function SetMenuDefaultItem Lib "user32" (ByVal hMenu As Long, ByVal _
uItem As Long, ByVal fByPos As Long) As Long
Declare Function SetMenuItemInfo Lib "user32" Alias "SetMenuItemInfoA" (ByVal _
hMenu As Long, ByVal un As Long, ByVal bool As Long, lpcMenuItemInfo As _
MENUITEMINFO) As Long

#Else
```

```
Declare Function GetVersion& Lib "Kernel" ()
Declare Function DeleteDC% Lib "GDI" (ByVal hdc%)
Declare Function BitBlt% Lib "GDI" (ByVal hDestDC%, ByVal x%, ByVal y%, ByVal _
nWidth%, ByVal nHeight%, ByVal hSrcDC%, ByVal xSrc%, ByVal ySrc%, ByVal dwRop&)
Declare Function SelectObject% Lib "GDI" (ByVal hdc%, ByVal hObject%)
Declare Function CreateCompatibleDC% Lib "GDI" (ByVal hdc%)
Declare Function CreateBitmapIndirect% Lib "GDI" (lpBitmap As BITMAP)
Declare Function GetObjectAPI% Lib "GDI" Alias "GetObject" (ByVal hObject%, _
ByVal nCount%, lpObject As Any)
Declare Function DeleteObject% Lib "GDI" (ByVal hObject%)
Declare Sub GetCursorPos Lib "User" (lpPoint As POINTAPI)
Declare Function LoadMenu% Lib "User" (ByVal hInstance%, ByVal lpstring$)
Declare Function GetMenu% Lib "User" (ByVal hwnd%)
Declare Function GetMenuCheckMarkDimensions& Lib "User" ()
Declare Function GetMenuItemCount% Lib "User" (ByVal hMenu%)
Declare Function GetMenuItemID% Lib "User" (ByVal hMenu%, ByVal nPos%)
Declare Function GetMenuState% Lib "User" (ByVal hMenu%, ByVal wID%, ByVal _
wFlags%)
Declare Function GetMenuString% Lib "User" (ByVal hMenu%, ByVal wIDItem%, ByVal _
lpstring$, ByVal nMaxCount%, ByVal wFlag%)
Declare Function GetSubMenu% Lib "User" (ByVal hMenu%, ByVal nPos%)
Declare Function GetSystemMenu% Lib "User" (ByVal hwnd%, ByVal bRevert%)
Declare Function HiliteMenuItem% Lib "User" (ByVal hwnd%, ByVal hMenu%, ByVal _
wIDHiliteItem%, ByVal wHilite%)
Declare Function InsertMenu% Lib "User" (ByVal hMenu%, ByVal nPosition%, ByVal _
wFlags%, ByVal wIDNewItem%, ByVal lpNewItem As Any)
Declare Function InsertMenuBynum% Lib "User" Alias "InsertMenu" (ByVal hMenu%, _
ByVal nPosition%, ByVal wFlags%, ByVal wIDNewItem%, ByVal lpNewItem&)
Declare Function InsertMenuBystring% Lib "User" Alias "InsertMenu" (ByVal _
hMenu%, ByVal nPosition%, ByVal wFlags%, ByVal wIDNewItem%, ByVal lpNewItem$)
Declare Function IsMenu% Lib "User" (ByVal hMenu%)
Declare Function ModifyMenu% Lib "User" (ByVal hMenu%, ByVal nPosition%, ByVal _
wFlags%, ByVal wIDNewItem%, ByVal lpstring As Any)
Declare Function ModifyMenuBynum% Lib "User" Alias "ModifyMenu" (ByVal hMenu%, _
ByVal nPosition%, ByVal wFlags%, ByVal wIDNewItem%, ByVal lpstring&)
Declare Function ModifyMenuBystring% Lib "User" Alias "ModifyMenu" (ByVal _
hMenu%, ByVal nPosition%, ByVal wFlags%, ByVal wIDNewItem%, ByVal lpstring$)
Declare Function RemoveMenu% Lib "User" (ByVal hMenu%, ByVal nPosition%, ByVal _
wFlags%)
Declare Function SetMenu% Lib "User" (ByVal hwnd%, ByVal hMenu%)
Declare Function SetMenuItemBitmaps% Lib "User" (ByVal hMenu%, ByVal _
nPosition%, ByVal wFlags%, ByVal hBitmapUnchecked%, ByVal hBitmapChecked%)
```

```
Declare Function TrackPop-upMenu% Lib "User" (ByVal hMenu%, ByVal wFlags%, _
ByVal x%, ByVal y%, ByVal nReserved%, ByVal hwnd%, lpRect As Any)
Declare Function TrackPop-upMenuBynum% Lib "User" Alias "TrackPop-upMenu" _
(ByVal hMenu%, ByVal wFlags%, ByVal x%, ByVal y%, ByVal nReserved%, ByVal _
hwnd%, ByVal lpRect&)
Declare Function CreateSolidBrush% Lib "GDI" (ByVal crColor&)
Declare Function Rectangle% Lib "GDI" (ByVal hdc%, ByVal X1%, ByVal Y1%, ByVal _
X2%, ByVal Y2%)


#End If
```

On load, the application determines if it is running in the Windows 95 environment and saves this information in the IsWindows95 public variable. This is used to select between two possible approaches to analyzing a menu hierarchy. On Unload, the program deletes any bitmap objects that it has created.

Listing 10.3   MENULOOK.FRM

```
Option Explicit
Dim IsWindows95 As Boolean

Private Sub Form_Load()
#If Win32 Then
    Dim os As OSVERSIONINFO
    Dim di&
    Print "Click anywhere on the form to"
    Print "bring up a tracked pop-up menu"
    Randomize
    os.dwOSVersionInfoSize = Len(os)
    di = GetVersionEx(os)
    If os.dwPlatformId = VER_PLATFORM_WIN32_WINDOWS Then IsWindows95 = True
#End If
' We never let IsWindows95 get set to True in 16 bits, because
    ' it is only used for Win32 specific APIs
End Sub



Private Sub Form_Unload(Cancel As Integer)
    Dim x%, di&
    ' If a new check bitmap was set, we need to destroy it
    ' otherwise the resources used by the bitmap will not
    ' be freed.
    If NewCheck <> ¯ Then
        di = DeleteObject(NewCheck)
    End If
    ' The same applies to the random menu bitmaps
```

Listing 10.3   MENULOOK.FRM (Continued)

```
For x% = ¯ To 32
    If BMHandles(x%) <> ¯ Then
        di = DeleteObject(BMHandles(x%))
    End If
Next x%
If FloatBitmap <> Ø Then
    Call DeleteObject(FloatBitmap)
End If

End Sub
```

The Label1 control is used to indicate which menu has been clicked. This lets you verify that a menu entry is, in fact, still generating a Visual Basic click event even after it has been changed into a bitmap or customized in some other fashion. All of the menu click events are displayed in this control. Some of the click events also toggle the check state of the entry.

```
' Let the system know this menu has been clicked
'
Private Sub MenuArray1_Click(Index As Integer)
    Label1.Caption = "Array1(" + Str$(Index) + ") selected."

End Sub


'
' Let the system know this menu has been clicked'
'
Private Sub MenuArt_Click(Index As Integer)
    Label1.Caption = "Menu Random Art (" + Str$(Index) + ") selected."

End Sub


'
' Let the system know this menu has been clicked'
'
Private Sub MenuEntry1_Click()
    ' Check or uncheck the menu each time it is clicked
    Label1.Caption = "Entry1 selected."
    MenuEntry1.Checked = Not MenuEntry1.Checked
End Sub


'
' Let the system know this menu has been clicked'
'
Private Sub MenuEntry2_Click()
    ' Check or uncheck the menu each time it is clicked
    If MenuEntry2.Checked Then MenuEntry2.Checked = ¯ Else MenuEntry2.Checked = -1
```

```
        Label1.Caption = "Entry2 selected."

End Sub

'

' Let the system know this menu has been clicked'

'

Private Sub MenuFloat_Click()
    Label1.Caption = "Floating selected."

End Sub

'

' Let the system know this menu has been clicked'

'

Private Sub MenuFloat1_Click(Index As Integer)
    Label1.Caption = "Float1(" + Str$(Index) + ") selected."
End Sub

'

' Let the system know this menu has been clicked'

'

Private Sub MenuRandomTop_Click()
    Label1.Caption = "Menu Random selected."
End Sub

'

' Let the system know this menu has been clicked'

'

Private Sub MenuSub1Entry1_Click()
    Label1.Caption = "Sub1Entry1 selected."
End Sub

'

' Let the system know this menu has been clicked'

'

Private Sub MenuSub1Entry2_Click()
    Label1.Caption = "Sub1Entry2 selected."
End Sub

'

' Let the system know this menu has been clicked'

'

Private Sub MenuSub-menu1_Click()
    Label1.Caption = "Sub-menu1 selected."
End Sub

'

' Let the system know this menu has been clicked'

'

Private Sub MenuTop_Click()
```

```
        Label1.Caption = "MenuTop selected."
End Sub
```

The CmdEntry2Chk_Click function demonstrates several important techniques. First, it shows how to obtain the handle to the forms top level menu and how to obtain one of the pop-up menus that belong to the top level menu entries. This technique is repeated throughout the application.

It is critical, when setting a bitmap into a menu entry, that the bitmap not change or be destroyed while it is in use by the menu. This function obtains a new bitmap for use as a checkmark by calling the GetNewCheck function. In this case the unchecked state is left at its default (nothing shown); however, it is possible to set a checkmark for both the checked and unchecked states. A handle to the bitmap is stored for destruction when the form is unloaded.

```
'
' Create a box checkmark bitmap for the Entry2 menu
'
Private Sub CmdEntry2Chk_Click()
#If Win32 Then
    Dim topmenuhnd&
    Dim floatmenu&
    Dim NewCheck&
#Else
    Dim NewCheck%
    Dim topmenuhnd%
    Dim floatmenu%
#End If
    Dim oldbkcolor&
    Dim di&

    ' Get the new checkmark bitmap
    NewCheck = GetNewCheck()
    ' Get a handle to the top level menu
    topmenuhnd = GetMenu(Menulook.hwnd)
    ' Get a handle to the first popup
    floatmenu = GetSubMenu(topmenuhnd, ¯)
    ' And set the new check bitmap for the first (entry1) menu item
    di = SetMenuItemBitmaps(floatmenu, 1, MF_BYPOSITION, ¯, NewCheck)
    ' Check the entry
    MenuEntry2.Checked = -1
    ' Remind the user to look at it.
    MsgBox "Look at the Menu1 - Entry2 menu"
End Sub
```

The GetNewCheck function creates a device-dependent bitmap using the same techniques demonstrated in Chapter 9. It starts by determining the standard checkmark dimensions to use. It shrinks this rectangle by two pixels on a side for aesthetic reasons—there is no Windows requirement to reduce the size of the bitmap. It draws the image that it will use on the Picture2 control.

The CreateBitmapIndirect function then creates a bitmap, and CreateCompatibleDC creates a memory device context with which it can be accessed. The copy is accomplished with a simple BitBlt operation, after which the device context is deleted. The function returns the bitmap handle, which should be destroyed by the application before it terminates.

```
' Create a custom bitmap checkmark and return a
' handle to that bitmap.
'
Private Function GetNewCheck&()
    Dim bm As BITMAP
    Dim pt As POINTS
    #If Win32 Then
    Dim newbm&
    Dim tdc&, oldbm&
    Dim br&, oldbrush&
    #Else
    Dim newbm%
    Dim tdc%, oldbm%
    Dim br%, oldbrush%
    #End If
    Dim markdims&
    Dim di&

    ' Find out how big the checkmark should be.
    markdims& = GetMenuCheckMarkDimensions()
    agDWORDto2Integers markdims&, pt.x, pt.y

    ' And create a magenta brush (the checkmark will be
    ' a magenta filled rectangle
    br = CreateSolidBrush(QBColor(5))

    Picture2.Cls
    oldbrush = SelectObject(Picture2.hdc, br)
    ' Draw the rectangle.
    di = Rectangle(Picture2.hdc, 2, 2, pt.x - 2, pt.y - 2)
    di = SelectObject(Picture2.hdc, oldbrush)
    di = DeleteObject(br) ' Dump the brush.

    ' Create a compatible bitmap of the right size
    ' was: di% = GetObjectAPI(Picture2.Image, 14, agGetAddressForObject&(bm))
    di = GetObjectAPI(Picture2.Image, Len(bm), bm)
    bm.bmBits = ¯
    bm.bmWidth = pt.x
    bm.bmHeight = pt.y
    newbm = CreateBitmapIndirect(bm)
    ' And create a memory device context to use
    tdc = CreateCompatibleDC(Picture2.hdc)
    oldbm = SelectObject(tdc, newbm)
    ' Copy in the new checkmark
    di = BitBlt(tdc, ¯, ¯, pt.x, pt.y, Picture2.hdc, ¯, ¯, SRCCOPY)
```

```
    oldbm = SelectObject(tdc, oldbm)
    di = DeleteDC(tdc)
    GetNewCheck = newbm

End Function
```

The CmdAddBitmap_Click function sets a bitmap into the entry for a menu. In the past, this example has used the Picture1 control's Picture property because that bitmap remained unchanged through the life of the program. On some operating system configurations, this no longer seems to be the case. For this reason, the example has been modified for this edition to use the CopyPictureImage function to make a copy of the bitmap.

This function creates a menu to modify by using standard Visual Basic menu control array techniques. This ensures that a VB menu control is assigned to the entry that is to be modified. The GetMenuItemID API function is used to obtain the menu ID for the new menu entry. This menu ID is used later when calling the ModifyMenu command to make sure that all WM_COMMAND messages from the modified menu entry will continue to go to the VB menu control.

```
' This command adds the bitmap that is in the Picture1
' control to the Floating menu.
'
Private Sub CmdAddBitmap_Click()
#If Win32 Then
    Dim topmenuhnd&
    Dim floatmenu&
    Dim menuid&
#Else
    Dim topmenuhnd%
    Dim floatmenu%
    Dim menuid%
#End If
    Dim di&

    ' Get a handle to the top level menu
    topmenuhnd = GetMenu(Menulook.hwnd)
    ' And get a handle to the Floating popup menu.
    floatmenu = GetSubMenu(topmenuhnd, 1)
    ' If 3rd (bitmap) entry is already loaded, exit now
    ' (we only load the bitmap once)
    If GetMenuItemCount(floatmenu) >= 3 Then Exit Sub

    ' First, add a menu entry under VB - this provides us
    ' with a menu entry that can be replaced with a bitmap,
    ' but whose menu ID will be the same (so it will work
    ' properly)
    Load MenuFloat1(2)
    ' Now get the ID of that entry
    menuid = GetMenuItemID(floatmenu, 2)
```

```
        If FloatBitmap = Ø Then FloatBitmap = CopyPictureImage(Picturel)
        ' And replace it with a bitmap.
        di = ModifyMenuBynum(floatmenu, 2, MF_BITMAP Or MF_BYPOSITION, menuid, _
        FloatBitmap)


End Sub
```

This function combines the techniques shown by the CmdAddBitmap_Click and CmdEntry2Chk_Click functions to create custom bitmap menu entries. For this program, a number of random rectangles are drawn into an empty bitmap (the Picture2) control for use as a menu entry bitmap. Note how a copy of the picture control's bitmap is used. The bitmap is stored in a global array for destruction when the form is unloaded.

```
'
' This command creates a random bitmap and loads it into
' the Random popup menu.
'
Private Sub CmdAddRandom_Click()
#If Win32 Then
    Dim topmenuhnd&
    Dim floatmenu&
    Dim menuid&
    Dim newmenupos&
    Dim newbm&
#Else
    Dim topmenuhnd%
    Dim floatmenu%
    Dim menuid%
    Dim newmenupos%
    Dim newbm%
#End If
    Dim pw!, ph!
    Dim x%, di&

    ' First get the width and height of the picture2 control
    pw! = Picture2.ScaleWidth
    ph! = Picture2.ScaleHeight
    ' Get a handle to the Random popup menu
    topmenuhnd = GetMenu(Menulook.hwnd)
    floatmenu = GetSubMenu(topmenuhnd, 2)
    ' Find out how many menu items are already in the popup
    newmenupos = GetMenuItemCount(floatmenu)

    ' Load a VB menu entry at that position
    Load MenuArt(newmenupos)
    ' And get the MenuID for that entry
    menuid = GetMenuItemID(floatmenu, newmenupos)
```

```
' Draw some stuff on picture2
Picture2.Cls
For x% = ¯ To 5 ' Random rectangles
    Picture2.Line (Rnd * pw!, Rnd * ph!)-(Rnd * pw!, Rnd * ph!), _
    QBColor(CInt(Rnd * 15)), B
Next x%
' Get a bitmap that is a copy of the picture2 control
newbm = CopyPictureImage(Picture2)
For x% = ¯ To 32
    If BMHandles(x%) = ¯ Then Exit For
Next x%
If x% = 32 Then ' No room to store the bitmap handle
    di = DeleteObject(newbm)
    Exit Sub
End If
BMHandles(x%) = newbm
' And place that bitmap in the menu
di = ModifyMenuBynum(floatmenu, newmenupos, MF_BITMAP Or MF_BYPOSITION, _
menuid, newbm)

End Sub
```

When using a bitmap in a menu entry it is important that the bitmap not be destroyed while the menu is using it. The MenuLook program uses the Picture2 control as a source for images. However, we cannot simply use the bitmap property returned by the Image property of the control—that bitmap changes as the application executes. This function makes a copy of a bitmap contained in a picture control. The techniques shown here are based on the information in Chapter 9.

```
'
'   This function makes a copy of the Image property
'   of the specified image control and returns a handle to that bitmap
'
Private Function CopyPictureImage(SourceImage As PictureBox) As Long
    Dim bm As BITMAP
    #If Win32 Then
    Dim newbm&
    Dim tdc&, oldbm&
    #Else
    Dim newbm%
    Dim tdc%, oldbm%
    #End If
    Dim di&

    ' First get the information about the image bitmap
    di = GetObjectAPI(SourceImage.Image, Len(bm), bm)
    bm.bmBits = 0
    ' Create a new bitmap with the same structure and size
    ' of the image bitmap
    newbm = CreateBitmapIndirect(bm)
```

```
      ' Create a temporary memory device context to use
      tdc = CreateCompatibleDC(SourceImage.hdc)
      ' Select in the newly created bitmap
      oldbm = SelectObject(tdc, newbm)

      ' Now copy the bitmap from the persistant bitmap in
      ' picture 2 (note that picture2 has AutoRedraw set TRUE
      di = BitBlt(tdc, 0, 0, bm.bmWidth, bm.bmHeight, SourceImage.hdc, 0, 0, _
      SRCCOPY)
      ' Select out the bitmap and delete the memory DC
      oldbm = SelectObject(tdc, oldbm)
      di = DeleteDC(tdc)

      ' And return the new bitmap
      CopyPictureImage = newbm
End Function
```

The CmdTrack_Click function demonstrates two techniques. First it shows how to temporarily hide a menu by setting the caption to the empty string. In practice you would probably want to disable the menu entry as well, and to position it to the right of all other menus. Even when hidden, the menu takes up space. Keep in mind that you cannot hide the menu by setting the menu control's Visible property to FALSE—that causes the menu entry and associated pop-up to be destroyed.

Second, this function demonstrates how to bring up a tracked pop-up menu at the cursor position.

```
'
'    Hides the Floating menu entry in the caption,
'    and turns it into a tracked popup menu
'
Private Sub CmdTrack_Click()
#If Win32 Then   ' Port to correct handle type
    Dim topmenuhnd&
    Dim floatmenu&
#Else
    Dim topmenuhnd%
    Dim floatmenu%
#End If
    Dim oldcap$, di&
    Dim pt As POINTAPI

    ' Get a handle to the popup menu
    topmenuhnd = GetMenu(Menulook.hwnd)
    floatmenu = GetSubMenu(topmenuhnd, 1)

    ' Hide the menu entry by clearing the string
    ' temporarily. Note, don't make it invisible or the
    ' menu will go away!
```

```
        oldcap$ = MenuFloat.Caption
        MenuFloat.Caption = ""
        ' Find where the mouse cursor is and place the
        ' popup at that point
        GetCursorPos pt
        di = TrackPop-upMenuBynum(floatmenu, TPM_CENTERALIGN, pt.x, pt.y, ¯, _
        Menulook.hwnd, ¯&)
        ' Restore the original popup name
        MenuFloat.Caption = oldcap$
End Sub


'
' Clicking anywhere on the form triggers the CmdTrack command
' button.
'

Private Sub Form_MouseUp(Button As Integer, Shift As Integer, x As Single, y As _
Single)
        ' Clicking anywhere on the form triggers the CmdTrack button
        CmdTrack.value = -1
End Sub
```

The CmdAnalyze_Click function obtains a handle to the top level menu for a form, then calls the ViewMenu command to display the structure of the menu in the List1 control. ViewMenu is recursive (meaning it can make additional calls to itself to analyze sub-menus), so this single call will cause the entire menu structure to be displayed.

```
'
'    Get the form's menu and analyze it.
'
Private Sub CmdAnalyze_Click()
#If Win32 Then
        Dim menuhnd&
#Else
        Dim menuhnd%
#End If

        ' Clear the listbox
        'dl& = SendMessage(List1.hwnd, LB_RESETCONTENT, ¯, ¯&)
        List1.Clear
        ' Get a handle to the top level menu for this window
        menuhnd = GetMenu(Menulook.hwnd)
        ' And analyze it
        ViewMenu menuhnd
End Sub
```

The ViewMenu function has the ability to add to the List1 list box a description of the menu whose handle is passed to it as a parameter. It shows how to obtain the number of menu entries in a menu, and how to obtain information about each menu entry including the menu ID and state information.

This function makes a list of all pop-up menus attached to this menu, and after completing the description of each entry proceeds to recursively call itself for each pop-up sub-menu.

This function uses two different techniques for analyzing a menu. Under Win16 and Windows NT, it uses the standard menu API commands. Under Windows 95 it uses the extended menu API commands that work with the MENUITEMINFO structure. It is important to stress that Windows 95 is fully compatible with the standard menu API command set and that absolutely no benefit is gained in this example by using the new functions—on the contrary, it requires substantially more sophisticated string handling than is needed by the standard functions. The only reason that it is used in this example is because this is a sample program—and a good example of some of the techniques involved in working with complex structures. Also, keep in mind that the new functions, while only demonstrated under this example with Windows 95, work equally well on NT 4.0 and later.

The portions of this function that discuss the use of a byte array to retrieve string information from the MENUITEMINFO structure are examined in detail in Chapter 15 under the section titled "Dynamic Strings In Structures." If you wish to pursue this subject further, you might want to skip ahead to read that section before continuing.

```
' '
'    This function loads into list1 an analysis of the
'    specified menu
'

Private Sub ViewMenu(ByVal menuhnd&)
Dim menulen&
    Dim di&
#If Win32 Then
    Dim thismenu&
    Dim menuid&
    Dim currentpopup&
    Dim menuinfo As MENUITEMINFO
#Else
    Dim thismenu%
    Dim menuid%
    Dim currentpopup%
#End If
    Dim db%
    Dim menuflags%
    Dim flagstring$
    Dim menustring(128) As Byte
    Dim menustring2 As String * 128
    Dim context&

    ' This routine can analyze up to 32 popup sub-menus
    ' for each menu. We keep track of them here so that
    ' we can recursively analyze the popups after we
```

```
' analyze the main menu.
Dim trackpopups&(32)


currentpopup = ¯

List1.AddItem "Analysis of Menu handle# " & Hex$(menuhnd)

' Find out how many entries are in the menu.
menulen = GetMenuItemCount(menuhnd)
List1.AddItem "# of entries = " & Str$(menulen)

#If Win32 Then
context& = GetMenuContextHelpId(menuhnd)
If context& > ¯ Then List1.AddItem "Help Context ID = " & Str$(context&)
#End If

If IsWindows95 Then
    #If Win32 Then
        menuinfo.cbSize = Len(menuinfo)

        For thismenu = ¯ To menulen - 1
            ' cch field is reset each time
            menuinfo.cch = 127
            menuinfo.dwTypeData = agGetAddressForObject(menustring(¯))
            menuinfo.fMask = MIIM_DATA Or MIIM_ID Or MIIM_STATE Or _
            MIIM_SUB-MENU Or MIIM_TYPE Or MIIM_CHECKMARKS

            ' Get the ID for this menu
            ' It's a command ID, -1 for a popup, ¯ for a separator
            di = GetMenuItemInfo(menuhnd, thismenu, True, menuinfo)
            If di = ¯ Then
                List1.AddItem "Entry #" + Str$(thismenu) + _
                " is  unaccessable via GetMenuItemInfo"
            Else
                With menuinfo
                    ' Obtain all information about a menu
                    If .hSub-menu <> ¯ Then
                        ' Save it in the list of popups
                        trackpopups&(currentpopup) = thismenu
                        currentpopup = currentpopup + 1
                        ' Why do we use left$?
                        List1.AddItem "Entry #" + Str$(thismenu) + _
                        " is a sub-menu. Handle = " + Hex$(.hSub-menu) +  _
                        " is " + Left$(StrConv(menustring, vbUnicode), .cch)
                        List1.AddItem "Flags: " + GetFlagStringNew$(.fType, _
                        .fState)
                    Else
```

```
                              If .fType = MFT_STRING Then
                                  List1.AddItem "Entry #" + Str$(thismenu) + _
                                  " is a string = " + Left$(StrConv(menustring, _
                                  vbUnicode), .cch)
                                  List1.AddItem "Flags:" _
                                  + GetFlagStringNew$(.fType, .fState)
                              Else
                                  ' Menu type is a bitmap, or otherwise not _
                                  supported by this application
                                  List1.AddItem "Entry #" & Str$(thismenu) & _
                                  "has flags: " + GetFlagStringNew$(.fType, _
                                  .fState)
                              End If


                          End If

                  End With
              End If
          Next thismenu
      #End If
  Else
      For thismenu = ¯ To menulen - 1
          ' Get the ID for this menu
          ' It's a command ID, -1 for a popup, ¯ for a separator
          menuid = GetMenuItemID(menuhnd, thismenu)
          Select Case menuid
              Case ¯ ' It's a seperator
                  List1.AddItem "Entry #" + Str$(thismenu) + "is a separator"
              Case -1 ' It's a popup menu
                  ' Save it in the list of popups
                  trackpopups&(currentpopup) = thismenu
                  currentpopup = currentpopup + 1
                  ' And report that it's here
                  db = GetMenuString(menuhnd, thismenu, menustring2, 127, _
                  MF_BYPOSITION)
                  menuflags = GetMenuState(menuhnd, thismenu, MF_BYPOSITION)
                  List1.AddItem "Entry #" + Str$(thismenu) + _
                  " is a sub-menu.
                  Handle = " + Hex$(GetSubMenu(menuhnd, thismenu)) _
                  + " is " + Left$(menustring2, db)
                  List1.AddItem "Flags: " + GetFlagString$(menuflags)

              Case Else ' A regular entry
                  db = GetMenuString(menuhnd, menuid, menustring2, 127, _
                  MF_BYCOMMAND)
                  List1.AddItem "Entry #" + Str$(thismenu) + " cmd = " + _
                  Str$(menuid) + " is " + Left$(menustring2, db)
                  menuflags = GetMenuState(menuhnd, menuid, MF_BYCOMMAND)
                  List1.AddItem "Flags: " + GetFlagString$(menuflags)
          End Select
```

```
        Next thismenu
    End If
    If currentpopup > ¯ Then ' At least one popup was found
        List1.AddItem "Sub menus:"
        For thismenu = ¯ To currentpopup - 1
            menuid = trackpopups&(thismenu)
            ' Recursively analyze the popup menu.
            ViewMenu GetSubMenu(menuhnd, menuid)
        Next thismenu
    End If


End Sub
```

The GetFlagString and GetFlagStringNew functions obtain a list of the flags that are set for a menu entry. The two different techniques correspond to the standard and extended menu functions.

```
'
'   Gets a string containing a description of the flags
'   set for this menu item.
'
Private Function GetFlagString$(menuflags%)
    Dim f$
    If (menuflags% And MF_CHECKED) <> ¯ Then
        f$ = f$ + "Checked "
    Else
        f$ = f$ + "Unchecked "
    End If
    If (menuflags% And MF_DISABLED) <> ¯ Then
        f$ = f$ + "Disabled "
    Else
        f$ = f$ + "Enabled "
    End If
    If (menuflags% And MF_GRAYED) <> ¯ Then f$ = f$ + "Grayed "
    If (menuflags% And MF_BITMAP) <> ¯ Then f$ = f$ + "Bitmap "
    If (menuflags% And MF_MENUBARBREAK) <> ¯ Then f$ = f$ + "Bar-break "
    If (menuflags% And MF_MENUBREAK) <> ¯ Then f$ = f$ + "Break "
    If (menuflags% And MF_SEPARATOR) <> ¯ Then f$ = f$ + "Seperator "
    GetFlagString$ = f$
End Function



Public Function GetFlagStringNew$(ByVal fType&, ByVal fState&)
    Dim f$
    If (fState And MFS_CHECKED) <> ¯ Then
        f$ = f$ + "Checked "
    Else
        f$ = f$ + "Unchecked "
    End If
    If (fState And MFS_DISABLED) <> ¯ Then
```

```
        f$ = f$ + "Disabled "
    Else
        f$ = f$ + "Enabled "
    End If
    If (fState And MFS_GRAYED) <> ¯ Then f$ = f$ + "Grayed "
    If (fType And MFT_BITMAP) <> ¯ Then f$ = f$ + "Bitmap "
    If (fType And MFT_MENUBARBREAK) <> ¯ Then f$ = f$ + "Bar-break "
    If (fType And MFT_RADIOCHECK) <> ¯ Then f$ = f$ + "Radio "
    If (fType And MFT_MENUBREAK) <> ¯ Then f$ = f$ + "Break "
    If (fType And MFT_SEPARATOR) <> ¯ Then f$ = f$ + "Separator "
    GetFlagStringNew$ = f$

End Function
```

Suggestions for Further Practice

Here are a number of suggestions for ways to improve the MenuLook program.

- In the example, the custom menu example always draws bitmaps with a white background into the menu. Modify the example to determine the background color for menus and use it as the background color for the bitmap. (Hint: Look at the GetSysColor function in Chapter 6, and the PatBlt or drawing functions in Chapter 9.)

- Try implementing the new radio menu capability under Windows 95 or NT 4.0.

- Modify the MenuLook program so that it will analyze the current system menu.

SysMenu—A System Menu and Context Menu Demonstration

The SysMenu program demonstrates how you can modify the system menu of a Visual Basic application and how you can implement true Context menu support (as compared to the partial support offered by Visual Basic).

There is a catch, though: Both of these techniques require that you use subclassing. Subclassing was not supported under Visual Basic 4.0 and thus required use of third party subclassing controls. It is possible to subclass a window within Visual Basic 5.0 using the SetWindowLong function. However, despite the directions given in the VB5 documentation, you should never subclass a window using this technique within a VB application. It will work—but you will run into severe problems debugging your application, for as soon as it enters break mode or the Stop command is invoked, the code that runs the window function stops running as well. Thus this technique can interfere with the normal operation of your system. You should always subclass windows in an application using an in-process DLL component (which can be written using VB5). This book includes a fully functional demonstration version of a subclassing OLE control dwsbc32d.ocx, which is one of two controls included in Desaware's Spyworks package (the other is written in VB and includes complete source code). This control will allow you to run the sample programs and learn how to take advantage of the capabilities that subclassing provides; but if you wish to do so in your own applications you will need to purchase a subclassing control that is licensed for distribution or write one yourself.

Using SysMenu

The SysMenu screen is shown in Figure 10.5. As you can see, a new menu entry was added to the system menu. You can enter any text into the text box (which is partially obscured by the dropped menu in the figure) and click on the "Add To System Menu" button to insert a new entry into the system menu.

Figure 10.5

SysMenu screen showing modified system menu

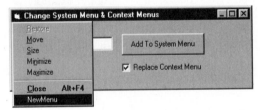

Context menus were discussed earlier in the chapter text. When you click the right mouse button on the form, a WM_CONTEXTMENU message is sent to the control that you clicked on. A control has the option of processing the message itself, or allowing it to be sent on to the container form. Most controls do not process the message themselves, but under Windows 95 and NT 4.0 the text control handles its own context menu. The dwsbc32d.ocx control uses subclassing to detect the WM_CONTEXTMENU message for both the form and the text control, thus allowing it to handle the default context menu for controls that do not have their own, and to override the context menu for the text control.

Project Description

The SysMenu project includes three files. SYSMENU.FRM is the only form used in the program. This program also uses MENULOOK.BAS which contains the constant type, variable, and function declarations. APIGID32.BAS contains the declarations for the APIGID32.DLL dynamic link library included with this book. Listing 10.4 contains the listing for SYSMENU.FRM. MENULOOK.BAS was listed in the previous section for the MenuLook.vbp example.

Listing 10.4   SYSMENU.FRM

```
VERSION5.¯¯
Begin VB.Form frmSysMenu
    Caption        =    "Change System Menu & Context Menus"
    ClientHeight   =    156¯
    ClientLeft     =    1¯95
    ClientTop      =    1515
    ClientWidth    =    579¯
    Height         =    1965
    Left           =    1¯35
    LinkTopic      =    "Form1"
    ScaleHeight    =    156¯
    ScaleWidth     =    579¯
    Top            =    117¯
    Width          =    591¯
    Begin VB.PictureBox picTarget
        Height         =    495
        Left           =    72¯
        ScaleHeight    =    465
        ScaleWidth     =    885
        TabIndex       =    3
        Top            =    84¯
        Visible        =    ¯      'False
        Width          =    915
    End
    Begin VB.CheckBox chkContext
        Caption        =    "Replace Context Menu"
        Height         =    255
        Left           =    27¯¯
        TabIndex       =    2
        Top            =    96¯
        Width          =    2115
    End
    Begin VB.CommandButton cmdAddSystem
        Caption        =    "Add To System Menu"
        Height         =    495
        Left           =    27¯¯
        TabIndex       =    1
        Top            =    3¯¯
        Width          =    1995
    End
    Begin VB.TextBox txtMenu
        Height         =    315
        Left           =    66¯
        TabIndex       =    ¯
        Text           =    "NewMenu"
        Top            =    36¯
        Width          =    1815
    End
```

The SubClass1 control Messages property contains a list of the messages that this control should intercept. You should set this to the WM_SYSCOMMAND, WM_COMMAND, and WM_CONTEXTMENU messages.

```
Begin DwsbcLib.SubClass SubClass1
        Left            =    5¯4¯
        Top             =    48¯
        _Version        =    262144
        _ExtentX        =    847
        _ExtentY        =    847
        _StockProps     =    ¯
        CtlParam        =    "frmSysMenu"
        Persist         =    ¯
        RegMessage1     =    ""
        RegMessage2     =    ""
        RegMessage3     =    ""
        RegMessage4     =    ""
        RegMessage5     =    ""
        Detect          =    ¯
        Messages        =    "SYSMENU.frx":¯¯¯¯
    End
End
Attribute VB_Name = "frmSysMenu"
Attribute VB_GlobalNameSpace = False
Attribute VB_Creatable = False
Attribute VB_PredeclaredId = TrueAttribute VB_Exposed = False
```

The NewContextMenu variable will hold a handle to a custom-created pop-up menu. This menu uses menu command IDs that start with &H2000. This number was chosen arbitrarily—as long as the menu ID is above WM_USER (&H400), it should not interfere with the normal behavior of the control.

```
Option Explicit
Dim CurrentID&
Dim NewContextMenu&

Const WM_CONTEXTMENU = &H7B
Const WM_SYSCOMMAND = &H112
Const WM_MENUBASE = &H2¯¯¯
Const WM_COMMAND = &H111

Const SCOFFSET = 2¯¯¯
```

During form load a new pop-up menu is created which has three entries. The control was set to subclass the form by setting the CtlParam parameter to frmSysMenu, the name of the form. The AddHwnd property is used to specify additional windows to subclass.

```
Private Sub Form_Load()
    Dim di&
```

```
    NewContextMenu = CreatePop-upMenu()
    di = AppendMenu(NewContextMenu, MF_STRING, WM_MENUBASE, "Entry 1")
    di = AppendMenu(NewContextMenu, MF_STRING, WM_MENUBASE + 1, "Entry 2")
    di = AppendMenu(NewContextMenu, MF_STRING, WM_MENUBASE + 2, "Entry 3")
    SubClass1.AddHwnd = txtMenu.hwnd
    SubClass1.AddHwnd = picTarget.hwnd
End Sub
```

Destroy the menu when the application is unloaded.

```
Private Sub Form_Unload(Cancel As Integer)
    If NewContextMenu Then Call DestroyMenu(NewContextMenu)
End Sub
```

Note the use of the **GetSystemMenu** API to retrieve the system menu.

```
Private Sub cmdAddSystem_Click()
    Dim sm&, di&
    If Len(txtMenu.Text) = ¯ Then
        MsgBox "Must specify menu text"
        Exit Sub
    End If
    sm& = GetSystemMenu(hwnd, False)
    di& = AppendMenu(sm, MF_STRING, SCOFFSET + CurrentID, txtMenu.Text)
    CurrentID = CurrentID + 1

End Sub
```

This particular application was set up so that one dwsbc32d.ocx control performs all of the subclassing. This means that the WndMessage event receives messages from every window that is being subclassed. You can use the hwnd property to determine which control a message is destined for.

The WM_SYSCOMMAND message is sent by the control menu messages. If the message number, which is in the wp parameter, is not one of the ones that we added, the function exits and the default operation for the message takes place. If it is a message from one of the menu entries we added, a message box is displayed indicating its receipt. The nodef property is then set to tell Windows that it need not process the message any further.

The WM_CONTEXTMENU message is sent when a context menu is requested. When this message is received, the function uses the TrackPopupMenu function to show a pop-up menu. Messages from this pop-up menu are directed to a picture box. This is necessary, as these messages can interfere with the behavior of other controls under Visual Basic (leading to fatal exceptions). Even so, you must intercept and block the WM_COMMAND messages coming into the picture control. Other messages (such as WM_MENUSELECT) are sent to a control while the pop-up menu is displayed. These, too, can cause problems with other controls, an issue that we avoid by using a picture control.

```
' This event is triggered for every WM_SYSCOMMAND message
```

```
'
Private Sub SubClass1_WndMessage(hwnd As Long, msg As Long, wp As Long, lp As _
Long, retval As Long, nodef As Integer)
    Dim sm&, di&
    Dim usestring$
    Dim usex%, usey%
    Select Case msg
        Case WM_COMMAND
            ' We only care about WM_COMMAND messages to picture control
            If hwnd <> picTarget.hwnd Then Exit Sub
            Call agDWORDto2Integers(wp, usex, usey)
            MsgBox "Received command # " & Hex$(usex)
            nodef = True
        Case WM_SYSCOMMAND
            ' If it's not one of the ones we added, just exit
            If wp < SCOFFSET Or wp >= (SCOFFSET + CurrentID) Then Exit Sub
            ' Get the text for this menu entry
            sm& = GetSystemMenu(hwnd, False)
            usestring$ = String$(128, ¯)
            di = GetMenuString(sm, wp, usestring, 127, MF_BYCOMMAND)
            MsgBox Left$(usestring, di), vbOKOnly, "System Menu Clicked is:"
            nodef = True
        Case WM_CONTEXTMENU
            ' Only trap the context menu if requested
            If chkContext.value = ¯ Then Exit Sub
            ' Get the location of the mouse click
            Call agDWORDto2Integers(lp, usex, usey)
            Call TrackPop-upMenuBynum(NewContextMenu, TPM_LEFTALIGN Or _
            TPM_RIGHTBUTTON, _
            usex, usey, ¯, picTarget.hwnd, ¯)
            nodef = True    ' Don't let control get the message!
    End Select
End Sub
```

Suggestions for Further Practice

This sample illustrates one of the simplest applications of subclassing. Here is
an experiment or two for you to try:

- What happens if you set the nodef property to TRUE to prevent the default processing of standard system menu messages? Could you prevent a
  window from being closed? Could you change the meaning of one of the
  standard messages?

- Chapter 6 showed how you can obtain the window handle for any window in the system. Can you add a system menu entry to another application and have it trigger an event in your application? (Hint: Yes, this is
  possible with the dwsbc32d.ocx control, though not with subclassing techniques written using VB5.)

Function Reference

■ AppendMenu

VB Declaration   `Declare Function AppendMenu& Lib "user32" Alias "AppendMenuA" (ByVal hMenu As _`
`Long, ByVal wFlags As Long, ByVal wIDNewItem As Long, ByVal lpNewItem As String)`

Description   This function adds a menu entry to the specified menu.

Use with VB   Refer to "How Visual Basic Menus Work," earlier in this chapter. Many of the changes made by this function will work, but will not be reflected by the VB menu object. The command ID added must be recognized by the VB menu system or intercepted using a subclassing control.

Parameter	Type/Description
hMenu	Long—Handle to a menu.
Wflags	Long—A combination of flags defined by constants in the file API32.TXT. Refer to Table 10.6 under the description for the Modify-Menu function for a list of the constants permitted.
WIDNewItem	Long—The new command ID for the specified menu entry. If the MF_POP-UP flag is specified in parameter wFlags, this should be a handle to a pop-up menu.
LpNewItem	String—If flag MF_STRING is set in parameter wFlags, this is the string to set into the menu. If flag MF_BITMAP is set, this is a long variable that contains a bitmap handle. If MF_OWNERDRAW is set, this value is included in the DRAWITEMSTRUCT and MEASUREITEMSTRUCT structures sent by Windows when the entry needs to be drawn.

Return Value   Long—Nonzero on success, zero on failure. Sets GetLastError.

Platform   Windows 95, Windows NT, Win16

Comments   Refer to the comments for the ModifyMenu function for more information.

Example   MenuLook.vbp, SysMenu.vbp

■ CheckMenuItem

VB Declaration   `Declare Function CheckMenuItem& Lib "user32" (ByVal hMenu As Long, ByVal _`
`wIDCheckItem As Long, ByVal wCheck As Long)`

Description   Checks or unchecks the specified menu entry.

Use with VB   Refer to "How Visual Basic Menus Work," earlier in this chapter. Changes made by this function will work, but will not be reflected by the VB menu Checked property.

Parameter	Type/Description
hMenu	Long—Handle to a menu.

Parameter	Type/Description
WIDCheckItem	Long—Identifier of the menu entry to check or uncheck. If the MF_BYCOMMAND flag is set in the wCheck parameter, this parameter refers to the command ID of the menu entry to change. If the MF_BYPOSITION flag is set, this parameter refers to the position of the entry in the menu (the first entry is zero).
Wcheck	Long—A combination of flags defined by constants in the file API32.TXT. Refer to Table 10.6 under the description of the Modify-Menu function for a list of menu constants. Only the following constants may be specified for this function: MF_BYCOMMAND, MF_BYPOSITION, MF_CHECKED, and MF_UNCHECKED.

Return Value   Long—MF_CHECKED if the previous state of the entry was checked, MF_UNCHECKED if it was unchecked. –1 if the menu entry does not exist.

Platform   Windows 95, Windows NT, Win16

■ CheckMenuRadioItem

VB Declaration
```
Declare Function CheckMenuRadioItem& Lib "user32" (ByVal hMenu As Long, ByVal _
un1 As Long, ByVal un2 As Long, ByVal un3 As Long, ByVal un4 As Long)
```

Description   Specifies that a menu entry be checked as a "radio" item. This is similar to an option button where only one item in a group may be checked. The group may be defined by position or by menu ID. An item checked with this function will display a circular "option button" style checkmark instead of a standard checkmark.

Use with VB   Refer to "How Visual Basic Menus Work," earlier in this chapter. Changes made by this function will work, but will not be reflected by the VB menu Checked property.

Parameter	Type/Description
hMenu	Long—A handle to a menu.
un1	Long—The first position or menu ID in the group.
un2	Long—The last position or menu ID in the group.
un3	Long—The position or menu ID to check.
un4	Long— One of the following flags: MF_BYPOSITION if un1, un2, and un3 refer to the position of the menu entry (the first is always zero). MF_BYCOMMAND if they refer to menu IDs.

Return Value   Long—TRUE (nonzero) on success, zero otherwise. Sets GetLastError.

Platform   Windows 95, Windows NT 4.0

Comments   An entry checked with this function will have the MFT_RADIOCHECK flag set as well as the MFT_CHECKED flag. Both of these flags will be cleared for all other entries in the group.

■ CreateMenu

VB Declaration   Declare Function CreateMenu& Lib "user32" ()

Description   Creates a new menu.

Use with VB   Refer to "How Visual Basic Menus Work," earlier in this chapter. Unlike pop-up menus, top level menus are unlikely to be useful to VB programmers.

Return Value   Long—A handle to a new top level menu on success, zero on error.

Platform   Windows 95, Windows NT, Win16

Comments   The menu is empty when created. Use menu API functions to insert menu entries. Use Destroy-Menu to destroy the menu when it is no longer needed.

■ CreatePopupMenu

VB Declaration   Declare Function CreatePop-upMenu& Lib "user32" ()

Description   Creates an empty pop-up menu. The AppendMenu or InsertMenu function may be used to add entries into the window and to add the pop-up to an existing menu and to add entries into the newly created menu.

Use with VB   Refer to "How Visual Basic Menus Work," earlier in this chapter. The use of this function to create alternate VB menus is not recommended, except when creating menus for the TrackPopup-Menu function. Command IDs used in this window must match those of existing VB menu controls or be handled using a subclasser.

Return Value   Long—A handle to a menu on success, zero on error.

Platform   Windows 95, Windows NT, Win16

Comments   This pop-up menu will be deleted automatically only if it is part of a higher level menu. Otherwise, it is the programmer's responsibility to destroy the handle returned by this function using the DestroyMenu function.

Example   SysMenu.vbp

■ DeleteMenu

VB Declaration   Declare Function DeleteMenu& Lib "user32" (ByVal hMenu As Long, ByVal nPosition _
As Long, ByVal wFlags As Long)

Description   Deletes the specified menu entry.

Use with VB   Refer to "How Visual Basic Menus Work," earlier in this chapter. It is strongly recommended that you use the VB menu Visible property to delete entries from a menu. Use of this function will cause the Visible property for other menu entries in the specified menu to affect the wrong menu entry.

Parameter	Type/Description
hMenu	Long—Handle to a menu.
NPosition	Long—Identifier of the menu entry to delete. If the MF_BYCOMMAND flag is set in the wFlags parameter, this parameter refers to the command ID of the menu entry to change. If the MF_BYPOSITION flag is set, this parameter refers to the position of the entry in the menu (the first entry is zero).
WFlags	Long—MF_BYCOMMAND or MF_BYPOSITION as specified for the nPosition parameter.

Return Value Long—Nonzero on success, zero on failure. Sets GetLastError.

Platform Windows 95, Windows NT, Win16

Comments If the entry has a pop-up menu attached, the pop-up menu is destroyed. Use the RemoveMenu API function to remove a pop-up menu entry without destroying the pop-up menu.

■ DestroyMenu

VB Declaration `Declare Function DestroyMenu& Lib "user32" (ByVal hMenu As Long)`

Description Destroys the specified menu. Note that menus that are part of another menu or assigned directly to a window are automatically destroyed when the window is destroyed.

Use with VB Refer to "How Visual Basic Menus Work," earlier in this chapter. This function is generally used on menus that were created with the CreateMenu and CreatePopupMenu functions.

Parameter	Type/Description
hMenu	Long—Handle of the menu to destroy.

Return Value Long—Nonzero on success, zero on failure. Sets GetLastError.

Platform Windows 95, Windows NT, Win16

Example SysMenu.vbp

■ DrawMenuBar

VB Declaration `Declare Function DrawMenuBar& Lib "user32" (ByVal hwnd As Long)`

Description Redraws the menu for the specified window. Use this when using API functions to change the contents of a window's menu.

Use with VB No problem, though it should rarely be necessary to use this function because you should not use API functions to change the top level menu bar of a window.

Parameter	Type/Description
hwnd	Long—A handle to the window whose menu bar is to be redrawn.

Return Value   Long—Nonzero on success, zero on failure. Sets GetLastError.

Platform   Windows 95, Windows NT, Win16

■ EnableMenuItem

VB Declaration   `Declare Function EnableMenuItem& Lib "user32" (ByVal hMenu As Long, ByVal _`
`wIDEnableItem As Long, ByVal wEnable As Long)`

Description   Enables or disables the specified menu entry.

Use with VB   Refer to "How Visual Basic Menus Work," earlier in this chapter. Changes made by this function will work, but will not be reflected by the VB menu Enabled property.

Parameter	Type/Description
hMenu	Long—Handle to a menu
wIDEnableItem	Long—Identifier of the menu entry to enable or disable. If the MF_BYCOMMAND flag is set in the wEnable parameter, this parameter refers to the command ID of the menu entry to change. If the MF_BYPOSITION flag is set, this parameter refers to the position of the entry in the menu (the first entry is zero).
wEnable	Long—A combination of flags defined by constants in the file API32.TXT. Refer to Table 10.6 under the description for the ModifyMenu function for a list of menu constants. Only the following constants may be specified for this function: MF_BYCOMMAND, MF_BYPOSITION, MF_ENABLED, MF_DISABLED, and MF_GRAYED.

Return Value   Long—One of the constants MF_ENABLED, MF_DISABLED, or MF_GRAYED that indicate the previous state of the entry. –1 if the menu entry does not exist.

Platform   Windows 95, Windows NT, Win16

Comments   If the entry specified has a pop-up menu attached, the entire pop-up menu is affected.

■ GetMenu

VB Declaration   `Declare Function GetMenu& Lib "user32" (ByVal hwnd As Long)`

Description   Retrieves the handle of the menu for a window.

Use with VB   No problem.

Parameter	Type/Description
hwnd	Long—A handle to a window. With VB, this should be a form handle. This may not be the handle of a child window.

Return Value   Long—The handle of the menu attached to the specified window, if one exists; zero otherwise.

Platform   Windows 95, Windows NT, Win16

■ GetMenuCheckMarkDimensions

VB Declaration Declare Function GetMenuCheckMarkDimensions& Lib "user32" ()

Description Returns the dimensions of a checkmark for a menu. Refer to the description for the SetMenu-ItemBitmaps for further information on use of this function.

Use with VB No problem.

Return Value Long—The high word (16 bits) contains the height of the menu checkmark in pixels; the low word contains the width. You can use the agDWORDto2Integers function to divide the result into two integers.

Platform Windows 95, Windows NT

Example MenuLook.vbp

■ GetMenuContextHelpId

VB Declaration Declare Function GetMenuContextHelpId& Lib "user32" (ByVal hMenu As Long)

Description Retrieves the help context ID assigned to a menu using the SetMenuContextHelpId function.

Use with VB No problem. The context ID value set using this function does not correspond to the help context ID assigned using the Visual Basic menu bar designer. Visual Basic stores its own help context ID values internally. The Visual Basic help context ID is preferred over use of this function due to its support for Windows NT 3.51.

Parameter	Type/Description
hMenu	Long—Handle to a menu.

Return Value Long—A help context ID if present, zero otherwise.

Platform Windows 95, Windows NT 4.0

■ GetMenuDefaultItem

VB Declaration Declare Function GetMenuDefaultItem& Lib "user32" (ByVal hMenu As Long, ByVal _
fByPos As Long, ByVal gmdiFlags As Long)

Description Allows you to determine which menu entry in a menu is the default entry. This entry corresponds by convention to the operation that is performed when the menu is double clicked.

Use with VB No problem.

Parameter	Type/Description
hMenu	Long—A handle to a menu.
fByPos	Long—TRUE to retrieve the position of the entry in the menu. FALSE to retrieve its menu ID.

Parameter	Type/Description
gmdiFlags	Long—One of the following flags: GMDI_GOINTOPOPUPS: If the default entry is a pop-up menu, the function will search for a default entry within the pop-up. GMDI_USEDISABLED: Specifies that you do not want to skip disabled menu entries in the search.

Return Value   Long—The position or identifier of the default menu entry. −1 if no default entry was found.

Platform   Windows 95, Windows NT 4.0

■ GetMenuItemCount

VB Declaration   `Declare Function GetMenuItemCount& Lib "user32" (ByVal hMenu As Long)`

Description   Returns the number of entries in a menu.

Use with VB   No problem.

Parameter	Type/Description
hMenu	Long—A handle to a menu.

Return Value   Long—The number of entries in the menu; −1 on error. Sets GetLastError.

Platform   Windows 95, Windows NT, Win16

Example   MenuLook.vbp

■ GetMenuItemID

VB Declaration   `Declare Function GetMenuItemID& Lib "user32" (ByVal hMenu As Long, ByVal nPos _`
`As Long)`

Description   Returns the menu ID of the entry at the specified position in a menu.

Use with VB   No problem.

Parameter	Type/Description
hMenu	Long—A handle to a menu.
nPos	Long—The position of the entry in the menu. The first entry is number zero.

Return Value   Long—The menu ID for the specified entry; −1 if the entry is a pop-up menu, 0 if the specified entry is a separator.

Platform   Windows 95, Windows NT, Win16

Example   MenuLook.vbp

■ GetMenuItemInfo

VB Declaration   Declare Function GetMenuItemInfo& Lib "user32" Alias "GetMenuItemInfoA" (ByVal _
hMenu As Long, ByVal un As Long, ByVal b As Long, lpMenuItemInfo As _
MENUITEMINFO)

Description   Retrieves requested information about a menu entry using a MENUITEMINFO structure.

Use with VB   No problem.

Parameter	Type/Description
hMenu	Long—Handle of a menu.
un	Long—The menu ID or position of a menu entry.
b	Long—TRUE if un specifies the position of the entry, FALSE if it is a menu ID.
lpMenuItemInfo	MENUITEMINFO—A MENUITEMINFO structure to load with requested information. Refer to Appendix B for further information on this structure.

Return Value   Long—TRUE (nonzero) on success, zero otherwise. Sets GetLastError.

Platform   Windows 95, Windows NT 4.0

Example   MenuLook.vbp

■ GetMenuItemRect

VB Declaration   Declare Function GetMenuItemRect& Lib "user32" (ByVal hWnd As Long, ByVal hMenu _
As Long, ByVal uItem As Long, lprcItem As RECT)

Description   Loads a rectangle with the screen coordinates for the specified menu entry.

Use with VB   No problem.

Parameter	Type/Description
hWnd	Long—The handle of the window that will contain the specified menu or pop-up menu.
hMenu	Long—Handle to the menu.
uItem	Long—Position or menu ID of the menu entry being examined.
lprcItem	RECT—A pointer to a RECT structure to load with the position and size of the menu entry in screen coordinates.

Return Value   Long—TRUE (nonzero) on success, zero otherwise. Sets GetLastError.

Platform   Windows 95, Windows NT 4.0

■ GetMenuState

VB Declaration   Declare Function GetMenuState& Lib "user32" (ByVal hMenu As Long, ByVal wID As _
                      Long, ByVal wFlags As Long)

Description   Retrieves information about the state of the specified menu entry.

Use with VB   Refer to "How Visual Basic Menus Work," earlier in this chapter.

Parameter	Type/Description
hMenu	Long—Handle to a menu.
wID	Long—Identifier of the menu entry to examine. If the MF_BY-COMMAND flag is set in the wFlags parameter, this parameter refers to the command ID of the menu entry. If the MF_BYPOSITION flag is set, this parameter refers to the position of the entry in the menu (the first entry is zero).
wFlags	Long—The constant MF_BYCOMMAND or MF_BYPOSITION as specified in the wId parameter.

Return Value   Long—A combination of flags defined by constants in the file API32.TXT as shown in Table 10.5.
                      If the entry is a pop-up menu, the lowest byte of the result contains state flags and the second
                      byte contains a count of the entries in the pop-up.

Table 10.5   **Menu Constants for GetMenuState**

Constant	Description
MF_HILITE	Menu entry is highlighted (selected).
MF_CHECKED	Menu entry is checked.
MF_DISABLED	Menu entry is disabled.
MF_GRAYED	Menu entry is gray and disabled.
MF_MENUBARBREAK	A bar break is specified for this entry. Refer to Table 10.6 under the ModifyMenu command for details.
MF_MENUBREAK	A menu break is specified for this entry. Refer to Table 10.6 under the ModifyMenu command for details.
MF_SEPARATOR	Menu entry is a separator.

Platform   Windows 95, Windows NT, Win16

Example   MenuLook.vbp

■ GetMenuString

VB Declaration   Declare Function GetMenuString& Lib "user32" Alias "GetMenuStringA" (ByVal _
hMenu As Long, ByVal wIDItem As Long, ByVal lpString As String, ByVal nMaxCount _
As Long, ByVal wFlag As Long)

Description   Retrieves the string for a specified menu entry.

Use with VB   Refer to "How Visual Basic Menus Work," earlier in this chapter.

Parameter	Type/Description
hMenu	Long—Handle to a menu.
wIDItem	Long—Identifier of the menu entry whose string you wish to retrieve. If the MF_BYCOMMAND flag is set in the wFlag parameter, this parameter refers to the command ID of the menu entry. If the MF_BYPOSITION flag is set, this parameter refers to the position of the entry in the menu (the first entry is zero).
lpString	String—A preinitialized string buffer to load with the string for the menu entry.
nMaxCount	Long—The maximum number of characters to load into lpString + 1.
wFlag	Long—The constant MF_BYCOMMAND or MF_BYPOSITION as specified in the wIDItem parameter.

Return Value   Long—The length of the string returned in lpString (not including the NULL terminating character). Zero on error.

Platform   Windows 95, Windows NT, Win16

Example   MenuLook.vbp

■ GetSubMenu

VB Declaration   Declare Function GetSubMenu& Lib "user32" (ByVal hMenu As Long, ByVal nPos As _
Long)

Description   Retrieves the handle of a pop-up menu that is located at the specified position in a menu.

Use with VB   No problem.

Parameter	Type/Description
hMenu	Long—A handle to a menu.
nPos	Long—The position of the entry in the menu. The first entry is number zero.

Return Value   Long—The handle of the pop-up menu at the specified position if one exists, zero otherwise.

Platform   Windows 95, Windows NT, Win16

Example   MenuLook.vbp

■ GetSystemMenu

VB Declaration   `Declare Function GetSystemMenu& Lib "user32" (ByVal hwnd As Long, ByVal bRevert _`
`As Long)`

Description   Retrieves the handle to the system menu for the specified window. This is referred to in VB as the control menu (the menu that appears when you click on the control box that exists on a form if the ControlBox property is TRUE).

Use with VB   System menus send WM_SYSCOMMAND messages to a window rather than WM_COMMAND messages. This means that they are not compatible with VB menu control objects. Thus, while you can change entries in the system menu if you wish, you cannot add new entries that will receive click events unless you use a subclassing control such as dwsbc32d.ocx. This command can also be used to remove entries from the system menu that you do not wish to make available to the user.

Parameter	Type/Description
hwnd	Long—A handle to a window.
bRevert	Long—Set TRUE to restore the original system menu.

Return Value   Long—A handle to the system menu on success, zero otherwise. Zero if bRevert is TRUE (the original system menu is simply restored).

Platform   Windows 95, Windows NT, Win16

Example   SysMenu.vbp

■ HiliteMenuItem

VB Declaration   `Declare Function HiliteMenuItem& Lib "user32" (ByVal hwnd As Long, ByVal hMenu _`
`As Long, ByVal wIDHiliteItem As Long, ByVal wHilite As Long)`

Description   Controls the highlight on a top level menu entry.

Use with VB   Refer to "How Visual Basic Menus Work," earlier in this chapter.

Parameter	Type/Description
hwnd	Long—A handle to a window that has a top level menu.
hMenu	Long—Handle to the top level menu for window hWnd.
wIDHiliteItem	Long—Identifier of the menu entry to highlight or unhighlight. If the MF_BYCOMMAND flag is set in the wHilite parameter, this parameter refers to the command ID of the menu entry to change. If the MF_BYPOSITION flag is set, this parameter refers to the position of the entry in the menu (the first entry is zero).
wHilite	Long—A combination of flags defined by constants in the file API32.TXT. Include MF_BYCOMMAND or MF_BYPOSITION to indicate the entry to change. Include MF_HILITE to set the highlight, or MF_UNHILITE to remove the highlight.

Return Value   Long—Nonzero on success, zero on failure.

Platform   Windows 95, Windows NT, Win16

■ InsertMenu

VB Declaration   `Declare Function InsertMenu& Lib "user32" Alias "InsertMenuA" (ByVal hMenu As _`
`Long, ByVal nPosition As Long, ByVal wFlags As Long, ByVal wIDNewItem As Long, _`
`ByVal lpNewItem As String)`

Description   This function inserts a menu entry at the specified location in a menu, moving other entries down as needed.

Use with VB   Refer to "How Visual Basic Menus Work," earlier in this chapter. Many of the changes made by this function will work but will not be reflected by the VB menu object. The command ID added must be recognized by the VB menu system.

Parameter	Type/Description
hMenu	Long—Handle to a menu.
nPosition	Long—Identifier to the menu entry specifying the insertion point of the new entry. If the MF_BYCOMMAND flag is set in the wFlags parameter, this parameter refers to the command ID of the menu entry to change. If the MF_BYPOSITION flag is set, this parameter refers to the position of the entry in the menu (the first entry is zero).
wFlags	Long—A combination of flags defined by constants in the file API32.TXT. Refer to Table 10.6 under the description for the Modify-Menu function for a list of the constants permitted.
wIDNewItem	Long—The new command ID for the specified menu entry. If the MF_POPUP flag is specified in parameter wFlags, this should be a handle to a pop-up menu.
lpNewItem	String—If flag MF_STRING is set in parameter wFlags, this is the string to set into the menu. If flag MF_BITMAP is set, this is a long variable that contains a bitmap handle (you will need to create an alias in which this parameter is defined as "ByVal as Long).”

Return Value   Long—Nonzero on success, zero on failure. Sets GetLastError.

Platform   Windows 95, Windows NT, Win16

Comments   Refer to the comments for the ModifyMenu function for more information.

■ InsertMenuItem

VB Declaration   `Declare Function InsertMenuItem& Lib "user32" Alias "InsertMenuItemA" (ByVal _`
`hMenu As Long, ByVal un As Long, ByVal bypos As Long, lpcMenuItemInfo As _`
`MENUITEMINFO)`

Description   Inserts a new menu entry with the characteristics specified in a MENUITEMINFO structure.

Use with VB	No problem.

Parameter	Type/Description
hMenu	Long—Handle of a menu.
un	Long—The menu ID or position of a menu entry. The new entry is inserted before the item specified by this parameter.
bypos	Long—TRUE if un specifies the position of the entry, FALSE if it is a menu ID.
lpMenuItemInfo	MENUITEMINFO—A MENUITEMINFO structure to use to set the characteristics of the specified menu entry. Refer to Appendix B for further information on this structure.

Return Value	Long—TRUE (nonzero) on success, zero otherwise. Sets GetLastError.
Platform	Windows 95, Windows NT 4.0

■ IsMenu

VB Declaration	`Declare Function IsMenu& Lib "user32" (ByVal hMenu As Long)`
Description	Determines if a handle is a handle to a menu..
Use with VB	No problem.

Parameter	Type/Description
hMenu	Long—The menu handle to test.

Return Value	Long—TRUE (nonzero) if the handle is a menu handle, zero if not.
Platform	Windows 95, Windows NT, Win16

■ LoadMenu

VB Declaration	`Declare Function LoadMenu& Lib "user32" Alias "LoadMenuA" (ByVal hInstance As _` `Long, ByVal lpString As String)`
Description	Loads a menu from the specified module or application instance.
Use with VB	Because of the inability of VB to handle menus that are not compatible with existing VB menus, use of this function is not recommended.

Parameter	Type/Description
hInstance	Long—Module handle for a dynamic link library, or instance handle that specifies the executable file that contains the menu resource.
lpString	String—As a String, specifies the name of the menu resource to load. As a Long, specifies the menu ID to load. You will need to create a type declaration that accepts a Long parameter for lpString to use the menu ID form of this function.

Return Value   Long—A handle to the loaded menu; zero on error. Sets GetLastError.

Platform   Windows 95, Windows NT, Win16

Comments   If the menu is not assigned to a window, it will be necessary to use the DestroyMenu function to destroy the menu before the application closes.

■ LoadMenuIndirect

VB Declaration   ```Declare Function LoadMenuIndirect& Lib "user32" Alias "LoadMenuIndirectA" _
(ByVal lpMenuTemplate As Long)```

Description   Loads a menu based on a memory block containing MENUITEMTEMPLATE data structures.

Use with VB   Refer to the description of the LoadMenu function.

Parameter	Type/Description
lpMenuTemplate	Long—A pointer to a MENUITEMTEMPLATEHEADER structure that is followed in memory by one or more MENUITEMTEMPLATE data structures. Refer to Appendix B for a description of these data structures. Under Windows 95 & NT 4.0, may be a pointer to a MENU-EX_HEADER_TEMPLATE structure that is followed by one or more MENUEX_HEADER_ITEM structures to specify extended menus.

Return Value   Long—A handle to the loaded menu; zero on error. Sets GetLastError.

Platform   Windows 95, Windows NT, Win16

Comments   If the menu is not assigned to a window, it will be necessary to use the DestroyMenu function to destroy the menu before the application closes.

Porting Notes   The string in the MENUITEMTEMPLATE and MENUEX_HEADER_ITEM structures are always Unicode strings under Win32 (even under Windows 95). Under Win16, they are ANSI.

■ MenuItemFromPoint

VB Declaration   ```Declare Function MenuItemFromPoint& Lib "user32" (ByVal hWnd As Long, ByVal _
hMenu As Long, ByVal ptx As Long, ByVal pty As Long)```

Description   Allows you to determine which menu entry contains a specified point on the screen.

Use with VB   No problem.

Parameter	Type/Description
hWnd	Long—A handle to the window that contains the specified menu.
hMenu	Long—Handle to a menu.
ptx, pty	Long—The X,Y position to test. If hMenu is a top level menu bar, this point is in window coordinates of window hWnd. Otherwise it is in client coordinates of the window.

Return Value   Long—The position of the entry containing the specified point. –1 if no entry contains the point.

Platform   Windows 95, Windows NT 4.0

■ ModifyMenu, ModifyMenuBynum

VB Declaration
```
Declare Function ModifyMenu& Lib "user32" Alias "ModifyMenuA" (ByVal hMenu As _
Long, ByVal nPosition As Long, ByVal wFlags As Long, ByVal wIDNewItem As Long, _
ByVal lpString As String)
Declare Function ModifyMenuBynum& Lib "user32" Alias "ModifyMenuA" (ByVal hMenu _
As Long, ByVal nPosition As Long, ByVal wFlags As Long, ByVal wIDNewItem As _
Long, ByVal lpString As Long)
```

Description   This function can be used to change a menu entry.

Use with VB   Refer to "How Visual Basic Menus Work," earlier in this chapter. Many of the changes made by this function will work, but will not be reflected by the VB menu object.

Parameter	Type/Description
hMenu	Long—Handle to a menu.
nPosition	Long—Identifier to the menu entry to change. If the MF_BYCOMMAND flag is set in the wFlags parameter, this parameter refers to the command ID of the menu entry to change. If the MF_BYPOSITION flag is set, this parameter refers to the position of the entry in the menu (the first entry is zero).
wFlags	Long—A combination of flags defined by constants in the file API32.TXT. Refer to Table 10.6 for a list of the constants permitted.
wIDNewItem	Long—The new command ID for the specified menu entry. If the MF_POPUP flag is specified in parameter wFlags, this should be a handle to a pop-up menu.
lpString	String—If flag MF_STRING is set in parameter wFlags, this is the string to set into the menu. If flag MF_BITMAP is set, this is a long variable that contains a bitmap handle. If MF_OWNERDRAW is set, this value is included in the DRAWITEMSTRUCT and MEASUREITEMSTRUCT structures sent by Windows when the entry needs to be drawn.

Return Value   Long—Nonzero on success, zero on failure. Sets GetLastError.

Table 10.6   Constant Menu Flag Definitions

Constant	Description
MF_BITMAP	Menu entry is a bitmap. This bitmap must not be deleted once set into the menu, so the value returned by the VB Image property should not be used.

Table 10.6   **Constant Menu Flag Definitions (Continued)**

Constant	Description
MF_BYCOMMAND	The menu entry is specified by the command ID of the menu.
MF_BYPOSITION	The menu entry is specified by the position of the entry in the menu. Zero specifies the first entry in the menu.
MF_CHECKED	Checks the specified menu entry. Not compatible with the VB Checked property.
MF_DISABLED	Disables the specified menu entry. Not compatible with the VB Enabled property.
MF_ENABLED	Enables the specified menu entry. Not compatible with the VB Enabled property.
MF_GRAYED	Disables the specified menu entry and draws it in light gray. Not compatible with the VB Enabled property.
MF_MENUBARBREAK	On pop-up menus, places the specified entry on a new column with a vertical bar separating the columns.
MF_MENUBREAK	On pop-up menus, places the specified entry on a new column. On top level menus, places the entry on a new line.
MF_OWNERDRAW	Creates an owner draw menu (one in which your program is responsible for drawing each menu entry). Requires use of a subclassing control.
MF_POP-UP	Places a pop-up menu at the specified entry. This may be used to create submenus and pop-up menus.
MF_SEPARATOR	Places a separator line at the specified entry.
MF_STRING	Places a string at the specified entry. Not compatible with the VB Caption property.
MF_UNCHECKED	Checks the specified menu entry. Not compatible with the VB Checked property.

Platform   Windows 95, Windows NT, Win16

Comments   The following combinations of flags are not allowed: MF_BYCOMMAND and MF_BYPOSITION; MF_CHECKED and MF_UNCHECKED; MF_MENUBARBREAK and MF_MENUBREAK; MF_DISABLED, MF_ENABLED, and MF_GRAYED; MF_BITMAP, MF_STRING, MF_OWNERDRAW, and MF_SEPARATOR.

Example   MenuLook.vbp

■ RemoveMenu

VB Declaration `Declare Function RemoveMenu& Lib "user32" (ByVal hMenu As Long, ByVal nPosition _`
`As Long, ByVal wFlags As Long)`

Description Removes the specified menu entry. If the removed entry is a pop-up menu, this function does not destroy the pop-up menu. You should first use the GetSubMenu function to obtain the handle of the pop-up menu, and destroy it later.

Use with VB Refer to "How Visual Basic Menus Work," earlier in this chapter. It is strongly recommended that you use the VB menu Visible property to delete entries from a menu instead of this function. Use of this function will cause the Visible property for other menu entries in the specified menu to affect the wrong menu entry.

Parameter	Type/Description
hMenu	Long—Handle to the menu.
nPosition	Long—Identifier to the menu entry to change. If the MF_BY-COMMAND flag is set in the wFlags parameter, this parameter refers to the command ID of the menu entry to change. If the MF_BY-POSITION flag is set, this parameter refers to the position of the entry in the menu (the first entry is zero).
wFlags	Long—The constant MF_BYCOMMAND or MF_BYPOSITION. See nPosition above.

Return Value Long—Nonzero on success, zero on failure. Sets GetLastError.

Platform Windows 95, Windows NT, Win16

■ SetMenu

VB Declaration `Declare Function SetMenu& Lib "user32" (ByVal hwnd As Long, ByVal hMenu As Long)`

Description Sets the menu for a window.

Use with VB Refer to "How Visual Basic Menus Work," earlier in this chapter. This function is not recommended for use with VB. If used, care must be taken that the command IDs in the new menu are compatible with the original VB window. Only form windows should be specified with this function.

Parameter	Type/Description
hwnd	Long—A handle to a window.
hMenu	Long—A handle to the new menu for the window. If zero, any existing menu for the window is removed.

Return Value Long—Nonzero on success, zero on failure. Sets GetLastError.

Platform Windows 95, Windows NT, Win16

Comments The previous menu for the window is not destroyed by this function.

■ SetMenuContextHelpId

VB Declaration   `Declare Function SetMenuContextHelpId& Lib "user32" (ByVal hMenu As Long, ByVal _`
`dw As Long)`

Description   Sets the help context ID assigned to a menu using the SetMenuContextHelpId function.

Use with VB   No problem. The context ID value set using this function does not correspond to the help context ID assigned using the Visual Basic menu bar designer. Visual Basic stores its own help context ID values internally. The Visual Basic help context ID is preferred over use of this function due to its support for Windows NT 3.51.

Parameter	Type/Description
hMenu	Long—Handle to a menu.
dw	Long—Help context ID to set.

Return Value   Long—TRUE (nonzero) on success, zero otherwise.

Platform   Windows 95, Windows NT 4.0

■ SetMenuDefaultItem

VB Declaration   `Declare Function SetMenuDefaultItem& Lib "user32" (ByVal hMenu As Long, ByVal _`
`uItem As Long, ByVal fByPos As Long)`

Description   Allows you to specify that a menu entry be the default entry. This entry corresponds by convention to the operation that is performed when the menu is double clicked.

Use with VB   No problem.

Parameter	Type/Description
hMenu	Long—A handle to a menu.
uItem	Long—The position or menu ID of the entry to set as a default menu entry. –1 to clear the current default entry.
fByPos	Long—TRUE if uItem is the position of the entry, FALSE if it is a menu ID.

Return Value   Long—TRUE (nonzero) on success, zero otherwise. Sets GetLastError.

Platform   Windows 95, Windows NT 4.0

■ SetMenuItemBitmaps

VB Declaration   `Declare Function SetMenuItemBitmaps& Lib "user32" (ByVal hMenu As Long, ByVal _`
`nPosition As Long, ByVal wFlags As Long, ByVal hBitmapUnchecked As Long, ByVal _`
`hBitmapChecked As Long)`

Description Sets the bitmaps to use for the specified menu entry in place of the standard checkmark. The bitmaps must be the correct size for menu checkmarks as obtained by the GetMenuCheckMarkDimensions function.

Use with VB No problem.

Parameter	Type/Description
hMenu	Long—Handle to a menu.
nPosition	Long—Identifier of the menu entry for which to set the bitmaps. If the MF_BYCOMMAND flag is set in the wFlags parameter, this parameter refers to the command ID of the menu entry to change. If the MF_BYPOSITION flag is set, this parameter refers to the position of the entry in the menu (the first entry is zero).
wFlags	Long—MF_BYCOMMAND or MF_BYPOSITION as specified for the nPosition parameter.
hBit-mapUnchecked	Long—Handle of a bitmap to use for the menu entry when unchecked. May be zero to specify no uncheck symbol.
hBit-mapChecked	Long—Handle of a bitmap to use for the menu entry when checked. May be zero to specify no symbol when checked. If both bitmap handle values are zero, the default check bitmap is restored for this entry.

Return Value Long—Nonzero on success, zero on failure. Sets GetLastError.

Platform Windows 95, Windows NT, Win16

Comments The bitmap used may be shared by multiple entries. The bitmap must be destroyed by the application when it is no longer needed, as it is not destroyed automatically by Windows.

Example MenuLook.vbp

■ SetMenuItemInfo

VB Declaration
```
Declare Function SetMenuItemInfo& Lib "user32" Alias "SetMenuItemInfoA" (ByVal _
hMenu As Long, ByVal un As Long, ByVal bypos As Long, lpcMenuItemInfo As _
MENUITEMINFO)
```

Description Sets the specified information for a menu entry using a MENUITEMINFO structure.

Use with VB No problem.

Parameter	Type/Description
hMenu	Long—Handle of a menu.
un	Long—The menu ID or position of a menu entry.
bypos	Long—TRUE if un specifies the position of the entry, FALSE if it is a menu ID.
lpMenuItemInfo	MENUITEMINFO—A MENUITEMINFO structure to use to set the characteristics of the specified menu entry. Refer to Appendix B for further information on this structure.

Return Value   Long—TRUE (nonzero) on success, zero otherwise. Sets GetLastError.

Platform   Windows 95, Windows NT 4.0

■ TrackPopupMenu, TrackPopupMenuBynum

VB Declaration
```
Declare Function TrackPop-upMenu& Lib "user32" (ByVal hMenu As Long, ByVal _
wFlags As Long, ByVal x As Long, ByVal y As Long, ByVal nReserved As Long, _
ByVal hwnd As Long, lprc As Rect)
Declare Function TrackPop-upMenuBynum& Lib "user32" Alias "TrackPop-upMenu" _
(ByVal hMenu As Long, ByVal wFlags As Long, ByVal x As Long, ByVal y As Long, _
ByVal nReserved As Long, ByVal hwnd As Long, ByVal lprc As Long)
```

Description   Displays a pop-up menu anywhere on the screen.

Use with VB   Refer to "How Visual Basic Menus Work," earlier in this chapter. You may use a VB pop-up menu or create one yourself. If you create one, be careful that the command IDs in the menu match those expected by Visual Basic.

Parameter	Type/Description
hMenu	Long—A handle to a pop-up menu.
wFlags	Long—A combination of position flags and mouse tracking flags as shown in Table 10.7.
x,y	Long—A point specifying the location of the pop-up menu in screen coordinates.
nReserved	Long—Not used; set to zero.
hwnd	Long—A handle of the window to receive the pop-up menu commands. You should use the window handle of the form that has a menu that accepts the same set of command IDs as the pop-up menu.
lprc	Rect—A pointer to a RECT structure that specifies a rectangle in screen coordinates. If the user clicks within this rectangle, the pop-up menu will not be closed. Clicking anywhere else outside of the pop-up menu will close the menu. May be NULL.

Return Value   Long—Nonzero on success, zero on failure. Sets GetLastError.

Table 10.7   **Position and Mouse Tracking Flags**

Position Flags	Description
TPM_CENTERALIGN	The menu is horizontally centered at the specified position.
TPM_LEFTALIGN	The left side of the menu is placed at the horizontal x coordinate.
TPM_RIGHTALIGN	The right side of the menu is placed at the horizontal x coordinate.

Table 10.7 **Position and Mouse Tracking Flags (Continued)**

Mouse Tracking Flags	Description
TPM_LEFTBUTTON	Normal operation with the left mouse button.
TPM_RIGHTBUTTON	The menu tracks using the right mouse button.

Platform   Windows 95, Windows NT, Win16

Example   MenuLook.vbp, SysMenu.vbp

■ TrackPopupMenuEx

VB Declaration
```
Declare Function TrackPop-upMenuEx& Lib "user32" (ByVal hMenu As Long, ByVal un _
As Long, ByVal n1 As Long, ByVal n2 As Long, ByVal hWnd As Long, lpTPMParams As _
TPMPARAMS)
```

Description   Similar to TrackPopupMenu except that it provides additional functionality.

Use with VB   No problem.

Parameter	Type/Description
hMenu	Long—A handle to a pop-up menu.
un	Long—A combination of position flags and mouse tracking flags as shown in Table 10.7 as well as the following two flags: TPM_HORIZONTAL or TPM_VERTICAL. See the lpTPMParams parameter for a description of these parameters.
n1, n2	Long—An x,y point (n1,n2) specifying the location of the pop-up menu in screen coordinates.
hWnd	Long—A handle of the window to receive the pop-up menu commands. You should use the window handle of the form that has a menu that accepts the same set of command IDs as the pop-up menu.
lpTPMParams	TPMPARAMS—A pointer to a TPMPARAMS structure. This structure contains a rectangle that specifies in screen coordinates a rectangle that should not be covered by this pop-up menu. If the TPM_HORIZONTAL flag is specified in the un parameter, Windows will try to set the horizontal position, moving the pop-up vertically to position it outside of this rectangle. If TPM_VERTICAL is specified, Windows will try to shift the pop-up position horizontally.

Return Value   Long—Nonzero on success, zero on failure. Sets GetLastError.

Platform   Windows 95, Windows NT 4.0

Example   Similar to the TrackPopupMenu examples in MenuLook.vbp and SysMenu.vbp

11

Text and Fonts

F
ONT AND TEXT MANIPULATION IS ONE OF THE MOST COMPLEX PARTS OF the Windows system. Fortunately, you do not need to be an expert to use this technology effectively in Visual Basic.

This chapter will focus on two areas. First, the chapter includes a brief overview of fonts in general, and Windows font technology in particular. A sample program, FontView, shows how to select and use a font, and how to obtain information about a font. Second, the chapter describes the use of the powerful Windows API text output functions. A sample program, TextDemo, illustrates the use of some of these functions. Other examples include the EnmFntX and DrawText projects that demonstrate font enumeration and additional drawing functions, respectively.

If you are planning to write a complete WYSIWYG ("What you see is what you get") word processor in Visual Basic (which *is* possible), or another application that requires an in-depth understanding of the internal functioning of scalable fonts, you are advised to seek out additional sources. It is possible to find entire books that deal with the problems of handling fonts, text output, typesetting, and performing WYSIWYG text editing.

Under Visual Basic, the text API drawing functions provide a good intermediate step between the minimal print functionality provided in the language and the capability of a rich text control.

For those who are porting applications from 16 bits to 32 bits, or writing code to run on both 16- and 32-bit platforms, the news regarding text is good. Changes to the font and text drawing capabilities for Win32 are evolutionary and have maintained a very high degree of compatibility.

A Note on the Chapter Structure

Throughout this book, the chapters are structured to present background information on the subject first, followed by example code, and then a reference section. Detailed information on function parameters and data structures has been left to the function reference and Appendix B (which contains a reference for the data structures used by the Windows API).

Fonts have numerous attributes, many of which are too complex to explain in a few words or even sentences. These attributes are used in many cases as function parameters or as fields in data structures. In order to bring all of the information on these attributes to one place, and eliminate the necessity of attempting to define them for each function, all of the parameters and data structure fields are defined later in this chapter in the section titled "Font Parameters." The function reference and data structure reference will refer to this section rather than attempt to describe each parameter.

Using Fonts

This section describes the attributes and characteristics of fonts. It also lists the fields to the Windows API font data structures, such as LOGFONT and TEXTMETRIC, and parameters to the font API functions, such as CreateFont.

Introduction to Fonts

A font describes the way a text string will appear on a device. Figure 11.1 shows how the choice of font can affect the appearance of the uppercase letter A.

Figure 11.1

The letter A in different fonts

As you can see, the fonts can vary a great deal. Some are simple line characters. Some are highly decorative. They vary in size and in weight. For example, a bold font is considered to have a heavier weight than a normal or light font.

You might be wondering what the hand symbol is doing in the middle of the array of As. One of the attributes of a font is the character set used. Character sets, which define the symbols used for each ASCII value, are described in Chapter 6. The letter A has the ASCII value of 65. The symbol just happens to be assigned to ASCII value 65 for the character set in that particular font.

A number of fonts will be installed on any given Windows system. Windows automatically installs a dozen or so standard fonts, but there are literally thousands of fonts available that may be installed on a system. In the world of traditional typography, a font is called a typeface. Fonts are typically known by their typeface name and attributes; for example, *Courier Bold 12 point* is a commonly used fixed-pitch font. The types and attributes of fonts will be covered through the course of this chapter.

Consider the case of a standard word processor document that uses several fonts. What happens when the document is transferred to another system that does not have the same fonts installed? If the document required that the exact font be present, it would be virtually impossible to transfer documents from one system to another.

One solution would be to include the font information in the document. Unfortunately, not only does this approach increase the size of each document, but in many cases it violates the copyright restrictions on the font. Windows does support this approach by supporting embedded fonts; however, for most cases Windows provides a much more flexible and powerful solution.

Windows avoids the problem that results when a font makes a document device-specific in much the same way as it provides other device-independent drawing capabilities. Instead of specifying an actual physical font, the programmer specifies an entity known as a *logical font*. A logical font can be thought of as the font that is ideal for a particular task. For example, the original manuscript for this book used a Courier font that is readable and makes it easy to calculate word counts. All of the fonts requested by a document are logical fonts rather than specific physical fonts.

Windows takes the requested logical font information and maps it into a physical font by finding the physical font that most closely matches the requested logical font. This mapping process is described later in this chapter.

It is important to recognize that each change in characteristic defines a different font. For example, say you have a normal Helvetica font such as that provided with Windows. The italicized version of that font is in fact a different font, even though only one attribute (italics) has changed. The same applies to other characteristics such as normal versus bold, normal versus underlined, and so on. And, with nonscalable fonts, each character size demands a different font.

In many cases, Windows can synthesize one font out of another. For example, Windows can usually do a good job of creating an underlined font out of a normal font, so you rarely need to purchase separate underlined fonts. In other cases, there is a significant drop in quality. For example, when Windows scales a raster font from a small size to a very large one, the result can be truly ugly because slight imperfections in a letter's form become pronounced as the letter increases in size.

Understanding Font Attributes

Before considering the font function parameters and data structure fields, it is important to understand some of the basic characteristics and dimensions of fonts, and to define some of the terms that are used in describing these attributes.

Font Technology

Windows uses a number of different font technologies, each with different advantages and disadvantages:

- *Raster fonts*. A raster font is defined as a series of character bitmaps. Whenever a character needs to be displayed, the bitmap for that character is copied to the device. A raster font is usually defined for a particular device and resolution. The primary advantage of raster fonts is that the font can be optimized to look good on the device for which it was designed. The disadvantage is that the font is not easily scalable—you need a separate set of character bitmaps for each font size you wish to use. Although Windows can scale raster fonts to create a synthesized font in a different size, the results are often of very poor quality.

- *Vector (or stroke) fonts*. These fonts are made up of graphic elements represented by GDI function calls. Because the vectors can be described mathematically (by numbers), they can be scaled through a fairly wide range while maintaining a reasonable quality. They have been superseded by TrueType fonts and are thus rarely used.

- *Scalable fonts*. With scalable fonts, the lines describing the character are defined mathematically using vectors and curves. There are several add-on packages to Windows that provide scalable font technology, but this chapter will deal exclusively with the TrueType scaling technology that is built into Windows 95 and Windows NT. The primary advantage of scalable fonts is their flexibility—these fonts may be scaled to virtually any size with little loss of quality. There are two disadvantages. First, at small sizes scalable fonts rarely look as good as a well-designed raster font. Second, scalable fonts are more complex and somewhat slower to draw than corresponding raster fonts.

Windows also differentiates between Windows fonts and device fonts. A *Windows font* is part of the Windows environment and may be used on the display and in most cases on the device. A *device font* is optimized for a particular device and may not be displayed on the screen. When drawing on the screen using a logical font that specifies a device font, Windows will display the closest available match to the requested font from those that it can display.

Font Pitch

Both raster and scalable fonts may be of either fixed pitch or variable pitch. In a *fixed pitch* font, the width of each character cell is equal—this means that the distance between any two characters is the same. In a *variable pitch* font, the spacing varies depending on the character. A narrow character such as the letter I will take up less space than a wide character such as W. Variable pitch fonts are also known as proportionally spaced fonts.

Font Dimensions

A character has a certain width and height. Sounds simple, doesn't it? If only it were so. The simple character cell actually has a great many attributes and characteristics. Table 11.1 and Figure 11.2 illustrate the parts of a character cell and define the terms used to describe them.

Table 11.2 and Figure 11.3 define the dimensions used for character cells and those used to determine character spacing both vertically and horizontally.

Table 11.1   Parts of a Character Cell

Font Attribute	Description
Baseline	An imaginary line within a character cell that indicates the base of a character. See Descender.
BlackRect	The smallest rectangle that fully encloses the character symbol (also known as the glyph).
Cell	A rectangular cell that contains the glyph.
Cell Origin	The upper-left corner of the character cell.
Descender	The part of the character that drops beneath the baseline.
Glyph	The actual character symbol.

Figure 11.2
Parts of a character cell

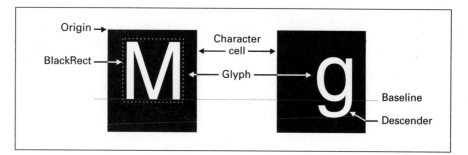

Table 11.2   Character Cell Dimensions

Font Attribute	Description
A-B-C	Character spacing for TrueType fonts. Refer to Figure 11.4.
Ascent	The height that a character rises above the baseline. The ascent for a font is usually defined by the letter M.
Average character width	The average width of the character (glyph) within the character cell.
Character width	The actual width of a character. This can vary with variable width fonts. For TrueType fonts, use the A-B-C dimensions.
Descent	The distance that a character descender drops below the baseline.

Table 11.2 **Character Cell Dimensions**

Font Attribute	Description
External leading	The recommended vertical spacing between character cells. (It's called leading because in the old days a typesetter adjusted the space between the lines by inserting slugs of lead.)
Height	The height of a character cell.
Internal leading	The distance from the top of the character to the top of the character cell. This area may be used by the character.
Maximum character width	The width of the widest character in the font. With fixed pitch fonts, all characters have the same width.
Width	The width of a character cell.

Figure 11.3

Character cell dimensions

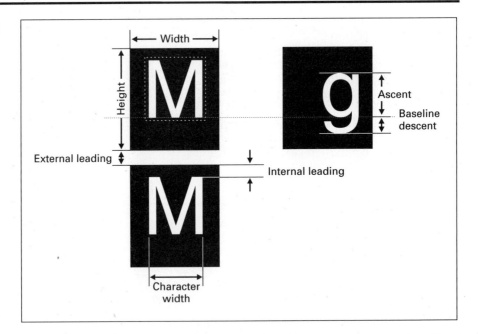

Spacing for variable pitch fonts varies for each character in the font. It is possible for part of one character to overhang or underhang another character. In order to provide this capability, Windows defines three width parameters for TrueType fonts. These are referred to as the A-B-C dimensions for the font. The B dimension defines the width of the glyph. The A dimension represents the distance from the left edge of the character cell to the left of the glyph. This may be a negative number, in which case the glyph will partially overlap the previous character. The C dimension describes the distance from the right edge of the character cell to the right of the glyph. This number may also be negative. Figure 11.4 illustrates the use of the A-B-C dimensions.

Figure 11.4

A-B-C dimensions

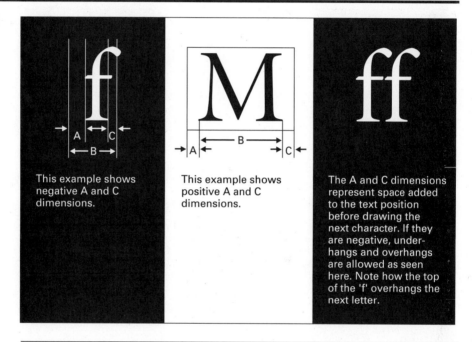

This example shows negative A and C dimensions.

This example shows positive A and C dimensions.

The A and C dimensions represent space added to the text position before drawing the next character. If they are negative, under-hangs and overhangs are allowed as seen here. Note how the top of the 'f' overhangs the next letter.

Windows provides a number of API functions to determine character spacing, as shown in Table 11.3. The space taken up by one or more characters is called the *extent* of the text. When two characters are printed near each other, the distance between them depends not only on the size of the character itself, but also on the two characters involved. A font may dictate that two characters be placed closer to each other than normal in order to provide a more pleasing look. The process of adjusting character position is known as *kerning*. A font may contain a kerning table that defines the kerning values for pairs of characters.

For this reason, it is not possible to determine the space required by a string of text by simply adding up the character spacing. You must call one of the extent calculation functions and specify the entire string for which extents are needed.

Table 11.3 **Font Extent Functions**

Function	Description
GetCharABCWidths	Retrieves the A-B-C dimensions for one or more characters in a TrueType font.
GetCharABCWidthsFloat	Retrieves the A-B-C dimensions into floating point variables. This can provide more accurate results depending on the mapping mode in effect.
GetCharacterPlacement	Retrieves detailed information about characters within a font. Win95 and NT 4.0.
GetCharWidth	Retrieves the widths of one or more characters in a font.
GetCharWidth32	An improved version of GetCharWidth that is preferred for use under the Win32 API.
GetCharWidthFloat	Retrieves the width of one or more characters in a font into a floating point variable. Provides more accurate results under certain mapping modes and when used with non-TrueType fonts.
GetKerningPairs	Retrieves kerning information for a font.
GetTabbedTextExtent	Retrieves the width and height of a text string as it will appear on a device. This function takes tabs into account.
GetTextCharacterExtra	Retrieves the amount of extra intercharacter spacing used by Windows when drawing text. This is usually zero.
GetTextExtentExPoint GetTextExtentPoint GetTextExtentPoint32	Retrieves the width and height of a text string as it will appear on a device. GetTextExtentPoint32 is preferred to GetTextExtentPoint. The Win16 GetTextExtent function is not supported.
SetTextCharacterExtra	Sets the amount of extra intercharacter spacing used by Windows when drawing text.

Font Families

A family describes a general class of fonts. Figure 11.5 shows the font families that are used by Windows. Every font should fall into one of these categories.

The decorative family is used for special applications. For example, an elegant "antique styled" invitation could be created using a decorative gothic font. This is the catch-all family that describes any font that does not fall into one of the other categories.

Modern fonts are the simplest family of fonts. They use constant width lines and may or may not have *serifs*, the small decorative lines or hooks that appear at the ends of the lines. For example, the bottom of the two vertical

Figure 11.5

Windows font families

 Decorative: Any decorative font used for special applications.

 Modern: Fixed pitch font where the stroke width of the font is constant.

 Roman: Proportionally spaced font with serifs. The stroke width may vary.

 Script: Proportionally spaced font that looks like handwriting. The stroke width may vary.

 Swiss: Proportionally spaced font without serifs. The stroke width may vary.

strokes on the M character have tiny horizontal serifs. Typewriter style fonts such as Courier and other fixed pitch fonts fall into this category.

Roman fonts are probably the most commonly used fonts for general text applications. The line or stroke width may vary, as can be seen in the legs of the letter M for this family. These fonts also have serifs.

Script fonts are fonts that are designed to look like handwriting. These fonts are often used to provide a handwritten or personalized look.

Swiss fonts are similar to Roman fonts except that they do not have the serifs (thus these are often referred to as *sans serif* fonts). These fonts are frequently used for headlines or captions in a document, or to provide a modern look.

In Windows, the term *family* is used to describe classifications of fonts and the term *typeface* or *facename* is used to identify a set of fonts that shares a common character set and design but varies in attributes such as size, weight, slant, and so on. The term *family* in the world outside of Windows typically refers to the typeface of the font. For example, in Windows, a Helvetica bold 10 point font and Helvetica normal 12 point font have the same typeface (Helvetica) and are part of the Swiss family. A commercial font package or printer may refer to these fonts as belonging to the Helvetica font family.

Character Set

Figure 11.1 showed the effect that character set has on a font and introduced the idea that fonts may have different character sets. (Refer to Chapter 6 for an in-depth explanation of character sets.) Windows defines three standard character sets for fonts:

- ANSI_CHARSET is the standard Windows character set.

- SYMBOL_CHARSET is a symbol character set in which each ASCII value represents an arbitrary symbol. Note that each symbol font will probably have different sets of symbols.

- OEM_CHARSET is the OEM character set. This set is system-dependent.

When Windows chooses a physical font based on a requested logical font, it gives highest priority to obtaining the requested character set.

Weight, Italics, and Underlines

Table 11.4 describes additional font attributes that are commonly used.

Table 11.4   **Other Font Attributes**

Attribute	Description
Aspect Ratio	Each raster font is designed for a specific display aspect ratio. Displaying the font on a device with a different aspect ratio will cause it to appear taller or shorter than it should be.
Escapement	The rotation of the font.
FaceName	Also knows as the "Typeface" of the font, the name of the font. Each font has a name which is usually copyrighted. For example, the most common Swiss family sans serif font is referred to as HELV, Ariel, Universe, Helvetica, Swiss, and other names, depending on who created the font.
Italic	The font is italicized (slanted).
Quality	Some fonts are defined as draft or proof (letter) quality. This is especially common for dot-matrix printer fonts.
StrikeOut	The font has a horizontal line through each character.
Underlined	The font is underlined.
Weight	Specifies how dark the font looks. A light font will appear light with thin character strokes. A heavy font will appear darker. The terms Normal and Bold are generally used to describe two commonly defined standard weights for a font. The Windows font functions define weight as a number from 100 to 900, where 400 is normal and 700 is bold.

TrueType fonts may define additional styles (OUTLINE, for example).

Diacritics, Ligation, and Kashida

As you have seen, a font is really a tool that takes a character as input, and allows you to determine how that character should be displayed in a given device context. In most cases, each character will map into a single glyph in the font (a glyph, you will recall, is the graphic image of the character within a character cell). However, for some fonts and languages there are exceptions. For example, it is possible for multiple characters to map into a single glyph. The glyph "Ã" may be represented by two characters, the first one being a diacritic—a dead character that indicates that the A is being modified. Or, consider the glyph "Æ"—a combination of two characters called a ligature. The text extent API functions take these situations into account when calculating extents and when drawing text, so in most cases you will not need to worry about them. These situations do emphasize the importance of using the API functions to calculate extents instead of trying to do so yourself. The location and distance between characters depends not only on the width of the original characters, but also on the values of neighboring characters and neighboring glyphs.

Windows 95 provides improved support for the Semitic languages: Hebrew and Arabic. Fonts for these languages add some additional excitement to the process of text output. For one thing, text is arranged from right to left (right to left reading). Even more confusing, in Arabic fonts the glyph used by a character can depend on the location of the character within a word (a font attribute called Kashida allows you to deal with this type of situation). In-depth information about the handling of these types of font information is beyond the scope of this book, but is included in the software development kits for versions of Windows that are found locally where these languages are used.

Creating Logical Fonts

Before drawing text under Windows, it is necessary to request a font to use by specifying a logical font. A logical font is a Windows GDI object that defines the attributes for the desired font. Table 11.5 shows the functions used to create a logical font.

The API DeleteObject function can be used to delete a logical font.

GDI Font Mapping

When an application requests a particular font from Windows, it provides a logical font that Windows uses to select a physical font. If the exact physical

Table 11.5   Font Creation Functions

Function	Description
CreateFont	Creates a logical font according to a specified set of attribute values.
CreateFontIndirect	Creates a logical font based on attribute values specified in a LOG-FONT data structure.

font requested does not exist, the Windows Graphics Device Interface (GDI) will choose or synthesize a font to use in its place. This process of mapping a logical to a physical font involves looking at attributes according to a set priority. Each attribute is assigned a penalty value. GDI examines each available physical font and scores each attribute according to how closely it matches the requested value. The physical font with the lowest penalty value is actually selected.

The order of priorities for attributes is listed in Table 11.6. In most cases, it is possible to specify a "don't care" value for an attribute, in which case GDI does not consider that particular attribute.

Table 11.6   Attribute Priorities

Attribute	Comments
Character set	The most important attribute for font mapping.
Pitch	Variable pitch fonts are highly penalized if a fixed pitch font is requested as the application may not be able to handle variable width fonts.
Family	The family of the font (see Figure 11.5)
FaceName	The name of the typeface of the font.
Height	GDI will never choose a font with a greater height than requested.
Width	GDI will never choose a font that is wider than requested.
Weight	GDI will always prefer an actual bold font to a synthesized bold font.
Slant	GDI will always prefer an actual italic font over a synthesized italic font.
Underline	GDI will always prefer an actual underline font over a synthesized underline font.
StrikeOut	GDI will always prefer an actual strikeout font over a synthesized strikeout font.

Scalable fonts can be scaled to match the requested font size.

Windows provides several API functions that allow you to influence the mapping process. These are shown in Table 11.7.

Table 11.7   **GDI Mapping Control Functions**

Function	Description
SetMapperFlags	Allows you to specify whether or not font mapping should take the device aspect ratio into account. Not used for TrueType fonts.
GetAspectRatioFilterEx	Determines the aspect ratio to be used when mapping fonts.
GetRasterizerCaps	Determines if TrueType fonts are installed in the system.

Windows performs mapping to obtain a physical font when the logical font is selected into a device context using the SelectObject API function. As with all GDI drawing objects, be sure to select the font out of the device context and select the original font back into the DC before deleting the font or the device context.

Font Information Functions

Table 11.8 lists the API functions that may be used to retrieve information about a font.

Table 11.8   **Font Information Functions**

Function	Description
EnumFontFamilies EnumFontFamiliesEx EnumFonts	Enumerates available fonts based on one or more criteria depending on the function from a specified family. Requires use of the dwcbk32d.ocx custom control.
GetFontData	Extracts font data that can be embedded in an application.
GetFontLanguageInfo	Allows you to determine if the font contains support for diacritics, ligature, kerning, and other advanced capabilities.
GetGlyphOutline	Retrieves information about the glyph of a TrueType font.
GetOutlineTextMetrics	Retrieves information about a TrueType font.

Table 11.8   **Font Information Functions (Continued)**

Function	Description
GetTextCharset GetTextCharsetInfo	Retrieves the character set of the specified font.
GetTextFace	Retrieves the face (font name) of the font selected into a device context.
GetTextMetrics	Retrieves information about the font selected into a device context.

Adding and Removing Fonts

In order to use a font, the font must be installed in the Windows system. This is generally accomplished using the control panel application provided with Windows.

It is possible to add or remove fonts from the Windows system using the functions listed in Table 11.9. Fonts can be contained in any executable file including dynamic link libraries. They may also be kept in a special font resource file identified with the extension .FON, .FOT, or .FOR (for FONt, FOntTruetype, and FOntReadonly, respectively). TrueType font files cannot directly be loaded by Windows, so an interface resource file must be created using the CreateScalableFontResources API function.

Table 11.9   **Font Resource Functions**

Function	Description
AddFontResource	Adds a font resource to Windows. It may then be used by any application.
CreateScalableFontResource	Creates a font resource file for a TrueType font.
RemoveFontResource	Removes a font resource from Windows.

After you add or remove a font from Windows, it is important that you notify other applications about the change. This is accomplished by sending the WM_FONTCHANGE to all of the top level Windows in the system as shown in the comments section for the AddFontResource function in the reference section for this chapter.

Font Parameters Used in Functions and Data Structures

The font attributes described to this point are used by the programmer in two ways. Information functions return structures that contain fields that indicate the state of a font attribute. The CreateFont function and LOGFONT data structure contain fields that specify the attributes for a logical font. This section lists the common parameters and structure data fields that correspond to these attributes.

The LOGFONT Structure Fields and CreateFont Function Parameters

The following fields are used in the LOGFONT and ENUMLOGFONT data structures and the CreateFont API function. They are used to specify the attributes of a logical font. GDI uses the information in this structure to choose a physical font. (Note: The ENUMLOGFONT structure in Win32 was called a NEWLOGFONT structure in Win16.)

All units are in the logical units of the device context for the logical font. All parameters are longs unless otherwise specified (for the CreateFont structure) or as defined in the LOGFONT data structure.

- lfCharSet. Specifies the character set (see Chapter 6). The following constants define the most common character sets:

    - ANSI_CHARSET: The Windows character set.

    - DEFAULT_CHARSET: Use any character set.

    - SYMBOL_CHARSET: Symbol character set.

    - OEM_CHARSET: System-dependent character set.

    The API32.TXT file lists additional constants in the form ???_CHARSET.

- lfClipPrecision. Defines the precision for clipping the font when a character is partly outside of the clipping region. Defined by the CLIP_???_PRECIS constants in file API32.TXT. Default is specified by the constant CLIP_DEFAULT_PRECIS.

- lfEscapement. Defines the angle for drawing text by specifying the angle between the font baseline and the X axis in one-tenth degree increments. If Y increases in the downward direction, this angle is measured from the baseline up. Otherwise it is measured from the baseline down. Escapement describes the angle at which a string is drawn. Under Windows NT, if the graphics mode is set to GM_ADVANCED, it is possible to set the orientation of each character separately from the orientation of the entire string. For example, the string could be set to draw at a 45 degree angle upward, but each character in the string could be rotated 30 degrees clockwise from the character's baseline. In this case, the character orientation is set using the lfOrientation field. Normally, you will set the lfOrientation value equal to the lfEscapement value.

- lfFaceName. String: Specifies the name of the typeface. If NULL, GDI attempts to select the default device typeface.

- lfFullName. String: The full face name and style name for a TrueType font. Used only in the NEWLOGFONT structure.

- lfHeight, lfWidth. The height and width of the font in logical units. Refers to the cell dimensions if positive, character (glyph) dimensions if negative. Refers to average character width for variable pitch fonts. GDI will always choose a physical font with dimensions equal to or smaller than those specified if such a font is available. If lfWidth is zero, the system uses the current device aspect ratio to find a close match based on the requested height.

- The following equation can be used to determine the height of a logical font given a point size.

Height = PointSize / 72 * (#Pixels/Vertical Logical Inch)

or in code:

lfHeight = -MulDiv(PointSize, GetDeviceCaps (hDC, LOGPIXELSY), 72);

- lfItalic. Nonzero to specify an italic font.

- lfOrientation. See the description for the lfEscapement field.

- lfOutPrecision. Provides guidelines to GDI to use for matching the font. Defined by the OUT_???_PRECIS constants in file API32.TXT. Default is specified by the constant OUT_DEFAULT_PRECIS. The OUT_TT_ONLY_PRECIS constant can be used to request only True-Type fonts.

- lfPitchAndFamily. Integer: A combination of the pitch and family. Pitch and family are specified by constants that are ORed together. The pitch constants are:

  - DEFAULT_PITCH: Use the default for the system.

  - FIXED_PITCH: Request a fixed pitch font. GDI will never return a variable pitch font if this is specified unless there are no fixed pitch fonts in the requested character set.

  - VARIABLE_PITCH: Request a variable pitch font.

- The family is specified by the constants FF_DECORATIVE, FF_MODERN, FF_ROMAN, FF_SCRIPT, FF_SWISS, or FF_DONTCARE if any family is acceptable.

- lfQuality. One of the following constants:

  - DEFAULT_QUALITY: Don't care.

  - DRAFT_QUALITY: Request a draft quality font.

  - PROOF_QUALITY: Request a proof quality font.

- lfStrikeOut. Nonzero to specify a strike-out font.

- lfStyle. String: The style of a TrueType font. TrueType fonts may define unique styles such as OUTLINE. This string allows you to determine the style of a TrueType font.

- lfUnderline. Nonzero to specify an underline font.

- lfWeight. The character weight ranging from 100 to 900. Example values are 100 for light, 400 for normal, 700 for bold. Refer to the FW_??? constants for a complete list of values.

The TEXTMETRIC and NEWTEXTMETRIC Structure Fields

The following fields are used in the TEXTMETRIC and NEWTEXTMETRIC data structures. These structures return the attributes of an actual physical font selected into a device context. All units specified are in logical units of the device context unless specified otherwise. Most of these attributes are defined earlier in this chapter.

- ntmAvgWidth. The average character width for a TrueType font given in EM logical units. The EM is the approximate width of the letter M in that font.

- ntmCellHeight. The height of a TrueType character cell given in EM logical units.

- ntmFlags. Specifies font style using the constants NTM_??? from the file API32.TXT. This is only used for TrueType fonts.

- ntmSizeEM. Specifies the EM square size of the font. It represents the logical units in which a TrueType font was laid out. The EM is the approximate width of the letter M in that font.

- tmAscent. The ascent of the character cell.

- tmAveCharWidth. The average width of the characters in the font. For ANSI fonts, only letters and the space character are used.

- tmBreakChar. The character used to define word breaks when text is justified. Usually the space character.

- tmCharSet. Specifies the character set for the font.

- tmDefaultChar. The ASCII value of the character that will be displayed whenever a character that is not defined for the font is requested.

- tmDescent. The descent of the character cell.

- tmDigitizedAspectX, tmDigitizedAspectY. The horizontal and vertical aspect ratio for which the font was designed.

- tmExternalLeading. The external leading dimension of the character cell.

- tmFirstChar. The ASCII value of the first character defined for the font (not all fonts define all 255 ASCII characters).

- tmHeight. The height of a character cell.

- tmInternalLeading. The internal leading dimension of the character cell.

- tmItalic. TRUE if this is an italic font.

- tmLastChar. The ASCII value of the last character defined for the font.

- tmMaxCharWidth. Specifies the width of the widest character in the font. This refers to the B spacing of the character for TrueType fonts.

- tmOverhang. This attribute is used when GDI synthesizes fonts that require a change in the intercharacter spacing. For example, when GDI synthesizes an italic or bold font, this represents the change in spacing. When you have a character in a normal font next to one in an italic font, this can be used to calculate the spacing between the two.

- tmPitchAndFamily. The family is defined by constants FF_DECORATIVE, FF_MODERN, FF_ROMAN, FF_SCRIPT, and FF_SWISS in the same manner as the lfPitchAndFamily attribute described in the previous section. FF_DONTCARE indicates the font is not assigned to a family. Four constants define the bit flags for the pitch as follows:

  - TMPF_FIXED_PITCH: This is a variable pitch font. (Note that the meaning is the exact opposite of the name!)

  - TMPF_VECTOR: This is a vector or TrueType font.

  - TMPF_TRUETYPE: This is a TrueType font.

- TMPF_DEVICE: This is a device font.

These bits may be combined; for example, a TrueType variable pitch font would have the TMPF_TRUETYPE and TMPF_FIXED_PITCH flag bits set.

- tmStruckOut. TRUE if this is a strikeout font.

- tmUnderlined. TRUE if this is an underlined font.

- tmWeight. See the lfWeight attribute in the previous section.

The key fact to keep in mind when dealing with the LOGFONT and TEXT-METRIC data structures is this: Logical fonts reflect the ideal font requested for a particular drawing operation and are specified using the LOGFONT structure. Physical fonts reflect the actual font that the system has selected based on a logical font request. Information about physical fonts is found in the TEXTMETRIC structure. In other words: The font described by the LOGFONT structure is what you ask for; a TEXTMETRIC structure describes the font you actually get.

TrueType Specification

This overview of font technology and the font API functions should prove adequate for most VB applications. The TrueType font specification is available directly from Microsoft for those who wish to explore the internals of font technology, use embedded fonts in their applications, or use some of the advanced TrueType API functions.

Drawing Text

Windows provides a number of powerful text drawing functions, all of which are compatible with Visual Basic.

The Process of Drawing Text

The most important thing to realize about text output under Windows is that the process is identical to any other graphic output. This can be seen in Table 11.10, which compares the process of drawing a rectangle with that of drawing a line of text.

Table 11.10   Comparison of Graphics versus Text Output

Drawing a Rectangle	Drawing Text
Obtain a device context to draw into.	Same.

Table 11.10   **Comparison of Graphics versus Text Output (Continued)**

Obtain a pen to draw with.	Obtain a font to draw with.
Select the pen into the device context.	Select the font into the device context.
Decide where to place the rectangle.	Decide the starting point for the text.
Draw the rectangle.	Draw the text.
Restore the original pen into the device context.	Restore the original font into the device context.
Free GDI objects as needed (pen, device context).	Free GDI objects as needed (font, device context).

There are two differences between the actual drawing of the rectangle and the drawing of the text. First, unlike the rectangle, you do not always know how much space is needed to contain a particular block of text. Second, the rectangle origin is always aligned at a rectangle corner (upper left or upper right depending on the coordinate system). With text, you have a number of alignment options depending on the output function used.

Text Extents and Alignment

Text extents refer to the size that a particular block of text will take up on the output device. This size is influenced by many factors including the font, the text to be displayed, and the coordinate system of the device context. Windows provides a number of functions to help calculate text extents as shown in Table 11.3. When drawing text, it is common to calculate the extent of a block of text before drawing it, and use that value to determine the location of the next block of text. For more complex situations where multiple fonts are combined on a line, you may need to use the text metrics for the font to calculate the spacing between individual characters.

In most cases you also have control over the alignment of text output. The first alignment issue relates to what part of text the drawing coordinate applies to. If you are trying to fit text into a particular rectangle, you will probably want the origin to refer to the upper-left or lower-left corner of the character cell depending on the coordinate system in use. If, however, you are combining several fonts on a line, you will probably want to align all of the characters to a single baseline, thus the drawing coordinate should be aligned to the font baseline.

A formatting rectangle is used by some of the text drawing functions. This allows you to specify a rectangle in which the text will be drawn, and provides the ability to specify additional formatting options. These include left,

center, and right alignment for a line, automatic word breaks at rectangle boundaries, and more. Table 11.11 lists the text output API functions and their supporting functions, along with some additional text manipulation routines.

Table 11.11 **Text Output and Support Functions**

Function	Description
DrawText DrawTextEx	The most powerful text output functions with formatting. Includes tabbing, automatic word wrap, and more.
ExtTextOut	An extended text output function that provides the ability to specify the exact location of every character.
GetTextAlign	Retrieves the current text alignment.
GetTextColor	Retrieves the current text drawing color.
GreyString	A function to draw gray strings. This is most frequently used to draw text on disabled controls.
PolyTextOut	A text drawing function that can draw multiple strings at once.
SetTextAlign	Sets the text alignment.
SetTextColor	Sets the drawing color for text.
SetTextJustification	Supports text justification while drawing text.
TabbedTextOut	Text output function that supports user-definable tab stops.
TextOut	The most basic text output function.

Examples

This chapter contains a number of sample programs that illustrate how to work with fonts and how to draw text.

The FontView Example

FontView is a program that allows you to modify the attributes of a logical font, then display the resulting font using a user-defined text sample. It then allows you to view text metric information about the actual physical font selected.

Using FontView

The FontView runtime screen is shown in Figure 11.6. The list box is loaded with the available font typeface names. The Height and Width text boxes specify the requested font width and height in pixels. The font returned will not be larger than these dimensions, even if GDI needs to select a different typeface in order to meet these requirements.

Figure 11.6

Main FontView project form

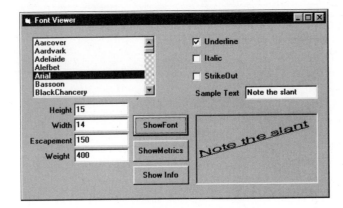

The Escapement text box allows you to specify the angle of the text drawing in tenths of a degree. The Underline, Italic, and StrikeOut check boxes are self-explanatory. The Sample Text text box allows you to specify the text to display.

The ShowFont command button causes the logical font to be selected into the picture control and the sample text drawn. The ShowMetrics command button brings up a message box that displays information about the physical font that was actually selected, as shown in Figure 11.7. The Show-Info command button brings up a listing of additional information about the font, as shown in Figure 11.8.

Figure 11.7

Display of physical font characteristics

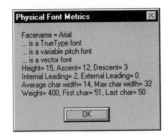

Project Description

The FontView project includes four files. FONTVIEW.FRM is the main form for the project. FNTVIEW2.FRM is a secondary form used to display font

Figure 11.8

Additional font
information

information results. FONTVIEW.BAS contains the constant type and function
declarations. APIGID32.BAS contains the declarations for the APIGID32.DLL
dynamic link library.

FontView Listings

Module FONTVIEW.BAS contains the constant declarations and function
declarations used by the program and is shown in Listing 11.1.

Listing 11.1   Module FONTVIEW.BAS

```
Attribute VB_Name = "FONTVIEW1"
' FontView Sample Application
' Copyright (c) 1995-1997, by Desaware

Option Explicit
```

The API Constants used by this sample application can be found in the sample program on the CD-ROM and in file API32.txt. This application uses constants with the following prefixes: OUT_, CLIP_, TMPF_, NTM_, FF_, FW_, and
GCP_. (The constants have been left out of the book in order to save space.)

The declarations for the following structures have also been left out to save
space: LOGFONT, RECT, TEXTMETRIC, and NEWTEXTMETRIC. These
declarations can be found in the sample on the CD-ROM and in Appendix B.

```
Public Const DEFAULT_QUALITY = ¯
Public Const DRAFT_QUALITY = 1
Public Const PROOF_QUALITY = 2
Public Const DEFAULT_PITCH = ¯
Public Const FIXED_PITCH = 1
Public Const VARIABLE_PITCH = 2
Public Const ANSI_CHARSET = ¯
```

```
Public Const DEFAULT_CHARSET = 1
Public Const SYMBOL_CHARSET = 2
Public Const SHIFTJIS_CHARSET = 128
Public Const OEM_CHARSET = 255
Public Const LF_FULLFACESIZE = 64
Public Const RASTER_FONTTYPE = 1
Public Const DEVICE_FONTTYPE = 2
Public Const TRUETYPE_FONTTYPE = 4
Public Const LF_FACESIZE = 32
Public Const FLI_MASK = &H1~3B
Public Const FLI_GLYPHS = &H4~~~~


' Public Variables

#If Win32 Then
Public FontToUse& ' The font in use
#Else
Public FontToUse% ' The font in use
#End If



#If Win32 Then

Declare Function CreateFontIndirect& Lib "gdi32" Alias "CreateFontIndirectA" _
(lpLogFont As LOGFONT)
Declare Function SelectObject& Lib "gdi32" (ByVal hdc As Long, ByVal hObject As _
Long)
Declare Function GetClientRect& Lib "user32" (ByVal hwnd As Long, lpRect As _
RECT)
Declare Function GetTextMetrics& Lib "gdi32" Alias "GetTextMetricsA" (ByVal hdc _
As Long, lpMetrics As TEXTMETRIC)
Declare Function GetTextFace& Lib "gdi32" Alias "GetTextFaceA" (ByVal hdc As _
Long, ByVal nCount As Long, ByVal lpFacename As String)
Declare Function DeleteObject& Lib "gdi32" (ByVal hObject As Long)
Declare Function TextOut Lib "gdi32" Alias "TextOutA" (ByVal hdc As Long, ByVal _
x As Long, ByVal y As Long, ByVal lpstring As String, ByVal nCount _
As Long) As Long
Declare Function GetFontLanguageInfo& Lib "gdi32" (ByVal hdc As Long)

#Else
Declare Function GetClientRect% Lib "User" (ByVal hwnd%, lpRect As RECT)
Declare Function CreateFontIndirect% Lib "GDI" (lpLogFont As LOGFONT)
Declare Function SelectObject% Lib "GDI" (ByVal hdc%, ByVal hObject%)
Declare Function GetTextMetrics% Lib "GDI" (ByVal hdc%, lpMetrics As TEXTMETRIC)
Declare Function GetTextFace% Lib "GDI" (ByVal hdc%, ByVal nCount%, ByVal _
lpFacename$)
Declare Function DeleteObject% Lib "GDI" (ByVal hObject%)
Declare Function TextOut% Lib "GDI" (ByVal hdc%, ByVal x%, ByVal y%, ByVal _
```

```
lpstring$, ByVal nCount%)

#End If
```

Listing 11.2 shows Form FONTVIEW.FRM.

Listing 11.2   Form FONTVIEW.FRM

```
VERSION 5.¯¯
Begin VB.Form Form1
    Caption          =    "Font Viewer"
    ClientHeight     =    4¯2¯
    ClientLeft       =    3735
    ClientTop        =    165¯
    ClientWidth      =    7365
    BeginProperty Font
        name         =    "MS Sans Serif"
        charset      =    1
        weight       =    7¯¯
        size         =    8.25
        underline    =    ¯    'False
        italic       =    ¯    'False
        strikethrough =   ¯    'False
    EndProperty
    ForeColor        =    &H8¯¯¯¯¯¯8&
    Height           =    4425
    Left             =    3675
    LinkMode         =    1    'Source
    LinkTopic        =    "Form1"
    ScaleHeight      =    4¯2¯
    ScaleWidth       =    7365
    Top              =    13¯5
    Width            =    7485
    Begin VB.CommandButton cmdFontInfo
        Caption      =    "Show Info"
        Height       =    435
        Left         =    27¯¯
        TabIndex     =    17
        Top          =    33¯¯
        Width        =    1335
    End
    Begin VB.TextBox TxtWeight
        Height       =    315
        Left         =    126¯
        TabIndex     =    8
        Text         =    "4¯¯"
        Top          =    288¯
        Width        =    1335
```

Listing 11.2   Form FONTVIEW.FRM (Continued)

```
  End
  Begin VB.CommandButton CmdShowMetrics
      Appearance      =       ‾  'Flat
      BackColor       =       &H8‾‾‾‾‾‾5&
      Caption         =       "ShowMetrics"
      Height          =       495
      Left            =       27‾‾
      TabIndex        =       16
      Top             =       27‾‾
      Width           =       1335
  End
  Begin VB.TextBox TxtEscapement
      Height          =       315
      Left            =       126‾
      TabIndex        =       6
      Text            =       "‾"
      Top             =       252‾
      Width           =       1335
  End
  Begin VB.CommandButton CmdShowFont
      Appearance      =       ‾  'Flat
      BackColor       =       &H8‾‾‾‾‾‾5&
      Caption         =       "ShowFont"
      Default         =       -1 'True
      Height          =       495
      Left            =       27‾‾
      TabIndex        =       13
      Top             =       21‾‾
      Width           =       1335
  End
  Begin VB.TextBox TxtWidth
      Height          =       315
      Left            =       126‾
      TabIndex        =       4
      Text            =       "1‾"
      Top             =       216‾
      Width           =       1335
  End
  Begin VB.PictureBox PicText
      Height          =       1635
      Left            =       42‾‾
      ScaleHeight     =       16‾5
      ScaleWidth      =       2925
      TabIndex        =       9
      Top             =       21‾‾
      Width           =       2955
  End
  Begin VB.TextBox TxtHeight
```

Listing 11.2 Form FONTVIEW.FRM (Continued)

```
         Height        =    315
         Left          =    126⁻
         TabIndex      =    1
         Text          =    "1⁻"
         Top           =    18⁻⁻
         Width         =    1335
      End
      Begin VB.TextBox TxtSample
         Height        =    315
         Left          =    54⁻⁻
         TabIndex      =    14
         Text          =    "ABC"
         Top           =    144⁻
         Width         =    1755
      End
      Begin VB.CheckBox ChkStrikeout
         Caption       =    "StrikeOut"
         Height        =    375
         Left          =    414⁻
         TabIndex      =    12M
         Top           =    1⁻2⁻
         Width         =    1575
      End
      Begin VB.CheckBox ChkItalic
         Caption       =    "Italic"
         Height        =    375
         Left          =    414⁻
         TabIndex      =    11
         Top           =    6⁻⁻
         Width         =    1575
      End
      Begin VB.CheckBox ChkUnderline
         Caption       =    "Underline"
         Height        =    315
         Left          =    414⁻
         TabIndex      =    1⁻
         Top           =    24⁻
         Width         =    1635
      End
      Begin VB.ListBox FontList
         Height        =    1395
         Left          =    24⁻
         Sorted        =    -1   'True
         TabIndex      =    ⁻
         Top           =    24⁻
         Width         =    3⁻15
      End
      Begin VB.Label Label4
         Alignment     =    1    'Right Justify
```

Listing 11.2   **Form FONTVIEW.FRM (Continued)**

```
      Appearance      =     ‾  'Flat
      BackColor       =     &H8‾‾‾‾‾‾5&
      BackStyle       =     ‾  'Transparent
      Caption         =     "Weight"
      ForeColor       =     &H8‾‾‾‾‾‾8&
      Height          =     315
      Left            =     12‾
      TabIndex        =     7
      Top             =     294‾
      Width           =     1‾35
   End
   Begin VB.Label Label3
      Alignment       =     1  'Right Justify
      Appearance      =     ‾  'Flat
      BackColor       =     &H8‾‾‾‾‾‾5&
      BackStyle       =     ‾  'Transparent
      Caption         =     "Escapement"
      ForeColor       =     &H8‾‾‾‾‾‾8&
      Height          =     315
      Left            =     6‾
      TabIndex        =     5
      Top             =     258‾
      Width           =     1155
   End
   Begin VB.Label Label2
      Alignment       =     1  'Right Justify
      Appearance      =     ‾  'Flat
      BackColor       =     &H8‾‾‾‾‾‾5&
      BackStyle       =     ‾  'Transparent
      Caption         =     "Width"
      ForeColor       =     &H8‾‾‾‾‾‾8&
      Height          =     255
      Left            =     54‾
      TabIndex        =     3
      Top             =     222‾
      Width           =     675
   End
   Begin VB.Label Label1
      Alignment       =     1  'Right Justify
      Appearance      =     ‾  'Flat
      BackColor       =     &H8‾‾‾‾‾‾5&
      BackStyle       =     ‾  'Transparent
      Caption         =     "Height"
      ForeColor       =     &H8‾‾‾‾‾‾8&
      Height          =     255
      Left            =     54‾
      TabIndex        =     2
      Top             =     186‾
```

Listing 11.2   Form FONTVIEW.FRM (Continued)

```
        Width         =     675
      End
      Begin VB.Label Label5
        Appearance    =    ¯   'Flat
        BackColor     =    &H8¯¯¯¯¯¯5&
        BackStyle     =    ¯   'Transparent
        Caption       =    "Sample Text"
        ForeColor     =    &H8¯¯¯¯¯¯8&
        Height        =    255
        Left          =    42¯¯
        TabIndex      =    15
        Top           =    15¯¯
        Width         =    1¯95
      End
   End
Attribute VB_Name = "Form1"
Attribute VB_GlobalNameSpace = False
Attribute VB_Creatable = False
Attribute VB_PredeclaredId = True Attribute VB_Exposed = False


Option Explicit
```

This function shows how you can create a logical font by filling in entries in a LOGFONT data structure. This example does not cover all of the fields—you might want to experiment with some of the others such as precision and font family. The SelectObject API function causes Windows to find a physical font that is as close as possible to the logical font you specified.

Under Win16 it was necessary to define bytes within a structure as single character fixed length strings. This also made it necessary to use the Asc and Chr$ functions to access values within these fields. With the appearance of the numeric Byte data type in VB4, this is no longer necessary, as shown in the listing.

```
' Creates a logical font based on the various control
' settings. Then displays a sample string in that font.
'
Private Sub CmdShowFont_Click()
    Dim lf As LOGFONT
    #If Win32 Then
    Dim oldhdc&
    #Else
    Dim oldhdc%
    #End If
    Dim TempByteArray() As Byte
    Dim dl&, x%
```

```
        Dim ByteArrayLimit&
        Dim rc As RECT
        PicText.Cls
        If FontToUse <> ˉ Then dl = DeleteObject(FontToUse)
        lf.lfHeight = Val(TxtHeight.Text)
        lf.lfWidth = Val(TxtWidth.Text)
        lf.lfEscapement = Val(TxtEscapement.Text)
        lf.lfWeight = Val(TxtWeight.Text)
        If (ChkItalic.value = 1) Then lf.lfItalic = 1
        If (ChkUnderline.value = 1) Then lf.lfUnderline = 1
        If (ChkStrikeout.value = 1) Then lf.lfStrikeOut = 1
        lf.lfOutPrecision = OUT_DEFAULT_PRECIS
        lf.lfClipPrecision = OUT_DEFAULT_PRECIS
        ' This kind of chr$ assignment is no longer necessary and
        ' is not advisable
        ' lf.lfQuality = Chr$(DEFAULT_QUALITY)
        lf.lfQuality = DEFAULT_QUALITY
        lf.lfPitchAndFamily = DEFAULT_PITCH Or FF_DONTCARE
        lf.lfCharSet = DEFAULT_CHARSET

        ' When we change this to a byte array, we
        ' no longer can assign a text string to a fixed
        ' length byte array.
        ' lf.lfFaceName = FontList.Text & Chr$(ˉ)

        #If Win32 Then
            TempByteArray = StrConv(FontList.Text & Chr$(ˉ), vbFromUnicode)
        #Else
            TempByteArray = FontList.Text & Chr$(ˉ)
        #End If
        ByteArrayLimit = UBound(TempByteArray)
        For x% = ˉ To ByteArrayLimit
            lf.lfFaceName(x%) = TempByteArray(x%)
        Next x%
        FontToUse = CreateFontIndirect(lf)
        If FontToUse = ˉ Then Exit Sub
        oldhdc = SelectObject(PicText.hdc, FontToUse)

        ' Get the client rectangle in order to place the
        ' text midway down the box
        dl& = GetClientRect(PicText.hwnd, rc)
        dl& = TextOut(PicText.hdc, 1, rc.Bottom / 2, (TxtSample.Text), _
        Len(TxtSample.Text))
        dl& = SelectObject(PicText.hdc, oldhdc)
End Sub
```

The GetTextMetrics function retrieves information about a physical font.
The message box brought up by this function presents the text metrics that
can be compared with the requested logical font.

```
'
Private Sub CmdShowMetrics_Click()
```

```
    Dim tm As TEXTMETRIC
    Dim r$
    Dim crlf$
#If Win32 Then
    Dim oldfont&
#Else
    Dim oldfont%
#End If
    Dim di&
    Dim tbuf As String * 8⁻
    crlf$ = Chr$(13) + Chr$(1⁻)
    If FontToUse = ⁻ Then
        MsgBox "Font not yet selected"
        Exit Sub
    End If
    oldfont = SelectObject(PicText.hdc, FontToUse)
    di = GetTextMetrics(PicText.hdc, tm)
    di = GetTextFace(PicText.hdc, 79, tbuf)
    ' Add to r$ only the part up to the null terminator
    r$ = "Facename = " + agGetStringFromLPSTR$(tbuf) + crlf$
    ' No need to have Asc conversions here
    If (tm.tmPitchAndFamily And TMPF_TRUETYPE) <> ⁻ Then r$ = r$ + "... is a _
TrueType font" + crlf$
    If (tm.tmPitchAndFamily And TMPF_DEVICE) <> ⁻ Then r$ = r$ + "... is a _
Device font" + crlf$
    ' Curiously enough, this bit is set for variable width fonts.
    If (tm.tmPitchAndFamily And TMPF_FIXED_PITCH) <> ⁻ Then
        r$ = r$ + "... is a variable pitch font" + crlf$
    Else
        r$ = r$ + "... is a fixed pitch font" + crlf$
    End If
    If (tm.tmPitchAndFamily And TMPF_VECTOR) <> ⁻ Then r$ = r$ + "... is a _
vector font" + crlf$
    r$ = r$ + "Height=" + Str$(tm.tmHeight) + ", Ascent=" + Str$(tm.tmAscent) + _
", Descent=" + Str$(tm.tmDescent) + crlf$
    r$ = r$ + "Internal Leading=" + Str$(tm.tmInternalLeading) + ", External _
Leading=" + Str$(tm.tmExternalLeading) + crlf$
    r$ = r$ + "Average char width=" + Str$(tm.tmAveCharWidth) + ", Max char _
width=" + Str$(tm.tmMaxCharWidth) + crlf$
    r$ = r$ + "Weight=" + Str$(tm.tmWeight) + ", First char=" + _
Str$(Asc(tm.tmFirstChar)) + ", Last char=" + Str$(Asc(tm.tmLastChar)) + crlf$

    MsgBox r$, ⁻, "Physical Font Metrics"
    di = SelectObject(PicText.hdc, oldfont)
End Sub
```

```
Private Sub FontList_Click()
    CmdShowFont_Click
End Sub

'   Load the font list dialog box with the available fonts
'
Private Sub Form_Load()
    Dim x%
    Dim a$
    #If Win16 Then
        ' This functionality is disabled for Win16
        cmdFontInfo.Visible = False
    #End If

    Screen.MousePointer = 11
    For x% = 1 To Screen.FontCount
        a$ = Screen.Fonts(x%)
        If a$ <> "" Then FontList.AddItem a$
    Next x%
    Screen.MousePointer = ‾
End Sub

Private Sub Form_Unload(Cancel As Integer)
    ' Be sure to clean up GDI objects when leaving the program
    Dim di&
    If FontToUse& <> ‾ Then di = DeleteObject(FontToUse)
```

The cmdFontInfo_Click command brings up the frmInfo form to display additional information about a font.

```
Private Sub cmdFontInfo_Click()
    If FontToUse = ‾ Then
        MsgBox "Select a font"
        Exit Sub
    End If
    frmInfo.Show 1
End Sub
```

Listing 11.3 shows Form FNTVIEW2.FRM.

Listing 11.3   Form FNTVIEW2.FRM

```
VERSION 5.‾‾
Begin VB.Form frmInfo
    BorderStyle     =   3  'Fixed Dialog
    Caption         =   "Form2"
    ClientHeight    =   279‾
    ClientLeft      =   1365
```

Listing 11.3   Form FNTVIEW2.FRM (Continued)

```
        ClientTop       =   2895
        ClientWidth     =   573⁻
        Height          =   3195
        Left            =   13⁻5
        LinkTopic       =   "Form2"
        MaxButton       =   ⁻     'False
        MinButton       =   ⁻     'False
        ScaleHeight     =   279⁻
        ScaleWidth      =   573⁻
        ShowInTaskbar   =   ⁻     'False
        Top             =   255⁻
        Width           =   585⁻
        Begin VB.TextBox Text1
            Height          =   1755
            Left            =   42⁻
            MultiLine       =   -1 'True
            TabIndex        =   1
            Text            =   "FNTVIEW2.frx":⁻⁻⁻⁻
            Top             =   18⁻
            Width           =   4995
        End
        Begin VB.CommandButton Command1
            Caption         =   "Ok"
            Height          =   435
            Left            =   246⁻
            TabIndex        =   ⁻
            Top             =   228⁻
            Width           =   975
        nd
End
Attribute VB_Name = "frmInfo"
Attribute VB_GlobalNameSpace = False
Attribute VB_Creatable = False
Attribute VB_PredeclaredId = True Attribute VB_Exposed = False
Option Explicit


Private Sub Command1_Click()
    ]nload Me
End Sub

Private Sub Form_Load()
    Dim oldfont&
    Die info&
    Dim t$
    Caption = Form1!FontList.Text
    oldfont& = SelectObject(hdc, FontToUse)
    info = GetFontLanguageInfo(hdc)
```

Listing 11.3   **Form FNTVIEW2.FRM (Continued)**

```
' Restore the original font
Call SelectObject(hdc, oldfont&)
 If info = ¯ Then
     Text1.Text = "Standard Latin Font"
 Else
     If (info And GCP_DBCS) <> ¯ Then t$ = t$ & "Double Byte Character Set" _
     & vbCrLf
     If (info And GCP_DIACRITIC) <> ¯ Then t$ = t$ & _
     "Contains diacritic characters" & vbCrLf
     If (info And FLI_GLYPHS) <> ¯ Then t$ = t$ & _
     "Font contains non- displaying glyphs" & vbCrLf_
     If (info And GCP_GLYPHSHAPE) <> ¯ Then t$ = t$ & _
     "Font contains special glyph shapes" & vbCrLf
     If (info And GCP_KASHIDA) <> ¯ Then t$ = t$ & _
     "Font supports Kashida glyphs" & vbCrLf
     If (info And GCP_LIGATE) <> ¯ Then t$ = t$ & _
     "Font supports Kashida" & vbCrLf
     If (info And GCP_USEKERNING) <> ¯ Then t$ = t$ & _
     "Font contains kerning tables" & vbCrLf
     If (info And GCP_REORDER) <> ¯ Then t$ = t$ & _
     "Characters need to be reordered for this font" & vbCrLf_
     Text1.Text = t$
 End If

End Sub
```

The TextDemo Example

TextDemo shows several techniques relating to drawing text and demonstrates use of two of the text output functions.

Using TextDemo

Figure 11.9 shows the TextDemo program in action. The list box is loaded with the typeface names of the available screen fonts. The lower picture box shows a text string using the default font for the control scaled to different sizes. Contrast this with the screen shown in Figure 11.10, which shows the scaling for a TrueType font.

The picture box at the upper right in Figure 11.10 shows a text string displayed using automatic word wrapping. It also demonstrates the use of tab stops.

The only user control for this program is the selection of the typeface to display.

Figure 11.9

The main form of the TextDemo project shown with a raster font

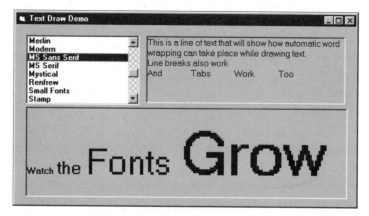

Figure 11.10

The main form of the TextDemo project shown with a TrueType font

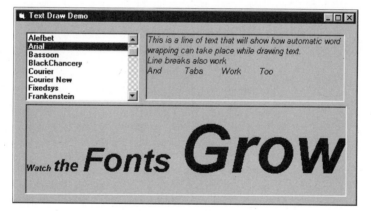

Project Description

The TextDemo project includes two files. TEXTDEMO.FRM is the only form used in the program. TEXTDEMO.BAS is the only module in the program and contains the constant type and function declarations.

The listing for the TEXTDEMO.BAS module is not included here in order to conserve space. The file is virtually identical to FONTVIEW.BAS except that it includes additional constants.

Listing 11.4 shows the TEXTDEMO.FRM file including the header which describes the control layout for the form.

Listing 11.4   **TEXTDEMO.FRM**

```
VERSION 5.¯¯
Begin VB.Form TextDemo
    Caption         =   "Text Draw Demo"
    ClientHeight    =   4185
    ClientLeft      =   1¯95
    ClientTop       =   1485
    ClientWidth     =   819¯
    BeginProperty Font
        name            =   "MS Sans Serif"
        charset         =   1
        weight          =   7¯¯
        size            =   8.25
        underline       =   ¯   'False
        italic          =   ¯   'False
        strikethrough   =   ¯   'False
    EndProperty
    ForeColor       =   &H8¯¯¯¯¯¯8&
    Height          =   459¯
    Left            =   1¯35
    LinkMode        =   1   'Source
    LinkTopic       =   "Form1"
    ScaleHeight     =   4185
    ScaleWidth      =   819¯
    Top             =   114¯
    Width           =   831¯
    Begin VB.PictureBox PicText
        Height          =   2115
        Left            =   24¯
        ScaleHeight     =   2¯55
        ScaleWidth      =   7695
        TabIndex        =   1
        Top             =   192¯
        Width           =   7755
    End
    Begin VB.PictureBox PicFrame
        BeginProperty Font
            name            =   "MS Sans Serif"
            charset         =   1
            weight          =   4¯¯
            size            =   9.75
            underline       =   ¯   'False
            italic          =   ¯   'False
            strikethrough   =   ¯   'False
        EndProperty
        Height          =   1575
        Left            =   312¯
        ScaleHeight     =   1515
        ScaleWidth      =   4755
```

Listing 11.4   TEXTDEMO.FRM (Continued)

```
            TabIndex        =    2
            Top             =    24¯
            Width           =    4815
        End
        Begin VB.ListBox FontList
            Height          =    162¯
            Left            =    24¯
            Sorted          =    -1   'True
            TabIndex        =    ¯
            Top             =    24¯
            Width           =    2715
        End
    End
End
Attribute VB_Name = "TextDemo"
Attribute VB_GlobalNameSpace = False
Attribute VB_Creatable = False
Attribute VB_PredeclaredId = True Attribute VB_Exposed = False
Option Explicit
' Redraw the demo pictures in the new font
'
Private Sub FontList_Click()
    PicText.FontName = FontList.Text
    PicFrame.FontName = FontList.Text
    PicText.Refresh
    PicFrame.Refresh
End Sub


'    Load the font list dialog box with the available fonts
'
Private Sub Form_Load()
    Dim x%
    Dim a$
    Screen.MousePointer = 11
    For x% = 1 To Screen.FontCount
        a$ = Screen.Fonts(x%)
        If a$ <> "" Then FontList.AddItem a$
    Next x%
    Screen.MousePointer = ¯
    FontList.ListIndex = ¯
End Sub
```

This function demonstrates how the DrawText API function can perform complex text formatting including word wrapping and handling of line breaks. It then follows with a demonstration of tab expansion to a tab interval that the user can set.

```
'    Use of drawtext to do some powerful text drawing
'
```

```
Private Sub PicFrame_PAINT()
    Dim demo$, demo2$
    Dim rc As RECT
    Dim atab$
    Dim heightused%
    Dim crlf$
    Dim di&

    atab$ = Chr$(9)
    crlf$ = Chr$(13) + Chr$(1¯)

    demo$ = "This is a line of text that will show how "
    demo$ = demo$ + "automatic word wrapping can take place while drawing text."
    demo$ = demo$ + crlf$ + "Line breaks also work"

    demo2$ = "And" + atab$ + "Tabs" + atab$ + "Work" + atab$ + "Too" + atab$

    ' Get the dimensions of the control
    di = GetClientRect(PicFrame.hWnd, rc)

    heightused% = DrawText(PicFrame.hDC, demo$, -1, rc, DT_WORDBREAK)

    rc.Top = heightused%

    ' Tabs are set 1¯ characters apart (based on average char width)
    heightused% = DrawText(PicFrame.hDC, demo2$, -1, rc, DT_EXPANDTABS Or _
    DT_TABSTOP Or &HA¯¯)


End Sub
```

The following function illustrates several interesting techniques. First, it shows how to obtain the default font for a device context by temporarily selecting into the context a temporary stock font. This can be especially useful for printer devices if you wish to determine the default font for a printer DC.

Next, the function shows how the LOGFONT structure obtained can be modified in order to change selected attributes, in this case, the size of the font. The CreateFontIndirect function may then be used to request the modified font.

This function also demonstrates use of GDI's text alignment capabilities to have the coordinate refer to the text block's baseline instead of the top or bottom of the character cell.

Finally, the function shows how you may use the current position for the device context to allow text output without having to calculate the extents manually for each text block.

```
' Draw a multiple font demo in the picture control
'
Private Sub PicText_Paint()
    ReDim demo$(4)
```

```
Dim lf As LOGFONT
#If Win32 Then
    Dim oldfont&, newfont&
    Dim alignorig&
    Dim vpos&
#Else
    Dim oldfont%, newfont%
    Dim alignorig%
    Dim vpos%
#End If
Dim rc As RECT
Dim todraw%
Dim di&
Dim prevpoint As POINTAPI

demo$(1) = "Watch "
demo$(2) = "the "
demo$(3) = "Fonts "
demo$(4) = "Grow "

' Get the dimensions of the control
di = GetClientRect(PicText.hWnd, rc)

' We get the current logical font by selecting in
' temporarily a stock font
oldfont = SelectObject(PicText.hDC, GetStockObject(SYSTEM_FONT))
di = GetObjectAPI(oldfont, Len(lf), lf)
' Restore the original font
di = SelectObject(PicText.hDC, oldfont)

' Reset current position and alignment
' Be sure to keep the original alignment
' Since we're changing font sizes, align to the baseline
' To make life easier, we use the current position
alignorig = SetTextAlign(PicText.hDC, TA_LEFT Or TA_BASELINE Or TA_UPDATECP)

' Draw the text about 3/4 of the way down.
vpos = rc.Bottom - rc.Bottom / 4
di = MoveToEx(PicText.hDC, 0, vpos, prevpoint)

' Draw the first word
di = TextOut(PicText.hDC, 0, 0, demo$(1), Len(demo$(1)))

' Now start drawing the rest of the words
For todraw% = 2 To 4
    ' Debug.Print lf.lfHeight
    lf.lfHeight = lf.lfHeight * 2
    newfont = CreateFontIndirect(lf)
    oldfont = SelectObject(PicText.hDC, newfont)
    di = TextOut(PicText.hDC, 0, 0, demo$(todraw%), Len(demo$(todraw)))
    newfont = SelectObject(PicText.hDC, oldfont)
    di = DeleteObject(newfont)
```

```
        Next todraw%

        di = SetTextAlign(PicText.hDC, alignorig)

    End Sub
```

The DrawText.vbp Example

The DrawText sample program allows you to experiment with some of the options available for the DrawText function. The main form of the project is shown in Figure 11.11. A rectangular shaded area shows the rectangle provided to the DrawText functions. This allows you to easily see the effect of the rectangle when clipping or using the function's word wrap capability.

Figure 11.11

The main form of the DrawText project

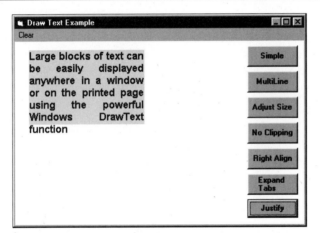

The DrawText example is, for the most part, extremely simple, thus only a partial listing is included here. The only part which deserves additional attention is the text justification algorithm shown in Listing 11.5. This function illustrates some of the techniques that are often used to perform text output under Windows.

Listing 11.5   **The CmdJustify_Click function from DRAWTEXT.FRM**

```
Private Sub cmdJustify_Click()
    Dim LineWidth%
    Dim CurrentLineWidth%
    Dim StartOfCurrentLine%
```

Listing 11.5   The CmdJustify_Click function from DRAWTEXT.FRM (Continued)

```
Dim CurrentPosition%
Dim NextPosition%
Dim BreakCharCount%
Dim CurrentYLocation%
Dim di%
Dim OutputString$

' Determine the maximum length
LineWidth% = OutputRect.right - OutputRect.left

StartOfCurrentLine% = 1
CurrentPosition% = 1
BreakCharCount% = 0
CurrentYLocation% = OutputRect.top

Do
    ' Find the next space
    NextPosition% = InStr(CurrentPosition%, Sample1$, " ")
    ' We're done with the loop
    If NextPosition% <= CurrentPosition% Then
        CurrentLineWidth = TextWidth(Mid$(Sample1$, StartOfCurrentLine%))
    Else
        CurrentLineWidth = TextWidth(Mid$(Sample1$, StartOfCurrentLine%, _
        NextPosition% - StartOfCurrentLine%))
    End If

    ' Does the current line fit?
    If CurrentLineWidth < LineWidth Then
        ' This word fit into the line
        ' Add to the count of break characters
        BreakCharCount% = BreakCharCount% + 1
        ' and set the new current position
        If NextPosition > 0 Then
            CurrentPosition% = NextPosition% + 1
        Else
            ' The final line fits on one line -
            ' print it without justification
            Exit Do
        End If
    Else
        ' The new word does not fit - print the line
        OutputString$ = Mid$(Sample1$, StartOfCurrentLine%, _
        CurrentPosition% - StartOfCurrentLine% - 1)
        ' Set the new current position
        StartOfCurrentLine% = CurrentPosition%
```

Listing 11.5   The CmdJustify_Click function from DRAWTEXT.FRM (Continued)

```
                    ' If there is at least one break character, set the correct count
                    If BreakCharCount% > 1 Then BreakCharCount% = BreakCharCount% - 1

                    ' Set the text justification
                    di% = SetTextJustification(hDC, LineWidth - _
                    TextWidth(OutputString$), BreakCharCount%)

                    ' And display the line
                    di% = TextOut(hDC, OutputRect.left, CurrentYLocation%, _
                    OutputString$, Len(OutputString$))
                    CurrentYLocation% = CurrentYLocation% + TextHeight(OutputString$)
                    BreakCharCount% = 0
                    ' Clear the text justification value
                    di% = SetTextJustification(hDC, 0, BreakCharCount%)

            End If
        Loop While CurrentPosition% < Len(Sample1$)

        If CurrentPosition% < Len(Sample1$) Then
            ' Print the rest of the last line - no justification
            OutputString$ = Mid$(Sample1$, StartOfCurrentLine%)
            di% = TextOut(hDC, OutputRect.left, CurrentYLocation%, OutputString$, _
            Len(OutputString$))
        End If

End Sub
```

Under DOS, text output was almost trivial—characters almost always had a fixed width, so justification and word wrap were simple. You could accurately place a character by simply multiplying its position in a line by the character width. Under Windows, each character can be placed anywhere on the device, and the position of a character usually depends on all of the characters that precede it in a line.

The Windows text output functions are capable, and handle many tasks, but they do not come close to handling the kinds of flexible text output that even a simple word processor must implement. In the justification example shown here, you can see how it is necessary to build each line one word at a time, testing the extents of the resulting line each time.

Once you have a line that fits, and have counted the number of break characters (spaces) in the line, Windows makes it easy to justify the line by extending the width of the break characters.

The EnmFntX Example

The EnmFntX sample program demonstrates the use of font enumeration functions to obtain information about the fonts that are available on a system. It also illustrates some interesting API programming techniques with regard to use of structures.

Using EnmFntX

Figure 11.12 shows the EnmFntX program in action. The upper list box is loaded with the font face name and full name separated by a "--". You can choose to load all fonts or only TrueType fonts. The lower list box displays all of the fonts available for a given font face name.

Figure 11.12
The main form of
the EnmFntX project

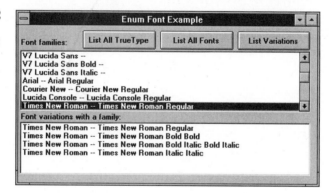

Project Description

The EnmFntX project includes two files. ENMFNTX.FRM is the only form used in the program. ENMFNTX.BAS is the only module in the program and contains the constant type and function declarations. The Visual Basic 4.0 version of this program requires the use of the dwcbk32d.ocx demonstration callback control included with this book. Listing 11.6 shows the ENMFNTX.BAS file.

Listing 11.6   ENMFNTX.BAS

```
Attribute VB_Name = "ENMFNTX1"
Option Explicit

' Logical Font
Public Const LF_FACESIZE = 32
Public Const LF_FULLFACESIZE = 64
```

Listing 11.6   ENMFNTX.BAS (Continued)

```
Type LOGFONT
        lfHeight As Long
        lfWidth As Long
        lfEscapement As Long
        lfOrientation As Long
        lfWeight As Long
        lfItalic As Byte
        lfUnderline As Byte
        lfStrikeOut As Byte
        lfCharSet As Byte
        lfOutPrecision As Byte
        lfClipPrecision As Byte
        lfQuality As Byte
        lfPitchAndFamily As Byte
        lfFaceName(LF_FACESIZE - 1) As Byte
End Type


' This used to be a NEWLOGFONT in Win16
Type ENUMLOGFONT
        elfLogFont As LOGFONT
        elfFullName(LF_FULLFACESIZE - 1) As Byte
        elfStyle(LF_FACESIZE - 1) As Byte
End Type

' Structure passed to FONTENUMPROC
' NOTE: NEWTEXTMETRIC is the same as TEXTMETRIC plus 4 new fields
Type NEWTEXTMETRIC
        tmHeight As Long
        tmAscent As Long
        tmDescent As Long
        tmInternalLeading As Long
        tmExternalLeading As Long
        tmAveCharWidth As Long
        tmMaxCharWidth As Long
        tmWeight As Long
        tmOverhang As Long
        tmDigitizedAspectX As Long
        tmDigitizedAspectY As Long
        tmFirstChar As Byte
        tmLastChar As Byte
        tmDefaultChar As Byte
        tmBreakChar As Byte
        tmItalic As Byte
        tmUnderlined As Byte
        tmStruckOut As Byte
        tmPitchAndFamily As Byte
```

Listing 11.6   ENMFNTX.BAS (Continued)

```
        tmCharSet As Byte
        ntmFlags As Long
        ntmSizeEM As Long
        ntmCellHeight As Long
        ntmAveWidth As Long
End Type


Public nlf As ENUMLOGFONT

Public ntm As NEWTEXTMETRIC

Public Const TMPF_TRUETYPE = 4

'  EnumFonts Masks
Public Const RASTER_FONTTYPE = &H1
Public Const DEVICE_FONTTYPE = &H2
Public Const TRUETYPE_FONTTYPE = &H4

Declare Function EnumFontFamilies Lib "gdi32" Alias "EnumFontFamiliesA" (ByVal _
hdc As Long, ByVal lpszFamily As String, ByVal lpEnumFontFamProc As Long, _
ByVal Param As Long) As Long
Declare Function EnumFontFamiliesEx Lib "gdi32" Alias "EnumFontFamiliesExA" _
(ByVal hdc As Long, lpLogFont As LOGFONT, ByVal lpEnumFontProc As Long, ByVal _
lParam As Long, ByVal dw As Long) As Long
Declare Function EnumFonts Lib "gdi32" Alias "EnumFontsA" (ByVal hdc As Long, _
ByVal lpsz As String, ByVal lpFontEnumProc As Long, ByVal lParam As Long) _
As Long
```

One subtle aspect of the declarations for the ENUMLOGFONT structure is the need to subtract 1 from the size specified in the equivalent C documentation or in the original Win16 declaration in order to take into account the fact that the first array index is entry zero. Refer to the section in Chapter 15 titled "Fixed Strings in Structures" for further information on this subject. Listing 11.7 shows form ENMFNTX.FRM.

Listing 11.7   ENMFNTX.FRM

```
VERSION 5.00
Begin VB.Form enmfntx
    Caption         =   "Enum Font Example"
```

Listing 11.7 ENMFNTX.FRM (Continued)

```
ClientHeight    =   3690
ClientLeft      =   1095
ClientTop       =   1500
ClientWidth     =   7215
BeginProperty Font
    name        =   "MS Sans Serif"
    charset     =   0
    weight      =   700
    size        =   8.25
    underline   =   0   'False
    italic      =   0   'False
    strikethrough = 0   'False
EndProperty
ForeColor       =   &H80000008&
Height          =   4095
Left            =   1035
LinkTopic       =   "Form1"
ScaleHeight     =   3690
ScaleWidth      =   7215
Top             =   1155
Width           =   7335
Begin VB.ListBox List2
    Height      =   1395
    Left        =   60
    TabIndex    =   4
    Top         =   600
    Width       =   6975
End
Begin VB.CommandButton cmdListTrueType
    Appearance  =   0   'Flat
    BackColor   =   &H80000005&
    Caption     =   "List All TrueType"
    Height      =   435
    Left        =   1560
    TabIndex    =   3
    Top         =   120
    Width       =   1755
End
Begin VB.CommandButton CmdListVariations
    Appearance  =   0   'Flat
    BackColor   =   &H80000005&
    Caption     =   "List Variations"
    Height      =   435
    Left        =   5280
    TabIndex    =   2
    Top         =   120
    Width       =   1755
End
```

Listing 11.7   ENMFNTX.FRM (Continued)

```
Begin VB.CommandButton CmdListFonts
      Appearance      =   Ø   'Flat
      BackColor       =   &H8ØØØØØØ5&
      Caption         =   "List All Fonts"
      Height          =   435
      Left            =   342Ø
      TabIndex        =   1
      Top             =   12Ø
      Width           =   1755
   End
   Begin VB.ListBox List1
      Height          =   12ØØ
      Left            =   6Ø
      TabIndex        =   Ø
      Top             =   228Ø
      Width           =   6975
   End
   Begin VB.Label Label2
      BackStyle       =   Ø   'Transparent
      Caption         =   "Font variations with a family:"
      Height          =   255
      Left            =   6Ø
      TabIndex        =   6
      Top             =   2Ø4Ø
      Width           =   2595
   End
   Begin VB.Label Label1
      BackStyle       =   Ø   'Transparent
      Caption         =   "Font families:"
      Height          =   255
      Left            =   6Ø
      TabIndex        =   5
      Top             =   3ØØ
      Width           =   1395
   End
End
Attribute VB_Name = "enmfntx"
Attribute VB_GlobalNameSpace = False
Attribute VB_Creatable = False
Attribute VB_PredeclaredId = True
Attribute VB_Exposed = False

Option Explicit
```

The following two functions demonstrate the use of the user-defined parameter to the EnumFontFamilies function. This value is passed directly to the callback control event which can then use that value to decide what operation to perform.

```
Private Sub CmdListFonts_Click()
    Dim di&
    list1.Clear
    List2.Clear
    ' This gets one font for each family
    di = EnumFontFamilies(hdc, vbNullString, AddressOf Callback1_EnumFonts, 0)
End Sub

Private Sub cmdListTrueType_Click()
    Dim di&
    list1.Clear
    List2.Clear
    ' This gets one font for each family
    ' Danger - be sure to use vbNullString, not 0!  Nasty VB type conversion!
    di = EnumFontFamilies(hdc, vbNullString, AddressOf Callback1_EnumFonts, 1)

End Sub
```

Within each font family (or face name) there may be many different fonts. This usage of EnumFontFamilies allows you to enumerate all of the fonts in a particular font family.

```
Private Sub CmdListVariations_Click()
    Dim di&
    Dim fname$
    Dim f%
    list1.Clear
    fname$ = List2.Text
    f% = InStr(fname$, " -- ")
    If f% > 0 Then
        fname$ = Left$(fname$, f% - 1)
    End If

    ' This gets Arial only (all styles)
    di = EnumFontFamilies(hdc, fname$, AddressOf Callback1_EnumFonts, 2)

End Sub
```

The lpData value determines what operation to perform—it is defined entirely by the application; Windows does not use it at all. In this case, a value of zero indicates that the program is enumerating all fonts, one indicates that it should ignore non-TrueType fonts, and two indicates that the results should be placed in the lower list box. The following functions are found in the ENM-FNTX.BAS file in the Visual Basic 5.0 version of the program.

```
Public Function Callback1_EnumFonts(ByVal lpLogFont As Long, ByVal
lpTextMetrics As Long, ByVal nFontType As Long, ByVal lpData As Long) As Long
    Dim fullname$, stylename$, facename$
```

```
' agCopyData copies the data referenced by the pointer
' provided into a structure
agCopyData ByVal lpLogFont, nlf, Len(nlf)
agCopyData ByVal lpTextMetrics, ntm, Len(ntm)

' Only look at TrueType fonts.
If (lpData = 1) And ((nFontType And TRUETYPE_FONTTYPE) = 0) Then
  Callback1_EnumFonts = True
  Exit Function
  End If

If (nFontType And TRUETYPE_FONTTYPE) <> 0 Then
    fullname$ = GetNameFromByteArray(nlf.elfFullName)
    stylename$ = GetNameFromByteArray(nlf.elfStyle)
End If
If lpData = 2 And (nFontType And RASTER_FONTTYPE) <> 0 Then
    fullname$ = " Height,Width: " & ntm.tmHeight & "," & ntm.tmAveCharWidth
End If

' Non truetype fonts do not have a valid lfFullname and lfStyle field
facename$ = GetNameFromByteArray(nlf.elfLogFont.lfFaceName)

If lpData = 2 Then
    enmfntx.List1.AddItem facename$ & " -- " & fullname$ & " " & stylename$
Else
    enmfntx.List2.AddItem facename$ & " -- " & fullname$ & " " & stylename$
End If
Callback1_EnumFonts = True
End Function
```

While you can perform assignments between byte arrays and strings, the data is copied directly into the string. VB strings are Unicode internally, and since the original byte data was in ANSI, it is necessary to explicitly convert it. This function also strips off the trailing NULL characters.

```
'
' Retrieves a string from a byte array which contains
' a null terminated ANSI string
'
Public Function GetNameFromByteArray$(src() As Byte)
    Dim t$, zeropos%
    ' The array is ANSI, and needs to be converted into Unicode
    ' to fit VB's internal format
    t$ = StrConv(CStr(src), vbUnicode)
    ' And remove the null terminating character and any trailing characters
    zeropos% = InStr(t$, Chr$(0))
    If zeropos% > 1 Then t$ = Left$(t$, zeropos% - 1)
    GetNameFromByteArray$ = t$
End Function
```

```
Private Sub List2_Click()
    CmdListVariations_Click
End Sub
```

Suggestions for Further Practice

- Extend FontView to allow you to set all of the parameters to the LOG-FONT structure.

- Extend FontView to display all of the TEXTMETRIC information.

- Try the TextDemo program with different text alignment settings.

Function Reference

■ AddFontResource

VB Declaration   Declare Function AddFontResource& Lib "gdi32" Alias "AddFontResourceA" (ByVal _
  lpFileName As String)

Description   Adds a font resource to the Windows system. Once added, a font is accessible by any application.

Use with VB   No problem. .

Parameter	Type/Description
lpFileName	String—The file name of a font resource file. This can be a .FON, .FNT, .TTF, or .FOT file.

Return Value   Long—The number of fonts added. Zero on error. Sets GetLastError.

Platform   Windows 95, Windows NT, Win16

Comments   You must call the following API function after adding a resource:
di% = SendMessageBynum(HWND_BROADCAST, WM_FONTCHANGE,Ø,Ø)

where HWND_BROADCAST and WM_FONTCHANGE use the values from file API32.TXT. This informs all Windows applications that a change to the font list has occurred.

Porting Notes   This function no longer takes a module handle of a loaded font resource as a parameter.

Example   Call AddFontResource("myfont.ttf")
Call SendMessage(HWND_BROADCAST, WM_FONTCHANGE, Ø, Ø)

■ CreateFont

VB Declaration   Declare Function CreateFont& Lib "gdi32" Alias "CreateFontA" (ByVal H As Long, _
  ByVal W As Long, ByVal E As Long, ByVal O As Long, ByVal W As Long, ByVal I As _
  Long, ByVal u As Long, ByVal S As Long, ByVal C As Long, ByVal OP As Long, _
  ByVal CP As Long, ByVal Q As Long, ByVal PAF As Long, ByVal F As String)

Description   Creates a logical font with the attributes specified.

Use with VB   No problem, though the Visual Basic font properties are quite effective at selecting fonts. The parameters are described in detail earlier in this chapter. The declaration here uses single characters to reduce the line length. The letters correspond to parameters as follows:

Parameter	Type/Description
H	Long—lfHeight
W	Long—lfWidth
E	Long—lfEscapement
O	Long—lfOrientation

Parameter	Type/Description
W	Long—lfWeight
I	Long—lfItalic
u	Long—lfUnderline
S	Long—lfStrikeOut
C	Long—lfCharSet
OP	Long—lfOutputPrecision
CP	Long—lfClipPrecision
Q	Long—lfQuality
PAF	Long—lfPitchAndFamily
F	String—lfFaceName

Return Value Long—A handle to a logical font on success, zero otherwise. Sets GetLastError.

Platform Windows 95, Windows NT, Win16

Example FontView.vbp demonstrates CreateFontIndirect, which is similar.

■ CreateFontIndirect

VB Declaration
```
Declare Function CreateFontIndirect& Lib "gdi32" Alias "CreateFontIndirectA" _
(lpLogFont As LOGFONT)
```

Description Creates a logical font with the specified attributes.

Use with VB No problem, though the Visual Basic font properties are quite effective at selecting fonts.

Parameter	Type/Description
lpLogFont	LOGFONT—A LOGFONT structure defining the requested attributes for the logical font.

Return Value Long—A handle to a logical font on success, zero otherwise.

Platform Windows 95, Windows NT, Win16

Example FontView.vbp

■ CreateScalableFontResource

VB Declaration
```
Declare Function CreateScalableFontResource& Lib "gdi32" Alias _
"CreateScalableFontResourceA" (ByVal fHidden As Long, ByVal lpszResourceFile As _
String, ByVal lpszFontFile As String, ByVal lpszCurrentPath As String)
```

Description Creates a resource file for a TrueType font so that it may be added into Windows using the Add-FontResource API function. The font information is not itself copied into the font resource file; instead, the resource file contains the name of the TrueType file to use.

Use with VB   No problem.

Parameter	Type/Description
fHidden	Long—Zero to create a normal font resource, one to create a read only font resource that can be embedded in a document.
lpszResourceFile	String—The name of the resource file to create. Use the .FOT extension for normal files, .FOR for read only files.
lpszFontFile	String—The file name of the TrueType font file. If this contains a full path, the font file will be expected to be at that location and the lpszCurrentPath parameter is not used. If this contains a name and extension only, the font file is assumed to currently be at the location specified by the lpszCurrentPath parameter, and that the font will be copied into the Windows SYSTEM directory before the AddFontResource function is called.
lpszCurrentPath	String—As described under the lpszFontFile parameter.

Return Value   Long—Nonzero on success, zero on failure. Sets GetLastError.

Platform   Windows 95, Windows NT, Win16

■ DrawText

VB Declaration
```
Declare Function DrawText& Lib "user32" Alias "DrawTextA" (ByVal hdc As Long, _
ByVal lpStr As String, ByVal nCount As Long, lpRect As RECT, ByVal wFormat As _
Long)
```

Description   Draws text into the specified rectangle.

Use with VB   No problem.

Parameter	Type/Description
hdc	Long—A handle to a device context on which to draw.
lpStr	String—The text string to draw.
nCount	Long—The number of characters to draw. If the entire string is to be drawn (up to the NULL terminator), this may be set to –1.
lpRect	RECT—The formatting rectangle to use for drawing (logical coordinates).
wFormat	Long—An array of flag bits that determines how the drawing will be performed. Refer to the list of constants in Table 11.12.

Return Value   Long—The height of the text drawn.

Platform   Windows 95, Windows NT, Win16

Example   TextDemo.vbp, DrawText.vbp

Table 11.12 **Text Drawing Flags**

Flag Constant	Description
DT_BOTTOM	DT_SINGLE must also be specified. Aligns text with the bottom of the formatting rectangle.
DT_CALCRECT	Calculates the formatting rectangle as follows: On multiline drawing, the bottom of the rectangle is extended as needed to hold the text; on single-line drawing the right of the rectangle is extended. No text is drawn. The rectangle specified by the lpRect parameter is loaded with the calculated values.
DT_CENTER	Text is centered horizontally.
DT_EXPANDTABS	Tabs are expanded when text is drawn. The default tab spacing is eight characters; however, this may be changed using the DT_TABSTOP flag.
DT_EXTERNALLEADING	Use the external leading attribute of the current font when calculating the line height.
DT_LEFT	Text is left-aligned.
DT_NOCLIP	Draws without clipping to the specified rectangle.
DT_NOPREFIX	Normally, this function assumes that the "&" character indicates that the next character should be underlined. This flag turns off this behavior.
DT_RIGHT	Text is right-aligned.
DT_SINGLELINE	Draws a single line only.
DT_TABSTOP	Specifies the new tab spacing in the high eight bits of this integer.
DT_TOP	DT_SINGLE must also be specified. Aligns text with the top of the formatting rectangle.
DT_VCENTER	DT_SINGLE must also be specified. Aligns text at the center of the formatting rectangle.
DT_WORDBREAK	Performs word wrapping. Starts a new line whenever a word would exceed the rectangle boundary or a carriage return linefeed sequence is met. Has no effect if the TA_UPDATECP flag has been set using the SetTextAlign function.

■ DrawTextEx

VB Declaration   Declare Function DrawTextEx& Lib "user32" Alias "DrawTextExA" (ByVal hDC As _
Long, ByVal lpsz As String, ByVal n As Long, lpRect As RECT, ByVal un As Long, _
lpDrawTextParams As DRAWTEXTPARAMS)

Description	Similar to DrawText with additional capabilities.
Use with VB	No problem

Parameter	Type/Description
hDC	Long—A handle to a device context on which to draw.
lpsz	String—The text string to draw.
n	Long—The number of characters to draw. If the entire string is to be drawn (up to the NULL terminator), this may be set to –1.
lpRect	RECT—The formatting rectangle to use for drawing (logical coordinates).
un	Long—An array of flag bits that determines how the drawing will be performed. Includes all of the constants listed in Table 11.12 plus additional constants listed in Table 11.13.
lpDraw-TextParams	DRAWTEXTPARAMS—A structure containing additional drawing parameters. This structure is described in Appendix B.

Return Value	Long—The height of the text drawn.
Platform	Windows 95, Windows NT 4.0

Table 11.13 **Additional Text Drawing Flags**

Flag Constant	Description
DT_EDITCONTROL	Display mimics that of a multiline edit control. A partially visible line is not displayed.
DT_ENDELLIPSES	The end of a line is replaced with ellipses if the string will not fit into the rectangle. For example, ...
DT_PATHELLIPSES	If the string contains the "\" character, ellipses are substituted within the string in order to make it fit into the rectangle. For example: a long path name might be displayed thus— c:\windows\....\doc\readme.txt
DT_MODIFYSTRING	If DT_ENDELLIPSES or DT_PATHELLIPSES is specified, the string is modified to match the string actually displayed.
DT_RTLREADING	Draws text right to left if the font selected into the device context is Hebrew or Arabic.

■ EnumFontFamilies

VB Declaration
```
Declare Function EnumFontFamilies& Lib "gdi32" Alias "EnumFontFamiliesA" (ByVal _
hdc As Long, ByVal lpszFamily As String, ByVal lpEnumFontFamProc As Long, ByVal _
lParam As Long)
```

Description   Enumerates the available fonts for a given device.

Use with VB   VB 4.0 programs require the dwcbk32d.ocx custom control provided with this book.

Parameter	Type/Description
hdc	Long—Handle to a device context.
LpszFamily	String—The family of the fonts to be enumerated. Specify vb-NULLString to enumerate one font from each available font family.
lpEnumFont-FamProc	Long—Function address to call obtained using the AddressOf operator on a function from a standard module or the ProcAddress property of the dwcbk32d.ocx control.
lParam	Long—A user-defined value that you wish to pass to the callback function.

Return Value   Long—The last value returned by the callback function.

Platform   Windows 95, Windows NT, Win16

Comments   Refer to Appendix A for details on using the dwcbk32d.ocx custom control with enumeration functions under VB 4.0. This function supersedes the EnumFonts API function due to its ability to handle TrueType font style descriptions.

Only actual existing fonts are enumerated. Fonts that may be synthesized by GDI are not included. Use the Type property of the dwcbk32d.ocx control to EnumFonts when used with this function.

Example   EnumFntX.vbp

■ EnumFontFamiliesEx

VB Declaration
```
Declare Function EnumFontFamiliesEx& Lib "gdi32" Alias "EnumFontFamiliesExA" _
(ByVal hdc As Long, lpLogFont As LOGFONT, ByVal lpEnumFontProc As Long, ByVal _
lParam As Long, ByVal dw As Long)
```

Description   Enumerates the available fonts for a given device based on information provided in a LOGFONT structure.

Use with VB   VB 4.0 programs require the dwcbk32d.ocx custom control provided with this book.

Parameter	Type/Description
hdc	Long—Handle to a device context.
lpLogFont	LOGFONT—A LOGFONT structure specifying which fonts to enumerate. The fields used in this case include: lfCharSet, lfFaceName, and lfPitchAndFamily. All other fields are ignored.
lpEnumFontProc	Long—Function address to call obtained using the AddressOf operator or the ProcAddress property of the dwcbk32d.ocx control.
lParam	Long—A user-defined value that you wish to pass to the callback function.
dw	Long—Reserved, set to zero.

Return Value   Long—The last value returned by the callback function.

Platform	Windows 95, Windows NT 4.0
Comments	See Notes for EnumFontFamilies.
Example	EnumFntX.vbp demonstrates the EnumFontFamilies function which is similar.

■ EnumFonts

VB Declaration
```
Declare Function EnumFonts& Lib "gdi32" Alias "EnumFontsA" (ByVal hDC As Long, _
ByVal lpsz As String, ByVal lpFontEnumProc As Long, ByVal lParam As Long)
```

Description Enumerates the available fonts for a given device. This function has the same parameters and works in much the same way as the EnumFontFamilies function, except that EnumFontFamilies passes additional information to the callback function by using the ENUMLOGFONT and NEWTEXTMETRIC structures instead of the LOGFONT and structures. Refer to the Enum-FontFamilies function for a detailed explanation on using this function.

■ ExtTextOut

VB Declaration
```
Declare Function ExtTextOut& Lib "gdi32" Alias "ExtTextOutA" (ByVal hdc As _
Long, ByVal x As Long, ByVal y As Long, ByVal wOptions As Long, lpRect As Rect, _
ByVal lpString As String, ByVal nCount As Long, lpDx As Long)
```

Description Extended text drawing function. Refer also to the SetTextAlign function.

Use with VB No problem.

Parameter	Type/Description
hdc	Long—A handle to a device context.
x,y	Long—Point in logical coordinates specifying the starting position for drawing.
wOptions	Long—Any combination of the following flag constants: ETO_CLIPPED: Clips text output to the specified rectangle. ETO_GLPYH_INDEX: lpString is an array of glyph indexes. Refer to the description of the GetCharacterPlacement function for additional information. Win95 only. ETO_OPAQUE: Fills the rectangle with the current background color before drawing the text.
lpRect	RECT—A rectangle to use for formatting the text. May specify the Long value zero to draw text without using a rectangular region.
lpString	String—The string to draw.
nCount	Long—The number of characters in the string to draw.
lpDx	Long—If not zero, this is a pointer to an array of longs describing the spacing between each pair of characters in logical units. The first entry is the space between the first and second character, and so on. If zero, the function uses the default spacing for the font. Chapter 3 discusses techniques for passing pointers to arrays to a DLL function.

Return Value   Long—Nonzero on success, zero on failure. Sets GetLastError.

Platform   Windows 95, Windows NT, Win16

■ GetAspectRatioFilterEx

VB Declaration   `Declare Function GetAspectRatioFilterEx& Lib "gdi32" (ByVal hdc As Long, _`
`lpAspectRatio As SIZE)`

Description   The SetMapperFlags function can be used to request that Windows select only raster fonts that match the current aspect ratio of a device. This function can be used to determine the aspect ratio that is being used for this selection process.

Use with VB   No problem.

Parameter	Type/Description
hdc	Long—A handle to a device context.
lpAspectRatio	SIZE—A structure to load with the aspect ratio.

Return Value   Long—Nonzero on success, zero on failure. Sets GetLastError.

Platform   Windows 95, Windows NT, Win16

■ GetCharABCWidths

VB Declaration   `Declare Function GetCharABCWidths& Lib "gdi32" Alias "GetCharABCWidthsA" (ByVal _`
`hdc As Long, ByVal uFirstChar As Long, ByVal uLastChar As Long, lpabc As ABC)`

Description   Retrieves the A-B-C dimensions of one or more characters in a TrueType font.

Use with VB   No problem.

Parameter	Type/Description
hdc	Long—A handle to a device context.
uFirstChar	Long—The ASCII value of the first character for which to obtain A-B-C dimensions.
uLastChar	Long—The ASCII value of the last character for which to obtain A-B-C dimensions.
lpabc	ABC—The first entry in an array of ABC structures to fill with the dimensions of the characters specified. This array must be long enough to hold the dimensions of all of the characters requested.

Return Value   Long—Nonzero on success, zero on failure. Sets GetLastError.

Platform   Windows 95, Windows NT, Win16

Comments   Use the GetCharWidth function for non-TrueType fonts.

GetCharABCWidthsFloat

VB Declaration
```
Declare Function GetCharABCWidthsFloat& Lib "gdi32" Alias _
"GetCharABCWidthsFloatA" (ByVal hdc As Long, ByVal iFirstChar As Long, ByVal _
iLastChar As Long, lpABCF As ABCFLOAT)
```

Description Retrieves the A-B-C dimensions of one or more characters in a font.

Use with VB No problem.

Parameter	Type/Description
hdc	Long—A handle to a device context.
iFirstChar	Long—The ASCII value of the first character for which to obtain A-B-C dimensions.
iLastChar	Long—The ASCII value of the last character for which to obtain A-B-C dimensions.
lpABCF	ABCFLOAT—The first entry in an array of ABCFLOAT structures to fill with the dimensions of the characters specified. This array must be long enough to hold the dimensions of all of the characters requested.

Return Value Long—Nonzero on success, zero on failure. Sets GetLastError.

Platform Windows NT

Comments Unlike GetCharABCWidths, this function works on any font. The ABC values are returned as floating point numbers and may not be integers depending on the transform in effect when this function is used with non-TrueType fonts.

GetCharacterPlacement

VB Declaration
```
Declare Function GetCharacterPlacement& Lib "gdi32" Alias " _
GetCharacterPlacementA" (ByVal hdc As Long, ByVal lpsz As String, ByVal n1 As _
Long, ByVal n2 As Long, lpGcpResults As GCP_RESULTS, ByVal dw As Long)
```

Description This function retrieves information on how a string will be displayed under a given font.

Use with VB No problem.

Parameter	Type/Description
hdc	Long—A handle to a device context.
lpsz	String—The string to analyze.
n1	Long—The length of the string.
n2	Long—If the GCP_MAXEXTENT constant is specified in the dw parameter, once the displayed string exceeds the width specified by this parameter (in logical units), the function stops processing the string.
lpGcpResults	GCP_RESULTS—A GCP_RESULTS structure to load with information calculated for this string.

Parameter	Type/Description
dw	Long—One or more of the following constants: GCP_CLASSIN: The lpClass array in the lpGcpResults structure contains classifications for the characters in the string. GCP_DIACRITIC: Includes diacritic or "dead" characters in the calculations. GCP_DISPLAYZWG: Displays invisible characters used by some character sets to modify characters depending on their position within a word. GCP_GLPYPHSHAPE: Enables specialized processing of glyphs. Use as specified by the results of the GetFontLanguageInfo function. GCP_JUSTIFY: Adjusts the glyph positions to justify the string to fill the extents specified by the n2 parameter. GCP_JUSTIFYIN: The lpDX parameter in the lpGcpResults structure contains justification weights to use during the calculation. GCP_LIGATE: Use ligation to combine characters into a single ligated glyph if supported by the current font. GCP_MAXEXTENT: See the n2 parameter description. GCP_USERKERNING: Use the font kerning table in calculating character locations if one is available. Additional flags are available that enable specialized processing of Hebrew and Arabic, languages which display from right to left and for which the glyph displayed may depend on the location of a character

Return Value   Long—TRUE (nonzero) on success, zero on error. Sets GetLastError.

Platform   Windows 95, Windows NT 4.0

■ GetCharWidth, GetCharWidth32, GetCharWidthFloat

VB Declaration
```
Declare Function GetCharWidth& Lib "gdi32" Alias "GetCharWidthA" (ByVal hDC As _
Long, ByVal iFirstChar As Long, ByVal iLastChar As Long, lpBuffer As Long)
Declare Function GetCharWidth32& Lib "gdi32" Alias "GetCharWidth32A" (ByVal hdc _
As Long, ByVal iFirstChar As Long, ByVal iLastChar As Long, lpBuffer As Long)
Declare Function GetCharWidthFloat& Lib "gdi32" Alias "GetCharWidthFloatA" _
(ByVal hdc As Long, ByVal iFirstChar As Long, ByVal iLastChar As Long, pxBuffer As
Single)
```

Description   Retrieves the widths of one or more characters in a font. Use GetCharWidth32 under Win32. Use GetCharWidthFloat to obtain fractional widths.

Use with VB   No problem.

Parameter	Type/Description
hDC	Long—A handle to a device context.
iFirstChar	Long—The ASCII value of the first character for which to obtain a character width.
iLastChar	Long—The ASCII value of the last character for which to obtain a character width.

Parameter	Type/Description
lpBuffer	Long—The first entry in an array of long values to load with the character widths for the font.
pxBuffer	Single—The first entry in an array of single values to load with the character widths for the font.

Return Value Long—Nonzero on success, zero on failure. Sets GetLastError.

Platform Windows 95, Windows NT, Win16

Comments GetCharABCWidths obtains more detailed information for TrueType fonts.

■ GetFontData

VB Declaration `Declare Function GetFontData& Lib "gdi32" (ByVal hdc As Long, ByVal dwTable As _`
`Long, ByVal dwOffset As Long, lpvBuffer As Any, ByVal cbData As Long)`

Description Retrieves the data for a scalable font file. This data may then be used to embed font information into a document. This can be useful in cases where a document requires a specific font that is not commonly available on systems and the programmer wishes to include the font information with the document.

A full discussion of font embedding is beyond the scope of this book. Refer to the TrueType Fonts specification published by Microsoft for further information.

Use with VB Untested.

■ GetFontLanguageInfo

VB Declaration `Declare Function GetFontLanguageInfo& Lib "gdi32" (ByVal hdc As Long)`

Description Returns information about the font currently selected into the specified device context.

Use with VB No problem.

Parameter	Type/Description
hdc	Long—A handle to a device context.

Return Value Long—Zero for simple fonts, GCP_ERROR on error. Otherwise, one or more of the following flags:

1. GCP_DBCS: Double byte character set.

2. GCP_DIACRITIC: Font contains diacritic characters.

3. FLI_GLYPHS: Font contains glyphs that are not normally displayed.

4. GCP_GLYPHSHAPE: Font contains specialized glyphs for use where the glyph displayed depends on factors other than the character value, for example: if the glyph depends on the position of a character within a word, or ligation in which a single glyph is displayed to indicate a combination of two character values.

5. GCP_KASHIDA: Used in Arabic fonts.

6. GCP_LIGATE: Font contains ligated glyphs.

7. GCP_USERKERNING: Font contains a kerning table.

8. GCP_REORDER: Font must be reordered to display properly: Used with Hebrew and Arabic fonts.

Platform   Windows 95, Windows NT 4.0

Comments   The value returned from this function may be used to set the flags for the GetCharacterPlacement function.

Example   FontView.vbp

■ GetGlyphOutline

VB Declaration   Declare Function GetGlyphOutline& Lib "gdi32" Alias "GetGlyphOutlineA" (ByVal _
hdc As Long, ByVal uChar As Long, ByVal fuFormat As Long, lpgm As GLYPHMETRICS, _
ByVal cbBuffer As Long, lpBuffer As Any, lpmat2 As MAT2)

Description   Retrieves information about the curves that make up a character in a TrueType font. It is primarily useful for converting text into curves or manipulating fonts (tasks for which a programmer would require advanced references on font technology anyway). Refer to the TrueType Font specification published by Microsoft for further information on this function.

■ GetKerningPairs

VB Declaration   Declare Function GetKerningPairs& Lib "gdi32" Alias "GetKerningPairsA" (ByVal _
hdc As Long, ByVal cPairs As Long, lpkrnpair As KERNINGPAIR)

Description   Retrieves kerning information for the specified font.

Use with VB   No problem.

Parameter	Type/Description
hdc	Long—Handle to a device context
cPairs	Long—The number of KERNINGPAIR structures in the array referenced by the lpkrnpair parameter. Set this parameter and lpkernpair to zero to determine the size of the kerning table.
lpkrnpair	KERNINGPAIR—The first entry in an array of KERNINGPAIR structures.

Return Value   Long—The number of kerning pairs returned, zero on error. Sets GetLastError.

Platform   Windows 95, Windows NT

Comments   A KERNINGPAIR structure is defined as follows:
Type KERNINGPAIR
        wFirst As Integer

```
        wSecond As Integer
        iKernAmount As Long
End Type
```

On return, the structure will have fields set for each entry in the array as follows: wFirst specifies the first character in a two character sequence; wSecond specifies the second character. The iKernAmount field will specify the kerning distance between these two characters. For example: If the first letter is "f" and the second is "i," The kerning distance will be the logical distance added to the default character spacing when these two characters appear one after the other. This value is typically negative, as kerning typically moves characters closer together.

Example   Ex11A.vbp

GetOutlineTextMetrics

VB Declaration
```
Declare Function GetOutlineTextMetrics& Lib "gdi32" Alias _
"GetOutlineTextMetricsA" (ByVal hdc As Long, ByVal cbData As Long, lpotm As _
OUTLINETEXTMETRIC)
```

Description   Retrieves detailed information about the internal characteristics of a TrueType font. Refer to the TrueType Font specification published by Microsoft for further information on this function.

GetRasterizerCaps

VB Declaration
```
Declare Function GetRasterizerCaps& Lib "gdi32" (lpraststat As _
RASTERIZER_STATUS, ByVal cb As Long)
```

Description   Retrieves information about the ability of the system to support scalable fonts. This can be used to determine if TrueType fonts are enabled for the system.

Use with VB   No problem.

Parameter	Type/Description
lpraststat	RASTERIZER_STATUS—A structure to load with the rasterizer information. Refer to Appendix B for further information.
cb	Long—The number of bytes to copy into the structure.

Return Value   Long—Nonzero on success, zero on failure. Sets GetLastError.

Platform   Windows 95, Windows NT, Win16

Comments   The size of the structure is currently six bytes and is contained in the first integer in the RASTERIZERSTATUS structure.

GetTabbedTextExtent

VB Declaration   `Declare Function GetTabbedTextExtent& Lib "user32" Alias "GetTabbedTextExtentA" _`

```
(ByVal hdc As Long, ByVal lpString As String, ByVal nCount As Long, ByVal _
nTabPositions As Long, lpnTabStopPositions As Long)
```

Description Determines the extents of a string taking tab expansion into account. Refer also to the Tabbed-TextOut function.

Use with VB No problem.

Parameter	Type/Description
hdc	Long—A handle to a device context.
lpString	String—The string to calculate.
nCount	Long—The number of characters in the string.
nTabPositions	Long—The number of tabs in the lpnTabStopPositions array. If zero, the lpnTabStopPositions should also be NULL (you will need to create a declaration where this parameter is declared as ByVal nTabPositions&), in which case tabs will be set to a default eight-character spacing based on the average character width of the current font. If nTabPositions is one, tab spacing will be according to the first entry in the lpnTabStopPositions array.
lpnTabStop-Positions	Long—The first element in an array of tab stop positions specified in device coordinates in ascending order.

Return Value Long—The low 16 bits contain the text width in logical coordinates in the device context. The high 16 bits contain the text height. Zero on error.

Platform Windows 95, Windows NT, Win16

Comments The clipping region is not taken into account during this calculation.

■ GetTextAlign

VB Declaration `Declare Function GetTextAlign& Lib "gdi32" (ByVal hdc As Long)`

Description Retrieves the current text alignment flags for a device context.

Use with VB No problem.

Parameter	Type/Description
hdc	Long—A handle to a device context.

Return Value Long—The current text alignment flags. GDI_ERROR on error. Sets GetLastError.
 The text alignment consists of a combination of one constant from each of the groups below. The text alignment flags are shown in Table 11.14.

Platform Windows 95, Windows NT, Win16

Comments Refer to the description of the SetTextAlign function for information on text alignment flags.

Table 11.14   **Text Alignment Flags**

Horizontal Alignment Flags	TA_CENTER: Center the text within the bounding rectangle. TA_LEFT: Left-align the text within the bounding rectangle. This is the default. TA_RIGHT: Right-align the text within the bounding rectangle.
Vertical Alignment Flags	Define the meaning of the Y parameter of the text output functions. TA_BASELINE: The Y parameter specifies placement of the baseline of the font. TA_BOTTOM: The Y parameter specifies the placement of the bottom of the bounding rectangle. TA_TOP: The Y parameter specifies the placement of the top of the bounding rectangle. This is the default.
Current Position	TA_NOUPDATECP: Text output functions do not use the device context's current drawing position. TA_UPDATECP: Text output functions use the device's current position. The output function updates the current position after drawing. The X and Y parameters of the text output functions are ignored—drawing begins instead at the current position.
Other	TA_RTLREADING: Text output is right to left. Applies only to Hebrew and Arabic fonts under Windows 95.

■ GetTextCharacterExtra

VB Declaration   `Declare Function GetTextCharacterExtra& Lib "gdi32" (ByVal hdc As Long)`

Description   Retrieves the current value of the extra character spacing. Refer to the SetTextCharacterExtra function for further information.

Use with VB   No problem.

Parameter	Type/Description
hdc	Long—A handle to a device context.

Return Value   Long—The extra space between characters is added when Windows draws text.

Platform   Windows 95, Windows NT, Win16

■ GetTextCharset

VB Declaration   `Declare Function GetTextCharset& Lib "gdi32" (ByVal hdc As Long)`

Description   Retrieves the character set identifier for the font currently selected into the specified device context.

Use with VB	No problem.

Parameter	Type/Description
hdc	Long—Handle to a device context.

Return Value   Long—The character set identifier. DEFAULT_CHARSET is the default. –1 on error.

Platform   Windows 95, Windows NT 4.0

■ GetTextCharsetInfo

VB Declaration   `Declare Function GetTextCharsetInfo& Lib "gdi32" (ByVal hdc As Long, lpSig As_ FONTSIGNATURE, ByVal dwFlags As Long)`

Description   Retrieves detailed information about the character set for the currently selected font.

Use with VB   No problem.

Parameter	Type/Description
hdc	Long—Handle to a device context.
lpSig	FONTSIGNATURE—Structure to load with character set information. Information on Unicode font signatures can be found in the Unicode specification.
dwFlags	Long—Reserved. Set to zero.

Return Value   Long—The character set identifier. DEFAULT_CHARSET is the default. –1 on error.

Platform   Windows 95, Windows NT 4.0

■ GetTextColor

VB Declaration   `Declare Function GetTextColor& Lib "gdi32" (ByVal hdc As Long)`

Description   Retrieves the current text color. This is also known as the foreground color.

Use with VB   No problem. Set for picture controls and forms by the VB ForeColor property.

Parameter	Type/Description
hdc	Long—A handle to a device context.

Return Value   Long—The current RGB color setting for the text color. CLR_INVALID on error. Sets GetLastError.

Platform   Windows 95, Windows NT, Win16

■ GetTextExtentExPoint

VB Declaration
```
Declare Function GetTextExtentExPoint& Lib "gdi32" Alias _
"GetTextExtentExPointA" (ByVal hdc As Long, ByVal lpszStr As String, ByVal _
cchString As Long, ByVal nMaxExtent As Long, lpnFit As Long, alpDx As Long, _
lpSize As SIZE)
```

Description
Determines the number of characters that will fit into a specified area. Also loads an array with the extent for each character.

Use with VB
No problem.

Parameter	Type/Description
hdc	Long—A handle to a device context.
lpszStr	String—The string whose extents are being measured.
cchString	Long—The length of the lpszStr string.
nMaxExtent	Long—The horizontal extent in logical units.
lpnFit	Long—A long value to load with the number of characters that will fit into the specified extent. May be NULL (use an aliased declaration set to ByVal As Long) in which case nMaxExtent is ignored.
alpDx	Long—The first entry in an array of cchString long values. Each entry is loaded with the distance in logical units from the start of the string to this character. May be NULL (use an aliased declaration set to ByVal As Long) if you do not need this information.
lpSize	SIZE—A SIZE structure that is loaded with the height and width of the string extents.

Return Value
Long—Nonzero on success, zero on failure. Sets GetLastError.

Platform
Windows 95, Windows NT

Comments
This function can be used to calculate character positions for word wrapped text output.

■ GetTextExtentPoint, GetTextExtentPoint32

VB Declaration
```
Declare Function GetTextExtentPoint& Lib "gdi32" Alias "GetTextExtentPointA" _
(ByVal hdc As Long, ByVal lpszString As String, ByVal cbString As Long, lpSize _
As SIZE)
Declare Function GetTextExtentPoint32& Lib "gdi32" Alias _
"GetTextExtentPoint32A" (ByVal hdc As Long, ByVal lpsz As String, ByVal _
cbString As Long, lpSize As SIZE)
```

Description
Determines the extents of a string. GetTextExtentPoint32 is preferred for use under Win32 and provides more accurate results.

Use with VB   No problem.

Parameter	Type/Description
hdc	Long—A handle to a device context.
lpszString	String—The string whose extents are being measured.
cbString	Long—The length of the lpszStr string.
lpSize	SIZE—A SIZE structure that is loaded with the height and width of the string extents.

Return Value   Long—Nonzero on success, zero on failure. Sets GetLastError.

Platform   Windows 95, Windows NT, Win16 (GetTextExtentPoint only)

Comments   This function does not take clipping regions into account, but does take into account any extra space set by the SetTextCharacterExtra function.

■ GetTextFace

VB Declaration   Declare Function GetTextFace& Lib "gdi32" Alias "GetTextFaceA" (ByVal hdc As _
Long, ByVal nCount As Long, ByVal lpFacename As String)

Description   Retrieves the name of the typeface for a font.

Use with VB   No problem. This is similar to reading the VB FontName property.

Parameter	Type/Description
hdc	Long—A handle to a device context.
nCount	Long—The size of the lpFacename property.
lpFacename	String— A string to load with the typeface name of the currently selected font. This buffer must be preinitialized to at least nCount+1 characters.

Return Value   Long—The number of bytes loaded into the buffer. Zero on error. Sets GetLastError.

Platform   Windows 95, Windows NT, Win16

■ GetTextMetrics

VB Declaration   Declare Function GetTextMetrics& Lib "gdi32" Alias "GetTextMetricsA" (ByVal hdc _
As Long, lpMetrics As TEXTMETRIC)

Description   Retrieves information about the physical font selected for a device context.

Use with VB   No problem.

Parameter	Type/Description
hdc	Long—A handle to a device context.

Parameter	Type/Description
lpMetrics	TEXTMETRIC—A structure to fill with the metrics of the physical font. Refer to the TEXTMETRIC and NEWTEXTMETRIC structure fields, earlier in this chapter.

Return Value   Long—Nonzero on success, zero on failure. Sets GetLastError.

Platform   Windows 95, Windows NT, Win16

Example   FontView.vbp

■ GrayString, GrayStringByString

VB Declaration
```
Declare Function GrayString& Lib "user32" Alias "GrayStringA" (ByVal hDC As _
Long, ByVal hBrush As Long, ByVal lpOutputFunc As Long, ByVal lpData As Long, _
ByVal nCount As Long, ByVal X As Long, ByVal Y As Long, ByVal nWidth As Long, _
ByVal nHeight As Long)
Declare Function GrayStringByString& Lib "user32" Alias "GrayStringA" (ByVal _
hDC As Long, ByVal hBrush As Long, ByVal lpOutputFunc As Long, ByVal lpData As _
String, ByVal nCount As Long, ByVal X As Long, ByVal Y As Long, ByVal nWidth As _
Long, ByVal nHeight As Long)
```

Description   Draws a "grayed" string like that used by Windows to indicate the disabled state. This function uses the current font, but ignores the background and text color.

Use with VB   No problem.

Parameter	Type/Description
hDC	Long—A handle to a device context.
hBrush	Long—A brush to use for the graying. If zero, uses the current brush.
lpOutputFunc	Long—A pointer to a function to output the text. Normally use zero to use the TextOut function. Otherwise this may be a procedure address as returned by the AddressOf operator using a standard function or the ProcAddress property of the dwcbk32d.ocx custom control. Refer to Appendix A for further details.
lpData	Long—As a string (when lpOutputFunc is NULL), this is the string to gray. Otherwise it's a long variable that will be passed to the callback function.
nCount	Long—The number of characters to print. If zero and lpData is a string, this calculates the length of the string.
X,Y	Long—The X,Y coordinates of the rectangle that bounds the string.
nWidth	Long—The width of the rectangle that bounds the string in device units. If zero, the value is calculated based on the string.
nHeight	Long—The height of the rectangle that bounds the string in device units. If zero, the value is calculated based on the string.

Return Value	Long—TRUE (nonzero) on success, zero if the TextOut function or the dwcbk32d.ocx text drawing event returns zero.
Platform	Windows 95, Windows NT, Win16
Porting Notes	The hBrush parameter is new to Win32

■ PolyTextOut

VB Declaration   `Declare Function PolyTextOut& Lib "gdi32" Alias "PolyTextOutA" (ByVal hdc As _`
`Long, pptxt As POLYTEXT, cStrings As Long)`

Description   Draws a series of strings.

Use with VB   No problem.

Parameter	Type/Description
hdc	Long—A device context to draw into.
pptxt	POLYTEXT—The first entry in an array of POLYTEXT structures describing the location and contents of strings to draw.
cStrings	Long—The number of entries in the pptxt array.

Return Value   Long—Nonzero on success, zero on failure. Sets GetLastError.

Platform   Windows NT

Comments   A POLYTEXT structure is defined as follows:
```
Type POLYTEXT
        x As Long
        y As Long
        n As Long
        lpStr As String
        uiFlags As Long
        rcl As Rect
        pdx As Long
End Type
```

x,y specifies the reference location for the string. The string is aligned to this reference point according to the current text alignment settings for the device context.

n is the number of characters in the string.

lpStr is the string to draw. Refer to Chapter 15 for information on handling strings in structures.

uiFlags can be one or more of the following: ETO_CLIPPED to clip the output to the rectangle specified by the rcl field. ETO_OPAQUE to fill the rcl rectangle with the current background color.

rcl is the bounding rectangle if ETO_CLIPPED is specified.

pdx contains the address of a block of memory that contains an array of long values to load with the width of each character.

■ RemoveFontResource

VB Declaration   `Declare Function RemoveFontResource& Lib "gdi32" Alias "RemoveFontResourceA" _`
`(ByVal lpFileName As String)`

Description   Removes a font resource from the Windows system. The font will not be removed immediately if it is currently in use by another application.

Use with VB   No problem.

Parameter	Type/Description
lpFileName	String—The file name of a font resource file.

Return Value   Long—Nonzero on success, zero on failure. Sets GetLastError.

Platform   Windows 95, Windows NT, Win16

Comments   You must call the following API function after removing a resource:
`di% = SendMessageBynum(HWND_BROADCAST, WM_FONTCHANGE,0,0)`

where HWND_BROADCAST and WM_FONTCHANGE are constant values from file API32.TXT. This informs all Windows applications that a change to the font list has occurred. The font file on disk is not deleted by this function.

■ SetMapperFlags

VB Declaration   `Declare Function SetMapperFlags& Lib "gdi32" (ByVal hdc As Long, ByVal dwFlag _`
`As Long)`

Description   When Windows is mapping fonts, this function may be used to select raster fonts that match the aspect ratio of the device. Not used for TrueType fonts. Refer to function GetAspectRatioFilter for further information.

Use with VB   No problem.

Parameter	Type/Description
hdc	Long—A handle to a device context.
dwFlag	Long—Use the constant ASPECT_FILTERING to request that GDI select fonts that match the aspect ratio of the device.

Return Value   Long—The previous value of the font mapping flag. GDI_ERROR on error. Sets GetLastError.

Platform   Windows 95, Windows NT, Win16

■ SetTextAlign

VB Declaration   `Declare Function SetTextAlign& Lib "gdi32" (ByVal hdc As Long, ByVal wFlags As _`
`Long)`

Description Sets the text alignment and specifies the use of the device context current position during text output.

Use with VB Be sure to restore the original alignment to any VB form or control that you modify. You can obtain the existing alignment using the GetTextAlign function.

The alignment specified here is used in the TextOut, ExtTextOut, and TabbedTextOut functions.

Parameter	Type/Description
hdc	Long—A handle to a device context.
wFlags	Long—As shown in Table 11.14 under the GetTextAlign function.

Return Value Long—The previous text alignment flags. GDI_ERROR on error. Sets GetLastError.

Platform Windows 95, Windows NT, Win16

■ SetTextCharacterExtra

VB Declaration
```
Declare Function SetTextCharacterExtra& Lib "gdi32" (ByVal hdc As Long, ByVal _
nCharExtra As Long)
```

Description Specifies the extra spacing to insert between characters when drawing text.

Use with VB Be sure to restore the original character spacing for a VB form or control if you change this setting.

Parameter	Type/Description
hdc	Long—A handle to a device context.
nCharExtra	Long—The extra space to add between characters specified in logical coordinates in the device context.

Return Value Long—The previous extra spacing for this device context.

Platform Windows 95, Windows NT, Win16

■ SetTextColor

VB Declaration
```
Declare Function SetTextColor& Lib "gdi32" (ByVal hdc As Long, ByVal crColor As _
Long)
```

Description Sets the current text color. This is also known as the foreground color.

Use with VB Be sure to restore the original text color for VB forms and controls if you change this setting.

Parameter	Type/Description
hdc	Long—A handle to a device context.
crColor	Long—The new text color.

Return Value Long—The previous RGB color setting for the text color. CLR_INVALID on error. Sets GetLastError.

Platform   Windows 95, Windows NT, Win16

■ SetTextJustification

VB Declaration
```
Declare Function SetTextJustification& Lib "gdi32" (ByVal hdc As Long, ByVal _
nBreakExtra As Long, ByVal nBreakCount As Long)
```

Description   This function is used to justify lines by specifying the extra space that a line should take. The extra space is divided among the break characters in the line. The break character is defined by the font but is usually the space character. You can use the GetTextMetrics function to determine the break character for a font. The normal sequence of operations when you wish to justify text is as follows:

    1. Calculate the extent of the string using the GetTextExtentPoint32 API function.

    2. Determine how much space (in logical coordinates) to add to the line in order to justify it. This is typically the right margin minus the horizontal extent of the text.

    3. Count the number of break characters in the line of text.

    4. Call the SetTextJustification function using the extra space and number of break characters as parameters.

    5. Call the text-drawing function.

    This function maintains an error term internally to correct for round-off errors during justification. This allows you to distribute the extra spacing between different parts of a line (if the line contains several fonts) by breaking the line into segments and calling this function for each segment. This error term must be cleared for a new line by calling the function with a zero value for the nBreakExtra and nBreakCount parameters.

Use with VB   No Problem—but be sure to clear the error term for a VB form or control if you use this function.

Parameter	Type/Description
hdc	Long—A handle to a device context.
nBreakExtra	Long—The amount of extra space to add to the string when drawing.
nBreakCount	Long—The number of break characters in which to distribute the extra space.

Return Value   Long—Nonzero on success, zero on failure. Sets GetLastError.

Platform   Windows 95, Windows NT, Win16

Example   DrawText.vbp

■ TabbedTextOut

VB Declaration
```
Declare Function TabbedTextOut& Lib "user32" Alias "TabbedTextOutA" (ByVal hdc _
As Long, ByVal x As Long, ByVal y As Long, ByVal lpString As String, ByVal _
nCount As Long, ByVal nTabPositions As Long, lpnTabStopPositions As Long, ByVal _
nTabOrigin As Long)
```

Description	Text-drawing function that supports tabs. Refer also to the SetTextAlign function.
Use with VB	No problem.

Parameter	Type/Description
hdc	Long—A handle to a device context.
x,y	Long—Point in logical coordinates specifying the starting position for drawing.
lpString	String—The string to draw.
nCount	Long—The number of characters in the string to draw.
nTabPositions	Long—The number of tabs in the lpnTabStopPositions array. If zero, the lpnTabStopPositions should also be NULL (you will need to create a declaration where this parameter is declared as ByVal nTabPositions&) in which case tabs will be set to a default eight-character spacing based on the average character width of the current font. If nTabPositions is one, tab spacing will be according to the first entry in the lpnTabStopPositions array.
lpnTabStop-Positions	Long—The first element in an array of tab stop positions specified in device coordinates in ascending order. A negative value indicates that the text should be right-aligned on the tab stop instead of the default left alignment (Win95 only).
nTabOrigin	Long—Specifies the origin to use for tabbing. This is useful if you call the function several times for the same line and wish to maintain the same tab origin.

Return Value	Long—The extents of the string, with the height in the high 16 bits and the width in the low 16 bits of the result.
Platform	Windows 95, Windows NT, Win16
Example	DrawText.vbp

■ TextOut

VB Declaration	Declare Function TextOut& Lib "gdi32" Alias "TextOutA" (ByVal hdc As Long, _ ByVal x As Long, ByVal y As Long, ByVal lpString As String, ByVal nCount As _ Long)
Description	Text-drawing function. Refer also to the SetTextAlign function.
Use with VB	No problem.

Parameter	Type/Description
hdc	Long—A handle to a device context.
x,y	Long—Point in logical coordinates specifying the starting position for drawing.

Parameter	Type/Description
lpString	String—The string to draw.
nCount	Long—The number of characters in the string to draw.

Return Value   Long—Nonzero on success, zero on failure. Sets GetLastError.

Platform   Windows 95, Windows NT, Win16

Comments   Within a path, if the drawing background mode is opaque (see the SetBkMode function), the outline created will consist of the character cell minus the character. When the background mode is transparent, the outline will consist of the character glyph itself.

Example   FontView.vbp, DrawText.vbp, TextDemo.vbp

12

Printing

PRINTING IS ONE AREA WHERE DRAMATIC CHANGES HAVE BEEN MADE recently both in Windows and in Visual Basic. The printer object in Visual Basic 4.0 and later versions is substantially improved over earlier versions. It makes it easy to select printers, to display graphics on printers, and to change printer settings. At first glance, a Visual Basic programmer might be tempted to believe that it is no longer necessary to use the Windows API for printing, and in many situations this will be true.

But at the same time that Visual Basic has improved its printing support, Windows itself has evolved, adding new capabilities that once again can only be accessed using API function calls. Specifically, Win32 provides a great deal of control over the printing subsystems—far more than was available under Win16. In fact, the Win32 printing system has changed dramatically from Win16.

In addition to taking advantage of the new Win32 features, there are other situations where you may want to use API printing functions instead of those built into Visual Basic. One is where you are taking advantage of API drawing functions. Another is where you are using a VBA-based application that does not provide extensive printer object support.

The Windows API is so flexible, however, that some of its features are beyond the scope of this book. For example, an in-depth discussion of relative kerning of device fonts is probably of interest only to those writing their own high-end desktop publishing applications. Also, Win32 provides a great deal of low-level direct access to the print spooler—more than a typical Visual Basic programmer would ever need. In fact, you can even create your own print manager using the API functions that are available. An in-depth discussion of all of the spooler functions would take far more space than is available here, so the emphasis will be on explaining some of the key concepts relating to the printing subsystem and illustrating some of the fundamental techniques that you will need to take advantage of them.

This chapter contains three sample programs. PicPrint demonstrates a number of techniques for configuring a printer and printing graphical information. Spooler.vbp illustrates a number of techniques that are commonly used when working with the print spooler functions, and introduces some new approaches towards implementing complex API calls. DocJob.vbp shows you how you can bypass GDI to write your own print job directly to the spooler. prWatch.vpb shows one technique for monitoring the state of a printer.

Printing in Windows

Before going into detail on how to perform certain printing tasks under Visual Basic, it is important to discuss how printing works in the Windows environment. This section will also describe the key differences between Win16 and Win32.

Printer Device Contexts

A printer device context can be used in exactly the same way as any other device context. This means that all of the graphic functions described in previous chapters work the same way for printers as they do for display devices. This device independence is one of the powerful features that Windows provides. It is possible to create a drawing function that accepts a device context as a parameter. The function will draw on either the screen or the printer depending on the device context used.

The Win32 Printing Subsystem

The heart of the Win32 printing system is the spooler. The spooler driver, Winspool.drv, coordinates the entire printing process. Figure 12.1 illustrates what happens when you print a document under 32-bit Windows. First, your application requests a printer device context from the spooler. When you perform graphic operations on the device context, those operations are recorded in the form of journal records. This is similar to the way a metafile records graphic operations that can be played back as needed. There are a number of types of journal records which are supported under Win32. These data types include GDI graphic commands, Postscript commands, and raw data. You can specify the type of journaling that a printer should use, though in most cases you will just accept the defaults set via the print manager.

After a page has been completed, the graphic commands are run through a print processor. This is a driver that converts the journal records into device driver instructions that are supported by a particular printer's device driver. Next, the graphics engine for the printer converts the device driver instructions into the raw binary data that is required by the particular printer. This conversion process can be very slow or extremely fast, depending on the printer. For example, on a Postscript printer, the conversion process is extremely fast at this point because the printer is able to handle the postscript commands directly. On a dot matrix printer this process can be extremely slow, as the graphics engine converts the graphic instructions into individual printer bands.

The spooler then sends the final output to whichever printer was originally selected for output using this device context. This is accomplished by way of a DLL called a port monitor.

There are some crucial differences between this system and the one used under Windows 3.x. Under 16-bit Windows applications, worked closely with individual printer drivers—in fact, it was common for applications to directly call driver functions that were responsible for printer configuration. When creating a printer device context, it was necessary to specify the printer driver to use, the name of the individual printer (for drivers that supported more than one printer), and the port to which the printer was connected. Win16 applications made frequent use of the Escape function—a function that bypassed the GDI system to allow applications to directly access the printer driver.

Figure 12.1

The Win32 printing subsystem

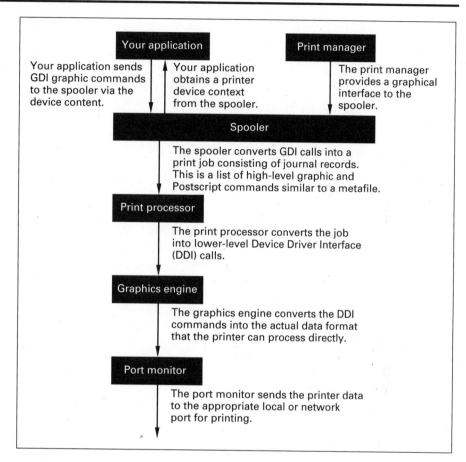

Win32 increases the separation between the application and the individual printer drivers. This is evident from a number of subtle changes in the Win32 functions and parameters. For example, you no longer specify the name of the printer driver when calling the CreateDC function to obtain a printer device context. Instead, you simply use the name of the print spooler itself: WINSPOOL. The device name is no longer the name of the specific printer type, but rather the name assigned to the printer using the print manager. It is no longer necessary to specify the output port to use—the spooler uses the current printer connection. The Win32 API contains additional API functions to control printer connections.

Also, it is no longer necessary to call functions within the individual printer drivers in order to configure a printer (a task that required use of an interface dynamic link library since Visual Basic cannot choose at runtime which driver to call). Instead, an application calls functions in the standard Winspool driver.

Another interesting change from Win16 relates to the role of the print manager. Under Windows 3.*x*, if the print manager application was closed, it was possible for an application to print directly to a printer without spooling. Under Win32, the print manager application is little more than a user interface to the print spooler. The print spooler driver itself is always active and cannot be bypassed (though it can be configured to send documents directly to a printer or port without creating a spool file, in which case the spooler is essentially duplicating the behavior that you would expect if no spooler was present).

In other words, you must differentiate between the spooler as a dynamic link library that controls the entire process of printing under Win32, and spooling as the process of creating a print queue that holds a number of print documents in a queue prior to printing them. The spooler is always present, but whether it actually performs a spooling operation for a printer depends on how the printer is configured.

The Default Printer and Others

The system registry contains information describing the printers connected to the system and which one is the default printer. You can print into the default printer or any printer connected to the system (including print servers on a network). The easiest way to determine the default printer is by reading the WIN.INI initialization file using the GetProfileString function (which under Win32 automatically references the system registry). This is the technique used in the samples for this chapter. Chapter 13 describes how initialization files and the system registry can be accessed.

The default printer settings for a driver are also kept in the system registry, and can be easily modified using the capabilities provided by the Win32 API.

Printer Configuration

Each printer driver provides a setup dialog box that allows the user to configure the printer. This dialog box is accessed by way of the spooler using the DeviceCapabilties, DocumentProperties, and AdvancedDocumentProperties functions. The features provided by these functions include:

- The ability to determine the capabilities of a printer.

- The ability to retrieve the current settings of the printer.

- The ability to temporarily change the printer configuration without affecting other applications. This may be accomplished under program control or via the printer setup dialog box.

■ The ability to keep a copy of printer settings unique to your application in a private initialization file or the system registry so that you can preserve a printer configuration required for a particular application or document.

Many of these techniques are demonstrated in the PicPrint example program and are described in detail in the reference section of this chapter.

The DocumentProperties and AdvancedDocumentProperties functions replace the DeviceMode and ExtDevMode functions in the Win16 API.

Table 12.1 lists the printer configuration functions.

Table 12.1 **Printer Configuration Functions**

Function Attribute	Description
AdvancedDocumentProperties	Brings up a dialog box for document settings.
ConfigurePort	Brings up a dialog box for port configuration.
ConnectToPrinterDlg	Brings up a dialog box for connecting to a network printer.
DeviceCapabilties	Determines current settings and capabilities for a printer.
DocumentProperties	A general-purpose routine for retrieving and setting printer configuration for a document.
PrinterProperties	Brings up a dialog box for printer property configuration.
ResetPrinter	Sets the default printer settings that are used with documents printed using the StartDocPrinter function.

Printer Objects

Each printer in the system is considered a type of object, and like other objects, it is possible to open a printer and obtain a handle to an open printer object. Printer handles are required by many of the functions that are used to obtain information about a printer or to control its behavior. It is also possible to use this object for synchronization, for example, to suspend an operation until a printer-related event such as the addition or completion of a job occurs. System objects are described in more detail in Chapter 14. Printer handles should be closed using the ClosePrinter API when they are no longer needed.

Keep in mind that a printer object from the Windows perspective is not the same thing as the printer object that you work with under Visual Basic.

The Printing Sequence

Once a device context has been obtained for a printer, there are several steps that need to be performed before drawing begins. Consider the differences between a printer and a screen display.

A screen has a single drawing area, which can be erased. A printer page cannot be erased, but you can print multiple pages. Applications share the display by drawing into windows that are owned by the application. This approach is clearly not applicable to printers where it is necessary to keep all of the pages grouped by application and by document. A printer needs a mechanism for controlling paging and for managing documents so that applications do not conflict with each other.

Figure 12.2 illustrates the sequence used in printing under Windows. Note that the actual drawing commands are identical to those used for display devices.

Windows deals with printing on both a page and document level. On the document level, the StartDoc API function informs Windows that you are beginning a document. Windows will make sure that all pages in a document are printed together. Without this capability, if more than one application was printing it would be possible for pages from different applications to be mixed with each other during printing. The EndDoc API function informs Windows that the document is complete. Windows will then begin the process of spooling data from the disk to the printer.

The StartPage and EndPage API functions bracket the graphics operations on a page. There is one interesting subtlety to printing that has a significant impact on the ability to abort printing operations. When you perform a graphics operation to a display device, the operation takes place immediately. This is possible because the entire screen is available to a display device context at all times. A printer device driver, on the other hand, generally needs to prepare the entire page in memory before sending it to the printer. Once a page is printed, no further printing to that page is possible.

A printer device context must accumulate all of the information required to print a page before it actually begins to send output to the printer. As a result, all graphics operations to a printer are in fact stored by the spooler in a series of journal records until the EndPage API function is executed. At that time, the records are processed by the print processor and graphics engine and converted into output data in the format or language expected by the printer.

Windows also supports a technique known as *banding*, which allows you to print under limited memory situations by dividing the print area into bands. This technique was used frequently in earlier versions of Windows, and in fact was often implemented manually by programmers. Windows 3.0 significantly improved the performance of printers, mostly by providing sufficient memory to hold entire pages of data in memory when necessary. In addition, many printers now support advanced page description languages that accept graphics

Figure 12.2

Printing under
windows

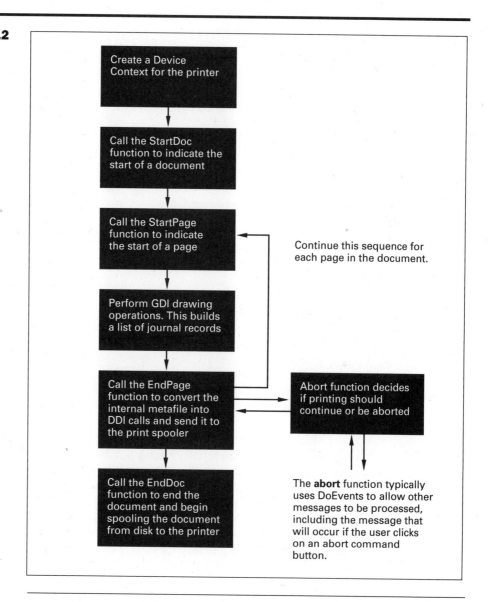

information, eliminating the need to draw all of the graphics into memory before sending it to the printer. As a result, banding is rarely handled on the programmer's level. This book assumes that you will draw graphics on a page level and allow Windows to perform any internal banding, if necessary.

Table 12.2 lists the functions used for most printing operations.

Table 12.2 **High-level Printing Functions**

Function Attribute	Description
AbortDoc	Aborts printing of the current document
EndDocAPI	Signals that a document is complete
EndPage	Signals the end of a page
Escape	Sends raw data to the printer
ResetDC	Resets the document device mode settings for a device context
SetAbortProc	Sets a printer abort procedure that allows a long print job to be aborted
StartDoc	Signals the start of a new document
StartPage	Indicates the start of a new page

Aborting the Print Operation

As you have seen, Windows creates a series of journal records for graphic commands that are executed as needed during the EndPage function. Building a journal—a process that is little more than recording GDI graphics functions—is a very fast operation. Converting the graphics into the format required for the printer may be extremely time-consuming. As a result, the EndPage function can take a very long time to finish.

In order to make it possible to abort a print operation in progress, Windows allows you to specify a special abort function using the SetAbortProc API function. This function is called by Windows during execution of the EndPage function. The abort function returns a value indicating whether printing should continue. Visual Basic does not directly support function callbacks of this type; however, this book provides the dwcbk32d.ocx custom control, which can be used to trigger an event whenever the abort function is called.

One technique that is frequently used is the creation of a dialog box that has a button for aborting the print job. The abort function periodically allows events to be processed, so a button click can be detected. The PicPrint example program demonstrates this technique.

Low-level Spooler Control

Win32 provides direct access to many spooler functions. Normally, when you write data to a device context, the spooler is responsible for translating graphic commands into data that is placed into a file for spooling to a printer. It is possible for you to directly access these low-level functions to open a printer, create a spool document, and write data directly into the spool file. This is demonstrated in the DocJob.vbp example later in this chapter. Table 12.3 lists these low-level functions. Generally speaking, these functions should be avoided.

Table 12.3 **Low-level Printing Functions**

Function Attribute	Description
EndDocPrinter	Terminates a print document that was started with the Start-DocPrinter function
EndPagePrinter	Signals the end of a page started with the StartPagePrinter function
ReadPrinter	Allows you to read information sent by a printer
StartDocPrinter	Starts spooling a new print document
StartPagePrinter	Informs the spooler that a new page is being sent to the spooler
WritePrinter	Writes spooled data to a printer

Printing and Visual Basic

The Windows API functions are generally compatible with Visual Basic. There are, however, areas where conflicts can occur that should be avoided.

Compatibility Issues

Visual Basic provides an object called the *printer object* that supports printing to the any of the printers on the system. The printer object provides access to the printer device context via the hDC property, which may be used as a parameter to most API graphics functions. This provides the first and most common level of API support for printing.

When using the hDC property of the printer object for API printing the same rules apply that were described in earlier chapters with regard to window device contexts. You must be careful to restore the device context to its original state when you are finished drawing with API functions. Remember that changing the mapping mode or other device context attributes can interfere with the Visual Basic drawing commands, so mix the two with caution.

Unlike Visual Basic 3.0, Visual Basic 4.0 and later will not print a page correctly if you use only API functions to draw on the printer device context. For this reason, it is necessary to perform a Visual Basic printer operation before calling API graphic commands. The printer operation need not actually draw anything—in the PicPrint example, the program simply prints a space character, which will have no effect on the final output.

Even though Visual Basic provides NewPage and EndDoc methods for the printer object device context, you should not attempt to mix the Windows API printer control functions with those methods. In other words, the Start-Doc, StartPage, EndPage, and EndDocAPI API functions should not be used on the printer object or the device context, nor should the SetAbortProc function be used to attempt to create a printer abort capability to the printer object. The reason for this is that the Visual Basic methods do not correspond directly to the API functions. The PicPrint sample application demonstrates two approaches for printing, one which uses the Visual Basic printer object, the other which uses only API functions.

Printer Configuration and Visual Basic

The Visual Basic printer object exposes a great deal of information via properties including metrics (such as width and height) and information about the printer configuration. In many cases this information is stored internally within Visual Basic and is not read dynamically from the printer. This means that if you modify the characteristics of the printer object by modifying the device context state, these changes will not necessarily be reflected in the Visual Basic properties. A classic example of this is the fact that using the ResetDC function to change a printer from portrait to landscape mode will not update the Scale-Width and ScaleHeight properties. Fortunately, Visual Basic now allows you a great deal of control over the printer using the printer object itself, so in most cases you will not need to modify the configuration using the API.

Driver Quirks

One of the great strengths of Windows is its ability to provide device-independent output. In theory, once you have written a printer output routine that works with one printer, it will work perfectly with all printers.

In practice, this is not always the case. Each printer has its own printer driver, and some printer drivers can be extremely sophisticated. Each one is therefore prone to its own set of potential bugs or features.

To create a robust printing application using API calls, there are a number of steps you can take. First, before performing raster operations, verify that the printer has in fact implemented the appropriate commands. The GetDevice-Caps function described in Chapter 7 allows you to obtain information on the features supported by the device. This includes the device's ability to support BitBlt transfers or device-independent bitmap (DIB) functions. You can also determine if the printer can transfer bitmaps over 64K in size. If not, you may find it necessary to divide the bitmap into smaller segments for transfer.

You may create memory device contexts that are compatible with a printer. These device contexts use the same printer driver and thus have the same feature set as the actual printer device context.

Printer Settings and the DEVMODE Structure

There are hundreds of printers available that work with Windows, each of which has its own unique features. It is the responsibility of the printer driver to support these features and provide a way for a Windows application to modify them. This is accomplished primarily via the DocumentProperties function and a special data structure known as the DEVMODE structure.

It is possible to use the DEVMODE structure to change the printer configuration during printing by using the ResetDC function between pages. This function also works on the Visual Basic printer object, though the changes may not be reflected in the printer object properties.

The definition of the DEVMODE structure appears in Listing 12.1. It is important to keep in mind that in addition to the standard fields defined in the listing, each printer driver may define its own private data area. The fields in this private data area are not accessible to the programmer, but it is necessary to allocate sufficient buffer space to include this data area when using the DocumentProperties function. Some printer drivers will fail if this extra space is not present. You can use the DocumentProperties function to determine the exact size of the DEVMODE structure. As you will see in the PicPrint example, the variable nature of this structure requires additional effort to handle correctly in Visual Basic.

The DEVMODE structure can also be used with display devices, though this is rather uncommon.

Listing 12.1   The DEVMODE structure

```
Type DEVMODE
        dmDeviceName As String * CCHDEVICENAME
        dmSpecVersion As Integer
        dmDriverVersion As Integer
        dmSize As Integer
        dmDriverExtra As Integer
        dmFields As Long
        dmOrientation As Integer
        dmPaperSize As Integer
        dmPaperLength As Integer
        dmPaperWidth As Integer
        dmScale As Integer
        dmCopies As Integer
        dmDefaultSource As Integer
```

Listing 12.1   The DEVMODE structure (Continued)

```
            dmPrintQuality As Integer
            dmColor As Integer
            dmDuplex As Integer
            dmYResolution As Integer
            dmTTOption As Integer
            dmCollate As Integer
            dmFormName As String * CCHFORMNAME
            dmUnusedPadding As Integer
            dmBitsPerPel As Integer
            dmPelsWidth As Long
            dmPelsHeight As Long
            dmDisplayFlags As Long
            dmDisplayFrequency As Long
End Type
```

Under Windows 95 and NT 4.0, add the following fields to the DEV-MODE structure after the dmDisplayFrequency field:

```
dmICMMethod As Long
dmICMIntent As Long
dmMediaType As Long
dmDitherType As Long
dmReserved1 As Long
dmReserved2 As Long
```

Table 12.4 describes the fields of the DEVMODE structure. Not all fields apply to every printer. You can use the dmFields field to determine which fields in a particular structure are valid.

Table 12.4   DEVMODE Structure Fields

Field	Description
dmDeviceName	The name of the printer. This is the name shown by the print manager.
dmSpecVersion	The DEVMODE version. You should set this to &H320 under Win32 if you are creating a structure from scratch, but should not otherwise rely on this value for useful information.
dmDriverVersion	The version of the printer driver.
dmSize	The total size of the DEVMODE structure not including the private data area.
dmDriverExtra	The size of the private data area of the DEVMODE structure.
dmFields	Specifies which entries in the DEVMODE structure are valid. Refer to the API32.TXT field for a list of flag constants with the prefix DM_

Table 12.4   **DEVMODE Structure Fields (Continued)**

Field	Description
dmOrientation	One of the following two constants: DMORIENT_PORTRAIT for portrait mode, or DMORIENT_LANDSCAPE for landscape mode.
dmPaperSize	Specifies the current paper size. If zero, the dmPaperLength and dmPaperWidth fields are used to set the paper size. Otherwise, this field refers to one of the constant values as defined in file API32.TXT with the prefix DMPAPER_.
dmPaperLength	The paper length measured in tenths of a millimeter. This field takes precedence over the dmPaperSize field.
dmPaperWidth	The paper width measured in tenths of a millimeter. This field takes precedence over the dmPaperSize field.
dmScale	Scales the page size by a factor of X/100. For example, if the paper size is 8 1/2 x 11 and the dmScale is 4, the application will see a page size of 34 x 44. All output will be scaled to fit on the paper.
dmCopies	Specifies the number of copies to print.
dmDefaultSource	Reserved—set to zero.
dmPrintQuality	Specifies the print quality to use for printers that support multiple resolutions. These may be specified by the constants in file API32.TXT that begin with the prefix DMRES_. If the dmYResolution field is not zero, this field contains the horizontal resolution in dots per inch and the dmYResolution field contains the vertical resolution in dots per inch.
dmColor	One of the following constants: DMCOLOR_COLOR for color printers, DMCOLOR_MONOCHROME for monochrome printers.
dmYResolution	Refer to the description of the dmPrintQuality field.
dmTTOption	Specifies how to print TrueType fonts. It is one of the following constants: DMTT_BITMAP prints TrueType fonts as graphics. This is used for most dot matrix printers. DMTT_DOWNLOAD downloads TrueType fonts to the printer. This is used for most PCL (LaserJet-compatible) printers. DMTT_SUBDEV uses a device font if available. This is used for most PostScript printers.
dmUnusedPadding	Reserved—do not use.
dmCollate	One of the constants: DMCOLLATE_TRUE or DMCOLLATE_FALSE. When TRUE, the driver will ask the printer to collate multiple copies if it supports that capability.
dmFormName	The name of the printer form to use (NT only).
dmLogPixels	Specifies the number of pixels in a logical inch for this device.
dmBitsPerPel	The number of bits per pixel for display devices. Not used with printers.

Table 12.4 **DEVMODE Structure Fields (Continued)**

Field	Description
dmPelsWidth, dmPelsHeight	The width and height of the display in pixels. Not used with printers.
dmDisplayFlags	If DM_GRAYSCALE, indicates a monochrome or gray scale device. If DM_INTERLACED, indicates an interlaced display. Not used with printers.
dmDisplay Frequency	Specifies the frequency of the display. Not used with printers.
dmICMMethod	One of the constants DMICM_? from file API32.TXT. Determines if internal color matching is in effect, and if so whether it is being handled at the application, printer, or driver level. Win95 & NT 4.0 only.
dmICMIntent	One of the constants: DMICM_SATURATE to minimize dithering. DMICM_CONTRAST to match the requested contrast. DMICM_COLORMETRIC to match colors as closely as possible. DMICM_USER or greater for device driver specified values. Win95 & NT4.0 only.
dmMediaType	One of the constants DMMEDIA_?? from file API32.TXT, indicating the type of paper or media in use.
dmDitherType	One of the constants DMDITHER_?? from file API32.TXT, indicating the type of dithering to use.

Table 12.1 lists the functions that work with the DEVMODE structure to retrieve and set the printer configuration.

Printer Escapes

Under Win16, it was common to use printer escapes to directly access specialized printer capabilities that were not directly accessible by way of API functions. Under Win32, the Escape function is rarely used. Most of the frequently used escapes have been replaced by Win32 API functions or new parameters to existing functions. For example, the GETPHYSPAGESIZE escape has been replaced by the PHYSICALWIDTH and PHYSICAL-HEIGHT options in the GetDeviceCaps function (described in Chapter 7).

Controlling the Print Spooler

The functions listed in Table 12.5 summarize the functions that are available for directly controlling all aspects of the printing subsystem from spooler job management to printer configuration. The Spooler.vbp and DocJob.vbp samples illustrate some of the techniques that you will need to work with these functions. In addition, you should keep the following points in mind:

- Many of the printer configuration functions are restricted by Windows NT security and require that the calling application have sufficient permission for them to work.

- Many functions use data structures that contain pointers to string information or data structures. Refer to the section titled "Spooler Functions and Structures" that follows later in this chapter.

- By necessity, the descriptions of these functions in this book are limited, with an emphasis on issues relating to using the functions from within Visual Basic. Additional information can be found in the Win32 online help files. The Microsoft Developer's Network CD-ROM is also an indispensable resource for working with these functions (the Windows NT resource kit and Windows NT Device Driver Developer Kit included therein contain extensive information on the printing subsystem).

Table 12.5   Spooler Control Functions

Function Attribute	Description
AbortPrinter	Deletes the current spool file for a printer
AddForm	Adds a new form to a printer
AddJob	A low-level function for creating your own spool file for a job
AddMonitor	Installs a printer monitor
AddPort	Makes the specified port accessible to the current system
AddPrinter	Adds a new printer to the system
AddPrinterConnection	Adds a printer connection—typically to a printer on a remote server
AddPrinterDriver	Installs a new printer driver
AddPrintProcessor	Installs a print processor
AddPrintProvidor	Installs a print providor
DeleteForm	Deletes a form from a printer
DeleteMonitor	Removes a print monitor
DeletePort	Removes access to the specified port

Table 12.5   Spooler Control Functions (Continued)

Function Attribute	Description
DeletePrinter	Disconnects or removes a printer from the system
DeletePrinterConnection	Disconnects from a remote printer
DeletePrinterDriver	Removes a printer driver
DeletePrintProcessor	Removes a print processor added with AddPrintProcessor
DeletePrintProvidor	Removes a providor added with AddPrintProvidor
EnumForms	Enumerates the forms that are available to a printer
EnumJobs	Enumerates the print jobs queued for a specified printer
EnumMonitors	Enumerates the available print monitors
EnumPorts	Enumerates the available local ports
EnumPrinterDrivers	Enumerates the available printer drivers
EnumPrinters	Enumerates the available printers
EnumPrintProcessorDatatypes	Enumerates the datatypes supported by a print processor
EnumPrintProcessors	Enumerates the print processors
FindClosePrinterNotification	Closes a printer notification object
FindFirstPrinterChangeNotification	Creates a printer change notification object
FindNextPrinterNotification	Retrieves information about a signaled printer notification object
FreePrinterNotifyInfo	Frees a system buffer allocated by FindNextPrinterNotification
GetJob	Retrieves information about a print job
GetPrinter	Retrieves information about a printer
GetPrinterData	Retrieves printer configuration information from the system registry
GetPrinterDriver	Retrieves information about the driver for a specified printer
GetPrinterDriverDirectory	Retrieves the directory that should hold all printer driver DLLs
GetPrintProcessorDirectory	Retrieves the directory that should hold all print processor DLLs

Table 12.5   **Spooler Control Functions (Continued)**

Function Attribute	Description
PrinterMessageBox	Displays a message box indicating a printer error on the system which owns a specified print job
ScheduleJob	Schedules a specified print job
SetForm	Sets the current form for a printer
SetJob	Allows you to control a print job (start, stop, or suspend)
SetPrinter	Allows you to control a printer
SetPrinterData	Sets printer configuration information into the system registry

Spooler Functions and Structures

Many of the spooler functions work with structures that are used to set and retrieve information. These functions tend to follow a standard format that is important to understand before you attempt to use them. Consider the Get-Printer function, which is defined thus:

```
Declare Function GetPrinter& Lib "spoolss.dll" Alias "GetPrinterA" (ByVal _
hPrinter As Long, ByVal Level As Long, pPrinter As Byte, ByVal cbBuf As Long, _
pcbNeeded As Long)
```

Parameter	Type/Description
hPrinter	Long—A handle to an open printer. This handle is obtained using the OpenPrinter function.
Level	Long—The level of structure requested.
pPrinter	Byte—A pointer to the first byte in an array to load with the requested information.
cbBuf	Long—The number of bytes in the pPrinter buffer.
pcbNeeded	Long—A pointer to a long variable to load with the number of the required buffer size, or the number of bytes actually read.
pcReturned	Long—Not used in this example, it is set to the number of structures loaded into the buffer for those functions that can return more than one structure.

This function can obtain different types of information by loading a buffer with a structure containing printer information. Consider these two structures:

```
Type PRINTER_INFO_1
        flags As Long
        pDescription As Long
        pName As Long
        pComment As Long
End Type

Type PRINTER_INFO_4
        pPrinterName As Long
        pServerName As Long
        Attributes As Long
End Type
```

The GetPrinter function can load either of these structures (not to mention a few others that are not described here). How does it know which structure you want? That's the job of the Level parameter. If the Level parameter is 1, the function assumes that you want to load a PRINTER_INFO_1 structure, 4 indicates a PRINTER_INFO_4 structure, and so on. Note that not every operating system supports every type of printer information structure. This technique for specifying structure type makes it possible for Microsoft to add additional structure types in the future.

Your first reaction might be to ask, Why not just create some aliased declarations, one for each structure? To see the answer, consider the PRINTER_INFO_1 structure. It is true that this structure is only 16 bytes in size, but the buffer needed to hold the result is 120 bytes! Why? Because the Long variables such as pDescription and pName are pointers to strings, and those strings are placed in the buffer that you create. This makes it necessary to allocate a byte array that is large enough to hold both the strings and the structure. The size can be determined by calling the function first with the cbBuf parameter set to zero. In this case the function will return an error result (zero), but will load into the pcbNeeded variable the required buffer size. This value is then used to redim the byte array. The function is then called again with pPrinter set to the first element in the byte array (element zero), and cbBuf to the size of the array. This time the function should succeed.

The following sample code from the project Ex12A.vbp demonstrates this procedure.

```
Dim pi As PRINTER_INFO_1
    Dim hPrinter&, res&
    Dim needed&

    res = OpenPrinter(txtPRName.Text, hPrinter, 0)
    If res = 0 Then
        MsgBox "Can't open printer - Specify a valid printer name"
```

```
        Exit Sub
    End If
    ' Find out how large the buffer needs to be
    res = GetPrinter(hPrinter, 1, 0, 0, needed)
    ReDim buffer(needed) As Byte
    res = GetPrinter(hPrinter, 1, buffer(0), needed, needed)
    ' Copy to a structure
    agCopyData buffer(0), pi, Len(pi)
    txtDescription.Text = agGetStringFromPointer(pi.pDescription)

    Call ClosePrinter(hPrinter)
```

As you see, the beginning of the buffer is copied to a local copy of the PRINTER_INFO_1 structure. This makes it possible to access individual fields within the structure. The long value pi.pDescription is an address of a NULL terminated string. This can easily be converted to a Visual Basic string using the agGetStringFromPointer function that is part of the APIGID32.DLL support DLL that comes with this book.

You may be wondering, why use long variables for these string addresses? Why not use strings? As you will see in Chapter 15, it is sometimes possible to define structures with string variables and have them work correctly—in fact, we do this in other samples in this chapter when passing information to the API function. However, when it comes to returning information from an API function, the string type is not compatible with the API—in this case Visual Basic would interpret the pointer values as BSTR string types, leading to an instant memory exception after the data copy. You can find additional information on working with strings within structures in Chapter 15.

The technique shown here applies to many of the functions described in this chapter, and this description is referenced by their descriptions in the function reference in order to conserve space. In those cases, the Byte parameter always refers to the first byte in a buffer to load with the desired information, the cbBuf and pcbNeeded parameters are as described here. Some functions can return more than one of a given structure (the spooler enumeration functions). These functions also have a parameter called pcReturned that is set to the number of structures loaded into the buffer. The Spooler.vbp example illustrates this.

Examples

This chapter contains a number of sample programs that illustrate how to work with the printer and print spooler. The Spooler.vbp project also demonstrates a new approach to working with API functions.

The prWatch.vbp example is not included in the text of this book but may be found on the CD-ROM. This example shows how you can monitor a printer for changes. Some of the techniques used in this example will not be described until Chapter 14, so you may wish to hold off reviewing this example until after you have covered synchronization techniques that are described there.

Due to the fact that each printer has a different driver, and that drivers vary in quality, it is impossible to guarantee that this code will run correctly on every printer. These samples have been tested on both Windows NT and Windows 95 (where appropriate—some samples are specific to Windows NT), and for three different printer configurations: an HP LaserJet 5P under both PCL and Postscript mode, and an Epson Color Stylus. This is based on the idea that if a program runs correctly on an industry standard PCL printer, a Postscript printer and a color printer, any problems that occur with other printers are more likely to be in the individual printer driver than in the program itself.

These sample programs make no effort to verify if a function is valid under the operating system that you are using—their focus is entirely on demonstrating printing and spooling functionality.

PicPrint—Prints a Bitmap and Shows Printer Configuration

PicPrint is a program that demonstrates a number of the techniques described in this chapter. It illustrates a method for printing a bitmap to a printer that will work successfully with most printers and accurately preserves the color of the bitmap. It shows how to read the printer configuration information and change it temporarily during printing.

Using PicPrint

The PicPrint screen has a single picture control, which holds the bitmap to print. Figure 12.3 shows the PicPrint program in action. The ConfigPrinter menu provides a number of different configuration options and demonstrates how to display various configuration dialog boxes. The PrinterProperties and DocumentProperties commands bring up the printer configuration and default document configuration dialog boxes respectively under Windows NT 3.51. Both bring up the same tabbed printer setup dialog under Windows 95 and NT 4.0 as shown in Figure 12.4. The DocumentProperties command also demonstrates how to read the current DEVMODE settings for a printer and displays information about the printer as shown in Figure 12.5. The ConfigureLPT1 command brings up a port configuration dialog box. The ConnectToPrinter brings up the remote printer connection dialog under Windows NT but has no effect on Windows 95. The PaperSizes command shows how to read a DEVMODE structure and extract information on available paper sizes from the structure as shown in Figure 12.6.

Note that not all of these functions are supported by every print driver. You may wish to temporarily load a LaserJet or PostScript printer driver to demonstrate these functions.

Figure 12.3

Mail form for the
PicPrint example

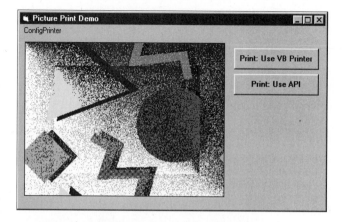

Figure 12.4

Printer configuration
dialog box

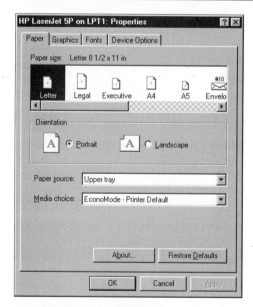

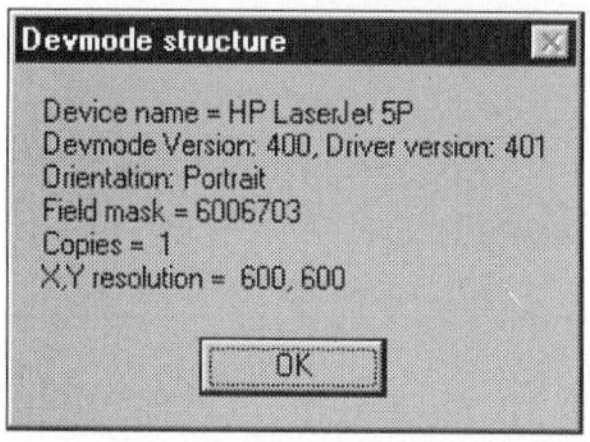

Figure 12.5

Summary of
DEVMODE
information in the
PicPrint example

Devmode structure

```
Device name = HP LaserJet 5P
Devmode Version: 400, Driver version: 401
Orientation: Portrait
Field mask = 6006703
Copies = 1
X,Y resolution = 600, 600
```

OK

Figure 12.6

Summary of paper sizes in the PicPrint example

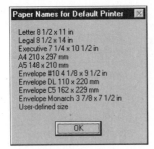

The two command buttons shown in Figure 12.3 print the bitmap in the picture control. The bitmap is actually printed twice on the same page: One version is a direct unscaled copy, the other stretches the bitmap to fill the rest of the page. The API printing function also shows how to temporarily set the printer into landscape mode. The latter function also demonstrates how to display an abort printing dialog box that allows you to cancel printing if necessary.

In many cases you will find that printing is so fast that the abort printing dialog is shown only briefly. One of the advantages of the new Win32 printing architecture is that much of the work of printing is offloaded from the application very quickly. In some cases (depending on your printer configuration) you may find that when you click on the abort printing button there is a delay before the printing is actually canceled; depending on the size of the bitmap being printed and the speed of the system, this could be several minutes. During the end of page processing, the internal journal records are converted into a series of graphic calls to the printer. Windows does not call the abort function during individual graphic calls. The StretchDIBits function is extremely slow in this application and an abort command received while this function is in progress will not be processed until it is complete.

Project Description

The PicPrint project includes five files. PICPRINT.FRM is the main form used in the program. The ABORTFOR.FRM form is used to allow the user to abort printing. PICPRINT.BAS contains the constant type and function declarations. APIGID32.BAS contains the declarations for the APIGID32.DLL dynamic link library. dwcbk32d.ocx is the generic callback custom control included on the program disk of this book, which enables use of callback functions with Visual Basic 4.0. This custom control is described in detail in Appendix A.

Even though the PicPrint example was ported from the original 16-bit API guide, no effort was made in this case to support both 16- and 32-bit code—this was a straight port to 32 bits. During porting, the greatest changes related to the printer configuration routines, which were completely different from those used under Win16. The actual drawing code ported very easily.

PicPrint Form Descriptions

Listing 12.2 contains the headers from file PicPrint.frm and ABORT-FOR.FRM that describe the control setup for the forms.

Listing 12.2   PicPrint form definitions

```
VERSION 5.00
Begin VB.Form Picprint
    Caption         =   "Picture Print Demo"
    ClientHeight    =   4005
    ClientLeft      =   1380
    ClientTop       =   2055
    ClientWidth     =   7365
    BeginProperty Font
        name            =   "MS Sans Serif"
        charset         =   0
        weight          =   700
        size            =   8.25
        underline       =   0   'False
        italic          =   0   'False
        strikethrough   =   0   'False
    EndProperty
    ForeColor       =   &H80000008&
    Height          =   4695
    Left            =   1320
    LinkMode        =   1   'Source
    LinkTopic       =   "Form1"
    ScaleHeight     =   4005
    ScaleWidth      =   7365
    Top             =   1425
    Width           =   7485
    Begin VB.CommandButton CmdPrintAPI
        Appearance      =   0   'Flat
        BackColor       =   &H80000005&
        Caption         =   "Print: Use API"
        Height          =   495
        Left            =   5160
        TabIndex        =   2
        Top             =   840
        Width           =   2055
    End
    Begin VB.CommandButton CmdPrint
        Appearance      =   0   'Flat
        BackColor       =   &H80000005&
        Caption         =   "Print: Use VB Printer"
        Height          =   495
        Left            =   5160
        TabIndex        =   1
        Top             =   240
```

Listing 12.2   PicPrint form definitions (Continued)

```
        Width           =   2055
      End
      Begin VB.PictureBox Picture1
         Appearance     =   0  'Flat
         AutoRedraw     =   -1  'True
         BackColor      =   &H80000005&
         ForeColor      =   &H80000008&
         Height         =   3615
         Left           =   120
         Picture        =   "PICPRINT.frx":0000
         ScaleHeight    =   3585
         ScaleWidth     =   4785
         TabIndex       =   0
         Top            =   120
         Width          =   4815
      End
      Begin VB.Menu MenuConfigPrinter
         Caption        =   "ConfigPrinter"
         Begin VB.Menu mnuPrinterProperties
            Caption      =   "PrinterProperties"
         End
         Begin VB.Menu mnuConfigurePort
            Caption      =   "Configure LPT1"
         End
         Begin VB.Menu mnuConnectToPrinter
            Caption      =   "ConnectToPrinter"
         End
         Begin VB.Menu mnuDocProperties
            Caption      =   "DocumentProperties"
         End
         Begin VB.Menu MenuPaperSizes
            Caption      =   "PaperSizes"
         End
      End
   End
Attribute VB_Name = "Picprint"
Attribute VB_GlobalNameSpace = False
Attribute VB_Creatable = False
Attribute VB_PredeclaredId = True Attribute VB_Exposed = False
```

File PICPRINT.FRX is the binary file for this form. It contains the definition of the Picture property for control Picture1. You may remove the line

```
Picture = PICPRINT.FRX:0000
```

in which case you should load a bitmap into the control's Picture property in Visual Basic design mode. The sample program uses the bitmap PARTY.BMP, which goes back to Windows 3.1.

The ABORTFOR.FRM form is defined as follows:

```
VERSION 5.00
Begin VB.Form AbortForm
    Caption         =   "Abort Printing"
    ClientHeight    =   1695
    ClientLeft      =   2235
    ClientTop       =   2340
    ClientWidth     =   3795
    BeginProperty Font
        name            =   "MS Sans Serif"
        charset         =   0
        weight          =   700
        size            =   8.25
        underline       =   0   'False
        italic          =   0   'False
        strikethrough   =   0   'False
    EndProperty
    ForeColor       =   &H80000008&
    Height          =   2100
    Left            =   2175
    LinkMode        =   1   'Source
    LinkTopic       =   "Form1"
    ScaleHeight     =   1695
    ScaleWidth      =   3795
    Top             =   1995
    Visible         =   0   'False
    Width           =   3915
    Begin VB.CommandButton CmdAbort
        Appearance      =   0   'Flat
        BackColor       =   &H80000005&
        Caption         =   "Press to Abort Print Job"
        Height          =   495
        Left            =   600
        TabIndex        =   0
        Top             =   480
        Width           =   2535
    End
End
Attribute VB_Name = "AbortForm"
Attribute VB_GlobalNameSpace = False
Attribute VB_Creatable = False
Attribute VB_PredeclaredId = True Attribute VB_Exposed = False
```

PicPrint Listings

Module PICPRINT.BAS (Listing 12.3) contains the constant, type, and function declarations used by the program.

The following public constants from file API32.TXT are used in this application and are not shown here in order to conserve space:

- All trinary raster operations (SRCCOPY, SRCPAINT, and so forth).

Listing 12.3	**Listing for file PICPRINT.BAS**

```
Attribute VB_Name = "PICPRINT1"
Option Explicit

' Global constants
```

- All DEVMODE constants with the prefix DM_, DMORIENT_, DMPAPER_, DMBIN_, DMRES_, DMCOLOR_, DMDUP_, DMTT_, DC_, and DCTT.

- Function error codes with the prefix SP_.

- GetDeviceCaps constants such as BITSPIXEL, PLANES, and so on.

- Global memory constants with the prefix GMEM_.

```
Public Const DIB_RGB_COLORS = Ø
Public Const DIB_PAL_COLORS = 1

' Global variables
Public AbortPrinting%
Public UseHourglass%

'  size of a device name string
Public Const CCHDEVICENAME = 32

'  size of a form name string
Public Const CCHFORMNAME = 32

Public Const BI_RGB = Ø&

Type POINTAPI
        x As Long
        y As Long
End Type

Type DEVMODE
        dmDeviceName As String * CCHDEVICENAME
        dmSpecVersion As Integer
        dmDriverVersion As Integer
        dmSize As Integer
        dmDriverExtra As Integer
        dmFields As Long
        dmOrientation As Integer
        dmPaperSize As Integer
        dmPaperLength As Integer
        dmPaperWidth As Integer
        dmScale As Integer
```

```
            dmCopies As Integer
            dmDefaultSource As Integer
            dmPrintQuality As Integer
            dmColor As Integer
            dmDuplex As Integer
            dmYResolution As Integer
            dmTTOption As Integer
            dmCollate As Integer
            dmFormName As String * CCHFORMNAME
            dmUnusedPadding As Integer
            dmBitsPerPel As Integer
            dmPelsWidth As Long
            dmPelsHeight As Long
            dmDisplayFlags As Long
            dmDisplayFrequency As Long
    End Type


Type PRINTER_DEFAULTS
            pDatatype As String
            pDevMode As Long
            DesiredAccess As Long
    End Type


Type DOCINFO
            cbSize As Long
            lpszDocName As String
            lpszOutput As String
    End Type


Type BITMAPINFOHEADER '40 bytes
            biSize As Long
            biWidth As Long
            biHeight As Long
            biPlanes As Integer
            biBitCount As Integer
            biCompression As Long
            biSizeImage As Long
            biXPelsPerMeter As Long
            biYPelsPerMeter As Long
            biClrUsed As Long
            biClrImportant As Long
    End Type


Type RGBQUAD
            rgbBlue As Byte
            rgbGreen As Byte
            rgbRed As Byte
            rgbReserved As Byte
    End Type
```

This example is hard coded for a 16-color bitmap.

```
' BITMAPINFO for this example is for 16 color bitmap
Type BITMAPINFO
        bmiHeader As BITMAPINFOHEADER
        bmiColors(15) As RGBQUAD
End Type

Type BITMAP
        bmType As Long
    '   bmWidth As Long
        bmHeight As Long
        bmWidthBytes As Long
        bmPlanes As Integer
        bmBitsPixel As Integer
        bmBits As Long
End Type

Public Const PRINTER_ACCESS_ADMINISTER = &H4

Public Declare Function GetProfileString Lib "kernel32" Alias _
"GetProfileStringA" (ByVal lpAppName As String, ByVal lpKeyName As String, _
ByVal lpDefault As String, ByVal lpReturnedString As String, ByVal nSize As _
Long) As Long
Declare Function OpenPrinter Lib "winspool.drv" Alias "OpenPrinterA" (ByVal _
pPrinterName As String, phPrinter As Long, pDefault As PRINTER_DEFAULTS) As Long
Declare Function OpenPrinterBynum Lib "winspool.drv" Alias "OpenPrinterA" _
(ByVal pPrinterName As String, phPrinter As Long, ByVal pDefault As Long) AsLong
Declare Function ResetPrinter Lib "winspool.drv" Alias "ResetPrinterA" (ByVal _
hPrinter As Long, pDefault As PRINTER_DEFAULTS) As Long
Declare Function ClosePrinter Lib "winspool.drv" (ByVal hPrinter As Long) As Long
Declare Function PrinterProperties Lib "winspool.drv" (ByVal hwnd As Long, _
ByVal hPrinter As Long) As Long
Declare Function DocumentProperties Lib "winspool.drv" Alias _
"DocumentPropertiesA" (ByVal hwnd As Long, ByVal hPrinter As Long, ByVal _
pDeviceName As String, ByVal pDevModeOutput As _
Long, ByVal pDevModeInput As Long, ByVal fMode As Long) As Long
Declare Function AdvancedDocumentProperties Lib "winspool.drv" Alias _
"AdvancedDocumentPropertiesA" (ByVal hwnd As Long, ByVal hPrinter As Long, _
ByVal pDeviceNameAs String, pDevModeOutput As DEVMODE, ByVal pDevModeInput _
As Long) As Long
Declare Function ConnectToPrinterDlg Lib "winspool.drv" (ByVal hwnd As Long, _
ByVal flags As Long) As Long
Declare Function ConfigurePort Lib "winspool.drv" Alias "ConfigurePortA" (ByVal _
```

```
pName As String, ByVal hwnd As Long, ByVal pPortName As String) As Long
Declare Function DeviceCapabilities Lib "winspool.drv" Alias _
"DeviceCapabilitiesA" (ByVal lpDeviceName As String, ByVal lpPort As String, _
ByVal iIndex As Long, ByVal lpOutput As String, ByVal lpDevMode As Long) As Long
Declare Function CreateDCBynum Lib "gdi32" Alias "CreateDCA" (ByVal _
lpDriverName As String, ByVal lpDeviceName As String, ByVal lpOutput As String, _
ByVal lpInitData As Long) As Long
Declare Function BringWindowToTop Lib "user32" (ByVal hwnd As Long) As Long
Declare Function StartDoc Lib "gdi32" Alias "StartDocA" (ByVal hdc As Long, _
lpdi As DOCINFO) As Long
Declare Function StartPage Lib "gdi32" (ByVal hdc As Long) As Long
Declare Function EndPage Lib "gdi32" (ByVal hdc As Long) As Long
Declare Function EndDocAPI Lib "gdi32" Alias "EndDoc" (ByVal hdc As Long) As _
Long
Declare Function AbortDoc Lib "gdi32" (ByVal hdc As Long) As Long
Declare Function SetAbortProc Lib "gdi32" (ByVal hdc As Long, ByVal lpAbortProc _
As Long) As Long
Declare Function CreateCompatibleDC Lib "gdi32" (ByVal hdc As Long) As Long
Declare Function GetObjectAPI Lib "gdi32" Alias "GetObjectA" (ByVal hObject As _
Long, ByVal nCount As Long, lpObject As Any) As Long
Declare Function GetDeviceCaps Lib "gdi32" (ByVal hdc As Long, ByVal nIndex As _
Long) As Long
Declare Function GlobalAlloc Lib "kernel32" (ByVal wFlags As Long, ByVal _
dwBytes As Long) As Long
Declare Function GlobalFree Lib "kernel32" (ByVal hMem As Long) As Long
Declare Function GlobalLock Lib "kernel32" (ByVal hMem As Long) As Long
Declare Function GetDIBits Lib "gdi32" (ByVal aHDC As Long, ByVal hBitmap As _
Long, ByVal nStartScan As Long, ByVal nNumScans As Long, lpBits As Any, lpBI _
AsBITMAPINFO, ByVal wUsage As Long) As Long
Declare Function SetDIBitsToDevice Lib "gdi32" (ByVal hdc As Long, ByVal x As _
Long, ByVal y As Long, ByVal dx As Long, ByVal dy As Long, ByVal SrcX As Long, _
ByVal SrcY As Long, ByVal Scan As Long, ByVal NumScans As Long, Bits As Any, _
BitsInfo As BITMAPINFO, ByVal wUsage As Long) As Long
Declare Function StretchDIBits Lib "gdi32" (ByVal hdc As Long, ByVal x As Long, _
ByVal y As Long, ByVal dx As Long, ByVal dy As Long, ByVal SrcX As Long, ByVal _
SrcY As Long, ByVal wSrcWidth As Long, ByVal wSrcHeight As Long, lpBits As Any, _
lpBitsInfo As BITMAPINFO, ByVal wUsage As Long, ByVal dwRop As Long) As Long
Declare Function GlobalUnlock Lib "kernel32" (ByVal hMem As Long) As Long
Declare Function DeleteDC Lib "gdi32" (ByVal hdc As Long) As Long
```

Listing 12.4 is the form listing for PICPRINT.FRM.

Listing 12.4 **Form listing PICPRINT.FRM**

Function GetDefPrinter$ can be used to extract the definition of the default printer from the system registry. The GetDeviceDriver$, GetDeviceName$, and GetDeviceOutput$ functions divide this string into its driver, description, and output port components.

```
Option Explicit

'    This function retrieves the definition of the default
'    printer on this system
'
Private Function GetDefPrinter$()
    Dim def$
    Dim di&

    def$ = String$(128, 0)
    di = GetProfileString("WINDOWS", "DEVICE", "", def$, 127)
    def$ = agGetStringFromLPSTR$(def$)
    GetDefPrinter$ = def$

End Function

'    This function returns the driver module name
'
Private Function GetDeviceDriver$(dev$)
    Dim firstpos%, nextpos%
    firstpos% = InStr(dev$, ",")
    nextpos% = InStr(firstpos% + 1, dev$, ",")
    GetDeviceDriver$ = Mid$(dev$, firstpos% + 1, nextpos% - firstpos% - 1)
End Function

'    Retrieves the name portion of a device string
'
Private Function GetDeviceName$(dev$)
    Dim npos%
    npos% = InStr(dev$, ",")
    GetDeviceName$ = Left$(dev$, npos% - 1)
End Function

'    Returns the output destination for the specified device
'
Private Function GetDeviceOutput$(dev$)
    Dim firstpos%, nextpos%
    firstpos% = InStr(dev$, ",")
    nextpos% = InStr(firstpos% + 1, dev$, ",")
    GetDeviceOutput$ = Mid$(dev$, nextpos% + 1)
End Function
```

Several of the configuration commands require a handle to a printer. OpenDefaultPrinter uses the GetDefPrinter function to obtain information about the default printer, then opens it. The optional DeviceName parameter is passed by reference from the calling function and is set to the printer name on exit. Note that this sample program is assumed to be running on an administrator access account when run under Windows NT. If your account does not have administrator access, parts of the application will not be fully functional and an error may occur.

```
Public Function OpenDefaultPrinter(Optional DeviceName) As Long
    Dim dev$, devname$, devoutput$
    Dim hPrinter&, res&
    Dim pdefs As PRINTER_DEFAULTS

    pdefs.pDatatype = vbNullString
    pdefs.pDevMode = 0
    pdefs.DesiredAccess = PRINTER_ACCESS_ADMINISTER


    dev$ = GetDefPrinter$()  ' Get default printer info

    If dev$ = "" Then Exit Function
    devname$ = GetDeviceName$(dev$)
    devoutput$ = GetDeviceOutput$(dev$)

    If Not IsMissing(DeviceName) Then
        DeviceName = devname$
    End If

    ' You can use OpenPrinterBynum to pass a zero as the
    ' third parameter, but you won't have full access to
    ' edit the printer properties
    res& = OpenPrinter(devname$, hPrinter, pdefs)
    If res <> 0 Then OpenDefaultPrinter = hPrinter
End Function
```

The mnuDocProperties_Click function demonstrates a number of important techniques. The function first calls DocumentProperties without specifying any buffers in order to determine the size of the DEVMODE structure for this device. Two byte buffers are dimensioned to this size. It is critical that these buffers be allocated dynamically in this manner—memory exceptions can occur if you try to use just a DEVMODE structure without allocating sufficient space for the printer specific information that follows it in memory.

Once the buffers are created, a second call is made using the DM_IN_PROMPT and DM_OUT_BUFFER flags. The prompt flag causes the printer configuration dialog to be shown. Any changes that you make to the printer settings are then combined into the current device settings and output to the dmOutBuf buffer. Note that the dmInBuf buffer is not actually used in this particular function. The output buffer data is copied into DEVMODE data structures, which can be easily accessed under program control in BASIC.

```
'    Demonstration of the Document Properties function
'
Private Sub mnuDocProperties_Click()
    Dim dm As DEVMODE, dmout As DEVMODE
    Dim bufsize&, res&
    Dim dmInBuf() As Byte
    Dim dmOutBuf() As Byte
    Dim hPrinter&
    Dim DeviceName$

    hPrinter = OpenDefaultPrinter(DeviceName$)
    If hPrinter = 0 Then
        MsgBox "Unable to open default printer"
        Exit Sub
    End If

    ' The output DEVMODE structure will reflect any changes
    ' made by the printer setup dialog box.
    ' Note that no changes will be made to the default
    ' printer settings!
    bufsize = DocumentProperties(hwnd, hPrinter, DeviceName$, 0, 0, 0)
    ReDim dmInBuf(bufsize)
    ReDim dmOutBuf(bufsize)

    res = DocumentProperties(hwnd, hPrinter, DeviceName$, _
    agGetAddressForObject(dmOutBuf(0))_
    , agGetAddressForObject(dmInBuf(0)),   DM_IN_PROMPT Or DM_OUT_BUFFER)

    ' Copy the data buffer into the DEVMODE structure
    agCopyData dmOutBuf(0), dmout, Len(dmout)
    ShowDevMode dmout

    ClosePrinter hPrinter
End Sub

' Shows information about the current device mode
'
Private Sub ShowDevMode(dm As DEVMODE)
    Dim crlf$
    Dim a$

    crlf$ = Chr$(13) + Chr$(10)
    a$ = "Device name = " + agGetStringFromLPSTR$(dm.dmDeviceName) + crlf$
    a$ = a$ + "Devmode Version: " + Hex$(dm.dmSpecVersion) + _
    ", Driver version: " + Hex$(dm.dmDriverVersion) + crlf$
    a$ = a$ + "Orientation: "
    If dm.dmOrientation = DMORIENT_PORTRAIT Then a$ = a$ + "Portrait" Else a$ = _
    a$ + "Landscape"
```

```
        a$ = a$ + crlf$
        a$ = a$ + "Field mask = " + Hex$(dm.dmFields) + crlf$
        a$ = a$ + "Copies = " + Str$(dm.dmCopies) + crlf$
        If dm.dmFields And DM_YRESOLUTION <> 0 Then
            a$ = a$ + "X,Y resolution = " + Str$(dm.dmPrintQuality) + "," + _
            Str$(dm.dmYResolution) _
            + crlf$
        End If
        MsgBox a$, 0, "Devmode structure"
End Sub
```

The other port configuration and printer configuration functions are very straightforward.

```
Private Sub mnuConfigurePort_Click()
    Dim dev$, devname$, devoutput$
    Dim hPrinter&, res&
    dev$ = GetDefPrinter$() ' Get default printer info

    If dev$ = "" Then Exit Sub
    devname$ = GetDeviceName$(dev$)
    devoutput$ = GetDeviceOutput$(dev$)
    Call ConfigurePort(vbNullString, hwnd, "LPT1:")
End Sub

Private Sub mnuConnectToPrinter_Click()
    Call ConnectToPrinterDlg(hwnd, 0)
End Sub

Private Sub mnuPrinterProperties_Click()
    Dim hPrinter&

    hPrinter& = OpenDefaultPrinter()
    If hPrinter = 0 Then
        MsgBox "Can't open default printer"
        Exit Sub
    End If
    Call PrinterProperties(hwnd, hPrinter)
    Call ClosePrinter(hPrinter)
End Sub
```

The MenuPaperSizes_Click function retrieves a list of paper sizes available to the printer. The routine first determines the number of paper sizes supported, then allocates a string that has 64 characters per paper size. In this case we use a string buffer rather than a byte buffer because we are retrieving text information. Unlike binary data, the internal conversion by Visual Basic of text strings into Unicode does no harm. The string is scanned in 64 character blocks. For each block the agGetStringFromLPSTR function extracts a Visual Basic string that consists of the string up until the NULL termination character.

```
'    This function shows how to use the DeviceCapabilities
'    function to find out how many paper names the device
'    supports. This technique can be used for any
'    device capability
'
Private Sub MenuPaperSizes_Click()
    Dim dev$, devname$, devoutput$
    Dim papercount&
    Dim papername$
    Dim a$, tname$
    Dim x&, di&

    dev$ = GetDefPrinter$() ' Get default printer info
    If dev$ = "" Then Exit Sub
    devname$ = GetDeviceName$(dev$)
    devoutput$ = GetDeviceOutput$(dev$)

    ' Find out how many paper names there are
    papercount = DeviceCapabilities(devname$, devoutput$, DC_PAPERNAMES, _
    vbNullString, 0)
    If papercount = 0 Then
        MsgBox "No paper names available", 0, "Paper name capability"
        Exit Sub
    End If

    ' Now dimension the string large enough to hold them all
    papername$ = String$(64 * papercount, 0)
    di = DeviceCapabilities(devname$, devoutput$, DC_PAPERNAMES, papername$, 0)

    ' Now display the results
    For x = 1 To papercount
        tname$ = Mid$(papername$, (x - 1) * 64 + 1)
        a$ = a$ + agGetStringFromLPSTR$(tname$) & vbCrLf
    Next x
    MsgBox a$, 0, "Paper Names for Default Printer"
End Sub
```

The PrintBitmap function prints the bitmap in the picture property of the Picture1 control twice. The first time it is printed at 1:1 scale using the SetDIBitsToDevice function. Next the function calculates how much space is left on the page and scales the bitmap to fill that space using the StretchDIBits function.

This function uses the techniques introduced in Chapter 9 for determining the size of a bitmap and for copying a bitmap into a device-independent bitmap. The function also uses the GetDeviceCaps function to find out if the printer driver supports the device-independent bitmap functions.

Device-independent bitmaps are the best way to print due to their ability to correctly handle color conversions. You are extremely unlikely to run into a raster printer driver under Win32 that does not support DIBs or that is limited to 64K bitmaps. If you do, it is still possible to print by using BitBlt or

StretchBlt to copy monochrome bitmaps (which are standard across all devices), or to break a large bitmap up into smaller segments.

Keep in mind, however, that there are some printer technologies that do not handle bitmaps at all (typewriter style printers or plotters, for example). Thus you should still test for these capabilities using the GetDeviceCaps function.

This function also uses the global memory allocation functions to create a buffer for the device-independent bitmap data. This is used instead of a Visual Basic string in order to avoid Unicode string conversions on binary data. Global memory functions are described in detail in Chapter 15.

Note how the PrintBitmap function can work with either the VB printer object or your own device context.

```
'   Prints the bitmap in the picture1 control to the
'   printer context specified.
'
Private Sub PrintBitmap(hdc&)
    Dim bi As BITMAPINFO
    Dim dctemp&, dctemp2&
    Dim msg$
    Dim bufsize&
    Dim bm As BITMAP
    Dim ghnd&
    Dim gptr&
    Dim xpix&, ypix&
    Dim doscale&
    Dim uy&, ux&
    Dim di&

    ' Create a temporary memory DC and select into it
    ' the background picture of the picture1 control.
    dctemp& = CreateCompatibleDC(picture1.hdc)

    ' Get the size of the picture bitmap
    di = GetObjectAPI(picture1.Picture, Len(bm), bm)

    ' Can this printer handle the DIB?
    If (GetDeviceCaps(hdc, RASTERCAPS)) And RC_DIBTODEV = 0 Then
        msg$ = "This device does not support DIB's" + vbCrLf + "See source code _
        for further info"
        MsgBox msg$, 0, "No DIB support"
    End If

    ' Fill the BITMAPINFO for the desired DIB
    bi.bmiHeader.biSize = Len(bi.bmiHeader)
    bi.bmiHeader.biWidth = bm.bmWidth
    bi.bmiHeader.biHeight = bm.bmHeight
    bi.bmiHeader.biPlanes = 1
    bi.bmiHeader.biBitCount = 4
    bi.bmiHeader.biCompression = BI_RGB
    ' Now calculate the data buffer size needed
```

```
bufsize& = bi.bmiHeader.biWidth

' Figure out the number of bytes based on the
' number of pixels in each byte. In this case we
' really don't need all this code because this example
' always uses a 16 color DIB, but the code is shown
' here for your future reference
Select Case bi.bmiHeader.biBitCount
    Case 1
        bufsize& = (bufsize& + 7) / 8
    Case 4
        bufsize& = (bufsize& + 1) / 2
    Case 24
        bufsize& = bufsize& * 3
End Select
' And make sure it aligns on a long boundary
bufsize& = ((bufsize& + 3) / 4) * 4
' And multiply by the # of scan lines
bufsize& = bufsize& * bi.bmiHeader.biHeight

' Now allocate a buffer to hold the data
' We use the global memory pool because this buffer
' could easily be above 64k bytes.
ghnd = GlobalAlloc(GMEM_MOVEABLE, bufsize&)
gptr& = GlobalLock&(ghnd)

di = GetDIBits(dctemp, picture1.Picture, 0, bm.bmHeight, ByVal gptr&, bi, _
DIB_RGB_COLORS)
di = SetDIBitsToDevice(hdc, 0, 0, bm.bmWidth, bm.bmHeight, 0, 0, 0, _
bm.bmHeight, ByVal gptr&, bi, DIB_RGB_COLORS)

' Now see if we can also print a scaled version
xpix = GetDeviceCaps(hdc, HORZRES)
' We subtract off the size of the bitmap already
' printed, plus some extra space
ypix = GetDeviceCaps(hdc, VERTRES) - (bm.bmHeight + 50)

' Find out the largest multiplier we can use and still
' fit on the page
doscale = xpix / bm.bmWidth
If (ypix / bm.bmHeight < doscale) Then doscale = ypix / bm.bmHeight
If doscale > 1 Then
    ux = bm.bmWidth * doscale
    uy = bm.bmHeight * doscale
    ' Now how this is offset a bit so that we don't
    ' print over the 1:1 scaled bitmap
    di = StretchDIBits(hdc, 0, bm.bmHeight + 50, ux, uy, 0, 0, bm.bmWidth, _
    bm.bmHeight, ByVal gptr&, bi, DIB_RGB_COLORS, SRCCOPY)
End If
' Dump the global memory block
```

```
    di = GlobalUnlock(ghnd)
    di = GlobalFree(ghnd)
    di = DeleteDC(dctemp)

End Sub
```

Printing from the VB printer object is very easy.

```
' Printing using the VB printer object
'
Private Sub CmdPrint_Click()
    Dim oldcursor&
    oldcursor = Screen.MousePointer
    Screen.MousePointer = 11
    Printer.Print " "    ' Convince VB that something should be printed
    PrintBitmap Printer.hdc
    Printer.NewPage
    Printer.EndDoc
    Screen.MousePointer = oldcursor
End Sub
```

Printing using a newly created Device Context is a bit more complex, but also provides additional capability.

Note how the DocumentProperties function may be used to set the configuration of a printer without affecting other applications. In this case the printer is set into landscape mode before printing.

Under Win32, the CreateDC function always specifies the same driver: "WinSpool." The spooler driver takes care of accessing individual printer drivers as necessary. Another change from Win16 is that this function no longer sets the system into a system modal state to prevent other applications from interfering with the printing. Instead, it simply disables the main form during printing.

```
' This function shows how you can use the API to obtain
'   a printer device context for printing.
'   Note how this function also switches to print in
'   landscape mode without changing the default printer
'   configuration.
'
Private Sub CmdPrintAPI_Click()
    Dim DeviceName$
    Dim dm As DEVMODE, dmout As DEVMODE
    Dim bufsize&
    Dim dmInBuf() As Byte
    Dim dmOutBuf() As Byte
    Dim prhdc&
    Dim dinfo As DOCINFO
    Dim docname$
    Dim oldcursor&
    Dim hPrinter&
    Dim res&, di&
```

```
hPrinter = OpenDefaultPrinter(DeviceName$)

' Get a copy of the DEVMODE structure for this printer
' First find out how big the DEVMODE structure is
bufsize& = DocumentProperties(hwnd, hPrinter, DeviceName$, Ø, Ø, Ø)

' Allocate buffers of that size
ReDim dmInBuf(bufsize&)
ReDim dmOutBuf(bufsize&)

' Get the output DEVMODE structure
res = DocumentProperties(hwnd, hPrinter, DeviceName$, _
agGetAddressForObject(_
dmOutBuf(Ø)), agGetAddressForObject(dmInBuf(Ø)), _
DM_OUT_BUFFER)

' Copy the data buffer into the DEVMODE structure
 agCopyData dmOutBuf(Ø), dmout, Len(dmout)

' Set the orientation, and set the dmField flag so that
' the function will know that it is valid.

dmout.dmOrientation = DMORIENT_LANDSCAPE
dmout.dmFields = dm.dmFields Or DM_ORIENTATION

' Now copy the data back to the buffer
agCopyData dmout, dmOutBuf(Ø), Len(dmout)


' We now have need DC to the default printer
' This DC is also initialized to landscape mode
prhdc = CreateDCBynum("WINSPOOL", DeviceName$, vbNullString, _
agGetAddressForObject&(dmOutBuf(Ø)))
If prhdc = Ø Then GoTo cleanup2

' The DOCINFO structure is the information that the
' print manager will show. This also gives you the
' opportunity of dumping output to a file.
docname$ = "Sample Document"
dinfo.cbSize = Len(dinfo)
dinfo.lpszDocName = docname$
dinfo.lpszOutput = vbNullString

' We set up the abort procdure here
AbortPrinting% = Ø
di = SetAbortProc(prhdc, AddressOf Callback1_AbortProc)

' And show the abort form which will be system modal
AbortForm.Show
Call BringWindowToTop(AbortForm.hwnd)
AbortForm.Refresh

Enabled = False ' Disable the main form
```

```
' The usual print sequence here
di = StartDoc(prhdc, dinfo)
di = StartPage(prhdc)
PrintBitmap prhdc

' The system will spend a long time in the EndPage
' function, but it will periodically call the Abort
' procedure which in turn triggers the Callback1
' AbortProc event.
di = EndPage(prhdc)
If di >= Ø Then di = EndDocAPI(prhdc)
Unload AbortForm
Enabled = True

cleanup2:
    If prhdc <> Ø Then di = DeleteDC(prhdc)
    If hPrinter <> Ø Then Call ClosePrinter(hPrinter)

End Sub
```

This event is triggered every time the abort function is called by Windows during page processing. The function calls the DoEvents function to allow system messages to be processed in the Abort dialog box (without it, a mouse click on the abort button would never be processed).

The following function looks at the AbortPrinting flag to determine if the user canceled the print operation. The retval parameter is set to 0 to terminate printing. The function is found in file PICPRINT.BAS.bas in the VB5 edition of this program.

```
Public Function Callback1_AbortProc(ByVal hPr As Long, ByVal code As Long) As
Long
    ' We must allow events to take place, otherwise the
    ' user button press on the abortform form will never
    ' be detected!
    DoEvents
    If code = SP_OUTOFDISK Or AbortPrinting% Then
        Callback1_AbortProc = Ø
        Exit Function
    End If
    Callback1_AbortProc = -1
End Function
```

The ABORTFOR.FRM form has a single command button with the following click event:

```
Private Sub CmdAbort_Click()
    AbortPrinting = -1
End Sub
```

Suggestions for Further Practice

- Modify PicPrint to work with any color format (monochrome, 256 color or RGB color). Don't forget to dynamically allocate the BITMAPINFO structure as described in Chapter 9!

- Extend PicPrint to allow you to select the printer to use, both with the VB printer object and using API only techniques (hint: look at the Enum-Printers function).

- Experiment with the other spooler configuration routines.

DocJob.vbp—Direct Output to a Printer

DocJob is a simple example that will help you understand what is going on in the spooler, one level down from the way you normally print using a device context. It is important to stress that the techniques shown here are used by the spooler and print manager themselves to manage print jobs and send information to the printer. It is unlikely to be used by most programmers.

One interesting application for these techniques is as follows: Let's say you have a complex drawing or document that you wish to store on line. Instead of having to load the original application to print the document each time you need a copy, you can print the output to a file. Any time you need a copy of the document, you can use the techniques shown here to create a new job and write the data from the file to the job file for printing. This can save quite a bit of time, but it does assume that you will always be printing to the same printer or one that is compatible with the printer used on the original file.

The DocJob project consists of a form with a text box that is set to the name of a printer (you must enter a valid printer name on your system—the default is HPLJ which is a share printer name on our development system). A multiline textbox contains text to write to the printer, and a single command button starts the print operation. Listing 12.5 shows the file DOCJOB.FRM, which contains the entire project.

Listing 12.5   DOCJOB.FRM

```
VERSION 5.00
Begin VB.Form frmDocJob
    Caption         =   "Direct Spooler Access"
    ClientHeight    =   2700
    ClientLeft      =   1095
    ClientTop       =   1515
    ClientWidth     =   5250
    Height          =   3105
```

Listing 12.5   DOCJOB.FRM (Continued)

```
      Left            =    1035
      LinkTopic       =    "Form1"
      ScaleHeight     =    2700
      ScaleWidth      =    5250
      Top             =    1170
      Width           =    5370
      Begin VB.CommandButton .cmdPrint
         Caption      =    "Print"
         Height       =    375
         Left         =    3900
         TabIndex     =    3
         Top          =    240
         Width        =    915
      End
      Begin VB.TextBox txtText
         Height       =    855
         Left         =    960
         MultiLine    =    -1   'True
         TabIndex     =    2
         Text         =    "DocJob.frx":0000
         Top          =    72
         Width        =    3855
      End
      Begin VB.TextBox txtName
         Height       =    315
         Left         =    960
         TabIndex     =    0
         Text         =    "HPLJ"
         Top          =    240
         Width        =    1695
      End
      Begin VB.Label Label2
         Alignment    =    1    'Right Justify
         Caption      =    "Printer:"
         Height       =    195
         Left         =    120
         TabIndex     =    1
         Top          =    300
         Width        =    795
      End
   End
End
Attribute VB_Name = "frmDocJob"
Attribute VB_GlobalNameSpace = False
Attribute VB_Creatable = False
Attribute VB_PredeclaredId = TrueAttribute VB_Exposed = False
Option Explicit


'*********************************
```

Listing 12.5 **DOCJOB.FRM (Continued)**

```
'**  Type Definitions:

#If Win32 Then
Private Type DOC_INFO_1
    pDocName As String
    pOutputFile As String
    pDatatype As String
End Type

#End If 'WIN32 Types


'**********************************
'**  Function Declarations:

#If Win32 Then
Private Declare Function OpenPrinter& Lib "winspool.drv" Alias "OpenPrinterA" _
(ByVal pPrinterName As String, phPrinter As Long, ByVal pDefault As Long) _
' Third param changed to long
Private Declare Function StartDocPrinter& Lib "winspool.drv" Alias _
"StartDocPrinterA" (ByVal hPrinter As Long, ByVal Level As Long, _
pDocInfo As DOC_INFO_1)
Private Declare Function StartPagePrinter& Lib "winspool.drv" (ByVal hPrinter _
As Long)
Private Declare Function WritePrinter& Lib "winspool.drv" (ByVal hPrinter As _
Long, pBuf As Any, ByVal cdBuf As Long, pcWritten As Long)
Private Declare Function EndDocPrinter& Lib "winspool.drv" (ByVal hPrinter As _
Long)
Private Declare Function EndPagePrinter& Lib "winspool.drv" (ByVal hPrinter As _
Long)
Private Declare Function ClosePrinter& Lib "winspool.drv" (ByVal hPrinter As _
Long)
#End If 'WIN32
```

The sequence of operations here is very straightforward. A DOCINFO structure is set to write directly to the printer in much the same way as was done with the StartDoc function in the PicPrint example. StartDocPrinter and StartPagePrinter are the low-level document and page initialization functions. The data is written directly to the spool file using the WritePrinter function. Note that a vbFormFeed character is appended to force the page to eject.

It is important to stress that this example will only work correctly on a printer that can accept direct text to print (most dot matrix and PCL-based laser printers will work correctly with this example—Postscript printers will not).

```
Private Sub cmdPrint_Click()
```

```
        Dim hPrinter&
        Dim jobid&
        Dim res&
        Dim written&
        Dim printdata$
        Dim docinfo As DOC_INFO_1
        res& = OpenPrinter(txtName.Text, hPrinter, 0)
        If res = 0 Then
            MsgBox "Unable to open the printer"
            Exit Sub
        End If
        docinfo.pDocName = "MyDoc"
        docinfo.pOutputFile = vbNullString
        docinfo.pDatatype = vbNullString
        jobid = StartDocPrinter(hPrinter, 1, docinfo)
        Call StartPagePrinter(hPrinter)
        printdata$ = txtText.Text & vbFormFeed
        Call WritePrinter(hPrinter, ByVal printdata$, Len(printdata$), written)
        Call EndPagePrinter(hPrinter)
        Call EndDocPrinter(hPrinter)
        Call ClosePrinter(hPrinter) ' Close when done

End Sub
```

Suggestions for Further Practice

■ Create a program that archives printed output files that you can then print at your convenience.

Spooler.vbp—A Different Approach to Using API Functions

You have seen that some API functions are more difficult to use than others, requiring allocation and manipulation of buffers or blocks of memory. One technique that has already been discussed for making these functions practical to use is to create your own Visual Basic functions that encapsulate these functions and hide their complexity from the rest of the application. This is especially useful with regard to team software development efforts, where a more advanced programmer can create a library of functions that can be used by other programmers.

Starting with Visual Basic 4.0, it has become possible to take this a step further by creating class libraries that encapsulate API functionality in an easy-to-use manner. Several commercial class libraries are now available, but you can always create your own. An in-depth look at the principles involved in creating a class library can be found in Chapter 20, along with a subset of a sample commercial grade class library to get you started. The Spooler.vbp example provides a first taste of how a class library can make some of the more sophisticated API functions easier to use.

Spooler Project Description

Figure 12.7 shows the main form of the spooler sample program. This program demonstrates how you can do enumerations—obtain lists of the printers, ports, or monitors on the system.

If you look at the descriptions of the enumeration functions (EnumPrinters, for example), you will see that these functions work by loading into a buffer an array of printer information structures. Working with these structures can be tricky; you need to allocate the buffers, copy information from the appropriate location in a buffer to a data structure, and convert pointers within these structures into Visual Basic strings.

Figure 12.7

The main spooler form

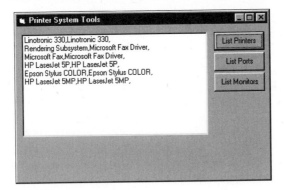

The Spooler example starts by creating a class module for each type of information structure. For example, the dwPrinterInfo class is used for printer information, corresponding to the PRINTER_INFO_x structures. It contains public properties that correspond to all of the fields available for the PRINTER_INFO_x structures, though not all of the properties will be set, depending on which level of printer information you are working with. The class has the ability to load itself given a byte array containing a sequence of PRINTER_INFO_x structures of any level, and an index into that byte array indicating which of the structures to load. This allows the class to handle the complexities of reading a structure out of an array and converting the pointers into the appropriate structures or strings and expose them as properties.

Still, the dwPrinterInfo class does not address the problem of allocating and loading the byte array—performing the actual enumeration. To do this, a higher-level class called dwSpool was created. This class exposes enumeration methods that can be called from outside the class. These methods call the API enumeration function and proceed to create a new dwPrinterInfo class (or appropriate object) for each of the printers that were found. These dwPRInfo class objects are loaded into a collection, which is returned to the calling function.

The result? dwSpool provides an easy-to-use way of obtaining collections of objects of different types, essentially hiding all of the complexity of the API from the high-level programmer. You can also turn these classes into an OLE DLL server, making it possible to access the capabilities provided from any application capable of using OLE automation servers.

The classes shown here are partial early implementations of classes from the Desaware API Class libraries. Full versions of some of the other classes are described in Chapter 20 and included with this book. Full versions of other classes (including these) are available as part of the SpyWorks 5.0 professional package.

Project Files

The Spooler project consists of eight files:

- FRMSPL.FRM is the main form of the project and contains a list box for results, and three buttons that trigger the enumerations.

- SPTYPES.BAS is a module that contains type definitions used by the classes that are intended to be accessible throughout the program.

- SPPRINT.BAS contains some constant declarations.

- DWPORT.CLS contains the dwPortInfo class, which encapsulates the PORT_INFO_x API structures.

- DWPRINFO.CLS contains the dwPrinterInfo class, which encapsulates the PRINTER_INFO_x API structures.

- DWPRMON.CLS contains the dwPrintMonitor class, which encapsulates the MONITOR_INFO_x API structures.

- DWSPOOL.CLS contains the dwSpool class, which provides high-level access to spooler functions, including the enumeration functions.

The listings that follow only illustrate the printer enumeration sequence from the form, through the dwSpool class through the dwPrinterInfo class. The implementation for the other classes is virtually identical. Listing 12.6 shows the relevant parts of the FRMSPL.FRM file.

Listing 12.6   **File FRMSPL.FRM (partial listing)**

```
VERSION 5.00
Begin VB.Form frmSpool
    Caption         =   "Printer System Tools"
    ClientHeight    =   3615
    ClientLeft      =   5385
    ClientTop       =   3180
```

Listing 12.6   File FRMSPL.FRM (partial listing) (Continued)

```
ClientWidth     =   6090
Height          =   4020
Left            =   5325
LinkTopic       =   "Form1"
ScaleHeight     =   3615
ScaleWidth      =   6090
Top             =   2835
Width           =   6210
Begin VB.CommandButton cmdMonitors
   Caption       =   "List Monitors"
   Height        =   435
   Left          =   4800
   TabIndex      =   3
   Top           =   1140
   Width         =   1215
End
Begin VB.ListBox lstResults
   Height        =   2565
   Left          =   120
   TabIndex      =   2
   Top           =   180
   Width         =   4515
End
Begin VB.CommandButton cmdPorts
   Caption       =   "List Ports"
   Height        =   435
   Left          =   4800
   TabIndex      =   1
   Top           =   660
   Width         =   1215
End
Begin VB.CommandButton cmdPrinters
   Caption       =   "List Printers"
   Height        =   435
   Left          =   4800
   TabIndex      =   0
   Top           =   180
   Width         =   1215
End
End
Attribute VB_Name = "frmSpool"
Attribute VB_GlobalNameSpace = False
Attribute VB_Creatable = False
Attribute VB_PredeclaredId = TrueAttribute VB_Exposed = False
' Desaware API Toolkit object library
' Copyright (c) 1995-1997 by Desaware
' All rights reserved
```

Listing 12.6   **File FRMSPL.FRM (partial listing) (Continued)**

```
' Preliminary demonstration edition

Option Explicit
```

From the form level, obtaining a collection of dwPrinterInfo objects is almost trivial. Simply create a new class of type dwSpool to work with (Listing 12.7). Variable c is a collection reference (no collection object is actually created). The EnumPrinters method of the dwSpool object returns a collection—not the use of the Set statement to assign the reference. The For Each loop simply adds the description of each dwPrinterInfo object into the list box.

One of the other nice features of using this approach relates to cleanup after the function is over. As soon as the object references and the collection go out of scope, all of the objects have their usage count decremented, which means in this case that they are all deleted.

```vb
Private Sub cmdPrinters_Click()
    Dim c As Collection
    Dim sp As New dwSpool
    Dim obj As Object
    lstResults.Clear
    Set c = sp.EnumPrinters(PRINTER_ENUM_LOCAL, "", 1)
    For Each obj In c
        lstResults.AddItem obj.pDescription
    Next
End Sub
```

Listing 12.7   **File DWSPOOL.CLS (partial listing)**

```vb
VERSION 1.0 CLASS
BEGIN
  MultiUse = -1  'True
END
Attribute VB_Name = "dwSpool"
Attribute VB_GlobalNameSpace = False
Attribute VB_Creatable = False
Attribute VB_PredeclaredId = False
Attribute VB_Exposed = False' Desaware API Toolkit object library
' Copyright (c) 1995-1997 by Desaware
' All rights reserved

' Preliminary demonstration edition

Option Explicit
```

The class contains private declarations of the API functions, thus hiding them from the rest of the application. Note the use of aliases to give the API functions different names internally. This allows the class to expose methods that have the same names as the API functions. For example, by changing the internal name of the EnumPrinters function to apiEnumPrinters, the class can expose a method called EnumPrinters.

```
Private Declare Function apiEnumPrinters Lib "winspool.drv" Alias _
"EnumPrintersA" (ByVal Flags As Long, ByVal Name As String, ByVal Level _
As Long, pPrinterEnum As Byte, ByVal cdBuf As Long, pcbNeeded As Long, _
pcReturned As Long) As Long
Private Declare Function apiEnumPorts Lib "winspool.drv" Alias "EnumPortsA" _
(ByVal pName As String, ByVal Level As Long, lpbPorts As Byte, ByVal cbBuf As _
Long, pcbNeeded As Long, pcReturned As Long) As Long
Private Declare Function apiEnumMonitors Lib "winspool.drv" Alias _
"EnumMonitorsA" (ByVal pName As String, ByVal Level As Long, pMonitors As Byte, _
ByVal cbBuf As Long, pcbNeeded As Long, pcReturned As Long) As Long

Private Declare Function GetLastError Lib "kernel32" () As Long
```

The technique used here for allocating a structure is virtually identical to that described in the "Spooler Functions and Structures" section earlier in this chapter. The new trick here relates to creating the individual objects. The returned parameter to the enumeration function tells you how many structures were loaded into the buffer. The function then proceeds to create dwPrinterInfo objects for each structure. The dwPrinterInfo object is responsible for loading itself from the buffer as shown in Listing 12.8.

```
' Retrieves a collection of printer objects
Public Function EnumPrinters(Flags As Long, Name As String, Level As Long) As
Collection
    Dim needed&
    Dim returned&
    Dim res&
    Dim tbt As Byte
    Dim usename$
    Dim cprinters As New Collection
    Dim x&
    Dim ppi As dwPrinterInfo
    If Name$ = "" Then usename$ = vbNullString Else usename$ = Name
    res& = apiEnumPrinters(Flags, usename$, Level, tbt, 0, needed, returned)
    If needed& = 0 Then
        Set EnumPrinters = cprinters
        Exit Function
    End If
```

```
        ReDim ResultBuffer(needed) As Byte
        res& = apiEnumPrinters(Flags, usename$, Level, ResultBuffer(0), needed, _
        needed, returned)

        ' Now enumerate create an object for each printer structure
        For x = 1 To returned
            Set ppi = New dwPrinterInfo
            Call ppi.LoadInfo(ResultBuffer(0), Level, x - 1)
            cprinters.Add ppi
        Next x
        Set EnumPrinters = cprinters
End Function
```

Listing 12.8   **File DWPRINFO.CLS (partial listing)**

```
VERSION 1.0 CLASS
BEGIN
  MultiUse = -1  'True
END
Attribute VB_Name = "dwPrinterInfo"
Attribute VB_GlobalNameSpace = False
Attribute VB_Creatable = False
Attribute VB_PredeclaredId = FalseAttribute VB_Exposed = True
' Desaware API Toolkit object library
' Copyright (c) 1995-1997 by Desaware
' All rights reserved

' Preliminary demonstration edition
```

The dwPrinterInfo class needs to use the PRINTER_INFO_x structures directly. The rest of the application can use the class and will not need access to these structures.

```
Option Explicit
Private Type PRINTER_INFO_1
        Flags As Long
        pDescription As Long
        pName As Long
        pComment As Long
End Type

Private Type PRINTER_INFO_2
        pServerName As Long
        pPrinterName As Long
        pShareName As Long
        pPortName As Long
        pDriverName As Long
        pComment As Long
```

```
        pLocation As Long
        pDevMode As Long      ' Pointer to DEVMODE
        pSepFile As String
        pPrintProcessor As Long
        pDatatype As Long
        pParameters As Long
        pSecurityDescriptor As Long ' Pointer to SECURITY_DESCRIPTOR
        Attributes As Long
        Priority As Long
        DefaultPriority As Long
        StartTime As Long
        UntilTime As Long
        Status As Long
        cJobs As Long
        AveragePPM As Long
End Type

Private Type PRINTER_INFO_3
        pSecurityDescriptor As Long ' Pointer to SECURITY_DESCRIPTOR
End Type

Private Type PRINTER_INFO_4
    pPrinterName As Long
    pServerName As Long
    Attributes As Long
End Type

Private Type PRINTER_INFO_5
        pPrinterName As Long
        pPortName As Long
        Attributes As Long
        DeviceNotSelectedTimeout As Long
        TransmissionRetryTimeout As Long
End Type
```

The class contains public properties that correspond to every possible field in the PRINTER_INFO_x structures. The only exception is the pDevMode field (structures cannot be exposed as public properties). A full implementation of this class actually contains a dwDEVMODE class object which can be referenced directly as a sub-object.

```
Public Flags&
Public pDescription$
Public pName$
Public pComment$
Public pServerName$
Public pPrinterName$
Public pShareName$
Public pPortName$
Public pDriverName$
```

```
Public pLocation$
Private pDevMode As DEVMODE
Public pSepFile$
Public pPrintProcessor$
Public pDatatype$
Public pParameters$
Public Attributes&
Public Priority&
Public DefaultPriority&
Public StartTime&
Public UntilTime&
Public Status&
Public cJobs&
Public AveragePPM&
Public DeviceNotSelectedTimeout&
Public TransmissionRetryTimeout&
Private pSecurityDescriptor As SECURITY_DESCRIPTOR
Public Level&    ' Level for which this object was created
```

The level information is required so that the class knows what type of structure is in the buffer.

```
' Load information from a byte structure
Public Sub LoadInfo(Buf As Byte, pLevel&, x&)
    Level = pLevel
    Select Case Level
        Case 1
            LoadPrinterInfo1 Buf, x&
        Case 2
            LoadPrinterInfo2 Buf, x&
        Case 4
            LoadPrinterInfo4 Buf, x&
        Case 5
            LoadPrinterInfo5 Buf, x&
    End Select
End Sub
' Load from PRINTER_INFO_1
```

All of the individual load functions follow the same principles. They start by calculating the start address for the structure in the buffer provided, and copy the structure into a local copy of the structure. The agGetStringFrom-Pointer function takes the string address in the structure and returns a Visual Basic string. You could duplicate this function in Visual Basic using the lstrlen and lstrcpy API functions, then converting the resulting buffer to Unicode, but this approach is far more efficient.

```
Public Sub LoadPrinterInfo1(Buf As Byte, x&)
    Dim pi As PRINTER_INFO_1
    Dim offset&
    Dim useaddr&
    offset& = x * Len(pi)
```

```
      useaddr& = agGetAddressForObject(Buf) + offset
      Call agCopyData(ByVal useaddr, pi, Len(pi))
      Flags = pi.Flags
      pDescription = agGetStringFromPointer(pi.pDescription)
      pName = agGetStringFromPointer(pi.pName)
      pComment = agGetStringFromPointer(pi.pComment)
  End Sub

  ' Load from PRINTER_INFO_2
  Public Sub LoadPrinterInfo2(Buf As Byte, x&)
      Dim pi As PRINTER_INFO_2
      Dim offset&
      Dim useaddr&
      offset& = x * Len(pi)
      useaddr& = agGetAddressForObject(Buf) + offset
      Call agCopyData(ByVal useaddr, pi, Len(pi))

      pServerName = agGetStringFromPointer(pi.pServerName)
      pPrinterName = agGetStringFromPointer(pi.pPrinterName)
      pShareName = agGetStringFromPointer(pi.pShareName)
      pPortName = agGetStringFromPointer(pi.pPortName)
      pDriverName = agGetStringFromPointer(pi.pDriverName)
      pComment = agGetStringFromPointer(pi.pComment)
      pLocation = agGetStringFromPointer(pi.pLocation)
      If pipDevMode Then
      agCopyData ByVal pi.pDevMode, pDevMode, Len(pDevMode)
      If pipSecurityDescriptor Then
      agCopyData ByVal pi.pSecurityDescriptor, pSecurityDescriptor, _
      Len(pSecurityDescriptor)
      pSepFile = agGetStringFromPointer(pi.pSepFile)
      pPrintProcessor = agGetStringFromPointer(pi.pPrintProcessor)
      pDatatype = agGetStringFromPointer(pi.pDatatype)
      pParameters = agGetStringFromPointer(pi.pParameters)
      Attributes = pi.Attributes
      Priority = pi.Priority
      DefaultPriority = pi.DefaultPriority
      StartTime = pi.StartTime
      UntilTime = pi.UntilTime
      Status = pi.Status
      cJobs = pi.cJobs
      AveragePPM = pi.AveragePPM
      Flags = pi.Flags
  End Sub
  ' Load from PRINTER_INFO_4
  Public Sub LoadPrinterInfo4(Buf As Byte, x&)
      Dim pi As PRINTER_INFO_4
      Dim offset&
      Dim useaddr&
      offset& = x * Len(pi)
      useaddr& = agGetAddressForObject(Buf) + offset
      Call agCopyData(ByVal useaddr, pi, Len(pi))
      pDescription = agGetStringFromPointer(pi.pDescription)
```

```
        pName = agGetStringFromPointer(pi.pName)
        Attributes = pi.Attributes
End Sub

Public Sub LoadPrinterInfo5(Buf As Byte, x&)
    Dim pi As PRINTER_INFO_5
    Dim offset&
    Dim useaddr&
    offset& = x * Len(pi)
    useaddr& = agGetAddressForObject(Buf) + offset
    Call agCopyData(ByVal useaddr, pi, Len(pi))
    Flags = pi.Flags
    pPrinterName = agGetStringFromPointer(pi.pPrinterName)
    pPortName = agGetStringFromPointer(pi.pPortName)
    Attributes = pi.Attributes
    DeviceNotSelectedTimeout = pi.DeviceNotSelectedTimeout
    TransmissionRetryTimeout = pi.TransmissionRetryTimeout
End Sub
```

Suggestions for Further Practice

- Extend the spooler project to enumerate jobs, forms, drivers, and print processors (and their data types).

- Modify the spooler classes to correctly handle levels that are specific to NT or Windows 95 depending on the system in use.

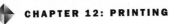

Function Reference

■ AbortDoc

VB Declaration Declare Function AbortDoc& Lib "gdi32" (ByVal hdc As Long)

Description Aborts printing of a document. All output since the last call to the StartDoc function is canceled. If the printer is configured to queue a document to the print spooler before it prints, no part of the document will print; otherwise it is possible that part of the document will already have been printed.

Use with VB If you use this function with the printer device context referred to by the hDC property of the printer object, it will work. You may, however, receive a printer error if you call the EndDoc method afterward.

It is strongly recommended that you trap printer errors when combining API printer functions with VB printer methods, or avoid such combinations.

Parameter	Type/Description
hdc	Long—A handle to a device context.

Return Value Long—Greater than zero on success, SP_ERROR on error. Sets GetLastError.

Platform Windows 95, Windows NT, Win16

■ AbortPrinter

VB Declaration Declare Function AbortPrinter& Lib "spoolss.dll" (ByVal hPrinter As Long)

Description Deletes the spool file associated with a printer.

Use with VB No problem.

Parameter	Type/Description
hPrinter	Long—A handle to an open printer object (obtain using OpenPrinter).

Return Value Long—Nonzero on success, zero on failure. Sets GetLastError.

Platform Windows 95, Windows NT

Comments This function will have no effect if a printer has no spool file (for instance, the spooler is sending data directly to the printer).

■ AddForm

VB Declaration Declare Function AddForm& Lib "spoolss.dll" Alias "AddFormA" (ByVal hPrinter As _
Long, ByVal Level As Long, pForm As FORM_INFO_1)

Description Adds a new form to the form list for a printer. A form describes a page size and layout, providing a device-independent mechanism for standardizing on paper sizes under Windows NT.

Use with VB	No problem.

Parameter	Type/Description
hPrinter	Long—A handle to an open printer object (obtain using OpenPrinter).
Level	Long—Set to 1.
pForm	FORM_INFO_1—A structure describing the form. See "Comments."

Return Value	Long—Nonzero on success, zero on failure. Sets GetLastError.
Platform	Windows NT
Comments	The FORM_INFO_1 structure is defined as follows:

```
Type FORM_INFO_1
    Flags As Long
    pName As String
    Size As SIZEL
    ImageableArea As RECTL
End Type
```

Flags = The constant FORM_BUILTIN if the form is built into the printer.
pName = The name of the form.
Size = The media dimensions in thousandths of a millimeter.
ImageableArea = The actual area that can be drawn on in thousandths of a millimeter.

■ AddJob

VB Declaration	`Declare Function AddJob& Lib "spoolss.dll" Alias "AddJobA" (ByVal hPrinter As _`
	`Long, ByVal Level As Long, pData As Byte, ByVal cdBuf As Long, pcbNeeded As _`
	`Long)`

Description	Used to retrieve a valid path name that can be used to create a spool file for a job. It also assigns a job number to the job.
Use with VB	No problem.

Parameter	Type/Description
hPrinter	Long—A handle to an open printer object (obtain using OpenPrinter).
Level	Long—Set to 1.
pData	Byte—See "Spooler Functions and Structures" in the chapter text. The buffer will reference a ADDJOB_INFO_1 structure.
cdBuf	Long—See "Spooler Functions and Structures" in the chapter text.
pcbNeeded	Long—See "Spooler Functions and Structures" in the chapter text.

Return Value	Long—Nonzero on success, zero on failure. Sets GetLastError.
Platform	Windows 95, Windows NT

Comments   The ADDJOB_INFO_1 structure is defined as follows:

```
Type ADDJOB_INFO_1
        Path As String
        JobId As Long
End Type
```

Path = A path to a file name.
JobId = A Job number.
After calling this function you can create the specified file, write data to it, then use the ScheduleJob API to turn it to send the data to the printer.

■ AddMonitor

VB Declaration   Declare Function AddMonitor& Lib "spoolss.dll" Alias "AddMonitorA" (ByVal pName _
As String, ByVal Level As Long, pMonitors As Byte)

Description   Adds a printer monitor to the system.

Use with VB   No problem.

Parameter	Type/Description
pName	String—The name of the server on which to install the monitor. Set to vbNullString for a local monitor.
Level	Long—Set to 2.
pMonitors	Byte—The first byte in a structure containing a MONITOR_INFO_2 structure.

Return Value   Long—Nonzero on success, zero on failure. Sets GetLastError.

Platform   Windows 95, Windows NT. For NT 3.51, only local monitors are supported.

Comments   The MONITOR_INFO_2 structure is defined as follows:

```
Type MONITOR_INFO_2
        pName As String
        pEnvironment As String
        pDLLName As String
End Type
```

pName = The name of the monitor.
pEnvironment = The environment for which the monitor was designed (example: "Windows NT x86"). Use vbNullString for the environment of the local system.
pDLLName = The name of the DLL for the monitor.

■ AddPort

VB Declaration   Declare Function AddPort& Lib "spoolss.dll" Alias "AddPortA" (ByVal pName As _
String, ByVal hwnd As Long, ByVal pMonitorName As String)

Description   Brings up the Add port dialog box that allows a user to add a port to the list of ports available to the system.

Use with VB   No problem.

Parameter	Type/Description
pName	String—The name of the server on which to install the port. Set to vbNullString for a local port
hwnd	Long—A handle of a parent window for the AddPort dialog box.
pMonitorName	String—The name of the monitor to use for the specified port.

Return Value   Long—Nonzero on success, zero on failure. Sets GetLastError.

Platform   Windows 95, Windows NT

■ AddPrinter

VB Declaration
```
Declare Function AddPrinter& Lib "spoolss.dll" Alias "AddPrinterA" (ByVal pName _
As String, ByVal Level As Long, pPrinter As Byte)
```

Description   Adds a new printer to the system.

Use with VB   No problem.

Parameter	Type/Description
pName	String—The name of the server on which to install the print processor. Set to vbNullString for a local printer.
Level	Long—Set to 2.
pPrinter	Byte—First entry in a buffer containing a PRINTER_INFO_2 structure that has the fields pPrinterName, pPortName, pDriverName, pPrintProcessor, and pDataType set to valid values. pPrinter can also be defined to be As PRINTER_INFO_2. The fields Attributes, DefaultPriority, pComment, pDevMode, pLocation, pParameters, Priority, pSecurityDescriptor, pSepFile, pShareName, StartTime, and UntilTime may also be set. Other fields should be left empty.

Return Value   Long—A handle to a new printer on success, zero on failure. Sets GetLastError.

Platform   Windows 95, Windows NT. Under NT, the caller must have sufficient privilege to configure printers on the specified server.

■ AddPrinterConnection

VB Declaration
```
Declare Function AddPrinterConnection& Lib "spoolss.dll" Alias _
"AddPrinterConnectionA" (ByVal pName As String)
```

Description   Connects to the specified printer.

Use with VB   No problem.

Parameter	Type/Description
pName	String—The name of a printer on the network.

Return Value   Long—Nonzero on success, zero on failure. Sets GetLastError.

Platform   Windows 95, Windows NT

■ AddPrinterDriver

VB Declaration
```
Declare Function AddPrinterDriver& Lib "spoolss.dll" Alias "AddPrinterDriverA" _
    (ByVal pName As String, ByVal Level As Long, pDriverInfor As Byte)
```

Description   Adds a new print driver to the specified system.

Use with VB   No problem.

Parameter	Type/Description
pName	String—The name of the server on which to install the driver. Set to vbNullString for the local system.
Level	Long—2 or 3 (2 only on NT 3.51).
pDriverInfor	Byte—A buffer containing a DRIVER_INFO_2 or DRIVER_INFO_3 structure specifying the driver to add. Refer to Appendix B and your online Win32 API reference for additional information on these structures.

Return Value   Long—Nonzero on success, zero on failure. Sets GetLastError.

Platform   Windows 95, Windows NT

Comments   All driver files must be in the appropriate directories before calling this function.

■ AddPrintProcessor

VB Declaration
```
Declare Function AddPrintProcessor& Lib "spoolss.dll" Alias _
    "AddPrintProcessorA" (ByVal pName As String, ByVal pEnvironment As String, _
    ByVal pPathName As String, ByVal pPrintProcessorName As String)
```

Description   Adds a print processor to the specified system.

Use with VB   No problem.

Parameter	Type/Description
pName	String—The name of the server on which to install the print processor. Set to vbNullString for the local system.
pEnvironment	String—The environment of the print processor being added (for example: Windows NT x86). vbNullString for the current (local) system environment.

Parameter	Type/Description
pPathName	String—The file containing the print processor. The file must be in the print processor directory.
pPrintProcessor-Name	String—The name of the print processor.

Return Value Long—Nonzero on success, zero on failure. Sets GetLastError.

Platform Windows 95, Windows NT

■ AddPrintProvidor

VB Declaration
```
Declare Function AddPrintProvidor& Lib "spoolss.dll" Alias "AddPrintProvidorA" _
(ByVal pName As String, ByVal Level As Long, pProvidorInfo As Byte)
```

Description Adds a print providor to the system.

Use with VB No problem.

Parameter	Type/Description
pName	String—The name of the server on which to install the print providor. Set to vbNullString for the local system.
Level	Long—Set to 1.
pProvidorInfo	Byte—A buffer containing a PROVIDER_INFO_1 structure.

Return Value Long—Nonzero on success, zero on failure. Sets GetLastError.

Platform Windows 95, Windows NT

Comments The PROVIDER_INFO_1 is defined as follows:
```
Type PROVIDOR_INFO_1
        pName As String
        pEnvironment As String
        pDLLName As String
End Type
```

pName = The name of the providor.
pEnvironment = The environment for which the providor was designed (example: "Windows NT x86"). Use vbNullString for the environment of the local system.
pDLLName = The name of the DLL for the providor.

■ AdvancedDocumentProperties

VB Declaration
```
Declare Function AdvancedDocumentProperties& Lib "winspool.dll" Alias _
"AdvancedDocumentPropertiesA" (ByVal hwnd As Long, ByVal hPrinter As Long, _
ByVal pDeviceName As String, ByVal pDevModeOutput As Long, ByVal pDevModeInput _
As Long)
```

Description	Brings up the Printer document settings dialog box. This function is virtually identical to calling the DocumentProperties function with fMode set to DM_IN_PROMPT. Refer to the Document-Properties function description for details on parameters for this function.
Use with VB	No problem.
Return Value	Long—Nonzero on success, zero on failure. Sets GetLastError.
Comments	Set pDevModeOutput to 0 to obtain the size of the required DEVMODE structure.
Porting Notes	Similar to the Win16 ExtDeviceMode function.

■ ClosePrinter

VB Declaration	`Declare Function ClosePrinter& Lib "spoolss.dll" (ByVal hPrinter As Long)`
Description	Closes an open printer object.
Use with VB	No problem.

Parameter	Type/Description
hPrinter	Long—A handle to an open printer object.

Return Value	Long—Nonzero on success, zero on failure. Sets GetLastError.
Platform	Windows 95, Windows NT
Example	Spooler.vbp

■ ConfigurePort

VB Declaration	`Declare Function ConfigurePort& Lib "spoolss.dll" Alias "ConfigurePortA" (ByVal _` `pName As String, ByVal hwnd As Long, ByVal pPortName As String)`
Description	Brings up the port configuration dialog box for the specified port.
Use with VB	No problem.

Parameter	Type/Description
pName	String—The name of the server whose port is being configured. vbNullString to specify the local system.
hwnd	Long—A parent window handle for the dialog box.
pPortName	String—The name of the port.

Return Value	Long—Nonzero on success, zero on failure. Sets GetLastError.
Platform	Windows 95, Windows NT
Example	PicPrint.vbp demonstrates use of similar spooler dialog boxes.

■ ConnectToPrinterDlg

VB Declaration Declare Function ConnectToPrinterDlg& Lib "winspool.dll" (ByVal hwnd As Long, _
ByVal flags As Long)

Description Brings up the printer connection dialog box which is used to connect to printers across a network.

Use with VB No problem.

Parameter	Type/Description
hwnd	Long—A parent window handle for the dialog box.
flags	Long—Reserved: Set to zero.

Return Value Long—A handle to the connected or selected printer. Zero on failure or if the user cancels the operation.

Platform Windows 95, Windows NT

Example PicPrint.vbp

■ DeleteForm

VB Declaration Declare Function DeleteForm& Lib "spoolss.dll" Alias "DeleteFormA" (ByVal _
hPrinter As Long, ByVal pFormName As String)

Description Deletes a form from the list of forms available to a printer.

Use with VB No problem.

Parameter	Type/Description
hPrinter	Long—A handle to an open printer (obtain using OpenPrinter).
pFormName	String—The name of the form to delete.

Return Value Long—Nonzero on success, zero on failure. Sets GetLastError.

Platform Windows NT

Comments You cannot delete built-in forms. Refer to the AddForm function for additional information.

■ DeleteMonitor

VB Declaration Declare Function DeleteMonitor& Lib "spoolss.dll" Alias "DeleteMonitorA" (ByVal _
pName As String, ByVal pEnvironment As String, ByVal pMonitorName As String)

Description Deletes the specified print monitor.

Use with VB	No problem.	

Parameter	Type/Description
pName	String—The name of the server for the monitor. vbNullString to specify the local system.
pEnvironment	String—The environment of the monitor being removed. vbNullString to use the current system.
pMonitorName	String—The name of the monitor to remove.

Return Value   Long—Nonzero on success, zero on failure. Sets GetLastError.

Platform   Windows 95, Windows NT

Comments   Refer to the AddMonitor function for further information.

■ DeletePort

VB Declaration   Declare Function DeletePort& Lib "spoolss.dll" Alias "DeletePortA" (ByVal pName _
As String, ByVal hwnd As Long, ByVal pPortName As String)

Description   Brings up the DeletePort dialog box that lets the user delete a port from the current system.

Use with VB   No problem.

Parameter	Type/Description
pName	String—The name of the server on which to delete the port. Set to vbNullString for a local port.
hwnd	Long—A handle of a parent window for the DeletePort dialog box.
pPortName	String—The name of the port to delete.

Return Value   Long—Nonzero on success, zero on failure. Sets GetLastError.

Platform   Windows 95, Windows NT

Comments   This function will fail if a printer is connected to the port.

■ DeletePrinter

VB Declaration   Declare Function DeletePrinter& Lib "spoolss.dll" (ByVal hPrinter As Long)

Description   Marks the specified printer for deletion from the system.

Use with VB   No problem.

Parameter	Type/Description
hPrinter	Long—A handle to an open printer object.

Return Value   Long—Nonzero on success, zero on failure. Sets GetLastError.

Platform	Windows 95, Windows NT
Comments	The printer will not be deleted until any pending jobs are finished.

■ DeletePrinterConnection

VB Declaration
```
Declare Function DeletePrinterConnection Lib "winspool.drv" Alias _
    "DeletePrinterConnectionA" (ByVal pName As String) As Long
```

Description   Removes a connection to the specified printer.

Use with VB   No problem.

Parameter	Type/Description
pName	String—The printer connection to remove.

Return Value   Long—Nonzero on success, zero on failure. Sets GetLastError.

Platform   Windows 95, Windows NT

■ DeletePrinterDriver

VB Declaration
```
Declare Function DeletePrinterDriver& Lib "spoolss.dll" Alias _
    "DeletePrinterDriverA" (ByVal pName As String, ByVal pEnvironment As String, _
    ByVal pDriverName As String)
```

Description   Removes a printer driver from the system.

Use with VB   No problem.

Parameter	Type/Description
pName	String—The name of the server. Set to vbNullString for a local driver.
pEnvironment	String—The environment of the driver to remove (for example, Windows NT x86). vbNullString for the current (local) system environment.
pDriverName	String—The name of the driver to delete.

Return Value   Long—Nonzero on success, zero on failure. Sets GetLastError.

Platform   Windows 95, Windows NT

Comments   The driver files are not actually deleted from the system. The driver just becomes unavailable.

■ DeletePrintProcessor

VB Declaration
```
Declare Function DeletePrintProcessor& Lib "spoolss.dll" Alias _
    "DeletePrintProcessorA" (ByVal pName As String, ByVal pEnvironment As String, _
    ByVal pPrintProcessorName As String)
```

Description   Deletes a print processor from the specified system.

Use with VB   No problem.

Parameter	Type/Description
pName	String—The name of the server. Set to vbNullString for a local port.
pEnvironment	String—The environment of the print processor to remove (for example, Windows NT x86). VbNullString for the current (local) system environment.
pPrintProcessor-Name	String—The name of the print processor to remove.

Return Value   Long—Nonzero on success, zero on failure. Sets GetLastError.

Platform   Windows 95, Windows NT

■ DeletePrintProvidor

VB Declaration
```
Declare Function DeletePrintProvidor& Lib "spoolss.dll" Alias _
"DeletePrintProvidorA" (ByVal pName As String, ByVal pEnvironment As String, _
ByVal pPrintProvidorName As String)
```

Description   Removes a print providor from the system.

Use with VB   No problem.

Parameter	Type/Description
pName	String—The name of the server. Set to vbNullString for a local port.
pEnvironment	String—The environment of the print providor to remove (for example, Windows NT x86). vbNullString for the current (local) system environment.
pPrintProvidor-Name	String—The name of the printer providor to remove.

Return Value   Long—Nonzero on success, zero on failure. Sets GetLastError.

Platform   Windows 95, Windows NT

■ DeviceCapabilities

VB Declaration
```
Declare Function DeviceCapabilities& Lib "winspool.dll" Alias _
"DeviceCapabilitiesA" (ByVal lpDeviceName As String, ByVal lpPort As String, _
ByVal iIndex As Long, ByVal lpOutput As String, ByVal lpDevMode As Long)
```

Description   This function allows you to obtain information about the capabilities of a device.

Use with VB	No problem.	
	Parameter	**Type/Description**
	lpDeviceName	String—The name of a device.
	lpPort	String—The port to which a device is connected.
	iIndex	Long—The capability to test. Refer to Table 12.7 for a list of possible values.
	lpOutput	String—A pointer to a buffer to load with the capabilities data. The contents of this buffer for each value of fwCapability is described in Table 12.7. The table also describes those cases when this parameter should be set to vbNullString.
	lpDevMode	DEVMODE—The address of a DEVMODE structure or zero. If present, this function will retrieve information based on the settings of this structure. If zero, this function will retrieve information based on the default values for the printer driver.

Return Value
Long—Depends on the value of the iIndex parameter. Refer to Table 12.7 for details. The function will return –1 if the function fails or if the printer driver does not support this function.

Platform
Windows 95, Windows NT, Win16

Comments
Table 12.7 lists the possible values of the iIndex field.

Table 12.7 **Device Capabilities Constants**

fwCapabilities	Description
DC_BINADJUST	Returns one of the constants from API32.TXT with the prefix DCBA_?? indicating the correct orientation for paper for the current paper source. Win95 only.
DC_BINNAMES	If lpszOutput is zero, returns the number of bins supported by the printer. Otherwise, lpszOutput should point to a buffer of at least (24* # of bins) bytes. Each 24 bytes will be loaded with the NULL terminated name of a paper bin.
DC_BINS	If lpszOutput is zero, returns the number of bins supported by the printer. Otherwise, lpszOutput is a pointer to an integer array of at least (# of bins) entries. The values correspond to the DMBIN_??? constants defined for the DEVMODE structure.
DC_COPIES	Returns the maximum number of copies the printer can print.
DC_DATATYPE_ PRODUCED	Obtains a list of data types supported by the printer. These types can be provided as the output data type for the DOCINFO structure used by the StartDoc API function. If this function returns –1, the only data type supported is "RAW". Win95 only.
DC_DRIVER	Returns the version number of the printer driver.

Table 12.7   Device Capabilities Constants (Continued)

fwCapabilities	Description
DC_DUPLEX	Returns 1 if the printer can print on both sides of a page at once, zero otherwise.
DC_EMF_COMPLIANT	Returns TRUE if the printer can directly support enhanced metafiles. Windows 95 only.
DC_ENUM RESOLUTIONS	If lpszOutput is zero, returns the number of printer resolutions supported by the printer. Otherwise, lpszOutput is a pointer to a Long array of at least (2 * # of resolutions) entries. Each pair of entries reflects a horizontal and vertical resolution in dots per inch.
DC_EXTRA	Returns the number of device-specific bytes appended to the DEVMODE structure for this device.
DC_FIELDS	Returns the value of the dmFields field for the device's default DEVMODE data structure.
DC_FILE DEPENDENCIES	If lpszOutput is zero, returns the number of files required by the printer driver. Otherwise, lpszOutput should point to a buffer of at least (64* # of files) bytes. Each 64 bytes will be loaded with the NULL terminated name of a required file.
DC_MAXEXTENT	Returns Long value containing the maximum length and width of paper supported by the printer. The low word contains the width value. These are the maximum values of the dmPaperWidth and dmPaperLength DEVMODE fields.
DC_MINEXTENT	Returns Long value containing the minimum length and width of paper supported by the printer. The low word contains the width value. These are the minimum values of the dmPaperWidth and dmPaperLength DEVMODE fields.
DC_ORIENTATION	Returns the rotation in degrees between landscape mode and portrait mode. Zero indicates that the driver does not support landscape mode. 90 is common for laser printers, 270 for dot-matrix printers.
DC_PAPERNAMES	If lpszOutput is zero, returns the number of paper sizes supported by the printer driver. Otherwise, lpszOutput should point to a buffer of at least (64* # of paper sizes) bytes. Each 64 bytes will be loaded with the NULL terminated name of a supported paper size.
DC_PAPERS	If lpszOutput is zero, returns the number of paper sizes supported by the printer. Otherwise, lpszOutput is a pointer to an integer array of at least (# of paper sizes) entries. The values correspond to the DMPAPER_??? constants defined for the DEVMODE structure.
DC_SIZE	Returns the dmSize field of the printer DEVMODE data structure.

Table 12.7	Device Capabilities Constants (Continued)	
fwCapabilities	**Description**	
DC_TRUETYPE	One of the following constants:	
	DCTT_BITMAP: Device can print TrueType fonts as graphics.	
	DCTT_DOWNLOAD: Device can download TrueType fonts.	
	DCTT_OUTLINE: Device can download outlined TrueType fonts.	
	DCTT_SUBDEV: Device can substitute built-in fonts that are compatible with corresponding TrueType fonts.	
DC_VERSION	Returns the version of the specification for the device driver.	

Note on use of lpszOutput: In many cases this function returns a list of names; for example, when the fwCapabilities flag is DC_PAPERNAMES, a list of names of supported paper sizes is obtained. In these cases the lpszOutput buffer should be a string variable preallocated to the length specified in Table 12.7. The function will load the buffer with all of the names, with each name taking the specified fixed space in the string. It is then possible to extract each entry using the Mid$ function. The PicPrint sample program shows how this is done for paper names, but the technique is identical for other capabilities.

In some cases lpszOutput needs to point to a numeric array. This address may be obtained by using the agGetAddressForInteger or agGetAddressForLong API function using the first entry in a numeric array as the object parameter.

Porting Notes
Under Win16 it was necessary to use a helper DLL under Visual Basic because this function was part of the individual printer drivers. It is now part of the Win32 spooler and is directly accessible.

Example
PicPrint.vbp

■ DocumentProperties

VB Declaration
```
Declare Function DocumentProperties& Lib "winspool.dll" Alias _
"DocumentPropertiesA" (ByVal hwnd As Long, ByVal hPrinter As Long, ByVal _
pDeviceName As String, ByVal pDevModeOutput As Long, ByVal pDevModeInput As _
Long, ByVal fMode As Long)
```

Description
This is a flexible printer configuration control function that replaces the ExtDeviceMode function in Windows 3.x, which in turn replaced the DeviceMode function in version 2.0 of Windows. It defines two DEVMODE data structures: one for input and one for output. The fwMode field determines how these data structures are used.

This function allows you to bring up the printer settings dialog box to change the settings in these data structures. The DEVMODE structure can then be used during the creation of a device context to change the printer setting for a single application, or even to change printer settings during the course of printing a document.

Use with VB   This function may be used with the Visual Basic printer object to change some settings while printing (for example, to switch between portrait and landscape mode).

Refer also to the section "Printing and Visual Basic" earlier in this chapter.

Parameter	Type/Description
hwnd	Long—A handle to the parent window for the dialog box. This will typically be the current active form.
hPrinter	Long—A handle to an open printer object.
pDeviceName	String—The name of the printer.
pDevMode-Output	Long—Pointer to a DEVMODE data structure for the device. Refer to Table 12.8 for further information. Note that this pointer must refer to a buffer that is large enough to include the private printer driver data as well as the standard DEVMODE structure. Use the agGetAddressForObject function to obtain the address of a structure or byte array, or pass the address of a memory block allocated using GlobalAlloc.
pDevModeInput	Long—Pointer to a DEVMODE data structure for the device. Refer to Table 12.8 for further information. See the description of the pDevModeOutput structure for additional information.
fMode	Long—Mode flags that determine the operation of this function as shown in Table 12.8.

Return Value   Long—Depends on the value of the fwMode field as follows:

If fwMode is zero, this function returns the size of the DEVMODE structure for this device. Note that this structure may be larger than the size specified in the type definition file API32.TXT.

If fwMode has the DM_IN_PROMPT constant flag set, the printer settings dialog box will appear. In this case, the return value will be the constant IDOK or IDCANCEL depending on which button the user presses to close the dialog box.

In all other cases, this function returns IDOK on success. For all cases, this function returns a negative value on error.

Platform   Windows 95, Windows NT

Comments   Table 12.8 describes the use of the fMode command.

Table 12.8   DocumentProperties Operating Modes

Constant Flag	Operation
None	pDevModeInput is not used; pDevModeOutput may be zero. The function returns the required size of the DEVMODE structures referenced by these two parameters.
DM_IN_BUFFER	The pDevModeInput buffer should be loaded with new settings for the printer driver. The dmFields field of the structure should be set before calling this function to determine which fields in the structure will be used.

Table 12.8 **DocumentProperties Operating Modes (Continued)**

Constant Flag	Operation
DM_IN_PROMPT	The printer setup dialog box is displayed allowing the user to specify printer settings for output. If DM_IN_BUFFER is specified, any fields specified in the input buffer are combined with the current printer DEVMODE structure before the dialog box is displayed.
DM_OUT_BUFFER	Causes the printer settings to be output to the buffer referred to by the pDevModeOutput parameter. These settings will be determined by the two input flags and may thus reflect the original input structure, the current printer settings, and any user modifications entered through the printer setup dialog box. If this flag is not specified, the lpdmOutput parameter may be set to zero.

Porting Notes   This function replaces the ExtDeviceMode function.

Example   PicPrint.vbp

■ EndDocAPI

VB Declaration   `Declare Function EndDocAPI& Lib "gdi32" Alias "EndDoc" (ByVal hDC As Long)`

Description   This function is used to end a successful print job.

Use with VB   No problem.

Parameter	Type/Description
hDC	Long—A handle to a device context.

Return Value   Long—Greater than zero on success, less than or equal to zero otherwise. Sets GetLastError.

Platform   Windows 95, Windows NT, Win16

Example   PicPrint.vbp

■ EndDocPrinter

VB Declaration   `Declare Function EndDocPrinter& Lib "spoolss.dll" (ByVal hPrinter As Long)`

Description   Specifies the end of a document at the spooler level.

Use with VB   No problem.

Parameter	Type/Description
hPrinter	Long—A handle to an open printer (obtain using OpenPrinter).

Return Value	Long—Nonzero on success, zero on failure. Sets GetLastError.
Platform	Windows 95, Windows NT
Comments	Not typically used at the application level, this is used by the spooler to indicate the end of a document in a print job.
Example	DocJob.vbp

■ EndPage

VB Declaration	`Declare Function EndPage& Lib "gdi32" (ByVal hdc As Long)`
Description	This function is used to complete printing on a page and prepare the device context for printing on the next page.
Use with VB	When using the Visual Basic Printer object, you should use the NewPage method instead of this function.

Parameter	Type/Description
hdc	Long—Handle to a device context.

Return Value	Long—Greater than zero on success, less than or equal to zero on failure. Sets GetLastError.
Platform	Windows 95, Windows NT, Win16
Comments	This function may take a very long time to execute, depending on the complexity of the drawing that is taking place, the operating system in use and whether the printer is local or on a network. In order to allow the user to abort the printing operation, this function calls the abort procedure specified by the SetAbortProc API call periodically during its operation.
Porting Notes	Under Win16, the attributes of the device context would be reset to their defaults after both this function and the StartPage function. Under Windows 95, the StartPage function resets the device context but this function does not. Under Windows NT 3.51 and later, neither function resets the device context.
Example	PicPrint.vbp

■ EndPagePrinter

VB Declaration	`Declare Function EndPagePrinter& Lib "spoolss.dll" (ByVal hPrinter As Long)`
Description	Specifies the end of a page in a print job.
Use with VB	No problem.

Parameter	Type/Description
hPrinter	Long—A handle to an open printer (obtain using OpenPrinter).

Return Value	Long—Nonzero on success, zero on failure. Sets GetLastError.

Platform	Windows 95, Windows NT
Comments	Not typically used at the application level, this is used by the spooler to indicate the end of a page in the actual printer data.
Example	DocJob.vbp

■ EnumForms

VB Declaration
```
Declare Function EnumForms& Lib "spoolss.dll" Alias "EnumFormsA" (ByVal _
hPrinter As Long, ByVal Level As Long, pForm As Byte, ByVal cbBuf As Long, _
pcbNeeded As Long, pcReturned As Long)
```

Description   Enumerates the available forms for a printer.

Use with VB   No problem.

Parameter	Type/Description
hPrinter	Long—A handle to an open printer (obtain using OpenPrinter).
Level	Long—Set to 1.
pForm	Byte—See "Spooler Functions and Structures" in the chapter text. Buffer will contain FORM_INFO_1 structures.
cbBuf	Long—See "Spooler Functions and Structures" in the chapter text.
pcbNeeded	Long—See "Spooler Functions and Structures" in the chapter text.
pcReturned	Long—See "Spooler Functions and Structures" in the chapter text.

Return Value   Long—Nonzero on success, zero on failure. Sets GetLastError.

Platform   Windows NT

Comments   See the AddForm function for additional information.

Example   Enumeration techniques are demonstrated in the Spooler.vbp example.

■ EnumJobs

VB Declaration
```
Declare Function EnumJobs& Lib "spoolss.dll" Alias "EnumJobsA" (ByVal hPrinter _
As Long, ByVal FirstJob As Long, ByVal NoJobs As Long, ByVal Level As Long, _
pJob As Byte, ByVal cdBuf As Long, pcbNeeded As Long, pcReturned As Long)
```

Description   Enumerates jobs in the print queue.

Use with VB   No problem.

Parameter	Type/Description
hPrinter	Long—A handle to an open printer (obtain using OpenPrinter).

Parameter	Type/Description
FirstJob	Long—The zero-based index of the first job in the job list to enumerate.
NoJobs	Long—The number of jobs to enumerate.
Level	Long—1 or 2 (JOB_INFO_1 or JOB_INFO_2).
pJob	Byte—See "Spooler Functions and Structures" in the chapter text. Buffer will contain JOB_INFO_1 or JOB_INFO_2 structures. Refer to Appendix B and your online Win32 API reference for further information on these structures.
cdBuf	Long—See "Spooler Functions and Structures" in the chapter text.
pcbNeeded	Long—See "Spooler Functions and Structures" in the chapter text.
pcReturned	Long—See "Spooler Functions and Structures" in the chapter text.

Return Value   Long—Nonzero on success, zero on failure. Sets GetLastError.

Platform   Windows 95, Windows NT

Example   Enumeration techniques are demonstrated in the Spooler.vbp example.

■ EnumMonitors

VB Declaration   Declare Function EnumMonitors& Lib "spoolss.dll" Alias "EnumMonitorsA" (ByVal _
pName As String, ByVal Level As Long, pMonitors As Byte, ByVal cbBuf As Long, _
pcbNeeded As Long, pcReturned As Long)

Description   Enumerates the available print monitors.

Use with VB   No problem.

Parameter	Type/Description
pName	String—The server name. vbNullString to specify the local system.
Level	Long—Set to 1.
pMonitors	Byte—See "Spooler Functions and Structures" in the chapter text. Buffer will contain MONITOR_INFO_1 structures.
cbBuf	Long—See "Spooler Functions and Structures" in the chapter text.
pcbNeeded	Long—See "Spooler Functions and Structures" in the chapter text.
pcReturned	Long—See "Spooler Functions and Structures" in the chapter text.

Return Value   Long—Nonzero on success, zero on failure. Sets GetLastError.

Platform   Windows 95, Windows NT

Comments   The MONITOR_INFO_1 structure has one field containing the name of the print monitor.

Example   Spooler.vbp

◼ EnumPorts

VB Declaration

```
Declare Function EnumPorts& Lib "spoolss.dll" Alias "EnumPortsA" (ByVal pName _
As String, ByVal Level As Long, ByVal lpbPorts As Long, ByVal cbBuf As Long, _
pcbNeeded As Long, pcReturned As Long)
```

Description   Enumerates the ports available to a system.

Use with VB   No problem.

Parameter	Type/Description
pName	String—The server name. vbNullString to specify the local system.
Level	Long— 1 or 2 (1 for NT 3.51). Specifies PORT_INFO_1 or PORT_INFO_1.
lpbPorts	Long—See "Spooler Functions and Structures" in the chapter text. The buffer will be loaded with PORT_INFO_1 or PORT_INFO_1 structures. Refer to Appendix B and your Windows online reference for additional information on these structures.
cbBuf	Long — See "Spooler Functions and Structures" in the chapter text.
pcbNeeded	Long — See "Spooler Functions and Structures" in the chapter text.
pcReturned	Long — See "Spooler Functions and Structures" in the chapter text.

Return Value   Long—Nonzero on success, zero on failure. Sets GetLastError.

Platform   Windows 95, Windows NT

Comments   Refer to the AddPorts function for additional information.

Example   Spooler.vbp

◼ EnumPrinterDrivers

VB Declaration

```
Declare Function EnumPrinterDrivers& Lib "spoolss.dll" Alias _
"EnumPrinterDriversA" (ByVal pName As String, ByVal pEnvironment As String, _
ByVal Level As Long, pDriverInfo As Byte, ByVal cdBuf As Long, pcbNeeded As _
Long, pcReturned As Long)
```

Description   Enumerates the installed printer drivers on the specified system.

Use with VB   No problem.

Parameter	Type/Description
pName	String—The server name. vbNullString to specify the local system.
pEnvironment	String—The environment of the driver to enumerate (for example, Windows NT x86). vbNullString for the current (local) system environment.

Parameter	Type/Description
Level	Long—1, 2, or 3 (3 is Windows 95 & NT 4.0 only).
pDriverInfo	Byte—See "Spooler Functions and Structures" in the chapter text. Buffers will be loaded with DRIVER_INFO_1, DRIVER_INFO_2, DRIVER_INFO_3 structures. Refer to Appendix B and your online Win32 reference for additional information on these structures.
cdBuf	Long—See "Spooler Functions and Structures" in the chapter text.
pcbNeeded	Long—See "Spooler Functions and Structures" in the chapter text.
pcRetruned	Long—See "Spooler Functions and Structures" in the chapter text.

Return Value   Long—Nonzero on success, zero on failure. Sets GetLastError.

Platform   Windows 95, Windows NT

Example   Enumeration techniques are demonstrated in the Spooler.vbp example.

■ EnumPrinters

VB Declaration
```
Declare Function EnumPrinters& Lib "spoolss.dll" Alias "EnumPrintersA" (ByVal _
flags As Long, ByVal name As String, ByVal Level As Long, pPrinterEnum As Byte, _
ByVal cdBuf As Long, pcbNeeded As Long, pcReturned As Long)
```

Description   Enumerates the printers installed on the system.

Use with VB   No problem.

Parameter	Type/Description
flags	Long—One or more of the following flags: PRINTER_ENUM_LOCAL: Enumerates local printers (including network printers on Windows 95). Name is ignored. PRINTER_ENUM_NAME: Enumerates the printer specified by the name parameter where the name is a providor, domain or server. If name is NULL, the available providors are enumerated. PRINTER_ENUM_SHARE: Enumerates shared printers (must be combined with other constant). PRINTER_ENUM_CONNECTIONS: Enumerates printers in the network connection list (even if not currently connected—NT only). PRINTER_ENUM_NETWORK: Enumerates printers connected across the network. Level must be 1. NT only. PRINTER_ENUM_REMOTE: Enumerates printers and print servers connected across the network. Level must be 1. NT only.
name	String—vbNullString to enumerate printers on the local machine. Otherwise depends on the flags and level.

Parameter	Type/Description
Level	Long—1, 2, 4, or 5 (4 NT only, 5 Win95 & NT 4.0 only) to specify the type of structure to enumerate. If 1, the name parameter depends on the flags settings. If 2 or 5, name is the server whose printers are being enumerated or vbNullString. If 4, Only PRINTER_ENUM_LOCAL and PRINTER_ENUM_CONNECTIONS is valid. Name must be vbNullString.
pPrinterEnum	Byte—See "Spooler Functions and Structures" in the chapter text. Buffer will contain PRINTER_ENUM_x structures where x is the level.
cdBuf	Long—See "Spooler Functions and Structures" in the chapter text.
pcbNeeded	Long—See "Spooler Functions and Structures" in the chapter text.
pcReturned	Long—See "Spooler Functions and Structures" in the chapter text.

Return Value Long—Nonzero on success, zero on failure. Sets GetLastError.

Platform Windows 95, Windows NT

Comments Level 4 and 5 base their results on the system registry and are much faster than level 2, which requires that each printer be opened.

Refer to the Microsoft Win32 documentation for additional information on this function.

Example Spooler.vbp

■ EnumPrintProcessorDatatypes

VB Declaration
```
Declare Function EnumPrintProcessorDatatypes& Lib "spoolss.dll" Alias _
"EnumPrintProcessorDatatypesA" (ByVal pName As String, ByVal _
pPrintProcessorName As String, ByVal Level As Long, pDatatypes As Byte, ByVal _
cdBuf As Long, pcbNeeded As Long, pcRetruned As Long)
```

Description Enumerates the datatypes supported by a print processor.

Use with VB No problem.

Parameter	Type/Description
pName	String—The server name. vbNullString to specify the local system.
pPrintProcessor- Name	String—The name of the print processor whose datatypes you are enumerating.
Level	Long—Set to 1.
pDatatypes	Byte—See "Spooler Functions and Structures" in the chapter text. Buffer will be loaded with DATATYPES_INFO_1 structures.
cdBuf	Long—See "Spooler Functions and Structures" in the chapter text.

Parameter	Type/Description
pcbNeeded	Long—See "Spooler Functions and Structures" in the chapter text.
pcReturned	Long—See "Spooler Functions and Structures" in the chapter text.

Return Value   Long—Nonzero on success, zero on failure. Sets GetLastError.

Platform   Windows 95, Windows NT

Comments   The DATATYPES_INFO_1 structure contains a single field containing the name of the datatype.

Example   Enumeration techniques are demonstrated in the Spooler.vbp example.

■ EnumPrintProcessors

VB Declaration
```
Declare Function EnumPrintProcessors& Lib "spoolss.dll" Alias _
"EnumPrintProcessorsA" (ByVal pName As String, ByVal pEnvironment As String, _
ByVal Level As Long, pPrintProcessorInfo As Byte, ByVal cdBuf As Long, _
pcbNeeded As Long, pcReturned As Long)
```

Description   Enumerates the available print processors on a system.

Use with VB   No problem.

Parameter	Type/Description
pName	String—The server name. vbNullString to specify the local system.
pEnvironment	String—The environment of the print processor to enumerate (for example, Windows NT x86). vbNullString for the current (local) system environment.
Level	Long—Set to 1.
pPrintProcessorInfo	Byte—See "Spooler Functions and Structures" in the chapter text. Buffer will be loaded with PRINTPROCESSOR_INFO_1 structures.
cdBuf	Long—See "Spooler Functions and Structures" in the chapter text.
pcbNeeded	Long—See "Spooler Functions and Structures" in the chapter text.
pcReturned	Long—See "Spooler Functions and Structures" in the chapter text.

Return Value   Long—Nonzero on success, zero on failure. Sets GetLastError.

Platform   Windows 95, Windows NT

Example   Enumeration techniques are demonstrated in the Spooler.vbp example.

■ Escape

VB Declaration
```
Declare Function Escape& Lib "gdi32" (ByVal hdc As Long, ByVal nEscape As Long, _
ByVal nCount As Long, lpInData As Any, lpOutData As Any)
```

Description	A flexible device control function.	
Use with VB	No problem.	

Parameter	Type/Description
hdc	Long—A handle to a device context.
nEscape	Long—The number of the escape as defined by a constant in file API32.TXT. This determines the operation that will take place. See "Comments."
nCount	Long—The size in bytes of the lpInData buffer
lpInData	Any—Depends on the Escape Type. For QUERYESCSUPPORT, this is a pointer to an integer variable containing the value of the escape to test. For PASSTHROUGH, this is a pointer to a block of data which contains in the first 16 bits the number of bytes of data to send. The remainder of the block contains the actual data buffer to send to the printer.
lpOutData	Any—An output buffer whose use depends on the escape. It is not used by QUERYESCSUPPORT or PASSTHROUGH and should be set to NULL (ByVal 0&).

Return Value
Long—For QUERYESCSUPPORT, TRUE (nonzero) if the escape is supported, zero if not. For PASSTHROUGH, greater than zero on success, zero if not implemented, and negative on error.

Platform
Windows 95, Windows NT, Win16

Comments
Only two escapes are commonly used under Win32. Use the QUERYESCSUPPORT escape to determine if an escape is supported by a driver. Use the PASSTHROUGH escape to send raw data directly to a printer. Other escapes are supported under Win32 for backwards compatibility with Win16—documentation on these escapes can be found in the Visual Basic Programmer's Guide to the Windows API (16-bit edition), and Windows documentation.

Porting Notes
Unless you are writing code for both Win16 and Win32, you should switch over to the Win32 API functions that replace the old escape types. Most escapes are holdovers from as far back as Windows 1.0 and it is definitely time to move on.

■ FindClosePrinterChangeNotification

VB Declaration
```
Declare Function FindClosePrinterChangeNotification& Lib "spoolss.dll" (ByVal _
hChange As Long)
```

Description
Closes a printer notification object obtained using FindFirstPrinterChangeNotification.

Use with VB
No problem.

Parameter	Type/Description
hChange	Long—A printer notification object handle to close.

Return Value
Long—TRUE (nonzero) on success, zero on failure. Sets GetLastError.

Platform	Windows NT
Example	prWatch.vbp

■ FindFirstPrinterChangeNotification

VB Declaration
```
Declare Function FindFirstPrinterChangeNotification& Lib "winspool.dll" (ByVal _
hPrinter As Long, ByVal fdwFlags As Long, ByVal fdwOptions As Long, _
pPrinterNotifyOptions As Byte)
```

Description Creates a new change notification object that allows you to watch for a variety of changes to the state of a printer.

Use with VB No problem.

Parameter	Type/Description
hPrinter	Long—A handle to an open printer (obtain using OpenPrinter).
fdwFlags	Long—One of the constants with the prefix PRINTER_CHANGE_?? from file API32.TXT that describes which changes to watch for. May be zero if pPrinterNotifyOptions is not zero.
fdwOptions	Long—Reserved: Set to zero.
pPrinterNotify-Options	Byte—A buffer containing a PRINTER_NOTIFY_OPTIONS structure which in turn contains pointers to one or more PRINTER_NOTIFY_OPTIONS_TYPE structures. This can be NULL (change the declaration to ByVal As Long and pass zero) to use the fdwFlags field to specify the changes to watch for. Refer to Appendix B and your online Win32 API reference for additional information on this structure.

Return Value Long—A handle to the change notification object on success. INVALID_HANDLE_VALUE on error. Sets GetLastError.

Platform Windows NT

Comments Refer to Chapter 14 for information on synchronization of objects and processes.

Example prWatch.vbp

■ FindNextPrinterChangeNotification

VB Declaration
```
Declare Function FindNextPrinterChangeNotification& Lib "winspool.dll" (ByVal _
hChange As Long, pdwChange As Long, ByVal pvReserved As Long, ByVal _
ppPrinterNotifyInfo As Long)
```

Description Allows you to determine the reasons that a printer change notification object was signaled.

Use with VB	No problem.

Parameter	Type/Description
hChange	Long—A handle to a printer notification change object.
pdwChange	Long—A long to load with flags indicating the source of the signal. These constants from file API32.TXT have the prefix PRINTER_CHANGE_???.
pvReserved	Long—The address of a PRINTER_NOTIFY_OPTIONS structure. If the Flags field of this structure is set to PRINTER_NOTIFY_OPTIONS_REFRESH, the ppPrinterNotifyInfo buffer will contain the current state of all events being monitored—not just those that are signaled. Other fields in the structure are ignored. May be NULL (zero) to return information only on signaled states.
ppPrinterNotify-Info	Long—The address of a buffer allocated by the system. This buffer should be deleted with the FreePrinterNotifyInfo function when done. The buffer contains a PRINTER_NOTIFY_INTO structure followed by a series of PRINTER_NOTIFY_INFO_DATA structures (the number is determined by the first structure). Refer to Appendix B and your online Win32 API reference for information on these structures.

Return Value Long—Nonzero on success, zero on failure. Sets GetLastError.

Platform Windows NT

Example prWatch.vbp

■ FreePrinterNotifyInfo

VB Declaration `Declare Function FreePrinterNotifyInfo Lib "winspool.drv" (ByVal addr As Long) _`
`As Long`

Description Frees a buffer allocated by the FindNextPrinterNotification function.

Use with VB No problem.

Parameter	Type/Description
addr	Long—The address of a system buffer allocated by the FindNextPrinterNotification function.

Return Value Long—Nonzero on success, zero on failure. Sets GetLastError.

Platform Windows NT

Example PrWatch.vbp

■ GetForm

VB Declaration   Declare Function GetForm& Lib "spoolss.dll" Alias "GetFormA" (ByVal hPrinter As _
Long, ByVal pFormName As String, ByVal Level As Long, pForm As Byte, ByVal _
cbBuf As Long, pcbNeeded As Long)

Description   Retrieves information about the specified form.

Use with VB   No problem.

Parameter	Type/Description
hPrinter	Long—A handle to an open printer (obtain using OpenPrinter).
pFormName	String—The name of the form whose information you wish to retrieve.
Level	Long—Set to 1
pForm	Byte—See "Spooler Functions and Structures" in the chapter text. The buffer will be loaded with a FORM_INFO_1 structure.
cbBuf	Long—See "Spooler Functions and Structures" in the chapter text.
pcbNeeded	Long—See "Spooler Functions and Structures" in the chapter text.

Return Value   Long—Nonzero on success, zero on failure. Sets GetLastError.

Platform   Windows NT

Comments   Refer to the AddForm function for additional information.

Example   Ex12A.vbp demonstrates GetPrinter, which is similar.

■ GetJob

VB Declaration   Declare Function GetJob& Lib "spoolss.dll" Alias "GetJobA" (ByVal hPrinter As _
Long, ByVal JobId As Long, ByVal Level As Long, pJob As Byte, ByVal cdBuf As _
Long, pcbNeeded As Long)

Description   Retrieves information on the specified job.

Use with VB   No problem.

Parameter	Type/Description
hPrinter	Long—A handle to an open printer (obtain using OpenPrinter).
JobId	Long—A job number.
Level	Long—1 or 2
pJob	Byte—See "Spooler Functions and Structures" in the chapter text. The buffer will contain a JOB_INFO_1 or JOB_INFO_2 structure containing information about the job. Refer to Appendix B for information on these structures.

Parameter	Type/Description
cdBuf	Long—See "Spooler Functions and Structures" in the chapter text.
pcbNeeded	Long—See "Spooler Functions and Structures" in the chapter text.

Return Value   Long—Nonzero on success, zero on failure. Sets GetLastError.

Platform   Windows 95, Windows NT

Example   Ex12A.vbp demonstrates GetPrinter, which is similar.

■ GetPrinter

VB Declaration
```
Declare Function GetPrinter& Lib "spoolss.dll" Alias "GetPrinterA" (ByVal _
hPrinter As Long, ByVal Level As Long, pPrinter As Byte, ByVal cbBuf As Long, _
pcbNeeded As Long)
```

Description   Retrieve information about the specified printer.

Use with VB   No problem.

Parameter	Type/Description
hPrinter	Long—A handle to an open printer (obtain using OpenPrinter).
Level	Long—1, 2, 3, 4 (NT only), or 5 (Win95 & NT 4.0).
pPrinter	Byte—See "Spooler Functions and Structures" in the chapter text. Buffer will be loaded with a PRINTER_INFO_x structure where x is the level.
cbBuf	Long—See "Spooler Functions and Structures" in the chapter text.
pcbNeeded	Long—See "Spooler Functions and Structures" in the chapter text.

Return Value   Long—Nonzero on success, zero on failure. Sets GetLastError.

Platform   Windows 95, Windows NT

Comments   Some fields in the PRINTER_INFO_x structure will only be read if the calling application has permission to do so based on current security settings.

Example   Ex12A.vbp

■ GetPrinterData

VB Declaration
```
Declare Function GetPrinterData& Lib "spoolss.dll" Alias "GetPrinterDataA" _
(ByVal hPrinter As Long, ByVal pValueName As String, pType As Long, pData As _
Byte, ByVal nSize As Long, pcbNeeded As Long)
```

Description   Sets registry configuration information for the printer.

Use with VB　No problem.

Parameter	Type/Description
hPrinter	Long—A handle to an open printer (obtain using OpenPrinter).
pValueName	String—The name of the registry value to set.
pType	Long—The type of data. One of the constants REG_?? from file API32.TXT. Refer to Chapter 13 for information on registry data types.
pData	Byte—See "Spooler Functions and Structures" in the chapter text.
nSize	Long—See "Spooler Functions and Structures" in the chapter text.
pcbNeeded	Long—See "Spooler Functions and Structures" in the chapter text.

Return Value　Long—Nonzero on success, zero on failure. Sets GetLastError.

Platform　Windows 95, Windows NT

■ GetPrinterDriver

VB Declaration
```
Declare Function GetPrinterDriver& Lib "spoolss.dll" Alias "GetPrinterDriverA" _
(ByVal hPrinter As Long, ByVal pEnvironment As String, ByVal Level As Long, _
pDriverInfo As Byte, ByVal cdBuf As Long, pcbNeeded As Long)
```

Description　Obtains information about the printer driver for the specified printer.

Use with VB　No problem.

Parameter	Type/Description
hPrinter	Long—A handle to an open printer (obtain using OpenPrinter).
pEnvironment	String—The environment of the driver to retrieve (for example, Windows NT x86). vbNullString for the current (local) system environment.
Level	Long — 1, 2, or 3 (Win95 & NT 4.0 only).
pDriverInfo	Byte—See "Spooler Functions and Structures" in the chapter text. The buffer will be loaded with a DRIVER_INFO_x structure where x is the level.
cdBuf	Long—See "Spooler Functions and Structures" in the chapter text.
pcbNeeded	Long—See "Spooler Functions and Structures" in the chapter text.

Return Value　Long—Nonzero on success, zero on failure. Sets GetLastError.

Platform　Windows 95, Windows NT

■ GetPrinterDriverDirectory

VB Declaration
```
Declare Function GetPrinterDriverDirectory& Lib "spoolss.dll" Alias _
"GetPrinterDriverDirectoryA" (ByVal pName As String, ByVal pEnvironment As _
```

```
String, ByVal Level As Long, pDriverDirectory As Byte, ByVal cdBuf As Long, _
pcbNeeded As Long)
```

Description Determines the directory on the specified system that contains printer drivers.

Use with VB No problem.

Parameter	Type/Description
pName	String—The name of the server. Set to vbNullString for a local port.
pEnvironment	String—The environment of the directory to retrieve (for example, Windows NT x86). vbNullString for the current (local) system environment.
Level	Long—Set to 1.
pDriverDirectory	Byte—See "Spooler Functions and Structures" in the chapter text. This buffer will be loaded with the full path of the printer driver directory. This can be defined ByVal As String to eliminate the need to perform an ANSI-to-Unicode conversion when assigning the byte array to a string.
cdBuf	Long—See "Spooler Functions and Structures" in the chapter text.
pcbNeeded	Long—See "Spooler Functions and Structures" in the chapter text.

Return Value Long—Nonzero on success, zero on failure. Sets GetLastError.

Platform Windows 95, Windows NT

■ GetPrintProcessorDirectory

VB Declaration
```
Declare Function GetPrintProcessorDirectory& Lib "spoolss.dll" Alias _
"GetPrintProcessorDirectoryA" (ByVal pName As String, ByVal pEnvironment As _
String, ByVal Level As Long, ByVal pPrintProcessorInfo As String, ByVal cdBuf _
As Long, pcbNeeded As Long)
```

Description Determines the directory on the specified system that contains printer processor drivers and files.

Use with VB No problem.

Parameter	Type/Description
pName	String—The name of the server. Set to vbNullString for a local port.
pEnvironment	String—The environment of the directory to retrieve (for example, Windows NT x86). vbNullString for the current (local) system environment.
Level	Long—Set to 1.
pPrintProcessorInfo	Byte—See "Spooler Functions and Structures" in the chapter text. This buffer will be loaded with the full path of the printer processor directory. This can be defined ByVal As String to eliminate the need to perform an ANSI-to-Unicode conversion when assigning the byte array to a string.

Parameter	Type/Description
cdBuf	Long—See "Spooler Functions and Structures" in the chapter text.
pcbNeeded	Long—See "Spooler Functions and Structures" in the chapter text.

Return Value Long—Nonzero on success, zero on failure. Sets GetLastError.

Platform Windows 95, Windows NT

■ OpenPrinter

VB Declaration
```
Declare Function OpenPrinter& Lib "spoolss.dll" Alias "OpenPrinterA" (ByVal _
pPrinterName As String, phPrinter As Long, pDefault As PRINTER_DEFAULTS)
```

Description Opens the specified printer and obtains a handle to the printer.

Use with VB No problem.

Parameter	Type/Description
pPrinterName	String—The name of the printer to open.
phPrinter	Long—A long variable that will be loaded with the printer handle.
pDefault	PRINTER_DEFAULTS—A structure containing information on the printer to load. See "Comments."

Return Value Long—TRUE (nonzero) on success. Zero on error. Sets GetLastError.

Platform Windows 95, Windows NT

Comments The PRINTER_DEFAULTS structure is defined as follows:
```
Type PRINTER_DEFAULTS
        pDatatype As String
        pDevMode As Long
        DesiredAccess As Long
End Type
```

pDatatype is the name of the default datatype to use for the printer. May be vbNullString to use the current configured default.

pDevMode is an address of the default configuration information for the printer. May be zero to use the current defaults.

DesiredAccess is PRINTER_ACCESS_ADMINISTER or PRINTER_ACCESS_USER or a generic security value (depending on whether you need to configure the printer, or just access it).

Example DocJob.vbp, PicPrint.vbp

■ PrinterMessageBox

VB Declaration
```
Declare Function PrinterMessageBox& Lib "spoolss.dll" Alias _
"PrinterMessageBoxA" (ByVal hPrinter As Long, ByVal error As Long, ByVal hwnd _
As Long, ByVal pText As String, ByVal pCaption As String, ByVal dwType As Long)
```

Description	Posts a printer error message box on the system that owns the specified print job. Useful when a user is logged on remotely.
Use with VB	No problem.

Parameter	Type/Description
hPrinter	Long—The handle of the printer on which the error occurred.
error	Long—ERROR_OUT_OF_PAPER or ERROR_NOT_READY.
hwnd	Long—The parent window of the message box. May be NULL.
pText	String—The message text to display.
pCaption	String — The caption of the message box.
dwType	Long—Any of the standard MessageBox flags. MB_ICONSTOP or MB_RETRYCANCEL or MB_SETFOREGROUND is recommended.

Return Value	Long—IDOK, IDRETRY, or IDCANCEL, depending on user input (always IDOK if the message box went to a remote system).
Platform	Windows NT

PrinterProperties

VB Declaration	`Declare Function PrinterProperties& Lib "winspool.dll" (ByVal hwnd As Long, _` `ByVal hPrinter As Long)`
Description	Brings up the printer properties dialog box for configuring a printer.
Use with VB	No problem.

Parameter	Type/Description
hwnd	Long—The parent window for the dialog box.
hPrinter	Long—A handle to an open printer.

Return Value	Long—Nonzero on success, zero on failure. Sets GetLastError.
Platform	Windows 95, Windows NT
Comments	Some of the features of the dialog box will be disabled if the printer was not opened with sufficient access permission.
Example	PicPrint.vbp

ReadPrinter

VB Declaration	`Declare Function ReadPrinter& Lib "spoolss.dll" (ByVal hPrinter As Long, pBuf _` `As Any, ByVal cdBuf As Long, pNoBytesRead As Long)`

Description	Reads data from a printer.
Use with VB	No problem.

Parameter	Type/Description
hPrinter	Long—A handle to an open printer (obtain using OpenPrinter).
pBuf	Any—A buffer or structure to load with data from the printer.
cdBuf	Long—The size of the buffer or number of bytes to read.
pNoBytesRead	Long—A long variable loaded with the number of bytes actually read.

Return Value	Long—Nonzero on success, zero on failure. Sets GetLastError.
Platform	Windows 95, Windows NT
Comments	The port must be bidirectional for this function to work.

■ ResetDC

VB Declaration

```
Declare Function ResetDC& Lib "gdi32" Alias "ResetDCA" (ByVal hdc As Long, _
lpInitData As Byte)
```

Description   Resets a device context according to the DEVMODE structure provided. This allows you to change the configuration of the printer during printing. For example, you can change a single page in a document to landscape mode using this function. You may use the DocumentProperties function to obtain the default DEVMODE structure for a device.

Use with VB   No problem.

Parameter	Type/Description
hdc	Long—A handle to a device context.
lpInitData	Byte—The first byte in a buffer containing a valid DEVMODE structure for the device. Remember to include the private data area for the device in this buffer.

Return Value   Long—A handle to the device context on success, zero on error.

Platform   Windows 95, Windows NT, Win16

Comments   Experimentation indicates that this function can be used successfully on the device context returned by the hDC property of the Visual Basic Printer object.

Be sure to set the dmFields field of lpdm correctly. Refer to "Printer Settings and the DEVMODE Structure," earlier in this chapter.

This function is disabled between the StartPage and EndPage functions—in other words, you can only call this function between pages.

The driver, device, and output port cannot be changed with this function.

Example   PicPrint.vbp

■ ResetPrinter

VB Declaration `Declare Function ResetPrinter& Lib "spoolss.dll" Alias "ResetPrinterA" (ByVal _`
`hPrinter As Long, pDefault As PRINTER_DEFAULTS)`

Description Changes the default data type and document settings for the specified printer.

Use with VB No problem.

Parameter	Type/Description
hPrinter	Long—A handle of a printer to modify.
pDefault	PRINTER_DEFAULTS—A structure defining the new settings for the printer. Refer to the OpenPrinter function description for details on this structure. The DesiredAccess field in the structure is ignored.

Return Value Long—Nonzero on success, zero on failure. Sets GetLastError.

Platform Windows NT

■ ScheduleJob

VB Declaration `Declare Function ScheduleJob& Lib "spoolss.dll" (ByVal hPrinter As Long, ByVal _`
`JobId As Long)`

Description Submits a job for printing.

Use with VB No problem.

Parameter	Type/Description
hPrinter	Long—An open handle to a printer (obtain using OpenPrinter).
JobId	Long—A Job number obtained earlier using the AddJob function.

Return Value Long—Nonzero on success, zero on failure. Sets GetLastError.

Platform Windows 95, Windows NT

Comments Refer to the AddJob function for additional information.

■ SetAbortProc

VB Declaration `Declare Function SetAbortProc& Lib "gdi32" (ByVal hDC As Long, ByVal _`
`lpAbortProc As Long)`

Description It is possible to provide Windows with a function to call during extended print operations. This function is known as an abort function. The result of the abort function informs Windows whether it should continue the print operation or abort it.

The SetAbortProc function specifies the address of the abort function to Windows. Since Visual Basic does not support function addresses, it is necessary to use the dwcbk32d.ocx generic callback custom control provided with this book in order to use this function.

Use with VB Use of this function with the Visual Basic printer object may interfere with the normal VB print mechanism. It has been demonstrated to work, but will lead to printer errors that must be trapped on the next occurrence of the Printer.NewPage method. It is recommended that you thoroughly test code that attempts to install an abort function for the Visual Basic Printer object.

There are no problems using this function when you print to a device context that you create.

Parameter	Type/Description
hDC	Long—A handle to a device context.
lpAbortProc	Long—The address of an abort function. This can be obtained from the ProcAddress property of the dwcbk32d.ocx custom control.

Return Value Long—Result greater than zero on success, SP_ERROR on error. Sets GetLastError.

Platform Windows 95, Windows NT, Win16

Comments Refer to Appendix A for details on using the dwcbk32d.ocx custom control.

Example PicPrint.vbp

■ SetForm

VB Declaration
```
Declare Function SetForm& Lib "spoolss.dll" Alias "SetFormA" (ByVal hPrinter As _
Long, ByVal pFormName As String, ByVal Level As Long, pForm As Byte)
```

Description Sets the information for the specified form.

Use with VB No problem.

Parameter	Type/Description
hPrinter	Long—A handle to an open printer (obtain using OpenPrinter).
pFormName	String—The name of the form to set.
Level	Long—Set to 1
pForm	Byte—A buffer containing a valid FORM_INFO_1 structure.

Return Value Long—Nonzero on success, zero on failure. Sets GetLastError.

Platform Windows NT

Comments Refer to the AddForm function for additional information.

■ SetJob

VB Declaration
```
Declare Function SetJob& Lib "spoolss.dll" Alias "SetJobA" (ByVal hPrinter As _
Long, ByVal JobId As Long, ByVal Level As Long, pJob As Byte, ByVal Command As _
Long)
```

Description Allows you to control the state of a print job.

Use with VB   No problem.

Parameter	Type/Description
hPrinter	Long—A handle to an open printer (obtain using OpenPrinter).
JobId	Long—The job number to modify.
Level	Long—0, 1, or 2
pJob	Byte—A buffer containing a JOB_INFO_1 or JOB_INFO_1 structure if level is 1 or 2. NULL (change to ByVal As Long and pass zero) if level is 0. If a structure is specified, information from the structure will be used to change the settings of the print job (except for the JobId, pPrinterName, pMachineName, pDriverName, Size, Submitte, and Time fields).
Command	Long—One of the following: JOB_CONTROL_CANCEL: Cancels the job. JOB_CONTROL_PAUSE: Pauses a job. JOB_CONTROL_RESTART: Restarts a job that has already started printing. JOB_CONTROL_RESUME: Resumes a paused job.

Return Value   Long—Nonzero on success, zero on failure. Sets GetLastError.

Platform   Windows 95, Windows NT

■ SetPrinter

VB Declaration
```
Declare Function SetPrinter& Lib "spoolss.dll" Alias "SetPrinterA" (ByVal _
    hPrinter As Long, ByVal Level As Long, pPrinter As Byte, ByVal Command As Long)
```

Description   Provides control of the state of a printer.

Use with VB   No problem.

Parameter	Type/Description
hPrinter	Long—A handle to an open printer (obtain using OpenPrinter).
Level	Long—0, 2, or 3 (4 or 5 for Windows 95, 5 or 6 for NT 4.0). Must be zero if Command is not zero.
pPrinter	Byte—A buffer containing a PRINTER_INFO_x structure where x is the level. If level is zero and command is PRINTER_CONTROL_SET_STATUS, the buffer contains a PRINTER_CONTROL_STATUS structure. Otherwise if level is zero, set to NULL (change to ByVal As Long and pass zero).

Parameter	Type/Description
Command	Long—One of the following: Zero—Change printer according to the PRINTER_INFO_x structure. PRINTER_CONTROL_PAUSE: Pauses the printer. PRINTER_CONTROL_PURGE: Deletes all jobs for the printer. PRINTER_CONTROL_RESUME: Resumes a paused printer. PRINTER_CONTROL_SET_STATUS: Loads PRINTER_CONTROL_STATUS structure for the printer (N/A on NT 3.51).

Return Value Long—Nonzero on success, zero on failure. Sets GetLastError.

Platform Windows 95, Windows NT

Comments When setting the printer status based on a PRINTER_INFO_2 structure, the pServerName, AveragePPM, Status, and cJobs fields are ignored. Refer to the Microsoft Win32 documentation for additional information.

■ SetPrinterData

VB Declaration
```
Declare Function SetPrinterData& Lib "spoolss.dll" Alias "SetPrinterDataA" _
(ByVal hPrinter As Long, ByVal pValueName As String, ByVal dwType As Long, _
pData As Byte, ByVal cbData As Long)
```

Description Sets registry configuration information for the printer.

Use with VB No problem.

Parameter	Type/Description
hPrinter	Long—A handle to an open printer (obtain using OpenPrinter).
pValueName	String—The name of the registry value to set.
dwType	Long—The type of data. One of the constants REG_?? from file API32.TXT. Refer to Chapter 13 for information on registry data types.
pData	Byte—The first entry in a buffer containing the appropriate data type to set.
cbData	Long—The length of buffer pData.

Return Value Long—ERROR_SUCCESS on success, an error value on failure.

Platform Windows 95, Windows NT

■ StartDoc

VB Declaration
```
Declare Function StartDoc& Lib "gdi32" Alias "StartDocA" (ByVal hdc As Long, _
lpdi As DOCINFO)
```

Description Begins a print job.

Use with VB	No problem.

Parameter	Type/Description
hdc	Long—A handle to a device context.
lpdi	DOCINFO—A structure defining a document. A description of this structure follows.

Return Value	Long—The job number for the document on success, the constant SP_ERROR on error. Sets GetLastError.
Platform	Windows 95, Windows NT, Win16
Comments	The DOCINFO structure is defined as follows:

```
Type DOCINFO      ' 12 Bytes
   cbSize As Long
   lpszDocName As String
   lpszOutput As String
End Type
```

The structure fields are defined as follows:

Field	Type/Description
cbSize	Long—The size of the structure, currently 12 bytes.
lpszDocName	Long—Pointer to a string containing the name of the document. This document name will be shown by the print manager application.
lpszOutput	Long—Pointer to a string containing the name of an output file if you wish to redirect printer output to a disk file. Set to vbNullString to send the output to the device.

Porting Notes	The size of the DOCINFO structure has changed from Win16.
Example	PicPrint.vbp

■ StartDocPrinter

VB Declaration	`Declare Function StartDocPrinter& Lib "spoolss.dll" Alias "StartDocPrinterA" _` `(ByVal hPrinter As Long, ByVal Level As Long, pDocInfo As Byte)`
Description	Starts a new document at the spooler level.
Use with VB	No problem.

Parameter	Type/Description
hPrinter	Long—A handle to an open printer (obtain using OpenPrinter).
Level	Long— 1 or 2 (Win95 only)
pDocInfo	Byte—A buffer containing a DOC_INFO_1 or DOC_INFO_1 structure. Refer to the chapter text describing the DocJob.vbp example for further information. Also see Appendix B for information on these structures.

Return Value	Long—Nonzero on success, zero on failure.
Platform	Windows 95, Windows NT
Comments	Not typically used at the application level, this is used by the spooler to indicate the start of a document at the spooler level.
Example	DocJob.vbp

■ StartPage

VB Declaration	`Declare Function StartPage& Lib "gdi32" (ByVal hdc As Long)`
Description	This function is called before printing into a new page.
Use with VB	When printing with the Visual Basic printer object, do not use this function.

Parameter	Type/Description
hdc	Long—Handle to a device context.

Return Value	Long—TRUE (nonzero) on success, zero otherwise.
Platform	Windows 95, Windows NT
Porting Notes	See the porting notes for the EndPage function.
Example	PicPrint.vbp

■ StartPagePrinter

VB Declaration	`Declare Function StartPagePrinter& Lib "spoolss.dll" (ByVal hPrinter As Long)`
Description	Specifies the start of a new page in a print job.
Use with VB	No problem.

Parameter	Type/Description
hPrinter	Long—A handle to an open printer (obtain using OpenPrinter).

Return Value	Long—Nonzero on success, zero on failure. Sets GetLastError.
Platform	Windows 95, Windows NT
Comments	Not typically used at the application level, this is used by the spooler to indicate the start of a page in the actual printer data.
Example	DocJob.vbp

■ WritePrinter

VB Declaration
```
Declare Function WritePrinter& Lib "spoolss.dll" (ByVal hPrinter As Long, pBuf _
As Any, ByVal cdBuf As Long, pcWritten As Long)
```

Description   Writes data to be sent directly to a printer.

Use with VB   No problem.

Parameter	Type/Description
hPrinter	Long—A handle to an open printer (obtain using OpenPrinter).
pBuf	Any—A buffer or structure containing data to write to the printer.
cdBuf	Long—The length of the pBuf buffer.
pcWritten	Long—A long variable to be loaded with the number of bytes actually written.

Return Value   Long—Nonzero on success, zero on failure. Sets GetLastError.

Platform   Windows 95, Windows NT

Example   DocJob.vbp

13

File Operations

I F THE ULTIMATE PURPOSE OF ALMOST ANY APPLICATION IS TO PROCESS information, then clearly one of the most important issues any programmer has to deal with is how to go about storing information on disk. This issue can be surprisingly complex. Applications that need to work with a few very large sets of archived information have completely different requirements from applications that need to process large numbers of smaller documents. The techniques used to work with document files are often different from those needed to save application configuration information that may need to be saved from one session to the next.

Windows and Visual Basic together provide a wealth of capability in this area, and Win32 improves substantially on Win16 when it comes to file-related operations. This chapter starts out with a review of initialization files and the system registry. It discusses the use of version resources to determine the version of an executable file, DLL, or other executable software component.

This chapter also describes general-purpose file operations, including those necessary to read and write file data, manipulate file systems, and work with compressed files. The concept of file mappings is introduced—a powerful new technique for working with files and sharing large blocks of information between processes.

Finally, FileDemo and a few other sample programs are included to illustrate many of the techniques introduced in this chapter. Most of the file access functions are very easy to use, so the examples focus on some of the more sophisticated file operations.

What Type of File Access Should You Use?

Windows and Visual Basic provide many different ways to store data on disk—so many that sometimes it is hard to know what the best approach is for any given application. This is made even more difficult by the recommendations that may be found in magazine articles and even in the system documentation. For example, although the Win32 documentation recommends that you use the Registry instead of private initialization files, is this approach better in every case, or are they just advocating the use of the new technology for marketing reasons?

Here then are some suggestions for where you may wish to use particular storage technologies.

Private Initialization Files

Private initialization files are useful for storing application configuration information. Though they are part of an older technology, they have the advantage of being easily edited using Windows Notepad or any text editor. Of course, this can also be a disadvantage, depending upon your application. Initialization files are very easy to use with the aid of a few simple functions.

The System Registry

The registry is also good for storing application configuration information. Its hierarchical nature makes it possible to create a more complex data organization. It can save data in formats other than the simple string format provided by initialization files. You can also save multiple sets of data under different keys. Its disadvantage is that the registry is difficult to edit by the casual user. Microsoft recommends that individual entries in the registry not exceed 2,048 bytes.

Private File Formats

Private document files are used by many applications and come in many forms: word processing documents, spreadsheets, and so on. Visual Basic and Windows both provide extensive functionality for reading and writing disk files directly. Private file formats provide high performance and complete flexibility. Unfortunately, implementing software support for complex file formats can be a great deal of work. Private file formats also provide no standard way for exposing public information, and no easy way for embedding other standard object types.

Databases

Databases provide a powerful mechanism for storing and archiving many different types of information. They are ideal for repositories of information that need to be shared among applications or systems. They are not suitable for a more "docucentric" approach—where you might want to have separate documents or configuration sets in individual files. They also suffer from potentially high overhead in terms of performance and the need to distribute a database engine with the application.

OLE Structured Storage

This is an implementation of the Compound Document standard used by Microsoft in their own Office applications. Each file contains an unlimited number of *storages* and *streams* of data in a hierarchy—in a sense, an entire file system within each file. A storage is similar to a directory, each having a name and supporting a complete hierarchy. A stream is read and written as if it were a standard disk file using simple read and write operations. Structured storage files have the advantage of making it easy to work with very complex file formats (the system is responsible for allocating space within the file for each stream). It is relatively easy to embed standard objects into a compound document, and compound documents make it possible to expose public information about the file as well as to maintain proprietary information in other parts of the file. Compound documents also provide support for *transactioning*—the ability to undo changes to the files.

OLE structured storage suffers from two disadvantages. First, the performance, while good, is not *as* good as direct file access. Second, Visual Basic cannot use OLE structured storage without the assistance of a third-party product such as Desaware's StorageTools.

Initialization Files

Windows provides the capability for applications to easily save initialization or status information in standard format text files known as initialization files. The best known of these is the WIN.INI initialization file. This file is used by some versions of Windows to save system settings such as font and device information, and by some applications to save their own initialization data. Windows allows each application to create and maintain its own initialization files as well.

Initialization files, or profile files as they are sometimes called, have a standard format. This format is described in your Windows documentation.

Each initialization file is divided into sections. Each section is marked by the name of the section in brackets, as shown here:

```
[section name]
```

Within the section, entries are formed of two parts separated by an equal sign. The first part is called the *key name* or *entry name*. The second part is the string for that key. This is the format of an entry:

```
keyname=string for this key
```

For example, the WIN.INI file has a section for various sounds that the system will play during certain events. The default "beep" sound is specified using the SystemDefault key. The string defined for that entry is the name of a sound file, in this case, DING.WAV, followed by a description of the entry as shown here.

```
[sounds]
SystemDefault=ding.wav, Default Beep
```

On Windows NT, most of the sections in both WIN.INI and other system initialization files are mapped to the registry. You can determine which sections of which files are mapped to the registry by looking at the HKEY_LOCAL_MACHINE\Software\Microsoft\Windows NT\CurrentVersion\IniFileMapping entry in the registry. When a section in an INI file is mapped to the registry, the INI file functions read and write the registry entries directly and the values will never appear in the initialization file. This mapping is entirely transparent to the programmer, so you can go ahead and use the initialization file functions safely without worrying about which operating system you are using and whether the data is actually stored in the file or in the system registry.

Visual Basic programs can easily use the initialization file functions both to support private initialization files and to read or set entries in the WIN.INI file. The available API functions are shown in Table 13.1.

Table 13.1 **Initialization File Functions**

Function	Description
GetProfileInt	Retrieves an integer setting from the WIN.INI initialization file
GetProfileSection	Retrieves data for an entire section from the WIN.INI initialization file
GetProfileString	Retrieves a string from the WIN.INI initialization file
GetPrivateProfileInt	Retrieves an integer setting from a private initialization file
GetPrivateProfileSection	Retrieves data for an entire section from a private initialization file
GetPrivateProfileString	Retrieves a string from a private initialization file
WritePrivateProfileSection	Writes data for an entire section from a private initialization file
WritePrivateProfileString	Sets a string into a private initialization file
WriteProfileSection	Writes data for an entire section from the WIN.INI initialization file
WriteProfileString	Sets a string into the WIN.INI initialization file

The WIN.INI initialization file contains configuration information that is used by Windows and is accessible to many files. If you change an entry in WIN.INI that is not unique to your application, it is important to notify the other applications in the system that WIN.INI has changed. This can be accomplished by posting a WM_WININICHANGE message to all applications as follows:

```
di% = PostMessageBystring(HWND_BROADCAST, WM_WININICHANGE, ˉ, sectionname$)
```

where *sectionname$* is the name of the section that was changed.

On Windows 95 if you change a setting that corresponds to one of the SPI_ settings set using the SystemParametersInfo function, you should post the WM_SETTINGCHANGE message described in Chapter 16.

Once again, keep in mind that some of your changes will not actually appear in WIN.INI because they are mapped to the system registry.

The System Registry

If there is one thing that is absolutely clear about the evolution of Windows, it is that the evolution of Windows will continue. This book focuses on part of that evolution—from 16 bits and the Win16 API to 32-bit operating systems and the new functionality provided by the Win32 API. But it is worth taking a moment to examine another part of that evolution that is a bit more subtle.

One of the characteristics of DOS and similar operating systems is that users work with applications that in turn work with data. In other words, when you have a task to do, you choose the application to work with. This application then allows you to access disk files that contain the data that you want to work with.

Windows has gradually been evolving towards a more docucentric approach of computing. Instead of choosing an application, you choose the data that you want to work with. It is then up to the operating system to choose the appropriate application. For example, if you have a document that contains an image that you want to edit, instead of launching a paint program you can simply open the document. Windows then searches your system for a paint program that can handle the image format in the document, launch the program, and open the document for editing. With the new OLE technology, a document can contain many different types of data, each of which might be editable using a different application. With in-place editing, your main application window can be temporarily taken over by these different applications, allowing you to edit all of the different types of data in a document using a single window that provides an interface to many different applications. For example, if you use Microsoft Word for Windows to edit a document that also contains an Excel spreadsheet, when you click on the spreadsheet Word will allow the Excel menus and interface to become active within the document window.

With future versions of Windows the operating system will provide even more support for this type of object linking. You might have a document that consists of many objects of different types in different disk files. Windows will keep track of the links between these objects and the document, making it easy to share objects among many different documents, and ensuring that the links remain valid even if individual disk files are moved.

But what does this have to do with the system registry?

In order for the operating system to be able to figure out which applications are associated with which types of objects, it must have access to a great deal of information about both objects and applications on the system. There needs to be a way to uniquely register and identify any type of object—both those defined by the system and those defined by individual applications. There needs to be a way to keep track of which applications work with which objects. There needs to be a way to keep track of where documents and objects are on disk so that they can be found quickly. There needs to be a way to keep track of shared components so that when one application is removed, components that it uses that are used by other applications are not deleted.

The amount and types of information that need to be stored now and that will need to be stored as Windows continues to evolve go beyond what can be stored effectively using initialization files. For this reason, Microsoft has created the system registry, or registration database. The registry can handle substantially more data than initialization files and is not restricted to string data. It is more secure and robust than individual initialization files, and is hard to edit or delete. The registry also includes some system configuration information, depending on the operating system. On Windows 3.x, almost all of the system configuration information is kept in initialization files—you can delete the registry and you will lose very little information. Under Windows 95 some system configuration information is kept in the registry, but if the registry becomes corrupt or is deleted, your system will still run. Under Windows NT if you lose the registry all bets are off—you either need to reinstall it from an emergency rescue disk or reinstall from scratch, since Windows NT stores very little information in initialization files.

The Win32 documentation suggests that initialization files are obsolete and that you should only use registry functions. This is not the case. There are situations where initialization files are a better choice; for example, where you want the user to be able to directly edit the configuration information. You should choose between the registry and initialization files based on the needs of your particular application.

Registry Architecture

The registry can best be thought of as a miniature file system. Instead of files, it contains "values." Instead of directories, it contains keys. These keys form a hierarchy of information. Instead of a single root directory, Windows 95 and Windows NT provide a number of predefined keys. Functions that accept handles to keys will, in most cases, also accept these predefined key constants as parameters. These are listed in Table 13.2.

Table 13.2 **Predefined Keys**

Key	Description
HKEY_CLASSES_ROOT	This key is used to store information about classes of files and objects. Associations between document types and applications are kept here, as are class identifiers used by OLE objects. This key can also be accessed as HKEY_LOCAL_MACHINE\SOFTWARE\Classes.
HKEY_CURRENT_USER	This key is used to access configuration information for the current user.

Table 13.2   **Predefined Keys (Continued)**

Key	Description
HKEY_LOCAL_MACHINE	This top-level key contains in-depth information about the hardware and software configuration of the system.
HKEY_USERS	This top-level key contains software and system configuration information that is unique to a particular user. The HKEY_USERS\Default key contains the default settings for new users, and the settings for users who have not made any user-specific configuration changes.
HKEY_CURRENT_CONFIG	This key is used to store general system configuration information. It is not available under NT 3.51. It also appears as a sub-key to HKEY_LOCAL_MACHINE.
HKEY_DYN_DATA	This key is used to hold data that is used in the current session but does not actually need to be saved between Windows sessions. For example, performance data relating to the current session can be found here. This key is not available under NT 3.51.

Figure 13.1 shows a view of the registry editor for Windows 95. As you can see, the six predefined keys appear as top-level keys (even though some of them actually map into other subkeys of other top-level keys). The currently selected key in this figure is HKEY_CURRENT_USER\Control Panel\desktop\WindowMetrics.

Figure 13.1

A view of the
Windows 95 registry

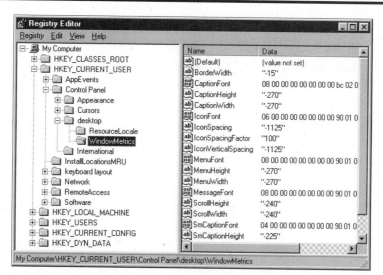

Each of these terms represents a key. Thus, HKEY_CURRENT_USER is the root key. "Control Panel" is a subkey, "desktop" is a subkey of "Control Panel," and "WindowMetrics" is a subkey of "desktop." "WindowMetrics" has no subkeys, but it does have a number of values associated with it. Each key can have a default value. This value does not have a name and must always be a string if present. Windows 3.1 only supported a single default value for each key, severely limiting the use of the registry when compared to Win32. The "WindowMetrics" key has a large number of values, divided between string data and binary data. You might recognize some of the key names as closely related to parameters that can be retrieved and set using the functions found in Chapter 6. You should avoid changing system parameters using registry functions. Always use API functions if they exist (and if they don't exist, chances are good that changing a parameter in the registry directly can lead to unintended results).

Registry values can contain many types of data, as shown in Table 13.3.

Table 13.3   **Registry Data Types**

Data type	Description
REG_BINARY	Binary data
REG_DWORD	32-bit long
REG_DWORD_BIGENDIAN	A 32-bit long with bytes organized so the high order byte is at the lowest address (see Chapter 4 for a discussion and examples of Big-Endian and Little-Endian values)
REG_DWORD_LITTLE_ENDIAN	A 32-bit long with bytes organized so the low order byte is at the lowest address (Intel X86 standard)
REG_EXPAND_SZ	An environment string that is not expanded (refer to the ExpandEnvironmentStrings function in Chapter 6 for details)
REG_LINK	A symbolic link
REG_MULTI_SZ	A list of strings that are separated by NULL characters and terminated by two NULL characters
REG_NONE	Undefined
REG_RESOURCE_LIST	A resource list for a device driver
REG_SZ	A string with a NULL termination

Strings in the registry are always stored in Unicode format internally, but you need not worry about that, as Visual Basic uses the ANSI registry functions, which always access the strings as ANSI strings. Unfortunately, this means that every string access from Visual Basic involves a conversion from Unicode to ANSI and back to Unicode.

Win32 provides a large number of functions for working with the registry. These are listed in Table 13.4.

Table 13.4 **Registry Functions**

Function	Description
RegCloseKey	Closes an open key
RegConnectRegistry	Opens a key on a remote system
RegCreateKey, RegCreateKeyEx	Creates a new key
RegDeleteKey	Deletes a key
RegDeleteValue	Deletes a value
RegEnumKey, RegEnumKeyEx	Enumerates the subkeys of a given key
RegEnumValue	Enumerates the values for a key
RegFlushKey	Ensures that changes to a key have been written to disk
RegGetKeySecurity	Obtains the security information for a key
RegLoadKey	Loads registry information that had been saved to a file
RegNotifyChangeKeyValue	Allows your application to be notified when a key's value or other information changes
RegOpenKey, RegOpenKeyEx	Opens a key
RegQueryInfoKey	Obtains information about a key
RegQueryValue, RegQueryValueEx	Retrieves value data
RegReplaceKey	Replaces registry information with information that had been saved to a file
RegRestoreKey	Restores registry information from information that had been saved to a file
RegSaveKey	Saves registry information to a file
RegSetKeySecurity	Sets the security for a key
RegSetValue, RegSetValueEx	Sets a value for a key
RegUnLoadKey	Disconnects an open registry key on a remote system

File and Directory Operations

Windows provides a set of API functions for file operations. With Windows 3.x and Visual Basic 3.0, while the Windows API did provide a few functions that went beyond the capability of Visual Basic, overall VB provided much more powerful file manipulation functions than were present in the Windows API. While Visual Basic has improved its file handling capability somewhat, it is negligible compared to the vast improvements in the Win32 API with regard to file handling. While the Visual Basic file functions will be adequate for most situations, you are encouraged to review the capabilities of the Win32 functions—even when they seem at first glance to be equivalent, so that you will be aware of the additional functionality that Win32 can provide should you need it.

Win32 File Functions

The vast majority of Win32 file functions are straightforward and easy to understand. There are, however, a few areas that deserve some in-depth attention.

Asynchronous File Operations

One of the most intriguing and potentially useful new features supported by Win32 is the ability to overlap file operations. Under Win16, any time you transferred data to or from a file using an API command (or Visual Basic command, for that matter), the transfer was performed synchronously. (This means that when you call a function to perform a data transfer, the function will not return until the transfer is complete.) On long I/O operations, this could cause a noticeable delay in the program's operation.

Win32 allows you to specify that a file operation be asynchronous—the transfer function returns immediately and the operating system completes the operation in the background. This type of operation is called an overlapped operation and requires the use of an OVERLAPPED structure which is defined as follows:

```
Type OVERLAPPED
        Internal As Long
        InternalHigh As Long
        offset As Long
        OffsetHigh As Long
        hEvent As Long
End Type
```

The Internal and InternalHigh fields are used internally by the system and should not be modified by the user. The offset and OffsetHigh fields are set to the offset in the file at which reading or writing should take place.

When you enable overlapped operations on a file, the system does not keep track of a file pointer for the file—since you effectively need a separate file pointer for each overlapped operation that you perform. The hEvent field is a handle to an event object—a special type of object that allows you to determine when an overlapped operation has finished. Event objects are discussed further in Chapter 14. The event object must be set to "manual reset" type and should be nonsignaled when the I/O operation is called (these terms will also be explained in Chapter 14).

File Times

Chapter 6 introduced the ideas of system and local time. Windows provides a mechanism for recording the time and date of file access and creation. This information is stored under Win32 as a 64-bit value that measures the number of 100ns intervals that have passed since January 1, 1601. This value is stored in a FILETIME structure that is defined as follows:

```
Type FILETIME
        dwLowDateTime As Long
        dwHighDateTime As Long
End Type
```

File times are generally stored in the system in Coordinated Universal Time (UTC), but functions are provided to convert to and from UTC and local time. A FILETIME structure can contain UTC or local time—it is up to you to keep track of which time the structure contains. Also keep in mind that not every file system saves the same time information or uses the same resolution. For example, Windows 95 records file times with two-second resolution. FAT file systems only record last modification time.

Win32 also provides conversion functions that work with DOS file times. DOS file times are defined as two 16-bit values. The first value specifies the date where bits 0–4 are the day (1–31), bits 5–8 are the month (1 = January, 12 = December, and so forth), and bits 9–15 are the year, where zero is 1980. The second value specifies the time where bits 0–4 are the number of seconds divided by 2, bits 5–10 are the number of minutes (0–59), and bits 11–15 are the number of hours (0–23). Refer to the Chapter 3 description of bitfields for a description of how numbers can be packed into an integer in this manner.

Table 13.5 summarizes the functions used to manipulate FILETIME structures.

Table 13.5   **File Time Functions**

Function	Description
CompareFileTime	Compares two FILETIME structures

Table 13.5 **File Time Functions (Continued)**

Function	Description
DosDateTimeToFileTime	Converts a DOS file time to a FILETIME
FileTimeToDosDateTime	Converts a FILETIME to a DOS file time
FileTimeToLocalFileTime	Converts a FILETIME structure from UTC to local time
FileTimeToSystemTime	Loads a SYSTEMTIME structure with the time specified by a FILE-TIME structure
GetFileTime	Obtains the creation, access, and modification time of a file
SetFileTime	Sets the creation, access, and modification time of a file
SystemTimeToFileTime	Loads a FILETIME structure with the time specified by a SYSTEM-TIME structure

Device I/O Control

Win32 includes a function that allows you to perform a variety of direct operations on a device that do not fall into the typical category of opening, reading, writing, and closing files. These are accomplished with the DeviceIoControl function.

This function takes as parameters a handle to a device, a constant that specifies the operation to perform, an input buffer, and an output buffer (refer to the Function Reference section for this chapter). Each type of operation has associated with it a structure that defines the operation to perform.

Security

Under Windows NT, files and other Windows system objects all have associated security attributes. The Win32 API file functions allow you to both retrieve and set the security of various objects (assuming, of course, that you have the security to do so). In virtually all cases, you can pass a NULL value where a function accepts a security descriptor to use the default security for the object. This lets you create applications that are essentially not security aware (though they are, of course, subject to the security already set for the system).

Security is a somewhat complex subject, and since it is only supported under Windows NT, it is one of those subjects that is covered very lightly in this book. You can use the techniques covered in this book to interpret the Win32 documentation on security based on your own needs.

Summary of File and Directory Functions

Table 13.6 lists the Windows API functions related to file and directory operations.

Table 13.6 **File and Directory API Functions**

Function	Description
CloseHandle	Closes a file handle (and many other types of handles as well)
CopyFile	Copies a file
CreateDirectory, CreateDirectoryEx	Creates a new directory
CreateFile	Creates or opens a file
DeleteFile	Deletes a file
DeviceIoControl	Allows low-level operations on a disk volume (and other device operations)
FindClose, FindFirstFile, FindNextFile	Functions that make it easy to search for files
FlushFileBuffers	Ensures that changes to a file have been written to disk
GetBinaryType	Determines if a file is executable
GetCompressedFileSize	Determines the amount of space that a compressed file takes up on disk
GetCurrentDirectory	Determines the current directory
GetDiskFreeSpace	Determines how much free space is available on a disk
GetDriveType	Determines the type of a specified disk drive
GetFileAttributes	Retrieves attributes of a file
GetFileInformationByHandle	Retrieves information about a file
GetFileSize	Determines the size of a file
GetFileType	Determines the type of file given a file handle
GetFullPathName	Obtains the full path name of a file
GetLogicalDrives, GetLogicalDriveStrings	Obtains a list of logical drives defined for a system
GetOverlappedResult	Obtains the result of an asynchronous file operation

Table 13.6   File and Directory API Functions (Continued)

Function	Description
GetShortPathName	Retrieves the short name for a file
GetSystemDirectory	Retrieves the path of the Windows system directory
GetTempDrive	Obsolete under Win32
GetTempFileName	Retrieves the name of a unique temporary file
GetTempPath	Determines the path of the directory assigned for use by temporary files
GetVolumeInformation	Retrieves information about a disk volume
GetWindowsDirectory	Retrieves the path of the Windows directory
lclose	Closes a file
lcreat	Creates a file
llseek	Seeks to a position in a file
LockFile, LockFileEx	Locks a region in a file
lopen	Opens a file
lread, hread	Reads from a file
lwrite, hwrite	Writes to a file
MoveFile, MoveFileEx	Moves a file
OpenFile	Flexible file open function
QueryDosDevice	Obtains information about the logical DOS device names present on a system
ReadFile, ReadFileEx	Reads from a file
RemoveDirectory	Deletes a directory
SearchPath	Searches for a file using the standard Windows search sequence
SetCurrentDirectory	Sets the current directory
SetEndOfFile	Sets the location of the end of a file
SetFileAttributes	Sets the attributes of a file
SetFilePointer	Sets the current file pointer location in a file

Table 13.6 **File and Directory API Functions (Continued)**

Function	Description
SetVolumeLabel	Sets the name of a volume
UnlockFile, UnlockFileEx	Unlocks a region in a file
WriteFile, WriteFileEx	Writes a file

Compressed File Operations

Windows provides support for expansion of compressed files. These functions, listed in Table 13.7, are designed for use by installation programs and require that files be compressed by the Microsoft COMPRESS.EXE program. This program is included in the professional version of Visual Basic.

Table 13.7 **File Expansion Functions**

Function	Description
CopyLZFile	Obsolete under Win32 (use LZCopy)
GetExpandedName	Determines the original name of a compressed file
LZClose	Closes a compressed file
LZCopy	Copies a single file
LZDone	Obsolete under Win32
LZInit	Initializes the internal data buffers required for use with compressed files
LZOpenFile	Opens or performs other operations on compressed files (similar to the OpenFile API function except that it is compatible with compressed files)
LZRead	Reads and decompresses data from a compressed file
LZSeek	Seeks to a new position in a compressed file
LZStart	Obsolete under Win32

The decompression library provides several techniques for reading from and copying compressed files. In most cases, these techniques involve use of special file handles that access internal buffers used to decompress the file. Up to 16 of these handles may be open at once.

The decompression functions can determine if a file is compressed. If the file is not compressed, the functions call the appropriate standard API functions to perform the requested operation. This means that you may use these functions to copy uncompressed files as well.

Copying a Single File

A single file can be copied using the LZCopy function as follows:

1. Open the source file and destination file using the LZOpenFile function.

2. Copy the source to the destination using the LZCopy function.

3. Close the source and destination file using the LZClose function.

Reading Data from a Compressed File

It is possible to read decompressed data from a compressed file as follows:

1. Open the file that you want to read using the LZOpenFile function. Or you can open the file with the normal OpenFile function and then use the LZInit function to obtain a compressed file handle for that file.

2. You may use the GetExpandedName function to determine the original name of a compressed file.

3. The LZRead function may be used to read from the file. The LZSeek function may be used to set the current position in the file.

4. Use the LZClose function to close the file handle.

File Mappings (Is It File, or Is It Memory?)

There is really no difference between a file and memory. Ah, I know what you're thinking: Surely such a statement is the product of a hallucination. We all know that these are two different things.

A file represents a block of data on disk that you access using file operations. First you open a file, then you use special functions to read and write data to the file, then you close the file when you are done with it. Memory corresponds to physical memory in your computer. In languages such as C++ you can access memory directly using pointers. In Visual Basic, you need to use DLL functions that can copy blocks of memory from Visual Basic objects to and from a specified address in memory. Memory blocks are allocated differently from files, they are accessed differently, and the data is stored differently. They are not the same. There is a difference.

It is true that once upon a time (say, a few months ago), there was quite a large difference between files and memory—but the lines had become increasingly blurred. For example, Windows has long supported virtual memory in which your system has access to more memory than is physically present in your system. Windows accomplishes this by allocating a paging file on disk. When you try to access an address in memory that is not physically present in your system, an error called a "page fault" occurs. The system loads the page of memory from the system paging file. If necessary, it frees space in physical memory by writing one of the other memory pages to the system paging file.

So when you access memory on a Windows system, you can't really be sure if the data you are looking at is actually in memory or on disk—nor would you care, in most cases.

But virtual memory has been around for a long time, and certainly is not enough to support a claim that files and memory are the same things. You still can't access files using memory pointers, right?

Well, actually, under Win32, you can. Consider again the concept of virtual memory. Virtual memory works by giving the system an address space that is greater than the available physical memory. Under Win32, the address space for each application is 2 gigabytes, even though it is unlikely that your typical desktop system will support that much physical memory for at least another few years. What could be the point of having such a large address space? Consider how it might be used: Portions of that 2GB address space might be mapped to physical memory, and parts to the system paging file. Since the operating system already knows how to map part of the address space to one file, how difficult would it be to map other portions of that address space to any arbitrary disk file? As it turns out, it's not hard at all. Under Win32 this is accomplished using an object called a memory mapped file, or "file mapping." A file mapping object can take a disk file and make it appear as if it was mapped into your application's address space. You can then read and optionally modify the contents of the file as easily as you would modify a block of memory. Figure 13.2 illustrates how files are mapped into your address space. (Purists will note that this figure is a vast oversimplification of the way Win32 actually manages memory—the point here is to communicate the concept of a file mapping, not to provide an in-depth look at the actual implementation of the Win32 memory management system under a particular operating system, a subject that will be covered further in Chapter 15.)

Why Memory Mapped Files Are Important

You may be wondering why memory mapped files are important to Visual Basic programmers. At first glance, it seems to relate to lower level aspects of the operating system that are not easily used from Visual Basic. After all, it is still difficult to access memory directly using Visual Basic so there really is no benefit to accessing files as memory instead of using file operations. Or is there?

Figure 13.2

How files are mapped into your address space

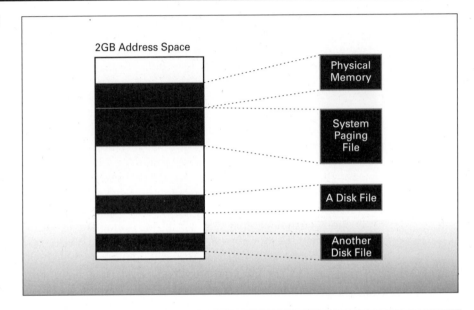

Take a look at the compile tab of the project-options dialog box for an ActiveX DLL project. You will see an option that lets you set the DLL base address. The Visual Basic online help explains that assigning a unique base address can speed the load time for your DLL. Why is this? Because Win32 uses a new executable format that takes advantage of the file mapping capabilities built into the operating system. Under Win16, when you loaded a DLL the operating system would open the file, load whatever segments are necessary for the program to start running into memory, then fix up any pointers in the program so that they would be correct for the address at which the program was actually loaded (a process called relocation). Only after all of these steps were complete would code in the newly loaded DLL actually begin executing.

Under Win32, the operating system looks at the file to see if it specified a preferred loading address. If that address is not currently in use by another DLL, the system simply maps the file into your address space and starts executing it. No time-consuming relocation, no need to preload large parts of the DLL—the operating system will load additional pages of memory as necessary. If the address requested by the DLL is already in use by another DLL or application, relocation is necessary, but the process is still relatively fast and file mapping is still used to map the DLL into the memory address space of your application. This process is also used to load executable files, though it is not as critical there since each process tends to have only a single executable file.

Why Memory Mapped Files Are Really Important

The fact that Win32 uses file mappings to load DLLs and executables is a nice tidbit of knowledge, but there is a far more important use for memory mapped files.

You see, memory mapped files provide the most efficient way to share large amounts of data between Win32 applications. If you've been using global memory to transfer blocks of memory between Win16 applications, you may have found that the technique no longer works with 32-bit Visual Basic. This is because these global memory blocks are no longer shared. You see, when we say that each application has a 2GB address space, it truly means that each application has its own 2GB address space. Memory allocated in one application's address space simply does not exist in the address space of any other application. (Note: This explanation is a bit of a simplification as well, as there are some code and memory objects which appear in the same address space for all applications—especially under Windows 95 which does not provide the high level of security offered by Windows NT.)

Under Win32 you share memory by creating a file mapping object. The handle to that object can be duplicated and passed to another application in order to share the underlying file, or you can take the easier approach of assigning the file mapping object a name. This allows other applications to access the object using the unique object name. Once you have a handle to a file mapping object, you can map the object into your application's address space, making the underlying file appear to the program as a block of memory. If multiple applications are accessing the same file mapping object, Win32 makes sure that the object remains coherent—that the contents of the object are identical for all of the applications (though this does not apply if you have opened the object remotely across a network or if you mix memory access to the file mapping object with file commands on the underlying disk file).

You may be wondering if this scheme is not, in a sense, a step backward—after all, one of the advantages of sharing global memory blocks was that they provided excellent performance when compared to writing and reading a disk file. Fear not, the Win32 designers took this into account as well. You see, a file mapping object need not actually reference a disk file— you can create a file mapping object that references a block of memory. This effectively lets you share a memory block among applications. There's just one catch though—you can't count on the block of memory being at the same address for each process. (Though they will be the same under Windows 95, they are often different under Windows NT.) This means that each process must keep track individually of where in memory a particular file mapping object appears.

The functions used for file mappings are shown in Table 13.8.

Table 13.8   **File Mapping Functions**

Function	Description
CreateFileMapping	Creates a file mapping object
FlushViewOfFile	Ensures that all changes to a file mapping have been written
MapViewOfFile, MapViewOfFileEx	Maps a file mapping object into the address space of the current process
OpenFileMapping	Opens an existing file mapping object
UnmapViewOfFile	Unmaps a file mapping object from the address space of the current process

Version Stamping

In the DOS world, software upgrades are traditionally not a big problem. When upgrading the DOS operating system, the upgrade generally included new copies of all of the files required by the system. When upgrading an application, the application had its own set of files, so one rarely needed to be concerned that something loaded by one application might affect another.

With Windows, the situation is more complex. For one thing, the Windows environment contains literally hundreds of files. In addition, many files under Windows can be shared among applications. Consider the following situation: You have an application that uses a particular dynamic link library or custom control. You then purchase a second application that uses the same DLL or custom control. When installing the second application, how can you be certain that the version of the DLL or control provided is in fact the latest version of the file? Perhaps that second application has been sitting on the shelf for a while—or perhaps its vendor never bothered to update those files, figuring that as long as they worked with their software there would be no problem.

If the second application simply copies over its version of the DLL or controls, there is a chance that the first application, which may depend on some new feature or fix in the newer version of those files, will stop working properly.

Windows solved this problem through a technique called *version stamping*. A special version resource was defined that can be examined by an installation program to determine which version of the file is the latest. Version stamping may also be used to verify that the new file matches the target operating system, that it supports the correct language for the version of Windows running, and so on.

Version Stamping and Visual Basic

Visual Basic supports version stamping when an executable is created. It does not, however, provide any built-in mechanism for reading the version resources of other applications, DLLs, or custom controls.

The functions listed in Table 13.9 are used to support version resources and to aid in the installation of files based on their version stamp.

Table 13.9 **Version Control API Functions**

Function	Description
GetFileVersionInfo	Loads a version information resource block
GetFileVersionInfoSize	Determines the size of a version information resource block
VerFindFile	Determines the recommended destination directory in which to install a file
VerInstallFile	A powerful function for installing a file onto a system; supports expansion of compressed files and version checking
VerLanguageName	Determines the text name of a language based on a standard language code
VerQueryValue	Determines the value of a version attribute for a file

The Version Resource Data Structures

The version stamp for a file can have many different components, depending on the file. Three of these are commonly used by installing programs and are used in virtually all programs that use version stamping. The first component is a data structure known as the VS_FIXEDFILEINFO structure. (Note: This structure was simply called FIXEDFILEINFO under Win16.) It contains numeric version information and flags defining the type of the file. The second component defines the language and code page translations that exist in the version resource. The third component consists of one or more strings called StringFileInfo attributes.

The VS_FIXEDFILEINFO Structure

The VS_FIXEDFILEINFO data structure is present in every file that has a version stamp. It is defined below.

```
VB Declaration
Type VS_FIXEDFILEINFO ' 52 Bytes
    dwSignature As Long
```

```
        dwStrucVersion As Long
        dwFileVersionMS As Long
        dwFileVersionLS As Long
        dwProductVersionMS As Long
        dwProductVersionLS As Long
        dwFileFlagsMask As Long
        dwFileFlags As Long
        dwFileOS As Long
        dwFileType As Long
        dwFileSubtype As Long
        dwFileDateMS As Long
        dwFileDateLS As Long
End Type
```

Field	Type/Description
dwSignature	Long—Always contains &HFEEF04BD.
dwStrucVersion	Long—The version of this structure. Will be greater than &H29.
dwFileVersionMS	Long—The high 32 bits of the file version number.
dwFileVersionLS	Long—The low 32 bits of the file version number.
dwProductVersionMS	Long—The high 32 bits of the product version number.
dwProductVersionLS	Long—The low 32 bits of the product version number.
dwFileFlagsMask	Long—Any combination of the constants in Table 13.10. The presence of a flag in this parameter indicates that the value of the dwFileFlags parameter for that bit is valid.
dwFileFlags	Long—Any combination of the constants in Table 13.10.
dwFileOS	Long—One of the constants defined in Table 13.11 to specify the operating system for which this file was designed.
dwFileType	Long—One of the constants defined in Table 13.12 to specify the type of file.
dwFileSubtype	Long—One of the constants defined in the API32.TXT file that begin with the VFT2_ prefix.

Field	Type/Description
dwFileDataMS	Long—The high 32 bits that specify the date and time of the file's creation. There is no guarantee that this field will be set by the compiler.
dwFileDataLS	Long—The low 32 bits that specify the date and time of the file's creation. There is no guarantee that this field will be set by the compiler.

Version numbers are typically 64-bits long to allow for numeric comparisons of versions. However, the internal structure of these numbers deserves further clarification.

On the most significant 32 bits, the high 16 bits comprise the major revision number, and the low 16 bits comprise the minor revision number. Thus Windows 3.10 will have &H0003000A in its major version number. The 3 in the high-order word indicates version 3, and the hexadecimal A represents the number 10 for a minor revision number of .10. This technique is used on the lower 32 bits to allow even finer resolution of versions, but these numbers are typically used only in a development environment and are rarely used by either application programmers or users. It is essential that you use the revision numbers from the VS_FIXEDFILEINFO structure when comparing file versions—do not use the FileVersion text string that will be described shortly. A text comparison on that string will not reliably compare file versions.

Table 13.10 lists the flags that are used in the dwFileFlags parameter to specify general information about the file.

Table 13.10   Version File Flags

Constants	Description
VS_FF_DEBUG	This file contains debugging information.
VS_FF_INFOINFERRED	The version resource for this file is dynamically allocated and some of the blocks in the resource may be incorrect.
VS_FF_PATCHED	This file has been patched. It may differ from the original file that has the same version number.
VS_FF_PRERELEASE	This is a prerelease version of the file.
VS_FF_PRIVATEBUILD	This version of the file is built specially as defined by the Private-Build StringFileInfo string.
VS_FF_SPECIALBUILD	This version of the file is built specially as defined by the Special-Build StringFileInfo string.

Table 13.11 lists the constants that are used in the dwFileType parameter to specify the file type.

Table 13.11   **Version File Operating System Types**

Constant	Target Operating System for This File
VOS_UNKNOWN	Undefined or unknown
VOS_DOS	MS-DOS
VOS_DOS_WINDOWS16	16-bit Windows on DOS (Windows 3.0, 3.1)
VOS_DOS_WINDOWS32	32-bit Windows on DOS (Win32s)
VOS_NT	Windows NT
VOS_OS216	16-bit OS/2
VOS_OS232	32-bit OS/2
VOS_OS216_PM16	16-bit Presentation Manager on 16 bit OS/2
VOS_OS232_PM32	32-bit Presentation Manager on 32 bit OS/2
VOS_PM16	16-bit Presentation Manager
VOS_PM32	32-bit Presentation Manager
VOS_WINDOWS32	32-bit Windows
VOS_NT_WINDOWS32	Win32 API on Windows NT

Table 13.12 lists the constants that are used in the dwFileOS parameter to specify the target operating system for the file.

Table 13.12   **Version File Types**

Constant	Type of File
VFT_UNKNOWN	Unknown
VFT_APP	Application
VFT_DLL	Dynamic link library—this includes most Visual Basic custom controls
VFT_DRV	Driver type is specified by the dwFileSubType parameter

Table 13.12	**Version File Types (Continued)**

Constant	Type of File
VFT_FONT	Font type is specified by the dwFileSubType parameter
VFT_VXD	Virtual device driver
VFT_STATIC_LIB	A static link library

The Translation Table

The translation table in a version stamp defines the language and code page combinations that are included in the version stamp. It takes the form of an array of integer pairs. The first integer is the language code as listed in Table 13.20 under the description of the VerLanguageName API function in this chapter's Function Reference. The second integer defines the character set or code page to use for that language.

Unfortunately, the language and code page definitions are not followed consistently by every application. For this reason, it is important to look at the translation table if one exists. You need accurate language and code page information to access the StringFileInfo strings that are defined in the next section.

If a translation table is not defined, the most common language/code combinations are &H040904E4, indicating U.S. English and the standard multilingual Windows character set, and &H04090000, which indicates U.S. English and the seven-bit ASCII character set. Table 13.13 lists the available character set identifiers.

Table 13.13	**Windows Character Sets**

Identifier Value	Character Set
0	Seven-bit ASCII
&H3A4	Windows—Japan
&H3B5	Windows—Korea
&H3B6	Windows—Taiwan
&H4B0	Unicode
&H4E2	Windows—Latin (Eastern Europe)

Table 13.13   **Windows Character Sets (Continued)**

Identifier Value	Character Set
&H4E3	Windows—Cyrillic
&H4E4	Windows—Multilingual (U.S. Standard)
&H4E5	Windows—Greek
&H4E6	Windows—Turkish
&H4E7	Windows—Hebrew
&H4E8	Windows—Arabic

The FileDemo example program illustrates how the translation table for a version resource can be read, and shows how to find the U.S. English entry in the table.

StringFileInfo Data

The StringFileInfo entries in a version resource are strings that describe certain characteristics of the file. A file may contain unique strings for each language supported; thus the language/code page information is used to access this data as well. Refer to the description of the VerQueryValue function for further information on retrieving these values.

The standard StringFileInfo strings are listed in Table 13.14. Not all of the strings defined are present in every file.

Table 13.14   **Version StringFileInfo Data Names**

StringFileInfo Name	Description
Comments	General comments
CompanyName	The name of the company
FileDescription	A description of the file
FileVersion	The version of the file in string form—do NOT use this string to compare file versions

Table 13.14   Version StringFileInfo Data Names (Continued)

StringFileInfo Name	Description
InternalName	The internal module or application name
LegalCopyright	A copyright notice
LegalTrademarks	Trademark notices
OLESelfRegister	Presence of this string indicates that this is an OLE control that can register itself into the system registry (the string itself is empty)
OriginalFilename	The original name of the file—useful in determining if the file has been renamed
PrivateBuild	A description of this build if the VS_FF_PRIVATEBUILD flag was set in the dwFileFlags field of the VS_FIXEDFILEINFO structure
ProductName	The name of the product to which this file belongs
ProductVersion	The version of the product to which this file belongs
SpecialBuild	A description of this build if the VS_FF_SPECIALBUILD flag was set in the dwFileFlags field of the VS_FIXEDFILEINFO structure

Examples

The sample programs described here illustrate some of the key concepts for this chapter. Most of the file API functions are very easy to understand and do not have specific example programs. In addition to the FileDemo and client/server sample described here, you will find the following sample programs on the CD-ROM that comes with this book:

- Async: Demonstrates asynchronous file reads. A better example of overlapped file operations will follow in Chapter 14.

- LogDrvs: Obtains a list of logical drives and information about each drive on the system.

- QryDos: Obtains the DOS device names and associated system devices on NT.

- FileInfo: Obtains various types of information about a file.

FileDemo—Initialization File, Registry, and Version Stamping Program

FileDemo is a program that demonstrates how to access initialization files from Visual Basic, and how to read the version stamping information for those files that have it. It also demonstrates how to read either the WIN.INI initialization file or the system registry to obtain a list of available printers on the system. This project has been ported from the original Win16 FileDemo example and all features except for the registry access code runs under both 16- and 32-bit Visual Basic (version 4.0 example only). It is, of course, possible to use the Win16 registry functions to modify this example so that it works identically under both Win16 and Win32, but that is left as an exercise to the reader.

Using FileDemo

The FileDemo screen shown in Figure 13.3 allows you to select an executable file, DLL, or custom control and determine the version information for that file. The menu also allows you to invoke commands to display the printers available on the system by reading either the devices section of the WIN.INI file or the system registry.

Figure 13.3

Main program screen for the FileDemo project

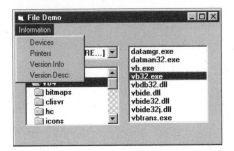

Version information is obtained in two parts. The Version Info menu command accesses the VS_FIXEDFILEINFO structure in the file's version resource to show the type of the file and the file and product version numbers. The Version Desc menu command accesses the StringFileInfo strings in the version resource to obtain the company, file description, and copyright notice for a file.

Project Description

The FileDemo project includes three files. FILEDEMO.FRM is the only form used in the program. FILEDEMO.BAS is the only module in the program and contains the constant type, function, and public declarations. APIGID32.BAS contains the declarations for the APIGID32.DLL dynamic link library.

File Descriptions

Listing 13.1 contains the FILEDEMO.BAS declaration file. The declarations for the following structures have also been left out to save space: VFT, HKEY, STANDARD_RIGHTS, and KEY. These declarations can be found in the sample on the CD-ROM.

Listing 13.1   FILEDEMO.BAS

```
Attribute VB_Name = "FILEDEMO1"
Option Explicit

#If Win32 Then
Declare Function GetFileVersionInfoSize Lib "version.dll" Alias _
"GetFileVersionInfoSizeA" (ByVal lptstrFilename As String, lpdwHandle _
As Long) As Long
Declare Function GetFileVersionInfo Lib "version.dll" Alias _
"GetFileVersionInfoA" (ByVal lptstrFilename As String, ByVal dwHandle As Long, _
ByVal dwLen As Long, lpData As Byte) As Long
Declare Function VerLanguageName Lib "version.dll" Alias "VerLanguageNameA" _
(ByVal wLang As Long, ByVal szLang As String, ByVal nSize As Long) As Long
Declare Function VerQueryValue Lib "version.dll" Alias "VerQueryValueA" (pBlock _
As Byte, ByVal lpSubBlock As String, lplpBuffer As Long, puLen As Long) As Long
Declare Function GetProfileString Lib "kernel32" Alias ðGetProfileStringA" _
(ByVal lpAppName As String, ByVal lpKeyName As String, ByVal lpDefault As _
String, ByVal lpReturnedString As String, ByVal nSize As Long) As Long
Declare Function RegOpenKey Lib "advapi32.dll" Alias "RegOpenKeyA" (ByVal hKey _
As Long, ByVal lpSubKey As String, phkResult As Long) As Long
Declare Function RegOpenKeyEx Lib "advapi32.dll" Alias "RegOpenKeyExA" (ByVal _
hKey As Long, ByVal lpSubKey As String, ByVal ulOptions As Long, ByVal _
samDesired As Long, phkResult As Long) As Long
Declare Function RegCloseKey Lib "advapi32.dll" (ByVal hKey As Long) As Long
Declare Function RegQueryValueEx Lib "advapi32.dll" Alias "RegQueryValueExA" _
(ByVal hKey As Long, ByVal lpValueName As String, ByVal lpReserved As Long, _
lpType As Long, lpData As Any, lpcbData As Long) As Long
Declare Function RegEnumKey Lib "advapi32.dll" Alias "RegEnumKeyA" (ByVal hKey _
As Long, ByVal dwIndex As Long, ByVal lpname As String, ByVal cbName _
As Long) As Long
```

Listing 13.1   FILEDEMO.BAS (Continued)

```
Declare Function RegEnumKeyEx Lib "advapi32.dll" Alias "RegEnumKeyExA" (ByVal _
hKey As Long, ByVal dwIndex As Long, ByVal lpname As String, lpcbName As Long, _
ByVal lpReserved As Long, ByVal lpClass As String, lpcbClass As Long, _
lpftLastWriteTime As FILETIME) As Long
#Else
Declare Function GetFileVersionInfo% Lib "ver.dll" (ByVal lpszFileName$, ByVal _
handle&, ByVal cbBuf&, lpvData As Byte)
Declare Function GetFileVersionInfoSize% Lib "ver.dll" (ByVal lpszFileName$, _
lpdwHandle&)
Declare Function VerLanguageName% Lib "ver.dll" (ByVal Lang%, ByVal lpszLang$, _
ByVal cbLang%)
Declare Function VerQueryValue% Lib "ver.dll" (lpvBlock As Byte, ByVal _
SubBlock$, lpBuffer&, lpcb%)
Declare Function GetProfileString% Lib "Kernel" (ByVal lpAppName$, ByVal _
lpKeyName As String, ByVal lpDefault$, ByVal lpReturnedString$, ByVal nSize%)
#End If


'-----------------------------------------------
'
'    Public Constants

Public Type VS_FIXEDFILEINFO
        dwSignature As Long
        dwStrucVersion As Long          ' e.g. ¯x¯¯¯¯¯¯42 = "¯.42"
        dwFileVersionMS As Long         ' e.g. ¯x¯¯¯3¯¯75 = "3.75"
        dwFileVersionLS As Long         ' e.g. ¯x¯¯¯¯¯¯31 = "¯.31"
        dwProductVersionMS As Long      ' e.g. ¯x¯¯¯3¯¯1¯ = "3.1¯"
        dwProductVersionLS As Long      ' e.g. ¯x¯¯¯¯¯¯31 = "¯.31"
        dwFileFlagsMask As Long         ' = ¯x3F for version "¯.42"
        dwFileFlags As Long             ' e.g. VFF_DEBUG Or VFF_PRERELEASE
        dwFileOS As Long                ' e.g. VOS_DOS_WINDOWS16
        dwFileType As Long              ' e.g. VFT_DRIVER
        dwFileSubtype As Long           ' e.g. VFT2_DRV_KEYBOARD
        dwFileDateMS As Long            ' e.g. ¯
        dwFileDateLS As Long            ' e.g. ¯
End Type

Public Type FILETIME
        dwLowDateTime As Long
        dwHighDateTime As Long
End Type

Public Const SYNCHRONIZE = &H1¯¯¯¯¯
```

Listing 13.1   FILEDEMO.BAS (Continued)

```
Public Const ERROR_SUCCESS = ¯&

'---------------------------------------------------
'
'    Public Variables
'
' We changed this to Byte to prevent the string
' mangling of the buffer
Public verbuf() As Byte        ' Version buffer
Public FileName$       ' Current file to examine
```

Listing 13.2 contains the file FILEDEMO.FRM, including the header that describes the control setup for the form.

Listing 13.2   FILEDEMO.FRM

```
VERSION 5.¯¯
Begin VB.Form FileDemo
    Caption         =    "File Demo"
    ClientHeight    =    252¯
    ClientLeft      =    1¯95
    ClientTop       =    177¯
    ClientWidth     =    498¯
    BeginProperty Font
        name            =    "MS Sans Serif"
        charset         =    1
        weight          =    7¯¯
        size            =    8.25
        underline       =    ¯    'False
        italic          =    ¯    'False
        strikethrough   =    ¯    'False
    EndProperty
    ForeColor       =    &H8¯¯¯¯¯¯8&
    Height          =    321¯
    Left            =    1¯35
    LinkMode        =    1  'Source
    LinkTopic       =    "Form1"
    ScaleHeight     =    252¯
    ScaleWidth      =    498¯
    Top             =    114¯
    Width           =    51¯¯
    Begin VB.DirListBox Dir1
        Height          =    138¯
        Left            =    24¯
```

Listing 13.2   FILEDEMO.FRM (Continued)

```
                    TabIndex        =   1
                    Top             =   72⁻
                    Width           =   2295
                End
                Begin VB.FileListBox File1
                    Height          =   1815
                    Left            =   276⁻
                    Pattern         =   "*.exe;*.dll;*.vbx"
                    TabIndex        =   2
                    Top             =   24⁻
                    Width           =   1935
                End
                Begin VB.DriveListBox Drive1
                    Height          =   315
                    Left            =   24⁻
                    TabIndex        =   ⁻
                    Top             =   24⁻
                    Width           =   2295
                End
                Begin VB.Menu MenuInformation
                    Caption         =   "Information"
                    Begin VB.Menu MenuDevices
                        Caption     =   "Devices"
                    End
                    Begin VB.Menu MenuPrinters
                        Caption     =   "Printers"
                    End
                    Begin VB.Menu MenuVersionInfo
                        Caption     =   "Version Info"
                    End
                    Begin VB.Menu MenuVersionDesc
                        Caption     =   "Version Desc:"
                    End
                End
            End
Attribute VB_Name = "FileDemo"
Attribute VB_GlobalNameSpace = False
Attribute VB_Creatable = False
Attribute VB_PredeclaredId = TrueAttribute VB_Exposed = False
Option Explicit


Private Sub MenuDevices_Click()
    ShowDevices
End Sub


Private Sub MenuPrinters_Click()
    ShowPrinters
```

Listing 13.2   FILEDEMO.FRM (Continued)

```
End Sub

Private Sub MenuVersionDesc_Click()
    ShowDescInfo
End Sub

Private Sub MenuVersionInfo_Click()
    ShowVersionInfo
End Sub

Private Sub Dir1_Change()
    File1.Path = Dir1.Path
End Sub

Private Sub Drive1_Change()
    Dir1.Path = drive1.Drive
End Sub
```

This function shows how the GetProfileString function is used to obtain a list of the key names for a section in the WIN.INI file. If a string was specified instead of vbNullString for the second parameter, the function would fill the buffer with the entire value of the specified key string.

Private initialization files can be accessed using the GetPrivateProfileString function, which works the same way. You can find a more in-depth review of initialization files in Chapter 4.

```
'
'   Lists all devices in the WIN.INI file
'
Private Sub ShowDevices()
    Dim devstring As String * 4096
    Dim startpos%, endpos%
    Dim crlf$
    Dim res$
    Dim di&

    crlf$ = Chr$(13) + Chr$(10)

    di = GetProfileString("devices", 0&, "", devstring, 4095)
    If di = 0 Then
        MsgBox "Win.ini does not contain devices field under this OS"
        Exit Sub
    End If
    startpos% = 1
    Do While (Asc(Mid$(devstring, startpos%, 1)) <> 0)
        endpos% = InStr(startpos%, devstring, Chr$(0))
```

```
            res$ = res$ + Mid$(devstring, startpos%, endpos% - startpos%) + crlf$
            startpos% = endpos% + 1
     Loop
     MsgBox res$, ¯, "Devices"
End Sub
```

Under Windows NT and Windows 95, the list of available printers is kept in the registry rather than in the WIN.INI file. The key that contains the list of printers is HKEY_LOCAL_MACHINE\SYSTEM\CurrentControlSet\Control\Print\Printers. Under this key you will find a key for each printer on the system. This function enumerates those keys and retrieves their names.

```
Private Sub ShowPrinters()
#If Win32 Then
     Dim ft As FILETIME
     Dim keyhandle&
     Dim res&
     Dim curidx&
     Dim keyname$, classname$
     Dim keylen&, classlen&
     Dim msg$
     Dim reserved&
     res& = RegOpenKeyEx(HKEY_LOCAL_MACHINE,
     "SYSTEM\CurrentControlSet\Control\Print\Printers", _
     ¯, KEY_READ, keyhandle)
     If res <> ERROR_SUCCESS Then
         MsgBox "Can't open key"
         Exit Sub
     End If
     Do
         keylen& = 2¯¯¯
         classlen& = 2¯¯¯
         keyname$ = String$(keylen, ¯)
         classname$ = String$(classlen, ¯)
         res = RegEnumKeyEx(keyhandle, curidx, keyname$, keylen, reserved, _
         classname$, classlen, ft)
         curidx = curidx + 1
         If res = ERROR_SUCCESS Then msg$ = msg$ & Left$(keyname$, keylen) + _
         vbCrLf
     Loop While res = ERROR_SUCCESS

     Call RegCloseKey(keyhandle)
     MsgBox msg$, ¯, "Printers"
#Else
     MsgBox "This function is not supported under Win16 in this example."
#End If
End Sub
```

The File_Click function demonstrates how the version resource information is loaded into a Visual Basic string buffer. In this example, the file version

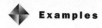

buffer is loaded any time you click on a file in the file list box. Note how the GetFileVersionInfoSize function is used to determine the required size for the string buffer. The biggest change to this function from the previous version is the use of a byte array instead of a string to hold the version resource buffer. This is critical in this case because the conversion to and from Unicode that occurs when you use a string buffer could possibly corrupt the binary data in this buffer.

```
Private Sub File1_Click()
    Dim fressize&
    Dim freshnd&
    Dim di&

    ' Build the file name
    If Right$(Dir1.Path, 1) = "\" Then
        FileName$ = Dir1.Path + File1.FileName
    Else
        FileName$ = Dir1.Path + "\" + File1.FileName
    End If

    ' Determine if version information is present, and
    ' if so how large a buffer is needed to hold it.
    fressize& = GetFileVersionInfoSize(FileName$, freshnd&)

    ' The following code from the VB3 version is no longer needed
    'If fressize& = ¯ Then
    '    verbuf$ = ""
    '    Exit Sub
    'End If

    ' Version info is unlikely to ever be greater than 64k
    ' but check anyway. If it was larger than 64k, we would
    ' need to allocate a huge buffer instead.  Note, we
    ' are only using an approximation to 64k here to take
    ' into account the VB string overhead.
    If fressize& > 64¯¯¯ Then fressize& = 64¯¯¯

    'Was: verbuf$ = String$(CInt(fressize&) + 1, Chr$(¯))
    ReDim verbuf(fressize + 1)

    ' Load the string with the version information

    ' In Win16, we used the address of the string
    ' Was: di% = GetFileVersionInfo(FileName$, freshnd&, fressize&, _
    agGetAddressForVBString&(verbuf$))

    di = GetFileVersionInfo(FileName$, freshnd&, fressize&, verbuf(¯))

    ' The menu commands will use the information global
    ' in this global version buffer.
```

```
        If di = ¯ Then ReDim verbuf(1)    ' Error occured
End Sub
```

The ShowVersionInfo function demonstrates how a VS_FIXEDFILEINFO block is loaded from the version resource buffer. The version resource buffer verbuf is loaded by the File1_Click function each time a file is selected. It will be a single byte if the file has no version information.

```
'
' Show information from the fixed version info for the
'   current file.
'
Private Sub ShowVersionInfo()
    Dim ffi As VS_FIXEDFILEINFO
    Dim fiiaddr&
    #If Win32 Then
        Dim fiilen&
        Dim di&
    #Else
        Dim fiilen%
        Dim di%
    #End If
    Dim res$, crlf$

    crlf$ = Chr$(13) + Chr$(1¯)

    If UBound(verbuf) <= 1 Then
        MsgBox "No version information available for this file"
        Exit Sub
    End If

    di = VerQueryValue(verbuf(¯), "\", fiiaddr&, fiilen)
    If di = ¯ Then
        MsgBox "No fixed version information in this file"
        Exit Sub
    End If

    ' Copy the fixed file info into the structure
    agCopyData ByVal fiiaddr&, ffi, 52

    ' Now build the output report
    res$ = "File Version " + CalcVersion$(ffi.dwFileVersionMS) + "." + _
    CalcVersion$(ffi.dwFileVersionLS) + crlf$
    res$ = res$ + "Product Version " + CalcVersion$(ffi.dwProductVersionMS) + _
    crlf$
    res$ = res$ + "File type is: "
    Select Case ffi.dwFileType
        Case VFT_UNKNOWN
                res$ = res$ + "unknown"
        Case VFT_APP
                res$ = res$ + "application"
```

```
        Case VFT_DLL
                    res$ = res$ + "dynamic link library"
        Case VFT_DRV
                    res$ = res$ + "device driver"
        Case VFT_FONT
                    res$ = res$ + "Font resource"
        Case VFT_VXD
                    res$ = res$ + "virtual device"
        Case VFT_STATIC_LIB
                    res$ = res$ + "static link library"
    End Select
    res$ = res$ + crlf$

    MsgBox res$, ¯, "Fixed Version Info"

End Sub


'
'   Breaks a 32 bit version into major and minor revs, then
'   then returns the string representation.
'
Private Function CalcVersion$(vernum&)
    Dim major%, minor%
    major% = CInt(vernum& / &H1¯¯¯¯)
    minor% = CInt(vernum& And &HFFFF&)
    CalcVersion$ = Str$(major%) + "." + LTrim$(Str$(minor%))
End Function
```

The ShowDescInfo and GetInfoString functions work together to obtain string information from the version resource for a file. Only a few of the strings are examined by these functions, but they can be easily extended to read all of the file version information using the same techniques.

The GetInfoString function first retrieves the translation array for the version resource, then demonstrates how you can look for the U.S. English entry in the table. It then builds the eight-character hexadecimal string required by the VerQueryValue function to obtain StringFileInfo strings.

The VerQueryValue function sets the value of a long address and integer variables with the address and size of the string, respectively, if it is found. The string is then copied into a Visual Basic string for display in a message box.

```
'
' This function shows how to obtain other information about
' a file.
'
Private Sub ShowDescInfo()
    Dim res$, crlf$

    crlf$ = Chr$(13) + Chr$(1¯)

    If UBound(verbuf) < 2 Then
```

```
        MsgBox "No version information available for this file"
     .  Exit Sub
    End If

    res$ = "Company: " + GetInfoString$("CompanyName") + crlf$
    res$ = res$ + "File Desc: " + GetInfoString$("FileDescription") + crlf$
    res$ = res$ + "Copyright: " + GetInfoString$("LegalCopyright") + crlf$
    res$ = res$ + "FileVersion: " + GetInfoString$("FileVersion") + crlf$

    MsgBox res$, ¯, "Fixed Version Info"


End Sub

Private Function GetInfoString$(stringtoget$)
    Dim tbuf$
    Dim nullpos%
    Dim xlatelang%
    Dim xlatecode%
    Dim numentries%
    Dim fiiaddr&
    Dim xlatestring$
    Dim xlateval&
    #If Win32 Then
        Dim fiilen&
        Dim di&
    #Else
        Dim fiilen%
        Dim di%
    #End If
    Dim x%

    di = VerQueryValue(verbuf(¯), "\VarFileInfo\Translation", fiiaddr&, fiilen)
    If (di <> ¯) Then ' Translation table exists
        numentries% = fiilen / 4
        xlateval& = ¯
        For x% = 1 To numentries%
            ' Copy the 4 byte tranlation entry for the first
            agCopyData ByVal fiiaddr&, xlatelang%, 2
            agCopyData ByVal (fiiaddr& + 2), xlatecode%, 2
            ' Exit if U.S. English was found
            If xlatelang% = &H4¯9 Then Exit For
            fiiaddr& = fiiaddr& + 4
        Next x%
    Else
        ' No translation table - Assume standard ASCII
        xlatelang% = &H4¯9
        xlatecode% = ¯
    End If

    xlatestring$ = Hex$(xlatecode%)
    ' Make sure hex string is 4 chars long
```

```
While Len(xlatestring$) < 4
    xlatestring$ = "‾" + xlatestring$
Wend
xlatestring$ = Hex$(xlatelang%) + xlatestring$
' Make sure hex string is 8 chars long       ·
While Len(xlatestring$) < 8
    xlatestring$ = "‾" + xlatestring$
Wend

di = VerQueryValue(verbuf(‾), "\StringFileInfo\" + xlatestring$ + "\" + _
stringtoget$, fiiaddr&, fiilen)
If di = ‾ Then
    GetInfoString$ = "Unavailable"
    Exit Function          ·
End If

tbuf$ = String$(fiilen + 1, Chr$(‾))

' Copy the fixed file info into the structure
agCopyData ByVal fiiaddr&, ByVal tbuf$, fiilen

nullpos% = InStr(tbuf$, Chr$(‾))
If (nullpos% > 1) Then
    GetInfoString$ = Left$(tbuf$, nullpos% - 1)
Else
    GetInfoString$ = "None"
End If

End Function
```

Suggestions for Further Practice

- Extend FileDemo so that it can obtain a list of printers from the registry under 16-bit Visual Basic as well.

- Extend the printer listing capability to display information about each printer in addition to the printer's key name.

- Extend the version information part of the FileDemo example to display all of the version information.

CkServe/CkClient: Cooperating Applications

One of the classic examples of a client/server simulation that demonstrates use of shared memory is that of a supermarket. The server is the checkstand that waits for a customer to arrive, then totals up their purchases and reports a total. The client is a customer that waits for a checkstand to be open, then presents their purchases to the server. Figure 13.4 shows a screen shot of the two programs, ckClient and ckServe. The ckClient, or "Customer" application has a text box that lets you assign a customer number, and a checkbox that determines if the program should actually be shopping. A listbox is loaded with the total for each successful checkout. The ckServe or "CheckStand" application has a text box that lets you assign a checkstand number and a checkbox that determines if the checkstand is open. It also lists each successful checkout (the totals for the customer and the checkstand should, of course, match). Each of these applications has a simple state machine inside that controls its operation during events triggered by a timer control. This is done to slow down the applications to more clearly demonstrate what is actually going on. Note that these are both very simple programs with minimal error checking and are certainly not rigorous simulations of the shopping experience.

Figure 13.4
ckServe and ckClient program screens

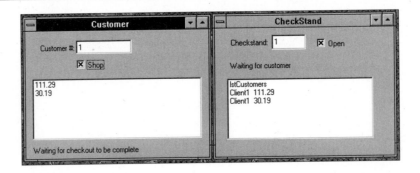

Project Description

The ckServe project includes three files. FRMSERVE.FRM is the only form used in the program. CHKSTAND.BAS is the only module in the program and contains the constant type, function, and public declarations. APIGID32.BAS contains the declarations for the APIGID32.DLL dynamic link library.

The ckClient project also includes three files. FCLIENT.FRM is the only form used in the program. The other two files are the same as those used by ckServe.

Listing 13.3 shows the shared CHKSTAND.BAS module. Listing 13.4 shows the frmServe.frm form. Listing 13.5 shows the FCLIENT.FRM form.

The most important structure defined in the CHKSTAND.BAS module is the CheckStand structure. This structure is used by the client and server application to exchange information. The client application checks the Total field to determine if the checkstand is available. If it is zero, the client loads a series of prices (the Prices array) of the items being purchased, then sets the Done field to let the server know that it is ready. The server then totals the items. When it is finished it sets the Total field and clears the Done field. The client clears the

Total field to indicate that the customer has left the checkstand and that the checkstand is again ready for another customer. The client also sets the Client field so that the server can record the client name in its list box.

Listing 13.3   CHKSTAND.BAS

```
Attribute VB_Name = "CheckStandModule"
Option Explicit
Type CheckStand
    Prices(99) As Single
    Done As Long      ' Indication that client is done
    Total As Single ' Set when server is done
    Client As String * 8
End Type

Type SECURITY_ATTRIBUTES
        nLength As Long
        lpSecurityDescriptor As Long
        bInheritHandle As Long
End Type

Public Const DELETE = &H1----
Public Const READ_CONTROL = &H2----
Public Const WRITE_DAC = &H4----
Public Const WRITE_OWNER = &H8----
Public Const SYNCHRONIZE = &H1-----
Public Const FILE_SHARE_READ = &H1
Public Const FILE_SHARE_WRITE = &H2

Public Const STANDARD_RIGHTS_READ = (READ_CONTROL)
Public Const STANDARD_RIGHTS_WRITE = (READ_CONTROL)
Public Const STANDARD_RIGHTS_EXECUTE = (READ_CONTROL)
Public Const STANDARD_RIGHTS_REQUIRED = &HF----
Public Const STANDARD_RIGHTS_ALL = &H1F----

Public Const SECTION_QUERY = &H1
Public Const SECTION_MAP_WRITE = &H2
Public Const SECTION_MAP_READ = &H4
Public Const SECTION_MAP_EXECUTE = &H8
Public Const SECTION_EXTEND_SIZE = &H1-
Public Const SECTION_ALL_ACCESS = STANDARD_RIGHTS_REQUIRED Or SECTION_QUERY Or _
SECTION_MAP_WRITE Or SECTION_MAP_READ Or SECTION_MAP_EXECUTE Or _
SECTION_EXTEND_SIZE
```

Listing 13.3   CHKSTAND.BAS (Continued)

```
Public Const FILE_MAP_COPY = SECTION_QUERY
Public Const FILE_MAP_WRITE = SECTION_MAP_WRITE
Public Const FILE_MAP_READ = SECTION_MAP_READ
Public Const FILE_MAP_ALL_ACCESS = SECTION_ALL_ACCESS

Public Const GENERIC_READ = &H8-------
Public Const GENERIC_WRITE = &H4-------
Public Const CREATE_ALWAYS = 2
Public Const FILE_ATTRIBUTE_NORMAL = &H8-
Public Const FILE_FLAG_RANDOM_ACCESS = &H1-------
Public Const PAGE_READWRITE = 4&


Declare Function CreateFile Lib "kernel32" Alias "CreateFileA" (ByVal _
lpFileName As String, ByVal dwDesiredAccess As Long, ByVal dwShareMode As Long, _
lpSecurityAttributes As SECURITY_ATTRIBUTES, ByVal dwCreationDisposition As _
Long, ByVal dwFlagsAndAttributes As Long, ByVal hTemplateFile As Long) As Long
Declare Function CloseHandle Lib "kernel32" (ByVal hObject As Long) As Long
Declare Function CreateFileMapping Lib "kernel32" Alias "CreateFileMappingA" _
(ByVal hFile As Long, lpFileMappigAttributes As SECURITY_ATTRIBUTES, ByVal _
flProtect As Long, ByVal dwMaximumSizeHigh As Long, ByVal dwMaximumSizeLow _
As Long, ByVal lpname As String) As Long
Declare Function WriteFile Lib "kernel32" (ByVal hFile As Long, lpBuffer As _
Any, ByVal nNumberOfBytesToWrite As Long, lpNumberOfBytesWritten As Long, ByVal _
lpOverlapped As Long) As Long
Declare Function ReadFile Lib "kernel32" (ByVal hFile As Long, lpBuffer As Any, _
ByVal nNumberOfBytesToRead As Long, lpNumberOfBytesRead As Long, ByVal _
lpOverlapped As Long) As Long
Declare Function FlushFileBuffers Lib "kernel32" (ByVal hFile As Long) As Long
Declare Function MapViewOfFile Lib "kernel32" (ByVal hFileMappingObject As _
Long, ByVal dwDesiredAccess As Long, ByVal dwFileOffsetHigh As Long, ByVal _
dwFileOffsetLow As Long, ByVal dwNumberOfBytesToMap As Long) As Long
Declare Function UnmapViewOfFile Lib "kernel32" (ByVal lpBaseAddress As Long) _
As Long
Declare Function OpenFileMapping Lib "kernel32" Alias "OpenFileMappingA" (ByVal _
dwDesiredAccess As Long, ByVal bInheritHandle As Long, ByVal lpname As String) _
As Long
Declare Function GetLastError Lib "kernel32" () As Long
```

Listing 13.4   FRMSERVE.FRM

```
VERSION 5.¨¨
Begin VB.Form frmServer
    Caption         =   "CheckStand"
    ClientHeight    =   2865
    ClientLeft      =   5475
    ClientTop       =   177¨
    ClientWidth     =   42¨¨
    Height          =   327¨
    Left            =   5415
    LinkTopic       =   "Form1"
    ScaleHeight     =   2865
    ScaleWidth      =   42¨¨
    Top             =   1425
    Width           =   432¨
    Begin VB.ListBox lstCustomers
        Height          =   1395
        ItemData        =   "frmServ.frx":¨¨¨¨
        Left            =   3¨¨
        List            =   "frmServ.frx":¨¨¨7
        TabIndex        =   3
        Top             =   12¨¨
        Width           =   3495
    End
    Begin VB.Timer Timer1
        Enabled         =   ¨    'False
        Interval        =   4¨¨
        Left            =   -12¨
        Top             =   78¨
    End
    Begin VB.CheckBox chkOpen
        Caption         =   "Open"
        Height          =   255
        Left            =   246¨
        TabIndex        =   2
        Top             =   24¨
        Width           =   915
    End
    Begin VB.TextBox txtCheck
        Height          =   315
        Left            =   138¨
        TabIndex        =   ¨
        Text            =   "1"
        Top             =   18¨
        Width           =   795
    End
    Begin VB.Label lblStatus
        Height          =   195
        Left            =   36¨
        TabIndex        =   4
```

Listing 13.4   FRMSERVE.FRM (Continued)

```
        Top            =   78˜
        Width          =   3495
    End
    Begin VB.Label Label1
        Alignment      =   1   'Right Justify
        Caption        =   "Checkstand:"
        Height         =   255
        Left           =   18˜
        TabIndex       =   1
        Top            =   24˜
        Width          =   1˜95
    End
End
Attribute VB_Name = "frmServer"
Attribute VB_GlobalNameSpace = False
Attribute VB_Creatable = False
Attribute VB_PredeclaredId = TrueAttribute VB_Exposed = False
Option Explicit
```

The server has four form level variables. It keeps track of the open file, the handle of the file mapping object associated with the file, and the address of the file mapping itself. The Security object is just a dummy structure used to set default security when creating the file.

```
Dim FileHandle As Long      ' Handle of open file
Dim MappingHandle As Long   ' Handle to file mapping
Dim MappingAddress As Long  ' Address of file mapping
Dim Security As SECURITY_ATTRIBUTES
```

The bulk of the work involved in initializing and terminating the server is done in the chkOpen check box. Note that while the sample program does clean up after itself, it is not designed to properly cut off the current client. In other words, instead of checking to see if a customer is in the process of checking out and finishing that operation, the server closes immediately, leaving the customer client application hanging forever (and probably quite irate). The exercise of redesigning the sample to close properly is left to the reader—a task that should not be too difficult considering that one good solution is demonstrated in the ckClient application.

If the checkstand is being opened, the application starts by creating a new file that will hold a single CheckStand data structure. The file is opened for exclusive use—the contents will be editable by other applications via the file mapping object, but the file object itself is private to the server and cannot be accessed by another application.

The server then writes a single blank CheckStand structure to the file to initialize it to the correct size, and flushes the file buffers to make sure that

the file is written. It is advisable to do this before creating the file mapping object because Win32 does not guarantee coherence of the file if you mix file I/O operations and file mapping operations after the file mapping object is created (in other words, if you mix memory access operations on a file mapping with file I/O on the underlying file, your data may become scrambled—especially under Windows 95).

The file mapping object is created with a unique name, in this case the file name, followed by the word "map." Once the file mapping object is created, it is mapped into the address space of the application using the MapViewOfFile function.

You should be careful to use unique names when creating file mappings, as the CreateFIleMapping function will open an existing file mapping with the specified name if one exists. In this case the function will succeed, but GetLastError will be set to ERROR_ALREADY_EXISTS.

```
Private Sub chkOpen_Click()
    Dim usename$
    Dim InitialStand As CheckStand
    Dim written&
    ' Note lack of error checking here
    usename$ = "ChkStd" & txtCheck.Text
    If chkOpen.value = 1 Then
        If FileHandle <> ¯ Then Exit Sub
        ' Create new file, read write access, exclusive use,
        FileHandle = CreateFile(usename$, GENERIC_READ Or GENERIC_WRITE, ¯, _
        Security, CREATE_ALWAYS, FILE_ATTRIBUTE_NORMAL Or    _
        FILE_FLAG_RANDOM_ACCESS, ¯)
        If FileHandle = -1 Then
            MsgBox "Can't create file"
            FileHandle = ¯
            Exit Sub
        End If
        ' Write the initial file info
        Call WriteFile(FileHandle, InitialStand, Len(InitialStand), written, ¯)
        Call FlushFileBuffers(FileHandle)
        ' Now we need a mapping
        MappingHandle = CreateFileMapping(FileHandle, Security, PAGE_READWRITE, _
        ¯, ¯, usename$ & "map")
        If MappingHandle = ¯ Then
            MsgBox "Can't create file mapping"
            Exit Sub
        End If
        MappingAddress = MapViewOfFile(MappingHandle, FILE_MAP_ALL_ACCESS, ¯, _
        ¯, ¯)
        If MappingAddress = ¯ Then
            MsgBox "Can't map view of the file"
            Exit Sub
        End If
```

```
        Timer1.Enabled = True    ' Start watching for customers
    Else
        CleanUp
        lblStatus.Caption = "Closed"
    End If
End Sub
```

Loading and unloading the application is straightforward. During load, a default security object is created. This is ignored under Windows 95. During unload, any open handles are closed. You should be careful when experimenting with these programs always to close the form by using the close menu command or close button—not by using the Visual Basic stop command. This is because when you stop a program from the VB environment, the form's unload event is not triggered, so the open handles will not be closed until you terminate Visual Basic.

```
Private Sub Form_Load()
    With Security
        .nLength = Len(Security)
        .lpSecurityDescriptor = ¯
        .bInheritHandle = True    ' Doesn't really matter
    End With
End Sub

Private Sub Form_Unload(Cancel As Integer)
    ' Remember, this won't get called if you Stop without
    ' closing the main window.
    CleanUp
End Sub
```

The CleanUp function reverses the process of mapping a file into the address space, first unmapping it, then closing the file mapping object, then closing the file. File mapping objects are system objects, meaning that the object is not actually destroyed until all of the handles to that object are closed. This is important because it means that the client application can actually hold the file mapping object open even after the server closes it.

```
Private Sub CleanUp()
    ' Remember, this won't get called if you Stop without
    ' closing the main window.
    Timer1.Enabled = False
    If MappingAddress <> ¯ Then
        Call UnmapViewOfFile(MappingAddress)
        MappingAddress = ¯
    End If
    If MappingHandle <> ¯ Then
        Call CloseHandle(MappingHandle)
        MappingHandle = ¯
    End If
    If FileHandle <> ¯ Then
```

```
        Call CloseHandle(FileHandle)
        FileHandle = ¯
    End If
End Sub
```

The timer is active any time the checkstand is either waiting for a client or processing a purchase. It reads the current state of the CheckStand structure by doing a memory copy to a local copy of the structure. Synchronization between the client and the server is accomplished by way of the Done and Total fields of the structure as described in the structure description earlier. Once a client is done, the function starts adding the items, one item on each timer event. The current item number and current total are kept in static variables. Once all of the items are totaled, the function sets the total field and clears the Done field. The new information is written back into the file.

```
Private Sub Timer1_Timer()
    Dim cs As CheckStand
    Static item%
    Static tot As Single

    ' Look at the checkstand
    agCopyData ByVal MappingAddress, cs, Len(cs)
    If cs.Done Then
        If cs.Total <> ¯ Then Exit Sub ' Waiting for payment
        If item = ¯ Then lblStatus.Caption = "Checking out " & cs.Client
        tot = tot + cs.Prices(item)
        item = item + 1
        ' Stop at free item anyway
        If item > UBound(cs.Prices) Or cs.Prices(item - 1) = ¯ Then ' Done
            lstCustomers.AddItem cs.Client & " " & Format$(tot, "¯.¯¯")
            cs.Total = tot
            cs.Done = ¯
            item = ¯
            tot = ¯
            lblStatus.Caption = "Waiting to pay"
        End If
        agCopyData cs, ByVal MappingAddress, Len(cs)
    Else
        lblStatus.Caption = "Waiting for customer"
    End If

End Sub
```

Listing 13.5   FCLIENT.FRM

```
VERSION 5.¯¯
Begin VB.Form frmClient
    Caption         =   "Customer"
```

Listing 13.5   FCLIENT.FRM (Continued)

```
      ClientHeight    =   3---
      ClientLeft      =   84-
      ClientTop       =   1785
      ClientWidth     =   447-
      Height          =   34-5
      Left            =   78-
      LinkTopic       =   "Form1"
      ScaleHeight     =   3---
      ScaleWidth      =   447-
      Top             =   144-
      Width           =   459-
      Begin VB.Timer Timer1
         Interval     =   5--
         Left         =   336-
         Top          =   24-
      End
      Begin VB.ListBox lstPurchase
         Height       =   1395
         Left         =   18-
         TabIndex     =   3
         Top          =   114-
         Width        =   4-95
      End
      Begin VB.CheckBox chkShop
         Caption      =   "Shop"
         Height       =   255
         Left         =   126-
         TabIndex     =   2
         Top          =   66-
         Width        =   1335
      End
      Begin VB.TextBox txtClient
         Height       =   285
         Left         =   126-
         MaxLength    =   1
         TabIndex     =   -
         Text         =   "1"
         Top          =   24-
         Width        =   1335
      End
      Begin VB.Label lblStatus
         Height       =   195
         Left         =   18-
         TabIndex     =   4
         Top          =   27--
         Width        =   4-95
      End
      Begin VB.Label Label1
         Alignment    =   1   'Right Justify
```

Listing 13.5   FCLIENT.FRM (Continued)

```
          Caption        =    "Customer #:"
          Height         =    195
          Left           =    12⁻
          TabIndex       =    1
          Top            =    3⁻⁻
          Width          =    1⁻95
      End
   End
End
Attribute VB_Name = "frmClient"
Attribute VB_GlobalNameSpace = False
Attribute VB_Creatable = False
Attribute VB_PredeclaredId = TrueAttribute VB_Exposed = False
Option Explicit
```

The client application implements a simple state machine that describes the current operation of the program. In fact, this program is a fairly pure implementation of a state machine—the only operation that is not part of the timer loop is the termination routine.

Turning on shopping via the chkShop option button causes the program to enter state 1. In this state, the program tries to open a file mapping object for a checkstand. In this implementation, only a single checkstand is supported. If you uncheck the chkShop button, the application will not actually enter the idle state until the current set of data has been processed.

```
' Simple state machine
'  ⁻ - Idle
' 1 - Looking for checkstand
' 2 - Waiting for checkstand to be free
' 3 - Checkstand is free, data loaded
' 4 - Waiting for checkout complete
Dim CurrentState%
Dim CurrentTotal As Single
Dim MappingHandle As Long
Dim MappingAddress As Long

Private Sub Form_Unload(Cancel As Integer)
    CleanUp
End Sub

Private Sub Timer1_Timer()
    Dim usename$
    Dim newtotal&
    Dim cs As CheckStand
    Dim x%

    Select Case CurrentState
```

```
        Case ¯
            If chkShop.value = 1 Then
                CurrentState = 1
            End If
        Case 1
            usename$ = GetMappingName$()
            ' Right now we only use checkstand 1
            MappingHandle = OpenFileMapping(FILE_MAP_WRITE, False, usename$)
            If MappingHandle = ¯ Then Exit Sub
            MappingAddress = MapViewOfFile(MappingHandle, FILE_MAP_ALL_ACCESS, _
            ¯, ¯, ¯)
            CurrentState = 2
        Case 2
            agCopyData ByVal MappingAddress, cs, Len(cs)
            If cs.Total = ¯ Then CurrentState = 3
        Case 3
            CurrentTotal = ¯
            For x = ¯ To CInt(Rnd(99))
                cs.Prices(x) = 1¯¯ * Rnd()
                CurrentTotal = CurrentTotal + cs.Prices(x)
            Next x
            cs.Done = True
            cs.Client = "Client" & txtClient.Text
            agCopyData cs, ByVal MappingAddress, Len(cs)
            CurrentState = 4
        Case 4
            agCopyData ByVal MappingAddress, cs, Len(cs)
            If cs.Total <> ¯ Then
                For x = ¯ To 99
                    newtotal = newtotal + cs.Prices(x)
                Next x
                cs.Total = ¯
                lstPurchase.AddItem Format$(CurrentTotal, "¯.¯¯")
                agCopyData cs, ByVal MappingAddress, Len(cs)
                If chkShop.value = ¯ Then
                    CurrentState = ¯
                Else
                    CurrentState = 1
                End If
            ' Clear file mapping handles, etc.
            CleanUp
            End If
    End Select
    Select Case CurrentState
        Case ¯
            lblStatus.Caption = "Idle"
        Case 1
            lblStatus.Caption = "Looking for checkstand"
        Case 2
            lblStatus.Caption = "Waiting in line at checkstand"
        Case 3
            lblStatus.Caption = "Loading items onto checkstand"
```

```
        Case 4
            lblStatus.Caption = "Waiting for checkout to be complete"
        End Select
End Sub

Public Function GetMappingName() As String
    GetMappingName = "ChkStdlmap"
End Function

Private Sub CleanUp()
    ' Remember, this won't get called if you Stop without
    ' closing the main window.
    If MappingAddress <> ¯ Then
        Call UnmapViewOfFile(MappingAddress)
        MappingAddress = ¯
    End If
    If MappingHandle <> ¯ Then
        Call CloseHandle(MappingHandle)
        MappingHandle = ¯
    End If
End Sub
```

Suggestions for Further Practice

- Fix ckServe so that it can safely be terminated regardless of the state of the client transaction.

- What happens if you open a server program and then run two separate client applications? You'll see that they very quickly get confused as to who actually checked out with which totals. You see, there is nothing in place here to make one client wait in line for a previous one to finish. This problem, called a synchronization problem, is a very serious issue on multitasking systems such as Windows 95 and Windows NT. The solution to the problem in this case will be presented in Chapter 14.

Disk.vbp—Disk Free Space Utility

The Disk.vbp project is a very simple example that determines the amount of free space on disk using the GetDiskFreeSpace function. The main screen for this program is shown in Figure 13.5.

Determining the amount of free disk space has been difficult in previous versions of Visual Basic, mostly because there was no function in either Visual Basic or the Win16 API to perform this task. The most common solution was to use a function in the Visual Basic setup kit to determine the free space on a disk, but it was subject to one major limitation—it turns out that the amount of free disk space available is not necessarily the information that you really need.

Figure 13.5

Disk.vbp program at
runtime

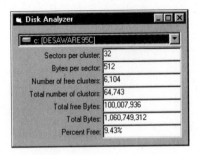

Listing 13.6 shows the only form in this project, FRMDISK.FRM.

Listing 13.6   FRMDISK.FRM

```
VERSION 5.¯¯
Begin VB.Form frmDisk
    Caption         =    "Disk Analyzer"
    ClientHeight    =    279¯
    ClientLeft      =    1¯95
    ClientTop       =    1515
    ClientWidth     =    4215
    Height          =    3195
    Left            =    1¯35
    LinkTopic       =    "Form1"
    ScaleHeight     =    279¯
    ScaleWidth      =    4215
    Top             =    117¯
    Width           =    4335
    Begin VB.DriveListBox Drive1
        Height          =    315
        Left            =    12¯
        TabIndex        =    ¯
        Top             =    18¯
        Width           =    3975
    End
    Begin VB.Label lblPercent
        BackColor       =    &H¯¯FFFFFF&
        BorderStyle     =    1  'Fixed Single
        Height          =    315
        Left            =    216¯
        TabIndex        =    14
        Top             =    234¯
        Width           =    1935
    End
    Begin VB.Label Label1
```

Listing 13.6 FRMDISK.FRM (Continued)

```
         Alignment       =    1  'Right Justify
         Caption         =    "Percent Free:"
         Height          =    255
         Index           =    6
         Left            =    12⁻
         TabIndex        =    13
         Top             =    24⁻⁻
         Width           =    1995
      End
      Begin VB.Label lblTotalBytes
         BackColor       =    &H⁻⁻FFFFFF&
         BorderStyle     =    1  'Fixed Single
         Height          =    315
         Left            =    216⁻
         TabIndex        =    12
         Top             =    2⁻4⁻
         Width           =    1935
      End
      Begin VB.Label lblTotalFree
         BackColor       =    &H⁻⁻FFFFFF&
         BorderStyle     =    1  'Fixed Single
         Height          =    315
         Left            =    216⁻
         TabIndex        =    11
         Top             =    174⁻
         Width           =    1935
      End
      Begin VB.Label Label1
         Alignment       =    1  'Right Justify
         Caption         =    "Total Bytes:"
         Height          =    255
         Index           =    5
         Left            =    12⁻
         TabIndex        =    1⁻
         Top             =    21⁻⁻
         Width           =    1995
      End
      Begin VB.Label Label1
         Alignment       =    1  'Right Justify
         Caption         =    "Total free Bytes:"
         Height          =    255
         Index           =    4
         Left            =    12⁻
         TabIndex        =    9
         Top             =    18⁻⁻
         Width           =    1995
      End
      Begin VB.Label lblClusters
```

Listing 13.6   FRMDISK.FRM (Continued)

```
        BackColor       =   &H¯¯FFFFFF&
        BorderStyle     =   1  'Fixed Single
        Height          =   315
        Left            =   216¯
        TabIndex        =   8
        Top             =   144¯
        Width           =   1935
    End
    Begin VB.Label lblFree
        BackColor       =   &H¯¯FFFFFF&
        BorderStyle     =   1  'Fixed Single
        Height          =   315
        Left            =   216¯
        TabIndex        =   7
        Top             =   114¯
        Width           =   1935
    End
    Begin VB.Label lblBytes
        BackColor       =   &H¯¯FFFFFF&
        BorderStyle     =   1  'Fixed Single
        Height          =   315
        Left            =   216¯
        TabIndex        =   6
        Top             =   84¯
        Width           =   1935
    End
    Begin VB.Label lblSectors
        BackColor       =   &H¯¯FFFFFF&
        BorderStyle     =   1  'Fixed Single
        Height          =   315
        Left            =   216¯
        TabIndex        =   5
        Top             =   54¯
        Width           =   1935
    End
    Begin VB.Label Label1
        Alignment       =   1  'Right Justify
        Caption         =   "Total number of clusters:"
        Height          =   255
        Index           =   3
        Left            =   12¯
        TabIndex        =   4
        Top             =   15¯¯
        Width           =   1995
    End
    Begin VB.Label Label1
        Alignment       =   1  'Right Justify
        Caption         =   "Number of free clusters:"
```

Listing 13.6   FRMDISK.FRM (Continued)

```
            Height          =    255
           .Index           =    2
            Left            =    12⁻
            TabIndex        =    3
            Top             =    12⁻⁻
            Width           =    1995
         End
         Begin VB.Label Label1
            Alignment       =    1    'Right Justify
            Caption         =    "Bytes per sector:"
            Height          =    255
            Index           =    1
            Left            =    12⁻
            TabIndex        =    2
            Top             =    9⁻⁻
            Width           =    1995
         End
         Begin VB.Label Label1
            Alignment       =    1    'Right Justify
            Caption         =    "Sectors per cluster:"
            Height          =    255
            Index           =    ⁻
            Left            =    12⁻
            TabIndex        =    1
            Top             =    6⁻⁻
            Width           =    1995
         End
      End
   End
Attribute VB_Name = "frmDisk"
Attribute VB_GlobalNameSpace = False
Attribute VB_Creatable = False
Attribute VB_PredeclaredId = TrueAttribute VB_Exposed = False
Option Explicit
Private Declare Function GetDiskFreeSpace Lib "kernel32" Alias _
"GetDiskFreeSpaceA" (ByVal lpRootPathName As String, lpSectorsPerCluster As _
Long, lpBytesPerSector As Long, lpNumberOfFreeClusters As Long, _
lpTotalNumberOfClusters As Long) As Long
Dim SectorsPerCluster&, BytesPerSector&, NumberOfFreeClustors&, _
TotalNumberOfClustors&
Dim BytesFree&, BytesTotal&
Dim PercentFree&

Private Sub Drive1_Change()
    DisplayResults
End Sub


Public Sub DisplayResults()
```

Listing 13.6   FRMDISK.FRM (Continued)

```
        Dim dl&
        Dim s$
        Dim spaceloc%
        Dim FreeBytes&, TotalBytes&
        s$ = Drive1.Drive
        ' Is there a space? Strip off the volume name if so
        spaceloc = InStr(s$, " ")
        If spaceloc > ¯ Then
            s$ = Left$(s$, spaceloc - 1)
        End If
        If Right$(s$, 1) <> "\" Then s$ = s$ & "\"
        dl& = GetDiskFreeSpace(s$, SectorsPerCluster, BytesPerSector, _
        NumberOfFreeClustors, TotalNumberOfClustors)
        lblSectors = Format(SectorsPerCluster, "#,¯")
        lblBytes = Format(BytesPerSector, "#,¯")
        lblFree = Format(NumberOfFreeClustors, "#,¯")
        lblClusters = Format(TotalNumberOfClustors, "#,¯")
        TotalBytes = TotalNumberOfClustors * SectorsPerCluster * BytesPerSector
        lblTotalBytes = Format(TotalBytes, "#,¯")
        FreeBytes = NumberOfFreeClustors * SectorsPerCluster * BytesPerSector
        lblTotalFree = Format(FreeBytes, "#,¯")
        lblPercent = Format(FreeBytes / TotalBytes, "Percent")
End Sub

Private Sub Form_Load()
    DisplayResults
End Sub
```

As you can see, the GetDiskFreeSpace function does not actually retrieve the number of bytes free on a disk—it actually retrieves the number of free clusters. At first glance, you might think that this is just the whim of some designer to help complicate things, but in fact there is a good reason for returning the free space data in the way that it is done here.

Consider a disk that holds a gigabyte of data—that's 1,073,741,824 bytes.

As a programmer or computer user, you need to divide this space up into usable areas, and the most common division is, of course, the disk file. Naturally, you would want files to be any size, from one byte to the size of the disk. And it goes without saying that you would want it to be possible for a disk to hold many different files.

Now consider these requirements from the operating system's point of view, for it is the operating system that is responsible for organizing information on the disk. In order to fulfill the requirements listed above, one thing is clear: The operating system must be able to keep track of the status of each and every byte on the system—whether it is free or in use by a file. If it is part

of a file, the system needs to know which file, and which byte follows it in the file (since files are often fragmented on disk).

It takes quite a bit of space to hold all of that status information. Even if you could cram it into 20 bytes or so, if the operating system allocated bytes one at a time, you would need 20 gigabytes of space to hold the information needed to organize that one gigabyte drive. Even with today's rapidly declining drive prices, this is not terribly practical.

You could turn to a more sophisticated scheme which maintains lists of bytes, keeping track of the start and end byte number for portions of files or free space. Even so, the effort to deal with individual bytes is significant.

Since it is not practical for an operating system to track individual bytes, it instead tracks blocks of bytes called clusters. The number of clusters on a FAT file system such as that used by DOS is limited to 64K—a very manageable number. On a 1 gigabyte disk this makes each cluster 16K in size. The NT file system uses a much more sophisticated allocation scheme and can support over 64K clusters, thus you will tend to see smaller clusters—512 bytes on a 1 gigabyte drive.

The cluster is the smallest block of data that can be managed by the operating system. If you create a file, the system allocates it an entire cluster, even if the file only uses a single byte in the cluster. The operating system does keep track of how much space is used within the cluster, but unused space is not available to other applications. This also means that the maximum number of files that you can store on a disk is equal to the number of clusters (less actually, as some clusters are used to manage the file system, directories, and so on). Each cluster may contain one or more logical sectors—but sector information is not terribly useful to programmers since the operating system works on a cluster basis.

Which brings us to the results of the GetDiskFreeSpace function. Why go to the trouble of returning the number of free clusters and then the number of sectors and bytes in a cluster? Why not just return the number of free bytes? The answer is that the number of free bytes on a disk is not enough information in many cases. The number of clusters allows you to determine not only if there is space for the data but also if the drive can hold the number of files you wish to create. Knowing the cluster size can allow you to accurately calculate how much real disk space a file needs. For example, lets say you wish to create ten files that are each 1K in size. If the GetDiskFreeSpace function returned only the number of free bytes and returned 16K bytes of free space, your first conclusion would be that there is plenty of space for the files. But this might be incorrect. If your cluster size was 512 bytes or 1,024 bytes, the files would fit. But if the cluster size was 16K (the cluster size for a one gigabyte drive under the FAT file system), only one file would fit on the disk even though the total number of free bytes was larger than all of the files put together. In fact, with a 16K cluster size, those ten 1K files (10K total space) require a whopping 160K bytes of disk space! This is a good argument for using the NT file system if you are planning to use Windows NT anyway.

The DisplayResults function does go on to calculate how many bytes are free and how many are in use and displays them along with the percentage of free space—but now you see that those figures are virtually worthless in real applications. More important—you'll know how to use the important results correctly for your own application.

By the way, purists will note that this entire discussion dealt with logical sectors and clusters as seen by the operating system—hardware issues were not covered at all. You see, at the hardware level you need to deal with cylinders, heads, physical sectors, bad block mapping, and so on—issues which are mercifully hidden from programmers (other than those brave souls who write the device drivers themselves).

Function Reference

This section contains an alphabetical reference for the functions described in this chapter.

■ CloseHandle

VB Declaration   Declare Function CloseHandle& Lib "kernel32" (ByVal hObject As Long)

Description   Closes a kernel object. These include files, file mappings, processes, threads, security, and synchronization objects.

Use with VB   No problem in general. With regard to files, it is similar to the Visual Basic Close command. It is generally better to use Close because it supports Visual Basic error handling. Note that the file handle used by this function is not the same as the Visual Basic file number.

Parameter	Type/Description
hObject	Long—A handle of an object to close.

Return Value   Long—Nonzero on success, zero on failure. Sets GetLastError.

Platform   Windows 95, Windows NT

Comments   A kernel object is not deleted until all references to the object are closed.

Porting Notes   Under Win16 it was possible to use the Visual Basic FileAttr function to retrieve the system file handle for a Visual Basic file. This is not possible under Win32.

Example   FileDemo.vbp

■ CompareFileTime

VB Declaration   Declare Function CompareFileTime& Lib "kernel32" (lpFileTime1 As FILETIME, _
                      lpFileTime2 As FILETIME)

Description   Compares two file times as specified by FILETIME structures.

Use with VB   No problem.

Parameter	Type/Description
lpFileTime1	FILETIME—First FILETIME structure.
lpFileTime2	FILETIME—Second FILETIME structure.

Return Value   Long—0 if the two times are equal. –1 if lpFileTime1 is less than lpFileTime2. 1 if lpFileTime1 is more than lpFileTime2.

Platform   Windows 95, Windows NT

■ CopyFile

VB Declaration
```
Declare Function CopyFile& Lib "kernel32" Alias "CopyFileA" (ByVal _
lpExistingFileName As String, ByVal lpNewFileName As String, ByVal _
bFailIfExists As Long)
```

Description   Copies a file.

Use with VB   No problem. Similar to the Visual Basic FileCopy command.

Parameter	Type/Description
lpExistingFile-Name	String—Source file name.
lpNewFileName	String—Destination file name.
bFailIfExists	Long—If TRUE (nonzero), the function will fail if the destination file already exists. Otherwise the destination file will be overwritten.

Return Value   Long—Nonzero on success, zero on failure. Sets GetLastError.

Platform   Windows 95, Windows NT

■ CreateDirectory, CreateDirectoryEx

VB Declaration
```
Declare Function CreateDirectory& Lib "kernel32" Alias "CreateDirectoryA" _
(ByVal lpNewDirectory As String, lpSecurityAttributes As SECURITY_ATTRIBUTES) _
Declare Function CreateDirectoryEx& Lib "kernel32" Alias "CreateDirectoryExA" _
(ByVal lpTemplateDirectory As String, ByVal lpNewDirectory As String, _
lpSecurityAttributes As SECURITY_ATTRIBUTES)
```

Description   Creates a new directory.

Use with VB   No problem. Similar to the MkDir function, but provides more capability.

Parameter	Type/Description
lpTemplateDi-rectory	String—Name of a template directory from which to copy default attributes (such as the default compression for files in the directory). vbNullString to specify no template.
lpNewDirectory	String—The name of the new directory.
lpSecurityAt-tributes	SECURITY_ATTRIBUTES—SECURITY_ATTRIBUTES structure defining security for the directory if supported by the operating system.

Return Value   Long—TRUE (nonzero) on success, FALSE on error. Sets GetLastError.

Platform   Windows 95, Windows NT

■ CreateFile

VB Declaration
```
Declare Function CreateFile& Lib "kernel32" Alias "CreateFileA" (ByVal _
lpFileName As String, ByVal dwDesiredAccess As Long, ByVal dwShareMode As Long, _
lpSecurityAttributes As SECURITY_ATTRIBUTES, ByVal dwCreationDisposition As _
Long, ByVal dwFlagsAndAttributes As Long, ByVal hTemplateFile As Long)
```

Description   All purpose routine for opening and creating files, pipes, mailslots, communication services, devices, and consoles.

Use with VB   No problem.

Parameter	Type/Description
lpFileName	String—The name of the file to open.
dwDesired-Access	Long—GENERIC_READ to allow read access to a device, GENERIC_WRITE to allow write access to a device (may be combined). Zero to allow you to obtain information for a device only.
dwShareMode	Long—0 for no sharing, FILE_SHARE_READ and/or FILE_SHARE_WRITE to allow shared access to the file.
lpSecurity-Attributes	SECURITY_ATTRIBUTES—Pointer to a SECURITY_ATTRIBUTES structure defining security for the file (if supported by the operating system).
dwCreation-Disposition	Long—One of the following constants: CREATE_NEW: Create the file. Error occurs if file exists. CREATE_ALWAYS: Create the file. Overwrites previous file. OPEN_EXISTING: File must already exist. Required for devices. OPEN_ALWAYS: Creates the file if it does not already exist. TRUNCATE_EXISTING: Truncates an existing file to zero length.
dwFlagsAnd-Attributes	Long—One or more of the following constants: FILE_ATTRIBUTE_ARCHIVE: Marks the archive attribute. FILE_ATTRIBUTE_COMPRESSED: Marks the file to be compressed, or the default compression for files in a directory. FILE_ATTRIBUTE_NORMAL: Default attributes. FILE_ATTRIBUTE_HIDDEN: File or directory is hidden. FILE_ATTRIBUTE_READONLY: File is read only. FILE_ATTRIBUTE_SYSTEM: File is a system file. FILE_FLAG_WRITE_THROUGH: Operating system does not defer write operations on the file. FILE_FLAG_OVERLAPPED: Enables overlapped operations on the file (see chapter text). FILE_FLAG_NO_BUFFERING: Disables buffering of the file. Files can only be written in volume sector blocks. FILE_FLAG_RANDOM_ACCESS: File buffering is optimized for random access. FILE_FLAG_SEQUENTIAL_SCAN: File buffering is optimized for sequential access. FILE_FLAG_DELETE_ON_CLOSE: Files is deleted when last open handle is closed. Ideal for temporary files.

Parameter	Type/Description
dwFlagsAnd-Attributes (Continued)	You may also combine in the following constant flags under Windows NT: SECURITY_ANONYMOUS, SECURITY_IDENTIFICATION, SECURITY_IMPERSONATION, SECURITY_DELEGATION, SECURITY_CONTEXT_TRACKING, SECURITY_EFFECTIVE_ONLY.
hTemplateFile	Long—If not zero, the handle to a file from which the new file will copy extended attributes.

Return Value   Long—A file handle on success. INVALID_HANDLE_VALUE on error. Sets GetLastError. GetLastError will be set to ERROR_ALREADY_EXISTS even if the function succeeds if the file exists and CREATE_ALWAYS or OPEN_ALWAYS is specified.

Platform   Windows 95, Windows NT

Comments   When opening a communication port (such as "Com1") always specify OPEN_EXISTING. Refer to the online Win32 API reference for additional information on advanced features of this function.

Porting Notes   This function replaces and is preferred to the lOpen and lCreate functions.

Example   ckServe.vbp, fileinfo.vbp

■ CreateFileMapping

VB Declaration
```
Declare Function CreateFileMapping& Lib "kernel32" Alias "CreateFileMappingA" _
(ByVal hFile As Long, lpFileMappingAttributes As SECURITY_ATTRIBUTES, ByVal _
flProtect As Long, ByVal dwMaximumSizeHigh As Long, ByVal dwMaximumSizeLow As _
Long, ByVal lpName As String)
```

Description   Creates a new file mapping object.

Use with VB   No problem.

Parameter	Type/Description
hFile	Long — A file handle to a file on which to create the mapping. &HFFFFFFFF& to create a file mapping on memory.
lpFileMappingAttributes	SECURITY ATTRIBUTE—A security object to use in creating the file mapping. NULL (use ByVal As Long and pass zero) to use default security.
flProtect	Long — One of the following constants: PAGE_READONLY—Mapping is opened as read only. PAGE_READWRITE—Mapping is opened for reading and writing. PAGE_WRITECOPY—Copy on write is enabled. You may combine in one or more of the following constants: SEC_COMMIT—Allocates memory for all pages in a section of the file mapping. SEC_IMAGE—The file is an executable file. SEC_RESERVE—Reserves virtual memory space for a section without allocating actual memory.

Parameter	Type/Description
dwMaximum-SizeHigh	Long—The maximum size of the file mapping (high 32 bits).
dwMaximum-SizeLow	Long—The maximum size of the file mapping (low 32 bits). If this parameter and dwMaximumSizeHigh are both zero, the actual size of the disk file is used.
lpName	String—The name of the file mapping object. If a mapping exists with this name, the function opens it. Use vbNullString to create a file mapping with no name.

Return Value   Long—A handle to the newly created file mapping object. Zero on error. Sets GetLastError. GetLastError will be set to ERROR_ALREADY_EXISTS even on success if the handle returned is that of an existing file mapping object. In that case, the size of the file mapping will be the size of the existing object, not that specified by this function.

Platform   Windows 95, Windows NT

Comments   Refer to the chapter text for additional information on file mappings.

Example   ckServe.vbp

■ DeleteFile

VB Declaration
```
Declare Function DeleteFile& Lib "kernel32" Alias "DeleteFileA" (ByVal _
    lpFileName As String)
```

Description   Deletes the specified file.

Use with VB   No problem. Similar to the Kill statement.

Parameter	Type/Description
lpFileName	String—Name of the file to delete.

Return Value   Long—Nonzero on success, zero on failure. Sets GetLastError.

Platform   Windows 95, Windows NT

Comments   Be careful when using this function under Windows 95—it will delete files even if the file is currently opened by an application.

■ DeviceIoControl

VB Declaration
```
Declare Function DeviceIoControl& Lib "kernel32" (ByVal hDevice As Long, ByVal _
    dwIoControlCode As Long, lpInBuffer As Any, ByVal nInBufferSize As Long, _
    lpOutBuffer As Any, ByVal nOutBufferSize As Long, lpBytesReturned As Long, _
    lpOverlapped As OVERLAPPED)
```

Description   Performs a specified operation on a device.

Use with VB	No problem.	
	Parameter	**Type/Description**
	hDevice	Long—Handle to a device.
	dwIoControl-Code	Long—Constant with the prefix FSCTL_. See Table 13.15.
	lpInBuffer	Any—Varies depending on the dwIoControlCode parameter. See Table 13.15.
	nInBufferSize	Long—The length of the input buffer
	lpOutBuffer	Any—Varies depending on the dwIoControlCode parameter. See Table 13.15.
	nOutBufferSize	Long—Size of the output buffer
	lpBytesReturned	Long—Number of bytes actually loaded into the output buffer.
	lpOverlapped	OVERLAPPED—OVERLAPPED structure for overlapped operations. Change to ByVal As Long and pass zero for synchronous operation.

Return Value Long—Nonzero on success, zero on failure. Sets GetLastError.

Platform Windows 95, Windows NT. Not all of the operations are supported under both operating systems.

Example Devio.vbp

Table 13.15 **Partial List of Device Control Options**

Operation	Parameter	Set to...
Dismount a volume	dwIoControlCode	FSCTL_DISMOUNT_VOLUME
	lpInBuffer	ByVal 0
	lpInBufferSize	0
	lpOutBuffer	ByVal 0
	lpOutBufferSize	0
Get volume compression	dwIoControlCode	FSCTL_GET_COMPRESSION
	lpInBuffer	ByVal 0
	lpInBufferSize	0
	lpOutBuffer	Integer variable to load with a constant with the prefix COMPRESSION_VALUE_???
	lpOutBufferSize	2

Table 13.15   Partial List of Device Control Options (Continued)

Operation	Parameter	Set to...
Lock a volume	dwIoControlCode	FSCTL_LOCK_VOLUME
	lpInBuffer	ByVal 0
	lpInBufferSize	0
	lpOutBuffer	ByVal 0
	lpOutBufferSize	0
Set volume compression	dwIoControlCode	FSCTL_SET_COMPRESSION
	lpInBuffer	Integer variable to load with a constant with the prefix COMPRESSION_VALUE_???
	lpInBufferSize	2
	lpOutBuffer	ByVal 0
	lpOutBufferSize	0
	lpBytesReturned	Long variable to load with results of the operation
Unlock a volume	dwIoControlCode	FSCTL_UNLOCK_VOLUME
	lpInBuffer	ByVal 0
	lpInBufferSize	0
	lpOutBuffer	ByVal 0
	lpOutBufferSize	0
Check if media is present and readable in a removable media device	dwIoControlCode	IOCTL_DISK_CHECK_VERIFY
	lpInBuffer	ByVal 0
	lpInBufferSize	0
	lpOutBuffer	ByVal 0
	lpOutBufferSize	0
	Function Return value	TRUE if device is accessible and media is present

Table 13.15 **Partial List of Device Control Options (Continued)**

Operation	Parameter	Set to...
Eject media on SCSI device	dwIoControlCode	IOCTL_DISK_EJECT_MEDIA
	lpInBuffer	ByVal 0
	lpInBufferSize	0
	lpOutBuffer	ByVal 0
	lpOutBufferSize	0
Format tracks on a device	dwIoControlCode	IOCTL_DISK_FORMAT_TRACKS
	lpInBuffer	A FORMAT_PARAMETERS data structure containing information on the tracks to format
	lpInBufferSize	Length of a FORMAT_PARAMETERS structure
	lpOutBuffer	ByVal 0
	lpOutBufferSize	0
Determine a drives geometry	dwIoControlCode	IOCTL_DISK_GET_DRIVE_GEOMETRY
	lpInBuffer	ByVal 0
	lpInBufferSize	0
	lpOutBuffer	A DISK_GEOMETRY data structure to load with information about a disk drive
	lpOutBufferSize	Length of a DISK_GEOMETRY structure
Determine a drive's partition layout	dwIoControlCode	IOCTL_DISK_GET_DRIVE_LAYOUT
	lpInBuffer	ByVal 0
	lpInBufferSize	0
	lpOutBuffer	A DRIVE_LAYOUT_INFORMATION structure followed by one or more PARTITION_INFORMATION structures to load with information about the layout of a disk drive
	lpOutBufferSize	Size of the buffer allocated

Table 13.15 Partial List of Device Control Options (Continued)

Operation	Parameter	Set to...
Determine the types of media supported by a drive	dwIoControlCode	IOCTL_DISK_GET_MEDIA_TYPES
	lpInBuffer	ByVal 0
	lpInBufferSize	0
	lpOutBuffer	An array of DISK_GEOMETRY data structures to load with information about the media supported by a disk drive
	lpOutBufferSize	Length of the output buffer
Retrieve information about a partition	dwIoControlCode	IOCTL_DISK_GET_PARTITION_INFO
	lpInBuffer	ByVal 0
	lpInBufferSize	0
	lpOutBuffer	A PARTITION_INFORMATION structure to load with information about a partition
	lpOutBufferSize	Size of the buffer allocated
Load media on a device	dwIoControlCode	IOCTL_DISK_LOAD_MEDIA
	lpInBuffer	ByVal 0
	lpInBufferSize	0
	lpOutBuffer	ByVal 0
	lpOutBufferSize	0
Enable or disable media removal	dwIoControlCode	IOCTL_DISK_MEDIA_REMOVAL
	lpInBuffer	A PREVENT_MEDIA_REMOVAL data structure containing information on whether to enable or disable media removal
	lpInBufferSize	Length of a PREVENT_MEDIA_REMOVAL structure
	lpOutBuffer	ByVal 0
	lpOutBufferSize	0

Table 13.15   Partial List of Device Control Options (Continued)

Operation	Parameter	Set to...
Determine a drive's performance	dwIoControlCode	IOCTL_DISK_PERFORMANCE
	lpInBuffer	ByVal 0
	lpInBufferSize	0
	lpOutBuffer	A DISK_PERFORMANCE structure to load with information about the performance of a drive
	lpOutBufferSize	Size of the buffer allocated
Control appearance of modem status data in a data stream	dwIoControlCode	IOCTL_SERIAL_LSRMST_INSERT
	lpInBuffer	A Byte variable—If nonzero, the escape character to use; if zero, inline status is disabled
	lpInBufferSize	1
	lpOutBuffer	ByVal 0
	lpOutBufferSize	0

■ DosDateTimeToFileTime

VB Declaration   `Declare Function DosDateTimeToFileTime& Lib "kernel32" (ByVal wFatDate As Long, _`
`ByVal wFatTime As Long, lpFileTime As FILETIME)`

Description   Converts DOS date and time values to a Win32 FILETIME value.

Use with VB   No problem.

Parameter	Type/Description
wFatDate	Long—The 16-bit DOS date value.
wFatTime	Long—The 16-bit DOS time value.
lpFileTime	FILETIME—Structure to load with the Win32 time.

Return Value   Long—Nonzero on success, zero on failure. Sets GetLastError.

Platform   Windows 95, Windows NT

Comments   Refer to the chapter text for information on the format of DOS date and time values.

■ FileTimeToDosDateTime

VB Declaration   Declare Function FileTimeToDosDateTime& Lib "kernel32" (lpFileTime As FILETIME, _
lpFatDate As Integer, lpFatTime As Integer)

Description   Converts a Win32 FILETIME value to DOS date and time values.

Use with VB   No problem.

Parameter	Type/Description
lpFileTime	FILETIME—A FILETIME structure containing the time to convert.
lpFatDate	Long—The 16-bit DOS date value.
lpFatTime	Long—The 16-bit DOS time value.

Return Value   Long—Nonzero on success, zero on failure. Sets GetLastError.

Platform   Windows 95, Windows NT

Comments   Refer to the chapter text for information on the format of DOS date and time values.

■ FileTimeToLocalFileTime

VB Declaration   Declare Function FileTimeToLocalFileTime& Lib "kernel32" (lpFileTime As _
FILETIME, lpLocalFileTime As FILETIME)

Description   Converts a FILETIME structure to local time.

Use with VB   No problem.

Parameter	Type/Description
lpFileTime	FILETIME—Structure containing time in UTC.
lpLocalFileTime	FILETIME—Structure to load with the converted local time.

Return Value   Long—Nonzero on success, zero on failure. Sets GetLastError.

Platform   Windows 95, Windows NT

■ FileTimeToSystemTime

VB Declaration   Declare Function FileTimeToSystemTime& Lib "kernel32" (lpFileTime As FILETIME, _
lpSystemTime As SYSTEMTIME)

Description   Loads a SYSTEMTIME structure based on the contents of a FILETIME structure.

Use with VB   No problem.

Parameter	Type/Description
lpFileTime	FILETIME—FILETIME structure containing a file time.
lpSystemTime	SYSTEMTIME—Structure to load with system time information.

Return Value   Long—Nonzero on success, zero on failure. Sets GetLastError.

Platform   Windows 95, Windows NT

Comments   Refer to Chapter 6 for information on system times.

Example   FileInfo.vbp

■ FindClose

VB Declaration   `Declare Function FindClose& Lib "kernel32" (ByVal hFindFile As Long)`

Description   Closes a search handle created by the FindFirstFile function.

Use with VB   No problem.

Parameter	Type/Description
hFindFile	Long—A search handle provided by the FindFirstFile function.

Return Value   Long—Nonzero on success, zero on failure. Sets GetLastError.

Platform   Windows 95, Windows NT

■ FindFirstFile

VB Declaration   `Declare Function FindFirstFile& Lib "kernel32" Alias "FindFirstFileA" (ByVal _`
`lpFileName As String, lpFindFileData As WIN32_FIND_DATA)`

Description   Searches for a file based on a file name.

Use with VB   No problem.

Parameter	Type/Description
lpFileName	String—The name of the file to search for. May include wild card characters. May include a path or relative path name.
lpFindFileData	WIN32_FIND_DATA—A structure to load with information about the file that was found. This structure is used on subsequent searches.

Return Value   Long—A search handle on success, INVALID_HANDLE_VALUE on error. The handle should be closed using the FindClose function when it is no longer needed.

Platform   Windows 95, Windows NT

Comments   The handle returned from this function is used as a parameter to the FindNextFile function. This allows you to enumerate all files that match the file name specified by the lpFileName parameter.

■ FindNextFile

VB Declaration   ```
Declare Function FindNextFile& Lib "kernel32" Alias "FindNextFileA" (ByVal _
hFindFile As Long, lpFindFileData As WIN32_FIND_DATA)
```

**Description**    Searches for the next file based on a file name specified during a call to the FindFirstFile function.

**Use with VB**    No problem.

| Parameter | Type/Description |
|---|---|
| hFindFile | Long—A search handle returned by the FindFirstFile function. |
| lpFindFileData | WIN32_FIND_DATA—A structure to load with information about the file that was found. |

**Return Value**    Long—TRUE (nonzero) on success, zero on error. Sets GetLastError to ERROR_NO_MORE_FILES when no files remain to be enumerated.

**Platform**    Windows 95, Windows NT

## ■ FlushFileBuffers

**VB Declaration**    ```
Declare Function FlushFileBuffers& Lib "kernel32" (ByVal hFile As Long)
```

Description   Flushes the internal file buffers for the specified file handle.

Use with VB   No problem.

Parameter	Type/Description
hFile	Long—A file handle.

Return Value   Long—Nonzero on success, zero on failure. Sets GetLastError.

Platform   Windows 95, Windows NT

Example   ckServe.vbp

■ FlushViewOfFile

VB Declaration   ```
Declare Function FlushViewOfFile& Lib "kernel32" (ByVal lpBaseAddress As Long, _
ByVal dwNumberOfBytesToFlush As Long)
```

**Description**    Flushes any data that has been written into file mapping buffers onto disk.
```

Use with VB	No problem.	

Parameter	Type/Description
lpBaseAddress	Long—A long value containing the base address to flush.
dwNumber-OfBytesToFlush	Long—The number of bytes to flush.

Return Value Long—Nonzero on success, zero on failure. Sets GetLastError.

Platform   Windows 95, Windows NT

Comments If the file mapping is on a remote system, this function guarantees that the data has been written from current system, but it does not guarantee that the data is actually written to the remote system's disk unless the file was opened with the FILE_FLAG_WRITE_THROUGH option, which disables deferred writes.

■ GetBinaryType

VB Declaration
```
Declare Function GetBinaryType& Lib "kernel32" Alias "GetBinaryTypeA" (ByVal _
    lpApplicationName As String, lpBinaryType As Long)
```

Description Determines if a file is executable.

Use with VB No problem.

Parameter	Type/Description
lpApplication-Name	String—The full path name of the file to test.
lpBinaryType	Long—A variable to load with the file type as defined by one of the following constants: SCS_32BIT_BINARY: A Win32 executable. SCS_DOS_BINARY: A DOS executable. SCS_OS216_BINARY: A 16-bit OS/2 executable. SCS_PIF_BINARY: A PIF file to execute a DOS executable. SCS_POSIX_BINARY: A Posix application. SCS_WOW_BINARY: A 16-bit Windows executable.

Return Value Long—TRUE (nonzero) on success, zero on error.

Platform   Windows NT

Example   FileInfo.vbp

■ GetCompressedFileSize

VB Declaration
```
Declare Function GetCompressedFileSize& Lib "kernel32" Alias _
    "GetCompressedFileSizeA" (ByVal lpFileName As String, lpFileSizeHigh As Long)
```

Description   Determines the number of bytes actually taken up on disk by a compressed file.

Use with VB   No problem.

Parameter	Type/Description
lpFileName	String—The name of the file to test.
lpFileSizeHigh	Long—A long value to load with the high 32 bits of a 64-bit file size. May be NULL (Change to ByVal) if the size will not exceed 2^32 bytes.

Return Value   Long—The size of the file. &HFFFFFFFF on error. Note that if lpFileSizeHigh is not NULL and the result is &HFFFFFFFF, you must call GetLastError to determine if an error actually occurred, since this may be a valid result.

Platform   Windows NT

Comments   If a volume is compressed, you can determine if a file is compressed by checking if the result of this function differs from the result of the GetFileSize function (if they differ, the file is compressed).

■ GetCurrentDirectory

VB Declaration
```
Declare Function GetCurrentDirectory& Lib "kernel32" Alias _
"GetCurrentDirectoryA" (ByVal nBufferLength As Long, ByVal lpBuffer As String)
```

Description   Loads a buffer with the current directory.

Use with VB   No problem.

Parameter	Type/Description
nBufferLength	Long—The length of the lpBuffer buffer.
lpBuffer	String—A preinitialized string to load with the current directory.

Return Value   Long—The number of bytes loaded into lpBuffer. If nBufferLength is not large enough to hold the directory, the return value is the required buffer length including the NULL terminator character. Zero on error. Sets GetLastError.

Platform   Windows 95, Windows NT

■ GetDiskFreeSpace

VB Declaration
```
Declare Function GetDiskFreeSpace& Lib "kernel32" Alias "GetDiskFreeSpaceA" _
(ByVal lpRootPathName As String, lpSectorsPerCluster As Long, lpBytesPerSector _
As Long, lpNumberOfFreeClusters As Long, lpTotalNumberOfClusters As Long)
```

Description   Obtains information about the organization of a disk and the amount of free space remaining.

Use with VB	No problem.

Parameter	Type/Description
lpRootPathName	String—The root path for the disk without the volume name.
lpSectorsPerCluster	Long—A variable to load with the number of sectors in a cluster.
lpBytesPerSector	Long—A variable to load with the number of bytes in a sector.
lpNumberOfFreeClusters	Long—A variable to load with the number of free clusters on the disk.
lpTotalNumberOfClusters	Long—A variable to load with the number of clusters on the disk.

Return Value	Long—Nonzero on success, zero on failure. Sets GetLastError.
Platform	Windows 95, Windows NT
Comments	Refer to the chapter text for an in-depth look at this function and how it should be used to determine the amount of usable space available on a drive. This function should not be used on Windows 95 for drives over 2GB in size. It will cap the drive size at 2GB.
Example	Disk.vbp

■ GetDriveType

VB Declaration	`Declare Function GetDriveType& Lib "kernel32" Alias "GetDriveTypeA" (ByVal _` `nDrive As String)`
Description	Determines the type of a disk drive.
Use with VB	No problem.

Parameter	Type/Description
nDrive	String— A string containing the path to the root directory of the drive.

Return Value	Long—Zero if the drive cannot be identified, one if the specified directory does not exist. One of the constants DRIVE_REMOVABLE, DRIVE_FIXED, DRIVE_REMOTE, DRIVE_CDROM or DRIVE_RAMDISK specifying the drive type on success.
Platform	Windows 95, Windows NT, Win16

■ GetExpandedName

VB Declaration	`Declare Function GetExpandedName& Lib "lz32.dll" Alias "GetExpandedNameA" _` `(ByVal lpszSource As String, ByVal lpszBuffer As String)`
Description	Retrieves the full name of a compressed file. The file must have been compressed using the COMPRESS.EXE program using the /r option.

Use with VB	Refer to "Compressed File Operations," earlier in this chapter.

Parameter	Type/Description
lpszSource	String—The name of the compressed file.
lpszBuffer	String—A buffer to load with the full name of the file.

Return Value	Long—1 on success, LZERROR_BADVALUE on error.
Platform	Windows 95, Windows NT, Win16
Comments	Be sure the lpszBuffer string is preinitialized to a length long enough to handle the expanded name.

■ GetFileAttributes

VB Declaration	Declare Function GetFileAttributes& Lib "kernel32" Alias "GetFileAttributesA" _ (ByVal lpFileName As String)
Description	Determines the attributes of the specified file.
Use with VB	No problem.

Parameter	Type/Description
lpFileName	String—The name of the file whose attributes are being retrieved.

Return Value	Long— –1 on error. A long value containing flag bits specifying the attributes of the file where the flag bits correspond to constants with the FILE_ATTRIBUTE_??? prefix. Refer to Chapter 3 for information on extracting bit values from a numeric value.
Platform	Windows 95, Windows NT

■ GetFileInformationByHandle

VB Declaration	Declare Function GetFileInformationByHandle& Lib "kernel32" (ByVal hFile As _ Long, lpFileInformation As BY_HANDLE_FILE_INFORMATION)
Description	This function provides another mechanism for obtaining information about a file by loading a BY_HANDLE_FILE_INFORMATION structure with information about the file.
Use with VB	No problem.

Parameter	Type/Description
hFile	Long—A handle to the file.
lpFileInformation	BY_HANDLE_FILE_INFORMATION—Structure to load with file information.

Return Value	Long—Nonzero on success, zero on failure. Sets GetLastError.
Platform	Windows 95, Windows NT

Comments The BY_HANDLE_FILE_INFORMATION structure is defined as follows:

```
Type BY_HANDLE_FILE_INFORMATION
        dwFileAttributes As Long
        ftCreationTime As FILETIME
        ftLastAccessTime As FILETIME
        ftLastWriteTime As FILETIME
        dwVolumeSerialNumber As Long
        nFileSizeHigh As Long
        nFileSizeLow As Long
        nNumberOfLinks As Long
        nFileIndexHigh As Long
        nFileIndexLow As Long
End Type
```

Most of the fields are self-documenting. The dwFileAttributes field contains a combination of one or more constants with the FILE_ATTRIBUTES_?? prefix describing the attributes of the file. nNumberOfLinks lists the number of links to a file under NFS. The nFileIndexHigh and nFileIndexLow fields combine to form a 64-bit number that uniquely identifies a file on a volume.

Example FileInfo.vbp

■ GetFileSize

VB Declaration
```
Declare Function GetFileSize& Lib "kernel32" (ByVal hFile As Long, _
lpFileSizeHigh As Long)
```

Description Determines the size of a file.

Use with VB No problem.

Parameter	Type/Description
hFile	Long—A handle to a file.
lpFileSizeHigh	Long—A long value to load with the high 32 bits of a 64-bit file size. May be NULL (Change to ByVal) if the size will not exceed 2^{32} bytes.

Return Value Long—The size of the file. &HFFFFFFFF on error. Note that if lpFileSizeHigh is not NULL and the result is &HFFFFFFFF, you must call GetLastError to determine if an error actually occurred, since this may be a valid result.

Platform Windows 95, Windows NT

■ GetFileTime

VB Declaration
```
Declare Function GetFileTime& Lib "kernel32" (ByVal hFile As Long, _
lpCreationTime As FILETIME, lpLastAccessTime As FILETIME, lpLastWriteTime As _
FILETIME)
```

Description Retrieves time information for the specified file.

Use with VB	No problem.

Parameter	Type/Description
hFile	Long—A handle to a file.
lpCreationTime	FILETIME—A FILETIME structure to load with the creation time of the file.
lpLastAccess-Time	FILETIME—A FILETIME structure to load with the last access time of the file (not supported by FAT file systems).
lpLastWriteTime	FILETIME—A FILETIME structure to load with the last modification time of the file.

Return Value	Long—Nonzero on success, zero on failure. Sets GetLastError.
Platform	Windows 95, Windows NT
Comments	The lpCreationTime, lpLastAcccessTime and lpLastWriteTime can be set to zero (pass ByVal As Long) if you do not need that information. File times returned by this function are UTC.

■ GetFileType

VB Declaration	`Declare Function GetFileType& Lib "kernel32" (ByVal hFile As Long)`
Description	Determines the type of file given a file handle.
Use with VB	No problem.

Parameter	Type/Description
hFile	Long—The handle of the file to check.

Return Value	Long—One of the constants: FILE_TYPE_UNKNOWN if the file type is unknown, FILE_TYPE_DISK if it is a disk file, FILE_TYPE_CHAR if the file is a console or printer, FILE_TYPE_PIPE if the file is a pipe (see Chapter 14 for information on pipes).
Platform	Windows 95, Windows NT

■ GetFileVersionInfo

VB Declaration	`Declare Function GetFileVersionInfo& Lib "version.dll" Alias _`
	`"GetFileVersionInfoA" (ByVal lptstrFilename As String, ByVal dwHandle As Long, _`
	`ByVal dwLen As Long, lpData As Byte)`

Description	Retrieves the file version information from a module that supports version stamping.
Use with VB	Refer to "Version Stamping," earlier in this chapter, for additional information.

Parameter	Type/Description
lptstrFilename	String—The name of the file from which to load version information.

Parameter	Type/Description
dwHandle	Long—Not used under Win32.
dwLen	Long—The size of the byte array or buffer specified by the lpData parameter. Use the GetFileVersionInfoSize function to determine the required buffer size.
lpData	Byte—The first byte in a buffer to load with the file's version information.

Return Value   Long—Nonzero on success, zero on failure. Sets GetLastError.

Platform   Windows 95, Windows NT, Win16

Porting Notes   The dwHandle parameter is not used under Win32.

Example   FileDemo.vbp

■ GetFileVersionInfoSize

VB Declaration   Declare Function GetFileVersionInfoSize& Lib "version.dll" Alias _
"GetFileVersionInfoSizeA" (ByVal lptstrFilename As String, lpdwHandle As Long)

Description   Retrieves the size of the buffer required to hold the file version information for a file that contains a version resource.

Use with VB   Refer to "Version Stamping," earlier in this chapter, for additional information.

Parameter	Type/Description
lptstrFilename	String—The name of the file containing a version resource.
lpdwHandle	Long—A long variable that will be loaded with the value zero.

Return Value   Long—The length of the buffer needed to hold the version resource for a file. Zero if the file has no version information. Sets GetLastError.

Platform   Windows 95, Windows NT, Win16

Porting Notes   The lpdwHandle parameter is no longer used under Win32.

Example   FileDemo.vbp

■ GetFullPathName

VB Declaration   Declare Function GetFullPathName& Lib "kernel32" Alias "GetFullPathNameA" _
(ByVal lpFileName As String, ByVal nBufferLength As Long, ByVal lpBuffer As _
String, lpFilePart As Long)

Description   Retrieves the full path name for the specified file.

Use with VB   The lpFilePart parameter is difficult to use under Visual Basic. The problem is this: Windows loads this long with the address in the lpBuffer string where the filename portion of the path begins. Unfortunately, this will be the address into the temporary ANSI string buffer that Visual Basic created to pass to the API. By the time this function returns, Visual Basic will have copied the returned (lpBuffer) string back into its internal Unicode string buffer, so the lpFilePart address will no longer be valid.

Ultimately, this leaves you with two choices. First, you can simply not use the lpFilePart information (ignore the value loaded into the parameter by Windows). Second, you can change the lpBuffer parameter to a byte array (lpBuffer As Byte—pass the first element of the array as a parameter). In this case, you can calculate the start of the filename by using the agGetAddress-ForObject function to determine the address of the start of the byte array, and subtract it from the value loaded into the lpFilePart parameter (this will give you the offset in the array where the file name begins). Of course, the approach also implies that you will need to do an explicit Unicode conversion to actually read the path name in lpBuffer.

Parameter	Type/Description
lpFileName	String—The name of the file (long file names or 8.3 DOS file names are both allowed).
nBufferLength	Long—The length of the lpBuffer string.
lpBuffer	String—A preinitialized string to load with the drive and path name for the file. This will always be the long file name if present.
lpFilePart	Long—A long variable to load with the address where the file name begins. See the "Use with VB" notes above.

Return Value   Long—The number of characters loaded into lpBuffer (excluding the terminating NULL character). If the buffer is not long enough to hold the path, the return value will be the size of buffer required. Zero on error. Sets GetLastError.

Platform   Windows 95, Windows NT

■ GetLogicalDrives

VB Declaration   `Declare Function GetLogicalDrives& Lib "kernel32" ()`

Description   Determines which logical drive letters exist on a system.

Use with VB   No problem.

Return Value   Long—The bits in this result indicate which drives exist. For example, bit zero set to 1 indicates that drive A: exists on a system, bit one indicates B:, and so forth.

Platform   Windows 95, Windows NT

■ GetLogicalDriveStrings

VB Declaration   `Declare Function GetLogicalDriveStrings& Lib "kernel32" Alias _`
`"GetLogicalDriveStringsA" (ByVal nBufferLength As Long, ByVal lpBuffer As _`
`String)`

Description	Retrieves a string containing the root drive paths for all current logical drives.
Use with VB	No problem.

Parameter	Type/Description
nBufferLength	Long—The length of the lpBuffer string.
lpBuffer	String—A string to load with the logical drive names. Each name is separated by a NULL character, with two nulls after the last name.

Return Value	Long—The number of characters loaded into lpBuffer (excluding the terminating NULL character). If the buffer is not long enough to hold the path, the return value will be the size of buffer required. Zero on error. Sets GetLastError.
Platform	Windows 95, Windows NT
Example	logdrvs.vbp

■ GetOverlappedResult

VB Declaration	`Declare Function GetOverlappedResult& Lib "kernel32" (ByVal hFile As Long, _`
	`lpOverlapped As OVERLAPPED, lpNumberOfBytesTransferred As Long, ByVal bWait As _`
	`Long)`

Description	Determines the current state of an overlapped operation. Refer to the chapter text on asynchronous file operations.
Use with VB	No problem.

Parameter	Type/Description
hFile	Long—A handle to a file, pipe, or communications device.
lpOverlapped	OVERLAPPED—The Overlapped structure for the I/O operation being checked.
lpNumberOf-BytesTransferred	Long—A variable to load with the number of bytes transferred.
bWait	Long—TRUE to wait until the asynchronous operation is complete. FALSE to return immediately.

Return Value	Long—Nonzero on success, zero on failure. Sets GetLastError. If bWait is FALSE and the asynchronous operation is still in progress, the function will return zero and GetLastError will be set to ERROR_IO_INCOMPLETE.
Platform	Windows 95, Windows NT

■ GetPrivateProfileInt

VB Declaration	`Declare Function GetPrivateProfileInt& Lib "kernel32" Alias _` `"GetPrivateProfileIntA" (ByVal lpApplicationName As String, ByVal lpKeyName As _`

```
String, ByVal nDefault As Long, ByVal lpFileName As String)
```

Description   Retrieves an integer value for the specified entry in an initialization file.

Use with VB   No problem.

Parameter	Type/Description
lpApplicationName	String—The section to search for the entry. This string is not case-sensitive.
lpKeyName	String—The key name or entry to retrieve. This string is not case-sensitive.
nDefault	nDefault—The default value to return if the specified entry is not found.
lpFileName	String —The name of the private initialization file. If a full path name is not specified, Windows will search for the file in the Windows directory.

Return Value   Long—The value of the entry found, or the default value if the specified entry is not found. If the number found is not a legal integer, the function will return that portion that is legal. For example, the entry xyz=55zz will cause 55 to be returned.

This function also understands hexadecimal numbers in standard C format. A hex number will be prefixed by the characters 0x—thus 0x55ab would be equivalent to &H55AB in Visual Basic.

Platform   Windows 95, Windows NT, Win16

Comments   Under Windows NT, some private initialization files will actually be implemented in the registry. A list of these files can be found in the HKEY_LOCAL_MACHINE\Software\Microsoft\Windows NT\CurrentVersion\IniFileMapping key in the registry.

Example   vb4ini.vbp in Chapter 4.

■ GetPrivateProfileSection

VB Declaration
```
Declare Function GetPrivateProfileSection& Lib "kernel32" Alias _
"GetPrivateProfileSectionA" (ByVal lpAppName As String, ByVal lpReturnedString _
As String, ByVal nSize As Long, ByVal lpFileName As String)
```

Description   Retrieves a list of all key names and values for a specified section.

Use with VB   No problem.

Parameter	Type/Description
lpAppName	String—The section to retrieve. This string is not case-sensitive.
lpReturned-String	String—A list of key and value strings. Each string is separated by a NULL, with a double NULL after the final string.
nSize	Long—The size of the lpReturnedString buffer. Maximum of 32767 on Windows 95.

Parameter	Type/Description
lpFileName	String—The name of the private initialization file. If a full path name is not specified, Windows will search for the file in the Windows directory.

Return Value   Long—The number of characters loaded into the lpReturnedString buffer. nSize-2 if the buffer is not large enough to hold all of the information.

Platform   Windows 95, Windows NT

Comments   See comments for GetPrivateProfileInt.

■ GetPrivateProfileString

VB Declaration
```
Declare Function GetPrivateProfileString& Lib "kernel32" Alias _
"GetPrivateProfileStringA" (ByVal lpApplicationName As String, ByVal lpKeyName _
As String, ByVal lpDefault As String, ByVal lpReturnedString As String, ByVal _
nSize As Long, ByVal lpFileName As String)
```

Description   Retrieves the string for the specified entry in an initialization file.

Use with VB   No problem.

Parameter	Type/Description
lpApplication-Name	String—The section to search for the entry. This string is not case-sensitive. If vbNullString, the lpReturnedString buffer will be loaded with a list of all of the sections for this INI file.
lpKeyName	String—The key name or entry to retrieve. This string is not case-sensitive. If vbNullString, the lpReturnedString buffer will be loaded with a list of all of the keys for the specified section.
lpDefault	String—The default value to return if the specified entry is not found. This may be the empty string ("").
lpReturned-String	String—A string buffer preallocated to at least nSize bytes in length.
nSize	Long—The maximum number of characters to load into the lpReturnedString buffer.
lpFileName	String—The name of the private initialization file. If a full path name is not specified, Windows will search for the file in the Windows directory.

Return Value   Long—The number of bytes copied into the lpReturnedString buffer not counting the terminating NULL character. NSize-1 (nSize-2 if lpApplicationName or lpKeyName is NULL) if the lpReturnedString buffer is not large enough to hold the information.

Platform   Windows 95, Windows NT, Win16

Comments   If the lpKeyName parameter is vbNullString, the lpReturnedString buffer will be loaded with a list of all of the keys for the specified section. Each key will be terminated with a NULL character, with the final key being terminated with two NULL characters. Also refer to the comments for the GetPrivateProfileInt function.

Porting Notes   Setting lpApplicationName to NULL to obtain a list of sections is a new feature to Win32.

Example   vb4ini.vbp in Chapter 4.

▓ GetProfileInt

VB Declaration   Declare Function GetProfileInt& Lib "kernel32" Alias "GetProfileIntA" (ByVal _
lpAppName As String, ByVal lpKeyName As String, ByVal nDefault As Long)

Description   Retrieves an integer value for the specified entry in the WIN.INI initialization file.

Use with VB   No problem.

Parameter	Type/Description
lpAppName	String—The section to search for the entry. This string is not case-sensitive.
lpKeyName	String—The key name or entry to retrieve. This string is not case-sensitive.
nDefault	Long—The default value to return if the specified entry is not found.

Return Value   Long—The value of the entry found, or the default value if the specified entry is not found. If the number found is not a legal integer, the function will return that portion that is legal. For example, the entry xyz=55zz will cause 55 to be returned.

This function also understands hexadecimal numbers in standard C format. A hex number will be prefixed by the characters 0x—thus 0x55ab would be equivalent to &H55AB in Visual Basic.

Platform   Windows 95, Windows NT, Win16

Comments   Refer to the comments for the GetPrivateProfileInt function.

Example   FileDemo.vbp

▓ GetProfileSection

VB Declaration   Declare Function GetProfileSection& Lib "kernel32" Alias "GetProfileSectionA" _
(ByVal lpAppName As String, ByVal lpReturnedString As String, ByVal nSize As _
Long)

Description   Retrieves a list of all key names and values for a specified section.

Use with VB   No problem.

Parameter	Type/Description
lpAppName	String—The section to retrieve. This string is not case-sensitive.
lpReturned-String	String—A buffer to load with a list of key and value strings. Each string is separated by a NULL, with a double NULL after the final string.
nSize	Long—The size of the lpFileName buffer. Maximum of 32767 on Windows 95.

Return Value   Long—The number of characters loaded into the lpReturnedString buffer. nSize-2 if the buffer is not large enough to hold all of the information.

Platform   Windows 95, Windows NT

Comments   See comments for GetPrivateProfileInt.

■ GetProfileString

VB Declaration
```
Declare Function GetProfileString& Lib "kernel32" Alias "GetProfileStringA" _
(ByVal lpAppName As String, ByVal lpKeyName As String, ByVal lpDefault As _
String, ByVal lpReturnedString As String, ByVal nSize As Long)
```

Description   Retrieves the string for the specified entry in the WIN.INI initialization file.

Use with VB   No problem.

Parameter	Type/Description
lpAppName	String—The section to search for the entry. This string is not case-sensitive. If vbNullString, the lpReturnedString buffer will be loaded with a list of all of the sections for this INI file.
lpKeyName	String—The key name or entry to retrieve. This string is not case-sensitive. If vbNullString, the lpReturnedString buffer will be loaded with a list of all of the keys for the specified section.
lpDefault	String—The default value to return if the specified entry is not found. This may be the empty string ("").
lpReturned-String	String—A string buffer preallocated to at least nSize bytes in length.
nSize	Long—The maximum number of characters to load into the lpsz-ReturnedString buffer.

Return Value   Long—The number of bytes copied into the lpReturnedString buffer not counting the terminating NULL character. NSize-1 (nSize-2 if lpApplicationName or lpKeyName is NULL) if the lpReturnedString buffer is not large enough to hold the information.

Platform   Windows 95, Windows NT, Win16

Comments   If the lpKeyName parameter is zero, the lpReturnedString buffer will be loaded with a list of all of the keys for the specified section. Each key will be terminated with a NULL character, with the final key being terminated with two NULL characters.

Example   vb4ini.vbp in Chapter 4

■ GetShortPathName

VB Declaration
```
Declare Function GetShortPathName& Lib "kernel32" Alias "GetShortPathNameA" _
(ByVal lpszLongPath As String, ByVal lpszShortPath As String, ByVal cchBuffer _
As Long)
```

Description   Retrieves the short path name for the specified file.

Use with VB   No problem.

Parameter	Type/Description
lpszLongPath	String—The file name whose short path is being retrieved. May be a full path or based on the current directory.
lpszShortPath	String—A buffer to load with the short path and file name of the file.
cchBuffer	Long—The length of the lpszShortPath buffer.

Return Value   Long—The number of characters loaded into the lpszShortPath buffer. The required buffer length if lpszShortPath is not large enough for the file name.

Platform   Windows 95, Windows NT

■ GetSystemDirectory

VB Declaration
```
Declare Function GetSystemDirectory& Lib "kernel32" Alias "GetSystemDirectoryA" _
(ByVal lpBuffer As String, ByVal nSize As Long)
```

Description   This function retrieves the full path name of the Windows system directory. This is the directory that contains all of the system files. Microsoft has standardized on placing custom controls and other shared components in this directory as well. Generally, you should avoid creating files in this directory. On network windows you will typically need administrator privileges to write into this directory.

Use with VB   No problem.

Parameter	Type/Description
lpBuffer	String—A string buffer to load with the system directory name. It should be preallocated to at least nSize+1 characters long. You should usually allocate at least MAX_PATH characters for this buffer.
nSize	Long—The maximum length of the lpBuffer string.

Return Value   Long—The number of characters loaded into the lpBuffer buffer. The required buffer length if lpBuffer is not large enough for the file name.

Platform   Windows 95, Windows NT

■ GetTempFileName

VB Declaration
```
Declare Function GetTempFileName& Lib "kernel32" Alias "GetTempFileNameA" _
(ByVal lpszPath As String, ByVal lpPrefixString As String, ByVal wUnique As _
Long, ByVal lpTempFileName As String)
```

Description   This function obtains the name of a temporary file that can be used by an application.

Use with VB   No problem.

Parameter	Type/Description
lpszPath	String—A directory to use for the temporary file. Typically determined using the GetTempPath function.
lpPrefixString	String—The file name prefix to use. The first three characters are used as the file name prefix.
wUnique	Long—A number to append to the prefix string. If zero, this function will generate a file name using a random number. It will then see if a file by that name exists. If it does, the function will increment the number and continue with the attempt until a unique file name is generated. The file will remain on the drive with a length of zero bytes. If not zero, the file will not be created and the function will not check to see that it is a unique file name.
lpTempFileName	String—A buffer to load with the new temporary file name. This buffer should be at least MAX_PATH characters long.

Return Value   Long—The value of the wUnique number actually used to generate the file name. If the wUnique parameter was not zero, this will be the value of the parameter. Zero on error. Sets GetLastError.

Platform   Windows 95, Windows NT, Win16

Comments   File names used by the function always use the ANSI character set. Refer to Chapter 5 for information on use of character sets under Windows. Temporary files are not automatically deleted by Windows.

Porting Notes   The Win16 version of this function does not use the lpszPath parameter. Instead, it accepts a byte parameter specifying the drive to use for the temporary file.

■ GetTempPath

VB Declaration
```
Declare Function GetTempPath& Lib "kernel32" Alias "GetTempPathA" (ByVal _
nBufferLength As Long, ByVal lpBuffer As String)
```

Description   Retrieves the path that is designated for use by temporary files.

Use with VB   No problem.

Parameter	Type/Description
nBufferLength	Long—The length of the lpBuffer string.
lpBuffer	String—A preinitialized string to load with the temporary path.

Return Value   Long—The number of characters loaded into lpBuffer. The required size of lpBuffer if the current buffer is not long enough to hold the path. Zero on error. Sets GetLastError.

Platform   Windows 95, Windows NT

Comments	The temporary path is that specified by the TMP environment variable, the TEMP environment variable if TMP does not exist, or the current directory if neither environment variable exists.
Porting Notes	Replaces the GetTempDrive function.

■ GetVolumeInformation

VB Declaration

```
Declare Function GetVolumeInformation& Lib "kernel32" Alias _
"GetVolumeInformationA" (ByVal lpRootPathName As String, ByVal _
lpVolumeNameBuffer As String, ByVal nVolumeNameSize As Long, _
lpVolumeSerialNumber As Long, lpMaximumComponentLength As Long, _
lpFileSystemFlags As Long, ByVal lpFileSystemNameBuffer As String, ByVal _
nFileSystemNameSize As Long)
```

Description Retrieves information about a disk volume.

Use with VB No problem.

Parameter	Type/Description
lpRootPath-Name	String—Root path of the volume for which to obtain information.
lpVolumeName-Buffer	String—String to load with the name of the volume.
nVolumeName-Size	Long—Length of the lpVolumeNameBuffer string.
lpVolumeSerial-Number	Long—Long variable to load with the serial number of the volume.
lpMaximum-Compo-nentLength	Long—Long variable to load with the length of each part of a file name. For example, in the case of file c:\component1\component2.ext—this is the length of the component1 or component2 name.
lpFileSystem-Flags	Long—Long variable to load with one or more bit flags as indicated by the following constants: FS_CASE_IS_PRESERVED: Case of filenames is recorded in the file system. FS_CASE_SENSITIVE: Filenames are case-sensitive. FS_UNICODE_STORED_ON_DISK: Filenames are stored as Unicode. FS_PERSISTANT_ACLS: File system supports access control list security on files. FS_FILE_COMPRESSION: File system supports compression on a file-by-file basis. FS_VOL_IS_COMPRESSED: Entire volume is compressed.
lpFileSystem-NameBuffer	String—Buffer to load with the name of the file system (such as FAT, NTFS, and so on).
nFileSystem-NameSize	Long—The length of the lpFileSystemNameBuffer string.

Return Value Long—Nonzero on success, zero on failure. Sets GetLastError.

Platform	Windows 95, Windows NT
Example	logdrvs.vbp

■ GetWindowsDirectory

VB Declaration
```
Declare Function GetWindowsDirectory& Lib "kernel32" Alias _
"GetWindowsDirectoryA" (ByVal lpBuffer As String, ByVal nSize As Long)
```

Description
This function retrieves the full path name of the Windows directory. This is the directory that contains most Windows application files and initialization files.

Use with VB
No problem.

Parameter	Type/Description
lpBuffer	String—A string buffer to load with the Windows directory name. The directory will not have a terminating "\" character unless it is the root directory.
nSize	Long—The maximum length of the lpBuffer string.

Return Value
Long—The length of the string copied into lpBuffer. If lpBuffer is not large enough to hold the string, this will be the required size of lpBuffer. Zero on error. Sets GetLastError.

Platform
Windows 95, Windows NT, Win16

■ hread

VB Declaration
```
Declare Function hread& Lib "kernel32" Alias "_hread" (ByVal hFile As Long, _
lpBuffer As Any, ByVal lBytes As Long)
```

Description
See lread.

Porting Notes
This function was used under Win16 to read blocks of data greater than 64K in size. Win32 file I/O functions do not suffer from this 64K limitation.

■ hwrite

VB Declaration
```
Declare Function hwrite& Lib "kernel32" Alias "_hwrite" (ByVal hFile As Long, _
ByVal lpBuffer As String, ByVal lBytes As Long)
```

Description
See lwrite.

Porting Notes
This function was used under Win16 to write blocks of data greater than 64K in size. Win32 file I/O functions do not suffer from this 64K limitation.

■ lclose

VB Declaration   `Declare Function lclose& Lib "kernel32" Alias "_lclose" (ByVal hFile As Long)`

Description   Closes the specified file. Refer to the CloseHandle function for details.

■ lcreat

VB Declaration   `Declare Function lcreat& Lib "kernel32" Alias "_lcreat" (ByVal lpPathName As _`
`String, ByVal iAttribute As Long)`

Description   Creates a file. If the file already exists, it is truncated to a length of zero and opened for reading and writing.

Use with VB   This function duplicates functionality available in the Visual Basic Open statement.

Parameter	Type/Description
lpPathName	String—The name of the file to create.
iAttribute	Long—One of the following values: 0: File can be read or written. 1: Create a read-only file. 2: Create a hidden file. 3: Create a system file.

Return Value   Long—File handle to the open file on success, HFILE_ERROR on error.

Platform   Windows 95, Windows NT, Win16

Comments   This function can open files that have already been opened by other applications, so use it with caution. The Win32 CreateFile function replaces this function.

■ llseek

VB Declaration   `Declare Function llseek& Lib "kernel32" Alias "_llseek" (ByVal hFile As Long, _`
`ByVal lOffset As Long, ByVal iOrigin As Long)`

Description   Sets the current position for reading or writing in a file.

Use with VB   This function is similar to the Visual Basic Seek statement. Do not use on files opened using the Visual Basic open command.

Parameter	Type/Description
hFile	Long—A system file handle.
lOffset	Long—The offset in bytes.

Parameter	Type/Description
iOrigin	Long—One of the following constants: FILE_BEGIN: lOffset specifies the new position as an offset from the start of the file. FILE_CURRENT: lOffset specifies the new position as an offset from the current position. FILE_END: lOffset specifies the new position as an offset from the end of the file.

Return Value   Long—The new position as an offset in bytes from the start of the file. HFILE_ERROR on error. Sets GetLastError.

Platform   Windows 95, Windows NT, Win16

Comments   Refer to the SetFilePointer function for a similar function that can work on larger files.

■ LockFile

VB Declaration
```
Declare Function LockFile& Lib "kernel32" (ByVal hFile As Long, ByVal _
dwFileOffsetLow As Long, ByVal dwFileOffsetHigh As Long, ByVal _
nNumberOfBytesToLockLow As Long, ByVal nNumberOfBytesToLockHigh As Long)
```

Description   Under Windows, it is possible for files to be opened in shared mode—under which multiple processes can access the file at once. This function makes it possible for an application that has read or write access to a file to lock a region in the file so that it cannot be accessed by other applications.

Use with VB   No problem.

Parameter	Type/Description
hFile	Long—A handle of the file to lock.
dwFileOffsetLow	Long—The low 32 bits of the start location of the region to lock.
dwFileOffsetHigh	Long—The high 32 bits of the start location of the region to lock.
nNumberOfBytes-ToLockLow	Long—The low 32 bits of the number of bytes in the locked region.
nNumberOfBytes-ToLockHigh	Long—The high 32 bits of the number of bytes in the locked region.

Return Value   Long—Nonzero on success, zero on failure. Sets GetLastError.

Platform   Windows 95, Windows NT

Comments   Locked regions may not overlap. Depending on the operating system, SHARE.EXE may need to be running in order for this function to work.

■ LockFileEx

VB Declaration   `Declare Function LockFileEx& Lib "kernel32" (ByVal hFile As Long, ByVal dwFlags _`

```
As Long, ByVal dwReserved As Long, ByVal nNumberOfBytesToLockLow As Long, ByVal _
nNumberOfBytesToLockHigh As Long, lpOverlapped As OVERLAPPED)
```

Description   Similar to LockFile, except that it provides additional capability.

Use with VB   No problem.

Parameter	Type/Description
hFile	Long—A handle of the file to lock.
dwFlags	Long— One or both of the following constants: LOCKFILE_FAIL_IMMEDIATELY: Specifies that if the lock fails the function should return an error. Otherwise the application thread will be suspended and will wait until the lock is possible. LOCKFILE_EXCLUSIVE_LOCK: Specifies that the locked region may not be read or written by any other thread or process. Otherwise, the region will only be protected from writing—other processes will be able to read the locked area.
dwReserved	Long—Unused; set to zero.
nNumberOfBytes-ToLockLow	Long—The low 32 bits of the number of bytes in the locked region.
nNumberOfBytes-ToLockHigh	Long—The high 32 bits of the number of bytes in the locked region.
lpOverlapped	OVERLAPPED—An OVERLAPPED structure containing the offset in the file to the start of the region to lock.

Return Value   Long—Nonzero on success, zero on failure. Sets GetLastError.

Platform   Windows NT

Comments   Locked regions may not overlap.

▪ lopen

VB Declaration
```
Declare Function lopen& Lib "kernel32" Alias "_lopen" (ByVal lpPathName As _
String, ByVal iReadWrite As Long)
```

Description   Opens the specified file in binary mode.

Use with VB   The Visual Basic Open command is recommended due to its flexibility and compatibility with the Visual Basic error handler.

Parameter	Type/Description
lpPathName	String—The name of the file to open.

Parameter	Type/Description
iReadWrite	Long—A combination of the access mode and share mode constants as follows: *Access Mode* READ: File is open for reading. READ_WRITE: File is open for reading and writing. WRITE: File is open for writing. *Share Mode* OF_SHARE_COMPAT, OF_SHARE_DENY_NONE, OF_SHARE_DENY_READ, OF_SHARE_DENY_WRITE, OF_SHARE_EXCLUSIVE, as defined in Table 13.17.

Return Value   Long—A file handle to the open file on success, HFILE_ERROR on error. Sets GetLastError.

Platform   Windows 95, Windows NT, Win16

Comments   The CreateFile function provides additional capability under Win32.

■ lread

VB Declaration
```
Declare Function lread& Lib "kernel32" Alias "_lread" (ByVal hFile As Long, _
lpBuffer As Any, ByVal wBytes As Long)
```

Description   Reads data from a file into a memory buffer.

Use with VB   No problem, but the Visual Basic file functions are more flexible.

Parameter	Type/Description
hFile	Long—A file handle.
lpBuffer	Any—Pointer to a block of memory into which data is read.
wBytes	Long—Number of bytes to read.

Return Value   Long—The number of bytes read, HFILE_ERROR on error. If this number is fewer than wBytes, the end of the file has been reached. Sets GetLastError.

Platform   Windows 95, Windows NT, Win16

Example   picprint.vbp in Chapter 12 and others.

■ lwrite

VB Declaration
```
Declare Function lwrite& Lib "kernel32" Alias "_lwrite" (ByVal hFile As Long, _
ByVal lpBuffer As Any, ByVal wBytes As Long)
```

Description   Writes data to a file from a memory buffer.

Use with VB	No problem, but the Visual Basic file functions are more flexible.

Parameter	Type/Description
hFile	Long—A file handle.
lpBuffer	Any—Pointer to a block of memory from which data is written.
wBytes	Long—Number of bytes to write.

Return Value	Long—The number of bytes written, HFILE_ERROR on error. Sets GetLastError.
Platform	Windows 95, Windows NT, Win16
Example	QuikDraw.vbp in Chapter 8 demonstrates hread, which is identical to this function.

■ LZClose

VB Declaration	`Declare Sub LZClose Lib "lz32.dll" (ByVal hfFile As Long)`
Description	Closes a file opened by the LZOpenFile or LZInit functions.
Use with VB	No problem.

Parameter	Type/Description
hfFile	Long—Handle to close. This is a handle returned by the LZOpenFile or LZInit functions—not a normal system file handle.

Platform	Windows 95, Windows NT, Win16

■ LZCopy

VB Declaration	`Declare Function LZCopy& Lib "lz32.dll" (ByVal hfSource As Long, ByVal hfDest _` `As Long)`
Description	Copies a file. If the source file is compressed, it will be decompressed during the copy process. The file must have been compressed using the Microsoft COMPRESS.EXE utility or its equivalent.
Use with VB	No problem.

Parameter	Type/Description
hfSource	Long—A handle to the source file. This handle is provided by the LZOpenFile or LZInit function.
hfDest	Long—A handle to the destination file. This handle is provided by the LZOpenFile or LZInit function.

Return Value	Long—The size of the destination files in bytes on success. A constant smaller than zero on error as shown in Table 13.16.
Platform	Windows 95, Windows NT, Win16

Table 13.16   LZCopy Error Codes

Error Code Constant	Description
LZERROR_BADINHANDLE	Source is invalid
LZERROR_BADOUTHANDLE	Destination is invalid
LZERROR_GLOBALLOC	Insufficient memory for the internal decompression buffers
LZERROR_GLOBLOCK	The handles to the internal decompression buffers are not valid
LZERROR_READ	Invalid source file format
LZERROR_UNKNOWNALG	The decompression DLL does not recognize the compression algorithm used by the source file
LZERROR_WRITE	Error writing the output file, typically caused by insufficient disk space

■ LZInit

VB Declaration   `Declare Function LZInit& Lib "lz32.dll" (ByVal hfSrc As Long)`

Description   This function initializes the internal buffers required to decompress a file given an open file handle to that file.

Use with VB   No problem.

Parameter	Type/Description
hfSrc	Long—A handle to a file.

Return Value   Long—A special handle to the file used by the lz32.dll library. This file handle compatible with the LZCopy, CopyLZFiles, LZRead, and LZSeek functions. On error, this function will return one of the error constants listed in Table 13.16. Be sure to close this handle using the LZClose command when done.

Platform   Windows 95, Windows NT, Win16

Comments   Only 16 compressed file handles can be open at one time.

■ LZOpenFile

VB Declaration   `Declare Function LZOpenFile& Lib "lz32.dll" Alias "LZOpenFileA" (ByVal lpszFile _`
`As String, lpOf As OFSTRUCT, ByVal style As Long)`

Description   This function performs a number of different file operations and is compatible with compressed files. Refer to "File and Directory Operations," earlier in this chapter.

Use with VB

No problem.

Parameter	Type/Description
lpszFile	String—The name of the file to open.
lpOf	OFSTRUCT—OFSTRUCT structure to fill with data including information about the file and results of the operation.
style	Long—A combination of flag constants specifying the operation to perform as described in Table 13.17 under the description of the OpenFile function.

Return Value

Long—A normal file handle as described under the description of the OpenFile function if the file is successful and the style is not OF_READ. If the style parameter is OF_READ and the file is compressed, this function returns a special file handle that may be used by the LZCopy, LZRead, and LZSeek functions. On error, one of the constants in Table 13.16.

Platform

Windows 95, Windows NT, Win16

Comments

Refer to the comments for the OpenFile function later in this section.

■ LZRead

VB Declaration

```
Declare Function LZRead& Lib "lz32.dll" (ByVal hfFile As Long, ByVal lpvBuf As _
String, ByVal cbread As Long)
```

Description

Reads data from a file into a memory buffer. If hFile is a handle to a compressed file opened by the LZOpenFile or LZInit functions, this function will decompress the data as it is read.

Use with VB

No problem.

Parameter	Type/Description
hfFile	Long—A special handle to the source file. This handle is provided by the LZOpenFile or LZInit function.
lpvBuf	String—Pointer to a block of memory into which data is read.
cbread	Long—The size of the lpvBuf buffer.

Return Value

Long—The number of bytes read. If this number is fewer than cbread, the end of the file has been reached. On error, this function will return one of the error constants listed in Table 13.16.

Platform

Windows 95, Windows NT, Win16

■ LZSeek

VB Declaration

```
Declare Function LZSeek& Lib "lz32.dll" (ByVal hfFile As Long, ByVal lOffset As _
Long, ByVal nOrigin As Long)
```

Description

Sets the current position for reading or writing in a file. If hfFile is a handle to a compressed file opened by the LZOpenFile or LZInit function, this function will seek based on the decompressed version of the file.

Use with VB	No problem.

Parameter	Type/Description
hfFile	Long—A special handle to the source file. This handle is provided by the LZOpenFile or LZInit function.
lOffset	Long—The offset in bytes.
nOrigin	Long—One of the following values: 0: lOffset specifies the new position as an offset from the start of the file. 1: lOffset specifies the new position as an offset from the current position. 2: lOffset specifies the new position as an offset from the end of the file.

Return Value
Long—The new position as an offset in bytes from the start of the file. On error, this function will return one of the error constants listed in Table 13.16.

Platform	Windows 95, Windows NT, Win16

■ MapViewOfFile, MapViewOfFileEx

VB Declaration
```
Declare Function MapViewOfFile& Lib "kernel32" (ByVal hFileMappingObject As _
Long, ByVal dwDesiredAccess As Long, ByVal dwFileOffsetHigh As Long, ByVal _
dwFileOffsetLow As Long, ByVal dwNumberOfBytesToMap As Long)
Declare Function MapViewOfFileEx& Lib "kernel32" (ByVal hFileMappingObject As _
Long, ByVal dwDesiredAccess As Long, ByVal dwFileOffsetHigh As Long, ByVal _
dwFileOffsetLow As Long, ByVal dwNumberOfBytesToMap As Long, lpBaseAddress As Any)
```

Description	Maps a file mapping object into the address space of the current application. Refer to the discussion of file mappings in the chapter. MapViewOfFileEx allows you to specified a base address for the mapping.
Use with VB	No problem.

Parameter	Type/Description
hFileMappingObject	Long—A handle to a file mapping object.
dwDesiredAccess	Long—One of the following constants: FILE_MAP_WRITE: Mapping can be read or written. File mapping object must be created with PAGE_READWRITE access. FILE_MAP_READ: Mapping is read only. File mapping object must be created with PAGE_READ or PAGE_READWRITE access. FILE_MAP_ALL_ACCESS: Same as FILE_MAP_WRITE. FILE_MAP_COPY: Mapping is copy on write. File mapping object must be created with PAGE_WRITECOPY access under Windows 95.
dwFileOffsetHigh	Long—The high 32 bits of the start location in the file to map.
dwFileOffsetLow	Long—The low 32 bits of the start location in the file to map.
dwNumberOf-BytesToMap	Long—The number of bytes in the file to map. Use zero to map the entire file mapping object.

Parameter	Type/Description
lpBaseAddress	Long—The address at which to map the file mapping object. Map-ViewOfFileEx will fail if adequate memory space is not available at this address if specified. Zero to allow Windows to find an address.

Return Value Long—The start address of the file mapping in memory. Zero on error. Sets GetLastError.

Platform Windows 95, Windows NT

Comments dwFileOffsetLow and dwFileOffsetHigh must reflect an offset that lies on the memory allocation granularity of the system. In other words, if the memory granularity of the system is 64K (allocations are on a 64K boundary), these values must be multiples of 64K. Use the GetSystemInfo function to determine the memory allocation granularity for the system. Most applications will simply use zero to start the mapping at the beginning of the file. lpBaseAddress must also be a multiple of the memory allocation granularity.

Example ckServe.vbp, ckClient.vbp

■ MoveFile, MoveFileEx

VB Declaration
```
Declare Function MoveFile& Lib "kernel32" Alias "MoveFileA" (ByVal _
lpExistingFileName As String, ByVal lpNewFileName As String)
Declare Function MoveFileEx& Lib "kernel32" Alias "MoveFileExA" (ByVal _
lpExistingFileName As String, ByVal lpNewFileName As String, ByVal dwFlags As _
Long)
```

Description Moves a file. MoveFile is identical to MoveFileEx when dwFlags is zero.

Use with VB No problem.

Parameter	Type/Description
lpExistingFileName	String—File to move.
lpNewFileName	String—New file name.
dwFlags	Long—One or more of the following constants: MOVEFILE_REPLACE_EXISTING: Replaces destination file if it exists. MOVEFILE_COPY_ALLOWED: If moving to a different volume, copies the file and deletes the original. MOVEFILE_DELAY_UNTIL_REBOOT: The move operation takes place next time the system is booted. This allows replacement of system files under Windows NT.

Return Value Long—Nonzero on success, zero on failure. Sets GetLastError.

Platform Windows 95 (MoveFile only), Windows NT

Comments These commands cannot normally move files from one volume to another. MoveFileEx can do so if the MOVEFILE_COPY_ALLOWED flag is set.

■ OpenFile

VB Declaration
```
Declare Function OpenFile& Lib "kernel32" (ByVal lpFileName As String, _
lpReOpenBuff As OFSTRUCT, ByVal wStyle As Long)
```

Description
This function performs a number of different file operations. The Win32 CreateFile function is preferred to this function (it can open named pipes, handle Unicode file names, and does not suffer the 128-character path limitation).

Use with VB
No problem.

Parameter	Type/Description
lpFileName	String—The name of the file to open.
lpReOpenBuff	OFSTRUCT—OFSTRUCT structure to fill with data including information about the file and results of the operation.
wStyle	Long—A combination of flag constants specifying the operation to perform as described in Table 13.17.

Return Value
Long—A file handle on success. Note that the file handle is not necessarily valid; for example, if the OF_EXIST flag is specified, the file is closed before the function returns, but the handle that was used when it was open is nevertheless returned. The function returns HFILE_ERROR on error, in which case the nErrCode of the OFSTRUCT structure specified by lpReOpenBuff is set to the error that occurred. Errors are listed in Table 13.18. Sets GetLastError.

Platform
Windows 95, Windows NT, Win16

Comments
The OFSTRUCT structure is defined in Visual Basic as follows:
```
Type OFSTRUCT
        cBytes As Byte
        fFixedDisk As Byte
        nErrCode As Integer
        Reserved1 As Integer
        Reserved2 As Integer
        szPathName As String * 128
End Type
```

Field	Type/Description
cBytes	Byte—Set to the length of this structure (currently 136).
fFixedDisk	String—The value of this byte will be nonzero if the file is on a fixed disk.
nErrCode	Integer—An error code as shown in Table 13.18.
szPathName	String—The full path name of the file. This string uses the OEM character set (see Chapter 6 for further information on character sets).

If the file name is specified without a full path name, or the OF_SEARCH flag is specified, the file will be searched for in the following locations:

1. The current directory.

2. The Windows system directory. Under Windows NT the 32-bit system directory will be searched, then the 16-bit system directory.

3. The Windows directory.

4. Directories specified in the PATH environment variable.

Porting Notes The OF_CANCEL flag is not supported under Win32. The message box brought up by the OF_PROMPT flag differs from Win16. The search order for OF_SEARCH differs from Win16.

Table 13.17 **OpenFile API Function Styles**

wStyle Constant	Description
OF_CREATE	Creates the specified file. Truncates it to zero length if it already exists.
OF_DELETE	Deletes the specified file.
OF_EXIST	Determines if a file exists by attempting to open the file. If the file exists, it is closed. The function will return the file handle used when the file was opened if the file exists, but the handle will not be valid. A negative number will be returned if the file does not exist.
OF_PARSE	Fills the lpReOpenBuff structure, but performs no other operation.
OF_PROMPT	If the file does not exist, a message box appears with a retry and cancel prompt.
OF_READ	File is opened for reading only.
OF_READWRITE	File is opened for reading and writing.
OF_REOPEN	Opens the file specified in the lpReOpenBuff structure rather than using the lpFileName parameter.
OF_SEARCH	Forces Windows to search for the file even if a path is specified.
OF_SHARE_COMPAT	File can be opened multiple times by multiple applications.
OF_SHARE_DENY_NONE	File can be opened for reading or writing by other programs.
OF_SHARE_DENY_READ	Other programs may not read the file.
OF_SHARE_DENY_WRITE	Other programs may read, but may not write to this file.
OF_SHARE_EXCLUSIVE	No other program may open this file.
OF_WRITE	File is opened for writing only.

Table 13.18   **OFSTRUCT Error Codes**

Value in Hexadecimal	Description
1	Invalid function
2	File not found
3	Path not found
4	No file handle available
5	Access denied
6	Handle is invalid
7	DOS memory corrupted
8	Insufficient memory for the operation
9	Invalid block
A	Illegal environment
B	Invalid format
C	Invalid access
D	Invalid data
F	Invalid drive
10	Invalid current directory
11	Device is different
12	No more files
13	Write protect error
14	Illegal unit
15	Drive not ready
16	Invalid command
17	CRC validation error
18	Invalid length
19	Seek error
1A	Disk is not MS-DOS compatible
1B	Sector not found

Table 13.18   OFSTRUCT Error Codes (Continued)

Value in Hexadecimal	Description
1C	Out of paper
1D	Write fault
1E	Read fault
1F	General failure of the drive
20	Sharing violation
21	File lock violation
22	Incorrect disk
23	No file control block available
24	Sharing buffer exceeded
32	Device not supported
33	Remote device unavailable
34	Duplicate name
35	Bad network path
36	Network is busy
37	Illegal device
38	Too many commands
39	Hardware error on the network adapter
3A	Network response error
3B	Other network error
3C	Remote adapter error
3D	Full print queue
3E	Print spooler full
3F	Print canceled
40	Deleted netname
41	Network access denied
42	Invalid device type

Table 13.18 **OFSTRUCT Error Codes (Continued)**

Value in Hexadecimal	Description
43	Invalid network name
44	Too many names
45	Too many sessions
46	Sharing paused
47	Request not accepted
48	Redirection paused
50	File exists
51	Duplicate file control block
52	Cannot make
53	Interrupt 24 failure
54	Out of structures
55	Already assigned
56	Invalid password
57	Invalid parameter
58	Network write fault

■ OpenFileMapping

VB Declaration
```
Declare Function OpenFileMapping& Lib "kernel32" Alias "OpenFileMappingA" _
(ByVal dwDesiredAccess As Long, ByVal bInheritHandle As Long, ByVal lpName As _
String)
```

Description   Opens an existing named file mapping object.

Use with VB   No problem.

Parameter	Type/Description
dwDesiredAccess	Long— One of the constants with the prefix FILE_MAP_???. Refer to the description of the dwDesiredAccess parameter for the MapViewOfFile function for further information.

Parameter	Type/Description
bInheritHandle	Long—TRUE if the handle returned by this function can be inherited by new processes launched by the current process.
lpName	String—The name of the file mapping object to open.

Return Value Long—A handle to a file mapping object. Zero on error. Sets GetLastError.

Platform Windows 95, Windows NT

Example ckClient.vbp

■ QueryDosDevice

VB Declaration
```
Declare Function QueryDosDevice& Lib "kernel32" Alias "QueryDosDeviceA" (ByVal _
lpDeviceName As String, ByVal lpTargetPath As String, ByVal ucchMax As Long)
```

Description Under Windows NT, DOS device names map into NT system device names. This function can be used to determine the current device mappings.

Use with VB No problem.

Parameter	Type/Description
lpDeviceName	String—If vbNullString, lpTargetPath is loaded with a list of currently mapped MS-DOS names. If an MS-DOS name, lpTargetPath is loaded with a list of device mappings (the first name is the active mapping, subsequent names are prior mappings that have not been deleted).
lpTargetPath	String—A list of names according to the lpDeviceName parameter. The names are separated by NULL characters. The list is terminated by two consecutive NULL characters.
ucchMax	Long—The size of the lpTargetPath buffer.

Return Value Long—Zero on error. The number of characters stored in lpTargetPath on success. Sets GetLastError.

Platform Windows NT

Comments The DefineDosDevice command can be used to change mappings to DOS device names. This function is not documented in this book, but can be found in the online Win32 API reference.

Example QueryDos.vbp

■ ReadFile

VB Declaration
```
Declare Function ReadFile& Lib "kernel32" (ByVal hFile As Long, lpBuffer As _
Any, ByVal nNumberOfBytesToRead As Long, lpNumberOfBytesRead As Long, _
lpOverlapped As OVERLAPPED)
```

Description   Reads data from a file. This function is more flexible than the lread function. This function works on communication devices, pipes, sockets, and mailslots as well.

Use with VB   No problem.

Parameter	Type/Description
hFile	Long—A handle to a file.
lpBuffer	Any—A buffer for the data being read.
nNumberOfBytesToRead	Long—Number of bytes of data to read.
lpNumberOfBytesRead	Long—The number of bytes actually read from the file.
lpOverlapped	OVERLAPPED—If the file was opened with FILE_FLAG_OVERLAPPED specified, this parameter must reference a structure defining an asynchronous read operation. Otherwise, this parameter should be NULL (change the declaration to ByVal lpOverlapped As Long and pass zero).

Return Value   Long—Nonzero on success, zero on failure. Sets GetLastError. If an asynchronous read is started, the function returns zero and sets ERROR_IO_PENDING as the result for GetLast-Error. If the result is nonzero but the number of bytes read is fewer than the nNumberOfBytes-ToRead parameter, the end of the file has been reached.

Platform   Windows 95, Windows NT

Comments   Not every operating system supports asynchronous operations for every type of device. For example, Windows 95 does not support an overlapped read on a disk file.

Example   Async.vbp

■ ReadFileEx

VB Declaration
```
Declare Function ReadFileEx& Lib "kernel32" (ByVal hFile As Long, lpBuffer As _
Any, ByVal nNumberOfBytesToRead As Long, lpOverlapped As OVERLAPPED, ByVal _
lpCompletionRoutine As Long)
```

Description   Similar to ReadFile, except that it is intended to be used only for asynchronous read operations and includes a completion callback.

Use with VB   Requires use of the dwcbk32d.ocx control to handle the completion callback.

Parameter	Type/Description
hFile	Long—A handle to a file.
lpBuffer	Any—A buffer for the data being read. Do not access this buffer until the read operation is complete.
nNumberOf-BytesToRead	Long—Number of bytes of data to read.

Parameter	Type/Description
lpOverlapped	OVERLAPPED—A structure defining an asynchronous read operation. The hEvent field in the structure is ignored when this function is used.
lpCompletion-Routine	Long—The value returned by the ProcAddress property of the dwcbk32d.ocx control.

Return Value   Long—Nonzero on success, zero on failure. Sets GetLastError.

Platform   Windows 95, Windows NT

Comments   Use the cbxLLL callback type of dwcbk32d.ocx. The cbxLLL event will be called with the following parameters once the current thread is open to being signaled: lval1—zero on success, ERROR_HANDLE_EOF if an attempt was made to read past the end of the file; lval2—the number of bytes actually transferred; lval3—the address of the OVERLAPPED structure from the original call to ReadFileEx. Use agCopyData to copy memory from this address to a locally declared OVERLAPPED structure.

■ RegCloseKey

VB Declaration   `Declare Function RegCloseKey& Lib "advapi32.dll" (ByVal hKey As Long)`

Description   Closes a key in the system registry.

Use with VB   No problem.

Parameter	Type/Description
hKey	Long—The key to close.

Return Value   Long—Zero (ERROR_SUCCESS) on success. All other values indicate an error code.

Platform   Windows 95, Windows NT, Win16

Example   FileDemo.vbp

■ RegConnectRegistry

VB Declaration   `Declare Function RegConnectRegistry& Lib "advapi32.dll" Alias _`
`"RegConnectRegistryA" (ByVal lpMachineName As String, ByVal hKey As Long, _`
`phkResult As Long)`

Description   Allows you to access parts of the registry on a remote system.

Use with VB   No problem.

Parameter	Type/Description
lpMachineName	String—The name of the system to connect to. This is in the form \\computername.

Parameter	Type/Description
hKey	Long—HKEY_LOCAL_MACHINE or HKEY_USERS
phkResult	Long—A variable to load with a handle to the specified key.

Return Value Long—Zero (ERROR_SUCCESS) on success. All other values indicate an error code.

Platform Windows 95, Windows NT

■ RegCreateKey

VB Declaration `Declare Function RegCreateKey& Lib "advapi32.dll" Alias "RegCreateKeyA" (ByVal _`
`hKey As Long, ByVal lpSubKey As String, phkResult As Long)`

Description Creates a new key under the specified key. If the key already exists, this function opens the existing key.

Use with VB No problem.

Parameter	Type/Description
hKey	Long—Handle of an open key or one of the standard key names (see chapter text).
lpSubKey	String—Name of the new subkey to create. You can create multiple keys at once by separating them with backslashes, for example, level1\level2\newkey.
phkResult	Long—A variable to load with a handle to the new subkey.

Return Value Long—Zero (ERROR_SUCCESS) on success. All other values indicate an error code.

Platform Windows 95, Windows NT, Win16

■ RegCreateKeyEx

VB Declaration `Declare Function RegCreateKeyEx& Lib "advapi32.dll" Alias "RegCreateKeyExA" _`
`(ByVal hKey As Long, ByVal lpSubKey As String, ByVal Reserved As Long, ByVal _`
`lpClass As String, ByVal dwOptions As Long, ByVal samDesired As Long, _`
`lpSecurityAttributes As SECURITY_ATTRIBUTES, phkResult As Long, lpdwDisposition _`
`As Long)`

Description A more sophisticated way to create a new key under a specified key. Recommended for use under Win32. If the key already exists, this function opens the existing key.

Use with VB No problem.

Parameter	Type/Description
hKey	Long—Handle of an open key or one of the standard key names (see chapter text).

Parameter	Type/Description
lpSubKey	String—Name of the new subkey to create.
Reserved	Long—Set to zero.
lpClass	String—A class name for the key.
dwOptions	Long—Zero or the following constant: REG_OPTION_VOLATILE—This key is not saved and will vanish when the system is restarted.
samDesired	Long—One or more constants with the prefix KEY_?? combined to describe which operations are allowed for this key.
lpSecurityAttributes	SECURITY ATTRIBUTES—A structure describing security for this key. May be NULL (redefine to be ByVal as Null). Not applicable to Windows 95.
phkResult	Long—A variable to load with a handle to the new subkey.
lpdwDisposition	Long—A variable to load with one of the following constants: REG_CREATED_NEW_KEY—A new key was created. REG_OPENED_EXISTING_KEY—An existing key was opened.

Return Value Long—Zero (ERROR_SUCCESS) on success. All other values indicate an error code.

Platform Windows 95, Windows NT. REG_OPTION_VOLATILE is not applicable to Windows 95.

■ RegDeleteKey

VB Declaration
```
Declare Function RegDeleteKey& Lib "advapi32.dll" Alias "RegDeleteKeyA" (ByVal _
hKey As Long, ByVal lpSubKey As String)
```

Description Deletes the specified subkey under an existing key.

Use with VB No problem.

Parameter	Type/Description
hKey	Long—Handle of an open key or one of the standard key names (see chapter text).
lpSubKey	String—The name of the key to delete. Any subkeys of this key are also deleted.

Return Value Long—Zero (ERROR_SUCCESS) on success. All other values indicate an error code.

Platform Windows 95, Windows NT

■ RegDeleteValue

VB Declaration
```
Declare Function RegDeleteValue& Lib "advapi32.dll" Alias "RegDeleteValueA" _
(ByVal hKey As Long, ByVal lpValueName As String)
```

Description	Deletes a value under a specified key.
Use with VB	No problem.

Parameter	Type/Description
hKey	Long—Handle of an open key or one of the standard key names (see chapter text).
lpValueName	String—The name of the value to delete. May be vbNullString or an empty string to delete the default value for the key.

Return Value	Long—Zero (ERROR_SUCCESS) on success. All other values indicate an error code.
Platform	Windows 95, Windows NT, Win16

■ RegEnumKey

VB Declaration
```
Declare Function RegEnumKey& Lib "advapi32.dll" Alias "RegEnumKeyA" (ByVal hKey _
As Long, ByVal dwIndex As Long, ByVal lpName As String, ByVal cbName As Long)
```

Description	Enumerates subkeys for a given key. Win32 functions should use RegEnumKeyEx.
Use with VB	No problem.

Parameter	Type/Description
hKey	Long—Handle of an open key or one of the standard key names (see chapter text).
dwIndex	Long—The index of the subkey to retrieve. The first subkey is at zero.
lpName	String—A buffer to load with the key name at the specified index.
cbName	Long—The length of the lpName buffer.

Return Value	Long—Zero (ERROR_SUCCESS) on success. All other values indicate an error code.
Platform	Windows 95, Windows NT, Win16
Comments	Use RegQueryInfoKey to determine the length of buffer needed to hold the longest key.
Example	FileDemo.vbp demonstrates RegEnumKeyEx which is similar.

■ RegEnumKeyEx

VB Declaration
```
Declare Function RegEnumKeyEx& Lib "advapi32.dll" Alias "RegEnumKeyExA" (ByVal _
hKey As Long, ByVal dwIndex As Long, ByVal lpName As String, lpcbName As Long, _
ByVal lpReserved As Long, ByVal lpClass As String, lpcbClass As Long, _
lpftLastWriteTime As FILETIME)
```

Description	Enumerates subkeys for a given key.

Use with VB   No problem.

Parameter	Type/Description
hKey	Long—Handle of an open key or one of the standard key names (see chapter text).
dwIndex	Long—The index of the subkey to retrieve. The first subkey is at zero.
lpName	String—A buffer to load with the key name at the specified index.
lpcbName	Long—A variable that should be loaded with the length of the lpName buffer (including the NULL character). On return it is set to the number of characters actually loaded into the lpName buffer.
lpReserved	Long—Unused, set to zero.
lpClass	String—A class name to use for the key. May be vbNullString.
lpcbClass	Long—A variable that should be loaded with the length of the lpClass buffer. On return it is set to the number of characters actually loaded into the buffer.
lpftLastWriteTime	FILETIME—The last modification time of the enumerated subkey.

Return Value   Long—Zero (ERROR_SUCCESS) on success. All other values indicate an error code.

Platform   Windows 95, Windows NT

Example   FileDemo.vbp

■ RegEnumValue

VB Declaration
```
Declare Function RegEnumValue& Lib "advapi32.dll" Alias "RegEnumValueA" (ByVal _
hKey As Long, ByVal dwIndex As Long, ByVal lpValueName As String, lpcbValueName _
As Long, lpReserved As Long, lpType As Long, lpData As Byte, lpcbData As Long)
```

Description   Enumerates the values for the specified key.

Use with VB   No problem.

Parameter	Type/Description
hKey	Long—Handle of an open key or one of the standard key names (see chapter text).
dwIndex	Long—The index of the value to retrieve. The first value is at zero.
lpValueName	String—A buffer to load with the value name at the specified index.
lpcbValueName	Long—A variable that should be loaded with the length of the lpValueName buffer. On return it is set to the number of characters actually loaded into the buffer.
lpReserved	Long—Unused, set to zero.
lpType	Long—A variable to load with the type code for the value (see chapter text).

Parameter	Type/Description
lpData	Byte—A buffer to load with the data for this value.
lpcbData	Long—A variable that should be loaded with the length of the lpData buffer. On return it is set to the number of bytes actually loaded into the buffer.

Return Value   Long—Zero (ERROR_SUCCESS) on success. All other values indicate an error code.

Platform   Windows 95, Windows NT

■ RegFlushKey

VB Declaration   `Declare Function RegFlushKey& Lib "advapi32.dll" (ByVal hKey As Long)`

Description   Flushes changes to a key and its subkeys to disk.

Use with VB   No problem.

Parameter	Type/Description
hKey	Long—A handle of a key to flush or one of the standard key names (see chapter text).

Return Value   Long—Zero (ERROR_SUCCESS) on success. All other values indicate an error code.

Platform   Windows 95, Windows NT

Comments   Some operating systems delay writing changes to the registry to disk in order to improve performance. This function ensures that the data has been written to disk, but should be avoided where possible as it can severely impact performance of an application.

■ RegGetKeySecurity

VB Declaration   `Declare Function RegGetKeySecurity& Lib "advapi32.dll" (ByVal hKey As Long, _`
`ByVal SecurityInformation As Long, pSecurityDescriptor As SECURITY_DESCRIPTOR, _`
`lpcbSecurityDescriptor As Long)`

Description   Retrieves security information about a registry key.

Use with VB   No problem.

Parameter	Type/Description
hKey	Long—A handle of a key or one of the standard key names (see chapter text).
SecurityInformation	Long—A flag describing the information to request.
pSecurityDescriptor	SECURITY_DESCRIPTOR—A structure to load with security information for the key.

Parameter	Type/Description
lpcbSecurityDescriptor	Long—A variable that should be loaded with the length of the pSecurityDescriptor buffer. On return it is set to the number of bytes actually loaded into the buffer.

Return Value   Long—Zero (ERROR_SUCCESS) on success. All other values indicate an error code.

Platform   Windows NT

Comments   Refer to the online Win32 API reference for information on security under Windows NT.

■ RegLoadKey

VB Declaration
```
Declare Function RegLoadKey& Lib "advapi32.dll" Alias "RegLoadKeyA" (ByVal hKey _
As Long, ByVal lpSubKey As String, ByVal lpFile As String)
```

Description   Loads registration information from a file that previously was created using the RegSaveKey function. The information is saved into a new subkey created under hKey.

Use with VB   No problem.

Parameter	Type/Description
hKey	Long—HKEY_LOCAL_MACHINE, HKEY_USERS or a key created using RegConnectRegistry.
lpSubKey	String—The name of the new subkey to create.
lpFile	String—The name of the file containing registration information.

Return Value   Long—Zero (ERROR_SUCCESS) on success. All other values indicate an error code.

Platform   Windows 95, Windows NT

■ RegNotifyChangeKeyValue

VB Declaration
```
Declare Function RegNotifyChangeKeyValue& Lib "advapi32.dll" (ByVal hKey As _
Long, ByVal bWatchSubtree As Long, ByVal dwNotifyFilter As Long, ByVal hEvent _
As Long, ByVal fAsynchronus As Long)
```

Description   Provides a mechanism to be notified when a registry key or any of its subkeys has been changed.

Use with VB   No problem.

Parameter	Type/Description
hKey	Long—A handle of a key to watch or one of the standard key names (see chapter text).
bWatchSubtree	Long—TRUE (nonzero) to watch subkeys as well as the specified key.

Parameter	Type/Description
dwNotifyFilter	Long—One or more of the following constants: REG_NOTIFY_CHANGE_NAME: Detects changes to names, creation or deletion of keys. REG_NOTIFY_CHANGE_ATTRIBUTES: Detects changes in attributes. REG_NOTIFY_CHANGE_LAST_SET: Detects changes in the last modification time. REG_NOTIFY_CHANGE_SECURITY: Detects changes in security.
hEvent	Long—A handle to an event. Ignored if fAsynchronus is FALSE.
fAsynchronus	Long—If zero, the function does not return until a change is detected. Otherwise, the function returns immediately and the event specified by hEvent is signaled when a change occurs. See Chapter 14 for information on events.

Return Value   Long—Zero (ERROR_SUCCESS) on success. All other values indicate an error code.

Platform   Windows NT

■ RegOpenKey

VB Declaration   `Declare Function RegOpenKey& Lib "advapi32.dll" Alias "RegOpenKeyA" (ByVal hKey _`
`As Long, ByVal lpSubKey As String, phkResult As Long)`

Description   Opens an existing key.

Use with VB   No problem.

Parameter	Type/Description
hKey	Long—Handle of an open key or one of the standard key names (see chapter text).
lpSubKey	String—Name of the key to open.
phkResult	Long—A variable to load with a handle to the open key.

Return Value   Long—Zero (ERROR_SUCCESS) on success. All other values indicate an error code.

Platform   Windows 95, Windows NT, Win16

Comments   Under NT, this function uses the default security mask.

■ RegOpenKeyEx

VB Declaration   `Declare Function RegOpenKeyEx& Lib "advapi32.dll" Alias "RegOpenKeyExA" (ByVal _`
`hKey As Long, ByVal lpSubKey As String, ByVal ulOptions As Long, ByVal _`
`samDesired As Long, phkResult As Long)`

Description   Opens an existing key. This function is recommended for use under Win32.

Use with VB   No problem.

Parameter	Type/Description
hKey	Long—Handle of an open key or one of the standard key names (see chapter text).
lpSubKey	String—Name of the key to open.
ulOptions	Long—Unused, set to zero.
samDesired	Long—One or more constants with the prefix KEY_?? combined to describe which operations are allowed for this key.
phkResult	Long—A variable to load with a handle to the open key.

Return Value   Long—Zero (ERROR_SUCCESS) on success. All other values indicate an error code.

Platform   Windows 95, Windows NT

■ RegQueryInfoKey

VB Declaration
```
Declare Function RegQueryInfoKey& Lib "advapi32.dll" Alias "RegQueryInfoKeyA" _
(ByVal hKey As Long, ByVal lpClass As String, lpcbClass As Long, lpReserved As _
Long, lpcSubKeys As Long, lpcbMaxSubKeyLen As Long, lpcbMaxClassLen As Long, _
lpcValues As Long, lpcbMaxValueNameLen As Long, lpcbMaxValueLen As Long, _
lpcbSecurityDescriptor As Long, lpftLastWriteTime As FILETIME)
```

Description   Obtain information about a key.

Use with VB   No problem.

Parameter	Type/Description
hKey	Long—Handle of an open key or one of the standard key names (see chapter text).
lpClass	String—A string to load with the class name for this key.
lpcbClass	Long—A variable that should be loaded with the length of the lpClass buffer. On return it is set to the number of bytes actually loaded into the buffer.
lpReserved	Long—Not used, set to zero.
lpcSubKeys	Long—A variable to load with the number of subkeys for this key.
lpcbMaxSub-KeyLen	Long—A variable to load with length of the longest subkey name for this key (not including the terminating NULL character).
lpcbMax-ClassLen	Long—A variable to load with the length of the longest class name for subkeys for this key (not including the terminating NULL character).
lpcValues	Long—A variable to load with the number of values for this key.
lpcbMaxValue-NameLen	Long—A variable to load with the length of the longest value name for subkeys for this key (not including the terminating NULL character).

Parameter	Type/Description
lpcbMax-ValueLen	Long—A variable to load with the buffer size required to hold the largest value data for this key.
lpcbSecurity-Descriptor	Long—A variable to load with the length of the key's security descriptor.
lpftlast-WriteTime	FILETIME—A structure to load with the last modification time for this key.

Return Value   Long—Zero (ERROR_SUCCESS) on success. All other values indicate an error code. The function returns ERROR_MORE_DATA if one of the buffers is not long enough to hold the returned data.

Platform   Windows 95, Windows NT

■ RegQueryValue

VB Declaration
```
Declare Function RegQueryValue& Lib "advapi32.dll" Alias "RegQueryValueA" _
(ByVal hKey As Long, ByVal lpSubKey As String, ByVal lpValue As String, _
lpcbValue As Long)
```

Description   Retrieves the default (unnamed) value for the specified key or subkey.

Use with VB   No problem.

Parameter	Type/Description
hKey	Long—Handle of an open key or one of the standard key names (see chapter text).
lpSubKey	String—Subkey for which to retrieve a value. May be vbNullString to retrieve the value for hKey.
lpValue	String—A string to load with the value for the specified key.
lpcbValue	Long—A variable that should be loaded with the length of the lpValue buffer. On return it is set to the number of bytes actually loaded into the buffer.

Return Value   Long—Zero (ERROR_SUCCESS) on success. All other values indicate an error code.

Platform   Windows 95, Windows NT, Win16

Comments   Win32 Applications should use RegQueryValueEx. lpValue is defined as a string to maintain compatibility with Win16 (under which values are always strings).

■ RegQueryValueEx

VB Declaration
```
Declare Function RegQueryValueEx& Lib "advapi32.dll" Alias "RegQueryValueExA" _
(ByVal hKey As Long, ByVal lpValueName As String, ByVal lpReserved As Long, _
lpType As Long, lpData As Any, lpcbData As Long)
```

Description   Retrieves a value for a key.

Use with VB   No problem.

Parameter	Type/Description
hKey	Long—Handle of an open key or one of the standard key names (see chapter text).
lpValueName	String—The name of the value to retrieve.
lpReserved	Long—Not used, set to zero.
lpType	Long—A variable to load with the type of data retrieved (refer to the chapter text).
lpData	Any—A buffer to load with the value specified.
lpcbData	Long—A variable that should be loaded with the length of the lpData buffer. On return it is set to the number of bytes actually loaded into the buffer.

Return Value   Long—Zero (ERROR_SUCCESS) on success. All other values indicate an error code.

Platform   Windows 95, Windows NT

■ RegReplaceKey

VB Declaration
```
Declare Function RegReplaceKey& Lib "advapi32.dll" Alias "RegReplaceKeyA" _
(ByVal hKey As Long, ByVal lpSubKey As String, ByVal lpNewFile As String, ByVal _
lpOldFile As String)
```

Description   Replaces registry information with information stored in a disk file, and creates a backup containing the current registry information.

Use with VB   No problem.

Parameter	Type/Description
hKey	Long—Handle of an open key or one of the standard key names (see chapter text).
lpSubKey	String—The name of the subkey to replace. It must be directly under HKEY_LOCAL_MACHINE or HKEY_USERS.
lpNewFile	String—The name of the file containing registration information. This file is created using the RegSaveKey function.
lpOldFile	String—The name of a file in which to backup the current registration information.

Return Value   Long—Zero (ERROR_SUCCESS) on success. All other values indicate an error code.

Platform   Windows 95, Windows NT

■ RegRestoreKey

VB Declaration `Declare Function RegRestoreKey& Lib "advapi32.dll" Alias "RegRestoreKeyA" _`
`(ByVal hKey As Long, ByVal lpFile As String, ByVal dwFlags As Long)`

Description Restores registration information from a disk file.

Use with VB No problem.

Parameter	Type/Description
hKey	Long—Handle of an open key or one of the standard key names (see chapter text).
lpFile	String—The name of the file from which to restore registration information.
dwFlags	Long—Zero for a regular restore. REG_WHOLE_HIVE_VOLATILE to make the restored information temporary (not saved when the system is restarted). In this case hKey must refer to HKEY_LOCAL_MACHINE or HKEY_USERS.

Return Value Long—Zero (ERROR_SUCCESS) on success. All other values indicate an error code.

Platform Windows NT

■ RegSaveKey

VB Declaration `Declare Function RegSaveKey& Lib "advapi32.dll" Alias "RegSaveKeyA" (ByVal hKey _`
`As Long, ByVal lpFile As String, lpSecurityAttributes As SECURITY_ATTRIBUTES)`

Description Saves a key and all its subkeys into a disk file.

Use with VB No problem.

Parameter	Type/Description
hKey	Long—Handle of an open key or one of the standard key names (see chapter text).
lpFile	String—The name of the disk file in which to save registry information.
lpSecurity-Attributes	SECURITY_ATTRIBUTES—Security information for the saved information. May be NULL to use default security information (change to ByVal As Long and pass zero).

Return Value Long—Zero (ERROR_SUCCESS) on success. All other values indicate an error code.

Platform Windows 95, Windows NT

■ RegSetKeySecurity

VB Declaration `Declare Function RegSetKeySecurity& Lib "advapi32.dll" (ByVal hKey As Long, _`

```
ByVal SecurityInformation As Long, pSecurityDescriptor As SECURITY_DESCRIPTOR)
```

Description	Sets the security for a specified key.
Use with VB	No problem.

Parameter	Type/Description
hKey	Long—A handle of a key or one of the standard key names (see chapter text).
SecurityInformation	Long—A flag describing the information to save.
pSecurityDescriptor	SECURITY_DESCRIPTOR—A structure containing new security information for the key.

Return Value	Long—Zero (ERROR_SUCCESS) on success. All other values indicate an error code.
Platform	Windows NT

■ RegSetValue

VB Declaration	`Declare Function RegSetValue& Lib "advapi32.dll" Alias "RegSetValueA" (ByVal _`
	`hKey As Long, ByVal lpSubKey As String, ByVal dwType As Long, ByVal lpData As _`
	`String, ByVal cbData As Long)`

Description	Sets the default value for the specified key or subkey.
Use with VB	No problem.

Parameter	Type/Description
hKey	Long—Handle of an open key or one of the standard key names (see chapter text).
lpSubKey	String—The name of the subkey whose value needs to be set. Set to vbNullString to set the default value for hKey. This subkey will be created if it does not exist.
dwType	Long—Must be REG_SZ.
lpData	String—The new value.
cbData	Long—The length of lpData not including the NULL termination character.

Return Value	Long—Zero (ERROR_SUCCESS) on success. All other values indicate an error code.
Platform	Windows 95, Windows NT, Win16

■ RegSetValueEx

VB Declaration	`Declare Function RegSetValueEx& Lib "advapi32.dll" Alias "RegSetValueExA" _`

```
(ByVal hKey As Long, ByVal lpValueName As String, ByVal Reserved As Long, ByVal _
dwType As Long, lpData As Byte, ByVal cbData As Long)
```

Description   Sets the value for the specified key.

Use with VB   No problem.

Parameter	Type/Description
hKey	Long—Handle of an open key or one of the standard key names (see chapter text).
lpValueName	String—The name of the value to set.
Reserved	Long—Not used, set to zero.
dwType	Long—The type of data to set (see chapter text).
lpData	Byte—The first byte in a buffer containing the data.
cbData	Long—The length of the lpData buffer.

Return Value   Long—Zero (ERROR_SUCCESS) on success. All other values indicate an error code.

Platform   Windows 95, Windows NT

■ RegUnLoadKey

VB Declaration
```
Declare Function RegUnLoadKey& Lib "advapi32.dll" Alias "RegUnLoadKeyA" (ByVal _
hKey As Long, ByVal lpSubKey As String)
```

Description   Unloads the specified key and all of its subkeys.

Use with VB   No problem.

Parameter	Type/Description
hKey	Long—HKEY_LOCAL_MACHINE, HKEY_USERS, or a key opened using RegConnectRegistry.
lpSubKey	String—The name of the subkey to unload. Must have been loaded earlier using the RegLoadKey function.

Return Value   Long—Zero (ERROR_SUCCESS) on success. All other values indicate an error code.

Platform   Windows 95, Windows NT

■ RemoveDirectory

VB Declaration
```
Declare Function RemoveDirectory& Lib "kernel32" Alias "RemoveDirectoryA" _
(ByVal lpPathName As String)
```

Description   Removes the specified directory.

Use with VB   No problem.

Parameter	Type/Description
lpPathName	String—The name of the directory to delete.

Return Value   Long—Nonzero on success, zero on failure. Sets GetLastError.

Platform   Windows 95, Windows NT

Comments   The directory must be empty before calling this function.

■ SearchPath

VB Declaration
```
Declare Function SearchPath& Lib "kernel32" Alias "SearchPathA" (ByVal lpPath _
As String, ByVal lpFileName As String, ByVal lpExtension As String, ByVal _
nBufferLength As Long, ByVal lpBuffer As String, lpFilePart As Long)
```

Description   Searches for the specified file.

Use with VB   See the notes for the GetFullPathName function.

Parameter	Type/Description
lpPath	String—Path to search. If vbNullString, uses the Windows search path will be used. Refer to the order described for the OF_SEARCH flag in the OpenFile function.
lpFileName	String—The name of the file to search for.
lpExtension	String—The extension of the file. Must begin with a period. Use vbNullString if the file has no extension or if lpFileName includes an extension.
nBufferLength	Long—The length of the lpBuffer string.
lpBuffer	String—A string to load with the filename.
lpFilePart	Long—A long variable to load with the address of the filename part of the buffer. Not generally useful from Visual Basic (see notes under the GetFullPathName function).

Return Value   Long—The number of characters loaded into the lpBuffer string. If larger than nBufferLength, the required buffer size. Zero on error. Sets GetLastError.

Platform   Windows 95, Windows NT

■ SetCurrentDirectory

VB Declaration
```
Declare Function SetCurrentDirectory& Lib "kernel32" Alias _
"SetCurrentDirectoryA" (ByVal lpPathName As String)
```

Description   Sets the current directory.

Use with VB	No problem.

Parameter	Type/Description
lpPathName	String—The path of the new current directory.

Return Value   Long—Nonzero on success, zero on failure. Sets GetLastError.

Platform   Windows 95, Windows NT

■ SetEndOfFile

VB Declaration   `Declare Function SetEndOfFile& Lib "kernel32" (ByVal hFile As Long)`

Description   Sets the current file position to be the end of file for an open file.

Use with VB   No problem.

Parameter	Type/Description
hFile	Long—A handle to a file. The current location of the file is set to be the end of file. The file is truncated as necessary.

Return Value   Long—Nonzero on success, zero on failure. Sets GetLastError.

Platform   Windows 95, Windows NT

Comments   Do not use this function on a file that is being used as the base for open file mapping objects.

■ SetFileAttributes

VB Declaration   `Declare Function SetFileAttributes& Lib "kernel32" Alias "SetFileAttributesA" _`
    `(ByVal lpFileName As String, ByVal dwFileAttributes As Long)`

Description   Sets the attributes for a file.

Use with VB   No problem.

Parameter	Type/Description
lpFileName	String—The name of the file whose attributes are being set.
dwFileAttributes	Long—One or more of the constants with the FILE_ATTRIBUTE_?? prefix.

Return Value   Long—Nonzero on success, zero on failure. Sets GetLastError.

Platform   Windows 95, Windows NT

■ SetFilePointer

VB Declaration   `Declare Function SetFilePointer& Lib "kernel32" (ByVal hFile As Long, ByVal _`

```
lDistanceToMove As Long, lpDistanceToMoveHigh As Long, ByVal dwMoveMethod As _
Long)
```

Description Sets the current position for reading or writing in a file.

Use with VB This function is similar to the Visual Basic Seek statement. Do not use on files opened using the Visual Basic open command.

Parameter	Type/Description
hFile	Long—A system file handle.
lDistanceTo-Move	Long—The offset in bytes.
lpDistanceTo-MoveHigh	Long—A long variable containing a high double word offset to use. May be zero (change declaration to ByVal) to use only lDistanceToMove.
dwMoveMethod	Long—One of the following constants: FILE_BEGIN: lOffset specifies the new position as an offset from the start of the file. FILE_CURRENT: lOffset specifies the new position as an offset from the current position. FILE_END: lOffset specifies the new position as an offset from the end of the file.

Return Value Long—The new position as an offset in bytes from the start of the file. HFILE_ERROR on error. Sets GetLastError.

Platform Windows 95, Windows NT

Comments This function allows you to work with files up to 2^64 in size.

■ SetFileTime

VB Declaration
```
Declare Function SetFileTime& Lib "kernel32" (ByVal hFile As Long, _
lpCreationTime As FILETIME, lpLastAccessTime As FILETIME, lpLastWriteTime As _
FILETIME)
```

Description Sets the file creation, access, and last modification time.

Use with VB No problem.

Parameter	Type/Description
hFile	Long—A system file handle.
lpCreationTime	FILETIME—A FILETIME structure containing the new creation time of the file.
lpLastAccess-Time	FILETIME—A FILETIME structure containing the new last access time of the file.
lpLastWriteTime	FILETIME—A FILETIME structure containing the new modification time of the file.

Return Value Long—Nonzero on success, zero on failure. Sets GetLastError.

Platform Windows 95, Windows NT

■ SetHandleCount

VB Declaration `Declare Function SetHandleCount& Lib "kernel32" (ByVal wNumber As Long)`

Description This function is not necessary under Win32 and has no effect.

■ SetVolumeLabel

VB Declaration `Declare Function SetVolumeLabel& Lib "kernel32" Alias "SetVolumeLabelA" (ByVal _`
`lpRootPathName As String, ByVal lpVolumeName As String)`

Description Sets the volume label of a disk.

Use with VB No problem.

Parameter	Type/Description
lpRootPathName	String—The root path of the volume.
LpVolumeName	String—The new volume label. vbNullString to delete the current volume name.

Return Value Long—TRUE (nonzero) on success, zero on error. Sets GetLastError.

Platform Windows 95, Windows NT

■ SystemTimeToFileTime

VB Declaration `Declare Function SystemTimeToFileTime& Lib "kernel32" (lpSystemTime As _`
`SYSTEMTIME, lpFileTime As FILETIME)`

Description Loads aSYSTEMTIME structure based on the contents of a FILETIME structure.

Use with VB No problem.

Parameter	Type/Description
lpSystemTime	SYSTEMTIME—Structure containing system time information.
lpFileTime	FILETIME—A FILETIME structure to load with a file time.

Return Value Long—Nonzero on success, zero on failure. Sets GetLastError.

Platform Windows 95, Windows NT

Comments Refer to Chapter 6 for information on system times.

■ UnlockFile

VB Declaration
```
Declare Function UnlockFile& Lib "kernel32" (ByVal hFile As Long, ByVal _
dwFileOffsetLow As Long, ByVal dwFileOffsetHigh As Long, ByVal _
nNumberOfBytesToUnlockLow As Long, ByVal nNumberOfBytesToUnlockHigh As Long)
```

Description   Unlocks a file.

Use with VB   No problem.

Parameter	Type/Description
hFile	Long—A handle of the file to unlock.
dwFileOffsetLow	Long—The low 32 bits of the start location of the region to unlock.
dwFileOffsetHigh	Long—The high 32 bits of the start location of the region to unlock.
nNumberOfBytes-ToLockLow	Long—The low 32 bits of the number of bytes in the locked region.
nNumberOfBytes-ToLockHigh	Long—The high 32 bits of the number of bytes in the locked region.

Return Value   Long—Nonzero on success, zero on failure. Sets GetLastError.

Platform   Windows 95, Windows NT

Comments   The region being unlocked must correspond exactly to a region that was locked earlier. Your application should be sure to unlock any locked regions in the file before it is closed. See the Lock-File command for additional information.

■ UnlockFileEx

VB Declaration
```
Declare Function UnlockFileEx& Lib "kernel32" (ByVal hFile As Long, ByVal _
dwReserved As Long, ByVal nNumberOfBytesToUnlockLow As Long, ByVal _
nNumberOfBytesToUnlockHigh As Long, lpOverlapped As OVERLAPPED)
```

Description   Unlocks a file.

Use with VB   No problem.

Parameter	Type/Description
hFile	Long—A handle of the file to unlock.
dwReserved	Long—Unused; set to zero.
nNumberOf-BytesToLockLow	Long—The low 32 bits of the number of bytes in the locked region.
nNumberOfBytes-ToLockHigh	Long—The high 32 bits of the number of bytes in the locked region.
lpOverlapped	OVERLAPPED—An OVERLAPPED structure containing the offset in the file to the start of the region to unlock.

Return Value	Long—Nonzero on success, zero on failure. Sets GetLastError.
Platform	Windows NT
Comments	The region being unlocked must correspond exactly to a region that was locked earlier. Your application should be sure to unlock any locked regions in the file before it is closed. See the Lock-FileEx command for additional information.

■ UnmapViewOfFile

VB Declaration	`Declare Function UnmapViewOfFile& Lib "kernel32" (ByVal lpBaseAddress As Long)`
Description	Unmaps a file mapping object from the current application's memory address space.
Use with VB	No problem.

Parameter	Type/Description
lpBaseAddress	Long—The base address of the file mapping to unmap that was obtained earlier using the MapViewOfFile function.

Return Value	Long—Nonzero on success, zero on failure. Sets GetLastError.
Example	ckServe.vbp, ckClient.vbp

■ VerFindFile

VB Declaration	`Declare Function VerFindFile& Lib "version.dll" Alias "VerFindFileA" (ByVal _`
	`uFlags As Long, ByVal szFileName As String, ByVal szWinDir As String, ByVal _`
	`szAppDir As String, ByVal szCurDir As String, lpuCurDirLen As Long, ByVal _`
	`szDestDir As String, lpuDestDirLen As Long)`

Description	This function is used to determine where a file should be installed.
Use with VB	Refer to "Version Stamping," earlier in this chapter.

Parameter	Type/Description
uFlags	Long—Currently only VFFF_ISSHAREDFILE is defined to indicate that the file can be shared by multiple applications. If this flag is specified, this function will recommend that the file be installed in the Windows or system directory. If this parameter is zero, the function will recommend that the file be installed in the application directory.
szFileName	String—The name of the file to be installed. This string should not include the path of the file.
szWinDir	String—Set to the windows directory as retrieved using the GetWindowsDirectory function.
szAppDir	String—The full path name of the directory in which the application and all its related files are being installed.

Parameter	Type/Description
szCurDir	String—A buffer to load with the directory containing the existing version of the file. If a version of the file is not already present, the buffer will be loaded with the directory of the source file. Must be allocated to be at least MAX_PATH characters long.
lpuCurDirLen	Long—The length of the szCurrDir buffer. This variable will be set to the actual number of characters loaded to the buffer.
szDestDir	String—A buffer to load with the directory in which the new file should be installed. Must be allocated to be at least MAX_PATH characters long.
lpuDestDirLen	Long—The length of the DestDir buffer. This variable will be set to the actual number of characters loaded to the buffer.

Return Value   Long—One of the following values:

VFF_CURNEDEST: Indicates that the existing version of the file is not in the directory specified by DestDir, which is where this function recommends that the new version be installed.

VFF_FILEINUSE: Indicates that the existing file is currently in use and that it may not be deleted at this time.

VFF_BUFFTOOSMALL: Indicates that one or both of the DestDir or CurrDir buffers are too small to hold the directory name.

Platform   Windows 95, Windows NT, Win16

■ VerInstallFile

VB Declaration
```
Declare Function VerInstallFile& Lib "version.dll" Alias " VerInstallFileA" _
(ByVal uFlags As Long, ByVal szSrcFileName As String, ByVal szDestFileName As _
String, ByVal szSrcDir As String, ByVal szDestDir As String, ByVal szCurDir As _
String, ByVal szTmpFile As String, lpuTmpFileLen As Long)
```

Description   This function is used to install a file. It uses the information provided by the VerFindFile function to determine where a file should be installed. The function works by first comparing the version stamps of the two files. If the source file is a newer and compatible version, the source file is copied to a temporary file in the destination directory, decompressing the file if it is compressed. Then the existing version of the file is deleted and the temporary file is renamed to match the destination file name.

Use with VB   Refer to "Version Stamping," earlier in this chapter.

Parameter	Type/Description
uFlags	Long—A combination of the following constant values: VIFF_FORCEINSTALL: Forces installation of the source file without version checking. VIFF_DONTDELETEOLD: Does not delete the existing version of the file if it is not in the destination directory. If it is in the destination directory, it will be overwritten by the new file.
szSrcFileName	String—The name of the file to install. This should not include the path name for the file.

Parameter	Type/Description
szDestFileName	String—The name that should be given to the file once it is installed. This is usually the same as szSrcFileName.
szSrcDir	String—The source directory from which the new version of the file is copied.
szDestDir	String—The directory in which to install the new version of the file. The DestDir buffer returned by the VerFindFile function is typically used for this parameter.
szCurDir	String—The directory that contains the current version of the file. The CurrDir buffer returned by the VerFindFile function is typically used for this parameter. If the string is empty, no previous version of the file exists on the system.
szTmpFile	String—A buffer to load with the name of a temporary copy of the source file. Must be allocated to be at least MAX_PATH characters long.
lpuTmpFileLen	Long—The length of the TmpFile buffer. This variable will be set to the actual number of characters loaded to the buffer including the terminating NULL character. If VIFF_FORCEINSTALL is specified and TmpFileLen is not zero, the temporary file will be renamed to the name specified in the SrcFile parameter.

Return Value   Long—An integer that contains a combination of one or more of the constants listed in Table 13.19.

Table 13.19   **VerInstallFile Result Constants**

Constant	Description
VIF_TEMPFILE	A temporary file that is a copy of the new file is present in the destination directory and needs to be deleted.
VIF_MISMATCH	The existing file differs from the new file in one or more version attributes. Can be overridden by specifying VIFF_FORCEINSTALL in the uFlags parameter.
VIF_SRCOLD	The new version of the file is older than the existing file based on the version stamping of the files. Can be overridden by specifying VIFF_FORCEINSTALL in the uFlags parameter.
VIF_DIFFLANG	The new version of the file has a different language or code page value from the existing file. Can be overridden by specifying VIFF_FORCEINSTALL in the uFlags parameter.
VIF_DIFFCODEPG	The new version of the file needs a code page that is not present on the version of Windows now running. Can be overridden by specifying VIFF_FORCEINSTALL in the uFlags parameter.
VIF_DIFFTYPE	The new version of the file differs in type, subtype, or target operating system from the existing version. Can be overridden by specifying VIFF_FORCEINSTALL in the uFlags parameter.

Table 13.19   VerInstallFile Result Constants (Continued)

Constant	Description
VIF_WRITEPROT	The preexisting file is write-protected.
VIF_FILEINUSE	The existing file is in use.
VIF_OUTOFSPACE	There is insufficient disk space on the destination drive.
VIF_ACCESSVIOLATION	Operation failed due to an access violation.
VIF_SHARINGVIOLATION	Operation failed due to a sharing violation.
VIF_CANNOTCREATE	The temporary file could not be created.
VIF_CANNOTDELETE	The existing version of the file could not be deleted.
VIF_CANNOTDELETECUR	The existing version of the file could not be deleted and VIFF_DONTDELETEOLD was not specified in the uFlags parameter.
VIF_CANNOTRENAME	The temporary file could not be renamed to the name of the existing file. The existing file has already been deleted.
VIF_OUTOFMEMORY	Operation failed due to lack of memory.
VIF_CANNOTREADSRC	The source file could not be read.
VIF_CANNOTREADDEST	The existing destination file cannot be read (thus version information can not be checked).
VIF_BUFFTOOSMALL	The TmpFileLen parameter is too small to hold the name of the temporary file.

Platform   Windows 95, Windows NT, Win16

■ VerLanguageName

VB Declaration
```
Declare Function VerLanguageName& Lib "version.dll" Alias "VerLanguageNameA" _
(ByVal wLang As Long, ByVal szLang As String, ByVal nSize As Long)
```

Description   This function retrieves the name of a language based on the 16-bit language code. Language codes are used in the version resource for a file to determine the language for which the file was written. Table 13.20 lists the language codes supported by Win32.

Use with VB   Refer to "Version Stamping," earlier in this chapter.

Parameter	Type/Description
wLang	Long—The language ID.

Parameter	Type/Description
szLang	String—A buffer to load with the text name of the specified language. This buffer should be preallocated to at least cbLang+1 bytes.
nSize	Long—The length of the szLang buffer.

Return Value   Long—The number of characters loaded into the lpszLang buffer. If the buffer is not large enough to hold the name, the function returns the required buffer size. Zero on error.

Table 13.20   **Language Codes Supported by Win32**

Language Value	Language
&H400	The default language for the process
&H401	Arabic
&H402	Bulgarian
&H403	Catalan
&H404	Traditional Chinese
&H405	Czech
&H406	Danish
&H407	German
&H408	Greek
&H409	U.S. English
&H40A	Castilian Spanish
&H40B	Finnish
&H40C	French
&H40D	Hebrew
&H40E	Hungarian
&H40F	Icelandic
&H410	Italian
&H411	Japanese
&H412	Korean
&H413	Dutch

Table 13.20   **Language Codes Supported by Win32 (Continued)**

Language Value	Language
&H414	Norwegian—Bokmål
&H415	Polish
&H416	Brazilian Portugese
&H417	Rhaeto-Romanic
&H418	Romanian
&H419	Russian
&H41A	Croato-Serbian (Latin)
&H41B	Slóvak
&H41C	Albanian
&H41D	Swedish
&H41E	Thai
&H41F	Turkish
&H420	Urdu
&H421	Bahasa
&H804	Simplified Chinese
&H807	Swiss German
&H809	U.K. English
&H80A	Mexican Spanish
&H80C	Belgian French
&H810	Swiss Italian
&H813	Belgian Dutch
&H814	Norwegian—Nynorsk
&H816	Portugese
&H81A	Serbo-Croatian (Cyrillic)
&HC0C	Canadian French
&H100C	Swiss French

Platform   Windows 95, Windows NT, Win16

■ VerQueryValue

VB Declaration

```
Declare Function VerQueryValue& Lib "version.dll" Alias "VerQueryValueA" _
(pBlock As Byte, ByVal lpSubBlock As String, lplpBuffer As Long, puLen As Long)
```

Description   This function is used to retrieve information from the version resource. Before calling this function, the version resource information must be retrieved using the GetFileVersionInfo function. This function examines the resource information and copies the requested data into a buffer.

Use with VB   Refer to "Version Stamping," earlier in this chapter.

Parameter	Type/Description
pBlock	Byte—The address of the first byte in a block of memory containing version information data as retrieved by the GetFileVersionInfo function.
lpSubBlock	String—One of the following: "\": To retrieve the VS_FIXEDFILEINFO structure for this file. "\VarFileInfo\Translation": To retrieve the translation table for this file. "\StringFileInfo\....": To retrieve string information for a file. Refer to the Comments section for a full description.
lplpBuffer	Long—The address of the long variable to load with the address of a buffer to load with the requested version information.
puLen	Long—The length, in bytes, of value data referenced by the lplpBuffer parameter.

Return Value   Long—TRUE (nonzero) on success, zero if the requested information does not exist or pBlock is not valid version information.

Platform   Windows 95, Windows NT, Win16

Comments   When the lpSubBlock parameter is "\VarFileInfo\Translation", the buffer will be loaded with an integer array. Each pair of integers represents a language and code page pair describing available string information. The StringFileInfo string data is retrieved by specifying a string with three parts as follows:

```
"\StringFileInfo\languagecodepage\stringname"
```

languagecodepage is an eight-character hex number in string form. If the language code page entry in the translation table is &H04090000, then this string should be "04090000". *stringname* is a string name from those listed in Table 13.14 in "Version Stamping," earlier in this chapter. An example of this parameter would be:

```
"\StringFileInfo\04090000\CompanyName"
```

Example   FileDemo.vbp

■ WriteFile

VB Declaration   `Declare Function WriteFile& Lib "kernel32" (ByVal hFile As Long, lpBuffer As _`

```
Any, ByVal nNumberOfBytesToWrite As Long, lpNumberOfBytesWritten As Long, _
lpOverlapped As OVERLAPPED)
```

Description   Writes data to a file. This function is more flexible than the lwrite function. This function works on communication devices, pipes, sockets, and mailslots as well.

Use with VB   No problem.

Parameter	Type/Description
hFile	Long—A handle to a file.
lpBuffer	Any—A buffer of data to write.
nNumberOf-BytesToWrite	Long—Number of bytes of data to write. Writing zero bytes causes nothing to be written but the file modified time is updated. Limited to 65,535 bytes for named pipes on remote systems.
lpNumberOf-BytesWritten	Long—The number of bytes actually written to the file.
lpOverlapped	OVERLAPPED—If the file was opened with FILE_FLAG_OVERLAPPED specified, this parameter must reference a structure defining an asynchronous write operation. Otherwise, this parameter should be NULL (change the declaration to ByVal lpOverlapped As Long and pass zero).

Return Value   Long—Nonzero on success, zero on failure. Sets GetLastError.

Platform   Windows 95, Windows NT

Comments   Not every operating system supports asynchronous operations for every type of device. For example, Windows 95 does not support an overlapped read on a disk file.

■ WriteFileEx

VB Declaration
```
Declare Function WriteFileEx& Lib "kernel32" (ByVal hFile As Long, lpBuffer As _
Any, ByVal nNumberOfBytesToWrite As Long, lpOverlapped As OVERLAPPED, ByVal _
lpCompletionRoutine As Long)
```

Description   Similar to WriteFile, except that it is intended to be used only for asynchronous write operations and includes a completion callback.

Use with VB   No problem.

Parameter	Type/Description
hFile	Long—A handle to a file.
lpBuffer	Any—A buffer for the data being read. Do not access this buffer until the write operation is complete.
nNumberOf-BytesToWrite	Long—Number of bytes of data to write.
lpOverlapped	OVERLAPPED—A structure defining an asynchronous write operation. The hEvent field in the structure is ignored when this function is used.

Parameter	Type/Description
lpCompletion-Routine	Long—The value returned by the ProcAddress property of the dwcbk32d.ocx control.

Return Value   Long—Nonzero on success, zero on failure. Sets GetLastError.

Platform   Windows 95, Windows NT

Comments   Use the cbxLLL callback type of dwcbk32d.ocx. The cbxLLL event will be called with the following parameters once the current thread is open to being signaled:

lval1—Zero on success, an error code on error.

lval2—The number of bytes actually transferred.

lval3—The address of the OVERLAPPED structure from the original call to WriteFileEx. Use agCopyData to copy memory from this address to a locally declared OVERLAPPED structure.

Not every operating system supports asynchronous operations for every type of device. For example, Windows 95 does not support an overlapped read on a disk file.

■ WritePrivateProfileSection

VB Declaration
```
Declare Function WritePrivateProfileSection& Lib "kernel32" Alias _
"WritePrivateProfileSectionA" (ByVal lpAppName As String, ByVal lpString As _
String, ByVal lpFileName As String)
```

Description   Sets all of the key names and values for a specified section in a private initialization file.

Use with VB   No problem.

Parameter	Type/Description
lpAppName	String—The section to set. This string is not case-sensitive.
lpString	String—A list of key and value strings. Each string is separated by a NULL, with a double NULL after the final string. If the section specified by lpAppName does not exist, a new section with that name is appended to the file. If it exists, all current key names and values are replaced by those specified in this buffer.
lpFileName	String—The name of the private initialization file. If a full path is specified and the file does not exist, an error will occur. If a file name only is specified and the file does not exist, it will be created in the current windows directory.

Return Value   Long—Nonzero on success, zero on failure. Sets GetLastError.

Platform   Windows 95, Windows NT

■ WritePrivateProfileString

VB Declaration
```
Declare Function WritePrivateProfileString& Lib "kernel32" Alias _
"WritePrivateProfileStringA" (ByVal lpApplicationName As String, ByVal _
lpKeyName As Any, ByVal lpString As String, ByVal lpFileName As String)
```

Description	Sets a string in the specified section of a private initialization file.
Use with VB	No problem.

Parameter	Type/Description
lpApplication-Name	String—The section in which to write the new string. This string is not case-sensitive.
lpKeyName	String—The key name or entry to set. This string is not case-sensitive. Use vbNullString to delete all of the keys for this section.
lpString	String—The value to write for this key. Use vbNullString to delete the existing string for this key.
lpFilename	String—The name of the private initialization file. If a full path name is not specified, Windows will search for the file in the Windows directory. If the file is not found, this function will create the file.

Return Value	Long—Nonzero on success, zero on failure. Sets GetLastError.
Platform	Windows 95, Windows NT, Win16
Example	vb4ini.vbp in Chapter 4.

■ WriteProfileSection

VB Declaration	`Declare Function WriteProfileSection& Lib "kernel32" Alias _` `"WriteProfileSectionA" (ByVal lpAppName As String, ByVal lpString As String)`
Description	Sets all of the key names and values for a specified section in the WIN.INI initialization file.
Use with VB	No problem. Keep in mind that changes to the WIN.INI file may affect other applications. If you are modifying a section that is used by other programs, be sure to send the WM_WININICHANGE message to all windows as described in "Initialization Files," earlier in this chapter.

Parameter	Type/Description
lpAppName	String—The section to set. This string is not case-sensitive.
lpString	String—A list of key and value strings. Each string is separated by a NULL, with a double NULL after the final string. If the section specified by lpAppName does not exist, a new section with that name is appended to the file. If it exists, all current key names and values are replaced by those specified in this buffer.

Return Value	Long—Nonzero on success, zero on failure. Sets GetLastError.
Platform	Windows 95, Windows NT

■ WriteProfileString

VB Declaration   ```
Declare Function WriteProfileString& Lib "kernel32" Alias "WriteProfileStringA" _
(ByVal lpszSection As String, ByVal lpszKeyName As String, ByVal lpszString As _
String)
```

**Description**    Sets a string in the specified section of the WIN.INI initialization file.

**Use with VB**    No problem. Keep in mind that changes to the WIN.INI file may affect other applications. If you are modifying a section that is used by other programs, be sure to send the WM_WININICHANGE message to all windows as described in "Initialization Files," earlier in this chapter.

| Parameter | Type/Description |
|-----------|------------------|
| lpszSection | String—The section in which to write the new string. The section will be created if it does not yet exist. This string is not case-sensitive. |
| lpszKeyName | String—The key name or entry to set. This string is not case-sensitive. Use vbNullString to delete all of the keys for this section. |
| lpszString | String—The value to write for this key. Use vbNullString to delete the existing string for this key. |

**Return Value**    Long—Nonzero on success, zero on failure. Sets GetLastError.

**Platform**    Windows 95, Windows NT, Win16

**Example**    vb4ini.vbp in Chapter 4 uses WritePrivateProfileString which is similar to this function.
```

14

Processes and Threads

Processes, Threads, and Instances

System and Synchronization Objects

Launching Applications

Interprocess Communication

Examples

Function Reference

WHEN YOU CONSIDER THE CHANGES FROM 16-BIT WINDOWS TO 32-BIT Windows several things come to mind: the change of handles and most function parameters from 16 to 32 bits, the large number of new functions, and increased overall capability. But as great as these changes are, they pale in significance to the differences in the way Win32 handles processes and memory, the subjects of the next two chapters. Here the changes are neither minor nor cosmetic—they reflect fundamental shifts in the underlying system architecture, and these are reflected in the API functions. Some Win16 functions are missing, and a great many new functions have been added.

This chapter starts with a discussion of these architectural changes and why they have occurred. It then moves into an in-depth discussion of system objects, with an emphasis on those objects that can be used to synchronize different applications. The task of launching processes and determining when they terminate is covered, along with mechanisms by which processes can communicate with each other. Finally, a number of examples are presented that demonstrate the principles and techniques covered in the chapter.

Processes, Threads, and Instances

Chapter 13 focused on various ways of working with files using the Win32 API. And while most of the functions did discuss files, you may have noticed an occasional hint or mention of other objects such as pipes, mailslots, and communication devices. Even the ckServe/ckClient example, while focusing on file mappings, touched lightly on the subject of processes and the interprocess communication and synchronization problems that can occur when more than one client or server is running.

Pipes? Mailslots? Processes? Synchronization? These are all terms that will be new to many Win32 programmers, and terms that are foreign to the world of Visual Basic. Yet these terms describe concepts and features in Win32 that are incredibly powerful and potentially very useful to VB programmers.

So this chapter begins with a discussion of some of the fundamental concepts that you will need to understand in order to take full advantage of the API functions that will be described later in the chapter. It continues with a review of the functions that apply to each of the concepts, and, as always, a set of demonstration programs.

On Multitasking

Multitasking is actually a very simple concept. It defines the ability of an operating system to run more than one program at the same time.

But what do we mean when we say an operating system can run more than one program at once? After all, it only has one central processing unit

(CPU). We will conveniently ignore, for the sake of this discussion, multiprocessor systems, as they have not yet become common on the desktop. How can one CPU run more than one application at a time? The answer is, of course, that it can't.

What you perceive as multitasking is actually the ability of the system to switch quickly between applications. In fact, the ideal multitasking system can switch between applications so quickly that as far as the user can tell, all of the programs appear to be running at the same time.

Consider the following simple program. Create a new VB project and place a button and label control on the form. Then add the following code to the button click event:

```
Private Sub Command1_Click()
    Dim cnt&
    For cnt& = 1 To 25``
        Label1.Caption = cnt&
        Label1.Refresh
    Next cnt&
End Sub
```

When you click on the button, the counter will display an incrementing count from 1 to 2,500 in the label control. Compile the program to an executable and run two instances of the program and rearrange them so that they are side by side. Now click on the command button of one application. While it is counting, try clicking on the command button of the other application. Try clicking on the forms to activate the two applications while they are counting.

The results of this test will depend on what operating system you are running and whether you are running 16-bit or 32-bit Visual Basic. The results also illustrate the key differences between operating systems when it comes to multitasking.

Windows 3.x supports a type of multitasking called "nonpreemptive" or "cooperative" multitasking. In this type of multitasking, applications are expected to cooperate with one another. The operating system assigns the CPU to one application and that application has full use of the CPU until it is ready to let other applications run. The tight loop shown in this sample effectively ties up the system, preventing other applications from running. Other applications are frozen until the program relinquishes the processor either by exiting the Command1_Click event, or by explicitly releasing the CPU by using a DoEvents command. You will see this clearly with the counter example if you used Windows 3.x or 16-bit Visual Basic on Windows 95 or Windows NT (as long as the two counter examples were not set to run in separate memory spaces). When one counter is counting, the other is frozen. It does not count and you cannot click on its command button.

Programming on a nonpreemptive multitasking system requires a certain amount of self-discipline on the part of programmers, who must be very careful not to tie up the system for long periods of time. There are some cases, however, where even the system or system utilities tie up the CPU. For example, try doing anything else on Windows 3.x while formatting a floppy disk.

If it sounds like this type of multitasking has severe limitations, you're right. But it is still true multitasking. You are running more than one application at once and, assuming the applications are well-designed, you can effectively have operations taking place in the background while you work.

If you try running the counter example on Windows NT or Windows 95 using 16-bit Visual Basic, and tried clicking on a 32-bit application such as the Start menu or Program Manager, you may have noticed that those applications were not frozen. And if you used 32-bit Visual Basic to create the sample, you would have found radically different behavior. When you click on the second counter while the first one is counting, the second counter starts going at full speed and the first one slows down (but does not stop completely, depending on how much priority your system gives to foreground applications). In fact, you can keep activating the different counters and see how the one that is active counts faster—but note that the inactive one is never frozen as it was in the 16-bit example. You can always activate it.

Since the sample program remains unchanged, and does not release the CPU by either exiting the click event or executing a DoEvents command, clearly some other mechanism for having an application release the CPU must exist. Well, actually it's not so much a matter of the application releasing the CPU as it is the operating system grabbing it away. This is a form of multitasking called "preemptive" multitasking, in which CPU time is allocated exclusively by the operating system. When the operating system has decided that an application has had its scheduled time allotment, it suspends the program, saves the state of all of the processor's internal registers, and turns it over to the next application. Applications also have the ability to suspend themselves whenever they don't need CPU time. From a programmer's perspective, while it is still worthwhile to keep the application from performing long continuous operations, the impact of such operations is entirely on the application, not on the entire system. This means that the need to avoid long operations is not as critical and the DoEvents command is needed even less frequently than it was under Visual Basic 3.0.

Tasks, Processes, and Synchronization

Under 16-bit Windows, each running application is called a task. It has a unique task identifier that the operating system uses to keep track of the application in terms of allocating memory and resources to it and deciding which application should be the next to receive CPU time when the current application is kind enough to allow other programs to run.

Under 32-bit Windows, each running application is called a process (task = process).

Now consider some of the implications of the way processes are handled under Win16 versus Win32. Under Win16 the operating system lets a task run, then waits for the task to release the CPU. The system then lets another task run, and so on. Under Win32, the operating system grants time to the different processes, generally giving priority to the one that is in the foreground, under the assumption that it is the process that the user is working with at the moment. The actual priority of different processes can be controlled through both system utilities and using the Win32 API. The system allocates CPU time as it wills, shifting processor time between the processes with little regard to what the application might be doing at any given time.

Now, if you are experienced with Win16 API programming, you know that there are many objects and resources that are shared between applications. Memory is shared (more rather than less). Drawing objects such as pens and brushes are shared. Programs can call API functions that often share memory within the operating system. For example, all applications use the same resource heaps. All of this sharing can lead to problems if an application accidentally trashes some system object or memory address that other applications need, but as long as all of the programs in the system are working correctly, this won't occur. You see, if an application calls an API function, that function is absolutely guaranteed to return without another application having a chance to run. This is because an application holds on to the CPU until it explicitly releases it (the one exception being API calls that explicitly allow other applications to run). Why is this important? Consider the simple task of adding 1 to an integer that is potentially shared between applications.

```
X = X+1
```

In Visual Basic, this looks like one operation, but conceptually it can be broken up into the following low-level operations:

```
Read the value of X into a CPU register.
Add 1 to the register holding X.
Store the register value back into variable X.
```

Now imagine what could happen if two programs need to increment the value of X and they try to do it at the same time.

Process #1   **Process #2**

Read value of X into a CPU register

Add 1 to the register holding X

Operating system switches to
process 2

Process #1	**Process #2**
	Read value of X into a CPU register
	Add 1 to the register holding X
	Operating system switches to process 1
Store the register value back into variable X	
Operating system switches to process 2	
	Store the register value back into variable X

If you walk through the example you will see that X only gets incremented once.

This might not be a fatal problem in Visual Basic, but imagine that this particular variable represents the usage count of a file or segment in memory that is shared by the two applications. If the object is referenced twice, but the usage count was only incremented once, then, as soon as one process terminates, the object will be freed—even though it is needed by the second process. The result: a system error, memory exception, or worse.

This type of problem is called a "synchronization" problem, and it can't happen on 16-bit Windows because the operating system can't switch between processes unless the process allows it.

But what about Win32? It's a problem. A very big problem.

There are two fundamental approaches for solving synchronization problems. The first is to come up with a special type of object that can arbitrate between processes. Imagine what would happen in our simple example if there was an object that could be "owned" by only one process at a time. You could call this the "increment" object and only the object that owned it could increment variable X. The first process would ask the system for the "increment" object and take ownership of the object. It could now start incrementing X. Meanwhile, process 2 asks the system for the "increment" object. Since it is in use, the operating system suspends process 2 until the object becomes available. Once the first process releases the object, the operating system sees that process 2 is waiting for it, suspends process 1 and activates process 2, which can now safely increment the variable. Win32 supports a number of types of synchronization objects, a subject that will be covered later in this chapter.

The second approach for solving these types of problems is, in a way, more important. In this approach the system avoids sharing objects wherever possible.

After all, synchronization is only a problem with a shared object or resource. If you don't share, the problem goes away. This approach is fundamental to Win32, especially as implemented by Windows NT. Under Win32, GDI objects such as pens and brushes are no longer shared. Each application has its own memory space that is completely protected from other applications (partially protected under Windows 95). Some objects can be shared, but in most cases you must explicitly share them, minimizing the chance that one application can accidentally modify an object used by another application.

But what about API functions? After all, in a preemptive operating system a process can be interrupted while executing a low level system function as well as application code. Windows NT and Windows 95 took different approaches in this regard. Windows NT was written from scratch to be reentrant; the operating system code is written to handle preemptive multitasking from the ground up. Windows 95 uses a synchronization object to protect parts of the system code so that only one application can use it at a time. In other words, while Windows 95 may not protect your code from being interrupted by another process, it does ensure that many API functions will not be interrupted (or if interrupted, cannot be entered again by another application). This is one of the reasons that multitasking under Windows 95 is not quite as smooth as it is under Windows NT. But don't rush to accuse the Windows 95 developers of laziness—the choice to use a synchronization object instead of rewriting large portions of the operating system was necessary to maximize the number of old 16-bit applications that could run successfully on Windows 95.

Threads

You've now seen how preemptive multitasking differs from cooperative multitasking, and how this raises new problems of synchronization. But it also presents interesting new opportunities. So far we have discussed how part of the nature of a preemptive multitasking system is that the operating system decides which task receives CPU time. Now here's a thought: As long as the operating system is allocating CPU time anyway, wouldn't it be interesting if you could set up your application so that it can do two things at once? For example, you could create a communications program that would have a nice user interface operating at the same time as it handles a complex communications protocol to transfer a file. Instead of writing your program to somehow manage both tasks, you could simply tell the operating system that there was a function that you want to run at the same time as the main program. The operating system would then start a separate execution path beginning with that function and it would allocate time between the two execution paths in the application in exactly the same way as it allocates time between processes. Each of these separate execution paths is called a "thread of execution" or simply a "thread." Each application has at least one thread, but an application can create as many threads at it needs (or as the operating system can provide).

Sounds great, doesn't it? But there is one important thing you should know about threads: When you create a new thread in a program, that thread has full access to all of the memory, variables, and resources of the main program. All of them. Now backtrack a few paragraphs and you'll see the problem. As you may recall, sharing objects, memory, and resources is, if not the root of all evil, then surely the root of all synchronization problems.

There's more bad news: Visual Basic does not allow you to create multithreaded applications. Of course, whether this is actually bad news is a matter of opinion. Take another look at the problem that we used earlier to illustrate synchronization problems. Now imagine, if you will, how you would go about debugging this type of problem. If you have been using Visual Basic for a while, you may recall the difficult transition that many programmers had to go through to understand how to write event-driven software. I assure you that learning to write reliable multithreaded applications is considerably worse. Visual Basic 5.0 does, however, allow you to create multithreaded components. An ActiveX EXE component can expose objects that run in independent threads. An ActiveX DLL component can allow objects that it creates to run in independent threads under multithreaded applications. In these cases, VB uses a model of multithreading called the "apartment model" in which synchronization problems are avoided by giving each thread its own copy of the component's global variables and eliminating global resources (such as forms) entirely. This subject is covered in depth in my book "Developing ActiveX Components for Visual Basic 5.0: A Guide to the Perplexed." Later in this chapter you will also see that it is possible to achieve many of the effects of multithreading using Visual Basic by creating an out-of-process ActiveX server and using ActiveX automation to work with it. Since it is a separate process, it naturally runs in a separate thread.

What about Instances?

Under Win16 it was not uncommon to refer to applications by their instance handle. The instance handle could be used to distinguish between applications and between multiple instances of the same application. (Thus, if you ran three copies of NotePad, each would have its own instance handle.) You could determine how many instances of an application were open using the GetModuleUsage function and monitor the value returned by this function to determine when an application closed.

You cannot use instance handles this way under Win32.

To understand why, you need to know what an instance handle actually is. Under Win16, an instance handle is the segment selector of the default data segment for the task. A module handle is also a segment selector to a code or data segment, thus an instance handle is just a specialized form of a module handle (that is why GetModuleUsage and other module functions accept instance handles as parameters). Every task has at least one data segment by default—this is the segment out of which the application allocates local memory. It was not unreasonable to use the instance handle to identify tasks, because no two applications would share data segments.

But what does the term "selector to a data segment" actually mean? Ultimately it is a memory address. As long as all of the applications in the system share the same address space, every instance handle is sure to be unique, but under Win32 memory is not shared. Each application has its own address space. The instance handle of an application is the base address at which the application loaded. As such, instance handles of different processes can easily be identical (and often are). This means that under Win32 you cannot identify a process by its instance handle. You must use a process identifier. How is this done? This subject will be covered later in this chapter.

System and Synchronization Objects

Windows uses a great many types of objects, as you have already seen. In earlier chapters you read about graphic objects (graphical device interface, or GDI, objects) that are private to each application. Windows also supports a number of system objects that come into play when working with processes and threads. You have already learned about file objects and file mapping objects. Unlike GDI objects, system objects are potentially shareable. This is not to say that you can somehow send a handle to an object from one process to another and always have it work—this is rarely the case. But you can often create a second handle in another application that refers to the same object, thus allowing two processes to access the same object. In other words: Objects are often shareable, but handles usually are not. The degree to which a system object can be shared depends upon the type of object, whether the object is inheritable, the operating system, and the type of security in effect.

Table 14.1 illustrates this with some examples.

Table 14.1 **Examples of Object Usage**

Object Type	Object Ownership	Object Usage
Pen Brush	Win32: Process Win16: System	Win32: Cannot be shared. Win16: Fully shareable. Each object has one handle which is valid in all applications.
Window	System	Shareable. Each object has one handle which is valid in all applications.

Table 14.1   **Examples of Object Usage (Continued)**

Object Type	Object Ownership	Object Usage
Process	System	Win32: Shareable if security allows. Each process must obtain its own handle to the process.Win16: Shareable. Each object has one handle which is valid in all applications.
Memory	Win32: Process Win16: System	Win32: Cannot be shared—memory addresses are separate. Win16: Shareable. Global handles and memory addresses are valid in all applications.

Most Win32 system objects, including files, file mappings, and synchronization objects, work like processes. The objects are owned by the system and each application must obtain its own handle to the shared object. The system keeps track of how many open handles exist for an object and deletes the object automatically when the last handle to the object is closed. When a process terminates normally, all of the system object handles that it opened are automatically closed.

Working with System Objects

Objects are created using the creation function for the object in question. Examples of these include CreateProcess, CreateFile, CreateMapping, CreateNamedPipe, and so on. These functions create a new object or open an existing object (depending on the function, parameters, and object type) and return a handle to that object.

The object handle is usually valid only within the context of the process that created it. One exception to this is when an object is transferred to a child process using inheritance. To do this the object must be defined as inheritable when it is created and the handle must be passed to the child process. This is typically done using one of the standard input or output handles, or by passing it as a parameter to the new process.

It is often possible for another application to create or obtain a new handle to the same object. There are a number of ways to accomplish this. The DuplicateHandle function takes an object handle and creates a new handle in a different process that refers to the same object. In some cases an object-specific function exists. For example, the OpenProcess function obtains a new handle for a process given its unique process identifier. This will be discussed further in the "Launching Applications" section that follows later in this chapter.

Object Security

All system objects have an associated security descriptor that describes how they may be accessed by other processes. This is set using the SECURITY_ATTRIBUTES structure in the creation process. System security is not described in detail in this book for two reasons: First, most of its features only work under Windows NT; and second, it is rarely used. Refer to your Microsoft Win32 SDK online help for additional information on security (Chapters 3, 4, and 15 will help you translate the information for use with Visual Basic) if you need this capability.

There are, however, two things that you do need to know about security when working with objects. The first is how to handle the parameter in each function that sets the security. In most cases, the easiest approach is to change the function declaration so that you can pass a null as the parameter. This is done, of course, by changing the declaration from "lpSecurity as SECURITY_ATTRIBUTES" to "ByVal lpSecurity As Long" and passing a zero to the function.

The second thing you need to know relates to inheritance. If you wish any child processes to inherit handles from your main process (meaning that you can pass the handle value to them and have it work correctly without them needing to use the DuplicateHandle function to create their own copy), you must pass the SECURITY_ATTRIBUTES structure to the function. In the structure, you must set the nLength field to the length of the structure (use the Len function to obtain the size of the structure), set the lpSecurityDescriptor field to zero, and set the bInheritHandle field to TRUE. This is necessary because the default security descriptor assigned to an object when you pass a null parameter instead of a SECURITY_ATTRIBUTES structure has inheritance disabled. Most of the declarations for object function in this book leave the security parameter as a structure in order to prevent confusion on the part of the casual user, so you will need to change it yourself to pass null values.

Object Access

Each system object has certain capabilities associated with it. For example, you can read to a file mapping object or write to it. This does not mean that you can perform both of these tasks using any handle to that object. Each handle has specific access rights to the object that determine what operations it can perform on the object. In other words: Access security is associated with the handle to the object, not the object itself. You can use the DuplicateHandle function to create a new handle to an object that has different access rights from the original. Refer to the description of this function for additional information.

Object Signals

Most system objects can exist in two states: signaled and nonsignaled. You can think of this as a toggle switch that each object holds. The switch can be toggled manually and is sometimes toggled when a particular event occurs. For example, a process object is signaled when the process terminates. Why is signaling important? Because Win32 provides functions that allow you to not only test the signaled state of an object, but to suspend an application until an object becomes signaled. Thus it is actually very simple for one process to determine when another process terminates—it only needs to obtain a handle to the other process and watch for that object to become signaled.

Refer back for a moment to the incrementing problem discussed earlier in this chapter, where we needed to create a hypothetical "increment" object in order to prevent two threads from interfering with each other. One of the characteristics of this hypothetical object was that it could be owned by only one application at a time. When an application requested ownership of this object while it was in use by another, the system would suspend the application until the object was available.

Now let's change this description slightly to use the actual Win32 terms. This "increment" object is actually a system object that can be owned by only one process at a time. While the object is owned, its state is nonsignaled, so any application requesting the object will be suspended. As soon as it is released by the application that is using it, this object will become signaled. The operating system will then wake up one of the processes that is waiting for the object, and set the object back to nonsignaled (so that only one waiting process will be activated—any other processes waiting for the same object will remain suspended).

This type of synchronization object exists and is called a "Mutex."

Mutexes, Semaphores, Events, and Waitable Timers

Synchronization objects allow two or more processes to define and enter a known state in their relationship to each other. This is a fancy way of saying that processes can use synchronization objects to signal each other when particular events occur, or to restrict access to some shared resource or object by requiring that each process gain access to a synchronization object before working with that shared resource or object.

Win32 supports three types of synchronization objects, though other objects can also be signaled and used for synchronization. Table 14.2 lists those synchronization functions that are common to most system objects.

Table 14.2	General Synchronization Functions

Function	Description
DuplicateHandle	Creates a new handle to a system object. You can specify the process for which the new handle will be valid.

Table 14.2   **General Synchronization Functions**

Function	Description
GetHandleInformation	Obtains information about a handle to a system object.
MsgWaitForMultipleObjects	Suspends a thread until either one or more of a group of objects are signaled, or a specified type of message arrives in the thread's input queue.
WaitForInputIdle	Suspends a thread until another process has become idle (defined as the process being ready to process input messages, but no messages are available). This function is often used for one process to wait until another process has completed its initialization.
SetHandleInformation	Changes some system object settings.
WaitForMultipleObjects WaitForMultipleObjectsEx	Suspends a thread until either one or more of a group of objects are signaled.
WaitForSingleObject WaitForSingleObjectEx	Suspends a thread until an object has been signaled.

Mutexes

A mutex is very much like the hypothetical "increment" object that was discussed earlier in this chapter. A mutex can be owned by one process at a time. While a mutex is owned, it is not signaled and thus can be waited on by other processes. When the mutex is released it becomes signaled and a waiting process can become active. When a process waits on a mutex that it already owns, the wait function returns immediately—however, a process must be careful to release the mutex the same number of times that it claims ownership of that mutex using one of the wait functions.

A process can obtain a handle to an existing mutex in three ways: It can have a handle duplicated from an existing one, it can inherit a mutex handle from a parent process, or it can open a mutex based on its name. Every process should be careful to release ownership of any mutexes that it owns before it terminates. If a process terminates while owning a mutex, that mutex becomes abandoned. This also signals the mutex, so other processes will become active—but because the mutex was abandoned they cannot be certain that the shared resource whose access is being synchronized by the mutex is in a defined state.

Mutexes, semaphores, events, and file mappings all use the same internal name table, thus you cannot have two objects of different types that have the same name. Names of these objects are case-sensitive.

Table 14.3 lists the functions used to work with mutexes.

Table 14.3	**Mutex Functions**

Function	Description
CreateMutex	Creates a mutex. If a mutex of the given name already exists, it is opened.
OpenMutex	Opens an existing mutex.
ReleaseMutex	Releases a mutex that is owned by the current process.

Semaphores

A semaphore is a special kind of shared counter that is signaled as long as its value is above zero. A semaphore has a maximum value that is set by the creator of the semaphore. When a process waits on a semaphore, the wait function returns immediately if the semaphore value is greater than zero (signaled) and the semaphore count is decremented by 1. When a process releases a semaphore, the count is incremented by 1 up to the maximum value of the semaphore. Semaphores are typically set to their maximum count on creation, though sometimes a process will create one with a count of zero, complete its initialization, then increment the count to maximum once it is ready for other applications to access the semaphore.

One caution to keep in mind: Windows does not keep track of which processes access a semaphore, thus any process can release a semaphore even if it never waited on it. This makes it especially important to be careful to release only a semaphore that your application has accessed using a wait function.

Processes obtain semaphore handles in the same way that they obtain mutex handles: by duplication, inheritance, or by opening one by name. Table 14.4 lists the functions used to work with semaphores.

Table 14.4	**Semaphore Functions**

Function	Description
CreateSemaphore	Creates a semaphore. If a semaphore of the given name already exists, it is opened.
OpenSemaphore	Opens an existing semaphore.
ReleaseSemaphore	Releases a semaphore by incrementing its count.

Events

An event object's signaled state can be set explicitly by an application. The ResetEvent function sets its state to nonsignaled and the SetEvent function sets it to signaled. These objects are typically used to indicate the occurrence of an event in an application or in the system. It should go without saying that the use of the term "events" in the context of the Event system object has absolutely nothing to do with Visual Basic events.

Events come in two flavors: manual- and auto-reset. Manual-reset events change their signal event only under program control (either by the application or a system background operation). When a manual-reset event is signaled, all threads that are waiting on that event are activated and the event remains signaled until reset by an application. When an auto-reset event is signaled, a single waiting thread is activated and the event is reset to nonsignaled (the operating system can choose any waiting thread). Any other waiting threads remain suspended.

Processes obtain event handles in the same way that they obtain mutex handles: by duplication, inheritance, or by opening one by name. Table 14.5 lists the functions used to work with events.

Table 14.5   **Event Functions**

Function	Description
CreateEvent	Creates an event object. If an event of the given name already exists, it is opened.
OpenEvent	Opens an existing event.
PulseEvent	Sets then resets the signaled state of an event.
ResetEvent	Resets an event state to nonsignaled.
SetEvent	Sets an event state to signaled.

Waitable Timers

A waitable timer is a new type of synchronization object that is supported under Windows NT 4.0 and later. This type of timer is different from the kind of system timer that the VB timer control supports. It is a full-fledged synchronization object that can be used to establish a time delay for one or more applications simultaneously.

A waitable timer can operate in three modes. In "manual reset" mode, the timer is signaled when the specified delay elapses and remains signaled until a new delay is specified using the SetWaitableTimer function. In "automatic reset" mode, the timer is signaled when the delay elapses, and remains signaled until the first successful wait function is called for the object. This is similar to the Event object's auto-reset mode, in which only a single thread will be allowed to execute each time the timer elapses. Finally, a waitable timer can be configured as a periodic timer that restarts the timer with a specified interval each time the object is triggered.

The main feature that distinguishes waitable timers from other system timers is the fact that they can be shared among applications. For example: you could have a set of applications suspended in the background that you "wake up" every few hours to perform an operation. This is demonstrated in the sleeper.vbp project included on the CD-ROM (VB 5.0 version only).

Processes obtain waitable timer handles in the same way that they obtain mutex handles: by duplication, inheritance, or by opening one by name. Table 14.6 lists the functions used to work with events.

Table 14.6 **Event Functions**

Function	Description
CancelWaitableTimer	Cancels a waitable timer operation. The timer is left in its current signal state.
CreateWaitableTimer	Creates a waitable timer object. If an event of the given name already exists, it is opened.
OpenWaitableTimer	Opens an existing waitable timer.
SetWaitableTimer	Starts a waitable timer with the duration and period specified.

Other Synchronization Functions

There are a number of other functions that can be used to either detect changes or synchronize between processes. These are listed in Table 14.7.

Synchronization and Visual Basic

So far we've discussed the different types of synchronization objects, how they work, and the concept of signaling. Now consider how they are used in practice. Let's say you have a shared resource (such as a shared memory space) that is protected by a mutex. Each application that uses this block of

Table 14.7   **Other Synchronization Functions**

Function	Description
FindCloseChangeNotification FindFirstChangeNotification FindNextChangeNotification	Creates and works with a file system change notification object. This object can be used to watch for changes in the file system including deleting, copying, and renaming of files.
InterlockedDecrement InterlockedExchange InterlockedIncrement	Allows a process to increment, decrement, or set the value of a variable in shared memory (typically memory backed by a file mapping object). These functions can be used to in effect create your own synchronization techniques—since they also solve the variable incrementing problem described earlier in the chapter.
ResumeThread	Allows one thread to reactivate another thread that had been suspended earlier.
Sleep, SleepEx	Allows a thread to suspend itself either for a specified duration or until receipt of a completion callback from ReadFileEx or WriteFileEx.
SuspendThread	Allows one thread to suspend another.

memory must open a named mutex and call one of the wait functions such as WaitForSingleObject in order to obtain ownership of the mutex.

When you call a wait function, you can specify a timeout. This means that you ultimately have two choices—to use a long (or infinite) timeout to suspend the thread until the mutex becomes available, or to use a short timeout and repeatedly call the wait function until it succeeds.

At first glance, these choices may seem somewhat limiting. Suspending an application is a poor approach. You will see through the sample applications for this chapter that a suspended application is truly frozen. No user input is possible, the window cannot be close or resized, and so on. Why then does Win32 provide this capability? Because Windows applications written in other languages can have multiple threads in one application. It is not uncommon for an application to create a separate thread to perform the background operation. The user interface can continue to run in the main thread while the memory access thread remains suspended until the mutex becomes available. Visual Basic applications support only a single thread, thus suspending the thread suspends the entire application and should be avoided. If you do suspend your application, you should hide its forms and set it's App.TaskVisible property to FALSE.

This leaves the polling technique, which works very well with the aid of a timer. You can implement a simple state machine that periodically checks for the mutex to become available, or even creates a tight loop that uses the DoEvents function to allow the application to run while waiting for the mutex.

One can't help but think how convenient it would be to simply create a function in your application that would magically be called when the mutex became available.

The good news is, you can accomplish this with very little trouble.

All you need to do is create a second Visual Basic program that is an OLE server. It must be an executable—not a DLL, as an executable is a separate program and thus runs in a separate thread. By making it run without a window (or at least a visible window), you won't care if it becomes suspended. You can pass a reference to a class or form in your application to the OLE server. As soon as the mutex becomes available, the server can call a function in the object from your main application.

You can take a more sophisticated approach by building a state machine into an OLE server application that polls for one or more system objects to be signaled and calls an appropriate function at that time. This approach has the advantage of allowing a single OLE server to support multiple applications—a far more efficient approach than launching a separate executable each time you need a thread. The dwWatch.vbp sample project described in this chapter is a preliminary version of the dwWatch server included in Desaware's API class library which is included with this book and is described further in Chapter 20.

Synchronization and Deadlock

Imagine the case where you have two different shared resources, each of which has a mutex controlling access to the resource, and two processes using these resources. Imagine that the first process owns one mutex and the second process owns the other mutex. Now the first process requests the second mutex as well so that it can access both shared resources at once. The application is, of course, immediately suspended. Now let's say the second application decides to request the first mutex because it also wants to access both shared resources at once. It becomes suspended, waiting on the first mutex. The two applications are now waiting for a mutex that will never be released because the thread that owns it is suspended. This situation is known as a "deadlock."

If you do choose to suspend your applications while waiting for objects, you should be aware of the possibility of entering a deadlocked state and take steps to avoid it. Appropriate uses of timeouts is one approach. Designing cooperating applications carefully with the possibility of deadlock in mind is strongly recommended.

Launching Applications

Win32 offers several techniques for launching applications. The Visual Basic Shell command will handle most simple application launching tasks, but the

Win32 functions provide additional capability in some cases. Before going into the details of how applications are launched under Win32, it is worth taking a closer look at the process and thread system objects.

Process and Thread Objects

A process corresponds to a single application running in its own separate address space. You can refer to a process object in several different ways. An application can obtain a handle to a process which can be used as a parameter to many process-information and control functions. Note that this handle is private to an application—process handles cannot be shared. However, it is possible for an application to open its own private handle to a different process using the OpenProcess or DuplicateHandle functions.

A process may be terminated, but the process object is not deleted until all open handles to the process have been closed. This means that it is important for your application to close any extra process handles when they are no longer needed. Failure to do so can prevent system memory and resources from being freed. The exception to this is the pseudo-handle returned by the GetCurrentProcess function. This handle is not a real handle to the process—just a temporary handle to the current process that can be used only within the context of the current process. It can be used any place that a true process handle can be used, but is automatically discarded when it is no longer needed.

Process handles are signaled when the process terminates.

In addition to process handles, every process has a unique process identifier. This process ID is valid throughout the system.

This same pattern of process handle, process pseudo-handle, and process ID is duplicated for threads. You can have thread handles, thread pseudo-handles, and thread identifiers—but these are rarely used by Visual Basic programmers due to VB's inability to launch multiple threads in one application.

Modules and Libraries

Earlier in this chapter you read that modules and instances under 16-bit Windows are essentially memory addresses. Under Win32, this is still the case—but that fact is not nearly as significant because these handles are much less important than they were.

Under Win16, every application would have a unique instance handle, and every dynamic link library that was loaded would have a unique module handle—in each case the handle would consist of the selector to the default data segment for the application or DLL. Because memory was shared, these handles were unique and were also shared. This had profound implications with regard to the necessity of carefully managing instances and modules.

Consider the case of a shared DLL. Every time an application loaded the DLL, the usage count for that DLL would be incremented. The DLL would appear at the same address for every application that was running. If an application loaded a DLL (or incremented its usage count) using the LoadLibrary function, and failed to free it because of a bug or a GPF (general protection fault), the DLL would never be unloaded. If (God forbid) the DLL became corrupted due to a bug or GPF, it was often necessary to restart Windows to clean up the problem. If the DLL that was corrupted was one of the core Windows DLLs, rebooting the system was inevitable.

Under Win32, the situation has changed dramatically. When an application loads a shared DLL, the system simply maps the DLL into the address space of the application using the same file mapping technology described in Chapter 13. The DLL does not generally share any data with other mappings of the DLL, so if one mapping of a DLL becomes corrupted, it will probably have no impact on other applications. (The exceptions are those DLLs that intentionally share data using their own file mappings or shared data segments.) Each application will usually have only one mapping of a particular DLL, thus the usage count of the DLL for any application will always be one. This makes the GetModuleUsage function useless for determining how many times a DLL is used in the system. In fact, this function is not supported under Win32.

Another change from Win16 is that it is possible to load two different instances of the same DLL in certain situations. Consider what happens if you have two copies of the same DLL in two different directories, where one of the copies is an older version than the other. Under Win16, once one of the DLLs was loaded, the other would never be loaded—even if it was a later version. Under Win32, one process can load one of the DLLs and another process can load the other. Because of the separation of memory address spaces they will not interfere with each other. Not only that, but it is possible for one process to actually load both copies of the DLL at once! Each will appear mapped into a different location in memory. Depending on the DLL and how it is used, this can lead to problems running the application.

Win32 Process and Thread Functions

Win32 provides a number of functions for working with processes and threads. These are listed in Table 14.8.

Determining When Other Applications Close

When using cooperating applications or a complex system where one application can launch other processes, it is often necessary to know when another application has closed. Under Win16 there were two common ways for applications to

Table 14.8   Process and Thread Functions

Function	Description
CreateProcess	Launches an application
ExitProcess	Closes a process in a clean manner
FindExecutable	Finds a program that is associated with the specified file
FreeLibrary	Frees a DLL that was loaded using LoadLibrary
GetCurrentProcess	Obtains a pseudo-handle to the current process
GetCurrentProcessId	Obtains the unique process identifier for the current process
GetCurrentThread	Obtains a pseudo-handle to the current thread
GetCurrentThreadId	Obtains the unique process identifier for the current thread
GetExitCodeProcess	Obtains the exit code and status for the specified process
GetExitCodeThread	Obtains the exit code and status for the specified thread
GetModuleFileName	Retrieves the executable file name of the specified module
GetModuleHandle	Retrieves the module handle for a loaded module given its file name
GetPriorityClass	Obtains the priority level of the specified process
GetProcessShutdownParameters	Determines the order in which processes are closed during system shutdown
GetProcessTimes	Obtains timing statistics on the specified process
GetProcessVersion	Determines the version of Windows that a process was designed for based on the information stamped in the executable file for the process
GetProcessWorkingSetSize	Determines the minimum and maximum amounts of physical memory used by a process
GetStartupInfo	Obtains a copy of the STARTUPINFO structure used to start the specified process
GetThreadPriority	Determines the priority of a thread
GetThreadTimes	Obtains timing statistics on the specified thread

Table 14.8	**Process and Thread Functions (Continued)**

Function	Description
GetWindowThreadProcessId	Obtains the process and thread identifiers for the thread that owns the specified window
LoadLibrary LoadLibraryEx	Loads a DLL or executable file into the address space of the current process
LoadModule	A limited form of the CreateProcess function
SetPriorityClass	Sets the priority of a process
SetProcessShutdownParameters	Specifies when this process will be terminated relative to other processes during system shutdown
SetProcessWorkingSetSize	Specifies the minimum and maximum amounts of physical memory used by a process
SetThreadPriority	Sets the priority of a thread
ShellExecute	Executes a program either by name, or by association to a document file
TerminateProcess	Terminates a process immediately
WinExec	Executes a program

accomplish this task. One common method was to call the GetModuleUsage function after launching an application to determine how many instances of the application are running. As soon as the function returned a value that was one fewer than the initial value (zero in most cases), you would know that the program had ended. This method was fine for most cases where you could be sure that only one instance of an application would run, but could fail if it was possible for multiple instances to be launched. A second method involved finding the window handle of the newly launched application and subclassing it, watching for the WM_DESTROY message. This latter method is still possible under Win32 given the appropriate subclassing tool such as the sample dwsbc32d.ocx control included with this book (you need a cross-task subclasser in cases such as this one, which is a specialized type of subclassing that is not easily accomplished in Visual Basic).

But Win32 offers a better solution, which you have probably guessed already. You have seen that Win32 supports synchronization objects along with several methods for watching for them to be signaled. You have also seen that a process object is signaled when it is terminated. The principles involved are clear. The Launch.vbp sample program described later demonstrates several practical ways to launch an application and determine when it is closed.

Interprocess Communication

One of the reasons that Microsoft's 32-bit operating systems are more stable than 16-bit Windows is the increased isolation between processes. Now that memory and most objects are unique to individual applications, it is much more difficult for applications to interfere with each other's operation. You might think that this makes it more difficult for applications to communicate with each other, but that is not the case. The Win32 API supports a number of mechanisms for applications to exchange data. In fact, these new mechanisms have a number of features that make them far superior to anything available on 16-bit Windows. For example, Win32 interprocess communication is frequently not restricted to a local system. You can communicate between processes running on different machines on a network.

Most Win32 interprocess communication mechanisms support overlapped (asynchronous) operations. This means that an application can call a function that starts an operation such as a data transfer and returns immediately. The application can then proceed to run while the operation continues in the background. The application can then wait for the operation to complete or wait for a notification.

You have already read in Chapter 13 about using file mapping objects to communicate between processes. Win32 also provides support for two additional sharing mechanisms called pipes and mailslots.

Pipes

Pipes are one of the most intriguing new features for Win32, providing an efficient and easy-to-use mechanism for communicating between processes. Win32 named pipes can even be used between processes on different systems, making them ideal for many client/server applications. There are two types of pipes: anonymous pipes and named pipes. Anonymous pipes are unnamed and are used on local systems primarily to allow a parent process to communicate with child processes that it launches. Named pipes are more advanced and are identified by a name so that client and server applications can communicate with each other.

The best way to understand pipes is to remember that their name describes their operation very nicely. Just as a water pipe connects two locations and transports water, a software pipe connects two processes and transports data. Once a pipe is created it is accessed very much like a file and uses many of the same functions. You must obtain a handle to an opened pipe using the CreateFile function or be given a handle from another process. You write data into a pipe using the WriteFile function which can then be read by the other process using the ReadFile function. Pipes are system objects and thus handles to pipes must be closed using the CloseHandle function when they are no longer needed.

Pipes generally connect two applications—they are rarely shared. Anonymous pipes can transfer data in one direction; named pipes may be bi-directional. Pipes can transfer arbitrary amounts of data as streams of bytes. Named pipes are also able to group data into blocks called messages.

When discussing pipes, it is common to refer to the two processes involved as a client and server process. The server is the one responsible for creating the pipe. The client connects to the pipe. A server can create multiple instances of a pipe, thus supporting multiple clients.

Named pipes, with their powerful ability to connect multiple processes, even across a network, would be one of the most exciting new features of Win32 except for one detail: While named pipe clients are supported by Windows 95, named pipes can only be created under Windows NT. This severely limits their use in the real world for general application development. Named pipes are covered in this chapter with the hope that this disappointing limitation will be corrected in future versions of Windows.

The functions listed in Table 14.9 are used to work with pipes.

Table 14.9   Pipe Functions

Function	Description
CallNamedPipe	Called by a client process to connect to a named pipe configured for message transfer mode. It then reads and writes a message.
ConnectNamedPipe	Called by a server process to prepare a pipe to connect to a client process and optionally wait until a client process is connected.
CreateNamedPipe	Creates a named pipe.
CreatePipe	Creates an anonymous pipe.
DisconnectNamedPipe	Called by a server process to disconnect a pipe from a client. The server can then call ConnectNamedPipe again to connect to another client (or wait until the same client reconnects).
GetNamedPipeHandleState	Obtains information about the state of a named pipe.
GetNamedPipeInfo	Obtains information about a named pipe.
PeekNamedPipe	Determines if any data is available in a pipe and optionally previews the data without removing it from the pipe.

Table 14.9	Pipe Functions (Continued)	
Function	**Description**	
SetNamedPipeHandleState	Allows you to control certain named pipe settings, including the blocking mode and whether the pipe is configured to transfer bytes or messages.	
TransactNamedPipe	Reads and writes a message to a named pipe configured in message mode. Supports both synchronous and asynchronous operation.	
WaitNamedPipe	Called by a client process to connect to a named pipe.	

Working with Anonymous Pipes

Anonymous pipes are used on a local system in cases where applications are co-operating closely with each other. A parent application creates a pipe using the CreatePipe function. This function returns two pipe handles, one for the read side and one for the write side. For bi-directional communication you must create two pipes. You will almost certainly need to specify that the pipe handles are inheritable when calling the CreatePipe function—this ensures that the handles will be usable by any processes launched by the parent process.

Next you have to somehow pass the handle to the other process. The easiest way to do this is to use the standard input and output handles that every application has by default. You can set the standard handle before launching the other application. The child application will then inherit the standard handle from its parent. By setting the standard handles for child processes to the appropriate pipe handles, it is possible for a parent application to communicate with child processes or for child processes to communicate with each other. The PipeSrc.vbp and PipeDest.vbp sample applications demonstrate how this can be accomplished.

Pipes have internal buffers that hold the data during the transfer process. When a program writes into a pipe, the data is generally written into this buffer and the write operation returns immediately. The other application will then read data from the pipe at its convenience. If the pipe buffer is full, the writing application will be suspended until there is enough room in the buffer to hold the data.

Working with Named Pipes

When a server application creates a named pipe using the CreateNamedPipe function, it has a number of configuration options that must be specified. First and foremost is the name of the pipe. From the server's perspective, a pipe name always has the form "\\.\pipe\myname". The "\\.\pipe\" component indicates that the pipe is on the local system. When the pipe is opened by a client using the CreateFile function, it will specify "\\.\pipe\" if it is on the same system as the server, or "*systemname*\pipe\" where *systemname* is the name of the computer on which the server is running.

The server also specifies the direction of data flow in the pipe and tells if the pipe is bi-directional and whether data is transferred as bytes or as messages. The term "messages" in this context is potentially confusing but is actually quite simple. All it does is provide an easy mechanism for grouping blocks of data. When in byte mode, the server writes blocks of data into the pipe. When the client reads information from the pipe, all it sees is a single stream of data made up of all of the blocks of data in sequence. In some cases this is not a problem; for example, a communications server might want to send a stream of data to a client. Since the client will be reading individual bytes, there is no need to group the data into messages. However, consider the case where the server is sending instructions to the client where each instruction is made up of a block of data where the blocks can be of variable length. In byte mode this would require the client to somehow find out the length of each instruction, perhaps by using PeekNamedPipe to preview the data or read it in several parts. By configuring the pipe for message mode, each time the server writes data into the pipe it is considered a message. The client can simply request the next message and the pipe will provide the correct number of bytes.

Named pipes can be set to run in blocking and nonblocking mode. Nonblocking mode is a form of asynchronous operation that is provided to remain backward-compatible with Microsoft LAN Manager 2.0. Microsoft recommends that you use pipes in blocking mode. Note that you can still perform asynchronous operations on these pipes using the standard Win32 asynchronous operations.

A server can create multiple instances of a named pipe, each of which can connect to a different client. The number of instances of a pipe allowed are specified during the first call to the CreateNamedPipe function. Named pipe operations are demonstrated in the PipeClnt.vbp and PipeSrv.vbp sample programs.

Mailslots

A pipe forms a direct connection between two processes. A mailslot can best be thought of as somewhat like the U.S. Postal Service. You can send messages from many different locations that are all addressed to the same mailbox, but you can't be absolutely certain that they will all arrive safely.

An application establishes a mailslot on its own system with a unique name. The name takes the form "\\.\mailslot\path\mailslotname." The server application (the one that creates the mailslot) can only create it on its own system, but client applications can write to mailslots throughout their domain. A mailslot name can have a pseudo path, for example, \\.\mailslot\ de-saware\user\marketing. This path does not correspond to any real path on a file system—it is merely a handy way to categorize mailslots into groups.

When a client opens a mailslot using the CreateFile function, it can use "\\.\mailslot\..." if the client and the server are running on the same system, "\\computername\mailslot\..." to open a mailslot on a remote system, or "\\domainname\mailslot\..." to open every mailslot with the specified name on the specified domain (use "*" for the domain name to specify the primary domain). The client should specify (FILE_SHARE_READ or FILE_SHARE_WRITE) for the file-sharing mode when using mailslots so that more than one client can write to the same server.

Multiple clients can open the same mailslot, in which case each client can write to the mailslot at will—the server will read messages from every client. When a client is connected to multiple mailslots, each active server will receive the message that it sends. Mailslot handles can be duplicated and shared among servers. The DuplicateHandle function can also be used. Table 14. 10 lists the functions related to using mailslots.

Table 14.10 **Mailslot Functions**

Function	Description
CreateMailslot	Used by a server application to create a mailslot
GetMailslotInfo	Used to obtain information about a mailslot
SetMailslotInfo	Sets the default timeout for a mailslot

Examples

This chapter includes a number of sample projects that demonstrate synchronization and interprocess communication. This section is divided into several parts, each of which includes several sample programs. This is necessary, as most of the examples require two or more applications to be running simultaneously in order to demonstrate the principles involved. You may also wish to set up a second system on a network to experiment with interprocess communication across a network.

In addition to the samples described here, the CD-ROM that comes with this book includes MailSlot.vbp, a sample project that illustrates the use of mailslots, and Sleeper.vbp, a sample project that illustrates the use of waitable timers.

ckServe/ckClient: Cooperating Applications Revisited

The client/server applications in Chapter 13 demonstrated a simple supermarket simulation in which two applications communicated using a file mapping. The only problem with the simulation was that it failed as soon as two client applications tried to run simultaneously. The purchases and sales would no longer match—in effect, the purchases of the two clients would get mixed up.

The solution to this problem is remarkably simple and is shown in the ckServe.vbp and ckClient.vbp projects located on the CD-ROM in the directory for this chapter. The following section summarizes the modifications that were made from the version of these applications presented in Chapter 13.

Modifying ckServe.vbp

Add the following functions and constant declarations to the CHK-STAND.BAS module.

Add the following code to the declaration section for the form:

```
Dim MutexHandle As Long        ' Handle of mutex for this server
```

Add the following code to the Cleanup subroutine for the form:

```
If MutexHandle <> ⁻ Then
    Call CloseHandle(MutexHandle)
    MutexHandle = ⁻
End If
```

The chkOpen_Click( ) function is modified as shown below. The server creates a mutex with a unique name. Note that the server application does not itself synchronize on the mutex—it is merely responsible for creating it and making it available to the client programs.

```
Private Sub chkOpen_Click()
    Dim usename$
    Dim InitialStand As CheckStand
    Dim written&
    ' Note lack of error checking here
    usename$ = "ChkStd" & txtCheck.Text
    If chkOpen.value = 1 Then
        If FileHandle <> ⁻ Then Exit Sub
        ' Create new file, read write access, exclusive use,
        FileHandle = CreateFile(usename$, GENERIC_READ Or GENERIC_WRITE, ⁻, _
        Security, CREATE_ALWAYS, FILE_ATTRIBUTE_NORMAL Or _
        FILE_FLAG_RANDOM_ACCESS, ⁻)
        If FileHandle = -1 Then
            MsgBox "Can't create file"
            FileHandle = ⁻
            Exit Sub
        End If
        ' Write the initial file info
```

```
        Call WriteFile(FileHandle, InitialStand, Len(InitialStand), written, ¯)
        Call FlushFileBuffers(FileHandle)
        ' Now we need a mapping
        MappingHandle = CreateFileMapping(FileHandle, Security, PAGE_READWRITE, _
        ¯, ¯, usename$ & "map")
        If MappingHandle = ¯ Then
            MsgBox "Can't create file mapping"
            Exit Sub
        End If
        MappingAddress = MapViewOfFile(MappingHandle, FILE_MAP_ALL_ACCESS, ¯, _
        ¯, ¯)
        If MappingAddress = ¯ Then
            MsgBox "Can't map view of the file"
            Exit Sub
        End If
        ' Don't get initial ownership
        MutexHandle = CreateMutexBynum(¯, False, usename$ & "mutex")
        Timer1.Enabled = True    ' Start watching for customers
    Else
        CleanUp
        lblStatus.Caption = "Closed"
    End If
End Sub
```

Modifying ckClient.vbp

Add the following code to the declaration section for the form:

```
Dim MutexHandle As Long
```

Add the following code to the Cleanup subroutine for the form:

```
If MutexHandle <> ¯ Then
        Call CloseHandle(MutexHandle)
        MutexHandle = ¯
End If
```

Modify the Timer1_Timer() function as shown and add the GetMutex-Name function. The only real difference from the original program is that an additional condition has been added at state 2 that prevents the application from entering state 3 unless it owns the mutex. Since only one application can own the mutex at a time, this ensures that only one application can access the memory shared via the file mapping object at once.

Once the application no longer needs to access the shared memory, the mutex is released, allowing another application to access the server.

```
Private Sub Timer1_Timer()
    Dim usename$
    Dim newtotal&
    Dim cs As CheckStand
    Dim x%
    Dim res&
```

```vb
Select Case CurrentState
    Case 0
        If chkShop.value = 1 Then
            CurrentState = 1
        End If
    Case 1
        usename$ = GetMappingName$()
        ' Right now we only use checkstand 1
        MappingHandle = OpenFileMapping(FILE_MAP_WRITE, False, usename$)
        MutexHandle = OpenMutex(MUTEX_ALL_ACCESS, False, GetMutexName$())
        If MappingHandle = 0 Or MutexHandle = 0 Then Exit Sub
        MappingAddress = MapViewOfFile(MappingHandle, FILE_MAP_ALL_ACCESS, _
        0, 0, 0)
        CurrentState = 2
    Case 2
        ' Obtain exclusive ownership
        res = WaitForSingleObject(MutexHandle, 0)
        If res <> WAIT_TIMEOUT Then
            agCopyData ByVal MappingAddress, cs, Len(cs)
            If cs.Total = 0 Then CurrentState = 3 else _
            ReleaseMutex(MutexHandle)
        End If
    Case 3
        CurrentTotal = 0
        For x = 0 To CInt(Rnd(99))
            cs.Prices(x) = 100 * Rnd()
            CurrentTotal = CurrentTotal + cs.Prices(x)
        Next x
        cs.Done = True
        cs.Client = "Client" & txtClient.Text
        agCopyData cs, ByVal MappingAddress, Len(cs)
        CurrentState = 4
    Case 4
        agCopyData ByVal MappingAddress, cs, Len(cs)
        If cs.Total <> 0 Then
            For x = 0 To 99
                newtotal = newtotal + cs.Prices(x)
            Next x
            cs.Total = 0
            lstPurchase.AddItem Format$(CurrentTotal, "0.00")
            agCopyData cs, ByVal MappingAddress, Len(cs)
            ' Release the mutex
            Call ReleaseMutex(MutexHandle)
            If chkShop.value = 0 Then
                CurrentState = 0
            Else
                CurrentState = 1
            End If
            ' Clear file mapping handles, etc.
            CleanUp
        End If
```

```
        End Select
        Select Case CurrentState
            Case ¯
                lblStatus.Caption = "Idle"
            Case 1
                lblStatus.Caption = "Looking for checkstand"
            Case 2
                lblStatus.Caption = "Waiting in line at checkstand"
            Case 3
                lblStatus.Caption = "Loading items onto checkstand"
            Case 4
                lblStatus.Caption = "Waiting for checkout to be complete"
        End Select
End Sub

Public Function GetMutexName() As String
    GetMutexName = "ChkStd1mutex"
End Function
```

Suggestions for Further Practice

The ckClient.vbp and ckServe.vbp applications evolved from a simple example and were not really designed with synchronization in mind.

- Redesign the state machine so that there is an additional state that requests access to the shared memory space instead of combining it with state 2.

- How would you go about implementing the programs to run with multiple servers (multiple checkstands)? Clearly some "seeking" mechanism can be given to the clients. This could take several forms. You could just assign a random number. You could try different servers in sequence. Since each server has a unique name (both a file mapping name and a mutex name), it should not be difficult to determine if a particular server number exists.

- Once you implement multiple servers, try using semaphores to limit the number of clients that each server supports at any given time (the number of customers that can wait in one line).

- After examining the Launch application, how would you go about redesigning these samples to use the dwWatch program instead of the polling technique shown here?

Launch.vbp: Launching Applications

This sample consists of three separate projects. The Shelled1.vbp application is a simple program that when executed displays its own process identifier,

thread identifier, and the window handle of the form. It is launched by the Launch.vbp application. The dwWatch.vbp project demonstrates an elegant synchronization technique using callbacks and is described in the next section.

The Launch.vbp project demonstrates a number of different techniques for launching applications and determining when they terminate. The main form for the project contains four buttons that demonstrate the various techniques, and three label controls to display the status of the project. Listing 14.1 contains the listing for the only form for this project.

Listing 14.1 **LAUNCH.FRM**

```
VERSION 5.¯¯
Begin VB.Form frmLaunch
   Caption         =    "Launch Shelled1.exe"
   ClientHeight    =    288¯
   ClientLeft      =    1¯95
   ClientTop       =    1515
   ClientWidth     =    414¯
   Height          =    3285
   Left            =    1¯35
   LinkTopic       =    "Form1"
   ScaleHeight     =    288¯
   ScaleWidth      =    414¯
   Top             =    117¯
   Width           =    426¯
   Begin VB.CommandButton cmdShell2
      Caption      =    "Shell with Callback"
      Height       =    495
      Left         =    24¯
      TabIndex     =    6
      Top          =    156¯
      Width        =    1755
   End
   Begin VB.CommandButton cmdShellExecute
      Caption      =    "Using ShellExecute"
      Height       =    495
      Left         =    24¯
      TabIndex     =    3
      Top          =    222¯
      Width        =    1755
   End
   Begin VB.CommandButton cmdCreateProcess
      Caption      =    "Using CreateProcess"
      Height       =    495
      Left         =    24¯
      TabIndex     =    2
      Top          =    9¯¯
      Width        =    1755
```

Listing 14.1   LAUNCH.FRM (Continued)

```
        End
        Begin VB.CommandButton cmdShell
            Caption         =   "Using Shell"
            Height          =   495
            Left            =   24‾
            TabIndex        =   ‾
            Top             =   24‾
            Width           =   1755
        End
        Begin VB.Label lblStatus
            Height          =   255
            Index           =   2
            Left            =   21‾‾
            TabIndex        =   5
            Top             =   168‾
            Width           =   1875
        End
        Begin VB.Label lblStatus
            Height          =   255
            Index           =   1
            Left            =   21‾‾
            TabIndex        =   4
            Top             =   1‾2‾
            Width           =   1875
        End
        Begin VB.Label lblStatus
            Height          =   255
            Index           =   ‾
            Left            =   21‾‾
            TabIndex        =   1
            Top             =   3‾‾
            Width           =   1875
        End
    End
End
Attribute VB_Name = "frmLaunch"
Attribute VB_GlobalNameSpace = False
Attribute VB_Creatable = False
Attribute VB_PredeclaredId = TrueAttribute VB_Exposed = False
Option Explicit


Private Const SYNCHRONIZE = &H1‾‾‾‾‾
Private Const INFINITE = &HFFFFFFFF        '  Infinite timeout
Private Const DEBUG_PROCESS = &H1
Private Const DEBUG_ONLY_THIS_PROCESS = &H2

Private Const CREATE_SUSPENDED = &H4
```

Listing 14.1 **LAUNCH.FRM (Continued)**

```
Private Const DETACHED_PROCESS = &H8

Private Const CREATE_NEW_CONSOLE = &H1⁻

Private Const NORMAL_PRIORITY_CLASS = &H2⁻
Private Const IDLE_PRIORITY_CLASS = &H4⁻
Private Const HIGH_PRIORITY_CLASS = &H8⁻
Private Const REALTIME_PRIORITY_CLASS = &H1⁻⁻

Private Const CREATE_NEW_PROCESS_GROUP = &H2⁻⁻

Private Const CREATE_NO_WINDOW = &H8⁻⁻⁻⁻⁻⁻

Private Const WAIT_FAILED = -1&
Private Const WAIT_OBJECT_⁻ = ⁻
Private Const WAIT_ABANDONED = &H8⁻&
Private Const WAIT_ABANDONED_⁻ = &H8⁻&
Private Const WAIT_TIMEOUT = &H1⁻2&

Private Const SW_SHOW = 5

Dim DemoDirectory$
```

The PROCESS_INFORMATION structure is used by the CreateProcess function to return information about the newly created process. The two handles that are returned in this structure are open handles to the new process and its primary thread. In most cases you will close these two handles immediately (this does *not* terminate the application—these are extra handles).

```
Private Type PROCESS_INFORMATION
        hProcess As Long
        hThread As Long
        dwProcessId As Long
        dwThreadId As Long
End Type
```

The STARTUPINFO structure allows the CreateProcess function to control many aspects of the creation process. This structure is described in Appendix B.

```
Private Type STARTUPINFO
        cb As Long
        lpReserved As String
        lpDesktop As String
```

```
        lpTitle As String
        dwX As Long
        dwY As Long
        dwXSize As Long
        dwYSize As Long
        dwXCountChars As Long
        dwYCountChars As Long
        dwFillAttribute As Long
        dwFlags As Long
        wShowWindow As Integer
        cbReserved2 As Integer
        lpReserved2 As Long
        hStdInput As Long
        hStdOutput As Long
        hStdError As Long
End Type

Private Declare Function OpenProcess Lib "kernel32" (ByVal dwDesiredAccess As _
Long, ByVal bInheritHandle As Long, ByVal dwProcessId As Long) As Long
Private Declare Function CloseHandle Lib "kernel32" (ByVal hObject As Long) As _
Long
Private Declare Function WaitForSingleObject Lib "kernel32" (ByVal hHandle As _
Long, ByVal dwMilliseconds As Long) As Long
Private Declare Function CreateProcessBynum Lib "kernel32" Alias _
"CreateProcessA" (ByVal lpApplicationName As String, ByVal lpCommandLine As _
String, ByVal lpProcessAttributes As Long, ByVal lpThreadAttributes As Long, _
ByVal bInheritHandles As Long, ByVal dwCreationFlags As Long, lpEnvironment _
As Any, ByVal lpCurrentDirectory As String, lpStartupInfo As _
STARTUPINFO, lpProcessInformation As PROCESS_INFORMATION) As Long
Private Declare Function WaitForInputIdle Lib "user32" (ByVal hProcess As Long, _
ByVal dwMilliseconds As Long) As Long
Private Declare Function ShellExecute Lib "shell32.dll" Alias "ShellExecuteA" _
(ByVal hwnd As Long, ByVal lpOperation As String, ByVal lpFile As String, _
ByVal lpParameters As String, ByVal lpDirectory As String, ByVal nShowCmd _
As Long) As Long
```

A more robust program would bring up a common dialog or form to let you choose the application to shell. Modifying the application in that manner is left as an exercise for the reader.

```
Private Sub Form_Load()
    DemoDirectory = InputBox$("Enter path of directory containing _
    Shelled1.exe", , "d:\zdbook3\sourcev5\ch14\")
End Sub
```

One of the easiest ways to launch an application is to use the Visual Basic Shell command. Under Win32, this function returns the process identifier of the new process. If the application is shelled successfully, it then calls the first of our synchronizing functions: WaitForTerm1.

```
Private Sub cmdShell_Click()
    Dim pid&
    lblStatus(¯).Caption = "Launching"
    lblStatus(¯).Refresh
    pid = Shell(DemoDirectory & "Shelled1.exe", vbNormalFocus)
    If pid <> ¯ Then
        lblStatus(¯).Caption = "Launched"
        lblStatus(¯).Refresh
        WaitForTerm1 pid
    End If
    lblStatus(¯).Caption = "Terminated"
End Sub
```

The WaitForTerm1 example takes a process identifier as its parameter. The process identifier is unique throughout the system, but cannot be used directly by the wait functions because it is not itself an object. The OpenProcess function obtains an actual process handle to the newly created process. This function can fail on NT systems which have increased security in place, but will work in most cases. The WaitForSingleObject function suspends the thread until the other process closes. Note how the application is truly frozen in this case. The Sleeper.vbp example on the CD-ROM demonstrates a better way to suspend an application, should you choose to do so. The WaitForTerm1 function returns after the process object is signaled, which occurs when the application is closed. The process handle must then be closed in order to allow Windows to delete the process object.

```
' This wait routine freezes the application
' It's clearly not a good way to wait for process
' termination - though if you hid the application
' first it could be very effective.
Private Sub WaitForTerm1(pid&)
    Dim phnd&
    phnd = OpenProcess(SYNCHRONIZE, ¯, pid)
    If phnd <> ¯ Then
        lblStatus(¯).Caption = "Waiting for termination"
        lblStatus(¯).Refresh
        Call WaitForSingleObject(phnd, INFINITE)
        Call CloseHandle(phnd)
    End If
End Sub
```

The CreateProcess example must first initialize a STARTUPINFO structure with the creation parameters. You must set the cb field in the structure to the length of the structure before using it. The initialization to null strings and zero shown here is not actually necessary, since Visual Basic initializes members of newly created structures to zero automatically. The function then calls the WaitForTerm2 function to wait until the shelled application is closed.

```
Private Sub cmdCreateProcess_Click()
    Dim res&
    Dim sinfo As STARTUPINFO
    Dim pinfo As PROCESS_INFORMATION
    sinfo.cb = Len(sinfo)
    sinfo.lpReserved = vbNullString
    sinfo.lpDesktop = vbNullString
    sinfo.lpTitle = vbNullString
    sinfo.dwFlags = ¯

    lblStatus(1).Caption = "Launching"
    lblStatus(1).Refresh
    res = CreateProcessBynum(DemoDirectory & "Shelled1.exe", vbNullString, ¯, _
    ¯, True, NORMAL_PRIORITY_CLASS, ByVal ¯&, vbNullString, sinfo, pinfo)
    If res Then
        lblStatus(1).Caption = "Launched"
        WaitForTerm2 pinfo
    End If
    lblStatus(1).Caption = "Terminated"

End Sub
```

The WaitForTerm2 function takes the PROCESS_INFORMATION structure returned by the CreateProcess function as its parameter. The first step it takes is to wait until the process has actually finished initializing using the WaitForInputIdle function. This is not actually necessary in this case, but if we were going to perform any interprocess communication, this would assure that the application had completed its initialization. Next, the thread handle is closed—it is not needed for this sample. Once again, closing the thread handle has no impact on the application; this is an extra handle to the thread.

This function uses the polling approach for waiting for the application to terminate, using a DoEvents function instead of a timer with state machine (the approach that was used in the ckclient example for waiting for a mutex). You will see that in this case the Launch application will continue to run. In order to prevent possible reentrancy problems, we disable the cmdCreateProcess button before entering the DoEvents loop. It should be stressed that this is a rather poor design, since it depends on the DoEvents function.

```
' This wait routine allows other application events
' to be processed while waiting for the process to
' complete.
Private Sub WaitForTerm2(pinfo As PROCESS_INFORMATION)
    Dim res&
    ' Let the process initialize
```

```
        Call WaitForInputIdle(pinfo.hProcess, INFINITE)
        ' We don't need the thread handle
        Call CloseHandle(pinfo.hThread)
        ' Disable the button to prevent reentrancy
        cmdCreateProcess.Enabled = False
        lblStatus(1).Caption = "Waiting for termination"
        lblStatus(1).Refresh
        Do
            res = WaitForSingleObject(pinfo.hProcess, ¯)
            If res <> WAIT_TIMEOUT Then
                ' No timeout, app is terminated
                Exit Do
            End If
            DoEvents
        Loop While True

        cmdCreateProcess.Enabled = True
        ' Kill the last handle of the process
        Call CloseHandle(pinfo.hProcess)
End Sub
```

The cmdShell2 button uses the Visual Basic Shell command again to launch an application, but uses the dwWatcher OLE server to implement a very elegant technique for watching for the application to terminate. The function creates a dwAppWatch object in the dwWatcher server. You should run a second instance of Visual Basic, open the dwWatch.vbp project, and run it before executing this function (or create the dwWatcher server executable if you wish).

The SetAppWatch object method sets the process identifier of the application to watch. The SetAppCallback function passes a reference to the form for this application to the dwWatcher project. The command button is once again disabled to prevent reentrancy problems; however, it probably is not necessary in this case—this function and the dwWatcher server are reentrant.

When the application terminates, the dwAppTerminated function for the form is called, receiving as a parameter a reference to the dwAppWatch object itself. This allows the function to determine which process was terminated (in the event that you are watching for the termination of more than one application).

It must be stressed that the dwWatch.vpb project included in this chapter is a preliminary version of the dwWatcher server that can be found with version 1.0 of the Desaware API Class library, included with this book.

```
Private Sub cmdShell2_Click()
    Dim pid&
    Dim obj As Object
    lblStatus(2).Caption = "Launching"
    lblStatus(2).Refresh
    pid = Shell(DemoDirectory & "Shelled1.exe", vbNormalFocus)
    If pid <> ¯ Then
        Set obj = CreateObject("dwWatcher.dwAppWatch")
        obj.SetAppWatch pid
```

```
        obj.SetAppCallback Me
        lblStatus(2).Caption = "Waiting for termination"
        cmdShell2.Enabled = False
    End If
End Sub

Public Sub dwAppTerminated(obj As Object)
    lblStatus(2).Caption = "Terminated"
    cmdShell2.Enabled = True
End Sub
```

The cmdShellExecute_Click() function demonstrates use of the ShellExecute function. Though used in this case to launch the same executable program, this function understands the file associations defined in the system registry. This means that you can pass a document file (such as a word document or excel spreadsheet) to the function and it will automatically launch the associated application and perform the desired operation. Unfortunately, the ShellExecute function does not return the process handle or identifier, making it difficult to determine which process was actually launched by the function.

```
Private Sub cmdShellExecute_Click()
    Dim res&
    Dim obj As Object
    res& = ShellExecute(hwnd, "open", DemoDirectory & "Shelled1.exe", _
    vbNullString, CurDir$, SW_SHOW)
    If res < 32 Then
        MsgBox "Unable to shell applicatin"
    End If
End Sub
```

dwWatch.vbp: Synchronization with OLE Callbacks

One of the unfortunate side effects of the increasing complexity of Windows is that we seem to run out of words to describe things. This is well illustrated by the use of the term "object" to refer to almost anything.

When talking about Windows, the term "callback" is clearly defined as what happens when an application passes a function address to Windows or a DLL so that Windows or the DLL can call that function at some future time. Callbacks of this type are implemented using the AddressOf operator in Visual Basic 5.0 or with the dwcbk32d.ocx control included with this book under Visual Basic 4.0.

But in addition to being tied closely to Win32, Visual Basic is also tied closely to OLE—Microsoft's object linking and embedding technology. In OLE it is also possible to use the term "callback" to describe what happens when you pass an object to an ActiveX server (also called an OLE server) so that the server can call one of the methods of that object at some future time. This type of callback is fully supported by Visual Basic and enables one of the most elegant solutions to performing interprocess synchronization using Visual Basic.

The dwWatch.vbp project included with this chapter is a preliminary version of the dwWatcher server that is included with version 1.0 of the Desaware API class library that is included with this book (later versions are available with Desaware's SpyWorks product line). dwWatcher is a general purpose state machine whose purpose is to monitor system objects and call specific functions in your application's forms or classes when those objects are signaled. A single dwWatcher server can support virtually any number of objects and applications at once.

The version of dwWatch.vbp shown here lacks some of the features and error checking that are present in the version in the class library directory on your CD-ROM. But the principles described are identical.

dwWatch.vbp has one form, one module, and two classes, and makes use of the APIGID32.BAS module that provides access to the APIGID32.DLL dynamic link library provided with this book.

Listing 14.2 shows the WATCH.BAS module. Listing 14.3 shows the WATCH.FRM form.

Listing 14.2   WATCH.BAS

```
Attribute VB_Name = "modWatcher"
Option Explicit
Public Const SYNCHRONIZE = &H1
Public Const PROCESS_DUP_HANDLE = &H4
Public Const INFINITE = &HFFFFFFFF        '  Infinite timeout
Public Const DEBUG_PROCESS = &H1
Public Const DEBUG_ONLY_THIS_PROCESS = &H2

Public Const CREATE_SUSPENDED = &H4

Public Const DETACHED_PROCESS = &H8

Public Const CREATE_NEW_CONSOLE = &H1

Public Const NORMAL_PRIORITY_CLASS = &H2
Public Const IDLE_PRIORITY_CLASS = &H4
Public Const HIGH_PRIORITY_CLASS = &H8
Public Const REALTIME_PRIORITY_CLASS = &H1

Public Const CREATE_NEW_PROCESS_GROUP = &H2

Public Const CREATE_NO_WINDOW = &H8

Public Const WAIT_FAILED = -1&
```

Listing 14.2   **WATCH.BAS (Continued)**

```
Public Const WAIT_OBJECT_¯ = ¯
Public Const WAIT_ABANDONED = &H8¯&
Public Const WAIT_ABANDONED_¯ = &H8¯&
Public Const WAIT_TIMEOUT = &H1¯2&


Public Declare Function OpenProcess Lib "kernel32" (ByVal dwDesiredAccess As _
Long, ByVal bInheritHandle As Long, ByVal dwProcessId As Long) As Long
Public Declare Function CloseHandle Lib "kernel32" (ByVal hObject As Long) As _
Long
Public Declare Function WaitForSingleObject Lib "kernel32" (ByVal hHandle As _
Long, ByVal dwMilliseconds As Long) As Long
Public Declare Function CreateProcessBynum Lib "kernel32" Alias _
"CreateProcessA" (ByVal lpApplicationName As String, ByVal lpCommandLine _
As String, ByVal lpProcessAttributes As Long, ByVal lpThreadAttributes As Long, _
ByVal bInheritHandles As Long, ByVal dwCreationFlags As Long, lpEnvironment As _
Any, ByVal lpCurrentDirectory As String, lpStartupInfo As STARTUPINFO, _
lpProcessInformation As PROCESS_INFORMATION) As Long
Public Declare Function WaitForInputIdle Lib "user32" (ByVal hProcess As Long, _
ByVal dwMilliseconds As Long) As Long
Public Declare Function DuplicateHandle Lib "kernel32" (ByVal _
hSourceProcessHandle As Long, ByVal hSourceHandle As Long, ByVal _
hTargetProcessHandle As Long, lpTargetHandle As Long, ByVal dwDesiredAccess _
As Long, ByVal bInheritHandle As Long, ByVal dwOptions As Long) As Long
Public Declare Function GetCurrentProcess Lib "kernel32" () As Long
```

This module has two important local variables. frmptr references a form that must be created to hold the timer that will be used for polling. WatchCollection will contain references to each class object that needs to be tested to see if its associated system object has been signaled.

```
Public frmptr As frmWatcher
Public WatchCollection As New Collection
```

The dwWatch program is set to start up with the Main routine. If the program is launched as a standalone application, it displays a form showing information about the application. Otherwise the form is created, but remains hidden.

```
Public Sub Main()
    Set frmptr = New frmWatcher
    Load frmptr ' Make sure form is loaded (but invisible)
```

```
    If App.StartMode = vbSModeStandalone Then
        ' Show the form if created standalone
        frmptr.Show
    End If
End Sub
```

RaiseError is a simple utility function to raise errors if necessary in the various classes. The RemovingClass function is called to remove objects from the WatchCollection collection when they are no longer needed.

```
' Raise an error
Public Sub RaiseError(errnum&, cls$, desc$)
    Dim usenum&
    usenum& = errnum& + vbObjectError
    Err.Raise Number:=usenum, source:="dwWatcher." & cls, Description:=desc
End Sub

Public Sub RemovingClass(o As Object)
    Dim obj As Object
    Dim counter&
    For counter = 1 To WatchCollection.Count
        If WatchCollection.Item(counter) Is o Then
            WatchCollection.Remove counter
        End If
    Next counter

End Sub
```

The header for this form (Listing 14.3) is very simple, consisting of just a few label controls with text and a timer. When the form unloads, the frmptr variable is cleared to make sure memory is released properly. The main purpose for this form is the Timer routine which simply calls the TimerEvent function in each class object. This approach allows a single timer to support many applications and class objects.

Listing 14.3   Form WATCH.FRM

```
Private Sub Form_Unload(Cancel As Integer)
    Set frmptr = Nothing    ' Free object
End Sub

' Call the timer event for each object
Private Sub Timer1_Timer()
    Dim obj As Object
    For Each obj In WatchCollection
        obj.TimerEvent
    Next obj
End Sub
```

The dwAppWatch class is used to watch for the termination of another process. It is shown in Listing 14.4.

Listing 14.4   Class dwAppWatch

```
VERSION 1.¯ CLASS
BEGIN
  MultiUse = -1  'True
END
Attribute VB_Name = "dwAppWatch"
Attribute VB_Creatable = True
Attribute VB_Exposed = True
Option Explicit
```

The class keeps a reference to the object provided by the other application. It also keeps track of the identifier of the process that it is watching for. The class maintains an internal state machine in which it is either idling, waiting for a process to terminate, or idling after a process has terminated.

```
Private CallbackObject As Object

' Process handle to watch
Private processhnd As Long
Private nprocessid As Long

' Internal state machine for dwAppWatch object
' ¯ - Idle
' 1 - Waiting on process to terminate
' 2 - Process has terminated
Private state As Integer
```

The client application can take an object containing a method to call back when the process terminates. The function uses the agIsValidName function in APIGID.DLL to make sure that the object actually has a dwAppTerminated function defined. An error occurs if the function is not defined. You don't actually have to call this function to use the class—it can be used without callbacks by just polling the Signaled property—but this type of polling can be accomplished easily from within an application and there is no benefit in doing it with a separate application.

```
' Set the callback object - make sure it is valid
Public Sub SetAppCallback(o As Object)
    If agIsValidName(o, "dwAppTerminated") = Ø Then
        RaiseError 3, "dwAppWatch", "Callback object function undefined"
        Exit Sub
    End If
```

```
    Set CallbackObject = o
End Sub
```

The dwAppWatch class has two properties: Signaled, which returns TRUE if the process has terminated, and ProcessId, which can be used by the client on receipt of the dwAppTerminated function to determine which process terminated.

```
Public Property Get Signaled() As Boolean
    If state = 2 Then Signaled = True Else Signaled = False
End Property

Public Property Get ProcessId() As Long
    ProcessId = nprocessid
End Property
```

The SetAppWatch function initializes the class and starts the process of watching for termination. An error occurs if the object is already being used to watch for a process to terminate or if a process handle cannot be obtained. As soon as the object is added to the WatchCollection class, the TimerEvent function for the class will be called repeatedly by the timer control on the watch form.

```
Public Sub SetAppWatch(ByVal pid&)
    ' If we're already watching a process, error
    If state = 1 Then
        RaiseError 1, "dwAppWatch", "Application already attached"
        Exit Sub
    End If
    processhnd = OpenProcess(SYNCHRONIZE, True, pid)
    If processhnd = ˉ Then
        RaiseError 2, "dwAppWatch", "Unable to open specified process"
        Exit Sub
    End If
    ' Set the new state
    nprocessid = pid
    state = 1
    ' Add this object to main collection
    WatchCollection.Add Me
End Sub
```

The timer event polls the state of the watched process using WaitForSingleObject. When the process is signaled, the handle to the process is closed and the object enters the idle signaled state. If a callback has been defined, the class tries to call the callback function. This will fail if the parent application has been closed. The class ignores this error. Once the process is signaled, the object is removed from the collection.

```
' Called by the timer routine
Public Sub TimerEvent()
```

```
        Dim res&
        If state = ¯ Or state = 2 Then Exit Sub
        res = WaitForSingleObject(processhnd, ¯)
        Select Case res
            Case WAIT_OBJECT_¯
                Call CloseHandle(processhnd)
                state = 2
                On Error GoTo cantcallback
                If Not (CallbackObject Is Nothing) Then
                    CallbackObject.dwAppTerminated Me
                End If
                On Error GoTo ¯
                ' Pull object off the timer list
                RemovingClass Me

            Case WAIT_FAILED
                Call CloseHandle(processhnd)
                state = ¯
        End Select
        Exit Sub
cantcallback:
        Resume Next
End Sub
```

Whereas the dwAppWatch project is designed specifically to watch for the termination of a process, the dwSyncWatch class (Listing 14.5) is designed to watch for the signaling of any system object. It is very similar to dwApp-Watch with the following exceptions:

- It keeps track of the original handle which can be retrieved using the ObjectHandle property. This allows the called application to determine which callback was invoked in cases where multiple callback objects are in use.

- The SetObjectWatch function requires two parameters: the object handle and the process identifier of the source project. The function uses these parameters with the DuplicateHandle function to obtain a duplicate handle to the system object that is local to the server process.

- The calling application should implement function dwSyncWatch which will be called when the system object is signaled.

Listing 14.5   Class dwSyncWatch

```
VERSION 1.¯ CLASS
BEGIN
  MultiUse = -1  'True
END
Attribute VB_Name = "dwSyncWatch"
```

Listing 14.5   Class dwSyncWatch (Continued)

```
Attribute VB_Creatable = True
Attribute VB_Exposed = True
Option Explicit

Private CallbackObject As Object

' Synchronization Object handle to watch
Private synchnd As Long
' Original object handle as known in the source
' process - for identification purposes only.
Private originalhnd As Long

' Internal state machine for dwSyncWatch object
' ¯ - Idle
' 1 - Waiting on object to signal
' 2 - Object has been signalled
Private state As Integer

Public Property Get Signaled() As Boolean
    If state = 2 Then Signaled = True Else Signaled = False
End Property

' Called by the timer routine
Public Sub TimerEvent()
    Dim res&
    If state = ¯ Or state = 2 Then Exit Sub
    res = WaitForSingleObject(synchnd, ¯)
    Select Case res
        Case WAIT_OBJECT_¯
            Call CloseHandle(synchnd)
            state = 2
            On Error GoTo synccallerr
            If Not (CallbackObject Is Nothing) Then
                CallbackObject.dwSignaled Me
            End If
            On Error GoTo ¯
            ' Pull object off the timer list
            RemovingClass Me

        Case WAIT_FAILED
            Call CloseHandle(synchnd)
            state = ¯
    End Select
    Exit Sub
synccallerr:
    Resume Next
End Sub
```

Listing 14.5   Class dwSyncWatch (Continued)

```
' pid = Process ID of calling process
' objhnd = Handle of object to watch
Public Sub SetObjectWatch(ByVal pid&, ByVal objhnd&)
    Dim srcprocesshnd&
    Dim res&
    ' If we're already watching a process, error
    If state = 1 Then
        RaiseError 1, "dwSyncWatch", "Object already being watched"
        Exit Sub
    End If
    originalhnd = objhnd
    ' Open the process as a source for DuplicaeHandle
    srcprocesshnd = OpenProcess(PROCESS_DUP_HANDLE, True, pid)
    If srcprocesshnd = ¯ Then
        RaiseError 2, "dwSyncWatch", "Unable to open the source process"
        Exit Sub
    End If
    res = DuplicateHandle(srcprocesshnd, objhnd, GetCurrentProcess(), synchnd, _
SYNCHRONIZE, False, ¯)
    ' Close the source process handle
    Call CloseHandle(srcprocesshnd)
    If res = ¯ Then
        RaiseError 4, "dwSyncWatch", "Unable to duplicate source handle"
        Exit Sub
    End If
    ' Set the new state
    state = 1
    ' Add this object to main collection
    WatchCollection.Add Me
End Sub

Public Property Get ObjectHandle() As Long
    ObjectHandle = originalhnd
End Property


' Set the callback object - make sure it is valid
Public Sub SetAppCallback(o As Object)
    If agIsValidName(o, "dwSignaled") = ¯ Then
        RaiseError 3, "dwSyncWatch", "Callback object function undefined"
        Exit Sub
    End If

    Set CallbackObject = o
End Sub
```

PipeSrc.vbp/PipeDest.vpb: Anonymous Pipes Example

The PipeSrc and PipeDest projects demonstrate the use of anonymous pipes to allow a process to communicate with a child process. Both samples use file pipe.bas which contains the function declarations and constants for the projects. Both projects include a single form that includes a text box and a label control. The PipeSrc program launches the PipeDest application and opens a pipe to that program. Set the focus to the text box on the PipeSrc program. As you type into the text box, you'll see the text appear in the text box for the PipeDest program. Listing 14.6 shows the code for PIPE.BAS. Listing 14.7 shows the code for form PIPESRC.FRM and Listing 14.8 shows PIPEDEST.FRM.

Listing 14.6   **PIPE.BAS**

```
Attribute VB_Name = "Pipe"
Option Explicit

Type STARTUPINFO
        cb As Long
        lpReserved As String
        lpDesktop As String
        lpTitle As String
        dwX As Long
        dwY As Long
        dwXSize As Long
        dwYSize As Long
        dwXCountChars As Long
        dwYCountChars As Long
        dwFillAttribute As Long
        dwFlags As Long
        wShowWindow As Integer
        cbReserved2 As Integer
        lpReserved2 As Long
        hStdInput As Long
        hStdOutput As Long
        hStdError As Long
End Type

Type PROCESS_INFORMATION
        hProcess As Long
        hThread As Long
        dwProcessId As Long
        dwThreadId As Long
End Type

Type SECURITY_ATTRIBUTES
        nLength As Long
        lpSecurityDescriptor As Long
```

Listing 14.6   PIPE.BAS (Continued)

```
        bInheritHandle As Long
End Type

Type OVERLAPPED
        Internal As Long
        InternalHigh As Long
        offset As Long
        OffsetHigh As Long
        hEvent As Long
End Type

Declare Function CreatePipe Lib "kernel32" (phReadPipe As Long, phWritePipe As _
Long, lpPipeAttributes As SECURITY_ATTRIBUTES, ByVal nSize As Long) As Long
Declare Function ConnectNamedPipe Lib "kernel32" (ByVal hNamedPipe As Long, _
ByVal lpOverlapped As Long) As Long
Declare Function DisconnectNamedPipe Lib "kernel32" (ByVal hNamedPipe As Long) _
As Long
Declare Function SetNamedPipeHandleState Lib "kernel32" (ByVal hNamedPipe As _
Long, lpMode As Long, lpMaxCollectionCount As Long, lpCollectDataTimeout _
As Long) As Long
Declare Function GetNamedPipeInfo Lib "kernel32" (ByVal hNamedPipe As Long, _
lpFlags As Long, lpOutBufferSize As Long, lpInBufferSize As Long, _
lpMaxInstances As Long) As Long
Declare Function PeekNamedPipe Lib "kernel32" (ByVal hNamedPipe As Long, _
lpBuffer As Any, ByVal nBufferSize As Long, lpBytesRead As Long, _
lpTotalBytesAvail As Long, lpBytesLeftThisMessage As Long) As Long
Declare Function GetStdHandle Lib "kernel32" (ByVal nStdHandle As Long) As Long
Declare Function SetStdHandle Lib "kernel32" (ByVal nStdHandle As Long, ByVal _
nHandle As Long) As Long
Declare Function WriteFile Lib "kernel32" (ByVal hFile As Long, lpBuffer As _
Any, ByVal nNumberOfBytesToWrite As Long, lpNumberOfBytesWritten As Long, _
ByVal lpOverlapped As Long) As Long
Declare Function WriteFileAsync Lib "kernel32" Alias "WriteFile" (ByVal hFile _
As Long, lpBuffer As Any, ByVal nNumberOfBytesToWrite As Long, _
lpNumberOfBytesWritten As Long, lpOverlapped As OVERLAPPED) As Long
Declare Function ReadFileAsync Lib "kernel32" (ByVal hFile As Long, lpBuffer _
As Any, ByVal nNumberOfBytesToRead As Long, lpNumberOfBytesRead As Long, _
lpOverlapped As OVERLAPPED) As Long
```

Listing 14.6   PIPE.BAS (Continued)

```
Declare Function ReadFile Lib "kernel32" (ByVal hFile As Long, lpBuffer As Any, _
ByVal nNumberOfBytesToRead As Long, lpNumberOfBytesRead As Long, ByVal _
lpOverlapped As Long) As Long
Declare Function CreateProcess Lib "kernel32" Alias "CreateProcessA" (ByVal _
lpApplicationName As String, ByVal lpCommandLine As String, lpProcessAttributes _
As SECURITY_ATTRIBUTES, lpThreadAttributes As SECURITY_ATTRIBUTES, ByVal _
bInheritHandles As Long, ByVal dwCreationFlags As Long, lpEnvironment As Any, _
ByVal lpCurrentDirectory As String, lpStartupInfo As STARTUPINFO, _
lpProcessInformation As PROCESS_INFORMATION) As Long
Declare Function CloseHandle Lib "kernel32" (ByVal hObject As Long) As Long
Declare Function DuplicateHandle Lib "kernel32" (ByVal hSourceProcessHandle As _
Long, ByVal hSourceHandle As Long, ByVal hTargetProcessHandle As Long, _
lpTargetHandle As Long, ByVal dwDesiredAccess As Long, ByVal bInheritHandle _
As Long, ByVal dwOptions As Long) As Long
Declare Function WaitNamedPipe Lib "kernel32" Alias "WaitNamedPipeA" (ByVal _
lpNamedPipeName As String, ByVal nTimeOut As Long) As Long
Declare Function CreateFile Lib "kernel32" Alias "CreateFileA" (ByVal _
lpFileName As String, ByVal dwDesiredAccess As Long, ByVal dwShareMode _
As Long, ByVal lpSecurityAttributes As Long, ByVal dwCreationDisposition As _
Long, ByVal dwFlagsAndAttributes As Long, ByVal hTemplateFile As Long) As Long
Declare Function CreateNamedPipe Lib "kernel32" Alias "CreateNamedPipeA" (ByVal _
lpName As String, ByVal dwOpenMode As Long, ByVal dwPipeMode As Long, ByVal _
nMaxInstances As Long, ByVal nOutBufferSize As Long, ByVal nInBufferSize As _
Long, ByVal nDefaultTimeOut As Long, ByVal lpSecurityAttributes As Long) As Long
Declare Function WaitForSingleObject Lib "kernel32" (ByVal hHandle As Long, _
ByVal dwMilliseconds As Long) As Long
Declare Function CreateEvent Lib "kernel32" Alias "CreateEventA" (ByVal _
lpEventAttributes As Long, ByVal bManualReset As Long, ByVal bInitialState _
As Long, ByVal lpName As String) As Long
Declare Function GetLastError Lib "kernel32" () As Long
Declare Function GetCurrentProcessId Lib "kernel32" () As Long


Public Const STD_INPUT_HANDLE = -1&
Public Const STD_OUTPUT_HANDLE = -11&
Public Const STD_ERROR_HANDLE = -12&
Public Const NORMAL_PRIORITY_CLASS = &H2
Public Const GENERIC_READ = &H8
```

Listing 14.6   PIPE.BAS (Continued)

```
Public Const GENERIC_WRITE = &H4-------
Public Const GENERIC_EXECUTE = &H2-------
Public Const GENERIC_ALL = &H1-------
Public Const OPEN_EXISTING = 3
Public Const FILE_ATTRIBUTE_NORMAL = &H8-
Public Const INVALID_HANDLE_VALUE = -1
Public Const PIPE_ACCESS_INBOUND = &H1
Public Const PIPE_ACCESS_OUTBOUND = &H2
Public Const PIPE_ACCESS_DUPLEX = &H3
Public Const FILE_FLAG_OVERLAPPED = &H4-------
Public Const PIPE_TYPE_BYTE = &H-
Public Const PIPE_TYPE_MESSAGE = &H4
Public Const WAIT_FAILED = -1&
Public Const WAIT_OBJECT_- = -
Public Const WAIT_ABANDONED = &H8-&
Public Const WAIT_ABANDONED_- = &H8-&
Public Const WAIT_TIMEOUT = &H1-2&
Public Const WAIT_IO_COMPLETION = &HC-&
Public Const STILL_ACTIVE = &H1-3&
Public Const INFINITE = -1&
Public Const ERROR_PIPE_CONNECTED = 535&
```

Listing 14.7   PIPESRC.FRM

```
VERSION 5.--
Begin VB.Form frmPipeSource
    Caption        =   "Pipe Source"
    ClientHeight   =   22-5
    ClientLeft     =   1-95
    ClientTop      =   1515
    ClientWidth    =   378-
    Height         =   261-
    Left           =   1-35
    LinkTopic      =   "Form1"
    ScaleHeight    =   22-5
    ScaleWidth     =   378-
    Top            =   117-
    Width          =   39--
    Begin VB.TextBox txtSrc
        Height       =   1215
        Left         =   18-
        TabIndex     =   -
        Top          =   72-
        Width        =   3315
    End
    Begin VB.Label Label1
```

Listing 14.7   PIPESRC.FRM (Continued)

```
            Caption         =    "Type into the text box:"
            Height          =    255
            Left            =    18¯
            TabIndex        =    1
            Top             =    24¯
            Width           =    3375
      End
End
Attribute VB_Name = "frmPipeSource"
Attribute VB_GlobalNameSpace = False
Attribute VB_Creatable = False
Attribute VB_PredeclaredId = TrueAttribute VB_Exposed = False
Option Explicit

Dim destdir$

Dim hPipeRead&
Dim hPipeWrite&
```

On load, the application starts by creating an anonymous pipe using the CreatePipe function which returns handles to the input and output side of the pipe. It then sets the standard input handle to the output (read) side of the pipe. The PIPEDEST.EXE child application is launched using the CreateProcess function. This function must be used because it allows you to use a security descriptor object that tells windows that the child should inherit the object handles of the parent application. In this case, the child will inherit the standard input handle which contains the output side of the pipe. The application should then close the handles to the process and thread.

Whenever a key is entered into the text box, the character value is written into the input side of the pipe.

```
Private Sub Form_Load()
    Dim si As STARTUPINFO
    Dim pi As PROCESS_INFORMATION
    Dim sa As SECURITY_ATTRIBUTES
    Dim res&
    Dim holdstd&
    destdir$ = InputBox$("Enter directory containing PipeDest.exe", , _
    "d:\zdbook3\source\ch14\")
    sa.nLength = Len(sa)
    sa.bInheritHandle = True
    si.cb = Len(si)
    res = CreatePipe(hPipeRead, hPipeWrite, sa, ¯)
    If res = ¯ Then
        MsgBox "Can't create the pipe"
```

```
            Exit Sub
        End If
        Call SetStdHandle(STD_INPUT_HANDLE, hPipeRead)
        ' The child process inherits the handle
        res = CreateProcess(destdir & "PipeDest.exe", vbNullString, sa, sa, _
        True, NORMAL_PRIORITY_CLASS, ByVal ¯&, vbNullString, si, pi)
        If res = ¯ Then
            MsgBox "Can't create process"
            Unload Me
            Exit Sub
        End If
        ' Always close the process handles
        Call CloseHandle(pi.hProcess)
        Call CloseHandle(pi.hThread)

End Sub


Private Sub Form_Unload(Cancel As Integer)
    If hPipeWrite <> ¯ Then
        Call CloseHandle(hPipeWrite)
    End If
End Sub


Private Sub txtSrc_KeyPress(KeyAscii As Integer)
    Dim char As Byte
    Dim res&
    char = KeyAscii
    Dim written&
    res = WriteFile(hPipeWrite, char, 1, written, ¯)
    KeyAscii = ¯
End Sub
```

Listing 14.8   PIPEDEST.FRM

```
VERSION 5.¯¯
Begin VB.Form frmPipeDest
    Caption         =   "Pipe Destination"
    ClientHeight    =   294¯
    ClientLeft      =   1155
    ClientTop       =   486¯
    ClientWidth     =   4725
    Height          =   3345
    Left            =   1¯95
    LinkTopic       =   "Form1"
    ScaleHeight     =   294¯
    ScaleWidth      =   4725
    Top             =   4515
    Width           =   4845
```

Listing 14.8   PIPEDEST.FRM (Continued)

```
Begin VB.Timer Timer1
   Enabled       =   ¯     'False
   Interval      =   1¯¯
   Left          =   432¯
   Top           =   ¯
End
Begin VB.TextBox txtDest
   Height        =   2295
   Left          =   18¯
   MultiLine     =   -1    'True
   TabIndex      =   ¯
   Top           =   48¯
   Width         =   4335
End
Begin VB.Label Label1
   Caption       =   "Incoming Data:"
   Height        =   255
   Left          =   18¯
   TabIndex      =   1
   Top           =   12¯
   Width         =   3375
End
End
Attribute VB_Name = "frmPipeDest"
Attribute VB_GlobalNameSpace = False
Attribute VB_Creatable = False
Attribute VB_PredeclaredId = TrueAttribute VB_Exposed = False
Option Explicit
Dim PipeHandle As Long
```

The destination application starts by retrieving the inherited input handle.

```
Private Sub Form_Load()
    PipeHandle = GetStdHandle(STD_INPUT_HANDLE)
    Timer1.Enabled = True
End Sub
Private Sub Form_Unload(Cancel As Integer)
    If PipeHandle <> ¯ Then
        Call CloseHandle(PipeHandle)
    End If
End Sub
```

This sample uses the polling technique to prevent the application from being suspended by the read operation. It uses the PeekNamePipe function to see if any data has been entered into the pipe. If it finds any information, it reads the available data from the pipe, moves it into a string buffer (since we only wrote single bytes into the pipe), then converts it into Unicode and appends it to the contents of the text box.

```
Private Sub Timer1_Timer()
    Dim res&
    Dim x&
    Dim t$
    Dim lread&, lavail&, lmessage&
    res = PeekNamedPipe(PipeHandle, ByVal ¯&, ¯, lread, lavail, lmessage)
    ' MsgBox res & lread & lavail & lmessage & " E: " & Hex$(GetLastError)
    If res <> ¯ And lavail > ¯ Then
        ReDim inbuf(lavail) As Byte
        res = ReadFile(PipeHandle, inbuf(¯), lavail, lread, ¯)
        ' MsgBox "read: " & lavail, lread
        ' We need to convert into Unicode here.
        t$ = inbuf()
        t$ = StrConv(t$, vbUnicode)
        txtDest = txtDest & t$
    End If
End Sub



Private Sub txtDest_KeyPress(KeyAscii As Integer)
    KeyAscii = ¯
End Sub
```

PipeClnt.vbp/PipeSrv.vpb: Named Pipes Example

The named pipes example demonstrates many of the techniques described in this chapter. First, it shows how to implement named pipes both locally and across a network. It also shows how to perform asynchronous data transfer operations using overlapped write operations, expanding on the Chapter 13 Asynch.vbp example.

The PipeSrv program creates a named pipe into which it can write data to any connected client. The program has a timer that continuously increments and displays a counter value. This serves as an indicator that the main application thread is running. The project has three options which are triggered using command buttons, and a label control that displays the current status (see Figure 14.1). Each button triggers a transfer of 200 bytes which are read by the client application one byte at a time (in order to slow the process down and thus emphasize the differences between each type of data transfer). The PipeSrv project can only run successfully on Windows NT, since Windows 95 is not able to create named pipes. The PipeClnt program can run on either platform.

This project has a single form, PIPESRV.FRM, and uses the same PIPE.BAS module as the previous example. Listing 14.9 shows the code for form PIPESRV.FRM.

Figure 14.1
Main form for the
PipeSrv project

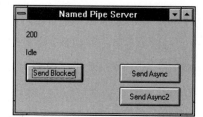

Listing 14.9   PIPESRV.FRM

```
VERSION 5.⁻⁻
Begin VB.Form frmserver
   Caption         =    "Named Pipe Server"
   ClientHeight    =    2175
   ClientLeft      =    1⁻95
   ClientTop       =    1515
   ClientWidth     =  , 426⁻
   Height          =    258⁻
   Left            =    1⁻35
   LinkTopic       =    "Form1"
   ScaleHeight     =    2175
   ScaleWidth      =    426⁻
   Top             =    117⁻
   Width           =    438⁻
   Begin VB.CommandButton cmdAsync2
      Caption      =    "Send Async2"
      Height       =    435
      Left         =    252⁻
      TabIndex     = ,  4
      Top          =    156⁻
      Width        =    1455
   End
   Begin VB.CommandButton sndAsync
      Caption      =    "Send Async"
      Height       =    435
      Left         =    252⁻
      TabIndex     =    3
      Top          =    1⁻2⁻
      Width        =    1455
   End
   Begin VB.CommandButton sndBlocked
      Caption      =    "Send Blocked"
      Height       =    435
      Left         =    24⁻
      TabIndex     =    1
      Top          =    1⁻2⁻
```

Listing 14.9   PIPESRV.FRM (Continued)

```
        Width           =   1395
     End
     Begin VB.Timer Timer1
        Interval        =   5˜
        Left            =   294˜
        Top             =   18˜
     End
     Begin VB.Label lblStat
        Caption         =   "Idle"
        Height          =   195
        Left            =   24˜
        TabIndex        =   2
        Top             =   66˜
        Width           =   1755
     End
     Begin VB.Label Label1
        Caption         =   "Label1"
        Height          =   255
        Left        ,   =   24˜
        TabIndex        =   ˜
        Top             =   24˜
        Width           =   1635
     End
  End
End
Attribute VB_Name = "frmserver"
Attribute VB_GlobalNameSpace = False
Attribute VB_Creatable = False
Attribute VB_PredeclaredId = TrueAttribute VB_Exposed = False
Option Explicit
Dim ctr&
Dim pipehnd&
Dim buffer$
```

The application includes two examples of asynchronous data transfers using an OVERLAPPED structure. Each example uses a different structure to avoid confusion.

```
Dim ol As OVERLAPPED
Dim ol2 As OVERLAPPED
Dim callbackobj As Object
```

On load, the application creates a named pipe. The pipe must be created on the local system. This is a unidirectional pipe which is designed to transfer data only from the server to the client (PIPE_ACCESS_OUTBOUND). Named pipes can also be created as duplex (bi-directional). The pipe is also opened in overlapped mode which means that the pipe supports (but does

not require) asynchronous data transfers. This sample uses a byte type pipe.
On unload the pipe handle is closed.

```
Private Sub Form_Load()
    pipehnd& = CreateNamedPipe("\\.\pipe\vbpgpipe1", PIPE_ACCESS_OUTBOUND _
    Or FILE_FLAG_OVERLAPPED, PIPE_TYPE_BYTE, 1, ¯, ¯, ¯, ¯)
    If pipehnd = ¯ Then
        sndBlocked.Enabled = False
        sndAsync.Enabled = False
        cmdAsync2.Enabled = False
        lblStat.Caption = "Can't create pipe"
    End If

End Sub

Private Sub Form_Unload(Cancel As Integer)
    If pipehnd& <> ¯ Then
        Call CloseHandle(pipehnd)
    End If
End Sub
```

The timer in this application serves two purposes. First, it increments and
displays a counter in the Label1 control. This allows you to see that the primary thread is active and allowing events to be processed. The sndAsync example uses the ol OVERLAPPED structure to control the background data
transfer. A transfer is in progress any time the ol.hEvent object exists (is nonzero) and is not yet signaled. The timer checks for this condition and watches
for the event to be signaled, indicating the end of the data transfer. At that
time the event handle is closed (which also deletes the event), and the caption is reset to indicate that the pipe is idle.

```
Private Sub Timer1_Timer()
    Dim res&
    Label1.Caption = ctr&
    ctr& = ctr& + 1
    If ol.hEvent <> ¯ Then
        ' Async operation is in progress
        res = WaitForSingleObject(ol.hEvent, ¯)
        If res = WAIT_OBJECT_¯ Then
            ' Async read is done
            Call CloseHandle(ol.hEvent)
            ol.hEvent = ¯
            lblStat.Caption = "Idle"
            sndAsync.Enabled = True
        End If
    End If
End Sub
```

The sndBlocked_Click function performs a synchronous data transfer. It
first calls the ConnectNamedPipe function which waits until a client connects

to the pipe. For the sake of this application, you should be sure the PipeClnt example is running and connected before the function is called. The WriteFile function does not return until all 200 bytes are written, which can take quite a while. You will see that while the data is being transferred, the label1 counter stops incrementing, showing that the thread has been blocked.

```
Private Sub sndBlocked_Click()
    Dim res&
    Dim written&
    ' Wait for a client to appear
    sndBlocked.Enabled = False
    lblStat.Caption = "Waiting for client"
    lblStat.Refresh
    res = ConnectNamedPipe(pipehnd, ¯)
    If res <> ¯ Or (res = ¯ And GetLastError() = ERROR_PIPE_CONNECTED) Then
        lblStat.Caption = "Sending data"
        lblStat.Refresh
        ' Pipe is connected
        buffer$ = String$(2¯¯, ¯)
        res = WriteFile(pipehnd, ByVal buffer, 2¯¯, written, ¯)
    Else
        MsgBox "Client has disconnected"
    End If
    lblStat.Caption = "Idle"
    sndBlocked.Enabled = True
End Sub
```

The sndAsync function creates an event for the ol OVERLAPPED structure which doubles as an indication that a data transfer is in progress. The WriteFile function returns immediately as the data transfer continues in the background. You will see that the label1 counter continues to increment during this operation.

```
Private Sub sndAsync_Click()
    Dim res&
    Dim written&
    ' Wait for a client to appear
    sndAsync.Enabled = False
    ol.hEvent = CreateEvent(¯, True, False, vbNullString)
    If ol.hEvent = ¯ Then
        MsgBox "Can't create event"
        Exit Sub
    End If
    lblStat.Caption = "Waiting for client"
    lblStat.Refresh
    res = ConnectNamedPipe(pipehnd, ¯)

    If res <> ¯ Or (res = ¯ And GetLastError() = ERROR_PIPE_CONNECTED) Then
        lblStat.Caption = "Sending data"
        lblStat.Refresh
```

```
            ' Pipe is connected
            buffer$ = String$(2¯¯, ¯)
            res = WriteFileAsync(pipehnd, ByVal buffer, 2¯¯, written, ol)
        Else
            Call CloseHandle(ol.hEvent)
            ol.hEvent = ¯
            MsgBox "Client has disconnected"
            lblStat.Caption = "Idle"
            sndAsync.Enabled = True
        End If

End Sub
```

The cmdAsync2 function is virtually identical to the sndAsync function. The only difference is that it uses the dwWatcher OLE server to set the dwSignaled callback to indicate when the data transfer is complete. This avoids the need to use a timer to watch for the completion status.

```
Private Sub cmdAsync2_Click()
    Dim res&
    Dim written&
    Set callbackobj = CreateObject("dwWatcher.dwSyncWatch")
    ' Wait for a client to appear
    cmdAsync2.Enabled = False
    ol2.hEvent = CreateEvent(¯, True, False, vbNullString)
    If ol2.hEvent = ¯ Then
        MsgBox "Can't create event"
        Exit Sub
    End If
    lblStat.Caption = "Waiting for client"
    lblStat.Refresh
    res = ConnectNamedPipe(pipehnd, ¯)

    If res <> ¯ Or (res = ¯ And GetLastError() = ERROR_PIPE_CONNECTED) Then
        lblStat.Caption = "Sending data"
        lblStat.Refresh
        ' Pipe is connected
        buffer$ = String$(2¯¯, ¯)
        res = WriteFileAsync(pipehnd, ByVal buffer, 2¯¯, written, ol2)
        ' Turn on the callback object
        Call callbackobj.SetAppCallback(Me)
        Call callbackobj.SetObjectWatch(GetCurrentProcessId(), ol2.hEvent)
    Else
        Call CloseHandle(ol2.hEvent)
        ol2.hEvent = ¯
        MsgBox "Client has disconnected"
        lblStat.Caption = "Idle"
        cmdAsync2.Enabled = True
    End If

End Sub
```

```
Public Sub dwSignaled(o As Object)
    Call CloseHandle(ol2.hEvent)
    ol2.hEvent = ¯
    lblStat.Caption = "Idle"
    cmdAsync2.Enabled = True
End Sub
```

The PipeClnt.vbp Example

Figure 14.2 shows the main form of the PipeClnt project and Listing 14.10 shows the form's code. This client displays the number of bytes received from the pipe. You must click on the check box to connect the client to the pipe and specify the name of the pipe. One interesting experiment is to run the client program on a different computer on the same network as the PipeSrv program and specify the computer name of the server in the pipe name—use the form *servercomputer*\pipe\vbpgpipe1 where *servercomputer* is the name of the computer on which the server is running. You will see that the client connects to the pipe across the network with no trouble.

Figure 14.2

Main form for the PipeClnt project

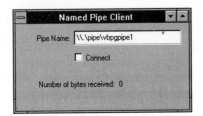

Listing 14.10   FRMCLNT.FRM

```
VERSION 5.¯¯
Begin VB.Form frmClient
    Caption         =    "Named Pipe Client"
    ClientHeight    =    2¯4¯
    ClientLeft      =    1¯95
    ClientTop       =    1515
    ClientWidth     =    423¯
    Height          =    2445
    Left            =    1¯35
    LinkTopic       =    "Form1"
    ScaleHeight     =    2¯4¯
    ScaleWidth      =    423¯
    Top             =    117¯
    Width           =    435¯
```

Listing 14.10   FRMCLNT.FRM (Continued)

```
Begin VB.CheckBox chkConnect
    Caption         =   "Connect"
    Height          =   255
    Left            =   144⁻
    TabIndex        =   4
    Top             =   66⁻
    Width           =   2175
End
Begin VB.Timer Timer1
    Enabled         =   ⁻   'False
    Interval        =   1⁻⁻
    Left            =   36⁻⁻
    Top             =   12⁻⁻
End
Begin VB.TextBox txtPipe
    Height          =   315
    Left            =   144⁻
    TabIndex        =   ⁻
    Text            =   "\\.\pipe\vbpgpipe1"
    Top             =   18⁻
    Width           =   2595
End
Begin VB.Label Label2
    Alignment       =   1  'Right Justify
    Caption         =   "Number of bytes received:"
    Height          =   195
    Left            =   48⁻
    TabIndex        =   3
    Top             =   132⁻
    Width           =   1935
End
Begin VB.Label lblCount
    Caption         =   "⁻"
    Height          =   255
    Left            =   252⁻
    TabIndex        =   2
    Top             =   132⁻
    Width           =   975
End
Begin VB.Label Label1
    Alignment       =   1  'Right Justify
    Caption         =   "Pipe Name:"
    Height          =   255
    Left            =   6⁻
    TabIndex        =   1
    Top             =   24⁻
    Width           =   1275
End
```

Listing 14.10 FRMCLNT.FRM (Continued)

```
End
Attribute VB_Name = "frmClient"
Attribute VB_GlobalNameSpace = False
Attribute VB_Creatable = False
Attribute VB_PredeclaredId = TrueAttribute VB_Exposed = False
Option Explicit
Dim pipehandle&
Dim totalread&
```

When you click on the connect check box, the client waits up to ten seconds for the server to create a pipe that it can connect to. Once it determines that the pipe is available, it uses the CreateFile function to actually open the pipe. If it succeeds, it turns on the timer which will actually read the data from the pipe. The CreateFile function can fail (though it is unlikely) if another client grabs the pipe.

```
Private Sub chkConnect_Click()
    Dim res&
    If chkConnect.Value = 1 Then
        ' Connect to pipe
        res = WaitNamedPipe(txtPipe.Text, 1¯¯¯¯)
        If res = ¯ Then
            MsgBox "Pipe is not available at this time"
            chkConnect.Value = ¯
            Exit Sub
        End If
        ' This could fail if server deletes pipe or other client
        ' grabs it during this time.
        pipehandle = CreateFile(txtPipe.Text, GENERIC_READ, ¯, ¯, _
        OPEN_EXISTING, FILE_ATTRIBUTE_NORMAL, ¯)
        If pipehandle = INVALID_HANDLE_VALUE Then
            MsgBox "Can't open named pipe"
            chkConnect.Value = ¯
            Exit Sub
        End If
        Timer1.Enabled = True
    Else
        Timer1.Enabled = ¯
        If pipehandle <> ¯ Then
            Call CloseHandle(pipehandle)
            pipehandle = ¯
        End If
    End If
End Sub
```

The timer function reads no more than a single byte during each timer event. This is, of course, an extremely poor design since it makes reading data from the pipe extremely slow. The intent here is to clearly illustrate the differences between synchronous and asynchronous data transfers, not to provide efficient data transfer between the processes. The function uses the PeekNamedPipe function to determine if any data is present in the pipe buffer.

```
Private Sub Timer1_Timer()
    Dim inbuf As Byte
    Dim res&
    Dim bytesread&, bytesavail&, bytesleft&
    ' See if any data is waiting in the pipe
    res = PeekNamedPipe(pipehandle, ByVal ¯&, ¯, bytesread, bytesavail, _
    bytesleft)
    If res <> ¯ And bytesavail > ¯ Then
        ' Read a byte off the pipe
        res = ReadFile(pipehandle, inbuf, 1, bytesread, ¯)
        If res And bytesread = 1 Then
            lblCount.Caption = totalread
            totalread = totalread + 1
        End If
    End If
End Sub

Private Sub Form_Unload(Cancel As Integer)
    If pipehandle <> ¯ Then
        Call CloseHandle(pipehandle)
        pipehandle = ¯
    End If
End Sub
```

Suggestions for Further Practice

- Once the PipeSrv example connects to a client program and the client is terminated, the server will not connect again to the client until the program is closed. Modify the program so that you can alternate between multiple clients. (See the DisconnectNamedPipe function.)

- Modify the server so that it can transfer data to several clients at once. (You'll need to create multiple instances of the pipe).

Function Reference

This section contains an alphabetical reference for the functions described in this chapter.

■ CancelWaitableTimer

VB Declaration   `Declare Function CancelWaitableTimer Lib "kernel32" (ByVal hTimer As Long)`

Description   This function cancels a waitable timer operation. The timer remains in its current state and will not restart until explicitly started using the SetWaitableTimer function.

Use with VB   No problem.

Parameter	Type/Description
hTimer	Long—A handle to a waitable timer.

Return Value   Long—Nonzero on success, zero on failure. Sets GetLastError.

Platform   Windows NT 4.0

■ CallNamedPipe

VB Declaration   `Declare Function CallNamedPipe& Lib "kernel32" Alias "CallNamedPipeA" (ByVal _`
`lpNamedPipeName As String, lpInBuffer As Any, ByVal nInBufferSize As Long, _`
`lpOutBuffer As Any, ByVal nOutBufferSize As Long, lpBytesRead As Long, ByVal _`
`nTimeOut As Long)`

Description   This function is called by a client process that wishes to communicate via a pipe. It connects to a pipe if available (waiting for the pipe to become available if necessary). It then reads and writes the data specified, and closes the pipe.

The named pipe must be opened as a message type pipe.

Use with VB   No problem.

Parameter	Type/Description
lpNamedPipeName	String—The name of the pipe to open.
lpInBuffer	Any—A memory buffer containing data to write into the pipe.
nInBufferSize	Long—The number of bytes in the lpInBuffer buffer.
lpOutBuffer	Any—A memory buffer to load with data read from the pipe.
nOutBufferSize	Long—A long variable that will be loaded with data from the pipe.
lpBytesRead	Long—The number of bytes read from the pipe. A single message will be read. If lpOutBuffer is not large enough to hold the entire message, the function will return False and GetLastError will be set to ERROR_MORE_DATA (any bytes left in the message will be lost).

Parameter	Type/Description
nTimeOut	Long—One of the following constants: NMPWAIT_NOWAIT: Returns with an error immediately if the pipe is not available. NMPWAIT_WAIT_FOREVER: Waits forever for the pipe. NMPWAIT_USE_DEFAULT_WAIT: Uses the default timeout for the pipe specified by the CreateNamedPipe function.

Return Value Long—Nonzero on success, zero on failure. Sets GetLastError.

Platform Windows 95, Windows NT

■ ConnectNamedPipe

VB Declaration
```
Declare Function ConnectNamedPipe& Lib "kernel32" (ByVal hNamedPipe As Long, _
lpOverlapped As OVERLAPPED)
```

Description Causes a server to wait until a client connects to a named pipe.

Use with VB No problem.

Parameter	Type/Description
hNamedPipe	Long—A handle to the pipe.
lpOverlapped	OVERLAPPED—Set to null (pass ByVal As Long) to suspend the thread until a client connects to the pipe. Otherwise returns immediately, in which case if the pipe is not already connected, the event object in the lpOverlapped structure will be signaled when the client connects to the pipe. You can then use one of the wait functions to watch for the connection.

Return Value Long—If lpOverlapped is NULL:

Returns TRUE (nonzero) if the pipe is connected, zero if an error occurs or if the pipe is already connected (GetLastError will return ERROR_PIPE_CONNECTED in this case).

If lpOverlapped is valid, returns zero. GetLastError will return ERROR_PIPE_CONNECTED if the pipe is already connected, ERROR_IO_PENDING if the overlapped operation succeeded.

In either case, GetLastError will return ERROR_NO_DATA if a client has closed the pipe and the server has not yet disconnected from the client using the DisconnectNamedPipe function.

Platform Windows NT

Comments You can switch a pipe to connect to another client using this function, but you must first disconnect from the current process using the DisconnectNamedPipe function.

Example PipeSrv.vbp

■ CreateEvent

VB Declaration `Declare Function CreateEvent& Lib "kernel32" Alias "CreateEventA" _`

```
(lpEventAttributes As SECURITY_ATTRIBUTES, ByVal bManualReset As Long, ByVal _
bInitialState As Long, ByVal lpName As String)
```

Description   Creates an event object. Refer to the chapter text for a description of event objects.

Use with VB   No problem.

Parameter	Type/Description
lpEventAttributes	SECURITY_ATTRIBUTES—A structure to set the security of the object. Change to ByVal As Long and pass zero to use default security for the object.
bManualReset	Long—TRUE to create a manual reset event. FALSE to create an auto-reset event.
bInitialState	Long—TRUE if the event should initially be in the signaled state.
lpName	String—The name of the event object. Use vbNullString to create an unnamed event object. If an event with this name already exists, the existing named event is opened. This name may not match the name of an existing mutex, semaphore, waitable timer, or file mapping.

Return Value   Long—A handle to the event object on success, zero on error. Sets GetLastError. GetLastError will be set to ERROR_ALREADY_EXISTS even when a valid handle is returned to indicate that an event with the specified name already existed.

Platform   Windows 95, Windows NT

Comments   Be sure to use CloseHandle to close the event handle when it is no longer needed. The object will be deleted when all handles to it are closed.

Example   PipeSrv.vbp, PipeClnt.vbp, Asynch.vbp (see Chapter 13).

■ CreateMailslot

VB Declaration
```
Declare Function CreateMailslot& Lib "kernel32" Alias "CreateMailslotA" (ByVal _
lpName As String, ByVal nMaxMessageSize As Long, ByVal lReadTimeout As Long, _
lpSecurityAttributes As SECURITY_ATTRIBUTES)
```

Description   Creates a mailslot. The handle returned is used by the mailslot server (message recipient).

Use with VB   No problem.

Parameter	Type/Description
lpName	String—The name of the mailslot in the form \\.\mailslot\[path\]mailslotname. Refer to the chapter text for information on valid mailslot names.
nMaxMessageSize	Long—The maximum length of a mailslot message. Zero for unlimited. Note that the maximum length is 400 for messages broadcast across a network domain to multiple mailslots.

Parameter	Type/Description
lReadTimeout	Long—The default timeout to use on a mailslot read operation when waiting for data specified in milliseconds. Zero for no wait. The constant MAILSLOT_WAIT_FOREVER to wait until data arrives.
lpSecurity-Attributes	SECURITY_ATTRIBUTES—A SECURITY_ATTRIBUTES structure or pass zero (declare the parameter as ByVal As Long and pass zero) to use a default descriptor that does not allow inheritance.

Return Value Long—A handle to the mailslot on success, INVALID_HANDLE_VALUE on error. Sets GetLastError.

Platform Windows 95, Windows NT

Comments Refer to the chapter text for additional information on mailslots.

Example MailSlot.vbp

■ CreateMutex

VB Declaration
```
Declare Function CreateMutex& Lib "kernel32" Alias "CreateMutexA" _
(lpMutexAttributes As SECURITY_ATTRIBUTES, ByVal bInitialOwner As Long, ByVal _
lpName As String)
```

Description Creates a mutex.

Use with VB No problem.

Parameter	Type/Description
lpMutexAt-tributes	SECURITY ARRTIBUTES—SECURITY_ATTRIBUTES structure or pass zero (declare the parameter as ByVal As Long and pass zero) to use a default descriptor that does not allow inheritance.
bInitialOwner	Long—TRUE if the creating process wishes to own the mutex immediately. A mutex may be owned by only one thread at a time.
lpName	String—The name of the mutex object. Use vbNullString to create an unnamed mutex object. If an event with this name already exists, the existing named mutex is opened. This name may not match the name of an existing event, semaphore, waitable timer, or file mapping.

Return Value Long—A handle to the mutex object on success, zero on error. Sets GetLastError. GetLastError will be set to ERROR_ALREADY_EXISTS even when a valid handle is returned to indicate that a mutex with the specified name already existed.

Platform Windows 95, Windows NT

Comments Be sure to use CloseHandle to close the mutex handle when it is no longer needed. The object will be deleted when all handles to it are closed.

Be sure to release the mutex before the process terminates. Failing to do so will mark the mutex as abandoned and release ownership automatically. Other applications sharing the mutex may still use it, but will receive an abandoned status that suggests that the last owning process did not shut down normally. Whether this matters or not depends on the applications involved.

Example ckClient.vbp, ckServe.vbp

■ CreateNamedPipe

VB Declaration
```
Declare Function CreateNamedPipe& Lib "kernel32" Alias "CreateNamedPipeA" _
(ByVal lpName As String, ByVal dwOpenMode As Long, ByVal dwPipeMode As Long, _
ByVal nMaxInstances As Long, ByVal nOutBufferSize As Long, ByVal nInBufferSize _
As Long, ByVal nDefaultTimeOut As Long, lpSecurityAttributes As _
SECURITY_ATTRIBUTES)
```

Description Creates a named pipe. The handle returned is used by the server side of the pipe.

Use with VB No problem.

Parameter	Type/Description
lpName	String—The name of the pipe in the form \\.\pipe*pipename*. May be up to 256 characters long and is not case-sensitive. If a pipe with this name already exists, a new instance of the pipe is created.
dwOpen-Mode	Long—A combination of the following groups of constants: One of the following (must be the same for all instances of the pipe): PIPE_ACCESS_DUPLEX: The pipe is bi-directional. PIPE_ACCESS_INBOUND: Data flows from the client to the server. PIPE_ACCESS_OUTBOUND: Data flows from the server to the client. Any combination of the following: FILE_FLAG_WRITE_THROUGH: On byte-type pipes across a network, forces data to be transferred across the network on each read or write operation. Otherwise, transfer may be delayed. FILE_FLAG_OVERLAPPED: Enables (but does not require) asynchronous (overlapped) operations using this pipe. The constants WRITE_DAC, WRITE_OWNER, and ACCESS_SYSTEM_SECURITY that provide additional security options.
dwPipeMode	Long—A combination of the following groups of constants: One of the following constants (all instances of a pipe must specify the same constant here): PIPE_TYPE_BYTE: Data is written to the pipe as a continuous byte data stream. PIPE_TYPE_MESSAGE: Data is written to the pipe in blocks of data called messages. One of the following constants: PIPE_READMODE_PIPE: Data is read from the pipe as individual bytes. PIPE_READMODE_MESSAGE: Data is read from the pipe in blocks of data called messages (requires that PIPE_TYPE_MESSAGE be specified). One of the following constants: PIPE_WAIT: Synchronous operations suspend the thread while waiting. PIPE_NOWAIT: (Not recommended!) Synchronous operations return immediately. This provides an obsolete method for asynchronous transfers and has been replaced by the Win32 overlapped transfer mechanism.

Parameter	Type/Description
nMax-Instances	Long—The maximum number of instances of this pipe that can be created. Must be a value between 1 and the constant. PIPE_UNLIMITED_INSTANCES. Must be the same for all instances of the pipe.
nOutBuffer-Size	Long—The recommended output buffer size. Zero for default.
nInBufferSize	Long—The recommended input buffer size. Zero for default.
nDefault-TimeOut	Long—The default wait timeout for the pipe. Must be the same for all instances of a pipe.
lpSecurity-Attributes	SECURITY_ATTRIBUTES—SECURITY_ATTRIBUTES structure or pass zero (declare the parameter as ByVal As Long and pass zero) to use a default descriptor that does not allow inheritance.

Return Value Long—The pipe handle on success. INVALID_HANDLE_VALUE on error. Sets GetLastError.

Platform Windows NT only (unfortunately)

Example PipeSrv.vbp, PipeClnt.vbp

■ CreatePipe

VB Declaration `Declare Function CreatePipe& Lib "kernel32" (phReadPipe As Long, phWritePipe As _`
`Long, lpPipeAttributes As SECURITY_ATTRIBUTES, ByVal nSize As Long)`

Description Creates an anonymous pipe.

Use with VB No problem.

Parameter	Type/Description
phReadPipe	Long—A variable that will be set to a handle to the read (output) side of the pipe.
phWritePipe	Long—A variable that will be set to a handle to the write (input) side of the pipe.
lpPipeAttributes	SECURITY_ATTRIBUTES—A SECURITY_ATTRIBUTES structure or pass zero (declare the parameter as ByVal As Long and pass zero) to use a default descriptor that does not allow inheritance.
nSize	Long—Recommended size for the pipe buffer. Zero to use default.

Return Value Long—Nonzero on success, zero on failure. Sets GetLastError.

Platform Windows 95, Windows NT

Comments   Anonymous pipes do not support asynchronous operations, so if you write into a pipe and the buffer is full, the write function will not return until the other process reads data from the pipe to clear space in the buffer.

Example   PipeSrc.vbp, PipeDest.vbp

■ CreateProcess

VB Declaration
```
Declare Function CreateProcess& Lib "kernel32" Alias "CreateProcessA" (ByVal _
   lpApplicationName As String, ByVal lpCommandLine As String, lpProcessAttributes _
   As SECURITY_ATTRIBUTES, lpThreadAttributes As SECURITY_ATTRIBUTES, ByVal _
   bInheritHandles As Long, ByVal dwCreationFlags As Long, lpEnvironment As Any, _
   ByVal lpCurrentDirectory As String, lpStartupInfo As STARTUPINFO, _
   lpProcessInformation As PROCESS_INFORMATION)
```

Description   Creates a new process (for example, executes a program).

Use with VB   No problem.

Parameter	Type/Description
lpApplication-Name	String—The name of the application to execute. May be vbNullString, in which case the application name should appear at the start of the lp-CommandLine parameter.
lpCommandLine	String—The command line to execute. The command line for a process may be retrieved using the GetCommandLine function. Windows will use the following standard Windows search sequence to find the executable if necessary: 1. The directory containing the executable of the parent process. 2. The current directory of the parent process. 3. The system directory as returned by GetSystemDirectory. 4. On Windows NT only: The 16-bit system directory. 5. The Windows directory as returned by GetWindowsDirectory. 6. The directories specified by the PATH environment variable.
lpProcess-Attributes	SECURITY_ATTRIBUTES—A SECURITY_ATTRIBUTES structure or pass zero (declare the parameter as ByVal As Long and pass zero) to use a default descriptor that does not allow inheritance. This defines the security for the process.
lpThread-Attributes	SECURITY_ATTRIBUTES—A SECURITY_ATTRIBUTES structure or pass zero (declare the parameter as ByVal As Long and pass zero) to use a default descriptor that does not allow inheritance. This defines security for the primary thread of the process.
bInheritHandles	Long—TRUE to allow all handles in the current process to be inherited by the newly created child process.

Parameter	Type/Description
dwCreationFlags	Long—One or more of the constants defined in API32.TXT with the prefix CREATE_???. The following are of use to VB programmers: CREATE_SEPARATE_WOW_VDM: (NT only) When launching a 16-bit Windows application, forces it to run in its own memory space. CREATE_SHARED_WOW_VDM: (NT only) When launching a 16-bit Windows application, forces it to run in the shared 16-bit virtual machine. CREATE_SUSPENDED: Suspends the new process immediately. It does not run until the ResumeThread function is called. Refer to your online Win32 documentation for information on the ResumeThread function. Also one of the following constants specifying the priority class: IDLE_PRIORITY_CLASS: The new process should have very low priority—running only when the system is idle. Base value 4. HIGH_PRIORITY_CLASS: The new process should have very high priority, preempting most applications. Base value 13. Avoid using this priority. NORMAL_PRIORITY_CLASS: Standard priority. Base value 9 if the process is in the foreground, 7 if in the background. Do not use REALTIME_PRIORITY_CLASS with Visual Basic.
lpEnvironment	Any—A pointer to an environment block (the first byte in an environment buffer, or an address to an environment block). Refer to Chapter 6 for information on environment blocks and functions to work with them.
lpCurrent-Directory	String—The path of the current directory for the new process. Use vbNullString to specify the current directory in use when the function is called.
lpStartupInfo	STARTUPINFO—A STARTUPINFO structure containing additional information used in creating the process. This structure is defined in Appendix B.
lpProcessInformation	PROCESS_INFORMATION—A structure to load with the process and thread identifiers of the new process, and a new process and thread handle for the new process. In most cases, the parent application will close the two handles immediately on return of this function. Refer to the chapter text for additional information.

Return Value   Long—Nonzero on success, zero on failure. Sets GetLastError.

Platform   Windows 95, Windows NT

Example   Launch.vbp

■ CreateSemaphore

VB Declaration
```
Declare Function CreateSemaphore& Lib "kernel32" Alias "CreateSemaphoreA" _
(lpSemaphoreAttributes As SECURITY_ATTRIBUTES, ByVal lInitialCount As Long, _
ByVal lMaximumCount As Long, ByVal lpName As String)
```

Description   Creates a new semaphore.

Use with VB   No problem.

Parameter	Type/Description
lpSemaphore-Attributes	SECURITY_ATTRIBUTES—A SECURITY_ATTRIBUTES structure or pass zero (declare the parameter as ByVal As Long and pass zero) to use a default descriptor that does not allow inheritance.
lInitialCount	Long—Sets the initial count of the semaphore. May be zero to lMaximumCount.
lMaximumCount	Long—Sets the maximum count of the semaphore.
lpName	String—The name of the semaphore object. Use vbNullString to create an unnamed semaphore object. If a semaphore with this name already exists, the existing named semaphore is opened. This name may not match the name of an existing mutex, event, waitable timer, or file mapping.

Return Value   Long—A handle to the semaphore object on success, zero on error. Sets GetLastError. GetLastError will be set to ERROR_ALREADY_EXISTS even when a valid handle is returned to indicate that a semaphore with the specified name already existed.

Platform   Windows 95, Windows NT

Comments   Be sure to use CloseHandle to close the semaphore handle when it is no longer needed. The object will be deleted when all handles to it are closed.

The semaphore will be signaled whenever its value is greater than zero. The ReleaseSemaphore function increments the semaphore's count, calling a wait function on a semaphore decrements its count when it succeeds.

■ CreateWaitableTimer

VB Declaration
```
Declare Function CreateWaitableTimer Lib "kernel32" Alias _
"CreateWaitableTimerA" (lpSemaphoreAttributes As SECURITY_ATTRIBUTES, _
ByVal bManualReset As Long, ByVal lpName As String) As Long
```

Description   Creates a waitable timer object. Refer to the chapter text for a description of waitable timer objects.

Use with VB   No problem.

Parameter	Type/Description
lpTimerAt-tributes	SECURITY_ATTRIBUTES—A structure to set the security of the object. Change to ByVal As Long and pass zero to use default security for the object.
bManualReset	Long—TRUE to create a manual reset timer. FALSE to create an auto-reset timer.
lpName	String—The name of the waitable timer object. Use vbNullString to create an unnamed event object. If a waitable timer with this name already exists, the existing named waitable timer is opened. This name may not match the name of an existing event, mutex, semaphore, or file mapping.

Return Value   Long—A handle to the waitable timer object on success, zero on error. Sets GetLastError. Get-LastError will be set to ERROR_ALREADY_EXISTS even when a valid handle is returned to indicate that an event with the specified name already existed.

Platform   Windows NT 4.0

Comments   Be sure to use CloseHandle to close the event handle when it is no longer needed. The object will be deleted when all handles to it are closed.

Example   sleeper.vbp.

■ DisconnectNamedPipe

VB Declaration   `Declare Function DisconnectNamedPipe& Lib "kernel32" (ByVal hNamedPipe As Long)`

Description   Disconnects a client from a named pipe.

Use with VB   No problem.

Parameter	Type/Description
hNamedPipe	Long—A handle to a pipe.

Return Value   Long—Nonzero on success, zero on failure. Sets GetLastError.

Platform   Windows NT

Comments   If the client has not yet closed the pipe handle from its end, an error will occur next time it tries to access the pipe.

■ DuplicateHandle

VB Declaration   `Declare Function DuplicateHandle& Lib "kernel32" (ByVal hSourceProcessHandle As _`
`Long, ByVal hSourceHandle As Long, ByVal hTargetProcessHandle As Long, _`
`lpTargetHandle As Long, ByVal dwDesiredAccess As Long, ByVal bInheritHandle As _`
`Long, ByVal dwOptions As Long)`

Description   Creates a new handle to an existing system object given an existing handle to that object. The existing handle may be in a different process.

Use with VB   No problem.

Parameter	Type/Description
hSourceProcess-Handle	Long—A handle to the process that owns the source handle. Use the GetCurrentProcess if the source handle belongs to the current process.
hSourceHandle	Long—An existing handle to the object.
hTargetProcess-Handle	Long—A handle to the process that will own the new object handle. Use the GetCurrentProcess if the source handle belongs to the current process.

Parameter	Type/Description
lpTargetHandle	Long—A long variable to load with the new handle.
dwDesired-Access	Long—The level of security access desired for the new handle. Ignored if dwOptions has DUPLICATE_SAME_ACCESS specified. Possible access depends on the type of object and is listed in Table 14.10.
bInheritHandle	Long—TRUE if the new handle is inheritable by child processes of hSourceProcessHandle.
dwOptions	Long—One or both of the following constants: DUPLICATE_SAME_ACCESS: The new handle has the same security access as the original. DUPLICATE_CLOSE_SOURCE: The original handle is closed. It is closed even if an error occurs.

Return Value   Long—Nonzero on success, zero on failure. Sets GetLastError.

Platform   Windows 95, Windows NT

Comments   This function can create a new handle in one process based on an existing handle in a different process. The function may be called from either process. The process handles must provide PROCESS_DUP_HANDLE access for the function to succeed.

Objects whose handles may be duplicated include consoles, files (including communication devices), file mappings, events, waitable timers, mutexes, pipes, processes, registry keys, semaphores, and threads.

Example   dwWatch.vbp

Table 14.10   Access Constants for Different System Objects

System Objects	Access Constants
Files, consoles, pipes, and communication devices	GENERIC_READ, GENERIC_WRITE (see CreateFile for descriptions)
File mappings	FILE_MAP_READ, FILE_MAP_WRITE, FILE_MAP_ALL_ACCESS (see MapViewOfFile for descriptions)
Mutexes	MUTEX_ALL_ACCESS, SYNCHRONIZE (see OpenMutex for descriptions)
Semaphores	SEMAPHORE_ALL_ACCESS, SEMAPHORE_MODIFY_STATE, SYNCHRONIZE (see OpenSemaphore for descriptions)
Events	EVENT_ALL_ACCESS, EVENT_MODIFY_STATE, SYNCHRONIZE (see OpenEvent for descriptions)
Registry Keys	KEY_??? constants—see API32.TXTSYNCHRONIZE
Process	PROCESS_??? constants—see API32.TXT SYNCHRONIZE

Table 14.10   Access Constants for Different System Objects (Continued)

System Objects	Access Constants
Thread	THREAD_??? constants—see API32 TXTSYNCHRONIZE
Waitable Timers	TIMER_ALL_ACCESS, TIMER_MODIFY_STATE, SYNCHRO-NIZE (see OpenWaitableTimer for descriptions)

■ ExitProcess

VB Declaration   `Declare Sub ExitProcess Lib "kernel32" (ByVal uExitCode As Long)`

Description   Terminates a process.

Use with VB   You should avoid trying to close processes using this function. Do not use on your own VB applications. Instead, try posting a WM_CLOSE message to the main window of the application you wish to close. This message is discussed further in Chapter 16.

Parameter	Type/Description
uExitCode	Long—An exit code for the terminating process.

■ FindCloseChangeNotification

VB Declaration   `Declare Function FindCloseChangeNotification& Lib "kernel32" (ByVal _`
`hChangeHandle As Long)`

Description   Closes a change notification object.

Use with VB   No problem.

Parameter	Type/Description
hChangeHandle	Long—A handle to a file change notification object to close.

Return Value   Long—Nonzero on success, zero on failure. Sets GetLastError.

Platform   Windows 95, Windows NT

■ FindExecutable

VB Declaration   `Declare Function FindExecutable& Lib "shell32.dll" Alias "FindExecutableA" _`
`(ByVal lpFile As String, ByVal lpDirectory As String, ByVal lpResult As String)`

Description   Finds the file name of the program that is associated with a specified file. The Windows registration editor can be used to associate types of files with particular applications. For example, text files that have the extension .TXT are typically associated with the Windows Notepad (NOTEPAD.EXE). Selecting any file with the .TXT extension in the file manager causes the file manager to load it into Notepad.

Use with VB	No problem.

Parameter	Type/Description
lpFile	String—A program name or a file name for which to find an associated program.
lpDirectory	String—The full path of the default directory to use.
lpResult	String—A string buffer to load with the name of the executable program. found for lpszFile. This string should be preallocated to be at least MAX_PATH characters long.

Return Value	Long—Greater than 32 on success. 31 if no association exists. 0 if the system is out of memory or resources. ERROR_FILE_NOT_FOUND if the file does not exist. ERROR_PATH_NOT_FOUND if the path does not exist. ERROR_BAD_FORMAT if the executable format is invalid.
Platform	Windows 95, Windows NT, Win16

■ FindFirstChangeNotification

VB Declaration	Declare Function FindFirstChangeNotification& Lib "kernel32" Alias _ "FindFirstChangeNotificationA" (ByVal lpPathName As String, ByVal bWatchSubtree _ As Long, ByVal dwNotifyFilter As Long)
Description	Creates a file notification object. This object is used to watch for changes in the file system.
Use with VB	No problem.

Parameter	Type/Description
lpPathName	String—The directory path to watch.
bWatchSubtree	Long—TRUE to watch all subdirectories of lpPathName.
dwNotifyFilter	Long—One or more of the constants with the prefix FILE_NOTIFY_CHANGE_??? specifying the conditions that will signal the object.

Return Value	Long—The handle of a change notification object on success. INVALID_HANDLE_VALUE on failure. Sets GetLastError.
Platform	Windows 95, Windows NT
Comments	Use the FileCloseChangeNotification function to close this handle, not the CloseHandle function.

■ FindNextChangeNotification

VB Declaration	Declare Function FindNextChangeNotification& Lib "kernel32" (ByVal _ hChangeHandle As Long)
Description	Resets a file change notification object to watch for the next change.

Use with VB	No problem.

Parameter	Type/Description
hChangeHandle	Long—A handle of a file change notification object to reset.

Return Value	Long—Nonzero on success, zero on failure. Sets GetLastError.
Platform	Windows 95, Windows NT

■ FreeLibrary

VB Declaration	`Declare Function FreeLibrary& Lib "kernel32" (ByVal hLibModule As Long)`
Description	Frees the specified dynamic link library that has been loaded using the LoadLibrary API function.
Use with VB	This function should be used only to free DLLs that were explicitly loaded by your application. Each call to LoadLibrary should be balanced with a matching FreeLibrary call.

Parameter	Type/Description
hLibModule	Long—A handle to a library module.

Return Value	Long—Nonzero on success, zero on failure. Sets GetLastError.
Platform	Windows 95, Windows NT, Win16

■ GetCurrentProcess

VB Declaration	`Declare Function GetCurrentProcess& Lib "kernel32" ()`
Description	Obtains a pseudohandle to the current process.
Use with VB	No problem.
Return Value	Long—A pseudohandle to the current process.
Platform	Windows 95, Windows NT
Comments	This handle may be used anywhere a process handle to the current process is needed. The handle may be duplicated but may not be inherited. There is no need to call the CloseHandle function to close this handle.
Example	dwWatch.vbp

■ GetCurrentProcessId

VB Declaration	`Declare Function GetCurrentProcessId& Lib "kernel32" ()`
Description	Obtains the unique process identifier of the current process.

Use with VB	No problem.
Return Value	Long—The current process identifier.
Platform	Windows 95, Windows NT
Example	Shelled1.vbp

■ GetCurrentThread

VB Declaration	`Declare Function GetCurrentThread& Lib "kernel32" ()`
Description	Obtains a pseudohandle to the current thread.
Use with VB	No problem.
Return Value	Long—A pseudohandle to the current thread.
Platform	Windows 95, Windows NT
Comments	This handle may be used anywhere a thread handle to the current thread is needed (it is not valid in the context of any other thread). The handle may be duplicated but may not be inherited. There is no need to call the CloseHandle function to close this handle.

■ GetCurrentThreadId

VB Declaration	`Declare Function GetCurrentThreadId& Lib "kernel32" ()`
Description	Obtains the unique process identifier of the current thread.
Use with VB	No problem.
Return Value	Long—The current thread identifier.
Platform	Windows 95, Windows NT

■ GetExitCodeProcess

VB Declaration	`Declare Function GetExitCodeProcess& Lib "kernel32" (ByVal hProcess As Long, _` `lpExitCode As Long)`
Description	Retrieves the exit code of a terminated process.
Use with VB	No problem.

Parameter	Type/Description
hProcess	Long—A handle of the process whose exit code you wish to obtain.
lpExitCode	Long—A long variable to load with the process exit code. Set to the constant STILL_ACTIVE if the process has not yet terminated.

Return Value Long—Nonzero on success, zero on failure. Sets GetLastError.

Platform Windows 95, Windows NT

■ GetExitCodeThread

VB Declaration `Declare Function GetExitCodeThread& Lib "kernel32" (ByVal hThread As Long, _`
`lpExitCode As Long)`

Description Retrieves the exit code of a terminated thread.

Use with VB No problem.

Parameter	Type/Description
hThread	Long—A handle of the thread whose exit code you wish to obtain.
lpExitCode	Long—A long variable to load with the thread exit code. Set to the constant STILL_ACTIVE if the thread has not yet terminated.

Return Value Long—Nonzero on success, zero on failure. Sets GetLastError.

Platform Windows 95, Windows NT

■ GetHandleInformation

VB Declaration `Declare Function GetHandleInformation& Lib "kernel32" (ByVal hObject As Long, _`
`lpdwFlags As Long)`

Description Retrieves information about a system object handle.

Use with VB No problem.

Parameter	Type/Description
hObject	Long—The handle to test.
lpdwFlags	Long—A bit flag with one or more of the following constants set: HANDLE_FLAG_INHERIT: This object can be inherited by a child process. HANDLE_FLAG_PROTECT_FROM_CLOSE: The handle cannot be closed using the CloseHandle function.

Return Value Long—Nonzero on success, zero on failure. Sets GetLastError.

Platform Windows NT

■ GetMailslotInfo

VB Declaration `Declare Function GetMailslotInfo& Lib "kernel32" (ByVal hMailslot As Long, _`
`lpMaxMessageSize As Long, lpNextSize As Long, lpMessageCount As Long, _`
`lpReadTimeout As Long)`

Description   Obtains information about a mailslot.

Use with VB   No problem.

Parameter	Type/Description
hMailslot	Long—A handle to a mailslot.
lpMaxMessage-Size	Long—A long variable to load with the maximum message size for this mailslot.
lpNextSize	Long—A long variable to load with the size of the next message. May be the constant MAILSLOT_NO_MESSAGE if no message is ready.
lpMessageCount	Long—A long variable to load with the number of messages ready in the mailslot.
lpReadTimeout	Long—A long variable to load with the default read timeout for the mailslot.

Return Value   Long—Nonzero on success, zero on failure. Sets GetLastError.

Platform   Windows 95, Windows NT

■ GetModuleFileName

VB Declaration   `Declare Function GetModuleFileName& Lib "kernel32" Alias "GetModuleFileNameA" _`
`(ByVal hModule As Long, ByVal lpFileName As String, ByVal nSize As Long)`

Description   Retrieves the full path name of a loaded module.

Use with VB   No problem.

Parameter	Type/Description
hModule	Long—A handle to a module. This can be a DLL module or the instance handle of an application.
lpFileName	String—String buffer to load with the NULL terminated path name to the file from which module hModule was loaded. This string should be preallocated to be at least nSize+1 characters long.
nSize	Long—The maximum number of characters to load into buffer lpFileName.

Return Value   Long—The actual number of bytes copied into lpFileName on success, zero on error. Sets GetLastError.

Platform   Windows 95, Windows NT, Win16

Comments   Under Windows 95, the function checks to see if the internal version number of the application is 4.0 or greater. If so, a long file name is returned, otherwise a short file name is returned.

■ GetModuleHandle

VB Declaration   Declare Function GetModuleHandle& Lib "kernel32" Alias "GetModuleHandleA" _
                      (ByVal lpModuleName As String)

Description   Retrieves the module handle for an application or dynamic link library.

Use with VB   No problem.

Parameter	Type/Description
lpModuleName	String—The name of the module. This is usually the same as the name of the module's file name. For example, the NOTEPAD.EXE program has the module file name of NOTEPAD.

Return Value   Long—The module handle on success, zero on error. Sets GetLastError.

Platform   Windows 95, Windows NT, Win16

Comments   This handle is only valid within the context of the current process.

■ GetNamedPipeHandleState

VB Declaration   Declare Function GetNamedPipeHandleState& Lib "kernel32" Alias _
                      "GetNamedPipeHandleStateA" (ByVal hNamedPipe As Long, lpState As Long, _
                      lpCurInstances As Long, lpMaxCollectionCount As Long, lpCollectDataTimeout As _
                      Long, ByVal lpUserName As String, ByVal nMaxUserNameSize As Long)

Description   Use to obtain current state information about a named pipe.

Use with VB   No problem.

Parameter	Type/Description
hNamedPipe	Long—A handle to a named pipe.
lpState	Long—A variable to load with one or more of the following constants: PIPE_NOWAIT: The pipe is set to never block. This mode is rarely used. PIPE_READMODE_MESSAGE: The pipe is set to read messages.
lpCurInstances	Long—A variable to load with the number of instances of this pipe that currently exist.
lpMaxCollectionCount	Long—A variable to load with the maximum amount of data that can be queued before being sent through the pipe if the pipe is set to transfer data across a network.
lpCollectDataTimeout	Long—A variable to load with the longest time that will elapse before a network data transfer if this pipe is set to transfer data across a network.
lpUserName	String—If this is the server handle, this a buffer that will be loaded with the user name of the client application. May be vbNullString in which case the information will not be retrieved.
nMaxUserNameSize	Long—The length of the lpUserName buffer. May be zero.

Return Value	Long—Nonzero on success, zero on failure. Sets GetLastError.
Platform	Windows 95, Windows NT

■ GetNamedPipeInfo

VB Declaration
```
Declare Function GetNamedPipeInfo& Lib "kernel32" (ByVal hNamedPipe As Long, _
lpFlags As Long, lpOutBufferSize As Long, lpInBufferSize As Long, _
lpMaxInstances As Long)
```

Description Use to obtain information about a named pipe.

Use with VB No problem.

Parameter	Type/Description
hNamedPipe	Long—A handle to a named pipe.
lpFlags	Long—One or more of the following constants: PIPE_CLIENT_END: This handle is the client side of a pipe. N/A for NT 3.51. PIPE_SERVER_END: This handle is the server side of a pipe. N/A for NT 3.51. PIPE_TYPE_MESSAGE: This pipe is configured to transfer blocks of data as messages.
lpOutBufferSize	Long—A variable to load with the output buffer size. Set to zero if the buffer is allocated by the system as necessary.
lpInBufferSize	Long—A variable to load with the input buffer size. Set to zero if the buffer is allocated by the system as necessary.
lpMaxInstances	Long—A variable to load with the maximum number of instances of this pipe that can be created. PIPE_UNLIMITED_INSTANCES if there is no limit.

Return Value	Long—Nonzero on success, zero on failure. Sets GetLastError.
Platform	Windows 95, Windows NT

■ GetPriorityClass

VB Declaration
```
Declare Function GetPriorityClass& Lib "kernel32" (ByVal hProcess As Long)
```

Description Retrieves the current priority class of a process.

Use with VB No problem.

Parameter	Type/Description
hProcess	Long—A handle to a process.

Return Value Long—The priority class of the process. Zero on error. Sets GetLastError.

Platform   Windows 95, Windows NT

Comments Refer to the dwCreationFlags parameter of the CreateProcess function for a description of priority classes.

■ GetProcessShutdownParameters

VB Declaration
```
Declare Function GetProcessShutdownParameters& Lib "kernel32" (lpdwLevel As _
Long, lpdwFlags As Long)
```

Description Retrieves information regarding when this process would be shut down relative to other processes when the system closes.

Use with VB No problem.

Parameter	Type/Description
lpdwLevel	Long—A value from 0 to &H4FF. Higher numbered applications are closed first during system shutdown. Default is &H280.
lpdwFlags	Long—SHUTDOWN_NORETRY. When a process shutdown times out, a retry dialog box is normally displayed. Setting this flag prevents the dialog from appearing and the process is shut down directly.

Return Value Long—Nonzero on success, zero on failure.

Platform   Windows NT

■ GetProcessTimes

VB Declaration
```
Declare Function GetProcessTimes& Lib "kernel32" (ByVal hProcess As Long, _
lpCreationTime As FILETIME, lpExitTime As FILETIME, lpKernelTime As FILETIME, _
lpUserTime As FILETIME)
```

Description Obtain information about elapsed time for a process.

Use with VB No problem.

Parameter	Type/Description
hProcess	Long—A handle to a process.
lpCreationTime	FILETIME—A FILETIME structure to load with the time at which the process was created.
lpExitTime	FILETIME—A FILETIME structure to load with the time at which the process was terminated (undefined if the process is still running).
lpKernelTime	FILETIME—A FILETIME structure to load with the total amount of time that the process has spent running in kernel mode.
lpUserTime	FILETIME—A FILETIME structure to load with the total amount of time that the process has spent running in user mode.

Return Value	Long—TRUE (nonzero) on success, zero on error. Sets GetLastError.
Platform	Windows NT

■ GetProcessWorkingSetSize

VB Declaration
```
Declare Function GetProcessWorkingSetSize& Lib "kernel32" (ByVal hProcess As _
Long, lpMinimumWorkingSetSize As Long, lpMaximumWorkingSetSize As Long)
```

Description   Retrieves information about the amount of memory committed to an application while it is running.

Use with VB   No problem.

Parameter	Type/Description
hProcess	Long—A handle to a process.
lpMinimumWorkingSetSize	Long—A variable to load with the minimum working set for the process.
lpMaximumWorkingSetSize	Long—A variable to load with the maximum working set for the process.

Return Value   Long—TRUE (nonzero) on success, zero on error. Sets GetLastError.

Platform   Windows NT

Comments   The operating system's virtual memory system will try to keep at least as much memory as specified as the minimum working set committed to the application while it is running. It will not try to allocate more than the maximum working set unless there is free memory available.

■ GetStartupInfo

VB Declaration
```
Declare Sub GetStartupInfo Lib "kernel32" Alias "GetStartupInfoA" _
(lpStartupInfo As STARTUPINFO)
```

Description   Retrieves the startup information for a process.

Use with VB   No problem.

Parameter	Type/Description
lpSartupInfo	STARTUPINFO—A STARTUPINFO structure to load with the start up information for the process.

Platform   Windows 95, Windows NT

■ GetThreadPriority

VB Declaration   `Declare Function GetThreadPriority& Lib "kernel32" (ByVal hThread As Long)`

Description   Retrieves the priority setting for the specified thread.

Use with VB	No problem.

Parameter	Type/Description
hThread	Long—A handle to a thread.

Return Value   Long—One of the constants with the prefix THREAD_PRIORITY_??? specifying the priority of the thread. **THREAD_PRIORITY_ERROR_RETURN** on error.

Platform   Windows 95, Windows NT

Comments   The thread priority is combined with the priority class for the process to set the actual priority of the thread.

■ GetThreadTimes

VB Declaration
```
Declare Function GetThreadTimes& Lib "kernel32" (ByVal hThread As Long, _
lpCreationTime As FILETIME, lpExitTime As FILETIME, lpKernelTime As FILETIME, _
lpUserTime As FILETIME)
```

Description   Obtains information about elapsed time for a thread.

Use with VB   No problem.

Parameter	Type/Description
hThread	Long—A handle to a thread.
lpCreationTime	FILETIME—A FILETIME structure to load with the time at which the thread was created.
lpExitTime	FILETIME—A FILETIME structure to load with the time at which the thread was terminated (undefined if the thread is still running).
lpKernelTime	FILETIME—A FILETIME structure to load with the total amount of time that the thread has spent running in kernel mode.
lpUserTime	FILETIME—A FILETIME structure to load with the total amount of time that the thread has spent running in user mode.

Return Value   Long—TRUE (nonzero) on success, zero on error. Sets GetLastError.

Platform   Windows NT

■ GetWindowThreadProcessId

VB Declaration
```
Declare Function GetWindowThreadProcessId& Lib "user32" (ByVal hwnd As Long, _
lpdwProcessId As Long)
```

Description   Obtain the identifiers of a thread and process that are associated with a window.

Use with VB	No problem.	
	Parameter	**Type/Description**
	hwnd	Long—A window handle.
	lpdwProcessId	Long—A variable to load with the process identifier of the process that owns a window.

Return Value   Long—The identifier of the thread that owns a window.

Platform   Windows 95, Windows NT

■ InterlockedDecrement

VB Declaration   `Declare Function InterlockedDecrement& Lib "kernel32" (lpAddend As Long)`

Description   Decrements a long variable.

Use with VB	No problem.	
	Parameter	**Type/Description**
	lpAddend	Long—A long variable to decrement.

Return Value   Long—The previous value of the variable.

Platform   Windows 95, Windows NT

Comments   The decrement operation performed by this function is safe from synchronization problems, even if it is a shared variable.

■ InterlockedExchange

VB Declaration   `Declare Function InterlockedExchange& Lib "kernel32" (Target As Long, ByVal _`
`Value As Long)`

Description   Sets the value of a long variable.

Use with VB	No problem.	
	Parameter	**Type/Description**
	Target	Long—The variable to set.
	Value	Long—The new value for the variable.

Return Value   Long—The previous value of the variable.

Platform   Windows 95, Windows NT

Comments   The operation performed by this function is safe from synchronization problems, even if it is a shared variable.

InterlockedIncrement

VB Declaration Declare Function InterlockedIncrement& Lib "kernel32" (lpAddend As Long)

Description Increments a long variable.

Use with VB No problem.

Parameter	Type/Description
lpAddend	Long—A long variable to increment.

Return Value Long—The previous value of the variable.

Platform Windows 95, Windows NT

Comments The increment operation performed by this function is safe from synchronization problems, even if it is a shared variable.

LoadLibrary

VB Declaration Declare Function LoadLibrary& Lib "kernel32" Alias "LoadLibraryA" (ByVal _
lpLibFileName As String)

Description Loads the specified dynamic link library and maps it into the address space for the current process. Once loaded, it is possible to access resources in the library.

Use with VB No problem.

Parameter	Type/Description
lpLibFileName	String—The name of the dynamic link library to load. Follows the same search sequence as that specified by the lpCommandLine parameter of the CreateProcess function.

Return Value Long—A handle to the library module on success, zero on error. Sets GetLastError.

Platform Windows 95, Windows NT, Win16

Comments Use the FreeLibrary function to free the DLL when it is no longer needed. Windows keeps track of how many times a DLL has been loaded and does not actually unmap the DLL from memory until the module usage count is reduced to zero.

LoadLibraryEx

VB Declaration Declare Function LoadLibraryEx& Lib "kernel32" Alias "LoadLibraryExA" (ByVal _
lpLibFileName As String, ByVal hFile As Long, ByVal dwFlags As Long)

Description Loads the specified dynamic link library and maps it into the address space for the current process. Once loaded, it is possible to access resources in the library.

Use with VB	No problem.

Parameter	Type/Description
lpLibFileName	String—The name of the dynamic link library to load. Follows the same search sequence as that specified by the lpCommandLine parameter of the CreateProcess function.
hFile	Long—Unused, set to zero.
dwFlags	Long—One or more of the following constants: DONT_RESOLVE_DLL_REFERENCES: Does not initialize the DLL. NT only. LOAD_LIBRARY_AS_DATAFILE: Does not prepare the DLL for execution. Can improve performance when loading a DLL only to access its resources. LOAD_WITH_ALTERED_SEARCH_PATH: If lpLibFileName includes a path, and the DLL needs to load additional DLLs, they are first searched for in the path included in the lpLibFileName directory instead of first searching the directory from which the application was loaded.

Return Value	Long—A handle to the library module on success, zero on error. Sets GetLastError.
Platform	Windows 95, Windows NT
Comments	Use the FreeLibrary function to free the DLL when it is no longer needed. Windows keeps track of how many times a DLL has been loaded and does not actually unmap the DLL from memory until the module usage count is reduced to zero.

■ LoadModule

VB Declaration	`Declare Function LoadModule& Lib "kernel32" (ByVal lpModuleName As String, _` `lpParameterBlock As Any)`
Description	Loads a Windows application and executes it in the environment specified.
Use with VB	No problem.

Parameter	Type/Description
lpModuleName	String—The name of the executable to load. Follows the same search sequence as that specified by the lpCommandLine parameter of the CreateProcess function.
lpParameter-Block	Any—A structure specifying the parameters for loading the new application. This structure is described in Appendix B.

Return Value	Long—Greater than 32 on success. See the return value of the FindExecutable function for additional information.
Platform	Windows 95, Windows NT, Win16

■ MsgWaitForMultipleObjects

VB Declaration
```
Declare Function MsgWaitForMultipleObjects& Lib "user32" (ByVal nCount As Long, _
pHandles As Long, ByVal fWaitAll As Long, ByVal dwMilliseconds As Long, ByVal _
dwWakeMask As Long)
```

Description
Waits for either a single object or an entire list of objects to become signaled, for the specified timeout to elapse, or for a specified type of message to arrive in the input queue for the thread. Returns immediately if the return condition is already met.

Use with VB
No problem.

Parameter	Type/Description
nCount	Long—The number of handles in the list.
pHandles	Long—The first element in an array of object handles.
fWaitAll	Long—TRUE to wait until all of the objects are signaled simultaneously. FALSE to wait until any one object is signaled.
dwMilliseconds	Long—The number of milliseconds to wait. Returns immediately if zero. Waits forever if necessary if the constant INFINITE is specified.
dwWakeMask	Long—One or more of the constants with the prefix QS_??? indicating the type of message whose arrival can cause this function to return.

Return Value
Long—If bWaitAll is true, one of the following constants on success.
WAIT_ABANDONED_0 if all of the objects are signaled and one or more of them is a mutex that became signaled when the process that owned it terminated.
WAIT_TIMEOUT if the objects remain unsignaled and the wait function timed out.
WAIT_OBJECT_0 if all of the objects are signaled.
WAIT_IO_COMPLETION (WaitForSingleObjectEx only)—Function returned because an I/O completion operation is ready to be executed.
Returns WAIT_FAILED on failure and sets GetLastError.
If bWaitAll is false, the results are similar except that it might also be a positive offset from either WAIT_ABANDONED_0 or WAIT_OBJECT_0 indicating which object was either abandoned or signaled. For example, a result of WAIT_OBJECT_0 + 5 indicates that the fifth object in the list was signaled.
WAIT_OBJECT_0 + nCount if the function returned because of the arrival of a message that met the criteria specified by dwWakeMask.

Platform
Windows 95, Windows NT. On Windows NT the object handles must have SYNCHRONIZE access specified.

Comments
If the function returns because an object was signaled, this function has additional effects depending on the type of object as follows:

- Semaphore: Increments the semaphore count.

- Mutex: Grants ownership of the mutex to the calling thread.

- Auto-Reset event: Sets the event signaled state back to false.

- Auto-Reset waitable timers: Sets the timer state back to false.

This function ignores messages that are already present in the input queue—it only returns on receipt of a new message.

■ OpenEvent

VB Declaration   Declare Function OpenEvent& Lib "kernel32" Alias "OpenEventA" (ByVal _
dwDesiredAccess As Long, ByVal bInheritHandle As Long, ByVal lpName As String)

Description   Creates a new handle to an existing named event object.

Use with VB   No problem.

Parameter	Type/Description
dwDesired-Access	Long—One of the following constants: EVENT_ALL_ACCESS: Requests full access to the event object. EVENT_MODIFY_STATE: Enables the SetEvent and ResetEvent functions. SYNCHRONIZE: Allows use of the event object for synchronization.
bInheritHandle	Long—TRUE if you want child processes to be able to inherit the handle.
lpName	String—The name of the object to open.

Return Value   Long—A handle to the object on success, zero on error. Sets GetLastError.

Platform   Windows 95, Windows NT

Comments   Be sure to use CloseHandle to close the event handle when it is no longer needed. The object will be deleted when all handles to it are closed.

Example   Similar to the OpenMutex function demonstrated in ckClient.vbp.

■ OpenMutex

VB Declaration   Declare Function OpenMutex& Lib "kernel32" Alias "OpenMutexA" (ByVal _
dwDesiredAccess As Long, ByVal bInheritHandle As Long, ByVal lpName As String)

Description   Creates a new handle to an existing named mutex object.

Use with VB   No problem.

Parameter	Type/Description
dwDesired-Access	Long—One of the following constants: MUTEX_ALL_ACCESS: Requests full access to the mutex object. SYNCHRONIZE: Allows use of the event object for synchronization and the ReleaseMutex function.
bInheritHandle	Long—TRUE if you want child processes to be able to inherit the handle.
lpName	String—The name of the object to open.

Return Value   Long—A handle to the object on success, zero on error. Sets GetLastError.

Platform   Windows 95, Windows NT

Comments	Be sure to use CloseHandle to close the mutex handle when it is no longer needed. The object will be deleted when all handles to it are closed.
Example	ckClient.vbp

■ OpenProcess

VB Declaration

```
Declare Function OpenProcess& Lib "kernel32" (ByVal dwDesiredAccess As Long, _
ByVal bInheritHandle As Long, ByVal dwProcessId As Long)
```

Description   Opens a handle to an existing process.

Use with VB   No problem.

Parameter	Type/Description
dwDesired-Access	Long—The access requested for this handle. One or more of the constants specified by the prefix PROCESS_??? as listed in API32.TXT.
bInheritHandle	Long—TRUE if the handle can be inherited by child processes.
dwProcessId	Long—The process identifier of the process to open.

Return Value   Long—A handle to the process on success. Zero on error. Sets GetLastError.

Platform   Windows 95, Windows NT

Comments   This function is frequently used to open a process for synchronization.

Example   dwWatch.vbp, Launch.vbp

■ OpenSemaphore

VB Declaration

```
Declare Function OpenSemaphore& Lib "kernel32" Alias "OpenSemaphoreA" (ByVal _
dwDesiredAccess As Long, ByVal bInheritHandle As Long, ByVal lpName As String)
```

Description   Creates a new handle to an existing named semaphore object.

Use with VB   No problem.

Parameter	Type/Description
dwDesiredAccess	Long—One of the following constants: SEMAPHORE_ALL_ACCESS: Requests full access to the event object. SEMAPHORE_MODIFY_STATE: Enables the ReleaseSemaphore function. SYNCHRONIZE: Allows use of the event object for synchronization.
bInheritHandle	Long—TRUE if you want child processes to be able to inherit the handle.
lpName	String—The name of the object to open.

Return Value   Long—A handle to the object on success, zero on error. Sets GetLastError.

Platform   Windows 95, Windows NT

Comments   Be sure to use CloseHandle to close the semaphore handle when it is no longer needed. The object will be deleted when all handles to it are closed.

Example   Similar to the OpenMutex function demonstrated in ckClient.vbp.

■ OpenWaitableTimer

VB Declaration
```
Declare Function OpenWaitableTimer Lib "kernel32" Alias "OpenWaitableTimerA" _
(ByVal dwDesiredAccess As Long, ByVal bInheritHandle As Long, ByVal lpName As _
String) As Long
```

Description   Creates a new handle to an existing waitable timer object.

Use with VB   No problem.

Parameter	Type/Description
dwDesired-Access	Long—One of the following constants: TIMER_ALL_ACCESS: Requests full access to the event object. EVENT_MODIFY_STATE: Enables the SetWaitableTimer and CancelWaitableTimer functions. SYNCHRONIZE: Allows use of the waitable timer object for synchronization.
bInheritHandle	Long—TRUE if you want child processes to be able to inherit the handle.
lpName	String—The name of the object to open.

Return Value Long—A handle to the object on success, zero on error. Sets GetLastError.

Platform   Windows NT 4.0

Comments   Be sure to use CloseHandle to close the waitable timer handle when it is no longer needed. The object will be deleted when all handles to it are closed.

Example   Sleeper.vbp

■ PeekNamedPipe

VB Declaration
```
Declare Function PeekNamedPipe& Lib "kernel32" (ByVal hNamedPipe As Long, _
lpBuffer As Any, ByVal nBufferSize As Long, lpBytesRead As Long, _
lpTotalBytesAvail As Long, lpBytesLeftThisMessage As Long)
```

Description   Previews data in a pipe or obtains information about data in a pipe.

Use with VB   No problem.

Parameter	Type/Description
hNamedPipe	Long—A handle to a pipe. This does not have to be a handle to a named pipe—anonymous pipes work as well.

Parameter	Type/Description
lpBuffer	Any—The first byte in a buffer to load with data. May be zero (use ByVal 0&)
nBufferSize	Long—The size of the lpBuffer buffer.
lpBytesRead	Long—A variable to load with the number of bytes loaded into the buffer.
lpTotalBytesAvail	Long—A variable to load with the number of bytes available in the pipe.
lpBytesLeftThis-Message	Long—A variable to load with the number of bytes that remain in the message after this read operation. Set for message-based named pipes only.

Return Value   Long—Nonzero on success, zero on failure. Sets GetLastError.

Platform   Windows 95, Windows NT

Comments   Data read by this function is not actually removed from the pipe. This function is ideal for polling a pipe to see if data is available.

Example   PipeClnt.vbp, PipeDest.vbp

■ PulseEvent

VB Declaration   `Declare Function PulseEvent& Lib "kernel32" (ByVal hEvent As Long)`

Description   Sets the specified event to the signaled state. If the event is a manual-reset event, all threads that are suspended waiting for the event are activated. The function then sets the event back to the nonsignaled state and returns.

        If the event is an auto-reset event, a single thread that is suspended waiting on the event is activated, the event is set back to nonsignaled, and the function returns.

Use with VB   No problem.

Parameter	Type/Description
hEvent	Long—A handle of the event to pulse.

Return Value   Long—Nonzero on success, zero on failure. Sets GetLastError.

Platform   Windows 95, Windows NT

Comments   If a thread is waiting on more than one synchronization object, and the other objects are not already signaled, the thread will not be activated by this function.

■ ReleaseMutex

VB Declaration   `Declare Function ReleaseMutex& Lib "kernel32" (ByVal hMutex As Long)`

Description   Releases a mutex that is owned by a thread.

Use with VB	No problem.	
	Parameter	**Type/Description**
	hMutex	Long—A handle to a mutex.

Return Value	Long—Nonzero on success, zero on failure. Sets GetLastError.
Platform	Windows 95, Windows NT
Comments	A thread gains ownership of a mutex by calling a wait function on the mutex.
Example	ckClient.vbp

◼ ReleaseSemaphore

VB Declaration	``Declare Function ReleaseSemaphore& Lib "kernel32" (ByVal hSemaphore As Long, _`` ``ByVal lReleaseCount As Long, lpPreviousCount As Long)``
Description	Increments a semaphore count.

Use with VB	No problem.	
	Parameter	**Type/Description**
	hSemaphore	Long—A handle to a semaphore.
	lReleaseCount	Long—The amount to add to the semaphore count. Must be at least 1, and must not be large enough to cause the semaphore to exceed its maximum count (the function will fail if this is the case and the count will be unchanged).
	lpPreviousCount	Long—A variable to load with the previous semaphore count.

Return Value	Long—Nonzero on success, zero on failure. Sets GetLastError.
Platform	Windows 95, Windows NT
Comments	Refer to the CreateSemaphore function and chapter text for information on semaphores.

◼ ResetEvent

VB Declaration	``Declare Function ResetEvent& Lib "kernel32" (ByVal hEvent As Long)``
Description	Sets the specified event to the nonsignaled state.

Use with VB	No problem.	
	Parameter	**Type/Description**
	hEvent	Long—A handle to an event.

Return Value	Long—Nonzero on success, zero on failure. Sets GetLastError.

Platform	Windows 95, Windows NT
Comments	This function is not generally used with auto-reset event objects because they reset automatically as soon as a thread that is blocked waiting for a signaled event is released.

■ ResumeThread

VB Declaration   `Declare Function ResumeThread& Lib "kernel32" (ByVal hThread As Long)`

Description   Resumes execution of a thread that was suspended using SuspendThread.

Use with VB   No problem, but not particularly useful.

Parameter	Type/Description
hThread	Long—The handle of the thread to resume.

Return Value   Long—The suspend count before this function was called. &HFFFFFFFF on error. Sets GetLastError.

Platform   Windows 95, Windows NT

Comments   See SuspendThread.

■ SetEvent

VB Declaration   `Declare Function SetEvent& Lib "kernel32" (ByVal hEvent As Long)`

Description   Sets an event to the signaled state.

Use with VB   No problem.

Parameter	Type/Description
hEvent	Long—A handle to an event.

Return Value   Long—Nonzero on success, zero on failure. Sets GetLastError.

Platform   Windows 95, Windows NT

Comments   Manual-reset events remain signaled until explicitly set to non-signaled using the ResetEvent function. AutoReset events will remain signaled until a single thread calls a wait function on the event object.

■ SetHandleInformation

VB Declaration   `Declare Function SetHandleInformation& Lib "kernel32" (ByVal hObject As Long, _`
`ByVal dwMask As Long, ByVal dwFlags As Long)`

Description   Allows you to set certain system object settings.

Use with VB   No problem.

Parameter	Type/Description
hObject	Long—A handle whose settings are being changed.
dwMask	Long—One or more of the mask constants specified by the dwFlags parameter indicating which bits to set.
dwFlags	Long—A bit flag with one or more of the following constants set: HANDLE_FLAG_INHERIT: This object can be inherited by a child process. HANDLE_FLAG_PROTECT_FROM_CLOSE: The handle cannot be closed using the CloseHandle function.

Return Value   Long—Nonzero on success, zero on failure. Sets GetLastError.

Platform   Windows NT

■ SetMailslotInfo

VB Declaration   `Declare Function SetMailslotInfo& Lib "kernel32" (ByVal hMailslot As Long, _`
`ByVal lReadTimeout As Long)`

Description   Allows you to change the default timeout for read operations on a mailslot.

Use with VB   No problem.

Parameter	Type/Description
hMailslot	Long—A handle to the mailslot.
lReadTimeout	Long—The new default timeout in milliseconds. Zero to never wait. MAILSLOT_WAIT_FOREVER to specify an infinite timeout.

Return Value   Long—Nonzero on success, zero on failure. Sets GetLastError.

Platform   Windows 95, Windows NT

■ SetNamedPipeHandleState

VB Declaration   `Declare Function SetNamedPipeHandleState& Lib "kernel32" (ByVal hNamedPipe As _`
`Long, lpMode As Long, lpMaxCollectionCount As Long, lpCollectDataTimeout As _`
`Long)`

Description   Sets information about the operation of a named pipe.

Use with VB   No problem.

Parameter	Type/Description
hNamedPipe	Long—A handle to a named pipe.

lpMode	Long—One or more of the following constants: PIPE_WAIT, PIPE_NOWAIT, PIPE_READMODE_BYTE, PIPE_READMODE_MESSAGE. Refer to the CreateNamedPipe function for information on these flags.
lpMaxCollection Count	Long—The maximum amount of data that can be queued before being sent through the pipe if the pipe is set to transfer data across a network.
lpCollectData-Timeout	Long—The longest time that will elapse before a network data transfer if this pipe is set to transfer data across a network.

Return Value Long—Nonzero on success, zero on failure. Sets GetLastError.

Platform Windows 95, Windows NT

■ SetPriorityClass

VB Declaration `Declare Function SetPriorityClass& Lib "kernel32" (ByVal hProcess As Long, _`
`ByVal dwPriorityClass As Long)`

Description Sets the priority class for a process.

Use with VB No problem.

Parameter	Type/Description
hProcess	Long—A handle to a process.
dwPriorityClass	Long—A constant specifying the new priority class. Refer to the dwCreationFlags parameter of the CreateProcess function for a list of priority classes.

Return Value Long—Nonzero on success, zero on failure. Sets GetLastError.

Platform Windows 95, Windows NT

■ SetProcessShutdownParameters

VB Declaration `Declare Function SetProcessShutdownParameters& Lib "kernel32" (ByVal dwLevel As _`
`Long, ByVal dwFlags As Long)`

Description Sets the order in which this process will be closed during system shutdown relative to other applications in the system.

Use with VB No problem.

Parameter	Type/Description
lpdwLevel	Long—A value from 0 to &H4FF. Higher numbered applications are closed first during system shutdown. Default is &H280.
lpdwFlags	Long—SHUTDOWN_NORETRY. When a process shutdown times out, a retry dialog box is normally displayed. Setting this flag prevents the dialog from appearing and the process is shut down directly.

Return Value   Long—Nonzero on success, zero on failure.

Platform   Windows NT

■ SetProcessWorkingSetSize

VB Declaration   Declare Function SetProcessWorkingSetSize& Lib "kernel32" (ByVal hProcess As _
Long, ByVal dwMinimumWorkingSetSize As Long, ByVal dwMaximumWorkingSetSize As _
Long)

Description   Sets the amount of memory that the operating system will commit to a process.

Use with VB   No problem.

Parameter	Type/Description
hProcess	Long—A handle to a process.
lpMinimum-WorkingSetSize	Long—A variable to load with the minimum working set for the process.
lpMaximum-WorkingSetSize	Long—A variable to load with the maximum working set for the process.

Return Value   Long—TRUE (nonzero) on success, zero on error. Sets GetLastError.

Platform   Windows NT

Comments   The operating system's virtual memory system will try to keep at least as much memory as specified as the minimum working set committed to the application while it is running. It will not try to allocate more than the maximum working set unless there is free memory available.

■ SetThreadPriority

VB Declaration   Declare Function SetThreadPriority& Lib "kernel32" (ByVal hThread As Long, _
ByVal nPriority As Long)

Description   Sets the priority setting for the specified thread.

Use with VB   No problem.

Parameter	Type/Description
hThread	Long—A handle to a thread.
nPriority	Long—One of the constants with the prefix THREAD_PRIORITY_??? specifying the priority of the thread.

Return Value   Long—Nonzero on success, zero on failure. Sets GetLastError.

Platform   Windows 95, Windows NT

Comments   The thread priority is combined with the priority class for the process to set the actual priority of the thread.

■ SetWaitableTimer

VB Declaration
```
Declare Function SetWaitableTimer Lib "kernel32" (ByVal hTimer As Long, _
lpDueTime As FILETIME, ByVal lPeriod As Long, ByVal pfnCompletionRoutine As _
Long, ByVal lpArgToCompletionRoutine As Long, ByVal fResume As Long) As Long
```

Description   Starts a waitable timer. Sets its state to unsignaled.

Use with VB   No problem.

Parameter	Type/Description
hTimer	Long—A handle to a waitable timer.
lpDueTimer	FILETIME—A structure containing a 64-bit time value. If positive, this represents the time at which the timer will be triggered. If negative, this is a duration from the time the function is called. Times are specified in units of 100ns.
lPeriod	Long—If zero, this timer triggers once only. Otherwise the timer will automatically restart with this duration (specified in milliseconds).
pfnCompletion-Routine	Long—Zero or the address of a function to call when the timer triggers. This can be provided using the AddressOf operator using a function in a standard module, or using the dwcbk32d.ocx control provided with this book when used with VB 4.0. The completion routine takes the form: Sub myfunc(ByVal lpArgToCompletion&, ByVal dwTimerLow&, ByVal dwTimerHigh&).
lpArgToCompletionRoutine	Long—A value to pass to the completion routine if specified.
fResume	Long—If TRUE, and the system supports power management, the system will exit power conservation mode when the timer is triggered. GetLastError will be ERROR_NOT_SUPPORTED if this is TRUE and the system does not support power conservation mode.

Return Value   Long—Nonzero on success, zero on failure. Sets GetLastError.

Platform   Windows NT 4.0

■ ShellExecute

VB Declaration
```
Declare Function ShellExecute& Lib "shell32.dll" Alias "ShellExecuteA" (ByVal _
hwnd As Long, ByVal lpOperation As String, ByVal lpFile As String, ByVal _
lpParameters As String, ByVal lpDirectory As String, ByVal nShowCmd As Long)
```

Description   Finds the file name of the program that is associated with a specified file and either runs the program for the file or prints the file. The Windows registration editor can be used to associate types of files with particular applications. For example, text files that have the extension .TXT are typically associated with the Windows Notepad (NOTEPAD.EXE). Specifying any file with the .TXT extension to this function will either launch the Notepad program using the file name as a parameter, or will print the specified file.

Use with VB   No problem.

Parameter	Type/Description
hwnd	Long—A handle to a window. Sometimes it is necessary for a Windows application to show a message box before it has created its own main window. If this occurs, the window specified by this parameter will be used as the parent window of the message box. Under Visual Basic you would usually use the window handle of the active form for this parameter.
lpOperation	String—The string "Open" to open the lpFile document or "Print" to print it. This may be vbNullString to default to "Open."
lpFile	String—A program name or the name of a file to print or open using the associated program.
lpParameters	String—A string containing parameters to pass to the executable file if lpszFile is an executable file. vbNullString if lpszFile refers to a document file or if no parameters are used.
lpDirectory	String—The full path of the default directory to use.
nShowCmd	Long—A constant value specifying how to show the launched program. This matches the nCmdShow parameter to the ShowWindow API function described in Chapter 5.

Return Value   Long—Greater than 32 on success. Refer to the description of the FindExecutable function for a list of error codes.

Platform   Windows 95, Windows NT, Win16

Example   Launch.vbp

■ Sleep, SleepEx

VB Declaration
```
Declare Sub Sleep Lib "kernel32" (ByVal dwMilliseconds As Long)
Declare Function SleepEx& Lib "kernel32" (ByVal dwMilliseconds As Long, ByVal _
bAlertable As Long)
```

Description   Suspends operation of a thread for the specified time.

Use with VB   No problem.

Parameter	Type/Description
dwMilliseconds	Long—The time to suspend the thread in milliseconds. The constant INFINITE to put a thread permanently to sleep.
bAlertable	Long—SleepEx only. Set to TRUE if an asynchronous I/O transfer has been initiated with a ReadFileEx or WriteFileEx function call, and you want the function to return so that the I/O completion routine specified by those functions may execute.

Return Value   Long—SleepEx only. Zero if the timeout elapses, WAIT_IO_COMPLETION if the function returned because of the completion of an asynchronous I/O operation.

Platform   Windows 95, Windows NT

■ SuspendThread

VB Declaration   `Declare Function SuspendThread& Lib "kernel32" (ByVal hThread As Long)`

Description   Suspends execution of the specified thread.

Use with VB   No problem, but unlikely to be of use.

Parameter	Type/Description
hThread	Long—A handle of the thread to suspend.

Return Value   Long—The suspend count before this function was called. &HFFFFFFFF on error. Sets GetLastError.

Platform   Windows 95, Windows NT

Comments   Each call of this function increments the suspend count. The count is decremented by the ResumeThread function. The thread executes only when the count is zero.

■ TerminateProcess

VB Declaration   `Declare Function TerminateProcess& Lib "kernel32" (ByVal hProcess As Long, _`
`ByVal uExitCode As Long)`

Description   Kills a process.

Use with VB   Works, but should be avoided. Post a WM_CLOSE message to the main window of an application to close it.

Parameter	Type/Description
hProcess	Long—The handle of the process to terminate.
uExitCode	Long—An exit code for the process.

Return Value   Long—Nonzero on success, zero on failure. Sets GetLastError.

Platform   Windows 95, Windows NT

■ TransactNamedPipe

VB Declaration   `Declare Function TransactNamedPipe& Lib "kernel32" (ByVal hNamedPipe As Long, _`
`lpInBuffer As Any, ByVal nInBufferSize As Long, lpOutBuffer As Any, ByVal _`
`nOutBufferSize As Long, lpBytesRead As Long, lpOverlapped As OVERLAPPED)`

Description   This function combines a read and write pipe operation into a single function. It can be used by both client and server processes.

Use with VB   No problem.

Parameter	Type/Description
hNamedPipe	Long—A handle to a message type named pipe.
lpInBuffer	Any—A memory buffer containing data to write into the pipe.
nInBufferSize	Long—The number of bytes in the lpInBuffer buffer.
lpOutBuffer	Any—A memory buffer to load with data read from the pipe.
nOutBufferSize	Long—A long variable that will be loaded with data from the pipe.
lpBytesRead	Long—The number of bytes read from the pipe. A single message will be read. If lpOutBuffer is not large enough to hold the entire message, the function will return FALSE and GetLastError will be set to ERROR_MORE_DATA (any bytes left in the message will be lost).
lpOverlapped	OVERLAPPED—May be NULL (Change to ByVal As Long and pass zero), or an OVERLAPPED structure containing an event object.

Return Value   Long—TRUE (nonzero) if the operation is completed. Zero otherwise. In asynchronous mode, Get-LastError will be set to ERROR_IO_PENDING and the operation will continue in the background. The event object in the lpOverlapped structure can be tested for completion of the operation.

Platform   Windows 95, Windows NT

Comments   The function will not return until both the write and read operation are complete if lpOverlapped is NULL or if the handle was not created with the FILE_FLAG_OVERLAPPED style.

■ WaitForInputIdle

VB Declaration   `Declare Function WaitForInputIdle& Lib "user32" (ByVal hProcess As Long, ByVal _`
`dwMilliseconds As Long)`

Description   Waits until the specified process is in an idle state. Idle is defined as the state where the process is ready to process a message but no message is pending.

Use with VB   No problem. This function is useful to detect when a child process has completed its initialization.

Parameter	Type/Description
hProcess	Long—A handle to a process.
dwMilliseconds	Long—A timeout in milliseconds. The constant INFINITE to wait as long as necessary.

Return Value   Long—Zero on success. WAIT_TIMEOUT if the timeout elapsed without the process entering the idle state. &HFFFFFFFF on error. Sets GetLastError.

Platform   Windows 95, Windows NT

Example   Launch.vbp

■ WaitForMultipleObjects, WaitForMultipleObjectsEx

VB Declaration
```
Declare Function WaitForMultipleObjects& Lib "kernel32" (ByVal nCount As Long, _
lpHandles As Long, ByVal bWaitAll As Long, ByVal dwMilliseconds As Long)
Declare Function WaitForMultipleObjectsEx& Lib "kernel32" (ByVal nCount As _
Long, lpHandles As Long, ByVal bWaitAll As Long, ByVal dwMilliseconds As Long, _
ByVal bAlertable As Long)
```

Description
Waits for either a single object, or an entire lists of objects to become signaled or for the specified timeout to elapse. Returns immediately if the return condition is already met.

Use with VB
No problem.

Parameter	Type/Description
nCount	Long—The number of handles in the list.
lpHandles	Long—The first element in an array of object handles.
bWaitAll	Long—TRUE to wait until all of the objects are signaled simultaneously. FALSE to wait until any one object is signaled.
dwMilliseconds	Long—The number of milliseconds to wait. Returns immediately if zero. Waits forever if necessary if the constant INFINITE is specified.
bAlertable	Long—WaitForMultipleObjectsEx only. Set to TRUE if an asynchronous I/O transfer has been initiated with a ReadFileEx or WriteFileEx function call, and you want the function to return so that the I/O completion routine specified by those functions may execute.

Return Value
Long—If bWaitAll is true, one of the following constants on success.
WAIT_ABANDONED_0 if all of the objects are signaled and one or more of them is a mutex that became signaled when the process that owned it terminated.
WAIT_TIMEOUT if the objects remain unsignaled and the wait function timed out.
WAIT_OBJECT_0 if all of the objects are signaled.
WAIT_IO_COMPLETION (WaitForMultipleObjectEx only)—Function returned because an I/O completion operation is ready to be executed.
Returns WAIT_FAILED on failure and sets GetLastError.
If bWaitAll is false, the results are similar except that it might also be a positive offset from either WAIT_ABANDONED_0 or WAIT_OBJECT_0 indicating which object was either abandoned or signaled. For example, a result of WAIT_OBJECT_0 + 5 indicates that the fifth object in the list was signaled.

Platform
Windows 95, Windows NT. On Windows NT the object handles must have SYNCHRONIZE access specified.

Comments
If the function returns because an object was signaled, this function has additional effects depending on the type of object as follows:

- ■ Semaphore: Increments the semaphore count.

- ■ Mutex: Grants ownership of the mutex to the calling thread.

- ■ Auto-Reset event: Sets the event signaled state back to false.

Example
Async.vbp in Chapter 13.

■ WaitForSingleObject, WaitForSingleObjectEx

VB Declaration
```
Declare Function WaitForSingleObject& Lib "kernel32" (ByVal hHandle As Long, _
ByVal dwMilliseconds As Long)
Declare Function WaitForSingleObjectEx& Lib "kernel32" (ByVal hHandle As Long, _
ByVal dwMilliseconds As Long, ByVal bAlertable As Long)
```

Description
Waits for the specified object to become signaled or for the specified timeout to elapse. Returns immediately if the object is already signaled.

Use with VB
No problem.

Parameter	Type/Description
hHandle	Long—The handle to wait for. May be a change notification object, a console input object, an event, a mutex, a semaphore, a process, or a thread.
dwMilliseconds	Long—The number of milliseconds to wait. Returns immediately if zero. Waits forever if necessary if the constant INFINITE is specified.
bAlertable	Long—WaitForSingleObjectEx only. Set to TRUE if an asynchronous I/O transfer has been initiated with a ReadFileEx or WriteFileEx function call, and you want the function to return so that the I/O completion routine specified by those functions may execute.

Return Value
Long—One of the following constants on success:

- WAIT_ABANDONED if the object is a mutex that became signaled when the process that owned it terminated.

- WAIT_TIMEOUT if the object remains unsignaled and the wait function timed out.

- WAIT_OBJECT_0 if the object is signaled.

- WAIT_IO_COMPLETION (WaitForSingleObjectEx only)—Function returned because an I/O completion operation is ready to be executed.

- Returns WAIT_FAILED on failure and sets GetLastError.

Platform
Windows 95, Windows NT. On Windows NT the object handle must have SYNCHRONIZE access specified.

Comments
If the function returns because the object was signaled, this function has additional effects depending on the type of object as follows:

- Semaphore: Increments the semaphore count.

- Mutex: Grants ownership of the mutex to the calling thread.

- Auto-Reset event: Sets the event signaled state back to false.

Example
dwWatch.vbp, ckClient.vbp, Sleeper.vbp and others

■ WaitNamedPipe

VB Declaration
```
Declare Function WaitNamedPipe& Lib "kernel32" Alias "WaitNamedPipeA" (ByVal _
```

lpNamedPipeName As String, ByVal nTimeOut As Long)

Description · Called by a client process to wait until a pipe is available (for example, the server has called the ConnectNamedPipe function to connect to a client).

Use with VB No problem.

Parameter	Type/Description
lpNamedPipeName	String—The name of the pipe to connect to.
nTimeOut	Long—The time to wait in milliseconds or one of the following constants: NMPWAIT_USE_DEFAULT_WAIT: Use the default timeout specified when the pipe was created. NMPWAIT_WAIT_FOREVER: Wait forever.

Return Value Long—Nonzero on success, zero on failure or if the pipe does not exist. Sets GetLastError.

Platform Windows 95, Windows NT

Comments Use CreateFile to open the pipe after this function. Note that this CreateFile call can fail if another process connects to the pipe between the time this function returns and the time CreateFile is called.

Example PipeClnt.vbp

■ WinExec

VB Declaration Declare Function WinExec& Lib "kernel32" (ByVal lpCmdLine As String, ByVal _
nCmdShow As Long)

Description Runs the specified program.

Use with VB This function is essentially identical to the Visual Basic Shell command. Refer to the description for the CreateProcess, LoadModule, and ShellExecute functions for information on other methods for launching applications.

Parameter	Type/Description
lpCmdLine	String—Contains the command line to execute.
nCmdShow	Long—A constant value specifying how to show the launched program. This matches the nCmdShow parameter to the ShowWindow API function described in Chapter 4.

Return Value Long—Greater than 32 on success. Refer to the description of the FindExecutable function for a list of error codes.

Platform Windows 95, Windows NT, Win16

Comments Refer to the description of the CreateProcess function for a description of the order in which directories are searched for the specified program file.

This function does not return until the launched program starts processing messages or a timeout occurs.

15

Memory, Strings, Structures, and Resources

NE OF THE CONSISTENT THEMES WHEN WORKING WITH THE WINDOWS API is the need to allocate and use blocks of memory. In some cases, this is as easy as allocating a string buffer and passing it "By-Val" to the API function. In other cases, this involves building complex structures that contain embedded structures and sometimes even pointers to other structures.

This chapter explores many of the various ways that you can work with memory using Visual Basic and the Win32 API. You will see how Visual Basic works with various types of memory, how it works internally with different types of strings, and how it organizes data inside of structures (user-defined types).

The concept of resources will be introduced. Although many resource functions for particular Windows objects have already been demonstrated, this chapter will explain more thoroughly why resources exist and how they may be used. In that respect you will find this particular chapter a bit long on theory and short on example, but that is only because the principles discussed have been demonstrated many times in earlier chapters.

Memory and Strings

Many of the Windows API functions require the use of memory buffers. These blocks of memory may vary from short buffers for strings to extremely large buffers for device-independent bitmaps.

Using Visual Basic to Create Buffers

There are two easy ways to obtain memory buffers using Visual Basic. One is to use a string, the other is to use a byte array. A string buffer of a specified length can be created in two ways: first, by creating a fixed length string using

```
Dim FixedSample As String * N
```

where N is the length of the string and second, by using the Visual Basic **String$** function on a variable-length string variable as follows:

```
Dim VarSample As String
VarSample = String$(N,0)
where N is the number of bytes in the string.
```

The API functions that require pointers to buffers expect 32-bit address parameters. Under Win16 it was possible to obtain the address of a string using any popular Visual Basic support DLL, including the APIGUIDE.BAS dynamic link library that was provided with the Visual Basic Programmer's Guide to the Windows API. You could then pass the address as a long (By-Val) to the function that needed a memory buffer. The only caveat was that you could not hold onto the address for long periods of time because of Visual Basic's tendency to relocate strings in memory as needed. However, as long as you used the address immediately after calling the function to obtain the address, this was a safe approach.

This approach does not work with 32-bit Visual Basic.

The reason for this is simple and goes back to the discussion in Chapter 3. Visual Basic stores strings internally as Unicode strings. When you call a DLL function, VB makes a temporary ANSI copy of the string. When the function returns, it converts this temporary ANSI string back into Unicode. The problem? The DLL function receives the address of the ANSI string, which is the address of a temporary buffer. As soon as the function returns, the buffer is no longer valid. Thus, any function that obtains the address of a string by passing the string to a DLL will not return a useful value.

There are several approaches that you can take to solve this problem. The first is to simply change the declaration of the function that requires a buffer to "ByVal As String" and pass it the string buffer. This will work in many cases—especially when the buffer is designed to hold text, but don't forget that Visual Basic will be converting the data to and from Unicode. If the buffer is intended to hold binary data, this conversion could corrupt the information in the buffer.

Another approach is to use a byte array. You can obtain the address of a byte array in memory by using the agGetAddressForObject function in APIGID32.DLL and passing it the first element in the byte array by reference as follows:

```
arrayaddress& = agGetAddressForObject(myarray(¯))
```

Note that byte arrays—like all VB arrays—start at index zero. You can, of course, pass the address of the second byte (in this case, myarray(1)) and everything will work properly as long as you remain consistent and don't try to perform a conversion of the array to a string. Byte arrays are safe from conversions and provide a very easy way to obtain memory buffers. If a DLL or API function loads a string into a byte buffer, you can convert it to a string using a simple assignment; however, you will need to perform an explicit conversion to Unicode in that case.

Finally, you can allocate your own global memory buffers using API functions and pass addresses to those buffers to the function using long parameters (ByVal As Long).

Using Windows to Create Buffers

Before looking at the Win32 functions used to allocate memory, it is interesting to consider for a moment what actually takes place when you access memory in a Windows application. It might be even more interesting to consider how this process has evolved. This is shown in Figure 15.1.

Under DOS, each application had direct access to physical memory. A 32-bit memory address actually formed a physical address of only 20 bits, which is enough to address only 1MB of memory. DOS extenders have to go through all sorts of convolutions to allow applications to access additional memory.

Figure 15.1

Memory
organization in
Windows 3.x

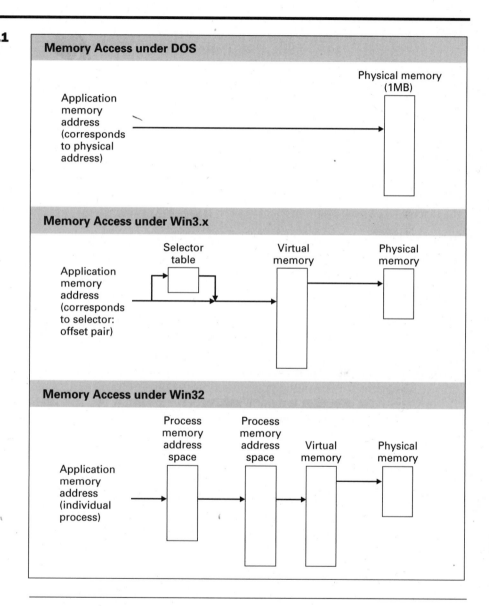

By the time Windows 3.1 rolled around, a more sophisticated memory address scheme was in place. The memory system was first divided into two levels. At the higher level, the application address consisted of a selector-offset pair. The high 16 bits was a selector into a table of segments of arbitrary length. The segment address was obtained from the selector table and combined with the offset to form an address in virtual memory. Virtual memory was in turn divided into pages of memory that could be in physical memory or swapped out to disk. All memory under Windows 3.x is shared—each application could access memory regardless of which application was using it.

A key point to remember even with Windows 3.x is this: The address that the application saw (a selector and an offset) did not correspond to any particular physical address.

Under Win32, yet another layer has been added. Each process is given its own 2 gigabyte address space. When an application addresses memory within this space, the operating system checks first to see if the addressed location has been allocated. If it has, it determines what address in the system memory address space corresponds to the address in process memory. This system memory address space corresponds to virtual memory, which works in much the same way as it did on 16-bit Windows.

The big change here is the difference between process address space and system address space. This is illustrated further in Figure 15.2. This figure shows the organization of memory on a hypothetical system that has 16MB of virtual memory (not physical memory). The system is running two applications under Windows NT: The file manager and a user application. Under Windows 3.x, both applications appear in shared memory. Under Win32, each application sees only those components that it needs. Also, the various modules may appear at different addresses in each process address space.

You might ask: What happens if a buggy process tries to write over a portion of one of the operating system DLLs or its data? The answer depends on the operating system. Windows NT implements two approaches. The operating system modules are placed in their own 2 gigabyte address space that is completely inaccessible to your application code. Thus the total address space seen by the application is 4GB, of which the upper 2GB is reserved for the operating system and is totally inaccessible. For other shared dynamic link libraries, a "copy on write" scheme is implemented. As long as each application is only reading the shared DLL, it can read it out of the same memory location (even though that location might be accessed using different addresses in each application). As soon as one of the applications tries to write into this shared data, Windows NT makes a copy of the memory that belongs only to the process that performed the write operation. Thus the changes appear only in that one application and other processes continue to see the original DLL. This is why Windows NT is able to recover from almost any crash—it is extremely difficult for one application to interfere with another. Windows 95, on the other hand, is a compromise on these principles. While each application does have its own 2GB process space, it can access a total of 4GB. Operating system DLLs and other DLLs are loaded into the upper 2GB space, which is shared, and they appear at the same address in each running process. This is still an enormous improvement over Windows 3.x, but it is not nearly as good as Windows NT.

Figure 15.2

Memory
organization in Win32

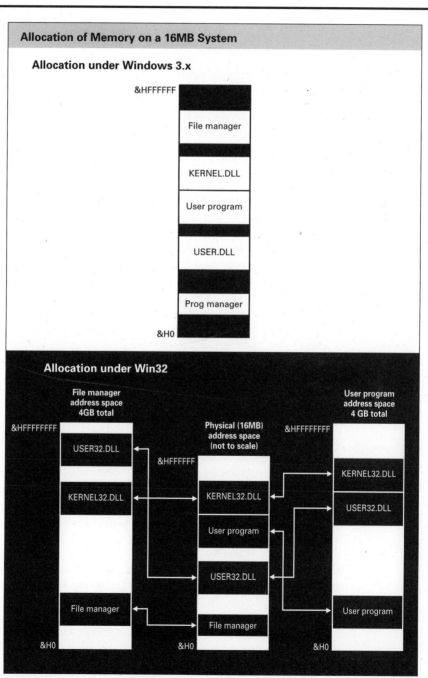

Windows Memory and Visual Basic

Now that you know a little bit about the organization of memory under Windows, one question you may ask is: Why is this important to Visual Basic programmers?

You have already read about the impact of some of these changes on VB API programming in previous chapters. These include

- The use of file mappings to share blocks of memory (and the fact that a block of memory shared in this manner may appear at different locations to each process)

- The fact that GDI objects are no longer shareable between processes

- The fact that memory addresses cannot be shared between processes

- The fact that instance handles are useless for identifying applications

Windows memory allocation has traditionally been used under Visual Basic for two main reasons. First, under Win16 it provided a mechanism for allocating blocks of memory over 64K in size. Second, memory allocated by Windows appeared at a fixed address (unless explicitly allowed to move) and thus memory addresses obtained through this mechanism could be held safely without concern that Visual Basic would move them.

These advantages still exist, but to a lesser degree. 32-bit Visual Basic can allocate buffers greater than 64K in size, but you will still need to use the Windows allocation functions if you want to create programs that are compatible with both 16- and 32-bit Windows. The advantage of being able to allocate fixed blocks of memory remains.

Win32 provides three main mechanisms for allocating memory. The global memory handler is discussed first. This is the same mechanism used under Win16 to allocate global blocks of memory and is provided for backward compatibility. A set of new heap functions is available to create and manage allocation from one or more heaps. This is the preferred mechanism for new applications. Finally, a set of virtual allocation functions exists that provides lower-level control over allocation of memory in your application's address space.

Global Memory Handles

Global memory blocks are Windows objects, and as such they have handles associated with them. You obtain a handle to a memory block using the GlobalAlloc API function. This function provides you with a number of options that specify the type of memory block. The complete list of memory block types is included in the function reference for the GlobalAlloc function; however, only a few are of use to the Visual Basic programmer:

■ *Fixed memory blocks.* These memory blocks are fixed in memory. This means that once you obtain an address pointer to allocated memory, it is guaranteed not to change.

■ *Moveable memory blocks.* These memory blocks are allowed to move in memory as long as they are not explicitly locked. Under 16-bit Windows this was the preferred type of memory block to use, as it provided Windows with the most flexibility in terms of managing memory in all memory modes. Win32 is unlikely to move these memory blocks except possibly when they are resized.

■ Discardable memory blocks. These memory blocks may be discarded if Windows needs additional memory. A mechanism exists by which an application can determine if the memory block has been discarded. This kind of memory block is commonly used for resources and other data that is not changed by the application.

Keep in mind that, under Win32, global memory handles are private to an application and cannot be shared.

Global Memory Pointers

Once you have allocated a global memory block, you can use the GlobalLock function to obtain the 32-bit address of the memory block. This function also locks moveable memory blocks in memory so that the returned address is guaranteed to remain valid until the memory block is explicitly unlocked using the GlobalUnlock function. Each memory block has a lock count. GlobalLock increments the lock count and GlobalUnlock decrements it. You should be careful to match every GlobalLock function with a GlobalUnlock function.

The sequence of operations for using global memory blocks is as follows:

1. Allocate the global memory block using the GlobalAlloc function.

2. Obtain an address for the global memory block using the GlobalLock function.

3. Use the memory as desired.

4. Unlock the memory block using the GlobalUnlock function.

5. Repeat steps 2–4 as needed. The GlobalReAlloc function may be used to change the size of the global memory block.

6. Use the GlobalFree function to free the global memory block when it is no longer needed.

Global memory blocks allocated in the manner described here belong to the calling application. This means that they will be automatically freed when the application terminates. Nevertheless, it is good programming practice to explicitly free any memory blocks that your program uses. Table 15.1 lists the most commonly used global memory API functions.

Table 15.1 **Global Memory API Functions**

Function	Description
GlobalAlloc	Allocates a global memory block
GlobalFlags	Determines the type and state of a global memory block
GlobalFree	Frees a global memory block
GlobalHandle	Retrieves a memory handle for a memory address
GlobalLock	Locks a global memory block in memory and retrieves a 32-bit address pointer to the locked memory
GlobalReAlloc	Changes the size of a global memory block
GlobalSize	Determines the size of a global memory block
GlobalUnlock	Unlocks a global memory block

Controlling the Global Memory Heap

There are a number of Win16 functions that were used to control the global memory heap including GlobalCompact, GlobalFix, GlobalLRUNewest, GlobalLRUOldest, and GlobalUnfix. These functions are not necessary under Win32 and are not supported.

Win32 Heap Functions

In addition to the global memory heap, Win32 allows you to create additional heaps, each of which can be privately managed. To work with private heaps, use the HeapCreate function to obtain a handle to a new heap. You can then use the HeapAlloc function to obtain the address in memory of a block of newly allocated memory in the private heap. All memory blocks in private heaps are fixed. The HeapLock and HeapUnlock functions are *not* at all like the GlobalLock and GlobalUnlock functions. These functions are actually used for synchronization. When a thread locks a heap, it prevents any other thread in a process from allocating or releasing memory in the heap. Since

Visual Basic only supports a single thread, there is no need to use these functions. Table 15.2 summarizes the heap allocation functions.

Table 15.2	Win32 Heap Functions	

Function	Description
GetProcessHeap GetProcessHeaps	Obtains information about heaps currently allocated for a process
HeapAlloc	Allocates a block of memory
HeapCompact	Compacts a heap
HeapCreate	Creates a new heap
HeapDestroy	Destroys a heap
HeapFree	Frees a block of memory
HeapLock	Used to lock heap allocation/deallocation to a single thread
HeapReAlloc	Reallocates and changes the size of a block of memory
HeapSize	Determines the size of a block of memory on the heap
HeapUnlock	Releases a heap locked using HeapLock
HeapValidate	Tests the heap to make sure it is not corrupted

Virtual Memory Functions

As mentioned earlier, each Win32 process is given its own 2GB process space. Win32 includes a number of functions that provide advanced control over the use of this memory space. They allow you, for example, to reserve a part of the address space without actually allocating physical memory, to specify that a block of memory is read only, and more. All memory addresses within the address space for a process can be in one of three states. It can be free, in which case it is available to be allocated by any of the memory allocation functions. It can be reserved, in which case no memory is actually allocated but the reserved space will not be used by any other memory allocation functions, or it can be committed, in which case the space is reserved and has virtual memory allocated for the space.

The virtual memory functions are listed in Table 15.3.

Table 15.3   **Virtual Memory Functions**

Function	Description
VirtualAlloc	Allocates or reserves a block of memory
VirtualFree	Frees or decommits a block of memory
VirtualLock	Locks a block of virtual memory into physical memory
VirtualProtect VirtualProtectEx	Changes the protection of a block of virtual memory
VirtualQuery VirtualQueryEx	Obtains information about a block of virtual memory
VirtualUnlock	Unlocks a block of virtual memory

Using Global Memory Blocks from Visual Basic

Using global memory from Visual Basic requires a good understanding of the use of 32-bit addresses. This subject was covered in Chapter 9 in the section titled "Dynamically Sized Structures," which you should review, if necessary, before continuing.

Under Win16, it was important to differentiate between small memory blocks (under 64K in size) and huge memory blocks (over 64K in size). Each type of memory also required a different memory copy routine. Data could be transferred to and from small memory blocks using the agCopyData function in APIGUIDE.DLL and address calculations could be performed using simple addition. Huge memory blocks under Win16 required a separate 1hmemcpy function to copy huge data and the agHugeOffset function in APIGUIDE.DLL to perform arithmetic on memory addresses. Details on handling these different types of memory blocks can be found in the 16-bit Visual Basic Programmer's Guide to the Windows API.

Under Win32, there is no difference between small and huge memory blocks. All memory blocks are in the single 2GB address space provided to the process and you can perform direct arithmetic on memory addresses safely. The hmemcpy function that was often used to copy a block of memory from one location to another is no longer exported from Windows. 32-bit C and C++ programs use memory copy routines that are built into the language libraries. The agCopyData function included in APIGUIDE.DLL has been extended to handle data transfers over 64K bytes in size.

Listing 15.1 shows how a function can allocate a large block of memory, which can be subdivided into smaller blocks and how those blocks can be accessed. Variable Glblhnd contains the handle to the global memory block. Global-Lock is used to obtain the actual memory address to use. It is good practice to check the result after locking the memory with GlobalLock. In this example, the function will always return a valid address. If it returns zero, you can assume a serious error has occurred and terminate the application as quickly as possible.

However, if the memory block had been defined as discardable by specifying the GMEM_DISCARDABLE flag to the GlobalAlloc function, a return value of zero for the GlobalLock function would indicate to the program that the memory block has been discarded by Windows. In this case the global handle remains valid. You have two choices as to how to proceed. You could just free the handle using the GlobalFree function and reallocate a new buffer. Or, you could use the GlobalReAlloc function to reallocate the global memory block.

Listing 15.1   Memory Access Example

```
'
' Typical code to access memory in a buffer
' In this case, the buffer is used to hold 1¯¯¯ x 256 byte
' fixed length strings.
'
Sub AllocArray()
Dim GlblAddr&, GlblAddr2&
Dim tstring As String * 256

Glblhnd& = GlobalAlloc(GMEM_ZEROINIT Or GMEM_MOVEABLE, CLng(1¯¯¯ * 256))

If Glblhnd& = ¯ Then
    ' Perform appropriate error handling here. Do not
    ' continue to the next line!
End If

GlblAddr& = GlobalLock(Glblhnd&)

' Here's how you retrieve one of the 256 byte strings
' from the huge memory block -
' In this case, the 5¯¯th entry

GlblAddr2& = GlblAddr& + 5¯¯ * 256

' Now extract the string
Call agCopyData(ByVal GlblAddr2&, ByVal tstring, 256)

di& = GlobalUnlock(Glblhnd&)

'The memory block is still available.


End Sub
```

You can free the memory block when it is no longer needed using the following line:

```
GlblHnd = GlobalFree(GlblHnd)
```

Note how the GlblHnd variable is set back to zero (which is the result after a successful GlobalFree operation). This is important in order to prevent other functions from trying to access a freed memory block.

Note also how each GlobalLock function is balanced with a matching GlobalUnlock operation.

In order to help prevent errors in accessing memory, Windows provides a number of functions to test and access memory addresses. These functions are shown in Table 15.4.

Table 15.4   **Memory Access Functions**

Function	Description
IsBadCodePtr	Determines if a block of memory is valid and executable
IsBadHugeReadPtr	Obsolete: Use IsBadReadPtr
IsBadHugeWritePtr	Obsolete: Use IsBadWritePtr
IsBadReadPtr	Determines if a block of memory is valid and readable
IsBadStringPtr	Determines if a block of memory is valid, can be read and written, and is a NULL terminated string
IsBadWritePtr	Determines if a block of memory is valid and writable
ReadProcessMemory	Allows you to copy memory from the address space of another process
WriteProcessMemory	Allows you to write memory to the address space of another process

---

String Functions

The Windows API provides a number of functions to perform common string operations. These functions are rarely needed from within Visual Basic because Visual Basic provides a powerful set of string operations that are much easier to use and pose no risk of system errors caused by copying data into invalid memory addresses. These are most often used when performing operations on buffers that you allocate directly or on structures within global memory blocks. Some of these functions are dependent on the locale information—a subject that is covered in Chapter 6. These Windows API string functions are summarized in Table 15.5.

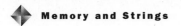

Table 15.5 **Windows API String Functions**

Function	Description
AnsiNext	Obsolete—replaced by CharNext
AnsiPrev	Obsolete—replaced by CharPrev
CharLower CharLowerBuff	Converts a character to lowercase
CharNext	Finds the next character in a string
CharPrev	Finds the previous character to a specified character in a string
CharUpper CharUpperBuff	Converts a character to uppercase
CompareString	Compares two strings based on the current locale settings
FoldString	Performs a number of string conversions
GetStringType GetStringTypeEx	Retrieves information about the types of characters in a string
IsCharAlpha	Determines if a character is a letter
IsCharAlphaNumeric	Determines if a character is a letter or number
IsCharLower	Determines if a character is lowercase
IsCharUpper	Determines if a character is uppercase
IsDBCSLeadByte IsDBSCLeadByteEx	Determines if a byte is the first byte in a double-byte character in a DBCS character set
IsTextUnicode	Determines the likelihood that a string consists of Unicode characters
LCMapString	Performs a specified mapping between character sets
lstrcat	Appends (concatenates) one string to another
lstrcmp	Compares two strings
lstrcmpi	Compares two strings, ignoring their case
lstrcpy, lstrcpyn	Copies one string to another
lstrlen	Determines the length of a string
MultiByteToWideChar	Converts an ANSI or DBCS string to Unicode
WideCharToMultiByte	Converts a Unicode string to ANSI or DBCS

The Visual Basic-Windows Interface: The Hardcore Version

As you may recall, Chapter 3 was entitled "The Visual Basic-Windows Interface." Chapter 4, "Real World API Programming," was really a continuation of the subject focusing in on practical applications.

Why then, has this subject returned to haunt this book, and why is it appearing so late in the text?

By now you have had the opportunity to look at and experiment with hundreds of API functions, and as you have seen, most of them are remarkably easy to use. Simply plug in one of the declarations that are provided in the API32.TXT file, follow one of the numerous examples, and chances are very good that your program will work.

But the APIDATA.MDB database included with this book includes over 1,500 functions, of which about half are documented in the text. Not only that, but those 1,500 Win32 functions still represent only a fraction of the functions in the Win32 API and its myriad extension libraries. In other words, sooner or later, many Visual Basic programmers are going to need to create their own declarations based on sometimes sparse and confusing C or C++ documentation. In addition, they will need to be able to evaluate existing declarations intelligently, because despite my best efforts to improve on the WIN32API.TXT file provided with Visual Basic, there are without doubt still errors in this book's declaration file. Also, as you have seen, it is sometimes possible to use several different declarations correctly with a single API function depending on the parameter types—using an existing declaration blindly may not work for your application in those cases.

The first four chapters of this book were intended to help any Visual Basic programmer deal with those situations by covering the fundamentals of the Visual Basic to Windows interface in enough depth to handle almost any situation that can arise. The other chapters and sample programs up to this point hopefully provided additional information to fill in some of the blanks.

This chapter is intended to take you the rest of the way. After mastering this chapter, you should be a true Win32/Visual Basic API guru—able to go into enough depth to handle anything that comes along.

Why wait until this late in the book to cover this information? Frankly, if I were a beginner and reached this material right after working through Chapter 4 of this book, I would probably drop the book and run away screaming, swearing to avoid Windows programming forever.

Fortunately, as a Win32 expert, you will be able to both follow and appreciate some of the subtle issues covered in this section.

Advanced Structure Techniques

Chapter 3 discussed the use of Visual Basic data types as parameters to API functions and how Visual Basic structures can be created to match Windows data structures. This section shows how the data in several Visual Basic data types is organized in memory.

There are two situations where this information is used. First, there are cases where you may be reading raw data into a string buffer or global memory block that does not correspond to a structure. In most cases it will be a simple matter to copy the data from the buffer to a Visual Basic variable, but on occasion the numeric format of the data structure may not match the numeric format used on your PC. For example, you may notice this when you examine a data file from a system that is not based on 80x86 technology. There may also be cases where you wish to examine a particular byte in a numeric variable without first copying it into a variable of that type. In such cases, you will need to know how to determine which byte in memory corresponds to a particular byte in a numeric data type.

The other, more common, situation occurs when accessing fixed-length strings inside of Visual Basic structures. These strings are not handled in the same way as regular string variables, and it is important to understand how to use them.

Organization of Data in Variables

Ultimately, every variable that is stored in memory is a sequence of 8-bit bytes. The order in which the bytes of a numeric variable are placed in memory varies depending on the type of computer. Figure 15.3 illustrates the byte order used on 80x86-based computers and thus under Windows.

In Figure 15.3, you can see how the bytes of integer variables are swapped so that the low-order byte is at the lowest memory address. The same applies to both bytes and words in a long variable.

Figure 15.3

Organization of bytes within numeric variables

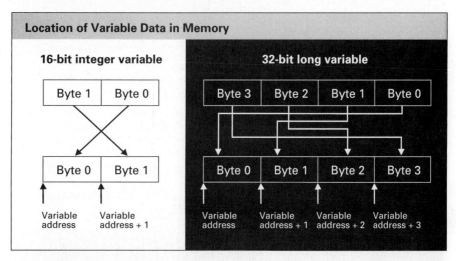

This information is also important when you refer to the address of a variable. The address of a variable in memory is defined as the lowest memory location that holds a byte from that variable.

Organization of Data in Structures

Working with structures under 32-bit Visual Basic presents some subtle but crucial challenges that you will need to understand in order to use them effectively. The most important thing to consider is that the way a structure is stored internally by Visual Basic is not always the same way it is stored when passed as a parameter to a function. When you pass a structure as a parameter to a DLL function, in many cases Visual Basic makes a temporary copy of the structure, in much the same way as Visual Basic has to make a temporary copy of strings in order to convert them from their internal Unicode format to ANSI. The structure is copied back when the function returns.

Visual Basic needs to perform this conversion for two reasons. The first case is when there are strings defined in the structure. Visual Basic must create a copy of the structure that refers to ANSI string copies of the Unicode strings that are kept in the structure's internal format. The second case is when alignment issues exist. As mentioned in Chapter 3, all variables within a structure must be aligned on their natural boundary.

One side effect of this conversion is that if you wish to obtain the address of a structure as it is stored internally in Visual Basic, you cannot simply pass the structure itself to the agGetAddressForObject function (the function in APIGID32.DLL that can generally be used to obtain function addresses). That would give you the address of the temporary buffer holding the converted structure. Instead, you must pass one of the numeric variables in the structure to the agGetAddressForObject function and calculate the structure address based on that. You must use a numeric variable instead of a string variable because string variables go through their own conversion process which would, once again, give you the address of a temporary buffer instead of the variable itself.

Not only is there a difference between the way a structure is stored internally and the way it is passed as a parameter to a DLL, there is yet another possible format used when a structure is stored in a file! In that case, all of the variables in the structure are packed together with single-byte alignment. To summarize:

- When saved in a file: Structures use one-byte alignment, and fixed length strings take one byte per character (see Figure 15.4).

- Inside Visual Basic: Structures use four-byte alignment, and fixed length strings take two bytes per character (see Figure 15.5).

- As a DLL parameter: Structures use natural boundary alignment, and fixed length strings take one byte per character (same as Figure 15.5,

Type SampleType
Logical organization of data. The letter indicates the variable name, the number indicates the byte number.
VarA as Integer
A-1 A-0
VarB as Long
B-3 B-2 B-1 B-0
VarC as String * 5
C-4 C-3 C-2 C-1 C-0
VarD as Byte
D-0
End Type
Corresponding Organization in Memory
A-0 A-1 B-0 B-1 B-2 B-3 C-0 C-1 C-2 C-3 C-4 D-0
Start address of the structure
Start address of string
Calculate using agGetAddressForObject(structurename)+6
Do not use agGetAddressFor LPSTR(structurename.VarC)

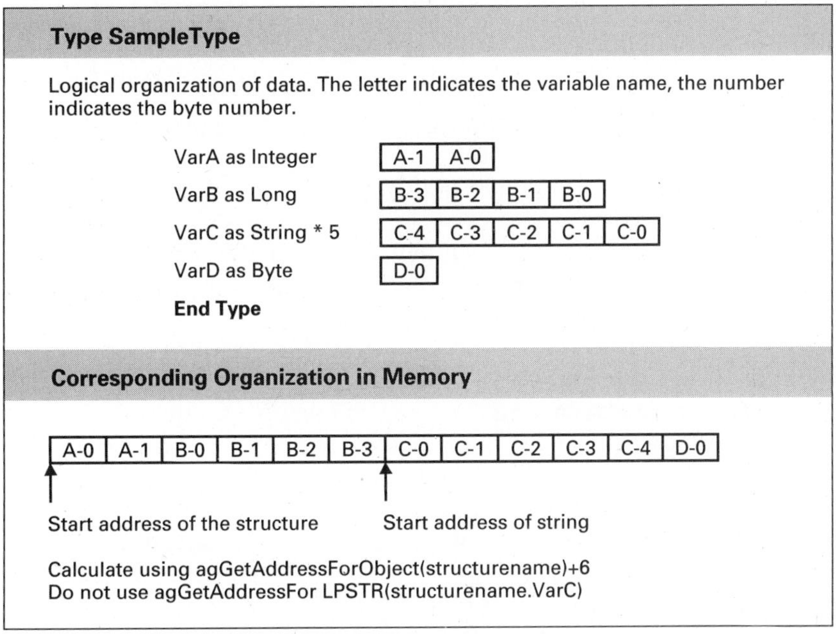

Figure 15.4 Organization of variables in a structure as they appear when written to a file. It takes up 12 bytes as shown by the Len function.

Type SampleType
Logical organization of data. The letter indicates the variable name, the number indicates the byte number.
VarA as Integer
A-1 A-0 Unused
VarB as Long
B-3 B-2 B-1 B-0
The long variable must be aligned on a 4-byte boundary.
VarC as String * 5
C-4 C-4 C-3 C-3 C-2 C-2 C-1 C-1 C-0 C-0
Strings are stored internally in Unicode.
VarD as Byte
D-0
End Type
Corresponding Organization in Memory
A-0 A-1 Unused B-0 B-1 B-2 B-3 C-4 C-4 C-3 C-3 C-2 C-2 C-1 C-1 C-0 C-0 D-0
Start address of the structure
Start address of string

Figure 15.5 Organization of variables in a structure as stored internally in Visual Basic. It takes up 19 bytes as shown by the LenB function. When passed to a DLL, each character takes one byte, and the entire structure takes up 14 bytes.

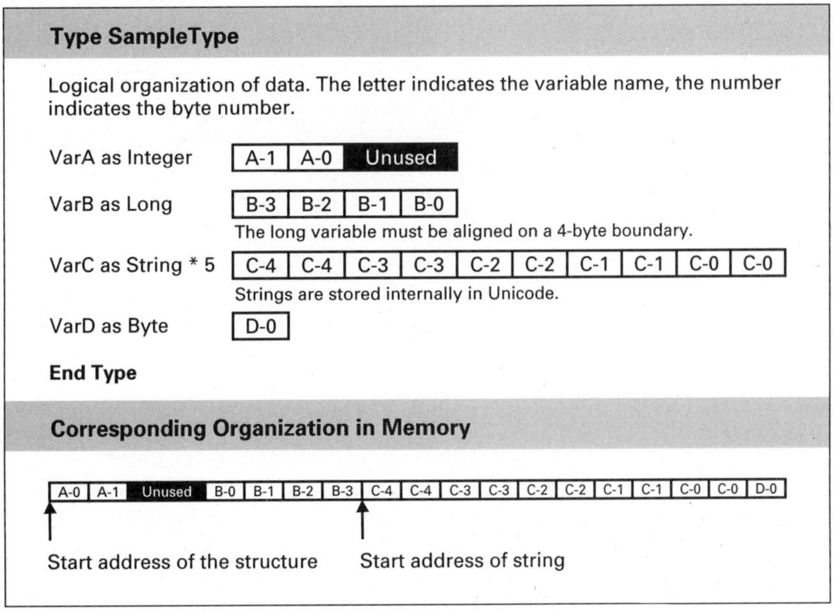

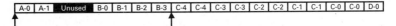

except that each string takes one character). Natural boundary means that a variable within a structure starts at a boundary that depends on the variable size. Bytes variables can start at any address, integer variables at even addresses, and long variables at 32 bit boundaries.

If you wish to obtain the address of a structure within Visual Basic, and you have a structure of this type named mystruct, you can calculate it as agGetAddressForObject(mystruct.VarA) or agGetAddressForObject(mystruct.VarB)-4. The string address would be agGetAddressForObject(mystruct.VarA)+8 or agGetAddressForObject(mystruct.VarB)+4. You cannot call agGetAddressForObject(mystruct.VarC) because that would obtain the address of a temporary ANSI copy of the string.

Once again, these issues only come into play on those rare occasions when you need to work with the addresses of structures and variables within structures. In most cases you will simply pass the structure or the structure's variables directly as parameters to API functions and allow Visual Basic to pass the correct address to the function.

Virtually all API functions that take structures as parameters use structures that are aligned on natural boundaries. There are a few structures, however, that require single byte alignment and thus cannot be passed correctly as parameters from Visual Basic. Consider, for example, the following structure:

```
Type mytype
    A As Byte
    B As Integer
End Type
```

This structure takes 8 bytes while stored within Visual Basic (4 byte packing), 5 bytes in a disk file (single byte packing) and will be passed to a DLL as 6 bytes (variable B will be aligned to its natural boundary of 2). This means that the structure cannot be passed successfully to a DLL which requires single byte packing. To get around this problem you have two choices. You can create a byte array and copy the variables from the structure into the correct locations in the array—essentially doing your own packing. Or you can use a third party tool such as SpyWorks that includes User Defined Type packing functions to handle this type of situation.

Fixed Strings in Structures

Figure 15.5 demonstrated the conversion that is applied to fixed strings inside of structures when they are passed as parameters to functions. Consider what happens when an API function needs to load data into a structure that contains a fixed-length string. As long as you are passing the structure directly as a parameter, you will have no problems because the string will be converted into the internal Unicode format. Do not try passing the address of the structure as stored internally by Visual Basic—as you have seen, the structure format will not match the format expected by the function.

One subtle aspect of declaring strings inside of structures is the need to subtract 1 from the size specified in the equivalent C documentation or in the original Win16 declaration. For example, a 32-byte string inside of a structure can be defined as follows:

C: char mystring[32];

VB old   mystring As String * 32

VB new   mystring(31) As Byte

You should avoid the old VB declaration from VB3 in most cases, because it will lead to incorrect results if you perform a direct memory copy to a structure using a pointer to the structure. Also, you run the risk of errors due to Unicode <-> ANSI conversions if the string contains binary data instead of simple text strings.

You must remember to define the byte array to one fewer than the equivalent C declaration to take into account the fact that in Visual Basic the array index sets the highest index value of the array, not the size of the array. Since the first array entry is entry zero, the size of the array is one more than the dimensioned parameter.

Dynamic Strings in Structures

Under Visual Basic 3.0, you would virtually never use a dynamic string inside of a structure that was passed to an API or DLL function. The only time you would do this is if you were calling a DLL that was specifically designed to handle Visual Basic strings, as a dynamic string inside of a structure was stored as a 32-bit internal Visual Basic handle called an HLSTR. Most API and DLL functions could not use this value.

The way dynamic strings are stored in structures has changed dramatically for 32 bit editions of Visual Basic, with significant consequences with regard to API and DLL calls.

Consider the following C declaration for the MENUITEM structure. The contents of this structure are described in Appendix B and Chapter 10. Functions that use this structure are described in Chapter 10 as well.

```
typedef struct tagMENUITEMINFOA
{
    UINT    cbSize;
    UINT    fMask;
    UINT    fType;          // used if MIIM_TYPE
    UINT    fState;         // used if MIIM_STATE
    UINT    wID;            // used if MIIM_ID
```

```
    HMENU    hSubMenu;         // used if MIIM_SUBMENU
    HBITMAP  hbmpChecked;      // used if MIIM_CHECKMARKS
    HBITMAP  hbmpUnchecked;    // used if MIIM_CHECKMARKS
    DWORD    dwItemData;       // used if MIIM_DATA
    LPSTR    dwTypeData;       // used if MIIM_TYPE
    UINT     cch;              // used if MIIM_TYPE
}   MENUITEMINFOA, FAR *LPMENUITEMINFOA;
```

Now take a look at two possible Visual Basic declarations for this structure:

```
Type MENUITEMINFO
    cbSize As Long
    fMask As Long
    fType As Long
    fState As Long
    wID As Long
    hSubMenu As Long
    hbmpChecked As Long
    hbmpUnchecked As Long
    dwItemData As Long
    dwTypeData As Long
    cch As Long
End Type


Type MENUITEMINFO
    cbSize As Long
    fMask As Long
    fType As Long
    fState As Long
    wID As Long
    hSubMenu As Long
    hbmpChecked As Long
    hbmpUnchecked As Long
    dwItemData As Long
    dwTypeData As String
    cch As Long
End Type
```

Note the difference in the dwTypeData field. Under Visual Basic 3.0 you would have to use the first declaration—under no circumstances could the functions that use this structure handle the internal Visual Basic string handle (HLSTR type).

But under Visual Basic 4.0 and later, a dynamic string is an OLE string—BSTR type. A BSTR value is a pointer to a location in memory that is the beginning of a string. The 32 bits before the address contained in the BSTR contains the length of the string. Though BSTR strings are often NULL terminated, Visual Basic does not guarantee that a BSTR string will, in fact, be NULL terminated. Figure 15.6 illustrates how Visual Basic stores the MENUITEMINFO structure internally when you use the second declaration—dwTypeData declared as a string, and how the structure appears when it is passed to a DLL or API function.

Figure 15.6

Passing the
MENUITEMINFO
structure to a DLL

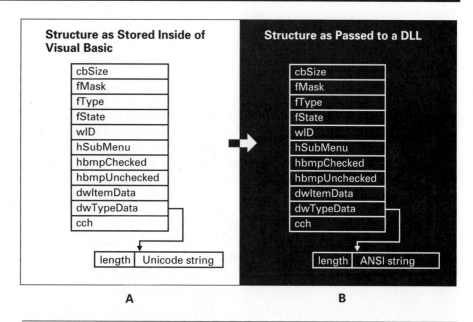

Visual Basic stores the structure internally as shown in Figure 15.6A. Assuming that the dwTypeData field contains a string, the dwTypeData field will contain a 32-bit pointer to a Unicode string. The pointer contains the memory address of the start of the string itself, the length appearing before the text.

When Visual Basic passes a structure to a DLL, it creates a copy of the structure as shown in Figure 15.6B. The dwTypeData field is loaded with a pointer to an ANSI string that was converted from the Unicode string.

Now consider the GetMenuItemInfo API function documented in Chapter 10. This function has the ability to return string information by loading the string referenced by the dwTypeData string with new information. When the function looks at the dwTypeData value, it will see a valid 32-bit memory address. If you have preallocated the string to an adequate length to hold the string, this will work in exactly the same way as a regular string. For example, if you have the following code:

```
Dim menuinfo As MENUITEMINFO
menuinfo.dwTypeData = string$(128," )
menuinfo.cch = 127
di = GetMenuItemInfo(MenuHandle, OffsetInMenu, True, menuinfo)
```

When GetMenuItemInfo is called, it receives a pointer to the menuinfo structure. The dwTypeData field contains a pointer to a 128-byte string filled with zeros. The function looks at that pointer, and loads up to 127 characters of data into the string. It loads the cch field with the actual length of the string (not including the NULL terminator character, which the function also places into the string).

When the function returns, Visual Basic looks at the dwTypeData field and converts the string that it points to back into Unicode. You can then perform the following function:

```
result$ = left$(menuinfo.dwTypeData, menuinfo.cch)
```

This extracts the string loaded by the function. Visual Basic will see the length of the string as 128 if you perform a Len(menuinfo.dwTypeData) call. Why isn't the Visual Basic Len function aware that the length of the string has changed? Because the GetMenuItemInfo function merely copied data into the string buffer, it did not change the length value that appears before the string data. The API function has no knowledge of OLE2 BSTR strings, so it treats the pointer as a simple memory pointer to a text string. If this was an OLE function, this might not be the case—OLE API functions often work with BSTR variables and can manipulate them directly in a way that is perfectly compatible with Visual Basic.

Still, this is a minor problem; as long as you pre-allocate the string, you can safely use the GetMenuItemInfo structure.

Or can you?

It turns out that this structure does not always return a string—in some cases, say, if the menu entry is a separator or a bitmap, it uses the dwTypeData field to return other, nonstring, information to the calling function. Figure 15.7 illustrates what can happen when this occurs. If the function sets the dwTypeData field to zero, when the function returns Visual Basic sees a NULL, or empty, string. When you try to reference the dwTypeData string you will find that it is empty. But what happened to the ANSI string? When the API function cleared the dwTypeData field, it also deleted Visual Basic's reference to the string. As a result, the string will never be freed—at least not until the application exits. And what happens if the dwTypeData field is set to some other value? Who knows? Whatever happens, you can count on it not being a correct result.

While you can use dynamic strings in structures that are passed to API and DLL functions, you can only do so safely when you are absolutely certain that the function will not modify the contents of the 32-bit string pointer itself; it can only modify the contents of the string that the pointer references.

And what about cases where Windows allocates its own string and places a pointer to that string into the structure? Unless it is an OLE API function, the results of doing this are almost sure to be fatal. Visual Basic will assume that the pointer is a valid BSTR (which will not be the case), it will look for the length before the text part of the string (sure to be an invalid value), and will ultimately try to free the string. The likely result will be a memory exception or other serious error.

Figure 15.7

Potential memory allocation problem with dynamic strings

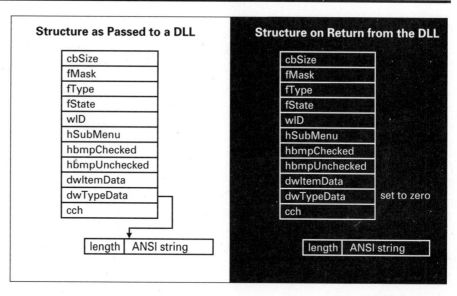

Another problem can arise when using block memory copies. Sometimes you will use memory buffers (either global memory blocks or byte arrays) to load information from an API function. In these cases it is common to copy all or part of the buffer into a locally allocated structure to make it easy to access individual fields within the structure. This can be seen in many of the examples in Chapter 12. If you try to perform a block memory copy into a structure that has dynamic strings defined, you are likely to cause an immediate memory exception, as Visual Basic will expect a valid BSTR in those fields and will not find one.

- To summarize, the only time it is safe to use a dynamic string inside of a structure is when:

- The API function expects a pointer to a string (LPSTR) that it will not modify.

- The API function expects a pointer to a string, and is sure to load the contents of the string buffer that you provide, but will not under any circumstances change the value of the pointer variable in the structure.

- You will not be using memory copy techniques to copy the structure to and from a memory buffer.

Using Long Variables for Dynamic Strings Inside Structures

In cases where it is not safe to use a String declaration, the solution is to declare the variable as a long as shown in the first MENUITEMINFO structure above.

In this case you must allocate your own buffer to use to hold the string and perform any necessary string conversions yourself. You can allocate a memory buffer using the techniques described earlier in this chapter. Or you can use a byte array. Take a close look at this partial code from the Menu-Look.vbp sample application from Chapter 10:

```
Private Sub ViewMenu(ByVal menuhnd&)
    Dim menulen&
    Dim di&
#If Win32 Then
    Dim thismenu&
    Dim menuid&
    Dim currentpopup&
    Dim menuinfo As MENUITEMINFO
#End If
    Dim db%
    Dim menuflags%
    Dim flagstring$
    Dim menustring(128) As Byte
    Dim context&

' Find out how many entries are in the menu.
menulen = GetMenuItemCount(menuhnd)
menuinfo.cbSize = Len(menuinfo)
' Note - this way of returning a string will not work on VB3

        For thismenu = ¯ To menulen - 1
            ' cch field is reset each time
            menuinfo.cch = 127
            menuinfo.dwTypeData = agGetAddressForObject(menustring(¯))
            menuinfo.fMask = MIIM_DATA Or MIIM_ID Or MIIM_STATE Or MIIM_SUBMENU _
            Or MIIM_TYPE Or MIIM_CHECKMARKS

            ' Get the ID for this menu
            ' It's a command ID, -1 for a popup, ¯ for a seperator
            di = GetMenuItemInfo(menuhnd, thismenu, True, menuinfo)
            With menuinfo
                If .hSubMenu <> ¯ Then
                    List1.AddItem "Entry #" + Str$(thismenu) + _
                    " is a submenu. Handle = " + Hex$(.hSubMenu) + " is " _
                    + Left$(StrConv(menustring, vbUnicode), .cch)
```

The function creates a byte array called menustring to hold the string information. You can obtain the address of the start of an array by using the agGetAddressForObject function and passing it the first element in the array. When the GetMenuItemInfo function is called one of two things can happen. If it needs to return a string, the byte array will be loaded with the ANSI string. But what happens if the function sets the dwTypeData field to zero or some other value?

Nothing. The field will be set to the new value. The menustring array is defined and managed by Visual Basic—so there is no chance of a memory leak. It is, of course, your responsibility to determine the meaning of the dwTypeData field based on the result of the function. In this case, if the hSubMenu field is nonzero, you can assume that there is a valid string in the menustring array.

Visual Basic makes it easy to convert between strings and byte arrays—you can simply assign one to another. If you pass a byte array to a function expecting a string, it is converted automatically. But remember the earlier process in which Visual Basic converted the string to and from Unicode? This does not occur automatically in this case: When you convert a byte array to a string it simply copies the data. It is your responsibility to convert the data to the internal Unicode format required by Visual Basic. This is accomplished using the StrConv function. The Left$ function is used to extract the correct number of characters.

Can you avoid the Unicode conversions? Sure, all you need to do is use a type library that lets you access the Unicode entry point for the API function (this is discussed briefly in Chapter 3). Of course, the program will no longer work under Windows 95, but that is just another of the trade-offs involved.

Other Samples

Additional information on using strings within structures can be found in Chapter 9 under the heading "Dynamically Sized Structures" and in Chapter 12 under the heading "Spooler Functions and Structures."

Resources

Resources provide a mechanism for including various objects and data in an executable file. Visual Basic is able to add many types of resources to an application by way of a resource file. In order to understand both the features and limitations of the resource mechanism, it is first necessary to understand what resources are and how they work with regular Windows applications.

Resources and Windows Applications

Some of the objects that are used under Windows can have a great deal of data associated with them. Consider, for example, the case of a font.

A font has associated with it all the data in the TEXTMETRIC structure introduced in Chapter 11. It also contains all the information needed to actually draw each character, and the spacing information needed to draw a text string. This can easily total thousands of bytes of data.

Icons are another example of an object that requires a fair amount of data. On a 16-color VGA monitor, the typical 32x32 pixel icon requires 512 bytes for one device-independent bitmap, an additional 128 bytes for the monochrome mask, and additional space for the icon header information.

Other objects that can take large amounts of data are bitmaps, strings, and cursors.

In many cases, it is desirable to include one or more of these objects in an executable file. This poses an interesting problem. In C or Pascal it is possible to hard code the data—to create static data structures that have the binary data defined. But this approach is tricky. First, it can be excruciatingly difficult to program. Imagine writing out the pattern for a bitmap in hexadecimal! Second, this approach makes it extremely difficult to change the object, a problem if you need to support several languages in your program for use in foreign countries.

Windows solves this problem through a mechanism called Windows resources. A resource is a block of data that represents a Windows object such as a cursor, icon, bitmap, font, or string. Each Windows executable file contains a resource table that lists the resources in the file. The Windows API contains functions that allow you to load these resources.

Each resource is created using an appropriate tool. Icons, bitmaps, and cursors are created with specialized image drawing programs. The Iconwrks program provided with Visual Basic is an example of an icon editor. Strings are created using a text editor. Fonts are created using special font editing programs.

Once the data for each object is created, a special tool known as a resource compiler combines the objects into a single resource file. The resource editor can then be used to insert the resource file into an executable file. Figure 15.8 illustrates the sequence of operations needed to add resources to an executable file.

The resource compiler makes use of a special resource definition file that lists the resources to include. It can also be used to define dialog boxes, menus, and even user-defined resources.

You might consider the entire concept of resources to be an incredibly powerful and flexible equivalent to the BASIC "Data" statement, except that you can save not only strings, but virtually any type of data object. Once resources are included in an executable file, they can be loaded by the application as needed.

One of the powerful subtleties of this approach becomes clear when you consider the fact that any application can load the resources contained in *any* executable file, including dynamic link libraries. For example, it is possible to create a dynamic link library that has no functions or program code at all—only hundreds of icon resources that are available to any application.

One of the other advantages of the Windows resource mechanism is that resources are loaded only as needed. Not only that, but Windows can discard them if necessary and reload them automatically when they are again required.

Resources and Visual Basic

In addition to Visual Basic's ability to work with resource files, the resource API functions are generally compatible with Visual Basic, thus your VB application can easily access resources in dynamic link libraries or executable files.

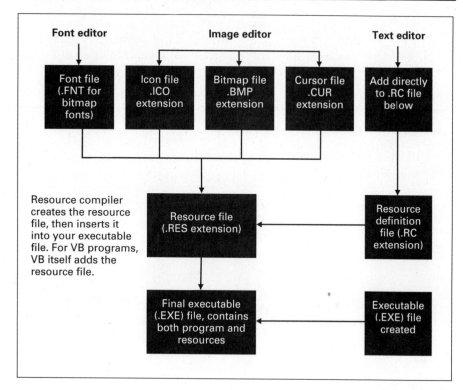

Figure 15.8

Creating resources

There are several approaches you can take to use resources under Visual Basic. The most common use will be to take advantage of the standard "stock" (built-in) Windows resources such as icons or bitmaps. The StockBms sample application described in Chapter 9 shows how this is accomplished.

Another approach is to create your own executable files that contain resources. To do this you will need a set of resource development tools that are capable of creating resource files, and the appropriate object generation or editing programs. These are available from a number of vendors, for example: Desaware's StorageTools includes a resource compiler that works as an add-in within Visual Basic.

A third approach is to extract resources from existing executable files. The Windows API provides a powerful set of functions for loading or directly reading resources from an executable file if you know that it is there—in other words, if you know the name or identifier of the resource. For example, the ExtraIcon function allows you to rapidly scan through any icon resources in a file.

Resource API Functions

Every resource must have a unique type and a unique name or identifier, each of which can take two forms: a string or an integer. Windows defines a number of standard resource types, which are listed in Table 15.6. These types are integer constants with the constant names shown in the table.

Table 15.6   **Resource Types**

Constant Value	Description
RT_ACCELERATOR	An accelerator table. Not useful in Visual Basic.
RT_BITMAP	A bitmap. May be loaded with the Loadbitmap function.
RT_DIALOG	A dialog box. Dialog resources are not useful in Visual Basic.
RT_FONT	A font. Can be used with the AddFontResource function.
RT_FONTDIR	A font directory.
RT_MENU	A menu resource. Not useful in Visual Basic.
RT_RCDATA	Raw data stream.
RT_STRING	A string resource. May be loaded with the LoadString function.
RT_MESSAGETABLE	A message table.
RT_CURSOR	A cursor. May be loaded with the LoadCursor function.
RT_GROUP_CURSOR	A cursor (hardware independent).
RT_ICON	An icon. May be loaded with the LoadIcon function.
RT_GROUP_ICON	An icon (hardware independent).
RT_VERSION	A version resource. Use the version API functions described in Chapter 13 to access these resources.
Other integer value 0–32767	Either a standard resource type not defined here, or an application defined resource type.
Any string	A standard resource type, such as "TYPELIB," which identifies a type library, or an application defined resource type.

An application can define its own resource types using other integer values or type names. Each resource must also have a unique name. For example, an icon resource can have the name "Icon1." You would pass the string "Icon1" to the resource API functions when you wish to access or load this icon.

In order to save space, however, most resources are identified by an integer. Most of the resource API functions expect the resource identifier to be a 32-bit long parameter. If the high-order 16 bits are zero, the function assumes that the low-order 16 bits contain the integer identifier. Otherwise the function assumes that the parameter is a 32-bit pointer to a NULL terminated string containing the name of the resource.

Win32 has improved on Win16 with regard to its ability to browse through existing resources in a file, eliminating the need to examine an executable directly to determine what resources it contains.

Most of the resource access functions that a Visual Basic programmer would use are defined in the chapters that describe the associated Windows object. For example, the LoadBitmap API function used to load bitmap resources is described in Chapter 9 with the other bitmap functions.

Most of the resource API functions described in Table 15.7 are thus rarely used in Visual Basic. These functions are used internally by Windows to implement specific resource functions such as LoadBitmap and LoadIcon. They are made available through the Windows API primarily in order to support user-defined resources. Refer to the function reference for an outline of how they are used.

Table 15.7   General Resource Functions

Function	Description
BeginUpdateResource	Starts a resource update operation
CreateIconFromResource CreateIconFromResourceEx	Creates an icon handle given a block of memory in a resource file
EndUpdateResource	Ends a resource update operation
EnumResourceLanguages	Enumerates all of the languages for a particular resource
EnumResourceNames	Enumerates all of the resources for a given resource type
FindResource FindResourceEx	Finds a resource in an executable file
FreeResource	Frees a resource
LoadResource	Loads a resource into memory
LoadString	Loads a string resource
LockResource	Obtains a pointer to a resource in memory
LookupIconIdFromDirectory LookupIconIdFromDirectoryEx	Finds the icon resource that best suits the current display

Table 15.7	**General Resource Functions (Continued)**	
SizeofResource		Determines the size of a resource
UpdateResource		Updates a resource in a file

The general sequence of operations is as follows:

1. Use the FindResource function to obtain a resource information handle.

2. Use the LoadResource function to obtain a handle to the resource and to load the resource.

3. Use the LockResource function to lock the resource and obtain a pointer to the resource data.

4. Use the GlobalUnlock function to unlock the resource.

5. Use the FreeResource function to free the memory used by the resource and the resource handle.

A simple font resource browser project, resource.vbp, is included on the CD-ROM source code directory for this chapter. Extending this sample to actually show the resources that it lists is left as an exercise for the reader.

Atoms and Properties

You've seen that Windows makes extensive use of handles to identify objects. You've also seen that many objects, such as windows, can have data associated with them as attributes. It should be no surprise that Windows also provides the ability to use these techniques for user-defined data.

This takes two forms. The Windows atom functions make it possible to assign a handle to any string. The Windows property functions make it possible to associate a handle with a window.

Atoms

An *atom* is a handle to a string. There are two types of atoms, local atoms and global atoms. A local atom is accessible only by the application that created it. A global atom is accessible by any application in the system.

An atom is created using the AddAtom or GlobalAddAtom function. These functions take a string as a parameter and return the integer atom value. The string may then be retrieved using the GetAtomName or Global-GetAtomName function. If an attempt is made to create another atom using the same string, the same integer atom value will be returned—in other words, a given string can have only one atom value. Strings used in atoms are not case-sensitive.

The most common use for global atoms is to transfer data between applications. The dynamic data exchange (DDE) system uses them extensively. Otherwise they are not of much use to the Visual Basic programmer. Table 15.8 lists the local and global atom functions.

Table 15.8   **Atom Functions**

Function	Description
AddAtom	Creates an atom
DeleteAtom	Deletes an atom
FindAtom	Retrieves the atom number for a string
GetAtomName	Retrieves the string given an atom number
GlobalAddAtom	Creates a global atom
GlobalDeleteAtom	Deletes a global atom
GlobalFindAtom	Retrieves the global atom number for a string
GlobalGetAtomName	Retrieves the string given a global atom number
InitAtomTable	Changes the size of a local atom hash table

Property Functions

The term *property* under Windows does not refer to the properties that each Visual Basic control possesses. Property here refers to the ability to associate any integer data value with a window based on the name of the property. For example, you can create a property for a window named PenToUse, which has an integer handle to a pen object as its value. Once you have created the property, you can retrieve the pen handle at any time by referencing property PenToUse.

The name of the property can be specified using a global atom instead of a string.

Any application can access window properties, thus this is another mechanism that can be used to share data. However, be careful: An application can access the values of the property but should only use those handles that are legally accessible to it.

Another common use of properties is to identify a window as belonging to a common set of applications. For example, let's say you have created a series of programs. You would like to set things up so that if any one of these programs is opened, the other programs will be minimized.

Chapter 5 showed how you can enumerate windows to find out which applications are open. There also needs to be a way to identify which programs belong to that series of applications. You could examine the application name, but this works only if you know in advance the name of every program that you wish to belong to the series.

A better approach is to define a property—for example, you could define a property called MinimizeOnRequest for the main form of each program in the series. Now all you need to do is enumerate all of the top-level windows and minimize any window that has the property MinimizeOnRequest defined. You could even get more sophisticated and base the operation on the value of the property; for example, you could define property HandleOnRequest for which the value 0 indicates no operation, 1 indicates to minimize the window, 2 indicates to redraw the window, and so on.

Properties for a window should be removed using the RemoveProperty function before a window is destroyed. One way to do this is to remove the properties for a form and any controls on that form during the form's Unload event.

The property functions are listed in Table 15.9.

Table 15.9   **Property Functions**

Function	Description
EnumProps	Enumerates all the properties for a window. This function requires use of the dwcbk32d.ocx custom control.
GetProp	Retrieves the value of a property.
RemoveProp	Removes a property.
SetProp	Creates a property.

Function Reference

This section contains an alphabetical reference for the functions described in this chapter.

■ AddAtom

VB Declaration
```
Declare Function AddAtom% Lib "kernel32" Alias "AddAtomA" (ByVal lpString As _
String)
```

Description   Adds an atom to the local atom table.

Use with VB   No problem.

Parameter	Type/Description
lpString	String—The string associated with the atom, also known as the name of the atom.

Return Value   Integer—The atom value on success, zero on error.

Platform   Windows 95, Windows NT, Win16

Comments   You should always check the result to make sure that the atom was allocated successfully. Also note that atoms are not case-sensitive.

■ BeginUpdateResource

VB Declaration
```
Declare Function BeginUpdateResource& Lib "kernel32" Alias _
"BeginUpdateResourceA" (ByVal pFileName As String, ByVal _
bDeleteExistingResources As Long)
```

Description   Use to begin the process of updating resources in an executable file.

Use with VB   No problem.

Parameter	Type/Description
pFileName	String—The name of the executable or DLL whose resources are being updated. The file must not be executing when this function is called.
bDeleteExistin-gResources	Long—True (nonzero) to delete all current resources in the file. If False, existing resources will only be changed if specified during an UpdateResource call.

Return Value   Long—A handle to use with the UpdateResource function to update the resources in the file.

Platform   Windows NT

Comments   Resources in an executable file or DLL can be updated by first calling BeginUpdateResource, then calling UpdateResource for each resource to modify, then closing EndUpdateResource to conclude the update operation.

■ CharLower

VB Declaration   `Declare Function CharLower& Lib "user32" Alias "CharLowerA" (ByVal lpsz As _`
`String)`

Description   Converts a string to lowercase based on the current locale or language driver.

Use with VB   No problem, but the VB LCase function is roughly equivalent.

. Parameter	Type/Description
lpsz	String—String to convert to lowercase. The string is converted in place. If you create an alias that takes a long parameter, the low 16 bits of lpsz can be a single character to convert to lowercase (the high 16 bits must be zero). In this case, the return value is the value of the lowercase character.

Return Value   Long—No meaning under VB if converting a string. The value of the lowercase character if converting a single character.

Platform   Windows 95, Windows NT

Porting Notes   Replaces the AnsiLower Win16 function.

■ CharLowerBuff

VB Declaration   `Declare Function CharLowerBuff& Lib "user32" Alias "CharLowerBuffA" (ByVal lpsz _`
`As String, ByVal cchLength As Long)`

Description   Converts a string to lowercase based on the current locale or language driver.
This function converts the number of characters specified and will ignore any NULL characters in the buffer.

Use with VB   No problem.

Parameter	Type/Description
lpsz	String—A string or pointer to a memory block to convert to lowercase.
cchLength	Long—The number of characters to convert.

Return Value   Long—The number of characters converted.

Platform   Windows 95, Windows NT

Porting Notes   Replaces the AnsiLowerBuff Win16 function.

■ CharNext

VB Declaration   `Declare Function CharNext& Lib "user32" Alias "CharNextA" (ByVal lpsz As String)`

Description	Returns a pointer to the next character in a string. Under a double-byte character set, each character may take one or two bytes, thus adding 1 to the location if one character does not always point to the next character.
Use with VB	This function provided one way to retrieve the address of a string in memory under Win16. Under Win32, however, it retrieves the address of the temporary copy of a string created by Visual Basic when it converts an internal Unicode string to ANSI for use with DLL calls. This value (and thus the entire function) is therefore worthless to Visual Basic programmers under Win32.

■ CharPrev

VB Declaration	```Declare Function CharPrev& Lib "user32" Alias "CharPrevA" (ByVal lpszStart _ As String, ByVal lpszCurrent As String)```
Description	Similar to CharNext, except that it retrieves the location of the previous character in a DBCS string.
Use with VB	See the CharNext function.

■ CharUpper

VB Declaration	```Declare Function CharUpper& Lib "user32" Alias "CharUpperA" (ByVal lpsz As _ String)```
Description	Converts a string to uppercase based on the current locale or language driver.
Use with VB	No problem, but the VB UCase function is roughly equivalent.

Parameter	Type/Description
lpsz	String—String to convert to uppercase. The string is converted in place. If you create an alias that takes a long parameter, the low 16 bits of lpsz can be a single character to convert to uppercase (the high 16 bits must be zero). In this case, the return value is the value of the uppercase character.

Return Value	Long—No meaning under VB if converting a string. The value of the uppercase character if converting a single character.
Platform	Windows 95, Windows NT
Porting Notes	Replaces the AnsiUpper Win16 function.

■ CharUpperBuff

VB Declaration	```Declare Function CharUpperBuff& Lib "user32" Alias "CharUpperBuffA" (ByVal lpsz _ As String, ByVal cchLength As Long)```
Description	Converts a string to uppercase based on the current locale or language driver. This function converts the number of characters specified and will ignore any NULL characters in the buffer.

Use with VB	No problem.	
	Parameter	**Type/Description**
	lpsz	String—A string or pointer to a memory block to convert to uppercase.
	cchLength	Long—The number of characters to convert.

Return Value   Long—The number of characters converted.

Platform   Windows 95, Windows NT

Porting Notes   Replaces the AnsiUpperBuff Win16 function.

■ CompareString

VB Declaration
```
Declare Function CompareString& Lib "kernel32" Alias "CompareStringA" (ByVal _
Locale As Long, ByVal dwCmpFlags As Long, ByVal lpString1 As String, ByVal _
cchCount1 As Long, ByVal lpString2 As String, ByVal cchCount2 As Long)
```

Description   Compares two strings based on the text comparison settings for a specified locale.

Use with VB	No problem.	
	Parameter	**Type/Description**
	Locale	Long—The locale identifier to use for the comparison.
	dwCmpFlags	Long—One or more of the constants with the prefix NORM_??? that specifies options such as ignoring case.
	lpString1	String—The first string to compare.
	cchCount1	Long—The length of the string in bytes (not characters in the case of DBCS strings). –1 to calculate automatically (based on the NULL terminator).
	lpString2	String—The second string to compare.
	cchCount2	Long—The length of the second string (see notes for cchCount1).

Return Value   Long—1 if lpString1<lpString2, 2 if they are equal, 3 if lpString1>lpString2. Sets GetLastError.

Platform   Windows 95, Windows NT

Comments   This function performs a language dependent comparison, not one based strictly on the character values.

■ CreateIconFromResource, CreateIconFromResourceEx

VB Declaration
```
Declare Function CreateIconFromResource& Lib "user32" (presbits As Byte, ByVal _
dwResSize As Long, ByVal fIcon As Long, ByVal dwVer As Long)
Declare Function CreateIconFromResourceEx Lib "user32" (presbits As Byte, ByVal _
dwResSize As Long, ByVal fIcon As Long, ByVal dwVer As Long, ByVal cxDesired As _
```

Long, ByVal cyDesired As Long, ByVal uFlags As Long) As Long

Description	Creates an icon or cursor given raw data from a resource file.
Use with VB	No problem.

Parameter	Type/Description
presbits	Byte—The first byte in a buffer containing raw resource data. Change to ByVal As Long to pass a memory address of a block of memory containing icon data.
dwResSize	Long—The size of the icon data.
fIcon	Long—TRUE (nonzero) to create an icon. Zero to create a cursor.
dwVer	Long—&H20000& to create a Windows 2.x icon. &H30000& for Win32 and Win3.x icons.
cxDesiredcy-Desired	Long—CreateIconFromResourceEx only. The requested width and height for the icon or cursor. Zero to use the standard values as returned by the GetSystemMetrics function.
uFlags	Long—CreateIconFromResourceEx only. One of the following: LR_DEFAULTCOLOR: Uses the default color format for the object. LR_LOADREALSIZE: Uses the size specified in the data structures in the data stream. LR_MONOCHROME: Forces the object to be monochrome.

Return Value	Long—A handle to the newly created icon or cursor. Zero on error. Sets GetLastError.
Platform	Windows 95, Windows NT
Comments	The LoadResource and LookupIconIdFromDirectoryEx can obtain a pointer to raw resource data.

■ DeleteAtom

VB Declaration	`Declare Function DeleteAtom% Lib "kernel32" (ByVal nAtom As Integer)`
Description	Deletes the specified atom.
Use with VB	No problem.

Parameter	Type/Description
nAtom	Integer—The atom number to delete.

Return Value	Integer—Zero on success, the atom number on failure.
Platform	Windows 95, Windows NT, Win16
Comments	If the atom has been allocated multiple times, the atom will not actually be deleted until this function has been called the same number of times. Windows maintains a reference count for each atom.

■ EndUpdateResource

VB Declaration `Declare Function EndUpdateResource& Lib "kernel32" Alias "EndUpdateResourceA" _`
`(ByVal hUpdate As Long, ByVal fDiscard As Long)`

Description Terminates a resource update operation started by the BeginUpdateResource function.

Use with VB No problem.

Parameter	Type/Description
hUpdate	Long—A handle returned by the BeginUpdateResource function.
fDiscard	Long—TRUE (nonzero) to discard all changes made by the UpdateResource function since the last call to BeginUpdateResource. If zero, the changes made by UpdateResource calls will be written into the file.

Return Value Long—TRUE (Nonzero) on success, zero on failure. Sets GetLastError.

Platform Windows NT

Comments See the BeginUpdateResource function.

■ EnumProps, EnumPropsEx

VB Declaration `Declare Function EnumProps& Lib "user32" Alias "EnumPropsA" (ByVal hWnd As _`
`Long, ByVal lpEnumFunc As Long)`
`Declare Function EnumPropsEx& Lib "user32" Alias "EnumPropsExA" (ByVal hWnd As _`
`Long, ByVal lpEnumFunc As Long, ByVal lParam As Long)`

Description Enumerates the properties of a window. For Visual Basic 4.0, this function requires use of the dwcbk32d.ocx custom control provided with this book. The EnumProps event of the control will be triggered for each property (use cbxLLLL for EnumPropsEx). Refer to Appendix A for further information.

Use with VB Requires use of the dwcbk32d.ocx demo custom control under VB 4.0.

Parameter	Type/Description
hWnd	Long—A handle of a window for which properties are to be enumerated.
lpEnumFunc	Long—A function address obtained using the AddressOf operator (VB 5 and later) or the ProcAddress property of the dwcbk32d.ocx custom control (VB 4).
lpParam	Long—(EnumPropsEx only) A user-defined value.

Return Value Long—1 if there were no properties to be enumerated. Otherwise returns the last value set by the callback function.

Platform Windows 95, Windows NT, Win16

Comments   The callback function should be defined as follows for EnumProps:

```
Public Function EnumPropCallback (ByVal hwnd&, ByVal lpString&, ByVal hData&) _
as Long
```

And as follows for EnumPropsEx:

```
Public Function EnumPropCallback (ByVal hwnd&, ByVal lpString&, ByVal hData&, _
ByVal lpParam&) as Long
```

hWnd is the hWnd parameter to the EnumProps function.

Use agGetStringFromPointer to retrieve a VB string from the lpString address retrieved from this function.

HData is the data handle or value associated with the property.

lpParam is the value passed to the EnumPropsEx function.

Under Visual Basic 4.0, use the EnumProps callback type #5 for EnumProps and callback type #24 (cbxLLLL) for EnumPropsEx.

Do not perform a DoEvents during the callback function or event.

Do not attempt to remove properties other than the one being enumerated during the callback function or event.

Do not add properties during the callback function or event.

Example   EnumProp.vbp.

■ EnumResourceLanguages

VB Declaration
```
Declare Function EnumResourceLanguages& Lib "kernel32" Alias _
"EnumResourceLanguagesA" (ByVal hModule As Long, ByVal lpType As String, ByVal _
lpName As String, ByVal lpEnumFunc As Long, ByVal lParam As Long)
```

Description   Enumerates the languages for a specified resource.

Use with VB   Under Visual Basic 4.0 requires use of the dwcbk32d.ocx demo control provided with this book.

Parameter	Type/Description
hModule	Long—A module containing a resource. Typically obtained using the LoadLibrary or LoadLibraryEx function.
lpType	String or Long—A resource type as described by Table 15.6.
lpName	String or Long—The identifier of the resource. Refer to the chapter text for details.
lpEnumFunc	Long—The address of an enumeration function obtained using the AddressOf function (VB5 or later) or as provided by the ProcAddress property of the dwcbk32d.ocx control (VB4).
lParam	Long—Any user-defined value.

Return Value   Long—Nonzero on success, zero on failure. Sets GetLastError.

Platform   Windows 95, Windows NT

Comments
It is possible for the resource part of a file to contain resources for different languages. When a resource exists for multiple languages, this function can be used to enumerate the languages for which it is available.

The callback function should be defined as follows:
```
Public Function ResourceLangCallback (ByVal hModule&, ByVal lpType&, ByVal _
lpName&, ByVal ival%, ByVal lParam&) As Long
```

hModule, lpName, lpType and lParam are the parameters passed to the EnumResourceLanguages function. Ival is the language identifier (see Table 13.20).

For VB4, use the cbxLLLIL callback type 34 for the Type property of the dwcbk32d.ocx control. Return TRUE to continue the enumeration process, zero to end it.

Example
The resource.vbp project demonstrates EnumResourceNames and EnumResourceTypes, which are similar.

■ EnumResourceNames

VB Declaration
```
Declare Function EnumResourceNames& Lib "kernel32" Alias "EnumResourceNamesA" _
(ByVal hModule As Long, ByVal lpType As String, ByVal lpEnumFunc As Long, ByVal _
lParam As Long)
```

Description
Enumerates the resources of a given type in a loaded module.

Use with VB
Under Visual Basic 4.0 requires use of the dwcbk32d.ocx demo control provided with this book.

Parameter	Type/Description
hModule	Long—A module containing a resource. Typically obtained using the LoadLibrary or LoadLibraryEx function.
lpType	String or Long—A resource type as described by Table 15.6.
lpEnumFunc	Long—The address of an enumeration function obtained using the AddressOf operator (VB5 and later) or provided by the ProcAddress property of the dwcbk32d.ocx control (VB4).
lParam	Long—Any user-defined value.

Return Value
Long—Nonzero on success, zero on failure. Sets GetLastError.

Platform
Windows 95, Windows NT

Comments
The callback function should be defined as follows:
```
Public Function ResourceNamesCallback (ByVal hModule&, ByVal lpType&, ByVal _
lpName&, ByVal lParam&) As Long
```

hModule, lpType, and lParam are the parameters passed to the EnumResourceNames function.

lval3—The name of the enumerated resource (may be an integer between 0 and 32K or the address of a string).

Return TRUE to continue the enumeration process, zero to end it.

For Visual Basic 4.0, use the cbxLLLL callback type 24 for the Type property of the dwcbk32d.ocx control.

Example   Resource.vbp

■ EnumResourceTypes

VB Declaration
```
Declare Function EnumResourceTypes& Lib "kernel32" Alias "EnumResourceTypesA" _
(ByVal hModule As Long, ByVal lpEnumFunc As Long, ByVal lParam As Long)
```

Description   Enumerates the types of resources available in a specified executable or DLL.

Use with VB   Under Visual Basic 4.0, this requires use of the dwcbk32d.ocx demo control provided with this book.

Parameter	Type/Description
hModule	Long—A module containing a resource. Typically obtained using the LoadLibrary or LoadLibraryEx function.
lpEnumFunc	Long—The address of an enumeration function obtained using the AddressOf operator (VB5 and later) or as provided by the ProcAddress property of the dwcbk32d.ocx control (VB4).
lParam	Long—Any user-defined value.

Return Value   Long—Nonzero on success, zero on failure. Sets GetLastError.

Platform   Windows 95, Windows NT

Comments   The callback function should be defined as follows:
```
Public Function ResourceTypesCallback (ByVal hModule&, ByVal lpType&, _
ByVal lParam&) As Long
```

hModule and lParam are the parameters passed to the EnumResourceTypes function.
LpType is the name of the enumerated resource (may be an integer between 0 and 32K or the address of a string).
Return TRUE to continue the enumeration process, zero to end it.
For Visual Basic 4.0, use the cbxLLLL callback type 23 for the Type property of the dwcbk32d.ocx control.

Example   Resource.vbp

■ FindAtom

VB Declaration
```
Declare Function FindAtom% Lib "kernel32" Alias "FindAtomA" (ByVal lpString As _
String)
```

Description   Retrieves the atom number for a string. The search is not case-sensitive.

Use with VB   No problem.

Parameter	Type/Description
lpString	String—The string to search for.

Return Value   Integer—The number of the atom for the string. Zero if there is no atom for the specified string. Sets GetLastError.

Platform   Windows 95, Windows NT, Win16

■ FindResource, FindResourceEx

VB Declaration
```
Declare Function FindResource& Lib "kernel32" Alias "FindResourceA" (ByVal _
hInstance As Long, ByVal lpName As String, ByVal lpType As String)
Declare Function FindResourceEx& Lib "kernel32" Alias "FindResourceExA" (ByVal _
hModule As Long, ByVal lpType As String, ByVal lpName As String, ByVal _
wLanguage As Integer)
```

Description   Finds the specified resource in an executable file and returns a resource handle that can be used by other functions to actually load the resource.

Use with VB   No problem.

Parameter	Type/Description
hInstance	Long—A handle to a loaded executable module that contains the desired resource.
lpName	String or Long—The identifier of the requested resource. Resources are identified either by a name (contained in a string) or an integer. If using a string and the first character is the "#" symbol, the string specifies an integer ID in string format (for example, #56 finds resource number 56).
lpType	String or Long—A resource type as defined in Table 15.6.
wLanguage	Integer—(FindResourceEx only). A language identifier.

Return Value   Long—A special handle to the resource that can be used by other resource functions such as LoadResource to access the resource. Zero on error. Sets GetLastError.

Platform   Windows 95, Windows NT, Win16

Comments   Use the LoadCursor, LoadIcon, and LoadString functions to load cursors, icons, and strings. It is recommended that you use the LoadBitmap function to load bitmaps instead of doing it manually using this function and the LoadResource function.
    Note the reversed parameter order of the lpType and lpName parameter between the two functions.

■ FoldString

VB Declaration
```
Declare Function FoldString& Lib "kernel32" Alias "FoldStringA" (ByVal _
dwMapFlags As Long, ByVal lpSrcStr As String, ByVal cchSrc As Long, ByVal _
lpDestStr As String, ByVal cchDest As Long)
```

Description   Performs a variety of string conversions.

Use with VB   Since most of the conversions specified here are in Unicode, the primary use of this function would be to use the FoldStringW entry instead of the ANSI FoldStringA constant and pass a byte buffer containing a Unicode string as the lpSrcStr parameter (declare it "As Byte" and pass the first byte of the array containing a Unicode string). Use a byte buffer for the output as well.

Parameter	Type/Description
dwMapFlags	Long—One or more of the following constants: MAP_FOLDZONE: Converts characters between &F900 and &FFEF into standard Unicode characters. MAP_FOLDDIGITS: Converts all digit characters into the standard Unicode 0–9 digits. MAP_PRECOMPOSED: Converts any characters composed of two characters (such as an accent mark with a character) into a single character. MAP_COMPOSED: Where possible, converts any characters that can be composed of two characters (such as an accent mark with a character) from a single character into two characters.
lpSrcStr	String—A source string.
cchSrc	Long—The number of bytes in the string. –1 to calculate automatically (based on the NULL terminator).
lpDestStr	String—An output buffer for the converted string.
cchDest	Long—The size of the lpDestStr buffer. If zero, the function will return the necessary buffer size.

Return Value   Long—The size in bytes of the destination buffer. Zero on error. Sets GetLastError.

Platform   Windows NT

■ FreeResource

VB Declaration   `Declare Function FreeResource& Lib "kernel32" (ByVal hResData As Long)`

Description   Use to free resources allocated using the LoadResource function.

Use with VB   No problem.

Parameter	Type/Description
hResData	Long—The handle returned by LoadResource.

Return Value   Long—Zero on success, nonzero on error.

Platform   Windows 95, Win16. You need not call this function under Windows NT.

■ GetAtomName

VB Declaration   `Declare Function GetAtomName& Lib "kernel32" Alias "GetAtomNameA" (ByVal nAtom _`
`As Integer, ByVal lpBuffer As String, ByVal nSize As Long)`

Description   Retrieves the string associated with an atom.

Use with VB   No problem.

Parameter	Type/Description
nAtom	Integer—An atom number.
lpBuffer	String—A string buffer to load with the string associated with an atom. This buffer should be preallocated to at least nSize+1 characters long.
nSize	Long—The maximum number of characters to load into the buffer.

Return Value   Long—The number of characters loaded into the lpBuffer string. Zero on error. Sets GetLastError.

Platform   Windows 95, Windows NT, Win16

■ GetProcessHeap

VB Declaration   `Declare Function GetProcessHeap& Lib "kernel32" ()`

Description   Retrieves the current default heap for the process.

Use with VB   No problem.

Return Value   Long—A handle to the current process heap.

Platform   Windows 95, Windows NT

■ GetProcessHeaps

VB Declaration   `Declare Function GetProcessHeaps& Lib "kernel32" (ByVal NumberOfHeaps As Long, _`
`ProcessHeaps As Long)`

Description   Retrieves a list of all of the heaps currently in use by a process.

Use with VB   No problem.

Parameter	Type/Description
NumberOfHeaps	Long—The size of the ProcessHeaps array.
ProcessHeaps	Long—The first entry in an array of long values. This array will be loaded with the handles to the heaps defined for this process.

Return Value   Long—The total number of heaps available to the current process.

Platform   Windows 95, Windows NT

■ GetProp

VB Declaration   `Declare Function GetProp& Lib "user32" Alias "GetPropA" (ByVal hwnd As Long, _`

```
ByVal lpString As String)
```

Description   Retrieves the integer data handle for the specified property.

Use with VB   No problem.

Parameter	Type/Description
hwnd	Long—A handle to a window.
lpString	String—The name of the property or an atom to use as the name of the property. If it is an atom, it must be a global atom and the high word of the parameter must be zero.

Return Value   Long—The 32-bit value or handle that was saved for the property using the SetProp function.

Platform   Windows 95, Windows NT, Win16

■ GetStringTypeEx

VB Declaration
```
Declare Function GetStringTypeEx& Lib "kernel32" Alias "GetStringTypeExA" _
(ByVal Locale As Long, ByVal dwInfoType As Long, ByVal lpSrcStr As String, _
ByVal cchSrc As Long, lpCharType As Integer)
```

Description   Allows you to obtain information about each character in a string.

Use with VB   No problem. You can use the GetStringTypeExW entry point and pass the first character of a byte buffer containing Unicode characters as the lpSrcStr parameter to perform type determination for characters in a Unicode string.

Parameter	Type/Description
Locale	Long—The locale to use for the type determination.
dwInfoType	Long—One of the following constants: CT_TYPE1: Sets the C1_??? type flags for each character. CT_TYPE2: Sets the C2_??? type flags for each character. CT_TYPE3: Sets the C3_??? type flags for each character.
lpSrcStr	String—The string to analyze.
cchSrc	Long—The length of the string in the lpSrcStr parameter. –1 to calculate this value automatically (the string must be NULL terminated).
lpCharType	Integer—An integer array with one entry for each character in the lpSrcStr string. This array will be loaded with a value for each character containing flags describing the character.

Return Value   Long—TRUE (nonzero) on success, zero on error. Sets GetLastError.

Platform   Windows 95, Windows NT

Comments   C1_??? type flags allow you to determine if a character is upper- or lowercase, is a character, number, or punctuation mark, and so on.
    C2_??? type flags allow you to determine the standard spacing and type direction of a character.

C3_??? type flags allow you to determine characteristics of characters for string processing operations using the standard C libraries and are not directly applicable to Visual Basic.

Refer to the declarations in the API32.TXT file for a list of the conversion constants. Refer to Chapter 3 for information on extracting bit values from flag variables.

■ GlobalAddAtom

VB Declaration
```
Declare Function GlobalAddAtom% Lib "kernel32" Alias "GlobalAddAtomA" (ByVal _
lpString As String)
```

Description   Adds an atom to the global atom table.

Use with VB   No problem, but the size of the global atom table is limited so it is suggested that you avoid holding atoms.

Parameter	Type/Description
lpString	String—The string associated with the atom, also known as the name of the atom.

Return Value   Integer—The atom value on success (&C000 through &FFFF), zero on error. Sets GetLastError.

Platform   Windows 95, Windows NT, Win16

Comments   You should always check the result to make sure that the atom was allocated successfully. Also note that atoms are not case-sensitive.

■ GlobalAlloc

VB Declaration
```
Declare Function GlobalAlloc& Lib "kernel32" (ByVal wFlags As Long, ByVal _
dwBytes As Long)
```

Description   Allocates a block of global memory.

Use with VB   Refer to "Using Global Memory Blocks from Visual Basic," earlier in this chapter.

Parameter	Type/Description
wFlags	Long—Constant flags that specify the type of memory to allocate as follows: GMEM_FIXED: Allocates a fixed memory block. GMEM_MOVEABLE: Allocates a moveable memory block. GMEM_DISCARDABLE: Allocates a discardable memory block. GMEM_NOCOMPACT: The heap will not be compacted during this function call. GMEM_NODISCARD: No memory blocks will be discarded during this function call. GMEM_ZEROINIT: The newly allocated memory block is initialized to all zeros.
dwBytes	Long—The number of bytes to allocate.

Return Value   Long—A global memory handle. Zero on error. Sets GetLastError.

Platform   Windows 95, Windows NT, Win16

Comments   If GMEM_FIXED is specified, the return value is the actual memory address to use (Global-Lock will return this same value)—thus you need not perform a GlobalLock/GlobalUnlock when using fixed memory blocks.

Due to Win32's advanced memory management scheme, there is no advantage to using move-able memory blocks.

Memory blocks allocated with this function are allowed on 8-byte boundaries.

Porting Notes Many Win16 wFlags constants have no meaning under Win32.

Remember that global memory handles under Win32 are private to an application—you can-not use global memory handles to exchange data between applications. Use file mappings (see Chapter 13) to transfer blocks of memory between processes.

Example   QuikDraw.vbp in Chapter 8. PicPrint.vbp in Chapter 12.

■ GlobalDeleteAtom

VB Declaration `Declare Function GlobalDeleteAtom% Lib "kernel32" (ByVal nAtom As Integer)`

Description   Deletes the specified global atom.

Use with VB   No problem.

Parameter	Type/Description
nAtom	Integer—The atom number to delete.

Return Value   Integer—Zero on success, the atom number on failure. Sets GetLastError.

Platform   Windows 95, Windows NT, Win16

Comments   If the atom has been allocated multiple times, the atom will not actually be deleted until this func-tion has been called the same number of times. Windows maintains a reference count for each atom.

■ GlobalFindAtom

VB Declaration `Declare Function GlobalFindAtom% Lib "kernel32" Alias "GlobalFindAtomA" (ByVal _`
`lpString As String)`

Description   Retrieves the global atom number for a string.

Use with VB   No problem.

Parameter	Type/Description
lpString	String—The string to search for.

Return Value   Integer—The number of the global atom for the string. Zero if there is no atom for the specified string. Sets GetLastError.

Platform	Windows 95, Windows NT, Win16

■ GlobalFlags

VB Declaration	`Declare Function GlobalFlags& Lib "kernel32" (ByVal hMem As Long)`
Description	Retrieves the global memory flags for a memory block.
Use with VB	No problem.

Parameter	Type/Description
hMem	Long—A handle to a global memory block.

Return Value	Long—The low 8 bits of the integer contain the current lock count for the memory block. Flag bits set as specified by the following constants: GMEM_DISCARDABLE: The memory block is discardable. GMEM_DISCARDED: The memory block has been discarded.
Platform	Windows 95, Windows NT, Win16

■ GlobalFree

VB Declaration	`Declare Function GlobalFree& Lib "kernel32" (ByVal hMem As Long)`
Description	Frees the specified global memory block. After calling this function, handle hMem will no longer be valid. Be sure that the memory block is not locked when this function is called.
Use with VB	Refer to "Using Global Memory Blocks from Visual Basic," earlier in this chapter.

Parameter	Type/Description
hMem	Long—A handle to a global memory block to free.

Return Value	Long—Zero on success, hMem on error.
Platform	Windows 95, Windows NT, Win16
Comments	Once memory has been freed, any attempt to write into that block of memory can corrupt the process heap, leading to a fatal exception.
Example	QuikDraw.vbp in Chapter 8. PicPrint.vbp in Chapter 12.

■ GlobalGetAtomName

VB Declaration	`Declare Function GlobalGetAtomName& Lib "kernel32" Alias "GlobalGetAtomNameA" _` `(ByVal nAtom As Integer, ByVal lpBuffer As String, ByVal nSize As Long)`
Description	Retrieves the string associated with a global atom.

Use with VB	No problem.

Parameter	Type/Description
nAtom	Integer—An atom number.
lpBuffer	String—A string buffer to load with the string associated with a global atom. This buffer should be preallocated to at least nSize+1 characters long.
nSize	Long—The maximum number of characters to load into the buffer.

Return Value Long—The number of characters loaded into the lpBuffer string. Sets GetLastError.

Platform Windows 95, Windows NT, Win16

■ GlobalHandle

VB Declaration `Declare Function GlobalHandle& Lib "kernel32" (wMem As Any)`

Description Determines the memory handle for a memory block given a selector.

Use with VB No problem.

Parameter	Type/Description
wMem	Any— A memory address—typically a long value (passed ByVal) to an address returned by a GlobalLock function.

Return Value Long—The memory handle. Zero if the wMem address is invalid. Sets GetLastError.

Platform Windows 95, Windows NT, Win16

■ GlobalLock

VB Declaration `Declare Function GlobalLock& Lib "kernel32" (ByVal hMem As Long)`

Description Locks the specified memory block in memory and returns an address value that points to the beginning of the memory block. The address will remain valid until the memory block is unlocked using the GlobalUnlock function. Windows maintains a lock count for each memory object. Each call to this function should have a matching call to GlobalUnlock.

Use with VB Refer to "Using Global Memory Blocks from Visual Basic," earlier in this chapter.

Parameter	Type/Description
hMem	Long—A handle to a global memory block.

Return Value Long—The address of the memory block on success. Zero if an error occurred or if this is a discardable block that has been discarded. Sets GetLastError.

Platform Windows 95, Windows NT, Win16

Example QuikDraw.vbp in Chapter 8. PicPrint.vbp in Chapter 12.

■ GlobalMemoryStatus

VB Declaration `Declare Sub GlobalMemoryStatus Lib "kernel32" (lpBuffer As MEMORYSTATUS)`

Description Loads a MEMORYSTATUS structure with information about the current state of the system's memory.

Use with VB No problem.

Parameter	Type/Description
lpBuffer	MEMORYSTATUS—A MEMORYSTATUS structure to load with information about system memory. Refer to Appendix B for additional information about this structure.

Platform Windows 95, Windows NT

Comments Be sure to load the dwLength parameter of the lpBuffer structure to the length of the MEMORYSTATUS structure before calling this function.

Porting Notes This function replaces the Win16 GetFreeSpace function.

Example ch01.vbp in Chapter 1.

■ GlobalReAlloc

VB Declaration `Declare Function GlobalReAlloc& Lib "kernel32" (ByVal hMem As Long, ByVal _`
`dwBytes As Long, ByVal wFlags As Long)`

Description Changes the size of a block of global memory.

Use with VB Refer to "Using Global Memory Blocks from Visual Basic," earlier in this chapter.

Parameter	Type/Description
hMem	Long—A handle to a global memory block.
dwBytes	Long—The size of the memory block. Zero to discard a memory block if it is discardable and not locked.
wFlags	Long—Constant flags that specify the type of memory to allocate as described for the GlobalAlloc function. Only the GMEM_DISCARDABLE, GMEM_MODIFY, GMEM_MOVEABLE, GMEM_NODISCARD, and GMEM_ZEROINIT flags may be used.

Return Value Long—A handle to the global memory block on success, zero on error or if the request cannot be fulfilled. Sets GetLastError.

Platform Windows 95, Windows NT, Win16

Comments Note that the handle returned may not be the same as the hMem parameter. Programs should take this into account. If an error occurs, the global handle referenced by the hMem parameter remains valid.

◼ GlobalSize

VB Declaration	Declare Function GlobalSize& Lib "kernel32" (ByVal hMem As Long)
Description	·Returns the minimum size of the specified global memory block. This value may be larger than the size of the block when it was allocated.
Use with VB	Refer to "Using Global Memory Blocks from Visual Basic," earlier in this chapter.

Parameter	Type/Description
hMem	Long—A handle to a global memory block.

Return Value	Long—The size of the memory block on success, zero on error or if the memory block has been discarded. Sets GetLastError.
Platform	Windows 95, Windows NT, Win16

◼ GlobalUnlock

VB Declaration	Declare Function GlobalUnlock& Lib "kernel32" (ByVal hMem As Long)
Description	Unlocks the specified memory block that had been previously locked using the GlobalLock function.
Use with VB	Refer to "Using Global Memory Blocks from Visual Basic," earlier in this chapter.

Parameter	Type/Description
hMem	Long—A handle to a global memory block.

Return Value	Long—TRUE if the lock count for the memory block is not zero, zero otherwise. Sets GetLastError to NO_ERROR on success.
Platform	Windows 95, Windows NT, Win16
Comments	Be careful that the number of GlobalUnlock calls matches the number of GlobalLock calls.
Example	QuikDraw.vbp in Chapter 8. PicPrint.vbp in Chapter 12.

◼ HeapAlloc

VB Declaration	Declare Function HeapAlloc& Lib "kernel32" (ByVal hHeap As Long, ByVal dwFlags _ As Long, ByVal dwBytes As Long)
Description	Allocates a block of memory off the specified heap.
Use with VB	No problem.

Parameter	Type/Description
hHeap	Long—A handle to the heap to use for this operation.

Parameter	Type/Description
dwFlags	Long— One or more of the following constants: HEAP_GENERATE_EXCEPTIONS: Causes this function to raise an exception instead of returning zero on error. Avoid using this option with Visual Basic. HEAP_NO_SERIALIZE: Prevents mutual exclusion on the heap during this function call. See the HeapCreate function. HEAP_ZERO_MEMORY: Initializes memory to zero on allocation.
dwBytes	Long—The size of the block to allocate.

Return Value Long—An address in memory to the newly allocated block of memory. Zero on error.

Platform Windows 95, Windows NT

■ HeapCompact

VB Declaration
```
Declare Function HeapCompact& Lib "kernel32" (ByVal hHeap As Long, ByVal _
dwFlags As Long)
```

Description As memory is allocated and freed off the heap, the heap can become fragmented. This function combines adjacent free blocks. Large blocks that were allocated may have their memory decommited as well.

Use with VB No problem.

Parameter	Type/Description
hHeap	Long—A handle to the heap to use for this operation.
dwFlags	Long—You may use the following constant: HEAP_NO_SERIALIZE: Prevents mutual exclusion on the heap during this function call. See the HeapCreate function.

Return Value Long—The size of the largest free space that is currently committed in memory.

Platform Windows NT

■ HeapCreate

VB Declaration
```
Declare Function HeapCreate& Lib "kernel32" (ByVal flOptions As Long, ByVal _
dwInitialSize As Long, ByVal dwMaximumSize As Long)
```

Description Creates a new private heap in the address space of the current application.

Use with VB	No problem.

Parameter	**Type/Description**
flOptions	Long—One or both of the following constants: HEAP_GENERATE_EXCEPTIONS: Causes heap functions to raise exceptions instead of returning zero on error. Avoid using this option with Visual Basic. HEAP_NO_SERIALIZE: Prevents mutual exclusion on the private heap. This can be safely used as long as a process has a single thread (as is the case with VB4) to improve performance. It can also be used on multithreaded applications as long as each thread only accesses its own heap or other synchronization techniques are applied.
dwInitialSize	Long—The initial size of the heap in bytes.
dwMaximumSize	Long—The maximum size for the heap (the size reserved in the processes address space for the heap). If zero, the heap can grow as needed. If nonzero, no allocated block can exceed &H7FFF8 bytes.

Return Value Long—A handle to the new heap. This handle is used by the other heap functions. Zero on error. Sets GetLastError.

Platform Windows 95, Windows NT

Comments The GetProcessHeap can be used to obtain the handle to the default heap for the process.

■ HeapDestroy

VB Declaration `Declare Function HeapDestroy& Lib "kernel32" (ByVal hHeap As Long)`

Description Destroys the specified heap.

Use with VB No problem.

Parameter	**Type/Description**
hHeap	Long—A handle to the heap to destroy.

Return Value Long—Nonzero on success, zero on failure.

Platform Windows 95, Windows NT

Comments You need not free the memory allocated in the heap before destroying it, but do not try to access any memory in a heap that has been destroyed. Do not try to destroy the default heap for a process.

■ HeapFree

VB Declaration `Declare Function HeapFree& Lib "kernel32" (ByVal hHeap As Long, ByVal dwFlags _`
`As Long, ByVal lpMem As Long)`

Description   Frees the specified memory block.

Use with VB   No problem.

Parameter	Type/Description
hHeap	Long—A handle to the heap to use for this operation.
dwFlags	Long—You may use the following constant: HEAP_NO_SERIALIZE: Prevents mutual exclusion on the heap during this function call. See the HeapCreate function.
lpMem	Long—The address of the memory block to release.

Return Value   Long—Nonzero on success, zero on failure.

Platform   Windows 95, Windows NT

■ HeapLock

VB Declaration   `Declare Function HeapLock& Lib "kernel32" (ByVal hHeap As Long)`

Description   Locks a heap for access by a single thread.

Use with VB   Works, but is not particularly useful.

Parameter	Type/Description
hHeap	Long—A handle to the heap to use for this operation.

Return Value   Long—TRUE (nonzero) on success, zero on error. Sets GetLastError.

Platform   Windows NT

■ HeapReAlloc

VB Declaration   `Declare Function HeapReAlloc& Lib "kernel32" (ByVal hHeap As Long, ByVal _`
`dwFlags As Long, ByVal lpMem As Long, ByVal dwBytes As Long)`

Description   Reallocates a block of memory on the heap to the specified size.

Use with VB   No problem.

Parameter	Type/Description
hHeap	Long— A handle to the heap to use for this operation.

Parameter	Type/Description
dwFlags	Long—One or more of the following constants: HEAP_GENERATE_EXCEPTIONS: Causes this function to raise an exception instead of returning zero on error. Avoid using this option with Visual Basic. HEAP_NO_SERIALIZE: Prevents mutual exclusion on the heap during this function call. See the HeapCreate function. HEAP_REALLOC_IN_PLACE_ONLY: Prevents the block of memory from being moved. This can increase the chance of the call failing. HEAP_ZERO_MEMORY: Initializes any additional memory allocated by this call to all zeros.
lpMem	Long—The address of the memory block to resize.
dwBytes	Long—The new desired length of the memory block.

Return Value Long—The address of the reallocated memory block. Any existing data in the block is preserved. Zero on error. Sets GetLastError.

Platform Windows 95, Windows NT

■ HeapSize

VB Declaration
```
Declare Function HeapSize& Lib "kernel32" (ByVal hHeap As Long, ByVal dwFlags _
As Long, ByVal lpMem As Long)
```

Description Determines the size of the specified memory block.

Use with VB No problem.

Parameter	Type/Description
hHeap	Long—A handle to the heap to use for this operation.
dwFlags	Long—You may use the following constant: HEAP_NO_SERIALIZE: Prevents mutual exclusion on the heap during this function call. See the HeapCreate function.
lpMem	Long—The address of the memory block to test.

Return Value Long—The number of bytes in the memory block. –1 on error.

Platform Windows 95, Windows NT

■ HeapUnlock

VB Declaration
```
Declare Function HeapUnlock& Lib "kernel32" (ByVal hHeap As Long)
```

Description Unlocks a heap that was locked using the HeapLock function.

Use with VB   Works, but is not particularly useful.

Parameter	Type/Description
hHeap	Long—A handle to the heap to use for this operation.

Return Value   Long—TRUE (nonzero) on success, zero on error. Sets GetLastError.

Platform   Windows NT

■ HeapValidate

VB Declaration   `Declare Function HeapValidate& Lib "kernel32" (ByVal hHeap As Long, ByVal _`
`dwFlags As Long, ByVal lpMem As Long)`

Description   Verifies that a heap or individual block in a heap is valid and has not been corrupted.

Use with VB   No problem.

Parameter	Type/Description
hHeap	Long—A handle to the heap to use for this operation.
dwFlags	Long—You may use the following constant: HEAP_NO_SERIALIZE: Prevents mutual exclusion on the heap during this function call. See the HeapCreate function.
lpMem	Long—If zero, the entire heap is validated. Otherwise, specify the address in memory of the block to validate.

Return Value   Long—TRUE (nonzero) if the heap or memory block is valid, zero otherwise.

Platform   Windows NT

■ InitAtomTable

VB Declaration   `Declare Function InitAtomTable& Lib "kernel32" (ByVal nSize As Long)`

Description   Changes the size of the local atom table. This is a hash table used to identify atoms with strings. Increasing the size of this table can improve performance for applications that use large numbers of atoms.

Use with VB   No known problems. It is unclear what effect this function actually has on the size of the atom hash table for VB applications, but it seems to do no harm.

Parameter	Type/Description
nSize	Long—The new size of the local atom hash table. The default size is 37.

Return Value   Long—Nonzero on success, zero on failure.

Platform   Windows 95, Windows NT, Win16

■ IsBadCodePtr

VB Declaration `Declare Function IsBadCodePtr& Lib "kernel32" (ByVal lpfn As Long)`

Description Determines if a memory address is readable and executable.

Use with VB No problem.

Parameter	Type/Description
lpfn	Long—Address of the start of a memory block.

Return Value Long—TRUE (nonzero) if the memory address is not readable/executable, zero otherwise. Sets GetLastError.

Platform Windows 95, Windows NT, Win16

■ IsBadReadPtr, IsBadHugeReadPtr

VB Declaration `Declare Function IsBadReadPtr& Lib "kernel32" (lp As Any, ByVal ucb As Long)`
`Declare Function IsBadHugeReadPtr& Lib "kernel32" (lp As Any, ByVal ucb As Long)`

Description Checks to make sure that the specified block of memory is valid and can be read.

Use with VB No problem.

Parameter	Type/Description
lp	Any—Address of the start of a memory block. Use ByVal As Long to pass a memory address in a long variable.
ucb	Long—The length of the memory block.

Return Value Long—TRUE (nonzero) if the memory address is not readable/executable, zero otherwise. Sets GetLastError.

Platform Windows 95, Windows NT, Win16

Porting Notes Under Win32, IsBadReadPtr and IsBadHugeReadPtr perform the same operation. Refer to the Visual Basic Programmer's Guide to the Windows API (16-bit edition) for information on working with memory on 16-bit systems.

■ IsBadStringPtr

VB Declaration `Declare Function IsBadStringPtr& Lib "kernel32" Alias "IsBadStringPtrA" (ByVal _`
`lpsz As String, ByVal ucchMax As Long)`

Description Checks to make sure that the specified block of memory is valid and contains a valid NULL terminated string.

Use with VB	No problem.	
	Parameter	**Type/Description**
	lpsz	String—Address of the start of a memory block. Change this to ByVal As Long to test an arbitrary memory address to see if it has a valid string.
	ucchMax	Long—The maximum length of the string.

Return Value   Long—TRUE (nonzero) if the memory address is not readable/executable up to the NULL terminator or ucchMax characters, zero otherwise. Sets GetLastError.

Platform   Windows 95, Windows NT, Win16

■ IsBadWritePtr, IsBadHugeWritePtr

VB Declaration
```
Declare Function IsBadWritePtr& Lib "kernel32" (lp As Any, ByVal ucb As Long)
Declare Function IsBadHugeWritePtr& Lib "kernel32" (lp As Any, ByVal ucb As _
Long)
```

Description   Checks to make sure that the specified block of memory is valid and can be written to.

Use with VB	No problem.	
	Parameter	**Type/Description**
	lp	Any—Address of the start of a memory block. Use ByVal As Long to pass a memory address in a long variable.
	ucb	Long—The length of the memory block.

Return Value   Long—TRUE (nonzero) if the memory address is not writable, zero otherwise. Sets GetLastError.

Platform   Windows 95, Windows NT, Win16

Porting Notes   Under Win32, IsBadWritePtr and IsBadHugeWritePtr perform the same operation. Refer to the Visual Basic Programmer's Guide to the Windows API (16-bit edition) for information on working with memory on 16-bit systems.

■ IsCharAlpha

VB Declaration
```
Declare Function IsCharAlpha& Lib "user32" Alias "IsCharAlphaA" (ByVal cChar As _
Byte)
```

Description   Determines if the specified character is an alphabetic character under the current language.

Use with VB	No problem.	
	Parameter	**Type/Description**
	cChar	Byte—The character to test.

Return Value   Long—TRUE (nonzero) if the character is alphabetic, zero otherwise. Sets GetLastError.

Platform   Windows 95, Windows NT, Win16

Example   Ex15A.vbp

■ IsCharAlphaNumeric

VB Declaration   `Declare Function IsCharAlphaNumeric& Lib "user32" Alias "IsCharAlphaNumericA" _`
                      `(ByVal cChar As Byte)`

Description   Determines if the specified character is an alphanumeric character under the current language.

Use with VB   No problem.

Parameter	Type/Description
cChar	Byte—The character to test.

Return Value   Long—TRUE (nonzero) if the character is alphanumeric, zero otherwise. Sets GetLastError.

Platform   Windows 95, Windows NT, Win16

Example   Ex15A.vbp

■ IsCharLower

VB Declaration   `Declare Function IsCharLower& Lib "user32" Alias "IsCharLowerA" (ByVal cChar As _`
                      `Byte)`

Description   Determines if the specified character is a lowercase character under the current language.

Use with VB   No problem.

Parameter	Type/Description
cChar	Byte—The character to test.

Return Value   Long—TRUE (nonzero) if the character is lowercase, zero otherwise. Sets GetLastError.

Platform   Windows 95, Windows NT, Win16

Example   Ex15A.vbp

■ IsCharUpper

VB Declaration   `Declare Function IsCharUpper& Lib "user32" Alias "IsCharUpperA" (ByVal cChar As _`
                      `Byte)`

Description   Determines if the specified character is an uppercase character under the current language.

Use with VB	No problem.

Parameter	Type/Description
cChar	Byte—The character to test.

Return Value	Long—TRUE (nonzero) if the character is uppercase, zero otherwise. Sets GetLastError.
Platform	Windows 95, Windows NT, Win16
Example	Ex15A.vbp

■ IsDBCSLeadByte, IsDBCSLeadByteEx

VB Declaration
```
Declare Function IsDBCSLeadByte& Lib "kernel32" (ByVal TestChar As Byte)
Declare Function IsDBCSLeadByteEx& Lib "kernel32" (ByVal codepage&, ByVal _
TestChar As Byte)
```

Description   Determines if the specified character is the first character in a double-byte character in a double-byte character set (DBCS) under the current language.

Use with VB   No problem.

Parameter	Type/Description
codepage	Long—The codepage identifier to test (Ex function only). Refer to Chapter 6 for a list of code page identifiers (see the GetACP and Get-OEMCP function descriptions), or use one of the constants: 0 or CP_ACP: Use the default ANSI code page. CP_OEMCP: Use the default OEM codepage.
TestChar	Byte—The character to test.

Return Value	Long—Nonzero on success, zero on failure. Sets GetLastError.
Platform	Windows 95, Windows NT, Win16

■ IsTextUnicode

VB Declaration
```
Declare Function IsTextUnicode& Lib "advapi32.dll" (lpBuffer As Any, ByVal cb _
As Long, lpi As Long)
```

Description   Attempts to determine if a buffer contains a Unicode string or an ANSI string. It is not always possible to determine this exactly, so you should not absolutely rely on the results of this function.

Use with VB   No problem.

Parameter	Type/Description
lpBuffer	Any—An address or buffer containing a string to test.

Parameter	Type/Description
cb	Long—The number of bytes in the buffer to test.
lpi	Long—A long variable that is initially set with flag bits specifying the tests to perform on the string. On return, each bit will be set to 1 if the test succeeded, 0 if it failed. Constants include: IS_TEXT_UNICODE_ASCII16: Text is Unicode but only contains ASCII characters. IS_TEXT_UNICODE_REVERSE_ASCII16: Same as previous, but bytes are reversed. IS_TEXT_UNICODE_STATISTICS: Text is Unicode based on a statistical analysis. IS_TEXT_UNICODE_REVERS_STATISTICS: Same as previous, but bytes are reversed. IS_TEXT_UNICODE_CONTROLS: Text contains control characters such as CR, LF, TAB. IS_TEXT_UNICODE_REVERSE_CONTROLS: Same as previous, but bytes are reversed. IS_TEXT_UNICODE_BUFFER_TO_SMALL: lpBuffer is too small to analyze. IS_TEXT_UNICODE_SIGNATURE: The first two bytes are the Unicode byte order mark &HFEFF. IS_TEXT_UNICODE_REVERSE_SIGNATURE: The first two bytes are the reversed Unicode byte order mark &HFFEF.

Return Value   Long—TRUE (nonzero) if all of the specified tests succeeded, zero otherwise.

Platform   Windows NT

■ LCMapString

VB Declaration
```
Declare Function LCMapString& Lib "kernel32" Alias "LCMapStringA" (ByVal Locale _
As Long, ByVal dwMapFlags As Long, ByVal lpSrcStr As String, ByVal cchSrc As _
Long, ByVal lpDestStr As String, ByVal cchDest As Long)
```

Description   Performs a locale-based string conversion.

Use with VB   No problem.

Parameter	Type/Description
Locale	Long—The locale on which to base the conversion.

Parameter	Type/Description
dwMapFlags	Long—One or more of the following constants: LCMAP_BYTEREV: (NT only) Reverses the orders of pairs of bytes. Good for converting Big-Endian to Little-Endian buffers. LCMAP_FULLWIDTH: Converts ANSI to DBCS. LCMAP_HALFWIDTH: Converts DBCS to ANSI. LCMAP_HIRAGANA: Converts double-byte characters from Katakana to Hiragana. LCMAP_KATAKANA: Converts double-byte characters from Hiragana to Katakana. LCMAP_LOWERCASE: Converts to lowercase. LCMAP_SORTKEY: See "Comments." NORM_IGNORECASE: Ignore case during conversion or sorting. NORM_IGNOREKANATYPE: Ignore differences between Katakana and Hiragana. NORM_IGNORENONSPACE: Ignore any character that doesn't take up space. NORM_IGNORESYMBOLS: Ignore symbol characters. NROM_IGNOREWIDTH: Single-byte and equivalent double-byte characters are treated identically. SORT_STRINGSORT: Punctuation characters are treated the same way as symbols when sorting.
lpSrcStr	String—A source string.
cchSrc	Long — The number of bytes in the string. –1 to calculate automatically (based on the NULL terminator).
lpDestStr	String—An output buffer for the converted string or sorting information.
cchDest	Long—The size of the lpDestStr buffer. If zero, the function will return the necessary buffer size.

Return Value Long—The size in bytes of the destination buffer. Zero on error. Sets GetLastError.

Platform Windows 95, Windows NT

Comments When LCMAP_SORTKEY is not specified, SORT_STRINGSORT, NORM_IGNOREKANATYPE, NORM_IGNOREWIDTH, and NORM_IGNORECASE are not allowed. The conversion specified is performed with the converted string going to the lpDestStr buffer.

When it is specified, no LCMAP options are allowed other than LCMAP_BYTEREV. lpDestStr is loaded with a sort key. This is a buffer formatted such that you can compare two sort keys using a simple numeric string comparison and achieve a valid locale specific comparison.

Consider the case where you want to sort an array of strings based on a specified locale. You could use the CompareString function every time you compare two strings, but this involves a locale-specific conversion each time—a slow process. A better approach would be to create a sort key for each string using this function. You can then compare the sort keys using the standard windows lstrcmp function, which is very fast.

■ LoadResource

VB Declaration Declare Function LoadResource& Lib "kernel32" (ByVal hInstance As Long, ByVal _

```
hResInfo As Long)
```

Description

This function returns a global memory handle to a resource in the specified module. The resource is not actually loaded until the LockResource function is called to obtain a pointer to the resource data.

Use with VB

No problem.

Parameter	Type/Description
hInstance	Long—A module handle to a loaded executable or DLL that contains the resource to read. Zero to use the instance of the current process.
hResInfo	Long—A handle to a resource as returned by the FindResource or FindResourceEx functions.

Return Value

Long—A global memory handle to the resource on success, zero on error. Sets GetLastError.

Platform

Windows 95, Windows NT, Win16

Comments

You should call the FreeResource function to free the handle returned by this function before the application terminates. This is especially important with Windows 95.

■ LoadString

VB Declaration

```
Declare Function LoadString& Lib "user32" Alias "LoadStringA" (ByVal hInstance _
As Long, ByVal wID As Long, ByVal lpBuffer As String, ByVal nBufferMax As Long)
```

Description

Loads a string resource from an executable module.

Use with VB

No problem.

Parameter	Type/Description
hInstance	Long—A handle to a loaded executable or DLL module that contains the string resource.
wID	String or Long—The name of the string resource to load.
lpBuffer	String—A string buffer to load with the string resource. The string must be preallocated to be at least nBufferMax characters long.
nBufferMax	Long—The maximum number of characters to load into the buffer.

Return Value

Long—The number of characters retrieved on success, zero if the string resource does not exist. Sets GetLastError.

Platform

Windows 95, Windows NT, Win16

■ LockResource

VB Declaration

```
Declare Function LockResource& Lib "kernel32" (ByVal hResData As Long)
```

Description Locks the specified resource. The function returns a 32-bit pointer to the data for the resource. This should be used for resources loaded with the LoadResource function.

Use with VB No problem.

Parameter	Type/Description
hResData	Long—A handle to a resource as returned by the LoadResource function.

Return Value Long—A 32-bit pointer to the resource data on success, zero on error.

Platform Windows 95, Windows NT, Win16

Porting Notes Unlike Win16 applications, Win32 applications need not use the GlobalUnlock function to unlock the resource.

■ LookupIconIdFromDirectory, LookupIconIdFromDirectoryEx

VB Declaration
```
Declare Function LookupIconIdFromDirectory& Lib "user32" (presbits As Byte, _
ByVal fIcon As Long)
Declare Function LookupIconIdFromDirectoryEx& Lib "user32" (presbits As Byte, _
ByVal fIcon As Long, ByVal cxDesired As Long, ByVal cyDesired As Long, ByVal _
Flags As Long)
```

Description Searches a block of resource data for the icon or cursor that best matches the current display device.

Use with VB No problem.

Parameter	Type/Description
presbits	Byte—The first byte in a buffer containing raw resource data for a cursor or icon directory (RT_GROUP_ICON or RT_GROUP_CURSOR). Change to ByVal As Long to pass a memory address of a block of memory containing directory data.
fIcon	Long—TRUE (nonzero) to search for an icon. Zero to search for a cursor.
cxDesiredcy-Desired	Long—LookupIconIdFromDirectoryEx only. The requested width and height for the icon or cursor. Zero to use the standard values as returned by the GetSystemMetrics function.
uFlags	Long—CreateIconFromResourceEx only. One of the following: LR_DEFAULTCOLOR: Uses the default color format for the object. LR_LOADREALSIZE: Uses the size specified in the data structures in the data stream. LR_MONOCHROME: Searches for a monochrome icon or cursor.

Return Value Long—The resource identifier of the icon or cursor that best matches the display. Zero if none is found.

Platform Windows 95, Windows NT

Comments These functions are used internally by Windows to implement the LoadIcon and LoadCursor functions.

■ lstrcat

VB Declaration
```
Declare Function lstrcat& Lib "kernel32" Alias "lstrcatA" (ByVal lpString1 As _
String, ByVal lpString2 As String)
```

Description Appends string lpString2 to string lpString1.

Use with VB Works fine, but be sure that lpString1 has been preallocated to a length adequate to hold the resulting string. The VB string operations are easier and safer to use.

Parameter	Type/Description
lpString1	String or Long—A string or address of a string buffer containing a NULL terminated string. The buffer referenced must be large enough to hold this string and lpString2.
lpString2	String or Long—A string or address of a string buffer containing a NULL terminated string to append to lpString1.

Return Value Long—The address of lpString1 on success. This is only of use when working with buffers directly allocated in memory. When used with VB strings, this will be the address of a temporary buffer that will no longer be valid. Zero on error. Sets GetLastError.

Platform Windows 95, Windows NT, Win16

Porting Notes Under Win32, there is no 64K limit to strings used with this function.

■ lstrcmp, lstrcmpi

VB Declaration
```
Declare Function lstrcmp& Lib "kernel32" Alias "lstrcmpA" (ByVal lpString1 As _
String, ByVal lpString2 As String)
Declare Function lstrcmpi& Lib "kernel32" Alias "lstrcmpiA" (ByVal lpString1 As _
String, ByVal lpString2 As String)
```

Description Compares string lpString2 to string lpString1. lstrcmpi is not case-sensitive.

Use with VB No problem. The VB string comparison operations are easier to use.

Parameter	Type/Description
lpString1	String or Long—A string or address of a string buffer containing a NULL terminated string.
lpString2	String or Long—A string or address of a string buffer containing a NULL terminated string to compare with lpString1.

Return Value Long—A negative value if lpString1 is less than lpString2, zero if the strings are equal, and a positive value if lpString1 is greater than lpString2. The absolute value is the difference between the two mismatched characters when the inequality is found.
The comparison is based on the current locale.

Platform Windows 95, Windows NT, Win16

Porting Notes Under Win32, hyphens and apostrophes are ignored in the comparison, assuring that hyphenated words such as "on-line" are treated like "online" when comparing them to other words. Under Win16 a simple string comparison is performed.

Under Win32, there is no 64K limit to strings used with this function.

■ lstrcpy, lstrcpyn

VB Declaration
```
Declare Function lstrcpy& Lib "kernel32" Alias "lstrcpyA" (ByVal lpString1 As _
String, ByVal lpString2 As String)
Declare Function lstrcpyn& Lib "kernel32" Alias "lstrcpynA" (ByVal lpString1 As _
String, ByVal lpString2 As String, ByVal iMaxLength As Long)
```

Description Copies string lpString2 to string lpString1.

Use with VB Works fine, but be sure that lpString1 has been preallocated to be at least as long as string lpString2. The VB string operations are easier and safer to use.

Parameter	Type/Description
lpString1	String or Long—A string or address of a string buffer containing a NULL terminated string. The buffer referenced must be large enough to hold string lpString2.
lpString2	String or Long—A string or address of a string buffer containing a NULL terminated string to copy to lpString1.
iMaxLength	Long—The maximum number of bytes to copy (lstrcpyn only).

Return Value Long—The address of lpString1 on success. This is only of use when working with buffers directly allocated in memory. When used with VB strings, this will be the address of a temporary buffer that will no longer be valid. Zero on error. Sets GetLastError.

Platform Windows 95, Windows NT, Win16

■ lstrlen

VB Declaration
```
Declare Function lstrlen& Lib "kernel32" Alias "lstrlenA" (ByVal lpString As _
String)
```

Description Determines the length of lpString.

Use with VB Works fine, but the VB Len operation is easier to use.

Parameter	Type/Description
lpString	String or Long—A string or address of a string buffer containing a NULL terminated string.

Return Value Long—The length of string lpString on success (in bytes). If you use the Unicode entry point (alias to lstrlenw) and pass a memory address of a Unicode string, you will obtain the length of the string in characters (not bytes).

Platform Windows 95, Windows NT, Win16

Porting Notes Under Win32, there is no 64K limit to strings used with this function.

■ MultiByteToWideChar

VB Declaration
```
Declare Function MultiByteToWideChar& Lib "kernel32" (ByVal CodePage As Long, _
ByVal dwFlags As Long, ByVal lpMultiByteStr As String, ByVal cchMultiByte As _
Long, ByVal lpWideCharStr As Long, ByVal cchWideChar As Long)
```

Description Converts an ANSI or DBCS string to Unicode.

Use with VB No problem. Similar to the VB StrConv function (which is easier to use).

Parameter	Type/Description
CodePage	Long—The code page identifier to use for the conversion (see Chapter 6), or one of the CP_??? constants.
dwFlags	Long—One or more of the following constants: MB_PRECOMPOSED: Convert composed characters (such as a letter with accent mark) into a single character where possible. This is the default. MB_COMPOSED: Leave composed characters as two characters. MB_ERR_INVALID_CHARS: An invalid character was found on the input. MB_USEGLPYHCHARS: Use glyph characters instead of control characters where possible.
lpMultiByteStr	String—The ANSI or DBCS string.
cchMultiByte	Long—The length of the lpMultiByteStr string. –1 to calculate automatically.
lpWideCharStr	Long—The address of a destination buffer for the converted Unicode string. You can use a string parameter here, but the additional conversion that VB applies to the string may cause errors. Must not be the same buffer as lpMultiByteStr.
cchWideChar	Long—The length of the lpWideCharStr buffer. Zero to find the required buffer length.

Return Value Long—The number of characters written into the lpWideCharStr buffer, or required if cchWideChar is zero. Zero on error. Sets GetLastError to: ERROR_INSUFFICIENT_BUFFER, ERROR_INVALID_PARAMETER, ERROR_INVALID_FLAGS, or ERROR_NO_UNICODE_TRANSLATION.

Platform Windows 95, Windows NT

■ ReadProcessMemory

VB Declaration
```
Declare Function ReadProcessMemory& Lib "kernel32" (ByVal hProcess As Long, _
ByVal lpBaseAddress As Long, lpBuffer As Any, ByVal nSize As Long, _
lpNumberOfBytesWritten As Long)
```

Description Reads memory from the address space of another process.

Use with VB   No problem. NT security may prevent this function from working. Use of this function to share memory between applications is strongly discouraged.

Parameter	Type/Description
hProcess	Long—A handle of a process whose memory you wish to read.
lpBaseAddress	Long—A memory address in the other process address space.
lpBuffer	Any—A buffer to load with a copy of memory from the other process.
nSize	Long—The number of bytes to copy.
lpNumberOf-BytesWritten	Long—A long variable to load with the number of bytes actually copied by this function.

Return Value   Long—Nonzero on success, zero on failure. Sets GetLastError.

Platform   Windows 95, Windows NT

■ RemoveProp

VB Declaration   `Declare Function RemoveProp& Lib "user32" Alias "RemovePropA" (ByVal hwnd As _`
`Long, ByVal lpString As String)`

Description   Deletes (or removes) a property for a window.

Use with VB   No problem.

Parameter	Type/Description
hwnd	Long—A handle to a window.
lpString	String or Long—The name of the property or an atom to use as the name of the property. If it is an atom, it must be a global atom and the high word of the parameter must be zero.

Return Value   Long—The 32-bit value or handle that was saved for the property using the SetProp function on success, zero on error.

Platform   Windows 95, Windows NT, Win16

Comments   You must remove any properties and handles associated with properties before the window is destroyed. This is typically done before unloading a form or control, or in the Unload event for the form. Do not remove properties from windows that you did not add.

■ SetProp

VB Declaration   `Declare Function SetProp& Lib "user32" Alias "SetPropA" (ByVal hwnd As Long, _`
`ByVal lpString As String, ByVal hData As Long)`

Description   Sets the data handle for the specified property.

Use with VB	No problem.	
	Parameter	**Type/Description**
	hwnd	Long—A handle to a window.
	lpString	String—The name of the property or an atom to use as the name of the property. If it is an atom, it must be a global atom and the high word of the parameter must be zero.
	hData	Long—A data handle or value to associate with the property.

Return Value	Long—Nonzero on success, zero on failure.
Platform	Windows 95, Windows NT, Win16
Comments	See comments for the RemoveProp function.

■ SizeofResource

VB Declaration
```
Declare Function SizeofResource& Lib "kernel32" (ByVal hInstance As Long, ByVal _
hResInfo As Long)
```

Description   Determines the size of a resource.

Use with VB	No problem.	
	Parameter	**Type/Description**
	hInstance	Long—A handle to a loaded executable module or DLL that contains the desired resource.
	hResInfo	Long—A handle to a resource as returned by the FindResource function.

Return Value	Long—The size of the resource, zero if the resource is not found. Sets GetLastError.
Platform	Windows 95, Windows NT, Win16

■ UpdateResource

VB Declaration
```
Declare Function UpdateResource& Lib "kernel32" Alias "UpdateResourceA" (ByVal _
hUpdate As Long, ByVal lpType As String, ByVal lpName As String, ByVal _
wLanguage As Long, lpData As Any, ByVal cbData As Long)
```

Description   Allows you to modify the resources in an executable file or DLL.

Use with VB	No problem.	
	Parameter	**Type/Description**
	hUpdate	Long—A handle returned by the BeginUpdateResource function.
	lpType	String or Long—A resource type as described in Table 15.6.

Parameter	Type/Description
lpName	String or Long—The new identifier of the resource. An existing resource of this type with this identifier will be replaced if necessary.
wLanguage	Long—The language identifier of the resource.
lpData	Any—The address of a block of data containing the raw resource data to embed in the file. Strings must be in Unicode. Use ByVal 0& to delete an existing resource with this identifier.
cbData	Long—The number of bytes in the buffer referenced by the lpData structure.

Return Value Long—Nonzero on success, zero on failure. Sets GetLastError.

Platform Windows NT

Comments Changes made by this function are not written into the file until the EndUpdateResource function is called.

■ VirtualAlloc

VB Declaration
```
Declare Function VirtualAlloc& Lib "kernel32" (ByVal lpAddress As Long, ByVal _
dwSize As Long, ByVal flAllocationType As Long, ByVal flProtect As Long)
```

Description Use to allocate memory in the address space of the process, or to reserve a range of memory for possible future allocation.

Use with VB No problem.

Parameter	Type/Description
lpAddress	Long—A requested start address to reserve. Zero to allow the system to set a start address. The actual address allocated will be rounded downward to the next page or 64K boundary depending on whether the memory is being allocated, or just reserved.
dwSize	Long—The amount of memory to allocate.
flAllocationType	Long—One or more of the following constants: MEM_COMMIT: Memory is allocated. MEM_RESERVE: The memory space specified is reserved. No other memory management functions will attempt to allocate memory out of this space. MEM_TOP_DOWN: Memory is allocated at the highest address possible. Use when lpAddress is zero.

Parameter	Type/Description
flProtect	Long—If MEM_COMMIT is specified, one or more of the following constants can be specified: PAGE_READONLY: The memory is read only. PAGE_READWRITE: The memory can be read and written. PAGE_EXECUTE: The memory can contain executable code. PAGE_EXECUTE_READ: The memory can be read and can contain executable code. PAGE_EXECUTE_READWRITE: Full read/write/execute access is allowed. PAGE_GUARD: Specifies that an exception will occur the first time memory on a given page is accessed. Not useful for VB. PAGE_NOACCESS: No access is allowed to the memory. The degree of protection actually supported depends on the operating system.

Return Value Long—The actual base address in memory allocated. Zero on error. Sets GetLastError.

Platform Windows 95, Windows NT

Comments This function may be called on an existing reserved memory range in order to actually commit memory within that range.

■ VirtualFree

VB Declaration `Declare Function VirtualFree& Lib "kernel32" (ByVal lpAddress As Long, ByVal _`
`dwSize As Long, ByVal dwFreeType As Long)`

Description Frees or decommits a range of memory.

Use with VB No problem.

Parameter	Type/Description
lpAddress	Long—The base address in memory to operate on. If MEM_RELEASE is specified, this value should have been returned earlier by VirtualAlloc.
dwSize	Long—Zero if MEM_RELEASE is specified. Otherwise, the amount of memory within an address range to free.
dwFreeType	Long—One of the following constants: MEM_DECOMMIT: Frees memory allocated within the specified range, but leaves the memory space reserved. MEM_RELEASE: Releases a memory range reserved earlier by the VirtualAlloc function.

Return Value Long—Nonzero on success, zero on failure. Sets GetLastError.

Platform Windows 95, Windows NT

■ VirtualLock

VB Declaration   `Declare Function VirtualLock& Lib "kernel32" (ByVal lpAddress As Long, ByVal _`
`dwSize As Long)`

Description   Normally, when you allocate memory you are allocating virtual memory. This means that Windows can swap memory to a page file on disk whenever it needs additional space. This function locks a range of memory into physical memory.

Use with VB   No problem. You should avoid use of this function as it can severely impact system performance.

Parameter	Type/Description
lpAddress	Long—The start address in memory to lock.
dwSize	Long—The length of the address range to lock.

Return Value   Long—Nonzero on success, zero on failure. Sets GetLastError.

Platform   Windows NT

■ VirtualProtect, VirtualProtectEx

VB Declaration   `Declare Function VirtualProtect& Lib "kernel32" (ByVal lpAddress As Long, ByVal _`
`dwSize As Long, ByVal flNewProtect As Long, lpflOldProtect As Long)`
`Declare Function VirtualProtectEx& Lib "kernel32" (ByVal hProcess As Long, _`
`ByVal lpAddress As Long, ByVal dwSize As Long, ByVal flNewProtect As Long, _`
`lpflOldProtect As Long)`

Description   Allows you to change the protection of a range of memory in the process address space. VirtualProtectEx can change the protection of a range of memory in the address space of any process.

Use with VB   No problem.

Parameter	Type/Description
hProcess	Long— Specifies the process whose address space is being accessed (VirtualProtectEx only).
lpAddress	Long—The start address of memory to modify.
dwSize	Long—The size of the memory range to modify.
flNewProtect	Long—The new protection values for the specified memory range. Use any of the constants specified in the flProtect parameter of the VirtualAlloc function.
lpflOldProtect	Long—A long variable to load with the previous protection for the specified memory range. Will be loaded with one of the constants specified in the flProtect parameter of the VirtualAlloc function.

Return Value   Long—Nonzero on success, zero on failure. Sets GetLastError.

Platform   Windows 95, Windows NT

■ VirtualQuery, VirtualQueryEx

VB Declaration
```
Declare Function VirtualQuery& Lib "kernel32" (lpAddress As Any, lpBuffer As _
MEMORY_BASIC_INFORMATION, ByVal dwLength As Long)
Declare Function VirtualQueryEx& Lib "kernel32" (ByVal hProcess As Long, ByVal _
lpAddress As Long, lpBuffer As MEMORY_BASIC_INFORMATION, ByVal dwLength As Long)
```

Description
Allows you to obtain information about a range of memory. It begins scanning from the address specified by the lpAddress parameter and continues until it finds a page that does not match the protection and allocation attributes of the first page, or until the specified number of bytes have been scanned.

Use with VB
No problem.

Parameter	Type/Description
hProcess	Long—(VirtualQueryEx only) Specifies the process whose address space is being accessed.
lpAddress	Long—The start address of memory to modify.
lpBuffer	MEMORY_BASIC_INFORMATION—A structure to load with information about the memory scanned.
dwLength	Long—The size of the memory address space to test.

Return Value
Long—The number of bytes loaded into the lpBuffer buffer.

Platform
Windows 95, Windows NT

Comments
The MEMORY_BASIC_INFORMATION structure is defined as follows:
```
Type MEMORY_BASIC_INFORMATION
    BaseAddress as Long
    AllocationBase as Long
    AllocationProtect As Long
    RegionSize As Long
    State As Long
    Protect As Long
    lType As Long
End Type
```

The parameters are as follows:
BaseAddress: The start address of the range being scanned.
AllocationBase: The base address used by the VirtualAlloc call that allocated this range of memory.
AllocationProtect: The protection flags as specified by constants with the PAGE_??? prefix describing the protection when the memory was allocated.
RegionSize: The number of bytes actually scanned. All of the memory in this range will have the same protection and allocation state.
State: MEM_COMMIT, MEM_FREE, or MEM_RESERVE depending on whether the memory is free, committed, or reserved but not committed.
Protect: The current protection flags for the range scanned as specified by constants with the PAGE_??? prefix.

Type: Typically MEM_PRIVATE indicating that the pages are private to this application. MEM_MAPPED if part of a file mapping.

■ VirtualUnlock

VB Declaration
```
Declare Function VirtualUnlock& Lib "kernel32" (ByVal lpAddress As Long, ByVal _
dwSize As Long)
```

Description   Unlocks a range of memory locked with VirtualLock.

Use with VB   No problem.

Parameter	Type/Description
lpAddress	Long—The start address in memory to unlock.
dwSize	Long—The length of the address range to unlock.

Return Value   Long—Nonzero on success, zero on failure. Sets GetLastError.

Platform   Windows 95, Windows NT

Comments   All pages in the range specified must be locked.

■ WideCharToMultiByte

VB Declaration
```
Declare Function WideCharToMultiByte& Lib "kernel32" (ByVal CodePage As Long, _
ByVal dwFlags As Long, ByVal lpWideCharStr As Long, ByVal cchWideChar As Long, _
ByVal lpMultiByteStr As String, ByVal cchMultiByte As Long, ByVal lpDefaultChar _
As String, ByVal lpUsedDefaultChar As Long)
```

Description   Converts the specified Unicode string to ANSI or DBCS based on the specified code page.

Use with VB   No problem. Similar to the VB StrConv function (which is easier to use).

Parameter	Type/Description
CodePage	Long—The codepage identifier to use for the conversion (see Chapter 6), or one of the CP_??? constants.
dwFlags	Long—Zero, or one or more of the following constants: WC_COMPOSITECHECK: Convert composed characters (such as a letter with accent mark) into a single character where possible. If WC_COMPOSITECHECK is specified, the following constants specify what to do with composite characters that cannot be converted into a single precomposed character. WC_DISCARDNS: Throw away the nonspacing characters (such as the accent mark). WC_SEPCHARS: Include both characters in the destination string.
lpWideCharStr	Long—The address of a source Unicode buffer. You can use a string parameter here, but the additional conversion that VB applies to the string may cause errors.

Parameter	Type/Description
cchWideChar	Long—The length of the lpWideCharStr buffer in characters (not bytes). –1 to calculate the required buffer length automatically.
lpMultiByteStr	String—A destination string buffer to load with the converted ANSI or DBCS string.
cchMultiByte	Long—The length of the lpMultiByteStr string. VbNullString to obtain the required length for this buffer.
lpDefaultChar	String—The first character of this string will be used for any character that cannot be converted. VbNullString to use the system default character.
lpUsedDefault-Char	Long—A long variable that will be loaded with a nonzero value if one or more characters in the source string could not be converted to ANSI or DBCS.

Return Value   Long—The number of characters written into the lpWideCharStr buffer, or required if cchWide-Char is zero. Zero on error. Sets GetLastError to: ERROR_INSUFFICIENT_BUFFER, ERROR_INVALID_PARAMETER, ERROR_INVALID_FLAGS.

■ WriteProcessMemory

VB Declaration
```
Declare Function WriteProcessMemory& Lib "kernel32" (ByVal hProcess As Long, _
ByVal lpBaseAddress As Long, lpBuffer As Any, ByVal nSize As Long, _
lpNumberOfBytesWritten As Long)
```

Description   Writes memory in the address space of another process.

Use with VB   No problem. NT security may prevent this function from working. Use of this function to share memory between applications is strongly discouraged.

Parameter	Type/Description
hProcess	Long—A handle of a process whose memory you wish to write.
lpBaseAddress	Long—A memory address in the other process address space.
lpBuffer	Any—A buffer containing data to a copy to the memory buffer in the other process.
nSize	Long—The number of bytes to copy.
lpNumberOf-BytesWritten	Long—A long variable to load with the number of bytes actually copied by this function.

Return Value   Long—Nonzero on success, zero on failure. Sets GetLastError.

Platform   Windows 95, Windows NT

General Windows Messages

Edit Control Messages

List Box, Combo Box, and Button Messages

3

Windows Messages

16

General Windows
Messages

Message Handling

*Messages That Are
Useful with Visual Basic*

*Visual Basic and
Subclassing*

THIS CHAPTER DESCRIBES THE STANDARD MESSAGES DEFINED BY THE Windows operating system. It begins with a review of what messages are and how they are used. Messages that are useful under Visual Basic are described. The concepts of messaging and subclassing were covered earlier in Chapter 2. You may wish to review them before continuing.

The chapter concludes with a reference section that describes most of the standard Windows messages that are likely to be used by even the most expert Visual Basic programmer using advanced subclassing techniques.

Message Handling

Under Windows, messages are used in two ways. First, they are sent by Windows to a window function to indicate that an event such as a mouse click or a keyboard press has occurred. A message can also be a notification by Windows of an internal event such as a change of focus. Finally, it can be a command from Windows that it is time for a window to perform some task such as erasing the background or painting the client area of the window.

Second, messages are often sent to a control or window to request it to perform a specified operation.

Windows Event Messages

Most Visual Basic events correspond to an internal Windows message; however, many Windows messages do not generate Visual Basic events. This is not surprising since there are dozens of Windows messages, many of which are rarely used by programmers. Supporting all Windows messages under Visual Basic would lead to a significant increase in the complexity of Visual Basic and would certainly impair the language's performance.

This has one unfortunate side effect: There is no easy way for a Visual Basic programmer to detect the occurrence of a Windows message, though there are times when the ability to do so would be very helpful. One classic example is detection of the WM_SYSCOMMAND messages that occur when clicking on the system menu. Access to this message allows you to create custom menu entries on the system menu or to block the operation of existing menu entries.

If you had the ability to intercept and modify Windows messages arriving at a control, you could customize every aspect of the operation of that control. This technique, described in Chapter 2, is known as subclassing.

Subclassing is accomplished by using the SetWIndowLong API function to replace the current window function for a window with a new one that you specify. From Visual Basic, there are two approaches to subclassing:

1. Use the AddressOf operator with the SetWindowLong function to specify a procedure in a standard module of your application to be the new window function for a window. This is possible only with Visual Basic 5.0 or later.

2. Create or use a subclassing component (DLL or OCX) to perform this task for you.

The VB5 documentation does describe how to take the first approach. This book strongly discourages that approach. The reason is simple: When you subclass a control, Windows expects that a valid window function always be available. However, when Visual Basic is in stop or break mode, any function that you have set to be a window function using SetWindowLong will be frozen as well. This can result in all sorts of problems ranging from freezing your application or the system to a memory exception. In other words, implementing subclassing code within your application makes it effectively impossible to debug using the Visual Basic environment.

Thus you should always use a DLL component to perform subclassing. You can write one yourself using the principles described here, or use a third party product. Use caution: performing safe subclassing can be notoriously difficult to do—especially when it comes to handling subclassing of multiple windows and avoiding conflicts with other controls or components that are simultaneously subclassing the same windows that you are. Desaware's Spy-Works includes a set of subclassing components written in Visual Basic 5.0 that include complete source code and demonstrate how to subclass safely.

You cannot use the AddressOf operator to subclass a window that is not part of your own process. To accomplish this type of cross-task subclassing you will need a third party component such as the dwsbc32d demonstration subclassing control from SpyWorks (this control is included with this book).

When subclassing a window, there are two ways to process each message that is received. You can allow the default processing for the message to continue and return the result of the default message, or you can handle the message directly. The reference section later in this chapter describes the values that must be returned when subclassing a message if default processing is not performed.

Messages That Perform Operations

There are a large number of messages that can be used to request a control to perform an operation. Examples of this include the WM_COPY message, which can be sent to some controls to instruct them to copy data into the clipboard. The WM_REDRAW message decides whether some controls update themselves each time they are changed.

These messages differ from event messages in that they are frequently sent to a control by applications, not just by Windows. They can also return values to an application, and can thus be used to retrieve information about a control. The following section describes in more detail how this type of message can be used.

Message Organization

Each message has a number. This value is the message parameter to the window function for a form or control. The messages numbered from 1 to &H400 are standard Windows messages. Not every control processes all of these messages, but no control may redefine them. Individual control messages also fall into this range under Win32. This is a change from Win16, which means that the numbers for standard control messages have changed.

The messages above &H400 are user-defined and their meaning depends on the class of the window.

The Visual Basic text and list controls are subclassed off of standard Windows controls and thus respond correctly to most of the messages for these controls, as was described earlier in Chapter 2.

Keep in mind that each application may define its own messages. Only the standard Windows messages are described in this book.

Sending Messages

Messages can be sent using either the SendMessage function (in all of its variations) or the PostMessage function. Both of these functions have additional type-safe aliases provided, as some messages use long parameters and others require string parameters.

The SendMessage function and its aliases are used to send a message by calling the Windows function for the window directly. The function does not return until the message has been completely processed. This function must be used for messages that return values.

The PostMessage function adds a message to the window queue for a window. The message will be processed during the normal course of event processing at some future time.

The behavior of the SendMessage functions under Win32 has changed slightly from Win16. Under Win16, a SendMessage call to a window in a different application executes immediately—Windows switches to the context of the other application, calls the window function for the specified window, and returns when the operation is complete. Under Win32, this could cause severe synchronization problems, since the process owning the target window is in an undefined state (remember that preemptive multitasking means that an application can be interrupted anywhere). In order to be sure that the other application is at a point where its window functions can be called safely, in this situation Windows will first suspend the thread making the SendMessage call. The function call will execute the next time the target application calls Get-Message or PeekMessage. Note that the Windows function for the other application will still be called directly—it will not actually be processed by GetMessage or PeekMessage. Windows simply uses the occurrence of the GetMessage or PeekMessage call to indicate that it is safe to process the message, and will proceed to do so at that time.

This change in message processing means that if you send a message to another application and that application is suspended for some reason (say it is in a tight loop, or has crashed), your application will be blocked as well. For this reason, Win32 adds a number of additional functions to send messages that incorporate time-outs or callbacks to prevent the calling process from being permanently blocked.

Table 16.1 lists the functions that can be used to send and post messages.

Table 16.1 **Message Functions**

Function	Description
BroadcastSystemMessage	Sends a message to all windows or applications of a specified type.
GetMessagePos	Obtains the coordinates for the cursor at the time the last message was processed.
GetMessageTime	Obtains the time at which the last message was processed.
PostMessage	Posts a message into a window's message queue.
PostThreadMessage	Posts a message into a thread's message queue.
RegisterWindowMessage	Obtains a message number that is uniquely associated with a specified name.
ReplyMessage	Allows an application to return a result to a SendMessage call without exiting the message function for the window.
SendMessage SendMessageBynum SendMessageBystring	Sends a message immediately by calling the window function of the specified window. Does not return until the message is processed. SendMessageBynum and SendMessageBystring are type-safe aliases for the function.
SendMessageCallback	Sends a message and returns immediately. Windows will call the specified callback function when the message has been processed.
SendMessageTimeout	Sends a message, returning when either the message has been processed or the specified time-out has elapsed.
SendNotifyMessage	Same as SendMessage except that it returns immediately if the window belongs to a different thread.

Message Parameters

Each message has two 32-bit-long parameters. The first parameter is typically known as the wParam parameter, the second parameter as the lParam parameter. Normally, the "w" prefix on the parameter would suggest that it is a 16-bit

integer, and in fact, wParam was a 16-bit integer under Win16. The parameter thus continues to be called wParam for historical reasons and to minimize the confusion arising during the switch to 32-bit Windows.

Under Win16, the lParam parameter was frequently used to transfer two 16-bit integer parameters: one in the high 16-bit word and the other in the low 16-bit word. This happens much less frequently under Win32 due to the switch to 32-bit handles. In fact, as you will see, the change to 32 bits has forced the meaning of the wParam and lParam parameters to many windows messages to change from their Win16 meanings.

Messages That Return Values

The SendMessage returns a long value. Since this function calls a window function directly, it is possible for the window function to return a value that appears as the result of the SendMessage function. The meaning of this value depends on the message. For the purposes of the message reference in this book, unless a message is listed as providing a return value, the result of the SendMessage function has no meaning and should be ignored.

When using SendMessageTimeout, you must be sure to test whether the time-out occurred or not, since a valid return value will only be provided if the message was completely processed.

Registered Messages

In most cases when you refer to a message, you refer to it by the name of the constant that is associated with the message. For example, the WM_SYSCOMMAND message described earlier is actually defined thus:

```
Public Const WM_SYSCOMMAND = &H112
```

This is because Windows processes messages by number. In most cases this is fine because the standard windows messages are all defined as constants and are known ahead of time. There are some cases, however, where you may wish for a message number to be defined dynamically. For example, say you have a group of cooperating applications and wish to be able to broadcast a message that only your applications will understand. You could search the system for each window belonging to your family of applications and send the message only to those applications; however, what happens if you add a new application? The earlier search programs would not recognize it. An easier approach is to simply broadcast a message (the SendMessage and PostMessage functions both provide the ability to send messages to all top level windows in one function call)—but if the message number that you use conflicts with a message number used by some other application, you could interfere with its operation and perhaps even cause a memory exception in that application.

The ideal solution would be to use the broadcasting capabilities of Send-Message or PostMessage, but to somehow be able to assign a unique message number to your group that would not be used by any other window in the system. This can be done with the RegisterWindowMessage function. This function takes a message name as its parameter and assigns a unique unused message number to that name. Any other applications using the same name will receive the same message number. Thus, all you need to do is define a unique string for your group of applications to be certain that they will share a unique message number for the duration of the current window session.

The WM_COMMAND Message

The WM_COMMAND message is somewhat unusual in that it actually reflects an entire set of messages. This message is used in two ways.

The WM_COMMAND message is sent to a window that owns a menu when a menu command occurs. This process is described at some length in Chapter 10. Or the WM_COMMAND message is sent by a control to its parent window when certain events occur. These are special messages known as notification messages.

Under Win16, the parameters of a notification message were as follows: The wParam parameter contains the identifier of the control sending the notification (you can obtain control identifiers using the GetWindowWord function). The low 16 bits of the lParam parameter contain the window handle of the control sending the notification and the high 16 bits contain the notification number.

Under Win32, the low 16 bits of the wParam parameter contains the identifier of the control sending the notification (use GetWindowLong to obtain this value under Win32). The high 16 bits of the wParam parameter contains the notification number. The lParam parameter contains the window handle of the control sending the notification. You can use the agDwordTo2Integers function in Apigid32.dll to split the wParam parameter into its two component integers.

Notification messages are listed for several of the standard Windows controls in Chapters 17 and 18.

Messages That Are Useful with Visual Basic

This section contains a reference and examples of standard Windows messages that are useful under Visual Basic. Messages that are specific to text, list, combo, and other controls are discussed in Chapters 17 and 18.

The messages listed here have been tested under the standard Visual Basic controls. They are likely to work with most custom controls as well, especially if they are subclassed from standard Windows controls.

Table 16. 2 summarizes a few of the messages that are most useful under Visual Basic. The detailed descriptions of each of these functions (and many others) can be found in the message reference section of this chapter.

Table 16.2   **Messages Useful under Visual Basic**

Message	Control	Description
WM_CLEAR	Text, combo	Clears the selected text
WM_CLOSE	Form	Closes the window or application
WM_COPY	Text, combo	Copies the selected text into the clipboard
WM_CUT	Text, combo	Cuts the selected text into the clipboard
WM_GETFONT	Most controls that show text	Retrieves a handle to the default logical font used by the control
WM_PASTE	Text, combo	Pastes text from the clipboard into the control
WM_SETFONT	Most controls that show text	Sets the default font that the control should use to display text
WM_SETREDRAW	List, combo, text	Determines whether a control should update its display when the contents of the control are changed
WM_SYSCOMMAND	Form	Can be used to execute system menu commands under program control
WM_UNDO	Text	Reverses the effect of the most recent editing operation

Visual Basic and Subclassing

Chapter 2 introduced the idea of subclassing—the ability to intercept windows messages before (or after) they are processed by the target window. This capability is provided by a type of control called a subclasser. The dwsbc32d.ocx control included with this book is a demonstration version of the subclasser from Desaware's SpyWorks. It is fully functional, but only works within the Visual Basic environment. With Visual Basic 5.0 you can write your own in-process subclasser as well. A high-quality VB5-authored subclasser with full source code is included in SpyWorks as well.

Subclassing has the potential of adding a great deal of flexibility to your Visual Basic applications. The message reference section includes suggestions for how each message can be used with a subclasser under the "Use with Sub-classing" section for each message.

The following section illustrates this with some simple code that can be used to add an image or logo to the background area of an MDI form—a task that is not supported directly by Visual Basic. More important, it ties together many of the concepts found throughout this book to illustrate one way that API techniques can be combined to perform powerful operations with very few lines of code.

A second version of this program, called MDIPntb.vbp, that uses the Ad-dressOf operator to perform the subclassing operation within Visual Basic, is included on the CD-ROM that comes with this book. The method shown in MdiPntb.vbp is discouraged because of the difficulty in developing and debug-ging applications that take this approach. You can demonstrate this for your-self by running this project within the VB environment and trying to step through the program.

Creating Custom MDI Form Backgrounds

In order to draw a picture on the background for an MDI form, it is first nec-essary to understand a little bit about how windows are updated and how an MDI form is structured. You can use the WinView application from Chapter 5 to analyze the structure of the MDI form. You'll quickly discover that every MDI form actually consists of two windows. The background area of the form is a separate window from the MDIform—it is a window with the class MDI-Client. The hWnd property for the form returns the form window handle, but in order to change the behavior of the background area of the form, you actu-ally need to subclass the MDIClient window. You can obtain the window han-dle of the MDIClient easily using the GetWindow function as follows:

```
GetWindow(MDIForm1.hwnd, GW_CHILD)
```

Subclassing is turned on during the form's load event using the following code:

```
SubClass1.HwndParam = GetWindow(hwnd, GW_CHILD)
```

The dwsbc32d.ocx control is placed on a picture control that is top-aligned to the MDI form. This picture control can be hidden if you do not in-tend to use it to hold a toolbar. In the MDIPaint example, this picture control also holds the logo image that is used by the application.

So how does one go about changing the behavior of this window in order to place an image on it? There are several approaches that you can use. One possibility is to watch for the WM_PAINT message that is received by the window any time all or part of the window needs to be updated. You could subclass the window after the window function has executed—thus the win-dow will first draw itself, then you can process the message by drawing the image at the desired location.

If you try this, you will find that two problems occur. First, there is a flicker due to the fact that every time the window is drawn it first fills the background color, than overlays the image. A worse problem occurs due to the MDIClient window's support for scrolling whenever an MDI child window is dragged outside of the client's boundaries. When you scroll the window, any existing image is shifted, but that part of the window is not redrawn during the WM_PAINT event. The result is that you quickly have fragments of the picture scrolling around the screen.

This sample avoids that problem by taking over the background painting for the MDIClient window. It does this by intercepting the WM_ERASEBKGND message and preventing the default background drawing from taking place.

The real work is done by the SubClass1_WndMessage event as shown in Listing 16.1. The device context for drawing is provided as the wp parameter for the function. Normally, this device context has a clipping region set so that only those areas that need to be drawn are accessible by the device context. In this case, we must clear the clipping region because we need to override the normal scrolling operation provided by the form (try commenting out the SelectClipRgn function and see what happens when you scroll the MDI form).

Create a temporary compatible device context and select into it the handle of the bitmap that you want to display. The FillRect function draws the main background area (outside of the bitmap area). The BitBlt function copies the bitmap into the desired location on the form.

Note how the bitmap and compatible device context are cleaned up after they are used. The retval event parameter is set to TRUE to notify Windows that the background has been erased. The nodef event parameter is set to TRUE to prevent the default WM_ERASEBKGND message processing from taking place.

Listing 16.1   Partial listing of project MDIPaint.vbp

```
Private Sub SubClass1_WndMessage(hwnd As OLE_HANDLE, msg As OLE_HANDLE, _
wp As OLE_HANDLE, lp As Long, retval As Long, nodef As Integer)
    Dim tdc&
    Dim usedc&
    Dim oldbm&
    Dim bm As BITMAP
    Dim rc As RECT
    Dim offsx&, offsy&
    Debug.Print "Erasebkgnd"
    ' Get a DC to draw into
    usedc = GetDC(hwnd)
    ' Create a compatible DC to use
    tdc = CreateCompatibleDC(usedc)
```

Listing 16.1   Partial listing of project MDIPaint.vbp (Continued)

```
        ' Gets the bitmap handle of the background bitmap
        oldbm = SelectObject(tdc, Picture1.Picture)
        Call GetObjectAPI(Picture1.Picture, Len(bm), bm)
        Call GetClientRect(hwnd, rc)
        ' Decide where to place the MDI client logo
        offsx = 20
        offsy = 20

        ' Set the clipping region to the entire window -
        ' necessary because the hDC provided has a clipping
        ' region set.
        Call SelectClipRgn(usedc, 0)

        ' We exclude the bitmap area - this reduces flicker (try removing it)
        Call ExcludeClipRect(usedc, offsx, offsy, offsx + bm.bmWidth, offsy + _
        bm.bmHeight)
        Call FillRect(usedc, rc, COLOR_BACKGROUND)

        ' And restore the clip region before painting the bitmap
        Call SelectClipRgn(usedc, 0)

        Call BitBlt(usedc, offsx, offsy, bm.bmWidth, bm.bmHeight, tdc, 0, 0, _
        SRCCOPY)

        Call ReleaseDC(hwnd, usedc)
        Call SelectObject(tdc, oldbm)
        Call DeleteDC(tdc)
        ' This was added for VB5
        Call ValidateRectBynum(hwnd, 0)
        nodef = True
        retval = True
End Sub
```

The CD-ROM for this book includes past issues of Desaware's Visual Basic bulletin which includes many additional samples of subclassing (even though some are from 16-bit Windows, the principles are easily adapted to Win32).

Function Reference

This section contains an alphabetical reference for the functions described in this chapter.

■ BroadcastSystemMessage

VB Declaration
```
Declare Function BroadcastSystemMessage& Lib "user32" (ByVal dw As Long, pdw As _
Long, ByVal un As Long, ByVal wParam As Long, ByVal lParam As Long)
```

Description   Broadcasts a system message to all top level windows in the system.

Use with VB   No problem, though it is quite rare for an application to define and use its own system messages.

Parameter	Type/Description
dw	Long—One or more of the following constants: BSF_FLUSHDISK: Disk is flushed each time a message is processed. BSF_FORCEIFHUNG: If target is hung, expires after a timeout. BSF_IGNORECURRENTTASK: Sending task does not receive the message. BSF_LPARAMBUFFER: lParam points to a memory buffer. BSF_NOHANG: Skips any processes that are hung. BSF_POSTMESSAGE: Message is posted. Not compatible with BSF_LPARAMBUFFER and BSF_QUERY. BSF_QUERY: Sends the message to processes in sequence, going to the next process only if the previous one returns TRUE.
pdw	Long—One or more of the following constants: BSF_ALLCOMPONENTS: Message goes to every system component that can receive a message. BSF_APPLICATIONS: Message goes to applications. BSF_INSTALLABLEDRIVERS: Message goes to installable drivers. BSF_NETDRIVERS: Message goes to network drivers. BSF_VXDS: Message goes to system device drivers.
un	Long—The message number.
wParam	Long—Depends on the message.
lParam	Long—Depends on the message. If BSF_LPARAMBUFFER is specified, this is the address of a memory buffer in the calling processes address space, and the first 16-bit word in the buffer contains the length of the buffer.

Return Value   Long—Greater than zero on success. –1 on error. Zero if BSF_QUERY is set and at least one message recipient returned zero.

Platform   Windows 95, Windows NT 4.0

■ GetMessagePos

VB Declaration
```
Declare Function GetMessagePos& Lib "user32" ()
```

Description	Retrieves the cursor screen coordinates at the time the most recent message in the message queue was processed.
Use with VB	No problem.
Return Value	Long—The X coordinate is in the lower order word of the result, the Y coordinate in the high word.
Platform	Windows 95, Windows NT, Win16

■ GetMessageTime

VB Declaration	`Declare Function GetMessageTime& Lib "user32" ()`
Description	Retrieves the time at which the most recent message in the message queue was processed.
Use with VB	No problem.
Return Value	Long—The time is specified in milliseconds from the time the system was started.
Platform	Windows 95, Windows NT, Win16

■ PostMessage, PostMessageBynum, PostMessageBystring

VB Declaration	`Declare Function PostMessage& Lib "user32" Alias "PostMessageA" (ByVal hwnd As _`
	`Long, ByVal wMsg As Long, ByVal wParam As Long, lParam As Any)`
	`Declare Function PostMessageByNum& Lib "user32" Alias "PostMessageA" (ByVal _`
	`hwnd As Long, ByVal wMsg As Long, ByVal wParam As Long, ByVal lParam As Long)`
	`Declare Function PostMessageByString& Lib "user32" Alias "PostMessageA" (ByVal _`
	`hwnd As Long, ByVal wMsg As Long, ByVal wParam As Long, ByVal lParam As String)`

Description	Posts a message to the message queue of the specified window. Posted messages are processed in due course during Windows event processing, at which time the Windows function for the specified window is called with the posted message. PostMessageBystring and PostMessageBynum are type-safe declarations of PostMessage.
Use with VB	Good for sending window messages that do not need to be processed immediately.

Parameter	Type/Description
hwnd	Long—Handle of the window to receive the message. HWND_BROADCAST to post to all top-level windows in the system. Zero to post a thread message (See PostThreadMessage).
wMsg	Long—Message identifier.
wParam	Long—Depends on the message.
lParam	Long—Depends on the message.

Return Value	Long—TRUE (nonzero) if the message is posted successfully. Sets GetLastError.
Platform	Windows 95, Windows NT, Win16

■ PostThreadMessage

VB Declaration   `Declare Function PostThreadMessage& Lib "user32" Alias "PostThreadMessageA" _`
`(ByVal idThread As Long, ByVal msg As Long, ByVal wParam As Long, ByVal lParam _`
`As Long)`

Description   Posts a message to an application. This message is retrieved by an application's internal GetMessage loop, but will not be sent to a particular window.

Use with VB   No problem, but unlikely to be particularly useful. Thread messages for VB applications can only be intercepted using windows hooks. Refer to your online Win32 reference for use of the SetWindowsHooksEx function, or use the sample hook control dwshk32d.ocx from Desaware's Spy-Works package.

Parameter	Type/Description
idThread	Long—Identifier of the thread to receive the message.
msg	Long—Message identifier.
wParam	Long—Depends on the message.
lParam	Long—Depends on the message.

Return Value   Long—TRUE (nonzero) if the message is posted successfully. Sets GetLastError.

Platform   Windows 95, Windows NT

Porting Notes   Replaces the Win16 PostAppMessage function.

■ RegisterWindowMessage

VB Declaration   `Declare Function RegisterWindowMessage& Lib "user32" Alias _`
`"RegisterWindowMessageA" (ByVal lpString As String)`

Description   Retrieves the message number assigned to a string identifier.

Use with VB   No problem, though not generally useful without the aid of a subclasser.

Parameter	Type/Description
lpString	String—The name of the registered message.

Return Value   Long—A message number between the range &C000 and &FFFF. Zero on error.

Platform   Windows 95, Windows NT, Win16

■ ReplyMessage

VB Declaration   `Declare Function ReplyMessage& Lib "user32" (ByVal lReply As Long)`

Description   When a message is sent to a window in a different process, normally the first process is suspended until the window function in the other process has completed operation. The other process can use this function to return a result to the first process (which will then continue to execute) before the window function in the target function finishes.

Use with VB   No problem.

Parameter	Type/Description
lReply	Long—The result to send to the calling process.

Return Value   Long—TRUE if the message you are replying to was sent by another process. FALSE if it was sent from within the same process (in which case the function has no effect).

Platform   Windows 95, Windows NT, Win16

■ SendMessage, SendMessageBynum, SendMessageBystring

VB Declaration   Declare Function SendMessage& Lib "user32" Alias "SendMessageA" (ByVal hwnd As _
Long, ByVal wMsg As Long, ByVal wParam As Long, lParam As Any)
Declare Function SendMessageBynum& Lib "user32" Alias "SendMessageA" (ByVal _
hwnd As Long, ByVal wMsg As Long, ByVal wParam As Long, ByVal lParam As Long)
Declare Function SendMessageByString& Lib "user32" Alias "SendMessageA" (ByVal _
hwnd As Long, ByVal wMsg As Long, ByVal wParam As Long, ByVal lParam As String)

Description   Sends a message to a window by calling the window function for that window. This function does not return until the message is processed. SendMessageBystring and SendMessageBynum are type-safe declarations of SendMessage.

Use with VB   No problem.

Parameter	Type/Description
hwnd	Long—Handle of the window to receive the message.
wMsg	Long—The identifier of the message.
wParam	Long—Depends on the message.
lParam	Long—Depends on the message.

Return Value   Long—Depends on the message.

Platform   Windows 95, Windows NT, Win16

■ SendMessageCallback

VB Declaration   Declare Function SendMessageCallback& Lib "user32" Alias "SendMessageCallbackA" _
(ByVal hwnd As Long, ByVal msg As Long, ByVal wParam As Long, ByVal lParam As _
Long, ByVal lpResultCallBack As Long, ByVal dwData As Long)

Description   Sends a message to a window. This function returns immediately. When the target window function has finished executing, it returns its result by way of a callback function.

Use with VB Requires the dwcbk32d.ocx callback control when used with Visual Basic 4.0.

Parameter	Type/Description
hwnd	Long—Handle of the window to receive the message.
msg	Long—The identifier of the message.
wParam	Long—Depends on the message.
lParam	Long—Depends on the message.
lpResultCall-Back	Long—A function address. Obtained using the AddressOf operator under VB5, or passing a value from the ProcAddress property of the dwcbk32d.ocx callback control under VB4.
dwData	Long—A user-defined value.

Return Value Long—TRUE on success, FALSE on error. Sets GetLastError.

Platform Windows 95, Windows NT

Comments The callback function is declared:

```
Public Function WndProc(ByVal hwnd&, ByVal msg&, ByVal wp&, ByVal lp&) As Long
```

The wp parameter will be the value passed as the dwData parameter. The lp parameter will contain the result from the window function.

Under VB4, set the type property of the dwcbk32d.ocx control to 9 (WndProc).

If the hwnd parameter of this function is HWND_BROADCAST, the callback event will be triggered once for each top level window in the system.

You may create type-safe aliases for the lParam parameter for this function.

■ SendMessageTimeout

VB Declaration
```
Declare Function SendMessageTimeout& Lib "user32" Alias "SendMessageTimeoutA" _
(ByVal hwnd As Long, ByVal msg As Long, ByVal wParam As Long, ByVal lParam As _
Long, ByVal fuFlags As Long, ByVal uTimeout As Long, lpdwResult As Long)
```

Description Sends a message to a window. If the window is in a different thread, this function allows you to specify a time-out value to prevent the calling thread from hanging indefinitely in the event the other thread is hung.

Use with VB No problem.

Parameter	Type/Description
hwnd	Long—Handle of a window to receive the message.
msg	Long—The identifier of the message.
wParam	Long—Depends on the message.
lParam	Long—Depends on the message.

Parameter	Type/Description
fuFlags	Long—One or more of the following constants: SMTO_ABORTIFHUNG: Function returns immediately if the target process is hung. SMTO_BLOCK: The calling thread cannot process messages until the function returns. SMTO_NORMAL: The calling thread is allowed to process messages while the function is in progress.
uTimeout	Long—The timeout value in milliseconds.
lpdwResult	Long—A long variable to load with the result of the function.

Return Value Long—TRUE on success, FALSE on error. Sets GetLastError.

Platform Windows 95, Windows NT

■ SendNotifyMessage

VB Declaration
```
Declare Function SendNotifyMessage& Lib "user32" Alias "SendNotifyMessageA" _
(ByVal hwnd As Long, ByVal msg As Long, ByVal wParam As Long, ByVal lParam As _
Long)
```

Description Sends a message to a window. If the target window belongs to the same thread as the caller, this function behaves like the SendMessage function and does not return until the message is processed. If the target window belongs to a different thread, the function returns immediately.

Use with VB No problem.

Parameter	Type/Description
hwnd	Long—Handle of a window to receive the message.
msg	Long—The identifier of the message.
wParam	Long—Depends on the message.
lParam	Long—Depends on the message.

Return Value Long—TRUE on success, FALSE on error. Sets GetLastError.

Platform Windows 95, Windows NT

Message Reference

This section contains a list of the most frequently used Windows messages. Many of these messages are either not directly accessible or useful under Visual Basic, or duplicate functionality provided by a Windows API function or Visual Basic property. They are described briefly here for two reasons.

First, you may choose to take advantage of technology to subclass Visual Basic forms or controls, in which case this reference can be extremely useful for modifying the behavior of the subclassed control.

Second, these messages provide a great deal of insight to the internal workings of Windows and Visual Basic.

Many of the message descriptions include a section on their use with subclassing, which describes briefly the functionality that is available using subclassing technology. Subclassing is described further in "Windows Event Messages," earlier in this chapter, and in Chapter 2.

■ WM_ACTIVATE

VB Declaration `Const WM_ACTIVATE = &H6`

Description Sent to a window when it is activated or deactivated.

Use with VB None. The Visual Basic Activate and Deactivate events are triggered by this message.

Parameter	Description
wParam	Low word is one of the following constants: WA_INACTIVE: Window is deactivated. WA_ACTIVE: Window is activated. WA_CLICKACTIVE: Window is activated after a mouse click. High word: Nonzero if window is minimized.
lParam	The handle of the window whose state is changing. May be zero.

■ WM_ACTIVATEAPP

VB Declaration `Const WM_ACTIVATEAPP = &H1C`

Description This message is sent to the active window of an application that is being activated or deactivated. WM_ACTIVATE is sent when switching between active windows within an application.

Use with VB None.

Use with Subclassing Used to determine when a user is switching between applications.

Parameter	Description
wParam	TRUE (nonzero) if the application is being activated.
lParam	A thread identifier. If the application is being activated, the thread identifier of the deactivated thread. If application is being deactivated, the thread identifier of the thread being activated.

■ WM_ASKCBFORMATNAME

VB Declaration `Const WM_ASKCBFORMATNAME = &H30C`

Description Sent to the clipboard owner when the clipboard contains data in the CF_OWNERDISPLAY format. The clipboard owner must copy the name of the format into the buffer pointed to by lParam.

Use with VB None.

Use with Subclassing   Makes possible use of the CF_OWNERDISPLAY format for VB applications.

Parameter	Description
wParam	The maximum number of bytes to copy.
lParam	The address of a buffer to load with the name of the buffer.

■ WM_CANCELJOURNAL

VB Declaration   Const WM_CANCELJOURNAL = &H4B

Description   Posted to an application when a user cancels the application's journaling activities.

Use with VB   None.

Use with Subclassing   The message is posted with a NULL window handle, therefore a hook must be used to intercept this notification.

■ WM_CANCELMODE

VB Declaration   Const WM_CANCELMODE = &H1F

Description   Informs a window that a dialog box or message box is about to be displayed.

Use with VB   None.

Use with Subclassing   Generally used to cancel modes such as the mouse capture. Return zero if this message is processed.

■ WM_CAPTURECHANGED

VB Declaration   Const WM_CAPTURECHANGED = &H215

Description   Informs a window when it loses the mouse capture.

Use with VB   None.

Use with Subclassing   Informs window of mouse capture state. Do not attempt to set the mouse capture while processing this message.

Platform   Windows 95, Windows NT 4.0

Parameter	Description
wParam	Not used—set to zero.
lParam	Handle of window receiving the mouse capture.

■ WM_CHANGECBCHAIN

VB Declaration   `Const WM_CHANGECBCHAIN = &H30D`

Description   Sent to the first window in the clipboard viewer chain when a window is being removed from the chain.

Use with VB   None.

Use with Subclassing   Notifies the window of changes to the clipboard contents.

Parameter	Description
wParam	The window handle of the window being removed from the clipboard viewer chain.
lParam	The window handle of the next window in the chain following the window being removed. Zero if window being removed is the last window in the chain.

Comments   Each window in the clipboard viewer chain must in turn send this message to the next window in the chain. Refer to your online Windows documentation for information on custom clipboard formats and the clipboard viewer chain.

■ WM_CHAR

VB Declaration   `Global Const WM_CHAR = &H102`

Description   Sent to a window when a character is received.

Use with VB   None. This message triggers the Visual Basic KeyPressed event on controls that support it.

Use with Subclassing   Allows detection of keyboard input on controls that do not support the KeyUp, KeyDown, and KeyPressed events.

Parameter	Description
wParam	The virtual key number of the character.
lParam	Bits 0–15: The number of repetitions of the character received (used during auto repeat). Bits 16–23: The device scan code of the key pressed. Bit 24: 1 if it is an extended key such as a function key or numeric keypad entry. Bit 29: 1 if the Alt key was held down when the key was pressed. Bit 30: 1 if the key was down before this message was added to the queue. This is common during auto-repeat. Bit 31: 0 if the key is being pressed, 1 if released.

Comments   The data in lParam only reflects the most recent key operation for this character and is rarely used.

■ WM_CHARTOITEM

VB Declaration   Const WM_CHARTOITEM = &H2F

Description   A list box with the LBS_WANTKEYBOARDINPUT style sends this to its parent in response to a WM_CHAR message.

Use with VB   None.

Use with Subclassing   Allows an application to perform special processing on the keyboard input before the listbox.

Parameter	Description
wParam	Low word: The virtual key number of the character. High word: The current caret position.
lParam	The window handle of the list box.

Comments   The application should return a negative value if it handled all aspects of selecting the item and requires no further action by the list box. The application should return 0 or greater to specify the index number of the list box entry for which the default action for the keystroke should take place.

■ WM_CHILDACTIVATE

VB Declaration   Const WM_CHILDACTIVATE = &H22

Description   This message is sent to Multiple Document Interface (MDI) controls when they are activated.

Use with VB   None.

Use with Subclassing   Return zero if this message is processed.

■ WM_CLEAR

VB Declaration   Const WM_CLEAR = &H303

Description   This message can be sent to a text box or combo box to clear the selected text.

Use with VB   No problem. This is equivalent to the Visual Basic command:
ctl.SelText = ""
where ctl is the name of the control.

■ WM_CLOSE

VB Declaration   Const WM_CLOSE = &H10

Description   This message is sent to indicate that a request has been made to close a window or application.

Use with VB   Posting this message to a form or window is equivalent to invoking the Close command on the system menu for that form or window.

Use with Subclassing

If you prevent default processing for this message from taking place, you can cause the system menu Close command to be ignored. In that case return zero.

Comments

The following line of code demonstrates use of this message to close a form:

```
di& = PostMessage(hWnd, WM_CLOSE, 0&, 0&)
```

■ WM_COMMAND

VB Declaration   `Const WM_COMMAND = &H111`

Description

This message is sent to a window when a message command is invoked, or when a control sends a notification message to a window. It is described in more detail in "The WM_COMMAND Message," earlier in this chapter. This message can be used to simulate the sending of menu commands to a form.

Use with VB   No problem.

Use with Subclassing

This message could be used to detect and intercept menu commands to a form.

Parameter	Description
wParam	Low word: The menu command ID if this is a menu command. The control identifier if this is a notification message. High word: The message number of the notification message. Notification messages for the several standard Windows controls can be found in the message reference sections of Chapters 17 and 18.
lParam	The window handle of a control if this is a notification message.

■ WM_COMPACTING

VB Declaration   `Const WM_COMPACTING = &H41`

Description   Sent to all top level windows when Windows is short on memory.

Use with VB   None.

Use with Subclassing   Frequently used as a signal to an application to free up any memory that it can.

Parameter	Description
wParam	N where N/&HFFFFFFFF is the percentage of time being spent compacting memory.

■ WM_COMPAREITEM

VB Declaration   `Const WM_COMPAREITEM = &H39`

Description   Sent by Windows to request that the application perform a comparison on two entries in a sorted owner draw listbox or combo box.

Use with VB None.

**Use with
Subclassing** Refer to your online Windows documentation or the documentation and sample code provided with your subclasser for further information on use of owner draw controls.

■ WM_COPY

VB Declaration `Const WM_COPY = &H301`

Description This message can be sent to a text box or combo box to copy the selected text into the clipboard.

Use with VB No problem. This is equivalent to the Visual Basic commands:
`Clipboard.SetText Text1.SelText`

■ WM_COPYDATA

VB Declaration `Const WM_COPYDATA = &H4A`

Description This message is sent when an application passes data to another application.

Use with VB Provides a mechanism for transferring blocks of data between processes.

**Use with
Subclassing** Provides one way to transfer data using private messaging if your subclasser does not include its own data exchange mechanism.

Parameter	Description
wParam	The window handle passing the data.
lParam	Pointer to a COPYDATASTRUCT structure containing the data passed as shown below.

```
Type COPYDATASTRUCT
        dwData As Long ' A user defined value
        cbData As Long ' The size of the buffer referenced by lpData
        lpData As Long ' A block of data to pass to the other process
End Type
```

The receiving process should not modify the block of data referenced. The lpData memory block must not contain object or memory references that are private to the originating process.

■ WM_CREATE

VB Declaration `Const WM_CREATE = &H1`

Description Sent to a window as soon as it is created.

Use with VB None.

**Use with
Subclassing**   Return –1 to destroy the window, in which case the calling CreateWindow or CreateWindowEx
                      function will return zero.

Parameter	Description
lParam	A pointer to a CREATESTRUCT data structure.

■ WM_CTLCOLOR

VB Declaration   `Const WM_CTLCOLOR = &H19`

Description   Sent by a standard Windows control to its parent window before the control is drawn.

Use with VB   None.

**Use with
Subclassing**   Typically used to set the background or foreground color for the control; this message probably
                      has no value under Visual Basic.

Parameter	Description
wParam	A device context for the control.
lParam	Low word: The control window handle. High word: The type of control. Refer to the constants with the CTLCOLOR_ prefix.

Comments   Return a handle to a brush to use for background fill or zero to use the default brush.

■ WM_CTLCOLORBTN, WM_CTLCOLORDLG, WM_CTLCOLOREDIT, WM_CTLCOLORLISTBOX, WM_CTLCOLORMSGBOX, WM_CTLCOLORSCROLLBAR, WM_CTLCOLORSTATIC

VB Declaration   `Const WM_CTLCOLORBTN = &H135`
                      `Const WM_CTLCOLORDLG = &H136`
                      `Const WM_CTLCOLOREDIT = &H133`
                      `Const WM_CTLCOLORLISTBOX = &H134`
                      `Const WM_CTLCOLORMSGBOX = &H132`
                      `Const WM_CTLCOLORSCROLLBAR = &H137`
                      `Const WM_CTLCOLORSTATIC = &H138`

Description   Sent by a Windows button control, dialog box, edit control, list box, message box, scrollbar, or
                      static control to its parent window before the control is drawn.

Use with VB   None.

**Use with
Subclassing**   Typically used to set the background or text color for the specified object; this message probably
                      has no value under Visual Basic.

Parameter	Description
wParam	Handle to a device context for the control.

Parameter	Description
lParam	The control window handle.

Comments Return a handle to a brush to use for background fill or zero to use the default brush.

■ WM_CUT

VB Declaration `Const WM_CUT = &H300`

Description This message can be sent to a text box or combo box to cut the selected text into the clipboard.

Use with VB No problem. This is equivalent to the Visual Basic commands:
```
Clipboard.SetText Text1.SelText
Text1.SelText = ""
```

■ WM_DEADCHAR

VB Declaration `Const WM_DEADCHAR = &H103`

Description This is similar to the WM_CHAR message except that it indicates that a character is to be combined with another character: for example, the accent mark used on many non-English character sets. Refer to the WM_CHAR message for information on use with VB, subclassing, and parameters.

■ WM_DELETEITEM

VB Declaration `Const WM_DELETEITEM = &H2D`

Description Used to delete items from owner draw listboxes and combo boxes.

Use with VB None.

Use with Subclassing Refer to your online Windows documentation or the documentation and sample code provided with your subclasser for further information on use of owner draw controls.

■ WM_DESTROY

VB Declaration `Const WM_DESTROY = &H2`

Description Sent to a window before it is destroyed, but after it has been hidden.

Use with VB None—the Visual Basic Unload event is triggered by this message.

Use with Subclassing A good opportunity to clean up any window properties.

Comments A window's child windows still exist when this message is received.

■ WM_DEVMODECHANGE

VB Declaration Const WM_DEVMODECHANGE = &H1B

Description Sent to all top level windows when the default configuration of a device has been changed.

Use with VB None.

Use with Subclassing Detects changes to device settings.

Parameter	Description
lParam	A string address containing the name of the device that has been reconfigured.

■ WM_DRAWCLIPBOARD

VB Declaration Const WM_DRAWCLIPBOAD = &H308

Description Sent to the first window in the clipboard viewer chain when the content of the clipboard changes.

Use with VB None.

Use with Subclassing Allows a clipboard viewer window to display the new contents of the clipboard.

Comments Each window in the clipboard viewer chain must in turn send this message to the next window in the chain.

■ WM_DRAWITEM

VB Declaration Const WM_DRAWITEM = &H2B

Description Sent to owner draw controls to indicate that all or part of the control needs to be redrawn.

Use with VB None

Use with Subclassing Refer to your online Windows documentation or the documentation and sample code provided with your subclasser for further information on use of owner draw controls.

■ WM_DROPFILES

VB Declaration Const WM_DROPFILES = &H233

Description Sent when the left mouse button is released while the cursor is in the window of an application that has registered itself as being able to receive dropped files.

Use with VB None.

**Use with
Subclassing**

Notifies you of dropped files for a window that has indicated to the system that it can accept file manager dropped files. Refer to online documentation for the DragAcceptFiles, DragFinish, DragQueryFile, and DragQueryPoint functions.

Parameter	Description
wParam	Handle to an internal structure describing the dropped files.
lParam	Not used—set to zero.

■ WM_ENABLE

VB Declaration `Const WM_ENABLE = &HA`

Description This message is sent to a window when it becomes enabled or disabled.

Use with VB None.

Parameter	Description
wParam	TRUE (nonzero) if the window is enabled.

Comments The WS_DISABLED style bit for the window has already been updated when this message is received.

■ WM_ENDSESSION

VB Declaration `Const WM_ENDSESSION = &H16`

Description Sent to the main window of an application before a Windows session ends.

Use with VB None.

**Use with
Subclassing** Can be used to perform cleanup operations before a Windows session ends.

Parameter	Description
wParam	TRUE (nonzero) if the session is ending.
lParam	Windows 95 & NT4.0: TRUE if logging off, FALSE if shutting down the system.

■ WM_ENTERIDLE

VB Declaration `Const WM_ENTERIDLE = &H121`

Description This message is sent to a window when a dialog box or menu for that window is idle (waiting for user input).

Use with VB	None.	
	Parameter	**Description**
	wParam	The constant MSGF_DIALOGBOX if a dialog box is displayed, MSGF_MENU if a menu is displayed.
	lParam	The dialog box handle, or handle of the window that owns the menu.

■ WM_ERASEBKGND

VB Declaration   Const WM_ERASEBKGND = &H14

Description   Sent to a window to inform it that it should erase its background.

Use with VB   None.

Use with Subclassing   The default operation is to erase the window background. This message can be intercepted to create a custom background.

	Parameter	**Description**
	wParam	A device context for the window.
	lParam	Not used—set to zero.

Comments   Return nonzero if you process the WM_ERASEBKGND message and erase the background; this tells Windows that it does not need to erase the background.

■ WM_FONTCHANGE

VB Declaration   Const WM_FONTCHANGE = &H1D

Description   This message is sent to all top level windows when the available system fonts change.

Use with VB   None.

Use with Subclassing   If your application displays a list of available fonts, this serves as notification that the list should change. If a window is using a font that is no longer available, it may be necessary to redraw the window.

	Parameter	**Description**
	wParam	Not used—set to zero.
	lParam	Not used—set to zero.

■ WM_GETFONT

VB Declaration   Const WM_GETFONT = &H31

Description   Retrieves the handle to the logical font used by a control. The logical font handle is returned in the result of the SendMessage function call. Logical fonts are described in Chapter 11.

Use with VB   Works with standard Visual Basic controls.

■ WM_GETMINMAXINFO

VB Declaration   `Const WM_GETMINMAXINFO = &H24`

Description   Sent to a window when Windows needs to determine the minimum or maximum sizes for the window.

Use with VB   None.

Use with Subclassing   Can be used to change the default minimum or maximum sizes for a window.

Parameter	Description
wParam	Not used—set to zero.
lParam	A pointer to a MINMAXINFO data structure as defined in the comments section below.

Comments   The MINMAXINFO is defined as follows:

```
Type MINMAXINFO
    ptReserved As POINTAPI
    ptMaxSize As POINTAPI
    ptMaxPosition As POINTAPI
    ptMinTrackSize As POINTAPI
    ptMaxTrackSize As POINTAPI
End Type
```

ptMaxSize specifies the maximum width and height of the window. ptMaxPosition specifies the maximum position of the upper left corner of the window. ptMinTrackSize and ptMaxTrackSize specify the minimum and maximum width and height of the window when sized by dragging the borders.

■ WM_GETTEXT

VB Declaration   `Const WM_GETTEXT = &HD`

Description   Sent to a window to retrieve the window text. Duplicates the functionality of the GetWindowText function.

Use with VB   No problem, but is rarely used due to the availability of the Visual Basic Text and Caption properties, and the GetWindowText function.

Parameter	Description
wParam	The size of the buffer.
lParam	An address of the buffer to load with the window text.

■ WM_GETTEXTLENGTH

VB Declaration   `Const WM_GETTEXTLENGTH = &HE`

Description Sent to a window to retrieve the length of the window text. Duplicates the functionality of the GetWindowTextLength function.

Use with VB No problem, but is rarely used due to the availability of the Visual Basic Text and Caption properties, and the GetWindowTextLength function.

Parameter	Description
wParam	Not used—set to zero.
lParam	Not used—set to zero.

Comments Under certain conditions, the return value may be larger than the actual length of the text.

■ WM_HSCROLL

VB Declaration `Const WM_HSCROLL = &H114`

Description This message is sent to a window when the user clicks on the window's horizontal scroll bar. It is also sent in response to user clicks on a horizontal scroll control.

Use with VB None.

Use with Subclassing Can be used to change the behavior of the window or scroll control. For example, if you intercept this message and do not send it to the control, you can manually control the thumb position instead of letting the normal positioning take effect. This could allow you to simulate scrolling through ranges greater than 64K in size.

Parameter	Description
wParam	Low word: One of the following constants:
	SB_ENDSCROLL: End of dragging.
	SB_TOP: Scroll all the way to the left.
	SB_LINELEFT: Scroll one unit to the left.
	SB_LINERIGHT: Scroll one unit to the right.
	SB_PAGELEFT: Scroll one page to the left.
	SB_PAGERIGHT: Scroll one page to the right.
	SB_BOTTOM: Scroll all the way to the right.
	SB_THUMBPOSITION: The thumb was dragged and released at the position specified in the high word of wParam. The possible values depend on the minimum and maximum settings as set by SetScrollRange.
	SB_THUMBTRACK: The thumb is in the process of being dragged. The current thumb position is specified in the high word of wParam.
	High word: Current thumb position if the low word is either SB_THUMBPOSITION or SB_THUMBTRACK; otherwise, not used.
lParam	If the scroll bar is a control, this is the handle of the control window. Zero otherwise.

■ WM_HSCROLLCLIPBOARD

VB Declaration `Const WM_HSCROLLCLIPBOARD = &H30E`

Description   Similar to the WM_HSCROLL message. This message is sent to the clipboard owner by a clipboard viewer window when the clipboard contains data in the CF_OWNERDISPLAY format and the user clicks on the window's horizontal scroll bar.

Use with VB   None.

Use with Subclassing   Can be used to change the behavior of the clipboard.

Parameter	Description
wParam	Handle to the clipboard viewer window.
lParam	Low word: One of the following constants: SB_ENDSCROLL: End of dragging. SB_TOP: Scroll all the way to the left. SB_LINELEFT: Scroll one unit to the left. SB_LINERIGHT: Scroll one unit to the right. SB_PAGELEFT: Scroll one page to the left. SB_PAGERIGHT: Scroll one page to the right. SB_BOTTOM: Scroll all the way to the right. SB_THUMBPOSITION: The thumb was dragged and released at the position specified in the low word of lParam. The possible values depend on the minimum and maximum settings as set by SetScrollRange. High word: Current thumb position if the low word is SB_THUMBPOSITION, otherwise not used.

■ WM_ICONERASEBKGND

VB Declaration   `Const WM_ICONERASEBKGND = &H27`

Description   This message is sent to a minimized window before drawing the icon for the window if a class icon is defined.

Use with VB   None.

Use with Subclassing   The default processing for this message uses the background brush or pattern of the parent window. Return zero if you process this message.

Parameter	Description
wParam	The device context on which the icon will be drawn.

■ WM_INITDIALOG

VB Declaration   `Const WM_INITDIALOG = &H110`

Description   This message is sent to a dialog box procedure immediately before the dialog box is displayed. The procedure typically carries out initialization for the dialog box when receiving this message.

Use with VB   None.

**Use with
Subclassing** May be used with callbacks to modify Windows common dialogs.

Parameter	Description
wParam	Handle to window receiving the keyboard focus. Windows will assign the keyboard focus to this window if the return value is TRUE.
lParam	Additional initialization information.

■ WM_INITMENU

VB Declaration `Const WM_INITMENU = &H116`

Description This message is sent to a window before its menu is displayed. Refer to Chapter 10 for more information on menus.

Use with VB None.

**Use with
Subclassing** Typically used to change the menu before it is displayed in response to the current state of the system. Also used to detect when a pop-up menu is activated in order to update a status bar.

Parameter	Description
wParam	The handle of the menu.

■ WM_INITMENUPOPUP

VB Declaration `Const WM_INITMENUPOPUP = &H117`

Description This message is sent to a window before a pop-up menu is displayed. Refer to Chapter 10 for more information on menus.

Use with VB None.

**Use with
Subclassing** Typically used to change the menu before it is displayed in response to the current state of the system. Also used to detect when a pop-up menu is activated in order to update a status bar.

Parameter	Description
wParam	Handle of the pop-up menu.
lParam	Low word: The index (position) of the pop-up menu in the top level menu. High word: TRUE (nonzero) if this is the system pop-up menu.

■ WM_KEYDOWN

VB Declaration `Const WM_KEYDOWN = &H100`

Description Posted to a window when a key is pressed that is not a system character. This message occurs when a window has the input focus and the Alt key is not pressed.

Use with VB   None. This message triggers the Visual Basic KeyDown event on controls that support it. Refer to the discussion of keyboard control in Chapter 6 for further information.

Use with Subclassing   Allows detection of keyboard input on controls that do not support the KeyUp, KeyDown, and KeyPressed events.

Parameter	Description
wParam	The virtual key number of the character.
lParam	Same as that defined for the WM_CHAR message except that bits 29 and 31 are always zero.

■ WM_KEYUP

VB Declaration   `Const WM_KEYUP = &H101`

Description   Posted to a window when a key is released that is not a system character. This message occurs when a window has the input focus and the Alt key is not pressed.

Use with VB   None. This message triggers the Visual Basic KeyUp event on controls that support it. Refer to the discussion of keyboard control in Chapter 6 for further information.

Use with Subclassing   Allows detection of keyboard input on controls that do not support the KeyUp, KeyDown, and KeyPressed events.

Parameter	Description
wParam	The virtual key number of the character.
lParam	Same as that defined for the WM_CHAR message except that bit 29 is always zero and bits 30 and 31 are always one.

■ WM_KILLFOCUS

VB Declaration   `Const WM_KILLFOCUS = &H8`

Description   This message is sent to a window before it loses the input focus.

Use with VB   None.

Use with Subclassing   Frequently used to destroy the caret when custom carets are used. Refer to the discussion of caret control in Chapter 6 for further information. Also used to detect the true lost focus event for a control.

Parameter	Description
wParam	The handle of the window gaining the focus. May be zero.

Comments   This differs from the Visual Basic LostFocus event, which actually occurs after the control has already lost the focus.

■ WM_LBUTTONDBLCLK

VB Declaration   Const WM_LBUTTONDBLCLK = &H203

Description   This message is sent to a window when the left mouse button is double-clicked inside a window. The window must belong to a class that has the CS_DBLCLKS style set.

Use with VB   May be used to simulate a mouse action. For example, sending a WM_LBUTTONDBLCLK message to a control will cause the control to behave as if it had actually been double-clicked. In order to use this successfully, you should simulate the entire sequence that is received by a control being double-clicked. This consists of a WM_LBUTTONDOWN message followed by a WM_LBUTTONUP message, a WM_LBUTTONDBLCLK message, and a WM_LBUTTONUP message.

Use with Subclassing   Very handy for detecting double-clicks in controls that do not support the DblClk event.

Parameter	Description
wParam	A combination of one or more of the following constants indicating the state of the shift, control keys, and other mouse buttons: MK_CONTROL: The control key is down. MK_LBUTTON: The left mouse button is down. MK_MBUTTON: The middle mouse button is down. MK_RBUTTON: The right mouse button is down. MK_SHIFT: The shift key is down.
lParam	Low word: The X coordinate of the cursor in window client coordinates. High word: The Y coordinate of the cursor in window client coordinates.

■ WM_LBUTTONDOWN

VB Declaration   Const WM_LBUTTONDOWN = &H201

Description   This message is sent to a window when the left mouse button is pressed inside a window.

Use with VB   May be used to simulate a mouse action. For example, sending a WM_LBUTTONDOWN message to a button control followed by a WM_LBUTTONUP message will cause the control to behave as if it had actually been clicked.

Use with Subclassing   Useful for detecting mouse events in controls that do not support the MouseDown event.

Parameter	Description
wParam	A combination of one or more of the following constants: MK_CONTROL: The control key is down. MK_MBUTTON: The middle mouse button is down. MK_RBUTTON: The right mouse button is down. MK_SHIFT: The shift key is down.
lParam	Low word: The X coordinate of the cursor in window client coordinates. High word: The Y coordinate of the cursor in window client coordinates.

■ WM_LBUTTONUP

VB Declaration Const WM_LBUTTONUP = &H202

Description This message is sent to a window when the left mouse button is released inside a window.

Use with VB May be used to simulate a mouse action. For example, sending a WM_LBUTTONDOWN message to a button control followed by a WM_LBUTTONUP message will cause the control to behave as if it had actually been clicked.

Use with Subclassing Useful for detecting mouse events in controls that do not support the MouseUp event.

Parameter	Description
wParam	Same as for the WM_LBUTTONDOWN message.
lParam	Same as for the WM_LBUTTONDOWN message.

■ WM_MBUTTONDBLCLK

VB Declaration Const WM_MBUTTONDBLCLK = &H209

Description This message is sent to a window when the center mouse button is double-clicked inside a window. The window must belong to a class that has the CS_DBLCLKS style set.

Use with VB May be used to simulate a mouse action. For example, sending a WM_MBUTTONDBLCLK message to a control will cause the control to behave as if it had actually been double-clicked with the middle mouse button. In order to use this successfully, you should simulate the entire sequence that is received by a control being double-clicked. This consists of a WM_MBUTTONDOWN message followed by a WM_MBUTTONUP message, a WM_MBUTTONDBLCLK message, and a WM_MBUTTONUP message.

Use with Subclassing Useful for detecting double-clicks in controls that do not support the DblClk event and for mouse buttons other than the left mouse button.

Parameter	Description
wParam	Same as for the WM_LBUTTONDBLCLK message.
lParam	Same as for the WM_LBUTTONDBLCLK message.

■ WM_MBUTTONDOWN

VB Declaration Const WM_MBUTTONDOWN = &H207

Description This message is sent to a window when the center mouse button is pressed inside a window.

Use with VB May be used to simulate a mouse action. For example, sending a WM_MBUTTONDOWN message to a control followed by a WM_MBUTTONUP message will cause the control to behave as if it had actually been clicked with the middle mouse button.

Subclassing   Useful for detecting mouse events in controls that do not support the MouseDown event.

Parameter	Description
wParam	A combination of one or more of the following constants: MK_CONTROL: The control key is down. MK_LBUTTON: The left mouse button is down. MK_RBUTTON: The right mouse button is down. MK_SHIFT: The shift key is down.
lParam	Low word: The X coordinate of the cursor in window client coordinates. High word: The Y coordinate of the cursor in window client coordinates.

■ WM_MBUTTONUP

VB Declaration   `Const WM_MBUTTONUP = &H208`

Description   This message is sent to a window when the center mouse button is released inside a window.

Use with VB   May be used to simulate a mouse action. For example, sending a WM_MBUTTONDOWN message to a button control followed by a WM_MBUTTONUP message will cause the control to behave as if it had actually been clicked with the middle mouse button.

Use with
Subclassing   Useful for detecting mouse events in controls that do not support the MouseUp event.

Parameter	Description
wParam	Same as for the WM_MBUTTONDOWN message.
lParam	Same as for the WM_MBUTTONDOWN message.

■ WM_MDIACTIVATE

VB Declaration   `Const WM_MDIACTIVATE = &H222`

Description   This message can be used to activate an MDI child window. It is also sent to MDI child windows when they are activated or deactivated. The active MDI child window is brought to the top of the display order and given the focus if the application is active.

Use with VB   This message must be sent to the MDIClient child window of an MDI form, not the form itself. Use the GetWindow function or hWnd property to find the window handle of this child window. Chapter 2 discusses the structure of MDI windows.

Use with
Subclassing   Can be used to monitor the activation of MDI child windows.
Sending WM_MDIACTIVATE to the MDIClient Window:

Parameter	Description
wParam	The handle of the window to activate.
lParam	Not used—set to zero.

WM_ MDIACTIVATE as Received by MDI Child Windows:

Parameter	Description
wParam	The window handle of the MDI child window being deactivated.
lParam	The window handle of the MDI child window being activated.

■ WM_MDICASCADE

VB Declaration   `Const WM_MDICASCADE = &H227`

Description   This message can be used to cascade the MDI child windows on an MDI form.

Use with VB   This message must be sent to the MDIClient child window of an MDI form, not the form itself. Use the GetWindow function to find the window handle of this child window. Chapter 2 discusses the structure of MDI windows.

The Visual Basic Arrange method provides this functionality and is easier to use.

Use with Subclassing   Not particularly useful.

Parameter	Description
wParam	The constant MDITILE_SKIPDISABLED may be specified to prevent the cascade of disabled MDI child windows.
lParam	Not used—set to zero.

■ WM_MDICREATE

VB Declaration   `Const WM_MDICREATE = &H220`

Description   This message can be used to create new MDI child windows on an MDI form.

Use with VB   This message must be sent to the MDIClient child window of an MDI form, not the form itself. Use the GetWindow function to find the window handle of this child window. Chapter 2 discusses the structure of MDI windows.

Use with Subclassing   Can be used to monitor the creation of MDI child windows.

Parameter	Description
wParam	Not used—set to zero.
lParam	Pointer to an MDICREATESTRUCT structure describing the new MDI child window.

■ WM_MDIDESTROY

VB Declaration   `Const WM_MDIDESTROY = &H221`

Description   This message can be used to close a MDI child window on an MDI form.

| **Use with VB** | This message must be sent to the MDIClient child window of an MDI form, not the form itself. Use the GetWindow function to find the window handle of this child window. Chapter 2 discusses the structure of MDI windows. |

Use with Subclassing Can be used to monitor when MDI child windows are closed.

Parameter	Description
wParam	The window handle of the MDI child window being closed.
lParam	Not used—set to zero.

■ WM_MDIGETACTIVE

VB Declaration   Const WM_MDIGETACTIVE = &H229

Description   This message can be used to retrieve the window handle of the currently active MDI child window.

Use with VB   This message must be sent to the MDIClient child window of an MDI form, not the form itself. Use the GetWindow function to find the window handle of this child window. Chapter 2 discusses the structure of MDI windows.

Parameter	Description
wParam	Not used—set to zero.
lParam	A pointer to a Long variable. On return, the Long will contain nonzero if the active MDI child window is maximized, zero if not. Set to zero if you do not need to know the maximized state of the active MDI child window.

Returns   Long—The window handle of the active MDI child window.

■ WM_MDIICONARRANGE

VB Declaration   Global Const WM_MDIICONARRANGE = &H228

Description   This message can be used to arrange the icons of all minimized MDI child windows on the MDI form.

Use with VB   This message must be sent to the MDIClient child window of an MDI form, not the form itself. Use the GetWindow function to find the window handle of this child window. Chapter 2 discusses the structure of MDI windows.

The Visual Basic Arrange method provides this functionality and is easier to use.

Parameter	Description
wParam	Not used—set to zero.
lParam	Not used—set to zero.

■ WM_MDIMAXIMIZE

VB Declaration   Const WM_MDIMAXIMIZE = &H225

Description	This message can be used to maximize an MDI child window within an MDI form.
Use with VB	This message must be sent to the MDIClient child window of an MDI form, not the form itself. Use the GetWindow function to find the window handle of this child window. Chapter 2 discusses the structure of MDI windows.

Parameter	Description
wParam	The window handle of the MDI child window to maximize.
lParam	Not used—set to zero.

■ WM_MDINEXT

VB Declaration   Const WM_MDINEXT = &H224

Description	This message can be used to activate the next or previous MDI child window within an MDI form.
Use with VB	This message must be sent to the MDIClient child window of an MDI form, not the form itself. Use the GetWindow function to find the window handle of this child window. Chapter 2 discusses the structure of MDI windows.

Parameter	Description
wParam	Zero to indicate the window handle of the active MDI child window. Otherwise, identifies the window handle for which to activate the next or previous MDI child window.
lParam	Zero if the next MDI child window of the specified window should be activated, nonzero if the previous MDI child window should be activated.

■ WM_MDIREFRESHMENU

VB Declaration   Const WM_MDIREFRESHMENU = &H234

Description	This message can be used to refresh the window menu of an MDI form.
Use with VB	This message must be sent to the MDIClient child window of an MDI form, not the form itself. Use the GetWindow function to find the window handle of this child window. Chapter 2 discusses the structure of MDI windows.

Parameter	Description
wParam	Not used—set to zero.
lParam	Not used—set to zero.

■ WM_MDIRESTORE

VB Declaration   Const WM_MDIRESTORE = &H223

Description	This message can be used to restore a minimized or maximized MDI child window to its previous state.

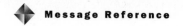

Use with VB   This message must be sent to the MDIClient child window of an MDI form, not the form itself. Use the GetWindow function to find the window handle of this child window. Chapter 2 discusses the structure of MDI windows.

Parameter	Description
wParam	The window handle of the MDI child window to restore.
lParam	Not used—set to zero.

■ WM_MDISETMENU

VB Declaration   Const WM_MDISETMENU = &H230

Description   This message can be used to replace the menu of a MDI form.

Use with VB   Visual Basic manages menus directly.

Parameter	Description
wParam	If nonzero, contains new menu handle for the MDI form.
lParam	If nonzero, contains new menu handle for the Window sub menu of the MDI form.

■ WM_MDITILE

VB Declaration   Const WM_MDITILE = &H226

Description   This message can be used to tile MDI child windows within an MDI form.

Use with VB   This message must be sent to the MDIClient child window of an MDI form, not the form itself. Use the GetWindow function to find the window handle of this child window. Chapter 2 discusses the structure of MDI windows.

The Visual Basic Arrange method provides the same functionality and is easier to use.

Parameter	Description
wParam	One of the following flags: MDITILE_HORIZONTAL: Tiles windows horizontally. MDITILE_SKIPDISABLED: Prevents tiling of disabled windows. MDITILE_VERTICAL: Tiles windows vertically.
lParam	Not used—set to zero.

■ WM_MEASUREITEM

VB Declaration   Const WM_MEASUREITEM = &H2C

Description   Used to determine the dimensions of owner draw controls.

Use with VB   None.

Use with Subclassing Refer to your online Windows documentation or the documentation and sample code provided with your subclasser for further information on use of owner draw controls.

■ WM_MENUCHAR

VB Declaration `Const WM_MENUCHAR = &H12Ø`

Description This message is sent to a window any time a character is entered while a menu is displayed and the character does not match a mnemonic (underlined) character for a menu entry. Refer to Chapter 10 for a detailed description of menus.

Use with VB None.

Use with Subclassing Typically used to allow mnemonic access to bitmap entries in a menu. Return one of the following values in the high order word: Zero if the character should be discarded and a short beep sounded on the speaker, one if Windows should close the menu, and two if the item specified in the low order word should be selected.

Parameter	Description
wParam	Low word: The ASCII value of the character. High word: The constant MF_POPUP if the menu is a pop-up menu, MF_SYSMENU if the menu is a system menu.
lParam	The handle of the menu.

■ WM_MENUSELECT

VB Declaration `Const WM_MENUSELECT = &H11F`

Description This message is sent to a window when the user selects a menu entry. Refer to Chapter 10 for a detailed description of menus.

Use with VB None.

Use with Subclassing Typically used to update a status bar as the user selects different entries in a menu.

Parameter	Description
wParam	Low word: The command identifier of the menu entry, or a menu index of the pop-up menu in the main menu if the entry is a pop-up menu. In the latter case, use the GetSubMenu function to get the menu handle of the pop-up menu. High word: A menu entry flag made up of one or more of the MF_ constants defined in Chapter 10.
lParam	If the MF_SYSMENU flag is specified in the high word of wParam, this is the handle of the system menu. Otherwise, this is the handle of the menu.

Comments If the high word of wParam contains &HFFFF and lParam is zero, then the menu was closed.

■ WM_MOUSEACTIVATE

VB Declaration   `Const WM_MOUSEACTIVATE = &H21`

Description   This message is sent to an inactive window when the user clicks a mouse button over the window.

Use with VB   None.

Use with Subclassing   Provides additional control over whether a window should be activated.

Parameter	Description
wParam	A handle to the top level window for the application of the window being activated.
lParam	Low word: A hit test code as defined in the return value of the WM_NCHITTEST message. High word: The value of the mouse message that caused this message.

Comments   The return value to this message is a constant that specifies the action to take as shown below.
MA_ACTIVATE: The window is activated.
MA_NOACTIVATE: The window is not activated.
MA_ACTIVATEANDEAT: The window is activated and the mouse message that caused it is discarded.
MA_NOACTIVATEANDEAT: The window is not activated and the mouse message that caused it is discarded.

■ WM_MOUSEMOVE

VB Declaration   `Const WM_MOUSEMOVE = &H200`

Description   This message is posted to a window when the mouse moves over the window or when the window has set the capture for the mouse cursor.

Use with VB   None.

Use with Subclassing   Frequently used for detecting the positioning of the mouse over a control.

Parameter	Description
wParam	A combination of one or more of the following constants indicating the state of the Shift key, Control key, and other mouse buttons: MK_CONTROL: The Control key is down. MK_LBUTTON: The left mouse button is down. MK_MBUTTON: The middle mouse button is down. MK_RBUTTON: The right mouse button is down. MK_SHIFT: The Shift key is down.
lParam	Low word: The X coordinate of the cursor in window client coordinates. High word: The Y coordinate of the cursor in window client coordinates.

■ WM_MOVE

VB Declaration	`Const WM_MOVE = &H3`
Description	This message is sent to a window when it has been moved.
Use with VB	None.
Use with Subclassing	Can be used for detecting when a form has been moved.

Parameter	Description
lParam	Low word: The X coordinate of the top-left corner of the window. High word: The Y coordinate of the top-left corner of the window. These values are in window client coordinates for child windows, and screen coordinates for pop-up and top-level windows.

■ WM_NCACTIVATE

VB Declaration	`Const WM_NCACTIVATE = &H86`
Description	This message is sent to a window when its caption or icon needs to be changed to indicate an active or inactive state.
Use with VB	None.
Use with Subclassing	Can be used to prevent the caption or icon from being set to the deactivate state.

Parameter	Description
wParam	Nonzero to indicate an active state, zero to indicate an inactive state.
lParam	Not used—set to zero.

■ WM_NCCALCSIZE

VB Declaration	`Const WM_NCCALCSIZE = &H83`
Description	This message is sent when the size and position of a window's client area must be calculated.
Use with VB	None.
Use with Subclassing	Can be used to control the size or position of the window's client area.

Parameter	Description
wParam	TRUE to specify that the application should indicate which part of the client area contains valid information. FALSE to specify that the application does not need to indicate the valid part of the client area.

Parameter	Description
lParam	If wParam is TRUE, points to a NCCALCSIZE_PARAMS structure that contains information concerning the new size and position of the client rectangle. If wParam is FALSE, lParam points to a RECT structure that contains the new coordinates of the window that has been moved or resized.

■ WM_NCCREATE

VB Declaration   Const WM_NCCREATE = &H81

Description   This is the first message sent to a window. This is the only time when the style of a window may be changed and guaranteed to take effect properly.

Use with VB   None.

Use with Subclassing   Difficult, as it is hard to obtain a handle for a newly created window to use in subclassing. When creating windows explicitly, this message indicates a safe time to change the styles of a window.

Parameter	Description
wParam	Not used—set to zero.
lParam	The address of the CREATESTRUCT structure for this window.

■ WM_NCDESTROY

VB Declaration   Const WM_NCDESTROY = &H82

Description   This message is sent to a window after the WM_DESTROY message. It notifies a window that its nonclient area is being destroyed.

Use with VB   None.

■ WM_NCHITTEST

VB Declaration   Const WM_NCHITTEST = &H84

Description   Used to determine what part of the nonclient area of a window contains the mouse cursor.

Use with VB   None.

Use with Subclassing   Usually used to examine the result after default processing occurs. The available areas are described by the constants beginning with the HT prefix in the file API32.TXT. These constants are self-explanatory. You can also intercept this message and return your own result to change the behavior of the window. For example, returning the constant HTCAPTION will cause Windows to think that you have clicked on a caption area in the window. This could let you implement window dragging on areas of the window other than the caption.

Parameter	Description
wParam	Not used—set to zero.
lParam	Low word: The horizontal position of the cursor in screen coordinates. High word: The vertical position of the cursor in screen coordinates.

■ WM_NCLBUTTONDBLCLK

VB Declaration   `Const WM_NCLBUTTONDBLCLK = &HA3`

Description   This message is posted to a window when the left mouse button is double-clicked in the nonclient area of a window. The window must belong to a class that has the CS_DBLCLKS style set. This message is not posted if a window has captured the mouse.

Use with VB   None.

Use with Subclassing   Used to detect double-clicks on nonclient areas.

Parameter	Description
wParam	Specifies the hit-test value returned by the DefWindowProc function as a result of processing the WM_NCHITTEST message. Refer to the constants beginning with the HT prefix in the file API32.TXT for a list of values.
lParam	Low word: The X coordinate of the cursor in window client coordinates. High word: The Y coordinate of the cursor in window client coordinates.

■ WM_NCLBUTTONDOWN

VB Declaration   `Const WM_NCLBUTTONDOWN = &HA1`

Description   This message is posted to a window when the left mouse button is pressed in the nonclient area of a window. This message is not posted if a window has captured the mouse.

Use with VB   None.

Use with Subclassing   Used to detect mouse down on nonclient areas.

Parameter	Description
wParam	Same as for the WM_NCLBUTTONDBLCLK.
lParam	Same as for the WM_NCLBUTTONDBLCLK.

■ WM_NCLBUTTONUP

VB Declaration   `Const WM_NCLBUTTONUP = &HA2`

Description   This message is posted to a window when the left mouse button is released in the nonclient area of a window. This message is not posted if a window has captured the mouse.

Use with VB   None.

Use with Subclassing   Used to detect mouse up on nonclient areas.

Parameter	Description
wParam	Same as for the WM_NCLBUTTONDBLCLK.
lParam	Same as for the WM_NCLBUTTONDBLCLK.

■ WM_NCMBUTTONDBLCLK

VB Declaration   `Const WM_NCMBUTTONDBLCK = &HA9`

Description   This message is posted to a window when the middle mouse button is double-clicked in the non-client area of a window. The window must belong to a class that has the CS_DBLCLKS style set. This message is not posted if a window has captured the mouse.

Use with VB   None.

Use with Subclassing   Used to detect double-clicks on nonclient areas.

Parameter	Description
wParam	Same as for the WM_NCLBUTTONDBLCLK.
lParam	Same as for the WM_NCLBUTTONDBLCLK.

■ WM_NCMBUTTONDOWN

VB Declaration   `Const WM_NCMBUTTONDOWN = &HA7`

Description   This message is posted to a window when the middle mouse button is pressed in the nonclient area of a window. This message is not posted if a window has captured the mouse.

Use with VB   None.

Use with Subclassing   Used to detect mouse down on nonclient areas.

Parameter	Description
wParam	Same as for the WM_NCLBUTTONDBLCLK.
lParam	Same as for the WM_NCLBUTTONDBLCLK.

■ WM_NCMBUTTONUP

VB Declaration   `Const WM_NCMBUTTONUP = &HA8`

Description   This message is posted to a window when the middle mouse button is released in the nonclient area of a window. This message is not posted if a window has captured the mouse.

Use with VB   None.

Use with Subclassing   Used to detect mouse up on nonclient areas.

Parameter	Description
wParam	Same as for the WM_NCLBUTTONDBLCLK.
lParam	Same as for the WM_NCLBUTTONDBLCLK.

■ WM_NCMOUSEMOVE

VB Declaration   Const WM_NCMOUSEMOVE = &HA0

Description   This message is posted to a window when the mouse moves over the nonclient area of a window. This message is not posted if a window has captured the mouse.

Use with VB   None.

Use with Subclassing   Used to detect mouse movement in nonclient areas.

Parameter	Description
wParam	Same as for the WM_NCLBUTTONDBLCLK.
lParam	Same as for the WM_NCLBUTTONDBLCLK.

■ WM_NCPAINT

VB Declaration   Const WM_NCPAINT = &H85

Description   This message is sent to a window when the window's frame has to be painted.

Use with VB   None.

Use with Subclassing   May intercept this message and paint custom window frame.

Parameter	Description
wParam	Handle containing the update region of the window. The update region is clipped to the window frame.
lParam	Not used—set to zero.

■ WM_NCRBUTTONDBLCLK

VB Declaration   Const WM_NCRBUTTONDBLCLK = &HA6

Description This message is posted to a window when the right mouse button is double-clicked in the nonclient area of a window. The window must belong to a class that has the CS_DBLCLKS style set. This message is not posted if a window has captured the mouse.

Use with VB None.

Use with Subclassing Used to detect double-clicks on nonclient areas.

Parameter	Description
wParam	Same as for the WM_NCLBUTTONDBLCLK.
lParam	Same as for the WM_NCLBUTTONDBLCLK.

■ WM_NCRBUTTONDOWN

VB Declaration Const WM_NCRBUTTONDOWN = &HA4

Description This message is posted to a window when the right mouse button is pressed in the nonclient area of a window. This message is not posted if a window has captured the mouse.

Use with VB None.

Use with Subclassing Used to detect mouse down on nonclient areas.

Parameter	Description
wParam	Same as for the WM_NCLBUTTONDBLCLK.
lParam	Same as for the WM_NCLBUTTONDBLCLK.

■ WM_NCRBUTTONUP

VB Declaration Const WM_NCRBUTTONUP = &HA5

Description This message is posted to a window when the right mouse button is released in the nonclient area of a window. This message is not posted if a window has captured the mouse.

Use with VB None.

Use with Subclassing Used to detect mouse up on nonclient areas.

Parameter	Description
wParam	Same as for the WM_NCLBUTTONDBLCLK.
lParam	Same as for the WM_NCLBUTTONDBLCLK.

■ WM_NOTIFY

VB Declaration Const WM_NOTIFY = &H4E

Description This message is sent by a child control to the parent when an event has occurred in the control or when the control requires some kind of information.

Use with VB None.

Use with Subclassing Detects additional events for edit controls.

Parameter	Description
wParam	ID of the control sending the message.
lParam	Address of a buffer containing a NMHDR structure that contains the notification code and additional information. For some notification messages, this parameter points to a larger structure that has the NMHDR structure as its first member.

Platform Windows NT.

■ WM_PAINT

VB Declaration `Const WM_PAINT = &HF`

Description This message is sent to a window when it is time for the window to update its client area.

Use with VB This message triggers the Visual Basic Paint event.

Use with Subclassing This is sometimes used to perform additional drawing on the window after the default processing for painting the window is complete. Also used to determine the portion of the window that actually needs to be drawn—this can be accomplished by calling the GetUpdateRect function during processing of this message.

■ WM_PARENTNOTIFY

VB Declaration `Const WM_PARENTNOTIFY = &H210`

Description Notifies a parent window when certain events take place in a child window unless the WS_EX_NOPARENTNOTIFY flag is set in the window's extended style.

Use with VB None.

Parameter	Description
wParam	Low word: The number of the message that has been received by the child window. This will be WM_CREATE, WM_DESTROY, WM_LBUTTONDOWN, WM_MBUTTONDOWN, or WM_RBUTTONDOWN. High word: The ID number of the child window if wParam is WM_CREATE or WM_DESTROY.
lParam	The handle of the child window if wParam is WM_CREATE or WM_DESTROY. Otherwise the low word contains the X coordinate of the cursor and the high word contains the Y coordinate of the cursor.

■ WM_PASTE

VB Declaration   Const WM_PASTE = &H302

Description   This message can be sent to a text box or combo box to paste the clipboard text into the control.

Use with VB   No problem. This is equivalent to the Visual Basic commands.
Text1.SelText = Clipboard.GetText

Comments   This function only has an effect if the clipboard contains text in the CF_TEXT format.

■ WM_POWER

VB Declaration   Const WM_POWER = &H48

Description   This message is sent to all top level windows to inform them that the system is entering or leaving a power conservation state. This is typically used only on battery-operated computers. Not all portable computers support this message.

Use with VB   None.

Parameter	Description
wParam	One of the following constants:
	PWR_SUSPENDREQUEST: System is about to be suspended or placed in a power conservation mode. You can return constant PWR_FAIL to prevent the system from entering the suspended condition, and should return PWR_OK otherwise.
	PWR_SUSPENDRESUME: System is resuming normal operation.
	PWR_CRITICALRESUME: System is resuming operation but a PWR_SUSPENDREQUEST message has not been sent.

Platform   Windows NT

Comments   Superseded by the WM_POWERBROADCAST message for a Windows 95 and NT4.0.

■ WM_POWERBROADCAST

VB Declaration   Const WM_POWERBROADCAST = &H218

Description   This message is sent to all top level windows to inform them that the system is entering or leaving a power conservation state. This is typically used only on battery-operated computers. Not all portable computers support this message.

Use with VB   None.

Parameter	Description
wParam	One of the following constants: PB_APMPOWERSTATUSCHANGED: Power status has changed. PB_APMQUERYSTANDBY: Requesting permission to standby. PB_APMQUERYSTANDBYFAILED: Standby request denied. PB_APMQUERYSUSPEND: Requesting permission to suspend. PB_APMQUERYSUSPENDFAILED: Suspension request denied. PB_APMRESUMECRITICAL: System is resuming normal operation after critical suspension. PB_APMRESUMESTANDBY: System is resuming normal operation after standby. PB_APMRESUMESUSPEND: System is resuming normal operation after being suspended. PB_APMSTANDBY: System is changing to standby. PB_APMSUSPEND: System is suspending operation.

Platform   Windows 95, Windows NT 4.0

Comments   Refer to the WM_POWER message for a Windows NT equivalent.

■ WM_QUERYDRAGICON

VB Declaration   Const WM_QUERYDRAGICON = &H37

Description   This message is sent to windows that do not have a class icon defined in order to display an icon.

Use with VB   None. Visual Basic draws the icon for a form on receipt of this message.

Use with Subclassing   Can be used to take over drawing of the form icon from VB when a form is minimized. To do so, do not allow default processing of the message. Return a cursor or icon handle in the result. The cursor or icon must be compatible with the display.

■ WM_QUERYENDSESSION

VB Declaration   Const WM_QUERYENDSESSION = &H11

Description   This message is sent to all top level windows to query if it is all right to end the Windows session.

Use with VB   None.

Use with Subclassing

Return TRUE if the application can be terminated, zero otherwise. A WM_ENDSESSION message will follow to inform the window if the Windows session may actually be ending (under Windows 95, the session is always ending when this message is received).

Parameter	Description
wParam	Zero if the request to end the Windows session occurred because the user clicked the Logoff or Shutdown button in the Shut Down Windows dialog box. Nonzero if the user clicked the End Task button in the Task List dialog box.
lParam	Windows 95 & NT4.0: TRUE if the user is logging off; FALSE if the user is shutting down the system.

■ WM_QUERYOPEN

VB Declaration   `Const WM_QUERYOPEN = &H13`

Description   This message is sent to a minimized window when the user has requested that the window be restored to its previous position and size.

Use with VB.   None.

Use with Subclassing   Allows the program to determine if the window should actually be restored or not. Return TRUE if the window can be restored, zero otherwise. The default operation is to return TRUE.

■ WM_RBUTTONDBLCLK

VB Declaration   `Const WM_RBUTTONDBLCLK = &H206`

Description   This message is sent to a window when the right mouse button is double-clicked inside a window. The window must belong to a class that has the CS_DBLCLKS style set.

Use with VB   May be used to simulate a mouse action. For example, sending a WM_RBUTTONDBLCLK message to a control will cause the control to behave as if it had actually been double-clicked with the right mouse button. In order to use this successfully, you should simulate the entire sequence that is received by a control being double-clicked. This consists of a WM_RBUTTONDOWN message followed by a WM_RBUTTONUP message, a WM_RBUTTONDBLCLK message, and a WM_RBUTTONUP message.

Use with Subclassing   Useful for detecting double-clicks in controls that do not support the DblClk event and for mouse buttons other than the left mouse button.

Parameter	Description
wParam	Same as for the WM_LBUTTONDBLCLK message.
lParam	Same as for the WM_LBUTTONDBLCLK message.

■ WM_RBUTTONDOWN

VB Declaration   `Const WM_RBUTTONDOWN = &H204`

Description   This message is sent to a window when the right mouse button is pressed inside a window.

Use with VB   May be used to simulate a mouse action. For example, sending a WM_RBUTTONDOWN message to a control followed by a WM_RBUTTONUP message will cause the control to behave as if it had actually been clicked with the right mouse button.

Use with Subclassing   Useful for detecting mouse events in controls that do not support the MouseDown event.

Parameter	Description
wParam	A combination of one or more of the following constants: MK_CONTROL: The Control key is down. MK_LBUTTON: The left mouse button is down. MK_MBUTTON: The center mouse button is down. MK_SHIFT: The Shift key is down.
lParam	Low word: The X coordinate of the cursor in window client coordinates. High word: The Y coordinate of the cursor in window client coordinates.

■ WM_RBUTTONUP

VB Declaration   `Const WM_RBUTTONUP = &H205`

Description   This message is sent to a window when the right mouse button is released inside a window.

Use with VB   May be used to simulate a mouse action. For example, sending a WM_RBUTTONDOWN message to a button control followed by a WM_RBUTTONUP message will cause the control to behave as if it had actually been clicked with the right mouse button.

Use with Subclassing   Useful for detecting mouse events in controls that do not support the MouseUp event.

Parameter	Description
wParam	Same as for the WM_MBUTTONDOWN message.
lParam	Same as for the WM_MBUTTONDOWN message.

■ WM_SETCURSOR

VB Declaration   `Const WM_SETCURSOR = &H20`

Description   This message is sent to a window when the mouse is over the window, and no other window has the mouse captured.

Use with VB   None.

Use with Subclassing	Can be used to modify the behavior of cursors. Return TRUE if a cursor has been selected.

Parameter	Description
wParam	The handle of the window that contains the cursor.
lParam	Low word: A hit test code as defined by the return values of the WM_NCHITTEST message. High word: The number of the mouse message that caused this message.

■ WM_SETFOCUS

VB Declaration	`Const WM_SETFOCUS = &H7`
Description	This message is sent to a window after it receives the input focus.
Use with VB	None.
Use with Subclassing	Frequently used to create the caret when custom carets are used. Refer to the discussion of caret control in Chapter 6 for further information. Can also be used to detect the TRUE GotFocus event for a control.

Parameter	Description
wParam	The handle of the window losing the focus. May be zero.
lParam	Not used.

■ WM_SETFONT

VB Declaration	`Const WM_SETFONT = &H30`
Description	Sets a logical font as the font to be used in a control. Logical fonts are described in Chapter 11.
Use with VB	Works with standard Visual Basic controls; however, the standard Visual Basic font properties are a preferred way to select fonts.

Parameter	Description
wParam	A handle to a logical font to use in this control. Zero to select the default system font.
lParam	Low word: TRUE (nonzero) to redraw the control when the font is changed.

■ WM_SETREDRAW

VB Declaration	`Const WM_SETREDRAW = &HB`
Description	This function controls the redraw operation on a control. Normally, each time a change is made to a control—for example, adding a string to a list box—the control is immediately updated to reflect the new state of the control. While this ensures that the current contents of a control are always displayed, it can slow down the process of changing a control when a large number of

changes are to be processed at once. This message can be used to turn off the redraw state. This allows changes to be made to a control without updating the control display. Once the redraw state is reenabled, the control can be updated.

Use with VB   Extremely useful for text, combo box, and list box controls.

Parameter	Description
wParam	TRUE (nonzero) to turn redraw on, zero to turn it off.
lParam	Not used—set to zero.

Comments   To take advantage of this function you may need to perform the modifications using Windows messages as described in Chapters 17 and 18 due to the fact that most modifications performed with Visual Basic property access cause an immediate update regardless of the state of the Redraw flag.

Normally under Windows, setting the Redraw flag back to TRUE after making modifications does not update the control—an explicit redraw operation is necessary using either the VB Refresh command or the Windows InvalidateRect function. Visual Basic seems to detect the setting of the Redraw flag using this message to automatically update the display.

■ WM_SETTEXT

VB Declaration   `Const WM_SETTEXT = &HC`

Description   Sent to a window to set the window text. Duplicates the functionality of the SetWindowText function.

Use with VB   No problem, but is rarely used due to the availability of the Visual Basic Text and Caption properties, and the SetWindowText function.

Parameter	Description
lParam	The string to set into the control.

■ WM_SETTINGCHANGE

VB Declaration   `Const WM_SETTINGCHANGE = &H1A`

Description   This message is sent to all top level windows when a systemwide change is made by using the SystemParametersInfo function.

Use with VB   None.

Use with Subclassing   Used to detect system-wide changes in Windows 95 and NT 4.0.

Parameter	Description
wParam	Specifies the systemwide parameter that has changed. Refer to the SystemParametersInfo function for a list.
lParam	Address of a buffer containing the string "WindowMetrics" if wParam specifies any of the following systemwide parameters. NULL, otherwise. SPI_SETANIMATION, SPI_SETNONCLIENTMETRICS, SPI_SETICONMETRICS, SPI_SETMINIMIZEDMETRICS.

Platform	Windows 95, Windows NT 4.0
Comments	Refer to the WM_WININICHANGE message for a Windows NT 3.51 equivalent.

■ WM_SHOWWINDOW

VB Declaration	`Const WM_SHOWWINDOW = &H18`
Description	This message is sent to a window when it is hidden or displayed.
Use with VB	None.
Use with Subclassing	Can be used to determine a change in the display state of a window.

Parameter	Description
wParam	TRUE (nonzero) if the window is being shown, zero if it is being hidden.
lParam	One of the following constants: SW_OTHERUNZOOM: Indicates that the window is being uncovered because a maximize window was restored or minimized. SW_OTHERZOOM: Indicates that the window is being covered by another window that has been maximized. SW_PARENTCLOSING: Indicates that the parent window is being hidden or minimized. SW_PARENTOPENING: Indicates that the parent window is being displayed.

■ WM_SIZE

VB Declaration	`Const WM_SIZE = &H5`
Description	This message is sent to a window when its size has been changed.
Use with VB	This message is used to trigger the Visual Basic Resize event.
Use with Subclassing	This can be used to restrict a control to certain sizes by calling the MoveWindow API function during the event processing.

Parameter	Description
wParam	One of the following constants: SIZE_MAXIMIZED: The window is maximized. SIZE_MINIMIZED: The window is minimized. SIZE_RESTORED: The window is restored. SIZE_MAXHIDE: Another window is being maximized. SIZE_MAXSHOW: Another maximized window has been restored.
lParam	Low word: The new width of the window. High word: The new height of the window. These values are in window client coordinates for child windows, and screen coordinates for pop-up and top level windows.

■ WM_SPOOLERSTATUS

VB Declaration   Const WM_SPOOLERSTATUS = &H2A

Description   This message is sent to applications to inform them that a print job has been added or removed from the print queue.

Use with VB   None.

Parameter	Description
wParam	Specifies the PR_JOBSTATUS flag.
lParam	Low word: The number of jobs remaining in the queue.

■ WM_SYSCHAR

VB Declaration   Const WM_SYSCHAR = &H106

Description   This is similar to the WM_CHAR message except that it detects Alt key combinations (characters entered when the Alt key is pressed) and characters entered when no window has the focus (in which case the message is sent to the active window).

■ WM_SYSCOLORCHANGE

VB Declaration   Const WM_SYSCOLORCHANGE = &H15

Description   This message is sent to applications to inform them that a system color has changed. System colors are those used for standard Windows objects.

Use with VB   None.

Use with Subclassing   Update any drawing that used colors based on system color settings.

■ WM_SYSCOMMAND

VB Declaration   Const WM_SYSCOMMAND = &H112

Description   This message is sent to an application when a system menu command has been selected by the user.

Use with VB   It is possible to execute system menu commands under program control by posting these messages to a form.

Use with Subclassing   Can be used to intercept system menu commands.

Parameter	Description
wParam	The system command posted. Refer to the constants with the SC_ prefix in the file API32.TXT. They are self-explanatory. The four low-order bits of wParam are used internally by Windows. Use the AND operator with &HFFF0 to obtain the correct SC_ value.

Parameter	Description
lParam	Low word: The X mouse coordinate if the mouse was used to trigger this system menu command. Otherwise this parameter is not used. High word: The Y mouse coordinate if the mouse was used to trigger this system menu command. -1 if the command is chosen using a system accelerator, or zero if using a mnemonic.

■ WM_SYSDEADCHAR

VB Declaration   Const WM_SYSDEADCHAR = &H107

Description   This is similar to the WM_CHAR message except that it indicates a character that is to be combined with another character; for example, the accent mark used on many non-English character sets. Refer to the WM_CHAR message for information on use with VB, subclassing, and parameters. This message only detects Alt key combinations or characters entered when no window has the focus.

■ WM_SYSKEYDOWN

VB Declaration   Const WM_SYSKEYDOWN = &H104

Description   Sent to a window when a key is pressed that is a system character. This message occurs when no window has the input focus or if the Alt key is pressed.

Use with VB   None. Refer to the discussion of keyboard control in Chapter 6 for further information.

Use with Subclassing   Allows detection of Alt key combinations.

Parameter	Description
wParam	The virtual key number of the character.
lParam	Same as that defined for the WM_CHAR message except that bit 31 is always zero. If bit 29 is zero, no window has the focus and this message is being received by the active window.

■ WM_SYSKEYUP

VB Declaration   Const WM_SYSKEYUP = &H105

Description   Sent to a window when a key is released that is a system character. This message occurs when no window has the input focus or if the Alt key is pressed.

Use with VB   None. Refer to the discussion of keyboard control in Chapter 6 for further information.

Use with Subclassing	Allows detection of Alt key combinations.

Parameter	Description
wParam	The virtual key number of the character.
lParam	Same as that defined for the WM_CHAR message except that bit 31 is always one. If bit 29 is zero, no window has the focus and this message is being received by the active window.

■ WM_TIMECHANGE

VB Declaration   `Const WM_TIMECHANGE = &H1E`

Description   This message is sent to all top level windows in the system when the system time has been changed.

Use with VB   If the system time is changed from Visual Basic, this message should be sent via the SendMessage function to all top level windows by setting the hwnd parameter to HWND_BROADCAST.

Use with Subclassing   Useful for applications that display the time.

■ WM_UNDO

VB Declaration   `Const WM_UNDO = &H304`

Description   This message can be sent to a text box to undo the effect of the most recent editing operation.

Use with VB   No problem; however, this function does not undo changes made by assigning a string to the Text or SelText property of the text box. It will undo the effects of the WM_CUT or WM_CLEAR message, and will undo the most recent keyboard operation.

■ WM_USER

VB Declaration   `Const WM_USER = &H400`

Description   Used as an offset to define private windows messages.

Use with VB   None.

Use with Subclassing   Can be used to communicate between applications.

Comments   There are five ranges of message numbers, 0 through WM_USER - 1 contain messages for use by Windows, WM_USER through &H7FFF contain integer messages for use by private window classes (listbox, text control, and so on), &H8000 through &HBFFF contain messages reserved for future use by Windows, &HC000 through &HFFFF contain string messages (registered messages) for use by applications, greater than &HFFFF contain messages reserved by Windows for future use.

■ WM_VSCROLL

VB Declaration   Const WM_VSCROLL = &H115

Description   This message is sent to a window when the user clicks on the window's vertical scroll bar. It is also sent in response to user clicks on a vertical scroll control.

Use with VB   None.

Use with Subclassing   Can be used to change the behavior of the window or scroll control. For example, if you intercept this message and do not send it to the control, you can manually control the thumb position instead of letting the normal positioning take effect. This could allow you to simulate scrolling through ranges greater than 64K in size.

Parameter	Description
wParam	Low word: One of the following constants: SB_BOTTOM: Scroll all the way to the bottom. SB_ENDSCROLL: End of dragging. SB_LINEDOWN: Scroll one unit down. SB_LINEUP: Scroll one unit up. SB_PAGEDOWN: Scroll one page down. SB_PAGEUP: Scroll one page up. SB_THUMBPOSITION: The thumb was dragged and released at the position specified in the highword of wParam. The possible values depend on the minimum and maximum settings as set by SetScrollRange. SB_THUMBTRACK: The thumb is in the process of being dragged. The current thumb position is specified in the high word of wParam. SB_TOP: Scroll all the way to the top. High word: Current thumb position if the low word is either SB_THUMBPOSITION or SB_THUMBTRACK otherwise not used.
lParam	If the scroll bar is a control, this is the handle of the control window. Zero otherwise.

■ WM_WINDOWPOSCHANGED

VB Declaration   Const WM_WINDOWPOSCHANGED = &H47

Description   This message is sent to a window whose size or position is changed after a call to the SetWindowPos function.

Use with VB   None.

Use with Subclassing   If this message is handled directly, it is up to the application to send WM_SIZE and WM_MOVE messages to the window.

Parameter	Description
lParam	The address of a WINDOWPOS structure. Refer to the Comments section for a definition of this structure.

Comments   The WINDOWPOS function is defined as follows:

```
Type WINDOWPOS
      hwnd As Long
      hwndInsertAfter As Long
      x As Long
      y As Long
      cx As Long
      cy As Long
      flags As Long
End Type
```

The meanings of these parameters are the same as the definitions of the parameters to the SetWindowPos function defined in Chapter 5.

■ WM_WINDOWPOSCHANGING

VB Declaration   `Const WM_WINDOWPOSCHANGING = &H46`

Description   This message is sent to a window whose size or position is about to change after a call to the SetWindowPos function.

Use with VB   None.

**Use with
Subclassing**   Changes made to the WINDOWPOS structure referred to by the lParam parameter at this time will be effective.

Parameter	Description
lParam	The address of a WINDOWPOS structure. Refer to the Comments section of the WM_WINDOWPOSCHANGED message for a definition of this structure.

■ WM_WININICHANGE

VB Declaration   `Const WM_WININICHANGE = &H1A`

Description   This message is sent to all top level windows when a change is made to the WIN.INI initialization file.

Use with VB   This message should be sent to all windows via the SendMessage function when changes are made to the WIN.INI file. Refer to the description of the WriteProfileString function in Chapter 13 and SystemParametersInfo function in Chapter 6 for further information.

Use with
Subclassing   Useful for programs that base any part of their display or execution on the contents of the
WIN.INI file.

Parameter	Description
lParam	A string containing the name of the section that has been changed.

Platform   Windows NT 3.51 (supported, but not recommended, for NT 4.0).

Comments   Superseded by WM_SETTINGCHANGE for Windows 95 and NT 4.0.

17

Edit Control Messages

The Text Control

*Example: TextMsgs—A
Demonstration of Edit
Control Messages*

THIS CHAPTER DISCUSSES MESSAGES THAT CAN BE USED WITH VISUAL Basic controls that are based on the Windows edit control, including the Visual Basic text control. These messages can significantly extend the capabilities of these controls. A sample program, TextMsgs, illustrates the use of many of these messages.

More important, this chapter and Chapter 18 both demonstrate how messages are used to work with windows controls in general. The techniques are directly applicable to other control types that are not documented in this book, including the Windows 95/NT 4.0 common controls.

The Text Control

The text control is typically used for entering and editing text. It is subclassed from the standard Windows edit control, so it supports all of the edit control messages. The techniques presented here will also work on other controls provided by third-party vendors that are based on the Windows edit control class.

The combo box control is a combination of a text control and list box. It supports combo box messages that are very similar to the edit control messages described in this chapter. These messages are reviewed in Chapter 18.

The edit control messages are divided into a number of functional groups, which are described below.

Undo Capability

Edit controls maintain a single-level undo buffer for most editing operations. This means that—in most cases—the previous editing operation can be reversed. The messages listed in Table 17.1 relate to the use of the undo buffer in edit controls.

Table 17.1 **Edit Control Undo Messages**

Message	Description
EM_CANUNDO	Determines if the last editing operation can be reversed
EM_EMPTYUNDOBUFFER	Clears the control's undo buffer, making it impossible to undo the previous editing operation
EM_UNDO	Reverses the previous editing operation

Text Formatting

The edit control messages provide a number of capabilities for internal formatting of data within the control.

Multiline edit controls maintain information internally regarding where soft line breaks occur. A soft line break is one that is inserted by the edit control in order to make the text fit within the control. Hard line breaks are those specified by the programmer by inserting a CR-LF (carriage return-line feed combination) into the text.

Edit controls keep track of soft line breaks by inserting a CR-CR-LF character sequence into the text string. Normally these soft line breaks are hidden from the programmer—they are not included in the text retrieved using the Visual Basic Text property.

You can force the edit control to include the soft line break characters in the text string by sending the EM_FMTLINES message to the control.

Each edit control has a formatting rectangle associated with it. On close examination of this type of control, you can see that the text does not extend all the way to the side of the control window. The formatting rectangle is the rectangle within the edit control that contains the text. Windows provides functions that allow you to determine the size of the formatting rectangle or to change it.

The edit control messages also provide the ability to set flexible tab stops for text within the control.

The messages listed in Table 17.2 are related to text formatting in edit controls.

Table 17.2   Text Formatting Messages for Edit Controls

Message	Description
EM_FMTLINES	Determines whether to include soft line breaks in retrieved text strings
EM_GETLIMITTEXT	Retrieves the maximum length of text for an edit control
EM_GETMARGINS	Retrieves the left and right margins for the edit control (N/A NT3.51)
EM_GETRECT	Retrieves the formatting rectangle for an edit control
EM_LIMITTEXT	Limits the length of text in an edit control
EM_SETLIMITTEXT	Limits the length of text in an edit control (not applicable in NT3.51)
EM_SETMARGINS	Sets the left and right margins for the edit control (not applicable in NT 3.51)
EM_SETRECT	Sets the formatting rectangle for an edit control
EM_SETRECTNP	Same as EM_SETRECT except that the control is not redrawn
EM_SETTABSTOPS	Sets tab spacing within an edit control

Selection and Display

The Visual Basic text control provides a flexible set of properties for controlling text selection and display. As always, it is generally better and easier to use a VB property when one is available rather than a Windows message.

There are, however, several areas where messages provide significantly improved capability when compared with the standard VB properties. This is especially true in the area of line versus character orientation on multiline edit controls.

The contents of an edit control can be thought of as a single string. This is the string that is set and retrieved using the Visual Basic Text property. Positions within the edit control can be described as an offset to a character from the start of the string. With multiline edit controls, the control breaks the string into lines, but this process is hidden from the programmer who still sees the text as a single string.

Windows provides a set of edit control messages that make it possible to treat a multiline edit control as a series of lines instead of a single string. Messages are provided that let you determine the number of lines in the control, the length of each line, and the offset of the first character in a given line from the start of the string. It is possible to retrieve individual lines from the control.

These messages also provide the important capability of determining the number of the first line that is actually visible. This, combined with the line-scrolling message EM_LINESCROLL, makes it possible to control most aspects of an edit control's display from a Visual Basic program. One example of where this might be useful is in an edit control to scroll through very large files. The TextMsgs demonstration program discussed later in this chapter illustrates some of the techniques that are possible using these messages.

Table 17.3 lists the selection and display messages that are available for edit controls.

Table 17.3 **Selection and Display Messages for Edit Controls**

Message	Description
EM_CHARFROMPOS	Determines the character at a specified location in an edit control (not applicable in NT 3.51)
EM_GETFIRSTVISIBLELINE	Determines the first line that is displayed in an edit control
EM_GETLINE	Retrieves a line from an edit control
EM_GETLINECOUNT	Determines the number of lines in an edit control
EM_GETMODIFY	Determines if the contents of an edit control have been changed
EM_GETPASSWORDCHAR	Retrieves the password character for an edit control

Table 17.3 **Selection and Display Messages for Edit Controls (Continued)**

Message	Description
EM_GETSEL	Determines the start and end locations of a selection in an edit control
EM_LINEFROMCHAR	Determines the line on which a specified character appears
EM_LINEINDEX	Determines the number of the first character on a specified line
EM_LINELENGTH	Determines the length of a line
EM_LINESCROLL	Scroll an edit control
EM_POSFROMCHAR	Determines the location of the specified character in an edit control (NT 3.51)
EM_REPLACESEL	Replaces the current selection in an edit control with the specified text
EM_SETMODIFY	Used to set or clear the modification flag for an edit control
EM_SETPASSWORDCHAR	Sets the password character for the specified control
EM_SETREADONLY	Specifies whether an edit control is read only or not
EM_SETSEL	Sets the start and end location of a selection in an edit control

Example: TextMsgs—A Demonstration of Edit Control Messages

TextMsgs is a program that demonstrates the use of edit control messages to perform a number of operations that are not possible using the standard Visual Basic Text control properties. It emphasizes use of line-oriented access to multi-line text controls. This project was ported directly from the original TextMsgs example in the Visual Basic Programmer's Guide to the Windows API (16-bit edition), and is compatible with both 16-bit VB4 and 32-bit Visual Basic.

Figure 17.1 shows the runtime screen for the TextMsgs program.

Using TextMsgs

The TextMsgs Setup menu has one entry, FillText, which is used to fill the text box with 20 lines of text for use in the demonstration. The Tests menu has entries for four different tests that can be performed.

The LineCount command determines the total number of lines in the text control and records the result in the LabelResult label control. The FirstVisible

Figure 17.1

Runtime screen for
TextMsgs.vbp

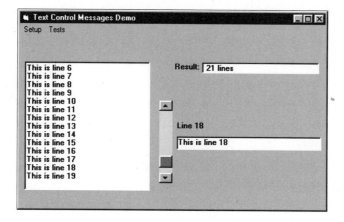

command displays the number of the first visible line. The Selected command
displays the start and end locations of the current selection. The LinesVisible
command (illustrated in Figure 17.1) calculates the number of lines that are
visible in the text control based on the size of the control and the current
font, and displays the result.

The VScroll1 and LabelShowline scroll and label controls demonstrate
how the programmer can take control of scrolling for a text control using a
standard vertical scroll bar control. The scroll bar is used to select a line to display in the LabelShowline label control. If the selected line is not visible, it
scrolls the text control to make sure the specified line is displayed.

Project Description

The TextMsgs project includes four files. TEXTMSGS.FRM is the only form
used in the program. TEXTMSGS.BAS is the only module in the program
and contains the constant type and global definitions. APIGID32.BAS contains the declarations for the APIGID32.DLL dynamic link library.

Form Description

Listing 17.1 contains the header from file TEXTMSGS.FRM that describes
the control setup for the form.

The VScroll1 control is used to scroll through lines from the Text1 control. The selected line is displayed in the LabelShowLine control.

The LabelResult label control is used to display the results of the various
Tests menu commands.

Listing 17.1   TextMsgs Form Header

```
VERSION 5.˜˜
Begin VB.Form TextMsgs
    Appearance      =   ˜  'Flat
    BackColor       =   &H8˜˜˜˜˜˜5&
    Caption         =   "Text Control Messages Demo"
    ClientHeight    =   4˜2˜
    ClientLeft      =   1˜95
    ClientTop       =   177˜
    ClientWidth     =   7365
    BeginProperty Font
        name        =   "MS Sans Serif"
        charset     =   1
        weight      =   7˜˜
        size        =   8.25
        underline   =   ˜  'False
        italic      =   ˜  'False
        strikethrough =  ˜  'False
    EndProperty
    ForeColor       =   &H8˜˜˜˜˜˜8&
    Height          =   471˜
    Left            =   1˜35
    LinkMode        =   1  'Source
    LinkTopic       =   "Form1"
    ScaleHeight     =   4˜2˜
    ScaleWidth      =   7365
    Top             =   114˜
    Width           =   7485
    Begin VB.VScrollBar VScroll1
        Height      =   1935
        LargeChange =   5
        Left        =   336˜
        Max         =   1
        TabIndex    =   4
        Top         =   15˜˜
        Width       =   315
    End
    Begin VB.TextBox Text1
        Appearance  =   ˜  'Flat
        Height      =   3˜15
        Left        =   12˜
        MultiLine   =   -1 'True
        TabIndex    =   ˜
        Text        =   "TEXTMSGS.frx":˜˜˜˜
        Top         =   6˜˜
        Width       =   3˜15
    End
    Begin VB.Label LabelShowLine
        Appearance  =   ˜  'Flat
```

Listing 17.1   TextMsgs Form Header (Continued)

```
            BackColor       =   &H8------5&
            BorderStyle     =   1  'Fixed Single
            ForeColor       =   &H8------8&
            Height          =   315
            Left            =   378-
            TabIndex        =   3
            Top             =   234-
            Width           =   3495
         End
         Begin VB.Label LabelLinenum
            Appearance      =   -  'Flat
            BackColor       =   &H8------5&
            ForeColor       =   &H8------8&
            Height          =   315
            Left            =   378-
            TabIndex        =   5
            Top             =   198-
            Width           =   1455
         End
         Begin VB.Label LabelResult
            Appearance      =   -  'Flat
            BackColor       =   &H8------5&
            BorderStyle     =   1  'Fixed Single
            ForeColor       =   &H8------8&
            Height          =   255
            Left            =   438-
            TabIndex        =   2
            Top             =   6--
            Width           =   2835
         End
         Begin VB.Label Label1
            Alignment       =   1  'Right Justify
            Appearance      =   -  'Flat
            BackColor       =   &H8------5&
            Caption         =   "Result:"
            ForeColor       =   &H8------8&
            Height          =   255
            Left            =   342-
            TabIndex        =   1
            Top             =   6--
            Width           =   915
         End
         Begin VB.Menu MenuSetup
            Caption         =   "Setup"
            Begin VB.Menu MenuFillText
               Caption         =   "FillText"
            End
         End
```

Listing 17.1   TextMsgs Form Header (Continued)

```
      Begin VB.Menu MenuTests
         Caption        =   "Tests"
         Begin VB.Menu MenuLineCount
            Caption        =   "LineCount"
         End
         Begin VB.Menu MenuFirstVisible
            Caption        =   "FirstVisible"
         End
         Begin VB.Menu MenuSelected
            Caption        =   "Selected"
         End
         Begin VB.Menu MenuLinesVisible
            Caption        =   "LinesVisible"
         End
      End
   End
End
Attribute VB_Name = "TextMsgs"
Attribute VB_GlobalNameSpace = False
Attribute VB_Creatable = False
Attribute VB_PredeclaredId = True Attribute VB_Exposed = False
```

TextMsgs Listings

Module TEXTMSGS.BAS contains the constant declarations and global variables used by the program. Specifically, it contains messages with both the WM_ prefix and the EM_ prefix, and function declarations for SendMessage and a few other functions. The complete listing is included on the CD-ROM and is not shown here. Listing 17.2 shows the listing for file TEXTMSGS.FRM.

There is no direct way to determine how many lines are actually visible in an edit control; however, Windows provides all the tools necessary to calculate this value. The number of lines displayed obviously depends on two factors: the size of the control and the height of the font used by the control.

In order to determine the size of the control, this function uses the EM_GETRECT message to determine the size of the internal formatting rectangle for the text. This allows you to determine the height, in pixels, of the area in which text is displayed.

Determining the height of a font is a bit trickier. Here we take advantage of the WM_GETFONT message to retrieve a handle to the logical font that the control is using. The font returned by this message is affected by the Visual Basic font properties, so there is no problem with compatibility with Visual Basic. Next, a device context is obtained for the text control. The SelectObject API function is used to select the logical font into the device context.

This makes it possible to retrieve the actual text metrics for the font including the font height. Chapter 10 describes this process in detail.

Once the height of the font has been obtained, it is very easy to calculate the number of lines that can actually be displayed by the control.

Listing 17.2   Listing for File TEXTMSGS.FRM

```
Private Sub Form_Load()
    ' Initialize the display line command
    UpdateDisplayLine
End Sub


'
' Determines the number of lines actually visible in the
' text control.
'
'
Private Function GetVisibleLines%()
    Dim rc As RECT
    #If Win32 Then
    Dim hDC&
    Dim lfont&, oldfont&
    Dim di&
    #Else
    Dim hDC%
    Dim lfont%, oldfont%
    Dim di%
    #End If
    Dim tm As TEXTMETRIC

    ' Get the formatting rectangle - this describes the
    ' rectangle in the control in which text is placed.
    lc% = SendMessage(Text1.hWnd, EM_GETRECT, ¯, rc)

    ' Get a handle to the logical font used by the control.
    ' The VB font properties are accurately reflected by
    ' this logical font.
    lfont = SendMessageBynum(Text1.hWnd, WM_GETFONT, ¯, ¯&)

    ' Get a device context to the text control.
    hDC = GetDC(Text1.hWnd)

    ' Select in the logical font to obtain the exact font
    ' metrics.
    If lfont <> ¯ Then oldfont = SelectObject(hDC, lfont)

    di = GetTextMetrics(hDC, tm)
    ' Select out the logical font
    If lfont <> ¯ Then lfont = SelectObject(hDC, oldfont)
```

Listing 17.2   Listing for File TEXTMSGS.FRM (Continued)

```
    ' The lines depend on the formatting rectangle and font height
    GetVisibleLines% = (rc.bottom - rc.top) / tm.tmHeight

    ' Release the device context when done.
    di = ReleaseDC(Text1.hWnd, hDC)
End Function

' Fill the text control with 2⁻ lines of text
'
Private Sub MenuFillText_Click()
    Dim x%
    Dim t$
    For x% = ⁻ To 19
        t$ = t$ + "This is line" + Str$(x%) + Chr$(13) + Chr$(1⁻)
    Next x%
    Text1.Text = t$

End Sub


' Determine the number of the first line visible in the text control
'
Private Sub MenuFirstVisible_Click()
    Dim lc%
    lc% = SendMessageBynum(Text1.hWnd, EM_GETFIRSTVISIBLELINE, ⁻, ⁻&)
    LabelResult.Caption = "Line" + Str$(lc%) + " at top"

End Sub


' Determine the number of lines of text in the text control
'
Private Sub MenuLineCount_Click()
    Dim lc%
    lc% = SendMessageBynum(Text1.hWnd, EM_GETLINECOUNT, ⁻, ⁻&)
    LabelResult.Caption = Str$(lc%) + " lines"
End Sub


' Determine the number of visibile lines in the text control.
'
Private Sub MenuLinesVisible_Click()
    LabelResult.Caption = Str$(GetVisibleLines()) + " lines visible"
End Sub


' Determine the start and end position of the current selection
'
```

Listing 17.2   **Listing for File TEXTMSGS.FRM (Continued)**

```
Private Sub MenuSelected_Click()
    Dim ls&
    ls& = SendMessageBynum&(Text1.hWnd, EM_GETSEL, ¯, ¯&)

    LabelResult.Caption = "Chars" + Str$(CInt(ls& And &HFFFF&)) + " to" + _
Str$(CInt(ls& / &H1¯¯¯¯))


End Sub


' Update the display line information on change
'
Private Sub Text1_Change()
    ' Make sure the vertical scroll range matches the number
    ' of lines in the text control
    lc% = SendMessageBynum(Text1.hWnd, EM_GETLINECOUNT, ¯, ¯&)
    VScroll1.Max = lc% - 1
    UpdateDisplayLine

End Sub
```

The UpdateDisplayLine function shows how individual lines can be extracted from an edit control. First the EM_LINEINDEX message is used to determine the offset in the edit control string to the first character in the line that you wish to retrieve. The EM_LINELENGTH message can then be used to determine the length of the line that contains that character.

The EM_GETLINE message requires that the first two bytes in the buffer represent the maximum length of the buffer. This function demonstrates how to load those bytes with the buffer length. Note how the first character contains the low-order byte of the integer and the second character contains the high-order byte. This is consistent with the byte ordering described in Chapter 15.

```
' This function updates the line displayed based on the
' current position of the scroll bar.
'
Private Sub UpdateDisplayLine()
    Dim linetoshow%, linelength%
    Dim linebuf$
    Dim lc%
    Dim linechar%

    linetoshow% = VScroll1.value
    ' Show the number of the line being displayed
    LabelLinenum.Caption = "Line" + Str$(linetoshow%)
```

```
        ' Find out the character offset to the first character
        ' in the specified line
        linechar% = SendMessageBynum(Text1.hWnd, EM_LINEINDEX, linetoshow%, ¯&)

        ' The character offset is used to determine the length of the line
        ' containing that character.
        lc% = SendMessageBynum(Text1.hWnd, EM_LINELENGTH, linechar%, ¯&) + 1

        ' Now allocate a string long enough to hold the result
        linebuf$ = String$(lc% + 2, ¯)
        Mid$(linebuf$, 1, 1) = Chr$(lc% And &HFF)
        Mid$(linebuf$, 2, 1) = Chr$(lc% \ &H1¯¯)

        ' Now get the line
        lc% = SendMessageBystring(Text1.hWnd, EM_GETLINE, linetoshow%, linebuf$)
        LabelShowLine.Caption = left$(linebuf$, lc%)

End Sub

' Whenever the scroll bar changes, display the requested
' line in the LabelShowLine label box
'
Private Sub VScroll1_Change()
    Dim lc%
    Dim dl&
    Dim firstvisible%, lastvisible%

    ' Make sure value is in range
    lc% = SendMessageBynum(Text1.hWnd, EM_GETLINECOUNT, ¯, ¯&)
    If VScroll1.value > lc% - 1 Then
        VScroll1.value = lc% - 1
        Exit Sub
    End If
    UpdateDisplayLine ' Update the display

    ' Get the number of the first and last visible line
    firstvisible% = SendMessageBynum(Text1.hWnd, EM_GETFIRSTVISIBLELINE, ¯, ¯&)
    lastvisible% = GetVisibleLines%() + firstvisible% - 1

    ' Scroll it into view if necessary
    If (VScroll1.value < firstvisible%) Then
        dl& = SendMessageBynum(Text1.hWnd, EM_LINESCROLL, ¯, _
        CLng(VScroll1.value - firstvisible%))
    End If
    If (VScroll1.value > lastvisible%) Then
        dl& = SendMessageBynum(Text1.hWnd, EM_LINESCROLL, ¯, _
        CLng(VScroll1.value - lastvisible%))
    End If

End Sub
```

Notification Messages (Edit)

Edit controls send WM_COMMAND messages to their parent window that notify it when certain events take place. Most of these messages are mapped into Visual Basic events for the VB text control. Those that are not cannot be accessed directly by the Visual Basic programmer, but may prove useful when using the advanced subclassing techniques described in Chapter 16.

All notification messages are sent using the WM_COMMAND message to the parent window of the control. The wParam parameter is divided into two parts. The low word refers to the numeric identifier of the control, a value that is not used in Visual Basic. The high word contains the notification type. In other words, the EN_KILLFOCUS notification would contain the constant EN_KILLFOCUS in the high-order word of the wParam parameter. The lParam parameter contains the window handle of the control. This can be used to determine which control sent the notification message.

■ EN_CHANGE

VB Declaration   Const EN_CHANGE = &H300

Description   Sent any time the contents of the edit control change.

Use with VB   This message generates a Change event in the standard text control. The message is sent after the changes have already been displayed.

■ EN_ERRSPACE

VB Declaration   Const EN_ERRSPACE = &H500

Description   Sent any time an editing operation fails because there is insufficient memory to perform the operation.

Use with VB   Visual Basic will trigger this type of error during assignment to the Text property through its normal error notification system.

■ EN_HSCROLL

VB Declaration   Const EN_HSCROLL = &H601

Description   Sent whenever the user clicks anywhere on the horizontal scroll bar belonging to an edit control. This message is sent before the control display is updated.

Use with VB   None.

Use with Subclassing   Could be used to control the behavior of the horizontal scroll bar or to perform other operations when scrolling takes place.

■ EN_KILLFOCUS

VB Declaration   Const EN_KILLFOCUS = &H200

Description   Sent when the control loses the input focus.

Use with VB   This message generates the VB LostFocus event.

Use with Subclassing   The Visual Basic LostFocus event is posted, so it occurs at some indeterminate time after this message is sent. This means that the VB event cannot be used to destroy a custom caret. Also, this event is not triggered when the focus is lost due to the activation of another application. The EN_KILLFOCUS message, however, can be used to provide full support of custom carets and to detect loss of focus in all circumstances.

■ EN_MAXTEXT

VB Declaration   Const EN_MAXTEXT = &H501

Description   Sent whenever the user attempts to enter text that exceeds the limit specified by the EM_LIMITTEXT message or VB MaxLength property. This message is also sent when automatic horizontal scrolling is not enabled and the insertion would exceed the width of the control, or automatic vertical scrolling is not enabled and the insertion would exceed the height of the control.

Use with VB   None.

Use with Subclassing   Could be used to provide a prompt to the user whenever this type of error occurred.

■ EN_SETFOCUS

VB Declaration   Const EN_SETFOCUS = &H100

Description   Sent when the control receives the input focus.

Use with VB   This message generates the VB GotFocus event.

Use with Subclassing   The Visual Basic GotFocus event is posted, so it occurs at some indeterminate time after this message is sent. This probably won't be a problem, so subclassing this message should not be necessary.

■ EN_UPDATE

VB Declaration   Const EN_UPDATE = &H400

Description   Sent before a control displays text that has been changed. This is similar to the EN_CHANGE notification except that it occurs before the text is displayed.

Use with VB   None.

| Use with Subclassing | Could be used to customize text display for an edit control. |

■ EN_VSCROLL

VB Declaration   `Const EN_VSCROLL = &H602`

Description   Sent whenever the user clicks anywhere on the vertical scroll bar belonging to an edit control. This message is sent before the control display is updated.

Use with VB   None.

Use with Subclassing   Could be used to control the behavior of the vertical scroll bar or to perform other operations when scrolling takes place.

Edit Control Messages

The following messages can be used to control the operation of any Visual Basic control based on the Windows edit class. This includes the standard Visual Basic text control.

As usual, the return value refers to the value returned by the SendMessage function used to send the message to the control.

Note that these message numbers are different from their Win16 declarations. Some of the message parameters have changes as well.

■ EM_CANUNDO

VB Declaration   `Const EM_CANUNDO = &HC6`

Description   Determines if the undo buffer for an edit control contains information that can be used to reverse the previous editing operation.

Use with VB   No problem.

Return Value   Long—TRUE (nonzero) on success, zero otherwise.

■ EM_CHARFROMPOS

VB Declaration   `Const EM_CHARFROMPOS = &HD7`

Description   Retrieves the character index and line index of the character nearest to a specified point in an edit control.

Use with VB   No problem.

Parameter	Description
wParam	Not used—set to zero.

Parameter	Description
lParam	Low word: Specifies the x-coordinate of a point. High word: Specifies the y-coordinate of a point. The coordinates are in device coordinates relative to the upper-left corner of the client area of the control.

Return Value   Long—Low word contains the character index. High word contains the line index. –1 if the point is outside of the client area of the control. References the last character if the position is beyond the last character.

Platform   Windows 95, Windows NT 4.0

■ EM_EMPTYUNDOBUFFER

VB Declaration   Const EM_EMPTYUNDOBUFFER = &HCD

Description   Clears the undo buffer for an edit control. After this message is sent, the previous editing operation for the control will not be reversible.

Use with VB   No problem.

■ EM_FMTLINES

VB Declaration   Const EM_FMTLINES = &HC8

Description   Determines whether soft line breaks are returned when the edit control string is read using the WM_GETTEXT message. This also applies to the Visual Basic Text property. A soft line break is indicated by the appearance of a CR-CR-LF sequence in the text string as follows: chr$(13)+chr$(13)+chr$(10)

Use with VB   No problem. Only applies to multiline edit controls.

Parameter	Description
wParam	TRUE (nonzero) to return soft line breaks. FALSE to return to normal operation.
lParam	Not used—set to zero.

■ EM_GETFIRSTVISIBLELINE

VB Declaration   Const EM_GETFIRSTVISIBLELINE = &HCE

Description   Retrieves the number of the first line that is visible in the edit control. Lines are numbered starting with zero. For single-line edit controls, retrieves the first visible character. Characters are numbered starting with zero.

Use with VB   No problem.

Return Value   Long—Contains the first visible line number for multiline edit controls. Contains the first visible character for single-line edit controls.

■ EM_GETHANDLE

VB Declaration   Const EM_GETHANDLE = &HBD

Description   Retrieves a memory handle allocated for a multiline edit control's text.

Use with VB   No problem. Valid only for multiline edit controls.

Return Value   Long—Memory handle on success, zero if error occurs.

■ EM_GETLIMITTEXT

VB Declaration   Const EM_GETLIMITTEXT = &HD5

Description   Retrieves the current text limit in characters for an edit control.

Use with VB   No problem.

Return Value   Long—Text limit of edit control.

Platform   Windows 95, Windows NT 4.0

■ EM_GETLINE

VB Declaration   Const EM_GETLINE = &HC4

Description   Retrieves a line from the edit control. Lines are numbered starting with zero.

Use with VB   No problem.

Parameter	Description
wParam	The number of the line to retrieve. Lines are numbered starting with zero. This value is not used on single-line edit controls.
lParam	The address of a string buffer to load with the line. The first two bytes of this string contain an integer representing the maximum number of characters that can be loaded into the buffer.

Return Value   Long—The number of characters loaded into the buffer. Zero is returned if an invalid line is specified.

Comments   The line copied does not include a terminating NULL. If linebuf is the string to load and lc% is the length of the buffer –1, the following lines can be used to load the string buffer with the value lc%:

```
linebuf(0) = Chr$(lc% And &HFF)
linebuf(1) = Chr$(lc% \ &H100)
```

You can substitute a byte array for the string buffer, in which case the normal ANSI to Unicode string conversion will need to be performed before assigning the array into a string variable.

■ EM_GETLINECOUNT

VB Declaration   Const EM_GETLINECOUNT = &HBA

Description	Retrieves the number of lines in an edit control.
Use with VB	No problem. Only applies to multiline edit controls.
Return Value	The number of lines in the edit control. Returns 1 even if there is no text in the control.

■ EM_GETMARGINS

VB Declaration	`Const EM_GETMARGINS = &HD4`
Description	Retrieves the widths of the left and right margins for an edit control.
Use with VB	No problem.
Return Value	Long—Width of the left margin in the low-order word, width of the right margin in the high-order word.
Platform	Windows 95, Windows NT 4.0

■ EM_GETMODIFY

VB Declaration	`Const EM_GETMODIFY = &HB8`
Description	Each edit class control has an internal flag called the modify flag. This flag bit is set to 1 any time the contents of the control are modified. You can use the EM_SETMODIFY message to clear this flag, then later use this message to determine if the contents of the control have changed.
Use with VB	The Visual Basic Change event provides an effective way to determine if the contents of an edit control are modified.
Return Value	Long—TRUE (nonzero) if the modify flag has been set, indicating that a change has occurred in the edit control since this flag was last cleared.

■ EM_GETPASSWORDCHAR

VB Declaration	`Const EM_GETPASSWORDCHAR = &HD2`
Description	Retrieves the current password character for an edit control. This is the character displayed in the control when the user enters text.
Use with VB	Works only with controls that have the ES_PASSWORD style. With Visual Basic 4.0 and later, you can use the PasswordChar property to retrieve the password character.
Return Value	The ASCII value of the password character. Zero if there is no password character set.

■ EM_GETRECT

VB Declaration	`Const EM_GETRECT = &HB2`

Description	Retrieves the formatting rectangle for an edit control. Refer to "Text Formatting," earlier in this chapter, for a description of formatting rectangles.
Use with VB	No problem.

Parameter	Description
wParam	Not used—set to zero.
lParam	An address of a RECT structure to load with the formatting rectangle.

■ EM_GETSEL

VB Declaration	`Const EM_GETSEL = &HB0`
Description	Retrieves the current selection state of the edit control.
Use with VB	No problem, but the standard SelStart and SelLength properties are easier to use.

Parameter	Description
wParam	Address of long value to hold the character offset of the start of the selection, may set this parameter to zero.
lParam	Address of long value to hold the character offset of the character after the last selected character, may set this parameter to zero.

Return Value	Long—The low word contains the character offset of the start of the selection; the high word contains the character offset of the character after the last selected character.

■ EM_GETTHUMB

VB Declaration	`Const EM_GETTHUMB = &HBE`
Description	Retrieves the position of the scroll box (thumb) in a multiline edit control.
Use with VB	No problem.

■ EM_LIMITTEXT

VB Declaration	`Const EM_LIMITTEXT = &HC5`
Description	Used to specify the maximum number of characters that can be contained in an edit control.
Use with VB	The Visual Basic MaxLength property serves this purpose and is the preferred way to set the maximum text length.

Parameter	Description
wParam	The maximum length of the text that can be entered into an edit control. Zero to set the length to 2,147,483,646 characters for a single-line edit control and 4,294,967,295 characters for a multiline edit control.
lParam	Not used—set to zero.

Comments   This message has been superseded by the EM_SETLIMITTEXT message.

■ EM_LINEFROMCHAR

VB Declaration   `Const EM_LINEFROMCHAR = &HC9`

Description   Determines the line number of the line containing the character specified.

Use with VB   No problem.

Parameter	Description
wParam	The offset of the character in the edit control text string to check. –1 to retrieve the offset of the start of the current line, or current selection if one exists.
lParam	Not used—set to zero.

Return Value   The number of the line containing the specified character. Lines are numbered from zero.

■ EM_LINEINDEX

VB Declaration   `Const EM_LINEINDEX = &HBB`

Description   Determines the character offset of the first character in the specified line.

Use with VB   No problem.

Parameter	Description
wParam	The number of a line in an edit control. Lines are numbered starting at zero. –1 specifies the number of the line containing the caret.
lParam	Not used—set to zero.

Return Value   The character offset of the first character in the line specified, –1 on error.

■ EM_LINELENGTH

VB Declaration   `Const EM_LINELENGTH = &HC1`

Description   Determines the length of the line containing the character specified.

Use with VB   No problem.

Parameter	Description
wParam	An offset of a character in the edit control text string. This message returns the length of the line containing that character. If –1, returns the number of unselected characters in all of the lines containing selected text.
lParam	Not used—set to zero.

Return Value   As specified in the description for the wParam parameter.

■ EM_LINESCROLL

VB Declaration   Const EM_LINESCROLL = &HB6

Description   Scrolls the contents of an edit control.

Use with VB   This is frequently used in conjunction with the EM_GETFIRSTVISIBLELINE message to display a particular line or lines in a multiline text control. This message is not supported for horizontal scrolling on single-line text controls.

Parameter	Description
wParam	Contains the number of characters to scroll horizontally: positive to scroll the display left, negative to scroll it right.
lParam	Contains the number of lines to scroll vertically: positive to scroll the display up, negative to scroll it down.

■ EM_POSFROMCHAR

VB Declaration   Const EM_POSFROMCHAR = &HD6

Description   Retrieves the coordinates of the specified character in an edit control.

Use with VB   No problem.

Parameter	Description
wParam	Character index. Characters are numbered starting at zero.
lParam	Not used—set to zero.

Return Value   Long—Returns the coordinates of the upper-left corner of the specified character. If the character index requested is beyond the last character, returns the position past the last character. Coordinates are relative to the upper-left corner of the client area of the control. May be negative if the character is outside the client area.

Platform   Windows 95, Windows NT 4.0

■ EM_REPLACESEL

VB Declaration   Const EM_REPLACESEL = &HC2

Description   Replaces the selected text in an edit control with the string specified.

Use with VB   No problem, but assignment to the SelText property is an easier way to perform this operation.

Parameter	Description
wParam	TRUE if the replacement operation can be undone. FALSE if the operation cannot be undone.
lParam	A pointer to a NULL terminated string.

Comments   If no text is selected, the specified string is inserted at the location of the caret.

▨ EM_SCROLL

VB Declaration	Const EM_SCROLL = &HB5

Description Scrolls the text vertically in a multiline edit control. This message is equivalent to sending a WM_VSCROLL message to the edit control.

Use with VB No problem.

Parameter	Description
wParam	SB_LINEDOWN: Scrolls down one line.
	SB_LINEUP: Scrolls up one line.
	SB_PAGEDOWN: Scrolls down one page.
	SB_PAGEUP: Scrolls up one page.
lParam	Not used—set to zero.

Return Value Long—High word contains TRUE on success. Low word contains the number of lines that were scrolled.

▨ EM_SCROLLCARET

VB Declaration	Const EM_SCROLLCARET = &HB7

Description Scrolls the caret into view in an edit control.

Use with VB No problem.

Parameter	Description
wParam	Not used—set to zero.
lParam	Not used—set to zero.

Return Value Long—Nonzero on success.

▨ EM_SETHANDLE

VB Declaration	Const EM_SETHANDLE = &HBC

Description Sets the memory handle that will be used by a multiline edit control.

Use with VB No problem. Prior to sending this message, the application should send an EM_GETHANDLE message to retrieve the handle of the current memory buffer and free that memory.

Parameter	Description
wParam	Memory handle that the edit control uses to store the text instead of allocating its own memory. If necessary, the control reallocates this memory.
lParam	Not used—set to zero.

■ EM_SETLIMITTEXT

VB Declaration   Const EM_SETLIMITTEXT = &HC5

Description   Used to specify the maximum number of characters that can be contained in an edit control.

Use with VB   The Visual Basic MaxLength property serves this purpose and is the preferred way to set the maximum text length.

Parameter	Description
wParam	The maximum length of the text that can be entered into an edit control. Zero to set the length to 32,766 characters for a single-line edit control and 65,535 characters for a multiline edit control.
lParam	Not used—set to zero.

Comments   This message supersedes the EM_LIMITTEXT message.

■ EM_SETMARGINS

VB Declaration   Const EM_SETMARGINS = &HD3

Description   Used to set the widths of the margins for an edit control. This message causes the control to redraw itself to reflect the new margins.

Use with VB   No problem.

Parameter	Description
wParam	One or more of the following: EC_LEFTMARGIN to set the left margin. EC_RIGHTMARGIN to set the right margin. EC_USEFONTINFO to use the edit control's font information to set the margins. Margins are set to the average width of characters in the font for a single-line edit control. For a multiline edit control, the right margin is set to the "A" width of the font (refer to Chapter 11), and the left margin is set to the "C" width (refer to Chapter 11).
lParam	Low word: Width of the left margin in pixels. Only valid if EC_LEFTMARGIN is specified and EC_USEFONTINFO is not specified. High word: Width of the right margin in pixels. Only valid if EC_RIGHTMARGIN is specified and EC_USEFONTINFO is not specified.

Platform   Windows 95, Windows NT 4.0

■ EM_SETMODIFY

VB Declaration   Const EM_SETMODIFY = &HB9

Description Each edit class control has an internal flag called the modify flag. This flag bit is set to 1 any time the contents of the control are modified. You can use the message to clear this flag, then later use the EM_GETMODIFY message to determine if the contents of the control have changed.

Use with VB The Visual Basic Change event provides an effective way to determine if the contents of an edit control are modified.

Parameter	Description
wParam	TRUE (nonzero) to set the modify flag bit to 1, zero to clear it.
lParam	Not used—set to zero.

■ EM_SETPASSWORDCHAR

VB Declaration `Const EM_SETPASSWORDCHAR = &HCC`

Description Sets the current password character for an edit control. This is the character displayed in the control when the user enters text.

Use with VB Works only with controls that have the ES_PASSWORD style. With Visual Basic, you can use the PasswordChar property to retrieve the password character.

Parameter	Description
wParam	The ASCII value of the new password character. Zero to display the text normally.
lParam	Not used—set to zero.

■ EM_SETREADONLY

VB Declaration `Const EM_SETREADONLY = &HCF`

Description Allows you to change an edit control's read only attribute. When a control is read only, it is not possible to edit the contents of the control.

Use with VB No problem.

Parameter	Description
wParam	TRUE (nonzero) to make the control read only. FALSE (zero) to clear the read only state.
lParam	Not used—set to zero.

Return Value Long—TRUE (nonzero) on success.

■ EM_SETRECT

VB Declaration `Const EM_SETRECT = &HB3`

Description Sets the formatting rectangle for an edit control. Refer to "Text Formatting," earlier in this chapter, for a description of formatting rectangles.

Use with VB	No problem.

Parameter	Description
wParam	Not used—set to zero.
lParam	An address of a RECT structure to set as the new formatting rectangle.

Comments   The formatting rectangle may exceed the size of the control, in which case text that is in the formatting rectangle but outside of the control's window will be clipped (not shown).

■ EM_SETRECTNP

VB Declaration   `Const EM_SETRECTNP = &HB4`

Description   Sets the formatting rectangle for an edit control. Refer to "Text Formatting," earlier in this chapter, for a description of formatting rectangles. This is the same as the EM_SETRECT message except that the control is not redrawn.

Use with VB   No problem.

Parameter	Description
wParam	Not used—set to zero.
lParam	An address of a RECT structure to set as the new formatting rectangle.

Comments   See the comments for the EM_SETRECT message.

■ EM_SETSEL

VB Declaration   `Const EM_SETSEL =&HB1`

Description   Sets the current selection state of the edit control.

Use with VB   No problem, but the standard SelStart and SelLength properties are easier to use.

Parameter	Description
wParam	The character offset of the first character in the selection. –1 to remove the current selection.
lParam	The character offset of the first character after the selection. If wParam is 0 and this parameter is –1, all the text in the edit control is selected.

Comments   The new caret location will be set to the wParam or lParam offset depending on which is greater. The meaning of the wParam parameter has changed from Win16.

■ EM_SETTABSTOPS

VB Declaration   `Const EM_SETTABSTOPS =&HCB`

Description Used to specify tab stops in an edit control. Tabs can be placed in a text string using the tab character chr$(9). Tab stops are specified in dialog base units, which are described earlier in this chapter. Each dialog base unit represents one-fourth of the average character width.

Use with VB No problem.

Parameter	Description
wParam	The number of tab stops to set. Zero to set the default of one tab stop every 32 dialog units. One to set tab stops every N dialog units where N is the first entry in an integer array specified by lParam. Otherwise, this specifies the number of tab stops to set based on the long array specified by lParam.
lParam	The address of the first entry in a long array containing tab stops to set. The tab stops should be given in order.

Comments This function does not redraw the control. Use InvalidateRect or the Visual Basic Refresh method to redraw the text control in order for the new tab stops to take effect.

The following code demonstrates how tab stops are set. In this example, the first tab stop is after the fourth character (16 dialog units divided by four is about four characters), followed by the sixth, eighth, and tenth character positions.

```
Sub Settabs
    ReDim tabvals&(8)
    tabvals&(0) = 16
    tabvals&(1) = 24
    tabvals&(2) = 32
    tabvals&(3) = 40

    di& = SendMessage(Text1.hWnd, EM_SETTABSTOPS, 4, tabvals&(0))
End Sub
```

■ EM_UNDO

VB Declaration `Const EM_UNDO =&HC7`

Description Reverses the most recent editing operation. The EM_CANUNDO buffer can be used to determine if the previous operation can be reversed. This message has the same effect as the WM_UNDO operation described in Chapter 16.

Use with VB No problem.

Return Value Always TRUE for single-line edit controls. TRUE on success, FALSE on error for multiline edit controls.

18

List Box, Combo Box, and Button Messages

The List Control
The Combo Box Control
Button Controls

T HIS CHAPTER DISCUSSES MESSAGES USED WITH VISUAL BASIC CONTROLS that are based on the Windows list box, combo box, and button controls. These include the Visual Basic list control, file control, combo controls, and all button-style controls including command buttons and check boxes. The messages described here can be used to provide features that are not supported by the standard Visual Basic events and properties for those controls. In many cases they will improve the performance of common operations.

Two small sample programs—ListTest.vbp and BtnTest.vbp—are included on the CD-ROM that comes with this book and are not covered in detail in this chapter.

The List Control

A list control is used to display and select lists of strings. The control can be configured in several different ways. The standard list control allows you to select only a single entry at a time. The Visual Basic MultiSelect property allows a standard list control to be configured as a multiple selection list box. These two configurations must be considered when using list control messages, as some messages are specific to one configuration or another.

The list control messages divide into a number of functional groups, which are described below.

Selection and Data Functions

The Visual Basic selection and item entry properties can be used to set and select individual entries in a list control, and are adequate for most applications. Though many of the list control messages duplicate this functionality, in some cases they can provide improved performance. For example, the LB_SELITEMRANGE message can be used to select a group of entries in a multiple selection list box.

The LB_FINDSTRING and LB_FINDSTRINGEXACT messages can be used to perform search operations on a list control that are significantly faster than those possible in Visual Basic.

Table 18.1 lists the messages associated with adding and deleting list box entries, and controlling the list selections.

Table 18.1	Selection and Data Messages
Message	**Description**
LB_ADDSTRING	Adds a string to the list control

Table 18.1   Selection and Data Messages (Continued)

Message	Description
LB_DELETESTRING	Removes a string from the list control
LB_DIR	Adds a list of files to a list control
LB_FINDSTRING	Finds an entry that matches a specified prefix
LB_FINDSTRINGEXACT	Finds an entry that matches a specified string
LB_GETCOUNT	Retrieves the number of entries in the list control
LB_GETCURSEL	Retrieves the index of the currently selected entry in a single selection list control
LB_GETSEL	Determines the selection state of an entry in a multiple selection list control
LB_GETSELCOUNT	Determines the number of entries that are selected in a multiple select list control
LB_GETSELITEMS	Loads an array with a list of selected items
LB_GETTEXT	Retrieves a text entry from the control
LB_GETTEXTLEN	Determines the length of a list control entry
LB_INSERTSTRING	Inserts a string into a list control at a specified location
LB_ITEMFROMPOINT	Determines the nearest entry to the specified point
LB_RESETCONTENT	Clears a list control
LB_SELECTSTRING	Searches a list control for a string and selects it if found
LB_SELITEMRANGE	Selects a range of entries in a list control
LB_SETCURSEL	Selects or deselects an entry in a single selection list control
LB_SETSEL	Selects or deselects an entry in a multiple selection list control

Display Functions

The API messages provide a great deal of flexibility in controlling the display of the contents of a list control.

The WM_SETREDRAW Message

The WM_SETREDRAW message defined in Chapter 16 is occasionally useful when performing long operations on a list control. Normally, any time a string is added, deleted, or changed, the control becomes invalidated—

flagged for update during event processing. If you are allowing events to run, you can improve performance by preventing update of the list control display until after all modifications have been completed. Note that this applies only when you are adding or deleting data using Windows messages. The Visual Basic AddItem and RemoveItem methods invalidate the control window and thus override the setting of the Redraw flag.

The ListTest.vbp sample project on the CD-ROM illustrates how the WM_SETREDRAW message can be used to disable the update of a list control during event processing.

Horizontal and Vertical Scrolling

List controls automatically display a vertical scroll bar when the number of entries exceeds those that can be displayed. Normally, when the length of an entry exceeds the width of the control window, it is clipped—in other words, the entry seems to go off the right side of the list control and cannot be seen.

It is possible to add a horizontal scroll bar to a list control in cases like this so that long entries can be viewed. This is accomplished by specifying an extent greater than the width of the control using the LB_SETHORIZONTALEXTENT message. For example, if a list box is 200 pixels wide, setting the extent to 300 will cause a horizontal scroll bar to appear and allow entries up to 300 pixels wide to be displayed.

The WS_HSCROLL style must be set for a list control in order for horizontal scrolling to work. This style bit is set by default for the Visual Basic list control.

Display Positioning Messages

Windows messages can also be used to control the list box display. The LB_GETCARETINDEX message allows you to determine which entry in a list control has the focus selection. The LB_SETCARETINDEX message can then be used to set the focus position.

The LB_GETITEMRECT and LB_GETITEMHEIGHT messages can be used to determine the size of each entry in the list control. This in turn can be used to determine the number of entries that can be displayed. The LB_SETITEMHEIGHT message can be used to change the height of each entry, in effect allowing you to control the amount of space between lines in the list control.

The LB_GETTOPINDEX and LB_SETTOPINDEX messages can be used to control which entry is displayed at the top of the list control. This allows you to scroll the list box under program control.

Finally, the LB_SETTABSTOPS message can be used to set tab stops in a list control in a manner identical to that described in Chapter 17 for edit controls.

Display Message Summary

Table 18.2 lists those list control messages related to control of the display.

Table 18.2 **Display Control Messages**

Message	Description
LB_GETCARETINDEX	Determines which entry is displaying the focus rectangle.
LB_GETHORIZONTALEXTENT	Determines the logical extent of an edit control. If this value is larger than the width of the control window, a horizontal scroll bar appears that allows viewing of the entire logical display.
LB_GETITEMHEIGHT	Determines the height of each list control entry.
LB_GETITEMRECT	Retrieves a bounding rectangle for the specified entry.
LB_GETTOPINDEX	Determines the number of the first entry displayed in the list control.
LB_SETCARETINDEX	Sets the focus rectangle to the specified entry.
LB_SETCOLUMNWIDTH	Allows you to change the width of each column when multicolumn mode is specified. Refer to the Column property in your Visual Basic manuals.
LB_SETHORIZONTALEXTENT	Sets the logical extent of an edit control. If this value is larger than the width of the control window, a horizontal scroll bar appears that allows viewing the entire logical display.
LB_SETITEMHEIGHT	Sets the height of each list control entry. This effectively controls spacing of the lines in the list box.
LB_SETTABSTOPS	Allows you to specify positions of tab stops in a list box.
LB_SETTOPINDEX	Sets the number of the first entry displayed in the list control.

The Combo Box Control

The combo box control is a combination of an edit control with an attached list control. The combo box messages thus combine many of the features of edit and list controls and in many cases are identical. Table 18.3 lists the combo box messages and the equivalent edit or list control message where appropriate. The list box messages affect the list box part of the combo box and the edit control messages affect the edit control portion of the combo box. Edit control message equivalents have an EM_ prefix; they can be found in Chapter 17. List control message equivalents have an LB_ prefix; they are described in this chapter.

The combo box control has several different styles available, as specified by the Visual Basic Style property. An extended user interface is available to combo boxes in which the list control drops down when the down arrow key is pressed. This extended mode is specified using the CB_SETEXTENDEDUI message.

Table 18.3   Combo Box Messages

Message	Description
CB_ADDSTRING	Equivalent to LB_ADDSTRING. Adds a string to the list control.
CB_DELETESTRING	Equivalent to LB_DELETESTRING. Removes a string from the list control.
CB_DIR	Equivalent to LB_DIR. Adds a list of files to the list control.
CB_FINDSTRING	Equivalent to LB_FINDSTRING. Finds an entry in the list control that matches a specified prefix.
CB_FINDSTRINGEXACT	Equivalent to LB_FINDSTRINGEXACT. Finds an entry that matches a specified string.
CB_GETCOUNT	Equivalent to LB_GETCOUNT. Retrieves the number of entries in the list control.
CB_GETCURSEL	Equivalent to LB_GETCURSEL. Retrieves the index of the currently selected entry in the list control.
CB_GETDROPPEDCONTROLRECT	Determines the size and position of the drop-down list box portion of a combo box.
CB_GETDROPPEDSTATE	Determines if the list box portion of a combo box is visible.
CB_GETDROPPEDWIDTH	Determines the width of the drop-down portion of a combo box.
CB_GETEDITSEL	Equivalent to EM_GETSEL. Determines the start and end locations of a selection in the edit control.
CB_GETEXTENDEDUI	Determines the user interface mode of the combo box.
CB_GETHORIZONTALEXTENT	Equivalent to LB_GETHORIZONTALEXTENT. Determines the logical extent of the combo box control.
CB_GETITEMHEIGHT	Equivalent to LB_GETITEMHEIGHT. Determines the height of each list control entry.
CB_GETLBTEXT	Equivalent to LB_GETTEXT. Retrieves a text entry from the list control.
CB_GETLBTEXTLEN	Equivalent to LB_GETTEXTLEN. Determines the length of a list control entry.
CB_GETTOPINDEX	Equivalent to LB_GETTOPINDEX. Retrieves the index of the top entry in the list box portion of the combo box.
CB_INSERTSTRING	Equivalent to LB_INSERTSTRING. Inserts a string into the list control at a specified location.

Table 18.3 **Combo Box Messages (Continued)**

Message	Description
CB_LIMITTEXT	Equivalent to EM_LIMITTEXT. Limits the length of text in the edit control.
CB_RESETCONTENT	Equivalent to LB_RESETCONTENT. Clears the list control.
CB_SELECTSTRING	Equivalent to LB_SELECTSTRING. Searches the list control for a string and selects it if found.
CB_SETCURSEL	Equivalent to LB_SETCURSEL. Selects or deselects an entry in a single selection list control.
CB_SETDROPPEDWIDTH	Sets the minimum width of the drop-down portion of a combo box.
CB_SETEDITSEL	Equivalent to EM_SETSEL. Sets the start and end location of a selection in an edit control.
CB_SETEXTENDEDUI	Sets the user interface mode of the combo box.
CB_SETHORIZONTALEXTENT	Equivalent to LB_SETHORIZONTALEXTENT. Sets the logical extents of the list box portion of a combo box.
CB_SETITEMHEIGHT	Equivalent to LB_SETITEMHEIGHT. Sets the height of each list control entry. This effectively controls spacing of the lines in the list control.
CB_SETTOPINDEX	Equivalent to LB_SETTOPINDEX. Sets the index of the top entry in the list box portion of the combo box.
CB_SHOWDROPDOWN	Used to show or hide the list box portion of the combo box.

The extended user interface affects the appearance of the drop-down box. Normally, the drop-down list box does not appear unless you either click on the drop-down arrow or press the F4 function key. If the drop-down list box is not visible, the up and down arrow keys scroll through the contents of the list box but do not cause the list box to appear.

When the extended user interface is enabled, the down arrow key causes the drop-down list box to appear. The F4 key is disabled. Clicking on the static control when the Combo Box Style property is set to 2 (Drop-down List) causes the drop-down list box to appear as well.

Button Controls

The Windows button-style controls include command buttons, check boxes, and option buttons (referred to in the Windows documentation as radio buttons).

These are among the simplest controls to use and the Windows messages provide little added functionality.

It is worthwhile to take a moment and review the difference between the *state* of a button and the *checked* status of a button. The checked status applies only to those buttons that can be checked or unchecked, such as the check box and option button. The general state of a button includes whether it is checked, but also other attributes such as whether the button is highlighted (pressed), or has the focus.

Table 18.4 lists the Windows messages that are used with button-style controls.

Table 18.4 **Button Control Messages**

Message	Description
BM_GETCHECK	Determines if a button-style control is checked or unchecked
BM_GETIMAGE	Retrieves the bitmap or icon handle for an image button
BM_GETSTATE	Determines the current state of a button-style control
BM_SETCHECK	Checks or unchecks a button-style control
BM_SETIMAGE	Sets the bitmap or icon handle for an image button
BM_SETSTATE	Sets the current state of a button-style control

One interesting application of these messages is to implement a "sticky" button—one that toggles between the pressed and unpressed appearance each time it is clicked.

In the following example, a static variable is used to keep track of the current state of the button. Each time the button is clicked, the variable is toggled. The BM_SETSTATE message is then sent to the command button to set it into either the normal (unpressed) or highlighted (pressed) state.

```
Private Sub Command2_Click()
    Static downstate&
    downstate = Not downstate
    Call SendMessageBynum(Command2.hwnd, BM_SETSTATE, downstate, ¯)

End Sub
```

Notification Messages (List, Combo, Button)

Combo and list box controls send WM_COMMAND messages to their parent window that notify it when certain events take place. Most of these messages are mapped into Visual Basic events for the VB list or combo control. Those that are not cannot be accessed directly by the Visual Basic programmer, but may prove useful when using the advanced subclassing techniques described in Chapter 16.

All notification messages are sent to the parent window of the control using the WM_COMMAND message. The wParam parameter is divided into two parts. The low word refers to the numeric identifier of the control, a value that is not used in Visual Basic. The high word contains the notification type. In other words, the LBN_KILLFOCUS notification would contain the constant LBN_KILLFOCUS in the high-order word of the wParam parameter. The lParam parameter contains the window handle of the control. This can be used to determine which control sent the notification message.

■ CBN_CLOSEUP

VB Declaration   Const CBN_CLOSEUP = 8

Description   Sent when the list box portion of a combo box is closed. The CBN_SELCHANGE message may be sent before or after this message if a change occurs when the list box is closed.

Use with VB   None.

Use with Subclassing   Could be used to detect a user action that closes the list box without causing a change to the contents.

■ CBN_DBLCLK

VB Declaration   Const CBN_DBLCLK = 2

Description   Sent when the user double-clicks on an entry in the list box part of a combo box. This notification is only sent with simple combo controls, as a click on a drop-down combo control causes the list box to be hidden.

Use with VB   This notification triggers the Visual Basic DblClick event.

■ CBN_DROPDOWN

VB Declaration   Const CBN_DROPDOWN = 7

Description   Sent when the list box portion of a drop-down combo box is about to be made visible.

Use with VB   This notification triggers the Visual Basic DropDown event.

■ CBN_EDITCHANGE

VB Declaration   Const CBN_EDITCHANGE = 5

Description   Sent any time the contents of the edit control part of a combo control change.

Use with VB   This message generates a Visual Basic Change event in the standard combo control. The message is sent after the changes have already been displayed.

■ CBN_EDITUPDATE

VB Declaration   Const CBN_EDITUPDATE = 6

Description   Sent before the edit control part of a combo control displays text that has been changed. This is similar to the CBN_EDITCHANGE notification except that it occurs before the text is displayed.

Use with VB   None.

Use with Subclassing   Could be used to customize text display for the edit control part of a combo box.

■ CBN_ERRSPACE

VB Declaration   Const CBN_ERRSPACE = (-1)

Description   Sent any time an operation fails because there is insufficient memory to perform the operation.

Use with VB   Visual Basic will trigger an error through its normal error notification system when this type of error occurs.

■ CBN_KILLFOCUS

VB Declaration   Const CBN_KILLFOCUS = 4

Description   Sent when the control loses the input focus.

Use with VB   This message generates the VB LostFocus event.

Use with Subclassing   The Visual Basic LostFocus event is posted, which means that it occurs at some indeterminate time after this message is sent. Also, this event is not sent when the focus is lost due to the activation of another application. This message, however, can be used to detect loss of focus in all circumstances.

■ CBN_SELCHANGE

VB Declaration   Const CBN_SELCHANGE = 1

Description   This message is sent any time the selection in the list control part of a combo control changes.

Use with VB	This message generates the Visual Basic Click event for combo box controls.

◼ CBN_SELENDCANCEL

VB Declaration	`Const CBN_SELENDCANCEL = 10`
Description	Sent before the CBN_CLOSEUP notification when the list box portion of a combo control is about to be hidden due to the user selecting or clicking outside of the combo control. This is used to indicate that the user's selection should be ignored. On simple combo boxes, this message is sent even though the list box is not hidden.
Use with VB	None.
Use with Subclassing	Can be used to detect the end of a list box selection operation.

◼ CBN_SELENDOK

VB Declaration	`Const CBN_SELENDOK = 9`
Description	Sent before the CBN_CLOSEUP notification when the list box portion of a combo control is about to be hidden due to the user pressing the Enter key or clicking inside a combo control. This is used to indicate that the user's selection is valid. On simple combo boxes, this message is sent even though the list box is not hidden.
Use with VB	None.
Use with Subclassing	Can be used to detect the end of a list box selection operation.

◼ CBN_SETFOCUS

VB Declaration	`Const CBN_SETFOCUS = 3`
Description	Sent when the control receives the input focus.
Use with VB	This message generates the VB GotFocus event.
Use with Subclassing	The Visual Basic GotFocus event is posted, which means that it occurs at some indeterminate time after this message is sent. This is unlikely to be a problem, so subclassing this message should not be necessary.

◼ LBN_DBLCLK

VB Declaration	`Const LBN_DBLCLK = 2`
Description	Sent when the user double-clicks on an entry in a list box.
Use with VB	This notification triggers the Visual Basic DblClick event.

■ LBN_ERRSPACE

VB Declaration   Const LBN_ERRSPACE = (-2)

Description   Sent any time an operation fails because there is insufficient memory to perform the operation.

Use with VB   Visual Basic will trigger an error through its normal error notification system when this type of error occurs.

■ LBN_KILLFOCUS

VB Declaration   Const LBN_KILLFOCUS = 5

Description   Sent when the control loses the input focus.

Use with VB   This message generates the VB LostFocus event.

Use with Subclassing   The Visual Basic LostFocus event is posted, which means that it occurs at some indeterminate time after this message is sent. Also, this event is not sent when the focus is lost due to the activation of another application. This message, however, can be used to detect loss of focus in all circumstances.

■ LBN_SELCANCEL

VB Declaration   Const LBN_SELCANCEL = 3

Description   Sent when a list box selection is canceled. This is typically due to the user selecting or clicking outside of the control.

Use with VB   None.

Use with Subclassing   Can be used to detect the end of a list box selection operation.

■ LBN_SELCHANGE

VB Declaration   Const LBN_SELCHANGE = 1

Description   This message is sent any time the selection in the list control changes except when the LB_SETCURSEL message changes the selection.

Use with VB   This message generates the Visual Basic Click event for list box controls.

■ LBN_SETFOCUS

VB Declaration   Const LBN_SETFOCUS = 4

Description   Sent when the control receives the input focus.

Use with VB   This message generates the VB GotFocus event.

**Use with
Subclassing**
The Visual Basic GotFocus event is posted, which means that it occurs at some indeterminate time after this message is sent. This is unlikely to be a problem, so subclassing this message should not be necessary.

Combo Box Control Messages

The following messages can be used to control the operation of any Visual Basic control based on the Windows Combo Box class. This includes the standard Visual Basic combo control.

Most of the messages defined here are exact duplicates of edit control messages defined in Chapter 17 or list control messages defined in the next section. In those cases, the entry simply refers you to the corresponding edit or list control message. The message applies to the corresponding part of the combo box (which consists of an edit control and a list box).

Note that these message numbers are different from their Win16 declarations. Some of the message parameters have changed as well.

■ CB_ADDSTRING

VB Declaration   `Const CB_ADDSTRING = &H143`

Description   See the description of the LB_ADDSTRING message in this chapter.

■ CB_DELETESTRING

VB Declaration   `Const CB_DELETESTRING = &H144`

Description   See the description of the LB_DELETESTRING message in this chapter.

■ CB_DIR

VB Declaration   `Const CB_DIR = &H145`

Description   See the description of the LB_DIR message in this chapter.

■ CB_FINDSTRING

VB Declaration   `Const CB_FINDSTRING = &H14C`

Description   See the description of the LB_FINDSTRING message in this chapter.

■ CB_FINDSTRINGEXACT

VB Declaration   `Const CB_FINDSTRINGEXACT = &H158`

Description   See the description of the LB_FINDSTRINGEXACT message in this chapter.

■ CB_GETCOUNT

VB Declaration   Const CB_GETCOUNT = &H146

Description   See the description of the LB_GETCOUNT message in this chapter.

■ CB_GETCURSEL

VB Declaration   Const CB_GETCURSEL = &H147

Description   See the description of the LB_GETCURSEL message in this chapter.

■ CB_GETDROPPEDCONTROLRECT

VB Declaration   Const CB_GETDROPPEDCONTROLRECT = &H152

Description   Determines the dimensions of the drop-down list box for a combo control. The dimensions are specified in pixel screen coordinates.

Use with VB   No problem.

Parameter	Description
wParam	Not used—set to zero.
lParam	The address of a RECT structure to load with the list box dimensions.

■ CB_GETDROPPEDSTATE

VB Declaration   Const CB_GETDROPPEDSTATE = &H157

Description   Determines if the list box portion of a combo box is visible.

Use with VB   No problem.

Return Value   Long—TRUE (nonzero) if the list box is visible, zero otherwise.

■ CB_GETDROPPEDWIDTH

VB Declaration   Const CB_GETDROPPEDCONTROLRECT = &H15F

Description   Retrieves the minimum width of the drop-down list box portion of a combo box.

Use with VB   No problem.

Parameter	Description
wParam	Not used—set to zero.
lParam	Not used—set to zero.

Return Value Long—The minimum width for the drop-down box.

Platform Windows 95, Windows NT 4.0

■ CB_GETEDITSEL

VB Declaration `Const CB_GETEDITSEL = &H140`

Description Equivalent to the EM_GETSEL message. Retrieves the current selection state of the edit control portion of the combo box.

Use with VB No problem, but the standard SelStart and SelLength properties are easier to use.

Parameter	Description
wParam	Address of long value to load with the character offset of the start of the selection, may be zero. To pass this value, either use agGetAddressForObject to obtain the address of a long variable, or use a SendMessage declaration that defines wParam as Long (no ByVal).
lParam	Address of long value to load with the character offset of the character after the last selected character, may be zero.

Return Value Long—The low word contains the character offset of the start of the selection, the high word contains the character offset of the character after the last selected character.

■ CB_GETEXTENDEDUI

VB Declaration `Const CB_GETEXTENDEDUI = &H156`

Description Determines if the combo control has the extended user interface enabled. The extended user interface is described in "The Combo Box Control," earlier in this chapter.

Use with VB No problem.

Return Value Long—Nonzero (TRUE) if the extended user interface is enabled.

■ CB_GETHORIZONTALEXTENT

VB Declaration `Const CB_GETHORIZONTALEXTENT =&H15D`

Description See the description of the LB_GETHORIZONTALEXTENT message in this chapter.

Platform Windows 95, Windows NT 4.0

■ CB_GETITEMDATA

VB Declaration `Const CB_GETITEMDATA = &H150`

Description See the description of the LB_GETITEMDATA message in this chapter.

■ CB_GETITEMHEIGHT

VB Declaration   Const CB_GETITEMHEIGHT = &H154

Description   See the description of the LB_GETITEMHEIGHT message in this chapter.

■ CB_GETLBTEXT

VB Declaration   Const CB_GETLBTEXT = &H148

Description   See the description of the LB_GETTEXT message in this chapter.

■ CB_GETLBTEXTLEN

VB Declaration   Const CB_GETLBTEXTLEN = &H149

Description   See the description of the LB_GETTEXTLEN message in this chapter.

■ CB_GETLOCALE

VB Declaration   Const CB_GETLOCALE = &H15A

Description   See the description of the LB_GETLOCALE message in this chapter.

■ CB_GETTOPINDEX

VB Declaration   Const CB_GETTOPINDEX = &H15B

Description   See the description of the LB_GETTOPINDEX message in this chapter.

Platform   Windows 95, Windows NT 4.0

■ CB_INSERTSTRING

VB Declaration   Const CB_INSERTSTRING = &H14A

Description   See the description of the LB_INSERTSTRING message in this chapter.

■ CB_LIMITTEXT

VB Declaration   Const CB_LIMITTEXT = &H141

Description   Used to specify the maximum number of characters that can be contained in the edit control portion of a combo box.

Use with VB   The standard Visual Basic combo box does not support the MaxLength property, so this message can be used to set the maximum length of text that can be entered into the edit control part of a combo control.

Parameter	Description
wParam	The maximum length of the text that can be entered into an edit control. Zero to set the length to 2,147,483,646 characters (64K under Windows 95).
lParam	Not used—set to zero.

■ CB_RESETCONTENT

VB Declaration   `Const CB_RESETCONTENT = &H14B`

Description   See the description of the LB_RESETCONTENT message in this chapter.

■ CB_SELECTSTRING

VB Declaration   `Const CB_SELECTSTRING = &H14D`

Description   See the description of the LB_SELECTSTRING message in this chapter.

■ CB_SETCURSEL

VB Declaration   `Const CB_SETCURSEL = &H14E`

Description   See the description of the LB_SETCURSEL message in this chapter.

■ CB_SETDROPPEDWIDTH

VB Declaration   `Const CB_SETDROPPEDCONTROLRECT = &H160`

Description   Sets the minimum width of the drop-down list box portion of a combo box.

Use with VB   No problem.

Parameter	Description
wParam	The width of the drop-down list box in pixels.
lParam	Not used—set to zero.

Return Value   Long—The new minimum width for the drop-down box. CB_ERR on error.

Platform   Windows 95, Windows NT 4.0

■ CB_SETEDITSEL

VB Declaration   `Const CB_SETEDITSEL = &H142`

Description	Sets the current selection for the edit control part of a combo box.
Use with VB	No problem, but the standard SelStart and SelLength properties are easier to use.

Parameter	Description
wParam	The character offset of the first character in the selection. –1 to remove the current selection.
lParam	The character offset of the first character after the selection. If wParam is 0 and this is –1, then the entire text is selected.

Return Value	Long—TRUE (nonzero) on success. CB_ERR on error.

■ CB_SETEXTENDEDUI

VB Declaration	`Const CB_SETEXTENDEDUI =&H155`
Description	Enables or disables the extended user interface for a combo control. The extended user interface is described in "The Combo Box Control," earlier in this chapter.
Use with VB	No problem.

Parameter	Description
wParam	One to enable the extended user interface for a combo control, zero to disable the extended user interface.
lParam	Not used—set to zero.

■ CB_SETHORIZONTALEXTENT

VB Declaration	`Const CB_GETHORIZONTALEXTENT =&H15E`
Description	See the description of the LB_SETHORIZONTALEXTENT message in this chapter.
Platform	Windows 95, Windows NT 4.0

■ CB_SETITEMDATA

VB Declaration	`Const CB_SETITEMDATA = &H151`
Description	See the description of the LB_SETITEMDATA message in this chapter.

■ CB_SETITEMHEIGHT

VB Declaration	`Const CB_SETITEMHEIGHT =&H153`
Description	See the description of the LB_SETITEMHEIGHT message in this chapter.

■ CB_SETLOCALE

VB Declaration   Const CB_SETLOCALE = &H159

Description   See the description of the LB_SETLOCALE message in this chapter.

■ CB_SETTOPINDEX

VB Declaration   Const CB_SETTOPINDEX = &H15C

Description   See the description of the LB_SETTOPINDEX message in this chapter.

Platform   Windows 95, Windows NT 4.0

■ CB_SHOWDROPDOWN

VB Declaration   Const CB_SHOWDROPDOWN =&H14F

Description   Used to show or hide the drop-down list box part of a combo control.

Use with VB   No problem.

Parameter	Description
wParam	TRUE (nonzero) to show the list box. Zero to hide it.
lParam	Not used—set to zero.

List Box Control Messages   The following messages can be used to control the operation of any Visual Basic control based on the Windows List class. This includes the standard Visual Basic list control and file control.

As usual, the return value refers to the value returned by the SendMessage function used to send the message to the control.

Note that these message numbers are different from their Win16 declarations. Some of the message parameters have changed as well.

■ LB_ADDFILE

VB Declaration   Const LB_ADDFILE =&H196

Description   Adds the specified filename to a directory list box.

Use with VB   No problem.

Parameter	Description
wParam	Not used—set to zero.
lParam	Address of a NULL terminated string containing the file name to add to the list box.

Return Value   The entry number of the new file name, where entry zero is the first string in the list box. –1 on error.

■ LB_ADDSTRING

VB Declaration   Const LB_ADDSTRING =&H180

Description   This message is used to add a string to a list box. If the list box is sorted, the new string will be inserted in the correct location. Otherwise, the string will be added to the end of the list box.

Use with VB   No problem. The Visual Basic AddItem method performs the same task.

Parameter	Description
wParam	Not used—set to zero.
lParam	Address of a NULL terminated string to add to the list box.

Return Value   The entry number of the new string, where entry zero is the first string in the list box. –1 on error.

■ LB_DELETESTRING

VB Declaration   Const LB_DELETESTRING =&H182

Description   Deletes a string from a list box.

Use with VB   No problem. The Visual Basic RemoveItem method performs the same task.

Parameter	Description
wParam	The entry number of the string to delete. Entry zero is the first entry in the list box. In Windows 95, only the low word of this parameter is used.
lParam	Not used—set to zero.

Return Value   The number of strings remaining in the list control. –1 on error.

■ LB_DIR

VB Declaration   Const LB_DIR =&H18D

Description   Fills a list control with a list of file names.

Use with VB   No problem. The Visual Basic file control is much easier to use for file management.

Parameter	Description
wParam	One or more of the following mask values can be combined to choose the files to load: &H1—Read only files. &H2—Hidden files. &H4—System files. &H10—lParam specifies a directory name. &H20—Files with the archive bit set. &H4000—All files matching the lParam specification are loaded. &H8000—Only files that match all of the attributes are loaded.
lParam	The address of a NULL terminated string specifying a DOS file specification. This can include the "?" and "*" wildcard characters.

Return Value   The entry number of the last file added to the list box. –1 on error.

■ LB_FINDSTRING

VB Declaration   Const LB_FINDSTRING =&H18F

Description   Finds an entry in a list box that matches the specified prefix. This search is not case-sensitive.

Use with VB   No problem.

Parameter	Description
wParam	The number of the list box entry from which to start the search. –1 to search the entire control starting from the beginning. The search will wrap around to the start if the last entry is reached without a match. In Windows 95, only the low word of this parameter is used.
lParam	The address of a NULL terminated string containing a prefix to search for.

Return Value   The entry number of the new string, where entry zero is the first string in the list box. –1 on error. For example, to search for a string in a list box that begins with the letters "LB_", starting the search from the sixth entry, you could use the command:
```
entrynum& = SendMessageByString(List1.hWnd, LB_FINDSTRING, 5, "LB_")
```

■ LB_FINDSTRINGEXACT

VB Declaration   Const LB_FINDSTRINGEXACT =&H1A2

Description   Finds an entry in a list box that matches the specified string. This search is not case-sensitive. This differs from LB_FINDSTRING in that the entire string must match.

Use with VB   No problem.

Parameter	Description
wParam	The number of the list box entry from which to start the search. –1 to search the entire control starting from the beginning. The search will wrap around to the start if the last entry is reached without a match. In Windows 95, only the low word of this parameter is used.
lParam	The address of a NULL terminated string to search for.

Return Value   The entry number of the new string, where entry zero is the first string in the list box. –1 on error.

■ LB_GETANCHORINDEX

VB Declaration   Const LB_GETANCHORINDEX =&H19D

Description   Retrieves the anchor entry number (the entry from which a multiple selection starts).

Use with VB   No problem.

Return Value   The entry number of the anchor.

▧ LB_GETCARETINDEX

VB Declaration   Const LB_GETCARETINDEX =&H19F

Description   When a multiple selection list box has the focus, a focus rectangle appears on one of entries. This message can be used to determine which entry has the focus rectangle.

Use with VB   No problem.

Return Value   The entry number of the string that has the focus, where entry zero is the first string in the list box. On single selection list boxes, the entry number of the selected string if one exists.

▧ LB_GETCOUNT

VB Declaration   Const LB_GETCOUNT =&H18B

Description   Used to determine the number of entries in a list box.

Use with VB   No problem. The Visual Basic ListCount property performs the same task and is easier to use.

Comments   The number of entries in the list box.

▧ LB_GETCURSEL

VB Declaration   Const LB_GETCURSEL =&H188

Description   Used to determine the entry number of the selected string if one exists in a single selection list box or the entry number of the first selected string if one exists in a multiple selection list box.

Use with VB   No problem. The Visual Basic ListIndex property performs the same task for a single select list box and is easier to use.

Return Value   The entry number of the current or first selection if one exists. –1 if no selection exists. The first entry in the list control is entry number zero.

▧ LB_GETHORIZONTALEXTENT

VB Declaration   Const LB_GETHORIZONTALEXTENT =&H193

Description   Determines the current horizontal extent of the list control. If this value is greater than the width of the list box, a horizontal list scroll bar appears that allows scrolling the contents of the control.

Use with VB   No problem.

Return Value   The horizontal extent of the list box in pixels.

▧ LB_GETITEMDATA

VB Declaration   Const LB_GETITEMDATA =&H199

Description Determines the user-defined 32-bit value associated with an entry in the list control.

Use with VB No problem. The Visual Basic ItemData property performs the same task and is easier to use.

Parameter	Description
wParam	The number of the entry for which to retrieve user defined data. The first entry is entry number zero. In Windows 95, only the low word of this parameter is used.
lParam	Not used—set to zero.

Return Value The user defined data for the specified entry, –1 on error.

■ LB_GETITEMHEIGHT

VB Declaration `Const LB_GETITEMHEIGHT =&H1A1`

Description Determines the height of each entry in the list control in pixels.

Use with VB No problem.

Parameter	Description
wParam	For the most part, it is not used—set to zero. It is used for owner draw list boxes to specify the entry number since each entry may have a different height.
lParam	Not used—set to zero.

Return Value The height of each entry in the list box in pixels.

■ LB_GETITEMRECT

VB Declaration `Const LB_GETITEMRECT =&H198`

Description Determines the dimensions of an entry in the list control. The dimensions are specified in list control client pixel coordinates.

Use with VB No problem.

Parameter	Description
wParam	The number of the entry for which to retrieve dimensions. The first entry is entry number zero. In Windows 95, only the low word of this parameter is used.
lParam	The address of a RECT structure to load with the entry dimensions.

Return Value –1 on error.

■ LB_GETLOCALE

VB Declaration `Const LB_GETLOCALE =&H1A6`

Description   Determines the current locale of the list box.

Use with VB   No problem. The locale is used to determine the correct sorting order of list boxes.

Return Value   Returns the locale of the list box. The high word contains the country code and the low word contains the language identifier (refer to Chapter 6 for information regarding country code and language ID).

■ LB_GETSEL

VB Declaration   `Const LB_GETSEL =&H187`

Description   Determines the selection state of an entry in a multiple select list box.

Use with VB   No problem. The Visual Basic Selected property performs the same task and is easier to use.

Parameter	Description
wParam	The number of the entry to check. The first entry is entry number zero. In Windows 95, only the low word of this parameter is used.
lParam	Not used—set to zero.

Return Value   A result greater than zero if the entry is selected, zero if it is not selected, and –1 on error.

■ LB_GETSELCOUNT

VB Declaration   `Const LB_GETSELCOUNT =&H190`

Description   Determines the total number of selected entries in a multiple select list box.

Use with VB   No problem. The Visual Basic SelCount property performs the same task and is easier to use.

Return Value   The number of selected entries selected in the list box. –1 on error or if it is a single selection list box.

■ LB_GETSELITEMS

VB Declaration   `Const LB_GETSELITEMS =&H191`

Description   Fills a long array with the numbers of all selected entries in a multiple selection list box.

Use with VB   No problem.

Parameter	Description
wParam	The maximum number of entries to load into the array specified by lParam. lParam must be large enough to contain this many longs. In Windows 95, only the low word of this parameter is used.
lParam	The address of the first entry in a long array that has at least wParam entries. After this message returns, this array will be loaded with the numbers of all selected entries up to the number of entries specified by the return value.

Return Value Number of entries loaded into the long array, –1 on error or if this message is sent to a single selection list box.

LB_GETTEXT

VB Declaration `Const LB_GETTEXT =&H189`

Description Retrieves the string for the specified list box entry.

Use with VB No problem. The Visual Basic List property performs the same task and is easier to use.

Parameter	Description
wParam	The number of the entry to retrieve. The first entry is entry number zero. In Windows 95, only the low word of this parameter is used.
lParam	The address of a string buffer to load with the list box text. This string must be preallocated to a length adequate to hold the string and NULL terminator. Use the LB_GETTEXTLEN message to determine the necessary buffer size.

Return Value The length of the string loaded.

LB_GETTEXTLEN

VB Declaration `Const LB_GETTEXTLEN =&H18A`

Description Retrieves the length of the string for the specified list box entry.

Use with VB No problem.

Parameter	Description
wParam	The number of the entry to check. The first entry is entry number zero. In Windows 95, only the low word of this parameter is used.
lParam	Not used—set to zero.

Return Value The length of the string for the specified entry. Under certain conditions, the return value is larger than the actual length of the string.

LB_GETTOPINDEX

VB Declaration `Const LB_GETTOPINDEX =&H18E`

Description Determines which entry appears at the top of the list control display.

Use with VB No problem. The Visual Basic TopIndex property performs the same task and is easier to use.

Comments The number of the first entry visible in the list box. The first string in the list box is entry zero.

■ LB_INSERTSTRING

VB Declaration   Const LB_INSERTSTRING =&H181

Description   This message is used to insert a string into a list box at a specified location. If the list box is
sorted, the new string will be inserted into the specified location without regard for the sort order.

Use with VB   No problem. The Visual Basic AddItem method performs the same task.

Parameter	Description
wParam	The entry location at which to insert this string. –1 to append the string to the end of the list box. The first entry is entry number zero.
lParam	Address of a NULL terminated string to insert into the list box.

Return Value   The entry number of the new string, where entry zero is the first string in the list box. The constant LB_ERR on error, LB_ERRSPACE if there is insufficient memory to insert the string.

■ LB_ITEMFROMPOINT

VB Declaration   Const LB_ITEMFROMPOINT =&H1A9

Description   Retrieves the index of the entry in the listbox that is closest to the specified point.

Use with VB   No problem. You can calculate this value yourself by obtaining the LB_GETITEMHEIGHT
message to find the height of each entry, GetClientRect to find the height of the list box, and the
LB_GETTOPINDEX message to find the first visible entry. This approach has the advantage of
working under Windows NT 3.51 as well.

Parameter	Description
wParam	Not used—set to zero.
lParam	A long variable that contains the X pixel coordinate to test in the low order word and the Y pixel coordinate to test in the high order word.

Return Value   The entry number closest to the specified point in the low word. The high word is zero if the
entry is visible.

Platform   Windows 95, Windows NT 4.0

■ LB_RESETCONTENT

VB Declaration   Const LB_RESETCONTENT =&H184

Description   Clears the contents of the list box.

Use with VB   No problem. The Visual Basic Clear method performs the same task and is easier to use.

■ LB_SELECTSTRING

VB Declaration   Const LB_SELECTSTRING =&H18C

Description   Finds an entry in a list box that matches the specified prefix and selects it. This search is not case-sensitive.

Use with VB   No problem.

Parameter	Description
wParam	The number of the list box entry from which to start the search. –1 to search the entire control starting from the beginning. The search will wrap around to the start if the last entry is reached without a match. In Windows 95, only the low word of this parameter is used.
lParam	The address of a NULL terminated string containing a prefix to search for.

Return Value   The entry number of the selected string if one is found, where entry zero is the first string in the list box. –1 if no match is found.

■ LB_SELITEMRANGE

VB Declaration   Const LB_SELITEMRANGE =&H19B

Description   Used to select or deselect a range of entries in a multiple select list box. This message can be used only on multiple selection list boxes.

Use with VB   No problem.

Parameter	Description
wParam	TRUE (nonzero) to select the specified entries, FALSE (zero) to clear the selection.
lParam	Low word: Specifies the first entry to select or deselect. High word: Specifies the last entry to select or deselect.

Return Value   –1 on error.

■ LB_SELITEMRANGEEX

VB Declaration   Const LB_SELITEMRANGEEX =&H183

Description   Similar to LB_SELITEMRANGE. This function can be used to select or deselect items beyond 32K under Windows NT.

Use with VB   No problem.

Parameter	Description
wParam	Specifies the first entry to select or deselect. If this entry number is less than the entry number specified in lParam, then the entries are selected. If this entry number is greater, then the entries are deselected. In Windows 95, only the low word of this parameter is used.
lParam	Specifies the last entry to select or deselect.

Return Value   –1 on error.

■ LB_SETANCHORINDEX

VB Declaration   Const LB_SETANCHORINDEX =&H19C

Description   Sets the anchor entry number (the entry from which a multiple selection starts).

Use with VB   No problem.

Parameter	Description
wParam	The entry number of the anchor. In Windows 95, only the low word of this parameter is used.
lParam	Not used—set to zero.

Return Value   0 on success, –1 on error.

■ LB_SETCARETINDEX

VB Declaration   Const LB_SETCARETINDEX =&H19E

Description   When a multiple selection list box has the focus, a focus rectangle appears on one of entries. This message can be used to set the focus rectangle to a particular entry. The string that is given the focus will be scrolled onto the display if necessary.

Use with VB   No problem.

Parameter	Description
wParam	The entry number that is to receive the focus rectangle.
lParam	The low 16 bits are set to FALSE to specify that the entire entry should be visible after this operation. Otherwise it is possible that it will be only partially visible after scrolling. The high 16 bits are not used and should be set to zero.

Return Value   –1 on error.

■ LB_SETCOLUMNWIDTH

VB Declaration   Const LB_SETCOLUMNWIDTH =&H195

Description   Sets the width of each column on a multiple column list control.

Use with VB   No problem. The Columns property of the standard list control must be greater than zero.

Parameter	Description
wParam	The width of each column in pixels.
lParam	Not used—set to zero.

■ LB_SETCOUNT

VB Declaration   Const LB_SETCOUNT =&H1A7

Description   Sets the number of items in an owner draw list box when Windows is not managing the data (LBS_NODATA style set).

Use with VB   None.

Parameter	Description
wParam	The number of items in the list box.
lParam	Not used—set to zero.

Return Value   LB_ERR on error.

■ LB_SETCURSEL

VB Declaration   Const LB_SETCURSEL =&H186

Description   Used to select an entry in a single selection list box. Do not use this message on multiple selection list boxes.

Use with VB   No problem. The Visual Basic ListIndex property performs the same task and is easier to use.

Parameter	Description
wParam	The entry number to select. The first entry in the list box is entry zero. -1 to clear any selection. In Windows 95, only the low word of this parameter is used.
lParam	Not used—set to zero.

■ LB_SETHORIZONTALEXTENT

VB Declaration   Const LB_SETHORIZONTALEXTENT =&H194

Description   Sets the current horizontal extent of the list control. If this value is greater than the width of the list box, a horizontal list scroll bar appears that allows scrolling the contents of the control.

Use with VB   No problem.

Parameter	Description
wParam	The new horizontal extent of the list control in pixels. In Windows 95, only the low word of this parameter is used.
lParam	Not used—set to zero.

■ LB_SETITEMDATA

VB Declaration   Const LB_SETITEMDATA =&H19A

Description   Sets a user-defined 32-bit value associated with the specified entry in a list box.

Use with VB	No problem. The Visual Basic ItemData property performs the same task and is easier to use.

Parameter	Description
wParam	The entry number to set the user defined data for. In Windows 95, only the low word of this parameter is used.
lParam	The value to associate the entry with.

Return Value	−1 on error.

■ LB_SETITEMHEIGHT

VB Declaration	Const LB_SETITEMHEIGHT =&H1A0
Description	Sets the height of each entry in the list control in pixels. This can be effectively used to set line spacing in a list control.
Use with VB	No problem.

Parameter	Description
wParam	Not used—set to zero. Set to the index number for the entry to set on variable height owner draw list box controls.
lParam	The low 16 bits are set to the height of each list box entry in pixels. The high 16 bits are not used and must be set to zero.

Return Value	−1 if the height specified is invalid.

■ LB_SETLOCALE

VB Declaration	Const LB_SETLOCALE =&H1A5
Description	Sets the current locale for the list box.
Use with VB	No problem. The locale is used to determine the correct sorting order of list boxes.

Parameter	Description
wParam	Locale ID to set to.
lParam	Not used—set to zero.

Return Value	Previous locale ID on success.

■ LB_SETSEL

VB Declaration	Const LB_SETSEL =&H185
Description	Sets the selection state of an entry in a multiple select list box.

Use with VB   No problem. The Visual Basic Selected property performs the same task and is easier to use.

Parameter	Description
wParam	TRUE (nonzero) to select the entry, FALSE to clear the entry.
lParam	The number of the entry to check. The first entry is entry number zero. −1 to apply the selection operation to all entries.

Return Value   −1 on error.
LB_SETTABSTOPS

VB Declaration   `Const LB_SETTABSTOPS =&H192`

Description   Used to specify tab stops in a list control. Tabs can be placed in a text string using the tab character, chr$(9). Tab stops are specified in dialog base units. Each dialog base unit represents one-fourth of the average character width in the current font.

Use with VB   No problems.

Parameter	Description
wParam	The number of tab stops to set. Zero to set the default of one tab stop every two dialog units. One to set tab stops every N dialog units where N is the first entry in a long array specified by lParam. Otherwise, this specifies the number of tab stops to set based on the long array specified by lParam.
lParam	The address of the first entry in a long array containing tab stops to set. The tab stops should be given in order.

Comments   This function does not redraw the control. Use InvalidateRect or the Visual Basic Refresh method to redraw the list control in order for the new tab stops to take effect. Refer to the List-Test.vbp example on the CD-ROM for a demonstration of the use of tab stops with list boxes.

■ LB_SETTOPINDEX

VB Declaration   `Const LB_SETTOPINDEX =&H197`

Description   Scrolls the list box so that the specified entry appears at the top of the list control display, or as close as possible to the top if the maximum scroll range has been reached.

Use with VB   No problem. The Visual Basic TopIndex property performs the same task and is easier to use.

Parameter	Description
wParam	The number of the entry to scroll to the top of the display. The first entry is entry number zero. In Windows 95, only the low word of this parameter is used.
lParam	Not used—set to zero.

Comments   −1 on error.

Button Control Messages

The following messages can be used to control the operation of any Visual Basic control based on the Windows Button class. This includes the standard Visual Basic command button, check box, and option buttons.

Note that these message numbers are different from their Win16 declarations.

■ BM_GETCHECK

VB Declaration Const BM_GETCHECK =&HF0

Description Used to determine if a button style control is checked or unchecked.

Use with VB No problem. The Visual Basic Value property performs this task and is easier to use.

Return Value 0 if the button is unchecked, 1 if checked, 2 if it is in a third state (typically grayed).

Comments This message has no effect on command buttons.

■ BM_GETIMAGE

VB Declaration Const BM_GETIMAGE =&HF6

Description Retrieves the bitmap or icon handle of an image button. Windows 95 and NT 4.0. The bitmap should have the BS_ICON or BS_BITMAP style set.

Use with VB Depends on the style chosen. You are encouraged to experiment. VB5 buttons support the Picture, DownPicture, and DisabledPicture properties which are a better choice for adding images to buttons.

Parameter	Description
wParam	Unused—set to zero.
lParam	Unused—set to zero.

■ BM_GETSTATE

VB Declaration Const BM_GETSTATE =&HF2

Description Used to determine the state of a button style control.

Use with VB No problem.

Return Value A bit field that is defined as follows:

- Bits 0–1: The checked state of the button. 0 if the button is unchecked, 1 if checked, 2 if it is in a third state (typically grayed).

- Bit 2: One if the button is highlighted (pressed).

- Bit 3: One if the button has the focus.

■ BM_SETCHECK

VB Declaration   Const BM_SETCHECK =&HF1

Description   Used to check or uncheck a button style control.

Use with VB   No problem. The Visual Basic Value property performs this task and is easier to use.

Parameter	Description
wParam	0 to uncheck the button. 1 to check the button. 2 to place it in its third state if applicable (gray, for example).
lParam	Not used—set to zero.

Comments   This message has no effect on command buttons.

■ BM_SETIMAGE

VB Declaration   Const BM_SETIMAGE =&HF7

Description   Sets the bitmap or icon handle of an image button. Windows 95 and NT4.0. The bitmap should have the BS_ICON or BS_BITMAP style set.

Use with VB   VB5 buttons support the Picture, DownPicture, and DisabledPicture properties which are a better choice for adding images to buttons.

Parameter	Description
wParam	Unused—set to zero.
lParam	The bitmap or icon handle for the button.

■ BM_SETSTATE

VB Declaration   Const BM_SETSTATE =&HF3

Description   Used to set the highlight state for a button style control. A button is highlighted when it is pressed; that is, the user clicks the left mouse button over the control. The button remains highlighted until the mouse button is released.

Use with VB   No problem.

Parameter	Description
wParam	0 to clear the highlighting. Nonzero to highlight the button.
lParam	Not used—set to zero.

■ BM_SETSTYLE

VB Declaration Const BM_SETSTYLE =&HF4

Description Changes the style of a button control. Refer to Chapter 5 for a list of available button styles.

Use with VB Depends on the style chosen. You are encouraged to experiment.

Parameter	Description
wParam	Low word is set to the new button style.
lParam	Low word is TRUE to redraw the control.

Using API Calls from VB: A Trade-off in Software Design

Building an API Class Library

4

**Real World API
Programming
Revisited**

19

Using API Calls from VB—A Trade-off in Software Design

Using the Windows API to Improve Performance

Power versus Safety When Using the Windows API

Design Choices

Learning through Experimentation

VISUAL BASIC REVOLUTIONIZED WINDOWS PROGRAMMING BY MAKING it easy to write Windows applications. Until Visual Basic appeared, Windows programming generally required the use of C or C++, and a good overall understanding of the Windows API. It would literally take months to train an experienced DOS programmer to be even minimally competent under Windows.

Visual Basic 1.0 was easy—you could learn to write Windows applications in days, and write small programs in a matter of hours. You could then learn to extend the power of Visual Basic gradually through use of custom controls and API calls.

While Visual Basic remains the easiest way to write Windows applications, it is no longer necessarily correct to call it "easy"—with classes, advanced database access, and OLE support, Visual Basic has grown into an extremely sophisticated and rather complex language. It would be easy to stop at this point in the book and simply say, "Here is the Win32 API—or at least the core parts of it—use it as you will," but this fails to address some key questions. When should you use API functions? What kind of performance trade-offs exist? How does one go about learning more about the Win32 extensions? What about Win32 object libraries or class libraries? This chapter addresses some of these questions. The chapter that follows demonstrates how you can encapsulate API functions in a class library and introduces a fairly comprehensive class library that is included with this book.

Using the Windows API to Improve Performance

One area where the Windows API can make a difference is with regard to performance—especially graphic performance. The potential for improved graphics performance is due to two key factors:

- Visual Basic graphic commands use floating-point parameters and scaling, whereas Windows API commands use long integer parameters and integer arithmetic for scaling.

- The Windows API includes a number of graphic commands, such as polygon commands, that do not exist as Visual Basic primitives.

But before demonstrating the potential improvement in performance, it is necessary to first find a way to measure that performance.

The Black Art of Benchmarking

Benchmarking is one of the most complex problems in computer science, in part because it is often difficult to figure out exactly what you are measuring. This is especially challenging in a preemptive multitasking operating system.

Because the resolution of the internal system timers is limited, one common technique for measuring performance of a piece of code is to run it multiple times and measure the total elapsed time. An easy way to calculate times is to use the GetTickCount function, which returns the number of milliseconds since the system was started—simply record the value at the beginning of the routine, run the code you wish to measure inside a loop, then measure the time again and compare with the original time. This works nicely on Windows 3.1, but in a preemptive multitasking system such as Windows 95 or Windows NT, this elapsed time will also include time spent running other applications and system services. This can compromise the accuracy of the measurements.

Fortunately, Win32 under Windows NT provides a mechanism for determining exactly how much time is being spent within a given process. This is accomplished with the GetProcessTimes function. This function loads various timing parameters for a process into a set of FILETIME structures. The FILETIME structure is defined as follows:

```
Private Type FILETIME
        dwLowDateTime As Long
        dwHighDateTime As Long
End Type
```

The two long variables combine to form a single 64-bit number that represents a time specified in 100-nanosecond increments. This is far more resolution than you are likely to need, and more than most systems can provide at this time, but at least one cannot accuse Microsoft of not thinking ahead. Still, as you will see, working with this type of structure poses its own unique challenges.

The GetProcessTimes function is defined as follows:

```
Declare Function GetProcessTimes Lib "kernel32" (ByVal hProcess As Long, _
lpCreationTime As FILETIME, lpExitTime As FILETIME, _
lpKernelTime As FILETIME, lpUserTime As FILETIME) As Long
```

The first parameter is a handle to the process. lpCreationTime references a FILETIME structure that will be loaded with the time that the process was started, and lpExitTime references a structure that will be loaded with the time that it was terminated (or an undefined value if the process is still running). To understand the lpKernelTime and lpUserTime you will need to know a little bit more about how Windows itself works. One of the ways that 32-bit Windows protects applications from interfering with each other is to isolate them in their own memory space. But how can an operating system really prevent an application from accessing all of the system's resources? After all, each application can access the same low-level computer instructions as the operating system—what's to stop them from executing the same commands that the operating system itself uses to manage applications and the system as a whole?

Clearly it couldn't, if the assumption about each application having access to all of a computer's instructions was accurate. As it turns out, the system processor used to support Win32 operating systems must be able to support two different modes. Kernel mode (also known as "privileged" mode) is the one used by the operating system itself. In this mode, all of the CPU's instructions are available. A second mode called User mode (nonprivileged) locks out a number of critical CPU instructions. This mode is used by applications and most system services. If an application tries to access one of the privileged instructions, an exception occurs and operating system code takes over.

Each process spends some time in user mode, but will also spend time in kernel mode when it is executing operating system code—which happens frequently during API calls. On a single tasking system, the total elapsed time for an application would equal the sum of the user time and the kernel time. As you will see, the total elapsed time in the examples shown in this chapter will exceed this value—the difference is time spent running other processes or system services.

In order to support these types of measurements, a simple benchmarking class was developed, portions of which are shown in Listing 19.1.

Listing 19.1 **dwBench.vbp**

```
VERSION 1.¯ CLASS
BEGIN
   MultiUse = -1  'True
END
Attribute VB_Name = "dwBenchMark"
Attribute VB_Creatable = True
Attribute VB_Exposed = True

' dwBenchMark - Benchmarking utility class
' Part of the Desaware API Class Library
' Copyright (c) 1996 by Desaware.
' All Rights Reserved

Option Explicit

Private Declare Function GetProcessTimes Lib "kernel32" (ByVal hProcess As _
Long, lpCreationTime As FILETIME, lpExitTime As FILETIME, lpKernelTime As _
FILETIME, lpUserTime As FILETIME) As Long
Private Declare Function GetTickCount Lib "kernel32" () As Long
Private Declare Function GetCurrentProcess Lib "kernel32" () As Long

Private Type FILETIME
        dwLowDateTime As Long
        dwHighDateTime As Long
```

Listing 19.1   dwBench.vbp (Continued)

```
End Type

' This is the reference user time as marked.
Private ReferenceTime As FILETIME
' This is the marked user time for comparisons.
Private MarkTime As FILETIME

' This is the reference kernel time as marked.
Private ReferenceKTime As FILETIME
' This is the marked kernel time for comparisons.
Private MarkKTime As FILETIME

' Reference TickCount
Private ReferenceTick As Long
' The marked tick count for comparisons
Private MarkTick As Long

' A variable to hold the current process handle to use
Private ThisProcess As Long

' Dummy filetime structures that we won't actually use
Private fcreate As FILETIME
Private fexit As FILETIME

Private Sub Class_Initialize()
    ' There is no need to close this pseudo handle
    ThisProcess = GetCurrentProcess()
End Sub

' Sets the reference time
Public Sub SetReference()
    ReferenceTick = GetTickCount
    Call GetProcessTimes(ThisProcess, fcreate, fexit, ReferenceKTime, _
    ReferenceTime)
End Sub


' Sets the mark time
Public Sub SetMark()
    MarkTick = GetTickCount
    Call GetProcessTimes(ThisProcess, fcreate, fexit, MarkKTime, MarkTime)
End Sub

' Subtracts MarkTime from ReferenceTime and returns the difference
Private Function CalculateDifference(ByVal timespec As Integer) As FILETIME
    Dim f As FILETIME
    Select Case timespec
        Case ˉ   ' User time
```

Listing 19.1   **dwBench.vbp (Continued)**

```
                Call agSubtractFileTimes(MarkTime, ReferenceTime, f)
        Case 1  ' Kernel time
                Call agSubtractFileTimes(MarkKTime, ReferenceKTime, f)
    End Select
    CalculateDifference = f
End Function


' Get the difference based on the tick count in ms
Public Function GetTickDifference() As Long
    GetTickDifference = MarkTick - ReferenceTick
End Function

' Get the difference based on user time in ms
Public Function GetuserDifferenceMS() As Double
    Dim diff As FILETIME
    Dim res As Double
    diff = CalculateDifference(¯)
    res = diff.dwLowDateTime / 1¯¯¯¯
    If diff.dwHighDateTime <> ¯ Then
        ' Add in the number of milliseconds for each high count
        res = res + diff.dwHighDateTime * 42949.67296
    End If
    GetuserDifferenceMS = res
End Function

Public Function GetkernelDifferenceMS() As Double
    Dim diff As FILETIME
    Dim res As Double
    diff = CalculateDifference(1)
    res = diff.dwLowDateTime / 1¯¯¯¯
    If diff.dwHighDateTime <> ¯ Then
        ' Add in the number of milliseconds for each high count
        res = res + diff.dwHighDateTime * 42949.67296
    End If
    GetkernelDifferenceMS = res
End Function
```

There are a few subtle aspects of this code that deserve further attention. The CalculateDifference function subtracts one FILETIME structure from another. Doing this in Visual Basic is quite tricky because VB does not support unsigned variables. This means that the relatively simple task of subtracting one long from another, determining if a carry is required, then subtracting the high order long fields, becomes a rather complex operation that must consider the signs of each variable and trap for overflow conditions as well.

Being rather lazy, it seemed to me far easier to implement this subtraction operation using the C language (which includes unsigned integers), so it is now part of the APIGID32.DLL dynamic link library included with this book.

The GetuserDifferenceMS() and GetkernelDifferenceMS() functions perform a rather odd calculation to convert a FILETIME structure into milliseconds. Keep in mind that this structure actually corresponds to a 64-bit value that measures 100ns units. To convert to milliseconds, you must divide this number by 10,000. Going back to basic number theory:

```
Elapsed time = dwHighDateTime * 2^32 + dwLowDateTime
```

To divide by 10,000 we have:

```
(dwHighDateTime * 2^32 + dwLowDateTime)/1⁻⁻⁻⁻ =
dwHighDateTime * 2^32/1⁻⁻⁻⁻ + dwLowDateTime/1⁻⁻⁻⁻ =
dwHighDateTime * 42949.67296 + dwLowDateTime/1⁻⁻⁻⁻
```

which is the calculation actually performed by the function.

If the user and kernel times are so valuable, why does the benchmarking class use the "tick count" elapsed time as well? An obvious reason is that the Get-ProcessTimes function is not implemented under Windows 95. But another reason is that total elapsed time can become useful when testing functionality that involves more than one process. For example, if you wanted to measure the performance of code that accesses an out-of-process OLE server, you would find that the process time functions do not include time spent in the OLE server—the process is suspended while it is waiting for the server to complete its operation and the elapsed time does not count as part of the process time. You could, perhaps, perform separate time measurements within the OLE server, but this presumes that you have access to the server code, and it still will not take into account overhead time spent within the server itself. In cases like this the total elapsed time can give a better indication of the overall code performance.

Elapsed time is also important for graphic operations which, under Windows NT, can occur in the background while your process is suspended. In cases like these the elapsed time can be substantially longer than the time spent within the process. Because of architectural differences between operating systems, it is crucial that you benchmark your application on all of the systems that you target.

A Benchmarking Example: Visual Basic versus API-Based Graphics

The Drawbnch.vbp sample project included on the CD-ROM that comes with this book demonstrates how you can perform your own comparisons between a pure Visual Basic graphics approach and one that includes API graphic commands. It also demonstrates use of the benchmarking class described earlier. Listing 19.2 shows a partial listing for the program.

Listing 19.2 **Partial listing for file FRMDRAW.FRM**

```
Dim CurrentOption%
Private Const LOOPS = 2¯¯
Dim bench As New dwBenchMark
Dim starpoints(12) As Long

Private Sub cmdExecute_Click()
    Dim rgt&
    Dim btm&
    Dim current&
    Dim loopcounter&
    Dim pt As POINTAPI
    Dim usedc&
    Dim oldbrush&
    Dim x&
    Picture1.Cls
    usedc = Picture1.hdc
    bench.SetReference
    For loopcounter = 1 To LOOPS
        Select Case CurrentOption
            Case ¯
                rgt = Picture1.ScaleWidth
                btm = Picture1.ScaleHeight
                If chkUseAPI Then
                    For current = ¯ To rgt
                        ' You'll see good performance here, but if you
                        ' used picture1.hdc as a parameter, it would be
                        ' slower than the VB code!  See chapter  text
                        Call MoveToEx(usedc, current&, ¯, pt)
                        Call LineTo(usedc, current, btm)
                    Next current
                Else
                    For current = ¯ To rgt
                        Picture1.Line (current, ¯)-(current, btm)
                    Next current
                End If
            Case 1
                rgt = Picture1.ScaleWidth
                btm = Picture1.ScaleHeight
                If chkUseAPI Then
                    oldbrush = SelectObject(usedc, GetStockObject(NULL_BRUSH))
                    For current = ¯ To rgt
                        Call Rectangle(usedc, ¯, ¯, current, current)
                    Next current
                    ' Restore the original brush
                    Call SelectObject(usedc, oldbrush)
                Else
                    For current = ¯ To rgt
                        Picture1.Line (¯, ¯)-(current, current), , B
                    Next current
```

Listing 19.2   Partial listing for file FRMDRAW.FRM (Continued)

```
                            End If
                        Case 2
                            rgt = Picture1.ScaleWidth
                            btm = Picture1.ScaleHeight
                            If chkUseAPI Then
                                oldbrush = SelectObject(usedc, GetStockObject(NULL_BRUSH))
                                For current = ¯ To rgt
                                    Call Ellipse(usedc, -current, -current, current,
current)
                                    ' Can perform the same task:
                                    ' Call Arc(usedc, -current, -current, current, current, _
                                    ¯, current, current, ¯)
                                Next current
                                ' Restore the original brush
                                Call SelectObject(usedc, oldbrush)
                            Else
                                For current = ¯ To rgt
                                    Picture1.Circle (¯, ¯), current
                                Next current
                            End If
                        Case 3
                            rgt = Picture1.ScaleWidth
                            btm = Picture1.ScaleHeight
                            If chkUseAPI Then
                                oldbrush = SelectObject(usedc, GetStockObject(NULL_BRUSH))
                                For current = 1 To rgt \ 4
                                    SetStarArray current
                                    Call Polygon(usedc, starpoints(¯), 6)
                                Next current
                                ' Restore the original brush
                                Call SelectObject(usedc, oldbrush)
                            Else
                                For current = 1 To rgt \ 4
                                    SetStarArray current
                                    For x = ¯ To 8 Step 2
                                        Picture1.Line (starpoints(x), starpoints(x + 1))-_
                                        (starpoints(x + 2), starpoints(x + 3))
                                    Next x
                                Next current
                            End If
                    End Select
                    Picture1.Cls
                Next loopcounter
                bench.SetMark
                lblUser.Caption = "User: " & bench.GetuserDifferenceMS()
                lblKernel.Caption = "Krnl: " & bench.GetkernelDifferenceMS()
                lblTicks.Caption = "Tot: " & bench.GetTickDifference()
            End Sub
```

As usual, the functions are placed within loops so that we have a long enough interval to obtain reasonably accurate measurements. You must never assume that simply using an API approach is enough to provide improved performance over Visual Basic. You must also be careful to avoid inefficient code. Consider the line examples:

```
API:
Call MoveToEx(usedc, current&, ¯, pt)
Call LineTo(usedc, current, btm)

VB equivalent:
Picture1.Line (current, ¯)-(current, btm)
```

The question is, can two API calls, with all of the overhead that Visual Basic imposes on a DLL call, still be faster than a single control method? The answer, as it turns out, is yes—at least as it is shown here.

However, if instead of saving the HDC property in a variable, you used the code

```
Call MoveToEx(Picture1.hdc, current&, ¯, pt)
Call LineTo(Picture1.hdc, current, btm)
```

you would find that the API approach is substantially slower than the Visual Basic only approach. The overhead of object access using OLE automation (even in-process) is still greater than the benefits of the faster API call.

So what are the potential performance benefits of using API graphics commands? They will vary based on the operating system, how well optimized your code is, the algorithm you are using, the type of operation, and so on. Based on this sample program, for graphic-intensive operations it is possible to see a threefold improvement in performance over pure VB code.

Power versus Safety When Using the Windows API

There are two overwhelming reasons to use the Windows API with Visual Basic: increased capability and improved performance. Increased capability results from the fact that the Visual Basic language does not provide a full encapsulation of all of the capabilities of Windows. Instead, it provides a good subset, and by encapsulating the functionality of Windows Visual Basic also succeeds in making Windows programming safe—or at least far safer than any other programming environment. In short, Visual Basic trades off the capability of Windows against safety.

As soon as you start working directly with the Win32 API, you essentially bypass the power versus safety trade-offs defined by Visual Basic in order to choose your own. In return for taking responsibility over the correct declaration and usage of the myriad API functions, you obtain nearly full access to the capability of Windows—and with the aid of third-party tools such as Desaware's SpyWorks, you can obtain just about as much low-level access as a C or C++ programmer can obtain.

In addition to capability, the Windows API can provide improved performance. API functions have been optimized for speed in many cases, and sometimes a single API function can perform the task of a complex series of Visual Basic commands. The drawing commands are a good example of this.

As it turns out, it is possible to control the power vs. performance trade-off closely when using API functions, not only by the functions that you choose to use, but by the way you design your application.

Inline Code, Functions, and Class Libraries

Consider a typical API function that can be used to obtain text information—GetWindowText, for example. Like other API functions, this one requires that you not only declare the function correctly, but also that you carefully preinitialize a string so that it will be long enough to hold the returned data. Failure to do so can lead to a corruption of memory that could crash your application, or worse, can introduce subtle bugs into your program's data.

One approach to making it safer to use these types of API functions is to isolate them into their own Visual Basic wrapper functions. You can write a Visual Basic function that initializes the string to the correct length, calls the API function, and returns the string. Naturally, there will be some compromise in performance, but the result will be as safe to use as the built-in VB functionality.

It is also possible to create classes that encapsulate portions of the Windows API functionality, and even to create OLE DLL server objects that do the same thing. When it comes to deciding the performance impact of some design decisions, Microsoft unfortunately gives you very little to go on. For example, we all know that an object implemented as an in-process OLE server (OLE DLL server) will provide good performance. But what does "good" mean in this context? Certainly the performance is outstanding when compared to an out-of-process object (OLE executable server)—by avoiding the need to switch between processes and transfer data across the process boundary, in-process servers are orders of magnitude faster than out-of-process servers. But how does it compare with the performance of a class within the project itself? And how does placing code within a class compare with placing code directly inline where it is used?

The answers to these questions are critical when it comes to designing your application. If OLE servers are as fast or faster than embedded classes, one could argue that an application should just be created from a whole bunch of stand-alone DLL servers which can be reused as needed. If, however, there is a performance impact, it might be better to create a library of reusable classes that can be added directly to your project as needed. And when it comes to designing classes, the traditional problem of deciding when to place a block of code in its own function versus keeping it inline comes into play.

There is no documentation available that discusses the performance trade-offs mentioned here, which means that it's up to us to figure it out through experimentation. The Bench1.vbp sample can be used to perform comparison measurements and illustrates the different approaches.

```
Private Sub cmdDirect_Click()
    Dim textlen As Long
    Dim usewnd As Long
    Dim counter As Long
    Dim marker As New dwBenchMark
    Dim res$
    usewnd = hwnd
    textlen = GetWindowTextLength(usewnd) + 1
    res$ = String$(textlen + 1, " ")
    Screen.MousePointer = vbHourglass
    marker.SetReference
    For counter = 1 To 1````
        Call GetWindowText(usewnd, res$, textlen)
    Next counter
    marker.SetMark
    Screen.MousePointer = vbDefault
    ShowDifference marker

End Sub
```

The marker object is used to measure the time it takes to perform 10,000 GetWindowText calls. The ShowDifference function loads the elapsed times into three label controls and is shown below:

```
Public Sub ShowDifference(marker As Object)
    lblTicks.Caption = "Ticks = " & marker.GetTickDifference() & " ms"
    lblUser.Caption = "User time = " & marker.GetuserDifferenceMS() & " ms"
    lblKernel.Caption = "Kernel time = " & marker.GetkernelDifferenceMS() & " _
    ms"

End Sub
```

As you can see, the inline function above must determine the length of the window caption, and allocate a buffer of the correct length in order to call the GetWindowText function safely. Failure to do so could lead to memory corruption. One obvious way to improve the safety of this function is to encapsulate it in its own function that performs the GetWindowTextLength call and buffer allocation, then returns a Visual Basic string directly. An example of this follows.

```
Public Function InternalGetWindowText(ByVal usewnd As Long) As String
    Dim textlen As Long
    Dim res$
```

```
    textlen = GetWindowTextLength(usewnd) + 1
    res$ = String$(textlen + 1, " )
    Call GetWindowText(usewnd, res$, textlen)
    InternalGetWindowText = res$
End Function

Private Sub cmdInFunction_Click()
    Dim marker As New dwBenchMark
    Dim res$
    Dim counter&
    Dim usewnd&
    usewnd = hwnd
    Screen.MousePointer = vbHourglass
    marker.SetReference
    For counter = 1 To 1----
        res$ = InternalGetWindowText(usewnd)
    Next counter
    marker.SetMark
    Screen.MousePointer = vbDefault
    ShowDifference marker
End Sub
```

What does it mean when I say this approach is "safer?" It certainly does not mean that this approach is less likely to fail—written correctly, both approaches are 100 percent safe. It does mean that you can implement this "canned" GetWindowText function once, put it in a module or class, and reuse it throughout your project or enterprise without worrying that you or some other programmer will accidentally use it in such a way that an exception might occur. (Note: For improved safety, you should use the IsWindow API to verify the window handle in the InternalGetWindowText function.)

What kind of performance impact might you expect from this approach? Clearly this particular example will run much more slowly than the inline version. It's not the overhead of the function that matters here, it's the fact that this approach in effect moves the GetWindowTextLength and buffer allocation into the loop. Instead of performing these tasks once and using the results 10,000 times, you are performing them 10,000 times.

But wait! you may ask, How can this be a fair comparison of performance?

The answer is, of course, that it isn't. The choice of which approach to take is not related to a Visual Basic technique at all; it isn't even related to Visual Basic other than the fact that VB is the implementation language. This is a straightforward software design trade-off. The latter approach provides safety with some sacrifice in performance. The former approach is more dangerous but allows you to maximize performance in cases where you can pull code out of a loop. For example, if you are retrieving a number of strings using API functions, you can preallocate a single large string and use it multiple times instead of calling functions that each preallocate their own string.

There is no right or wrong approach here—it is up to you to choose an approach based on the characteristics of your own application.

The next question of interest is, as long as you are using a function such as InternalGetText anyway, why not place it in an OLE server DLL so that it can be shared and the code hidden from other programmers (after all, classes are shareable, but do require that you provide the source code). Listing 19.3 is a simple class that exposes a GetWindowText method.

Listing 19.3   **TSTWND.BAS**

```
VERSION 1.¯ CLASS
BEGIN
  MultiUse = -1  'True
END
Attribute VB_Name = "App"
Attribute VB_Creatable = True
Attribute VB_Exposed = True
Option Explicit
Private Declare Function APIGetWindowText Lib "user32" Alias "GetWindowTextA" _
(ByVal hwnd As Long, ByVal lpString As String, ByVal cch As Long) As Long
Private Declare Function APIGetWindowTextLength Lib "user32" Alias _
"GetWindowTextLengthA" (ByVal hwnd As Long) As Long


Public Function GetWindowText(ByVal usewnd As Long) As String
    Dim textlen As Long
    Dim res$
    textlen = APIGetWindowTextLength(usewnd) + 1
    res$ = String$(textlen + 1, ¯)
    Call APIGetWindowText(usewnd, res$, textlen)
    GetWindowText = res$
End Function
You can then rewrite the function-based approach shown earlier as follows:
Private Sub cmdCallDLL_Click()
    Dim marker As New dwBenchMark
    Dim wintext As Object

    Dim res$
    Dim counter&
    Dim usewnd&
    usewnd = hwnd
    Set wintext = CreateObject("tstWindowText.App")
    Screen.MousePointer = vbHourglass
    marker.SetReference
    For counter = 1 To 1¯¯¯¯
        res$ = wintext.GetWindowText(usewnd)
```

Listing 19.3   TSTWND.BAS (Continued)

```
    Next counter
    marker.SetMark
    Screen.MousePointer = vbDefault
    ShowDifference marker

End Sub
```

Clearly, here we are comparing two virtually identical approaches, which means that any time difference between the embedded function or class approach and the DLL server approach will clearly indicate overhead due to the use of OLE automation and a DLL server. We will finally see how "fast" a DLL server really is. In order to see the impact of one of the well known "tips" for improving performance, a second DLL server example uses a direct reference to the object type and the "with" statement to reduce OLE overhead.

```
ç Dim wintext As tstWindowText.App ç
With wintext
    For counter = 1 To 1````
        res$ = .GetWindowText(usewnd)
    Next counter
End With
```

As a final bonus, the sample also includes a tight loop measurement of the use of the caption property to read the window text.

Results

The results are left for you to calculate, since they are totally dependent on your own system hardware and software configuration. If your results track our own tests, you should find the following:

- The inline example illustrates the obvious: Any time you hand-optimize code within a loop to remove everything possible from within the loop, performance will improve. The function approach was about five times slower than the inline approach in this example.

- Object references and string allocations are expensive. The caption property example is slower than performing the GetWindowText function by about a factor of two. This is both because it moves the string allocation out of the loop, and because it moves the object reference out of the loop.

- In-process DLL servers are as fast as including the function in the application if the reference uses early binding (which requires using a direct

reference to the object and adding a reference to the DLL to the application). Otherwise, the additional overhead of late binding to the function can be substantial.

The conclusion? The performance versus safety trade-off is real. Hand-optimized inline code can be dramatically faster than placing individual functions in an OLE server DLL—by a factor of 10 or more. In practice what does this mean? Only that you should consider the trade-offs involved carefully. Use a profiler to identify where your code is slow and hand-optimize those portions. If you are making relatively light use of the Windows API, don't waste time with entire API object libraries or classes—place the code inline or write a few functions. It is for this last reason that the Desaware API class library (a subset of which comes with this book) includes full source code. It is expected that in many cases you will simply cut out those functions that you need, using it as essentially a large sample code library.

Design Choices

So far this chapter has focused on techniques for evaluating some of the trade-offs involved in choosing to use API functions in your Visual Basic programs. It would take an entire book and numerous case studies to give this subject the coverage that it deserves. Even then, it would be up to you to make these choices based on your own application. Nevertheless, these techniques can help you, not only in tuning your code for performance, but in making fundamental design choices in your application.

This section will review some of the design trade-offs that you should consider, along with some of the advantages and disadvantages of each approach. Because the choice to use API calls does not exist in a vacuum, this section will examine a broad spectrum of design trade-offs.

Comparisons

Before comparing different architectures, it is worthwhile to examine some of the advantages and disadvantages of each approach. The question here is, given several ways to implement a given set of functionality, what are the advantages and disadvantages of each approach?

Visual Basic Code
Advantages:

- Maximum safety

- Easy to test and debug

- Predictable life cycle costs

- Platform independent

Disadvantages:

- May have lower performance than other approaches
- Often has higher development cost than using custom controls

Win32 API Code
Advantages:

- Maximum flexibility
- Thoroughly tested and documented
- Often provides improved performance
- Predictable life cycle costs

Disadvantages:

- Requires separate Win16 and Win32 code
- Often has higher development cost than using custom controls
- High learning curve may require more knowledgeable (read: expensive) programmers

Commercial Custom Controls and OLE Servers
Advantages:

- Extremely low entry cost (as compared to writing the functionality yourself)
- Easy to use
- Potentially excellent performance

Disadvantages:

- Dependency on third party vendor makes overall life cycle costs hard to estimate
- Requires distribution of additional software components
- Code bloat, as controls always contain functionality that you don't need

Custom Controls and OLE Servers Developed In-House
Advantages:

- Easy to use

- Potentially Excellent performance

- Predictable life cycle costs

Disadvantages:

- Potentially higher development cost depending on the technology chosen.

- Requires distribution of additional software components

Issues

Another way to look at the choices facing you as a software designer is to examine the issues individually and see how they might influence the choice of technology.

Life Cycle Cost

What does the term *life cycle costs* mean in this context? It derives from the fact that the cost of developing software includes much more than the initial development. You must also include the cost to test, support, and distribute the code, and the potential long term risks that could dramatically increase those costs. For example, let's say you use a custom control that was provided free with a book in a major project. Later in the project you find a bug in the control, or you need an updated version. Chances are that the control is unsupported, meaning that you now face the challenge of replacing it late in the development cycle (or after it has been released) when costs are greatest. (This is one reason that all of the controls provided in this book are demonstration versions for experimental use only—I know that "free" controls are ultimately more expensive than commercial controls for both the customer and the vendor and would never use them myself.) In this chaotic industry, with constant mergers and acquisitions, even a company's size is not a sure predictor of whether it will be around in a year or two to support your existing code. I realize that this may sound unusual coming from an individual who runs a company that develops and markets custom controls and VB add-ons. While I may not enjoy acknowledging the risks of using commercial controls, and do everything possible to eliminate the risks for our own customers—the truth is that those risks do exist and it is essential that you consider them in your own calculations.

The same problem also applies to controls developed in-house using a consultant—though the risk is not as great presuming that you keep ownership of the source code.

Performance

The performance of an application is dictated by many factors. While one might think that the choice of language is the major factor in determining performance, the truth is that in many cases the design of an application is the overriding issue. Choice of algorithms is beyond the scope of this book, but clearly the choice of technology bears discussion.

Prior to Visual Basic 5.0, custom controls had a potential performance advantage due to the fact that they were written in C or C++ and usually compiled to native code. Whether this potential advantage was achieved or not depended on the design of the custom control and the language under which it was implemented. Visual Basic 5.0's native compilation option eliminates much of this advantage, but does not change the fact that there is a performance cost in accessing a custom control or server—the samples in this chapter clearly demonstrate this. This overhead can be a substantial part of the execution time for very small functions.

In many cases, a relatively small investment in programmer time can eliminate the need for a control or server and improve performance at the same time. Classic examples include using API functions to determine the state of keys such as the NumLock key instead of using a keystate control, and using the Line command to draw a line instead of the line control.

In the case of some graphic operations, as you have seen, API functions can provide a dramatic improvement in performance if used carefully.

Developer Cost

Programmer time is expensive. If you are a hobbyist or are working for a company, you may not realize this or even consider it important. But if you are responsible for a software project (whether as an individual or as a part of or manager of a large team), you are probably well aware of this fact.

Visual Basic, due to its relative ease of use and lower learning curve, is one of the least expensive languages to develop in, which is why it is so incredibly widespread. This also means that the programmers writing solely in Visual Basic tend to cost less than those who are experienced at using API functions, and less again than those using C++.

This book presupposes that anyone can learn to make effective use of API functions, thus in effect making API use under VB almost equal in cost to pure VB development. However, C++ development is likely to continue to be very expensive.

Commercial custom controls and servers have the benefit of dramatically reducing developer cost, one of the reasons that they have become so popular.

Time Cost

Time to market is everything in these days of ever-shrinking product cycles. When deciding which technology to use, it is often more economical to use a readily available custom control than to take the time to write equivalent code on your own. One common approach used is to design applications initially using Visual Basic code and custom controls, then gradually to incorporate optimizations using API functions and custom code to both improve performance and reduce distribution size.

Learning through Experimentation

As heavy a tome as this book is, it does not come *close* to covering the entire Win32 API. Even if that was the intent it would not be possible, for Win32 is evolving rapidly and this book would have to go through monthly editions if it were to incorporate the new API functions as they were created.

So what do you do when faced with the task of learning or using an API function that is not covered in this book? What do you do when you are stuck and can't figure out how to solve a particular problem? Here are some suggestions that should help you on your way:

- **Don't panic**. If you have read through the text portions of this book and followed the examples, you are (though you may not believe it), a true API guru—for while this book did not cover all of the Win32 API, you can be sure that those parts that were covered were discussed in enough depth for you to handle anything else that comes along. This book places strong emphasis on understanding the underlying concepts of how Windows works and how API functions can be effectively used from Visual Basic—concepts which are applicable to all API or DLL functions.

- **Get MSDN**. The Microsoft Developer's Network level 1 is the one absolutely indispensable resource for Windows developers regardless of the language that they are using. This book will help you in understanding the concepts that are covered by MSDN, and will help you apply the C and C++ examples to Visual Basic.

- **Check in with us**. We're working in conjunction with Desaware to establish an ongoing online support and update service for this book. To receive the latest information you can visit www.desaware.com where you will find an area dedicated to this book. You can also subscribe to Desaware's mailing list by sending a message to listserv@desaware.com with "Subscribe" in the subject line. Finally, you can request a free subscription to our periodic newsletter which often has API related information (a recent issue had a Win32 API "cheat sheet")—just send your mailing address to support@desaware.com and request a subscription to the Desaware Visual Basic Bulletin.

■ **Experiment.** When in doubt, try it. There are very few API operations that can truly screw up your system (watch out when playing with the file system and registry functions). Take advantage of the fact that NT is extremely secure (and Windows 95 is fairly secure) and try things. Explore what is possible using both this book and MSDN. If you find something really cool, drop us a line. We're still learning too.

20

Building an API Class Library

THE APPEARANCE OF CLASSES IN VISUAL BASIC IS POSSIBLY THE SINGLE most significant development in the language since it first came out. While classes under Visual Basic do not meet the full definition of a class in a true object-oriented language, they do fill one of the important requirements: the ability to associate methods and properties with a structure that contains private and public data. A complete discussion of how to use classes effectively, and what it means to be a true object-oriented class, is a subject for an entire book, and beyond the scope of what can be covered here. You may wish to review the Visual Basic documentation regarding the use of classes before continuing.

Class Library Design

While there is a temptation to focus on the OLE aspects of classes—specifically the ability to use them to create OLE servers—for most programmers the real value of classes should be in their use within applications for general programming tasks. Chapter 19 has already introduced the idea of using a class library to encapsulate parts of the Win32 API in order to provide an additional degree of safety at the cost of some performance.

This book includes not one, but two implementations of an API class library to help you learn how to take advantage of the power of the Win32 API. First, you have the current edition of the Desaware API Class library. This is a commercial quality class library written in Visual Basic that you can use in the following ways:

- Add the classes to your application and use them directly.

- Compile the classes into your own ActiveX OLE DLL server for use by your applications.

- Look at the classes for examples of how to implement hundreds of API functions.

- Cut and paste sample code from the class library to add to your own application.

Because full source code for the class library is provided, you can use it in the ways that best suit your own needs.

This edition of the class library is fairly comprehensive in terms of covering the core Win32 API. It provides support for both 16-and 32-bit API calls (where appropriate) and includes complete source code. This class library is provided as is, without warranty or support. For information on obtaining support or updates for this class library, send e-mail to Desaware at support@desaware.com. Subscribers to Desaware's SpyWorks Professional will automatically receive the latest updates to the class library, including classes for subclassing, Windows hooks, and other advanced Win32 classes as they are developed—and, of course, technical support.

Design Criteria for an API Class Library

The critical first steps in any software project are to specify the requirements for the software, and choose design criteria. Without a good understanding of exactly what you want to accomplish, it will be impossible to make intelligent design trade-offs. Some of the questions that apply in this case are, How important is performance? How about safety and ease of use? How steep a learning curve is involved in using the classes, and how easy are they to use? And what about long term reliability and support?

The following choices were made in developing the Desaware API Class library as it is presented here.

Source Code Distribution

The Desaware API Class Library was designed from the start to be included with this book. This influenced the choice to write it in Visual Basic and to include complete source code. Even if you never use an API class or object library, the source code provides literally hundreds of examples of API function calls.

Including the source code also offers the greatest flexibility in terms of use. If you wish to deploy a standard library that is safe to use, is shareable among applications, and does not need to maximize performance, you can simply compile the class library into an OLE DLL server. If you do not wish to distribute another DLL and wish to achieve higher performance, you can include the classes directly into your application, cutting out those functions that you do not need in order to reduce the size of your program. For use of selected API functions with the best possible performance, you can cut and paste portions of the code from the class library into your own application as needed.

Safety, Performance, and Choice of Language

The Desaware API Class Library was designed to provide a safe layer for most API calls. In every case, safety was chosen over performance. Fairly robust error checking is implemented. At the same time, there are a number of "dangerous" functions included that provide additional flexibility for those who need it.

The choice to implement the library in Visual Basic (as opposed to C++) was dictated by the desire to provide additional sample code demonstrating the use of API functions from Visual Basic. With the introduction of native code compilation in Visual Basic 5.0, there is little or no performance cost in this approach. Finally, you can always gain improved performance by copying code from the class library into your program.

API Compatibility and Learning Curve

The Desaware API Class Library follows the philosophy set by Microsoft with their C++ Foundation Classes—the class function names match their corresponding API function names. Parameters are as similar as possible. This choice means that once you are acquainted with the use of the Windows API, it becomes fairly easy to find the equivalent class function and learn how to use it.

End User Support

It is my view that including unsupported software or components in an application is at least a mild form of insanity (or suicide, as the case may be). At the same time, the economics of book publishing make it impossible to provide free technical support or updates for this class library (or, for that matter, the rest of the sample code and information in the book).

One solution to this dilemma is provided by inclusion of the source code for the library—it allows you to support the code effectively yourself.

Regarding distribution, you are welcome to incorporate these classes into your own applications, or to cut and paste code from these classes into your own applications. You may create your own OLE server with these classes that is designed for use with your applications. In all of these cases, there are no restrictions or royalties on use of this class library. There are two exceptions: First, you may not distribute your own API class library or API object server that uses code from these classes without first obtaining a distribution license from Desaware. Second, if you distribute source code with your application and wish to include the source code for these classes, you must first contact Desaware for licensing information. Don't hesitate to call or send e-mail if you have any questions.

Choosing Classes

The next question that arises when designing a class library is how to define the initial classes and how they will encapsulate the various API objects and functions. When it comes to the core Windows API, this task is actually quite simple. The classes divide out as outlined below.

Classes That Represent Windows Objects and Architecture

The following classes are the "core" classes that reflect key Windows concepts or architecture.

dwSystem   This class is used to obtain information about the system and to retrieve and set system settings. It encapsulates key functions such as GetSystemMetrics and SystemParametersInfo. It also allows you to set and retrieve various system colors. Many of the functions defined in Chapter 6 will be found here.

dwWindow   This class encapsulates the functions that work with windows on the screen. Generally speaking, any function that takes a window handle as its first parameter will fit into this class. Most of the functions described in Chapter 5 will be found here.

dwDeviceContext   This class encapsulates the functions that work with device contexts. Generally speaking, any function that takes a device context as its first parameter will fit into this class. Most of the functions described in Chapters 7 and 8 will be found here.

Classes That Represent Windows Data Structures and Objects

The following classes correspond to commonly used Windows API data structures and are often used as parameters to methods of the core API classes.

Parameter	Description
dwRect	This object contains a RECT data structure that describes a rectangle.
dwPoint	This object contains a POINTAPI data structure that describes a point.
dwRegion	This object corresponds to region objects.
dwSize	This object contains a SIZE data structure that describes a size.

Classes That Represent GDI Objects

The following classes correspond to GDI graphic objects. They are often used as parameters to methods of the dwDeviceContext class.

Parameter	Description
dwBursh	Corresponds to a GDI brush object
dwPen	Corresponds to a GDI pen object
dwMetaFile	Corresponds to a GDI metafile object

Secondary Classes That Encapsulate Additional Functionality

The following classes are created and exposed by the core classes to encapsulate additional API functionality.

Parameter	Description
dwCPInfo	Used to retrieve information about code pages.
dwDevCaps	Used to obtain information about a device. Encapsulates the GetDeviceCaps function.
dwLogBrush	Used to obtain information about a logical brush.
dwMetrics	Used in conjunction with the dwSystem object to obtain information about the system. Encapsulates the GetSystemMetrics function.
dwOSVerInfo	Used in conjunction with the dwSystem object to obtain system version information.
dwSysColor	Used in conjunction with the dwSystem object to retrieve and set system colors.

Class Library Implementation

This section describes how the Desaware API Class library is implemented and explains the principles so that you can apply these techniques to your own classes or to modify the classes presented here. Note: Due to the production schedule, the version of the class library on the CD-ROM is slightly more recent than the one on which this chapter was based. In the event of differences between the listings in the book and those on the CD-ROM, the CD-ROM listings will be correct.

Function Names and Parameters

One of the best ways to make an API class library easy to learn is to have the class methods (class functions) match their corresponding API function names. Listing 20.1 shows a partial listing of the declaration section for the dwRECT class that encapsulates the API RECT structure, where you can see that this is the case. Each API function has been given a new name internal to Visual Basic that is the original API name with the prefix "api." Creating these new aliases makes it possible to use the actual API name as a class function name without conflict. Conditional compilation is used to allow the class to work with both Win16 and Win32. In fact, it is designed to eliminate the need to use conditional compilation elsewhere in the application.

Listing 20.1   Partial Listing of Declarations for Class dwRECT

```
Option Explicit

' Class dwRECT
' Desaware API Toolkit object library
' Copyright (c) 1996 by Desaware
' All rights reserved

Private InternalRect As RECT

#If Win32 Then
Private Declare Function apiCopyRect& Lib "user32" Alias _
 "CopyRect" (lpDestRect As RECT, lpSourceRect As RECT)
Private Declare Function apiInflateRect& Lib "user32" Alias _
 "InflateRect" (lpRect As RECT, ByVal x As Long, ByVal y As Long)
Private Declare Function apiIntersectRect& Lib "user32" Alias _
 "IntersectRect" (lpDestRect As RECT, lpSrc1Rect As RECT, _
 lpSrc2Rect As RECT)
#Else ' Win16
Private Declare Function apiCopyRect% Lib "user" Alias _
 "CopyRect" (lpDestRect As RECT, lpSourceRect As RECT)
Private Declare Function apiInflateRect% Lib "user" Alias _
 "InflateRect" (lpRect As RECT, ByVal x As Integer, ByVal y _
 As Integer)
Private Declare Function apiIntersectRect% Lib "user" Alias _
 "IntersectRect" (lpDestRect As RECT, lpSrc1Rect As RECT, _
 lpSrc2Rect As RECT)
#End If 'WIN32
```

Encapsulating Structures

As you can see in Listing 20.1, the dwRECT class contains an actual RECT structure called InternalRect. The structure defaults to the empty rectangle, because all of the variables in the InternalRect structure are initialized to zero by Visual Basic when the structure is created. Individual variables within the structure are accessed via Get/Let properties as shown in Listing 20.2. Note how the property names are identical to the standard RECT structure field names. This close correspondence between the class and the encapsulated structure helps make the class easy to use.

The InflateRect function demonstrates several important techniques. The class function name matches the API function name, eliminating the need to learn and remember a separate class function name.

The parameters are long variables instead of variants. This will work under Win16 even though the Win16 InflateRect function requires integer parameters. In that case, VB will automatically convert the long variables to

integers for the API call. This choice is dictated purely by performance—there is no benefit to using variant parameters in this case and there is a performance benefit to using long parameters.

If you compare the InflateRect class function with the API function, you will see that the only difference between their parameters is that the API function requires a RECT structure as a parameter. InflateRect assumes that when you call the InflateRect class function, you wish to operate on the internal rectangle encapsulated by the class. This is a very common convention in this type of class library.

The IntersectRect API function requires three separate RECT structures as parameters, the first of which is a destination rectangle for the result. Following this parameter convention, the first parameter is replaced by the InternalRect structure and the other two are replaced by dwRECT objects. The InflateRect function thus becomes, "Assign this dwRect object with the intersection of two other dwRect objects."

Listing 20.2   Partial Listing of Class dwRECT

```
Public Property Get left() As Long
    left = InternalRect.left
End Property

Public Property Let left(vNewValue As Long)
    InternalRect.left = vNewValue
End Property

Public Property Get right() As Long
    right = InternalRect.right
End Property

Public Property Let right(vNewValue As Long)
    InternalRect.right = vNewValue
End Property


Public Sub InflateRect(ByVal x As Long, ByVal y As Long)
    Dim dl&
    #If Win32 Then
        dl& = apiInflateRect(InternalRect, x, y)
        If dl = ¯ Then RaiseRectError
    #Else
        Call apiInflateRect(InternalRect, x, y)
    #End If
End Sub

Public Function IntersectRect(rcSrc1 As dwRECT, rcSrc2 As dwRECT) As Boolean
```

Listing 20.2   Partial Listing of Class dwRECT (Continued)

```
    Dim rc1 As RECT
    Dim rc2 As RECT
    rcSrc1.CopyToRECT agGetAddressForObject(rc1.left)
    rcSrc2.CopyToRECT agGetAddressForObject(rc2.left)
    IntersectRect = apiIntersectRect(InternalRect, rc1, rc2)
End Function
```

There will be cases where it is necessary to access the internal structure of an object directly. Visual Basic cannot expose structures as public members of classes, so this class library provides a mechanism to obtain the memory address of the internal structure using the GetAddress class member. The IntersectRect function is an example of this; the API function requires RECT structures as parameters, so it creates two temporary RECT structures and loads them based on the dwRECT objects passed as parameters. You could load these two structures (rc1 and rc2) one member at a time by accessing the properties of each dwRECT parameter, however, this will be rather slow and for some structures may not be possible. A more "dangerous" but faster approach is used here to copy the InternalRect structures of the two objects directly into the two local structures. The CopyToRECT function copies the InternalRect structure from the current object into a RECT structure at the address specified.

The principles for finding the address of a structure are covered in Chapter 3 and Chapter 15 (and various other places in this book). Now, it just happens that for the RECT structure, the way it is stored within Visual Basic is identical to the format of the structure as it would be passed to an API function. This will not always be the case—the alignment issues and string issues discussed in Chapter 15 explain why the organization of the structure within VB is often larger than it is when passed as a parameter. For those cases, you would need two separate functions: one similar to CopyToRECT that would copy data in the format expected by API functions, and a separate one that would copy data in the format used internally by Visual Basic. The CopyRect function shows how an internal format copy works (except that it copies into the InternalRect structure instead of out of the structure to another buffer).

```
Public Sub CopyToRECT(ByVal lprc As Long)
    If lprc = 0 Then RaiseRectError 5
    agCopyData InternalRect, ByVal lprc, Len(InternalRect)
End Sub

Public Function GetAddress() As Long
    GetAddress = agGetAddressForObject(InternalRect.left)
End Function
```

```
Public Sub CopyRect(rc As dwRECT)
    agCopyData ByVal rc.GetAddress, GetAddress(), LenB(InternalRect)
End Sub
```

Encapsulating Objects

When using a class to encapsulate an object, the general rule is to initialize the API object when the class is created or soon after, and to free or delete the object when the class object is destroyed. This approach allows the class library implementation to take responsibility for freeing any Windows objects or resources. This is illustrated by the dwBrush object, a partial listing for which is shown in Listing 20.3.

The dwBrush object can hold two types of brushes: those that it creates itself, and those that it receives from another source such as the system. The bCreated variable keeps track of the type of brush. If it is TRUE, the brush handle will be deleted by the Cleanup function. Cleanup is called any time the class is destroyed, or when the brush is changed. This helps prevent resource leaks—creation of resources that are not deleted. On rare occasions, you may need to assign the brush handle directly. In this case, the class assumes by default that the handle should not be deleted. The bCreated flag can be set to TRUE to force deletion of the object using the Created property (which can also read the bCreated variable). Note that you cannot set the bCreated variable to FALSE—once the class takes "ownership" of the object, it will not give it up. Of course, you can always change the code to make this possible if you prefer.

This class is defined to always contain a valid brush handle. It is initialized to the stock white brush when the class is created, and is careful to never set the brush handle to an invalid handle.

Listing 20.3   **Partial Listing of Class dwBrush**

```
Option Explicit

' Class dwBrush
' Brush drawing object control and configuration class
' Copyright (c) 1996 by Desaware
' Part of the Desaware API Classes Library

' Brush objects always reference a valid handle, stock or created

#If Win32 Then
Private ihBrush As Long
#Else
Private ihBrush As Integer
```

Listing 20.3   Partial Listing of Class dwBrush (Continued)

```
#End If

Private bCreated As Boolean    ' Brush was created

#If Win32 Then
Private Declare Function apiGetStockObject& Lib "gdi32" Alias "GetStockObject" _
(ByVal nIndex As Long)
Private Declare Function apiDeleteObject& Lib "gdi32" Alias "DeleteObject" _
(ByVal hObject As Long)
Private Declare Function apiCreateSolidBrush& Lib "gdi32" Alias _
"CreateSolidBrush" (ByVal crColor As Long)

#Else
Private Declare Function apiGetStockObject% Lib "gdi" Alias "GetStockObject" _
(ByVal nIndex As Integer)
Private Declare Function apiDeleteObject% Lib "gdi" Alias "DeleteObject" (ByVal _
hObject As Integer)
Private Declare Function apiCreateSolidBrush% Lib "gdi" Alias _
"CreateSolidBrush" (ByVal crColor As Long)
#End If 'WIN32

Public Property Get hBrush() As Long
    hBrush = ihBrush
End Property

Public Property Let hBrush(vNewValue As Long)
    #If Win32 Then
        If apiGetObjectType(vNewValue) <> OBJ_BRUSH Then
            RaiseBrushError DWERR_INVALIDPARAMETER
        End If
    #End If

    Cleanup
    ihBrush = vNewValue
End Property

Public Property Get Created() As Boolean
    Created = bCreated
End Property

Public Property Let Created(vNewValue As Boolean)
    If vNewValue Then bCreated = True
End Property
```

Listing 20.3   Partial Listing of Class dwBrush (Continued)

```
Private Sub Class_Initialize()
    ihBrush = apiGetStockObject(WHITE_BRUSH)
End Sub

' Delete any allocated objects
Public Sub Cleanup()
    If bCreated Then
        Call apiDeleteObject(ihBrush)
        bCreated = False
        ihBrush = apiGetStockObject(WHITE_BRUSH)
    End If
End Sub

Private Sub Class_Terminate()
    Cleanup
End Sub


Public Sub CreateSolidBrush(ByVal crColor As Long)
    Dim ret&
    ret& = apiCreateSolidBrush(crColor)
    If ret& = ¯ Then RaiseBrushError
    Cleanup
    ihBrush = ret&
    bCreated = True
End Sub


Private Sub RaiseBrushError(Optional errval)
' fix this so it can take no numbers
    Dim useerr%
    If IsMissing(errval) Then
        RaiseBrushError DWERR_APIRESULT
    Else
        RaiseError errval, "dwBrush"
    End If
End Sub

Public Property Get WHITE_BRUSH() As Integer
    WHITE_BRUSH = ¯
End Property

Public Property Get LTGRAY_BRUSH() As Integer
    LTGRAY_BRUSH = 1
End Property

Public Property Get GRAY_BRUSH() As Integer
    GRAY_BRUSH = 2
```

Listing 20.3   Partial Listing of Class dwBrush (Continued)

```
End Property

Public Property Get DKGRAY_BRUSH() As Integer
    DKGRAY_BRUSH = 3
End Property

Public Property Get BLACK_BRUSH() As Integer
    BLACK_BRUSH = 4
End Property

Public Property Get NULL_BRUSH() As Integer
    NULL_BRUSH = 5
End Property

Public Sub GetStockObject(idx%)
    Cleanup
    If idx < WHITE_BRUSH Or idx > NULL_BRUSH Then
        RaiseBrushError DWERR_INVALIDPARAMETER
    Else
        ihBrush = apiGetStockObject(idx)
    End If
End Sub
```

Working with Constants

The Windows API contains a number of functions whose behavior depends on a parameter that can take on the value of one of a set of constants. One example of this is the GetStockObject API function, which returns a stock pen, brush, or font based on a numeric parameter. The dwBrush object, like the other encapsulated objects, is set by calling functions belonging to the class. Thus, you create a brush by first creating a dwBrush object, then calling the CreateSolidBrush function for the class. This promotes a consistent and modular programming style.

To remain consistent with this approach, it stands to reason that the class should also have a GetStockObject function to initialize the object to one of the stock system brushes. There are two approaches one can take here. One is to create six different functions, one for each brush. You could thus call myop.WHITE_BRUSH() or perhaps myop.GetStockWhiteBrush to initialize the object to the white system brush. In this approach, the class would not actually expose the GetStockObject function.

As you will soon see, an approach similar to this is used elsewhere in the class library. In this case it was decided to expose GetStockObject in order to remain as close as possible to the API. The constants are exposed as read-only properties that return the constant values. If Visual Basic will, in the future, support public constants in classes, code that uses these classes should port easily (if not automatically) to work with those constants. Visual Basic 5.0 does support public enumerations which could be used to expose these constants as well. For now it was decided to continue the current approach both to ensure ongoing compatibility with VB4 and to keep the constants specific to the class (VB5 enumerations are always global). A stock white brush can be created for an object of this class using the syntax:

```
mybrush.GetStockObject(mybrush.WHITE_BRUSH)
```

Listing 20.4 demonstrates the other approach for working with constants. The dwSysColor class encapsulates the SetSysColors and GetSysColor functions, allowing you to set and retrieve system colors. Instead of exposing the constants as read-only properties that return constant values to use with the SetSysColors and GetSysColor functions, the constant names allow you to directly access the system colors.

For example, if you have an object of type dwSysColor called mysycolor, you can obtain the current setting of the button highlight color as follows:

```
ButtonHighlightColor = mysyscolor.BTNHIGHLIGHT
```

The property name corresponds to the constant name without the prefix. In this case COLOR_BTNHIGHLIGHT becomes the property BTNHIGH-LIGHT. COLOR_3DDKSHADOW becomes DKSHADOW3D due the inability of Visual Basic to accept property names that begin with a number. Why use this approach instead of the constant approach? Because it is hoped that code developed this way will be better structured and easier to read. This is especially true when you look at the way this particular class will most often be used. Generally speaking, you will never create an object in the dwSysColor class. Instead, you will access the SysColor object that is created as part of the dwSystem class. If you have a dwSystem object with the name mysysobject, you can read or set the button highlight color using the following code:

```
ButtonHighlightColor = mysysobject.SysColor.BTNHIGHLIGHT
mysysobject.SysColor.BTNHIGHLIGHT = NewButtonHighlightColor
```

This technique is also used to obtain system information using the dwMetrics class. The dwSystem object contains a public dwMetrics object named Metrics. You can, for example, obtain the horizontal and vertical screen resolution using the following code:

```
Dim sysobject As New dwSystem

MsgBox "Screen Resolution is: " & sysobject.Metrics.CXSCREEN & " X " & _
sysobject.Metrics.CYSCREEN
```

This provides a very concise and easy-to-use encapsulation of the Get-SystemMetrics function.

Listing 20.4   Partial Listing of Class dwSysColor

```
Option Explicit

' Class dwSysColor
' Desaware API Toolkit object library
' Copyright (c) 1996 by Desaware
' All rights reserved


#If Win32 Then
Private Declare Function apiGetSysColor Lib "user32" Alias _
"GetSysColor" (ByVal nIndex As Long) As Long
Private Declare Function apiSetSysColors Lib "user32" Alias _
"SetSysColors" (ByVal nChanges As Long, lpSysColor As Long, _
lpColorValues As Long) As Long
#Else
Private Declare Function apiGetSysColor& Lib "user" Alias _
"GetSysColor" (ByVal nIndex%)
Private Declare Sub apiSetSysColors Lib "user" Alias _
"SetSysColors" (ByVal nChanges%, lpSysColor%, lpColorValues&)
#End If

Private Const COLOR_BTNTEXT = 18
Private Const COLOR_INACTIVECAPTIONTEXT = 19
Private Const COLOR_BTNHIGHLIGHT = 2⁻
Private Const COLOR_3DDKSHADOW = 21
Private Const COLOR_3DFACE = COLOR_BTNFACE
Private Const COLOR_3DHIGHLIGHT = COLOR_BTNHIGHLIGHT
Private Const COLOR_3DHILIGHT = COLOR_BTNHIGHLIGHT

Private Sub RaiseSysColorError(Optional errval)
    If IsMissing(errval) Then
        RaiseError DWERR_APIRESULT, "dwSysColor"
    Else
        RaiseError errval, "dwSysColor"
    End If
End Sub

Private Function GetSysColor(ByVal iColor As Integer) As Long
    GetSysColor = apiGetSysColor(iColor)
End Function

Private Sub SetSysColors(ByVal lpSysColor As Integer, _
ByVal lpColorValue As Long)
    Dim newcolor&
    Dim idx&
    Dim res&

    idx& = lpSysColor
```

Listing 20.4 **Partial Listing of Class dwSysColor (Continued)**

```
        newcolor = lpColorValue
        res& = apiSetSysColors(1, idx, newcolor)
        If res& = ⁻ Then RaiseSysColorError DWERR_APIRESULT
End Sub


Public Property Get BTNHIGHLIGHT() As Long
    BTNHIGHLIGHT = GetSysColor(COLOR_BTNHIGHLIGHT)
End Property

Public Property Let BTNHIGHLIGHT(ByVal newcolor&)
    Call SetSysColors(COLOR_BTNHIGHLIGHT, newcolor&)
End Property

Public Property Get DKSHADOW3D() As Long
    c3DDKSHADOW = GetSysColor(COLOR_3DDKSHADOW)
End Property

Public Property Let DKSHADOW3D(ByVal newcolor&)
    Call SetSysColors(COLOR_3DDKSHADOW, newcolor&)
End Property
```

Error Handling

This class library takes a fairly aggressive stand with regard to verifying parameters and testing API function results in accordance with the original design criteria that makes safety a high priority. It uses the Visual Basic error object to raise errors when they occur. The advantage of this approach is that it is compatible with the use of the classes in an OLE DLL server.

In cases where a class object must be initialized, functions for the class test to make sure that the object is valid before calling the API function associated with the class. Error reporting is centralized to make it easy to change the error handling for the class library. Listing 20.3 included the function RaiseBrushError, which provides centralized error handling for the dwBrush class. This function in turn calls the RaiseError function in module DWERRORS.BAS.

It is a good idea to turn on error handling when using this class library. When an API result error occurs, you can use the GetLastError API function (also exposed in DWERROR.BAS) to determine the nature of the error.

Bringing It All Together : The dwDeviceContext Class

The dwDeviceContext class makes use of almost all of the techniques described earlier in this section. Listing 20.5 shows the private variables belonging to the class. The iHDC variable holds the handle to the device context. It is zero if the object is not initialized. Dcsource is a very important variable that keeps track of how the iHDC device context handle was obtained. If it was created by the class library, the class will call DeleteDC to free the handle when the object is destroyed. If it was obtained using the GetDC function, the handle will be released using ReleaseDC. If it was assigned from the Hdc property of a Visual Basic form or control, no clean up is required—it wouldn't do to try to delete a device context that is in use by Visual Basic. If the device context is that of a metafile, the metafile will be closed and deleted. The task of a programmer using this class is simplified by letting the class code keep track of the type of device context and perform the necessary clean up. However, you can see that there is a cost for this service in terms of performance and the additional code required to keep track of the object type and decide how to delete it.

The DeviceCaps object is used to encapsulate the GetDeviceCaps function. It makes it easy to obtain information about this dwDeviceContext object.

The iHDC property can be set directly using the class hDC property, in which case the class assumes that you are assigning the property from the Hdc property of a VB form or control. In this case, the class performs an immediate SaveDC operation and stores the result in the InitialSaveDC variable. A RestoreDC operation is performed automatically when the object is terminated. The device context is restored when the class is terminated. This means that if you create the dwDeviceContext object, perform operations, then delete it, you need not worry about restoring the initial device context state—critical when using API functions in Visual Basic, as you have seen throughout this book.

If you use the GetDC class member and pass it a dwWindow object, a reference to the dwWindow object is stored in the objwnd variable. This ensures that the dwWindow object is not destroyed before the associated dwDeviceContext object terminates.

Listing 20.5   Declaration Section for the dwDeviceContext Class

```
Option Explicit

' Class dwDeviceContext
' Device context object control and configuration class
' Copyright (c) 1996 by Desaware
' Part of the Desaware API Classes Library

#If Win32 Then
Private iHDC As Long
#Else
Private iHDC As Integer
#End If
```

Listing 20.5   Declaration Section for the dwDeviceContext Class (Continued)

```
' Who owns this DC?
' ¯ - This DC is via GetDC
' 1 - This DC is via CreateDC or CreateCompatibleDC
' 2 - This DC is via direct setting
' 3 - This DC is a regular metafile
' 4 - This DC is an enhanced metafile
Dim Dcsource%

Public DeviceCaps As New dwDevCaps

' InitialSaveDC - On assign or GetDC we do an initial SaveDC
' to store original VB state. This also makes sure
' all objects are selected out when we delete/destroy the DC
Private InitialSaveDC As Long

' Which window (if any) owns this device context?
Private objwnd As dwWindow


' Currently selected objects
Private iCurrentBrush As dwBrush
Private iCurrentBitmap As dwBitmap
Private iCurrentPen As dwPen

Private OriginalBrush As Long
Private OriginalPen As Long
Private OriginalBitmap As Long
```

Selecting Objects with dwDeviceContext

The process of selecting objects posed an interesting dilemma for this class. The SelectObject API function accepts pens, brushes, or bitmaps as parameters. It returns the original object selected so that you can reselect it later to restore the original object—important, since you do not want to delete GDI objects that are selected into device contexts, or destroy a device context that has selected an object that you need. This means that the use of SelectObject tends to follow the pseudocode shown here:

```
Oldobject = SelectObject (pen, brush or bitmap)
Use the device context
Call SelectObject(Oldobject) ò restore the original object
```

This class could easily have followed this technique. A single SelectObject method for the class could be defined to accept any object as a parameter. It could then test the type of object, perform the selection, and return an object of the appropriate type to the calling function.

This approach, while possible, involves quite a bit of overhead, and while performance was not the highest priority for this class library, it was certainly not ignored. As a result, this class takes a slightly different approach for selecting an object that strays only slightly from the API function and provides better performance and additional functionality. Instead of a single SelectObject function, there is a separate SelectObject function for each object type. Listing 20.6 shows the SelectObjectBrush function, which is used to select a brush object.

When you select a brush for the first time using this function, it stores the original default brush for the device context in the OriginalBrush member of the class. It also stores a reference to the dwBrush object that was used for the selection in the iCurrentBrush variable. If you then select a different brush, the OriginalBrush variable remains unchanged, but the iCurrentBrush reference is updated.

You may pass *Nothing* as a parameter of this function at any time to restore the original brush. Thus, selecting an object using this class takes the general sequence:

```
SelectObjectBrush mybrush
Use the device context
SelectObjectBrush Nothing
```

There is no need for the calling function to store the original brush in a temporary variable. Since the dwDeviceContext object holds a reference to each object in use, you need not worry about accidentally deleting a dwBrush object that is in use; it won't be deleted until it is released by the dwDeviceContext class.

Listing 20.6   Brush Selection Function for dwDeviceContext

```
Public Sub SelectObjectBrush(br As dwBrush)
    Dim oldbrush&
    If iHDC = ¯ Then RaiseHdcError DWERR_UNINITIALIZED

    If br Is Nothing Then    ' Clear existing brush
        ' No brush selected
        If iCurrentBrush Is Nothing Then Exit Sub
        Call apiSelectObject(iHDC, OriginalBrush)
        Set iCurrentBrush = Nothing
    Else
        oldbrush = apiSelectObject(iHDC, br.hBrush)
        If OriginalBrush = ¯ Then OriginalBrush = oldbrush
        Set iCurrentBrush = br
    Else
        RaiseHdcError DWERR_INVALIDPARAMETER
    End If
End Sub
```

Using the Class Library

Due to the close correspondence between the API functions described in the book and the class functions, you should find this class library extremely easy to use. A quick look at the source code, along with an understanding of the techniques described in this chapter, should serve to provide you with all of the information that you need to use it effectively. This section includes a number of trivial sample programs that illustrate some ways in which you can use the class library.

Using dwRECT

Listing 20.7 shows the typical way in which class objects are used within an application. You must use the New statement to actually create an instance of the class. If the class library is compiled into an OLE server, you will use the CreateObject function to create a new instance of each class object. Clearly, this will entail additional performance overhead, so if all you need are a few classes or functions you may prefer to add the classes directly into your project.

Listing 20.7   dwRECT Sample

```
Dim rc As New dwRECT
    Dim rc2 As New dwRECT
    Dim rc3 As New dwRECT
    Dim pt As New dwPoint
    rc.SetRect 5, 5, 1¯, 1¯
    rc2.CopyRect rc
    Debug.Print "rc2: " & rc2.left, rc2.top, rc2.right, rc2.bottom
    rc2.InflateRect 1¯, 1¯
    Debug.Print "rc2: " & rc2.left, rc2.top, rc2.right, rc2.bottom
    rc3.IntersectRect rc, rc2
    Debug.Print "rc3: " & rc3.left, rc3.top, rc3.right, rc3.bottom
    pt.x = 7
    pt.y = 7
    Debug.Print "pt in rect: " & rc3.PtInRect(pt)
    pt.x = 1
    Debug.Print "pt in rect: " & rc3.PtInRect(pt)
```

Using dwWindow

The dwWindow class provides an easy way to manipulate and interrogate windows. The class has a single property, the hWnd or window handle. To initialize the class, set the hWnd property to the window handle of the window you want the class to operate on. From then on, all of the class's methods operate on the specified window. No actions are required to clean up after you are done with the class. Listing 20.8 illustrates a typical application of this class.

Listing 20.8   dwWindow Sample

```
Dim window1 as New dwWindow
Dim window2 as New dwWindow

' This is how you would set up an instance of the dwWindow class.
window1.hWnd = form1.hWnd
window2.hWnd = button1.hWnd

' Now you can perform actions on each window.
' For example, you can move and resize the button with the line:
window2.MoveWindow 2¯, 2¯, 2¯¯, 2¯¯, True

' no cleanup needed
End Sub
```

Using dwSystem

The dwSystem class encapsulates many functions that apply to the overall system and environment. No set up or clean up actions are required. Methods of the dwSystem class either apply to the system as a whole, or simply are not related to any particular window or device context. The Metrics object is a sub-object of this class that can be used to access system metrics (corresponding to the GetSystemMetrics API function). The SysColor object is a sub-object of this class that can be used to set and retrieve system color settings. Listing 20.9 illustrates a typical application of this class.

Listing 20.9   dwSystem Sample

```
Dim system1 As New dwSystem
    Dim pnt As New dwPoint
    Dim oldcolor&

    ' no setup needed

    ' Here is an example of how you would use a system _
      class method.
    ' This gets the current position of the mouse cursor _
      (in pixels).
    Set pnt = system1.GetCursorPos()
    Debug.Print "Cusor Position: " & pnt.x, pnt.y

    ' Here are examples of how you would use the sub objects.
    ' This sets the caption bar of the active window to red.
    oldcolor = system1.SysColor.ACTIVECAPTION
```

Listing 20.9   **dwSystem Sample (Continued)**

```
      system1.SysColor.ACTIVECAPTION = &HFF&
      MsgBox "Caption color changed"
      system1.SysColor.ACTIVECAPTION = oldcolor

      ' This gets the width of icons.
      Debug.Print "Icon width: " & system1.Metrics.CXICON

      ' no cleanup needed
End Sub
```

Using dwDeviceContext

The dwDeviceContext class provides the methods for using device contexts, which are necessary for drawing, printing text, manipulating bitmaps, and other graphical tasks. There are a number of ways to create an instance of the dwDeviceContext class. The easiest is to use a window's device context, shown in Listing 20.10. As always, the object is designed to clean up after itself.

Listing 20.10   **dwDeviceContext Sample**

```
Dim window1 As New dwWindow
Dim dContext1 As dwDeviceContext
Dim ClientRect As dwRECT

window1.hwnd = frmTest.hwnd

Set dContext1 = window1.GetDC()

' You could also do this the other way around:
' Set dContext1 = new dwDeviceContext
' Call dContext.GetDC(window1)

Set ClientRect = window1.GetClientRect

dContext1.MoveTo MakePoint(¯, ¯)
dContext1.LineTo MakePoint(ClientRect.right, ClientRect.bottom)
```

You could also set up a device context by setting the hDC property to a device context handle if you already have one. dwDeviceContext objects can also be obtained from other dwDeviceContext objects using the CreateCompatibleDC method.

Using Callbacks, APIGID32.DLL, dwcbk32d.ocx, and dwsbc32d.ocx

Visual Basic can access the vast majority of the Windows API functions. There are, however, a significant number of API functions that are not directly compatible with Visual Basic, but can be used with the help of a few DLL functions that are not part of the Windows API or of Visual Basic.

The disk that comes with this book contains a dynamic link library, APIGID32.DLL, and two demonstration custom controls, dwcbk32d.ocx and dwsbc32d.ocx, which will both prove useful in accessing the Windows API functions.

The functions in APIGID32.DLL serve several purposes:

- Manipulate memory and obtain addresses of VB objects

- Port I/O

- Miscellaneous data manipulation functions

dwcbk32d.ocx is a custom control that enables use of Windows API functions that require callback function addresses under Visual Basic 4.0. It is superseded under VB5 by the AddressOf operator. dwsbc32d.ocx is a demonstration subclassing control. APIGID32.DLL can be used freely and distributed with your Visual Basic applications. The CD-ROM that comes with this book includes the source code for this DLL as well. dwcbk32d.ocx and dwsbc32d.ocx are fully functional controls that execute only within the Visual Basic design time environment. They are provided for educational purposes. Commercial versions of these controls (and other controls that are useful for low-level API access from Visual Basic including VB5 subclassers with source code) are available as part of Desaware's SpyWorks package.

dwcbk32d.ocx-Generic Callback Custom Control

dwcbk32d.ocx is a custom control that enables use of Windows API callback functions. This control is a demonstration version of the Generic Callback custom control provided with Desaware's SpyWorks program. A 16-bit VBX version of this control, cbk.vbx, is included in the *Visual Basic Programmer's Guide to the Windows API* (16-bit edition), along with documentation on using callbacks from 16-bit Windows. The documentation provided here only covers Win32 callbacks—there are significant differences in parameter types and, in some cases, in functionality as well.

How Do Callback Functions Work?

In a number of situations, you may wish to enumerate objects. Consider the problem of listing all of the top-level windows in the system. One way to do this is to use the EnumWindows API function. This function works by calling a

user-defined function for each window. Similar enumeration functions follow the same principle for enumerating fonts, properties, GDI objects, and so on.

How do enumeration functions know which user-defined function to call? Like data objects, the code for functions is present in memory and has a memory address associated with it. The enumeration functions require as one of their parameters the address of a user-defined function to call. Figure A.1 illustrates the program flow used during such enumeration. The Windows application passes the address of a callback function to Windows. Windows then calls the function for each object being enumerated.

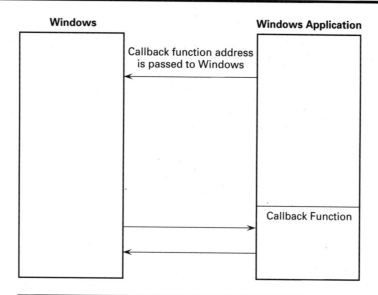

Figure A.1
Use of callback functions by traditional Windows applications

Visual Basic 5.0 allows you to obtain an address of a public VB function in a standard module to use as an enumeration function. For earlier versions of Visual Basic, the dwcbk32d.ocx custom control contains a built-in pool of function addresses that can be provided to an enumeration function. These addresses are obtained using the ProcAddress property. The Visual Basic application obtains the address of a callback function in dwcbk32d.ocx using the ProcAddress property, and passes it to Windows. Windows then calls the callback function, which in turn triggers a Visual Basic event for each object being enumerated.

Enumeration functions not only expect a function address, but they expect it to be a function of a certain type—it accepts certain parameters and returns certain values. The dwcbk32d.ocx custom control has a Type property that specifies the type of enumeration function in use. When the enumeration function calls the callback function address provided by the dwcbk32d.ocx custom control, the custom control triggers a Visual Basic event corresponding to the type of enumeration. Under VB5 it is the programmer's responsibility to declare the callback function correctly. Failure to do so will likely cause a memory exception.

Most enumeration functions provide a mechanism for stopping the enumeration process. dwcbk32d.ocx supports this capability by including a return value parameter to the Visual Basic event. This return value can be set by your program to specify the value that will be returned by the callback function. This return value usually determines whether the enumeration should continue. Refer to the description of each event in "Callback Types and Events," later in this appendix, for information on required return values.

Most enumeration functions provide a user-defined parameter that is passed to the enumeration function and in turn is passed to the callback function each time it is called. The value is then passed to the appropriate Visual Basic event. This parameter can be used in any way you choose. One common technique is to pass the address of a structure or block of memory. This block of memory can then be used to save information during the enumeration process so that when the original enumeration function returns it has all of the accumulated data available. This provides an alternative to using global variables to pass information back to the calling function.

Using dwcbk32d.ocx

The dwcbk32d.ocx custom control is added into your Visual Basic controls' toolbox using the Tools menu in the same way as any other Visual Basic custom control. Like the timer control, the dwcbk32d.ocx custom control is not displayed at runtime.

You can have as many controls loaded as you wish. The control does not actually obtain a function address from the pool until it is enabled using the Type property. The control maintains a pool of five function addresses that are shared by all controls in the application. If other programs are using all of the function addresses, an error will occur when the Type property is set.

When you wish to use an enumeration function, you simply set the Type property to the type of callback you wish to use. You can then use the ProcAddress property to obtain a long function address that can be passed as a parameter to the enumeration function. Table A.1 lists the most frequently used properties for the dwcbk32d.ocx custom control.

When you are finished with the enumeration, you can set the Type property back to 0 (disabled) to return the function address to the pool of callback functions.

During enumeration, the dwcbk32d.ocx event corresponding to the callback type will be triggered for each object being enumerated.

Table A.1 **dwcbk32d.ocx Properties**

Property	Description
(About)	When the "..." button in the property window is clicked, it will display information about the version and capabilities of the dwcbk32d.ocx custom control.
Convention	All API callbacks use the 'Pascal' or stdCall calling convention.
EventTrigger	Set to Immediate for use with API enumeration functions. Posted causes the dwcbk32d.ocx control to defer the actual event trigger by way of a posted message. This allows the control to work with some interrupt level callbacks. In this case the value of the PostedReturn property will be returned to windows.
Type	Refer to "Callback Types and Events," later in this appendix, for a description of the callback function types.
Type32Enabled	When TRUE, the Type will be set by the Type32 property instead of the Type property. This allows you to specify different callbacks for 16- and 32-bit versions of the control (only the 32-bit demo control is included with this book).
ProcAddress	When the Type property is not zero (disabled), this property returns the address of a callback function that can be passed to an enumeration function.

Callback Types and Events

This section describes the most frequently used types of callbacks supported by the version of the dwcbk32d.ocx custom control provided with this book. Each section describes the associated Type property value and corresponding Visual Basic event. You should not modify the values of parameters passed by this VB event unless otherwise noted in the description for that parameter.

■ AbortProc

```
Type property = 1ïAbortProc
```

Description The ProcAddress property provides the address for a function suitable for use with the SetAbortProc API function. Refer to the Chapter 12 function reference for more information on this function. The callback function is called periodically during printing to provide the user with the opportunity to cancel printing.

Visual Basic
Event Triggered AbortProc (hPr&, code&, retval&)

Visual Basic 5.0
Equivalent
Callback
Function

```
Public Function AbortProc(ByVal hPr&, ByVal code&) As Long
```

Event Parameter	Description
hPr	Long—A handle to a device context for the printer.
code	Long—Nonzero indicates that a printer error occurred. The constant SB_OUTOFDISK indicates that there is insufficient disk space for the output spool file on disk. When this occurs there is a chance that disk space will be freed up by other applications, so you need not abort printing.
retval	Long—Set this value to zero to cancel printing.

■ CommEvent

```
Type property = ¯ïDisabled
```

Description   This event is not used under Win32. The communications system for Win32 is substantially changed from Win16. Refer to the introductory section of the CD-ROM for information on serial communications under Win32.

■ Disabled

```
Type property = ¯ïDisabled
```

Description   This control is not active. No function is allocated from the internal function pool and the ProcAddress property value is not valid.

Visual Basic
Event Triggered   None.

■ EnumFonts

```
Type property = 2ïEnumFonts
```

Description   The ProcAddress property provides the address for a function suitable for use with the Enum-Fonts and EnumFontFamilies API functions. Refer to the Chapter 11 function reference for more information on these functions. This callback function is called for each font that is enumerated.

Visual Basic
Event Triggered

```
EnumFonts(lpLogFont&, lpTextMetrics&, nFontType&, lpData&, retval&)
```

Visual Basic 5.0
Equivalent
Callback
Function

```
Public Function EnumFontsProc(ByVal lpLogFont&, ByVal lpTextMetrics&, ByVal _
```

```
nFontType&, _ByVal lpData&) As Long
```

Event Parameter	Description
lpLogFont	Long—A 32-bit address to a LOGFONT data structure containing information about the enumerated font. A description of this structure can be found in Chapter 11.
lpTextMetrics	Long—A 32-bit address to a NEWTEXTMETRIC structure for TrueType fonts, or a TEXTMETRIC structure for non-TrueType fonts. A description of this structure can be found in Chapter 11.
nFontType	Long—A combination of zero or more of the following constants ORed together: DEVICE_FONTTYPE if this is a device font. RASTER_FONTTYPE if this is a bitmap raster font. TRUETYPE_FONTTYPE if this is a TrueType font.
lpData	Long—This is the same value passed by your program as the lPData parameter to the EnumFonts function. This is typically used to pass information to the callback function.
retval	Long—Set this value to zero to stop the enumeration.

■ EnumMetaFile

```
Type property = 3ïEnumMetaFile
```

Description

The ProcAddress property provides the address for a function suitable for use with the EnumMetaFile API function. Refer to the Chapter 8 function reference for more information on this function and sample code demonstrating its use. This callback function is called for each record in a metafile.

```
Visual Basic Event TriggeredEnumMetaFile (hDC&, lpHTable&, lpMFR&, nObj&, _
lpClientData&, retval&)
```

Visual Basic 5.0 Equivalent Callback Function

```
Public Function EnumMetaFileProc(ByVal hDC&, ByVal lpHTable&, ByVal lpMFR&, _
ByVal nObj&, ByVal lpClientData&) As Long
```

Event Parameter	Description
hDC	Long—A handle to the device context associated with the metafile.
lpHTable	Long—A 32-bit address to an integer table of GDI objects that are used by the metafile. This can include pens, brushes, and so on.
lpMFR	Long—A 32-bit address to a METARECORD structure defining a metafile record. A description of this structure can be found in Appendix B.
nObj	Long—The number of object handles contained in the object table referred to by lpHTable.

Event Parameter	Description
lpClientData	Long—This is the same value passed by your program as the lPClientData parameter to the EnumMetaFile function. This is typically used to pass information to the callback function.
retval	Long—Set this value to zero to stop the enumeration.

■ EnumObjects

`Type property = 4ïEnumObjects`

Description The ProcAddress property provides the address for a function suitable for use with the EnumObjects API function. Refer to the Chapter 8 function reference for more information on this function. This callback function is called for each GDI object that is enumerated.

Visual Basic Event Triggered `EnumObjects (lpLogObject&, lpData&, retval&)`

Visual Basic 5.0 Equivalent Callback Function `Public Function EnumObjectsProc(ByVal lpLogObject&, ByVal lpData&) As Long`

Event Parameter	Description
lpLogObject	Long—A 32-bit address to a LOGPEN or LOGBRUSH data structure depending on the type of object being enumerated. A description of this structure can be found in Appendix B.
lpData	Long—This is the same value passed by your program as the lPData parameter to the EnumObjects function. This is typically used to pass information to the callback function.
retval	Long—Set this value to zero to stop the enumeration.

■ EnumProps

`Type property = 5ïEnumProps`

Description The ProcAddress property provides the address for a function suitable for use with the EnumProps API function. Refer to the Chapter 15 function reference for more information on this function. This callback function is called for each property that is enumerated. Note that property in this case does not refer to Visual Basic properties but rather to Windows properties, as defined in Chapter 15.

Visual Basic Event Triggered `EnumProps (hWnd&, lpString$, hData&, retval&)`

Visual Basic 5.0
Equivalent
Callback
Function
```
Public Function EnumPropsProc(ByVal hWnd&, ByVal lpString&, ByVal hData&) As Long
```

Event Parameter	Description
hWnd	Long—A handle to the windows whose properties are being enumerated.
lpString	String—The string associated with the property being enumerated. Note: Under VB5, use the agGetStringFromPointer to convert the lpString address into a VB string.
hData	Long—The data associated with the property being enumerated.
retval	Long—Set this value to zero to stop the enumeration.

Warning

- Do not perform any operation that could yield control to other applications (such as the VB DoEvents function) during this event.

- Do not add new properties during this event.

- Do not remove properties during this event (except for the property being enumerated).

■ EnumWindows

```
Type property = 6ïEnumWindows
```

Description
The ProcAddress property provides the address for a function suitable for use with the Enum-Windows and other windows enumeration API functions. Refer to the Chapter 5 function reference for more information on these functions. This callback function is called for each window that is enumerated.

Visual Basic
Event Triggered
```
EnumWindows(hWnd&, lParam&, retval&)
```

Visual Basic 5.0
Equivalent
Callback
Function
```
Public Function EnumWindowsProc(ByVal hWnd&, ByVal lParam&) As Long
```

Event Parameter	Description
hWnd	Long—A handle to the window being enumerated.
lpParam	Long—This is the same value passed by your program as the lParam parameter to the EnumWindows function. This is typically used to pass information to the callback function.
retval	Long—Set this value to zero to stop the enumeration.

■ GrayString

```
Type property = 7ïGrayString
```

Description

The ProcAddress property provides the address for a function suitable for use with the Gray-String API function. Refer to the Chapter 11 function reference for more information on this function. This callback is typically used when you want to draw a grayed string (like those used when a control is disabled), but wish to customize the text output.

**Visual Basic
Event Triggered**

```
GrayString(hDC&, lpData&, nCount&, retval&)
```

**Visual Basic 5.0
Equivalent
Callback
Function**

```
Public Function GrayStringProc(ByVal hDC&, ByVal lpData&, ByVal nCount&) As Long
```

Event Parameter	Description
hDC	Long—A device context on which to draw the string. The string specified by lpData and nCount should be drawn at coordinates 0,0 of this device context.
lpData	Long—A 32-bit address of the string to draw.
nCount	Long—The number of characters to draw.
retval	Long—Set this value to TRUE (nonzero) to indicate that the drawing was successful. Zero on error. This result will be reflected in the result of the GrayString API function.

■ LineDDA

```
Type property = 8ïLineDDA
```

Description

The ProcAddress property provides the address for a function suitable for use with the LineDDA API function. Refer to the Chapter 8 function reference for more information on this function. This callback function is used to determine the x,y coordinates of each point in a line.

**Visual Basic
Event Triggered**

```
LineDDA (x&, y&, lpData&, retval&)
```

**Visual Basic 5.0
Equivalent
Callback
Function**

```
Public Function LineDDAProc(ByVal x&, ByVal y&, ByVal lpData&) As Long
```

Event Parameter	Description
x&, y&	Integer—The x and y coordinate of a point in a line specified by the LineDDA API function.
lpData	Long—This is the same value passed by your program as the lPData parameter to the LineDDA function. This is typically used to pass information to the callback function.
retval	Integer—Not used.

dwsbc32d.ocx-Subclassing Custom Control

dwsbc32d.ocx is a custom control that allows Visual Basic applications to subclass windows in their own or other applications. This control is a demonstration version of the dwsbc32.ocx subclassing custom control provided with Desaware's SpyWorks program. The CD-ROM for this book also includes the dwshk32d.ocx control which implements system hooks—a technique for intercepting messages on an application or system-wide basis.

Visual Basic 5.0 does make it possible to subclass in-process windows from within your application, however this book recommends that you continue to subclass windows from within a component, whether it is a commercial ActiveX control or DLL, or one that you author yourself.

The documentation given here provides a brief summary of how to use this control. Refer to Chapter 3 for an in-depth discussion of subclassing, and Chapter 16 for information on how subclassing can be used with individual messages and for sample programs.

Using dwsbc32d.ocx

The dwsbc32d.ocx custom control is added into your Visual Basic controls' toolbox using the File-Add command in the same way as any other Visual Basic custom control. Like the timer control, the dwcbk32d.ocx custom control is not displayed at runtime.

In general, using the dwsbc32d.ocx control requires three steps:

- Select the window to subclass either at design time (using the ctlParam property) or at runtime (by setting the HwndParam or AddHwnd property).

- Select the messages to detect using the Messages property.

- Add Code to the WndMessage or WndMessageX event to execute when the message is detected.

Use the Type property to specify if you wish to intercept the message before the default processing for the window, after the default processing for the window, or simply wish it to be posted as a notification.

When a message is detected by the dwsbc32d.ocx control, the WndMessage or WndMessageX events are triggered (depending on whether the message comes from the same application or a foreign application). This event contains all of the standard window function parameters (hWnd, msg, wparam, lparam), and two additional parameters: nodef and retval, which are described in Table A.2 under the description of the Type property.

A single dwsbc32d.ocx control can subclass any number of windows. A primary window to subclass may be specified using the CtlParam or HwndParam properties. Additional windows can be added to an internal subclassing array using the AddHwnd property. All windows subclass by a particular control share the same list of messages to detect.

Note: This control is provided for educational use and experimentation only. No technical support is available for this demonstration control at this time, though we may be able to provide limited online support at some future time (Send an e-mail message to support@desaware.com to receive updated information). This is especially important because subclassing is an extremely dangerous technology to use—it is safe and reliable once your code is correct, but it is common during the debugging process to crash not only your application, but others as well (not to mention, the entire system). This is especially true of this subclassing control, since it is capable of subclassing windows in other applications even under Windows NT.

There are many operations that cannot be performed safely during processing of messages, especially when the Type property is set to zero or one. You should especially avoid use of message boxes or breakpoints. For debugging, use the debug.print statement to obtain information on what is going on during your message routines.

Table A.2 lists the most frequently used properties for the dwsbc32d.ocx custom control.

Table A.2   **Most Frequently Used dwsbc32d.ocx Properties**

Property	Description
(About)	When the "..." button in the property window is clicked, it will display information about the version and capabilities of the dwsbc32d.ocx custom control.
AddHwnd	Assigns a window handle to this property to add the window to an internal array of windows to subclass.
ClearMessage	Assigns a message number to this property to remove the message from the list of messages to detect.
CtlParam	Sets this property to the name of a form or control to subclass.
HookCount	Reads this property to determine how many windows are being subclassed using the internal subclassing array.
HwndParam	Sets this property at runtime to the main window you wish to subclass if you do not use the CtlParam parameter to choose the window by name. This window is in addition to any windows specified by the internal subclassing array.
MessageArray	This property array contains all of the messages currently being detected.
MessageCount	This property contains the number of messages in the MessageArray.

Table A.2   Most Frequently Used dwsbc32d.ocx Properties (Continued)

Property	Description
Messages	This design time property is a placeholder. Click on the property select button in the property window to bring up the message selection dialog box.
PostEvent	Sets this property to a value to cause a message to be posted to the control. This will cause a DelayedEvent event to be triggered during the course of normal Windows processing with the long value set into this property as a parameter. This allows you to "do something later" without using a timer.
RegMessage1 through RegMessage5	These properties can be set to names of registered messages that will be detected.
RegMessageNum	This property array (with five entries) allows you to retrieve the numbers for registered messages RegMessage1 through RegMessage5 without calling the RegisterWindowMessage API function.
RemoveHwnd	Removes a window handle from the internal subclassing array. This stops subclassing on the specified window. To stop subclassing on the primary window (specified using the HwndParam or CtlParam properties), set the property to zero or the empty string respectively.
Type	Pre-Default: Intercept the message before sending it to the default window function. You can set the nodef parameter in the WndMessage or WndMessageX event to TRUE to prevent default processing from taking place. Set the RetVal parameter in these events to return a value to the calling routine.
	PostDefault: Intercept the message after default processing. The RetVal parameter contains the value returned by the default window function and may be modified.
	Posted: The WndMessage or WndMessageX events are triggered after the message has completed processing. The event is triggered during the normal course of message processing. Changing parameters has no effect. Any messages that use memory pointers may not refer to valid data at this time. This is the safest subclassing mode.
UseOnlyXEvent	All messages trigger the WndMessageX event regardless of whether they are in process or out of process.

APIGID32.DLL

The functions described in this section are part of the APIGID32.DLL dynamic link library. The source code for this library is included on the CD-ROM that comes with this book and is described further in Appendix D. The APIGID32.DLL project is designed to be compiled under Visual C++ 4.0 or later.

■ agCopyData, agCopyDataBynum

VB Declaration   Declare Sub agCopyData Lib "apigid32.dll"apigid32.dll" (source As Any, dest As _
Any, ByVal nCount&)
Declare Sub agCopyDataBynum Lib "apigid32.dll" Alias "agCopyData" (ByVal _
source&, ByVal dest&, ByVal nCount&)

Description   This function is provided to copy data from one object to another. Two forms of this function are
provided; the first accepts any type of object. If the two objects were of the same type, you could
simply use the Visual Basic LSet function; however, this function can be used for copying only
the specified part of the object.
     The second form accepts Long parameters. It is typically used to copy data between Visual
Basic structures and string buffers or memory blocks. Chapter 15 demonstrates the use of this
function for transferring data to and from global memory blocks.

Use with VB   No problem.

Parameter	Type/Description
source	Long—The address of the start of a block of memory to copy.
dest	Long—The address of the beginning of a destination block of memory.
nCount	Long—The number of bytes to copy.

Comments   Be very careful that the parameters to this function are valid and that the entire range specified
by nCount is also valid.
     This function under Win32 can handle blocks greater than 64K in size.
     The source and destination memory ranges may overlap.

■ agDWORDto2Integers

VB Declaration   Declare Function agDWORDto2Integers& Lib "apigid32.dll" (ByVal l&, lw%, lh%)

Description   Many Windows API functions return a long variable that contains two integers. This function provides an efficient way to separate the two integers.

Use with VB   No problem.

Parameter	Type/Description
l	Long—The source Long variable.
lw	Integer—This variable is set to the low 16 bits of parameter l.
lh	Integer—This variable is set to the high 16 bits of parameter l.

■ agGetAddressForObject, agGetAddressForInteger, agGetAddressForLong, agGetAddressForLPSTR, agGetAddressForVBString

VB Declaration   Declare Function agGetAddressForObject& Lib "apigid32.dll" (object As Any)
Declare Function agGetAddressForInteger& Lib "apigid32.dll" Alias _

```
"agGetAddressForObject" (intnum%)
Declare Function agGetAddressForLong& Lib "apigid32.dll" Alias _
"agGetAddressForObject" (intnum&)
Declare Function agGetAddressForLPSTR& Lib "apigid32.dll" Alias _
"agGetAddressForObject" (ByVal lpstring$) ò [See Warning!]
Declare Function agGetAddressForVBString& Lib "apigid32.dll" (vbstring$)
```

Description
Many of the API declarations found in this book require 32-bit (long) addresses as parameters. These functions can be used to determine the address of a Visual Basic variable. Three type-safe declarations are provided for integers, longs, and strings.

The function agGetAddressForObject is defined to retrieve the addresses of variables and user-defined structures. This should not be confused with the object type. Refer to Appendix D for a low-level look at how this function works.

Use with VB
Addresses obtained using this function should be used immediately because Visual Basic variable objects can move in memory. Generally, you should call these functions to obtain an address each time you need it. agGetAddressForLPSTR retrieves the address of a temporary ANSI buffer for a string and is thus useless under Win32. Refer to Chapter 15 for additional information.

Parameter	Type/Description
object	Any—The object for which to obtain an address.

Return Value
Long—The address of the object. agGetAddressForVBString returns the address of a location in memory that points to a BSTR (OLE string).

■ agGetInstance

VB Declaration
`Declare Function agGetInstance& Lib "apigid32.dll" ()`

Description
Retrieves the instance handle of the current application. The instance handle is used by a number of Windows API functions.

Use with VB
No problem.

Return Value
Long—A handle to the current instance.

■ agGetStringFrom2NullBuffer

VB Declaration
`Declare Function agGetStringFrom2NullBuffer$ Lib "apigid32.dll" (ByVal ptr&)`

Description
There are a number of API functions which load a buffer with a series of strings, where each string is separated from the next by a null character and the final string is followed by two null characters. Loading a buffer of this type into a Visual Basic string is possible to do using VB and API functions alone, but it is a complex task that includes using API functions to calculate the length of each string and copy each string individually. This function is able to load a VB string with all of the strings in a double NULL terminated buffer in a single operation. You can then parse the individual strings easily using the VB Instr and Mid$ functions.

Use with VB   No problem.

Parameter	Type/Description
ptr	Long—The address of a buffer containing a series of strings separated by NULL characters and terminated by two NULL characters.

Return Value   String—A string containing a series of strings separated by NULL characters

■ agGetStringFromPointer

VB Declaration
```
Declare Function agGetStringFromPointer$ Lib "apigid32.dll" Alias _
"agGetStringFromLPSTR" (ByVal ptr&)
```

Description   There are a number of API functions that return pointers to buffers containing strings. There are also other cases when working with the Windows API where you will have a string inside of a buffer. This function provides an easy way to convert that string into a Visual Basic string.

Use with VB   No problem.

Parameter	Type/Description
ptr	Long—The address of a buffer containing a string

Return Value   String—A VB string.

■ agInp, agInpw, agInpd

VB Declaration
```
Declare Function agInp% Lib "apigid32.dll" (ByVal portid%)
Declare Function agInpw% Lib "apigid32.dll" (ByVal portid%)
Declare Function agInpd& Lib "apigid32.dll" (ByVal portid%)
```

Description   These functions are used to input data from an I/O port.

Use with VB   No problem.

Parameter	Type/Description
portid	Integer—I/O port address.

Return Value   Integer or Long—The byte (agInp) or integer (agInpw) or long (agInpd) read from the port.

Comments   Direct port access under Windows may not work depending on the device and operating system that you are using. This function is typically used for accessing specialized interfaces for which a Windows driver does not exist.

■ agIsValidName

VB Declaration
```
Declare Function agIsValidName& Lib "apigid32.dll" (ByVal o As Object, ByVal _
lpname$)
```

Description   When working with Visual Basic objects and other OLE automation objects, it is often useful to be able to determine if a method or property name exists in the object before calling it. This function tests the object to see if the specified name is valid.

Use with VB   No problem.

Parameter	Type/Description
o	Object—A Visual Basic object.
lpname	String—The name of a method or property to test.

Return Value   Long—Nonzero (TRUE) if the method or property name is valid.

■ agOutp, agOutpw, agOutpd

VB Declaration
```
Declare Sub agOutp Lib "apigid32.dll" (ByVal portid%, ByVal outval%)
Declare Sub agOutpw Lib "apigid32.dll" (ByVal portid%, ByVal outval%)
Declare Sub agOutpd Lib "apigid32.dll" (ByVal portid%, ByVal outval&)
```

Description   These functions are used to send data to an I/O port.

Use with VB   No problem.

Parameter	Type/Description
portid	Integer—I/O port address.
outval	Integer or Long—The data to write out to the I/O port.

Comments   Direct port access under Windows may not work depending on the device and operating system that you are using. This function is typically used for accessing specialized interfaces for which a Windows driver does not exist.

■ agPOINTStoLong

VB Declaration   `Declare Function agPOINTStoLong& Lib "apigid32.dll" (pt As POINTS)`

Description   Converts a POINTS structure into a Long, placing the X field in the low 16 bits of the result and the Y field in the high 16 bits of the result. This function is convenient for Windows API functions that expect POINTS structures to be passed as Long parameters. The APIGUIDE.DLL 16-bit library that comes with the *Visual Basic Programmer's Guide to the Windows API* (16-bit edition) includes a similar function agPOINTAPItoLong. Under Win32, a POINTAPI structure takes 64 bits instead of 32 bits, hence the change in function. Refer to Chapter 4 for additional information on POINTAPI and POINTS structures.

Use with VB   No problem.

Parameter	Type/Description
pt	POINTS—A POINTS structure.

Return Value   Long—A long representation of the POINTS structure.

■ agSubtractFileTimes

VB Declaration

```
Declare Sub agSubtractFileTimes Lib "apigid32.dll" (f1 As Any, f2 As Any, f3 _
As Any)
```

Description Subtracts the contents of one FILETIME structure from another. Refer to Chapter 14 for details.

■ agSwapBytes, agSwapWords

VB Declaration
```
Declare Function agSwapBytes% Lib "apigid32.dll" (ByVal src%)
Declare Function agSwapWords& Lib "apigid32.dll" (ByVal src&)
```

Description In rare situations, you may need to swap the order of bytes in an integer or the integers in a long. This will typically occur when working with file formats defined originally for non-Intel processors. This function provides an easy way to accomplish this task. Refer to Chapter 4 for additional information. Use of this function eliminates the need to worry about overflow errors that can occur when attempting to perform this task using Visual Basic.

Use with VB No problem.

Parameter	Type/Description
src	Integer or Long—An integer or long variable whose bytes or words are to be swapped.

Return Value Integer or Long—The parameter with bytes or integers swapped.

Windows Data Structures

Appendix B, which appears on the CD-ROM edition of this book, lists the data structures used by Microsoft Windows that are useful under Visual Basic and are related to subjects that are covered in this book. These type definitions can be found in file API32.TXT provided with this book. API32.TXT contains declarations for many structures that are not covered in Appendix B. Refer to your online Win32 documentation or the MSDN CD-ROM for additional information.

Windows File Formats

This appendix describes the file formats for some of the common file types used under Windows. In most cases the file contains a series of data structures, some of which are described here and some of which are described in Appendix B. File formats are one of the few things that have generally remained unchanged from 16-bit Windows. This is not surprising considering the need for many of these files to be compatible with Windows 3.x, Windows 95, and Windows NT.

Bitmap File Format

Bitmap files—those with a .BMP extension—consist of three parts. The file begins with a BITMAPFILEHEADER structure that describes the file. It is followed by a BITMAPINFO structure (described in Appendix B and in Chapter 9). It contains the header and color table for a device-independent bitmap. The BITMAPINFO structure is followed by the bitmap data.

The BITMAPFILEHEADER structure is defined as follows:

■ BITMAPFILEHEADER

VB Declaration

```
Type BITMAPFILEHEADER    ' 14 Bytes
        bfType As Integer
        bfSize As Long
        bfReserved1 As Integer
        bfReserved2 As Integer
        bfOffBits As Long
End Type
```

Description   This structure appears at the beginning of a bitmap file.

Field	Type/Description
bfType	**Integer**—The string "BM" (hex value &H424D)
bfSize	**Long**—The size of the file, measured in bytes
bfReserved1	**Integer**—Not used, set to zero
bfReserved2	**Integer**—Not used, set to zero
bfOffBits	**Long**—The start offset of the bitmap data in the file

Icon File Format

An icon file, with an .ICO extension, can in fact contain any number of icons. Generally, each icon will be a rendition of an icon image designed for a particular display device. Thus a single icon file may contain icons for CGA, monochrome, VGA, and super VGA devices.

An icon file begins with an ICONDIR structure as described below:

■ ICONDIR

VB Declaration

```
Type ICONDIR    ' 6 Bytes
        idReserved As Integer
        idType As Integer
        idCount As Integer
End Type
```

Description

This structure appears at the beginning of an icon file.

Field	Type/Description
idReserved	**Integer**—Not used, set to zero
idType	**Integer**—1
idCount	**Integer**—The number of icons in the file. This specifies the number of ICON-DIRENTRY structures that follow this structure in the file.

A series of ICONDIRENTRY structures immediately follows the ICONDIR structure at the start of the file. Each of these structures defines the characteristics of one of the icons in the file. This structure is defined as follows:

■ ICONDIRENTRY

VB Declaration

```
Type ICONDIRENTRY
        bWidth As Byte
        bHeight As Byte
        bColorCount As Byte
        bReserved As Byte
        wPlanes As Integer
        wBitCount As Integer
        dwBytesInRes As Long
        dwImageOffset As Long
End Type
```

Description

Each icon in an icon file has an ICONDIRENTRY structure associated with it that describes the characteristics of the icon.

Field	Type/Description
bWidth	**Byte**—The width of the icon. This may be 16, 32, or 64. Most Windows icons are 32×32.
bHeight	**Byte**—The height of the icon. This may be 16, 32, or 64. Most Windows icons are 32×32.
bColorCount	**Byte**—The number of colors used by the icons. This may be 2, 8, or 16.
bReserved	**Byte**—Not used, set to zero

Field	Type/Description
wPlanes	**Integer**—The number of color planes in the icon
wBitCount	**Integer**—The number of bits per pixel in the icon
dwBytesInRes	**Long**—The size of the icon specified in bytes
dwImageOffset	**Long**—The offset of the specified icon from the beginning of the file

This structure provides enough information for Windows or an application to match the icon to the display device. You would usually choose the icon in the file that most closely matches the actual display.

The icon data appears after all of the ICONDIRENTRY structures. Each icon consists of two bitmaps: an XOR bitmap defining the exclusive-or part of the icon, and an AND bitmap defining the AND mask. These are defined in "Icons and Cursors" in Chapter 9. The XOR bitmap appears first and consists of a device-independent bitmap. This bitmap may be monochrome or color. (Device-independent bitmaps are described in Chapter 9. The data structures used by DIBs are listed in Appendix B.) Only the biSize through biBitCount fields of the DIB's BITMAPINFOHEADER structure are used with icons. The biHeight field of the BITMAPINFOHEADER structure is equal to the sum of the height of the DIB and mask bitmaps. Thus for a 32×32 pixel icon, the biHeight field will have a value of 64, not 32 as one might expect.

After the XOR bitmap DIB, the AND bitmap appears. This is a monochrome bitmap with the same dimensions as the XOR bitmap.

Cursor File Format

An icon file with a .CUR extension can also contain any number of cursors. Generally, each cursor will be a rendition of a cursor image designed for a particular display device.

A cursor file begins with a CURSORDIR structure as described here:

■ CURSORDIR

VB Declaration

```
Type CURSORDIR    ' 6 Bytes
    cdReserved As Integer
    cdType As Integer
    cdCount As Integer
End Type
```

Description

This structure appears at the beginning of a cursor file.

Field	Type/Description
idReserved	**Integer**—Not used, set to zero

Field	Type/Description
idType	**Integer**—2
idCount	**Integer**—The number of cursors in the file. This specifies the number of CURSORDIRENTRY structures that follow this structure in the file.

A series of CURSORDIRENTRY structures immediately follows the CURSORDIR structure at the start of the file. Each of these structures defines the characteristics of one of the cursors in the file. This structure is defined as follows:

■ CURSORDIRENTRY

VB Declaration
```
Type CURSORDIRENTRY
    bWidth As Byte
    bHeight As Byte
    bColorCount As Byte
    bReserved As Byte
    wXHotspot As Integer
    wYHotspot As Integer
    dwBytesInRes As Long
    dwImageOffset As Long
End Type
```

Description   Each cursor in a cursor file has a CURSORDIRENTRY structure associated with it that describes the characteristics of the cursor.

Field	Type/Description
bWidth	**Byte**—The width of the cursor. This may be up to 32 for Windows 3.*x*.
bHeight	**Byte**—The height of the cursor. This may be up to 32 for Windows 3.*x*.
bColorCount	**Byte**—The number of colors used by the cursor. This is 2 for Windows 3.*x*.
bReserved	**Byte**—Not used, set to zero
wXHotspot, wYHotspot	**Integers**—The offset of the hot spot for the cursor. This specifies the pixel within the cursor that the cursor is actually pointing to.
dwBytesInRes	**Long**—The size of the cursor specified in bytes
dwImageOffset	**Long**—The offset of the specified cursor from the beginning of the file

The rest of the cursor file is identical to that of an icon file with the exception that the XOR bitmap of a cursor must be monochrome.

Metafile Format (.WMF extension)

There are two types of metafiles, with the .WMF extension, available under Windows. The standard metafile begins with a METAHEADER structure, which was defined in Appendix B. This structure is followed by one or more METARECORD structures, each of which describes a GDI graphic command that is executed when the record is played.

The second type of metafile is known as a placeable metafile. Virtually every metafile you will find at this time on a typical system is a placeable metafile. This metafile contains additional information describing the desired appearance of the metafile drawing. The standard metafile is preceded with a METAFILEHEADER structure. The QuikDraw.vbp example in Chapter 8 shows how to read and write placeable metafiles.

Visual Basic-to-DLL Calling Conventions: A Technical Review

Chapter 3 of this book discusses in detail how a Visual Basic programmer can use the VB Declare statement to access virtually any dynamic link library function. This appendix reviews this same process from the other point of view—that of the C or C++ language programmer who wishes to write dynamic link library functions for use by Visual Basic applications. Even if you never expect to write your own DLL, this information can be useful in providing a better understanding of how the Visual Basic-to-DLL interface works.

Visual Basic comes with a file—VB4DLL.TXT—that discusses this issue in some depth. This appendix briefly summarizes the key concepts presented in that file and elaborates on those sections that deserve further discussion. You are encouraged to refer to VB4DLL.TXT as a supplement to this apendix.

The APIGID32.DLL dynamic link library contains file vbintf.cpp which exports many functions that, along with the VBDLL.VBP project, demonstrate most of the possible ways to pass parameters to DLLs from Visual Basic and return values from DLL functions to Visual Basic. Complete source code for APIGID32.DLL is included on the CD-ROM that comes with this book.

Calling Conventions

Visual Basic supports the standard Microsoft StdCall calling convention. This calling convention is of course supported by Microsoft's compilers, and should be supported by any other compiler that allows you to create Windows dynamic link libraries. Refer to the mixed-language guide for your compiler or contact your compiler vendor to verify compatibility.

Your DLL functions should be defined as extern "c" in the header file (use the stdcall specified to choose the calling convention) and exported in the .DEF file. This also prevents C++ name mangling from occurring.

Two calling conventions are supported in Visual Basic for data types other than strings. The default is known as *call by reference*. In this scheme your VB function actually transfers a pointer to the variable. The DLL function can then use the pointer to access the data. Any changes made to that data will be reflected in the Visual Basic variable once the function returns.

The second scheme is known as *call by value*. In this case, VB passes a copy of the data to the DLL function. Call by value is specified by placing the ByVal keyword before the variable name in the function declaration.

Calling Conventions by Data Type

All of Visual Basic's data types can be passed as parameters to DLL functions. Some of the data types, such as the Visual Basic string type and currency type, are not supported directly by the C language. However, in most cases it is possible to write additional code to handle those data types.

Numeric Data Types

The numeric data types Integer, Long, Single, and Double are easily handled from Visual Basic. Variables can be passed by value or by reference and DLL functions may return numeric values directly.

Currency Data Types

The currency data type has no direct equivalent in C. This type uses eight bytes in a fixed precision format. A DLL designed to handle currency could use a structure to define the variable as shown below:

```
typedef struct currencystruct {
   char cbuf[8];
} currency;

currency FAR PASCAL ReceivesCurrency(currency curr)
{
     // You can access the curr parameter within the
     // function and return it as well.
     return(curr);
}
```

This takes advantage of the fact that C supports passing of structures by value and returning structures as results of functions.

The eight bytes of the currency structure form a single 64-bit integer that is a fixed-point representation of a floating-point currency number with four digits after the decimal point. In other words, the value $12.53 would be represented by the number 125,300 in a 64-bit number.

String Data Types

Strings in Visual Basic are handled differently from numeric data. They are always called by reference. The ByVal keyword is still used, however, to differentiate between two types of strings. When ByVal is specified, Visual Basic makes a copy of the string that is null terminated. This produces a string in the standard format expected by Windows API functions. When the DLL function returns, Visual Basic copies the string data back into the string variable (hence the DLL can modify the string even though ByVal is specified). Note that Visual Basic strings may have embedded nulls. Passing such a string to a DLL using this method will lead to truncation of the string.

When modifying a string parameter in a DLL that was passed using this method, it is critical that you do not modify any data past the null terminator unless you are certain that enough space has been allocated in the string. Doing so will almost certainly cause a system error sooner or later. You must initialize the string to the largest length that you expect to need before passing it as a parameter. This is commonly accomplished by using fixed length strings or setting the string length with the **String$()** function before the DLL call.

When ByVal is absent, the string is passed as a pointer to a BSTR data type—or a handle to an OLE string. You must use the standard OLE BSTR string functions such as **SysAllocString** to work with this type of string.

There are a number of advantages in using Visual Basic strings directly. It allows you to use Visual Basic's string management facilities, eliminating the need to preallocate buffers of a particular length. Also, it is possible for a DLL function to be defined as a string type and thus have it return a string directly in the form

```
a$ = dllfunc$()
```

Be aware that Visual Basic strings may contain nulls. Your DLL code must take this into account. Also, destroying VB strings in a DLL that are passed as parameters from Visual Basic will probably lead to trouble.

Forms, Controls, and Objects

Forms, controls, and objects are available as parameter and return types in the Declare statement. They are all represented by an OLE interface. When ByVal is specified, an LPUNKNOWN interface pointer is passed to the DLL function. When it is not specified, a pointer to an LPUNKNOWN is passed, meaning that it is possible to change the object that is referenced by an object variable. Objects are returned by returning an LPUNKNOWN value (be sure that you have one reference on the object before returning it).

If you are not acquainted with OLE programming, the above paragraph will probably be totally cryptic. I could say "fear not, the OLE documentation will make this clear and easy to deal with," but that would be a lie. Unfortunately, the mysteries of OLE are well beyond the scope of this book. Kraig Brockschmidt's *Inside OLE2* from Microsoft Press is a good place to start.

User-Defined Types

User-defined types can be called by reference only and cannot be returned. The C or C++ function receives a pointer to the user-defined structure. The user-defined structures may contain strings; however, these strings will not be converted into null terminated strings. Dynamic strings will be BSTRs and thus can be worked with using the OLE string functions. Fixed-length strings in user-defined structures can be treated as arrays of characters of the specified length since Visual Basic allocates enough space for each fixed-length string inside the structure. Arrays in user-defined types can be accessed directly, as Visual Basic allocates enough space in the structure for the entire array. You will need to copy the fixed-length string to a temporary buffer and add a null terminating character before using the string. The Visual Basic documentation implies that a variable-length string entry in a user-defined type may have a null value if it is not yet initialized (though this has not been demonstrated by the author). If a string entry in a user-defined structure has a null value, you should be able to use **SysAllocString** function to insert the string into the structure.

User defined structures passed to DLL's use a structure member alignment of 4.

Arrays

There are two ways to work with arrays in Visual Basic. The first involves using the call-by-reference protocol and passing the first element in the array as a parameter to the DLL function. Be very careful when using this technique—it is easy to accidentally access memory outside the array boundaries (by not using the first element of the array in the VB call, or through an indexing error in the DLL). As usual, this type of error will likely cause a system error. Control arrays cannot be passed as parameters to a DLL using this technique. A sample declaration of this type is:

```
Declare Sub dllfunc Lib "dlllib.dll" (xentry As Integer)
```

Note that xentry is not defined as an array. This works because all of the elements in a numeric array are arranged in sequence in memory. Using this technique on string arrays passes the first element in an array of BSTR string handles.

If the DLL is designed for use with Visual Basic, it may be designed to accept OLE SAFEARRAY arrays as parameters. This is a typical declaration for using OLE arrays with DLL functions:

```
Declare Sub dllfunc Lib "dlllib.dll" (xentry() As Integer)
```

Note that the xentry parameter is an array rather than a single value. The DLL function receives a pointer to a pointer to a SAFEARRAY (SAFEARRAY **). When passing string arrays to a DLL, you should always use the latter technique.

You can return arrays to Visual Basic as part of a variant.

Variants

Visual Basic Variant types can be passed to DLL functions both by value and by reference and can be returned from DLL functions. Visual Basic 4.0 uses OLE variants. These are not compatible with the variants used in VB3.0 and earlier. Refer to Appendix D of the *Visual Basic Programmer's Guide to the Windows API* (16-bit edition) for information on use of variants under VB3.0.

VARIANTARG types can be passed as parameters by value or by reference, and can be returned using standard C++ declarations.

Summary of Parameter Passing Conventions

Table D.1 summarizes the legal calling conventions for the Visual Basic-to-DLL interface.

Table 8.1 **Visual Basic to DLL Calling Conventions**

Data Type	Convention	Parameter	Comments
Integer	By value	16-bit integer	—
Long	By value	32-bit long value	—
Single	By value	32-bit single (float) value	—
Double	By value	64-bit double	Points to temporary copy of double
Currency	By value	64-bit currency value	Points to temporary copy of a 64-bit currency variable
String	By value	32-bit address	Points to a null terminated copy of the string. Copy will be set into the VB variable on return (thus this is actually call by reference)
Integer	By reference	32-bit address	Points to 16-bit VB integer variable
Long	By reference	32-bit address	Points to 32-bit VB long variable
Single	By reference	32-bit address	Points to 32-bit VB single variable
Double	By reference	32-bit address	Points to 64-bit VB double variable
Currency	By reference	32-bit address	Points to 64-bit VB currency variable
String	By reference	32-bit address that points to an OLE BSTR	Refer to your OLE documentation for further details
Form, control, or object	By value	32-bit LPUNKNOWN OLE interface	Refer to your OLE documentation for further details
Form, control, or object	By reference	32-bit pointer to an LPUNKNOWN OLE interface	Refer to your OLE documentation for further details
User-defined type	By reference	32-bit address	Points to the structure

Table 8.1   Visual Basic to DLL Calling Conventions (Continued)

Data Type	Convention	Parameter	Comments
Array (first method)	By reference	32-bit address	Points to the first element of the array by reference
Array (second method)	By reference	32-bit address that points to an OLE SAFEARRAY pointer	Refer to your OLE documentation
Variant	By value	VARIANTARG structure	The actual VARIANTARG structure as defined in the OLE documentation
Variant	By reference	32-bit address	Points to a VARIANTARG structure as defined in the OLE documentation

Table D.2 summarizes the legal return conventions for the Visual Basic-to-DLL interface. Values are returned in the EAX and EDX registers as specified in the table. Address offset and selector combine to form a 32-bit FAR pointer.

Table 8.2   Visual Basic-to-DLL Function Return Conventions

Data Type	EAX	EDX	Comments
Integer	16-bit integer	—	—
Long	32-bit long	—	—
Single	—	—	Value returned on the floating point stack
Double	—	—	Value returned on the floating point stack
Currency	Low 32 bits of the currency value	High 32 bits of the currency value	—
String	32-bit BSTR (OLE string handle)	—	Refer to your OLE documentation for further information
Variant	32-bit Address	—	Points to a temporary copy of the variant result on the stack. Refer to your OLE documentation for further information
Object	LPUNKNOWN	—	Refer to your OLE documentation for further information

Avoiding Exceptions

Visual Basic guarantees that any DLL function calls in your program will match the expected parameters and return values in the declaration for that function. This means that if you have declared a function as accepting an integer parameter and call it from VB with a double parameter, VB will convert that parameter into an integer before calling the DLL function just as it would for any other VB function. Once a DLL function has been correctly declared, you are unlikely to run into any difficulties with general protection faults due to programming errors in Visual Basic unless you intentionally turned off error checking for a parameter by using the As Any type definition.

Visual Basic and Windows perform absolutely no error checking or detection when it comes to making sure that the VB declaration for a DLL function is in any way compatible with the DLL function itself. Given these facts, the following techniques should help when it comes to creating DLLs for use with Visual Basic.

- Save your work frequently!

- Declare VOID DLL functions as VB subroutines (SUB), and DLL functions returning values as VB functions (FUNCTION).

- Be sure that the DLL return value type matches the VB declaration. This is especially critical for the double, currency, and variant data types.

- Be sure that all DLL function parameters are defined correctly in the VB declaration. Pay special attention to call by value and call by reference considerations, and to the two string types available.

- When passing regular string parameters, be sure that your DLL does not modify any part of the string after the NULL terminator.

- When passing parameters by reference, be sure that your DLL does not exceed the boundaries of the data (especially for user-defined data types and arrays).

- Test your DLL thoroughly. If possible, use the debugging version of Windows in your testing—it detects error conditions that the retail version may miss.

- Generally speaking, Windows NT provides a more robust environment for writing and testing dynamic link libraries (and C/C++ code in general).

Raster Operation Table

Appendix E, which appears on the CD-ROM edition of this book, lists the raster operations available under Windows. Each has a 32-bit value that can be used as a parameter to functions that use raster-ops. The third column shows the constant name for those raster operations that are defined in the API32.TXT file. These are the operations most commonly used in Windows.

INDEX

ABOUT THE CD-ROM

The CD-ROM that comes with this book includes the full text of the book along with sample code, additional information, articles, and other items that I think you will find of interest. Refer to the introductory section on the CD-ROM for the latest information about the contents.

In order to run the CD-ROM, in addition to having a CD-ROM drive, your computer must have either Windows 95 or Windows NT installed. The multimedia components of the CD-ROM require a double-speed CD-ROM (or faster) and the ability to play AVI files.

To start exploring the CD-ROM, run the program VBPG32.EXE (this program will start automatically under Windows 95 if you have auto-run capability enabled for your CD-ROM).

The primary design consideration for the CD-ROM is that it not interfere with your system in any way. With one exception, it does not modify your registry or install any files on your system. The exception is that you have the opportunity of installing the demonstration custom controls on your system if you wish—otherwise, you can register them to run on the CD-ROM. You may, of course, copy the sample code to your system at will.

Portions of the CD first appeared in *Visual Basic Developer*. *Visual Basic Developer* is published monthly by Pinnacle Publishing Inc., PO Box 888, Kent, WA 98035; Telephone: (206) 251-1900, (800) 788-1900, fax: (206) 251-5057.

Some articles on the CD appear courtesy of Fawcette Technical Publications, publishers of *Visual Basic Programmer's Journal* and *Microsoft Interactive Developer*.